HARRAP'S FIVE LANGUAGE BUSINESS DICTIONARY

English-French-German-Italian-Spanish

HARRAP

FIVE-LANGUAGE BUSINESS DICTIONARY

Compilers: Monika Angerer, Martina Drux, Barbara Eder-Riegel,
Ursula Guidi, Nicola Petersen, Dr. Santiago Rodriguez de la Fuente
Designer: Inga Koch

First published in Great Britain 1991
by HARRAP BOOKS Ltd
Chelsea House, 26 Market Square, Bromley, Kent BR1 1NA

ISBN 0 245-60347-6

ISBN 0-13-387978-X (United States)

Printed in Germany

FOREWORD

The steady growth of international communications – particularly within today's unified Europe – means that knowledge of foreign languages is becoming an ever more important aspect of business life. This new dictionary meets the demand for a practical, up-to-date reference source by providing the user with access to a comprehensive business vocabulary of 20,000 headwords and 80,000 translations in five major European languages: English, French, German, Italian and Spanish.

The multilingual integration of all the headwords within a single alphabetical sequence makes it quick and easy to look up a particular word and its translations in any of the five languages.

This convenient international dictionary is designed to cover all areas of business and commerce – making it an ideal general reference source for office use or for overseas business trips.

ABBREVIATIONS

D= GERMAN
E= ENGLISH
F= FRENCH
I= ITALIAN
ES= SPANISH
f= feminine
m= masculine
n= neuter

	D	E	F	I	Es
abaratamiento (Es)	Verbilligung *f*	cheapening	réduction du prix *f*	ribasso *m*	—
abastecedor (Es)	Zulieferer *m*	supplier	sous-traitant *m*	fornitore *m*	—
abastecimiento (Es)	Versorgung *f*	supply	approvisionne-ment *m*	approvvigiona-mento *m*	—
abastecimiento energético (Es)	Energieversorgung *f*	energy supply	approvisionnement en énergie *m*	approvvigionamento d'energia *m*	—
abatement of an action (E)	Verfahrens-einstellung *f*	—	arrêt d'une procédure *m*	sospensione del procedimento *f*	sobreseimiento del proceso *m*
ab Bahnhof (D)	—	ex rail/free on rail	départ gare	franco stazione	puesto en estación
Abbau (D)	—	reduction/lay off	réduction *f*/ diminution *f*	riduzione *f*/ diminuzione *f*	reducción *f*/ disminución *f*
abbonamento (I)	Abonnement *n*	subscription	abonnement *m*	—	suscripción *f*
abbonato (I)	Abonnent *m*	subscriber	abonné *m*	—	suscriptor *m*
abbuono (I)	Bonifikation *f*	bonus	bonification *f*	—	bonificación *f*
ABC-Analyse (D)	—	ABC analysis	analyse ABC *f*	analisi ABC *f*	análisis ABC *m*
ABC analysis (E)	ABC-Analyse *f*	—	analyse ABC *f*	analisi ABC *f*	análisis ABC *m*
Abfall (D)	—	waste	déchet *m*	rifiuti *m pl*	desechos *m pl*
Abfallbeseitigung (D)	—	waste disposal	élimination de déchets *f*	smaltimento dei rifiuti *m*	evacuación de residuos *f*
Abfallbörse (D)	—	recycling exchange	bourse de recyclage *f*	borsa dei rifiuti *f*	bolsa de reciclaje *f*
Abfallexperte (D)	—	expert on waste products	expert de déchets *m*	esperto dei rifiuti *m*	experto de productos residuales *m*
Abfallwirtschaft (D)	—	waste management	industrie de déchets *f*	industria dei rifiuti *f*	industria de desperdicios *f*
Abfertigung (D)	—	dispatch/clearance	expédition *f*/expédition en douane *f*	spedizione *f*/ sdoganamento *m*	despacho *m*/des-pacho de aduana *m*
Abfindung (D)	—	indemnity/ compensation	indemnité *f*/ compensation *f*	indennità *f*/ compensazione *f*	indemnización *f*/ compensación *f*
Abfindungsangebot (D)	—	compensation offer	offre d'indemnité *f*	offerta d'indennità *f*	oferta de indemnización *f*
Abgabe (D)	—	tax/duty	taxe *f*	imposta *f*/dazio *m*	impuesto *m*/ arancel *m*
abgabenfrei (D)	—	tax-free/duty-free	exempt de taxes	esente da contributi	exento de impuestos/ exento de derechos
abgabenpflichtig (D)	—	liable to tax	soumis à l'impôt	soggetto a contributi	sujeto a impuestos
Abgrenzung (D)	—	demarcation	délimitation *f*	delimitazione *f*	delimitación *f*
Abgrenzungsposten (D)	—	deferred item	comptes transitoires *m pl*	ratei e risconti *m pl*	cuentas de orden *f pl*
abholbereit (D)	—	ready for collection	disponible	pronto per il ritiro	listo para la recogida
abilità nel trattare (I)	Verhandlungs-geschick *n*	negotiation skills	habileté en matière de négociation *f*	—	tino de negociar *m*
ability (E)	Fähigkeit *f*	—	capacité *f*	capacità *f*	capacidad *f*
abitazione (I)	Wohnung *f*	apartment	appartement *m*	—	vivienda *f*
ab Kai (D)	—	ex quay/f.a.s.	départ quai	franco banchina	ex muelle
Abkommen (D)	—	agreement	accord *m*	accordo *m*	acuerdo *m*
Abladegewicht (D)	—	shipping (delivered) weight	poids au déchargement *m*	peso di scarico *m*	peso de descarga *m*
Ablage (D)	—	file	collection des dossiers *f*	archivio *m*	archivo *m*
Ablauffrist (D)	—	time limit	délai *m*	termine di scadenza *m*	vencimiento *m*
Ablauforganisation (D)	—	scheduling organization	organisation fonction-nelle de l'entreprise *f*	organizzazione del lavoro *f*	organización funcional *f*
Ablehnung (D)	—	refusal/rejection	refus *m*/rejet *m*	rifiuto *m*/rigetto *m*	recusación *f*/repulsa *f*
abliefern (D)	—	hand over	livrer	consegnare	entregar
ablösen (D)	—	redeem	amortir	rimborsare	sustituir/amortizar
Ablösesumme (D)	—	redemption sum	montant de rachat *m*	importo di rimborso *m*	suma de amortización *f*
Ablösungs-finanzierung (D)	—	redemption financing	financement du rachat *m*	finanziamento del rimborso *m*	financiamiento de amortización *m*
Abnahme (D)	—	acceptance/decrease	réception *f*/ réduction *f*	accettazione *f*/ riduzione *f*	aceptación *f*/ disminución *f*

	D	E	F	I	Es
Abnahmemenge (D)	—	purchased quantity	quantité commercialisée *f*	quantità d'acquisto *f*	cantidad de compra *f*
Abnahmepflicht (D)	—	obligation to accept delivery	obligation d'acceptation de la marchandise *f*	obbligo di accettare la consegna *m*	obligación de recepción *f*
Abnehmer (D)	—	buyer/purchaser/ customer	acheteur *m*	acquirente *m*/ cliente *m*	tomador *m*
Abnehmerland (D)	—	buyer country	pays acheteur *m*	paese acquirente *m*	país comprador *m*
Abnutzung (D)	—	wear and tear	dépréciation *f*	usura *f*	desgaste *m*
abogado (Es)	Rechtsanwalt *m*	lawyer	avocat *m*	avvocato *m*	—
abonar en cuenta (Es)	gutschreiben	credit	créditer	accreditare	—
abondance de matières premières (F)	Rohstoffreichtum *m*	abundancy of raw materials	—	ricchezza di materie prime *f*	abundancia en materias primas *f*
abonné (F)	Abonnent *m*	subscriber	—	abbonato *m*	suscriptor *m*
Abonnement (D)	—	subscription	abonnement *m*	abbonamento *m*	suscripción *f*
abonnement (F)	Abonnement *n*	subscription	—	abbonamento *m*	suscripción *f*
Abonnent (D)	—	subscriber	abonné *m*	abbonato *m*	suscriptor *m*
abono (Es)	Gutschrift *f*	credit	crédit *m*	accredito *m*	—
Abrechnung (D)	—	settlement of accounts	règlement *m*	liquidazione *f*	liquidación *f*
Abrechnungstag (D)	—	settling day	jour de la liquidation *m*	giorno di liquidazione *m*	fecha de liquidación *f*
Abrechnungs-verfahren (D)	—	settling procedure	méthode de l'apurement des comptes	metodo di liquidazione *m*	operaciones de descuento *f pl*
Abrechnungs-zeitraum (D)	—	accounting period	période comptable *f*	periodo di liquidazione *m*	período contable *m*
Abreisedatum (D)	—	date of departure	date de départ *f*	data di partenza *f*	fecha de partida *f*
a breve scadenza (I)	kurzfristig	short-term	à court terme	—	a corto plazo
abroad (E)	im Ausland	—	à l'étranger	all'estero	en el extranjero
Abruf (D)	—	call	appel *m*	richiesta *f*	reclamación de la entrega de un pedido *f*
Absage (D)	—	refusal	refus *m*	risposta negativa *f*	negativa *f*
Absatz (D)	—	sale/distribution	volume des ventes *m*	vendita *f*	cifra de ventas *f*
Absatzanalyse (D)	—	sales analysis	analyse de la distribution *f*	analisi di mercato *f*	análisis de venta *m*
Absatzchance (D)	—	sales prospects	possibilités de réussite des ventes *f pl*	prospettive di smercio *f pl*	posibilidades de venta *f pl*
Absatzfinanzierung (D)	—	sales financing	financement des ventes *m*	finanziamento delle vendite *m*	financiación de las ventas *f*
Absatzförderung (D)	—	sales promotion	promotion des ventes *f*	promozione dello smercio *f*	promoción comercial *f*
Absatzkrise (D)	—	sales crisis	crise de vente *f*	crisi di mercato *f*	crisis en la venta *f*
Absatzorganisation (D)	—	sales organization	organisation de vente *f*	organizzazione di vendita *f*	organización de ventas *f*
Absatzplanung (D)	—	sales planning	planning de la distribution *m*	pianificazione delle vendite *f*	planificación de ventas *f*
Absatzpolitik (D)	—	marketing policy	politique de vente *f*	politica di vendita *f*	política de ventas *f*
Absatzsegment (D)	—	sales segment	segment de vente *m*	segmento di vendita *m*	segmento de venta *m*
Absatzstatistik (D)	—	sales statistics	statistique de la vente *f*	statistica delle vendite *f*	estadística de ventas *f*
Absatzstrategie (D)	—	sales strategy	stratégie de vente *f*	strategia di vendita *f*	estrategia de ventas *f*
Absatzweg (D)	—	channel of distribution	canal de distribution *m*	via della distribuzione *f*	medio de venta *f*
Absatzwirtschaft (D)	—	marketing	commercialisation *f*	marketing *m*	economía de distribución *f*
Absatzziel (D)	—	sales target	objectif de vente *m*	obbiettivo di vendita *m*	fin de venta *m*
ab Schiff (D)	—	ex ship	départ navire	franco bordo	ex vapor
Abschlag (D)	—	reduction	déduction *f*	detrazione *f*	descuento *m*

	D	E	F	I	Es
Abschlagszahlung (D)	—	partial payment/ payment on account	premier versement *m*/acompte *m*	pagamento a rate *m*/ pagamento in acconto *m*	pago parcial *m*/ pago a cuenta *m*
Abschluß (D)	—	conclusion	conclusion *f*	stipulazione *f*	contratación *f*/ conclusión *f*/cierre *m*
Abschlußprüfer (D)	—	auditor	vérificateur des comptes *m*	revisore *m*	revisor contable *m*
Abschlußprüfung (D)	—	audit	vérification des comptes *f*	revisione *f*	revisión contable *f*
Abschlußtechnik (D)	—	finishing technique	technique de conclusion *f*	metodo di chiusura *m*	técnica de conclusión *f*
Abschöpfungs-system (D)	—	absorption system	système d'absorption *m*	regime di prelievo *m*	sistema de gravámenes *m*
Abschreibung (D)	—	depreciation	amortissement *m*	ammortamento *m*	amortización *f*
Abschreibungs-fonds (D)	—	depreciation fund	fonds d'amortissement *m*	fondo ammortamenti *m*	fondo amortización *m*
Abschreibungs-gesellschaft (D)	—	project write-off company	société d'amortissement *f*	società di ammortamento *f*	sociedad de amortización *f*
Abschreibungs-objekt (D)	—	object of depreciation	objet d'amortissement *m*	oggetto da ammortizzare *m*	objeto de amortización *m*
Abschrift (D)	—	copy	copie *f*	copia *f*	copia *f*
Abschwung (D)	—	down-swing	dépression *f*	regresso *m*	baja *f*
Absender (D)	—	sender	envoyeur *m*	mittente *m*	remitente *m*
Absendung (D)	—	dispatch	expédition *f*	spedizione *f*	expedición *f*
absent (E)	abwesend	—	absent	assente	ausente
absent (F)	abwesend	absent	—	assente	ausente
absolutamente confidencial (Es)	streng vertraulich	strictly confidential	strictement confidentiel	strettamente confidenziale	—
absorción (Es)	Absorption *f*	absorption	absorption *f*	assorbimento *m*	—
Absorption (D)	—	absorption	absorption *f*	assorbimento *m*	absorción *f*
absorption (E)	Absorption *f*	—	absorption *f*	assorbimento *m*	absorción *f*
absorption (F)	Absorption *f*	absorption	—	assorbimento *m*	absorción *f*
absorption system (E)	Abschöpfungs-system *n*	—	système d'absorption *m*	regime di prelievo *m*	sistema de gravámenes *m*
Abstand (D)	—	distance	distance *f*	distanza *f*	distancia *f*
Abteilung (D)	—	division/department	service *m*	reparto *m*	sección *f*
Abteilungsleiter (D)	—	head of department	chef de service *m*	capo reparto *m*	jefe de sección *m*
Abteilungs-organisation (D)	—	department organization	organisation du service *f*	organizzazione reparto *f*	organización de sección *f*
Abtretung (D)	—	assignment	cession *f*	cessione *f*	cesión *f*
Abtretungsvertrag (D)	—	contract of assignment	contrat de cession *m*	contratto di cessione *m*	contrato de cesión *m*
abuso del computer (I)	Computer-kriminalität *f*	computer criminality	délits informatiques *m pl*	—	delincuencia informática *f*
abuso di fiducia (I)	Veruntreuung *f*	misappropriation	détournement *m*	—	malversación *f*
Abwärtstrend (D)	—	downward trend	baisse *f*	tendenza al ribasso *f*	tendencia bajista *f*
Abwasser (D)	—	waste water	eaux résiduelles *f pl*	acque di scarico *f pl*	aguas residuales *f pl*
Abwasserkosten (D)	—	sewage disposal costs	coûts de traitement des eaux usées *m pl*	costi per le acque di scarico *m pl*	gastos para aguas residuales *m pl*
Abwasserreinigung (D)	—	purification of sewage	clarification des eaux usées *f*	depurazione delle acque di scarico *f*	depuración de las aguas residuales *f*
Abweichung (D)	—	deviation	divergence *f*	deviazione *f*	diferencia *f*
Abwerbung (D)	—	pirating	débauchage *m*	accaparramento *m*	sonsacamiento *m*
ab Werk (D)	—	ex works	départ usine	franco fabbrica	ex fábrica
Abwertung (D)	—	devaluation	dévaluation *f*	svalutazione *f*	devaluación *f*
abwesend (D)	—	absent	absent	assente	ausente
Abwickler (D)	—	liquidator	liquidateur *m*	liquidatore *m*	liquidador *m*
Abwicklung (D)	—	settlement	exécution *f*	esecuzione *f*	ejecución *f*
Abwicklungskonto (D)	—	settlement account	compte de liquidation *m*	conto di liquidazione *f*	cuenta de liquidación *f*
abzahlen (D)	—	pay off	régler par compte	pagare a rate	pagar por cuotas

	D	E	F	I	Es
Abzahlung (D)	—	repayment	remboursement *m*	rimborso *m*	reintegro *m*/ pago a plazos *m*
Abzahlungs-geschäft (D)	—	hire purchase transaction	achat à tempérament *m*	operazione con pagamento a rate *f*	venta a plazos *f*
Abzinsung (D)	—	discounting	déduction des intérêts non courus *f*	deduzione di interessi *f*	deducción de intereses no acumulados *f*
Abzug (D)	—	deduction/discount	diminution *f*/ escompte *m*	detrazione *f*/ sconto *m*	deducción *f*/ descuento *m*
academia (Es)	Akademie *f*	academy	académie *f*	accademia *f*	—
académie (F)	Akademie *f*	academy	—	accademia *f*	academia *f*
academy (E)	Akademie *f*	—	académie *f*	accademia *f*	academia *f*
a cargo de (Es)	zu Lasten	chargeable to	à la charge de	a carico di	—
a carico di (I)	zu Lasten	chargeable to	à la charge de	—	a cargo de
accademia (I)	Akademie *f*	academy	académie *f*	—	academia *f*
accantonamento (I)	Rückstellung *f*	reserves	provision pour pertes et charges *f*	—	reserva *f*
accaparramento (I)	Abwerbung *f*	pirating	débauchage *m*	—	sonsacamiento *m*
acceleration principle (E)	Akzelerations-prinzip *n*	—	principe d'accélération *m*	principio di accelerazione *m*	principio de aceleración *m*
accelerato (I)	beschleunigt	speedy	accéléré	—	acelerado
accéléré (F)	beschleunigt	speedy	—	accelerato	acelerado
accensione di un mutuo (I)	Geldaufnahme *f*	raising of money	emprunt *m*	—	dinero tomado a préstamo *m*
acceptable (E)	akzeptabel	—	acceptable	accettabile	aceptable
acceptable (F)	akzeptabel	acceptable	—	accettabile	aceptable
acceptable risk (E)	Restrisiko *n*	—	risque acceptable *m*	rischio rimanente *m*	riesgo aceptable *m*
acceptance[1] (E)	Annahme *f*	—	acceptation *f*	accettazione *f*	aceptación *f*
acceptance[2] (E)	Abnahme *f*	—	réception *f*	accettazione *f*	aceptación *f*/ disminución *f*
acceptance credit[1] (E)	Wechselkredit *m*	—	crédit d'escompte *m*	credito cambiario *m*	crédito cambiario *m*
acceptance credit[2] (E)	Akzeptkredit *m*	—	crédit par traites acceptées *m*	credito d'accettazione *m*	crédito de aceptación *m*
acceptation (F)	Annahme *f*	acceptance	—	accettazione *f*	aceptación *f*
acceptation de prendre le risque en charge (F)	Deckungszusage *f*	confirmation of cover	—	impegno di copertura *m*	nota de cobertura *f*
accepted bill (E)	Akzept *n*	—	traite acceptée *f*	accettazione *f*	aceptación *f*
accertamento tributario (I)	Steuerveranlagung *f*	tax assessment	taxation fiscale *f*	—	tasación de los impuestos *f*
acceso (Es)	Zugang *m*	access	entrée *f*	accesso *m*	—
access (E)	Zugang *m*	—	entrée *f*	accesso *m*	acceso *m*
accesso (I)	Zugang *m*	access	entrée *f*	—	acceso *m*
accesso al mercato (I)	Marktzutritt *m*	access to the market	accès au marché *m*	—	acceso al mercado *m*
accettabile (I)	akzeptabel	acceptable	acceptable	—	aceptable
accettazione[1] (I)	Akzept *n*	accepted bill	traite acceptée *f*	—	aceptación *f*
accettazione[2] (I)	Annahme *f*	acceptance	acceptation *f*	—	aceptación *f*
accettazione[3] (I)	Abnahme *f*	acceptance	réception *f*	—	aceptación *f*
accident du travail (F)	Arbeitsunfall *m*	industrial injury	—	infortunio sul posto di lavoro *m*	accidente profesional *m*
accidente profesional (Es)	Arbeitsunfall *m*	industrial injury	accident du travail *m*	infortunio sul posto di lavoro *m*	—
acción (Es)	Aktie *f*	share	action *f*	azione *f*	—
acción al portador (Es)	Inhaberaktie *f*	bearer share	action au porteur *f*	azione al portatore *f*	—
acción de impugnación (Es)	Anfechtungsklage *f*	action for avoidance	action en annulation *f*	azione di impugnazione *f*	—
acciones[1] (Es)	Aktien *pl*	shares	actions *f pl*	azioni *f*	—
acciones[2] (Es)	Aktionen *pl*	actions	actions *f pl*	azioni *f pl*	—
acción especial (Es)	Sonderaktion *f*	special action	action spéciale *f*	azione speciale *f*	—
accionista (Es)	Aktionär *m*	shareholder	actionnaire *m*	azionista *m*	—
acción nominal (Es)	Namensaktie *f*	registered share	action nominative *f*	azione nominativa *f*	—

	D	E	F	I	Es
acción ordinaria (Es)	Stammaktie *f*	ordinary share	action ordinaire *f*	azione ordinaria *f*	—
acción preferente (Es)	Vorzugsaktie *f*	preference share	action privilégiée *f*	azione privilegiata *f*	—
accollamento (I)	Überwälzung *f*	passing on	répercussion *f*	—	traslación *f*
accommodating (E)	kulant	—	arrangement	corrente	de fácil avenencia
accommodation (E)	Kulanz *f*	—	souplesse en affaires *f*	correntezza *f*	facilidad en los negocios *f*
accompanying documents (E)	Begleitpapiere *pl*	—	pièces accompagnant l'envoi *f pl*	bolle di accompagnamento *f pl*	documentos adjuntos *m pl*
accoppiamento a reazione (I)	Rückkopplung *f*	feedback	accouplement réactif *m*	—	reacoplamiento *m*
accord[1] (F)	Abkommen *n*	agreement	—	accordo *m*	acuerdo *m*
accord[2] (F)	Zustimmung *f*	consent	—	consenso *m*	consentimiento *m*
accord de compensation de devises (F)	Devisenausgleichsabkommen *n*	foreign exchange offset agreement	—	accordo di clearing valutario *m*	acuerdo de compensación de divisas *m*
accord de contrôle (F)	Beherrschungsvertrag *m*	control agreement	—	contratto di controllo *m*	contrato de dominación *m*
accord de payement (F)	Zahlungsabkommen *n*	payments arrangement	—	accordo di pagamento *m*	acuerdo de pagos *m*
accord de salaires (F)	Lohnvereinbarung *f*	wage agreement	—	accordo salariale *m*	pacto salarial *m*
accord douanier (F)	Zollabkommen *n*	customs convention	—	accordo sulle tariffe doganali *m*	convenio aduanero *m*
accord monétaire (F)	Währungsabkommen *n*	currency agreement	—	accordo monetario *m*	acuerdo monetario *m*
accordo (I)	Abkommen *n*	agreement	accord *m*	—	acuerdo *m*
accordo di clearing valutario (I)	Devisenausgleichsabkommen *n*	foreign exchange offset agreement	accord de compensation de devises *m*	—	acuerdo de compensación de divisas *m*
accordo di pagamento (I)	Zahlungsabkommen *n*	payments arrangement	accord de payement *m*	—	acuerdo de pagos *m*
accordo monetario (I)	Währungsabkommen *n*	currency agreement	accord monétaire *m*	—	acuerdo monetario *m*
accordo salariale (I)	Lohnvereinbarung *f*	wage agreement	accord de salaires *m*	—	pacto salarial *m*
accordo speciale (I)	Sondervereinbarung *f*	special agreement	accord particulier *m*	—	acuerdo especial *m*
accordo sui prezzi (I)	Preisabsprache *f*	price fixing	accord sur les prix *m*	—	acuerdo de precios *m*
accordo sulle materie prime (I)	Rohstoffabkommen *n*	International Commodity Agreements	accord sur les matières premières *m*	—	acuerdo de materias primas *m*
accordo sulle tariffe doganali (I)	Zollabkommen *n*	customs convention	accord douanier *m*	—	convenio aduanero *m*
accord particulier (F)	Sondervereinbarung *f*	special agreement	—	accordo speciale *m*	acuerdo especial *m*
accords généraux de crédit (F)	allgemeine Kreditvereinbarungen *pl*	general borrowing agreements	—	condizioni generali di credito *f pl*	acuerdos generales de crédito *m pl*
accord sur les matières premières (F)	Rohstoffabkommen *n*	International Commodity Agreements	—	accordo sulle materie prime *m*	acuerdo de materias primas *m*
accord sur les prix (F)	Preisabsprache *f*	price fixing	—	accordo sui prezzi *m*	acuerdo de precios *m*
account (E)	Konto *n*	—	compte *m*	conto *m*	cuenta *f*
account book (E)	Kontobuch *n*	—	livre de compte *m*	libro dei conti *m*	libro de cuentas *m*
account books (E)	Geschäftsbücher *pl*	—	livres de commerce *m pl*	libri contabili *m pl*	libros de contabilidad *m pl*
account holder (E)	Kontoinhaber *m*	—	titulaire d'un compte *m*	titolare del conto *m*	titular de una cuenta *m*
accounting (E)	Buchhaltung *f*	—	comptabilité *f*	contabilità *f*	contabilidad *f*
accounting period (E)	Abrechnungszeitraum *m*	—	période comptable *f*	periodo di liquidazione *m*	período contable *m*
accounting system (E)	Rechnungswesen *n*	—	comptabilité *f*	ragioneria *f*	contabilidad *f*
account number (E)	Kontonummer *f*	—	numéro de compte *m*	numero di conto *m*	número de cuenta *m*
accouplement réactif (F)	Rückkopplung *f*	feedback	—	accoppiamento a reazione *m*	reacoplamiento *m*
accredit (E)	akkreditieren	—	accréditer	accreditare	acreditar
accreditare[1] (I)	akkreditieren	accredit	accréditer	—	acreditar
accreditare[2] (I)	gutschreiben	credit	créditer	—	abonar en cuenta
accréditer (F)	akkreditieren	accredit	—	accreditare	acreditar

	D	E	F	I	Es
accréditif (F)	Akkreditiv *n*	letter of credit	—	credito documentario *m*	crédito documentario *m*
accréditif bancaire (F)	Bankakkreditiv *n*	bank letter of credit	—	lettera di credito *f*	carta de crédito bancaria *f*
accréditif irrévocable (F)	unwiderrufliches Akkreditiv *n*	irrevocable letter of credit	—	apertura di credito *f* documentario irrevocabile	crédito documentario irrevocable *m*
accréditif payable en espèce (F)	Barakkreditiv	cash letter of credit	—	apertura di credito documentario semplice *f*	crédito simple *m*
accredito (I)	Gutschrift *f*	credit	crédit *m*	—	abono *m*
accreedor (Es)	Gläubiger *m*	creditor	créancier *m*	creditore *m*	—
accroissement constant (F)	lineares Wachstum *n*	linear growth	—	crescita lineare *f*	crecimiento lineal *m*
accroissement de la population (F)	Bevölkerungswachstum *m*	increase in population	—	incremento demografico *m*	crecimiento demográfico *m*
accroissement de valeur (F)	Wertzuwachs *m*	appreciation	—	incremento di valore *m*	plusvalía *f*
accumulation (E)	Akkumulation *f*	—	accumulation *f*	accumulazione *f*	acumulación *f*
accumulation (F)	Akkumulation *f*	accumulation	—	accumulazione *f*	acumulación *f*
accumulazione (I)	Akkumulation *f*	accumulation	accumulation *f*	—	acumulación *f*
accusé de réception (F)	Empfangsbestätigung *f*	acknowledgement of receipt	—	ricevuta *f*	recibo *m*
aceite usado (Es)	Altöl *n*	waste oil	huile usée *m*	olio usato *m*	—
acelerado (Es)	beschleunigt	speedy	accéléré	accelerato	—
aceptable (Es)	akzeptabel	acceptable	acceptable	accettabile	—
aceptación[1] (Es)	Akzept *n*	accepted bill	traite acceptée *f*	accettazione *f*	—
aceptación[2] (Es)	Annahme *f*	acceptance	acceptation *f*	accettazione *f*	—
aceptación[3] (Es)	Abnahme *f*	acceptance	réception *f*	accettazione *f*	—
achat[1] (F)	Kauf *m*	purchase	—	acquisto *m*	compra *f*
achat[2] (F)	Einkauf *m*	purchase	—	acquisto *m*	compra *f*
achat à crédit[1] (F)	Kreditgeschäft *n*	credit business	—	operazione di credito *f*	operaciones de crédito *f pl*
achat à crédit[2] (F)	Kreditkauf *m*	credit purchase	—	acquisto a credito *m*	compra de crédito *f*
achat à l'éssai (F)	Kauf auf Probe *m*	sale on approval	—	acquisto a titolo di prova *m*	compra a prueba *f*
achat à tempérament[1] (F)	Teilzahlungsgeschäft *n*	partial payment transaction	—	vendita a rate *f*	operación a plazo *f*
achat à tempérament[2] (F)	Ratenkauf *m*	hire-purchase transaction	—	acquisto a rate *m*	compra a plazo *f*
achat à tempérament[3] (F)	Abzahlungsgeschäft *n*	hire purchase transaction	—	operazione con pagamento a rate *f*	venta a plazos *f*
achat à terme (F)	Zielkauf *m*	purchase on credit	—	acquisto a termine *m*	compra a plazos *m*
achat de remplacement (F)	Ersatzkauf *m*	substitute purchase	—	acquisto di compensazione *m*	compra de sustitución *f*
achat de soutien (F)	Stützungskauf *m*	support buying	—	acquisto di sostegno *m*	compra para sostener precios *f*
achat d'impulsion (F)	Impulskauf *m*	impulse buying	—	acquisto impulsivo *m*	compra espontánea *f*
achat d'une quantité minimum (F)	Mindestabnahme *f*	minimum purchase	—	quantitativo minimo di fornitura *m*	recogida mínima *f*
achat intermédiaire (F)	Zwischenabnahme *f*	intermediate purchase	—	acquisto intermediario *m*	compra intermediaria *f*
achats d'intervention (F)	Interventionskäufe *pl*	intervention buying	—	acquisti d'intervento *m pl*	compras de intervención *f pl*
achats spéculatifs (F)	Meinungskäufe *pl*	speculative buying	—	acquisti speculativi *m pl*	compras especulativas *f pl*
acheter (F)	kaufen	buy	—	acquistare	comprar
acheteur[1] (F)	Abnehmer *m*	buyer/purchaser/ customer	—	acquirente *m*/ cliente *m*	tomador *m*
acheteur[2] (F)	Einkäufer *m*	buyer	—	acquirente *m*	comprador *m*
acheteur[3] (F)	Besteller *m*	customer	—	committente *m*	demandante *m*
acheteur[4] (F)	Käufer *m*	purchaser	—	acquirente *m*	adquirente *m*

	D	E	F	I	Es
acheteur en gros (F)	Großabnehmer *m*	bulk buyer	—	acquirente all'ingrosso *m*	comprador al por mayor *m*
achèvement (F)	Fertigstellung *f*	completion	—	completamento *m*	terminación total *f*
Ackerbau (D)	—	agriculture	agriculture *f*	agricoltura *f*	agricultura *f*
acknowledgement of a debt (E)	Schuldanerkennung *f*	—	reconnaissance de dette *f*	riconoscimento del debito *m*	reconocimiento de la deuda *m*
acknowledgement of receipt (E)	Empfangs-bestätigung *f*	—	accusé de réception *m*	ricevuta *f*	recibo *m*
a comisión (Es)	auf Provisionsbasis	on a commission basis	à la commission	a provvigione	—
acompte[1] (F)	Rate *f*	instalment/rate	—	rata *f*	plazo *m*
acompte[2] (F)	Anzahlung *f*	deposit	—	pagamento in acconto *m*	pago a cuenta *m*
acompte provisionnel sur l'imposition (F)	Steuer-vorauszahlung *f*	advanced payment of taxes	—	pagamento anticipato delle imposte *m*	impuestos adelantados *m pl*
a-conto-Zahlung (D)	—	payment on account	payement acompte *m*	pagamento a conto *m*	pago a cuenta *m*
à convenance (F)	auf Abruf	on call	—	su richiesta	a requerimiento
a corto plazo (Es)	kurzfristig	short-term	à court terme	a breve scadenza	—
à court terme (F)	kurzfristig	short-term	—	a breve scadenza	a corto plazo
acque di scarico (I)	Abwasser *n*	waste water	eaux résiduelles *f pl*	—	aguas residuales *f pl*
acque territoriali (I)	Küstengewässer *n*	coastal waters	eaux côtières *f pl*	—	zona costera *f*
acquirente[1] (I)	Einkäufer *m*	buyer	acheteur *m*	—	comprador *m*
acquirente[2] (I)	Abnehmer *m*	buyer/purchaser/ customer	acheteur *m*	—	tomador *m*
acquirente[3] (I)	Käufer *m*	purchaser	acheteur *m*	—	adquirente *m*
acquirente all'ingrosso (I)	Großabnehmer *m*	bulk buyer	acheteur en gros *m*	—	comprador al por mayor *m*
acquirente finale (I)	Endabnehmer *m*	ultimate buyer	preneur final *m*	—	comprador final *m*
acquisition[1] (E)	Anschaffung *f*	—	acquisition *f*	acquisto *m*	adquisición *f*
acquisition[2] (E)	Aquisition *f*	—	acquisition *f*	acquisizione *f*	adquisición *f*
acquisition[1] (F)	Aquisition *f*	acquisition	—	acquisizione *f*	adquisición *f*
acquisition[2] (F)	Anschaffung *f*	acquisition	—	acquisto *m*	adquisición *f*
acquisition value (E)	Anschaffungswert *m*	—	valeur d'acquisition *f*	valore d'acquisto *m*	valor de adquisición *m*
acquisizione (I)	Aquisition *f*	acquisition	acquisition *f*	—	adquisición *f*
acquistare (I)	einkaufen	buy	acheter	—	comprar
acquistare (I)	kaufen	buy	acheter	—	comprar
acquisti d'intervento (I)	Interventionskäufe *pl*	intervention buying	achats d'intervention *m pl*	—	compras de intervención *f pl*
acquisti speculativi (I)	Meinungskäufe *pl*	speculative buying	achats spéculatifs *m pl*	—	compras especulativas *f pl*
acquisto[1] (I)	Einkauf *m*	purchase	achat *m*	—	compra *f*
acquisto[2] (I)	Anschaffung *f*	acquisition	acquisition *f*	—	adquisición *f*
acquisto[3] (I)	Kauf *m*	purchase	achat *m*	—	compra *f*
acquisto a credito (I)	Kreditkauf *m*	credit purchase	achat à crédit *m*	—	compra de crédito *f*
acquisto a rate (I)	Ratenkauf *m*	hire-purchase transaction	achat à tempérament *m*	—	compra a plazo *f*
acquisto a termine (I)	Zielkauf *m*	purchase on credit	achat à terme *m*	—	compra a plazos *m*
acquisto a titolo di prova (I)	Kauf auf Probe *m*	sale on approval	achat à l'éssai *m*	—	compra a prueba *f*
acquisto di compensazione (I)	Ersatzkauf *m*	substitute purchase	achat de remplacement *m*	—	compra de sustitución *f*
acquisto di sostegno (I)	Stützungskauf *m*	support buying	achat de soutien *m*	—	compra para sostener precios *f*
acquisto di un'azienda (I)	Geschäfts-übernahme *f*	business acquisition	reprise d'une affaire *f*	—	adquisición de una empresa *f*
acquisto impulsivo (I)	Impulskauf *m*	impulse buying	achat d'impulsion *m*	—	compra espontánea *f*
acquisto intermediario (I)	Zwischenabnahme *f*	intermediate purchase	achat intermédiaire *m*	—	compra intermediaria *f*
acquit d'entrée (F)	Zolleinfuhrschein *m*	bill of entry	—	bolletta d'entrata *f*	certificado de aduana *m*

	D	E	F	I	Es
acquit de transit (F)	Durchgangsschein *m*	transit certificate	—	bolletta di transito *f*	pasavante *m*
acquittement (F)	Erfüllung *f*	compliance	—	adempimento *m*	cumplimiento *m*
acreditar (Es)	akkreditieren	accredit	acccréditer	accreditare	—
acreedor (Es)	Kreditor *pl*	creditor	créditeur *m*	creditore *m*	—
acreedor de la quiebra (Es)	Konkursgläubiger *m*	bankrupt's creditor	créancier de la faillite *m*	creditore della massa fallimentare *m*	—
acte administratif (F)	Verwaltungsakt *m*	administrative act	—	atto amministrativo *m*	acto administrativo *m*
acte de société (F)	Gesellschafts-vertrag *m*	shareholder's agreement	—	contratto di società *m*	contrato social *m*
acte juridique (F)	Rechtsgeschäft *n*	legal transaction	—	negozio giuridico *m*	negocio jurídico *m*
actif[1] (F)	erwerbstätig	gainfully employed	—	attivo	activo
actif[2] (F)	Aktivbestand *m*	assets	—	effetivo *m*	activo disponible *m*
action (F)	Aktie *f*	share	—	azione *f*	acción *f*
action au porteur (F)	Inhaberaktie *f*	bearer share	—	azione al portatore *f*	acción al portador *f*
action de presse (F)	Presseaktion *f*	press campaign	—	azione stampa *f*	campaña de prensa *f*
action en annulation (F)	Anfechtungsklage *f*	action for avoidance	—	azione di impugnazione *f*	acción de impugnación *f*
action en dommages-intérêts (F)	Schadens-ersatzklage *f*	action for damages	—	azione di risarcimen-to danni *f*	demanda de daños y perjuicios *f*
action en justice (F)	Klage *f*	legal action	—	citazione in giudizio *f*	demanda *f*
action for avoidance (E)	Anfechtungsklage *f*	—	action en annulation *f*	azione di impugnazione *f*	acción de impugnación *f*
action for damages (E)	Schadens-ersatzklage *f*	—	action en dommages-intérêts *f*	azione di risarcimen-to danni *f*	demanda de daños y perjuicios *f*
actionnaire (F)	Aktionär *m*	shareholder	—	azionista *m*	accionista *m*
action nominative (F)	Namensaktie *f*	registered shares	—	azione nominativa *f*	acción nominal *f*
action ordinaire (F)	Stammaktie *f*	ordinary shares	—	azione ordinaria *f*	acción ordinaria *f*
action parameter (E)	Aktionsparameter *m*	—	paramètre d'action *m*	parametro d'azione *m*	parámetro de acción *m*
action privilégiée (F)	Vorzugsaktie *f*	preference share	—	azione privilegiata *f*	acción preferente *f*
actions (E)	Aktionen *pl*	—	actions *f pl*	azioni *f pl*	acciones *f pl*
actions[1] (F)	Aktien *pl*	shares	—	azioni *f pl*	acciones *f pl*
actions[2] (F)	Aktionen *pl*	actions	—	azioni *f pl*	acciones *f pl*
action spéciale (F)	Sonderaktion *f*	special action	—	azione speciale *f*	acción especial *f*
action successorale (F)	Erbstreit *m*	dispute concerning an inheritance	—	causa ereditaria *f*	litigio hereditario *m*
active balance (E)	Aktivsaldo *m*	—	solde créditeur *m*	saldo attivo *m*	saldo activo *m*
active partner (E)	aktiver Teilhaber *m*	—	associé prenant part à la gestion *m*	socio attivo *m*	socio activo *m*
actividad del Estado (Es)	Staatstätigkeit *f*	state activity	activité de l'Etat *f*	attività pubblica *f*	—
activité de l'Etat (F)	Staatstätigkeit *f*	state activity	—	attività pubblica *f*	actividad del Estado *f*
activité professionnelle (F)	Gewerbe *n*	trade/industry/craft	—	commercio *m*/indu-stria *f*/artigianato *m*	industria *f*/comer-cio *m*/artesanía *f*
activity rate (E)	Erwerbsquote *f*	—	proportion de la population active *f*	quota della popolazione attiva *f*	proporción de la población activa *f*
activo[1] (Es)	Aktiva *pl*	assets	masse active *f*	attivo *m*	—
activo[2] (Es)	erwerbstätig	gainfully employed	actif	attivo	—
activo disponible (Es)	Aktivbestand *m*	assets	actif *m*	effettivo *m*	—
activo efectivo (Es)	Barvermögen *n*	cash assets	valeurs réalisables à court terme ou disponibles *f pl*	patrimonio in contanti *m*	—
activo exterior (Es)	Auslandsvermögen *n*	foreign assets	avoirs à l'étranger *m pl*	patrimonio estero *m*	—
activo fijo (Es)	Anlagevermögen *n*	fixed assets	valeurs immobilisées *f pl*	attivo fisso *m*	—
activo inmobiliario (Es)	Realvermögen *n*	real wealth	patrimoine réel *m*	patrimonio reale *m*	—
activo monetario (Es)	Geldvermögen *n*	financial assets	moyens financiers *m pl*	patrimonio monetario *m*	—
acto administrativo (Es)	Verwaltungsakt *m*	administrative act	acte administratif *m*	atto amministrativo *m*	—
actual costs (E)	Istkosten *pl*	—	coûts réels *m pl*	costi effettivi *m pl*	gastos efectivos *m pl*

	D	E	F	I	Es
actual figures (E)	Istzahlen *pl*	—	résultats effectifs *m pl*	dati effettivi *m pl*	cifras efectivas *f pl*
actual wage (E)	Effektivlohn *m*	—	salaire effectif *m*	salario effettivo *m*	salario efectivo *m*
acuerdo (Es)	Abkommen *n*	agreement	accord *m*	accordo *m*	—
acuerdo de apertura (Es)	Eröffnungs-beschluß *m*	order opening a trial	arrêt de mise en accusation *m*	decreto di citazione in giudizio *m*	—
acuerdo de compensación de divisas (Es)	Devisenausgleichs-abkommen *n*	foreign exchange offset agreement	accord de compensation de devises *m*	accordo di clearing valutario *m*	—
acuerdo de materias primas (Es)	Rohstoffabkommen *n*	International Commodity Agreements	accord sur les matières premières *m*	accordo sulle materie prime *m*	—
acuerdo de pagos (Es)	Zahlungs-abkommen *n*	payments arrangement	accord de payement *m*	accordo di pagamento *m*	—
acuerdo de precios (Es)	Preisabsprache *f*	price fixing	accord sur les prix *m*	accordo sui prezzi *m*	—
acuerdo especial (Es)	Sondervereinbarung *f*	special agreement	accord particulier *m*	accordo speciale *m*	—
acuerdo monetario (Es)	Währungs-abkommen *n*	currency agreement	accord monétaire *m*	accordo monetario *m*	—
acuerdos generales de crédito (Es)	allgemeine Kreditver-einbarungen *pl*	general borrowing agreements	accords généraux de crédit *f pl*	condizioni generali di credito *f pl*	—
acumulación (Es)	Akkumulation *f*	accumulation	accumulation *f*	accumulazione *f*	—
acuse de recibo (Es)	Rückschein *m*	advice of delivery	avis de réception *m*	ricevuta di ritorno *f*	—
ad alta incidenza di capitale (I)	kapitalintensiv	capital-intensive	avec grande intensité de capital	—	con gran intensidad de capital
ad alta incidenza di lavoro (I)	arbeitsintensiv	labour-intensive	déterminé par le facteur main-d'œuvre	—	con gran intensidad de mano de obra
ad alta incidenza salariale (I)	lohnintensiv	wage-intensive	déterminé par le facteur salaire	—	con gran intensidad de costos salariales
adaptación (Es)	Anpassung *f*	adaptation	adaptation *f*	adattamento *m*/ adeguamento *m*	—
adaptation (E)	Anpassung *f*	—	adaptation *f*	adattamento *m*/ adeguamento *m*	adaptación *f*/ajuste *m*
adaptation (F)	Anpassung *f*	adaptation	—	adattamento *m*/ adeguamento *m*	adaptación *f*/ajuste *m*
adattamento (I)	Anpassung *f*	adaptation	adaptation *f*	—	adaptación *f*/ajuste *m*
add (E)	addieren	—	additionner	addizionare	sumar
addebitare (I)	belasten	load/charge	débiter	—	cargar/adeudar
addebito[1] (I)	Belastung *f*	load	charge *f*	—	gravamen *m*
addebito[2] (I)	Lastschrift *f*	debit note	note de débit *f*	—	cargo en cuenta *m*
addestramento dei venditori (I)	Verkäuferschulung *f*	sales training	formation des vendeurs *f*	—	formación de los vendedores *f*
addieren (D)	—	add	additionner	addizionare	sumar
adding mistake (E)	Additionsfehler *m*	—	erreur d'addition *f*	errore di addizione *m*	error de adición *m*
Addition (D)	—	addition	addition *f*	addizione *f*	adición *f*
addition (E)	Addition *f*	—	addition *f*	addizione *f*	adición *f*
addition (F)	Addition *f*	addition	—	addizione *f*	adición *f*
additional burden (E)	Mehrbelastung *f*	—	surcharge *f*	onere supplementare *m*	carga suplementaria *f*
additional delivery (E)	Mehrlieferung *f*	—	livraison supplémentaire *f*	fornitura supplementare *f*	exceso *m*
additional freight charges (E)	Frachtzuschlag *m*	—	supplément de fret *m*	supplemento di nolo *m*	sobreporte *m*
additional payment of taxes (E)	Steuernachzahlung *f*	—	payement d'un rappel d'impôt *m*	pagamento arretrato delle imposte *m*	pago de impuestos atrasados *m*
additional period (E)	Nachfrist *f*	—	prolongation *f*	termine supplementare *m*	plazo de gracia *m*
additional sale (E)	Zusatzverkauf *m*	—	vente additionnelle *f*	vendita complementare *f*	venta adicional *f*
additional work (E)	Mehrarbeit *f*	—	travail supplémentaire *m*	lavoro supplementare *m*	trabajo extraordinario *m*
additionner (F)	addieren	add	—	addizionare	sumar
Additionsfehler (D)	—	adding mistake	erreur d'addition *f*	errore di addizione *m*	error de adición *m*
addizionare (I)	addieren	add	additionner	—	sumar

	D	E	F	I	Es
addizione (I)	Addition *f*	addition	addition *f*	—	adición *f*
address[1] (E)	Anschrift *f*	—	adresse *f*	indirizzo *m*	dirección *f*
address[2] (E)	adressieren	—	adresser	indirizzare	dirigir
address[3] (E)	Adresse *f*	—	adresse *f*	indirizzo *m*	dirección *f*
addressee (E)	Adressat *m*	—	destinataire *m*	destinatario *m*	destinatario *m*
adelanto (Es)	Vorauszahlung *f*	payment in advance	payement anticipé *m*	pagamento anticipato *m*	—
adempimento (I)	Erfüllung *f*	compliance	acquittement *m*	—	cumplimiento *m*
adición (Es)	Addition *f*	addition	addition *f*	addizione *f*	—
adjoint (F)	Stellvertreter *m*	deputy	—	sostituto *m*	sustituto *m*
adjudicated bankrupt (E)	Gemeinschuldner *m*	—	failli *m*	debitore fallito *m*	deudor común *m*
adjustment costs (E)	Anpassungskosten *pl*	—	coûts d'adaptation *m pl*	costi d'adattamento *m pl*	gastos de readaptación *m pl*
adjustment lag (E)	Anpassungs-verzögerung *f*	—	retard d'adaptation *m*	ritardo d'adattamento *m*	retraso de adaptación *m*
administered prices (E)	administrierte Preise *pl*	—	prix administrés *m pl*	prezzi amministrati *m pl*	precios administrados *m pl*
administración (Es)	Verwaltung *f*	administration	administration *f*	amministrazione *f*	—
administración de almacén (Es)	Lagerverwaltung *f*	stockkeeping	entreposage *m*	amministrazione del magazzino *f*	—
administración de hacienda (Es)	Steuerbehörden *pl*	tax authority	administration des contributions *f*	autorità fiscali *f pl*	—
administración del proyecto (Es)	Projekt-Management *n*	project management	gestion d'un projet *f*	management di progetto *m*	—
administración de una cuenta (Es)	Kontoführung *f*	keeping of an account	tenue de compte *f*	tenuta di un conto *f*	—
administración forzosa (Es)	Zwangsverwaltung *f*	receivership	séquestre judiciare *m*	amministrazione giudiziaria *f*	—
administrador (Es)	Verwalter *m*	administrator	administrateur *m*	amministratore *m*	—
administrador de la herencia (Es)	Nachlaßverwalter *m*	administrator of the deceased's estate	administrateur de la succession *m*	amministratore dell'eredità *m*	—
administrateur (F)	Verwalter *m*	administrator	—	amministratore *m*	administrador *m*
administrateur de la succession (F)	Nachlaßverwalter *m*	administrator of the deceased's estate	—	amministratore dell'eredità *m*	administrador de la herencia *m*
Administration (D)	—	administration	administration *f*	amministrazione *f*	administración *f*
administration (E)	Verwaltung *f*	—	administration *f*	amministrazione *f*	administración *f*
administration (F)	Verwaltung *f*	administration	—	amministrazione *f*	administración *f*
administration des contributions (F)	Steuerbehörden *pl*	tax authority	—	autorità fiscali *f pl*	administración de hacienda *f*
administration fee (E)	Bußgeld *n*	—	amende *f*	pena pecuniaria *f*	multa *f*
administration of justice (E)	Rechtsprechung *f*	—	jurisprudence *f*	giurisprudenza *f*	jurisprudencia *f*
administration of prices (E)	Preislenkung *f*	—	réglementation des prix *f*	gestione dei prezzi *f*	reglamentación de precios *f*
administrative act (E)	Verwaltungsakt *m*	—	acte administratif *m*	atto amministrativo *m*	acto administrativo *m*
administrator (E)	Verwalter *m*	—	administrateur *m*	amministratore *m*	administrador *m*
administrator in bankruptcy proceedings (E)	Konkursverwalter *m*	—	liquidateur de la faillite *m*	curatore fallimentare *m*	síndico de quiebra *m*
administrator of the deceased's estate (E)	Nachlaßverwalter *m*	—	administrateur de la succession *m*	amministratore dell'eredità *m*	administrador de la herencia *m*
administrierte Preise (D)	—	administered prices	prix administrés *m pl*	prezzi amministrati *m pl*	precios administrados *m pl*
admisión (Es)	Zulassung *f*	admission	admission *f*	ammissione *f*	—
admission (E)	Zulassung *f*	—	admission *f*	ammissione *f*	admisión *f*
admission (F)	Zulassung *f*	admission	—	ammissione *f*	admisión *f*
admission ticket (E)	Eintrittskarte *f*	—	billet *m*	biglietto d'ingresso *m*	entrada *f*
(ad)monición (Es)	Mahnung *f*	demand for payment	mise en demeure *f*	sollecito *m*	—
adorno del escaparate (Es)	Schaufenster-dekoration *f*	window dressing	décoration de vitrine *f*	allestimento di vetrina *m*	—
adquirente (Es)	Käufer *m*	purchaser	acheteur *m*	acquirente *m*	—

	D	E	F	I	Es
adquisición[1] (Es)	Aquisition *f*	acquisition	acquisition *f*	acquisizione *f*	—
adquisición[2] (Es)	Anschaffung *f*	acquisition	acquisition *f*	acquisto *m*	—
adquisición de una empresa (Es)	Geschäfts-übernahme *f*	business acquisition	reprise d'une affaire *f*	acquisto di un'azienda *m*	—
Adressat (D)	—	addressee	destinataire *m*	destinatario *m*	destinatario *m*
Adresse (D)	—	address	adresse *f*	indirizzo *m*	dirección *f*
adresse[1] (F)	Anschrift *f*	address	—	indirizzo *m*	dirección *f*
adresse[2] (F)	Adresse *f*	address	—	indirizzo *m*	dirección *f*
adresse de la maison (F)	Firmenanschrift *f*	company address	—	indirizzo della ditta *m*	dirección de la empresa *f*
adresser (F)	adressieren	address	—	indirizzare	dirigir
adressieren (D)	—	address	adresser	indirizzare	dirigir
aduana (Es)	Zoll *m*	customs	douane *f*	dogana *f*	—
aduana aparte (Es)	unverzollt	duty unpaid	non dédouané	non sdoganato	—
aduana proteccionista (Es)	Schutzzoll *m*	protective duty	droit de protection *m*	dazio protettivo *m*	—
aduanas ad valorem (Es)	Wertzoll *m*	ad valorem duty	taxe de douane ad valorem *f*	dazio ad valorem *m*	—
aduanas preferenciales (Es)	Präferenzzoll *m*	preferential duty	taxe préférentielle de douane *f*	dazio preferenziale *m*	—
aduanas uniformes (Es)	Einheitszoll *m*	uniform duty	droit unique *m*	dazio unitario *m*	—
ad valorem duty (E)	Wertzoll *m*	—	taxe de douane ad valorem *f*	dazio ad valorem *m*	aduanas ad valorem *f pl*
advance (E)	Vorschuß *m*	—	avance *f*	anticipo *m*	anticipo *m*
advanced payment of taxes (E)	Steuer-vorauszahlung *f*	—	acompte provisionnel sur l'imposition *m*	pagamento anticipato delle imposte *m*	impuestos adelantados *m pl*
advantage (E)	Vorteil *m*	—	avantage *m*	vantaggio *m*	ventaja *f*
advertisement[1] (E)	Anzeige *f*	—	annonce *f*	inserzione *f*	anuncio *m*
advertisement[2] (E)	Zeitungsanzeige *f*	—	annonce de journal *f*	inserzione sul giornale *f*	anuncio de prensa *m*
advertisement of a vacancy (E)	Stellen-ausschreibung *f*	—	mise au concours d'une place *f*	bando di concorso per impiegati *m*	convocatoria de oposiciones *f*
advertisement under a box number (E)	Chiffre-Anzeige *f*	—	annonce chiffrée *f*	inserzione in cifra *f*	anuncio codificado *m*
advertising (E)	Reklame *f*	—	publicité *f*	réclame *f*	publicidad *f*
advertising activity (E)	Werbeaktion *f*	—	campagne publicitaire *f*	azione pubblicitaria *f*	campaña publicitaria *f*
advertising agency (E)	Werbeagentur *f*	—	agence de publicité *f*	agenzia pubblicitaria *f*	agencia publicitaria *f*
advertising aids (E)	Werbemittel *n*	—	moyen publicitaire *m*	mezzo pubblicitario *m*	medio publicitario *m*
advertising bill (E)	Aktionsplakat *n*	—	affiche d'action *f*	manifesto promozionale *m*	cartel de acción *m*
advertising budget (E)	Werbebudget *n*	—	budget de publicité *m*	budget pubblicitario *m*	presupuesto publicitario *m*
advertising campaign (E)	Werbekampagne *f*	—	campagne publicitaire *f*	campagna pubblicitaria *f*	campaña publicitaria *f*
advertising control (E)	Werbeerfolgs-kontrolle *f*	—	contrôle du résultat de la publicité *m*	controllo del succes-so pubblicitario *m*	análisis del resultado publicitario *m*
advertising copy (E)	Werbetext *m*	—	texte publicitaire *m*	testo pubblicitario *m*	texto publicitario *m*
advertising expert (E)	Werbefachmann *m*	—	technicien publicitaire *m*	esperto di pubblicità *m*	perito publicitario *m*
advertising film (E)	Werbefilm *m*	—	film publicitaire *m*	film pubblicitario *m*	película promocional *f*
advertising frequency (E)	Werbefrequenz *f*	—	fréquence publicitaire *f*	frequenza della pubblicità *f*	frecuencia publicitaria *f*
advertising gift (E)	Werbegeschenk *n*	—	cadeau publicitaire *m*	omaggio pubblicitario *m*	regalo publicitario *m*
advertising letter (E)	Werbebrief *m*	—	lettre publicitaire *f*	lettera pubblicitaria *f*	circular de publicidad *m*
advertising media (E)	Werbemedien *pl*	—	médias publicitaires *m pl*	mezzi pubblicitari *m pl*	medios de publicidad *m pl*
advertising medium (E)	Werbeträger *m*	—	support publicitaire *m*	veicolo pubblicitario *m*	medio de publicidad *m*

	D	E	F	I	Es
advertising objectives (E)	Werbeziele *pl*	—	objectifs publicitaires *m pl*	obiettivi pubblicitari *m pl*	objetivos de la publicidad *m pl*
advertising spot (E)	Werbespot *m*	—	spot publicitaire *m*	spot pubblicitario *m*	spot publicitario *m*
advice[1] (E)	Beratung *f*	—	consultation *f*	consulenza *f*	asoramiento *m*
advice[2] (E)	Avis *m*	—	avis *m*	avviso *m*	aviso *m*
advice of delivery (E)	Rückschein *m*	—	avis de réception *m*	ricevuta di ritorno *f*	acuse de recibo *m*
adviser (E)	Berater *m*	—	conseiller *m*	consulente *m*	asesor *m*
affaire (F)	Geschäft *n*	business	—	negozio *m*	negocio *m*
affaire au comptant (F)	Tagesgeschäft *n*	day-to-day operations	—	contratto a contanti *m*	operación al contado *f*
affaire couplée (F)	Kopplungsgeschäft *n*	tie-in transaction	—	operazione abbinata *f*	negocio acoplado *m*
affaire de compensation (F)	Kompensations-geschäft *n*	barter transaction	—	operazione di compensazione *f*	operacion de compensación *f*
affaire déficitaire (F)	Verlustgeschäft *n*	losing business	—	affare in perdita *m*	venta con pérdida *f*
affaire d'exportation (F)	Exportgeschäft *n*	export business	—	operazione d'esportazione *f*	operación de exportación *f*
affaire d'immobilière (F)	Immobiliengeschäft *n*	property transactions	—	operazione immobiliare *f*	negocio de inmuebles *m*
affaire en commission (F)	Kommissions-geschäft *n*	commission business	—	operazione di commissione *f*	operación de comisión *f*
affaire spéculative (F)	Spekulations-geschäft *n*	speculative operations	—	operazione speculativa *f*	operación de especulación *f*
affare con l'estero (I)	Auslandsgeschäft *n*	foreign business	opération avec l'étranger *f*	—	negocio de exporta-ción o importación *m*
affare in perdita (I)	Verlustgeschäft *n*	losing business	affaire déficitaire *f*	—	venta con pérdida *f*
affectation (F)	Zuwendung *f*	bestowal	—	assegnazione *f*	gratificación *f*
affermato (I)	behauptet	maintained	affirmé	—	sostenido
affichage des prix (F)	Preisauszeichnung *f*	pricemarking	—	indicazione del prezzo *f*	indicación de precios *f*
affiche (F)	Plakat *n*	poster	—	manifesto *m*	cartel *m*
affiche d'action (F)	Aktionsplakat *n*	advertising bill	—	manifesto promozionale *m*	cartel de acción *m*
affidabile (I)	zuverlässig	reliable	de confiance	—	de confianza
affiliated company (E)	Schwester-gesellschaft *f*	—	société affiliée *f*	consorella *f*	compañía asociada *f*
affirmé (F)	behauptet	maintained	—	affermato	sostenido
affluent society (E)	Wohlstands-gesellschaft *f*	—	société de bien-être *f*	società del benessere *f*	sociedad de bienestar *f*
affrancare (I)	frankieren	prepay the postage	affranchir	—	franquear
affranchir (F)	frankieren	prepay the postage	—	affrancare	franquear
affrètement (F)	Verfrachtung *f*	carriage of goods by sea	—	trasporto marittimo *m*	expedición *f*
after-sale service (E)	Kundendienst *m*	—	service après-vente *m*	servizio d'assistenza *m*	servicio posventa *m*
after treatment (E)	Nachbereitung *f*	—	remise en ordre *f*	rielaborazione *f*	tratamiento ulterior *m*
against cash (E)	gegen Barzahlung	—	au comptant	contro pagamento in contanti	al contado
against letter of credit (E)	gegen Akkreditiv	—	contre accréditif	contro lettera di credito	con crédito documentario
age group (E)	Altersgruppe *f*	—	groupe d'âge *m*	gruppo d'età *m*	grupo según la edad *m*
age limit (E)	Altersgrenze *f*	—	limite d'âge *f*	limite d'età *m*	limite de edad *m*
agence[1] (F)	Zweigstelle *f*	branch	—	agenzia *f*	filial *f*
agence[2] (F)	Agentur *f*	agency	—	agenzia *f*	agencia *f*
agence[3] (F)	Geschäftsstelle *f*	office	—	ufficio *m*	oficina *f*
agence[4] (F)	Filiale *f*	branch	—	filiale *f*	filial *f*
agence à l'étranger (F)	Auslandsvertretung *f*	agency abroad	—	rappresentanza estera *f*	representación en el exterior *f*
agence de publicité (F)	Werbeagentur *f*	advertising agency	—	agenzia pubblicitaria *f*	agencia publicitaria *f*
agence de renseignements (F)	Auskunftei *f*	information bureau	—	agenzia d'informazioni *f*	oficina de información *f*

	D	E	F	I	Es
agence de voyages (F)	Reisebüro *n*	travel agency	—	ufficio viaggi *m*	agencia de viajes *f*
agence exclusive (F)	Alleinvertretung *f*	sole agency	—	rappresentanza esclusiva *f*	representación exclusiva *f*
agencia (Es)	Agentur *f*	agency	agence *f*	agenzia *f*	—
agencia de viajes (Es)	Reisebüro *n*	travel agency	agence de voyages *f*	ufficio viaggi *m*	—
agencia laboral (Es)	Arbeitsvermittlung *f*	employment agency	bureau de placement *m*	ufficio di collocamento *m*	—
agencia publicitaria (Es)	Werbeagentur *f*	advertising agency	agence de publicité *f*	agenzia pubblicitaria *f*	—
agency (E)	Agentur *f*	—	agence *f*	agenzia *f*	agencia *f*
agency abroad (E)	Auslandsvertretung *f*	—	agence à l'étranger *f*	rappresentanza estera *f*	representación en el exterior *f*
Agent (D)	—	agent	agent *m*	agente *m*	agente *m*
agent (E)	Agent *m*	—	agent *m*	agente *m*	agente *m*
agent (F)	Agent *m*	agent	—	agente *m*	agente *m*
agent d'assurance (F)	Versicherungs-agent *m*	insurance agent	—	agente d'assicurazione *m*	agente de seguros *m*
agente (Es)	Agent *m*	agent	agent *m*	agente *m*	—
agente (I)	Agent *m*	agent	agent *m*	—	agente *m*
agente cambio y bolsa (Es)	Kursmakler *m*	stock broker	courtier en bourse *m*	agente di borsa *m*	—
agente d'assicurazione (I)	Versicherungs-agent *m*	insurance agent	agent d'assurance *m*	—	agente de seguros *m*
agente de inmuebles (Es)	Immobilienmakler *m*	estate agent	courtier en affaires immoblières *m*	agente immobiliare *m*	—
agente de seguros (Es)	Versicherungs-agent *m*	insurance agent	agent d'assurance *m*	agente d'assicurazione *m*	—
agente di borsa (I)	Kursmakler *m*	stock broker	courtier en bourse *m*	—	agente cambio y bolsa *m*
agente di cambio (I)	Börsenmakler *m*	stock broker	courtier en bourse *m*	—	corredor de bolsa *m*
agente di zona (I)	Gebietsvertreter *m*	area representative	représentant régional *m*	—	representante regional *m*
agente immobiliare (I)	Immobilienmakler *m*	estate agent	courtier en affaires immoblières *m*	—	agente de inmuebles *m*
agente marittimo (I)	Schiffsmakler *m*	shipbroker	courtier maritime *m*	—	corredor marítimo *m*
agente regional (Es)	Bezirksvertreter *m*	local agent	agent local *m*	rappresentante di zona *m*	—
agent exclusif (F)	Alleinvertreter *m*	sole agent	—	rappresentante esclusivo *m*	representante exclusivo *m*
agent général (F)	Generalvertreter *m*	general agent	—	rappresentante generale *m*	representante general *m*
agent local (F)	Bezirksvertreter *m*	local agent	—	rappresentante di zona *m*	agente regional *m*
Agentur (D)	—	agency	agence *f*	agenzia *f*	agencia *f*
agenzia[1] (I)	Zweigstelle *f*	branch	agence *f*	—	filial *f*
agenzia[2] (I)	Agentur *f*	agency	agence *f*	—	agencia *f*
agenzia d'informazioni (I)	Auskunftei *f*	information bureau	agence de renseignements *f*	—	oficina de información *f*
agenzia pubblicitaria (I)	Werbeagentur *f*	advertising agency	agence de publicité *f*	—	agencia publicitaria *f*
agevolazione sugli interessi (I)	Zinserleichterung *f*	reduction of interest	minoration de l'intérêt *m*	—	reducción de intereses *f*
aggio[1] (I)	Aufgeld *n*	agio	prime *f*	—	agio *m*
aggio[2] (I)	Agio *n*	agio	agio *m*	—	agio *m*
aggiunta[1] (I)	Zugabe *f*	extra	prime *f*	—	suplemento *m*
aggiunta[2] (I)	Aufschlag *m*	surcharge	hausse *f*	—	recargo *m*
Agglomeration (D)	—	agglomeration	agglomération *f*	agglomerazione *f*	aglomeración *f*
agglomeration (E)	Agglomeration *f*	—	agglomération *f*	agglomerazione *f*	aglomeración *f*
agglomération (F)	Agglomeration *f*	agglomeration	—	agglomerazione *f*	aglomeración *f*
agglomerazione (I)	Agglomeration *f*	agglomeration	agglomération *f*	—	aglomeración *f*
Agio (D)	—	agio	agio *m*	aggio *m*	agio *m*
agio (F)	Agio *n*	agio	—	aggio *m*	agio *m*

	D	E	F	I	Es
agio[1] (E)	Aufgeld *n*	—	prime *f*	aggio *m*	agio *m*
agio[2] (E)	Agio *n*	—	agio *m*	aggio *m*	agio *m*
agio[1] (Es)	Agio *n*	agio	agio *m*	aggio *m*	—
agio[2] (Es)	Aufgeld *n*	agio	prime *f*	aggio *m*	—
a giro di posta (I)	postwendend	by return of post	par retour du courrier	—	a vuelta de correo
aglomeración (Es)	Agglomeration *f*	agglomeration	agglomération *f*	agglomerazione *f*	—
Agrarbetrieb (D)	—	agricultural enterprise	entreprise agricole *f*	azienda agricola *f*	empresa agrícola *f*
Agrarerzeugnis (D)	—	agricultural product	produit agricole *m*	prodotto agricolo *m*	producto agrícola *m*
Agrarexport (D)	—	farm exports	exportation de produits agricoles *f*	esportazione agricola *f*	exportación agrícola *f*
Agrargüter (D)	—	agricultural goods	produits agricoles *m pl*	beni agricoli *m pl*	bienes agrícolas *m pl*
Agrarimport (D)	—	farm imports	importation de produits agricoles *f*	importazione agricola *f*	importación agrícola *f*
Agrarkrise (D)	—	agricultural crisis	crise de l'agriculture *f*	crisi agricola *f*	crisis agrícola *f*
Agrarmarkt (D)	—	agricultural market	marché agricole *m*	mercato agrario *m*	mercado agrícola *m*
Agrarmarkt-ordnung (D)	—	agricultural market organization	organisation des marchés agricoles *f*	regolamento del mercato agrario *m*	reglamentación del mercado agrícola *f*
Agrarpolitik (D)	—	agricultural policy	politique agricole *f*	politica agraria *f*	política agrícola *f*
Agrarpreis (D)	—	prices of farm products	prix agricole *m*	prezzo agrario *m*	precio agrícola *m*
Agrarprodukt (D)	—	farm product	produit agricole *m*	prodotto agricolo *m*	producto agrario *m*
Agrarstaat (D)	—	agricultural state	état agricole *m*	paese agrario *m*	estado agrario *m*
Agrarstatistik (D)	—	agricultural statistics	statistique agricole *f*	statistica agraria *f*	estadística agrícola *f*
Agrarstruktur (D)	—	agricultural structure	structure agraire *f*	struttura agraria *f*	estructura agraria *f*
Agrarsubventionen (D)	—	agricultural subsidies	subventions de l'agriculture *f pl*	sovvenzioni agrarie *f pl*	subvención a la agricultura *f*
Agrarüberschüsse (D)	—	agricultural surpluses	excédents agricoles *m pl*	eccedenze agricole *f pl*	excedentes agrícolas *m pl*
Agrarunion (D)	—	agricultural union	union agricole *f*	unione agraria *f*	unión agrícola *f*
Agrarwirtschaft (D)	—	farming	économie agricole *f*	economia agraria *f*	economía agraria *f*
agreement (E)	Abkommen *n*	—	accord *m*	accordo *m*	acuerdo *m*
agricoltura (I)	Ackerbau *m*	agriculture	agriculture *f*	—	agricultura *f*
agricultura (Es)	Ackerbau *m*	agriculture	agriculture *f*	agricoltura *f*	—
agricultural crisis (E)	Agrarkrise *f*	—	crise de l'agriculture *f*	crisi agricola *f*	crisis agrícola *f*
agricultural enterprise (E)	Agrarbetrieb *m*	—	entreprise agricole *f*	azienda agricola *f*	empresa agrícola *f*
agricultural goods (E)	Agrargüter *pl*	—	produits agricoles *m pl*	beni agricoli *m pl*	bienes agrícolas *m pl*
agricultural market (E)	Agrarmarkt *m*	—	marché agricole *m*	mercato agrario *m*	mercado agrícola *m*
agricultural market organization (E)	Agrarmarktordnung *f*	—	organisation des marchés agricoles *f*	regolamento del mercato agrario *m*	reglamentación del mercado agrícola *f*
agricultural policy (E)	Agrarpolitik *f*	—	politique agricole *f*	politica agraria *f*	política agrícola *f*
agricultural produce (E)	Agrarerzeugnis *n*	—	produit agricole *m*	prodotto agricolo *m*	producto agrícola *m*
agricultural state (E)	Agrarstaat *m*	—	état agricole *m*	paese agrario *m*	estado agrario *m*
agricultural statistics (E)	Agrarstatistik *f*	—	statistique agricole *f*	statistica agraria *f*	estadística agrícola *f*
agricultural structure (E)	Agrarstruktur *f*	—	structure agraire *f*	struttura agraria *f*	estructura agraria *f*
agricultural subsidies (E)	Agrarsubventionen *pl*	—	subventions de l'agriculture *f pl*	sovvenzioni agrarie *f pl*	subvención a la agricultura *f*
agricultural surpluses (E)	Agrarüberschüsse *pl*	—	excédents agricoles *m pl*	eccedenze agricole *f pl*	excedentes agrícolas *m pl*
agricultural union (E)	Agrarunion *f*	—	union agricole *f*	unione agraria *f*	unión agrícola *f*
agriculture (E)	Ackerbau *m*	—	agriculture *f*	agricoltura *f*	agricultura *f*
agriculture (F)	Ackerbau *m*	agriculture	—	agricoltura *f*	agricultura *f*
aguas residuales (Es)	Abwasser *n*	waste water	eaux résiduelles *f pl*	acque di scarico *f pl*	—
ahorro[1] (Es)	Sparen *n*	saving	épargne *f*	risparmio *m*	—

	D	E	F	I	Es
ahorro² (Es)	Ersparnis *f*	savings	épargne *f*	risparmio *m*	—
ahorro forzoso (Es)	Zwangssparen *n*	compulsory saving	épargne forcée *f*	risparmio coatto *m*	—
aide (F)	Aushilfe *f*	auxiliary worker	—	aiuto *m*	ayudante *m*
aide au développement (F)	Entwicklungshilfe *f*	development aid	—	aiuto ai paesi in via di sviluppo *m*	ayuda al desarrollo *f*
aide financière (F)	Kapitalhilfe *f*	capital aid	—	aiuto finanziario *m*	ayuda financiera *f*
aide financière à l'exportation (F)	Außenhandels-finanzierung *f*	foreign trade financing	—	finanziamento del commercio estero *m*	financiación del comercio exterior *f*
aide sociale (F)	Sozialhilfe *f*	public assistance	—	assistenza sociale *f*	ayuda social *f*
air carrier (E)	Luftfrachtführer *m*	—	voiturier aérien *m*	vettore aereo *m*	transportista *m*
air freight (E)	Luftfracht *f*	—	fret aérien *m*	nolo aereo *m*	flete aéreo *m*
air freight traffic (E)	Luftfrachtverkehr *m*	—	transport aérien des marchandises *m*	traffico aereo commerciale *m*	tráfico de flete aéreo *m*
air mail (E)	Luftpost *f*	—	par avion	posta aerea *f*	correo aéreo *m*
air route (E)	Luftweg *m*	—	voie aérienne *f*	via aerea *f*	vía aérea *f*
airway bill (E)	Luftfrachtbrief *m*	—	lettre de transport aérien *f*	lettera di trasporto aereo *f*	transporte aéreo *m*
aiuto (I)	Aushilfe *f*	auxiliary worker	aide *m*	—	ayudante *m*
aiuto ai paesi in via di sviluppo (I)	Entwicklungshilfe *f*	development aid	aide au développement *f*	—	ayuda al desarrollo *f*
aiuto all'esportazione (I)	Exporthilfe *f*	export subsidy	subvention à l'exportatiion *f*	—	ayuda a la exportación *f*
aiuto finanziario (I)	Kapitalhilfe *f*	capital aid	aide financière *f*	—	ayuda financiera *f*
ajournement (F)	Vertagung *f*	postponement	—	rinvio *m*	aplazamiento *m*/ suspensión *f*
ajuste financiero (Es)	Finanzausgleich *m*	financial equalization	compensation financière *f*	compensazione finanziaria *f*	—
ajuste presupuestario (Es)	Planrevision *f*	budget adjustment	révision des coûts marginaux *f*	revisione del piano *f*	—
Akademie (D)	—	academy	académie *f*	accademia *f*	academia *f*
Akkord (D)	—	piece work	convention de salaire à la tâche *f*	cottimo *m*	destajo *m*
Akkordarbeit (D)	—	piecework	travail à la tâche *m*	lavora a cottimo *m*	trabajo a destajo *m*
Akkordlohn (D)	—	piece work wages	salaire à la pièce *m*	retribuzione per il lavoro a cottimo *f*	salario a destajo *m*
Akkordsystem (D)	—	piece work system	système du travail aux pièces *m*	sistema del lavoro a cottimo *m*	régimen de trabajo a destajo *m*
akkreditieren (D)	—	accredit	accréditer	accreditare	acreditar
Akkreditiv (D)	—	letter of credit	accréditif *m*	credito documentario *m*	crédito documentario *m*
Akkreditiv-abwicklung (D)	—	settlement by letter of credit	exécution par crédit documentaire *f*	procedura del credito documentario *f*	ejecución por crédito documentario *f*
Akkreditiv-eröffnung (D)	—	opening of a letter of credit	ouverture d'un accréditif *f*	apertura del credito documentario *f*	apertura de un crédito documentario *f*
Akkreditivklausel (D)	—	letter of credit clause	clause de payement par accréditif *f*	clausola del credito documentario *f*	cláusula de crédito documentario *f*
Akkreditivsumme (D)	—	amount of the letter of credit	montant de l'accréditif *m*	importo del credito documentario *m*	suma del crédito documentario *f*
Akkreditivzahlung (D)	—	payment by letter of credit	payement par accréditif *m*	pagamento contro credito documentario *m*	pago por crédito documentario *m*
Akkumulation (D)	—	accumulation	accumulation *f*	accumulazione *f*	acumulación *f*
Akte (D)	—	file	dossier *m*	pratica *f*	documento *m*
Aktenablage (D)	—	filing	archives *f pl*	archivio delle pratiche *m*	archivo *m*
Aktennotiz (D)	—	memorandum	note *f*	annotazione *f*	nota *f*
Aktie (D)	—	share	action *f*	azione *f*	acción *f*
Aktienausgabe (D)	—	share issue	émission d'actions *f*	emissione di azioni *f*	emisión de acciones *f*
Aktienbestand (D)	—	shareholding	portefeuille d'actions *m*	portafoglio di azioni *m*	cartera de acciones *f*
Aktiendepot (D)	—	share deposit	dépôt d'actions *m*	deposito di azioni *m*	depósitio de acciones *m*

	D	E	F	I	Es
Aktienemision (D)	—	share issue	émission d'actions *f*	emissione di azioni *f*	emisión de acciones *f*
Aktiengesellschaft (D)	—	joint stock company	société anonyme *f*	società per azioni *f*	sociedad anónima *f*
Aktiengesetz (D)	—	Companies Act	loi sur les sociétés par actions *f*	legge sulle società per azioni *f*	ley sobre sociedades anónimas *f*
Aktienhandel (D)	—	dealing in shares	négociation des actions *f*	commercio azionario *m*	contratación de acciones *f*
Aktienindex (D)	—	share index	indice du cours des actions *m*	indice azionario *m*	índice de cotización de acciones *m*
Aktienkapital (D)	—	share capital	fonds social *m*	capitale azionario *m*	capital en acciones *m*
Aktienkurs (D)	—	share price	cours des actions *m*	corso delle azioni *m*	cotización de las acciones *f*
Aktienmehrheit (D)	—	majority of shares	majorité d'actions *f*	maggioranza delle azioni *f*	mayoría de acciones *f*
Aktiennotierung (D)	—	share quotation	cotation des actions *f*	quotazione delle azioni *f*	cotización de acciones *f*
Aktienpaket (D)	—	block of shares	paquet d'actions *m*	pacchetto delle azioni *m*	paquete de acciones *m*
Aktienrecht (D)	—	company law	loi sur les sociétés anonymes *f pl*	diritto azionario *m*	derecho de sociedades anónimas *m*
Aktionär (D)	—	shareholder	actionnaire *m*	azionista *m*	accionista *m*
Aktionen (D)	—	actions	actions *f pl*	azioni *f pl*	acciones *f pl*
Aktionsfeld (D)	—	field of action	champ d'action *m*	campo d'azione *m*	campo de acción *m*
Aktionsparameter (D)	—	action parameter	paramètre d'action *m*	parametro d'azione *m*	parámetro de acción *m*
Aktionsplakat (D)	—	advertising bill	affiche d'action *f*	manifesto promozionale *m*	cartel de acción *m*
Aktiva (D)	—	assets	masse active *f*	attivo *m*	activo *m*
Aktivbestand (D)	—	assets	actif *m*	effettivo *m*	activo disponible *m*
aktiver Teilhaber (D)	—	active partner	associé prenant part à la gestion *m*	socio attivo *m*	socio activo *m*
Aktivgeschäft (D)	—	credit transaction	opération active *f*	operazione attiva *f*	operaciones activas *f pl*
Aktivsaldo (D)	—	active balance	solde créditeur *m*	saldo attivo *m*	saldo activo *m*
Akzelerationsprinzip (D)	—	acceleration principle	principe d'accélération *m*	principio di accelerazione *m*	principio de aceleración *m*
Akzept (D)	—	accepted bill	traite acceptée *f*	accettazione *f*	aceptación *f*
akzeptabel (D)	—	acceptable	acceptable	accettabile	aceptable
Akzepteinlösung (D)	—	honouring of an acceptance	honorer la traite acceptée	pagamento di un effetto *m*	descuento de una letra aceptada *m*
Akzeptkredit (D)	—	acceptance credit	crédit par traites acceptées *m*	credito d'accettazione *m*	crédito de aceptación *m*
a la atención (Es)	zu treuen Händen	for safekeeping	remettre en mains sûres	alla particolare attenzione	—
à la charge de (F)	zu Lasten	chargeable to	—	a carico di	a cargo de
à la commission (F)	auf Provisionsbasis	on a commission basis	—	a provvigione	a comisión
a largo plazo (Es)	langfristig	long-term	à long terme	a lunga scadenza	—
alarma de smog (Es)	Smogalarm *m*	smog warning	alerte au smog *f*	allarme smog *m*	—
a la vista (Es)	auf Sicht	at sight	à vue	a vista	—
alcance publicitario (Es)	Werbereichweite *f*	scope of advertising effect	zone de rayonnement de la publicité *f*	raggio d'azione della pubblicità *m*	—
alcista (Es)	Haussier *m*	bull	haussier *m*	speculatore al rialzo *m*	—
al contado (Es)	gegen Barzahlung	against cash	au comptant	contro pagamento in contanti	—
al contado contra documentos (Es)	Dokumente gegen Zahlung *pl*	documents against payments	documents contre payement *m pl*	pagamento contro documenti *m*	—
alerte au smog (F)	Smogalarm *m*	smog warning	—	allarme smog *m*	alarma de smog *f*
à l'essai (F)	auf Probe	on trial	—	in prova	a prueba
à l'étranger (F)	im Ausland	abroad	—	all'estero	en el extranjero
aliénation (F)	Veräußerung *f*	sale/alienation	—	alienazione *f*	enajenación *f*
alienazione (I)	Veräußerung *f*	sale/aleination	aliénation *f*	—	enajenación *f*

	D	E	F	I	Es
Alkoholsteuer (D)	—	tax on alcohol	impôt sur l'alcool *m*	imposta sugli alcolici *f*	impuesto sobre el alcohol *m*
alla particolare attenzione (I)	zu treuen Händen	for safekeeping	remettre en mains sûres	—	a la atención
allarme smog (I)	Smogalarm *m*	smog warning	alerte au smog *f*	—	alarma de smog *f*
allegato (I)	Anlage *f*	enclosure	pièce jointe *f*	—	anexo *m*
Alleininhaber (D)	—	sole owner	seul propriétaire *m*	titolare unico *m*	propietario exclusivo *m*
Alleinvertreter (D)	—	sole agent	agent exclusive *m*	rappresentante esclusivo *m*	representante exclusivo *m*
Alleinvertretung (D)	—	sole agency	agence exclusive *f*	rappresentanza esclusiva *f*	representación exclusiva *f*
Alleinvertretungs-recht (D)	—	sole and exclusive agency right	droit exclusif de représentation *m*	diritto di rappresen-tanza esclusiva *m*	derecho de representación exclusiva *m*
Alleinvertrieb (D)	—	exclusive distribution	vente exclusive *f*	vendita esclusiva *f*	distribución exclusiva *f*
all'estero (I)	im Ausland	abroad	à l'étranger	—	en el extranjero
allestimento di vetrina (I)	Schaufenster-dekoration *f*	window dressing	décoration de vitrine *f*	—	adorno del escaparate *m*
allgemeine Geschäfts-bedingungen (D)	—	general terms of contract	conditions générales de contrat *f pl*	condizioni generali di contratto *f pl*	condiciones generales de contrato *f pl*
allgemeine Kredit-vereinbarungen (D)	—	general borrowing agreements	accords généraux de crédit *f pl*	condizioni generali di credito *f pl*	acuerdos generales de crédito *m pl*
Allgemeinwohl (D)	—	public wellfare	bien général *m*	benestare pubblico *m*	bienestar público *m*
allocation[1] (E)	Allokation *f*	—	allocation *f*	allocazione *f*	alocación *f*
allocation[2] (E)	Zuteilung *f*	—	répartition *f*	attribuzione *f*/ ripartizione *f*	asignación *f*
allocation[1] (F)	Zuschuß *m*	allowance	—	sovvenzione *f*	subvención *f*
allocation[2] (F)	Allokation *f*	allocation	—	allocazione *f*	alocación *f*
allocazione (I)	Allokation *f*	allocation	allocation *f*	—	alocación *f*
Allokation (D)	—	allocation	allocation *f*	allocazione *f*	alocación *f*
allowance (E)	Zuschuß *m*	—	allocation *f*	sovvenzione *f*	subvención *f*
allowance for expenses (E)	Spesenpauschale *f*	—	forfait de frais *m*	forfait di spese *m*	suma global de gastos *f*
allowance per kilometre (E)	Kilometergeld *n*	—	indemnité par kilomètre *f*	indennità per chilometro *f*	kilometraje *m*
all-risks-clause (E)	all-risks-Klausel *f*	—	clause d'assurance (contre) tous (les) risques *f*	clausola tutti i rischi *f*	cláusula a todo riesgo *f*
all-risks-Klausel (D)	—	all-risks-clause	clause d'assurance (contre) tous (les) risques *f*	clausola tutti i rischi *f*	cláusula a todo riesgo *f*
almacén[1] (Es)	Lager *n*	warehouse	magasin *m*	magazzino *m*	—
almacén[2] (Es)	Lagerraum *m*	storage space	halle de dépôt *f*	magazzino *m*	—
almacenaje[1] (Es)	Lagerung *f*	storage	stockage *m*	magazzinaggio *m*	—
almacenaje[2] (Es)	Lagerhaltung *f*	stockkeeping	entreposage *m*	magazzinaggio *m*	—
almacenamiento (Es)	Einlagerung *f*	storage	entreposage *m*	immagazzina-mento *m*	—
almacén de entregas (Es)	Auslieferungslager *n*	distribution centre	entrepôt de distribution *m*	deposito di consegna *m*	—
al mejor cambio[1] (Es)	bestens	at best	au mieux	ottimo	—
al mejor cambio[2] (Es)	billigst	at best price	au meilleur prix	al prezzo più basso	—
al netto degli influssi stagionali (I)	saisonbereinigt	seasonally adjusted	corrigé du mouvement saisonnier	—	desestacionalizado
alocación (Es)	Allokation *f*	allocation	allocation *f*	allocazione *f*	—
à long terme (F)	langfristig	long-term	—	a lunga scadenza	a largo plazo
al più presto possibile (I)	schnellstmöglich	as quickly as possible	le plus vite possible	—	tan rápido como sea posible
al prezzo più basso (I)	billigst	at best price	au meilleur prix	—	al mejor cambio
alquiler (Es)	Miete *f*	rent	location *f*	canone di locazione *m*	—

	D	E	F	I	Es
alquiler de almacenaje (Es)	Lagermiete *f*	warehouse rent	location d'une surface pour magasinage *f*	spese di magazzinaggio *f pl*	—
Alta Autoridad (Es)	hohe Behörde *f*	high authority	haute autorité *f*	alta autorità *f*	—
alta autorità (I)	hohe Behörde *f*	high authority	haute autorité *f*	—	Alta Autoridad *f*
alta congiuntura (I)	Hochkonjunktur *f*	boom	haute conjoncture *f*	—	alta coyuntura *f*
alta coyuntura (Es)	Hochkonjunktur *f*	boom	haute conjoncture *f*	alta congiuntura *f*	—
alta dirección (Es)	Management *n*	management	management *m*	management *m*	—
alternativa (Es)	Alternative *f*	alternative	alternative *f*	alternativa *f*	—
alternativa (I)	Alternative *f*	alternative	alternative *f*	—	alternativa *f*
Alternative (D)	—	alternative	alternative *f*	alternativa *f*	alternativa *f*
alternative (E)	Alternative *f*	—	alternative *f*	alternativa *f*	alternativa *f*
alternative (F)	Alternative *f*	alternative	—	alternativa *f*	alternativa *f*
alternative planning (E)	Alternativplanung *f*	—	planification alternative *f*	pianificazione alternativa *f*	planificación alternativa *f*
Alternativkosten (D)	—	opportunity costs	coûts alternatifs *m pl*	costi alternativi *m pl*	coste alternativo *m*
Alternativplanung (D)	—	alternative planning	planification alternative *f*	pianificazione alternativa *f*	planificación alternativa *f*
Altersgrenze (D)	—	age limit	limite d'âge *f*	limite d'età *m*	limite de edad *m*
Altersgruppe (D)	—	age group	groupe d'âge *m*	gruppo d'età *m*	grupo según la edad *m*
Altersversicherung (D)	—	old age insurance	assurance-vieillesse *f*	assicurazione per la vecchiaia *f*	seguro de vejez *m*
Altersversorgung (D)	—	provision for old age	prévoyance vieillesse *f*	previdenza per la vecchiaia *f*	previsión para la vejez *f*
alto directivo (Es)	Manager *m*	manager	manager *m*	manager *m*	—
Altöl (D)	—	waste oil	huile usée *f*	olio usato *m*	aceite usado *m*
Altölbeseitigung (D)	—	disposal of waste oil	élimination d'huile usée *f*	smaltimento dell'olio usato *m*	eliminación de petróleo usado *f*
a lunga scadenza (I)	langfristig	long-term	à long terme	—	a largo plazo
alza (Es)	Hausse *f*	boom	hausse *f*	rialzo *m*	—
alza de las cotizaciones (Es)	Kurssteigerung *f*	price advance	hausse *f*	aumento dei corsi *m*	—
a macchina (I)	maschinell	by machine	mécanique	—	a máquina
a máquina (Es)	maschinell	by machine	mécanique	a macchina	—
ambiente de trabajo (Es)	Betriebsklima *n*	working conditions and human relations	climat social *m*	atmosfera di lavoro *f*	—
ambulantes Gewerbe (D)	—	itinerant trade	commerce ambulant *m*	commercio ambulante *m*	comercio ambulante *m*
a media scadenza (I)	mittelfristig	medium-term	à moyen terme	—	a medio plazo
a medio plazo (Es)	mittelfristig	medium-term	à moyen terme	a media scadenza	—
amélioration du rendement (F)	Leistungs-steigerung *f*	increase in efficiency	—	aumento della produttività *m*	incremento del rendimiento *m*
aménagement des espaces (F)	Raumordnung *f*	regional policy	—	ordinamento territoriale *m*	ordenación del territorio *f*
aménagement régional (F)	Regionalplanung *f*	regional planning	—	pianificazione regionale *f*	planificación regional *f*
amende[1] (F)	Bußgeld *n*	administration fee	—	pena pecuniaria *f*	multa *f*
amende[2] (F)	Geldbuße *f*	fine	—	pena pecuniaria *f*	multa *f*
amendement d'une loi (F)	Gesetzesänderung *f*	amendment of a law	—	emendamento di legge *m*	enmienda de la ley *f*
amendment of a law (E)	Gesetzesänderung *f*	—	amendement d'une loi *m*	emendamento di legge *m*	enmienda de la ley *f*
amendment of the statutes (E)	Satzungsänderung *f*	—	modification des statuts *f*	modificazione dello statuto *f*	modificación de los estatutos *f*
amministratore[1] (I)	Geschäftsführer *m*	manager	gérant d'une affaire *m*	—	gerente *m*
amministratore[2] (I)	Verwalter *m*	administrator	administrateur *m*	—	administrador *m*
amministratore dell'eredità (I)	Nachlaßverwalter *m*	administrator of the deceased's estate	administrateur de la succession *m*	—	administrador de la herencia *m*
amministrazione[1] (I)	Geschäftsführung *f*	management	gestion *f*	—	gestión *f*
amministrazione[2] (I)	Verwaltung *f*	administration	administration *f*	—	administración *f*

	D	E	F	I	Es
amministrazione del magazzino (I)	Lagerverwaltung *f*	stockkeeping	entreposage *m*	—	administración de almacén *f*
amministrazione giudiziaria (I)	Zwangsverwaltung *f*	receivership	séquestre judiciare *m*	—	administración forzosa *f*
ammissione (I)	Zulassung *f*	admission	admission *f*	—	admisión *f*
ammontare della fattura (I)	Rechnungsbetrag *m*	amount of invoice	montant de la facture *m*	—	importe de la factura *m*
ammortamenti straordinari (I)	Sonder-abschreibungen *pl*	special depreciation	amortissement extraordinaire *m*	—	amortización extraordinaria *f*
ammortamento[1] (I)	Tilgung *f*	redemption	amortissement *m*	—	amortización *f*
ammortamento[2] (I)	Amortisation *f*	amortization	amortissement *m*	—	amortización *f*
ammortamento[3] (I)	Abschreibung *f*	depreciation	amortissement *m*	—	amortización *f*
ammortamento decrescente (I)	degressive Abschreibung *f*	declining-balance depreciation	amortissement dégressif *m*	—	amortización decreciente *f*
ammortamento lineare (I)	lineare Abschreibung *f*	linear depreciation	amortissement constant *m*	—	amortización constante *f*
ammortamento progressivo (I)	progressive Abschreibung *f*	progressive depreciation	amortissement progressif *m*	—	amortización progresiva *f*
amortir (F)	ablösen	redeem	—	rimborsare	amortizar
Amortisation (D)	—	amortization	amortissement *m*	ammortamento *m*	amortización *f*
amortissement[1] (F)	Abschreibung *f*	depreciation	—	ammortamento *m*	amortización *f*
amortissement[2] (F)	Tilgung *f*	redemption	—	ammortamento *m*	amortización *f*
amortissement[3] (F)	Amortisation *f*	amortization	—	ammortamento *m*	amortizacion constante *f*
amortissement constant (F)	lineare Abschreibung *f*	linear depreciation	—	ammortamento lineare *m*	depreciación proporcional *f*
amortissement dégressif (F)	degressive Abschreibung *f*	declining-balance depreciation	—	ammortamento decrescente *m*	amortización decreciente *f*
amortissement extraordinaire (F)	Sonder-abschreibungen *pl*	special depreciation	—	deduzione per usura *f*	amortización extraordinaria *f*
amortissement progressif (F)	progressive Abschreibung *f*	progressive depreciation	—	ammortamento progressivo *m*	amortización progresiva *f*
amortización[1] (Es)	Abschreibung *f*	depreciation	amortissement *m*	ammortamento *m*	—
amortización[2] (Es)	Amortisation *f*	amortization	amortissement *m*	ammortamento *m*	—
amortización[3] (Es)	Tilgung *f*	redemption	amortissement *m*	ammortamento *m*	—
amortización constante (Es)	lineare Abschreibung *f*	linear depreciation	amortissement constant *m*	ammortamento lineare *m*	—
amortización decreciente (Es)	degressive Abschreibung *f*	declining-balance depreciation	amortissement dégressif *m*	ammortamento decrescente *m*	—
amortización extraordinaria (Es)	Sonder-abschreibungen *f*	special depreciation	amortissement extraordinaire *m*	ammortamenti straordinari *m pl*	—
amortización progresiva (Es)	progressive Abschreibung *f*	progressive depreciation	amortissement progressif *m*	ammortamento progressivo *m*	—
amortizar (Es)	ablösen	redeem	amortir	rimborsare	—
amortization (E)	Amortisation *f*	—	amortissement *m*	ammortamento *m*	amortización *f*
amount (E)	Betrag *m*	—	montant *m*	importo *m*	suma *f*
amount of invoice (E)	Rechnungsbetrag *m*	—	montant de la facture *m*	ammontare della fattura *m*	importe de la factura *m*
amount of money (E)	Geldbetrag *m*	—	somme d'argent *f*	somma di denaro *f*	suma de dinero *f*
amount of the letter of credit (E)	Akkreditivsumme *f*	—	montant de l'accréditif *m*	importo del credito documentario *m*	suma del crédito documentario *f*
à moyen terme (F)	mittelfristig	medium-term	—	a media scadenza	a medio plazo
ampliación de la capacidad (Es)	Kapazitäts-ausweitung *f*	increase in capacity	extension de la capacité *f*	ampliamento delle capacità *m*	—
ampliamento delle capacità (I)	Kapazitäts-ausweitung *f*	increase in capacity	extension de la capacité *f*	—	ampliación de la capacidad *f*
Amt (D)	—	office	bureau *m*	ufficio *m*	cargo *m*
analisi ABC (I)	ABC-Analyse *f*	ABC analysis	analyse ABC *f*	—	análisis ABC *m*
analisi aziendale (I)	Betriebsanalyse *f*	operation analysis	situation analytique de l'expoitation *f*	—	análisis de la empresa *m*
analisi congiunturale (I)	Konjunkturanalyse *f*	economic analysis	analyse de la conjoncture *f*	—	análisis de la situación económica *m*

	D	E	F	I	Es
analisi costi-benefici (I)	Kosten-Nutzen-Analyse *f*	cost-benefit analysis	analyse du ratio coût à profit *f*	—	análisis de coste-beneficio *m*
analisi del fabbisogno (I)	Bedarfsanalyse *f*	analysis of requirements	analyse des besoins *m*	—	análisis de las necesidades *m*
analisi dell'assortimento (I)	Sortimentsanalyse *f*	analysis of assortment	analyse d'assortiment *f*	—	análisis del surtido *m*
analisi delle tendenze (I)	Trendanalyse *f*	trend analysis	analyse de la tendence générale *f*	—	análisis de tendencia *m*
analisi delle vendite (I)	Verkaufsanalyse *f*	sales analysis	analyse des ventes *f*	—	análisis de las ventas *m*
analisi del potere d'acquisto (I)	Kaufkraftanalyse *f*	spending capacity analysis	analyse du pouvoir d'achat *f*	—	análisis del poder adquisitivo *m*
analisi di bilancio (I)	Bilanzanalyse *f*	balance analysis	analyse du bilan *f*	—	análisis de balance *m*
analisi di categoria (I)	Branchenanalyse *f*	trade analysis	analyse des branches *f*	—	análisis del ramo *m*
analisi di mercato[1] (I)	Absatzanalyse *f*	sales analysis	analyse de la distribution *f*	—	análisis de venta *m*
analisi di mercato[2] (I)	Marktuntersuchung *f*	market survey	étude de marché *f*	—	estudio del mercado *m*
analisi di mercato[3] (I)	Marktanalyse *f*	market analysis	analyse du marché *f*	—	análisis de mercado *m*
analisi di sistema (I)	Systemanalyse *f*	systems analysis	analyse du système *f*	—	análisis de los sistemas *m*
analisi economica (I)	Wirtschaftsanalyse *f*	economic analysis	analyse de l'économie *f*	—	análisis económico *m*
analisi input-output (I)	Input-Output-Analyse *f*	input-output analysis	tableau économique input-output *m*	—	análisis de input-output *m*
análisis ABC (Es)	ABC-Analyse *f*	ABC analysis	analyse ABC *f*	analisi ABC *f*	—
análisis de balance (Es)	Bilanzanalyse *f*	balance analysis	analyse du bilan *f*	analisi di bilancio *f*	—
análisis de coste-beneficio (Es)	Kosten-Nutzen-Analyse *f*	cost-benefit analysis	analyse du ratio coût à profit *f*	analisi costi-benefici *f*	—
análisis de costes (Es)	Kostenanalyse *f*	cost analysis	analyse des coûts *f*	analisi dei costi *f*	—
análisis de flujos monetarios (Es)	Finanzierungs-rechnung *f*	flow-of-funds analysis	analyse des flux monétaires *f*	calcolo di finanziamento *m*	—
análisis de input-output (Es)	Input-Output-Analyse *f*	input-output analysis	tableau économique input-output *m*	analisi input-output *f*	—
análisis de la empresa (Es)	Betriebsanalyse *f*	operation analysis	situation analytique de l'expoitation *f*	analisi aziendale *f*	—
análisis de la situación económica (Es)	Konjunkturanalyse *f*	economic analysis	analyse de la conjoncture *f*	analisi congiunturale *f*	—
análisis de las necesidades (Es)	Bedarfsanalyse *f*	analysis of requirements	analyse des besoins *m*	analisi del fabbisogno *f*	—
análisis de las ventas (Es)	Verkaufsanalyse *f*	sales analysis	analyse des ventes *f*	analisi delle vendite *f*	—
análisis de los sistemas (Es)	Systemanalyse *f*	systems analysis	analyse du système *f*	analisi di sistema *f*	—
análisis del poder adquisitivo (Es)	Kaufkraftanalyse *f*	spending capacity analysis	analyse du pouvoir d'achat *f*	analisi del potere d'acquisto *f*	—
análisis del ramo (Es)	Branchenanalyse *f*	trade analysis	analyse des branches *f*	analisi di categoria *f*	—
análisis del resultado publicitario (Es)	Werbeerfolgs-kontrolle *f*	advertising control	contrôle du résultat de la publicité *m*	controllo del succes-so pubblicitario *m*	—
análisis del surtido (Es)	Sortimentsanalyse *f*	analysis of assortment	analyse d'assortiment *f*	analisi dell'assortimento *f*	—
análisis de mercado (Es)	Marktanalyse *f*	market analysis	analyse du marché *f*	analisi di mercato *f*	—
análisis de tendencia (Es)	Trendanalyse *f*	trend analysis	analyse de la tendance générale *f*	analisi delle tendenze *f*	—
análisis de venta (Es)	Absatzanalyse *f*	sales analysis	analyse de la distribution *f*	analisi di mercato *f*	—
análisis económico (Es)	Wirtschaftsanalyse *f*	economic analysis	analyse de l'économie *f*	analisi economica *f*	—
analisi sul tempo impiegato (I)	Zeitstudie *f*	time study	étude des temps *f*	—	estudio de tiempo *m*
analyse ABC (F)	ABC-Analyse *f*	ABC analysis	—	analisi ABC *f*	análisis ABC *m*

	D	E	F	I	Es
analyse d'assortiment (F)	Sortimentsanalyse *f*	analysis of assortment	—	analisi dell'assortimento *f*	análisis del surtido *m*
analyse de la conjoncture (F)	Konjunkturanalyse *f*	economic analysis	—	analisi congiunturale *f*	análisis de la situación económica *m*
analyse de la distribution (F)	Absatzanalyse *f*	sales analysis	—	analisi di mercato *f*	análisis de venta *m*
analyse de la tendance générale (F)	Trendanalyse *f*	trend analysis	—	analisi delle tendenze *f*	análisis de tendencia *m*
analyse de l'économie (F)	Wirtschaftsanalyse *f*	economic analysis	—	analisi economica *f*	análisis económico *m*
analyse des besoins (F)	Bedarfsanalyse *f*	analysis of requirements	—	analisi del fabbisogno *f*	análisis de las necesidades *m*
analyse des branches (F)	Branchenanalyse *f*	trade analysis	—	analisi di categoria *f*	análisis del ramo *m*
analyse des flux monétaires (F)	Finanzierungsrechnung *f*	flow-of-funds analysis	—	calcolo di finanziamento *m*	análisis de flujos monetarios *m*
analyse des ventes (F)	Verkaufsanalyse *f*	sales analysis	—	analisi delle vendite *f*	análisis de las ventas *m*
analyse du bilan (F)	Bilanzanalyse *f*	balance analysis	—	analisi di bilancio *f*	análisis de balance *m*
analyse du marché (F)	Marktanalyse *f*	market analysis	—	analisi di mercato *f*	análisis de mercado *m*
analyse du pouvoir d'achat (F)	Kaufkraftanalyse *f*	spending capacity analysis	—	analisi del potere d'acquisto *f*	análisis del poder adquisitivo *m*
analyse du ratio coût à profit (F)	Kosten-Nutzen-Analyse *f*	cost-benefit analysis	—	analisi costi-benefici *f*	análisis de coste-beneficio *m*
analyse du système (F)	Systemanalyse *f*	systems analysis	—	analisi di sistema *f*	análisis de los sistemas *m*
analysis of assortment (E)	Sortimentsanalyse *f*	—	analyse d'assortiment *f*	analisi dell'assortimento *f*	análisis del surtido *m*
analysis of requirements (E)	Bedarfsanalyse *f*	—	analyse des besoins *f*	analisi del fabbisogno *f*	análisis de las necesidades *m*
Anbau-beschränkung (D)	—	restriction on cultivation	limitation des cultures *f*	restrizione di coltivazione *f*	limitación de cultivos *f*
Anbaufläche (D)	—	area under cultivation	surface plantée *f*	area coltivata *f*	superficie agrícola utilizada *f*
anbieten (D)	—	offer	offrir	offrire	ofrecer
ancillary costs (E)	Nebenkosten *pl*	—	coûts accessoires *m pl*	costi accessori *m pl*	gastos adicionales *m pl*
ancillary wage costs (E)	Lohnnebenkosten *pl*	—	charges salariales annexes *f pl*	costi complementari del lavoro *m pl*	cargas salariales accesorias *f pl*
andamento dell'economia (I)	Wirtschaftsverlauf *m*	course of the economic evolution	évolution économique *f*	—	evolución económica *f*
Anderkonto (D)	—	fiduciary account	compte de tiers *m*	conto per terzi *m*	cuenta fiduciaria de un abogado *f*
anexo (Es)	Anlage *f*	enclosure	pièce jointe *f*	allegato *m*	—
Anfangsbestand (D)	—	opening inventory	stock initial *m*	scorte iniziali *f pl*	existencias iniciales *f pl*
Anfangsgehalt (D)	—	starting salary	salaire initial *m*	stipendio iniziale *m*	salario inicial *m*
Anfangskapital (D)	—	opening capital	capital initial *m*	capitale iniziale *m*	capital inicial *m*
Anfechtungsklage (D)	—	action for avoidance	action en annulation *f*	azione di impugnazione *f*	acción de impugnación *f*
Anforderungs-merkmal (D)	—	requirement characteristics	caractéristique d'exigences *f*	caratteristica richiesta *f*	característica de requisitos *f*
Anfrage (D)	—	inquiry	demande *f*	richiesta *f*	demanda *f*
Anführer (D)	—	leader	chef *m*	leader *m*	líder *m*
Angebot (D)	—	offer	proposition *f*	offerta *f*	propuesta f/oferta *f*
Angebotsüberhang (D)	—	excess of supply over demand	excès de l'offre *m*	eccedenza d'offerta *f*	exceso de oferta *m*
angelernt (D)	—	semi-skilled	semi-qualifié	semi-qualificato	semicualificado
Angestellten-versicherung (D)	—	Salaried Employees' Pension Insurance	assurance invalidité-vieillesse des employés *f*	assicurazione degli impiegati *f*	seguro de empleados *m*
Angestellter (D)	—	employee	employé *m*	impiegato *m*	empleado *m*
animation d'innovation (F)	Innovationsschub *m*	technology push	—	spinta innovativa *f*	empuje innovador *m*

	D	E	F	I	Es
aniversario de la empresa (Es)	Geschäftsjubiläum *n*	jubilee	anniversaire de l'entreprise *m*	anniversario aziendale *m*	—
Ankauf (D)	—	purchase	achat *m*	acquisto *m*	compra *f*
Ankaufgarantie (D)	—	purchase guarantee	garantie d'achat *f*	garanzia d'acquisto *f*	garantía de compra *f*
Ankunftsdatum (D)	—	date of arrival	date d'arrivée *f*	data d'arrivo *f*	fecha de llegada *f*
Anlage (D)	—	enclosure/investment	pièce jointe *f*/ investissement *m*	allegato *m*/ investimento *m*	anexo *m*/ inversión *f*
Anlagegüter (D)	—	capital goods	valeur immoblisée *f*	beni d'investimento *m pl*	bienes de inversión *m pl*
Anlageinvestition (D)	—	investment in fixed assets	investissement productif *m*	investimento fisso *m*	inversión fija *f*
Anlagepapiere (D)	—	investment securities	valeurs de placement *f pl*	titoli d'investimento *m pl*	valores de inversión *m pl*
Anlagevermögen (D)	—	fixed assets	valeurs immobilisées *f pl*	attivo fisso *m*	activo fijo *m*
Anlaufperiode (D)	—	initial period	période de mise en marche *f*	periodo iniziale *m*	período de puesta en marcha *m*
Anleihe (D)	—	loan	emprunt *m*	prestito *m*	empréstito *m*
Anleitung (D)	—	instructions	instruction *f*	istruzione *f*	instrucción *f*
Anmeldefrist (D)	—	time for application	délai de déclaration *m*	termine di denuncia *m*	plazo de solicitud *m*
Anmeldung (D)	—	registration/ declaration	inscription *f*/ déclaration *f*	avviso *m*/ dichiarazione *f*	solicitud *f*/ declaración *f*
Annahme (D)	—	acceptance	acceptation *f*	accettazione *f*	aceptación *f*
Annahme-verweigerung (D)	—	refusal of delivery	refus d'acceptation *m*	rifiuto d'accettazione *m*	rehuso de aceptación *m*
année civile (F)	Kalenderjahr *n*	calendar year	—	anno solare *m*	año civil *m*
année de base (F)	Basisjahr *n*	base year	—	anno di base *m*	año básico *m*
anniversaire (F)	Geburtstag *m*	birthday	—	compleanno *m*	cumpleaños *m*
anniversaire de l'entreprise (F)	Geschäftsjubiläum *n*	jubilee	—	anniversario aziendale *m*	aniversario de la empresa *m*
anniversario aziendale (I)	Geschäftsjubiläum *n*	jubilee	anniversaire de l'entreprise *m*	—	aniversario de la empresa *m*
anno d'esercizio (I)	Rechnungsjahr *n*	financial year	exercice comptable *m*	—	ejercicio *m*
anno di base (I)	Basisjahr *n*	base year	année de base *f*	—	año básico *m*
anno finanziario (I)	Haushaltsjahr *n*	financial year	exercice budgétaire *m*	—	ejercicio *m*
annonce (F)	Anzeige *f*	advertisement	—	inserzione *f*	anuncio *m*
annonce chiffrée (F)	Chiffre-Anzeige *f*	advertisement under a box number	—	inserzione in cifra *f*	anuncio codificado *m*
annonce de journal (F)	Zeitungsanzeige *f*	advertisement	—	inserzione sul giornale *f*	anuncio de prensa *m*
annonce d'emploi (F)	Stellenanzeige *f*	position offered	—	inserzione d'impiego *f*	anuncio de empleo *m*
annonce de visiteurs (F)	Besuchsanmeldung *f*	announcement of a visitor	—	avviso di visita *m*	anuncio de visita *m*
anno solare (I)	Kalenderjahr *n*	calendar year	année civile *f*	—	año civil *m*
annotazione[1] (I)	Aktennotiz *f*	memorandum	note *f*	—	nota *f*
annotazione[2] (I)	Vermerk *m*	note	remarque *f*	—	nota *f*
annotazione[3] (I)	Notiz *f*	note	note *f*	—	noticia *f*
announcement of a visitor (E)	Besuchsanmeldung *f*	—	annonce de visiteurs *f*	avviso di visita *m*	anuncio de visita *m*
annual (E)	jährlich	—	annuel	annuale	anual
annual accounts (E)	Jahresabschluß *m*	—	clôture annuelle des comptes *f*	chiusura d'esercizio *f*	cierre de cuentas *m*
Annual Economic Report (E)	Jahreswirtschafts-bericht *m*	—	compte rendu d'activité économique annuel *m*	relazione generale sulla situazione economica *f*	informe económico anual *m*
annual holiday (E)	Betriebsferien *pl*	—	clôture annuelle de l'établissement *f*	ferie aziendali *f pl*	vacaciones de la empresa *f pl*
annual holidays (E)	Urlaub *m*	—	congé *m*/ vacances *f pl*	ferie *f pl*/ vacanze *f pl*	vacaciones *f pl*
annual hours of work (E)	Jahresarbeitszeit *f*	—	temps de travail annuel *m*	orario di lavoro annuale *m*	jornada anual *f*
annual income (E)	Jahreseinkommen *n*	—	revenu annuel *m*	reddito annuale *m*	renta anual *f*

	D	E	F	I	Es
annual meeting of shareholders (E)	Jahreshauptversammlung *f*	—	assemblée générale annuelle *f*	assemblea generale annuale *f*	junta general anual *f*
annual need (E)	Jahresbedarf *m*	—	besoin annuel *m*	bisogno annuale *m*	necesidad anual *f*
annual profit (E)	Jahresgewinn *m*	—	bénéfice annuel *m*	utile dell'anno *m*	beneficio del ejercicio *m*
annual surplus (E)	Jahresüberschuß *m*	—	excédent annuel *m*	surplus dell'anno *m*	superávit del ejercicio *m*
annuale (I)	jährlich	annual	annuel	—	anual
annualità (I)	Annuität *f*	annuity	annuité *f*	—	anualidad *f*
annuel (F)	jährlich	annual	—	annuale	anual
Annuität (D)	—	annuity	annuité *f*	annualità *f*	anualidad *f*
Annuitätendarlehen (D)	—	annuity loan	prêt amortissable par annuités *m*	prestito rimborsabile in annualità *m*	empréstito sin vencimiento *m*
annuité (F)	Annuität *f*	annuity	—	annualità *f*	anualidad *f*
annuity[1] (E)	Rente *f*	—	rente *f*/ pension de vieillesse *f*	rendita *f*/ pensione *f*	renta *f*/ pensión *f*
annuity[2] (E)	Annuität *f*	—	annuité *f*	annualità *f*	anualidad *f*
annuity bonds (E)	Rentenanleihe *f*	—	effet public *m*	prestito a reddito fisso *m*	empréstito por anualidades *m*
annuity loan (E)	Annuitätendarlehen *n*	—	prêt amortissable par annuités *m*	prestito rimborsabile in annualità *m*	empréstito por anualidades *m*
annul (E)	annullieren	—	annuler	annullare	anular
annulation (F)	Stornierung *f*	cancellation	—	storno *m*	cancelación *f*/ anulación *f*/ contrapartida *f*
annuler[1] (F)	annullieren	annul	—	annullare	anular
annuler[2] (F)	löschen	cancel	—	cancellare	cancelar
annullare (I)	annullieren	annul	annuler	—	anular
annullieren (D)	—	annul	annuler	annullare	anular
año básico (Es)	Basisjahr *n*	base year	année de base *f*	anno di base *m*	—
año civil (Es)	Kalenderjahr *n*	calendar year	année civile *f*	anno solare *m*	—
Anordnung (D)	—	order	ordre *m*	ordine *m*	orden *f*
Anpassung (D)	—	adaption	adaptation *f*	adattamento *m*	adaptación *f*
Anpassungskosten (D)	—	adjustment costs	coûts d'adaptation *m pl*	costi d'adattamento *m pl*	gastos readaptación *m pl*
Anpassungsverzögerung (D)	—	adjustment lag	retard d'adaptation *m*	ritardo d'adattamento *m*	retraso de adaptación *m*
Anrede (D)	—	form of address	début de lettre *m*	titolo *m*	tratamiento *m*
Anreiz (D)	—	incentive	incitation *f*	incentivo *m*	incentivo *m*
Anreizsystem (D)	—	incentive system	système d'incitation *m*	sistema d'incentivo *m*	sistema de incentivos *m*
Anrufbeantworter (D)	—	answering machine	répondeur automatique *m*	segreteria telefonica *f*	contestador de llamadas *m*
Anschaffung (D)	—	acquisition	acquisition *f*	acquisto *m*	adquisición *f*
Anschaffungskosten (D)	—	purchase costs	frais d'acquisition *m pl*	costi d'acquisto *m pl*	coste de adquisición *m*
Anschaffungswert (D)	—	acquisition value	valeur d'acquisition *f*	valore d'acquisto *m*	valor de adquisición *m*
Anschlußfinanzierung (D)	—	follow-up financing	financement successif *m*	finanziamento successivo *m*	financiación sucesiva *f*
Anschrift (D)	—	address	adresse *f*	indirizzo *m*	dirección *f*
Ansichtssendung (D)	—	consignment on approval	envoi à condition *m*	campione per esame *m*	envío para inspección *m*
Anspruch (D)	—	claim	prétention *f*	pretesa *f*	reivindicación *f*
anstehen (D)	—	be due	être échu	essere scaduto	estar pendiente
anstellen (D)	—	employ	employer	impiegare	emplear
Anstellung (D)	—	employment	emploi *m*	impiego *m*	empleo *m*
answering machine (E)	Anrufbeantworter *m*	—	répondeur automatique *m*	segreteria telefonica *f*	contestador de llamadas *m*
Anteilnahme (D)	—	sympathy	participation *f*	interesse *m*	participación *f*

	D	E	F	I	Es
anticipazioni (I)	Lombardgeschäft *n*	lending on securities	prêt sur gage *m*	—	operaciones de pignoración *f pl*
anticipo (Es)	Vorschuß *m*	advance	avance *f*	anticipo *m*	—
anticipo (I)	Vorschuß *m*	advance	avance *f*	—	anticipo *m*
antidated cheque (E)	vordatierter Scheck *m*	—	chèque antidaté *m*	assegno antidatato *m*	cheque de fecha adelantada *m*
Antrag (D)	—	application	demande *f*	domanda *f*	solicitud *f*
Antragsformular (D)	—	application form	formulaire de demande *m*	modulo di domanda *m*	formulario de solicitud *m*
Antwort (D)	—	reply	réponse *f*	risposta *f*	respuesta *f*
anual (Es)	jährlich	annual	annuel	annuale	—
anualidad (Es)	Annuität *f*	annuity	annuité *f*	annualità *f*	—
anular (Es)	annullieren	annul	annuler	annullare	—
anuncio (Es)	Anzeige *f*	advertisement	annonce *f*	inserzione *f*	—
anuncio codificado (Es)	Chiffre-Anzeige *f*	advertisement under a box number	annonce chiffrée *f*	inserzione in cifra *f*	—
anuncio de empleo (Es)	Stellenanzeige *f*	position offered	annonce d'emploi *f*	inserzione d'impiego *f*	—
anuncio de prensa (Es)	Zeitungsanzeige *f*	advertisement	annonce de journal *f*	inserzione sul giornale *f*	—
anuncio de visita (Es)	Besuchsanmeldung *f*	announcement of a visitor	annonce de visiteurs *f*	avviso di visita *m*	—
Anwalt (D)	—	lawyer	avocat *m*	avvocato *m*	abogado *m*
Anwaltskanzlei (D)	—	lawyer's office	cabinet d'avocat *m*	studio d'avvocato *m*	bufete de abogado *m*
Anwartschaft (D)	—	candidature	candidature *f*	candidatura *f*	expectativa de un futuro pago *f*
Anweisung (D)	—	transfer	mandat *m*	ordine di pagamento *m*	transferencia *f*
Anwerbung (D)	—	recruitment	recrutement *m*	reclutamento *m*	contratación *f*
Anzahlung (D)	—	deposit	acompte *m*	pagamento in acconto *m*	pago a cuenta *m*
Anzeige (D)	—	advertisement	annonce *f*	inserzione *f*	anuncio *m*
Anzeigenformat (D)	—	size of an advertisement	format de l'annonce *m*	formato dell'inserzione *m*	tamaño del anuncio *m*
Anzeigengestaltung (D)	—	lay-out of an advertisement	arrangement de l'annonce *m*	tipo d'inserzione *m*	estructuración del anuncio *f*
Anzeigenplazierung (D)	—	placing of an advertisement	disposition de l'annonce *f*	collocamento dell'inserzione *m*	colocación del anuncio *f*
Anzeigenschaltung (D)	—	insertion of an advertisement	placement de l'annonce *m*	posizionamento dell'inserzione *m*	inserción del anuncio *f*
Anzeigenwerbung (D)	—	newspaper and magazine advertising	publicité par la presse *f*	pubblicità per inserzione *f*	publicidad por anuncios *f*
Anzeigenwirkung (D)	—	effectiveness of an advertisement	effet de l'annonce *m*	effetto dell'inserzione *m*	efectividad del anuncio *f*
apartado postal (Es)	Postfach *n*	post office box	boîte postale *f*	casella postale *f*	—
apartment (E)	Wohnung *f*	—	appartement *m*	abitazione *f*	vivienda *f*
apertura del credito documentario (I)	Akkreditiveröffnung *f*	opening of a letter of credit	ouverture d'un accréditif *f*	—	apertura de un crédito documentario *f*
apertura de los establecimientos (Es)	Geschäftseröffnung *f*	opening of a business	ouverture d'une affaire *f*	apertura di un negozio *f*	—
apertura del testamento (I)	Testaments-eröffnung *f*	opening of the will	ouverture du testament *f*	—	apertura de testamento *f*
apertura de testamento (Es)	Testaments-eröffnung *f*	opening of the will	ouverture du testament *f*	apertura del testamento *f*	—
apertura de una cuenta (Es)	Kontoeröffnung *f*	opening of an account	ouverture de compte *f*	apertura di un conto *f*	—
apertura de un crédito documentario (Es)	Akkreditiveröffnung *f*	opening of a letter of credit	ouverture d'un accréditif *f*	apertura del credito documentario *f*	—
apertura di credito documentario (I)	Dokumenten-akkreditiv *n*	documentary letter of credit	crédit documentaire *m*	—	crédito documentario *m*
apertura di credito documentario irrevocabile (I)	unwiderrufliches Akkreditiv *n*	irrevocable letter of credit	accréditif irrévocable *m*	—	crédito documentario irrevocable *m*

	D	E	F	I	Es
apertura di credito documentario semplice (I)	Barakkreditiv	cash letter of credit	accréditif payable en espèce *m*	—	crédito simple *m*
apertura di mercato (I)	Markteintritt *m*	entry into the market	entrée dans le marché *f*	—	entrada en el mercado *f*
apertura di un conto (I)	Kontoeröffnung *f*	opening of an account	ouverture d'un compte *f*	—	apertura de una cuenta *f*
apertura di un negozio (I)	Geschäftseröffnung *f*	opening of a business	ouverture d'une affaire *f*	—	apertura de los establecimientos *f*
aplazamiento[1] (Es)	Aufschiebung *f*	postponement	remise *f*	rinvio *m*	—
aplazamiento[2] (Es)	Vertagung *f*	postponement	ajournement *m*	rinvio *m*	—
aplazamiento de gastos (Es)	Ausgaben-verzögerung *f*	expenditure delay	dépenses retardées *f pl*	dilazione delle spese *f*	—
aplicación de la garantía (Es)	Garantieleistung *f*	guarantee	fourniture sous garantie *f*	prestazione di garanzia *f*	—
aplicación de los resultatdos (Es)	Gewinnverwendung *f*	appropriation of net income	utilisation des bénéfices *f*	impiego dell'utile *m*	—
apoderado especial (Es)	Handlungsbevoll-mächtigter *m*	commercial agent	personne ayant le pouvoir commercial *f*	mandatario commerciale *m*	—
apoderado general (Es)	Prokurist *m*	"Prokurist" (authorized clerk)	fondé de procuration *m*	procuratore *m*	—
apoderamiento (Es)	Bevollmächtigung *f*	authorization	pouvoir *m*	autorizzazione *f*	—
aportación de cobertura (Es)	Deckungsbeitrag *m*	contribution margin	proportion de garantie *f*	contributo per copertura *m*	—
appalto (I)	Ausschreibung *f*	tender	soumission *f*	—	concurso-subasta *m*
appareil à dicter (F)	Diktiergerät *n*	dictaphone	—	dittafono *m*	máquina de dictar *f*
appareil automatique (F)	Automat *m*	vending machine	—	distributore automatico *m*	distribuidor automático *m*
appareil téléphonique (F)	Fernsprecher *m*	telephone	—	telefono *m*	teléfono *m*
appartamento in condominio (I)	Eigentumswohnung *f*	freehold flat	logement en propriété *m*	—	piso en propiedad *m*
appartement (F)	Wohnung *f*	apartment	—	abitazione *f*	vivienda *f*
appeal court (E)	Berufungsgericht *n*	—	tribunal d'appel *m*	corte d'appello *f*	tribunal de apelación *m*
appel (F)	Abruf *m*	call	—	richiesta *f*	reclamación de la entrega de un pedido *f*
applicant (E)	Bewerber *m*	—	candidat *m*	aspirante *m*	aspirante *m*
application[1] (E)	Bewerbung *f*	—	candidature *f*	domanda d'impiego *f*	candidatura *f*
application[2] (E)	Antrag *m*	—	demande *f*	domanda *f*	solicitud *f*
application documents (E)	Bewerbungs-unterlagen *pl*	—	dossier de candidature *m*	documenti della domanda d'impiego *m pl*	documentos de solicitud *m pl*
application form (E)	Antragsformular *n*	—	formulaire de demande *m*	modulo di domanda *m*	formulario de solicitud *m*
appointment (E)	Ernennung *f*	—	nomination *f*	nomina *f*	nombramiento *m*
appointment for a meeting (E)	Gesprächstermin *m*	—	date de conversation *f*	appuntamento per un colloquio *m*	fecha de cita *f*
apport personnel (F)	Privateinlagen *pl*	private contribution	—	depositi privati *m pl*	depósitos privados *m pl*
apport social (F)	Stammeinlage *f*	initial contribution	—	quota sociale *f*	capital suscrito *m*
appreciation (E)	Wertzuwachs *m*	—	accroissement de valeur *m*	incremento di valore *m*	plusvalía *f*
apprendistato (I)	Ausbildung *f*	apprenticeship	apprentissage *m*	—	aprendizaje *m*
apprendistato di commercio (I)	kaufmännische Lehre *f*	commercial apprenticeship	apprentissage commercial *m*	—	aprendizaje comercial *m*
apprenti (F)	Trainee *m*	trainee	—	trainee *m*	entrenamiento
apprenticeship (E)	Ausbildung *f*	—	apprentissage *m*	apprendistato *m*	aprendizaje *m*
apprentissage (F)	Ausbildung *f*	apprenticeship	—	apprendistato *m*	aprendizaje *m*
apprentissage commercial (F)	kaufmännische Lehre *f*	commercial apprenticeship	—	apprendistato di commercio *m*	aprendizaje comercial *m*
appropriation of income (E)	Einkommens-verwendung *f*	—	utilisation du revenu *f*	impiego dei redditi *m*	distribución de la renta *f*

	D	E	F	I	Es
appropriation of net income (E)	Gewinnverwendung *f*	—	utilisation des bénéfices *f*	impiego dell'utile *m*	aplicación de los resultados *f*
appropriazione indebita (I)	Unterschlagung *f*	embezzlement	détournement *m*	—	defraudación *f*
approvisionnement (F)	Versorgung *f*	supply	—	approvvigionamento *m*	abastecimiento *m*
approvisionnement de matières premières (F)	Rohstoffversorgung *f*	provisioning with raw materials	—	approvvigionamento di materie prime *m*	aprovisionamiento de materias primas *m*
approvisionnement en énergie (F)	Energieversorgung *f*	energy supply	—	approvvigionamento d'energia *m*	abastecimiento energético *m*
approvvigionamento (I)	Versorgung *f*	supply	approvisionnement *m*	—	abastecimiento *m*
approvvigionamento d'energia (I)	Energieversorgung *f*	energy supply	approvisionnement en énergie *m*	—	abastecimiento energético *m*
approvvigionamento di materie prime (I)	Rohstoffversorgung *f*	provisioning with raw materials	approvisionnement de matières premières *m*	—	aprovisionamiento de materias primas *m*
appuntamento di presentazione (I)	Vorstellungstermin *m*	date of interview	rendez-vous de présentation *m*	—	fecha de entrevista personal *f*
appuntamento per un colloquio (I)	Gesprächstermin *m*	appointment for a meeting	date de conversation *f*	—	fecha de cita *f*
aprendizaje (Es)	Ausbildung *f*	apprenticeship	apprentissage *m*	apprendistato *m*	—
aprendizaje comercial (Es)	kaufmännische Lehre *f*	commercial apprenticeship	apprentissage commercial *m*	apprendistato di commercio *m*	—
après avoir réçu la facture (F)	nach Erhalt der Rechnung	on receipt of the invoice	—	a ricevimento della fattura	después de haber recibo la factura
aprovisionamiento de materias primas (Es)	Rohstoffversorgung *f*	provisioning with raw materials	approvisionnement de matières premières *m*	approvvigionamento di materie prime *m*	—
a provvigione (I)	auf Provisionsbasis	on a commission basis	à la commission	—	a comisión
a prueba (Es)	auf Probe	on trial	à l'essai	in prova	—
a prueba de crisis (Es)	krisenfest	slump-proof	insensible aux influences de la crise économique	resistente alle crisi	—
Aquisition (D)	—	acquisition	acquisition *f*	acquisizione *f*	adquisición *f*
arancel aduanero cuantitativo (Es)	Mengenzoll *m*	specific duty	droit de douane par quantité *m*	dazio di quantità *m*	—
arancel de importación (Es)	Einfuhrzoll *m*	import duty	droit d'entrée *m*	dazio d'importazione *m*	—
Arbeit (D)	—	work	travail *m*	lavoro *m*	trabajo *m*
Arbeiter (D)	—	worker	travailleur *m*	operaio *m*	trabajador *m*
Arbeiterklasse (D)	—	working class	classe ouvrière *f*	classe degli operai *f*	clase obrera *f*
Arbeitgeber (D)	—	employer	employeur *m*	datore di lavoro *m*	patrón *m*
Arbeitnehmer (D)	—	employee	salarié *m*	prestatore d'opera *m*	empleado *m*
Arbeitnehmerbeteiligung (D)	—	worker participation	participation du personnel *f*	partecipazione dei prestatori d'opera *f*	participación de los empleados *f*
Arbeitsanfall (D)	—	volume of work	travail à exécuter *m*	volume di lavoro *m*	volumen de trabajo *m*
Arbeitsbewertung (D)	—	job evaluation	qualification du travail *f*	valutazione del lavoro *f*	evaluación del trabajo *f*
Arbeitserlaubnis (D)	—	work permit	permis de travail *m*	permesso di lavoro *m*	permiso de trabajo *m*
Arbeitsertrag (D)	—	work performed	rendement du travail *m*	rendimento del lavoro *m*	rendimiento del trabajo *m*
Arbeitsessen (D)	—	working lunch	déjeuner de travail *m*	pranzo di lavoro *m*	comida de trabajo *f*
arbeitsintensiv (D)	—	labour-intensive	déterminé par le facteur main-d'œuvre	ad alta incidenza di lavoro	con gran intensidad de mano de obra
Arbeitsleistung (D)	—	productivity	rendement *m*	produttività *f*	productividad *f*
Arbeitslosenunterstützung (D)	—	unemployment benefits	indemnité de chômage *f*	sussidio di disoccupazione *m*	prestaciones por desempleo *f pl*
Arbeitslosigkeit (D)	—	unemployment	chômage *m*	disoccupazione *f*	desempleo *m*
Arbeitsmarkt (D)	—	labour market	marché du travail *m*	mercato del lavoro *m*	mercado laboral *m*
Arbeitsnachfrage (D)	—	job demand	demande d'emploi *f*	domanda di lavoro *f*	demanda de trabajo *f*
Arbeitsnachweis (D)	—	employment vacancies	emploi vacant *m*	informazioni sui posti vacanti *f pl*	servicio de colocación *m*
Arbeitsnorm (D)	—	fair labour standards	norme de travail *f*	norma di lavoro *f*	norma de producción *f*

	D	E	F	I	Es
Arbeitsplatz (D)	—	place of employment	poste de travail *m*	posto di lavoro *m*	puesto de trabajo *m*
Arbeitsplatzwechsel (D)	—	change of employment	changement d'emploi *m*	cambiamento del posto di lavoro *m*	cambio de puesto *m*
Arbeitspsychologie (D)	—	industrial psychology	psychologie de travail *f*	psicologia del lavoro *f*	psicología laboral *f*
Arbeitsraum (D)	—	workroom	lieu de travail *m*	locale di lavoro *m*	sala de trabajo *f*
Arbeitsrecht (D)	—	labour law	législation industrielle *f*	diritto di lavoro *m*	derecho laboral *m*
Arbeitsrhythmus (D)	—	work rhythm	rythme de travail *m*	ritmo di lavoro *m*	ritmo de trabajo *m*
Arbeitsschutz (D)	—	employment protection	protection sociale du travail *f*	tutela del lavoro *f*	protección del trabajo *f*
Arbeitssicherheit (D)	—	safety at work	sécurité du travail *f*	sicurezza del lavoro *f*	seguridad del trabajo *f*
Arbeitstag (D)	—	working day	jour de travail *m*	giorno lavorativo *m*	día laboral *m*
Arbeitstechnik (D)	—	working technique	technique de travail *f*	tecnica lavorativa *f*	técnica del trabajo *f*
Arbeitsteilung (D)	—	division of labour	division du travail *f*	divisione del lavoro *f*	división del trabajo *f*
Arbeitsunfall (D)	—	industrial injury	accident du travail *m*	infortunio sul posto di lavoro *m*	accidente profesional *m*
Arbeitsverhältnis (D)	—	employee-employer relationship	rapport de travail *m*	rapporto di lavoro *m*	relación laboral *f*
Arbeitsverhältnis auf Probe (D)	—	employee-employer relationship on a trial basis	contrat de travail convenu à l'essai *m*	rapporto di lavoro in prova *m*	relación laboral a prueba *f*
Arbeitsvermittlung (D)	—	employment agency	bureau de placement *m*	ufficio di collocamento *m*	agencia laboral *f*
Arbeitsvertrag (D)	—	contract of employment	contrat de travail *m*	contratto di lavoro *m*	contrato laboral *m*
Arbeitsvorbereitung (D)	—	job preparation	préparation du travail *f*	preparazione del lavoro *f*	preparación laboral *f*
Arbeitswoche (D)	—	working week	semaine de travail *f*	settimana lavorativa *f*	semana laboral *f*
Arbeitszeit (D)	—	working hours	heures de travail *f pl*	orario di lavoro *m*	jornada laboral *f*
Arbeits-zufriedenheit (D)	—	job satisfaction	satisfaction de travail *f*	soddisfazione del lavoro *f*	satisfacción en el trabajo *f*
Arbitrage (D)	—	arbitration	arbitrage *m*	arbitraggio *m*	arbitraje *m*
arbitrage (F)	Arbitrage *f*	arbitration	—	arbitraggio *m*	arbitraje *m*
arbitrage sur les devises (F)	Devisenarbitrage *f*	exchange arbitrage	—	arbitraggio valutario *m*	arbitraje de divisas *m*
arbitraggio (I)	Arbitrage *f*	arbitration	arbitrage *m*	—	arbitraje *m*
arbitraggio valutario (I)	Devisenarbitrage *f*	exchange arbitrage	arbitrage sur les devises *m*	—	arbitraje de divisas *m*
arbitraje (Es)	Arbitrage *f*	arbitration	arbitrage *m*	arbitraggio *m*	—
arbitraje de divisas (Es)	Devisenarbitrage *f*	exchange arbitrage	arbitrage sur les devises *m*	arbitraggio valutario *m*	—
arbitration (E)	Arbitrage *f*	—	arbitrage *m*	arbitraggio *m*	arbitraje *m*
Archiv (D)	—	archives	archives *f pl*	archivio *m*	archivo *m*
archives (E)	Archiv *n*	—	archives *f pl*	archivio *m*	archivo *m*
archives[1] (F)	Aktenablage *f*	filing	—	archivio delle pratiche *m*	archivo *m*
archives[2] (F)	Archiv *n*	archives	—	archivio *m*	archivo *m*
archivio[1] (I)	Archiv *n*	archives	archives *f pl*	—	archivo *m*
archivio[2] (I)	Ablage *f*	file	collection des dossiers *f*	—	archivo *m*
archivio delle pratiche (I)	Aktenablage *f*	filing	archives *f pl*	—	archivo *m*
archivo[1] (Es)	Archiv *n*	archives	archives *f pl*	archivio *m*	—
archivo[2] (Es)	Aktenablage *f*	filing	archives *f pl*	archivio delle pratiche *m*	—
archivo[3] (Es)	Ablage *f*	file	collection des dossiers *f*	archivio *m*	—
archivo de datos (Es)	Datei *f*	file	fichier de données *m*	file *m*	—
area coltivata (I)	Anbaufläche *f*	area under cultivation	surface plantée *f*	—	superficie agrícola utilizada *f*

	D	E	F	I	Es
area doganale di confine (I)	Zollgrenzgebiet *n*	customs frontier district	territoire de surveillance douanière *m*	—	territorio aduanero fronterizo *m*
area edificabile (I)	Bauland *n*	building land	espace à bâtir *m*	—	terreno edificable *m*
área monetaria (Es)	Währungsgebiet *n*	currency area	zone monétaire *f*	area monetaria *f*	—
area monetaria (I)	Währungsgebiet *n*	currency area	zone monétaire *f*	—	área monetaria *f*
area representative (E)	Gebietsvertreter *m*	—	représentant régional *m*	agente di zona *m*	representante regional *m*
area sales manager (E)	Gebietsverkaufs-leiter *m*	—	chef de vente régionale *m*	direttore di vendita regionale *m*	jefe de venta regional *m*
area under cultivation (E)	Anbaufläche *f*	—	surface plantée *f*	area coltivata *f*	superficie agrícola utilizada *f*
a requerimiento (Es)	auf Abruf	on call	à convenance	su richiesta	—
argent[1] (F)	Silber *n*	silver	—	argento *m*	plata *f*
argent[2] (F)	Geld *n*	money	—	denaro *m*	dinero *m*/efectivo *m*
argent au jour le jour (F)	Tagesgeld *n*	day-to-day money	—	prestito giornaliero *m*	dinero de día a día *m*
argent bon marché (F)	billiges Geld *n*	easy money	—	crediti agevolati *m pl*	dinero barato *m*
argent comptant (F)	Bargeld *n*	cash	—	denaro contante *m*	dinero efectivo *m*
argent immobilisé (F)	Festgeld *n*	fixed deposit	—	denaro vincolato *m*	depósito a plazo *m*
argento (I)	Silber *n*	silver	argent *m*	—	plata *f*
argomentazione (I)	Argumentation *f*	argumentation	argumentation *f*	—	argumentación *f*
argumentación (Es)	Argumentation *f*	argumentation	argumentation *f*	argomentazione *f*	—
Argumentation (D)	—	argumentation	argumentation *f*	argomentazione *f*	argumentación *f*
argumentation (E)	Argumentation *f*	—	argumentation *f*	argomentazione *f*	argumentación *f*
argumentation (F)	Argumentation *f*	argumentation	—	argomentazione *f*	argumentación *f*
Argumentations-stärke (D)	—	talent for argumentation	capacité d'argumentation *f*	forza d'argomentazione *f*	fuerza de argumentación *f*
a ricevimento della fattura (I)	nach Erhalt der Rechnung	on receipt of the invoice	après avoir réçu la facture	—	después de haber recibido la factura
armador (Es)	Reeder *m*	shipowner	armateur *m*	armatore *m*	—
armateur (F)	Reeder *m*	shipowner	—	armatore *m*	armador *m*
armatore (I)	Reeder *m*	shipowner	armateur *m*	—	armador *m*
armonizado a nivel comunitario (Es)	EG-einheitlich	standardized within the European Community	uniforme au niveau communautaire	uniforme all'interno della CEE	—
arrangeant (F)	kulant	accommodating	—	corrente	de fácil avenencia
arrangement de l'annonce (F)	Anzeigengestaltung *f*	lay-out of an advertisement	—	tipo d'inserzione *m*	estructuración del anuncio *f*
arrangement forcé (F)	Zwangsvergleich *m*	compulsory settlement	—	concordato fallimentare *m*	convenio forzoso *m*
arranging for a credit (E)	Kreditvermittlung *f*	—	médiation du crédit *f*	intermediazione di crediti *f*	mediación de créditos *f*
arrears (E)	Rückstand *m*	—	arriéré *m*	arretrato *m*	pago atrasado *m*/ atraso *m*
arrendamiento (Es)	Mietzins *m*	rent	prix de location *m*	canone di locazione *m*	—
arrendatante financiero (Es)	Leasing-Nehmer *m*	lessee	preneur de leasing *m*	utente del leasing *m*	—
arrendatario financiero (Es)	Leasing-Geber *m*	lessor	donneur de leasing *m*	concedente del leasing *m*	—
arrêt de mise en accusation (F)	Eröffnungs-beschluß *m*	order opening a trial	—	decreto di citazione in giudizio *m*	acuerdo de apertura *m*
arrêt d'une procédure (F)	Verfahrens-einstellung *f*	abatement of an action	—	sospensione del procedimento *f*	sobreseimiento del proceso *m*
arretrato (I)	Rückstand *m*	arrears	arriéré *m*	—	pago atrasado *m*/ atraso *m*
arriéré (F)	Rückstand *m*	arrears	—	arretrato *m*	pago atrasado *m*/ atraso *m*
arriéré de payement (F)	Zahlungsrückstand *m*	payment in arrears	—	morosità di pagamento *f*	pago atrasado *m*
arriesgado (Es)	riskant	risky	risqué	rischioso	—
arrival of goods (E)	Wareneingang *m*	—	entrée de marchandises *f*	entrata merci *f*	entrada de mercancías *f*

	D	E	F	I	Es
art de vendre (F)	Verkaufstechnik *f*	sales technique	—	tecnica di vendita *f*	técnica de venta *f*
art director (E)	Art-director *m*	—	directeur artistique *m*	art director *m*	director artístico *m*
art director (I)	Art-director *m*	art director	directeur artistique *m*	—	director artístico *m*
Art-director (D)	—	art director	directeur artistique *m*	art director *m*	director artístico *m*
artesanía (Es)	Handwerk *n*	craft trade	artisanat *m*	artigianato *m*	—
article de mode (F)	Modeartikel *m*	fashion article	—	articolo di moda *m*	artículos de moda *m pl*
articolo di marca (I)	Markenartikel *m*	brandname article	produit de marque *m*	—	artículo de marca *m*
articolo di moda (I)	Modeartikel *m*	fashion article	article de mode *m*	—	artículos de moda *m pl*
artículo fundamental (Es)	Stapelware *f*	staple commodities	produit de stockage *m*	merce immagazzinata *f*	—
artículos de moda (Es)	Modeartikel *m*	fashion article	article de mode *m*	articolo di moda *m*	—
artigianato (I)	Handwerk *n*	craft trade	artisanat *m*	—	artesanía *f*
artisanat (F)	Handwerk *n*	craft trade	—	artigianato *m*	artesanía *f*
as agreed (E)	vereinbarungsgemäß	—	comme convenu	come convenuto	según lo acordado
ascendente (Es)	steigend	rising	croissant(e)	in aumento	—
ascenso (Es)	Beförderung *f*	promotion	nomination *f*	promozione *f*	—
asegurado (Es)	Versicherungs-nehmer *m*	insured person	souscripteur d'une assurance *m*	assicurato *m*	—
asesor (Es)	Berater *m*	adviser	conseiller *m*	consulente *m*	—
asesor de marketing (Es)	Marketingberater *m*	marketing consultant	conseiller de marketing *m*	consulente di marketing *m*	—
asesor fiscal (Es)	Steuerberater *m*	tax adviser	conseiller fiscal *m*	consulente fiscale *m*	—
asiento en otra cuenta (Es)	Umbuchung *f*	transfer of an entry	jeu d'écritures *m*	giro di partite *m*	—
asignación (Es)	Zuteilung *f*	allocation	répartition *f*	attribuzione *f*/ ripartizione *f*	—
asked price (E)	Briefkurs *m*	—	cours de vente *m*	prezzo d'offerta *m*	cotización ofrecida *f*
asociación[1] (Es)	Verband *m*	association	association *f*	associazione *f*	—
asociación[2] (Es)	Verein *m*	association	association *f*	associazione *f*	—
asociación con un fin determinado (Es)	Zweckverband *m*	special purpose association	association à but déterminé *f*	consorzio intercomunale *m*	—
asociación económica (Es)	Wirtschafts-verband *m*	trade association	association économique *f*	associazione economica *f*	—
asociación empresarial (Es)	Unternehmer-verband *m*	employers' association	association des chefs d'entreprise *f*	unione degli imprenditori *f*	—
asoramiento (Es)	Beratung *f*	advice	consultation *f*	consulenza *f*	—
aspirante (Es)	Bewerber *m*	applicant	candidat *m*	aspirante *m*	—
aspirante (I)	Bewerber *m*	applicant	candidat *m*	—	aspirante *m*
as quickly as possible (E)	schnellstmöglich	—	le plus vite possible	al più presto possibile	tan rápido como sea posible
assainissement (F)	Sanierung *f*	urban renewal	—	risanamento *m*	saneamiento *m*
assegnazione (I)	Zuwendung *f*	bestowal	affectation *f*	—	gratificación *f*
assegno (I)	Scheck *m*	cheque	chèque *m*	—	cheque *m*
assegno all'ordine (I)	Orderscheck *m*	order cheque	chèque à ordre *m*	—	cheque a la orden *m*
assegno al portatore[1] (I)	Inhaberscheck *m*	cheque payable to bearer	chèque au porteur *m*	—	cheque al portador *m*
assegno al portatore[2] (I)	Überbringerscheck *m*	bearer cheque	chèque au porteur *m*	—	cheque al portador *m*
assegno antidatato (I)	vordatierter Scheck *m*	antedated cheque	chèque antidaté *m*	—	cheque de fecha adelantada *m*
assegno circolare (I)	Barscheck *m*	open cheque	chèque non barré *m*	—	cheque de caja *m*
assegno falsificato (I)	gefälschter Scheck *m*	forged cheque	chèque maquillé *m*	—	cheque falsificado *m*
assegno in bianco (I)	Blankoscheck *m*	blank cheque	chèque en blanc *m*	—	cheque en blanco *m*
assegno postale (I)	Postscheck *m*	postal giro	chèque postal *m*	—	cheque postal *m*
assegno sbarrato[1] (I)	gekreuzter Scheck *m*	crossed cheque	chèque barré *m*	—	cheque cruzado *m*
assegno sbarrato[2] (I)	Verrechnungs-scheck *m*	crossed cheque	chèque à porter en compte *m*	—	cheque cruzado *m*
assegno turistico (I)	Reisescheck *m*	traveller's cheque	chèque de voyage *m*	—	cheque de viaje *m*

	D	E	F	I	Es
Assekuranz (D)	—	assurance	assurance *f*	assicurazione *f*	seguro *m*
assemblea dei soci (I)	Gesellschafter-versammlung *f*	meeting of shareholders	réunion des associés *f*	—	junta social *f*
assemblea generale annuale (I)	Jahreshaupt-versammlung *f*	annual meeting of shareholders	assemblée générale annuelle *f*	—	junta general anual *f*
assemblée des créanciers (F)	Gläubiger-versammlung *f*	creditors' meeting	—	riunione dei creditori *f*	junta de acreedores *f*
assemblée générale annuelle (F)	Jahreshaupt-versammlung *f*	annual meeting	—	assemblea generale annuale *f*	junta general anual *f*
assente (I)	abwesend	absent	absent	—	ausente
assets[1] (E)	Aktivbestand *m*	—	actif *m*	effettivo *m*	activo disponible *m*
assets[2] (E)	Aktiva *pl*	—	masse active *f*	attivo *m*	activo *m*
assets value (E)	Substanzwert *m*	—	valeur de remplacement *f*	valore sostanziale *m*	valor sustancial *m*
assicurato (I)	Versicherungs-nehmer *m*	insured person	souscripteur d'une assurance *m*	—	asegurado *m*
assicuratore diretto (I)	Erstversicherer *m*	direct insurer	assureur direct *m*	—	primer asegurador *m*
assicurazione[1] (I)	Assekuranz *f*	assurance	assurance *f*	—	seguro *m*
assicurazione[2] (I)	Versicherung *f*	insurance	assurance *f*	—	seguro *m*
assicurazione autoveicoli (I)	Kraftfahrzeug-versicherung *f*	motor insurance	assurance responsabilité civile automobile *f*	—	seguro de automóviles *m*
assicurazione contro il furto (I)	Diebstahl-versicherung *f*	theft insurance	assurance contre le vol *f*	—	seguro contra el robo *m*
assicurazione contro il furto con scasso (I)	Einbruch-versicherung *f*	housebreaking insurance	assurance contre le vol avec effraction *f*	—	seguro contra robo con fractura *m*
assicurazione contro incendi (I)	Feuerversicherung *f*	fire insurance	assurance contre l'incendie *f*	—	seguro contra incendios *m*
assicurazione contro infortuni (I)	Unfallversicherung *f*	personal accident insurance	assurance accidents corporels *f*	—	seguro de accidentes *m*
assicurazione contro le malattie (I)	Kranken-versicherung *f*	health insurance	assurance maladie *f*	—	seguro de enfermedad *m*
assicurazione corpi del ramo trasporto (I)	Kaskoversicherung *f*	comprehensive insurance	assurance tous risques *f*	—	seguro de casco *m*
assicurazione degli impiegati (I)	Angestellten-versicherung *f*	Salaried Employees' Pension Insurance	assurance invalidité-vieillesse des employés *f*	—	seguro de empleados *m*
assicurazione dei crediti (I)	Kreditversicherung *f*	credit insurance	assurance crédit *f*	—	seguro crediticio *m*
assicurazione dei fabbricati (I)	Gebäude-versicherung *f*	insurance on buildings	assurance des bâtiments *f*	—	seguro inmobiliario *m*
assicurazione dei trasporti (I)	Transport-versicherung *f*	transportation insurance	assurance transports *f*	—	seguro de transporte *m*
assicurazione del bagaglio (I)	Reisegepäck-versicherung *f*	baggage insurance	assurance des bagages *f*	—	seguro de equipajes *m*
assicurazione della responsabilità civile (I)	Haftpflicht-versicherung *f*	third party liability insurance	assurance respon-sabilité civile *f*	—	seguro de respon-sabilidad civil *m*
assicurazione delle macchine (I)	Maschinen-versicherung *f*	machine insurance	assurance des machines *f*	—	seguro de maquinaria *m*
assicurazione di cose (I)	Sachversicherung *f*	property insurance	assurance de choses *f*	—	seguro de cosas *m*
assicurazione di persone (I)	Personen-versicherung *f*	insurance of persons	assurance des personnes *f*	—	seguro personal *m*
assicurazione invalidità e vecchiaia (I)	Rentenversicherung *f*	old-age pension insurance	assurance sociale in-validité-vieillesse *f*	—	seguro de pensiones *m*
assicurazione per la vecchiaia (I)	Altersversicherung *f*	old age insurance	assurance-vieillesse *f*	—	seguro de vejez *m*
assicurazione privata (I)	Privatversicherung *f*	private insurance	assurance privée *f*	—	seguro privado *m*
assicurazione recessione viaggio (I)	Reiserücktritts-versicherung *f*	travel cancellation insurance	assurance de résilia-tion du voyage *f*	—	seguro de rescisión del viaje *m*
assicurazione rischio-vita (I)	Risiko-Lebens-versicherung *f*	term life insurance	assurance-vie temporaire *f*	—	seguro de vida temporal *m*
assicurazione sulla vita (I)	Lebens-versicherung *f*	life insurance	assurance vie *f*	—	seguro de vida *m*
assignee (E)	Zessionar *m*	—	cessionnaire *m*	cessionario *m*	cesionario *m*

	D	E	F	I	Es
assignment (E)	Abtretung *f*	—	cession *f*	cessione *f*	cesión *f*
assignor (E)	Zedent *m*	—	cédant *m*	cedente *m*	cedente *m*
assistenza sociale (I)	Sozialhilfe *f*	public assistance	aide sociale *f*	—	ayuda social *f*
association[1] (E)	Verband *m*	—	association *f*	associazione *f*	asociación *f*
association[2] (E)	Verein *m*	—	association *f*	associazione *f*	asociación *f*
association[1] (F)	Verein *m*	association	—	associazione *f*	asociación *f*
association[2] (F)	Verband *m*	association	—	associazione *f*	asociación *f*
association à but déterminé (F)	Zweckverband *m*	special purpose association	—	consorzio intercomunale *m*	asociación con un fin determinado *f*
association commerciale en participation (F)	stille Gesellschaft *f*	dormant partnership	—	associazione in partecipazione *f*	sociedad en participación *f*
association des chefs d'entreprise (F)	Unternehmerverband *m*	employers' association	—	unione degli imprenditori *f*	asociación empresarial *f*
association économique (F)	Wirtschaftsverband *m*	trade association	—	associazione economica *f*	asociación económica *f*
associazione[1] (I)	Verein *m*	association	association *f*	—	asociación *f*
associazione[2] (I)	Sozietät *f*	partnership	groupe de sociétaires *m*	—	sociedad *f*
associazione[3] (I)	Verband *m*	association	association *f*	—	asociación *f*
associazione di categoria (I)	Berufsgenossenschaft *f*	professional association	association professionnelle d'assurance accident *f*	—	mutua profesional *f*
associazione economica (I)	Wirtschaftsverband *m*	trade association	association économique *f*	—	asociación económica *f*
associazione in partecipazione (I)	stille Gesellschaft *f*	dormant partnership	association commerciale en participation *f*	—	sociedad en participación *f*
associé[1] (F)	Gesellschafter *m*	partner	—	socio *m*	socio *m*
associé[2] (F)	Geschäftspartner *m*	business partner	—	partner commerciale *m*	socio *m*
associé prenant part à la gestion (F)	aktiver Teilhaber *m*	active partner	—	socio attivo *m*	socio activo *m*
assorbimento (I)	Absorption *f*	absorption	absorption *f*	—	absorción *f*
assortiment (F)	Sortiment *n*	assortment	—	assortimento *m*	surtido *m*
assortimento (I)	Sortiment *n*	assortment	assortiment *m*	—	surtido *m*
assortment (E)	Sortiment *n*	—	assortiment *m*	assortimento *m*	surtido *m*
assortment policy (E)	Sortimentspolitik *f*	—	politique d'assortiment *f*	politica dell'assortimento *f*	política de surtido *f*
assortment structuring (E)	Sortimentsgestaltung *f*	—	structure d'assortiment *f*	composizione dell'assortimento *f*	configuración del surtido *f*
assujettissement obligatoire à l'assurance (F)	Versicherungspflicht *f*	liability to insure	—	obbligo d'assicurazione *m*	obligatoriedad del seguro *f*
assurance (E)	Assekuranz *f*	—	assurance *f*	assicurazione *f*	seguro *m*
assurance[1] (F)	Versicherung *f*	insurance	—	assicurazione *f*	seguro *m*
assurance[2] (F)	Assekuranz *f*	assurance	—	assicurazione *f*	seguro *m*
assurance accidents corporels (F)	Unfallversicherung *f*	personal accident insurance	—	assicurazione contro infortuni *f*	seguro de accidentes *m*
assurance contre le vol (F)	Diebstahlversicherung *f*	theft insurance	—	assicurazione contro il furto *f*	seguro contra el robo *m*
assurance contre le vol avec effraction (F)	Einbruchversicherung *f*	housebreaking insurance	—	assicurazione contro il furto con scasso *f*	seguro contra robo con fractura *m*
assurance contre l'incendie (F)	Feuerversicherung *f*	fire insurance	—	assicurazione contro incendi *f*	seguro contra incendios *m*
assurance crédit (F)	Kreditversicherung *f*	credit insurance	—	assicurazione dei crediti *f*	seguro crediticio *m*
assurance de choses (F)	Sachversicherung *f*	property insurance	—	assicurazione di cose *f*	seguro de cosas *m*
assurance de résiliation du voyage (F)	Reiserücktrittsversicherung *f*	travel cancellation insurance	—	assicurazione recessione viaggio *f*	seguro de rescisión del viaje *m*
assurance des bagages (F)	Reisegepäckversicherung *f*	baggage insurance	—	assicurazione del bagaglio *f*	seguro de equipajes *m*
assurance des bâtiments (F)	Gebäudeversicherung *f*	insurance on buildings	—	assicurazione dei fabbricati *f*	seguro inmobiliario *m*

	D	E	F	I	Es
assurance des machines (F)	Maschinen-versicherung *f*	machine insurance	—	assicurazione delle macchine *f*	seguro de maquinaria *m*
assurance des personnes (F)	Personen-versicherung *f*	insurance of persons	—	assicurazione di persone *f*	seguro personal *m*
assurance invalidité-vieillesse des employés (F)	Angestellten-versicherung *f*	Salaried Employees' Pension Insurance	—	assicurazione degli impiegati *f*	seguro de empleados *m*
assurance maladie (F)	Kranken-versicherung *f*	health insurance	—	assicurazione contro le malattie *f*	seguro de enfermedad *m*
assurance mutuelle (F)	Versicherung auf Gegenseitigkeit *f*	mutual insurance	—	mutua assicurazione *f*	caja de socorros mutuos *f*
assurance privée (F)	Privatversicherung *f*	private insurance	—	assicurazione privata *f*	seguro privado *m*
assurance responsabilité civile (F)	Haftpflicht-versicherung *f*	third party liability insurance	—	assicurazione della responsabilità civile *f*	seguro de responsabilidad civil *m*
assurance responsabilité civile automobile (F)	Kraftfahrzeug-versicherung *f*	motor insurance	—	assicurazione autoveicoli *f*	seguro de automóviles *m*
assurance sociale (F)	Sozialversicherung *f*	social security	—	previdenza sociale *f*	seguro social *m*
assurance sociale invalidité-vieillesse (F)	Rentenversicherung *f*	old-age pension insurance	—	assicurazione invalidità e vecchiaia *f*	seguro de pensiones *m*
assurance tous risques (F)	Kaskoversicherung *f*	comprehensive insurance	—	assicurazione ramo trasporto *f*	seguro de casco *m*
assurance transports (F)	Transport-versicherung *f*	transportation insurance	—	assicurazione dei trasporti *f*	seguro de transporte *m*
assurance vie (F)	Lebensversicherung *f*	life insurance	—	assicurazione sulla vita *f*	seguro de vida *m*
assurance-vieillesse (F)	Altersversicherung *f*	old age pension	—	assicurazione per *f* la vecchiaia	seguro de vejez *m*
assurance-vie temporaire (F)	Risiko-Lebens-versicherung *f*	term life insurance	—	assicurazione rischio-vita *f*	seguro de vida temporal *m*
assureur direct (F)	Erstversicherer *m*	direct insurer	—	assicuratore diretto *m*	primer asegurador *m*
asta (I)	Auktion *f*	auction	vente à l'enchère *f*	—	subasta *f*
asta giudiziaria (I)	Zwangs-versteigerung *f*	sale by court order	vente de biens par justice *f*	—	subasta forzosa *f*
at best (E)	bestens	—	au mieux	ottimo	al mejor cambio
at best price (E)	billigst	—	au meilleur prix	al prezzo più basso	al mejor cambio
a título de pago[1] (Es)	zahlungshalber	on account of payment	à titre de payement	a titolo di pagamento	—
a título de pago[2] (Es)	zahlungsstatt	in lieu of payment	à titre de payement	a titolo di pagamento	—
a titolo di pagamento[1] (I)	zahlungshalber	on account of payment	pour raison de payement	—	a título de pago
a titolo di pagamento[2] (I)	zahlungsstatt	in lieu of payment	à titre de payement	—	a título de pago
à titre de payement (F)	zahlungsstatt	in lieu of payment	—	a titolo di pagamento	a título de pago
à titre gracieux (F)	unentgeltlich	free of charge	—	gratuito	gratuito
atmósfera (Es)	Atmosphäre *f*	atmosphere	atmosphère *f*	atmosfera *f*	—
atmosfera (I)	Atmosphäre *f*	atmosphere	atmosphère *f*	—	atmósfera *f*
atmosfera di lavoro (I)	Betriebsklima *n*	working conditions and human relations	climat social *m*	—	ambiente de trabajo *m*
Atmosphäre (D)	—	atmosphere	atmosphère *f*	atmosfera *f*	atmósfera *f*
atmosphere (E)	Atmosphäre *f*	—	atmosphère *f*	atmosfera *f*	atmósfera *f*
atmosphère (F)	Atmosphäre *f*	atmosphere	—	atmosfera *f*	atmósfera *f*
Atomkraftwerk (D)	—	nuclear power plant	centrale nucléaire *f*	centrale nucleare *f*	central nuclear *f*
at sight (E)	auf Sicht	—	à vue	a vista	a la vista
attachment of earnings (E)	Lohnpfändung *f*	—	saisie-arrêt sur le salaire *f*	pignoramento del salario *m*	embargo de salario *m*
atteggiamento razionale (I)	Rationalverhalten *n*	rational behaviour	comportement rationnel *m*	—	comportamiento racional *m*
attività pubblica (I)	Staatstätigkeit *f*	state activity	activité de l'Etat *f*	—	actividad del Estado *f*
attivo[1] (I)	Haben *n*	credit side	avoir *m*	—	haber *m*
attivo[2] (I)	Aktiva *pl*	assets	masse active *f*	—	activo *m*
attivo[3] (I)	erwerbstätig	gainfully employed	actif	—	activo

	D	E	F	I	Es
attivo fisso (I)	Anlagevermögen *n*	fixed assets	valeurs immobilisées *f pl*	—	activo fijo *m*
atto amministrativo (I)	Verwaltungsakt *m*	administrative act	acte administratif *m*	—	acto administrativo *m*
attribuzione (I)	Zuteilung *f*	allocation	répartition *f*	—	asignación *f*
au comptant (F)	gegen Barzahlung	against cash	—	contro pagamento in contanti	al contado
au pair (F)	pari	at par	—	pari	a la par
auction[1] (E)	Versteigerung *f*	—	vente à l'enchère *f*	vendita all'asta *f*	subasta *f*
auction[2] (E)	Auktion *f*	—	vente à l'enchère *f*	asta *f*	subasta *f*
auction fees (E)	Auktionsgebühr *f*	—	droits de vente aux enchères *m pl*	diritto d'asta *m*	gastos de subasta *m pl*
audit[1] (E)	Abschlußprüfung *f*	—	vérification des comptes *f*	revisione *f*	revisión contable *f*
audit[2] (E)	Revision *f*	—	vérification *f*	revisione *f*	revisión *f*
auditing (E)	Wirtschaftsprüfung *f*	—	contrôle de la gestion et des comptes *m*	revisione *f*	revisoría *f*
auditor[1] (E)	Abschlußprüfer *m*	—	vérificateur des comptes *m*	revisore *m*	revisor contable *m*
auditor[2] (E)	Betriebsprüfer *m*	—	expert-comptable *m*	revisore aziendale *m*	contador público *m*
auditor[3] (E)	Wirtschaftsprüfer *m*	—	expert comptable économique et financier *m*	revisore dei conti *m*	revisor de cuentas *m*/ experto contable *m*
auditor[4] (E)	Rechnungsprüfer *m*	—	commissaire aux comptes *m*	revisore dei conti *m*	revisor contable *m*
auf Abruf (D)	—	on call	à convenance	su richiesta	a requerimiento
Aufbauphase (D)	—	development phase	phase d'organisation *f*	fase di costruzione *f*	fase de desarrollo *f*
aufbereiten (D)	—	process/prepare	élaborer/traiter	elaborare/lavorare	elaborar/tratar
Aufbewahrungs-pflicht (D)	—	obligation to preserve records	obligation de conservation *f*	obbligo di conservazione *m*	deber de conservación *m*
Aufenthalts-erlaubnis (D)	—	residence permit	autorisation de séjour *f*	permesso di soggiorno *m*	permiso de residencia *m*
Aufgeld (D)	—	agio	prime *f*	aggio *m*	agio *m*
Aufkleber (D)	—	sticker	étiquette *f*	eticchetta adesiva *f*	pegatina *f*
auf Kommissionsbasis (D)	—	on a commission basis	en commission	in base commissionaria	en comisión
auf Lager (D)	—	in stock	en stock	in magazzino	en almacén
auf Lager haben (D)	—	have in stock	avoir en stock	avere in magazzino	tener en almacén
Auflösung (D)	—	dissolution	liquidation *f*	scioglimento *m*	disolución *f*
Aufrechnung (D)	—	set-off	compensation *f*	compensazione *f*	compensación *f*
auf Probe (D)	—	on trial	à l'essai	in prova	a prueba
auf Provisionsbasis (D)	—	on a commission basis	à la commission	a provvigione	a comisión
Aufschiebung (D)	—	postponement	remise *f*	rinvio *m*	aplazamiento *m*
Aufschlag (D)	—	surcharge	hausse *f*	aggiunta *f*	recargo *m*
Aufsicht (D)	—	supervision	surveillance *f*	sorveglianza *f*	inspección *f*
auf Sicht (D)	—	at sight	à vue	a vista	a la vista
Aufsichtspflicht (D)	—	duty of supervision	obligation de surveillance *f*	obbligo di sorveglianza *m*	obligación de vigilancia *f*
Aufsichtsrat (D)	—	supervisory board	conseil de surveillance *m*	consiglio di sorveglianza *m*	consejo de vigilancia *m*
Aufsichtsrats-vorsitzender (D)	—	chairman of the supervisory board	président du conseil de surveillance *m*	presidente del consiglio di sorveglianza *m*	presidente del consejo de vigilancia *m*
Aufstiegs-möglichkeit (D)	—	promotion possibility	perspectives de promotion *f pl*	possibilità di carriera *f*	posibilidades de ascenso *f pl*
Auftrag (D)	—	order	commande *f*	ordine *m*	pedido *m*
Auftraggeber (D)	—	client	commettant *m*	committente *m*	mandante *m*
Auftragsabwicklung (D)	—	execution of the order	exécution d'une commande *f*	esecuzione ordini *f*	ejecución de pedidos *f*
Auftrags-bearbeitung (D)	—	order processing	réalisation d'une commande *f*	esecuzione ordini *f*	tramitación de pedidos *f*
Auftragsbestätigung (D)	—	confirmation of order	confirmation de commande *f*	conferma d'ordine *f*	confirmación de pedido *f*

	D	E	F	I	Es
Auftragserteilung (D)	—	placing of an order	passation d'une commande *f*	ordinazione *f*	otorgamiento de un pedido *m*
Auftragsnummer (D)	—	order number	numéro de commande *m*	numero d'ordine *m*	número de pedido *m*
Auftragsplanung (D)	—	order scheduling	planification des commandes *f*	pianificazione degli ordini *f*	planificación de la ejecución de pedidos *f*
Aufwand (D)	—	expenditure	dépenses *f pl*	spese *f pl*	gastos *m pl*
Aufwandsfaktor (D)	—	expenditure factor	facteur des frais *m*	fattore spese *m*	factor de gastos *m*
Aufwands-minimierung (D)	—	expenditure minimization	minimiser les frais	riduzione delle spese *f*	minimación de gastos *f*
Aufwärtstrend (D)	—	upward trend	mouvement ascendant *m*	tendenza al rialzo *f*	tendencia alcista *f*
Aufwendung (D)	—	expenditure	dépenses *f pl*	spese *f pl*	gastos *m pl*
Aufwertung (D)	—	revaluation	revalorisation *f*	rivalutazione *f*	revalorización *f*
augmentation de capital (F)	Kapitalerhöhung *f*	increase of the share capital	—	aumento del capitale *m*	aumento de capital *m*
augmentation des prix (F)	Preiserhöhung *f*	price increase	—	rialzo dei prezzi *m*	aumento de precios *m*
augmentation du chiffre d'affaires (F)	Umsatzanstieg *m*	turnover increase	—	aumento del fatturato *m*	aumento del volumen de facturación *m*
augmentation du revenu (F)	Einkommens-erhöhung *f*	rise in income	—	aumento del reddito *m*	aumento de salario *m*
augmentation du salaire (F)	Lohnerhöhung *f*	increase in wages	—	aumento salariale *m*	aumento de salario *m*
augmentation du traitement (F)	Gehaltserhöhung *f*	increase in salary	—	aumento dello stipendio *m*	aumento de sueldo *m*
auguri (I)	Glückwunsch *m*	congratulations	félicitations *f pl*	—	felicitaciones *f pl*
Auktion (D)	—	auction	vente à l'enchère *f*	asta *f*	subasta *f*
Auktionsgebühr (D)	—	auction fees	droits de vente aux enchères *m pl*	diritto d'asta *m*	gastos de subasta *m pl*
au meilleur prix (F)	billigst	at best price	—	al prezzo più basso	al mejor cambio
aumento de capital (Es)	Kapitalerhöhung *f*	increase of the share capital	augmentation de capital *f*	aumento del capitale *m*	—
aumento dei corsi (I)	Kurssteigerung *f*	price advance	hausse *f*	—	alza de las cotizaciones *f*
aumento dei prezzi (I)	Preissteigerung *f*	price increase	hausse des prix *f*	—	aumento de precios *m*
aumento del capitale (I)	Kapitalerhöhung *f*	increase of the share capital	augmentation de capital *f*	—	aumento de capital *m*
aumento del fatturato (I)	Umsatzanstieg *m*	turnover increase	augmentation du chiffre d'affaires *f*	—	aumento del volumen de facturación *m*
aumento delle imposte (I)	Steuererhöhung *f*	increase of taxes	relèvement des impôts *m*	—	aumento de los impuestos *m*
aumento dello stipendio (I)	Gehaltserhöhung *f*	increase in salary	augmentation du traitement *f*	—	aumento de sueldo *m*
aumento de los impuestos (Es)	Steuererhöhung *f*	increase of taxes	relèvement des impôts *m*	aumento delle imposte *m*	—
aumento del prezzo (I)	Preisanstieg *m*	price rise	hausse des prix *f*	—	aumento de precios *m*
aumento del reddito (I)	Einkommens-erhöhung *f*	rise in income	augmentation du revenu *f*	—	aumento de salario *m*
aumento del volumen de facturación (Es)	Umsatzanstieg *m*	turnover increase	augmentation du chiffre d'affaires *f*	aumento del fatturato *m*	—
aumento de precios[1] (Es)	Preiserhöhung *f*	price increase	augmentation des prix *f*	rialzo dei prezzi *m*	—
aumento de precios[2] (Es)	Preissteigerung *f*	price increase	hausse des prix *f*	aumento dei prezzi *m*	—
aumento de precios[3] (Es)	Preisanstieg *m*	price rise	hausse des prix *f*	aumento del prezzo *m*	—
aumento de salario[1] (Es)	Lohnerhöhung *f*	increase in wages	augmentation du salaire *f*	aumento salariale *m*	—
aumento de salario[2] (Es)	Einkommens-erhöhung *f*	rise in income	augmentation du revenu *f*	aumento del reddito *m*	—
aumento de sueldo (Es)	Gehaltserhöhung *f*	increase in salary	augmentation du traitement *f*	aumento dello stipendio *m*	—

	D	E	F	I	Es
aumento della produttività (I)	Leistungs-steigerung *f*	increase in efficiency	amélioration du rendement *f*	—	incremento del rendimiento *m*
aumento salariale (I)	Lohnerhöhung *f*	increase in wages	augmentation du salaire *f*	—	aumento de salario *m*
au mieux (F)	bestens	at best	—	ottimo	al mejor cambio
Ausbilder (D)	—	trainer	instructeur *m*	istruttore *m*	instructor *m*
Ausbildung (D)	—	apprenticeship	apprentissage *m*	apprendistato *m*	aprendizaje *m*
ausente (Es)	abwesend	absent	absent	assente	—
Ausfallbürgschaft (D)	—	deficiency guarantee	garantie de bonne fin *f*	fideiussione d'indennità *f*	fianza con beneficio de excusión *f*
Ausfallquote (D)	—	default rate	ratio de perte *m*	tasso di perdita *m*	cuota de pérdida *f*
Ausfallrisiko (D)	—	default risk	risque de perte *m*	rischio di perdita *m*	riesgo de pérdida *m*
Ausfuhr (D)	—	export	exportation *f*	esportazione *f*	exportación *f*
Ausfuhrabfertigung (D)	—	customs clearance of exports	formalités en douane à l'exportation *f pl*	sdoganamento delle esportazioni *m*	despacho de exportación *m*
Ausfuhr-beschränkung (D)	—	export restriction	contingentement de l'exportation *m*	restrizione delle esportazioni *f*	restricción a la exportación *f*
Ausfuhr-bestimmungen (D)	—	export regulations	dispositions d'exportation *f pl*	disposizioni per le esportazioni *f pl*	reglamiento de exportación *m*
Ausfuhr-finanzierung (D)	—	export financing	financement de l'exportation *m*	finanziamento delle esportazioni *m*	financiación de la exportación *f*
Ausfuhrförderung (D)	—	measures to encourage exports	encouragement à l'exportation *m*	promozione delle esportazioni *f*	fomento de la exportación *m*
Ausfuhr-genehmigung (D)	—	export licence	autorisation d'exportation *f*	autorizzazione per le esportazioni *f*	licencia de exportación *f*
Ausfuhrpapiere (D)	—	export documents	documents d'exportation *m pl*	documenti d'esportazione *m pl*	documentos de exportación *m pl*
Ausfuhrzoll (D)	—	export duty	taxe de sortie *f*	dazio sull'esportazione *m*	derechos de exportación *m pl*
Ausgaben (D)	—	expenses	dépenses *f pl*	spese *f pl*	gastos *m pl*
Ausgabenkontrolle (D)	—	expenditure control	contrôle des dépenses *m*	controllo delle spese *m*	control de gastos *m*
Ausgabensenkung (D)	—	drop in expenditure	diminution des dépenses *f*	riduzione delle spese *f*	reducción de gastos *f*
Ausgaben-verzögerung (D)	—	expenditure delay	dépenses retardées *f pl*	dilazione delle spese *f*	aplazamiento de gastos *m*
Ausgleichsfonds (D)	—	compensation fund	fonds de compensation *m*	fondo di compensazione *m*	fondo de compensación *m*
Ausgleichszahlung (D)	—	compensation payment	payement pour solde de compte *m*	conguaglio *m*	pago de compensación *m*
Aushilfe (D)	—	auxiliary worker	aide *m*	aiuto *m*	ayudante *m*
ausiliario (I)	Erfüllungsgehilfe *m*	vicarious agent	auxiliaire d'exécution *m*	—	auxiliar *m*
Auskunft (D)	—	information	renseignement *m*	informazione *f*	información *f*
Auskunftei (D)	—	information bureau	agence de renseignements *f*	agenzia d'informazioni *f*	oficina de información *f*
Auslage (D)	—	display	étalage *f*	vetrina *f*	vitrina *f*
Ausländer (D)	—	foreigner	étranger *m*	straniero *m*	extranjero *m*
ausländische Arbeitnehmer (D)	—	foreign worker	travailleur étranger *m*	prestatori d'opera stranieri *m pl*	trabajadores extranjeros *m*
Auslandsanleihe (D)	—	foreign bond	emprunt extérieur *m*	prestito estero *m*	empréstito exterior *m*
Auslandsgeschäft (D)	—	foreign business	opération avec l'étranger *f*	affare con l'estero *m*	negocio de exporta-ción o importación *m*
Auslandskapital (D)	—	foreign capital	capital étranger *m*	capitale estero *m*	capital extranjero *m*
Auslandskonto (D)	—	foreign account	compte d'étranger *m*	conto estero *m*	cuenta exterior *f*
Auslandskunde (D)	—	foreign customer	client étranger *m*	cliente estero *m*	cliente extranjero *m*
Auslandsmärkte (D)	—	foreign markets	marchés extérieurs *m pl*	mercati esteri *m pl*	mercado exterior *m*
Auslandsnachfrage (D)	—	foreign demand	demande en provenance de l'étranger *f*	domanda estera *f*	demanda exterior *m*
Auslands-niederlassung (D)	—	branch abroad	succursale à l'étranger *f*	succursale estera *f*	filial en el exterior *m*

	D	E	F	I	Es
Auslandsschulden (D)	—	foreign debts	dettes à l'étranger *f pl*	debiti con l'estero *m pl*	deudas exteriores *f pl*
Auslandsvermögen (D)	—	foreign assets	avoirs à l'étranger *m pl*	patrimonio estero *m*	activo exterior *m*
Auslands-vertretung (D)	—	agency abroad	agence à l'étranger *f*	rappresentanza estera *f*	representación en el exterior *f*
Auslandswechsel (D)	—	foreign bill of exchange	traite tirée sur l'étranger *f*	cambiale estera *f*	letra sobre el exterior *f*
Auslastungsgrad (D)	—	capacity utilisation rate	dégré de saturation *m*	grado di sfruttamento *m*	tasa de utilización *f*
Auslieferungslager (D)	—	distribution centre	entrepôt de distribution *m*	deposito di consegna *m*	almacén de entregas *m*
Ausnutzungsgrad (D)	—	utilization rate	taux d'utilisation *m*	grado di utilizzazione *m*	grado de utilización *m*
Ausschreibung (D)	—	tender	soumission *f*	appalto *m*	concurso-subasta *m*
Außendienst (D)	—	field work	service extérieur *m*	servizio esterno *m*	servicio exterior *m*
Außendienst-mitarbeiter (D)	—	field staff	personnel du service extérieur *m*	collaboratore del servizio esterno *m*	colaborador en el servicio exterior *m*
Außenhandel (D)	—	foreign trade	commerce extérieur *m*	commercio estero *m*	comercio exterior *m*
Außenhandels-defizit (D)	—	trade deficit	déficit de la balance du commerce extérieur *m*	deficit del commercio estero *m*	déficit del comercio exterior *m*
Außenhandels-finanzierung (D)	—	foreign trade financing	aide financière à l'exportation *m*	finanziamento del commercio estero *m*	financiación del comercio exterior *f*
Außenhandels-freiheit (D)	—	free trade	libre-échange *m*	libertà di commercio estero *f*	librecambio *m*
Außenhandels-kammer (D)	—	chamber of foreign trade	chambre du commerce extérieur *f*	camera di commercio estero *f*	cámara del comercio exterior *f*
Außenhandels-monopol (D)	—	foreign trade monopoly	monopole du commerce extérieur *m*	monopolio del commercio estero *m*	monopolio del comercio exterior *m*
Außenhandels-politik (D)	—	foreign trade policy	politique de commerce extérieur *f*	politica del commercio estero *f*	política comercial exterior *f*
Außenstände (D)	—	outstanding debts	dettes actives *f pl*	debiti insoluti *m pl*	cobros pendientes *m pl*
Außenwerbung (D)	—	outdoor publicity	publicité extérieure *f*	pubblicità all'aperto *f*	publicidad al aire libre *f*
außergerichtlich (D)	—	extrajudicial	extrajudiciaire	extragiudiziale	extrajudicial
außergewöhnliche Belastung (D)	—	extraordinary expenses	charges exceptionnelles *f pl*	oneri straordinari *m pl*	carga extraordinaria *f*
Aussperrung (D)	—	lockout	lock-out *m*	serrata *f*	cierre patronal *m*
Aussteller (D)	—	exhibitor	exposant *m*	espositore *m*	expositor *m*
Ausstellung (D)	—	exhibition	exposition *f*	esposizione *f*	exhibición *f*
Ausverkauf (D)	—	clearance sale	soldes *m pl*	svendita *f*	liquidación *f*
Auszahlung (D)	—	paying out	payement *m*	pagamento *m*	pago *m*
autenticazione (I)	Beglaubigung *f*	authentication	certification *f*	—	legalización *f*
auteur de la procuration (F)	Vollmachtgeber *m*	grantor of power of attorney	—	mandante *m*	poderdante *m*
authenticated copy (E)	beglaubigte Abschrift *f*	—	copie certifiée *f*	copia autenticata *f*	copia legalizada *f*
authentication (E)	Beglaubigung *f*	—	certification *f*	autenticazione *f*	legalización *f*
authoritarian (E)	autoritär	—	autoritaire	autoritario	autoritario
authority (E)	Behörde *f*	—	autorité *f*	autorità *f*	autoridad *f*
authority to sign (E)	Zeichnungs-berechtigung *f*	—	autorisation de signer *f*	diritto di firma *m*	facultad de firma *f*
authorization[1] (E)	Bevollmächtigung *f*	—	pouvoir *m*	autorizzazione *f*	apoderamiento *m*
authorization[2] (E)	Befugnis *f*	—	pouvoir *m*	prerogativa *f*	autorización *f*
authorization to receive (E)	Empfangs-berechtigung *f*	—	autorité pour recevoir *f*	autorizzazione di ricezione *f*	autorización de recibimiento *f*
authorized to represent (E)	Vertretungs-berechtigung *f*	—	autorisation de représentation *f*	autorizzazione alla rappresentanza *f*	derecho de representación *m*
authorized to under-take the collection (E)	inkassoberechtigt	—	autorisé à l'encaissement	autorizzato all'incasso	autorizado al encobro

	D	E	F	I	Es
autofinancement[1] (F)	Selbstfinanzierung *f*	self-financing	—	autofinanziamento *m*	autofinanciación *f*
autofinancement[2] (F)	Eigenfinanzierung *f*	self-financing	—	autofinanziamento *m*	financiación propia *f*
autofinanciación (Es)	Selbstfinanzierung *f*	self-financing	autofinancement *m*	autofinanziamento *m*	—
autofinanziamento[1] (I)	Selbstfinanzierung *f*	self-financing	autofinancement *m*	—	autofinanciación *f*
autofinanziamento[2] (I)	Eigenfinanzierung *f*	self-financing	autofinancement *m*	—	financiación propia *f*
Automat (D)	—	vending machine	appareil automatique *m*	distributore automatico *m*	distribuidor automático *m*
Automatenverkauf (D)	—	automatic vending	vente par distributeur automatique *f*	vendita per distributori automatici *f*	venta por distribuidores automáticos *f*
automatic vending (E)	Automatenverkauf *m*	—	vente par distributeur automatique *f*	vendita per distributori automatici *f*	venta por distribuidores automáticos *f*
Automation (D)	—	automation	automation *f*	automazione *f*	automatización *f*
automation (F)	Automation *f*	automation	—	automazione *f*	automatización *f*
automation[1] (E)	Automatisierung *f*	—	automatisation *f*	automatizzazione *f*	automatización *f*
automation[2] (E)	Automation *f*	—	automation *f*	automazione *f*	automatización *f*
automatisation (F)	Automatisierung *f*	automation	—	automatizzazione *f*	automatización *f*
Automatisierung (D)	—	automation	automatisation *f*	automatizzazione *f*	automatización *f*
automatización[1] (Es)	Automation *f*	automation	automation *f*	automazione *f*	—
automatización[2] (Es)	Automatisierung *f*	automation	automatisation *f*	automatizzazione *f*	—
automatizzazione (I)	Automatisierung *f*	automation	automatisation *f*	—	automatización *f*
automazione (I)	Automation *f*	automation	automation *f*	—	automatización *f*
automobile (I)	Kraftfahrzeug *n*	motor vehicle	véhicule à moteur *m*	—	automóvil *m*
automobile usata (I)	Gebrauchtwagen *m*	used car	voiture d'occasion *f*	—	coche de segunda mano *m*
automóvil (Es)	Kraftfahrzeug *n*	motor vehicle	véhicule à moteur *m*	automobile *f*	—
autonomía (Es)	Autonomie *f*	autonomy	autonomie *f*	autonomia *f*	—
autonomia (I)	Autonomie *f*	autonomy	autonomie *f*	—	autonomía *f*
Autonomie (D)	—	autonomy	autonomie *f*	autonomia *f*	autonomía *f*
autonomie (F)	Autonomie *f*	autonomy	—	autonomia *f*	autonomía *f*
autonomie d'administration (F)	Verwaltungshoheit *f*	power of administration	—	sovranità amministrativa *f*	soberanía administrativa *f*
autonomy (E)	Autonomie *f*	—	autonomie *f*	autonomia *f*	autonomía *f*
autoridad (Es)	Behörde *f*	authority	autorité *f*	autorità *f*	—
autoridad monetaria (Es)	Währungsbehörde *f*	monetary authority	autorité monétaire *f*	autorità monetaria *f*	—
autorisation (F)	Genehmigung *f*	permission	—	autorizzazione *f*	autorización *f*
autorisation de change (F)	Devisengenehmigung *f*	foreign exchange authorization	—	autorizzazione valutaria *f*	certificado de divisas *m*
autorisation de représentation (F)	Vertretungsberechtigung *f*	authorization to represent	—	autorizzazione alla rappresentanza *f*	derecho de representación *m*
autorisation de séjour (F)	Aufenthaltserlaubnis *f*	residence permit	—	permesso di soggiorno *m*	permiso de residencia *m*
autorisation de signer (F)	Zeichnungsberechtigung *f*	authority to sign	—	diritto di firma *m*	facultad de firma *f*
autorisation d'exportation (F)	Ausfuhrgenehmigung *f*	export licence	—	autorizzazione per le esportazioni *f*	licencia de exportación *f*
autorisation d'importation (F)	Einfuhrgenehmigung *f*	import licence	—	permesso d'importazione *m*	permiso de importación *m*
autorisé à l'encaissement (F)	inkassoberechtigt	authorized to undertake the collection	—	autorizzato all'incasso	autorizado al encobro
autorità (I)	Behörde *f*	authority	autorité *f*	—	autoridad *f*
autorità antimonopoli (I)	Kartellbehörde *f*	cartel authority	office de surveillance des cartels et ententes *m*	—	oficina de cártels *f*
autorità fiscali (I)	Steuerbehörden *pl*	tax authority	administration des contributions *f*	—	administración de hacienda *f*
autoritaire (F)	autoritär	authoritarian	—	autoritario	autoritario
autorità monetaria (I)	Währungsbehörde *f*	monetary authority	autorité monétaire *f*	—	autoridad monetaria *f*
autoritär (D)	—	authoritarian	autoritaire	autoritario	autoritario
autoritario (Es)	autoritär	authoritarian	autoritaire	autoritario	—

	D	E	F	I	Es
autoritario (I)	autoritär	authoritarian	autoritaire	—	autoritario
autorité (F)	Behörde *f*	authority	—	autorità *f*	autoridad *f*
autorité monétaire (F)	Währungsbehörde *f*	monetary authority	—	autorità monetaria *f*	autoridad monetaria *f*
autorité pour recevoir (F)	Empfangs-berechtigung *f*	authorization to receive	—	autorizzazione a ricevere *f*	autorización de recibimiento *f*
autorización[1] (Es)	Genehmigung *f*	permission	autorisation *f*	autorizzazione *f*	—
autorización[2] (Es)	Befugnis *f*	authorization	pouvoir *m*	prerogativa *f*	—
autorización de funcionamiento (Es)	Betriebserlaubnis *f*	operating permit	droit d'exploitation *m*	autorizzazione per l'esercizio *f*	—
autorización de recibimiento (Es)	Empfangs-berechtigung *f*	authorization to receive	autorité pour recevoir *f*	autorizzazione a ricevere *f*	—
autorizado al encobro (Es)	inkassoberechtigt	authorized to under-take the collection	autorisé à l'encaissement	autorizzato all'incasso	—
autorizzato all'incasso (I)	inkassoberechtigt	authorized to under-take the collection	autorisé à l'encaissement	—	autorizado al encobro
autorizzazione[1] (I)	Bevollmächtigung *f*	authorization	pouvoir *m*	—	apoderamiento *m*
autorizzazione[2] (I)	Genehmigung *f*	permission	autorisation *f*	—	autorización *f*
autorizzazione[3] (I)	Vollmacht *f*	full power/ power of attorney	plein pouvoir *m*/ mandat *m*	—	poder *m*/ autorización *f*
autorizzazione alla rappresentanza (I)	Vertretungs-berechtigung *f*	authorization to represent	autorisation de représentation *f*	—	derecho de representación *m*
autorizzazione di ricezione (I)	Empfangs-berechtigung *f*	authorization to receive	autorité pour recevoir *f*	—	autorización de recibimiento *f*
autorizzazione per l'esercizio (I)	Betriebserlaubnis *f*	operating permit	droit d'exploitation *m*	—	autorización de funcionamiento *f*
autorizzazione per le esportazioni (I)	Ausfuhr-genehmigung *f*	export licence	autorisation d'exportation *f*	—	licencia de exportación *f*
autorizzazione valutaria (I)	Devisen-genehmigung *f*	foreign exchange authorization	autorisation de change *f*	—	certificado de divisas *m*
autoservicio (Es)	Selbstbedienung *f*	self-service	self-service *m*	self service *m*	—
autumn fair (E)	Herbstmesse *f*	—	foire d'automne *f*	fiera autunnale *f*	feria de otoño *f*
auxiliary worker (E)	Aushilfe *f*	—	aide *m*	aiuto *m*	ayudante *m*
Aval (D)	—	guarantee of a bill	aval *m*	avallo *m*	aval *m*
aval (Es)	Aval *m*	guarantee of a bill	aval *m*	avallo *m*	—
aval (F)	Aval *m*	guarantee of a bill	—	avallo *m*	aval *m*
Avalkredit (D)	—	credit by way of bank guarantee	crédit d'escompte sur traite avalisée *m*	credito d'avallo *m*	crédito de aval *m*
avallo (I)	Aval *m*	guarantee of a bill	aval *m*	—	aval *m*
avance (F)	Vorschuß *m*	advance	—	anticipo *m*	anticipo *m*
avance sur compte courant (F)	Überziehungs-kredit *m*	credit by way of overdraft	—	credito allo scoperto *m*	crédito en descubierto *m*
avance sur marchandises (F)	Warenkredit *m*	trade credit	—	credito su merci *m*	crédito comercial *m*
avantage (F)	Vorteil *m*	advantage benefit	—	vantaggio *m*	ventaja *f*
avantage de concurrence (F)	Wettbewerbs-vorteil *m*	competitive advantage	—	vantaggio concorrenziale *m*	ventaja de competencia *f*
avantage de coût (F)	Kostenvorteil *m*	cost advantage	—	vantaggio di costo *m*	ventaja de costes *f*
avaria (I)	Havarie *f*	damage by sea	avarie *f*	—	avería *m*
avarie (F)	Havarie *f*	damage by sea	—	avaria *f*	avería *m*
avec grande intensité de capital (F)	kapitalintensiv	capital-intensive	—	ad alta incidenza di capitale	con gran intensidad de capital
average (E)	Durchschnitt *m*	—	moyenne *f*	media *f*	promedio *m*
average costs (E)	Durchschnitts-kosten *pl*	—	coût moyen *m*	costi medi *m pl*	gastos medios *m pl*
avere in magazzino (I)	auf Lager haben	have in stock	avoir en stock	—	tener en almacén
avería (Es)	Havarie *f*	damage by sea	avarie *f*	avaria *f*	—
Avis (D)	—	advice	avis *m*	avviso *m*	aviso *m*
avis[1] (F)	Nachricht *f*	news	—	notizia *f*	noticia *f*
avis[2] (F)	Avis *m*	advice	—	avviso *m*	aviso *m*
avis de chargement (F)	Ladeschein *m*	bill of lading	—	bolletta di carico *f*	póliza de carga *f*
avis de crédit (F)	Gutschriftsanzeige *f*	credit advice	—	nota di accredito *f*	aviso de abono *m*

	D	E	F	I	Es
avis de réception (F)	Rückschein *m*	advice of delivery	—	ricevuta di ritorno *f*	acuse de recibo *m*
avis d'imposition (F)	Steuerbescheid *m*	notice of assessment	—	cartella delle imposte *f*	liquidación de impuestos *f*
aviso[1] (Es)	Avis *m*	advice	avis *m*	avviso *m*	—
aviso[2] (Es)	Mitteilung *f*	information	notification *f*	comunicazione *f*	—
aviso bancario (Es)	Bankavis *m*	bank notification	confirmation banquaire *f*	avviso bancario *m*	—
aviso de abono (Es)	Gutschriftsanzeige *f*	credit advice	avis de crédit *m*	nota di accredito *f*	—
aviso de siniestro (Es)	Schadensmeldung *f*	notification of damage	déclaration du sinistre *f*	avviso di danni *m*	—
aviso de vicios (Es)	Mängelanzeige *f*	notice of defect	notification d'un vice *f*	denuncia dei vizi *f*	—
a vista (I)	auf Sicht	at sight	à vue	—	a la vista
avocat (F)	Rechtsanwalt *m*	lawyer	—	avvocato *m*	abogado *m*
avoir[1] (F)	Haben *n*	credit side	—	attivo *m*	haber *m*
avoir[2] (F)	Guthaben *n*	money owed	—	saldo attivo *m*	haber *m*
avoir en stock (F)	auf Lager haben	have in stock	—	avere in magazzino	tener en almacén
avoir net (F)	Reinvermögen *n*	net assets	—	patrimonio netto *m*	patrimonio neto *m*
avoirs à l'étranger (F)	Auslandsvermögen *n*	foreign assets	—	patrimonio estero *m*	activo exterior *m*
à vue[1] (F)	auf Sicht	at sight	—	a vista	a la vista
à vue[2] (F)	zur Ansicht	on approval	—	in visione	para examen
a vuelta de correo (Es)	postwendend	by return of post	par retour du courrier	a giro di posta	—
avviso[1] (I)	Avis *m*	advice	avis *m*	—	aviso *m*
avviso[2] (I)	Anmeldung *f*	registration	inscription *f*	—	solicitud *f*
avviso bancario (I)	Bankavis *m*	bank notification	confirmation bancaire *f*	—	aviso bancario *m*
avviso di danni (I)	Schadensmeldung *f*	notification of damage	déclaration du sinistre *f*	—	aviso de siniestro *m*
avviso di visita (I)	Besuchsanmeldung *f*	announcement of a visitor	annonce des visiteurs *f*	—	anuncio de visita *m*
avvocato (I)	Rechtsanwalt *m*	lawyer	avocat *m*	—	abogado *m*
ayuda a la exportación (Es)	Exporthilfe *f*	export subsidy	subvention à l'exportatiin *f*	aiuto all'esportazione *m*	—
ayuda al desarrollo (Es)	Entwicklungshilfe *f*	development aid	aide au développement *f*	aiuto ai paesi in via di sviluppo *m*	—
ayuda financiera (Es)	Kapitalhilfe *f*	capital aid	aide financière *f*	aiuto finanziario *m*	—
ayudante (Es)	Aushilfe *f*	auxiliary worker	aide *m*	aiuto *m*	—
ayuda social (Es)	Sozialhilfe *f*	public assistance	aide sociale *f*	assistenza sociale *f*	—
azienda (I)	Betrieb *m*	factory	usine *f*	—	fábrica *f*
azienda agricola (I)	Agrarbetrieb *m*	agricultural enterprise	entreprise agricole *f*	—	empresa agrícola *f*
azienda commerciale (I)	gewerblicher Betrieb *m*	industrial undertaking	établissement commercial	—	empresa industrial *f*
azienda di grande dimensione (I)	Großbetrieb *m*	large-scale operation	grande exploitation *f*	—	gran explotación *f*
azienda industriale (I)	Industriebetrieb *m*	industrial enterprise	entreprise industrielle *f*	—	establecimiento industrial *m*
aziende pubbliche (I)	öffentliche Betriebe *pl*	public sector industrial enterprises	entreprises *pl* publiques *f*	—	empresa pública *f*
aziende statali (I)	staatliche Betriebe *pl*	state-owned enterprise	entreprise publique *f*	—	empresas públicas *f pl*
azione (I)	Aktie *f*	share	action *f*	—	acción *f*
azione al portatore (I)	Inhaberaktie *f*	bearer share	action au porteur *f*	—	acción al portador *f*
azione di impugnazione (I)	Anfechtungsklage *f*	action for avoidance	action en annulation *f*	—	acción de impugnación *f*
azione di risarcimento danni (I)	Schadensersatzklage *f*	action for damages	action en dommages-intérêts *f*	—	demanda de daños y perjuicios *f*
azione nominativa (I)	Namensaktie *f*	registered shares	action nominative *f*	—	acción nominal *f*
azione ordinaria (I)	Stammaktie *f*	ordinary shares	action ordinaire *f*	—	acción ordinaria *f*
azione privilegiata (I)	Vorzugsaktie *f*	preference share	action privilégiée *f*	—	acción preferente *f*
azione pubblicitaria (I)	Werbeaktion *f*	advertising activity	campagne publicitaire *f*	—	campaña publicitaria *f*

	D	E	F	I	Es
azione speciale (I)	Sonderaktion *f*	special action	action spéciale *f*	—	acción especial *f*
azione stampa (I)	Presseaktion *f*	press campaign	action de presse *f*	—	campaña de prensa *f*
azioni[1] (I)	Aktionen *pl*	actions	actions *f pl*	—	acciones *f pl*
azioni[2] (I)	Aktien *pl*	shares	actions *f pl*	—	acciones *f pl*
azionista (I)	Aktionär *m*	shareholder	actionnaire *m*	—	accionista *m*
baby bonds (E)	Baby-Bonds *pl*	—	bons de petite valeur nominale *m pl*	baby bonds *m pl*	bonos de pequeño valor nominal *m pl*
baby bonds (I)	Baby-Bonds *pl*	baby bonds	bons de petite valeur nominale *m pl*	—	bonos de pequeño valor nominal *m pl*
Baby-Bonds (D)	—	baby bonds	bons de petite valeur nominale *m pl*	baby bonds *m pl*	bonos de pequeño valor nominal *m pl*
Bagatellschaden (D)	—	minimal damage	dommage mineur *m*	danno piccolo *m*	siniestro leve *m*
baggage insurance (E)	Reisegepäck-versicherung *f*	—	assurance des bagages *f*	assicurazione del bagaglio *f*	seguro de equipajes *m*
Bahnfracht (D)	—	rail freight	fret par rail *m*	nolo ferroviario *m*	transporte ferroviario *m*
bail (E)	Haftkaution *f*	—	caution pour être mis en liberté *f*	cauzione per la scarcerazione *f*	fianza de puesta en libertad *f*
bailiff (E)	Gerichtsvollzieher *m*	—	huissier de justice *m*	ufficiale giudiziario *m*	ejecutor judicial *m*
bailleur de fonds (F)	Geldgeber *m*	financial backer	—	finanziatore *m*	prestamista *m*
baisse (F)	Abwärtstrend *m*	downward trend	—	tendenza al ribasso *f*	tendencia bajista *f*
baisse de l'offre d'emploi (F)	Beschäftigungs-rückgang *m*	drop in employment	—	calo dell'occupazione *m*	descenso del empleo *m*
baisse des prix (F)	Preissenkung *f*	price reduction	—	riduzione dei prezzi *f*	redución de precios *f*
baisse sur les cours (F)	Kursverlust *m*	loss in exchange	—	perdita sul cambio *f*	pérdida en bolsa *f*
baja (Es)	Abschwung *m*	down-swing	dépression *f*	regresso *m*	—
balance[1] (E)	Gleichgewicht *n*	—	équilibre *m*	equilibrio *m*	equilibrio *m*
balance[2] (E)	Saldo *m*	—	solde *m*	saldo *m*	saldo *m*
balance (Es)	Bilanz *f*	balance sheet	bilan *m*	bilancio *m*	—
balance analysis (E)	Bilanzanalyse *f*	—	analyse du bilan *f*	analisi di bilancio *f*	análisis de balance *m*
balance consolidado (Es)	konsolidierte Bilanz *f*	consolidated balance sheet	bilan consolidé *m*	bilancio consolidato *m*	—
balance del consorcio (Es)	Konzernbilanz *f*	balance sheet of a group	bilan consolidé d'un groupement de sociétés *m*	bilancio del gruppo *m*	—
balance del presupuesto (Es)	Budgetausgleich *m*	balancing of the budget	équilibrage du budget *m*	pareggio di bilancio *m*	—
balance des opérations courantes (F)	Leistungsbilanz *f*	balance of goods and services	—	bilancia delle partite correnti *f*	balanza por cuenta corriente *f*
balance des opérations en capital (F)	Kapitalbilanz *f*	balance of capital transactions	—	bilancia dei capitali *f*	balanza de capitales *f*
balance des opérations en marchandises (F)	Handelsbilanz *f*	balance of trade	—	bilancia commerciale *f*	balanza comercial *f*
balance des payements (F)	Zahlungsbilanz *f*	balance of payments	—	bilancia dei pagamenti *f*	balanza de pagos *f*
balance des payements déficitaire (F)	Zahlungsbilanz-defizit *n*	deficit in the balance of payments	—	disavanzo della bilancia dei pagamenti *m*	déficit en la balanza de pagos *m*
balance des payements équilibrée (F)	Zahlungsbilanz-gleichgewicht *n*	equilibrium of the balance of payments	—	equilibrio della bilancia dei pagamenti *m*	balanza de pagos equilibrada *f*
balance des payements excédentaire (F)	Zahlungsbilanz-überschuß *m*	surplus in the balance of payments	—	eccedenza della bilancia dei pagamenti *f*	superávit en la balanza de pagos *m*
balance d'or et de devises (F)	Gold- und Devisenbilanz *f*	foreign exchange and gold balance	—	bilancia dell'oro e delle divise *f*	balanza de oro y divisas *f*
balance final (Es)	Schlußbilanz *f*	closing balance	bilan de clôture *m*	bilancio consuntivo *m*	—
balance impositivo (Es)	Steuerbilanz *f*	tax balance-sheet	bilan fiscal *m*	bilancio fiscale *m*	—
balance inicial (Es)	Eröffnungsbilanz *f*	opening balance sheet	bilan d'ouverture *m*	bilancio d'apertura *m*	—
balance intermedio (Es)	Zwischenbilanz *f*	interim balance sheet	bilan intermédiaire *m*	bilancio provvisorio *m*	—
balance of capital transactions (E)	Kapitalbilanz *f*	—	balance des opérations en capital *f*	bilancia dei capitali *f*	balanza de capitales *f*

	D	E	F	I	Es
balance of goods and services (E)	Leistungsbilanz *f*	—	balance des opérations courantes *f*	bilancia delle partite correnti *f*	balanza de cuentas *f*
balance of payments (E)	Zahlungsbilanz *f*	—	balance des payements *f*	bilancia dei pagamenti *f*	blanza de pagos *f*
balance of payments policy (E)	Zahlungsbilanzpolitik *f*	—	politique en matière de la balance des payements *f*	politica della bilancia dei pagamenti *f*	política en materia de balanza de pagos *f*
balance of trade (E)	Handelsbilanz *f*	—	balance des opérations en marchandises *f*	bilancia commerciale *f*	balanza comercial *f*
balance policy (E)	Bilanzpolitik *f*	—	politique du bilan *f*	politica di bilancio *f*	política en materia de balanzas *f*
balance sheet (E)	Bilanz *f*	—	bilan *m*	bilancio *m*	balance *m*
balance sheet of a group (E)	Konzernbilanz *f*	—	bilan consolidé d'un groupement de sociétés *m*	bilancio del gruppo *m*	balance del consorcio *m*
balance transparency (E)	Bilanzklarheit *f*	—	clarté du bilan *f*	trasparenza di bilancio *f*	claridad del balance *f*
balancing of the budget (E)	Budgetausgleich *m*	—	équilibrage du budget *m*	pareggio di bilancio *m*	balance del presupuesto *m*
balanza comercial (Es)	Handelsbilanz *f*	balance of trade	balance des opérations en marchandises *f*	bilancia commerciale *f*	—
balanza de capitales (Es)	Kapitalbilanz *f*	balance of capital transactions	balance des opérations en capital *f*	bilancia dei capitali *f*	—
balanza de divisas (Es)	Devisenbilanz *f*	foreign exchange balance	compte de devises *m*	bilancia delle divise *f*	—
balanza de oro y divisas (Es)	Gold- und Devisenbilanz *f*	foreign exchange and gold balance	balance d'or et de devises *f*	bilancia dell'oro e delle divise *f*	—
balanza de pagos (Es)	Zahlungsbilanz *f*	balance of payments	balance des payements *f*	bilancia dei pagamenti *f*	—
balanza de pagos equilibrada (Es)	Zahlungsbilanzgleichgewicht *n*	equilibrium of the balance of payments	balance des payements équilibrée *f*	equilibrio della bilancia dei pagamenti *m*	—
balanza por cuenta corriente (Es)	Leistungsbilanz *f*	balance of goods and services	balance des opérations courantes *f*	bilancia delle partite correnti *f*	—
Banca Centrale[1] (I)	Zentralbank *f*	central bank	banque centrale *f*	—	banco emisor *m*
Banca Centrale[2] (I)	Staatsbank *f*	state bank	banque nationale *f*	—	banco del Estado *m*
banca commerciale (I)	Handelsbank *f*	merchant bank	banque de commerce *f*	—	banco comercial *m*
banca d'emissione (I)	Notenbank *f*	central bank	banque d'émission *f*	—	banco emisor *m*
banca dati (I)	Datenbank *f*	data bank	banque de données *f*	—	banco de datos *m*
banca di credito (I)	Kreditbank *f*	commercial bank	banque de crédit *f*	—	banco de crédito *m*
banca d'investimento (I)	Investmentbank *f*	investment bank	banque d'investissement *f*	—	banco de inversiones *m*
banca di preferenza (I)	Hausbank *f*	company's bank	banque habituelle *f*	—	banco particular *m*
banca ipotecaria (I)	Hypothekenbank *f*	mortgage bank	banque hypothécaire *f*	—	banco hipotecario *m*
Banca Mondiale (I)	Weltbank *f*	World Bank	banque mondiale *f*	—	Banco Mundial *m*
banca regionale (I)	Regionalbank *f*	regional bank	banque régionale *f*	—	banco regional *m*
bancarotta (I)	Bankrott *m*	bankruptcy	banqueroute *f*	—	quiebra *f*
bancarotta fraudolenta (I)	betrügerischer Bankrott *m*	fraudulent bankruptcy	banqueroute frauduleuse *f*	—	quiebra fraudulenta *f*
banchiere (I)	Bankier *m*	banker	banquier *m*	—	banquero *m*
banco comercial (Es)	Handelsbank *f*	merchant bank	banque de commerce *f*	banca commerciale *f*	—
banco de crédito (Es)	Kreditbank *f*	commercial bank	banque de crédit *f*	banca di credito *f*	—
banco de datos (Es)	Datenbank *f*	data bank	banque de données *f*	banca dati *f*	—
banco de giros (Es)	Girobank *f*	clearing bank	banque de dépôts et de virements *f*	banca fungente da stanza di compensazione *f*	—
banco de inversiones (Es)	Investmentbank *f*	investment bank	banque d'investissement *f*	banca d'investimento *f*	—
banco del Estado (Es)	Staatsbank *f*	state bank	banque nationale *f*	Banca Centrale *f*	—
banco emisor[1] (Es)	Notenbank *f*	central bank	banque d'émission *f*	banca d'emissione *f*	—
banco emisor[2] (Es)	Zentralbank *f*	central bank	banque centrale *f*	Banca Centrale *f*	—

	D	E	F	I	Es
banco hipotecario (Es)	Hypothekenbank *f*	mortgage bank	banque hypothécaire *f*	banca ipotecaria *f*	—
bancomat (I)	Bankomat *m*	cash dispenser	billetterie *m*	—	cajero automático *m*
Banco Mundial (Es)	Weltbank *f*	World Bank	banque mondiale *f*	Banca Mondiale *f*	—
banconota (I)	Banknote *f*	bank-note	billet de banque *m*	—	billete de banco *m*
banconote (I)	Papiergeld *n*	paper money	monnaie de papier *f*	—	papel-moneda *m*
banco particular (Es)	Hausbank *f*	company's bank	banque habituelle *f*	banca di preferenza *f*	—
banco regional (Es)	Regionalbank *f*	regional bank	banque régionale *f*	banca regionale *f*	—
Bandbreite (D)	—	margin	marge *f*	margine *m*	margen de fluctuación *f*
bande étiquette (F)	Streifband *f*	postal wrapper	—	fascia *f*	precinto *m*
bando di concorso per impiegati (I)	Stellen-ausschreibung *f*	advertisement of a vacancy	mise au concours d'une place *f*	—	convocatoria de oposiciones *f*
bank account (E)	Bankkonto *n*	—	compte en banque *m*	conto bancario *m*	cuenta bancaria *f*
Bankakkreditiv (D)	—	bank letter of credit	accréditif bancaire *m*	lettera di credito *f*	carta de crédito bancaria *f*
Bankavis (D)	—	bank notification	confirmation bancaire *f*	avviso bancario *m*	aviso bancario *m*
bank charges[1] (E)	Kontogebühren *pl*	—	frais de tenue de compte *m pl*	diritti di conto *m pl*	gastos de administración de una cuenta *m pl*
bank charges[2] (E)	Bankspesen *pl*	—	frais de banque *m pl*	commissioni bancarie *f pl*	gastos bancarios *m pl*
Bankenaufsicht (D)	—	public supervision of banking	contrôle des banques *m*	commissione bancaria *f*	supervisión bancaria *f*
Bankenkonsortium (D)	—	banking syndicate	consortium des banques *m*	consorzio bancario *m*	consorcio bancario *m*
banker (E)	Bankier *m*	—	banquier *m*	banchiere *m*	banquero *m*
banker's duty of secrecy (E)	Bankgeheimnis *n*	—	secret bancaire *m*	segreto bancario *m*	secreto bancario *m*
Bankgarantie (D)	—	bank guarantee	garantie de banque *f*	garanzia bancaria *f*	garantía bancaria *f*
Bankgeheimnis (D)	—	banker's duty of secrecy	secret bancaire *m*	segreto bancario *m*	secreto bancario *m*
bank guarantee (E)	Bankgarantie *f*	—	garantie de banque *f*	garanzia bancaria *f*	garantía bancaria *f*
Bankier (D)	—	banker	banquier *m*	banchiere *m*	banquero *m*
banking syndicate (E)	Bankenkonsortium *n*	—	consortium des banques *m*	consorzio bancario *m*	consorcio bancario *m*
Bankkonto (D)	—	bank account	compte en banque *m*	conto bancario *m*	cuenta bancaria *f*
bank letter of credit (E)	Bankakkreditiv *n*	—	accréditif bancaire *m*	lettera di credito *f*	carta de crédito bancaria *f*
Banknote (D)	—	bank-note	billet de banque *m*	banconota *f*	billete de banco *m*
bank-note (E)	Banknote *f*	—	billet de banque *m*	banconota *f*	billete de banco *m*
bank notification (E)	Bankavis *m*	—	confirmation bancaire *f*	avviso bancario *m*	aviso bancario *m*
Bankomat (D)	—	cash dispenser	billetterie *m*	bancomat *m*	cajero automático *m*
Bankrott (D)	—	bankruptcy	banqueroute *f*	bancarotta *f*	quiebra *f*
bankruptcy[1] (E)	Konkurs *m*	—	faillite *f*	fallimento *m*	quiebra *f*
bankruptcy[2] (E)	Bankrott *m*	—	banqueroute *f*	bancarotta *f*	quiebra *f*
Bankruptcy Act (E)	Konkursordnung *f*	—	régime juridique de la faillite *m*	legge fallimentare *f*	ley de las quiebras *f*
bankruptcy court (E)	Konkursgericht *n*	—	tribunal de la faillite *m*	tribunale fallimentare *m*	tribunal de quiebras *m*
bankruptcy petition (E)	Konkursantrag *m*	—	demande en déclaration de faillite *f*	domanda di dichiarazione del fallimento *f*	petición de quiebra *f*
bankrupt's creditor (E)	Konkursgläubiger *m*	—	créancier de la faillite *m*	creditore della massa fallimentare *m*	acreedor de la quiebra *m*
bankrupt's estate (E)	Konkursmasse *f*	—	masse de la faillite *f*	massa fallimentare *f*	masa de la quiebra *f*
Bankspesen (D)	—	bank charges	frais de banque *m pl*	commissioni bancarie *f pl*	gastos bancarios *m pl*
bank transfer (E)	Banküberweisung *f*	—	virement bancaire *m*	rimessa bancaria *f*	transferencia bancaria *f*
Banküberweisung (D)	—	bank transfer	virement bancaire *m*	rimessa bancaria *f*	transferencia bancaria *f*

	D	E	F	I	Es
ban on advertising[1] (E)	Werbeverbot *n*	—	défense de publicité *f*	divieto di pubblicità *m*	prohibición de publicidad *f*
ban on advertising[2] (E)	Werbeverbot	—	défense de publicité *f*	divieto dei pubblicità *m*	prohibición de publicidad *f*
banque centrale (F)	Zentralbank *f*	central bank	—	Banca Centrale *f*	banco emisor *m*
banque centrale de virement (F)	Girozentrale *f*	central giro institution	—	stanza centrale di compensazione *f*	central de giros *f*
banque de commerce (F)	Handelsbank *f*	merchant bank	—	banca commerciale *f*	banco comercial *m*
banque de crédit (F)	Kreditbank *f*	commercial bank	—	banca di credito *f*	banco de crédito *m*
banque de données (F)	Datenbank *f*	data bank	—	banca dati *f*	banco de datos *m*
banque d'émission (F)	Notenbank *f*	central bank	—	banca d'emissione *f*	banco emisor *m*
banque d'investissement (F)	Investmentbank *f*	investment bank	—	banca d'investimento *f*	banco de inversiones *m*
banque habituelle (F)	Hausbank *f*	company's bank	—	banca di preferenza *f*	banco particular *m*
banque hypothécaire (F)	Hypothekenbank *f*	mortgage bank	—	banca ipotecaria *f*	banco hipotecario *m*
banque mondiale (F)	Weltbank *f*	World Bank	—	Banca Mondiale *f*	Banco Mundial *m*
banque nationale (F)	Staatsbank *f*	state bank	—	Banca Centrale *f*	banco del Estado *m*
banque régionale (F)	Regionalbank *f*	regional bank	—	banca regionale *f*	banco regional *m*
banquero (Es)	Bankier *m*	banker	banquier *m*	banchiere *m*	—
banqueroute (F)	Bankrott *m*	bankruptcy	—	bancarotta *f*	quiebra *f*
banqueroute frauduleuse (F)	betrügerischer Bankrott *m*	fraudulent bankruptcy	—	bancarotta fraudolenta *f*	quiebra fraudulenta *f*
banquier (F)	Bankier *m*	banker	—	banchiere *m*	banquero *m*
bar (D)	—	cash	comptant	in contanti	al contado
Barakkreditiv (D)	—	cash letter of credit	accréditif payable en espèce *m*	apertura di credito documentario semplice *f*	crédito simple *m*
Bargeld (D)	—	cash	argent comptant *m*	denaro contante *m*	dinero efectivo *m*
Bargeldbestand (D)	—	cash in hand	espèces en caisse *f pl*	denaro contante in cassa *m*	saldo en efectivo *m*
bargeldlos (D)	—	non-cash	par virement	mediante assegno	por transferencia
Barkredit (D)	—	cash credit	crédit de caisse *m*	credito per cassa *m*	crédito en efectivo *m*
barometer of public opinion (E)	Stimmungsbarometer *n*	—	baromètre de la tendance *m*	barometro economico *m*	barómetro de la opinión pública *m*
baromètre de la tendance (F)	Stimmungsbarometer *n*	barometer of public opinion	—	barometro economico *m*	barómetro de la opinión pública *m*
barómetro de la opinión pública (Es)	Stimmungsbarometer *n*	barometer of public opinion	baromètre de la tendance *m*	barometro economico *m*	—
barometro economico (I)	Stimmungsbarometer *n*	barometer of public opinion	baromètre de la tendance *m*	—	barómetro de la opinión pública *m*
Barrengold (D)	—	gold in bars	or en lingot *m*	oro in lingotti *m*	oro en barras *m*
Barscheck (D)	—	open cheque	chèque non barré *m*	assegno circolare *m*	cheque de caja *m*
barter transaction (E)	Kompensationsgeschäft *n*	—	affaire de compensation *f*	operazione di compensazione *f*	operacion de compensación *f*
Barvermögen (D)	—	cash assets	valeurs réalisables à court terme ou disponibles *f pl*	patrimonio in contanti *m*	activo efectivo *m*
Barzahlung (D)	—	cash payment	payement comptant *m*	pagamento in contanti *m*	pago al contado *m*
Barzahlungskonto (D)	—	cash discount	escompte de caisse *m*	sconto per pagamento in contanti *m*	descuento de pago al contado *f*
Barzahlungsnachlaß (D)	—	discount for cash payment	remise pour payement au comptant *f*	sconto per pagamento in contanti *m*	descuento por pago al contado *m*
Barzahlungsrabatt (D)	—	cash discount	remise pour payement comptant *f*	ribasso per pagamento in contanti *m*	descuento por pago al contado *m*
base (E)	Basis *f*	—	base *f*	base *f*	base *f*
base (Es)	Basis *f*	base	base *f*	base *f*	—
base (F)	Basis *f*	base	—	base *f*	base *f*
base (I)	Basis *f*	base	base *f*	—	base *f*
base de capital (Es)	Kapitalbasis *f*	capital base	base de capital *f*	base di capitale *f*	—

	D	E	F	I	Es
base de capital (F)	Kapitalbasis *f*	capital base	—	base di capitale *f*	base de capital *f*
base di capitale (I)	Kapitalbasis *f*	capital base	base de capital *f*	—	base de capital *f*
base period (E)	Basisperiode *f*	—	période de base *f*	periodo di base *m*	período básico *m*
base year (E)	Basisjahr *n*	—	année de base *f*	anno di base *m*	año básico *m*
basic income (E)	Basiseinkommen *n*	—	revenu de base *m*	introiti base *m pl*	salario base *m*
basic information (E)	Basisinformation *f*	—	information de base *f*	informazione base *f*	información básica *f*
basic knowledge (E)	Grundkenntnisse *pl*	—	connaissances fondamentales *f pl*	cognizioni elementari *f pl*	conocimientos básicos *m pl*
basic pension (E)	Grundrente *f*	—	pension de base *f*	pensione base *f*	pensión básica *f*
basic salary (E)	Grundgehalt *n*	—	traitement de base *m*	stipendio base *m*	salario base *m*
basic wage (E)	Basislohn *m*	—	salaire de référence *m*	salario base *m*	sueldo base *m*
Basis (D)	—	base	base *f*	base *f*	base *f*
Basiseinkommen (D)	—	basic income	revenu de base *m*	introiti base *m pl*	salario base *m*
Basisinformation (D)	—	basic information	information de base *f*	informazione base *f*	información básica *f*
Basisjahr (D)	—	base year	année de base *f*	anno di base *m*	año básico *m*
Basislohn (D)	—	basic wage	salaire de référence *m*	salario base *m*	sueldo base *m*
Basisperiode (D)	—	base period	période de base *f*	periodo di base *m*	período básico *m*
basura de embalaje (Es)	Verpackungsmüll *m*	packing waste	déchets d'emballage *m pl*	rifiuti da imballaggi *m pl*	—
basura especial (Es)	Sondermüll *m*	special refuse	détritus spéciaux *m pl*	rifiuti speciali *m pl*	—
Bau (D)	—	construction	construction *f*	costruzione *f*	construcción *f*
Baufinanzierung (D)	—	construction financing	financement à la construction *m*	finanziamento di costruzione *m*	financiación de la construcción *f*
Bauindustrie (D)	—	construction industry	industrie de sous-traitance du bâtiment *f*	industria edile *f*	industria de la construcción *f*
Bauinvestitionen (D)	—	structural investments	investissements à la construction *m pl*	investimenti edili *m pl*	inversión inmobiliaria *f*
Baukredit (D)	—	building loan	crédit à la construction *m*	credito edilizio *m*	crédito para la construcción *f*
Bauland (D)	—	building land	espace à bâtir *m*	area edificabile *f*	terreno edificable *m*
Bauwirtschaft (D)	—	building and construction industry	(industrie du) bâtiment *f*	edilizia *f*	ramo de la construcción *m*
Beamter (D)	—	official	fonctionnaire *m*	funzionario *m*	funcionario *m*
Beanstandung (D)	—	objection	objection *f*	reclamo *m*	queja *f*
bear sale (E)	Leerverkauf *m*	—	vente à découvert *f*	vendita allo scoperto *f*	venta al descubierto *f*
bearer (E)	Überbringer *m*	—	porteur *m*	portatore *m*	portador *m*
bearer cheque (E)	überbringerscheck *m*	—	chèque au porteur *m*	assegno al portatore *m*	cheque al portador *m*
bearer instrument (E)	Inhaberpapier *n*	—	titre souscrit au porteur *m*	titolo al portatore *m*	título al portador *m*
bearer share (E)	Inhaberaktie *f*	—	action au porteur *f*	azione al portatore *f*	acción al portador *f*
Bedarf (D)	—	need/demand	besoin *m*/demande *f*	fabbisogno *m*/ domanda *f*	necesidades *f pl*/ demanda *f*
Bedarfsanalyse (D)	—	analysis of requirements	analyse des besoins *m*	analisi del fabbisogno *f*	análisis de las necesidades *m*
Bedarfsfaktoren (D)	—	requirement factors	éléments pouvant influencer la demande *m pl*	fattori del fabbisogno *m pl*	factores determinantes de las necesidades *m pl*
Bedarfs-schwankung (D)	—	fluctuations in requirements	oscillations de demande *f pl*	oscillazioni del fabbisogno *f pl*	fluctuación de las necesidades *f*
Bedienungsgeld (D)	—	tip	pourboire *m*	diritto di servizio *m*	propina *f*
Bedingung (D)	—	condition	condition *f*	condizione *f*	condición *f*
be due (E)	anstehen	—	être échnu	essere scaduto	estar pendiente
Bedürfnis (D)	—	need	besoin *m*	bisogno *m*	necesidad *f*
Bedürfnis-befriedigung (D)	—	satisfaction of needs	satisfaction des besoins *f*	soddisfazione dei bisogni *f*	satisfacción de las necesidades *f*
beeidigte Erklärung (D)	—	sworn statement	déclaration sous serment *f*	dichiarazione giurata *f*	declaración jurada *f*
beeinflußbar (D)	—	be influenced	influençable	influenzabile	sugestionable

	D	E	F	I	Es
Beförderung (D)	—	promotion/transport	nomination *f*/ transport *m*	promozione *f*/ trasporto *m*	ascenso *m*/ transporte *m*
Beförderungs-bedingungen (D)	—	terms of conveyance	conditions de transport *f pl*	condizioni di trasporto *f pl*	condiciones de transporte *f pl*
Beförderungs-geschäfte (D)	—	transport services	transports *m pl*	operazioni di trasporto *f pl*	negocios de transporte *m pl*
before hours dealing (E)	Vorbörse *f*	—	marché avant le marché officiel *m*	mercato preborsistico *m*	operaciones antes de la apertura de la bolsa *f pl*
Befragung (D)	—	poll	enquête *f*	interrogazione *f*	encuesta *f*
Befugnis (D)	—	authorization	pouvoir *m*	prerogativa *f*	autorización *f*
beglaubigte Abschrift (D)	—	authenticated copy	copie certifiée *f*	copia autenticata *f*	copia legalizada *f*
Beglaubigung (D)	—	authentication	certification *f*	autenticazione *f*	legalización *f*
Begleitpapiere (D)	—	accompanying documents	pièces accompagnant l'envoi *f pl*	bolle di accompagnamento *f pl*	documentos adjuntos *m pl*
Begrüßung (D)	—	salutation	salutations *f pl*	saluto *m*	saludo *m*
Begünstigter (D)	—	beneficiary	bénéficiaire *m*	beneficiario *m*	favorecido *m*
Behälterverkehr (D)	—	container transport	transport utilisant des containers *m*	trasporto container *m*	transportación en contenedores *f*
behauptet (D)	—	maintained	affirmé	affermato	sostenido
Beherrschungs-vertrag (D)	—	control agreement	accord de contrôle *m*	contratto di controllo *m*	contrato de dominación *m*
Behörde (D)	—	authority	autorité *f*	autorità *f*	autoridad *f*
Beilage (D)	—	supplement	encart non broché à la revue *m*	inserto *m*	suplemento *m*
be influenced (E)	beeinflußbar	—	influençable	influenzabile	sugestionable
Beiträge (D)	—	contributions	participations *f pl*	contributi *m pl*	contribuciones *f pl*
belasten (D)	—	load/charge	débiter	addebitare	cargar/adeudar
Belastung (D)	—	load	charge *f*	addebito *m*	gravamen *m*
Beleg (D)	—	voucher	justificatif *m*	quietanza *f*	justificativo *m*
Belegschaft (D)	—	staff	personnel *m*	maestranza *f*	plantilla *f*
Beleihungswert (D)	—	sum as security for a loan	montant de la garantie *m*	valore finanziabile *m*	valor para préstamos *m*
Belieferungspflicht (D)	—	duty to supply	obligation de livraison *f*	obbligo di fornitura *m*	obligación de suministro *f*
bene economico (I)	Wirtschaftsgut *n*	economic good	bien économique *m*	—	bien económico *m*
bénéfice (F)	Gewinn *m*	profit/surplus	—	utile *m*	beneficio *m*/ superávit *m*
bénéfice annuel (F)	Jahresgewinn *m*	annual profit	—	utile dell'anno *m*	beneficio del ejercicio *m*
bénéfice brut[1] (F)	Handelsspanne *f*	trading margin	—	margine commerciale *m*	margen comercial *f*
bénéfice brut[2] (F)	Rohgewinn *m*	gross profit on sales	—	utile lordo *m*	ganancia bruta *f*
bénéfice comptable (F)	Buchgewinn *m*	book profit	—	utile contabile *m*	beneficio contable *m*
bénéfice d'exploitation (F)	Unternehmens-gewinn *m*	profit of the enterprise	—	utile d'impresa *m*	beneficio empresarial *m*
bénéfice net (F)	Reingewinn *m*	net profit	—	utile netto *m*	ganancia neta *f*
bénéficiaire (F)	Begünstigter *m*	beneficiary	—	beneficiario *m*	favorecido *m*
bénéficiaire d'un crédit (F)	Kreditnehmer *m*	borrower	—	beneficiario del credito *m*	prestatario *m*
bénéficiaire du payement (F)	Zahlungs-berechtigter *m*	beneficiary of payment	—	beneficiario del pagamento *m*	beneficiario del pago *m*
beneficial to the environment (E)	umweltfreundlich	—	favorable à l'environnement	ecologico	no contaminante
beneficiario[1] (I)	Begünstigter *m*	beneficiary	bénéficiaire *m*	—	favorecido *m*
beneficiario[2] (I)	Remittent *m*	payee	remettant *m*	—	remitente *m*
beneficiario del credito (I)	Kreditnehmer *m*	borrower	bénéficiaire d'un crédit *m*	—	prestatario *m*
beneficiario del pagamento (I)	Zahlungs-berechtigter *m*	beneficiary of payment	bénéficiaire du payement *m*	—	beneficiario del pago *m*
beneficiario del pago (Es)	Zahlungs-berechtigter *m*	beneficiary of payment	bénéficiaire du payement *m*	beneficiario del pagamento *m*	—

	D	E	F	I	Es
beneficiary (E)	Begünstigter *m*	—	bénéficiaire *m*	beneficiario *m*	favorecido *m*
beneficiary of payment (E)	Zahlungs-berechtigter *m*	—	bénéficiaire du payement *m*	beneficiario del pagamento *m*	beneficiario del pago *m*
beneficio[1] (Es)	Gewinn *m*	profit/surplus	bénéfice *m*	utile *m*	—
beneficio[2] (Es)	Erlös *m*	proceeds	produit des ventes *m*	ricavo *m*	—
beneficio[3] (Es)	Profit *m*	profit	profit *m*	profitto *m*	—
beneficio contable (Es)	Buchgewinn *m*	book profit	bénéfice comptable *m*	utile contabile *m*	—
beneficio del ejercicio (Es)	Jahresgewinn *m*	annual profit	bénéfice annuel *m*	utile dell'anno *m*	—
beneficio de racionalización (Es)	Rationalisierungs-gewinn *m*	rationalization profit	profit de rationalisation *m*	profitto di razionalizzazione *m*	—
beneficio empresarial (Es)	Unternehmens-gewinn *m*	profit of the enterprise	bénéfice d'exploitation *m*	utile d'impresa *m*	—
beneficio simulado (Es)	Scheingewinn *m*	fictitious profit	gain fictif *m*	utile fittizio *m*	—
benessere (I)	Wohlstand *m*	prosperity	prospérité *f*	—	bienestar *m*
benestare pubblico (I)	Allgemeinwohl *n*	public welfare	bien général *m*	—	bienestar público *m*
beni (I)	Güter *pl*	goods	biens *m pl*	—	bienes *m pl*
beni agricoli (I)	Agrargüter *pl*	agricultural goods	produits agricoles *m pl*	—	bienes agrícolas *m pl*
beni collettivi (I)	Kollektivgüter *pl*	collective goods	biens collectifs *m pl*	—	bienes sociales *m pl*
beni complementari (I)	komplementäre Güter *pl*	complementary goods	produits de complément *m pl*	—	bienes com-plementarios *m pl*
beni di consumo (I)	Konsumgüter *pl*	consumer goods	biens de consommation *m pl*	—	bienes de consumo *m pl*
beni di consumo durevoli (I)	Gebrauchsgüter *pl*	durable consumer goods	biens d'utilisation courante *m pl*	—	bienes de consumo duradero *m pl*
beni di investimento (I)	Investitionsgüter *pl*	capital goods	biens d'investissement *m pl*	—	bienes de inversión *m pl*
beni d'investimento (I)	Anlagegüter *pl*	capital goods	valeur immoblisée *f*	—	bienes de inversión *m pl*
beni di lusso (I)	Luxusgüter *pl*	luxury goods	produits de luxe *m pl*	—	bienes de lujo *m pl*
beni di massa (I)	Massengüter *pl*	bulk goods	marchandises en vrac *f pl*	—	productos a granel *m pl*
beni in conto deposito (I)	Kommissionsgüter *pl*	goods for sale on commission	marchandises en commission *f pl*	—	mercancías en comisión *f pl*
beni inferiori (I)	inferiore Güter *pl*	inferior goods	biens inférieurs *m pl*	—	bienes inferiores *m pl*
beni mobili (I)	bewegliche Güter	movable goods	biens meubles *m pl*	—	bienes muebles *m pl*
beni non durevoli (I)	Verbrauchsgüter *pl*	consumer goods	biens de consommation *m pl*	—	bienes de consumo *m pl*
beni pubblici (I)	öffentliche Güter *pl*	public goods	biens publics *m pl*	—	bienes públicos *m pl*
Benzin (D)	—	petrol	essence *f*	benzina *f*	gasolina *f*
benzina (I)	Benzin *n*	petrol	essence *f*	—	gasolina *f*
Benzingutscheine (D)	—	petrol voucher	bon d'essence *m*	coupons *m pl*	bono de gasolina *m*
Berater (D)	—	adviser	conseiller *m*	consulente *m*	asesor *m*
Beratung (D)	—	advice	consultation *f*	consulenza *f*	asesoramiento *m*
Berechnung (D)	—	computation	calcul *m*	calcolo *m*	calculación *f*
Bereitstellungs-kosten (D)	—	commitment fee	coûts administratifs *m pl*	spese di stanziamento *f pl*	gastos fijos *m pl*
Bereitstellungs-zinsen (D)	—	commitment interests	intérêts de disponibilité *m pl*	interessi per lo stanziamento *m pl*	interés de disponibilidad *m*
Bergbau (D)	—	mining	industrie extractive *f*	industria mineraria *f*	minería *f*
Bergung (D)	—	salvage	sauvetage *m*	ricupero *m*	salvamento *m*
Berichterstattung (D)	—	reporting	compte rendu *m*	relazione *f*	reportaje *m*
Berichtigung (D)	—	correction	rectification *f*	correzione *f*	rectificación *f*
Berichtspflicht (D)	—	obligation to report	obligation d'information *f*	obbligo di relazione *m*	obligación de información *f*
Beruf (D)	—	profession	profession *f*	professione *f*	profesión *f*
Berufsausbildung (D)	—	professional training	formation professionelle *f*	formazione professionale *f*	formación profesional *f*
Berufsgeheimnis (D)	—	professional secret	secret professionnel *m*	segreto professionale *m*	secreto profesional *m*

	D	E	F	I	Es
Berufsrisiko (D)	—	occupational hazard	risque professionnel *m*	rischio professionale *m*	riesgo profesional *m*
Berufungsgericht (D)	—	appeal court	tribunal d'appel *m*	corte d'appello *f*	tribunal de apelación *m*
Beschädigung (D)	—	damage	endommagement *m*	danno *m*	deterioración *f*
Beschäftigung (D)	—	employment	occupation *f*	occupazione *f*	ocupación *f*
Beschäftigungs-grad (D)	—	level of employment	taux d'emploi *m*	tasso d'occupazione *m*	grado de empleo *m*
Beschäftigungs-politik (D)	—	employment policy	politique d'emploi *f*	politica d'occupazione *f*	política de empleo *f*
Beschäftigungs-rückgang (D)	—	drop in employment	baisse de l'offre d'emploi *f*	calo dell'occupazione *m*	descenso del empleo *m*
Beschäftigungs-theorie (D)	—	employment theory	théorie d'emploi *f*	teoria dell'occupazione *f*	teoría del empleo *f*
Beschlagnahme (D)	—	confiscation	saisie *f*	sequestro *m*	confiscación *f*
beschleunigt (D)	—	speedy	accéléré	accelerato	acelerado
Beschluß (D)	—	decision	décision *f*	delibera *f*	decisión *f*
Beschwerde (D)	—	complaint	réclamation *f*	protesta *f*	recurso *m*
Besitz (D)	—	possession	possession *f*	possesso *m*	posesión *f*
Besitzeinkommen (D)	—	unearned income	revenu du patrimoine *m*	reddito da possesso *m*	renta de la propiedad *f*
Besitzgesellschaft (D)	—	controlling company	société contrôleuse *f*	società finanziaria *f*	sociedad controladora *f*
besoin[1] (F)	Bedarf *m*	need/demand	—	fabbisogno *m*/ domanda *f*	necesidades *f pl*/ demanda *f*
besoin[2] (F)	Bedürfnis *n*	need	—	bisogno *m*	necesidad *f*
besoin annuel (F)	Jahresbedarf *m*	annual need	—	bisogno annuale *m*	necesidad anual *f*
besoin d'information (F)	Informations-bedarf *m*	requirement of information	—	bisogno d'informazioni *m*	necesidad de información *f*
besoin en capital (F)	Kapitalbedarf *m*	capital requirements	—	domanda di capitale *m*	necesidad de capital *f*
besoin individuel (F)	Individualbedürfnis *n*	individual need	—	fabbisogno individuale *m*	necesidades individuales *f pl*
Besoldung (D)	—	pay	rétribution *f*	retribuzione *f*	sueldo *m*
Besprechung (D)	—	discussion	conférence *f*	colloquio *m*	conferencia *f*
Besprechungs-termin (D)	—	meeting date	date de la conférence *f*	termine del colloquio *m*	fecha de conferencia *f*
Bestandsgröße (D)	—	stock variable	stock variable *m*	entità dell'inventario *f*	magnitud *f*
Bestandskonto (D)	—	real account	compte d'existences *m*	conto merci *m*	cuenta de existencias *f*
Bestätigung (D)	—	confirmation	confirmation *f*	conferma *f*	confirmación *f*
Bestechung (D)	—	bribe	corruption *f*	corruzione *f*	soborno *f*
Bestelldaten (D)	—	details of order	références de commande *f pl*	dati delle ordinazioni *m pl*	datos de pedido *m pl*
Besteller (D)	—	customer	acheteur *m*	committente *m*	demandante *m*
Bestellformular (D)	—	order form	bon de commande *m*	modulo d'ordinazione *m*	formulario de pedido *m*
Bestellmenge (D)	—	ordered quantity	quantité commandée *f*	quantità d'ordinazione *f*	cantidad pedida *f*
Bestellschein (D)	—	order form	bulletin de commande *m*	bolletta d'ordinazione *f*	hoja de pedido *f*
Bestellung (D)	—	order	commande *f*	ordinazione *f*	pedido *m*
bestens (D)	—	at best	au mieux	ottimo	al mejor cambio
Bestensorder (D)	—	order at best	ordre non limité *m*	ordine al miglior corso *m*	orden al mejor cambio posible *f*
beste Qualität (D)	—	first class quality	première qualité *f*	qualità ottima *f*	primera calidad *f*
Bestimmungs-bahnhof (D)	—	station of destination	gare destinataire *f*	stazione di destinazione *f*	estación de destino *f*
Bestimmungsort (D)	—	place of destination	lieu de destination *m*	luogo di destinazione *m*	lugar de destino *m*
bestowal (E)	Zuwendung *f*	—	affectation *f*	assegnazione *f*	gratificación *f*
Besuchs-anmeldung (D)	—	announcement of a visitor	annonce de visiteurs *f*	avviso di visita *m*	anuncio de visita *m*

	D	E	F	I	Es
Beteiligung (D)	—	participation	participation *f*	partecipazione *f*	participación *f*
Betrag (D)	—	amount	montant *m*	importo *m*	suma *f*
Betrieb (D)	—	factory	usine *f*	azienda *f*	fábrica *f*
Betriebsanalyse (D)	—	operation analysis	situation analytique de l'expoitation *f*	analisi aziendale *f*	análisis de la empresa *m*
Betriebsausgaben (D)	—	(current) operational expenses	charges d'exploitation *f pl*	spese aziendali *f pl*	gastos de explotación *m pl*
Betriebsausweis (D)	—	staff identification card	pièce d'identité de l'entreprise *f*	tessera aziendale *f*	carné de empresa *f*
Betriebserlaubnis (D)	—	operating permit	droit d'exploitation *m*	autorizzazione per l'esercizio *f*	autorización de funcionamiento *f*
Betriebsferien (D)	—	annual holiday	clôture annuelle de l'établissement *f*	ferie aziendali *f pl*	vacaciones de la empresa *f pl*
Betriebsgeheimnis (D)	—	trade secret	secret d'exploitation *m*	segreto aziendale *m*	secreto empresarial *m*
Betriebs-gesellschaft (D)	—	operating company	entreprise d'exploitation *f*	società d'esercizio *f*	empresa de explotación *f*
Betriebsgröße (D)	—	size of the company	dimension de l'entreprise *f*	dimensione dell'azienda *f*	tamaño de la explotación *m*
Betriebskapital (D)	—	working capital	capital de roulement *m*	capitale d'esercizio *m*	capital de explotación *m*
Betriebsklima (D)	—	working conditions and human relations	climat social *m*	atmosfera di lavoro *f*	ambiente de trabajo *m*
Betriebskosten (D)	—	operating costs	charges d'exploitation *f pl*	spese d'esercizio *f pl*	gastos de explotación *m pl*
Betriebsprüfer (D)	—	auditor	expert-comptable *m*	revisore aziendale *m*	contador público *m*
Betriebsprüfung (D)	—	investigation by the tax authorities	vérification des livres de l'entreprise *f*	revisione aziendale *f*	inspección de la explotación *f*
Betriebsspionage (D)	—	industrial espionage	espionnage dans l'entreprise	spionaggio aziendale *m*	espionaje industrial *m*
Betriebsstatistik (D)	—	operational statistics	statistique commerciale et industrielle *f*	statistica aziendale *f*	estadística de la empresa *f*
Betriebswirtschafts-lehre (D)	—	business administration	(science de la) gestion industrielle et commerciale *f*	economia aziendale *f*	teoría de la empresa *f*
Betrug (D)	—	fraud	fraude *f*	frode *f*	fraude *m*
betrügerischer Bankrott (D)	—	fraudulent bankruptcy	banqueroute frauduleuse *f*	bancarotta fraudolenta *f*	quiebra fraudulenta *f*
Bevölkerung (D)	—	population	population *f*	popolazione *f*	población *f*
Bevölkerungsdichte (D)	—	density of population	densité da la population *f*	densità di popolazione *f*	densidad de la población *f*
Bevölkerungspolitik (D)	—	population policy	politique démographique populationniste *f*	politica demografica *f*	política demográfica *f*
Bevölkerungs-statistik (D)	—	population statistics	statistique démographique *f*	statistica demografica *f*	estadística de población *f*
Bevölkerungs-struktur (D)	—	population structure	structure démographique *f*	struttura demografica *f*	estructura demográfica *f*
Bevölkerungs-wachstum (D)	—	increase in population	accroissement de la population *m*	incremento demografico *m*	crecimiento vegetativo *m*
Bevollmächtigung (D)	—	authorization	pouvoir *m*	autorizzazione *f*	apoderamiento *m*
bewegliche Güter (D)	—	movable goods	biens meubles *m pl*	beni mobili *m pl*	bienes muebles *m pl*
Beweis (D)	—	proof	preuve *f*	prova *f*	prueba *f*
Beweislast (D)	—	burden of proof	charge de la preuve *f*	onere di prova *m*	carga de la prueba *f*
Bewerber (D)	—	applicant	candidat *m*	aspirante *m*	aspirante *m*
Bewerbung (D)	—	application	candidature *f*	domanda d'impiego *f*	candidatura *f*
Bewerbungs-schreiben (D)	—	letter of application	lettre de demande d'emploi *f*	domanda d'impiego *f*	carta de solicitud *f*
Bewerbungs-unterlagen (D)	—	application documents	dossier de candidature *m*	documenti della domanda d'impiego *m pl*	documentos de solicitud *m pl*
Bewertung (D)	—	valuation	valorisation *f*	valutazione *f*	valoración *f*
Bewirtung (D)	—	hospitality/ catering	hospitalité *f*/ accueil *m*	ospitalità *f*/ servizio *m*	hospedaje *m*/ atenciones *f pl*

	D	E	F	I	Es
bezahlter Urlaub (D)	—	paid vacation	congé payé *m*	ferie pagate *f pl*	vacaciones con goce de sueldo *f pl*
Bezirksvertreter (D)	—	local agent	agent local *m*	rappresentante di zona *m*	agente regional *m*
Bezogener (D)	—	drawee	tiré *m*	trattario *m*	librado *m*
Bezug (D)	—	reference	référence *f*	riferimento *m*	referencia *f*
Bezüge (D)	—	earnings	émoluments *m pl*	entrate *f pl*	retribuciones *f pl*
bezugnehmend (D)	—	referring to	se référant (à)	con riferimento a	con referencia a
Bezugskosten (D)	—	purchasing costs	coûts d'acquisition *m pl*	prezzo d'acquisto *m*	gastos de adquisición *m pl*
Bezugsquelle (D)	—	source of supply	source d'approvisionnement *f*	fonte d'acquisto *f*	fuente de suministro *f*
bien económico (Es)	Wirtschaftsgut *n*	economic good	bien économique *m*	bene economico *m*	—
bien économique (F)	Wirtschaftsgut *n*	economic good	—	bene economico *m*	bien económico *m*
bienes (Es)	Güter *pl*	goods	biens *m pl*	beni *m pl*	—
bienes agrícolas (Es)	Agrargüter *pl*	agricultural goods	produits agricoles *m pl*	beni agricoli *m pl*	—
bienes complementarios (Es)	komplementäre Güter *pl*	complementary goods	produits de complément *m pl*	beni complementari *m pl*	—
bienes de consumo[1] (Es)	Konsumgüter *pl*	consumer goods	biens de consommation *m pl*	beni di consumo *m pl*	—
bienes de consumo[2] (Es)	Verbrauchsgüter *pl*	consumer goods	biens de consommation *m pl*	beni non durevoli *m pl*	—
bienes de consumo duradero (Es)	Gebrauchsgüter *pl*	durable consumer goods	biens d'utilisation courante *m pl*	beni di consumo durevoli *m pl*	—
bienes de inversión[1] (Es)	Investitionsgüter *pl*	capital goods	biens d'investissement *m pl*	beni di investimento *m pl*	—
bienes de inversión[2] (Es)	Anlagegüter *pl*	capital goods	valeur immoblisée *f*	beni d'investimento *m pl*	—
bienes de lujo (Es)	Luxusgüter *pl*	luxury goods	produits de luxe *m pl*	beni di lusso *m pl*	—
bienes inferiores (Es)	inferiore Güter *pl*	inferior goods	biens inférieurs *m pl*	beni inferiori *m pl*	—
bienes muebles (Es)	bewegliche Güter	movable goods	biens meubles *m pl*	beni mobili *m pl*	—
bienes públicos (Es)	öffentliche Güter *pl*	public goods	biens publics *m pl*	beni pubblici *m pl*	—
bienes sociales (Es)	Kollektivgüter *pl*	collective goods	biens collectifs *m pl*	beni collettivi *m pl*	—
bienestar (Es)	Wohlstand *m*	prosperity	prospérité *f*	benessere *m*	—
bienestar público (Es)	Allgemeinwohl *n*	public welfare	bien général *m*	benestare pubblico *m*	—
bien général (F)	Allgemeinwohl *n*	public welfare	—	benestare pubblico *m*	bienestar público *m*
bien immobilier (F)	Immobilie *f*	item of real estate	—	immobile *m*	inmueble *m*
biens (F)	Güter *pl*	goods	—	beni *m pl*	bienes *m pl*
biens collectifs (F)	Kollektivgüter *pl*	collective goods	—	beni collettivi *m pl*	bienes sociales *m pl*
biens corporels (F)	Sachvermögen *n*	material assets	—	capitale reale *m*	patrimonio real *m*
biens corporels immobilisés (F)	Realkapital *n*	real capital	—	capitale reale *m*	capital real *m*
biens de consommation[1] (F)	Verbrauchsgüter *pl*	consumer goods	—	beni non durevoli *m pl*	bienes de consumo *m pl*
biens de consommation[2] (F)	Konsumgüter *pl*	consumer goods	—	beni di consumo *m pl*	bienes de consumo *m pl*
biens d'investissement (F)	Investitionsgüter *pl*	capital goods	—	beni di investimento *m pl*	bienes de inversión *m pl*
biens d'utilisation courante (F)	Gebrauchsgüter *pl*	durable consumer goods	—	beni di consumo durevoli *m pl*	bienes de consumo duradero *m pl*
biens inférieurs (F)	inferiore Güter *pl*	inferior goods	—	beni inferiori *m pl*	bienes inferiores *m pl*
biens meubles (F)	bewegliche Güter	movable goods	—	beni mobili *m pl*	bienes muebles *m pl*
biens publics (F)	öffentliche Güter *pl*	public goods	—	beni pubblici *m pl*	bienes públicos *m pl*
bien transporté (F)	Speditionsgut *n*	forwarding merchandise	—	merce spedita *f*	mercancía transportada *f*
Bietungsgarantie (D)	—	tender guarantee	cautionnement provisoire *m*	garanzia d'offerta *f*	caución de licitación *f*
biglietto di andata e ritorno (I)	Rückfahrkarte *f*	return ticket	billet d'aller et retour *m*	—	billete de ida y vuelta *m*
biglietto d'ingresso (I)	Eintrittskarte *f*	admission ticket	billet *m*	—	entrada *f*

	D	E	F	I	Es
biglietto gratuito (I)	Freikarte *f*	free ticket	billet de faveur *m*	—	entrada gratuita *f*
bilan (F)	Bilanz *f*	balance sheet	—	bilancio *m*	balance *m*
bilancia commerciale (I)	Handelsbilanz *f*	balance of trade	balance des opérations en marchandises *f*	—	balanza comercial *f*
bilancia dei capitali (I)	Kapitalbilanz *f*	balance of capital transactions	balance des opérations en capital *f*	—	balanza de capitales *f*
bilancia dei pagamenti (I)	Zahlungsbilanz *f*	balance of payments	balance des payements *f*	—	balanza de pagos *f*
bilancia delle divise (I)	Devisenbilanz *f*	foreign exchange balance	compte de devises *m*	—	balanza de divisas *f*
bilancia delle partite correnti (I)	Leistungsbilanz *f*	balance of goods and services	balance des opérations courantes *f*	—	balanza por cuenta corriente *f*
bilancia dell'oro e delle divise (I)	Gold- und Devisenbilanz *f*	foreign exchange and gold balance	balance d'or et de devises *f*	—	balanza de oro y divisas *f*
bilancia per corrispondenza (I)	Briefwaage *f*	letter scales	pèse-lettres *m*	—	pesacartas *m*
bilancio[1] (I)	Bilanz *f*	balance sheet	bilan *m*	—	balance *m*
bilancio[2] (I)	Budget n/Etat *m*	budget	budget *m*	—	presupuesto *m*
bilancio consolidato (I)	konsolidierte Bilanz *f*	consolidated balance sheet	bilan consolidé *m*	—	balance consolidado *m*
bilancio consuntivo (I)	Schlußbilanz *f*	closing balance	bilan de clôture *m*	—	balance final *m*
bilancio d'apertura (I)	Eröffnungsbilanz *f*	opening balance sheet	bilan d'ouverture *m*	—	balance inicial *m*
bilancio del gruppo (I)	Konzernbilanz *f*	balance sheet of a group	bilan consolidé d'un groupement de sociétés *m*	—	balance del consorcio *m*
bilancio fiscale (I)	Steuerbilanz *f*	tax balance sheet	bilan fiscal *m*	—	balance impositivo *m*
bilancio parziale (I)	Teilbilanz *f*	partial balance sheet	bilan partiel *m*	—	balance parcial *m*
bilancio preventivo (I)	Haushaltsplan *m*	budget	budget *m*	—	presupuesto *m*
bilancio provvisorio (I)	Zwischenbilanz *f*	interim balance sheet	bilan intermédiaire *m*	—	balance intermedio *m*
bilan consolidé (F)	konsolidierte Bilanz *f*	consolidated balance sheet	—	bilancio consolidato *m*	balance consolidado *m*
bilan consolidé d'un groupement de sociétés (F)	Konzernbilanz *f*	balance sheet of a group	—	bilancio del gruppo *m*	balance del consorcio *m*
bilan de clôture (F)	Schlußbilanz *f*	closing balance	—	bilancio consuntivo *m*	balance final *m*
bilan d'ouverture (F)	Eröffnungsbilanz *f*	opening balance sheet	—	bilancio d'apertura *m*	balance inicial *m*
bilan fiscal (F)	Steuerbilanz *f*	tax balance sheet	—	bilancio fiscale *m*	balance impositivo *m*
bilan intermédiaire (F)	Zwischenbilanz *f*	interim balance sheet	—	bilancio provvisorio *m*	balance intermedio *m*
Bilanz (D)	—	balance sheet	bilan *m*	bilancio *m*	balance *m*
Bilanzanalyse (D)	—	balance analysis	analyse du bilan *f*	analisi di bilancio *f*	análisis de balance *m*
Bilanzklarheit (D)	—	balance transparency	clarté du bilan *f*	trasparenza di bilancio *f*	claridad del balance *f*
Bilanzkontinuität (D)	—	formal identity	identité des bilans successifs *f*	continuità di bilancio *f*	identidad de los balances sucesivos *f*
Bilanzpolitik (D)	—	balance policy	politique du bilan *f*	politica di bilancio *f*	política en materia de balanzas *f*
Bilanzwahrheit (D)	—	truth in the balance sheet	sincérité du bilan *f*	chiarezza di bilancio *f*	sinceridad del balance *f*
bilateral (D)	—	bilateral	bilatéral	bilaterale	bilateral
bilateral (E)	bilateral	—	bilatéral	bilaterale	bilateral
bilateral (Es)	bilateral	bilateral	bilatéral	bilaterale	—
bilatéral (F)	bilateral	bilateral	—	bilaterale	bilateral
bilaterale (I)	bilateral	bilateral	bilatéral	—	bilateral
Bildschirm (D)	—	screen	écran *m*	video *m*	pantalla *f*
Bildschirmarbeit (D)	—	screen work	travail à l'écran	lavoro video *m*	trabajo de pantalla *m*
Bildschirmarbeitsplatz (D)	—	screen job	poste de travail à l'écran *f*	posto di lavoro video *m*	puesto de trabajo de pantalla *m*
Bildschirmtext (D)	—	videotext	videotex international *m*	videotex, Btx *m*	teletexto *m*
Bildung (D)	—	education	formation *f*	formazione *f*	educación *f*

	D	E	F	I	Es
bill of entry (E)	Zolleinfuhrschein *m*	—	acquit d'entrée *m*	bolletta d'entrata *f*	certificado de aduana *m*
bill of exchange (E)	Wechsel *m*	—	lettre de charge *f*	cambiale *f*	letra de cambio *f*
billet (F)	Eintrittskarte *f*	admission ticket	—	biglietto d'ingresso *m*	entrada *f*
billet d'aller et retour (F)	Rückfahrkarte *f*	return ticket	—	biglietto di andata e ritorno *m*	billete de ida y vuelta *m*
billet de banque (F)	Banknote *f*	bank-note	—	banconota *f*	billete de banco *m*
billet de créance (F)	Schuldschein *m*	certificate of indebtedness	—	certificato di debito *m*	pagaré *m*
billet de faveur (F)	Freikarte *f*	free ticket	—	biglietto gratuito *m*	entrada gratuita *f*
billete de banco (Es)	Banknote *f*	bank-note	billet de banque *m*	banconota *f*	—
billete de ida y vuelta (Es)	Rückfahrkarte *f*	return ticket	billet d'aller et retour *m*	biglietto di andata e ritorno *m*	—
billetterie (F)	Bankomat *m*	cash dispenser	—	bancomat *m*	cajero automático *m*
billiges Geld (D)	—	easy money	argent à bon marché *m*	crediti agevolati *m pl*	dinero barato *m*
billigst (D)	—	at best price	au meilleur prix	al prezzo più basso	al mejor cambio
bill of lading[1] (E)	Ladeschein *m*	—	avis de chargement *m*	bolletta di carico *f*	póliza de carga *f*
bill of lading[2] (E)	Seefrachtbrief *m*	—	connaissement maritime *m*	polizza di carico *f*	póliza *f*
bill of lading[3] (E)	Konnossement *n*	—	connaissement *m*	polizza di carico *f*	conocimiento *m*
bill of loading (E)	Ladeschein *m*	—	avis de chargement *m*	bolletta di carico *f*	póliza de carga *f*
binnen (D)	—	within	dans le délai de	entro	en el término de
Binnenhandel (D)	—	domestic trade	commerce intérieur *m*	commercio nazionale *m*	comercio interior *m*
Binnenmarkt (D)	—	home market	marché national *m*	mercato nazionale *m*	mercado interior *m*
Binnenschiffahrt (D)	—	inland navigation	navigation fluviale *f*	navigazione interna *f*	navegación fluvial *f*
Binnenwirtschaft (D)	—	domestic economy	économie nationale *f*	economia nazionale *f*	economía interior *f*
birthday (E)	Geburtstag *m*	—	anniversaire *m*	compleanno *m*	cumpleaños *m*
birth rate (E)	Geburtenrate *f*	—	taux de natalité *m*	tasso di natalità *m*	tasa de natalidad *f*
bisogno (I)	Bedürfnis *n*	need	besoin *m*	—	necesidad *f*
bisogno annuale (I)	Jahresbedarf *m*	annual need	besoin annuel *m*	—	necesidad anual *f*
bisogno d'informazioni (I)	Informationsbedarf *m*	requirement of information	besoin d'information *m*	—	necesidad de información *f*
black market (E)	Schwarzmarkt *m*	—	marché noir *m*	mercato nero *m*	mercado negro *m*
blank cheque (E)	Blankoscheck *m*	—	chèque en blanc *m*	assegno in bianco *m*	cheque en blanco *m*
blank form (E)	Blankoformular *n*	—	imprimé en blanc *m*	modulo in bianco *m*	formulario en blanco *m*
Blankoformular (D)	—	blank form	imprimé en blanc *m*	modulo in bianco *m*	formulario en blanco *m*
Blankokredit (D)	—	open credit	crédit en compte courant *m*	credito scoperto *m*	crédito en blanco *m*
Blankoscheck (D)	—	blank cheque	chèque en blanc *m*	assegno in bianco *m*	cheque en blanco *m*
Blankounterschrift (D)	—	blank signature	signature en blanc *f*	firma in bianco *f*	firma en blanco *f*
Blankoverkauf (D)	—	short sale	vente à découvert *f*	vendita allo scoperto *f*	venta al descubierto *f*
blank signature (E)	Blankounterschrift *f*	—	signature en blanc *f*	firma in bianco *f*	firma en blanco *f*
blocage de livraisons (F)	Liefersperre *f*	delivery ban	—	blocco delle forniture *m*	embargo *m*
blocage des prix (F)	Preisstopp *m*	price stop	—	blocco dei prezzi *m*	limitación de precios *f*
blocage des salaires (F)	Lohnstopp *m*	wage freeze	—	blocco dei salari *m*	congelación salarial *f*
bloccaggio (I)	Blockade *f*	blockade	blocus *m*	—	bloqueo *m*
blocco d'assegno (I)	Schecksperrung *f*	stopping payment of cheque	opposition au paye-ment d'un chèque *f*	—	bloqueo de un cheque *m*
blocco dei prezzi (I)	Preisstopp *m*	price stop	blocage des prix *m*	—	limitación de precios *f*
blocco dei salari (I)	Lohnstopp *m*	wage freeze	blocage des salaires *m*	—	congelación salarial *f*

	D	E	F	I	Es
blocco delle forniture (I)	Liefersperre *f*	delivery ban	blocage de livraisons *m*	—	embargo *m*
blocco marittimo (I)	Seeblockade *f*	naval blockade	blocus maritime *m*	—	bloqueo marítimo *m*
Blockade (D)	—	blockade	blocus *m*	bloccaggio *m*	bloqueo *m*
blockade (E)	Blockade *f*	—	blocus *m*	bloccaggio *m*	bloqueo *m*
blocked account[1] (E)	Sperrkonto *n*	—	compte bloqué *m*	conto vincolato *m*	fondos bloqueados *m pl*
blocked account[2] (E)	gesperrtes Konto *n*	—	compte bloqué *m*	conto bloccato *m*	cuenta congelada *f*
blocking minority (E)	Sperrminorität *f*	—	minorité suffisante pour bloquer qch. *f*	sindacato di blocco *m*	minoría de bloqueo *f*
block of shares (E)	Aktienpaket *n*	—	paquet d'actions *m*	pacchetto delle azioni *m*	paquete de acciones *m*
blocus (F)	Blockade *f*	blockade	—	bloccaggio *m*	bloqueo *m*
blocus maritime (F)	Seeblockade *f*	naval blockade	—	blocco marittimo *m*	bloqueo marítimo *m*
bloqueo (Es)	Blockade *f*	blockade	blocus *m*	bloccaggio *m*	—
bloqueo de un cheque (Es)	Schecksperrung *f*	stopping payment of cheque	opposition au payement d'un chèque *f*	blocco d'assegno *m*	—
bloqueo marítimo (Es)	Seeblockade *f*	naval blockade	blocus maritime *m*	blocco marittimo *m*	—
board (E)	Vorstand *m*	—	comité directeur *m*	consiglio di amministrazione *m*	consejo de dirección *m*
board of directors (E)	Direktion *f*	—	direction *f*	direzione *f*	junta directiva *f*
Boden (D)	—	ground/soil	sol m/terrain *m*	terra f/suolo *m*	suelo *m*/terreno *m*
Bodenpolitik (D)	—	land policy	politique de la terre *f*	politica del suolo *f*	política del suelo *f*
Bodenpreis (D)	—	land price	prix du terrain *m*	prezzo del suolo *m*	precio del suelo *m*
Bodenreform (D)	—	land reform	réforme agraire *f*	riforma agraria *f*	reforma agraria *f*
bogus firm (E)	Scheinfirma *f*	—	raison sociale imaginaire *f*	pseudoditta *f*	casa ficticia *f*
boicot (Es)	Boykott *m*	boycott	boycottage *m*	boicottaggio *m*	—
boicot económico (Es)	Wirtschaftsboykott *m*	economic boycott	boycottage économique *m*	boicottaggio economico *m*	—
boicottaggio (I)	Boykott *m*	boycott	boycottage *m*	—	boicot *m*
boicottaggio economico (I)	Wirtschaftsboykott *m*	economic boycott	boycottage économique *m*	—	boicot económico *m*
boîte aux lettres (F)	Briefkasten *m*	mail box	—	cassetta postale *f*	buzón *m*
boîte postale (F)	Postfach *n*	post office box	—	casella postale *f*	apartado postal *m*
boletín de cambios (Es)	Kurszettel *m*	stock exchange list	bulletin des cours *m*	listino di borsa *m*	—
bolle di accompagnamento (I)	Begleitpapiere *pl*	accompanying documents	pièces accompagnant l'envoi *f pl*	—	documentos adjuntos *m pl*
bolletta d'entrata (I)	Zolleinfuhrschein *m*	bill of entry	acquit d'entrée *m*	—	certificado de aduana *m*
bolletta di carico (I)	Ladeschein *m*	bill of lading	avis de chargement *m*	—	póliza de carga *f*
bolletta di consegna (I)	Lieferschein *m*	delivery note	bulletin de livraison *m*	—	recibo de entrega *m*
bolletta di transito (I)	Durchgangsschein *m*	transit certificate	acquit de transit *m*	—	pasavante *m*
bollette doganali (I)	Einfuhrpapiere *pl*	import documents	documents d'importation *m pl*	—	documentos de importación *m pl*
bolletta d'ordinazione (I)	Bestellschein *m*	order form	bulletin de commande *m*	—	hoja de pedido *f*
bolsa (Es)	Börse *f*	(stock) exchange	bourse *f*	borsa *f*	—
Bolsa de divisas (Es)	Devisenbörse *f*	foreign exchange market	bourse de devises *f*	borsa valutaria *f*	—
bolsa de mercancías (Es)	Warenbörse *f*	commodity exchange	bourse de marchandises *f*	borsa merci *f*	—
bolsa de mercancías a plazo (Es)	Warenterminbörse *f*	commodity forward exchange	bourse d'opérations à livrer *f*	borsa merci a termine *f*	—
bolsa de reciclaje (Es)	Abfallbörse *f*	recycling exchange	bourse de recyclage *f*	borsa dei rifiuti *f*	—
Bolsa de valores (Es)	Effektenbörse *f*	stock exchange	bourse des titres et valeurs mobilières *f*	borsa valori *f*	—
bolsa de valores a término (Es)	Terminbörse *f*	futures market	bourse à terme *f*	mercato a termine *m*	—

	D	E	F	I	Es
Bon (D)	—	voucher	bon *m*	buono *m*	bono *m*
bon (F)	Bon *m*	voucher	—	buono *m*	bono *m*
bona fide (E)	gutgläubig	—	de bonne foi	di buona fede	de buena fe
bon de commande (F)	Bestellformular *n*	order form	—	modulo d'ordinazione *m*	formulario de pedido *m*
bon d'essence (F)	Benzingutscheine *pl*	petrol voucher	—	coupons *m pl*	bono de gasolina *m*
bond market (E)	Rentenmarkt *m*	—	marché des effets publics *m*	mercato dei titoli a reddito fisso *m*	mercado de títulos de renta fija *m*
bonds (E)	Rentenpapiere *pl*	—	titres de rente *m pl*	titoli a reddito fisso *m pl*	títulos de renta fija *m pl*
bonificación (Es)	Bonifikation *f*	bonus	bonification *f*	abbuono *m*	—
bonification[1] (F)	Bonus *m*	bonus	—	premio *m*	gratificación *f*
bonification[2] (F)	Bonifikation *f*	bonus	—	abbuono *m*	bonificación *f*
bonifico postale (I)	Postüberweisung *f*	postal remittance	virement postal *m*	—	giro postal *m*
bonifico telegrafico (I)	Kabelüberweisung *f*	cable transfer	virement par câble *m*	—	giro telegráfico *m*
Bonifikation (D)	—	bonus	bonification *f*	abbuono *m*	bonificación *f*
Bonität (D)	—	solvency	solvabilité *f*	solvibilità *f*	solvencia *f*
bono (Es)	Bon *m*	voucher	bon *m*	buono *m*	—
bono de gasolina (Es)	Benzingutscheine *pl*	petrol voucher	bon d'essence *m*	coupons *m pl*	—
bonos de pequeño valor nominal (Es)	Baby-Bonds *pl*	baby bonds	bons de petite valeur nominale *m pl*	baby bonds *m pl*	—
bons de petite valeur nominale (F)	Baby-Bonds *pl*	baby bonds	—	baby bonds *m pl*	bonos de pequeño valor nominal *m pl*
Bonus (D)	—	bonus	bonification *f*	premio *m*	gratificación *f*
bonus[1] (E)	Bonifikation *f*	—	bonification *f*	abbuono *m*	bonificación *f*
bonus[2] (E)	Bonus *m*	—	bonification *f*	premio *m*	gratificación *f*
bonus[3] (E)	Prämie *f*	—	prime *f*	premio *m*	gratificación *f*/prima *f*
bonus[4] (E)	Gratifikation *f*	—	gratification *f*	gratificazione *f*	gratificación *f*
bonus system (E)	Prämiensystem *n*	—	système de primes *m*	sistema dei premi *m*	sistema de primas *m*
bookkeeper (E)	Buchhalter *m*	—	comptable *m*	ragioniere *m*	tenedor de libros *m*
bookkeeping (E)	Buchführung *f*	—	comptabilité *f*	contabilità *f*	contabilidad *f*
bookkeeping error (E)	Buchungsfehler *m*	—	erreur de comptabilité *f*	errore di contabilità *m*	error contable *m*
book profit (E)	Buchgewinn *m*	—	bénéfice comptable *m*	utile contabile *m*	beneficio contable *m*
book value (E)	Buchwert *m*	—	valeur comptable *f*	valore contabile *m*	valor contable *m*
boom[1] (E)	Hausse *f*	—	hausse *f*	rialzo *m*	alza *f*
boom[2] (E)	Hochkonjunktur *f*	—	haute conjoncture *f*	alta congiuntura *f*	alta coyuntura *f*
boom de inversión (Es)	Investitionsboom *m*	investment boom	boom d'investissement *m*	boom d'investimento *m*	—
boom d'investimento (I)	Investitionsboom *m*	investment boom	boom d'investissement *m*	—	boom de inversión *m*
boom d'investissement (F)	Investitionsboom *m*	investment boom	—	boom d'investimento *m*	boom de inversión *m*
boomerang effect (E)	Bumerang-Effekt *m*	—	effet boomerang *m*	effetto bumerang *m*	efecto bumerán *m*
border control (E)	Grenzkontrolle *f*	—	contrôle à la frontière *m*	controllo alla frontiera *m*	control fronterizo *m*
borrower (E)	Kreditnehmer *m*	—	bénéficiaire d'un crédit *m*	beneficiario del credito *m*	prestatario *m*
borrowing limit (E)	Kreditlimit *n*	—	plafond du crédit alloué *m*	limite di credito *m*	límite de crédito *m*
borsa (I)	Börse *f*	(stock) exchange	bourse *f*	—	bolsa *f*
borsa dei rifiuti (I)	Abfallbörse *f*	recycling exchange	bourse de recyclage *f*	—	bolsa de reciclaje *f*
borsa merci (I)	Warenbörse *f*	commodity exchange	bourse de marchandises *f*	—	bolsa de mercancías *f*
borsa merci a termine (I)	Warenterminbörse *f*	commodity forward exchange	bourse d'opérations à livrer *f*	—	bolsa de mercancías a plazo *f*
borsa valori[1] (I)	Wertpapierbörse *f*	securities market	bourse des titres et valeurs *f*	—	mercado de valores *m*
borsa valori[2] (I)	Effektenbörse *f*	stock exchange	bourse des titres et valeurs mobilières *f*	—	bolsa de valores *f*

	D	E	F	I	Es
borsa valutaria (I)	Devisenbörse *f*	foreign exchange market	bourse de devises *f*	—	bolsa de divisas *f*
Börse (D)	—	(stock) exchange	bourse *f*	borsa *f*	bolsa *f*
Börsengeschäfte (D)	—	stock market transactions	opérations de bourse *f pl*	operazioni di borsa *f pl*	operación bursátil *f*
Börsenhandel (D)	—	stock exchange transactions	transactions boursiaires *f pl*	commercio in borsa *m*	negociación bursátil *f*
Börsenindex (D)	—	stock exchange index	indice des cours des actions *m*	indice delle quotazioni *m*	índice bursátil *m*
Börsenkrach (D)	—	stockmarket crash	débâcle boursière *f*	crollo di borsa *m*	caída en picado de la bolsa *f*
Börsenkurs (D)	—	quotation on the stock exchange	cours de bourse *m pl*	corso di borsa *m*	cotización en bolsa *f*
Börsenmakler (D)	—	stockbroker	courtier en bourse *m*	agente di cambio *m*	corredor de bolsa *m*
Börsennotierung (D)	—	quotation on the stock exchange	cotation des cours en bourse *f*	quotazione di borsa *f*	cotización de bolsa *f*
Börsenplatz (D)	—	stock exchange centre	place boursière *f*	piazza *f*	plaza bursátil *f*
Börsentag (D)	—	market day	jour de bourse *m*	giorno di borsa *m*	sesión bursátil *f*
Börsenumsatzsteuer (D)	—	stock exchange turnover tax	droit de transaction sur les opérations boursières *m*	imposta sulle operazioni di borsa *f*	impuesto de negociación bursátil *m*
bosquejo (Es)	Konzept *n*	concept	brouillon *m*	piano *m*	—
bottleneck in capacity (E)	Kapazitätsengpaß *m*	—	goulot d'étranglement de capacité *m*	strettoia di capacità *f*	escasez de capacidad *f*
bourse (F)	Börse *f*	(stock) exchange	—	borsa *f*	bolsa *f*
bourse à terme (F)	Terminbörse *f*	futures market	—	mercato a termine *m*	bolsa de valores a término *f*
bourse de devises (F)	Devisenbörse *f*	foreign exchange market	—	borsa valutaria *f*	bolsa de divisas *f*
bourse de marchandises (F)	Warenbörse *f*	commodity exchange	—	borsa merci *f*	bolsa de mercancías *f*
bourse de recyclage (F)	Abfallbörse *f*	recycling exchange	—	borsa dei rifiuti *f*	bolsa de reciclaje *f*
bourse des titres et valeurs (F)	Wertpapierbörse *f*	securities market	—	borsa valori *f*	mercado de valores *m*
bourse des titres et valeurs mobilières (F)	Effektenbörse *f*	stock exchange	—	borsa valori *f*	bolsa de valores *f*
bourse d'opérations à livrer (F)	Warenterminbörse *f*	commodity forward exchange	—	borsa merci a termine *f*	bolsa de mercancías *f*
box (E)	Kiste *f*	—	caisse *f*	cassa *f*	caja *f*
boycott (E)	Boykott *m*	—	boycottage *m*	boicottaggio *m*	boicot *m*
boycottage (F)	Boykott *m*	boycott	—	boicottaggio *m*	boicot *m*
boycottage économique (F)	Wirtschaftsboykott *m*	economic boycott	—	boicottaggio economico *m*	boicot económico *m*
Boykott (D)	—	boycott	boycottage *m*	boicottaggio *m*	boicot *m*
branch[1] (E)	Filiale *f*	—	agence *f*	filiale *f*	filial *f*
branch[2] (E)	Zweigstelle *f*	—	agence *f*	agenzia *f*	filial *f*
branch abroad (E)	Auslandsniederlassung *f*	—	succursale à l'étranger *f*	succursale estera *f*	filial en el exterior *m*
branch business (E)	Zweigbetrieb *m*	—	établissement secondaire *m*	filiale *f*	sucursal *f*
branch manager (E)	Filialleiter *m*	—	directeur d'agence *m*	direttore della filiale *m*	jefe de sucursal *m*
branch network (E)	Filialnetz *n*	—	réseau de succursales *m*	rete delle filiali *f*	red de sucursales *f*
branch office (E)	Zweigniederlassung *f*	—	succursale *f*	succursale *f*	filial *f*
Branche (D)	—	line of business	branche *f*	categoria *f*	ramo *m*
branche (F)	Branche *f*	line of business	—	categoria *f*	ramo *m*
Branchenanalyse (D)	—	trade analysis	analyse des branches *f*	analisi di categoria *f*	análisis del ramo *m*
Branchenstatistik (D)	—	trade statistics	statistique sur les différentes branches économiques *f*	statistica di categoria *f*	estadística del ramo *f*

	D	E	F	I	Es
Branchenstruktur (D)	—	trade structure	structure de la branche *f*	struttura di categoria *f*	estructura del ramo *f*
Branchenvergleich (D)	—	trade comparison	comparaison des différentes branches *f*	comparazione delle categorie *f*	comparación de ramos *f*
brandname article (E)	Markenartikel *m*	—	produit de marque *m*	articolo di marca *m*	artículo de marca *m*
Brandschutz (D)	—	protection against fire	protection contre l'incendie *f*	protezione antincendio *f*	protección contra incendios *f*
Brandversicherung (D)	—	fire insurance	assurance contre l'incendie *f*	assicurazione contro incendio *f*	seguro contra incencios *f*
Braunkohle (D)	—	brown coal	lignite *m*	lignite *f*	lignito *m*
break-even point[1] (E)	Gewinnschwelle *f*	—	seuil de rentabilité *m*	soglia dell'utile *f*	umbral de la rentabilidad *m*
break-even point[2] (E)	Rentabilitätschwelle *f*	—	seuil de rentabilité *m*	soglia di redditività *f*	límite inferior de rentabilidad *m*
brevet d'invention (F)	Patent *n*	patent	—	brevetto *m*	patente *f*
brevet européen (F)	Europapatent *n*	European patent	—	brevetto europeo *m*	patente europea *f*
brevetto[1] (I)	Patent *n*	patent	brevet d'invention *m*	—	patente *f*
brevetto[2] (I)	Patenturkunde *f*	patent document	certificat d'attestation du brevet d'invention *m*	—	patente *f*
brevetto europeo (I)	Europapatent *n*	European patent	brevet européen *m*	—	patente europea *f*
bribe (E)	Bestechung *f*	—	corruption *f*	corruzione *f*	soborno *f*
bridging loan (E)	Überbrückungs-kredit *m*	—	crédit transitoire *m*	credito ponte *m*	crédito transitorio *m*
Brief (D)	—	letter	lettre *f*	lettera *f*	carta *f*
Briefkasten (D)	—	mail box	boîte aux lettres *f*	cassetta postale *f*	buzón *m*
Briefkastenfirma (D)	—	bubble company	entreprise fantôme *f*	società bucalettere *f*	empresa ficticia *f*
Briefkopf (D)	—	letterhead	en-tête *m*	intestazione *f*	encabezamiento *m*
Briefkurs (D)	—	ask(ed) price	cours de vente *m*	prezzo d'offerta *m*	cotización ofrecida *f*
Briefmarke (D)	—	stamp	timbre-poste *m*	francobollo *m*	sello *m*
Briefträger (D)	—	postman	facteur *m*	portalettere *m*	cartero *m*
Briefumschlag (D)	—	envelope	enveloppe de lettre *f*	busta *f*	sobre *m*
Briefwaage (D)	—	letter scales	pèse-lettres *m*	bilancia per corrispondenza *f*	pesacartas *m*
brochure (E)	Broschüre *f*	—	prospectus *m*	depliant *m*	folleto *m*
broken period interest (E)	Stückzinsen *f*	—	intérêts courus *m pl*	interessi maturati *m pl*	intereses por fracción de período *m pl*
Broker (D)	—	broker	courtier *m*	broker *m*	corredor de bolsa *m*
broker[1] (E)	Makler *m*	—	courtier *m*	mediatore *m*	corredor *m*
broker[2] (E)	Broker *m*	—	courtier *m*	broker *m*	corredor de bolsa *m*
broker (I)	Broker *m*	broker	courtier *m*	—	corredor de bolsa *m*
brokerage (E)	Courtage *f*	—	courtage *m*	courtage *f*	corretaje *m*
Broschüre (D)	—	brochure	prospectus *m*	depliant *m*	folleto *m*
brouillon (F)	Konzept *n*	concept	—	piano *m*	bisquejo *m*
brown coal (E)	Braunkohle *f*	—	lignite *m*	lignite *f*	lignito *m*
Bruchteil (D)	—	fraction	fraction *f*	frazione *f*	parte fraccionaria *f*
Bruchteils-eigentümer (D)	—	co-owner	copropriétaire d'une quote-part *m*	comproprietario di quota ideale *m*	copropietario de bienes indivisos *m*
Bruttoeinkommen (D)	—	gross income	revenu brut *m*	reddito lordo *m*	ingreso bruto *m*
Bruttoinlands-produkt (D)	—	gross domestic product	produit intérieur brut *m*	prodotto interno lordo *m*	producto interior bruto *m*
Bruttolohn (D)	—	gross pay	salaire brut *m*	salario lordo *m*	salario bruto *m*
Bruttopreis (D)	—	gross price	prix brut *m*	prezzo lordo *m*	precio bruto *m*
Bruttoproduktion (D)	—	gross production	production brute *f*	produzione lorda *f*	producción bruta *m*
Bruttoregistertonne (D)	—	gross register(ed) ton	tonneau de jauge brut *m*	tonnellata di stazza lorda *f*	tonelada de registro bruto *f*
Bruttosozialprodukt (D)	—	gross national product	produit national brut *m*	prodotto nazionale lordo *m*	producto nacional bruto *m*
bubble company (E)	Briefkastenfirma *f*	—	entreprise fantôme *f*	società bucalettere *f*	empresa ficticia *f*
Buchführung (D)	—	bookkeeping	comptabilité *f*	contabilità *f*	contabilidad *f*

	D	E	F	I	Es
Buchgeld (D)	—	money in account	monnaie de crédit *f*	moneta bancaria *f*	dinero bancario *m*
Buchgewinn (D)	—	book profit	bénéfice comptable *m*	utile contabile *m*	beneficio contable *m*
Buchhalter (D)	—	bookkeeper	comptable *m*	ragioniere *m*	tenedor de libros *m*
Buchhaltung (D)	—	accounting	comptabilité *f*	contabilità *f*	contabilidad *f*
Buchungsfehler (D)	—	bookkeeping error	erreur de comptabilité *f*	errore di contabilità *m*	error contable *m*
Buchwert (D)	—	book value	valeur comptable *f*	valore contabile *m*	valor contable *m*
Budget (D)	—	budget	budget *m*	bilancio *m*	presupuesto *m*
budget[1] (E)	Haushaltsplan *m*	—	budget *m*	bilancio preventivo *m*	presupuesto *m*
budget[2] (E)	Haushalt *m*	—	budget *m*	bilancio *m*	presupuesto *m*
budget[3] (E)	Budget *n*/Etat *m*	—	budget *m*	bilancio *m*	presupuesto *m*
budget[1] (F)	Haushaltsplan *m*	budget	—	bilancio preventivo *m*	presupuesto *m*
budget[2] (F)	Budget n/Etat *m*	budget	—	bilancio *m*	presupuesto *m*
budget[3] (F)	Haushalt *m*	budget	—	bilancio *m*	presupuesto *m*
budget adjustment (E)	Planrevision *f*	—	révision des coûts marginaux *f*	revisione del piano *f*	ajuste presupuestario *m*
budgetary control (E)	Finanzkontrolle *f*	—	contrôle de financement *m*	controllo finanziario *m*	control financiero *m*
budgetary deficit (E)	Haushaltsdefizit *n*	—	déficit budgétaire *m*	deficit del bilancio *m*	déficit presupuestario *m*
budgetary planning (E)	Budgetplanung *f*	—	planification du budget *f*	programmazione del bilancio *f*	planificación del presupuesto *m*
Budgetausgleich (D)	—	balancing of the budget	équilibrage du budget *m*	pareggio di bilancio *m*	balance del presupuesto *m*
budget control (E)	Budgetkontrolle *f*	—	contrôle du budget *m*	controllo del bilancio *m*	control del presupuesto *m*
budget de publicité (F)	Werbebudget *n*	advertising budget	—	budget pubblicitario *m*	presupuesto publicitario *m*
budgeted costs (E)	Sollkosten *pl*	—	coûts ex ante *m pl*	costi calcolati *m pl*	gastos precalculados *m pl*
Budgetgrundsätze (D)	—	budget principles	principes budgétaires	principi di bilancio *m pl*	principios presupuestarios *m pl*
Budgetierung (D)	—	budgeting	établissement du budget *m*	compilazione del bilancio *f*	establecimiento del presupuesto *m*
budgeting (E)	Budgetierung *f*	—	établissement du budget *m*	compilazione del bilancio *f*	establecimiento del presupuesto *m*
Budgetkontrolle (D)	—	budget control	contrôle du budget *m*	controllo del bilancio *m*	control del presupuesto *m*
Budgetplanung (D)	—	budgetary planning	planification du budget *f*	programmazione del bilancio *f*	planificación del presupuesto *f*
budget principles (E)	Budgetgrundsätze *f*	—	principes budgétaires	principi di bilancio *m pl*	principios presupuestarios *m pl*
budget pubblicitario (I)	Werbebudget *n*	advertising budget	budget de publicité *m*	—	presupuesto publicitario *m*
buena reputación (Es)	Seriosität *f*	seriousness	caractère sérieux *m*	serietà *f*	—
bufete de abogado (Es)	Anwaltskanzlei *f*	lawyer's office	cabinet d'avocat *m*	studio d'avvocato *m*	—
building and construction industry (E)	Bauwirtschaft *f*	—	(industrie du) bâtiment *f*	edilizia *f*	ramo de la construcción *m*
building land (E)	Bauland *n*	—	espace à bâtir *m*	area edificabile *f*	terreno edificable *m*
building loan (E)	Baukredit *m*	—	crédit à la construction *m*	credito edilizio *m*	crédito para la construcción *f*
bulk buyer (E)	Großabnehmer *m*	—	acheteur en gros *m*	acquirente all'ingrosso *m*	comprador al por mayor *m*
bulk goods (E)	Massengüter *pl*	—	marchandises en vrac *f pl*	beni di massa *m pl*	productos a granel *m pl*
bull (E)	Haussier *m*	—	haussier *m*	speculatore al rialzo *m*	alcista *m*
bulletin de commande (F)	Bestellschein *m*	order form	—	bolletta d'ordinazione *f*	hoja de pedido *f*
bulletin de livraison (F)	Lieferschein *m*	delivery note	—	bolletta di consegna *f*	recibo de entrega *m*
bulletin des cours (F)	Kurszettel *m*	stock exchange list	—	listino di borsa *m*	boletín de bolsa *m*

	D	E	F	I	Es
bulto (Es)	Paket *n*	parcel	colis *m*	pacco *m*	—
Bumerang-Effekt (D)	—	boomerang effect	effet boomerang *m*	effetto bumerang *m*	efecto bumerán *m*
buono (I)	Bon *m*	voucher	bon *m*	—	bono *m*
burden of proof (E)	Beweislast *f*	—	charge de la preuve *f*	onere di prova *m*	carga de la prueba *f*
bureau[1] (F)	Schreibtisch *m*	desk	—	scrivania *f*	escritorio *m*
bureau[2] (F)	Amt	office	—	ufficio *m*	cargo *m*
bureaucracy (E)	Bürokratie *f*	—	bureaucratie *f*	burocrazia *f*	burocracia *f*
bureaucratie (F)	Bürokratie *f*	bureaucracy	—	burocrazia *f*	burocracia *f*
bureaucratie communautaire (F)	EG-Bürokratie *f*	burocracy inside the European Communities	—	burocrazia CEE *f*	burocracia comunitaria *f*
bureau de chèques postaux (F)	Postscheckamt *n*	postal giro centre	—	ufficio dei conti correnti postali *m*	oficina de cheques postales *f*
bureau de déclaration de résidence (F)	Einwohnermeldeamt *n*	residents' registration office	—	ufficio anagrafe *m*	oficina del censo *f*
bureau de douane (F)	Zollstelle *f*	customs office	—	posto di dogana *m*	oficina de aduanas *f*
bureau de la paye (F)	Lohnbüro *n*	pay office	—	ufficio paga *m*	departamento de nóminas *m*
bureau de marketing (F)	Marketingabteilung *f*	marketing department	—	reparto marketing *m*	departamento de mercadeo *m*
bureau de placement (F)	Arbeitsvermittlung *f*	employment agency	—	ufficio di collocamento *m*	agencia laboral *f*
bureau de poste (F)	Postamt *n*	post office	—	ufficio postale *m*	correos *m pl*
bureau du personnel (F)	Personalbüro *n*	personnel office	—	ufficio del personale *m*	oficina de personal *f*
bureau juridique (F)	Rechtsabteilung *f*	legal department	—	ufficio legale *m*	sección jurídica *f*
Bürge (D)	—	guarantor	garant *m*	fideiussore *m*	fiador *m*
Bürgschaft (D)	—	guarantee	caution *f*	fideiussione *f*	fianza *f*
Bürgschaftskredit (D)	—	credit by way of bank guarantee	crédit cautionné *m*	credito di fideiussione *m*	crédito de garantía *m*
burocracia (Es)	Bürokratie *f*	bureaucracy	bureaucratie *f*	burocrazia *f*	—
burocrazia (I)	Bürokratie *f*	bureaucracy	bureaucratie *f*	—	burocracia *f*
Bürokratie (D)	—	bureaucracy	bureaucratie *f*	burocrazia *f*	burocracia *f*
business (E)	Geschäft *n*	—	affaire *f*	negozio *m*	negocio *m*
business acquisition (E)	Geschäftsübernahme *f*	—	reprise d'une affaire *f*	acquisto di un'azienda *m*	adquisición de una empresa *f*
business administration (E)	Betriebswirtschaftslehre *f*	—	(science de la) gestion industrielle et commerciale *f*	economia aziendale *f*	teoría de la empresa *f*
business concentration (E)	Unternehmenskonzentration *f*	—	concentration d'entreprises *f*	pool d'imprese *m*	concentración de empresas *f*
business concept (E)	Unternehmenskonzept *n*	—	stratégie de l'entreprise *f*	piano imprenditoriale *m*	concepto comercial *m*
business connections[1] (E)	Geschäftsbeziehung *f*	—	relations d'affaires *f pl*	rapporti d'affari *m pl*	relaciones comerciales *f pl*
business connections[2] (E)	Geschäftsverbindung *f*	—	relation d'affaires *f*	relazione d'affari *f*	relación comercial *f*
business cycle[1] (E)	Konjunktur *f*	—	conjoncture *f*	congiuntura *f*	conyuntura *f*
business cycle[2] (E)	Konjunkturzyklus *m*	—	cycle conjoncturel *m*	ciclo congiunturale *m*	ciclo económico *m*
business friend (E)	Geschäftsfreund *m*	—	correspondant *m*	partner d'affari *m*	corresponsal *m*
business hours (E)	Geschäftszeit *f*	—	heures d'ouverture *f pl*	orario d'apertura *m*	horas de despacho *f pl*
business papers (E)	Geschäftspapiere *pl*	—	papiers d'affaires *m pl*	documenti commerciali *m pl*	documentos comerciales *m pl*
business partner (E)	Geschäftspartner *m*	—	associé *m*	partner commerciale *m*	socio *m*
business practice (E)	Handelsbrauch *m*	—	usage commercial *m*	usanza commerciale *f*	uso comercial *m*
business premises (E)	Geschäftsräume *pl*	—	local à usage commercial *m*	locali commerciali *m pl*	local comercial *m*
business report (E)	Geschäftsbericht *m*	—	rapport de gestion *m*	relazione sull'esercizio commerciale *f*	informe *m*

	D	E	F	I	Es
business secret (E)	Geschäfts-geheimnis *n*	—	secret d'affaires *m*	segreto commerciale *m*	secreto comercial *m*
business year (E)	Wirtschaftsjahr *n*	—	exercice comptable *m*	esercizio *m*	ejercicio *m*
businessman (E)	Kaufmann *m*	—	négociant *m*	commerciante *m*	comerciante *m*
businessmen (E)	Kaufleute *pl*	—	commerçants *m pl*	commercianti *m pl*	comerciantes *m pl*
Bußgeld (D)	—	administration fee	amende *f*	pena pecuniaria *f*	multa *f*
busta[1] (I)	Briefumschlag *m*	envelope	enveloppe de lettre *f*	—	sobre *m*
busta[2] (I)	Kuvert *n*	envelope	enveloppe *f*	—	sobre *m*
but (F)	Ziel *n*	objective	—	obiettivo *m*	objetivo *m*
buy (E)	(ein-)kaufen	—	acheter	acquistare	comprar
buyer[1] (E)	Abnehmer *m*	—	acheteur *m*	acquirente *m*	tomador *m*
buyer[2] (E)	Einkäufer *m*	—	acheteur *m*	acquirente *m*/ cliente *m*	comprador *m*
buyer country (E)	Abnehmerland *n*	—	pays acheteur *m*	paese acquirente *m*	país comprador *m*
buyer's commission (E)	Käuferprovision *f*	—	commission d'acheteur *f*	provvigione dell'acquirente *f*	comisión al comprador *f*
buyer's market (E)	Käufermarkt *m*	—	marché d'acheteurs *m*	mercato favorevole all'acquirente *m*	mercado favorable al comprador *m*
buying motive (E)	Kaufanlaß *m*	—	motif d'achat *m*	motivo d'acquisto *m*	motivo de compra *m*
buying intention (E)	Kaufbereitschaft *f*	—	propension à l'achat *f*	propensione all'acquisto *f*	disposición a comprar *f*
buzón (Es)	Briefkasten *m*	mail box	boîte aux lettres *f*	cassetta postale *f*	—
by express (mail) (E)	per Express	—	par exprès	per espresso	por expreso
by lorry (E)	per Lastkraftwagen	—	par camion	per autocarro	por camión
by machine (E)	maschinell	—	mécanique	a macchina	a máquina
by order (E)	im Auftrag	—	par ordre	per ordine	por poder
by procuration (E)	per procura	—	par procuration	per procura	por poder
by-product (E)	Nebenprodukt *n*	—	produit dérivé *m*	prodotto secondario *m*	producto accesorio *m*
by registered post (E)	per Einschreiben	—	sous pli recommandé	per raccomandata	certificado
by return of post (E)	postwendend	—	par retour du courrier	a giro di posta	a vuelta de correo
cabinet d'avocat (F)	Anwaltskanzlei *f*	lawyer's office	—	studio d'avvocato *m*	bufete de abogado *m*
cablegram (E)	Kabeltelegramm *n*	—	câblogramme *m*	cablogramma *m*	cablegrama *f*
cablegrama (Es)	Kabeltelegramm *n*	cablegramm	câblogramme *m*	cablogramma *m*	—
cable television (E)	Kabelfernsehen *n*	—	télévision par câble *f*	televisione via cavo *f*	televisión por cable *f*
cable transfer (E)	Kabelüberweisung *f*	—	virement par câble *m*	bonifico telegrafico *m*	giro telegráfico *m*
cablogramma (I)	Kabeltelegramm *n*	cablegram	câblogramme *m*	—	cablegrama f
câblogramme (F)	Kabeltelegramm *n*	cablegram	—	cablogramma *m*	cablegrama f
cachet (F)	Gage *f*	salary	—	onorario *m*	remuneración *f*
cachet de la poste (F)	Poststempel *m*	postmark	—	timbro postale *m*	matasellos *m*
cadaster (E)	Kataster *m*	—	cadastre *m*	catasto *m*	catastro *m*
cadastre (F)	Kataster *m*	cadaster	—	catasto *m*	catastro *m*
cadeau publicitaire (F)	Werbegeschenk *n*	advertising gift	—	omaggio pubblicitario *m*	regalo publicitario *m*
cadre (F)	Führungsperson *f*	executive	—	dirigente *m*	ejecutivo *m*
caduta dei prezzi (I)	Preisverfall *m*	decline in prices	chute des prix *f*	—	caída de precios *f*
caída de los cambios (Es)	Kurs-zusammbruch *m*	collapse of prices	chute des cours *f*	crollo delle quotazioni *m*	—
caída de precios (Es)	Preisverfall *m*	decline in prices	chute des prix *f*	caduta dei prezzi *f*	—
caída en picado de la bolsa (Es)	Börsenkrach *m*	stockmarket crash	débâcle boursière *f*	crollo di borsa *m*	—
caisse (F)	Kiste *f*	box	—	cassa *f*	caja *f*
caissier (F)	Kassierer *m*	cashier	—	cassiere *m*	cajero *m*
caja (Es)	Kiste *f*	box	caisse *f*	cassa *f*	—
caja de ahorros (Es)	Sparkasse *f*	savings bank	institut bancaire d'épargne *m*	cassa di risparmio *f*	—
caja de seguridad (Es)	Safe *m*	safe	coffre-fort *m*	cassetta di sicurezza *f*	—

	D	E	F	I	Es
caja de socorros mutuos (Es)	Versicherung auf Gegenseitigkeit *f*	mutual insurance	assurance mutuelle *f*	mutua assicurazione *f*	—
caja fuerte (Es)	Tresor *m*	safe	coffre-fort *m*	cassaforte *f*	—
cajero (Es)	Kassierer *m*	cashier	caissier *m*	cassiere *m*	—
cajero automático (Es)	Bankomat *m*	cash dispenser	billetterie *m*	bancomat *m*	—
calcolatore (I)	Rechner *m*	computer/calculator	ordinateur *m*/ calculateur de poche *m*	—	ordenador *m*/ calculadora de bolsillo *f*
calcolazione (I)	Kalkulation *f*	calculation	calcul *m*	—	calculación *f*
calcolo (I)	Berechnung *f*	computation	calcul *m*	—	calculación *f*
calcolo degli interessi (I)	Zinsberechnung *f*	calculating the interest	calcul des intérêts *m*	—	cálculo de intereses *m*
calcolo dei costi pianificati (I)	Plankosten-rechnung *f*	calculation of the budget costs	calcul de l'écart sur cadence de fabrication *m*	—	cálculo de costes normalizados *m*
calcolo del contributo per copertura (I)	Deckungsbeitrags-rechnung *f*	contribution costing	calcul de la propor-tion de garantie *m*	—	factura de aportación de fondos *f*
calcolo della liquidità (I)	Liquiditätsrechnung *f*	liquidity calculation	compte de liquidité *m*	—	cálculo de liquidez *m*
calcolo della probabilità (I)	Wahrscheinlichkeits-rechnung *f*	calculation of probabilities	calcul des probabilités *m*	—	cálculo de probabilidades *m*
calcolo del patrimonio (I)	Vermögens-rechnung *f*	capital account	calcul du patrimoine *m*	—	cálculo del valor neto *m*
calcolo di finanziamento (I)	Finanzierungs-rechnung *f*	flow-of-funds analysis	analyse des flux monétaires *f*	—	análisis de flujos monetarios *m*
calcolo pianificato (I)	Plankalkulation *f*	target calculation	calcul des coûts prévisionnels *m*	—	cálculo de los objetivos *m*
calcolo preventivo (I)	Vorkalkulation *f*	estimation of cost	calcul des coûts a priori *m*	—	cálculo provisional *m*
calcul[1] (F)	Kalkulation *f*	calculation	—	calcolazione *f*	calculación *f*
calcul[2] (F)	Berechnung *f*	computation	—	calcolo *m*	calculación *f*
calculación[1] (Es)	Berechnung *f*	computation	calcul *m*	calcolo *m*	—
calculación[2] (Es)	Kalkulation *f*	calculation	calcul *m*	calcolazione *f*	—
calculating the interest (E)	Zinsberechnung *f*	—	calcul des intérêts *m*	calcolo degli interessi *m*	cálculo de intereses *m*
calculation (E)	Kalkulation *f*	—	calcul *m*	calcolazione *f*	calculación *f*
calculation of probabilities (E)	Wahrscheinlichkeits-rechnung *f*	—	calcul des probabilités *m*	calcolo della probabilità *m*	cálculo de probabilidades *m*
calculation of the budget costs (E)	Plankosten-rechnung *f*	—	calcul de l'écart sur cadence de fabrication *m*	calcolo dei costi pianificati *m*	cálculo de costes normalizados *m*
cálculo de costes a posteriori (Es)	Nachkalkulation *f*	historical costing	calcul des coûts a posteriori *m*	computisteria *f*	—
calcul de la proportion de garantie (F)	Deckungsbeitrags-rechnung *f*	contribution costing	—	calcolo del contributo per copertura *m*	factura de aportación de fondos *f*
calcul de l'écart sur cadence de fabrication (F)	Plankosten-rechnung *f*	calculation of the budget costs	—	calcolo dei costi pianificati *m*	cálculo de costes normalizados *m*
calcul des coûts a posteriori (F)	Nachkalkulation *f*	historical costing	—	computisteria *f*	cálculo de costes a posteriori *m*
calcul des coûts a priori (F)	Vorkalkulation *f*	estimation of cost	—	calcolo preventivo *m*	cálculo provisional *m*
calcul des coûts prévisionnels (F)	Plankalkulation *f*	target calculation	—	calcolo pianificato *m*	cálculo de los objetivos *m*
calcul des intérêts[1] (F)	Zinsberechnung *f*	calculating the interest	—	calcolo degli interessi *m*	cálculo de intereses *m*
calcul des intérêts[2] (F)	Zinsrechnung *f*	interest account	—	conteggio degli interessi *m*	cómputo de intereses *m*
calcul des probabilités (F)	Wahrscheinlichkeits-rechnung *f*	calculation of probabilities	—	calcolo della probabilità *m*	cálculo de probabilidades *m*
calcul du patrimoine (F)	Vermögens-rechnung *f*	capital account	—	calcolo del patrimonio *m*	cálculo del valor neto *m*
calculation unit (E)	Recheneinheit *f*	—	unité de calcul *f*	unità di conteggio *f*	unidad de cuenta *f*
cálculo de costes normalizados (Es)	Plankostenrechnung *f*	calculation of the budget costs	calcul de l'écart sur cadence de fabrication *m*	calcolo dei costi pianificati *m*	—

	D	E	F	I	Es
cálculo de intereses (Es)	Zinsberechnung *f*	calculating the interest	calcul des intérêts *m*	calcolo degli interessi *m*	—
cálculo de liquidez (Es)	Liquiditätsrechnung *f*	liquidity calculation	compte de liquidité *m*	calcolo della liquidità *m*	—
cálculo de los costes marginales (Es)	Grenzkosten-rechnung *f*	marginal costing	détermination du coût marginal *f*	conto dei costi limite *m*	—
cálculo de los objetivos (Es)	Plankalkulation *f*	target calculation	calcul des coûts prévisionnels *m*	calcolo pianificato *m*	—
cálculo del valor neto (Es)	Vermögens-rechnung *f*	capital account	calcul du patrimoine *m*	calcolo del patrimonio *m*	—
cálculo de probabilidades (Es)	Wahrscheinlichkeits-rechnung *f*	calculation of probabilities	calcul des probabilités *m*	calcolo della probabilità *m*	—
cálculo provisional (Es)	Vorkalkulation *f*	estimation of cost	calcul des coûts a priori *m*	calcolo preventivo *m*	—
calendar year (E)	Kalenderjahr *n*	—	année civile *f*	anno solare *m*	año civil *m*
calidad (Es)	Qualität *f*	quality	qualité *f*	qualità *f*	—
calidad del agua potable (Es)	Trinkwasserqualität *f*	drinking water quality	qualité de l'eau potable *f*	qualità dell'acqua potabile *f*	—
calidad de vida (Es)	Lebensqualität *f*	quality of life	qualité de la vie *f*	qualità di vita *f*	—
calidades aseguradas (Es)	zugesicherte Eigenschaften *pl*	warranted characteristics	qualité promise *f*	caratteristiche promesse *f pl*	—
call (E)	Abruf *m*	—	appel *m*	richiesta *f*	reclamación de la entrega de un pedido *f*
callable (E)	kündbar	—	résiliable/remboursable	risolubile/redimibile	revocable/rescindible
calle (Es)	Straße *f*	street/road	rue *f*/route *f*	via *f*/strada *f*	—
calo del fatturato (I)	Umsatzrückgang *m*	decrease of turnover	recul du chiffre d'affaires *m*	—	disminución de la cifra de facturación *f*
calo dell'occupazione (I)	Beschäftigungs-rückgang *m*	drop in employment	baisse de l'offre d'emploi *f*	—	descenso del empleo *m*
cámara de artesanía (Es)	Handwerkskammer *f*	chamber of handicrafts	chambre artisanale *f*	camera dell'artigianato *f*	—
cámara de comercio (Es)	Handelskammer *f*	Chamber of Commerce	chambre de commerce *f*	camera di commercio *f*	—
cámara de industria y comercio (Es)	Industrie- und Handelskammer *f*	Chamber of Industry and Commerce	chambre de com-merce et d'industrie *f*	camera di commercio e industria *f*	—
cámara del comercio exterior (Es)	Außenhandels-kammer *f*	chamber of foreign trade	chambre du com-merce extérieur *f*	camera di commercio estero *f*	—
cambiale (I)	Wechsel *f*	bill of exchange	lettre de change *f*	—	letra de cambio *f*
cambiale commerciale (I)	Warenwechsel *m*	commercial bill	traite commerciale *f*	—	letra comercial *f*
cambiale domiciliata (I)	Domizilwechsel *m*	domiciliary bill	effet domicilier *m*	—	letra domiciliada *f*
cambiale estera (I)	Auslandswechsel *n*	foreign bill of exchange	traite tirée sur l'étranger *f*	—	letra sobre el exterior *f*
cambiamenti strutturali (I)	Strukturwandel *m*	structural change	changement dans les structures *m*	—	cambio de estructuras *m*
cambiamento dell'abitazione (I)	Wohnungs-wechsel *m*	change of residence	transfert de résidence *m*	—	cambio de vivienda *m*
cambiamento del posto di lavoro (I)	Arbeitsplatz-wechsel *m*	change of employment	changement d'emploi *m*	—	cambio de puesto *m*
cambi fissi (I)	feste Wechselkurse *pl*	fixed exchange rates	taux de change fixe *m*	—	tipos de cambio fijos *m pl*
cambi multipli (I)	gespaltene Wechselkurse *pl*	two-tier exchange rate	cours du change multiple *m*	—	tipo de cambio múltiple *m*
cambio[1] (Es)	Umtausch *m*	exchange	échange *m*	cambio *m*	—
cambio[2] (Es)	Tausch *m*	exchange/barter	échange *m*/troc *m*	scambio *m*/baratto *m*	—
cambio[1] (I)	Wechselkurs *m*	exchange rate	cours du change *m*	—	tipo de cambio *m*
cambio[2] (I)	Umtausch *m*	exchange	échange *m*	—	cambio *m*/conversión *f*
cambio a término (Es)	Terminkurs *m*	forward price	cours de bourse à terme *m*	corso a termine *m*	—
cambio de divisas (Es)	Devisenkurs *m*	foreign exchange rate	taux de change *m*	cambio delle divise *m*	—

	D	E	F	I	Es
cambio de empleo (Es)	Stellungswechsel *m*	change of employment	changement d'emploi *m*	cambiamento del posto di lavoro *m*	—
cambio de estructuras (Es)	Strukturwandel *m*	structural change	changement dans les structures *m*	cambiamenti strutturali *m pl*	—
cambio del equipo de obreros (Es)	Schichtwechsel *m*	change of shift	relève d'équipe *f*	cambio di turno *m*	—
cambio delle divise (I)	Devisenkurs *m*	foreign exchange rate	taux de change *m*	—	cambio de divisas *m*
cambio del personale (I)	Personalwechsel *m*	staff changes	mouvements dans le personnel *m pl*	—	cambio de personal *m*
cambio de personal (Es)	Personalwechsel *m*	staff changes	mouvements dans le personnel *m pl*	cambio del personale *m*	—
cambio de puesto (Es)	Arbeitsplatzwechsel *m*	change of employment	changement d'emploi *m*	cambiamento del posto di lavoro *m*	—
cambio de vivienda (Es)	Wohnungswechsel *m*	change of residence	transfert de résidence *m*	cambiamento dell'abitazione *m*	—
cambio di turno (I)	Schichtwechsel *m*	change of shift	relève d'équipe *f*	—	cambio del equipo de obreros *m*
cambio en el poder adquisitivo (Es)	Kaufkraftänderung *f*	changes in purchasing power	modification du pouvoir d'achat *f*	mutamento del potere d'acquisto *m*	—
cambio flessibile (I)	flexibler Wechselkurs *m*	flexible exchange rate	taux de change flottant *m*	—	tipo flotante de cambio *m*
cambio reale (I)	Mengennotierung *f*	fixed exchange	cotation de quantité *f*	—	cotización real *f*
cambio unitario (I)	Einheitskurs *m*	spot price	cours unique *m*	—	cotización única *f*
cambio valuta (I)	Sortenhandel *m*	dealing in foreign notes and coins	commerce de change *m*	—	operación de moneda extranjera *f*
camera d'albergo (I)	Hotelzimmer *n*	hotel room	chambre d'hôtel *f*	—	habitación de hotel *f*
camera dell'artigianato (I)	Handwerkskammer *f*	chamber of handicrafts	chambre artisanale *f*	—	cámara de artesanía *f*
camera di commercio (I)	Handelskammer *f*	Chamber of Commerce	chambre de commerce *f*	—	cámara de comercio *f*
camera di commercio e industria (I)	Industrie- und Handelskammer *f*	Chamber of Industry and Commerce	chambre de commerce et d'industrie *f*	—	cámara de industria y comercio *f*
camera di commercio estero (I)	Außenhandelskammer *f*	chamber of foreign trade	chambre du commerce extérieur *f*	—	cámara del comercio exterior *f*
camionnage (F)	Rollgeld *n*	haulage	—	spese di trasporto *f pl*	derechos de acarreo *m pl*
campagna (I)	Kampagne *f*	campaign	campagne *f*	—	campaña *f*
campagna di vendita (I)	Verkaufskampagne *f*	sales campaign	campagne de vente *f*	—	campaña de venta *f*
campagna pubblicitaria (I)	Werbekampagne *f*	advertising campaign	campagne publicitaire *f*	—	campaña publicitaria *f*
campagne (F)	Kampagne *f*	campaign	—	campagna *f*	campaña *f*
campagne de vente (F)	Verkaufskampagne *f*	sales campaign	—	campagna di vendita *f*	campaña de venta *f*
campagne publicitaire[1] (F)	Werbekampagne *f*	advertising campaign	—	campagna pubblicitaria *f*	campaña publicitaria *f*
campagne publicitaire[2] (F)	Werbeaktion *f*	advertising activity	—	azione pubblicitaria *f*	campaña publicitaria *f*
campaign (E)	Kampagne *f*	—	campagne *f*	campagna *f*	campaña *f*
campaña (Es)	Kampagne *f*	campaign	campagne *f*	campagna *f*	—
campaña de prensa (Es)	Presseaktion *f*	press campaign	action de presse *f*	azione stampa *f*	—
campaña de venta (Es)	Verkaufskampagne *f*	sales campaign	campagne de vente *f*	campagna di vendita *f*	—
campaña publicitaria[1] (Es)	Werbekampagne *f*	advertising campaign	campagne publicitaire *f*	campagna pubblicitaria *f*	—
campaña publicitaria[2] (Es)	Werbeaktion *f*	advertising activity	campagne publicitaire *f*	azione pubblicitaria *f*	—
campione[1] (I)	Muster *n*	sample/pattern	échantillon *m*/ dessin *m*	—	muestra *f*/dibujo *m*
campione[2] (I)	(Waren-)Probe *f*	sample	échantillon *m*	—	muestra *f*
campione di merce (I)	Warenprobe *f*	sample	échantillon *m*	—	muestra de mercancía *f*
campione per esame (I)	Ansichtssendung *f*	consignment on approval	envoi à condition *m*	—	envío para inspección *m*
campione senza valore (I)	Muster ohne Wert *n*	sample, no commercial value	échantillon sans valeur *m*	—	muestra sin valor *f*

	D	E	F	I	Es
campioni (I)	Stichproben *pl*	random test	sondage *m*	—	prueba por sondeo *f*
campo d'azione[1] (I)	Tätigkeitsfeld *n*	field of activity	champ d'acitivité *m*	—	campo de actividad *m*
campo d'azione[2] (I)	Aktionsfeld *n*	field of action	champ d'action *m*	—	campo de acción *m*
campo de acción (Es)	Aktionsfeld *n*	field of action	champ d'action *m*	campo d'azione *m*	—
campo de actividad (Es)	Tätigkeitsfeld *n*	field of activity	champ d'acitivité *m*	campo d'azione *m*	—
canal de distribution[1] (F)	Vertriebsweg *m*	distribution channel	—	rete di distribuzione *f*	circuito de distribución *m*
canal de distribution[2] (F)	Absatzweg *m*	channel of distribution	—	via della distribuzione *f*	medio de venta *m*
cancel (E)	löschen	—	annuler	cancellare	cancelar
cancelación (Es)	Stornierung *f*	cancellation	annulation *f*	storno *m*	—
cancelar (Es)	löschen	cancel	annuler	cancellare	—
cancellare (I)	löschen	cancel	annuler	—	cancelar
cancellation (E)	Stornierung *f*	—	annulation *f*	storno *m*	cancelación *f*/ anulación *f*/ contrapartida *f*
candidat (F)	Bewerber *m*	applicant	—	aspirante *m*	aspirante *m*
candidatura (Es)	Bewerbung *f*	application	candidature *f*	domanda d'impiego *f*	—
candidatura (I)	Anwartschaft *f*	candidature	candidature *f*	—	expectativa de un futuro pago *f*
candidature (E)	Anwartschaft *f*	—	candidature *f*	candidatura *f*	expectativa de un futuro pago *f*
candidature[1] (F)	Anwartschaft *f*	candidature	—	candidatura *f*	expectativa de un futuro pago *f*
candidature[2] (F)	Bewerbung *f*	application	—	domanda d'impiego *f*	candidatura *f*
canone di locazione[1] (I)	Miete *f*	rent	location *f*	—	alquiler *m*
canone di locazione[2] (I)	Mietzins *m*	rent	prix de location *m*	—	arrendamiento *m*
cantidad (Es)	Menge *f*	quantity	quantité *f*	quantità *f*	—
cantidad de compra (Es)	Abnahmemenge *f*	purchased quantity	quantité commercialisée *f*	quantità d'acquisto *f*	—
cantidad mínima[1] (Es)	Mindestmenge *f*	minimum quantity	quantité minimum *f*	quantitativo minimo *m*	—
cantidad mínima[2] (Es)	Mindesthöhe *f*	minimum amount	montant minimum *m*	importo minimo *m*	—
cantidad mínima de pedido (Es)	Mindestbestell-menge *f*	minimum quantity order	quantité commandée minimum *f*	quantitativo minimo di ordine *m*	—
cantidad pedida (Es)	Bestellmenge *f*	ordering quantity	quantité commandée *f*	quantità d'ordinazione *f*	—
cantidad producida[1] (Es)	Fördermenge *f*	output	quantité extraite *f*	quantitativo d'estrazione *m*	—
cantidad producida[2] (Es)	Fertigungsmenge *f*	manufactured quantity	quantité fabriquée *f*	quantitativo di produzione *m*	—
capability of asserting one's rights (E)	Durchsetzungs-vermögen *n*	—	capacité de se faire valoir *f*	capacità di imporsi *f*	capacidad de imponerse *f*
capability to establish public relations (E)	Kontaktfähigkeit *f*	—	capacité d'entrer en contact *f*	comunicativa *f*	capacidad de anudar contactos *f*
capability to innovate (E)	Innovationsfähigkeit *f*	—	capacité d'innovation *f*	capacità innovativa *f*	capacidad de innovación *f*
capable de jouir des droits (F)	rechtsfähig	capable of acting in law	—	avendo capacità giuridica	jurídicamente capaz
capable of acting in law (E)	rechtsfähig	—	capable de jouir des droits	avendo capacità giuridica	jurídicamente capaz
capacidad[1] (Es)	Fähigkeit *f*	ability	capacité *f*	capacità *f*	—
capacidad[2] (Es)	Kapazität *f*	capacity	capacité *f*	capacità *f*	—
capacidad[3] (Es)	Leistung *f*	performance	prestation *f*	capacità *f*	—
capacidad de almacenaje (Es)	Lagerkapazität *f*	storage capacity	capacité de stockage *f*	capacità di magazzino *f*	—
capacidad de anudar contactos (Es)	Kontaktfähigkeit *f*	capability to estab-lish public relations	capacité d'entrer en contact *f*	comunicativa *f*	—
capacidad de entrega (Es)	Lieferkapazität *f*	delivery capacity	capacité de livraison *f*	capacità di fornitura *f*	—
capacidad de imponerse (Es)	Durchsetzungs-vermögen *n*	capability of asserting one's right	capacité de se faire valoir *f*	capacità di imporsi *f*	—

	D	E	F	I	Es
capacidad de innovación (Es)	Innovationsfähigkeit *f*	capability to innovate	capacité d'innovation *f*	capacità innovativa *f*	—
capacidad de memoria (Es)	Speicherkapazität *f*	storage capacity	capacité de mémoire *f*	capacità di memoria *f*	—
capacidad de producción (Es)	Produktions-kapazität *f*	production capacity	capacité de production *f*	capacità produttiva *f*	—
capacidad jurídica (Es)	Rechtsfähigkeit *f*	legal capacity	capacité de jouis-sance des droits *f*	capacità giuridica *f*	—
capacidad negocial (Es)	Geschäftsfähigkeit *f*	capacity to enter into legal transactions	capacité d'accomplir des actes juridiques *f*	capacità di agire *f*	—
capacidad productiva (Es)	Leistungsfähigkeit *f*	efficiency	efficience *f*	efficienza *f*	—
capacità[1] (I)	Fähigkeit *f*	ability	capacité *f*	—	capacidad *f*
capacità[2] (I)	Kapazität *f*	capacity	capacité *f*	—	capacidad *f*
capacità[3] (I)	Leistung *f*	performance	rendement *m*	—	rendimiento *m*
capacità di agire (I)	Geschäftsfähigkeit *f*	capacity to enter into legal transactions	capacité d'accomplir des actes juridiques *f*	—	capacidad negocial *f*
capacità di credito (I)	Kreditfähigkeit *f*	financial standing	solvabilité *f*	—	crédito *m*
capacità di fornitura (I)	Lieferkapazität *f*	delivery capacity	capacité de livraison *f*	—	capacidad de entrega *f*
capacità di imposizione (I)	Durchsetzungs-vermögen *n*	capability of asserting one's rights	capacité de se faire valoir *f*	—	capacidad de imponerse *f*
capacità di magazzino (I)	Lagerkapazität *f*	storage capacity	capacité de stockage *f*	—	capacidad de almacenaje *f*
capacità eccessiva (I)	Überkapazität *f*	overcapacity	surcapacité *f*	—	supercapacidad *f*
capacità giuridica (I)	Rechtsfähigkeit *f*	legal capacity	capacité de jouissance des droits *f*	—	capacidad jurídica *f*
capacità innovativa (I)	Innovationsfähigkeit *f*	capability to innovate	capacité d'innovation *f*	—	capacidad de innovación *f*
capacità produttiva (I)	Produktions-kapazität *f*	production capacity	capacité de production *f*	—	capacidad de producción *f*
capacité[1] (F)	Fähigkeit *f*	ability	—	capacità *f*	capacidad *f*
capacité[2] (F)	Kapazität *f*	capacity	—	capacità *f*	capacidad *f*
capacité d'accomplir des actes juridiques (F)	Geschäftsfähigkeit *f*	capacity to enter into legal transactions	—	capacità di agire *f*	capacidad negocial *f*
capacité d'argumentation (F)	Argumentations-stärke *f*	talent for argumentation	—	forza d'argomentazione *f*	fuerza de argumentación *f*
capacité de jouissance des droits (F)	Rechtsfähigkeit *f*	legal capacity	—	capacità giuridica *f*	capacidad jurídica *f*
capacité de livraison (F)	Lieferkapazität *f*	delivery capacity	—	capacità di fornitura *f*	capacidad de entrega *f*
capacité d'entrer en contact (F)	Kontaktfähigkeit *f*	capability to establish public relations	—	comunicativa *f*	capacidad de anudar contactos *f*
capacité de production (F)	Produktions-kapazität *f*	production capacity	—	capacità produttiva *f*	capacidad de producción *f*
capacité de se faire valoir (F)	Durchsetzungs-vermögen *n*	capability of asserting one's rights	—	capacità di imporsi *f*	capacidad de imponerse *f*
capacité de stockage (F)	Lagerkapazität *f*	storage capacity	—	capacità di magazzino *f*	capacidad de almacenaje *f*
capacité d'innovation (F)	Innovationsfähigkeit *f*	capability to innovate	—	capacità innovativa *f*	capacidad de innovación *f*
capacity (E)	Kapazität *f*	—	capacité *f*	capacità *f*	capacidad *f*
capacity to enter into legal transactions (E)	Geschäftsfähigkeit *f*	—	capacité d'accomplir des actes juridiques *f*	capacità di agire *f*	capacidad negocial *f*
capacity utilisation rate (E)	Auslastungsgrad *m*	—	dégré de saturation *m*	grado di sfruttamento *m*	tasa de utilización *f*
capa del ozono (Es)	Ozonschicht *f*	ozone layer	ozonosphère *f*	strato d'ozono *m*	—
capital (E)	Kapital *n*	—	capital *m*	capitale *m*	capital *m*
capital (Es)	Kapital *n*	capital	capital *m*	capitale *m*	—
capital (F)	Kapital *n*	capital	—	capitale *m*	capital *m*
capital account (E)	Vermögens-rechnung *f*	—	calcul du patrimoine *m*	calcolo del patrimonio *m*	cálculo del valor neto *m*
capital aid (E)	Kapitalhilfe *f*	—	aide financière *f*	aiuto finanziario *m*	ayuda financiera *f*

	D	E	F	I	Es
capital a largo plazo (Es)	langfristiges Kapital *n*	long-term capital	capital à long terme *m*	capitale a lungo termine *m*	—
capital à long terme (F)	langfristiges Kapital *n*	long-term capital	—	capitale a lungo termine *m*	capital a largo plazo *m*
capital base (E)	Kapitalbasis *f*	—	base de capital *f*	base di capitale *f*	base de capital *f*
capital circulante (Es)	Umlaufvermögen *n*	current assets/ floating assets	capital de roulement *m*	patrimonio circolante *m*	—
capital de explotación (Es)	Betriebskapital *n*	working capital	capital de roulement *m*	capitale d'esercizio *m*	—
capital de roulement[1] (F)	Umlaufvermögen *n*	current assets/ floating assets	—	patrimonio circolante *m*	capital circulante *m*
capital de roulement[2] (F)	Betriebskapital *n*	working capital	—	capitale d'esercizio *m*	capital de explotación *m*
capitale (I)	Kapital *n*	capital	capital *m*	—	capital *m*
capitale a lungo termine (I)	langfristiges Kapital *n*	long-term capital	capital à long terme *m*	—	capital a largo plazo *m*
capitale azionario (I)	Aktienkapital *n*	share capital	fonds social *m*	—	capital en acciones *m*
capitale d'esercizio (I)	Betriebskapital *n*	working capital	capital de roulement *m*	—	capital de explotación *m*
capitale estero (I)	Auslandskapital *n*	foreign capital	capital étranger *m*	—	capital extranjero *m*
capitale infruttifero (I)	totes Kapital *n*	unproductive capital	capital improductif *m*	—	capital improductivo *m*
capitale iniziale (I)	Anfangskapital *n*	opening capital	capital initial *m*	—	capital inicial *m*
capitale minimo (I)	Mindestkapital *n*	minimum capital	capital minimum *m*	—	capital mínimo *m*
capital en acciones (Es)	Aktienkapital *n*	share capital	fonds social *m*	capitale azionario *m*	—
capitale proprio (I)	Eigenkapital *n*	equity capital	capital propre *m*	—	capital propio *m*
capitale reale[1] (I)	Sachvermögen *n*	material assets	biens corporels *m pl*	—	patrimonio real *m*
capitale reale[2] (I)	Realkapital *n*	real capital	biens corporels immobilisés *m pl*	—	capital real *m*
capitale sociale[1] (I)	Stammkapital *n*	share capital/ nominal capital	capital social *m*	—	capital social *m*
capitale sociale[2] (I)	Grundkapital *n*	share capital	capital initial *m*	—	capital social *m*
capital étranger (F)	Auslandskapital *n*	foreign capital	—	capitale estero *m*	capital extranjero *m*
capitale versato (I)	eingezahltes Kapital *n*	paid-up capital	capital versé *m*	—	capital desembolsado *m*
capital export (E)	Kapitalexport *m*	—	exportation de capitaux *f*	esportazione di capitale *f*	exportación de capital *f*
capital extranjero (Es)	Auslandskapital *n*	foreign capital	capital étranger *m*	capitale estero *m*	—
capital formation (E)	Vermögensbildung *f*	—	formation de capital *f*	formazione del patrimonio *f*	formación de capital *f*
capital goods[1] (E)	Investitionsgüter *pl*	—	biens d'investissement *m pl*	beni di investimento *m pl*	bienes de inversión *m pl*
capital goods[2] (E)	Anlagegüter *pl*	—	valeur immoblisée *f*	beni d'investimento *m pl*	bienes de inversión *m pl*
capital import (E)	Kapitalimport *m*	—	importation de capitaux *f*	importazione di capitali *f*	importación de capital *f*
capital improductif (F)	totes Kapital *n*	unproductive capital	—	capitale infruttifero *m*	capital improductivo *m*
capital improductivo (Es)	totes Kapital *n*	unproductive capital	capital improductif *m*	capitale infruttifero *m*	—
capital inicial (Es)	Anfangskapital *n*	opening capital	capital initial *m*	capitale iniziale *m*	—
capital initial[1] (F)	Grundkapital *n*	share capital	—	capitale sociale *m*	capital social *m*
capital initial[2] (F)	Anfangskapital *n*	opening capital	—	capitale iniziale *m*	capital inicial *m*
capital-intensive (E)	kapitalintensiv	—	avec grande intensité de capital	ad alta incidenza di capitale	con gran intensidad de capital
capital investment (E)	Kapitalanlage *f*	—	investissement de capitaux *m*	investimento di capitale *m*	inversión de capital *f*
capitalisation (F)	Kapitalisierung *f*	capitalization	—	capitalizzazione *f*	capitalización *f*
capitalism (E)	Kapitalismus *m*	—	capitalisme *m*	capitalismo *m*	capitalismo *m*
capitalisme (F)	Kapitalismus *m*	capitalism	—	capitalismo *m*	capitalismo *m*
capitalismo (Es)	Kapitalismus *m*	capitalism	capitalisme *m*	capitalismo *m*	—
capitalismo (I)	Kapitalismus *m*	capitalism	capitalisme *m*	—	capitalismo *m*

	D	E	F	I	Es
capitalización (Es)	Kapitalisierung *f*	capitalization	capitalisation *f*	capitalizzazione *f*	—
capitalization (E)	Kapitalisierung *f*	—	capitalisation *f*	capitalizzazione *f*	capitalización *f*
capitalized value (E)	Ertragswert *m*	—	valeur d'une chose mesurée à son rendement *f*	valore del reddito *m*	valor de rendimiento *m*
capitalizzazione (I)	Kapitalisierung *f*	capitalization	capitalisation *f*	—	capitalización *f*
capital market (E)	Kapitalmarkt *m*	—	marché des capitaux *m*	mercato finanziario *m*	mercado financiero *m*
capital mínimo (Es)	Mindestkapital *n*	minimum capital	capital minimum *m*	capitale minimo *m*	—
capital minimum (F)	Mindestkapital *n*	minimum capital	—	capitale minimo *m*	capital mínimo *m*
capital productif (F)	Produktivvermögen *n*	productive property	—	patrimonio produttivo *m*	patrimonio productivo *m*
capital propio (Es)	Eigenkapital *n*	equity capital	capital propre *m*	capitale proprio *m*	—
capital propre (F)	Eigenkapital *n*	equity capital	—	capitale proprio *m*	capital propio *m*
capital real (Es)	Realkapital *n*	real capital	biens corporels immobilisés *m pl*	capitale reale *m*	—
capital requirements (E)	Kapitalbedarf *m*	—	besoin en capital *m*	domanda di capitale *m*	necesidad de capital *f*
capital resources (E)	Kapitalausstattung *f*	—	dotation en capital *f*	dotazione di capitale *f*	dotación de capital *f*
capital social (F)	Stammkapital *n*	share capital/ nominal capital	—	capitale sociale *m*	capital social *m*
capital social[1] (Es)	Stammkapital *n*	share capital/ nominal capital	capital social *m*	capitale sociale *m*	—
capital social[2] (Es)	Grundkapital *n*	share capital	capital initial *m*	capitale sociale *m*	—
capital stock (E)	Kapitalstock *m*	—	réserve de capital *f*	riserva di capitale *f*	fondo de capital *m*
capital suscrito[1] (Es)	eingezahltes Kapital *n*	paid-up capital	capital versé *m*	capitale versato *m*	—
capital suscrito[2] (Es)	Stammeinlage *f*	initial contribution	apport social *m*	quota sociale *f*	—
capital theory (E)	Kapitaltheorie *f*	—	théorie du capital *f*	teoria del capitale *f*	teoría financiera *f*
capital transactions (E)	Kapitalverkehr *m*	—	mouvement des capitaux *m*	movimento dei capitali *m*	circulación de capitales *f*
capital turnover (E)	Kapitalumschlag *m*	—	roulement des capitaux *m*	rotazione del capitale *f*	rotación del capital *f*
capital value (E)	Kapitalwert *m*	—	valeur en capital *f*	valore del capitale *m*	valor capitalizado *m*
capital versé (F)	eingezahltes Kapital *n*	paid-up capital	—	capitale versato *m*	capital desembolsado *m*
capo (I)	Chef *m*	head	chef *m*	—	jefe *m*
Capodanno (I)	Neujahr *n*	New Year	nouvel an *m*	—	(día de) Año Nuevo *m*
capo reparto (I)	Abteilungsleiter *m*	head of department	chef de service *m*	—	jefe de sección *m*
capo reparto personale (I)	Personalleiter *m*	staff manager	chef du personnel *m*	—	jefe de personal *m*
capo reparto spedizioni (I)	Versandleiter *m*	manager of shipping department	chef du service des expéditions *m*	—	jefe del departamento de expedición *m*
caractère sérieux (F)	Seriosität *f*	seriousness	—	serietà *f*	buena reputación *f*
característica (Es)	Marke *f*	mark	marque *f*	marca *f*	—
característica de requisitos (Es)	Anforderungs-merkmal *n*	requirement characteristics	caractéristique d'exigences *f*	caratteristica richiesta *f*	—
caractéristique d'exigences (F)	Anforderungs-merkmal *n*	requirement characteristics	—	caratteristica richiesta *f*	característica de requisitos *f*
carat (E)	Karat *n*	—	carat *m*	carato *m*	quilate *m*
carat (F)	Karat *n*	carat	—	carato *m*	quilate *m*
carato (I)	Karat *n*	carat	carat *m*	—	quilate *m*
caratteristica richiesta (I)	Anforderungs-merkmal *n*	requirement characteristics	caractéristique d'exigences *f*	—	característica de requisitos *f*
caratteristiche promesse (I)	zugesicherte Eigenschaften *pl*	warranted characteristics	qualité promise *f*	—	calidades aseguradas *f pl*
carbone fossile (I)	Steinkohle *f*	hard coal	houille *f*	—	hulla *f*
carburant (F)	Treibstoff *m*	fuel	—	carburante *m*	combustible *m*
carburante (I)	Treibstoff *m*	fuel	carburant *m*	—	combustible *m*
card-index (E)	Kartei *f*	—	cartothèque	schedario *m*	fichero *m*
carga (Es)	Fracht *f*	freight	fret *m*	nolo *m*	—

	D	E	F	I	Es
carga colectiva (Es)	Sammelladung *f*	collective consignment	envoi par groupage *m*	carico a collettame *m*	—
carga de la prueba (Es)	Beweislast *f*	burden of proof	charge de la preuve *f*	onere di prova *m*	—
carga de un vagón (Es)	Wagenladung *f*	lorryload	charge de voiture *f*	carico di autocarro *m*	—
carga extraordinaria (Es)	außergewöhnliche Belastung *f*	extraordinary expenses	charges exceptionnelles *f pl*	oneri straordinari *m pl*	—
carga por expreso (Es)	Expressgut *n*	express goods	colis express *m*	merce spedita per espresso *f*	—
cargar (Es)	belasten	load/charge	débiter	addebitare	—
cargas salariales accesorias (Es)	Lohnnebenkosten *pl*	ancillary wage costs	charges salariales annexes *f pl*	costi complementari del lavoro *m pl*	—
carga suplementaria (Es)	Mehrbelastung *f*	additional burden	surcharge *f*	onere supplementare *m*	—
cargo (E)	Frachtgut *n*	—	marchandise à transporter *f*	merce di trasporto *f*	mercancías en pequeña velocidad *f pl*
cargo (Es)	Amt *n*	office	bureau *m*	ufficio *m*	—
cargo en cuenta (Es)	Lastschrift *f*	debit note	note de débit *f*	addebito *m*	—
caricare (I)	verladen	load	charger	—	expedir
carico a collettame (I)	Sammelladung *f*	collective consignment	envoi par groupage *m*	—	carga colectiva *f*
carico di autocarro (I)	Wagenladung *f*	lorryload	charge de voiture *f*	—	carga de un vagón *f*
carico pesante (I)	Schwergut *n*	heavy freight	produit pondéreux *m*	—	mercancía pesada *f*
carné de empresa (Es)	Betriebsausweis *m*	staff identification card	pièce d'identité de l'entreprise *f*	tessera aziendale *f*	—
carné de identidad (Es)	Personalausweis *m*	identity card	pièce d'identité *f*	carta d'identità *f*	—
carnet de chèques (F)	Scheckheft *n*	cheque book	—	carnet degli assegni *m*	libreta de cheques *f*
carnet degli assegni (I)	Scheckheft *n*	cheque book	carnet de chèques *m*	—	libreta de cheques *f*
carriage of goods (E)	Güterbeförderung *f*	—	transport de marchandises *m*	trasporto di merci *m*	transporte de mercancías *m*
carriage of goods by sea (E)	Verfrachtung *f*	—	affrètement *m*	trasporto marittimo *m*	expedición *f*
carriage of passengers (E)	Personenbeförderung *f*	—	transport de personnes *m*	trasporto di persone *m*	transporte de personas *m*
carrier (E)	Frachtführer *m*	—	transporteur *m*	vettore *m*	transportista *m*
carta (Es)	Brief *m*	letter	lettre *f*	lettera *f*	—
carta (ad)monitoria (Es)	Mahnbrief *m*	reminder	lettre d'avertissement *f*	lettera di sollecito *f*	—
carta assegni (I)	Scheckkarte *f*	cheque card	carte d'identité eurochèque *f*	—	tarjeta de cheques *f*
carta certificada (Es)	Einschreibebrief *m*	registered letter	lettre recommandée *f*	lettera raccomandata *f*	—
carta certificada con talón de recibo (Es)	Einschreiben-Rückschein *m*	recorded registered letter (with advice)	lettre recommandée avec avis de réception *f*	lettera raccomandata con ricevuta di ritorno *f*	—
carta de agradecimiento (Es)	Dankschreiben *n*	letter of thanks	lettre de remerciement *f*	lettera di ringraziamento *f*	—
carta de confirmación (Es)	Schlußbrief *m*	letter of confirmation	lettre de confirmation des conditions *f*	lettera di conferma *f*	—
carta de crédito (Es)	Kreditbrief *m*	letter of credit	lettre de crédit *f*	lettera di credito *f*	—
carta de crédito bancaria (Es)	Bankakkreditiv *n*	bank letter of credit	accréditif bancaire *m*	lettera di credito bancario *f*	—
carta de crédito comercial (Es)	Handelskreditbrief *m*	commercial letter of credit	lettre de crédit commercial *f*	lettera di credito commerciale *f*	—
carta de pago (Es)	Zahlkarte *f*	money order	mandat-carte *m*	modulo di versamento *m*	—
carta de porte (Es)	Frachtbrief *m*	consignment note	lettre de voiture *f*	lettera di vettura *f*	—
carta de recomendación (Es)	Empfehlungsschreiben *n*	letter of recommendation	lettre de recommandation *f*	lettera di raccomandazione *f*	—
carta de solicitud (Es)	Bewerbungsschreiben *n*	letter of application	lettre de demande d'emploi *f*	domanda d'impiego *f*	—
carta di credito (I)	Kreditkarte *f*	credit card	carte accréditive *f*	—	tarjeta de crédito *f*
carta d'identità (I)	Personalausweis *m*	identity card	pièce d'identité *f*	—	carné de identidad *m*

	D	E	F	I	Es
carta urgente (Es)	Eilbrief *m*	express letter	lettre par exprès *f*	lettera espresso *f*	—
carte accréditive (F)	Kreditkarte *f*	credit card	—	carta di credito *f*	tarjeta de crédito *f*
carte de garantie (F)	Garantiekarte *f*	certificate of warranty	—	certificato di garanzia *m*	tarjeta de garantía *f*
carte d'identité eurochèque (F)	Scheckkarte *f*	cheque card	—	carta assegni *f*	tarjeta de cheques *f*
cartel (E)	Kartell *n*	—	cartel *m*	cartello *m*	cártel *m*
cartel (Es)	Plakat *n*	poster	affiche *f*	manifesto *m*	—
cartel (F)	Kartell *n*	cartel	—	cartello *m*	cártel *m*
cártel (Es)	Kartell *n*	cartel	cartel *m*	cartello *m*	—
cartel authority (E)	Kartellbehörde *f*	—	office de surveillance des cartels et ententes *m*	autorità antimonopoli *f pl*	oficina de cártels *f*
cartel de acción (Es)	Aktionsplakat *n*	advertising bill	affiche d'action *f*	manifesto promozionale *m*	—
cartel formation (E)	Kartellbildung *f*	—	cartellisation *f*	costituzione di cartelli *f*	formación de carteles *f*
cartella campioni (I)	Mustermappe *f*	sample bag	dossier à échantillons *m*	—	muestrario *m*
cartella delle imposte (I)	Steuerbescheid *m*	notice of assessment	avis d'imposition *m*	—	liquidación de impuestos *f*
Cartel Law (E)	Kartellgesetz *n*	—	loi sur les cartels *f*	legge sui cartelli *f*	ley relativa a los cártels *f*
cartellisation (F)	Kartellbildung *f*	cartel formation	—	costituzione di cartelli *f*	formación de carteles *f*
cartello (I)	Kartell *n*	cartel	cartel *m*	—	cártel *m*
carte postale (F)	Postkarte *f*	postcard	—	cartolina postale *f*	tarjeta postal *f*
cartera (Es)	Portfolio *n*	portfolio	portefeuille *m*	portafoglio *m*	—
cartera de acciones (Es)	Aktienbestand *m*	shareholding	portefeuille d'actions *m*	portafoglio di azioni *m*	—
cartero (Es)	Postbote *m*	postman	facteur *m*	portalettere *m*	—
cartolina postale (I)	Postkarte *f*	postcard	carte postale *f*	—	tarjeta postal *f*
cartothèque (F)	Kartei *f*	card-index	—	schedario *m*	fichero *m*
casa editrice (I)	Verlag *m*	publishing house	maison d'édition *f*	—	editorial *f*
casa ficticia (Es)	Scheinfirma *f*	bogus firm	raison sociale imaginaire *f*	pseudoditta *f*	—
casa madre¹ (I)	Mutterhaus *n*	mother house	maison mère *f*	—	casa matriz *f*
casa madre² (I)	Stammhaus *n*	parent company	maison mère *f*	—	casa matriz *f*
casa matriz¹ (Es)	Stammhaus *n*	parent company	maison mère *f*	casa madre *f*	—
casa matriz² (Es)	Mutterhaus *n*	mother house	maison mère *f*	casa madre *f*	—
casella postale (I)	Postfach *n*	post office box	boîte postale *f*	—	apartado postal *m*
cash¹ (E)	Bargeld *n*	—	argent comptant *m*	denaro contante *m*	dinero efectivo *m*
cash² (E)	bar	—	comptant	in contanti	al contado
cash-and-carry clause (E)	Cash-and-carry-Klausel *f*	—	clause de prix sur place comptant *f*	clausola cash-and-carry *f*	cláusula page y llévatelo *f*
Cash-and-carry-Klausel (D)	—	cash-and-carry clause	clause de prix sur place comptant *f*	clausola cash-and-carry *f*	cláusula page y llévatelo *f*
cash assets (E)	Barvermögen *n*	—	valeurs réalisables à court terme ou disponibles *f pl*	patrimonio in contanti *m*	activo efectivo *m*
cash book (E)	Kassenbuch *n*	—	compte de caisse *m*	libro di cassa *m*	libro de caja *m*
cash credit (E)	Barkredit *m*	—	crédit de caisse *m*	credito per cassa *m*	crédito en efectivo *m*
cash discount¹ (E)	Barzahlungsrabatt *m*	—	remise pour payement comptant *f*	ribasso per pagamento in contanti *m*	descuento por pago al contado *m*
cash discount² (E)	Barzahlungskonto *n*	—	escompte de caisse *m*	sconto per pagamento in contanti *m*	descuento de pago al contado *m*
cash dispenser (E)	Bankomat *m*	—	billetterie *m*	bancomat *m*	cajero automático *m*
cash forecasting plan (E)	Liquiditätsplan *m*	—	plan de liquidité *m*	piano della liquidità *m*	plan de liquidez *m*
cashier (E)	Kassierer *m*	—	caissier *m*	cassiere *m*	cajero *m*
cash in hand (E)	Bargeldbestand *m*	—	espèces en caisse *f pl*	denaro contante in cassa *m*	saldo en efectivo *m*

	D	E	F	I	Es
cash letter of credit (E)	Barakkreditiv	—	accréditif payable en espèce *m*	apertura di credito documentario semplice *f*	crédito simple *m*
cash on delivery[1] (E)	Nachnahme *f*	—	remboursement *m*	contrassegno *m*	reembolso *m*
cash on delivery[2] (E)	gegen Nachnahme	—	contre remboursement	contro assegno	contra rembolso
cash on delivery[3] (E)	Zahlung per Nachnahme *f*	—	payement contre remboursement *m*	pagamento contro assegno *m*	pago contra reembolso *m*
cash on delivery[4] (E)	Lieferung gegen Nachnahme *f*	—	livraison contre remboursement *f*	consegna contro assegno *f*	entrega contra reembolso *f*
cash payment (E)	Barzahlung *f*	—	payement comptant *m*	pagamento in contanti *m*	pago al contado *m*
caso di sinistro (I)	Versicherungsfall *m*	event insured against	sinistre *m*	—	situación de siniestro *f*
cassa (I)	Kiste *f*	box	caisse *f*	—	caja *f*
cassa continua (I)	Nachttresor *m*	night safe	dépôt de nuit *m*	—	depósito de noche *m*
cassa di risparmio (I)	Sparkasse *f*	savings bank	institut bancaire d'épargne *m*	—	caja de ahorros *f*
cassaforte (I)	Tresor *m*	safe	coffre-fort *m*	—	caja fuerte *f*
cassetta di sicurezza (I)	Safe *m*	safe	coffre-fort *m*	—	caja de seguridad *f*
cassetta postale (I)	Briefkasten *m*	mail box	boîte aux lettres *f*	—	buzón *m*
cassiere (I)	Kassierer *m*	cashier	caissier *m*	—	cajero *m*
catalizador (Es)	Katalysator *m*	catalytic converter	catalyseur *m*	catalizzatore *m*	—
catalizzatore (I)	Katalysator *m*	catalytic converter	catalyseur *m*	—	catalizador *m*
catálogo (Es)	Katalog *m*	catalogue	catalogue *m*	catalogo *m*	—
catalogo (I)	Katalog *m*	catalogue	catalogue *m*	—	catálogo *m*
catalogue (E)	Katalog *m*	—	catalogue *m*	catalogo *m*	catálogo *m*
catalogue (F)	Katalog *m*	catalogue	—	catalogo *m*	catálogo *m*
catalyseur (F)	Katalysator *m*	catalytic converter	—	catalizzatore *m*	catalizador *m*
catalytic converter (E)	Katalysator *m*	—	catalyseur *m*	catalizzatore *m*	catalizador *m*
catasto (I)	Kataster *m*	cadaster	cadastre *m*	—	catastro *m*
catastro (Es)	Kataster *m*	cadaster	cadastre *m*	catasto *m*	—
categoria[1] (I)	Sorte *f*	variety/foreign notes and coins	genre *m*/devises *f pl*	—	especie *f*/calidad *f*/ marca *f*/moneda extranjera *f*
categoria[2] (I)	Branche *f*	line of business	branche *f*	—	ramo *m*
categoria commerciale (I)	Handelsklasse *f*	grade	catégorie de produits *f*	—	clase *f*
categoría de calidad (Es)	Güteklasse *f*	grade	catégorie de qualité *f*	qualità *f*	—
categoría de mercancías (Es)	Warenart *f*	class of goods	catégorie de marchandise *f*	tipo di merce *m*	—
catégorie de marchandise (F)	Warenart *f*	class of goods	—	tipo di merce *m*	categoría de mercancías *f*
catégorie de produits (F)	Handelsklasse *f*	grade	—	categoria commerciale *f*	clase *f*
catégorie de qualité (F)	Güteklasse *f*	grade	—	qualità *f*	categoría de calidad *f*
category of goods (E)	Gütergruppe *f*	—	groupe de marchandises *m*	gruppo di merci *m*	grupo de mercancías *m*
caución (Es)	Kaution *f*	security/bond	caution *f*	cauzione *f*	—
caución de licitación (Es)	Bietungsgarantie *f*	tender guarantee	cautionnement provisoire *m*	garanzia d'offerta *f*	—
causa (I)	Rechtsstreit *m*	legal action	litige *m*	—	conflicto jurídico *m*
causa ereditaria (I)	Erbstreit *m*	dispute concerning an inheritance	action successorale *f*	—	litigio hereditario *m*
causing environmental damage (E)	umweltschädlich	—	nuisible à l'environnement	inquinante	contaminante
caution[1] (F)	Bürgschaft *f*	guarantee	—	fideiussione *f*	fianza *f*
caution[2] (F)	Kaution *f*	security/bond	—	cauzione *f*	caución *f*/garantía *f*
caution de garantie (F)	Gewährleistungsgarantie *f*	guarantee for proper execution	—	garanzia di esecuzione *f*	fianza de contratista *f*

	D	E	F	I	Es
cautionnement provisoire (F)	Bietungsgarantie *f*	tender guarantee	—	garanzia d'offerta *f*	caución de licitación *f*
caution pour être mis en liberté (F)	Haftkaution *f*	bail	—	cauzione per la scarcerazione *f*	fianza de puesta en libertad *f*
cauzione (I)	Kaution *f*	security/bond	caution *f*	—	caución *f*/garantía *f*
cauzione per la scarcerazione (I)	Haftkaution *f*	bail	caution pour être mis en liberté *f*	—	fianza de puesta en libertad *f*
cédant (F)	Zedent *m*	assignor	—	cedente *m*	cedente *m*
cedente (Es)	Zedent *m*	assignor	cédant *m*	cedente *m*	—
cedente (I)	Zedent *m*	assignor	cédant *m*	—	cedente *m*
cedola (I)	Coupon *m*	coupon	coupon *m*	—	cupón *m*
cédula hipotecaria (Es)	Pfandbrief *m*	mortgage bond	obligation hypothécaire *f*	titolo ipotecario *m*	—
ceiling (E)	Plafond *m*	—	plafond *m*	plafond *m*	límite máximo *m*
censimento (I)	Volkszählung *f*	census of population	recensement démographique *m*	—	censo *m*
censo (Es)	Volkszählung *f*	census of population	recensement démographique *m*	censimento *m*	—
census of population (E)	Volkszählung *f*	—	recensement démographique *m*	censimento *m*	censo *m*
central bank[1] (E)	Zentralbank *f*	—	banque centrale *f*	Banca Centrale *f*	banco emisor *m*
central bank[2] (E)	Notenbank *f*	—	banque d'émission *f*	banca d'emissione *f*	banco emisor *m*
Central Bank Council (E)	Zentralbankrat *m*	—	Conseil de la Banque Centrale *m*	consiglio superiore della Banca Centrale *m*	Consejo del Banco Central *m*
central de giros (Es)	Girozentrale *f*	central giro institution	banque centrale de virement *f*	stanza centrale di compensazione *f*	—
centrale nucléaire (F)	Atomkraftwerk *n*	nuclear power plant	—	centrale nucleare *f*	central nuclear *f*
centrale nucleare (I)	Atomkraftwerk *n*	nuclear power plant	centrale nucléaire *f*	—	central nuclear *f*
central giro institution (E)	Girozentrale *f*	—	banque centrale de virement *f*	stanza centrale di compensazione *f*	central de giros *f*
central interurbana (Es)	Fernmeldeamt *n*	telephone exchange	service de télécommunication *m*	ufficio telecomunicazioni *m*	—
centralisation (F)	Zentralisierung *f*	centralization	—	centralizzazione *f*	centralización *f*
centralización (Es)	Zentralisierung *f*	centralization	centralisation *f*	centralizzazione *f*	—
centralization (E)	Zentralisierung *f*	—	centralisation *f*	centralizzazione *f*	centralización *f*
centralizzazione (I)	Zentralisierung *f*	centralization	centralisation *f*	—	centralización *f*
centrally controlled economy (E)	zentrale Planwirtschaft *f*	—	économie planifiée centrale *f*	economia pianificata *f*	economía planificada central *f*
central nuclear (Es)	Atomkraftwerk *n*	nuclear power plant	centrale nucléaire *f*	centrale nucleare *f*	—
central rate (E)	Leitkurs *m*	—	taux central *m*	parità centrale *f*	tipo pivote *m*
central unit (E)	Zentraleinheit *f*	—	unité centrale *f*	unità centrale *f*	unidad central *f*
centre commercial (F)	Shopping Center *n*	shopping centre	—	centro commerciale *m*	centro comercial *m*
centre de calcul (F)	Rechenzentrum *n*	computer centre	—	centro da computer *m*	centro de computación *m*
centro comercial (Es)	Shopping Center *n*	shopping centre	centre commercial *m*	centro commerciale *m*	—
centro commerciale (I)	Shopping Center *n*	shopping centre	centre commercial *m*	—	centro comercial *m*
centro da computer (I)	Rechenzentrum *n*	computer centre	centre de calcul *m*	—	centro de computación *m*
centro de computación (Es)	Rechenzentrum *n*	computer centre	centre de calcul *m*	centro da computer *m*	—
certificado[1] (Es)	per Einschreiben	by registered post	sous pli recommandé	per raccomandata	—
certificado[2] (Es)	Zertifikat *n*	certificate	certificat *m*	certificato *m*	—
certificado[3] (Es)	Einschreiben *n*	Registered	en recommandé	raccomandata *f*	—
certificado de aduana (Es)	Zolleinfuhrschein *m*	bill of entry	acquit d'entrée *m*	bolletta d'entrata *m*	—
certificado de avería (Es)	Havariezertifikat *n*	survey/ damage report	certificat d'avarie *m*	certificato d'avaria *m*	—
certificado de divisas (Es)	Devisen-genehmigung *f*	foreign exchange authorization	autorisation de change *f*	autorizzazione valutaria *f*	—

	D	E	F	I	Es
certificado de escuela (Es)	Zeugnis *n*	school report	certificat scolaire *m*	pagella *f*	—
certificado de origen (Es)	Ursprungszeugnis *n*	certificate of origin	certificat d'origine *m*	certificato d'origine *m*	—
certificado de participación (Es)	Investmentzertifikat *n*	investment certificate	certificat émis par un fonds commun de placement *m*	certificato d'investimento *m*	—
certificado de sanidad (Es)	Gesundheits-zeugnis *n*	health certificate	certificat de santé *m*	certificato sanitario *m*	—
certificado policial (Es)	polizeiliches Führungszeugnis *n*	police certificate of good conduct	certificat de bonnes vie et mœurs *m*	certificato di buona condotta *m*	—
certificado provisional (Es)	Zwischenzeugnis *n*	interim report	certificat provisoire *m*	certificato provvisorio *m*	—
certificat (F)	Zertifikat *n*	certificate	—	certificato *m*	certificado *m*
certificat d'attestation du brevet d'invention (F)	Patenturkunde *f*	patent document	—	brevetto *m*	patente *f*
certificat d'avarie (F)	Havariezertifikat *n*	survey/ damage report	—	certificato d'avaria *m*	certificado de avería *m*
certificat de bonnes vie et mœurs (F)	polizeiliches Führungszeugnis *n*	police certificate of good conduct	—	certificato di buona condotta *m*	certificado policial *m*
certificat de dépot (F)	Lagerschein *m*	warehouse warrant	—	ricevuta di deposito *f*	resguardo de almacén *m*
certificat de santé (F)	Gesundheits-zeugnis *n*	health certificate	—	certificato sanitario *m*	certificado de sanidad *m*
certificat d'origine (F)	Ursprungszeugnis *n*	certificate of origin	—	certificato d'origine *m*	certificado de origen *m*
certificate (E)	Zertifikat *n*	—	certificat *m*	certificato *m*	certificado *m*
certificat émis par un fonds commun de placement (F)	Investmentzertifikat *n*	investment certificate	—	certificato d'investimento *m*	certificado de participación *m*
certificate of indebtedness (E)	Schuldschein *m*	—	billet de créance *m*	certificato di debito *m*	pagaré *m*
certificate of origin (E)	Ursprungszeugnis *n*	—	certificat d'origine *m*	certificato d'origine *m*	certificado de origen *m*
certificate of warranty (E)	Garantiekarte *f*	—	carte de garantie *f*	certificato di garanzia *m*	tarjeta de garantía *f*
certification (F)	Beglaubigung *f*	authentication	—	autenticazione *f*	legalización *f*
certificato (I)	Zertifikat *n*	certificate	certificat *m*	—	certificado *m*
certificato d'avaria (I)	Havariezertifikat *n*	survey/ damage report	certificat d'avarie *m*	—	certificado de avería *m*
certificato di buona condotta (I)	polizeiliches Führungszeugnis *n*	police certificate of good conduct	certificat de bonnes vie et mœurs *m*	—	certificado policial *m*
certificato di debito (I)	Schuldschein *m*	certificate of indebtedness	billet de créance *m*	—	pagaré *m*
certificato di garanzia (I)	Garantiekarte *f*	certificate of warranty	carte de garantie *f*	—	tarjeta de garantía *f*
certificato d'investimento (I)	Investmentzertifikat *n*	investment certificate	certificat émis par un fonds commun de placement *m*	—	certificado de participación *m*
certificato d'origine (I)	Ursprungszeugnis *n*	certificate of origin	certificat d'origine *m*	—	certificado de origen *m*
certificato provvisorio (I)	Zwischenzeugnis *n*	interim report	certificat provisoire *m*	—	certificado provisional *m*
certificato sanitario (I)	Gesundheitszeugnis *n*	health certificate	certificat de santé *m*	—	certificado de sanidad *m*
certificat provisoire (F)	Zwischenzeugnis *n*	interim report	—	certificato provvisorio *m*	certificado provisional *m*
certificat scolaire (F)	Zeugnis *n*	school report	—	pagella *f*	certificado de escuela *m*
cesión (Es)	Abtretung *f*	assignment	cession *f*	cessione *f*	—
cesionario (Es)	Zessionar *m*	assignee	cessionnaire *m*	cessionario *m*	—
cesión en bloque (Es)	Globalzession *f*	global assignment	cession globale *f*	cessione globale *f*	—
cessation of payments (E)	Zahlungseinstellung *f*	—	suspension de payement *f*	cessazione dei pagamenti *f*	suspensión de pagos *f*
cessazione dei pagamenti (I)	Zahlungseinstellung *f*	cessation of payments	suspension de payement *f*	—	suspensión de pagos *f*

	D	E	F	I	Es
cession (F)	Abtretung *f*	assignment	—	cessione *f*	cesión *f*
cessionario (I)	Zessionar *m*	assignee	cessionnaire *m*	—	cesionario *m*
cessione (I)	Abtretung *f*	assignment	cession *f*	—	cesión *f*
cessione globale (I)	Globalzession *f*	global assignment	cession globale *f*	—	cesión en bloque *f*
cession globale (F)	Globalzession *f*	global assignment	—	cessione globale *f*	cesión en bloque *f*
cessionnaire (F)	Zessionar *m*	assignee	—	cessionario *m*	cesionario *m*
ceto medio (I)	Mittelstand *m*	middle class(es)	classe moyenne *f*	—	clase media *f*
chairman of the board (E)	Vorstandsvorsitzender *m*	—	président du comité de direction *m*	presidente del consiglio di amministrazione *m*	presidente del consejo *m*
chairman of the supervisory board (E)	Aufsichtsratsvorsitzender *m*	—	président du conseil de surveillance *m*	presidente del consiglio di sorveglianza *m*	presidente del consejo de vigilancia *m*
chairmanship (E)	Vorsitz *m*	—	présidence *f*	presidenza *f*	presidencia *f*
Chamber of Commerce (E)	Handelskammer *f*	—	chambre de commerce *f*	camera di commercio *f*	cámara de comercio *f*
chamber of foreign trade (E)	Außenhandelskammer *f*	—	chambre du commerce extérieur *f*	camera di commercio estero *f*	cámara del comercio exterior *f*
chamber of handicrafts (E)	Handwerkskammer *f*	—	chambre artisanale *f*	camera dell'artigianato *f*	cámara de artesanía *f*
Chamber of Industry and Commerce (E)	Industrie- und Handelskammer *f*	—	chambre de commerce et d'industrie *f*	camera di commercio e industria *f*	cámara de industria y comercio *f*
chambre artisanale (F)	Handwerkskammer *f*	chamber of handicrafts	—	camera dell'artigianato *f*	cámara de artesanía *f*
chambre de commerce (F)	Handelskammer *f*	Chamber of Commerce	—	camera di commercio *f*	cámara de comercio *f*
chambre de commerce et d'industrie (F)	Industrie- und Handelskammer *f*	Chamber of Industry and Commerce	—	camera di commercio e industria *f*	cámara de industria y comercio *f*
chambre du commerce extérieur (F)	Außenhandelskammer *f*	chamber of foreign trade	—	camera di commercio estero *f*	cámara del comercio exterior *f*
champ d'acitivité (F)	Tätigkeitsfeld *n*	field of activity	—	campo d'azione *m*	campo de actividad *m*
champ d'action (F)	Aktionsfeld *n*	field of action	—	campo d'azione *m*	campo de acción *m*
changement dans les structures (F)	Strukturwandel *m*	structural change	—	cambiamenti strutturali *m pl*	cambio de estructuras *m*
changement d'emploi[1] **(F)**	Stellungswechsel *m*	change of employment	—	cambiamento del posto di lavoro *m*	cambio de empleo *m*
changement d'emploi[2] (F)	Arbeitsplatzwechsel *m*	change of employment	—	cambiamento del posto di lavoro *m*	cambio de puesto *m*
change of employment[1] (E)	Arbeitsplatzwechsel *m*	—	changement d'emploi *m*	cambiamento del posto di lavoro *m*	cambio de puesto *m*
change of employment[2] (E)	Stellungswechsel *m*	—	changement d'emploi *m*	cambiamento del posto di lavoro *m*	cambio de empleo *m*
change of residence[1] (E)	Umzug *m*	—	déménagement *m*	trasferimento *m*	mudanza *f*
change of residence[2] (E)	Wohnungswechsel *m*	—	transfert de résidence *m*	cambiamento dell'abitazione *m*	cambio de vivienda *m*
change of shift (E)	Schichtwechsel *m*	—	relève d'équipe *f*	cambio di turno *m*	cambio del equipo de obreros *m*
changes in purchasing power (E)	Kaufkraftänderung *f*	—	modification du pouvoir d'achat *f*	mutamento del potere d'acquisto *m*	cambio en el poder adquisitivo *m*
channel of distribution (E)	Absatzweg *m*	—	canal de distribution *m*	via della distribuzione *f*	medio de venta *f*
charge (F)	Belastung *f*	load	—	addebito *m*	gravamen *m*
chargeable to (E)	zu Lasten	—	à la charge de	a carico di	a cargo de
charge de la preuve (F)	Beweislast *f*	burden of proof	—	onere di prova *m*	carga de la prueba *f*
charge de voiture (F)	Wagenladung *f*	lorryload	—	carico di autocarro *m*	carga de un vagón *f*
charge levied (E)	Umlage *f*	—	répartition *f*	ripartizione *f*	reparto *m*
charge primaire (F)	Primäraufwand *m*	primary expenses	—	spese primarie *f pl*	gastos directos *m pl*
charger (F)	verladen	load	—	caricare	expedir
charges d'exploitation[1] (F)	Betriebsausgaben *f*	(current) operational expenses	—	spese aziendali *f pl*	gastos de explotación *m pl*
charges d'exploitation[2] (F)	Betriebskosten *pl*	operating costs	—	spese d'esercizio *f pl*	gastos de explotación *m pl*

	D	E	F	I	Es
charges exceptionnelles (F)	außergewöhnliche Belastung *f*	extraordinary expenses	—	oneri straordinari *m pl*	carga extraordinaria *f*
charges salariales annexes (F)	Lohnnebenkosten *pl*	ancillary wage costs	—	costi complementari del lavoro *m pl*	cargas salariales accesorias *f pl*
charter flight (E)	Charterflug *m*	—	vol charter *m*	volo charter *m*	vuelo fletado *m*
Charterflug (D)	—	charter flight	vol charter *m*	volo charter *m*	vuelo fletado *m*
charter party (E)	Chartervertrag *m*	—	contrat d'affrètement *m*	contratto di noleggio *m*	contrato de fletamento *m*
Chartervertrag (D)	—	charter party	contrat d'affrètement *m*	contratto di noleggio *m*	contrato de fletamento *m*
cheapening (E)	Verbilligung *f*	—	réduction du prix *f*	ribasso *m*	abaratamiento *m*
checklist (E)	Checkliste *f*	—	liste de contrôle *f*	lista di controllo *f*	lista de control *f*
Checkliste (D)	—	checklist	liste de contrôle *f*	lista di controllo *f*	lista de control *f*
Chef (D)	—	head	chef *m*	capo *m*	jefe *m*
chef[1] (F)	Chef *m*	head	—	capo *m*	jefe *m*
chef[2] (F)	Anführer *m*	leader	—	leader *m*	líder *m*
chef de service (F)	Abteilungsleiter *m*	head of department	—	capo reparto *m*	jefe de sección *m*
chef de vente régionale (F)	Gebietsverkaufs-leiter *m*	area sales manager	—	direttore di vendita regionale *m*	jefe de venta regional *m*
chef du personnel (F)	Personalleiter *m*	staff manager	—	capo reparto personale *m*	jefe de personal *m*
chef du service des expéditions (F)	Versandleiter *m*	manager of shipping department	—	capo reparto spedizioni *m*	jefe del departamento de expedición *m*
Chemie (D)	—	chemistry	chimie *f*	chimica *f*	química *f*
chemistry (E)	Chemie *f*	—	chimie *f*	chimica *f*	química *f*
cheque (Es)	Scheck *m*	cheque	chèque *m*	assegno *m*	—
chèque (F)	Scheck *m*	cheque	—	assegno *m*	cheque *m*
cheque (E)	Scheck *m*	—	chèque *m*	assegno *m*	cheque *m*
cheque a la orden (Es)	Orderscheck *m*	order cheque	chèque à ordre *m*	assegno all'ordine *m*	—
cheque al portador[1] (Es)	Inhaberscheck *m*	cheque payable to bearer	chèque au porteur *m*	assegno al portatore *m*	—
cheque al portador[2] (Es)	Überbringerscheck *m*	bearer cheque	chèque au porteur *m*	assegno al portatore *m*	—
chèque à ordre (F)	Orderscheck *m*	order cheque	—	assegno all'ordine *m*	cheque a la orden *m*
chèque à porter en compte (F)	Verrechnungs-scheck *m*	crossed cheque	—	assegno sbarrato *m*	cheque cruzado *m*
chèque antidaté (F)	vordatierter Scheck *m*	antedated cheque	—	assegno antidatato *m*	cheque de fecha adelantada *m*
chèque au porteur[1] (F)	Überbringerscheck *m*	bearer cheque	—	assegno al portatore *m*	cheque al portador *m*
chèque au porteur[2] (F)	Inhaberscheck *m*	cheque payable to bearer	—	assegno al portatore *m*	cheque al portador *m*
chèque barré (F)	gekreuzter Scheck *m*	crossed cheque	—	assegno sbarrato *m*	cheque cruzado *m*
cheque book[1] (E)	Scheckbuch *n*	—	livre d'enregistre-ment des chéques *m*	libretto degli assegni *m*	libro de cheques *m*
cheque book[2] (E)	Scheckheft *n*	—	carnet de chèques *m*	carnet degli assegni *m*	libreta de cheques *f*
cheque card (E)	Scheckkarte *f*	—	carte d'identité eurochèque *f*	carta assegni *f*	tarjeta de cheques *f*
cheque cruzado[1] (Es)	gekreuzter Scheck *m*	crossed cheque	chèque barré *m*	assegno sbarrato *m*	—
cheque cruzado[2] (Es)	Verrechnungs-scheck *m*	crossed cheque	chèque à porter en compte *m*	assegno sbarrato *m*	—
cheque de caja (Es)	Barscheck *m*	open cheque	chèque non barré *m*	assegno circolare *m*	—
cheque de fecha adelantada (Es)	vordatierter Scheck *m*	antedated cheque	chèque antitdaté *m*	assegno antidatato *m*	—
cheque de viaje (Es)	Reisescheck *m*	traveller's cheque	chèque de voyage *m*	assegno turistico *m*	—
chèque de voyage (F)	Reisescheck *m*	traveller's cheque	—	assegno turistico *m*	cheque de viaje *m*
chèque en blanc (F)	Blankoscheck *m*	blank cheque	—	assegno in bianco *m*	cheque en blanco *m*
cheque en blanco (Es)	Blankoscheck *m*	blank cheque	chèque en blanc *m*	assegno in bianco *m*	—
cheque falsificado (Es)	gefälschter Scheck *m*	forged cheque	chèque maquillé *m*	assegno falsificato *m*	—

	D	E	F	I	Es
cheque fraud (E)	Scheckbetrug *m*	—	irrégularité en matière de chèque *f*	emissione di assegno a vuoto *f*	falsificación de cheques *f*
chèque maquillé (F)	gefälschter Scheck *m*	forged cheque	—	assegno falsificato *m*	cheque falsificado *m*
chèque non barré (F)	Barscheck *m*	open cheque	—	assegno circolare *m*	cheque de caja *m*
cheque payable to bearer (E)	Inhaberscheck *m*	—	chèque au porteur *m*	assegno al portatore *m*	cheque al portador *m*
cheque postal (Es)	Postscheck *m*	postal giro	chèque postal *m*	assegno postale *m*	—
chèque postal (F)	Postscheck *m*	postal giro	—	assegno postale *m*	cheque postal *m*
chiarezza di bilancio (I)	Bilanzwahrheit *f*	truth in the balance sheet	sincérité du bilan *f*	—	sinceridad del balance *f*
Chiffre-Anzeige (D)	—	advertisement under a box number	annonce chiffrée *f*	inserzione in cifra *f*	anuncio codificado *m*
chiffre d'affaires (F)	Umsatz *m*	turnover	—	fatturato *m*	volumen de ventas *m*
chiffre d'affaires minimum (F)	Mindestumsatz *m*	minimum turnover	—	fatturato minimo *m*	cifra de venta mínima *f*
chiffre d'affaires net (F)	Nettoumsatz *m*	net turnover	—	fatturato netto *m*	ventas netas *f pl*
chiffres prévisionnels (F)	Sollzahlen *pl*	target figures	—	cifre calcolate *f pl*	cifras estimadas *f pl*
chiffres rouges (F)	rote Zahlen *pl*	(in) the red	—	conti in rosso *m pl*	cifras rojas *f pl*
chimica (I)	Chemie *f*	chemistry	chimie *f*	—	química *f*
chimie (F)	Chemie *f*	chemistry	—	chimica *f*	química *f*
chi si assume i costi (I)	Kostenträger *m*	unit assuming cost	poste de production absorbant des coûts *m*	—	que sufraga los costes
chiusura d'esercizio (I)	Jahresabschluß *m*	annual accounts	clôture annuelle des comptes *f*	—	cierre de cuentos *m*
choice of location (E)	Standortwahl *f*	—	choix du lieu d'implantation *m*	scelta dell'ubicazione *f*	elección de la ubicación *f*
choix du lieu d'implantation (F)	Standortwahl *f*	choice of location	—	scelta dell'ubicazione *f*	elección de la ubicación *f*
chômage (F)	Arbeitslosigkeit *f*	unemployment	—	disoccupazione *f*	desempleo *m*
chômage saisonnier (F)	saisonale Arbeitslosigkeit *f*	seasonal unemployment	—	disoccupazione stagionale *f*	paro estacional *m*
chômage structurel (F)	strukturelle Arbeitslosigkeit *f*	structural unemployment	—	disoccupazione strutturale *f*	paro estructural *m*
Christmas (E)	Weihnachten *n*	—	Noël *m*	Natale *m*	Navidad *f*
chute des cours (F)	Kurs-zusammenbruch *m*	collapse of prices	—	crollo delle quotazioni *m*	caída de los cambios *f*
chute des prix (F)	Preisverfall *m*	decline in prices	—	caduta dei prezzi *f*	caída de precios *f*
cibernética (Es)	Kybernetik *f*	cybernetics	cybernétique *f*	cibernetica *f*	—
cibernetica (I)	Kybernetik *f*	cybernetics	cybernétique *f*	—	cibernética *f*
ciclo (Es)	Zyklus *m*	cycle	cycle *m*	ciclo *m*	—
ciclo (I)	Zyklus *m*	cycle	cycle *m*	—	ciclo *m*
ciclo congiunturale (I)	Konjunkturzyklus *m*	business cycle	cycle conjoncturel *m*	—	ciclo económico *m*
ciclo de vida (Es)	Lebenszyklus *m*	life cycle	cycle de vie *m*	ciclo di vita *m*	—
ciclo di magazzinaggio (I)	Lagerzyklus *m*	stock cycle	cycle de stockage *m*	—	período de almacenaje *m*
ciclo di vita (I)	Lebenszyklus *m*	life cycle	cycle de vie *m*	—	ciclo de vida *m*
ciclo económico (Es)	Konjunkturzyklus *m*	business cycle	cycle conjoncturel *m*	ciclo congiunturale *m*	—
ciencias económicas[1] (Es)	Wirtschafts-wissenschaften *pl*	economics	sciences économiques *f pl*	scienze economiche *f pl*	—
ciencias económicas[2] (Es)	Volks-wirtschaftslehre *f*	economics	économie politique *f*	economia politica *f*	—
cierre de cuentas (Es)	Jahresabschluß *m*	annual accounts	clôture annuelle des comptes *f*	chiusura d'esercizio *f*	—
cierre patronal (Es)	Aussperrung *f*	lockout	lock-out *m*	serrata *f*	—
cifra de venta mínima (Es)	Mindestumsatz *m*	minimum turnover	chiffre d'affaires minimum *m*	fatturato minimo *m*	—
cifra de ventas (Es)	Absatz *m*	sale/distribution	volume des ventes *m*	vendita *f*	—
cifras efectivas (Es)	Istzahlen *pl*	actual figures	résultats effectifs *m pl*	dati effettivi *m pl*	—

	D	E	F	I	Es
cifras estimadas (Es)	Sollzahlen *pl*	target figures	chiffres prévisionnels *m pl*	cifre calcolate *f pl*	—
cifras índice (Es)	Kennziffern *pl*	code numbers	indice *m*	cifre d'identificazione *f pl*	—
cifras rojas (Es)	rote Zahlen *pl*	(in) the red	chiffres en déficit *m*	conti in rosso *m pl*	—
cifre calcolate (I)	Sollzahlen *pl*	target figures	chiffres prévisionnels *m pl*	—	cifras estimadas *f pl*
cifre d'identificazione (I)	Kennziffern *pl*	code numbers	indice *m*	—	cifras índice *f pl*
circolare (I)	Rundschreiben *n*	circular (letter)	lettre circulaire *f*	—	circular *m*
circolazione delle banconote (I)	Notenumlauf *m*	notes in circulation	circulation fiduciaire *f*	—	circulación fiduciaria *f*
circolazione delle merci (I)	Handelsverkehr *m*	commercial intercourse	échanges commerciaux *m pl*	—	comercio *m*
circolazione di denaro (I)	Geldumlauf *m*	circulation of money	circulation monétaire *f*	—	circulación monetaria *f*
circuit économique (F)	Wirtschafts-kreislauf *m*	economic cycle	—	circuito economico *m*	circuito económico *m*
circuito de distribución (Es)	Vertriebsweg *m*	distribution channel	canal de distribution *m*	rete di distribuzione *f*	—
circuito económico (Es)	Wirtschafts-kreislauf *m*	economic cycle	circuit économique *m*	circuito economico *m*	—
circuito economico (I)	Wirtschafts-kreislauf *m*	economic cycle	circuit économique *m*	—	circuito económico *m*
circulación[1] (Es)	Straßenverkehr *m*	road traffic	trafic routier *m*	traffico stradale *m*	—
circulación[2] (Es)	Verkehr *m*	traffic	circulation *f*	traffico *m*	—
circulación de capitales (Es)	Kapitalverkehr *m*	capital transactions	mouvement des capitaux *m*	movimento dei capitali *m*	—
circulación fiduciaria (Es)	Notenumlauf *m*	notes in circulation	circulation fiduciaire *f*	circolazione delle banconote *f*	—
circulación monetaria (Es)	Geldumlauf *m*	circulation of money	circulation monétaire *f*	circolazione di denaro *f*	—
circular (Es)	Rundschreiben *n*	circular (letter)	lettre circulaire *f*	circolare *f*	—
circular de publicidad (Es)	Werbebrief *m*	advertising letter	lettre publicitaire *f*	lettera pubblicitaria *f*	—
circular (letter) (E)	Rundschreiben *n*	—	lettre circulaire *f*	circolare *f*	circular *m*
circulation (F)	Verkehr *m*	traffic	—	traffico *m*	circulación *f*
circulation fiduciaire (F)	Notenumlauf *m*	notes in circulation	—	circolazione delle banconote *f*	circulación fiduciaria *f*
circulation monétaire (F)	Geldumlauf *m*	circulation of money	—	circolazione di denaro *f*	circulación monetaria *f*
circulation of money (E)	Geldumlauf *m*	—	circulation monétaire *f*	circolazione di denaro *f*	circulación monetaria *f*
citación (Es)	Ladung *f*	summons to appear	citation *f*	citazione *f*	—
citation (F)	Ladung *f*	summons to appear	—	citazione *f*	citación *f*
citazione (I)	Ladung *f*	summons to appear	citation *f*	—	citación *f*
citazione in giudizio (I)	Klage *f*	legal action	action en justice *f*	—	demanda *f*
claim (E)	Anspruch *m*	—	prétention *f*	pretesa *f*	reivindicación *f*
claim for damages[1] (E)	Schadensforderung *f*	—	prétention à dommages-intérêts *f*	credito da danni *m*	pretensión de indemnización *f*
claim for damages[2] (E)	Schadenersatz-ansprüche *pl*	—	droit à l'indemnité *m*	diritti al risarcimento danni *m pl*	derecho a indemnización por daños y perjuicios *m*
claim to subsequent delivery (E)	Nachlieferungs-anspruch *m*	—	droit à livraison complémentaire *m*	diritto alla fornitura supplementare *m*	derecho de suminis-tro adicional *m*
claridad del balance (Es)	Bilanzklarheit *f*	balance transparency	clarté du bilan *f*	trasparenza di bilancio *f*	—
clarification des eaux usées (F)	Abwasserreinigung *f*	purification of sewage	—	depurazione delle acque di scarico *f*	depuración de las aguas residuales *f*
clarté du bilan (F)	Bilanzklarheit *f*	balance transparency	—	trasparenza di bilancio *f*	claridad del balance *f*
clase (Es)	Handelsklasse *f*	grade	catégorie de produits *f*	categoria commerciale *f*	—
clase media (Es)	Mittelstand *m*	middle class(es)	classe moyenne *f*	ceto medio *m*	—

	D	E	F	I	Es
clase obrera (Es)	Arbeiterklasse *f*	working class	classe ouvrière *f*	classe degli operai *f*	—
clases de costes (Es)	Kostenarten *pl*	cost types	coûts par nature *m pl*	tipi di costi *m pl*	—
classe degli operai (I)	Arbeiterklasse *f*	working class	classe ouvrière *f*	—	clase obrera *f*
classe moyenne (F)	Mittelstand *m*	middle class(es)	—	ceto medio *m*	clase media *f*
classe ouvrière (F)	Arbeiterklasse *f*	working class	—	classe degli operai *f*	clase obrera *f*
class of goods (E)	Warenart *f*	—	catégorie de marchandise *f*	tipo di merce *m*	categoría de mercancías *f*
clause (E)	Klausel *f*	—	clause *f*	clausola *f*	cláusula *f*
clause (F)	Klausel *f*	clause	—	clausola *f*	cláusula *f*
clause commerciale (F)	Handelsklausel *f*	trade terms	—	clausola commerciale *f*	cláusula comercial *f*
clause d'assurance (contre) tous (les) risques (F)	all-risks-Klausel *f*	all-risks clause	—	clausola tutti i rischi *f*	cláusula a todo riesgo *f*
clause de la nation la plus favorisée (F)	Meistbegünstigungs-klausel *f*	most-favoured nation clause	—	clausola della nazione più favorita *f*	cláusula de la nación más favorecida *f*
clause de livraison (F)	Lieferklausel *f*	delivery clause	—	clausola di fornitura *f*	cláusula de entrega *f pl*
clause de payement par accréditif (F)	Akkreditivklausel *f*	letter of credit clause	—	clausola del credito documentario *f*	cláusula de crédito documentario *f*
clause de prix sur place comptant (F)	Cash-and-carry-Klausel *f*	cash-and-carry clause	—	clausola cash-and-carry *f*	cláusula page y llévatelo *f*
clause de résolution du contrat (F)	Rücktrittsklausel *f*	escape clause	—	clausola di recesso *f*	cláusula de arrepentimiento *f*
clause de révocation (F)	Widerrufsklausel *f*	revocation clause	—	clausola di revoca *f*	cláusula revocatoria *f*
clause de stabilité (F)	Wertsicherungs-klausel *f*	stable value clause	—	clausola di garanzia monetaria *f*	cláusula de índice variable *f*
clause de transit (F)	Transitklausel *f*	transit clause	—	clausola di transito *f*	cláusula de tránsito *f*
clause d'indexation (F)	Indexklausel *f*	index clause	—	clausola dell'indice *f*	cláusula de índice variable *f*
clause dollar (F)	Dollarklausel *f*	dollar clause	—	clausola dollaro *f*	cláusula dólar *f*
clause monétaire (F)	Währungsklausel *f*	currency clause	—	clausola monetaria *f*	cláusula monetaria *f*
clausola (I)	Klausel *f*	clause	clause *f*	—	cláusula *f*
clausola cash-and-carry (I)	Cash-and-carry-Klausel *f*	cash-and-carry clause	clause de prix sur place comptant *f*	—	cláusula page y llévatelo *f*
clausola commerciale (I)	Handelsklausel *f*	trade terms	clause commerciale *f*	—	cláusula comercial *f*
clausola del credito documentario (I)	Akkreditivklausel *f*	letter of credit clause	clause de payement par accréditif *f*	—	cláusula de crédito documentario *f*
clausola della nazione più favorita (I)	Meistbegünstigungs-klausel *f*	most-favoured nation clause	clause de la nation la plus favorisée *f*	—	cláusula de la nación más favorecida *f*
clausola dell'indice (I)	Indexklausel *f*	index clause	clause d'indexation *f*	—	cláusula de índice variable *f*
clausola di fornitura (I)	Lieferklausel *f*	delivery clause	clause de livraison *f*	—	cláusula de entrega *f pl*
clausola di garanzia monetaria (I)	Wertsicherungs-klausel *f*	stable value clause	clause de stabilité *f*	—	cláusula de índice variable *f*
clausola di recesso (I)	Rücktrittsklausel *f*	escape clause	clause de résolution du contrat *f*	—	cláusula de arrepentimiento *f*
clausola di revoca (I)	Widerrufsklausel *f*	revocation clause	clause de révocation *f*	—	cláusula revocatoria *f*
clausola di transito (I)	Transitklausel *f*	transit clause	clause de transit *f*	—	cláusula de tránsito *f*
clausola dollaro (I)	Dollarklausel *f*	dollar clause	clause dollar *f*	—	cláusula dólar *f*
clausola monetaria (I)	Währungsklausel *f*	currency clause	clause monétaire *f*	—	cláusula monetaria *f*
clausola tutti i rischi (I)	all-risks-Klausel *f*	all-risks clause	clause d'assurance (contre) tous (les) risques *f*	—	cláusula a todo riesgo *f*
cláusula (Es)	Klausel *f*	clause	clause *f*	clausola *f*	—
cláusula a todo riesgo (Es)	all-risks-Klausel *f*	all-risks clause	clause d'assurance (contre) tous (les) risques *f*	clausola tutti i rischi *f*	—
cláusula comercial (Es)	Handelsklausel *f*	trade terms	clause commerciale *f*	clausola commerciale *f*	—

	D	E	F	I	Es
cláusula de arrepentimiento (Es)	Rücktrittsklausel *f*	escape clause	clause de résolution du contrat *f*	clausola di recesso *f*	—
cláusula de crédito documentario (Es)	Akkreditivklausel *f*	letter of credit clause	clause de payement par accréditif *f*	clausola del credito documentario *f*	—
cláusula de entrega (Es)	Lieferklausel *f*	delivery clause	clause de livraison *f*	clausola di fornitura *f*	—
cláusula de índice variable[1] (Es)	Indexklausel *f*	index clause	clause d'indexation *f*	clausola dell'indice *f*	—
cláusula de índice variable[2] (Es)	Wertsicherungs-klausel *f*	stable value clause	clause de stabilité *f*	clausola di garanzia monetaria *f*	—
cláusula de la nación más favorecida (Es)	Meistbegünstigungs-klausel *f*	most-favoured nation clause	clause de la nation la plus favorisée *f*	clausola della nazione più favorita *f*	—
cláusula de tránsito (Es)	Transitklausel *f*	transit clause	clause de transit *f*	clausola di transito *f*	—
cláusula dólar (Es)	Dollarklausel *f*	dollar clause	clause dollar *f*	clausola dollaro *f*	—
cláusula monetaria (Es)	Währungsklausel *f*	currency clause	clause monétaire *f*	clausola monetaria *f*	—
cláusula page y llévatelo (Es)	Cash-and-carry-Klausel *f*	cash-and-carry clause	clause de prix sur place comptant *f*	clausola cash-and-carry *f*	—
cláusula revocatoria (Es)	Widerrufsklausel *f*	revocation clause	clause de révocation *f*	clausola di revoca *f*	—
clavier (F)	Tastatur *f*	keyboard	—	tastiera *f*	teclado *m*
clearance sale[1] (E)	Räumungsverkauf *m*	—	liquidation des stocks *f*	liquidazione totale *f*	venta total *f*
clearance sale[2] (E)	Ausverkauf *m*	—	soldes *m pl*	svendita *f*	liquidación *f*
clearing unit (E)	Verrechnungs-einheit *f*	—	unité de compte *f*	unità di compensazione *f*	unidad de compensación *f*
client (E)	Auftraggeber *m*	—	commettant *m*	committente *m*	mandante *m*
client (F)	Kunde *m*	customer	—	cliente *m*	cliente *m*
client étranger (F)	Auslandskunde *f*	foreign customer	—	cliente estero *m*	cliente extranjero *m*
client habituel (F)	Stammkunde *f*	regular customer	—	cliente fisso *m*	cliente habitual *m*
cliente (Es)	Kunde *m*	customer	client *m*	cliente *m*	—
cliente (I)	Kunde *m*	customer	client *m*	—	cliente *m*
cliente estero (I)	Auslandskunde *f*	foreign customer	client étranger *m*	—	cliente extranjero *m*
cliente extranjero (Es)	Auslandskunde *f*	foreign customer	client étranger *m*	cliente estero *m*	—
cliente fisso (I)	Stammkunde *f*	regular customer	client habituel *m*	—	cliente habitual *m*
cliente habitual (Es)	Stammkunde *f*	regular customer	client habituel *m*	cliente fisso *m*	—
clientela[1] (Es)	Klientel *f*	clientele	clients *m pl*	clientela *f*	—
clientela[2] (Es)	Kundenkreis *m*	clientele	clientèle *f*	clientela *f*	—
clientela[1] (I)	Klientel *f*	clientele	clients *m pl*	—	clientela *f*
clientela[2] (I)	Kundenkreis *m*	clientele	clientèle *f*	—	clientela *f*
clientela fija (Es)	Kundenstamm *m*	regular customers	clients en portefeuille *m pl*	clientela fissa *f*	—
clientela fissa (I)	Kundenstamm *m*	regular customers	clients en portefeuille *m pl*	—	clientela fija *f*
clientele[1] (E)	Klientel *f*	—	clients *m pl*	clientela *f*	clientela *f*
clientele[2] (E)	Kundschaft *f*	—	clientèle *f*	clientela *f*	clientela *f*
clientele[3] (E)	Kundenkreis *m*	—	clientèle *f*	clientela *f*	clientela *f*
clientèle[1] (F)	Kundschaft *f*	clientele	—	clientela *f*	clientela *f*
clientèle[2] (F)	Kundenkreis *m*	clientele	—	clientela *f*	clientela *f*
clients (F)	Klientel *f*	clientele	—	clientela *f*	clientela *f*
clients en portefeuille (F)	Kundenstamm *m*	regular customers	—	clientela fissa *f*	clientela fija *f*
climat social (F)	Betriebsklima *n*	working conditions and human relations	—	atmosfera di lavoro *f*	ambiente de trabajo *m*
closing balance (E)	Schlußbilanz *f*	—	bilan de clôture *m*	bilancio consuntivo *m*	balance final *m*/ balanza de saldos definitivos *f*
closing price (E)	Schlußkurs *m*	—	dernier cours *m*	quotazione di chiusura *f*	cotización final *f*
clôture annuelle de l'établissement (F)	Betriebsferien *pl*	annual holiday	—	ferie aziendali *f pl*	vacaciones de la empresa *f pl*

	D	E	F	I	Es
clôture annuelle des comptes (F)	Jahresabschluß *m*	annual accounts	—	chiusura d'esercizio *f*	cierre de cuentas *m*
Club (D)	—	club	club *m*	club *m*	club *m*
club (E)	Club *m*	—	club *m*	club *m*	club *m*
club (Es)	Club *m*	club	club *m*	club *m*	—
club (F)	Club *m*	club	—	club *m*	club *m*
club (I)	Club *m*	club	club *m*	—	club *m*
coastal waters (E)	Küstengewässer *n*	—	eaux côtières *f pl*	acque territoriali *f pl*	zona costera *f*
cobertura (Es)	Deckung *f*	cover	couverture *f*	copertura *f*	—
cobertura de seguro (Es)	Versicherungs-schutz *m*	insurance cover	couverture de l'assurana *f*	copertura assicurativa *f*	—
cobros pendientes (Es)	Außenstände *pl*	outstanding debts	dettes actives *f pl*	debiti insoluti *m pl*	—
coche de alquiler (Es)	Leihwagen *m*	hired car	voiture de location *f*	vettura da noleggio *f*	—
coche de empresa (Es)	Firmenwagen *m*	company car	voiture appartenant à l'entreprise *f*	vettura aziendale *f*	—
coche de segunda mano (Es)	Gebrauchtwagen *m*	used car	voiuture d'occasion *f*	automobile usata *f*	—
coche de servicio (Es)	Dienstwagen *m*	official car	voiture de service *f*	vettura di servizio *f*	—
cociente (Es)	Quotient *m*	quotient	quotient *m*	quoziente *m*	—
Code (D)	—	code	code *m*	codice *m*	código *m*
code (F)	Code *m*	code	—	codice *m*	código *m*
code[1] (E)	Code *m*	—	code *m*	codice *m*	código *m*
code[2] (E)	codieren	—	coder	codificare	codificar
code de commerce (F)	Handelsgesetzbuch *n*	Commercial Code	—	codice commerciale *m*	código mercantil *m*
code de l'artisanat (F)	Handwerksordnung *f*	Handicrafts Regulation Act	—	codice dell'artigianato *m*	reglamento del artesanado *m*
code numbers[1] (E)	Kennziffern *pl*	—	indice *m*	cifre d'identificazione *f pl*	cifras índice *f pl*
code numbers[2] (E)	Kennzahlen *pl*	—	numéros de référence *m pl*	numeri d'identificazione *m pl*	números índice *m pl*
code postal (F)	Postleitzahl *f*	postal code	—	codice d'avviamento postale *m*	código postal *m*
coder (F)	codieren	code	—	codificare	codificar
co-determination of labour (E)	Mitbestimmung *f*	—	cogestion *f*	cogestione *f*	cogestión *f*
codeword (E)	Codewort *n*	—	mot de code *m*	parola di codice *f*	palabra de clave *f*
Codewort (D)	—	codeword	mot de code *m*	parola di codice *f*	palabra de clave *f*
codice (I)	Code *m*	code	code *m*	—	código *m*
codice commerciale (I)	Handelsgesetzbuch *n*	Commercial Code	code de commerce *m*	—	código mercantil *m*
codice d'avviamento postale (I)	Postleitzahl *f*	postal code	code postal *m*	—	código postal *m*
codice dell'artigianato (I)	Handwerksordnung *f*	Handicrafts Regulation Act	code de l'artisanat *m*	—	reglamento del artesanado *m*
codieren (D)	—	code	coder	codificare	codificar
codificar (Es)	codieren	code	coder	codificare	—
codificare (I)	codieren	code	coder	—	codificar
código (Es)	Code *m*	code	code *m*	codice *m*	—
código mercantil (Es)	Handelsgesetzbuch *n*	Commercial Code	code de commerce *m*	codice commerciale *m*	—
código postal (Es)	Postleitzahl *f*	postal code	code postal *m*	codice d'avviamento postale *m*	—
coffre-fort[1] (F)	Safe *m*	safe	—	cassetta di sicurezza *f*	caja de seguridad *f*
coffre-fort[2] (F)	Tresor *m*	safe	—	cassaforte *f*	caja fuerte *f*
cogestión (Es)	Mitbestimmung *f*	co-determination of labour	cogestion *f*	cogestione *f*	—
cogestion (F)	Mitbestimmung *f*	co-determination of labour	—	cogestione *f*	cogestión *f*
cogestione (I)	Mitbestimmung *f*	co-determination of labour	cogestion *f*	—	cogestión *f*
cognizioni elementari (I)	Grundkenntnisse *pl*	basic knowledge	connaissances fondamentales *f pl*	—	conocimientos básicos *m pl*

	D	E	F	I	Es
cognizioni professionali (I)	Fachwissen *n*	professional knowledge	connaissances professionnelles *f pl*	—	conocimientos especializados *m pl*
coin (E)	Münze *f*	—	monnaie *f*	moneta *f*	moneda *f*
colaboración (Es)	Mitarbeit *f*	collaboration	collaboration *f*	collaborazione *f*	—
colaborador en el servicio exterior (Es)	Außendienst-mitarbeiter *m*	field staff	personnel du service extérieur *m*	collaboratore del servizio esterno *m*	—
cold storage lorry (E)	Kühlwagen *m*	—	wagon frigorifique *m*	vagone frigorifero *m*	vagón frigorífico *m*
colectivismo (Es)	Kollektivismus *m*	collectivism	collectivisme *m*	collettivismo *m*	—
colectivo (Es)	Kollektiv *n*	collective	collectif *m*	collettivo *m*	—
colis[1] (F)	Paket *n*	parcel	—	pacco *m*	bulto *m*
colis[2] (F)	Frachtstücke *pl*	packages	—	colli *m pl*	fardo *m*
colis de détail (F)	Stückgut *n*	mixed cargo	—	collettame *m*	fardos *m pl*
colis exprès (F)	Eilpaket *n*	express parcel	—	pacco espresso *m*	paquete urgente *m*
colis express (F)	Expressgut *n*	express goods	—	merce spedita per espresso *f*	carga por expreso *f*
collaboration (E)	Mitarbeit *f*	—	collaboration *f*	collaborazione *f*	colaboración *f*
collaboration[1] (F)	Zusammenarbeit *f*	cooperation	—	collaborazione *f*	cooperación *f*
collaboration[2] (F)	Mitarbeit *f*	collaboration	—	collaborazione *f*	colaboración *f*
collaboratore del servizio esterno (I)	Außendienst-mitarbeiter *m*	field staff	personnel du service extérieur *m*	—	colaborador en el servicio exterior *m*
collaborazione[1] (I)	Zusammenarbeit *f*	cooperation	collaboration *f*	—	cooperación *f*
collaborazione[2] (I)	Mitarbeit *f*	collaboration	collaboration *f*	—	colaboración *f*
collapse of prices (E)	Kurs-zusammenbruch *m*	—	chute des cours *f*	crollo delle quotazioni *m*	caída de los cambios *f*
collectif (F)	Kollektiv *n*	collective	—	collettivo *m*	colectivo *m*
collection (E)	Inkasso *n*	—	recouvrement *m*	incasso *m*	encobro *m*
collection des dossiers (F)	Ablage *f*	file	—	archivio *m*	archivo *m*
collective (E)	Kollektiv *n*	—	collectif *m*	collettivo *m*	colectivo *m*
collective advertisement (E)	Sammelwerbung *f*	—	publicité groupée *f*	pubblicità collettiva *f*	publicidad colectiva *f*
collective agreement (E)	Tarifvertrag *m*	—	convention collective *f*	contratto salariale *m*	contrato colectivo *m*
collective consignment (E)	Sammelladung *f*	—	envoi par groupage *m*	carico a collettame *m*	carga colectiva *f*
collective goods (E)	Kollektivgüter *pl*	—	biens collectifs *m pl*	beni collettivi *m pl*	bienes sociales *m pl*
collective property (E)	Gemeinschafts-eigentum *n*	—	propriété collective *f*	proprietà comunitaria *f*	propiedad colectiva *f*
collective transport (E)	Sammeltransport *m*	—	transport de groupage *m*	trasporto a collettame *m*	transporte colectivo *m*
collectivism (E)	Kollektivismus *m*	—	collectivisme *m*	collettivismo *m*	colectivismo *m*
collectivisme (F)	Kollektivismus *m*	collectivism	—	collettivismo *m*	colectivismo *m*
collectivité (F)	Körperschaft *f*	corporation	—	ente *m*	corporación *f*
collegamento telex (I)	Telexanschluß *m*	telex connection	communication de télex *f*	—	comunicación de télex *f*
collettame (I)	Stückgut *n*	mixed cargo	colis de détail *m*	—	fardos *m pl*
collettivismo (I)	Kollektivismus *m*	collectivism	collectivisme *m*	—	colectivismo *m*
collettivo (I)	Kollektiv *n*	collective	collectif *m*	—	colectivo *m*
colli (I)	Frachtstücke *pl*	packages	colis *m*	—	fardo *m*
collocamento[1] (I)	Plazierung *f*	placing	placement *m*	—	colocación *f*
collocamento[2] (I)	Placierung *f*	placement	placement *m*	—	colocación
collocamento dell'inserzione (I)	Anzeigenplazierung *f*	placing of an advertisement	disposition de l'annonce *f*	—	colocación del anuncio *f*
collocare (I)	plazieren	place	placer	—	colocar
colloquio[1] (I)	Besprechung *f*	discussion	conférence *f*	—	conferencia *f*
colloquio[2] (I)	Unterredung *f*	discussion	entretien *m*	—	conversación *f*
colloquio di vendita (I)	Verkaufsgespräch *n*	sales talk	conversation de vente *f*	—	conversación de venta *f*
colloquio personale (I)	persönliches Gespräch *n*	personal conversation	conversation personnelle *f*	—	conversación personal *f*

	D	E	F	I	Es
colocación[1] (Es)	Plazierung *f*	placing	placement *m*	collocamento *m*	—
colocación[2] (Es)	Placierung *f*	placement	placement *m*	collocamento *m*	—
colocación del anuncio (Es)	Anzeigenplazierung *f*	placing of an advertisement	disposition de l'annonce *f*	collocamento dell'inserzione *m*	—
colocar[1] (Es)	plazieren	place	placer	collocare	—
colocar[2] (Es)	placieren	place	placer	collocare	—
colposo (I)	schuldhaft	culpable	coupable	—	culpable
comanditario (Es)	Kommanditist *m*	limited partner	commanditaire *m*	socio accomandante *m*	—
combatting rising costs (E)	Kostendämpfung *f*	—	réduction des coûts *f*	contenimento dei costi *m*	disminución de costes *f*
combustible (Es)	Treibstoff *m*	fuel	carburant *m*	carburante *m*	—
combustión (Es)	Verbrennung *f*	incineration	combustion *f*	combustione *f*	—
combustion (F)	Verbrennung *f*	incineration	—	combustione *f*	combustión *f*
combustione (I)	Verbrennung *f*	incineration	combustion *f*	—	combustión *f*
come convenuto (I)	vereinbarungsgemäß	as agreed	comme convenu	—	según lo acordado
comerciable (Es)	marktfähig	marketable	vendable	smerciabile	—
comercialización de las materias primas (Es)	Rohstoff-vermarktung *f*	raw materials marketing	commercialisation des matières premières *f*	smercio delle materie prime *m*	—
comercialización directa (Es)	Direct-Marketing *n*	direct marketing	stratégie des ventes directes *f*	marketing in prima persona *m*	—
comercializar (Es)	vermarkten	market	commercialiser	lanciare sul mercato	—
comerciante[1] (Es)	Händler *m*	trader	commerçant *m*	commerciante *m*	—
comerciante[2] (Es)	Kaufmann *m*	businessman	négociant *m*	commerciante *m*	—
comerciante particular (Es)	Einzelhandels-kaufmann *m*	retail merchant	détaillant *m*	commerciante al dettaglio *m*	—
comerciantes (Es)	Kaufleute *pl*	businessmen	commerçants *m pl*	commercianti *m pl*	—
comercio[1] (Es)	Handel *m*	trade	commerce *m*	commercio *m*	—
comercio[2] (Es)	Handelsverkehr *m*	commercial intercourse	échanges commerciaux *m pl*	circolazione delle merci *f*	—
comercio[3] (Es)	Kommerz *m*	commerce	commerce *m*	commercio *m*	—
comercio al por menor (Es)	Einzelhandel *m*	retail trade	commerce de détail *m*	commercio al dettaglio *m*	—
comercio ambulante (Es)	ambulantes Gewerbe *n*	itinerant trade	commerce ambulant *m*	commercio ambulante *m*	—
comercio de comisión (Es)	Kommissionshandel	commission trade	commissionnage *m*	commercio di commissione *m*	—
comercio de exportación (Es)	Exporthandel *m*	export trade	commerce d'exportation *m*	esportazioni *f pl*	—
comercio de importación (Es)	Importhandel *m*	import trade	commerce d'importation *m*	commercio delle importazioni *m*	—
comercio de tránsito (Es)	Transithandel *m*	transit trade	commerce de transit *m*	commercio di transito *m*	—
comercio de ultramar (Es)	Überseehandel *m*	overseas trade	commerce d'outre-mer *m*	commercio d'oltremare *m*	—
comercio este-oeste (Es)	Ost-West-Handel *m*	East-West trade	commerce Est-Ouest *m*	scambio est-ovest *m*	—
comercio exterior (Es)	Außenhandel *m*	foreign trade	commerce extérieur *m*	commercio estero *m*	—
comercio interior (Es)	Binnenhandel *m*	domestic trade	commerce intérieur *m*	commercio nazionale *m*	—
comercio internacional (Es)	Welthandel *m*	world trade	commerce mondial *m*	commercio mondiale *m*	—
comercio mayorista (Es)	Großhandel *m*	wholesale trade	commerce de gros *m*	commercio all'ingrosso *m*	—
comida de trabajo (Es)	Arbeitsessen *n*	working lunch	déjeuner de travail *m*	pranzo di lavoro *m*	—
comisión[1] (Es)	Kommission *f*	commission	commission *f*	commissione *f*	—
comisión[2] (Es)	Provision *f*	commission	commission *f*	provvigione *f*	—
comisión al comprador (Es)	Käuferprovision *f*	buyer's commission	commission d'acheteur *f*	provvigione dell'acquirente *f*	—

	D	E	F	I	Es
comisión de apertura de crédito (Es)	Kreditprovision *f*	credit commission	frais de commissions d'ouverture de crédit *m pl*	provvigione di credito *f*	—
comisión de garantía (Es)	Delkredereprovision *f*	del credere commission	commission ducroire *f*	provvigione dello star del credere *f*	—
comisionista (Es)	Kommissionär *m*	commission agent	commissionnaire *m*	commissionario *m*	—
comisión sobre la cifra de ventas (Es)	Umsatzprovision *f*	commission on turnover	commission sur le chiffre d'affaires *f*	provvigione sul fatturato *f*	—
comisión sobre la venta (Es)	Verkäuferprovision *f*	sales commission	commission sur les ventes *f*	provvigione del venditore *f*	—
comité directeur (F)	Vorstand *m*	board	—	consiglio di amministrazione *m*	consejo de dirección *m*
commande[1] (F)	Bestellung *f*	order	—	ordinazione *f*	pedido *m*
commande[2] (F)	Auftrag *m*	order	—	ordine *m*	pedido *m*
commande consécutive (F)	Folgeauftrag *m*	follow-up order	—	ordine successivo *m*	orden sucesivo *f*
commande d'exportation (F)	Exportauftrag *m*	export order	—	ordine d'esportazione *m*	pedido destinado a la exportación *m*
commande directe (F)	Direktbestellung *f*	direct ordering	—	ordinazione diretta *f*	pedido directo *m*
commande préalable (F)	Vorbestellung *f*	reservation	—	ordinazione anticipata *f*	pedidio anticipado *m*
commanditaire (F)	Kommanditist *m*	limited partner	—	socio accomandante *m*	comanditario *m*
commandité (F)	Komplementär *m*	general partner	—	socio accomandatario *m*	socio colectivo *m*
comme convenu (F)	vereinbarungsgemäß	as agreed	—	come convenuto	según lo acordado
comment (E)	Stellungnahme *f*	—	prise de position *f*	presa di posizione *f*	dictamen *m*
commentaire de presse (F)	Pressemitteilung *f*	press release	—	comunicazione stampa *f*	remitido a la prensa *m*
commerçant (F)	Händler *m*	trader	—	commerciante *m*	comerciante *m*
commerçant détaillant (F)	Einzelhändler *m*	retailer	—	dettagliante *m*	minorista *m*
commerçants (F)	Kaufleute *pl*	businessmen	—	commercianti *m pl*	comerciantes *m pl*
commerce (E)	Kommerz *m*	—	commerce *m*	commercio *m*	comercio *m*
commerce[1] (F)	Kommerz *m*	commerce	—	commercio *m*	comercio *m*
commerce[2] (F)	Handel *m*	trade	—	commercio *m*	comercio *m*
commerce ambulant (F)	ambulantes Gewerbe *n*	itinerant trade	—	commercio ambulante *m*	comercio ambulante *m*
commerce de change (F)	Sortenhandel *m*	dealing in foreign notes and coins	—	cambio valuta *m*	operación de moneda extranjera *f*
commerce de détail (F)	Einzelhandel *m*	retail trade	—	commercio al dettaglio *m*	comercio al por menor *m*
commerce de gros (F)	Großhandel *m*	wholesale trade	—	commercio all'ingrosso *m*	comercio mayorista *m*
commerce des valeurs mobilières (F)	Effektengeschäft *n*	securities business	—	operazione su titoli *f*	operación de valores *f*
commerce de transit (F)	Transithandel *m*	transit trade	—	commercio di transito *m*	comercio de tránsito *m*
commerce de vente au détail par correspondance (F)	Versandhandel *m*	mail order business	—	vendita per corrispondenza *f*	venta por correspondencia *f*
commerce d'exportation (F)	Exporthandel *m*	export trade	—	esportazioni *f pl*	comercio de exportación *m*
commerce d'importation (F)	Importhandel *m*	import trade	—	commercio delle importazioni *m*	comercio de importación *m*
commerce d'opérations à terme (F)	Warentermin-handel *m*	commodity forward dealing	—	operazioni a termine su merci *f pl*	tráfico de futuro *m*
commerce d'outre-mer (F)	Überseehandel *m*	overseas trade	—	commercio d'oltremare *m*	comercio de ultramar *m*
commerce Est-Ouest (F)	Ost-West-Handel *m*	East-West trade	—	scambio est-ovest *m*	comercio este-oeste *m*
commerce extérieur (F)	Außenhandel *m*	foreign trade	—	commercio estero *m*	comercio exterior *m*
commerce intérieur (F)	Binnenhandel *m*	domestic trade	—	commercio nazionale *m*	comercio interior *m*
commerce libre (F)	Freihandel *m*	free trade	—	scambio libero *m*	librecambio *m*

	D	E	F	I	Es
commerce mondial (F)	Welthandel *m*	world trade	—	commercio mondiale *m*	comercio internacional *m*
commercial agency (E)	Handelsvertretung *f*	—	représentation commerciale *f*	rappresentanza commerciale *f*	representación comercial *f*
commercial agent[1] (E)	Handlungsbevollmächtigter *m*	—	personne ayant le pouvoir commercial *f*	mandatario commerciale *m*	apoderado especial *m*
commercial agent[2] (E)	Handelsvertreter *m*	—	représentant de commerce *m*	rappresentante commerciale *m*	representante comercial *m*
commercial apprenticeship (E)	kaufmännische Lehre *f*	—	apprentissage commercial *m*	apprendistato di commercio *m*	aprendizaje comercial *m*
commercial bank (E)	Kreditbank *f*	—	banque de crédit *f*	banca di credito *f*	banco de crédito *m*
commercial bill (E)	Warenwechsel *m*	—	traite commerciale *f*	cambiale commerciale *f*	letra comercial *f*
Commercial Code (E)	Handelsgesetzbuch *n*	—	code de commerce *m*	codice commerciale *m*	código mercantil *m*
commercial intercourse (E)	Handelsverkehr *m*	—	échanges commerciaux *m pl*	circolazione delle merci *f*	comercio *m*
commercial letter of credit (E)	Handelskreditbrief *m*	—	lettre de crédit commercial *f*	lettera di credito commerciale *f*	carta de crédito comercial *f*
commercialisation (F)	Absatzwirtschaft *f*	marketing	—	marketing *m*	economía de distribución *f*
commercialisation des matières premières (F)	Rohstoffvermarktung *f*	raw materials marketing	—	smercio delle materie prime *m*	comercialización de las materias primas *f*
commercialiser (F)	vermarkten	market	—	lanciare sul mercato	comercializar
commercial policy (E)	Handelspolitik *f*	—	politique commerciale *f*	politica commerciale *f*	política comercial *f*
commercial register (E)	Handelsregister *n*	—	registre du commerce *m*	registro commerciale *m*	registro mercantil *m*
commerciante[1] (I)	Kaufmann *m*	businessman	négociant *m*	—	comerciante *m*
commerciante[2] (I)	Händler *m*	trader	commerçant *m*	—	comerciante *m*
commerciante al dettaglio (I)	Einzelhandelskaufmann *m*	retail merchant	détaillant *m*	—	comerciante particular *m*
commercianti (I)	Kaufleute *pl*	businessmen	commerçants *m pl*	—	comerciantes *m pl*
commercio[1] (I)	Handel *m*	trade	commerce *m*	—	comercio *m*
commercio[2] (I)	Gewerbe *n*	trade/industry/craft	activité professionnelle *f*/ industrie *f*/artisanat *m*	—	industria *f*/ comercio *m*/ artesanía *f*
commercio[3] (I)	Kommerz *m*	commerce	commerce *m*	—	comercio *m*
commercio al dettaglio (I)	Einzelhandel *m*	retail trade	commerce de détail *m*	—	comercio al por menor *m*
commercio all'ingrosso (I)	Großhandel *m*	wholesale trade	commerce de gros *m*	—	comercio mayorista *m*
commercio ambulante (I)	ambulantes Gewerbe *n*	itinerant trade	commerce ambulant *m*	—	comercio ambulante *m*
commercio azionario (I)	Aktienhandel *m*	dealing in shares	négociation des actions *f*	—	contratación de acciones *f*
commercio dei cambi (I)	Devisenverkehr *m*	foreign exchange dealings	mouvement des devises *m*	—	tráfico de divisas *m*
commercio delle divise (I)	Devisenhandel *m*	foreign exchange dealings	marché des changes *m*	—	operaciones de divisas *f pl*
commercio delle importazioni (I)	Importhandel *m*	import trade	commerce d'importation *m*	—	comercio de importación *m*
commercio di commissione (I)	Kommissionshandel	commission trade	commissionnage *m*	—	comercio de comisión *m*
commercio di transito (I)	Transithandel *m*	transit trade	commerce de transit *m*	—	comercio de tránsito *m*
commercio d'oltremare (I)	Überseehandel *m*	overseas trade	commerce d'outre-mer *m*	—	comercio de ultramar *m*
commercio estero (I)	Außenhandel *m*	foreign trade	commerce extérieur *m*	—	comercio exterior *m*
commercio in borsa (I)	Börsenhandel *m*	stock exchange transactions	transactions boursiaires *f pl*	—	negociación bursátil *f*
commercio mondiale (I)	Welthandel *m*	world trade	commerce mondial *m*	—	comercio internacional *m*
commercio nazionale (I)	Binnenhandel *m*	domestic trade	commerce intérieur *m*	—	comercio interior *m*

	D	E	F	I	Es
commettant (F)	Auftraggeber *m*	client	—	committente *m*	mandante *m*
commissaire aux comptes (F)	Rechnungsprüfer *m*	auditor	—	revisore dei conti *m*	revisor contable *m*
commission[1] (E)	Kommission *f*	—	commission *f*	commissione *f*	comisión *f*
commission[2] (E)	Provision *f*	—	commission *f*	provvigione *f*	comisión *f*
commission[1] (F)	Provision *f*	commission	—	provvigione *f*	comisión *f*
commission[2] (F)	Kommission *f*	commission	—	commissione *f*	comisión *f*
commission agent (E)	Kommissionär *m*	—	commissionnaire *m*	commissionario *m*	comisionista *m*
commissionario (I)	Kommissionär *m*	commission agent	commissionnaire *m*	—	comisionista *m*
commission business (E)	Kommissions-geschäft *n*	—	affaire en commission	operazione di commissione *f*	operación de comisión *f*
commission d'acheteur (F)	Käuferprovision *f*	buyer's commission	—	provvigione dell'acquirente *f*	comisión al comprador *f*
commission ducroire (F)	Delkredereprovision *f*	del credere commission	—	provvigione dello star del credere *f*	comisión de garantía *f*
commissione (I)	Kommission *f*	commission	commission *f*	—	comisión *f*
commissione bancaria (I)	Bankenaufsicht *f*	public supervision of banking	contrôle des banques *m*	—	supervisión bancaria *f*
commission guarantee (E)	Provisionsgarantie *f*	—	garantie de commission *f*	garanzia di provvigione *f*	garantía de comisión *f*
commissioni bancarie (I)	Bankspesen *pl*	bank charges	frais de banque *m pl*	—	gastos bancarios *m pl*
commissionnage[1] (F)	Kommissionshandel	commission trade	—	commercio di commissione *m*	comercio de comisión *m*
commissionnaire[2] (F)	Kommissionär *m*	commission agent	—	commissionario *m*	comisionista *m*
commissionnaire de transport (F)	Spediteur *m*	forwarder	—	spedizioniere *m*	expeditor *m*
commission on turnover (E)	Umsatzprovision *f*	—	commission sur le chiffre d'affaires *f*	provvigione sul fatturato *f*	comisión sobre la cifra de ventas *f*
commission payment (E)	Provisionszahlung *f*	—	payement de commission *m*	pagamento di provvigione *m*	pago de comisión *m*
commission sur le chiffre d'affaires (F)	Umsatzprovision *f*	commission on turnover	—	provvigione sul fatturato *f*	comisión sobre la cifra de ventas *f*
commission sur les ventes (F)	Verkäuferprovision *f*	sales commission	—	provvigione del venditore *f*	comisión sobre la venta *f*
commission trade (E)	Kommissionshandel	—	commissionnage *m*	commercio di commissione *m*	comercio de comisión *m*
commitment fee (E)	Bereitstellungs-kosten *pl*	—	coûts administratifs *m pl*	spese di stanziamento *f pl*	gastos fijos *m pl*
commitment interests (E)	Bereitstellungs-zinsen *pl*	—	intérêts de disponibilité *m pl*	interessi per lo stanziamento *m pl*	interés de disponibilidad *m*
committente[1] (I)	Besteller *m*	customer	acheteur *m*	—	demandante *m*
committente[2] (I)	Auftraggeber *m*	client	commettant *m*	—	mandante *m*
commodity exchange (E)	Warenbörse *f*	—	bourse de marchandises *f*	borsa merci *f*	bolsa de mercancías *f*
commodity forward dealing (E)	Warentermin-handel *m*	—	commerce d'opérations à terme *m*	operazioni a termine su merci *f pl*	tráfico de futuro *m*
commodity forward exchange (E)	Warenterminbörse *f*	—	bourse d'opérations à livrer *f*	borsa merci a termine *f*	bolsa de mercancías a plazo *f*
commodity forward transaction (E)	Warentermin-geschäft *n*	—	opération de livraison à terme *f*	operazione a termine su merci *f*	operación a plazo de mercancías *f*
commodity market (E)	Rohstoffmarkt *m*	—	marchés des matières premières *m*	mercato delle materie prime *m*	mercado de materias primas *m*
common business-oriented language (E)	Programmier-sprache *f*	—	langage de programmation *m*	linguaggio di programmazione *m*	lenguaje de programación *m*
common market (E)	gemeinsamer Markt *m*	—	marché commun *m*	mercato comune *m*	mercado común *m*
communauté économique (F)	Wirtschafts-gemeinschaft *f*	economic community	—	comunità economica *f*	comunidad económica *f*
Communauté Européenne (F)	Europäische Gemeinschaft, EG *f*	European Community	—	Comunità Europea CEE *f*	Comunidad Europea, C.E. *f*
commune[1] (F)	Kommune *f*	municipality	—	comune *m*	municipalidad *f*
commune[2] (F)	Gemeinde *f*	community	—	comune *m*	comunidad *f*

	D	E	F	I	Es
communication de télex (F)	Telexanschluß *m*	telex connection	—	collegamento telex *m*	comunicación de télex *f*
community (E)	Gemeinde *f*	—	commune *f*	comune *m*	comunidad *f*
community of heirs (E)	Erbengemeinschaft *f*	—	communauté d'héritiers *f*	comunità degli eredi *f*	comunidad sucesoria *f*
compagnia armatoriale (I)	Reederei *f*	shipping company	société d'armateurs *f*	—	compañía naviera *f*
compagnia di assicurazione (I)	Versicherungs-gesellschaft *f*	insurance company	société d'assurance *f*	—	sociedad de seguros *f*
compañía asociada (Es)	Schwester-gesellschaft *f*	affiliated company	société affiliée *f*	consorella *f*	—
compañía distribuidora (Es)	Vertriebsfirma *f*	distributor	distributeur *m*	ditta di distribuzione *f*	—
compañía naviera (Es)	Reederei *f*	shipping company	société d'armateurs *f*	compagnia armatoriale *f*	—
Companies Act (E)	Aktiengesetz *n*	—	loi sur les sociétés par actions *f*	legge sulle società per azioni *f*	ley sobre sociedades anónimas *f*
company (E)	Firma *f*	—	entreprise *f*	impresa *f*	empresa *f*
company account (E)	Firmenkonto *n*	—	compte de maison *m*	conto intestato ad una ditta *m*	cuenta de la empresa *f*
company address (E)	Firmenanschrift *f*	—	adresse de la maison *f*	indirizzo della ditta *m*	dirección de la empresa *f*
company car (E)	Firmenwagen *m*	—	voiture appartenant à l'entreprise *f*	vettura aziendale *f*	coche de empresa *m*
company law (E)	Aktienrecht *n*	—	loi sur les sociétés anonymes *f pl*	diritto azionario *m*	derecho de socie-dades anónimas *m*
company limited by shares (E)	Kapitalgesellschaft *f*	—	société de capitaux *f*	società di capitale *f*	sociedad capitalista *f*
company name (E)	Firmenname *m*	—	nom de la maison *m*	denominazione *f*/ ragione sociale *f*	razón social *f*
company objective (E)	Unternehmensziel *n*	—	objectif de l'entreprise *m*	obiettivo imprenditoriale *m*	objetivo empresarial *m*
company's bank (E)	Hausbank *f*	—	banque habituelle *f*	banca di preferenza *f*	banco particular *m*
company's name plate (E)	Firmenschild *n*	—	enseigne commerciale *f*	insegna dell'impresa *f*	letrero de establecimiento *m*
comparación (Es)	Vergleich *m*	comparison	comparaison *f*	confronto *m*	—
comparación de las cotizaciones (Es)	Kursvergleich *m*	comparison of prices	comparaison des cours *f*	confronto dei corsi *m*	—
comparación de ramos (Es)	Branchenvergleich *m*	trade comparison	comparaison des différentes branches *f*	comparazione delle categorie *f*	—
comparación entre los resultados efectivos y las previsiones (Es)	Soll/Ist-Vergleich *m*	comparison of estimates with results	comparaison entre les résultats effectifs et les prévisions *f*	confronto costi calcolati/costi reali *m*	—
comparaison (F)	Vergleich *m*	comparison	—	confronto *m*	comparación *f*
comparaison des cours (F)	Kursvergleich *m*	comparison of prices	—	confronto dei corsi *m*	comparación de las cotizaciones *f*
comparaison des différentes branches (F)	Branchenvergleich *m*	trade comparison	—	comparazione delle categorie *f*	comparación de ramos *f*
comparaison entre les résultats effectifs et les prévisions (F)	Soll/Ist-Vergleich *m*	comparison of estimates with results	—	confronto costi calcolati/costi reali *m*	comparación entre los resultados efectivos y las previsiones *f*
comparative advertising (E)	vergleichende Werbung *f*	—	publicité comparative *f*	pubblicità comparativa *f*	publicidad comparativa *f*
comparazione delle categorie (I)	Branchenvergleich *m*	trade comparison	comparaison des différentes branches *f*	—	comparación de ramos *f*
comparison (E)	Vergleich *m*	—	comparaison *f*	confronto *m*	comparación *f*
comparison of estimates with results (E)	Soll/Ist-Vergleich *m*	—	comparaison entre les résultats effectifs et les prévisions *f*	confronto costi calcolati/costi reali *m*	comparación entre los resultados efectivos y las previsiones *f*
comparison of prices (E)	Kursvergleich *m*	—	comparaison des cours *f*	confronto dei corsi *m*	comparación de las cotizaciones *f*
compensación[1] (Es)	Verrechnung *f*	compensation	compensation *f*	compensazione *f*	—
compensación[2] (Es)	Kompensation *f*	compensation	compensation *f*	compensazione *f*	—
compensación[3] (Es)	Aufrechnung *f*	set-off	compensation *f*	compensazione *f*	—
compensation[1] (E)	Kompensation *f*	—	compensation *f*	compensazione *f*	compensación *f*

	D	E	F	I	Es
compensation[2] (E)	Entschädigung *f*	—	indemnité *f*	indennità *f*	indemnización *f*
compensation[3] (E)	Verrechnung *f*	—	compensation *f*	compensazione *f*	compensación *f*
compensation[1] (F)	Verrechnung *f*	compensation	—	compensazione *f*	compensación *f*
compensation[2] (F)	Aufrechnung *f*	set-off	—	compensazione *f*	compensación *f*
compensation[3] (F)	Kompensation *f*	compensation	—	compensazione *f*	compensación *f*
compensation financière (F)	Finanzausgleich *m*	financial equalization	—	compensazione finanziaria *f*	ajuste financiero *m*
compensation for loss suffered (E)	Schadensersatz *m*	—	dommages-intérêts *m pl*	risarcimento danni *m*	indemnización *f*
compensation fund (E)	Ausgleichsfonds *m*	—	fonds de compensation *m*	fondo di compensazione *m*	fondo de compensación *m*
compensation offer (E)	Abfindungsangebot *n*	—	offre d'indemnité *f*	offerta d'indennità *f*	oferta de indemnización *f*
compensation payment (E)	Ausgleichszahlung *f*	—	payement pour solde de compte *m*	conguaglio *m*	pago de compensación *m*
compensazione[1] (I)	Verrechnung *f*	compensation	compensation *f*	—	compensación *f*
compensazione[2] (I)	Kompensation *f*	compensation	compensation *f*	—	compensación *f*
compensazione[3] (I)	Aufrechnung *f*	set-off	compensation *f*	—	compensación *f*
compensazione finanziaria (I)	Finanzausgleich *m*	financial equalization	compensation financière *f*	—	ajuste financiero *m*
compenso straordinario (I)	Sondervergütung *f*	special remuneration	rémunération spéciale *f*	—	gratificación *f*
competence (E)	Kompetenz *f*	—	compétence *f*	competenza *f*	competencia *f*
compétence[1] (F)	Kompetenz *f*	competence	—	competenza *f*	competencia *f*
compétence[2] (F)	Sachkenntnis *f*	know-how	—	competenza *f*	conocimiento de causa *m*
compétence législative (F)	Gesetzgebungs-hoheit *f*	legislative sovereignty	—	sovranità legislativa *f*	soberanía legislativa *f*
competencia[1] (Es)	Konkurrenz *f*	competition	concurrence *f*	concorrenza *f*	—
competencia[2] (Es)	Kompetenz *f*	competence	compétence *f*	competenza *f*	—
competencia[3] (Es)	Wettbewerb *m*	competition	compétition *f*	concorrenza *f*	—
competencia de precios (Es)	Preiswettbewerb *m*	competition in prices	concurrence des prix *f*	competizione dei prezzi *f*	—
competencia desleal (Es)	unlauterer Wettbewerb *m*	unfair competition	concurrence déloyale *f*	concorrenza sleale *f*	—
competencia viable (Es)	funktionsfähiger Wettbewerb *m*	workable competition	concurrence viable *f*	concorrenza perfetta *f*	—
competenza[1] (I)	Sachkenntnis *f*	know-how	compétence *f*	—	conocimiento de causa *m*
competenza[2] (I)	Kompetenz *f*	competence	compétence *f*	—	competencia *f*
competición de vendedores (Es)	Verkäufer-wettbewerb *m*	sellers competition	compétition des vendeurs *f*	concorrenza dei venditori *f*	—
competidor (Es)	Konkurrent *m*	competitor	concurrent *m*	concorrente *m*	—
competing firm (E)	Konkurrenzfirma *f*	—	maison concurrente *f*	ditta concorrente *f*	empresa competidora *f*
compétition (F)	Wettbewerb *m*	competition	—	concorrenza *f*	competencia *f*
competition[1] (E)	Wettbewerb *m*	—	compétition *f*	concorrenza *f*	competencia *f*
competition[2] (E)	Konkurrenz *f*	—	concurrence *f*	concorrenza *f*	competencia *f*
compétition des vendeurs (F)	Verkäufer-wettbewerb *m*	sellers competition	—	concorrenza dei venditori *f*	competición de vendedores *f*
competition in prices (E)	Preiswettbewerb *m*	—	concurrence des prix *f*	competizione dei prezzi *f*	competencia de precios *f*
competition policy (E)	Wettbewerbspolitik *f*	—	politique de concurrence *f*	politica concorrenziale *f*	política de competencia *f*
competitive advantage (E)	Wettbewerbs-vorteil *m*	—	avantage de concurrence *m*	vantaggio concorrenziale *m*	ventaja de competencia *f*
competitiveness (E)	Wettbewerbs-fähigkeit *f*	—	compétitivité *f*	competitività *f*	competitividad *f*
competitive situation (E)	Konkurrenzsituation *f*	—	situation de concurrence *f*	situazione concorrenziale *f*	situación de competencia *f*
competitividad (Es)	Wettbewerbs-fähigkeit *f*	competitiveness	compétitivité *f*	competitività *f*	—

	D	E	F	I	Es
competitività (I)	Wettbewerbs-fähigkeit *f*	competitiveness	compétitivité *f*	—	competitividad *f*
compétitivité (F)	Wettbewerbs-fähigkeit *f*	competitiveness	—	competitività *f*	competitividad *f*
competitor[1] (E)	Konkurrent *m*	—	concurrent *m*	concorrente *m*	competidor *m*
competitor[2] (E)	Mitbewerber *m*	—	concurrent *m*	competitore *m*	contendiente *m*
competitore (I)	Mitbewerber *m*	competitor	concurrent *m*	—	contendiente *m*
competizione dei prezzi (I)	Preiswettbewerb *m*	competition in prices	concurrence des prix *f*	—	competencia de precios *f*
compettive undertaking (E)	Konkurrenz-unternehmen *n*	—	entreprise concurrente *f*	impresa concorrente *f*	empresa competitoria *f*
compilazione del bilancio (I)	Budgetierung *f*	budgeting	établissement du budget *m*	—	establecimiento del presupuesto *m*
complaint[1] (E)	Reklamation *f*	—	réclamation *f*	reclamo *m*	reclamación *f*
complaint[2] (E)	Beschwerde *f*	—	réclamation *f*	protesta *f*	recurso *m*
compleanno (I)	Geburtstag *m*	birthday	anniversaire *m*	—	cumpleaños *m*
complementary goods (E)	komplementäre Güter *pl*	—	produits de complément *m pl*	beni complementari *m pl*	bienes com-plementarios *m pl*
completamento (I)	Fertigstellung *f*	completion	achèvement *m*	—	terminación total *f*
completion (E)	Fertigstellung *f*	—	achèvement *m*	completamento *m*	terminación total *f*
compliance (E)	Erfüllung *f*	—	acquittement *m*	adempimento *m*	cumplimiento *m*
componenti essenziali (I)	wesentliche Bestandteile *pl*	integral parts	parties constitutives essentielles *f pl*	—	partes integrantes esencial *f pl*
comportamiento de compra (Es)	Kaufverhalten *n*	purchase pattern	comportement d'achat *m*	filosofia d'acquisto *f*	—
comportamiento racional (Es)	Rationalverhalten *n*	rational behaviour	comportement rationnel *m*	atteggiamento razionale *m*	—
comportement d'achat (F)	Kaufverhalten *n*	purchase pattern	—	filosofia d'acquisto *f*	comportamiento de compra *m*
comportement rationnel (F)	Rationalverhalten *n*	rational behaviour	—	atteggiamento razionale *m*	comportamiento racional *m*
composition proceedings (E)	Vergleichsverfahren *n*	—	procédure de conciliation *f*	procedura di concordato *f*	procedimiento conciliatorio *m*
composizione dell'assortimento (I)	Sortiments-gestaltung *f*	assortment structuring	structure du sortiment *f*	—	configuración del surtido *f*
compound interest (E)	Zinseszins *m*	—	intérêt composé *m*	interessi composti *m pl*	interés compuesto *m*
compra[1] (Es)	Ankauf *m*	purchase	achat *m*	acquisto *m*	—
compra[2] (Es)	Einkauf *m*	purchase	achat *m*	acquisto *m*	—
compra[3] (Es)	Kauf *m*	purchase	achat *m*	acquisto *m*	—
compra a plazo (Es)	Ratenkauf *m*	hire-purchase transaction	achat à tempérament *m*	acquisto a rate *m*	—
compra a plazos (Es)	Zielkauf *m*	purchase on credit	achat à terme *m*	acquisto a termine *m*	—
compra a prueba (Es)	Kauf auf Probe *m*	sale on approval	achat à l'éssai *m*	acquisto a titolo di prova *m*	—
compra de crédito (Es)	Kreditkauf *m*	credit purchase	achat à crédit *m*	acquisto a credito *m*	—
compra de sustitución (Es)	Ersatzkauf *m*	substitute purchase	achat de remplacement *m*	acquisto di compensazione *m*	—
comprador (Es)	Einkäufer *m*	buyer	acheteur *m*	acquirente *m*	—
comprador al por mayor (Es)	Großabnehmer *m*	bulk buyer	acheteur en gros *m*	acquirente all'ingrosso *m*	—
comprador final (Es)	Endabnehmer *m*	ultimate buyer	preneur final *m*	acquirente finale *m*	—
compra espontánea (Es)	Impulskauf *m*	impulse buying	achat d'impulsion *m*	acquisto impulsivo *m*	—
compra intermediaria (Es)	Zwischenabnahme *f*	intermediate purchase	achat intermédiaire *m*	acquisto intermediario *m*	—
compra para sostener precios (Es)	Stützungskauf *m*	support buying	achat de soutien *m*	acquisto di sostegno *m*	—
comprar[1] (Es)	einkaufen	buy	acheter	acquistare	—
comprar[2] (Es)	kaufen	buy	acheter	acquistare	—
compras de intervención (Es)	Interventionskäufe *pl*	intervention buying	achats d'intervention *m pl*	acquisti d'intervento *m pl*	—
compras de sostén (Es)	Kurspflege *f*	price nursing	soutien des cours *m*	sostegno dei corsi *m*	—

	D	E	F	I	Es
compras especulativas (Es)	Meinungskäufe *pl*	speculative buying	achats spéculatifs *m pl*	acquisti speculativi *m pl*	—
comprehensive insurance (E)	Kaskoversicherung *f*	—	assurance tous risques *f*	assicurazione corpi del ramo trasporto *f*	seguro de casco *m*
compromiso (Es)	Engagement *n*	engagement/ commitment	engagement *m*	impegno *m*	—
comproprietà (I)	Miteigentum *n*	co-ownership	copropriété *f*	—	copropiedad *f*
comproprietario di quota ideale (I)	Bruchteils-eigentümer *m*	co-owner	copropriétaire d'une quote-part *m*	—	copropietario de bienes indivisos *m*
comptabilisation économique (F)	Wirtschafts-rechnung *f*	economic account	—	conto economico *m*	contabilización económica *f*
comptabilité¹ (F)	Rechnungswesen *n*	accounting system	—	ragioneria *f*	contabilidad *f*
comptabilité² (F)	Buchhaltung *f*	accounting	—	contabilità *f*	contabilidad *f*
comptabilité³ (F)	Buchführung *f*	bookkeeping	—	contabilità *f*	contabilidad *f*
comptabilité en partie double (F)	doppelte Buchführung *f*	double entry bookkeeping	—	contabilità a partita doppia *f*	contabilidad por doble partida *f*
comptabilité financière (F)	Finanzbuchhaltung *f*	financial accounting	—	contabilità finanziaria *f*	contabilidad financiera *f*
comptabilité national (F)	Volkswirtschaftliche Gesamtrechnung *f*	national accounting	—	contabilità nazionale *f*	contabilidad nacional *f*
comptable (F)	Buchhalter *m*	bookkeeper	—	ragioniere *m*	tenedor de libros *m*
comptant¹ (F)	bar	cash	—	in contanti	al contado
comptant² (F)	in bar	in cash	—	in contanti	en efectivo
compte (F)	Konto *n*	account	—	conto *m*	cuenta *f*
compte anonyme (F)	Nummernkonto *n*	numbered account	—	conto cifrato *m*	cuenta cifrada *f*
compte bloqué¹ (F)	Sperrkonto *n*	blocked account	—	conto vincolato *m*	fondos bloqueados *m pl*
compte bloqué² (F)	gesperrtes Konto *n*	blocked account	—	conto bloccato *m*	cuenta congelada *f*
compte chèque postal (F)	Postscheckkonto *n*	(postal) giro account	—	conto corrente postale *m*	cuenta corriente postal *f*
compte courant¹ (F)	laufende Rechnung *f*	current account	—	conto corrente *m*	cuenta corriente *f*
compte courant² (F)	Kontokorrent *n*	account current	—	conto corrente *m*	cuenta corriente *f*
compte de caisse (F)	Kassenbuch *n*	cash book	—	libro di cassa *m*	libro de caja *m*
compte de dépôt à terme (F)	Festgeldkonto *n*	time deposit account	—	deposito vincolato *m*	cuenta a plazo *f*
compte de devises (F)	Devisenbilanz *f*	foreign exchange balance	—	bilancia delle divise *f*	balanza de divisas *f*
compte de domiciliation du salaire (F)	Gehaltskonto *n*	salary account	—	conto stipendi *m*	cuenta de salario *f*
compte de frais par secteurs (F)	Kostenstelle *f*	departmental expense account	—	posizione costi *f*	posición de costes *f*
compte de liquidation (F)	Abwicklungskonto *n*	settlement account	—	conto di liquidazione *f*	cuenta de liquidación *f*
compte de liquidité (F)	Liquiditätsrechnung *f*	liquidity calculation	—	calcolo della liquidità *m*	cálculo de liquidez *m*
compte de maison (F)	Firmenkonto *n*	company account	—	conto intestato ad una ditta *m*	cuenta de la empresa *f*
compte de pertes et profits (F)	Gewinn- und Verlustrechnung *f*	profit and loss account	—	conto profitti e perdite *m*	cuenta de pérdidas y ganancias *f*
compte de résultats (F)	Erfolgskonto *n*	profit account	—	conto profitti *m*	cuenta de beneficios y pérdidas *f*
compte de tiers (F)	Anderkonto *n*	fiduciary account	—	conto per terzi *m*	cuenta fiduciaria de un abogado *f*
compte d'étranger (F)	Auslandskonto *n*	foreign account	—	conto estero *m*	cuenta exterior *m*
compte d'existences (F)	Bestandskonto *n*	real account	—	conto merci *m*	cuenta de existencias *f*
compte en banque (F)	Bankkonto *n*	bank account	—	conto bancario *m*	cuenta bancaria *f*
compte en monnaies étrangères (F)	Währungskonto *n*	foreign currency account	—	conto in valuta *m*	cuenta de moneda extranjera *f*
compte privé (F)	Privatkonto *n*	private account	—	conto privato *m*	cuenta particular *f*
compte provisoire (F)	Zwischenkonto *n*	interim account	—	conto transitorio *m*	cuenta provisional *f*
compter des intérêts (F)	verzinsen	pay interest	—	pagare interessi	pagar interés
compte rendu (F)	Berichterstattung *f*	reporting	—	relazione *f*	reportaje *m*

	D	E	F	I	Es
compte rendu d'activité économique annuel (F)	Jahreswirtschafts-bericht *m*	Annual Economic Report	—	relazione generale sulla situazione economica *f*	informe económico anual *m*
comptes-transitoires (F)	Abgrenzungs-posten *m*	deferred item	—	ratei e risconti *m pl*	cuentas de orden *f pl*
compte tenu en compte courant (F)	Kontokorrentkonto *n*	current account	—	conto corrente *m*	cuenta corriente *f*
compte trimestriel (F)	Quartalsrechnung *f*	quarterly invoice	—	conto trimestrale *m*	cuenta trimestral *f*
compulsory consolida-tion of farmland (E)	Flurbereinigung *f*	—	remembrement parcellaire *m*	ricomposizione fondiaria *f*	concentración par celaria *f*
compulsory saving (E)	Zwangssparen *n*	—	épargne forcée *f*	risparmio coatto *m*	ahorro forzoso *m*
compulsory settlement (E)	Zwangsvergleich *m*	—	arrangement forcé *m*	concordato fallimentare *m*	convenio forzoso *m*
computation (E)	Berechnung *f*	—	calcul *m*	calcolo *m*	calculación *f*
Computer (D)	—	computer	ordinateur *m*	computer *m*	ordenador *m*
computer[1] (E)	Rechner *m*	—	ordinateur *m*/ calculateur de poche *m*	calcolatore *m*	ordenador *m*/ calculadora de bolsillo *f*
computer[2] (E)	Computer *m*	—	ordinateur *m*	computer *m*	ordenador *m*
computer (I)	Computer *m*	computer	ordinateur *m*	—	ordenador *m*
computer-aided information system (E)	computergestütztes Informationssystem *n*	—	système d'informa-tion assisté par ordinateur *m*	sistema di informazione computerizzato *m*	sistema de información asistido por ordenador *m*
computer centre (E)	Rechenzentrum *n*	—	centre de calcul *m*	centro da computer *m*	centro de computación *m*
computer criminality (E)	Computer-kriminalität *f*	—	délits informatiques *m pl*	abuso del computer *m*	delincuencia informática *f*
Computereinsatz (D)	—	use of computers	emploi d'ordinateurs *m*	impiego di computer *m*	utilización de ordenadores *f*
computergestützes Informations-system (D)	—	computer-aided information system	système d'informa-tion assisté par ordinateur *m*	sistema di informazione computerizzato *m*	sistema de información asistido por ordenador *m*
Computer-kriminalität (D)	—	computer criminality	délits informatiques *m pl*	abuso del computer *m*	delincuencia informática *f*
Computertechnik (D)	—	computer technology	technique informatique *f*	tecnica dei computer *f*	técnica informática *f*
computer technology (E)	Computertechnik *f*	—	technique informatique *f*	tecnica dei computer *f*	técnica informática *f*
computisteria (I)	Nachkalkulation *f*	historical costing	calcul des coûts a posteriori *m*	—	cálculo de costes a posteriori *m*
cómputo de intereses (Es)	Zinsrechnung *f*	interest account	calcul des intérêts *m*	conteggio degli interessi *m*	—
comune[1] (I)	Gemeinde *f*	community	commune *f*	—	comunidad *f*
comune[2] (I)	Kommune *f*	municipality	commune *f*	—	municipalidad *f*
comunicación de télex (Es)	Telexanschluß *m*	telex connection	communication de télex *f*	collegamento telex *m*	—
comunicaciones (Es)	Wegenetz *n*	road network	voirie *f*	rete stradale *f*	—
comunicativa (I)	Kontaktfähigkeit *f*	capability to establish public relations	capacité d'entrer en contact *f*	—	capacidad de anudar contactos *f*
comunicazione (I)	Mitteilung *f*	information	notification *f*	—	aviso *m*
comunicazione stampa (I)	Pressemitteilung *f*	press release	commentaire de presse *m*	—	remitido a la prensa *m*
comunidad (Es)	Gemeinde *f*	community	commune *f*	comune *m*	—
comunidad económica (Es)	Wirtschafts-gemeinschaft *f*	economic community	communauté économique *f*	comunità economica *f*	—
Comunidad Europea (Es)	Europäische Gemeinschaft, EG *f*	European Community	Communauté Européenne, EC *f*	Comunità Europea CEE *f*	—
comunidad sucesoria (Es)	Erbengemeinschaft *f*	community of heirs	communauté d'héritiers *f*	comunità degli eredi *f*	—
comunità degli eredi (I)	Erbengemeinschaft *f*	community of heirs	communauté d'héritiers *f*	—	comunidad sucesoria *f*
comunità economica (I)	Wirtschafts-gemeinschaft *f*	economic community	communauté économique *f*	—	comunidad económica *f*
Comunità Europea (I)	Europäische Gemeinschaft, EG *f*	European Community	Communauté Européenne, EC *f*	—	Comunidad Europea, C.E. *f*

	D	E	F	I	Es
concédant de licence (F)	Lizenzgeber *m*	licenser	—	concedente di licenza *m*	licitador *m*
concedente del leasing (I)	Leasing-Geber *m*	lessor	donneur de leasing *m*	—	arrendatario financiero *m*
concedente di licenza (I)	Lizenzgeber *m*	licenser	concédant de licence *m*	—	licitador *m*
concentración (Es)	Konzentration *f*	concentration	concentration *f*	concentrazione *f*	—
concentración de empresas (Es)	Unternehmens-konzentration *f*	business concentration	concentration d'entreprises *f*	pool d'imprese *m*	—
concentración económica (Es)	Wirtschafts-konzentration *f*	economic concentration	concentration économique *f*	concentrazione economica *f*	—
concentración parcelaria (Es)	Flurbereinigung *f*	compulsory consoli-dation of farmland	remembrement parcellaire *m*	ricomposizione fondiaria *f*	—
concentration (F)	Konzentration *f*	concentration	—	concentrazione *f*	concentración *f*
concentration (E)	Konzentration *f*	—	concentration *f*	concentrazione *f*	concentración *f*
concentration d'entreprises (F)	Unternehmens-konzentration *f*	business concentration	—	pool d'imprese *m*	concentración de empresas *f*
concentration économique (F)	Wirtschafts-konzentration *f*	economic concentration	—	concentrazione economica *f*	concentración económica *f*
concentrazione (I)	Konzentration *f*	concentration	concentration *f*	—	concentración *f*
concentrazione economica (I)	Wirtschafts-konzentration *f*	economic concentration	concentration économique *f*	—	concentración económica *f*
concepción (Es)	Konzeption *f*	conception	conception *f*	concezione *f*	—
concepción de venta (Es)	Verkaufskonzeption *f*	sales conception	conception de vente *f*	concezione di vendita *f*	—
concepción general (Es)	Gesamtkonzeption *f*	overall conception	conception générale *f*	concezione universale *f*	—
concept (E)	Konzept *n*	—	brouillon *m*	piano *m*	bosquejo *m*
conception (E)	Konzeption *f*	—	conception *f*	concezione *f*	concepción *f*
conception (F)	Konzeption *f*	conception	—	concezione *f*	concepción *f*
conceptional thinking (E)	konzeptionelles Denken *n*	—	penser conceptionnel *m*	mentalità concezionale *f*	pensar concepcional *m*
conception de vente (F)	Verkaufskonzeption *f*	sales conception	—	concezione di vendita *f*	concepción de venta *f*
conception générale (F)	Gesamtkonzeption *f*	overall conception	—	concezione universale *f*	concepción general *f*
concepto comercial (Es)	Unternehmens-konzept *n*	business concept	stratégie de l'entreprise *f*	piano imprenditoriale *m*	—
concesión (Es)	Konzession *f*	licence	concession *f*	concessione *f*	—
concesionario (Es)	Franchisenehmer *m*	concessionary	concessionnaire *m*	concessionarion *m*	—
concesionary (E)	Franchisenehmer *m*	—	concessionnaire *m*	concessionario *m*	concesionario *m*
concesión de un plazo (Es)	Fristgewährung *f*	granting a respite	octroi d'un délai *m*	concessione di un termine *f*	—
concession (F)	Konzession *f*	licence	—	concessione *f*	concesión *f*
concessionario (I)	Franchise-nehmer *m*	concessionary	concessionnaire *m*	—	concesionario *m*
concessionario di licenza (I)	Lizenznehmer *m*	licensee	preneur d'une licence *m*	—	licenciado *m*
concessione (I)	Konzession *f*	licence	concession *f*	—	concesión *f*
concessione di un termine (I)	Fristgewährung *f*	granting a respite	octroi d'un délai *m*	—	concesión de un plazo *f*
concessionnaire (F)	Franchisenehmer *m*	concessionary	—	concessionario *m*	concesionario *m*
concezione (I)	Konzeption *f*	conception	conception *f*	—	concepción *f*
concezione di vendita (I)	Verkaufskonzeption *f*	sales conception	conception de vente *f*	—	concepción de venta *f*
concezione universale (I)	Gesamtkonzeption *f*	overall conception	conception générale *f*	—	concepción general *f*
conclusion (E)	Abschluß *m*	—	conclusion *f*	stipulazione *f*	contratación *f*/ conclusión *f*/cierre *m*
conclusion (F)	Abschluß *m*	conclusion	—	stipulazione *f*	contratación *f*/ conclusión *f*/cierre *m*
conclusion d'une affaire (F)	Geschäftsabschluß *m*	conclusion of a deal	—	conclusione di un affare *f*	conclusión de un negocio *f*/cierre de cuentas *m*

	D	E	F	I	Es
conclusión de la venta (Es)	Verkaufsabschluß *m*	sales contract	contrat de vente *m*	conclusione di vendita *f*	—
conclusión de un contrato (Es)	Vertragsabschluß *m*	conclusion of a contract	conclusion du contrat *f*	stipulazione del contratto *f*	—
conclusión de un negocio (Es)	Geschäftsabschluß *m*	conclusion of a deal	conclusion d'une affaire *f*	conclusione di un affare *f*	—
conclusion du contrat (F)	Vertragsabschluß *m*	conclusion of a contract	—	stipulazione del contratto *f*	conclusión de un contrato *f*
conclusion du marché (F)	Kaufabschluß *m*	conclusion of a sales contract	—	conclusione d'acquisto *f*	convenio de compra *m*
conclusione d'acquisto (I)	Kaufabschluß *m*	conclusion of a sales contract	conclusion du marché *f*	—	convenio de compra *m*
conclusione di un affare (I)	Geschäftsabschluß *m*	conclusion of a deal	conclusion d'une affaire *f*	—	conclusión de un negocio *f*
conclusione di vendita (I)	Verkaufsabschluß *m*	sales contract	contract de vente *m*	—	conclusión de la venta *f*
conclusion of a contract (E)	Vertragsabschluß *m*	—	conclusion du contrat *f*	stipulazione del contratto *f*	conclusión de un contrato *f*
conclusion of a deal (E)	Geschäftsabschluß *m*	—	conclusion d'une affaire *f*	conclusione di un affare *f*	conclusión de un negocio *f*/cierre de cuentas *m*
conclusion of a sales contract (E)	Kaufabschluß *m*	—	conclusion du marché *f*	conclusione d'acquisto *f*	convenio de compra *m*
concordato fallimentare (I)	Zwangsvergleich *m*	compulsory settlement	arrangement forcé *m*	—	convenio forzoso *m*
concorrente (I)	Konkurrent *m*	competitor	concurrent *m*	—	competidor *m*
concorrenza[1] (I)	Wettbewerb *m*	competition	compétition *f*	—	competencia *f*
concorrenza[2] (I)	Konkurrenz *f*	competition	concurrence *f*	—	competencia *f*
concorrenza dei venditori (I)	Verkäufer-wettbewerb *m*	sellers competition	compétition des vendeurs *f*	—	competición de vendedores *f*
concorrenza sleale (I)	unlauterer Wettbewerb *m*	unfair competition	concurrence déloyale *f*	—	competencia desleal *f*
con crédito documentario (Es)	gegen Akkreditiv	against letter of credit	contre accréditif	contro lettera di credito	—
concurrence (F)	Konkurrenz *f*	competition	—	concorrenza *f*	competencia *f*
concurrence déloyale (F)	unlauterer Wettbewerb *m*	unfair competition	—	concorrenza sleale *f*	competencia desleal *f*
concurrence des prix (F)	Preiswettbewerb *m*	competition in prices	—	competizione dei prezzi *f*	competencia de precios *f*
concurrent (E)	Zug um Zug	—	de point en point	contestualmente	punto por punto
concurrent[1] (F)	Konkurrent *m*	competitor	—	concorrente *m*	competidor *m*
concurrent[2] (F)	Mitbewerber *m*	competitor	—	competitore *m*	contendiente *m*
concurso-subasta (Es)	Ausschreibung *f*	tender	soumission *f*	appalto *m*	—
condición (Es)	Bedingung *f*	condition	condition *f*	condizione *f*	—
condiciones comerciales (Es)	Handels-bedingungen *pl*	trading conditions	conditions commerciales *f pl*	condizioni commerciali *f pl*	—
condiciones contractuales (Es)	Vertragsbedingung *f*	term of contract	condition du contrat *f*	condizione del contratto *f*	—
condiciones de compra (Es)	Einkaufs-bedingungen *pl*	purchasing terms	conditions d'achat *f pl*	condizioni d'acquisto *f pl*	—
condiciones de pago (Es)	Zahlungsbedingung *f*	terms of payment	conditions de payement *f pl*	condizione di pagamento *f*	—
condiciones de suminstro (Es)	Lieferbedingungen *pl*	terms of delivery	conditions de livraison *f pl*	condizioni di consegna *f pl*	—
condiciones de transporte (Es)	Beförderungs-bedingungen *f*	terms of conveyance	conditions de transport *f pl*	condizioni di trasporto *f pl*	—
condiciones del mercado (Es)	Marktlage *f*	state of the market	situation du marché *f*	situazione di mercato *f*	—
condiciones generales de contrato (Es)	allgemeine Geschäfts-bedingungen *pl*	general terms	conditions générales de contract *f pl*	condizioni generali di contratto *f pl*	—
condición previa (Es)	Voraussetzung *f*	precondition	condition préalable *f*	presupposto *m*	—
condition[1] (E)	Bedingung *f*	—	condition *f*	condizione *f*	condición *f*
condition[1] (F)	Kondition *f*	condition	—	condizione *f*	condición *f*
condition[2] (E)	Kondition *f*	—	condition *f*	condizione *f*	condición *f*

	D	E	F	I	Es
condition[2] (F)	Bedingung *f*	condition	—	condizione *f*	condición *f*
condition du contrat (F)	Vertragsbedingung *f*	term of contract	—	condizione del contratto *f*	condiciones contractuales *f pl*
condition préalable (F)	Voraussetzung *f*	precondition	—	presupposto *m*	condición previa *f*
conditions commerciales (F)	Handels-bedingungen *pl*	trading conditions	—	condizioni commerciali *f pl*	condiciones comerciales *f pl*
conditions d'achat (F)	Einkaufs-bedingungen *pl*	purchasing terms	—	condizioni d'acquisto *f pl*	condiciones de compra *f pl*
conditions de livraison (F)	Lieferbedingungen *pl*	terms of delivery	—	condizioni di consegna *f pl*	condiciones de suminstro *f pl*
conditions de payement (F)	Zahlungsbedingung *f*	terms of payment	—	condizione di pagamento *f*	condiciones de pago *f pl*
conditions de transport (F)	Beförderungs-bedingungen *f*	terms of conveyance	—	condizioni di trasporto *f pl*	condiciones de transporte *f pl*
conditions générales de contract (F)	allgemeine Geschäfts-bedingungen *pl*	general terms	—	condizioni generali di contratto *f pl*	condiciones generales de contrato *f pl*
condizione[1] (I)	Kondition *f*	condition	condition *f*	—	condición *f*
condizione[2] (I)	Bedingung *f*	condition	condition *f*	—	condición *f*
condizione del contratto (I)	Vertragsbedingung *f*	term of contract	condition du contrat *f*	—	condiciones contractuales *f pl*
condizione di pagamento (I)	Zahlungsbedingung *f*	terms of payment	conditions de payement *f pl*	—	condiciones de pago *f pl*
condizioni commerciali (I)	Handels-bedingungen *pl*	trading conditions	conditions commerciales *f pl*	—	condiciones comerciales *f pl*
condizioni d'acquisto (I)	Einkaufs-bedingungen *pl*	purchasing terms	conditions d'achat *f pl*	—	condiciones de compra *f pl*
condizioni di consegna (I)	Liefer-bedingungen *pl*	terms of delivery	conditions de livraison *f pl*	—	condiciones de suminstro *f pl*
condizioni di trasporto (I)	Beförderungs-bedingungen *f*	terms of conveyance	conditions de transport *f pl*	—	condiciones de transporte *f pl*
condizioni generali di contratto (I)	allgemeine Geschäfts-bedingungen *pl*	general terms	conditions générales de contract *f pl*	—	condiciones generales de contrato *f pl*
condizioni generali di credito (I)	allgemeine Kreditver-einbarungen *pl*	general borrowing agreements	accords généraux de crédit *f pl*	—	acuerdos generales de crédito *m pl*
con effetto retroattivo (I)	rückwirkend	retrospective	rétroactif	—	retroactivo
con falta de objetividad (Es)	unsachgemäß	improper	non adéquat	non idoneo	—
conference (E)	Konferenz *f*	—	conférence *f*	conferenza *f*	conferencia *f*
conférence[1] (F)	Konferenz *f*	conference	—	conferenza *f*	conferencia *f*
conférence[2] (F)	Besprechung *f*	discussion	—	colloquio *m*	conferencia *f*
conférence de presse (F)	Pressekonferenz *f*	press conference	—	conferenza stampa *f*	rueda de prensa *f*
Conférence des Nations Unies sur le Commerce et le Développement (F)	Welthandels-konferenz *f*	United Nations Conference on Trade and Development	—	Comitato delle Nazioni Unite per il commercio e lo sviluppo *m*	Conferencia de las Naciones Unidas sobre el Comercio y el Desarrollo *f*
conference room[1] (E)	Sitzungszimmer *n*	—	salle de réunion *f*	sala riunioni *f*	sala de conferencia *f*
conference room[2] (E)	Konferenzraum *m*	—	salle de conférences *f*	sala conferenze *f*	sala de conferencia *f*
conferencia[1] (Es)	Besprechung *f*	discussion	conférence *f*	colloquio *m*	—
conferencia[2] (Es)	Konferenz *f*	conference	conférence *f*	conferenza *f*	—
Conferencia de las Naciones Unidas sobre el Comercio y el Desarrollo (Es)	Welthandels-konferenz *f*	United Nations Conference on Trade and Development	Conférence des Nations Unies sur le Commerce et le Développement	Comitato delle Nazioni Unite per il commercio e lo sviluppo *m*	—
conferencia de representantes (Es)	Vertretertagung *f*	sales meeting	réunion de représentants *f*	convegno dei rappresentanti *m*	—
Conferencia Internacional de Materias Primas (Es)	internationale Rohstoff-Konferenz *f*	International Resources Conference	Conférence Internationale des Matières Premières *f*	Conferenza Internazionale sulle Materie Prime *f*	—
conferencia telefónica (Es)	Telefongespräch *n*	telephone conversation	conversation téléphonique *f*	telefonata *f*	—
conferenza (I)	Konferenz *f*	conference	conférence *f*	—	conferencia *f*
conferenza stampa (I)	Pressekonferenz *f*	press conference	conférence de presse *f*	—	rueda de prensa *f*

	D	E	F	I	Es
conferma[1] (I)	Zusage *f*	promise	promesse *f*	—	promesa *f*
conferma[2] (I)	Bestätigung *f*	confirmation	confirmation *f*	—	confirmación *f*
conferma della prenotazione (I)	Reservierungs-bestätigung *f*	reservation confirmation	confirmation de réservation *f*	—	confirmación de la reservación *f*
conferma di pagamento (I)	Zahlungs-bestätigung *f*	receipt for payment	confirmation de payement *f*	—	confirmación de pago *f*
conferma d'ordine (I)	Auftragsbestätigung *f*	confirmation of order	confirmation de commande *f*	—	confirmación de pedido *f*
confezione campione (I)	Probepackung *f*	trial package	échantillon *m*	—	muestra *f*
confidencial (Es)	vertraulich	confidential	confidentiel	confidenziale	—
confidential (E)	vertraulich	—	confidentiel	confidenziale	confidencial
confidential relationship (E)	Vertrauens-verhältnis *n*	—	rapport de confiance *m*	rapporto di fiducia *m*	relación de confianza *f*
confidentiality (E)	Diskretion *f*	—	discrétion *f*	discrezione *f*	discreción *f*
confidentiel (F)	vertraulich	confidential	—	confidenziale	confidencial
confidenziale (I)	vertraulich	confidential	confidentiel	—	confidencial
configuración del surtido (Es)	Sortiments-gestaltung *f*	assortment structuring	structure du sortiment *f*	composizione dell'assortimento *f*	—
confine doganale (I)	Zollgrenze *f*	customs frontier	frontière douanière *f*	—	frontera aduanera *f*
confirmación (Es)	Bestätigung *f*	confirmation	confirmation *f*	conferma *f*	—
confirmación de la reservación (Es)	Reservierungs-bestätigung *f*	reservation confirmation	confirmation de réservation *f*	conferma della prenotazione *f*	—
confirmación de pago (Es)	Zahlungs-bestätigung *f*	receipt for payment	confirmation de payement *f*	conferma di pagamento *f*	—
confirmación de pedido (Es)	Auftragsbestätigung *f*	confirmation of order	confirmation de commande *f*	conferma d'ordine *f*	—
confirmation (E)	Bestätigung *f*	—	confirmation *f*	conferma *f*	confirmación *f*
confirmation (F)	Bestätigung *f*	confirmation	—	conferma *f*	confirmación *f*
confirmation bancaire (F)	Bankavis *m*	bank notification	—	avviso bancario *m*	aviso bancario *m*
confirmation de commande (F)	Auftragsbestätigung *f*	confirmation of order	—	conferma d'ordine *f*	confirmación de pedido *f*
confirmation de payement (F)	Zahlungs-bestätigung *f*	receipt for payment	—	conferma di pagamento *f*	confirmación de pago *f*
confirmation de réservation (F)	Reservierungs-bestätigung *f*	reservation confirmation	—	conferma della prenotazione *f*	confirmación de la reservación *f*
confirmation of cover (E)	Deckungszusage *f*	—	acceptation de prendre le risque en charge *f*	impegno di copertura *m*	nota de cobertura *f*
confirmation of order (E)	Auftragsbestätigung *f*	—	confirmation de commande *f*	conferma d'ordine *f*	confirmación de pedido *f*
confiscación (Es)	Beschlagnahme *f*	confiscation	saisie *f*	sequestro *m*	—
confiscation (E)	Beschlagnahme *f*	—	saisie *f*	sequestro *m*	confiscación *f*
conflicting goals (E)	Zielkonflikt *m*	—	conflit d'objectifs *m*	incompatibilità degli obiettivi *f*	conflicto de objectivos *m*
conflicto de objectivos (Es)	Zielkonflikt *m*	conflicting goals	conflit d'objectifs *m*	incompatibilità degli obiettivi *f*	—
conflicto jurídico (Es)	Rechtsstreit *m*	legal action	litige *m*	causa *f*	—
conflit d'objectifs (F)	Zielkonflikt *m*	conflicting goals	—	incompatibilità degli obiettivi *f*	conflicto de objectivos *m*
conforme al mercado (Es)	marktkonform	in conformity with market conditions	conforme au marché	conforme al mercato	—
conforme al mercato (I)	marktkonform	in conformity with market conditions	conforme au marché	—	conforme al mercado
conforme au marché (F)	marktkonform	in conformity with market conditions	—	conforme al mercato	conforme al mercado
confronto (I)	Vergleich *m*	comparison	comparaison *f*	—	comparación *f*
confronto costi calcolati/costi reali (I)	Soll/Ist-Vergleich *m*	comparison of estimates with results	comparaison entre les résultats effectifs et les prévisions *f*	—	comparación entre los resultados efectivos y las previsiones *f*
confronto dei corsi (I)	Kursvergleich *m*	comparison of prices	comparaison des cours *f*	—	comparación de las cotizaciones *f*

	D	E	F	I	Es
congé (F)	Urlaub *m*	annual holidays/ vacation	—	ferie *f pl*/vacanze *f pl*	vacaciones *f pl*/ vacaciones colectivas de la empresa *f pl*
congelación salarial (Es)	Lohnstopp *m*	wage freeze	blocage des salaires *m*	blocco dei salari *m*	—
congé non payé (F)	unbezahlter Urlaub *m*	unpaid vacation	—	ferie non pagate *f pl*	vacaciones no pagadas *f pl*
congé payé (F)	bezahlter Urlaub *m*	paid vacation	—	ferie pagate *f pl*	vacaciones con goce de sueldo *f pl*
congiuntura (I)	Konjunktur *f*	business cycle	conjoncture *f*	—	conyuntura *f*
congiuntura quantitativa (I)	Mengenkonjunktur *f*	quantitative boom	conjoncture de quantité *f*	—	coyuntura cuantitativa *f*
con gran intensidad de capital (Es)	kapitalintensiv	capital-intensive	avec grande intensité de capital	ad alta incidenza di capitale	—
con gran intensidad de costos salariales (Es)	lohnintensiv	wage-intensive	déterminé par le facteur salaire	ad alta incidenza salariale	—
con gran intensidad de mano de obra (Es)	arbeitsintensiv	labour-intensiv	déterminé par le facteur main-d'œuvre	ad alta incidenza di lavoro	—
congratulations (E)	Glückwunsch *m*	—	félicitations *f pl*	auguri *m pl*	felicitaciones *f pl*
congrès (F)	Tagung *f*	meeting	—	convegno *m*	reunión *f*
conguaglio (I)	Ausgleichszahlung *f*	compensation payment	payement pour solde de compte *m*	—	pago de compensación *m*
conjecture (E)	Mutmaßung *f*	—	présomption *f*	presunzione *f*	suposición *f*
conjoncture (F)	Konjunktur *f*	business cycle	—	congiuntura *f*	conyuntura *f*
conjoncture de quantité (F)	Mengenkonjunktur *f*	quantitative boom	—	congiuntura quantitativa *f*	coyuntura cuantitativa *f*
connaissances fondamentales (F)	Grundkenntnisse *pl*	basic knowledge	—	cognizioni elementari *f pl*	conocimientos básicos *m pl*
connaissances professionnelles (F)	Fachwissen *n*	professional knowledge	—	cognizioni professionali *f pl*	conocimientos especializados *m pl*
connaissement (F)	Konnossement *n*	bill of lading	—	polizza di carico *f*	conocimiento *m*
connaissement maritime (F)	Seefrachtbrief *m*	bill of lading	—	polizza di carico *f*	póliza *f*
connoisseur's price (E)	Liebhaberpreis *m*	—	prix d'amateur *m*	prezzo d'affezione *m*	precio afectivo *m*
conocimiento (Es)	Konnossement *n*	bill of lading	connaissement *m*	polizza di carico *f*	—
conocimiento de causa (Es)	Sachkenntnis *f*	know-how	compétence *f*	competenza *f*	—
conocimientos básicos (Es)	Grundkenntnisse *pl*	basic knowledge	connaissances fondamentales *f pl*	cognizioni elementari *f pl* -	—
conocimientos especializados (Es)	Fachwissen *n*	professional knowledge	connaissances professionnelles *f pl*	cognizioni professionali *f pl*	—
con referencia a (Es)	bezugnehmend	referring to	se référant (à)	con riferimento a	—
con riferimento a (I)	bezugnehmend	referring to	se référant (à)	—	con referencia a
con rispetto dell'ambiente (I)	umweltbewußt	environmental by aware	conscient de la réalité écologique	—	consciente del medio ambiente
conscient de la réalité écologique (F)	umweltbewußt	environmental-conscious	—	con rispetto dell'ambiente	consciente del medio ambiente
consciente del medio ambiente (Es)	umweltbewußt	environmental-conscious	conscient de la réalité écologique	con rispetto dell'ambiente	—
consegna (I)	Übergabe *f*	delivery	remise *f*	—	entrega *f*
consegna contro assegno (I)	Lieferung gegen Nachnahme *f*	cash on delivery	livraison contre remboursement *f*	—	entrega contra reembolso *f*
consegna immediata (I)	sofortige Lieferung *f*	immediate delivery	livraison immédiate *f*	—	entrega inmediata *f*
consegna per espresso (I)	Eilzustellung *f*	express delivery	remise par exprès *f*	—	entrega urgente *f*
consegnare (I)	abliefern	hand over	livrer	—	entregar
Conseil de la Banque Centrale (F)	Zentralbankrat *m*	Central Bank Council	—	consiglio superiore della Banca Centrale *m*	Consejo del Banco Central *m*
conseil de surveillance (F)	Aufsichtsrat *m*	supervisory board	—	consiglio di sorveglianza *m*	consejo de vigilancia *m*
conseiller (F)	Berater *m*	adviser	—	consulente *m*	asesor *m*
conseiller de marketing (F)	Marketingberater *m*	marketing consultant	—	consulente di marketing *m*	asesor de marketing *m*

	D	E	F	I	Es
conseiller fiscal (F)	Steuerberater *m*	tax adviser	—	consulente fiscale *m*	asesor fiscal *m*
consejero directivo (Es)	Vorstandsmitglied *n*	member of the managing board	membre du comité de direction *m*	membro del consiglio di amministrazione *m*	—
consejo de dirección (Es)	Vorstand *m*	board	comité directeur *m*	consiglio di amministrazione *m*	—
Consejo del Banco Central (Es)	Zentralbankrat *m*	Central Bank Council	Conseil de la Banque Centrale *m*	consiglio superiore della Banca Centrale *m*	—
consejo de vigilancia (Es)	Aufsichtsrat *m*	supervisory board	conseil de surveillance *m*	consiglio di sorveglianza *m*	—
consenso[1] (I)	Einwilligung *f*	consent	consentement *m*	—	consentimiento *m*
consenso[2] (I)	Zustimmung *f*	consent	accord *m*	—	consentimiento *m*
consenso di credito (I)	Kreditzusage *f*	promise of credit	promesse de crédit *f*	—	promesa de créditos *f*
consent[1] (E)	Einwilligung *f*	—	consentement *m*	consenso *m*	consentimiento *m*
consent[2] (E)	Zustimmung *f*	—	accord *m*	consenso *m*	consentimiento *m*
consentement (F)	Einwilligung *f*	consent	—	consenso *m*	consentimiento *m*
consentimiento[1] (Es)	Zustimmung *f*	consent	accord *m*	consenso *m*	—
consentimiento[2] (Es)	Einwilligung *f*	consent	consentement *m*	consenso *m*	—
consequential damages (E)	Folgeschäden *pl*	—	dommage consécutif *m*	danni indiretti *m pl*	daño consecuencial *m*
conservación de la sustancia (Es)	Substanzerhaltung *f*	maintaining the real value	maintien de la substance *m*	mantenimento della sostanza *m*	—
conservation du sevret (F)	Geheimhaltung *f*	maintenance of secrecy	—	segretezza *f*	mantenimiento del secreto *m*
conservative estimate (E)	vorsichtige Schätzung *f*	—	évaluation approximative *f*	valutazione approssimativa *f*	evaluación aproximativa *f*
consiglio di amministrazione (I)	Vorstand *m*	board	comité directeur *m*	—	consejo de dirección *m*
consiglio di sorveglianza (I)	Aufsichtsrat *m*	supervisory board	conseil de surveillance *m*	—	consejo de vigilancia *m*
consiglio superiore della Banca Centrale (I)	Zentralbankrat *m*	Central Bank Council	Conseil de la Banque Centrale *m*	—	Consejo del Banco Central *m*
consignment (E)	Sendung *f*	—	envoi *m*	spedizione *f*	envío *m*
consignment note (E)	Frachtbrief *m*	—	lettre de voiture *f*	lettera di vettura *f*	carta de porte *f*
consignment of goods (E)	Warensendung *f*	—	expédition de marchandises *f*	spedizione di merci *f*	envío de mercancías *m*
consignment on approval (E)	Ansichtssendung *f*	—	envoi à condition *m*	campione per esame *m*	envío para inspección *m*
consignment with value declared (E)	Wertsendung *f*	—	envoi avec valeur déclarée *m*	spedizione con valore dichiarato *f*	envío con valor declarado *m*
consolato (I)	Konsulat *n*	consulate	consulat *m*	—	consulado *m*
console (I)	Konsul *m*	consul	consul *m*	—	cónsul *m*
console onorario (I)	Wahlkonsul *m*	honorary consul	consul honoraire *m*	—	cónsul honorario *m*
consolidación (Es)	Konsolidierung *f*	consolidation	consolidation *f*	consolidamento *m*	—
consolidamento (I)	Konsolidierung *f*	consolidation	consolidation *f*	—	consolidación *f*
consolidated balance sheet (E)	konsolidierte Bilanz *f*	—	bilan consolidé *m*	bilancio consolidato *m*	balance consolidado *m*
consolidation (E)	Konsolidierung *f*	—	consolidation *f*	consolidamento *m*	consolidación *f*
consolidation (F)	Konsolidierung *f*	consolidation	—	consolidamento *m*	consolidación *f*
consommateur[1] (F)	Verbraucher *m*	consumer	—	consumatore *m*	consumidor *m*
consommateur[2] (F)	Konsument *m*	consumer	—	consumatore *m*	consumidor *m*
consommateur final (F)	Endverbraucher *m*	ultimate consumer	—	consumatore finale *m*	consumidor final *m*
consommation (F)	Konsum *m*, Verbrauch *m*	consumption	—	consumo *m*	consumo *m*
consommation personnelle (F)	Eigenverbrauch *m*	personal consumption	—	consumo proprio *m*	consumo propio *m*
consommer (F)	verbrauchen	consume	—	consumare	consumir
consorcio[1] (Es)	Konsortium *n*	consortium	consortium *m*	consorzio *m*	—
consorcio[2] (Es)	Konzern *m*	group/combine	groupe industriel *m*	gruppo *m*	—
consorcio bancario (Es)	Bankenkonsortium *n*	banking syndicate	consortium des banques *m*	consorzio bancario *m*	—

	D	E	F	I	Es
consorella (I)	Schwester-gesellschaft *f*	affiliated company	société affiliée *f*	—	compañía asociada *f*
consortium (E)	Konsortium *n*	—	consortium *m*	consorzio *m*	consorcio *m*
consortium (F)	Konsortium *n*	consortium	—	consorzio *m*	consorcio *m*
consortium des banques (F)	Bankenkonsortium *n*	banking syndicate	—	consorzio bancario *m*	consorcio bancario *m*
consorzio (I)	Konsortium *n*	consortium	consortium *m*	—	consorcio *m*
consorzio bancario (I)	Bankenkonsortium *n*	banking syndicate	consortium des banques *m*	—	consorcio bancario *m*
consorzio intercomunale (I)	Zweckverband *m*	special purpose association	association à but déterminé *f*	—	asociación con un fin determinado *f*
constitution (F)	Gründung *f*	formation	—	costituzione *f*	fundación *f*
constitution de capital par apport de tiers (F)	Fremdfinanzierung *f*	debt financing	—	finanziamento passivo *m*	financiación externa *f*
construcción (Es)	Bau *m*	construction	construction *f*	costruzione *f*	—
construcción de viviendas (Es)	Wohnungsbau *m*	housing construction	construction de logements *f*	edilizia abitativa *f*	—
construction (E)	Bau *m*	—	construction *f*	costruzione *f*	construcción *f*
construction (F)	Bau *m*	construction	—	costruzione *f*	construcción *f*
construction de logements (F)	Wohnungsbau *m*	housing construction	—	edilizia abitativa *f*	construcción de viviendas *f*
construction financiation (E)	Baufinanzierung *f*	—	financement à la construction *m*	finanziamento di costruzione *m*	financiación de la construcción *f*
construction industry (E)	Bauindustrie *f*	—	industrie de sous-traitance du bâtiment *f*	industria edile *f*	industria de la construcción *f*
consuetudine di pagamento (I)	Zahlungs-gewohnheit *f*	practice of payment	habitude de payement *f*	—	práctica de pago *f*
consul (E)	Konsul *m*	—	consul *m*	console *m*	cónsul *m*
cónsul (Es)	Konsul *m*	consul	consul *m*	console *m*	—
consul (F)	Konsul *m*	consul	—	console *m*	cónsul *m*
consulado (Es)	Konsulat *n*	consulate	consulat *m*	consolato *m*	—
consulat (F)	Konsulat *n*	consulate	—	consolato *m*	consulado *m*
consulate (E)	Konsulat *n*	—	consulat *m*	consolato *m*	consulado *m*
consulente (I)	Berater *m*	adviser	conseiller *m*	—	asesor *m*
consulente di marketing (I)	Marketingberater *m*	marketing consultant	conseiller de marketing *m*	—	asesor de marketing *m*
consulente fiscale (I)	Steuerberater *m*	tax adviser	conseiller fiscal *m*	—	asesor fiscal *m*
consulente legale (I)	Syndikus	legal adviser	syndic *m*	—	síndico *m*
consulenza (I)	Beratung *f*	advice	consultation *f*	—	asesoramiento *m*
consul honoraire (F)	Wahlkonsul *m*	honorary consul	—	console onorario *m*	cónsul honorario *m*
cónsul honorario (Es)	Wahlkonsul *m*	honorary consul	consul honoraire *m*	console onorario *m*	—
consultation (F)	Beratung *f*	advice	—	consulenza *f*	asesoramiento *m*
consumare (I)	verbrauchen	consume	consommer	—	consumir
consumatore (I)	Verbraucher *m*	consumer	consommateur *m*	—	consumidor *m*
consumatore finale (I)	Endverbraucher *m*	ultimate consumer	consommateur final *m*	—	consumidor final *m*
consume (E)	verbrauchen	—	consommer	consumare	consumir
consumer (E)	Verbraucher *m*	—	consommateur *m*	consumatore *m*	consumidor *m*
consumer credit (E)	Konsumkredit *m*	—	crédit à la consommation *m*	credito al consumatore *m*	crédito de consumo *m*
consumer goods[1] (E)	Verbrauchsgüter *pl*	—	biens de consommation *m pl*	beni non durevoli *m pl*	bienes de consumo *m pl*
consumer goods[2] (E)	Konsumgüter *pl*	—	biens de consommation *m pl*	beni di consumo *m pl*	bienes de consumo *m pl*
consumer goods industry (E)	Konsumgüter-industrie *f*	—	industrie des biens de consommation *f*	industria dei beni di consumo *f*	industria de bienes de consumo *f*
consumer information (E)	Verbraucher-information *f*	—	information des consommateurs *f*	informazione per i consumatori *f*	información de consumidores *f*
consumer market (E)	Verbrauchermarkt *m*	—	marché des consommateurs *m*	ipermercato *m*	mercado favorable al consumidor *m*

	D	E	F	I	Es
consumer protection (E)	Verbraucherschutz *m*	—	protection des consommateurs *f*	tutela dei consumatori *f*	protección de los consumidores *f*
consumer protection organization (E)	Verbraucher-organisation *f*	—	organisation des consommateurs *f*	organizzazione dei consumatori *f*	organización de defensa del consumidor *f*
consumer's information (E)	Konsumenten-information *f*	—	information des consommateurs *f*	informazione per i consumatori *f*	información a los comsumidores *f*
consumidor (Es)	Verbraucher *m*	consumer	consommateur *m*	consumatore *m*	—
consumidor final (Es)	Endverbraucher *m*	ultimate consumer	consommateur final *m*	consumatore finale *m*	—
consumir (Es)	verbrauchen	consume	consommer	consumare	—
consumo (Es)	Konsum *m*, Verbrauch *m*	consumption	consommation *f*	consumo *m*	—
consumo (I)	Konsum *m*, Verbrauch *m*	consumption	consommation *f*	—	consumo *m*
consumo propio (Es)	Eigenverbrauch *m*	personal consumption	consommation personnelle *f*	consumo proprio *m*	—
consumo proprio (I)	Eigenverbrauch *m*	personal consumption	consommation personnelle *f*	—	consumo propio *m*
consumption (E)	Konsum *m*, Verbrauch *m*	—	consommation *f*	consumo *m*	consumo *m*
consumption (E)	Konsumstruktur *f*	—	structure de consommation	struttura del consumo *f*	estructura del consumo *f*
contabilidad[1] (Es)	Buchführung *f*	bookkeeping	comptabilité *f*	contabilità *f*	—
contabilidad[2] (Es)	Buchhaltung *f*	accounting	comptabilité *f*	contabilità *f*	—
contabilidad[3] (Es)	Rechnungs-wesen *n*	accounting system	comptabilité *f*	ragioneria *f*	—
contabilidad financiera (Es)	Finanzbuchhaltung *f*	financial accounting	comptabilité financière *f*	contabilità finanziaria *f*	—
contabilidad nacional (Es)	Volkswirtschaftliche Gesamtrechnung *f*	national accounting	comptabilité nationale *f*	contabilità nazionale *f*	—
contabilidad por doble partida (Es)	doppelte Buchführung *f*	double entry bookkeeping	comptabilité en partie double *f*	contabilità a partita doppia *f*	—
contabilità[1] (I)	Buchhaltung *f*	accounting	comptabilité *f*	—	contabilidad *f*
contabilità[2] (I)	Buchführung *f*	bookkeeping	comptabilité *f*	—	contabilidad *f*
contabilità a partita doppia (I)	doppelte Buchführung *f*	double entry bookkeeping	comptabilité en partie double *f*	—	contabilidad por doble partida *f*
contabilità finanziaria (I)	Finanzbuchhaltung *f*	financial accounting	comptabilité financière *f*	—	contabilidad financiera *f*
contabilità nazionale (I)	Volkswirtschaftliche Gesamtrechnung *f*	national accounting	comptabilité nationale *f*	—	contabilidad nacional *f*
contabilización económica (Es)	Wirtschafts-rechnung *f*	economic account	comptabilisation économique *f*	conto economico *m*	—
contador público (Es)	Betriebsprüfer *m*	auditor	expert-comptable *m*	revisore aziendale *m*	—
Container (D)	—	container	container *m*	container *m*	contenedor *m*
container (E)	Container *m*	—	container *m*	container *m*	contenedor *m*
container (F)	Container *m*	container	—	container *m*	contenedor *m*
container (I)	Container *m*	container	container *m*	—	contenedor *m*
container di grande dimensione (I)	Großcontainer *m*	large container	conteneur à grand volume *m*	—	gran contenedor *m*
container transport (E)	Behälterverkehr *m*	—	transport utilisant des containers *m*	trasporto container *m*	transportación en contenedores *f*
contaminación (Es)	Kontamination *f*	contamination	contamination *f*	contaminazione *f*	—
contaminación del agua (Es)	Wasser-verschmutzung *f*	water pollution	contamination des eaux *f*	inquinamento delle acque *m*	—
contaminación del medio ambiente (Es)	Umwelt-verschmutzung *f*	environmental pollution	pollution de l'environnement *f*	inquinamento dell'ambiente *m*	—
contaminante (Es)	umweltschädlich	causing environ-mental damage	nuisible à l'environnement	inquinante	—
contamination (E)	Kontamination *f*	—	contamination *f*	contaminazione *f*	contaminación *f*
contamination (F)	Kontamination *f*	contamination	—	contaminazione *f*	contaminación *f*
contamination des eaux (F)	Wasser-verschmutzung *f*	water pollution	—	inquinamento delle acque *m*	contaminación del agua *f*
contaminazione (I)	Kontamination *f*	contamination	contamination *f*	—	contaminación *f*

	D	E	F	I	Es
conteggio degli interessi (I)	Zinsrechnung *f*	interest account	calcul des intérêts *m*	—	cómputo de intereses *m*
conteggio dei costi di viaggio (I)	Reisekosten-abrechnung *f*	travel expense accounting	règlement des frais de voyage *m*	—	liquidación de los gastos de viaje *f*
conteggio delle provvigioni (I)	Provisions-abrechnung *f*	statement of a commission	liquidation des commissions *f*	—	liquidación de la comisión *f*
conteggio delle spese (I)	Spesenabrechung *f*	statement of expenses	décompte des frais *m*	—	liquidación de gastos *f*
contendiente (Es)	Mitbewerber *m*	competitor	concurrent *m*	competitore *m*	—
contenedor (Es)	Container *m*	container	container *m*	container *m*	—
conteneur à grand volume (F)	Großcontainer *m*	large container	—	container di grande dimensione *m*	gran contenedor *m*
contenimento dei costi (I)	Kostendämpfung *f*	combatting rising costs	réduction des coûts *f*	—	disminución de costes *f*
contestador de llamadas (Es)	Anrufbeantworter *m*	answering machine	répondeur automatique *m*	segreteria telefonica *f*	—
contestualmente (I)	Zug um Zug	concurrent	de point en point	—	punto por punto
conti in nero (I)	schwarze Zahlen *pl*	surplus	excédent *m*	—	superávit *m*
conti in rosso (I)	rote Zahlen *pl*	(in) the red	chiffres en déficit *m*	—	cifras rojas *f pl*
contingent (F)	Kontingent *n*	quota	—	contingente *m*	contingente *m*
contingentación (Es)	Kontingentierung *f*	fixing of a quota	contingentement *m*	contingentamento *m*	—
contingentamento (I)	Kontingentierung *f*	fixing of a quota	contingentement *m*	—	contingentación *f*
contingent de marchandises (F)	Mengenkontingent *n*	quantity quota	—	contingente di quantità *m*	contingente cuantitativo *m*
contingent d'importation (F)	Importquote *f*	import quota	—	quota d'importazione *f*	cuota de importación *f*
contingente (Es)	Kontingent *n*	quota	contingent *m*	contingente *m*	—
contingente (I)	Kontingent *n*	quota	contingent *m*	—	contingente *m*
contingente cuantitativo (Es)	Mengenkontingent *n*	quantity quota	contingent de marchandises *m*	contingente di quantità *m*	—
contingente d'esportazione (I)	Exportquote *f*	export quota	quota d'exportation *m*	—	cupo de exportación *m*
contingente di quantità (I)	Mengenkontingent *n*	quantity quota	contingent de marchandises *m*	—	contingente cuantitativo *m*
contingentement (F)	Kontingentierung *f*	fixing of a quota	—	contingentamento *m*	contingentación *f*
contingentement de l'exportation (F)	Ausfuhr-beschränkung *f*	export restriction	—	restrizione delle esportazioni *f*	restricción a la exportación *f*
continuità di bilancio (I)	Bilanzkontinuität *f*	formal identity	identité des bilans successifs *f*	—	identidad de los balances sucsivos *f*
conto (I)	Konto *n*	account	compte *m*	—	cuenta *f*
conto aperto (I)	offene Rechnung *f*	unsettled account	facture pas encore payée *f*	—	factura pendiente *f*
conto bancario (I)	Bankkonto *n*	bank account	compte en banque *m*	—	cuenta bancaria *f*
conto bloccato (I)	gesperrtes Konto *n*	blocked account	compte bloqué *m*	—	cuenta congelada *f*
conto cifrato (I)	Nummernkonto *n*	numbered account	compte anonyme *m*	—	cuenta cifrada *f*
conto corrente[1] (I)	Kontokorrent *n*	current account	compte courant *m*	—	cuenta corriente *f*
conto corrente[2] (I)	laufende Rechnung *f*	current account	compte courant *m*	—	cuenta corriente *f*
conto corrente[3] (I)	Kontokorrentkonto *n*	current account	compte tenu en compte courant *m*	—	cuenta corriente *f*
conto corrente postale (I)	Postscheckkonto *n*	(postal) giro account	compte chèque postal *m*	—	cuenta corriente postal *f*
conto dei costi limite (I)	Grenzkosten-rechnung *f*	marginal costing	détermination du coût marginal *f*	—	cálculo de los costes marginales *m*
conto di liquidazione (I)	Abwicklungskonto *n*	settlement account	compte de liquidation *m*	—	cuenta de liquidación *f*
conto economico[1] (I)	Ertragsrechnung *f*	profit and loss account	solde net de l'exploitation *m*	—	cuenta de ganancias *f pl*
conto economico[2] (I)	Wirtschaftsrechnung *f*	economic account	comptabilisation économique *f*	—	contabilización económica *f*
conto estero (I)	Auslandskonto *n*	foreign account	compte d'étranger *m*	—	cuenta exterior *m*
conto intestato ad una ditta (I)	Firmenkonto *n*	foreign company account	compte de maison *m*	—	cuenta de la empresa *f*

	D	E	F	I	Es
conto in valuta (I)	Währungskonto *n*	currency account	compte en monnaies étrangères *m*	—	cuenta de moneda extranjera *f*
contol de planificación (Es)	Planungskontrolle *f*	planning control	contrôle de la planification *f*	controllo della programmazione *m*	—
conto merci (I)	Bestandskonto *n*	real account	compte d'existences *m*	—	cuenta de existencias *f*
conto per terzi (I)	Anderkonto *n*	fiduciary account	compte de tiers *m*	—	cuenta fiduciaria de un abogado *f*
conto privato (I)	Privatkonto *n*	private account	compte privé *m*	—	cuenta particular *f*
conto profitti (I)	Erfolgskonto *n*	profit account	compte de résultats *m*	—	cuenta de beneficios y pérdidas *f*
conto profitti e perdite (I)	Gewinn- und Verlustrechnung *f*	profit and loss account	compte de pertes et profits *m*	—	cuenta de pérdidas y ganancias *f*
conto stipendi (I)	Gehaltskonto *n*	salary account	compte de domiciliation du salaire *m*	—	cuenta de salario *f*
conto transitorio (I)	Zwischenkonto *n*	interim account	compte provisoire *m*	—	cuenta provisional *f*
conto trimestrale (I)	Quartalsrechnung *f*	quarterly invoice	compte trimestriel *m*	—	cuenta trimestral *f*
conto vincolato (I)	Sperrkonto *n*	blocked account	compte bloqué *m*	—	fondos bloqueados *m pl*
contrabando (Es)	Schmuggel *m*	smuggling	contrebande *f*	contrabbando *m*	—
contrabbando (I)	Schmuggel *m*	smuggling	contrebande *f*	—	contrabando *m*
contract[1] (E)	Vertrag *m*	—	contrat *m*/traité *m*/ accord *m*	contratto *m*	contrato m/tratado *m*/ acuerdo *m*
contract[2] (E)	Kontrakt *m*	—	contrat *m*	contratto *m*	contrato *m*
contract for work and services (E)	Werkvertrag *m*	—	contrat de louage d'ouvrage et d'industrie *m*	contratto d'appalto *m*	contrato de obra *m*
contract of assignment (E)	Abtretungsvertrag *m*	—	contrat de cession *m*	contratto di cessione *m*	contrato de cesión *m*
contract of employment (E)	Arbeitsvertrag *m*	—	contrat de travail *m*	contratto di lavoro *m*	contrato laboral *m*
contract of sale (E)	Kaufvertrag *m*	—	contrat de vente *m*	contratto di compravendita *m*	contrato de compraventa *m*
contract period (E)	Vertragsdauer *f*	—	durée du contrat *f*	durata del contratto *f*	duración del contrato *f*
contract services (E)	Auftragswesen *n*	—	services commandes *m pl*	settore ordini *m*	servicio de pedidos *m*
contractual penalty (E)	Konventionalstrafe *f*	—	pénalité *f*	penalità convenzionale *f*	pena convencional *f*
contrafirma (Es)	Gegenzeichnung *f*	countersignature	contreseing *m*	controfirma *f*	—
contraire à la loi (F)	ungesetzlich	illegal	—	illegale	ilegal
contra rembolso (Es)	gegen Nachnahme	cash on delivery	contre remboursement	contro assegno	—
contrassegno (I)	Nachnahme *f*	cash on delivery	remboursement *m*	—	reembolso *m*
contrastar (Es)	eichen	gauge	jauger	tarare	—
contrat[1] (F)	Vertrag *m*	contract/treaty	—	contratto *m*	contrato *m*/ tratado *m*
contrat[2] (F)	Kontrakt *m*	contract	—	contratto *m*	contrato *m*
contrata (Es)	Liefervertrag *m*	supply contract	contrat de fourniture *m*	contratto di consegna *m*	—
contrat à terme (F)	Terminkontrakt *m*	forward contract	—	contratto a termine *m*	contrato de entrega futura *m*
contratación[1] (Es)	Anwerbung *f*	recruitment	recrutement *m*	reclutamento *m*	—
contratación[2] (Es)	Abschluß *m*	conclusion	conclusion *f*	stipulazione *f*	—
contratación de acciones (Es)	Aktienhandel *m*	dealing in shares	négociation des actions *f*	commercio azionario *m*	—
contrat d'affrètement[1] (F)	Chartervertrag *m*	charter party	—	contratto di noleggio *m*	contrato de fletamento *m*
contrat d'affrètement[2] (F)	Frachtvertrag *m*	freight contract	—	contratto di trasporto *m*	contrato de transporte *m*
contrat d'assurance (F)	Versicherungs-vertrag *m*	insurance contract	—	contratto d'assicurazione *m*	contrato de seguro *m*
contrat de cession (F)	Abtretungsvertrag *m*	contract of assignment	—	contratto di cessione *m*	contrato de cesión *m*

	D	E	F	I	Es
contrat de concession de licence (F)	Lizenzvertrag *m*	licence agreement	—	contratto di licenza *m*	contrato de licencia *m*
contrat de fourniture (F)	Liefervertrag *m*	supply contract	—	contratto di consegna *m*	contrata *f*
contrat de leasing (F)	Leasing-Vertrag *m*	leasing contract	—	contratto leasing *m*	contrato de arrendamiento financiero *m*
contrat de louage d'ouvrage et d'industrie (F)	Werkvertrag *m*	contract for work and services	—	contratto d'appalto *m*	contrato de obra *m*
contrat de travail (F)	Arbeitsvertrag *m*	contract of employment	—	contratto di lavoro *m*	contrato laboral *m*
contrat de travail convenu à l'essai (F)	Arbeitsverhältnis auf Probe *n*	employee-employer relationship on a trial basis	—	rapporto di lavoro in prova *m*	relación laboral a prueba *f*
contrat de vente[1] (F)	Kaufvertrag *m*	contract of sale	—	contratto di compravendita *m*	contrato de compraventa *m*
contrat de vente[2] (F)	Verkaufsabschluß *m*	sales contract	—	conclusione di vendita *f*	conclusión de la venta *f*
contrato[1] (Es)	Kontrakt *m*	contract	contrat *m*	contratto *m*	—
contrato[2] (Es)	Vertrag *m*	contract	contrat *m*	contratto *m*	—
contrato colectivo (Es)	Tarifvertrag *m*	collective agreement	convention collective *f*	contratto salariale *m*	—
contrato de arrendamiento financiero (Es)	Leasing-Vertrag *m*	leasing contract	contrat de leasing *m*	contratto leasing *m*	—
contrato de cesión (Es)	Abtretungsvertrag *m*	contract of assignment	contrat de cession *m*	contratto di cessione *m*	—
contrato de compraventa (Es)	Kaufvertrag *m*	contract of sale	contrat de vente *m*	contratto di compravendita *m*	—
contrato de dominación (Es)	Beherrschungsvertrag *m*	control agreement	accord de contrôle *m*	contratto di controllo *m*	—
contrato de entrega futura (Es)	Terminkontrakt *m*	forward contract	contrat à terme *m*	contratto a termine *m*	—
contrato de fletamento (Es)	Chartervertrag *m*	charter party	contrat d'affrètement *m*	contratto di noleggio *m*	—
contrato de licencia (Es)	Lizenzvertrag *m*	licence agreement	contrat de concession de licence *m*	contratto di licenza *m*	—
contrato de obra (Es)	Werkvertrag *m*	contract for work and services	contrat de louage d'ouvrage et d'industrie *m*	contratto d'appalto *m*	—
contrato de seguro[1] (Es)	Versicherungsvertrag *m*	insurance contract	contrat d'assurance *m*	contratto d'assicurazione *m*	—
contrato de seguro[2] (Es)	Versicherungsschutz *m*	insurance cover	couverture de l'assurance *f*	copertura assicurativa *f*	—
contrato de transporte (Es)	Frachtvertrag *m*	freight contract	contrat d'affrètement *m*	contratto di trasporto *m*	—
contrato laboral (Es)	Arbeitsvertrag *m*	contract of employment	contrat de travail *m*	contratto di lavoro *m*	—
contrato social (Es)	Gesellschaftsvertrag *m*	shareholder's agreement/partnership agreement	acte de société *m*	contratto di società *m*	—
contratto[1] (I)	Kontrakt *m*	contract	contrat *m*	—	contrato *m*
contratto[2] (I)	Vertrag *m*	contract/treaty	contrat *m*/traité *m*/accord *m*	—	contrato *m*/tratado *m*
contratto a contanti (I)	Tagesgeschäft *n*	day-to-day operations	affaire au comptant *f*	—	operación al contado *f*
contratto a termine (I)	Terminkontrakt *m*	forward contract	contrat à terme *m*	—	contrato de entrega futura *m*
contratto d'appalto (I)	Werkvertrag *m*	contract for work and services	contrat de louage d'ouvrage et d'industrie *m*	—	contrato de obra *m*
contratto d'assicurazione (I)	Versicherungsvertrag *m*	insurance contract	contrat d'assurance *m*	—	contrato de seguro *m*
contratto di cessione (I)	Abtretungsvertrag *m*	contract of assignment	contrat de cession *m*	—	contrato de cesión *m*
contratto di compravendita (I)	Kaufvertrag *m*	contract of sale	contrat de vente *m*	—	contrato de compraventa *m*
contratto di consegna (I)	Liefervertrag *m*	supply contract	contrat de fourniture *m*	—	contrata *f*

	D	E	F	I	Es
contratto di controllo (I)	Beherrschungs-vertrag *m*	control agreement	accord de contrôle *m*	—	contrato de dominación *m*
contratto di lavoro (I)	Arbeitsvertrag *m*	contract of employment	contrat de travail *m*	—	contrato laboral *m*
contratto di licenza (I)	Lizenzvertrag *m*	licence agreement	contrat de concession de licence *m*	—	contrato de licencia *m*
contratto di noleggio (I)	Chartervertrag *m*	charter party	contrat d'affrètement *m*	—	contrato de fletamento *m*
contratto di società (I)	Gesellschafts-vertrag *m*	shareholder's agree-ment/partnership agreement	acte de société *m*	—	contrato social *m*
contratto di trasporto (I)	Frachtvertrag *m*	freight contract	contrat d'affrètement *m*	—	contrato do transporte *m*
contratto leasing (I)	Leasing-Vertrag *m*	leasing contract	contrat de leasing *m*	—	contrato de arrenda-miento financiero *m*
contratto salariale (I)	Tarifvertrag *m*	collective agreement	convention collective *f*	—	contrato colectivo *m*
contravalor (Es)	Gegenwert *m*	equivalent	contre-valeur *f*	controvalore *m*	—
contre accréditif (F)	gegen Akkreditiv	against letter of credit	—	contro lettera di credito	con crédito documentario
contrebande (F)	Schmuggel *m*	smuggling	—	contrabbando *m*	contrabando *m*
contre remboursement (F)	gegen Nachnahme	cash on delivery	—	contro assegno	contra rembolso
contreseing (F)	Gegenzeichnung *f*	countersignature	—	controfirma *f*	contrafirma *f*
contre-valeur (F)	Gegenwert *m*	equivalent	—	controvalore *m*	contravalor *m*
contribuable (F)	Steuerzahler *m*	taxpayer	—	contribuente *m*	contribuyente *m*
contribuciones (Es)	Beiträge *pl*	contributions	participations *f pl*	contributi *m pl*	—
contribuente (I)	Steuerzahler *m*	taxpayer	contribuable *m*	—	contribuyente *m*
contributi (I)	Beiträge *pl*	contributions	participations *f pl*	—	contribuciones *f pl*
contribution costing (E)	Deckungsbeitrags-rechnung *f*	—	calcul de la proportion de garantie *m*	calcolo del contri-buto per copertura *m*	factura de aportación de fondos *f*
contribution margin (E)	Deckungsbeitrag *m*	—	proportion de garantie *f*	contributo per copertura *m*	aportación de cobertura *f*
contributions (E)	Beiträge *pl*	—	participations *f pl*	contributi *m pl*	contribuciones *f pl*
contributo per copertura (I)	Deckungsbeitrag *m*	contribution margin	proportion de garantie *f*	—	aportación de cobertura *f*
contribuyente (Es)	Steuerzahler *m*	taxpayer	contribuable *m*	contribuente *m*	—
contro assegno (I)	gegen Nachnahme	cash on delivery	contre remboursement	—	contra rembolso
controfirma (I)	Gegenzeichnung *f*	countersignature	contreseing *m*	—	contrafirma *f*
control¹ (E)	Kontrolle *f*	—	contrôle *m*	controllo *m*	control *m*
control² (E)	Steuerung *f*	—	contrôle *f*	controllo *m*	control *m*
control¹ (Es)	Kontrolle *f*	control	contrôle *m*	controllo *m*	—
control² (Es)	Steuerung *f*	control	contrôle *f*	controllo *m*	—
control agreement (E)	Beherrschungs-vertrag *m*	—	accord de contrôle *m*	contratto di controllo *m*	contrato de dominación *m*
control de divisas¹ (Es)	Devisenkontrolle *f*	foreign exchange control	contrôle des changes *m*	controllo delle divise *m*	—
control de divisas² (Es)	Devisenbewirt-schaftung *f*	foreign exchange control	contrôle des devises *m*	controllo valutario *m*	—
control de eficiencia (Es)	Effizienzkontrolle *f*	efficiency control	contrôle de l'efficience *m*	controllo d'efficienza *m*	—
control de fusiones (Es)	Fusionskontrolle *f*	merger control	contrôle de fusion *m*	controllo delle fusioni *m*	—
control de gastos (Es)	Ausgabenkontrolle *f*	expenditure control	contrôle des dépenses *m*	controllo delle spese *m*	—
control de las inversiones (Es)	Investitionskontrolle *f*	investment control	contrôle d'investissement *m*	controllo degli investimenti *m*	—
control del presupuesto (Es)	Budgetkontrolle *f*	budget control	contrôle du budget *m*	controllo del bilancio *m*	—
control del sistema (Es)	Systemsteuerung *f*	system control	contrôle du système *m*	controllo del sistema *m*	—
control de precios (Es)	Preiskontrolle *f*	price control	contrôle des prix *m*	controllo dei prezzi *m*	—

	D	E	F	I	Es
control de producción (Es)	Produktions-kontrolle *f*	production control	contrôle de la production *m*	controllo della produzione *m*	—
contrôle[1] (F)	Kontrolle *f*	control	—	controllo *m*	control *m*
contrôle[2] (F)	Steuerung *f*	control	—	controllo *m*	control *m*
contrôle à la frontière (F)	Grenzkontrolle *f*	border control	—	controllo alla frontiera *m*	control fronterizo *m*
contrôle de financement (F)	Finanzkontrolle *f*	budgetary control	—	controllo finanziario *m*	control financiero *m*
contrôle de fusion (F)	Fusionskontrolle *f*	merger control	—	controllo delle fusioni *m*	control de fusiones *m*
contrôle de la gestion et des comptes (F)	Wirtschaftsprüfung *f*	auditing	—	revisione *f*	revisoría *f*
contrôle de la planification (F)	Planungskontrolle *f*	planning control	—	controllo della programmazione *m*	contol de planificación *m*
contrôle de la production (F)	Produktions-kontrolle *f*	production control	—	controllo della produzione *m*	control de producción *m*
contrôle de la qualité (F)	Qualitätskontrolle *f*	quality control	—	controllo di qualità *m*	verificación de la calidad *f*
contrôle de l'efficience (F)	Effizienzkontrolle *f*	efficiency control	—	controllo d'efficienza *m*	control de eficiencia *m*
contrôle des banques (F)	Bankenaufsicht *f*	public supervision of banking	—	commissione bancaria *f*	supervisión bancaria *f*
contrôle des changes (F)	Devisenkontrolle *f*	foreign exchange control	—	controllo delle divise *m*	control de divisas *m*
contrôle des dépenses (F)	Ausgabenkontrolle *f*	expenditure control	—	controllo delle spese *m*	control de gastos *m*
contrôle des devises (F)	Devisen-bewirtschaftung *f*	foreign exchange control	—	controllo valutario *m*	control de divisas *m*
contrôle des livres comptables (F)	Einsichtnahme *f*	inspection	—	presa visione *f*	inspección *f*
contrôle des prix (F)	Preiskontrolle *f*	price control	—	controllo dei prezzi *m*	control de precios *m*
contrôle d'investissement (F)	Investitionskontrolle *f*	investment control	—	controllo degli investimenti *m*	control de las inversiones *m*
contrôle du budget (F)	Budgetkontrolle *f*	budget control	—	controllo del bilancio *m*	control del presupuesto *m*
contrôle du résultat de la publicité (F)	Werbeerfolgs-kontrolle *f*	advertising control	—	controllo del successo pubblicitario *m*	análisis del resultado publicitario *m*
contrôle du système (F)	Systemsteuerung *f*	system control	—	controllo del sistema *m*	control del sistema *m*
contrôle final (F)	Endkontrolle *f*	final control	—	controllo finale *m*	control final *m*
contro lettera di credito (I)	gegen Akkreditiv	against letter of credit	contre accréditif	—	con crédito documentario
control final (Es)	Endkontrolle *f*	final control	contrôle final *m*	controllo finale *m*	—
control financiero (Es)	Finanzkontrolle *f*	budgetary control	contrôle de financement *m*	controllo finanziario *m*	—
control fronterizo (Es)	Grenzkontrolle *f*	border control	contrôle à la frontière *m*	controllo alla frontiera *m*	—
controlled economy (E)	Dirigismus *m*	—	dirigisme *m*	dirigismo *m*	dirigismo *m*
controlling company[1] (E)	herrschendes Unternehmen *n*	—	entreprise dirigeante *f*	impresa controllante *f*	empresa dominante *f*
controlling company[2] (E)	Besitzgesellschaft *f*	—	société contrôleuse *f*	società finanziaria *f*	sociedad controladora *f*
controllo[1] (I)	Steuerung *f*	control	contrôle *m*	—	control *m*
controllo[2] (I)	Kontrolle *f*	control	contrôle *m*	—	control *m*
controllo[3] (I)	Prüfung *f*	inspection/ examination	vérification *f*/ examen *m*	—	verificación *f*/ examen *m*
controllo alla frontiera (I)	Grenzkontrolle *f*	border control	contrôle à la frontière *m*	—	control fronterizo *m*
controllo d'efficienza (I)	Effizienzkontrolle *f*	efficiency control	contrôle de l'efficience *m*	—	control de eficiencia *m*
controllo degli investimenti (I)	Investitions-kontrolle *f*	investment control	contrôle d'investissement *m*	—	control de las inversiones *m*
controllo dei prezzi (I)	Preiskontrolle *f*	price control	contrôle des prix *m*	—	control de precios *m*
controllo del bilancio (I)	Budgetkontrolle *f*	budget control	contrôle du budget *m*	—	control del presupuesto *m*

	D	E	F	I	Es
controllo della produzione (I)	Produktions-kontrolle *f*	production control	contrôle de la production *m*	—	control de producción *m*
controllo della programmazione (I)	Planungskontrolle *f*	planning control	contrôle de la planification *f*	—	contol de planificación *m*
controllo delle divise (I)	Devisenkontrolle *f*	foreign exchange control	contrôle des changes *m*	—	control de divisas *m*
controllo delle fusioni (I)	Fusionskontrolle *f*	merger control	contrôle de fusion *m*	—	control de fusiones *m*
controllo delle spese (I)	Ausgabenkontrolle *f*	expenditure control	contrôle des dépenses *m*	—	control de gastos *m*
controllo del sistema (I)	Systemsteuerung *f*	system control	contrôle du système *m*	—	control del sistema *m*
controllo del successo pubblicitario (I)	Werbeerfolgs-kontrolle *f*	advertising control	contrôle du résultat de la publicité *m*	—	análisis del resultado publicitario *m*
controllo di qualità (I)	Qualitätskontrolle *f*	quality control	contrôle de la qualité *m*	—	verificación de la calidad *f*
controllo finale (I)	Endkontrolle *f*	final control	contrôle final *m*	—	control final *m*
controllo finanziario (I)	Finanzkontrolle *f*	budgetary control	contrôle de financement *m*	—	control financiero *m*
controllo globale (I)	Globalsteuerung *f*	global control	régulation globale *f*	—	regulación global *f*
controllo valutario (I)	Devisenbewirt-schaftung *f*	foreign exchange control	contrôle des devises *m*	—	control de divisas *m*
contro pagamento in contanti (I)	gegen Barzahlung	against cash	au comptant	—	al contado
controvalore (I)	Gegenwert *m*	equivalent	contre-valeur *f*	—	contravalor *m*
convegno (I)	Tagung *f*	meeting	congrès *m*	—	reunión *f*
convegno dei rappresentanti (I)	Vertretertagung *f*	sales meeting	réunion de représentants *f*	—	conferencia de representantes *f*
convenio aduanero (Es)	Zollabkommen *n*	customs convention	accord douanier *m*	accordo sulle tariffe doganali *m*	—
convenio de compra (Es)	Kaufabschluß *m*	conclusion of a sales contract	conclusion du marché *f*	conclusione d'acquisto *f*	—
convenio forzoso (Es)	Zwangsvergleich *m*	compulsory settlement	arrangement forcé *m*	concordato fallimentare *m*	—
convention collective (F)	Tarifvertrag *m*	collective agreement	—	contratto salariale *m*	contrato colectivo *m*
convention de salaire à la tâche (F)	Akkord *m*	piece work	—	cottimo *m*	destajo *m*
conversación (Es)	Unterredung *f*	discussion	entretien *m*	colloquio *m*	—
conversación de venta (Es)	Verkaufsgespräch *n*	sales talk	conversation de vente *f*	colloquio di vendita *m*	—
conversación personal (Es)	persönliches Gespräch *n*	personal conversation	conversation personnelle *f*	colloquio personale *m*	—
conversation de vente (F)	Verkaufsgespräch *n*	sales talk	—	colloquio di vendita *m*	conversación de venta *f*
conversation personnelle (F)	persönliches Gespräch *n*	personal conversation	—	colloquio personale *m*	conversación personal *f*
conversation téléphonique (F)	Telefongespräch *n*	telephone conversation	—	telefonata *f*	conferencia telefónica *f*
convertibile (I)	konvertibel	convertible	convertible	—	convertible
convertibilidad (Es)	Konvertibilität *f*	convertibility	convertibilité *f*	convertibilità *f*	—
convertibilità (I)	Konvertibilität *f*	convertibility	convertibilité *f*	—	convertibilidad *f*
convertibilité (F)	Konvertibilität *f*	convertibility	—	convertibilità *f*	convertibilidad *f*
convertibility (E)	Konvertibilität *f*	—	convertibilité *f*	convertibilità *f*	convertibilidad *f*
convertible (E)	konvertibel	—	convertible	convertibile	convertible
convertible (Es)	konvertibel	convertible	convertible	convertibile	—
convertible (F)	konvertibel	convertible	—	convertibile	convertible
convertible bonds (E)	Wandelschuld-verschreibung *f*	—	obligation convertible *f*	obbligazione convertibile *f*	obligaciones convertibles *f pl*
convocatoria de oposiciones (Es)	Stellen-ausschreibung *f*	advertisement of a vacancy	mise au concours d'une place *f*	bando di concorso per impiegati *m*	—
conyuntura (Es)	Konjunktur *f*	business cycle	conjoncture *f*	congiuntura *f*	—
cooperación[1] (Es)	Kooperation *f*	cooperation	coopération *f*	cooperazione *f*	—

	D	E	F	I	Es
cooperación² (Es)	Zusammenarbeit *f*	cooperation	collaboration *f*	collaborazione *f*	—
coopératif (F)	kooperativ	cooperative	—	cooperativo	cooperativo
cooperation¹ (E)	Zusammenarbeit *f*	—	collaboration *f*	collaborazione *f*	cooperación *f*
cooperation² (E)	Kooperation *f*	—	coopération *f*	cooperazione *f*	cooperación *f*
coopération (F)	Kooperation *f*	cooperation	—	cooperazione *f*	cooperación *f*
cooperativa (I)	Genossenschaft *f*	co-operative	société coopérative *f*	—	sociedad cooperativa *f*
cooperativa de producción (Es)	Produktions-genossenschaft *f*	producer cooperative	société coopérative de production *f*	cooperativa di produzione *f*	—
cooperativa di produzione (I)	Produktions-genossenschaft *f*	producer cooperative	société coopérative de production *f*	—	cooperativa de producción *f*
cooperative (E)	kooperativ	—	coopératif	cooperativo	cooperativo
co-operative (E)	Genossenschaft *f*	—	société coopérative *f*	cooperativa *f*	sociedad cooperativa *f*
cooperativo (Es)	kooperativ	cooperative	coopératif	cooperativo	—
cooperativo (I)	kooperativ	cooperative	coopératif	—	cooperativo
cooperazione (I)	Kooperation *f*	cooperation	coopération *f*	—	cooperación *f*
coordinación (Es)	Koordination *f*	coordination	coordination *f*	coordinazione *f*	—
coordination (E)	Koordination *f*	—	coordination *f*	coordinazione *f*	coordinación *f*
coordination (F)	Koordination *f*	coordination	—	coordinazione *f*	coordinación *f*
coordinazione (I)	Koordination *f*	coordination	coordination *f*	—	coordinación *f*
co-owner (E)	Bruchteils-eigentümer *m*	—	copropriétaire d'une quote-part *m*	comproprietario di quota ideale *m*	copropietario de bienes indivisos *m*
co-ownership (E)	Miteigentum *n*	—	copropriété *f*	comproprietà *f*	copropiedad *f*
copertura (I)	Deckung *f*	cover	couverture *f*	—	cobertura *f*
copertura assicurativa (I)	Versicherungs-schutz *m*	insurance cover	couverture de l'assurance *f*	—	cobertura de seguro *f*
copia¹ (Es)	Abschrift *f*	copy	copie *f*	copia *f*	—
copia² (Es)	Kopie *f*	copy	copie *f*	copia *f*	—
copia¹ (I)	Abschrift *f*	copy	copie *f*	—	copia *f*
copia² (I)	Kopie *f*	copy	copie *f*	—	copia *f*
copia autenticata (I)	beglaubigte Abschrift *f*	authenticated copy	copie certifiée *f*	—	copia legalizada *f*
copia legalizada (Es)	beglaubigte Abschrift *f*	authenticated copy	copie certifiée *f*	copia autenticata *f*	—
copialettere (I)	Fotokopierer *m*	photocopier	photocopieur *m*	—	fotocopiadora *f*
copie¹ (F)	Kopie *f*	copy	—	copia *f*	copia *f*
copie² (F)	Abschrift *f*	copy	—	copia *f*	copia *f*
copie certifiée (F)	beglaubigte Abschrift *f*	authenticated copy	—	copia autenticata *f*	copia legalizada *f*
coproducción (Es)	Koppel-produktion *f*	tied production	production couplée *f*	produzione abbinata *f*	—
copropiedad (Es)	Miteigentum *n*	co-ownership	copropriété *f*	comproprietà *f*	—
copropietario de bienes indivisos (Es)	Bruchteils-eigentümer *m*	co-owner	copropriétaire d'une quote-part *m*	comproprietario di quota ideale *m*	—
copropriétaire d'une quote-part (F)	Bruchteils-eigentümer *m*	co-owner	—	comproprietario di quota ideale *m*	copropietario de bienes indivisos *m*
copropriété (F)	Miteigentum *n*	co-ownership	—	comproprietà *f*	copropiedad *f*
copy¹ (E)	Abschrift *f*	—	copie *f*	copia *f*	copia *f*
copy² (E)	Kopie *f*	—	copie *f*	copia *f*	copia *f*
copyright (E)	Urheberrecht *n*	—	droit d'auteur *m*	diritto d'autore *m*	derecho del autor *m*
corpo (I)	Kasko *m*	comprehensive	sur corps	—	de casco
corporación (Es)	Körperschaft *f*	corporation	collectivité *f*	ente *m*	—
corporate strategy (E)	Unternehmens-strategie *f*	—	stratégie de l'entreprise *f*	strategia imprenditoriale *f*	estrategia empresarial *f*
corporation (E)	Körperschaft *f*	—	collectivité *f*	ente *m*	corporación *f*
corporation stock (E)	Kommunal-obligation *f*	—	obligation communale *f*	obbligazioni comunali *f pl*	obligación comunal *f*
corporation tax (E)	Körperschaftsteuer *f*	—	taxe sur les sociétés *f*	imposta sul reddito delle società *f*	impuesto de corporaciones *m*

	D	E	F	I	Es
corps de sécurité d'entreprise (F)	Werkschutz *m*	works protection force	—	servizio di sorveglianza aziendale *m*	policía de la empresa *f*
correct (E)	korrigieren	—	corriger	correggere	corrigir
correct (F)	ordnungsgemäß	orderly/duly	—	regolare	debidamente
correction (E)	Berichtigung *f*	—	rectification *f*	correzione *f*	rectificación *f*
corredor (Es)	Makler *m*	broker	courtier *m*	mediatore *m*	—
corredor de bolsa[1] (Es)	Börsenmakler *m*	stockbroker	courtier en bourse *m*	agente di cambio *m*	—
corredor de bolsa[2] (Es)	Broker *m*	broker	courtier *m*	broker *m*	—
corredor de seguros (Es)	Versicherungsmakler *m*	insurance broker	courtier en assurance *m*	mediatore d'assicurazione *m*	—
corredor marítimo (Es)	Schiffsmakler *m*	shipbroker	courtier maritime *m*	agente marittimo *m*	—
correggere (I)	korrigieren	correct	corriger	—	corrigir
correlación (Es)	Korrelation *f*	correlation	corrélation *f*	correlazione *f*	—
correlation (E)	Korrelation *f*	—	corrélation *f*	correlazione *f*	correlación *f*
corrélation (F)	Korrelation *f*	correlation	—	correlazione *f*	correlación *f*
correlazione (I)	Korrelation *f*	correlation	corrélation *f*	—	correlación *f*
corrente (I)	kulant	accommodating	arrangeant	—	de fácil avenencia
correntezza (I)	Kulanz *f*	accommodation	souplesse en affaires *f*	—	facilidad en los negocios *f*
correo aéreo (Es)	Luftpost *f*	air mail	par avion	posta aerea *f*	—
correos (Es)	Postamt *n*	post office	bureau de poste *m*	ufficio postale *m*	—
correspondant (F)	Geschäftsfreund *m*	business friend	—	partner d'affari *m*	corresponsal *m*
corresponsal (Es)	Geschäftsfreund *m*	business friend	correspondant *m*	partner d'affari *m*	—
corretaje (Es)	Courtage *f*	brokerage	courtage *m*	courtage *f*	—
correzione (I)	Berichtigung *f*	correction	rectification *f*	—	rectificación *f*
corriere (I)	Eilbote *m*	express messenger	facteur spécial *m*	—	expreso *m*
corrigé du mouvement saisonnier (F)	saisonbereinigt	seasonally adjusted	—	al netto degli influssi stagionali	desestacionalizado
corriger (F)	korrigieren	correct	—	correggere	corrigir
corrigir (Es)	korrigieren	correct	corriger	correggere	—
corruption (F)	Bestechung *f*	bribe	—	corruzione *f*	soborno *f*
corruzione (I)	Bestechung *f*	bribe	corruption *f*	—	soborno *f*
corso (I)	Kurs *m*	exchange rate	cours (du change) *m*	—	cotización *f*/tipo de cambio *m*
corso a pronti (I)	Kassakurs *m*	spot price	cours au comptant *m*	—	cotización al contado *f*
corso a termine (I)	Terminkurs *m*	forward price	cours de bourse à terme *m*	—	cambio a término *m*
corso dei cambi (I)	Sortenkurs *m*	rate for foreign notes and coins	cours des monnaies étrangères *m*	—	tipo de cambio de billetes y monedas extranjeras *m*
corso delle azioni (I)	Aktienkurs *m*	share price	cours des actions *m*	—	cotización de las acciones *f*
corso di borsa (I)	Börsenkurs *m*	quotation on the stock exchange	cours de bourse *m pl*	—	cotización en bolsa *f*
corso di cambio (I)	Umrechnungskurs *m*	rate of conversion	cours de conversion *m*	—	tasa de cambio *f*
corso massimo (I)	Höchstkurs *m*	highest rate	cours le plus haut *m*	—	cotización máxima *f*
corso minimo (I)	Niedrigstkurs *m*	floor price	cours le plus bas *m*	—	cotización mínima *f*
corte d'appello (I)	Berufungsgericht *n*	appeal court	tribunal d'appel *m*	—	tribunal de apelación *m*
Corte di Giustizia Europea (I)	Europäischer Gerichtshof *m*	European Court	Cour de Justice Européenne *f*	—	Tribunal de Justicia de las Comunidades Europeas *m*
cost (E)	Selbstkosten *pl*	—	coût de revient *m*	spese vive *f pl*	costes propios *m pl*
cost accounting system (E)	Kostenrechnungssystem *n*	—	méthode de calcul des coûts *f*	sistema dei costi *m*	sistema de costes *m*
cost advantage (E)	Kostenvorteil *m*	—	avantage de coût *m*	vantaggio di costo *m*	ventaja de costes *f*
cost allocation (E)	Kostenverrechung *f*	—	répartition des frais *f*	ripartizione dei costi *f*	repartición de costes *f*

	D	E	F	I	Es
cost analysis (E)	Kostenanalyse *f*	—	analyse des coûts *f*	analisi dei costi *f*	análisis de costes *m*
costas (Es)	Verfahrenskosten *pl*	costs of the proceedings	frais de procédure *m pl*	spese del procedimento *f pl*	—
cost-benefit analysis (E)	Kosten-Nutzen-Analyse *f*	—	analyse du ratio coût à profit *f*	analisi costi-benefici *f*	análisis de coste-beneficio *m*
cost degression (E)	Kostendegression *f*	—	dégressivité des coûts *f*	riduzione dei costi *f*	reducción de costes *f*
coste alternativo (Es)	Alternativkosten *pl*	opportunity costs	coûts alternatifs *m pl*	costi alternativi *m pl*	—
coste de adquisición (Es)	Anschaffungs-kosten *pl*	purchase costs	frais d'acquisition *m pl*	costi d'acquisto *m pl*	—
coste de material (Es)	Materialaufwand *m*	material expenditure	dépenses en matériel *f pl*	spese materiale *f pl*	—
coste de salarios (Es)	Lohnkosten *pl*	cost of wages	coût du travail *m*	costo del lavoro *m*	—
coste directo (Es)	direkte Kosten *pl*	direct cost	coûts directs *m pl*	costi diretti *m pl*	—
coste por unidad (Es)	Stückkosten *pl*	costs per unit	coût unitaire de production *m*	costi unitari *m pl*	—
cost escalation (E)	Kostenexplosion *f*	—	explosion des coûts *f*	esplosione dei costi *f*	incremento desmesu-rado de los costes *m*
costes de apelación al crédito (Es)	Kreditbeschaffungs-kosten *pl*	cost of borrowing	coûts d'obtention de crédits *m pl*	spese d'approvvi-gionamento di credito *f pl*	—
costes propios (Es)	Selbstkosten *pl*	cost	coût de revient *m*	spese vive *f pl*	—
costi (I)	Kosten *pl*	costs	coût *m*	—	gastos *m pl*
costi accessori (I)	Nebenkosten *pl*	ancillary costs	coûts accessoires *m pl*	—	gastos adicionales *m pl*
costi alternativi (I)	Alternativkosten *pl*	opportunity costs	coûts alternatifs *m pl*	—	coste alternativo *m*
costi calcolati (I)	Sollkosten *pl*	budgeted costs	coûts ex ante *m pl*	—	gastos precalculados *m pl*
costi complementari del lavoro (I)	Lohnnebenkosten *pl*	ancillary wage costs	charges salariales annexes *f pl*	—	cargas salariales accesorias *f pl*
costi comuni (I)	Gemeinkosten *pl*	overhead expenses	coûts indirects *m pl*	—	gastos generales *m pl*
costi d'acquisto (I)	Anschaffungs-kosten *pl*	purchase costs	frais d'acquisition *m pl*	—	coste de adquisición *m*
costi d'adattamento (I)	Anpassungskosten *pl*	adjustment costs	coûts d'adaptation *m pl*	—	gastos readaptación *m pl*
costi d'informazione (I)	Informationskosten *pl*	information costs	coûts d'information *m pl*	—	gastos de información *m pl*
costi della costituzione (I)	Gründungskosten *pl*	organization costs	frais de fondation *m pl*	—	gastos de fundación *m pl*
costi del materiale (I)	Materialkosten *pl*	material costs	frais coûts de matériel *m pl*	—	gastos de material *m pl*/coste de material *m*
costi di caricamento (I)	Verladekosten *pl*	loading charges	coût du chargement *m*	—	gastos de carga *m pl*
costi di produzione (I)	Herstellungskosten *pl*	production costs	frais de fabrication *m pl*	—	costo de la producción *m*
costi diretti (I)	direkte Kosten *pl*	direct cost	coûts directs *m pl*	—	coste directo *m*
costi di riproduzione (I)	Reproduktions-kosten *pl*	reproduction cost	coût de reproduction *m*	—	gastos de reproducción *m pl*
costi di risanamento (I)	Sanierungskosten *pl*	renewal costs	coûts d'assainissent *m pl*	—	gastos de saneamien-to *m pl*/gastos de rehabilitación *m pl*
costi di sviluppo (I)	Entwicklungs-kosten *pl*	development costs	coûts de développement *m pl*	—	gastos de desarrollo *m pl*
costi di viaggio (I)	Reisekosten *pl*	travelling expenses	frais de voyage *m pl*	—	gastos de viaje *m pl*
costi effettivi (I)	Istkosten *pl*	actual costs	coûts réels *m pl*	—	gastos efectivos *m pl*
costi fissi (I)	Fixkosten *pl*	fixed costs	coûts fixes *m pl*	—	gastos fijos *m pl*
costi fissi di utilizzo (I)	Nutzkosten *pl*	utility costs	coûts fixes utiles *m pl*	—	gastos fijos de utilización *m pl*
costi medi (I)	Durchschnitts-kosten *pl*	average costs	coût moyenne *m*	—	gastos medios *m pl*
costi per le acque di scarico (I)	Abwasserkosten *pl*	sewage disposal costs	coûts de traitement des eaux usées *m pl*	—	gastos para aguas residuales *m pl*
costi produttivi (I)	Produktionskosten *pl*	cost of production	coût de production *m*	—	gastos de producción *m pl*

	D	E	F	I	Es
costi sociali (I)	Sozialkosten *pl*	social insurance costs	coûts sociaux *m pl*	—	costo social *m*/ cargas sociales *f pl*
costi totali (I)	Gesamtkosten *pl*	total costs	coût total *m*	—	gastos generales *m pl*
costituzione di cartelli (I)	Kartellbildung *f*	cartel formation	cartellisation *f*	—	formación de carteles *f*
costituzione di un lavoro indipendente (I)	Existenzgründung *f*	setting up of new business	fondation d'existence *f*	—	fundación de existencia *f*
costituzione di un sindacato (I)	Syndizierung *f*	syndication	syndication *f*	—	sindicación *f*
costituzione nuova (I)	Neugründung *f*	new foundation	création d'une nouvelle société *f*	—	fundación nueva *f*
costi unitari (I)	Stückkosten *pl*	costs per unit	coût unitaire de production *m*	—	coste por unidad *m*
costi variabili (I)	variable Kosten *pl*	variable costs	coûts variables *m pl*	—	gastos variables *m pl*
costituzione (I)	Gründung *f*	formation	constitution *f*	—	fundación *f*
costo de la producción (Es)	Herstellungskosten *pl*	production costs	frais de fabrication *m pl*	costi di produzione *m pl*	—
costo del lavoro (I)	Lohnkosten *pl*	cost of wages	coût du travail *m*	—	coste de salarios *m*
cost of borrowing (E)	Kreditbeschaffungs-kosten *pl*	—	coûts d'obtention de crédits *m pl*	spese d'approvvi-gionamento di credito *f pl*	costes de apelación al crédito *m pl*
cost of production (E)	Produktionskosten *pl*	—	coût de production *m*	costi produttivi *m pl*	gastos de producción *m pl*
cost of wages (E)	Lohnkosten *pl*	—	coût du travail *m*	costo del lavoro *m*	coste de salarios *m*
costo social (Es)	Sozialkosten *pl*	social insurance costs	coûts sociaux *m pl*/ charges sociales *f pl*	costi sociali *m pl*	—
cost price[1] (E)	Selbstkostenpreis *m*	—	prix coûtant *m*	prezzo di costo *m*	precio de coste *m*
cost price[2] (E)	Einstandspreis *m*	—	prix coûtant *m*	prezzo di costo *m*	precio de coste *m*
cost reduction (E)	Kostensenkung *f*	—	diminution des coûts *f*	ribasso dei costi *m*	reducción de coste *f*
costruzione (I)	Bau *m*	construction	construction *f*	—	construcción *f*
costs (E)	Kosten *pl*	—	coût *m*	costi *m pl*	gastos *m pl*
cost schedule (E)	Kostenplan *m*	—	planning des coûts *m*	piano dei costi *m*	planilla de costas *f*
costs of the proceedings (E)	Verfahrenskosten *pl*	—	frais de procédure *m pl*	spese del procedimento *f pl*	costas *f pl*
costs per unit (E)	Stückkosten *pl*	—	coût unitaire de production *m*	costi unitari *m pl*	coste por unidad *m*
cost types (E)	Kostenarten *pl*	—	coûts par nature *m pl*	tipi di costi *m pl*	clases de costes *f pl*
cotation[1] (F)	Kursnotierung *f*	quotation of prices	—	quotazione dei corsi *f*	cotización *m*
cotation[2] (F)	Notierung *f*	quotation	—	quotazione *f*	cotización *f*
cotation de quantité (F)	Mengennotierung *f*	fixed exchange	—	cambio reale *m*	cotización real *f*
cotation des actions (F)	Aktiennotierung *f*	share quotation	—	quotazione delle azioni *f*	cotización de acciones *f*
cotation des cours en bourse (F)	Börsennotierung *f*	quotation on the stock exchange	—	quotazione di borsa *f*	cotización de bolsa *f*
cotation des prix (F)	Preisnotierung *f*	prices quoted	—	quotazione dei prezzi *f*	cotización de precios *f*
cotización[1] (Es)	Kurs *m*	exchange rate	cours (du change) *m*	corso *m*	—
cotización[2] (Es)	Kursnotierung *f*	quotation of prices	cotation *f*	quotazione dei corsi *f*	—
cotización[3] (Es)	Notierung *f*	quotation	cotation *f*	quotazione *f*	—
cotización al contado (Es)	Kassakurs *m*	spot price	cours au comptant *m*	corso a pronti *m*	—
cotización de acciones (Es)	Aktiennotierung *f*	share quotation	cotation des actions *f*	quotazione delle azioni *f*	—
cotización de bolsa (Es)	Börsennotierung *f*	quotation on the stock exchange	cotation des cours en bourse *f*	quotazione di borsa *f*	—
cotización de las acciones (Es)	Aktienkurs *m*	share price	cours des actions *m*	corso delle azioni *m*	—
cotización de precios (Es)	Preisnotierung *f*	prices quoted	cotation des prix *f*	quotazione dei prezzi *f*	—
cotización demandada (Es)	Geldkurs *m*	demand price	cours de la demande *m*	prezzo di domanda *m*	—

	D	E	F	I	Es
cotización en bolsa (Es)	Börsenkurs *m*	quotation on the stock exchange	cours de bourse *m pl*	corso di borsa *m*	—
cotización final (Es)	Schlußkurs *m*	closing price	dernier cours *m*	quotazione di chiusura *f*	—
cotización máxima (Es)	Höchstkurs *m*	highest rate	cours le plus haut *m*	corso massimo *m*	—
cotización mínima (Es)	Niedrigstkurs *m*	floor price	cours le plus bas *m*	corso minimo *m*	—
cotización ofrecida (Es)	Briefkurs *m*	ask price	cours de vente *m*	prezzo d'offerta *m*	—
cotización real (Es)	Mengennotierung *f*	fixed exchange	cotation de quantité *f*	cambio reale *m*	—
cotización única (Es)	Einheitskurs *m*	spot price	cours unique *m*	cambio unitario *m*	—
cottimo (I)	Akkord *m*	piece work	convention de salaire à la tâche *f*	—	destajo *m*
counter entry (E)	Storno *n*	—	écriture de contre-passation *f*	storno *m*	extorno *m*
countersignature (E)	Gegenzeichnung *f*	—	contreseing *m*	controfirma *f*	contrafirma *f*
country of origin[1] (E)	Herkunftsland *n*	—	pays de provenance *m*	paese d'origine *m*	país de origen *m*
country of origin[2] (E)	Ursprungsland *n*	—	pays d'origine *m*	paese d'origine *m*	país de origen *m*
country of purchase (E)	Einkaufsland *n*	—	pays où l'on achète *m*	paese acquirente *m*	país de compra *m*
coupable (F)	schuldhaft	culpable	—	colposo	culpable
Coupon (D)	—	coupon	coupon *m*	cedola *f*	cupón *m*
coupon (E)	Coupon *m*	—	coupon *m*	cedola *f*	cupón *m*
coupon (F)	Coupon *m*	coupon	—	cedola *f*	cupón *m*
coupons (I)	Benzingutscheine *pl*	petrol voucher	bon d'essence *m*	—	bono de gasolina *m*
Cour de Justice Européenne (F)	Europäischer Gerichtshof *m*	European Court	—	Corte di Giustizia Europea *f*	Tribunal de Justicia de la Comunidad Europea *m*
cours (F)	Kurs *m*	exchange rate	—	corso *m*/cambio *m*	cotización *f*/ tipo de cambio *m*
cours au comptant (F)	Kassakurs *m*	spot price	—	corso a pronti *m*	cotización al contado *f*
cours de bourse (F)	Börsenkurs *m*	quotation on the stock exchange	—	corso di borsa *m*	cotización en bolsa *f*
cours de bourse à terme (F)	Terminkurs *m*	forward price	—	corso a termine *m*	cambio a término *m*
cours de conversion (F)	Umrechnungskurs *m*	rate of conversion	—	corso di cambio *m*	tasa de cambio *f*
cours de la demande (F)	Geldkurs *m*	demand price	—	prezzo di domanda *m*	cotización demandada *f*/precio ofrecido *m*
cours d'émission (F)	Emissionskurs *m*	price of issue	—	prezzo d'emissione *m*	tipo de emisión *m*
cours des actions (F)	Aktienkurs *m*	share price	—	corso delle azioni *m*	cotización de las acciones *f*
cours des monnaies étrangères (F)	Sortenkurs *m*	rate for foreign notes and coins	—	corso dei cambi *m*	tipo de cambio de billetes y monedas extranjeras *m*
cours de vente (F)	Briefkurs *m*	ask price	—	prezzo d'offerta *m*	cotización ofrecida *f*
cours du change (F)	Wechselkurs *m*	exchange rate	—	cambio *m*	tipo de cambio *m*
cours du change multiple (F)	gespaltene Wechselkurse *pl*	two-tier exchange rate	—	cambi multipli *m pl*	tipo de cambio múltiple *m*
course des prix et des salaires (F)	Lohn-Preis-Spirale *f*	wage-price spiral	—	spirale prezzi-salari *f*	espiral salarios-precios *m*
course of the economic evolution (E)	Wirtschaftsverlauf *m*	—	évolution économique *f*	andamento dell'economia *m*	evolución económica *f*
cours le plus bas (F)	Niedrigstkurs *m*	floor price	—	corso minimo *m*	cotización mínima *f*
cours le plus haut (F)	Höchstkurs *m*	highest rate	—	corso massimo *m*	cotización máxima *f*
cours unique (F)	Einheitskurs *m*	spot price	—	cambio unitario *m*	cotización única *f*
court of arbitration (E)	Schiedsgericht *n*	—	tribunal d'arbitrage *m*	tribunale arbitrale *m*	tribunal arbitral *m*
Courtage (D)	—	brokerage	courtage *m*	courtage *f*	corretaje *m*
courtage (F)	Courtage *f*	brokerage	—	courtage *f*	corretaje *m*
courtage (I)	Courtage *f*	brokerage	courtage *m*	—	corretaje *m*
courtier[1] (F)	Broker *m*	broker	—	broker *m*	corredor de bolsa *m*
courtier[2] (F)	Makler *m*	broker	—	mediatore *m*	corredor *m*

	D	E	F	I	Es
courtier en affaires immoblières (F)	Immobilienmakler *m*	estate agent	—	agente immobiliare *m*	agente de inmuebles *m*
courtier en assurance (F)	Versicherungs-makler *m*	insurance broker	—	mediatore d'assicurazione *m*	corredor de seguros *m*
courtier en bourse[1] (F)	Börsenmakler *m*	stockbroker	—	agente di cambio *m*	corredor de bolsa *m*
courtier en bourse[2] (F)	Kursmakler *m*	stock broker/ exchange broker	—	agente di borsa *m*	agente cambio y bolsa *m*/corredor de cambios *m*
courtier maritime (F)	Schiffsmakler *m*	shipbroker	—	agente marittimo *m*	corredor marítimo *m*
coût (F)	Kosten *pl*	costs	—	costi *m pl*	gastos *m pl*
coût de production (F)	Produktionskosten *pl*	cost of production	—	costi produttivi *m pl*	gastos de producción *m pl*
coût de reproduction (F)	Reproduktions-kosten *pl*	reproduction cost	—	costi di riproduzione *m pl*	gastos de reproducción *m pl*
coût de revient (F)	Selbstkosten *pl*	cost	—	spese vive *f pl*	costes propios *m pl*
coût du chargement (F)	Verladekosten *pl*	loading charges	—	costi di caricamento *m pl*	gastos de carga *m pl*
coût du travail (F)	Lohnkosten *pl*	cost of wages	—	costo del lavoro *m*	coste de salarios *m*
coût du voyage (F)	Fahrgeld *n*	fare	—	spese di trasferta *f pl*	precio de la travesía *m*
coût moyen (F)	Durchschnitts-kosten *pl*	average costs	—	costi medi *m pl*	gastos medios *m pl*
coûts accessoires (F)	Nebenkosten *pl*	ancillary costs	—	costi accessori *m pl*	gastos adicionales *m pl*
coûts administratifs (F)	Bereitstellungs-kosten *pl*	commitment fee	—	spese di stanziamento *f pl*	gastos fijos *m pl*
coûts alternatifs (F)	Alternativkosten *pl*	opportunity costs	—	costi alternativi *m pl*	coste alternativo *m*
coûts d'acquisition (F)	Bezugskosten *pl*	purchasing costs	—	prezzo d'acquisto *m*	gastos de adquisición *m pl*
coûts d'adaptation (F)	Anpassungskosten *pl*	adjustment costs	—	costi d'adattamento *m pl*	gastos readaptación *m pl*
coûts d'assainissement (F)	Sanierungskosten *pl*	renewal costs/ construction costs	—	costi di risanamento *m pl*	gastos de saneamien-to *m pl*/gastos de rehabilitación *m pl*
coûts de déchargement (F)	Entladungskosten *pl*	discharging expenses	—	spese di scaricamento *f pl*	gastos de descargo *m pl*
coûts de développement (F)	Entwicklungs-kosten *pl*	development costs	—	costi di sviluppo *m pl*	gastos de desarrollo *m pl*
coûts de nuitée (F)	Übernachtungs-kosten *pl*	overnight expenses	—	spese di pernottamento *f pl*	gastos de alojamiento *m pl*
coûts de traitement des eaux usées (F)	Abwasserkosten *pl*	sewage disposal costs	—	costi per le acque di scarico *m pl*	gastos para aguas residuales *m pl*
coûts d'information (F)	Informations-kosten *pl*	information costs	—	costi d'informazione *m pl*	gastos de información *m pl*
coûts directs (F)	direkte Kosten *pl*	direct costs	—	costi diretti *m pl*	coste directo *m*
coûts d'obtention de crédits (F)	Kreditbeschaffungs-kosten *pl*	cost of borrowing	—	spese d'approvvi-gionamento di credito *f pl*	costes de apelación al crédito *m pl*
coûts ex ante (F)	Sollkosten *pl*	budgeted costs	—	costi calcolati *m pl*	gastos precalculados *m pl*
coûts fixes (F)	Fixkosten *pl*	fixed costs	—	costi fissi *m pl*	gastos fijos *m pl*
coûts fixes utiles (F)	Nutzkosten *pl*	utility costs	—	costi fissi di utilizzo *m pl*	gastos fijos de utilización *m pl*
coûts indirects (F)	Gemeinkosten *pl*	overhead expenses	—	costi comuni *m pl*	gastos generales *m pl*
coûts par nature (F)	Kostenarten *pl*	cost types	—	tipi di costi *m pl*	clases de costes *f pl*
coûts réels (F)	Istkosten *pl*	actual costs	—	costi effettivi *m pl*	gastos efectivos *m pl*
coûts sociaux (F)	Sozialkosten *pl*	social insurance costs	—	costi sociali *m pl*	costo social *m*/ cargas sociales *f pl*
coûts variables (F)	variable Kosten *pl*	variable costs	—	costi variabili *m pl*	gastos variables *m pl*
coût total (F)	Gesamtkosten *pl*	total costs	—	costi totali *m pl*	gastos generales *m pl*
coût unitaire de production (F)	Stückkosten *pl*	costs per unit	—	costi unitari *m pl*	coste por unidad *m*
couverture (F)	Deckung *f*	cover	—	copertura *f*	cobertura *f*
couverture de l'assurance (F)	Versicherungs-schutz *m*	insurance cover	—	copertura assicurativa *f*	cobertura de seguro *f*

	D	E	F	I	Es
cover (E)	Deckung *f*	—	couverture *f*	copertura *f*	cobertura *f*
coyuntura cuantitativa (Es)	Mengenkonjunktur *f*	quantitative boom	conjoncture de quantité *f*	congiuntura quantitativa *f*	—
craft trade (E)	Handwerk *n*	—	artisanat *m*	artigianato *m*	artesanía *f*
creación de dinero (Es)	Geldschöpfung *f*	money creation	création de trésorerie *f*	creazione di denaro *f*	—
creación de riqueza (Es)	Wertschöpfung *f*	value added	création de valeurs *f*	valore aggiunto *m*	—
créance douteuse (F)	zweifelhafte Forderung *f*	doubtful account	—	credito dubbio *m*	créditos dudosos *m pl*
créancier (F)	Gläubiger *m*	creditor	—	creditore *m*	accreedor *m*
créancier de la faillite (F)	Konkursgläubiger *m*	bankrupt's creditor	—	creditore della massa fallimentare *m*	acreedor de la quiebra *m*
créatif (F)	kreativ	creative	—	creativo	creativo
création de dinero (Es)	Geldschöpfung *f*	money creation	création de trésorerie *f*	creazione di denaro *f*	—
création de trésorerie (F)	Geldschöpfung *f*	money creation	—	creazione di denaro *f*	creación de dinero *f*
création de valeurs (F)	Wertschöpfung *f*	value added	—	valore aggiunto *m*	creación de riqueza *f*
création d'une nouvelle société (F)	Neugründung *f*	new foundation	—	costituzione nuova *f*	fundación nueva *f*
creative (E)	kreativ	—	créatif	creativo	creativo
creative thinking (E)	kreatives Denken *n*	—	créativité conceptionnelle *f*	mentalità creativa *f*	creatividad concepcional *f*
creatividad concepcional (Es)	kreatives Denken *n*	creative thinking	créativité conceptionnelle *f*	mentalità creativa *f*	—
créativité conceptionnelle (F)	kreatives Denken *n*	creative thinking	—	mentalità creativa *f*	creatividad concepcional *f*
creativo (Es)	kreativ	creative	créatif	creativo	—
creativo (I)	kreativ	creative	créatif	—	creativo
creazione del prodotto (I)	Produktgestaltung *f*	product design	présentation d'un produit *f*	—	diseño del producto *m*
creazione di denaro (I)	Geldschöpfung *f*	money creation	création de trésorerie *f*	—	creación de dinero *f*
crecimiento (Es)	Wachstum *n*	growth	croissance *f*	crescita *f*	—
crecimiento cero (Es)	Nullwachstum *n*	zero growth	croissance zéro *m*	crescita zero *f*	—
crecimiento económico (Es)	Wirtschafts-wachstum *n*	economic growth	croissance économique *f*	crescita economica *f*	—
crecimiento lineal (Es)	lineares Wachstum *n*	linear growth	accroissement constant *m*	crescita lineare *f*	—
crecimiento vegetativo (Es)	Bevölkerungs-wachstum *m*	increase in population	accroissement de la population *m*	incremento demografico *m*	—
credit[1] (E)	gutschreiben	—	créditer	accreditare	abonar en cuenta
credit[2] (E)	Gutschrift *f*	—	crédit *m*	accredito *m*	abono *m*
credit[3] (E)	Kredit *m*	—	crédit *m*	credito *m*	crédito *m*
crédit[1] (F)	Kredit *m*	credit	—	credito *m*	crédito *m*
crédit[2] (F)	Gutschrift *f*	credit	—	accredito *m*	abono *m*
crédit à court terme (F)	kurzfristiger Kredit *m*	short-term credit	—	credito a breve scadenza *m*	crédito a corto plazo *m*
credit advice (E)	Gutschriftsanzeige *f*	—	avis de crédit *m*	nota di accredito *f*	aviso de abono *m*
credit against securities (E)	Lombardkredit *m*	—	crédit garanti par nantissement *m*	credito su pegno *m*	crédito pignoraticio *m*
crédit à la consommation (F)	Konsumkredit *m*	consumer credit	—	credito al consumatore *m*	crédito de consumo *m*
crédit à la construction (F)	Baukredit *m*	building loan	—	credito edilizio *m*	crédito para la construcción *f*
crédit à long terme (F)	langfristiger Kredit *m*	long-term credit	—	credito a lunga scadenza *m*	crédito a largo plazo *m*
crédit à moyen terme (F)	mittelfristiger Kredit *m*	medium-term credit	—	credito a media scadenza *m*	crédito a medio plazo *m*
crédit-bail (F)	Leasing *n*	leasing	—	leasing *m*	leasing *m*
credit business (E)	Kreditgeschäft *n*	—	achat à crédit *m*	operazione di credito *f*	operaciones de crédito *f pl*

	D	E	F	I	Es
credit by way of bank guarantee[1] (E)	Bürgschaftskredit *m*	—	crédit cautionné *m*	credito di fideiussione *m*	crédito de garantía *m*
credit by way of bank guarantee[2] (E)	Avalkredit *m*	—	crédit d'escompte sur traite avalisée *m*	credito d'avallo *m*	crédito de aval *m*
credit by way of overdraft (E)	Überziehungskredit *m*	—	avance sur compte courant *f*	credito allo scoperto *m*	crédito en descubierto *m*
credit card (E)	Kreditkarte *f*	—	carte accréditive *f*	carta di credito *f*	tarjeta de crédito *f*
crédit cautionné (F)	Bürgschaftskredit *m*	credit by way of bank guarantee	—	credito di fideiussione *m*	crédito de garantía *m*
credit commission (E)	Kreditprovision *f*	—	frais de commissions d'ouverture de crédit *m pl*	provvigione di credito *f*	comisión de apertura de crédito *f*
crédit de caisse (F)	Barkredit *m*	cash credit	—	credito per cassa *m*	crédito en efectivo *m*
crédit de fournisseurs (F)	Lieferantenkredit *m*	supplier's credit	—	credito al fornitore *m*	crédito comercial *m*
crédit d'escompte (F)	Wechselkredit *m*	acceptance credit	—	credito cambiario *m*	crédito cambiario *m*
crédit d'escompte sur traite avalisée (F)	Avalkredit *m*	credit by way of bank guarantee	—	credito d'avallo *m*	crédito de aval *m*
crédit d'investissement (F)	Investitionskredit *m*	investment credit	—	credito d'investimento *m*	crédito de inversión *m*
crédit documentaire (F)	Dokumenten-akkreditiv *n*	documentary letter of credit	—	apertura di credito documentario *f*	crédito documentario *m*
crédit documentaire confirmé (F)	Rembourskredit *m*	documentary acceptance credit	—	credito di rimborso *m*	crédito de reembolso *m*
crédit en compte courant[1] (F)	Kontokorrentkredit *m*	current account credit	—	credito in conto corrente *m*	crédito en cuenta corriente *m*
crédit en compte courant[2] (F)	Blankokredit *m*	open credit	—	credito scoperto *m*	crédito en blanco *m*
créditer (F)	gutschreiben	credit	—	accreditare	abonar en cuenta
créditeur (F)	Kreditor *m*	creditor	—	creditore *m*	acreedor *m*
crédit garanti par nantissement (F)	Lombardkredit *m*	credit against securities	—	credito su pegno *m*	crédito pignoraticio *m*
crediti agevolati (I)	billiges Geld *n*	easy money	argent à bon marché *m*	—	dinero barato *m*
credit institution (E)	Kreditinstitut *n*	—	établissement de crédit *m*	istituto di credito *m*	instituto de crédito *m*
credit insurance (E)	Kreditversicherung *f*	—	assurance crédit *f*	assicurazione dei crediti *f*	seguro crediticio *m*
credit interest (E)	Habenzinsen *pl*	—	intérêts créditeur *m*	interessi creditori *m pl*	intereses acreedores *m pl*
crediti stand-by (I)	Stand-by-Kredite *pl*	stand-by credits	crédit stand-by *m*	—	créditos stand-by *m pl*
credit line (E)	Kreditlinie *f*	—	plafond du crédit accordé *m*	linea creditizia *f*	línea de crédito *f*
credit margin (E)	Kreditrahmen *m*	—	marge de crédit accordé *f*	plafond di credito *m*	margen de crédito *m*
crédito[1] (Es)	Kreditfähigkeit *f*	financial standing	solvabilité *f*	capacità di credito *f*	—
crédito[2] (Es)	Kreditwürdigkeit *f*	creditworthiness	solvabilité *f*	essere degno di credito	—
crédito[3] (Es)	Kredit *m*	credit	crédit *m*	credito *m*	—
credito (I)	Kredit *m*	credit	crédit *m*	—	crédito *m*
credito a breve scadenza (I)	kurzfristiger Kredit *m*	short-term credit	crédit à court terme *m*	—	crédito a corto plazo *m*
crédito a corto plazo (Es)	kurzfristiger Kredit *m*	short-term credit	crédit à court terme *m*	credito a breve scadenza *m*	—
crédito a largo plazo (Es)	langfristiger Kredit *m*	long-term credit	crédit à long terme *m*	credito a lunga scadenza *m*	—
credito a lunga scadenza (I)	langfristiger Kredit *m*	long-term credit	crédit à long terme *m*	—	crédito a largo plazo *m*
credito a media scadenza (I)	mittelfristiger Kredit *m*	medium-term credit	crédit à moyen terme *m*	—	crédito a medio plazo *m*
crédito a medio plazo (Es)	mittelfristiger Kredit *m*	medium-term credit	crédit à moyen terme *m*	credito a media scadenza *m*	—
credito al consumatore (I)	Konsumkredit *m*	consumer credit	crédit à la consommation *m*	—	crédito de consumo *m*

	D	E	F	I	Es
credito al fornitore (I)	Lieferantenkredit *m*	supplier's credit	crédit de fournisseurs *m*	—	crédito comercial *m*
credito allo scoperto (I)	Überziehungskredit *m*	credit by way of overdraft	avance sur compte courant *f*	—	crédito en descubierto *m*
credito al personale (I)	Personalkredit *m*	personal loan	crédit personnel *m*	—	crédito personal *m*
crédito cambiario (Es)	Wechselkredit *m*	acceptance credit	crédit d'escompte *m*	credito cambiario *m*	—
credito cambiario (I)	Wechselkredit *m*	acceptance credit	crédit d'escompte *m*	—	crédito cambiario *m*
crédito comercial[1] (Es)	Warenkredit *m*	trade credit	avance sur marchandises *f*	credito su merci *m*	—
crédito comercial[2] (Es)	Lieferantenkredit *m*	supplier's credit	crédit de fournisseurs *m*	credito al fornitore *m*	—
credito d'accettazione (I)	Akzeptkredit *m*	acceptance credit	crédit par traites acceptées *m*	—	crédito de aceptación *m*
credito da danni (I)	Schadensforderung *f*	claim for damages	prétention à dommages-intérêts *f*	—	pretensión de indemnización *f*
credito d'avallo (I)	Avalkredit *m*	credit by way of bank guarantee	crédit d'escompte sur traite avalisée *m*	—	crédito de aval *m*
crédito de aceptación (Es)	Akzeptkredit *m*	acceptance credit	crédit par traites acceptées *m*	credito d'accettazione *m*	—
crédito de aval (Es)	Avalkredit *m*	credit by way of bank guarantee	crédit d'escompte sur traite avalisée *m*	credito d'avallo *m*	—
crédito de consumo (Es)	Konsumkredit *m*	consumer credit	crédit à la consommation *m*	credito al consumatore *m*	—
crédito de garantía (Es)	Bürgschaftskredit *m*	credit by way of bank guarantee	crédit cautionné *m*	credito di fideiussione *m*	—
crédito de inversión (Es)	Investitionskredit *m*	investment credit	crédit d'investissement *m*	credito d'investimento *m*	—
crédito de reembolso (Es)	Rembourskredit *m*	documentary acceptance credit	crédit documentaire confirmé *m*	credito di rimborso *m*	—
credito di fideiussione (I)	Bürgschaftskredit *m*	credit by way of bank guarantee	crédit cautionné *m*	—	crédito de garantía *m*
credito d'investimento (I)	Investitionskredit *m*	investment credit	crédit d'investissement *m*	—	crédito de inversión *m*
credito di rimborso (I)	Rembourskredit *m*	documentary acceptance credit	crédit documentaire confirmé *m*	—	crédito de reembolso *m*
crédito documentario[1] (Es)	Akkreditiv *n*	letter of credit	accréditif *m*	credito documentario *m*	—
crédito documentario[2] (Es)	Dokumenten-akkreditiv *n*	documentary letter of credit	crédit documentaire *m*	apertura di credito documentario *f*	—
credito documentario (I)	Akkreditiv *n*	letter of credit	accréditif *m*	—	crédito documentario *m*
crédito documentario irrevocable (Es)	unwiderrufliches Akkreditiv *n*	irrevocable letter of credit	accréditif irrévocable *m*	apertura di credito documentario irrevocabile *f*	—
credito dubbio (I)	zweifelhafte Forderung *f*	doubtful account	créance douteuse *f*	—	créditos dudosos *m pl*
credito edilizio (I)	Baukredit *m*	building loan	crédit à la construction *m*	—	crédito para la construcción *m*
crédito en blanco (Es)	Blankokredit *m*	open credit	crédit en compte courant *m*	credito scoperto *m*	—
crédito en cuenta corriente (Es)	Kontokorrent-kredit *m*	current account credit	crédit en compte courant *m*	credito in conto corrente *m*	—
crédito en descubierto (Es)	Überziehungs-kredit *m*	credit by way of overdraft	avance sur compte courant *f*	credito allo scoperto *m*	—
crédito en efectivo (Es)	Barkredit *m*	cash credit	crédit de caisse *m*	credito per cassa *m*	—
credito in conto corrente (I)	Kontokorrentkredit *m*	current account credit	crédit en compte courant *m*	—	crédito en cuenta corriente *m*
crédito para la construcción (Es)	Baukredit *m*	building loan	crédit à la construction *m*	credito edilizio *m*	—
credito per cassa (I)	Barkredit *m*	cash credit	crédit de caisse *m*	—	crédito en efectivo *m*
crédito personal (Es)	Personalkredit *m*	personal loan	crédit personnel *m*	credito al personale *m*	—
crédito pignoraticio (Es)	Lombardkredit *m*	credit against securities	crédit garanti par nantissement *m*	credito su pegno *m*	—
credito ponte (I)	Überbrückungs-kredit *m*	bridging loan	crédit transitoire *m*	—	crédito transitorio *m*
creditor[1] (E)	Gläubiger *m*	—	créancier *m*	creditore *m*	accreedor *m*

	D	E	F	I	Es
creditor[2] (E)	Kreditor *m*	—	créditeur *m*	creditore *m*	accreedor *m*
creditore[1] (I)	Gläubiger *m*	creditor	créancier *m*	—	accreedor *m*
creditore[2] (I)	Kreditor *m*	creditor	créditeur *m*	—	accreedor *m*
crédito real (Es)	Realkredit *m*	credit secured by real property	crédit sur gage mobilier *m*	credito reale *m*	—
credito reale (I)	Realkredit *m*	credit secured by real property	crédit sur gage mobilier *m*	—	crédito real *m*
creditore della massa fallimentare (I)	Konkursgläubiger *m*	bankrupt's creditor	créancier de la faillite *m*	—	accreedor de la quiebra *m*
crédito roll over (Es)	Roll-over-Kredit *m*	roll-over credit	crédit roll-over *m*	credito roll-over *m*	—
credito roll-over (I)	Roll-over-Kredit *m*	roll-over credit	crédit roll-over *m*	—	crédito roll over *m*
crédito rotativo (Es)	Revolving-Kredit *m*	revolving credit	crédit rotatif *m*	credito rotativo *m*	—
credito rotativo (I)	Revolving-Kredit *m*	revolving credit	crédit rotatif *m*	—	crédito rotativo *m*
credito scoperto (I)	Blankokredit *m*	open credit	crédit en compte courant *m*	—	crédito en blanco *m*
crédito simple (Es)	Barakkreditiv	cash letter of credit	accréditif payable en espèce *m*	apertura di credito documentario semplice *f*	—
credito su merci (I)	Warenkredit *m*	trade credit	avance sur marchandises *f*	—	crédito comercial *m*
credito su pegno (I)	Lombardkredit *m*	credit against securities	crédit garanti par nantissement *m*	—	crédito pignoraticio *m*
crédito transitorio (Es)	Überbrückungs-kredit *m*	bridging loan	crédit transitoire *m*	credito ponte *m*	—
creditors' meeting (E)	Gläubiger-versammlung *f*	—	assemblée des créanciers *f*	riunione dei creditori *f*	junta de acreedores *f*
créditos dudosos (Es)	zweifelhafte Forderung *f*	doubtful account	créance douteuse *f*	credito dubbio *m*	—
créditos stand-by (Es)	Stand-by-Kredite *pl*	stand-by credits	crédit stand-by *m*	crediti stand-by *m pl*	—
crédit par traites acceptées (F)	Akzeptkredit *m*	acceptance credit	—	credito d'accettazione *m*	crédito de aceptación *m*
crédit personnel (F)	Personalkredit *m*	personal loan	—	credito al personale *m*	crédito personal *m*
credit policy (E)	Kreditpolitik *f*	—	politique favorisant le crédit *f*	politica creditizia *f*	política de crédito *f*
credit purchase (E)	Kreditkauf *m*	—	achat à crédit *m*	acquisto a credito *m*	compra de crédito *f*
credit restriction (E)	Kreditrestriktion *f*	—	restriction du crédit *f*	restrizione creditizia *f*	restricción de créditos *f*
crédit roll-over (F)	Roll-over-Kredit *m*	roll-over credit	—	credito roll-over *m*	crédito roll over *m*
crédit rotatif (F)	Revolving-Kredit *m*	revolving credit	—	credito rotativo *m*	crédito rotativo *m*
credit secured by real property (E)	Realkredit *m*	—	crédit sur gage mobilier *m*	credito reale *m*	crédito real *m*
credit side (E)	Haben *n*	—	avoir *m*	attivo *m*	haber *m*
crédit stand-by (F)	Stand-by-Kredite *pl*	stand-by credits	—	crediti stand-by *m pl*	créditos stand-by *m pl*
crédit sur gage mobilier (F)	Realkredit *m*	credit secured by real property	—	credito reale *m*	crédito real *m*
credit transaction (E)	Aktivgeschäft *n*	—	opération active *f*	operazione attiva *f*	operaciones activas *f pl*
credit transfer (E)	Giro *n*	—	virement *m*	giro *m*	giro *m*
crédit transitoire (F)	Überbrückungs-kredit *m*	bridging loan	—	credito ponte *m*	crédito transitorio *m*
creditworthiness (E)	Kreditwürdigkeit *f*	—	solvabilité *f*	essere degno di credito	crédito *m*
creditworthy (E)	kreditwürdig	—	solvable	degno di credito	solvente
creeping inflation (E)	schleichende Inflation *f*	—	inflation rampante *f*	inflazione strisciante *f*	inflación latente *f*
créneau du marché (F)	Marktlücke *f*	market gap	—	lacuna di mercato *f*	sector del mercado no abarcado por la oferta *m*
crescita (I)	Wachstum *n*	growth	croissance *f*	—	crecimiento *m*
crescita economica (I)	Wirtschaftswachs-tum *n*	economic growth	croissance économique *f*	—	crecimiento económico *m*
crescita lineare (I)	lineares Wachstum *n*	linear growth	accroissement linéaire *m*	—	crecimiento lineal *m*

	D	E	F	I	Es
crescita zero (I)	Nullwachstum *n*	zero growth	croissance zéro *f*	—	crecimiento cero *m*
cría de animales (Es)	Tierzucht *f*	livestock breeding	élevage *m*	zootecnia *f*	—
criminal (Es)	straffällig	liable to prosecution	encourir une peine	passibile di pena	—
criminalidad económica[1] (Es)	Wirtschafts-kriminalität *f*	white-collar crime	délinquence économique *f*	criminalità economica *f*	—
criminalidad económica[2] (Es)	White-collar-Kriminalität *f*	white-collar delinquency	délinquence économique *f*	criminalità dei colletti bianchi *f*	—
criminalità dei colletti bianchi (I)	White-collar-Kriminalität *f*	white-collar delinquency	délinquence économique *f*	—	criminalidad económica *f*
criminalità economica (I)	Wirtschafts-kriminalität *f*	white-collar crime	délinquence économique *f*	—	criminalidad económica *f*
crise (F)	Krise *f*	crisis	—	crisi *f*	crisis *f*
crise de l'agriculture (F)	Agrarkrise *f*	agricultural crisis	—	crisi agricola *f*	crisis agrícola *f*
crise de l'énergie (F)	Energiekrise *f*	energy crisis	—	crisi energetica *f*	crisis energética *f*
crise de vente (F)	Absatzkrise *f*	sales crisis	—	crisi di mercato *f*	crisis en la venta *f*
crise économique (F)	Wirtschaftskrise *f*	economic crisis	—	crisi economica *f*	crisis económica *f*
crise économique mondiale (F)	Weltwirtschaftskrise *f*	worldwide economic crisis	—	crisi dell'economia mondiale *f*	crisis económica internacional *f*
crisi (I)	Krise *f*	crisis	crise *f*	—	crisis *f*
crisi agricola (I)	Agrarkrise *f*	agricultural crisis	crise de l'agriculture *f*	—	crisis agrícola *f*
crisi dell'economia mondiale (I)	Weltwirtschaftskrise *f*	worldwide economic crisis	crise économique mondiale *f*	—	crisis económica internacional *f*
crisi di mercato (I)	Absatzkrise *f*	sales crisis	crise de vente *f*	—	crisis en la venta *f*
crisi economica (I)	Wirtschaftskrise *f*	economic crisis	crise économique *f*	—	crisis económica *f*
crisi energetica (I)	Energiekrise *f*	energy crisis	crise de l'énergie *f*	—	crisis energética *f*
crisis (E)	Krise *f*	—	crise *f*	crisi *f*	crisis *f*
crisis (Es)	Krise *f*	crisis	crise *f*	crisi *f*	—
crisis agrícola (Es)	Agrarkrise *f*	agricultural crisis	crise de l'agriculture *f*	crisi agricola *f*	—
crisis económica (Es)	Wirtschaftskrise *f*	economic crisis	crise économique *f*	crisi economica *f*	—
crisis económica internacional (Es)	Weltwirtschaftskrise *f*	worldwide economic crisis	crise économique mondiale *f*	crisi dell'economia mondiale *f*	—
crisis energética (Es)	Energiekrise *f*	energy crisis	crise de l'énergie *f*	crisi energetica *f*	—
crisis en la venta (Es)	Absatzkrise *f*	sales crisis	crise de vente *f*	crisi di mercato *f*	—
croissance (F)	Wachstum *n*	growth	—	crescita *f*	crecimiento *m*
croissance économique (F)	Wirtschafts-wachstum *n*	economic growth	—	crescita economica *f*	crecimiento económico *m*
croissance zéro (F)	Nullwachstum *n*	zero growth	—	crescita zero *f*	crecimiento cero *m*
croissant (F)	steigend	rising	—	in aumento	ascendente
crollo delle quotazioni (I)	Kurszusammen-bruch *m*	collapse of prices	chute des cours *f*	—	caída de los cambios *f*
crollo di borsa (I)	Börsenkrach *m*	stockmarket crash	débâcle boursière *f*	—	caída en picado de la bolsa *f*
crollo finanziario (I)	finanzieller Zusammenbruch *m*	financial failure	débâcle financière *f*	—	derrumbamiento financiero *m*
crossed cheque[1] (E)	gekreuzter Scheck *m*	—	chèque barré *m*	assegno sbarrato *m*	cheque cruzado *m*
crossed cheque[2] (E)	Verrechnungs-scheck *m*	—	chèque à porter en compte *m*	assegno sbarrato *m*	cheque cruzado *m*
crude oil (E)	Rohöl *n*	—	pétrole brut *m*	petrolio greggio *m*	crudo *m*
crude oil price (E)	Rohölpreis *m*	—	prix du pétrole brut *m*	prezzo del petrolio greggio *m*	precio del crudo *m*
crudo[1] (Es)	Rohöl *n*	crude oil	pétrole brut *m*	petrolio greggio *m*	—
crudo[2] (Es)	Erdöl *n*	mineral oil	pétrole *m*	petrolio *m*	—
cuadro (Es)	Schaubild *n*	graph	graphique *m*	diagramma *m*	—
cualificación (Es)	Qualifikation *f*	qualification	qualification *f*	qualificazione *f*	—
cualitativo (Es)	qualitativ	qualitative	qualitatif	qualitativo	—
cuantitativo (Es)	quantitativ	quantitative	quantitatif	quantitativo	—
cuenta (Es)	Konto *n*	account	compte *m*	conto *m*	—
cuenta a plazo (Es)	Festgeldkonto *n*	time deposit account	compte de dépôt à terme *m*	deposito vincolato *m*	—

	D	E	F	I	Es
cuenta bancaria (Es)	Bankkonto *n*	bank account	compte en banque *m*	conto bancario *m*	—
cuenta cifrada (Es)	Nummernkonto *n*	numbered account	compte anonyme *m*	conto cifrato *m*	—
cuenta congelada (Es)	gesperrtes Konto *n*	blocked account	compte bloqué *m*	conto bloccato *m*	—
cuenta corriente[1] (Es)	laufende Rechnung *f*	account current	compte courant *m*	conto corrente *m*	—
cuenta corriente[2] (Es)	Kontokorrent *n*	account current	compte courant *m*	conto corrente *m*	—
cuenta corriente[3] (Es)	Kontokorrentkonto *n*	current account	compte tenu en compte courant *m*	conto corrente *m*	—
cuenta corriente postal (Es)	Postscheckkonto *n*	(postal) giro account	compte chèque postal *m*	conto corrente postale *m*	—
cuenta de beneficios y pérdidas (Es)	Erfolgskonto *n*	profit account	compte de résultats *m*	conto profitti *m*	—
cuenta de existencias (Es)	Bestandskonto *n*	real account	compte d'existences *m*	conto merci *m*	—
cuenta de ganancias (Es)	Ertragsrechnung *f*	profit and loss account	solde net de l'exploitation *m*	conto economico *m*	—
cuenta de la empresa (Es)	Firmenkonto *n*	company account	compte de maison *m*	conto intestato ad una ditta *m*	—
cuenta de liquidación (Es)	Abwicklungskonto *n*	settlement account	compte de liquidation *m*	conto di liquidazione *f*	—
cuenta de moneda extranjera (Es)	Währungskonto *n*	foreign currency account	compte en monnaies étrangères *m*	conto in valuta *m*	—
cuenta de pérdidas y ganancias (Es)	Gewinn- und Verlustrechnung *f*	profit and loss account	compte de pertes et profits *m*	conto profitti e perdite *m*	—
cuenta de salario (Es)	Gehaltskonto *n*	salary account	compte de domiciliation du salaire *m*	conto stipendi *m*	—
cuenta exterior (Es)	Auslandskonto *n*	foreign account	compte d'étranger *m*	conto estero *m*	—
cuenta fiduciaria de un abogado (Es)	Anderkonto *n*	fiduciary account	compte de tiers *m*	conto per terzi *m*	—
cuenta particular (Es)	Privatkonto *n*	private account	compte privé *m*	conto privato *m*	—
cuenta provisional (Es)	Zwischenkonto *n*	interim account	compte provisoire *m*	conto transitorio *m*	—
cuenta trimestral (Es)	Quartalsrechnung *f*	quarterly invoice	compte trimestriel *m*	conto trimestrale *m*	—
cuentas de orden (Es)	Abgrenzungsposten *m*	deferred item	comptes transitoires *m pl*	ratei e risconti *m pl*	—
cuestionario (Es)	Fragebogen *m*	questionnaire	questionnaire *m*	questionario *m*	—
culpable (E)	schuldhaft	—	coupable	colposo	culpable
culpable (Es)	schuldhaft	culpable	coupable	colposo	—
cultura empresarial (Es)	Unternehmenskultur *f*	entrepreneurial culture	culture de l'entreprise *f*	cultura imprenditoriale *f*	—
cultura imprenditoriale (I)	Unternehmenskultur *f*	entrepreneurial culture	culture de l'entreprise *f*	—	cultura empresarial *f*
culture de l'entreprise (F)	Unternehmenskultur *f*	entrepreneurial culture	—	cultura imprenditoriale *f*	cultura empresarial *f*
cumpleaños (Es)	Geburtstag *m*	birthday	anniversaire *m*	compleanno *m*	—
cumplimiento (Es)	Erfüllung *f*	compliance	acquittement *m*	adempimento *m*	—
cuota (Es)	Quote *f*	quota	quota *m*	quota *f*	—
cuota del mercado (Es)	Marktanteil *m*	market share	participation au marché *f*	quota di mercato *f*	—
cuota de ahorro (Es)	Sparquote *f*	savings ratio	quote-part de revenu réservée à des fins d'épargne *f*	quota di risparmio *f*	—
cuota de importación (Es)	Importquote *f*	import quota	contingent d'importation *m*	quota d'importazione *f*	—
cuota de pérdida (Es)	Ausfallquote *f*	default rate	ratio de perte *m*	tasso di perdita *m*	—
cuota de producción (Es)	Förderquote *f*	production quota	quote-part de production *f*	quota d'estrazione *f*	—
cupo de exportación (Es)	Exportquote *f*	export quota	quota d'exportation *m*	contingente d'esportazione *m*	—
cupón (Es)	Coupon *m*	coupon	coupon *m*	cedola *f*	—
curatore fallimentare (I)	Konkursverwalter *m*	administrator in bankruptcy proceedings	liquidateur de la faillite *m*	—	síndico de quiebra *m*
currency (E)	Währung *f*	—	monnaie *f*	valuta f/moneta *f*	moneda *f*
currency agreement (E)	Währungsabkommen *n*	—	accord monétaire *m*	accordo monetario *m*	acuerdo monetario *m*

	D	E	F	I	Es
currency area (E)	Währungsgebiet *n*	—	zone monétaire *f*	area monetaria *f*	área monetaria *f*
currency clause (E)	Währungsklausel *f*	—	clause monétaire *f*	clausola monetaria *f*	cláusula monetaria *f*
currency risk (E)	Währungsrisiko *n*	—	risque de change *m*	rischio monetario *m*	riesgo monetario *m*
currency snake (E)	Währungsschlange *f*	—	serpent monétaire *m*	serpente monetario *m*	serpiente monetaria *f*
currency zone (E)	Währungszone *f*	—	zone monétaire *f*	zona monetaria *f*	zona monetaria *f*
current account[1] (E)	laufende Rechnung *f*	—	compte courant *m*	conto corrente *m*	cuenta corriente *f*
current account[2] (E)	Kontokorrentkonto *n*	—	compte tenu en compte courant *m*	conto corrente *m*	cuenta corriente *f*
current account credit (E)	Kontokorrentkredit *m*	—	crédit en compte courant *m*	credito in conto corrente *m*	crédito en cuenta corriente *m*
current account (E)	Kontokorrent *n*	—	compte courant *m*	conto corrente *m*	cuenta corriente *f*
current assets (E)	Umlaufvermögen *n*	—	capital de roulement *m*	patrimonio circolante *m*	capital circulante *m*
current market value (E)	Zeitwert *m*	—	valeur à une certaine date *f*	valore corrente *m*	valor actual *m*
(current) operational expenses (E)	Betriebsausgaben *f*	—	charges d'exploitation *f pl*	spese aziendali *f pl*	gastos de explotación *m pl*
current value (E)	Tageswert *m*	—	valeur du jour *f*	valore del giorno *m*	valor del día *m*
curriculum vitae (E)	Lebenslauf *m*	—	curriculum vitae *m*	curriculum vitae *m*	curriculum vitae *m*
curriculum vitae (Es)	Lebenslauf *m*	curriculum vitae	curriculum vitae *m*	curriculum vitae *m*	—
curriculum vitae (F)	Lebenslauf *m*	curriculum vitae	—	curriculum vitae *m*	curriculum vitae *m*
curriculum vitae (I)	Lebenslauf *m*	curriculum vitae	curriculum vitae *m*	—	curriculum vitae *m*
curriculum vitae écrit à la main (F)	handgeschriebener Lebenslauf *m*	hand-written curriculum vitae	—	curriculum vitae scritto a mano *m*	curriculum vitae escrito a mano *m*
curriculum vitae escrito a mano (Es)	handgeschriebener Lebenslauf *m*	hand-written curriculum vitae	curriculum vitae écrit à la main *m*	curriculum vitae scritto a mano *m*	—
curriculum vitae scritto a mano (I)	handgeschriebener Lebenslauf *m*	hand-written curriculum vitae	curriculum vitae écrit à la main *m*	—	curriculum vitae escrito a mano *m*
custodia (Es)	Verwahrung *f*	custody	dépôt *m*	custodia *f*	—
custodia (I)	Verwahrung *f*	custody	dépôt *m*	—	custodia *f*/ incautación *f*
custodia de valores (Es)	Depotgeschäft *n*	deposit banking	garde des titres *f*	operazione di deposito *f*	—
custody (E)	Verwahrung *f*	—	dépôt *m*	custodia *f*	custodia *f*/ incautación *f*
customer[1] (E)	Kunde *m*	—	client *m*	cliente *m*	cliente *m*
customer[2] (E)	Besteller *m*	—	acheteur *m*	committente *m*	demandante *m*
customer magazine (E)	Kundenzeitschrift *f*	—	journal destiné à la clientèle *m*	periodico per i clienti *m*	revista para los clientes *f*
customer's reference number (E)	Kundennummer *f*	—	numéro de référence du client *m*	numero di cliente *m*	número del cliente *m*
customer survey (E)	Kundenbefragung *f*	—	enquête parmi les clients *f*	intervista ai clienti *f*	encuesta entre los clientes *f*
customs (E)	Zoll *m*	—	douane *f*/droit de douane *m*	dogana *f*/dazio *m*	aduana *f*/arancel *m*
customs application (E)	Zollantrag *m*	—	demande de dédouanement *f*	domanda di sdoganamento *f*	solicitud de aduana *f*
customs clearance of exports (E)	Ausfuhrabfertigung *f*	—	formalités en douane à l'exportation *f pl*	sdoganamento delle esportazioni *m*	despacho de exportación *m*
customs convention (E)	Zollabkommen *n*	—	accord douanier *m*	accordo sulle tariffe doganali *m*	convenio aduanero *m*
customs declaration[1] (E)	Zollerklärung *f*	—	déclaration en douane *f*	dichiarazione doganale *f*	declaración arancelaria *f*
customs declaration[2] (E)	Zollanmeldung *f*	—	déclaration en douane *f*	dichiarazione doganale *f*	declaración arancelaria *f*
customs documents (E)	Zollpapiere *pl*	—	documents douaniers *m pl*	documenti doganali *m pl*	documentos aduaneros *m pl*
customs drawback (E)	Rückzoll *m*	—	ristourne des droits de douane *f*	restituzione di dazi *f*	drawback *m*
customs duties (E)	Zollgebühren *pl*	—	droit de douane *m*	diritti doganali *m pl*	derechos arancelarios *m pl*
customs formalities (E)	Zollformalität *f*	—	formalité douanières *f*	formalità doganale *f*	formalidades aduaneras *f pl*

	D	E	F	I	Es
customs frontier (E)	Zollgrenze *f*	—	frontière douanière *f*	confine doganale *m*	frontera aduanera *f*
customs frontier district (E)	Zollgrenzgebiet *n*	—	territoire de surveil-lance douanière *m*	area doganale di confine *f*	territorio aduanero fronterizo *m*
customs invoice (E)	Zollfaktura *f*	—	facture douanière *f*	fattura doganale *f*	factura arancelaria *f*
customs office (E)	Zollstelle *f*	—	bureau de douane *m*	posto di dogana *m*	oficina de aduanas *f*
customs procedure (E)	Zollverkehr m	—	régime douanier m	procedure doganali *f pl*	régimen aduanero de mercancías *m*
(customs) procedure (E)	Verfahren *n*	—	méthode *f*/ procédure *f*	procedimento *m*/ procedura *f*	proceso *m*/ procedimiento *m*
customs seal (E)	Zollverschluß *m*	—	fermeture douanière *f*	sigillo doganale *m*	precinto aduanero *m*
customs tariff (E)	Zolltarif *m*	—	tarif des douanes *m*	tariffa doganale *f*	tarifa arancelaria *f*
customs territory (E)	Zollgebiet *n*	—	territoire douanier *m*	territorio doganale *m*	distrito aduanero *m*
customs union (E)	Zollunion *f*	—	union douanière *f*	unione doganale *f*	unión aduanera *f*
customs warehouse procedure (E)	Zollagerung *f*	—	dépôt en entrepôt sous douane *m*	immagazzinamento doganale *m*	depósito de aduana *m*
cybernetics (E)	Kybernetik *f*	—	cybernétique *f*	cibernetica *f*	cibernética *f*
cybernétique (F)	Kybernetik *f*	cybernetics	—	cibernetica *f*	cibernética *f*
cycle (E)	Zyklus *m*	—	cycle *m*	ciclo *m*	ciclo *m*
cycle (F)	Zyklus *m*	cycle	—	ciclo *m*	ciclo *m*
cycle conjoncturel (F)	Konjunkturzyklus *m*	business cycle	—	ciclo congiunturale *m*	ciclo económico *m*
cycle de stockage (F)	Lagerzyklus *m*	stock cycle	—	ciclo di magazzinaggio *m*	período de almacenaje *m*
cycle de vie (F)	Lebenszyklus *m*	life cycle	—	ciclo di vita *m*	ciclo de vida *m*
d'accord avec (F)	im Einvernehmen mit	in agreement with	—	d'accordo con	de conformidad con
d'accordo con (I)	im Einvernehmen mit	in agreement with	d'accord avec	—	de conformidad con
Dachgesellschaft (D)	—	holding company	société holding *f*	società finanziaria *f*	sociedad holding *f*
daily (E)	täglich	—	quotidien	giornaliero	diario
damage[1] (E)	Schaden *m*	—	dommage *m*	danno *m*	daño *m*
damage[2] (E)	Beschädigung *f*	—	endommagement *m*	danno *m*	deterioración *f*
damage by sea (E)	Havarie *f*	—	avarie *f*	avaria *f*	avería *m*
damage caused by water (E)	Wasserschaden *m*	—	dommage causé par l'eau *m*	danno dovuto all'acqua *m*	daño causado por el agua *m*
damage in transit (E)	Transportschaden *m*	—	dommage au cours d'un transport *m*	danno di trasporto *m*	daño de transporte *m*
Damnum (D)	—	damnum	perte *f*	perdita *f*	pérdida *f*
damnum (E)	Damnum *n*	—	perte *f*	perdita *f*	pérdida *f*
danger (E)	Gefahr *f*	—	danger *m*	pericolo *m*	peligro *m*
danger (F)	Gefahr *f*	danger	—	pericolo *m*	peligro *m*
danger money (E)	Gefahrenzulage *f*	—	prime de danger *f*	premio di rischio *m*	incremento por peligrosidad *m*
Dankschreiben (D)	—	letter of thanks	lettre de remerciement *f*	lettera di ringraziamento *f*	carta de agradecimiento *f*
danni indiretti (I)	Folgeschäden *pl*	consequential damages	dommage consécutif *m*	—	daño consecuencial *m*
danno[1] (I)	Beschädigung *f*	damage	endommagement *m*	—	deterioración *f*
danno[2] (I)	Schaden *m*	damage	dommage *m*	—	daño *m*
danno di trasporto (I)	Transportschaden *m*	damage in transit	dommage au cours d'un transport *m*	—	daño de transporte *m*
danno dovuto all'acqua (I)	Wasserschaden *m*	damage caused by water	dommage causé par l'eau *m*	—	daño causado por el agua *m*
danno immateriale (I)	immaterieller Schaden *m*	non-material damage	dommage immatériel *m*	—	daño inmaterial *m*
danno piccolo (I)	Bagatell-schaden *m*	minimal damage	dommage mineur *m*	—	siniestro leve *m*
danno totale (I)	Totalschaden *m*	total loss	dommage total *m*	—	daño total *m*
daño (Es)	Schaden *m*	damage	dommage *m*	danno *m*	—
daño causado por el agua (Es)	Wasserschaden *m*	damage caused by water	dommage causé par l'eau *m*	danno dovuto all'acqua *m*	—
daño consecuencial (Es)	Folgeschäden *pl*	consequential damages	dommage consécutif *m*	danni indiretti *m pl*	—

	D	E	F	I	Es
daño de transporte (Es)	Transportschaden *m*	damage in transit	dommage au cours d'un transport *m*	danno di trasporto *m*	—
daño inmaterial (Es)	immaterieller Schaden *m*	non-material damage	dommage immatériel *m*	danno immateriale *m*	—
daño total (Es)	Totalschaden *m*	total loss	dommage total *m*	danno totale *m*	—
dans le délai de (F)	binnen	within	—	entro	en el término de
dans les délais[1] (F)	termingerecht	on schedule	—	puntuale	en la fecha fijada
dans les délais[2] (F)	fristgerecht	timely	—	entro il termine convenuto	dentro del plazo fijado
Darlehen (D)	—	loan	prêt *m*	mutuo *m*	préstamo *m*
data (E)	Daten *f*	—	données *f pl*	dati *m pl*	datos *m pl*
data (I)	Datum *n*	date	date *f*	—	fecha *f*
data bank (E)	Datenbank *f*	—	banque de données *f*	banca dati *f*	banco de datos *m*
data collection (E)	Datenerfassung *f*	—	saisie des données informatiques *f*	raccolta dati *f*	recogida de datos *f*
data d'arrivo (I)	Ankunftsdatum *n*	date of arrival	date d'arrivée *f*	—	fecha de llegada *f*
data di nascita (I)	Geburtsdatum *n*	date of birth	date de naissance *f*	—	fecha de nacimiento *f*
data di partenza (I)	Abreisedatum *n*	date of departure	date de départ *f*	—	fecha de partida *f*
data di scadenza (I)	Verfallsdatum *n*	expiry date	date d'échéance *f*	—	fecha de vencimiento *f*
data flow chart (E)	Datenflußplan *m*	—	organigramme de flux des données *m*	diagramma flusso dati *m*	organigrama de flujo de datos *m*
data medium (E)	Datenträger *m*	—	porteur des données *m*	supporto dati *m*	medio de datos *m*
data processing[1] (E)	Datenverarbeitung *f*	—	traitement des information *m*	elaborazione dati *f*	procesamiento de datos *m*
data processing[2] (E)	Informatik *f*	—	informatique *f*	informatica *f*	informática *f*
data processing system (E)	Datenverarbeitungs-anlage *f*	—	installation de traitement électronique des informations *f*	elaboratore elettronico di dati *m*	ordenador *m*
data protection (E)	Datensicherung *f*	—	protection de données *f*	protezione dei dati *f*	protección de datos *f*
Data Protection Act (E)	Datenschutzgesetz *n*	—	loi sur l'informatique *f*	legge sulla tutela dei dati *f*	ley de protección de datos *f*
data securing (E)	Datenschutz *m*	—	sauvegarde des données *f*	tutela dei dati *f*	protección de los datos *f*
data transmission (E)	Datenübertragung *f*	—	transmission de dates *f*	trasmissione dati *f*	transmisión de datos *f*
date (E)	Datum *n*	—	date *f*	data *f*	fecha *f*
date (F)	Datum *n*	date	—	data *f*	fecha *f*
date d'arrivée (F)	Ankunftsdatum *n*	date of arrival	—	data d'arrivo *f*	fecha de llegada *f*
date d'échéance (F)	Verfallsdatum *n*	expiry date	—	data di scadenza *f*	fecha de vencimiento *f*
date de conversation (F)	Gesprächstermin *m*	appointment for a meeting	—	appuntamento per un colloquio *m*	fecha de cita *f*
date de départ (F)	Abreisedatum *n*	date of departure	—	data di partenza *f*	fecha de partida *f*
date de la conférence (F)	Besprechungs-termin *m*	meeting date	—	termine del colloquio *m*	fecha de conferencia *f*
date de naissance (F)	Geburtsdatum *n*	date of birth	—	data di nascita *f*	fecha de nacimiento *f*
date limite (F)	Termin *m*	deadline	—	termine *m*	fecha *f*/cita *f*
date of arrival (E)	Ankunftsdatum *n*	—	date d'arrivée *f*	data d'arrivo *f*	fecha de llegada *f*
date of birth (E)	Geburtsdatum *n*	—	date de naissance *f*	data di nascita *f*	fecha de nacimiento *f*
date of delivery (E)	Liefertermin *m*	—	délai de livraison *m*	termine di consegna *m*	plazo de entrega *m*
date of departure (E)	Abreisedatum *n*	—	date de départ *f*	data di partenza *f*	fecha de partida *f*
date of interview (E)	Vorstellungstermin *m*	—	rendez-vous de présentation *m*	appuntamento di presentazione *m*	fecha de entrevista personal *f*
date of payment (E)	Zahlungstermin *m*	—	terme du payement *m*	termine di pagamento *m*	plazo de pago *m*
Datei (D)	—	file	fichier de données *m*	file *m*	archivo de datos *m*
Daten (D)	—	data	données *f pl*	dati *m pl*	datos *m pl*
Datenbank (D)	—	data bank	banque de données *f*	banca dati *f*	banco de datos *m*

	D	E	F	I	Es
Datenerfassung (D)	—	data collection	saisie des données informatiques *f*	raccolta dati *f*	recogida de datos *f*
Datenfern-übertragung (D)	—	remote of data transmission	télétransmission des données informatiques *f*	teletrasmissione dati *f*	transmisión de datos *f*
Datenflußplan (D)	—	data flow chart	organigramme de flux des données *m*	diagramma flusso dati *m*	organigrama de flujo de datos *m*
Datenschutz (D)	—	data securing	sauvegarde des données *f*	tutela dei dati *f*	protección de los datos *f*
Datenschutzgesetz (D)	—	Data Protection Act	loi sur l'informatique *f*	legge sulla tutela dei dati *f*	ley de protección de datos *f*
Datensicherung (D)	—	data protection	protection de données *f*	protezione dei dati *f*	protección de datos *f*
Datenträger (D)	—	data medium	porteur des données *m*	supporto dati *m*	medio de datos *m*
Datentypistin (D)	—	terminal operator	perforatrice *f*	dattilografa *f*	perforadora *f*
Datenübertragung (D)	—	data transmission	transmission de données *f*	trasmissione dati *f*	transmisión de datos *f*
Datenverarbeitung (D)	—	data processing	traitement des information *m*	elaborazione dati *f*	procesamiento de datos *m*
Datenverarbeitungs-anlage (D)	—	data processing system	installation de traitement électronique des informations *f*	elaboratore elettronico di dati *m*	ordenador *m*
dati (I)	Daten *f*	data	données *f pl*	—	datos *m pl*
dati delle ordinazioni (I)	Bestelldaten *pl*	details of order	références de commande *f pl*	—	datos de pedido *m pl*
dati di mercato (I)	Marktdaten *pl*	market details	données sur le marché *f pl*	—	datos del mercado *m pl*
dati effettivi (I)	Istzahlen *pl*	actual figures	résultats effectifs *m pl*	—	cifras efectivas *f pl*
datore di lavoro (I)	Arbeitgeber *m*	employer	employeur *m*	—	patrón *m*
datos (Es)	Daten *f*	data	données *f pl*	dati *m pl*	—
datos del mercado (Es)	Marktdaten *pl*	market details	données sur le marché *f pl*	dati di mercato *m pl*	—
datos de pedido (Es)	Bestelldaten *pl*	details of order	références de commande *f pl*	dati delle ordinazioni *m pl*	—
datos personales (Es)	Personalien *pl*	personal data	identité *f*	generalità *f pl*	—
dattilografa (I)	Datentypistin *f*	terminal operator	perforatrice *f*	—	perforadora *f*
Datum (D)	—	date	date *f*	data *f*	fecha *f*
Dauerauftrag (D)	—	standing order	ordre régulier *m*	ordine permanente *m*	órden permanente *f*
Dauerschuld-verschreibung (D)	—	unredeemable bond	obligation perpétuelle *f*	obbligazione perpetua *f*	obligación perpetua *f*
day of expiry (E)	Verfalltag *m*	—	jour de l'échéance *m*	giorno di scadenza *m*	día de vencimiento *m*
day-to-day money (E)	Tagesgeld *n*	—	argent au jour le jour *m*	prestito giornaliero *m*	dinero de día a día *m*
day-to-day operations (E)	Tagesgeschäft *n*	—	affaire au comptant *f*	contratto a contanti *m*	operación al contado *f*
dazio ad valorem (I)	Wertzoll *m*	ad valorem duty	taxe de douane ad valorem *f*	—	aduanas ad valorem *f pl*
dazio d'importazione (I)	Einfuhrzoll *m*	import duty	droit d'entrée *m*	—	arancel de importación *m*
dazio di quantità (I)	Mengenzoll *m*	specific duty	droit de douane par quantité *m*	—	arancel aduanero cuantitativo *m*
dazio preferenziale (I)	Präferenzzoll *m*	preferential duty	taxe préférentielle de douane *f*	—	aduanas preferenciales *f pl*
dazio proibitivo (I)	Prohibitivzoll *m*	prohibitive duty	droit prohibitif *m*	—	derechos prohibitivos *m pl*
dazio protettivo (I)	Schutzzoll *m*	protective duty	droit de protection *m*	—	aduana proteccionista *f*
dazio sull'esportazione (I)	Ausfuhrzoll *m*	export duty	taxe de sortie *f*	—	derechos de exportación *m pl*
dazio unitario (I)	Einheitszoll *m*	uniform duty	droit unique *m*	—	aduanas uniformes *f pl*
deadline (E)	Termin *m*	—	date limite *f*	termine *m*	fecha *f*/cita *f*

	D	E	F	I	Es
dealing in foreign notes and coins (E)	Sortenhandel *m*	—	commerce de change *m*	cambio valuta *m*	operación de moneda extranjera *f*
dealing in shares (E)	Aktienhandel *m*	—	négociation des actions *f*	commercio azionario *m*	contratación acciones *f*
débâcle boursière (F)	Börsenkrach *m*	stockmarket crash	—	crollo di borsa *m*	caída en picado de la bolsa *f*
débâcle fiancière (F)	Finanzdebakel *n*	financial debacle	—	dissesto finanziario *m*	descalabro financiero *m*
débâcle financière (F)	finanzieller Zusammenbruch *m*	financial failure	—	crollo finanziario *m*	derrumbamiento financiero *m*
débauchage (F)	Abwerbung *f*	pirating	—	accaparramento *m*	sonsacamiento *m*
debe (Es)	Soll *m*	debit/target	doit *m*	passivo *m*	—
debenture loan (E)	Obligationsanleihe *f*	—	emprunt obligataire *m*	prestito obbligazionario *m*	empréstito sobre obligaciones *m*
debenture stock (E)	Schuld-verschreibung *f*	—	obligation *f*	obbligazione *f*	obligación *f*
deber de conservación (Es)	Aufbewahrungs-pflicht *f*	obligation to preserve records	obligation de conservation *f*	obbligo di custodia *m*	—
debidamente (Es)	ordnungsgemäß	orderly	correct(e)	regolare	—
debit (E)	Soll *m*	—	doit *m*	passivo *m*	debe m
débiter (F)	belasten	load/charge	—	addebitare	cargar/adeudar
débiteur[1] (F)	Schuldner *m*	debtor	—	debitore *m*	deudor *m*/respons-able *m*/obligado *m*
débiteur[2] (F)	Debitor *m*	debtors	—	debitore *m*	deudor *m*
debiti (I)	Schulden *pl*	debts	dettes *f pl*	—	deudas *f pl*
debiti con l'estero (I)	Auslandsschulden *pl*	foreign debts	dettes à l'étranger *f pl*	—	deudas exteriores *f pl*
debiti insoluti (I)	Außenstände *pl*	outstanding debts	dettes actives *f pl*	—	cobros pendientes *m pl*
debit note (E)	Lastschrift *f*	—	note de débit *f*	addebito *m*	cargo en cuenta *m*
debito (I)	Schuld *f*	debt	dette *f*	—	deuda *f*/crédito pasivo *m*
debito fondiario (I)	Grundschuld *f*	mortgage	dette foncière *f*	—	hipoteca *f*
debito pubblico (I)	Staatsverschuldung *f*	state indebtedness	endettement de l'Etat *m*	—	endeudamiento público *m*
Debitor (D)	—	debtors	débiteur *m*	debitore *m*	deudor *m*
debitore[1] (I)	Schuldner *m*	debtor	débiteur *m*	—	deudor *m*/respons-able *m*/obligado *m*
debitore[2] (I)	Debitor *m*	debtors	débiteur *m*	—	deudor *m*
debitore fallito (I)	Gemeinschuldner *m*	adjudicated bankrupt	failli *m*	—	deudor común *m*
de bonne foi (F)	gutgläubig	bona fide	—	di buona fede	de buena fe
debt financing (E)	Fremdfinanzierung *f*	—	constitution de capi-tal par apport de tiers *f*	finanziamento passivo *m*	financiación externa *f*
debtor (E)	Schuldner *m*	—	débiteur *m*	debitore *m*	deudor *m*/respons-able *m*/obligado *m*
debtor countries (E)	Schuldnerländer *pl*	—	pays débiteurs *m pl*	paesi debitori *m pl*	países deudores *m pl*
debtor interest rates (E)	Sollzinsen *pl*	—	intérêt débiteur *m*	interessi debitori *m pl*	intereses deudores *m pl*
debtors (E)	Debitor *m*	—	débiteur *m*	debitore *m*	deudor *m*
debt ratio (E)	Verschuldungs-grad *m*	—	niveau de l'endettement *m*	tasso d'indebitamento *m*	grado de endeudamiento *m*
debts (E)	Schulden *pl*	—	dettes *f pl*	debiti *m pl*	deudas *f pl*
debt service (E)	Schuldendienst *m*	—	service de la dette *m*	servizio dei debiti *m*	servicio de la deuda *m*
début de lettre (F)	Anrede *f*	form of address	—	titolo *m*	tratamiento *m*
de buena fe (Es)	gutgläubig	bona fide	de bonne foi	di buona fede	—
décalage entre les prix et les salaires (F)	Lohnlag *m*	wage lag	—	lag salariale *m*	diferencial entre pre-cios y salarios *m*
de casco (Es)	Kasko *m*	comprehensive	sur corps	corpo *m*	—
deceit (E)	Täuschung *f*	—	tromperie *f*	inganno *m*	engaño *m*
décentralisation (F)	Dezentralisierung *f*	decentralization	—	decentralizzazione *f*	descentralización *f*
decentralization (E)	Dezentralisierung *f*	—	décentralisation *f*	decentralizzazione *f*	descentralización *f*

	D	E	F	I	Es
decentralizzazione (I)	Dezentralisierung *f*	decentralization	décentralisation *f*	—	descentralización *f*
décharge (F)	Entlastung *f*	discharge	—	sgravio *m*	desgravamen *m*
déchet[1] (F)	Abfall *m*	waste	—	rifiuti *m pl*	desechos *m pl*
déchet[2] (F)	Rückstände *pl*	residues	—	residui m p	residuos *m pl*
déchets d'emballage (F)	Verpackungsmüll *m*	packing waste	—	rifiuti da imballaggi *m pl*	basura de embalaje *f*
decision (E)	Beschluß *m*	—	décision *f*	delibera *f*	decisión *f*
decisión (Es)	Beschluß *m*	decision	décision *f*	delibera *f*	—
décision (F)	Beschluß *m*	decision	—	delibera *f*	decisión *f*
décision d'acheter (F)	Kaufentscheidung *f*	decision to purchase	—	decisione d'acquisto *f*	decisión de compra *f*
decisión de compra (Es)	Kaufentscheidung *f*	decision to purchase	décision d'acheter *f*	decisione d'acquisto *f*	—
décision de l'implantation (F)	Standort-entscheidung *f*	location decision	—	determinazione dell'ubicazione *f*	decisión de ubicación *f*
decisión de ubicación (Es)	Standort-entscheidung *f*	location decision	décision de l'implantation *f*	determinazione dell'ubicazione *f*	—
decisione d'acquisto (I)	Kaufentscheidung *f*	decision to purchase	décision d'acheter *f*	—	decisión de compra *f*
decision to purchase (E)	Kaufentscheidung *f*	—	décision d'acheter *f*	decisione d'acquisto *f*	decisión de compra *f*
Deckung (D)	—	cover	couverture *f*	copertura *f*	cobertura *f*
Deckungsbeitrag (D)	—	contribution margin	proportion de garantie *f*	contributo per copertura *m*	aportación de cobertura *f*
Deckungsbeitrags-rechnung (D)	—	contribution costing	calcul de la propor-tion de garantie *m*	calcolo del contri-buto per copertura *m*	factura de aportación de cobertura *f*
Deckungszusage (D)	—	confirmation of cover	acceptation de prendre le risque en charge *f*	impegno di copertura *m*	nota de cobertura *f*
declaración a efectos fiscales (Es)	Steuererklärung *f*	tax return	déclaration d'impôts *f*	dichiarazione dei redditi *f*	—
declaración arancelaria[1] (Es)	Zollerklärung *f*	customs declaration	déclaration en douane *f*	dichiarazione doganale *f*	—
declaración arancelaria[2] (Es)	Zollanmeldung *f*	customs declaration	déclaration en douane *f*	dichiarazione doganale *f*	—
declaración bajo juramento (Es)	eidesstattliche Erklärung *f*	declaration in lieu of an oath	déclaration formelle sans prestation de serment *f*	dichiarazione sostitu-tiva del giuramento *f*	—
declaración de importación (Es)	Einfuhrerklärung *f*	import declaration	déclaration d'entrée *f*	dichiarazione doganale *f*	—
declaración de la renta (Es)	Einkommens-erklärung *f*	income declaration	déclaration du revenue *f*	dichiarazione del reddito *f*	—
declaración de la voluntad (Es)	Willenserklärung *f*	declaration of intent	déclaration de volonté *f*	dichiarazione di volontà *f*	—
declaración jurada (Es)	beeidigte Erklärung *f*	sworn statement	déclaration sous serment *f*	dichiarazione giurata *f*	—
declarar (Es)	deklarieren	declare	déclarer	dichiarare	—
déclaration d'entrée (F)	Einfuhrerklärung *f*	import declaration	—	dichiarazione doganale *f*	declaración de importación *f*
déclaration de volonté (F)	Willenserklärung *f*	declaration of intent	—	dichiarazione di volontà *f*	declaración de la voluntad *f*
déclaration d'impôts (F)	Steuererklärung *f*	tax return	—	dichiarazione dei redditi *f*	declaración a efectos fiscales *f*
déclaration du revenue (F)	Einkommens-erklärung *f*	income declaration	—	dichiarazione del reddito *f*	declaración de la renta *f*
déclaration du sinistre (F)	Schadensmeldung *f*	notification of damage	—	avviso di danni *m*	aviso de siniestro *m*
déclaration en douane[1] (F)	Zollanmeldung *f*	customs declaration	—	dichiarazione doganale *f*	declaración arancelaria *f*
déclaration en douane[2] (F)	Zollerklärung *f*	customs declaration	—	dichiarazione doganale *f*	declaración arancelaria *f*
déclaration formelle sans prestation de serment (F)	eidesstattliche Erklärung *f*	declaration in lieu of an oath	—	dichiarazione sostitu-tiva del giuramento *f*	declaración bajo juramento *f*
declaration in lieu of an oath (E)	eidesstattliche Erklärung *f*	—	déclaration formelle sans prestation de serment *f*	dichiarazione sostitu-tiva del giuramento *f*	declaración bajo juramento *f*

	D	E	F	I	Es
declaration of intent (E)	Willenserklärung *f*	—	déclaration de volonté *f*	dichiarazione di volontà *f*	declaración de la voluntad *f*
déclaration sous serment (F)	beeidigte Erklärung *f*	sworn statement	—	dichiarazione giurata *f*	declaración jurada *f*
declare (E)	deklarieren	—	déclarer	dichiarare	declarar
déclarer (F)	deklarieren	declare	—	dichiarare	declarar
decline in prices (E)	Preisverfall *m*	—	chute des prix *f*	caduta dei prezzi *f*	caída de precios *f*
declining-balance depreciation (E)	degressive Abschreibung *f*	—	amortissement dégressif *m*	ammortamento decrescente *m*	amortización decreciente *f*
decode (E)	decodieren	—	décoder	decodificare	decodificar
décoder (F)	decodieren	decode	—	decodificare	decodificar
decodieren (D)	—	decode	décoder	decodificare	decodificar
decodificar (Es)	decodieren	decode	décoder	decodificare	—
decodificare (I)	decodieren	decode	décoder	—	decodificar
décompte des frais (F)	Spesenabrechung *f*	statement of expenses	—	conteggio delle spese *m*	liquidación de gastos *f*
de confiance (F)	zuverlässig	reliable	—	affidabile	de confianza
de confianza (Es)	zuverlässig	reliable	de confiance	affidabile	—
de conformidad con (Es)	im Einvernehmen mit	in agreement with	d'accord avec	d'accordo con	—
décoration de vitrine (F)	Schaufenster-dekoration *f*	window dressing	—	allestimento di vetrina *m*	adorno del escaparate *m*
découvert de compte (F)	Kontoüberziehung *f*	overdraft of an account	—	scoperto di conto *m*	descubierto *m*
decrease in demand (E)	Nachfragerückgang *m*	—	recul de la demande *m*	flessione della domanda *f*	disminución en la demanda *f*
decrease in value (E)	Wertminderung *f*	—	diminution de la valeur *f*	riduzione di valore *f*	depreciación *f*
decrease of turnover (E)	Umsatzrückgang *m*	—	recul du chiffre d'affaires *m*	calo del fatturato *m*	disminución de la cifra de facturación *f*
decree (E)	Verordnung *f*	—	décret *m*	regolamento *m*	ordenanza *f*
décret (F)	Verordnung *f*	decree	—	regolamento *m*	ordenanza *f*
decreto di citazione in giudizio (I)	Eröffnungs-beschluß *m*	order opening a trial	arrêt de mise en accusation *m*	—	acuerdo de apertura *m*
de derecho público (Es)	öffentlich-rechtlich	under public law	de droit public	di diritto pubblico	—
dédouané (F)	verzollt	duty paid	—	sdoganato	pagado
de droit public (F)	öffentlich-rechtlich	under public law	—	di diritto pubblico	de derecho público
deducción (Es)	Abzug *m*	deduction/discount	diminution *f*/ escompte *m*	detrazione *f*/ sconto *m*	—
deducción de intereses no acumulados (Es)	Abzinsung *f*	discounting	déduction des in-térêts non courus *f*	deduzione di interessi *f*	—
deducción del descuento (Es)	Skontoabzug *m*	discount deduction	déduction de l'escompte *f*	detrazione di sconto *f*	—
deducción de porte (Es)	Portoabzug *m*	postage deduction	déduction de port *f*	detrazione porto *f*	—
deduction (E)	Abzug *m*	—	diminution *f*/ escompte *m*	detrazione *f*/ sconto *m*	deducción *f*/ descuento *m*
déduction (F)	Abschlag *m*	reduction	—	detrazione *f*	descuento *m*
déduction de l'escompte (F)	Skontoabzug *m*	discount deduction	—	detrazione di sconto *f*	deducción del descuento *f*
déduction de port (F)	Portoabzug *m*	postage deduction	—	detrazione porto *f*	deducción de porte *f*
déduction des intérêts non courus (F)	Abzinsung *f*	discounting	—	deduzione di interessi *f*	deducción de intere-ses no acumulados *f*
deduzione di interessi (I)	Abzinsung *f*	discounting	déduction des intérêts non courus *f*	—	deducción de intere-ses no acumulados *f*
de facil avenencia (Es)	kulant	accommodating	arrangeant	corrente	—
default interest (E)	Verzugszinsen *pl*	—	intérêts moratoires *m pl*	interessi di mora *m pl*	intereses de demora *m pl*
default rate (E)	Ausfallquote *f*	—	ratio de perte *m*	tasso di perdita *m*	cuota de pérdida *f*
default risk (E)	Ausfallrisiko *n*	—	risque de perte *m*	rischio di perdita *m*	riesgo de pérdida *m*
défaut (F)	Mangel *m*	defect	—	vizio *m*	defecto *m*
defect (E)	Mangel *m*	—	défaut *m*	vizio *m*	defecto *m*/vicio *m*

	D	E	F	I	Es
defective (E)	fehlerhaft	—	défectueux	difettoso	defectuoso
defecto (Es)	Mangel *m*	defect	défaut *m*	vizio *m*	—
défectueux (F)	fehlerhaft	defective	—	difettoso	defectuoso
defectuoso (Es)	fehlerhaft	defective	défectueux	difettoso	—
défense de publicité (F)	Werbeverbot *n*	ban on advertising	—	divieto di pubblicità *m*	prohibición de publicidad *f*
deferred item (E)	Abgrenzungs-posten *m*	—	comptes transitoires *m pl*	ratei e risconti *m pl*	cuentas de orden *f pl*
défiant toute concurrence (F)	konkurrenzlos	without competition	—	senza concorrenza	sin competencia
deficiency guarantee (E)	Ausfallbürgschaft *f*	—	garantie de bonne fin *f*	fideiussione d'indennità *f*	fianza con beneficio de excusión *f*
déficit budgétaire (F)	Haushaltsdefizit *n*	budgetary deficit	—	deficit del bilancio *m*	déficit presupuestario *m*
déficit de la balance du commerce extérieur (F)	Außenhandels-defizit *n*	trade deficit	—	deficit del commercio estero *m*	déficit del comercio exterior *m*
deficit del bilancio (I)	Haushaltsdefizit *n*	budgetary deficit	déficit budgétaire *m*	—	déficit presupuestario *m*
déficit del comercio exterior (Es)	Außenhandels-defizit *n*	trade deficit	déficit de la balance du commerce extérieur *m*	deficit del commercio estero *m*	—
deficit del commercio estero (I)	Außenhandels-defizit *n*	trade deficit	déficit de la balance du commerce extérieur *m*	—	déficit del comercio exterior *m*
déficit en la balanza de pagos (Es)	Zahlungsbilanz-defizit *n*	deficit in the balance of payments	balance des paye-ments déficitaire *f*	disavanzo della bilancia dei pagamenti *m*	—
deficit financing (E)	Defizitfinanzierung *f*	—	financement du déficit *m*	finanziamento del deficit *m*	financiación del déficit *f*
deficit in the balance of payments (E)	Zahlungsbilanz-defizit *n*	—	balance des paye-ments déficitaire *f*	disavanzo della bilan-cia dei pagamenti *m*	déficit en la balanza de pagos *m*
déficit presupuestario (Es)	Haushaltsdefizit *n*	budgetary deficit	déficit budgétaire *m*	deficit del bilancio *m*	—
Defizitfinanzierung (D)	—	deficit financing	financement du déficit *m*	finanziamento del deficit *m*	financiación del déficit *f*
deflación (Es)	Deflation *f*	deflation	déflation *f*	deflazione *f*	—
Deflation (D)	—	deflation	déflation *f*	deflazione *f*	deflación *f*
deflation (E)	Deflation *f*	—	déflation *f*	deflazione *f*	deflación *f*
déflation (F)	Deflation *f*	deflation	—	deflazione *f*	deflación *f*
deflazione (I)	Deflation *f*	deflation	déflation *f*	—	deflación *f*
deflusso di divise (I)	Devisenabfluß *m*	foreign exchange outflow	sortie de devises *f*	—	drenaje de divisas *m*
defraudación[1] (Es)	Unterschlagung *f*	embezzlement	détournement *m*	appropriazione indebita *f*	—
defraudación[2] (Es)	Hinterziehung *f*	evasion of taxes	fraude fiscale *f*	evasione *f*	—
defraudación fiscal (Es)	Steuerhinterziehung *f*	tax evasion	dissimulation en matière fiscale *f*	evasione fiscale *f*	—
degno di credito (I)	kreditwürdig	creditworthy	solvable	—	solvente
dégré de saturation (F)	Auslastungsgrad *m*	capacity utilisation rate	—	grado di sfruttamento *m*	tasa de utilización *f*
degressive Abschreibung (D)	—	declining-balance depreciation	amortissement dégressif *m*	ammortamento decrescente *m*	amortización decreciente *f*
dégressivité des coûts (F)	Kostendegression *f*	cost degression	—	riduzione dei costi *f*	reducción de costes *f*
déjeuner de travail (F)	Arbeitsessen *n*	working lunch	—	pranzo di lavoro *m*	comida de trabajo *f*
deklarieren (D)	—	declare	déclarer	dichiarare	declarar
délai[1] (F)	Frist *f*	period	—	termine *m*	plazo *m*
délai[2] (F)	Ablauffrist *f*	time limit	—	termine di scadenza *m*	vencimiento *m*
délai de carence (F)	Karenzzeit *f*	qualifying period	—	periodo d'attesa *m*	período carencial *m*
délai de déclaration (F)	Anmeldefrist *f*	time for application	—	termine di denuncia *m*	plazo de solicitud *m*
délai d'engagement sur le taux d'intérêt accordé (F)	Zinsbindungsfrist *f*	lock-down period for interest rates	—	scadenza degli interessi vincolati *f*	plazo de vinculación al tipo de interés pactado *f*

	D	E	F	I	Es
délai de livraison[1] (F)	Lieferfrist *f*	time for delivery	—	termine di consegna *m*	plazo de entrega *m*
délai de livraison[2] (F)	Liefertermin *m*	date of delivery	—	termine di consegna *m*	plazo de entrega *m*
délai de payement[1] (F)	Zahlungsziel *n*	period for payment	—	termine di pagamento *m*	plazo de pago *m*
délai de payement[2] (F)	Zahlungsfrist *f*	terms of payment	—	scadenza di pagamento *f*	plazo de pago *m*
délai de préavis (F)	Kündigungsfrist *f*	period of notice	—	termine di preavviso per la disdetta *m*	plazo de preaviso *m*
délai de protection (F)	Schutzfrist *f*	term of protection	—	durata della protezione *f*	plazo de protección *m*
delay[1] (E)	Verzug *m*	—	demeure *f*	mora *f*	retraso *m*/demora *f*
delay[2] (E)	Verspätung *f*	—	retard *m*	ritardo *m*	retraso *m*
delay in delivery[1] (E)	Lieferverzug *m*	—	demeure du fournisseur *f*	mora nella consegna *f*	demora en la entrega *f*
delay in delivery[2] (E)	Lieferungsverzögerung *f*	—	retard dans la livraison *m*	ritardo della consegna *m*	demora en la entrega *f*
delcrédere (Es)	Delkredere *n*	del credere	ducroire *m*	star del credere *m*	—
del credere (E)	Delkredere *n*	—	ducroire *m*	star del credere *m*	delcrédere *m*
del credere commission (E)	Delkredereprovision *f*	—	commission ducroire *f*	provvigione dello star del credere *f*	comisión de garantía *f*
delegación (Es)	Delegation *f*	delegation	délégation *f*	delegazione *f*	—
delegar (Es)	delegieren	delegate	déléguer	delegare	—
delegare (I)	delegieren	delegate	déléguer	—	delegar
delegate (E)	delegieren	—	déléguer	delegare	delegar
Delegation (D)	—	delegation	délégation *f*	delegazione *f*	delegación *f*
delegation (E)	Delegation *f*	—	délégation *f*	delegazione *f*	delegación *f*
délégation (F)	Delegation *f*	delegation	—	delegazione *f*	delegación *f*
delegazione (I)	Delegation *f*	delegation	délégation *f*	—	delegación *f*
delegieren (D)	—	delegate	déléguer	delegare	delegar
déléguer (F)	delegieren	delegate	—	delegare	delegar
de l'Etat (F)	staatlich	state	—	statale	estatal
delibera (I)	Beschluß *m*	decision	décision *f*	—	decisión *f*
delimitación (Es)	Abgrenzung *f*	demarcation	délimitation *f*	delimitazione *f*	—
délimitation (F)	Abgrenzung *f*	demarcation	—	delimitazione *f*	delimitación *f*
delimitazione (I)	Abgrenzung *f*	demarcation	délimitation *f*	—	delimitación *f*
delincuencia informática (Es)	Computerkriminalität *f*	computer criminality	délits informatiques *m pl*	abuso del computer *m*	—
délinquance économique[1] (F)	White-collar-Kriminalität *f*	white-collar delinquency	—	criminalità dei colletti bianchi *f*	criminalidad económica *f*
délinquence économique[2] (F)	Wirtschaftskriminalität *f*	white-collar crime	—	criminalità economica *f*	criminalidad económica *f*
délits informatiques (F)	Computerkriminalität *f*	computer criminality	—	abuso del computer *m*	delincuencia informática *f*
deliverable (E)	lieferbar	—	livrable	disponibile	suministrable
delivery[1] (E)	Zustellung *f*	—	remise *f*	notifica *f*/recapito *m*	envío *m*
delivery[2] (E)	Übergabe *f*	—	remise *f*	consegna *f*	entrega *f*
delivery[3] (E)	Lieferung *f*	—	livraison *f*	fornitura *f*/consegna *f*	suminstro *m*
delivery ban (E)	Liefersperre *f*	—	blocage de livraisons *m*	blocco delle forniture *m*	embargo *m*
delivery capacity (E)	Lieferkapazität *f*	—	capacité de livraison *f*	capacità di fornitura *f*	capacidad de entrega *f*
delivery clause (E)	Lieferklausel *f*	—	clause de livraison *f*	clausola di fornitura *f*	cláusulas comerciales *f pl*
delivery note (E)	Lieferschein *m*	—	bulletin de livraison *m*	bolletta di consegna *f*	recibo de entrega *m*
delivery programme (E)	Lieferprogramm *n*	—	programme de livraison *m*	programma di fornitura *m*	programa de entrega *m*
Delkredere (D)	—	del credere	ducroire *m*	star del credere *m*	delcrédere *m*
Delkredereprovision (D)	—	del credere commission	commission ducroire *f*	provvigione dello star del credere *f*	comisión de garantía *f*

	D	E	F	I	Es
demand (E)	Nachfrage *f*	—	demande *f*	domanda *f*	demanda *f*
demanda[1] (Es)	Klage *f*	legal action	action en justice *f*	citazione in giudizio *f*	—
demanda[2] (Es)	Anfrage *f*	inquiry	demande *f*	richiesta *f*	—
demanda[3] (Es)	Nachfrage *f*	demand	demande *f*	domanda *f*	—
demanda de daños y perjuicios (Es)	Schadensersatz-klage *f*	action for damages	action en dommages-intérêts *f*	azione di risarcimento danni *f*	—
demanda de trabajo (Es)	Arbeitsnachfrage *f*	job demand	demande d'emploi *f*	domanda di lavoro *f*	—
demanda exterior (Es)	Auslandsnachfrage *f*	foreign demand	demande en provenance de l'étranger *f*	domanda estera *f*	—
demanda interior (Es)	Inlandsnachfrage *f*	home demand	demande intérieure *f*	domanda interna *f*	—
demanda monetaria (Es)	Geldnachfrage *f*	demand for money	demande sur le marché monétaire *f*	domanda di denaro *f*	—
demandante (Es)	Besteller *m*	customer	acheteur *m*	committente *m*	—
demande[1] (F)	Nachfrage *f*	demand	—	domanda *f*	demanda *f*
demande[2] (F)	Anfrage *f*	inquiry	—	richiesta *f*	demanda *f*
demande[3] (F)	Antrag *m*	application	—	domanda *f*	solicitud *f*
demande de dédouanement (F)	Zollantrag *m*	customs application	—	domanda di sdoganamento *f*	solicitud de aduana *f*
demande d'emploi[1] (F)	Stellengesuch *n*	situation wanted/ application for a job	—	domanda d'impiego *f*	solicitud de colocación *f*
demande d'emploi[2] (F)	Arbeitsnachfrage *f*	job demand	—	domanda di lavoro *f*	demanda de trabajo *f*
demande en déclaration de faillite (F)	Konkursantrag *m*	bankruptcy petition	—	domanda di dichiarazione del fallimento *f*	petición de quiebra *f*
demande en provenance de l'étranger (F)	Auslandsnachfrage *f*	foreign demand	—	domanda estera *f*	demanda exterior *m*
demande intérieure (F)	Inlandsnachfrage *f*	home demand	—	domanda interna *f*	demanda interior *f*
demande sur le marché monétaire (F)	Geldnachfrage *f*	demand for money	—	domanda di denaro	demanda monetaria *f*
demand for money (E)	Geldnachfrage *f*	—	demande sur le marché monétaire *f*	domanda di denaro	demanda monetaria *f*
demand for payment (E)	Mahnung *f*	—	mise en demeure *f*	sollecito *m*	(ad)monición *f*
demand price (E)	Geldkurs *m*	—	cours de la demande *m*	prezzo di domanda *m*	cotización demandada *f*/precio ofrecido *m*
demarcation (E)	Abgrenzung *f*	—	délimitation *f*	delimitazione *f*	delimitación *f*
déménagement (F)	Umzug *m*	change of residence/ parade/demonstration	—	trasferimento *m*	mudanza f/desfile *m*/ manifestación *f*
demeure (F)	Verzug *m*	delay	—	mora *f*	retraso *m*/demora *f*
demeure du débiteur (F)	Zahlungsverzug *m*	failure to pay on due date	—	morosità di pagamento *f*	retraso en el pago *m*
demeure du fournisseur (F)	Lieferverzug *m*	delay in delivery	—	mora nella consegna *f*	demora en la entrega *f*
démission (F)	Rücktritt *m*	resignation	—	dimissioni *f pl*	dimisión *f*
demografía (Es)	Demographie *f*	demography	démographie *f*	demografia *f*	—
demografia (I)	Demographie *f*	demography	démographie *f*	—	demografía *f*
Demographie (D)	—	demography	démographie *f*	demografia *f*	demografía *f*
démographie (F)	Demographie *f*	demography	—	demografia *f*	demografía *f*
demography (E)	Demographie *f*	—	démographie *f*	demografia *f*	demografía *f*
demora en el pago (Es)	Zahlungs-verzögerung *f*	delay in payment	retard dans le payement *m*	ritardo del pagamento *m*	—
demora en la entrega[1] (Es)	Lieferverzug *m*	delay in delivery	demeure du fournisseur *f*	mora nella consegna *f*	—
demora en la entrega[2] (Es)	Lieferungs-verzögerung *f*	delay in delivery	retard dans la livraison *m*	ritardo della consegna *m*	—
demoscopia (Es)	Demoskopie *f*	public opinion research	sondage de l'opinion publique *m*	demoscopia *f*	—
demoscopia (I)	Demoskopie *f*	public opinion research	sondage de l'opinion publique *m*	—	demoscopia *f*
Demoskopie (D)	—	public opinion research	sondage de l'opinion publique *m*	demoscopia *f*	demoscopia *f*
denaro (I)	Geld *n*	money	argent *m*	—	dinero *m*/efectivo *m*

	D	E	F	I	Es
denaro contante (I)	Bargeld *n*	cash	argent comptant *m*	—	dinero efectivo *m*
denaro contante in cassa (I)	Bargeldbestand *m*	cash in hand	espèces en caisse *f pl*	—	saldo en efectivo *m*
denaro vincolato (I)	Festgeld *n*	fixed deposit	argent immobilisé *m*	—	depósito a plazo *m*
dénationalisation (F)	Reprivatisierung *f*	reversion to private ownership	—	riprivatizzazione *f*	desnacionalización *f*
denationalization (E)	Privatisierung *f*	—	privatisation *f*	privatizzazione *f*	privatización *f*
denominazione (I)	Firmenname *m*	company name	nom de la maison *m*	—	razón social *f*
dénoncer (F)	kündigen	terminate	—	disdire	denunciar
densidad de la población (Es)	Bevölkerungsdichte *f*	density of population	densité de la population *f*	densità di popolazione *f*	—
densità di popolazione (I)	Bevölkerungsdichte *f*	density of population	densité de la population *f*	—	densidad de la población *f*
densité de la population (F)	Bevölkerungsdichte *f*	density of population	—	densità di popolazione *f*	densidad de la población *f*
density of population (E)	Bevölkerungsdichte *f*	—	densité de la population *f*	densità di popolazione *f*	densidad de la población *f*
dentro del plazo fijado (Es)	fristgerecht	timely	dans les délais	entro il termine convenuto	—
denuncia dei vizi (I)	Mängelanzeige *f*	notice of defect	notification d'un vice *f*	—	aviso de vicios *m*
denunciar (Es)	kündigen	terminate	dénoncer	disdire	—
denutrizione (I)	Unterernährung *f*	malnutrition	sous-alimentation *f*	—	subalimentación *f*
departamento de expedición (Es)	Versandabteilung *f*	dispatch department	service des expéditions *m*	reparto spedizioni *m*	—
departamento de exportación (Es)	Exportabteilung *f*	export department	service d'exportation *m*	reparto esportazioni *m*	—
departamento de mercadeo (Es)	Marketingabteilung *f*	marketing department	bureau de marketing *m*	reparto marketing *m*	—
departamento de nóminas (Es)	Lohnbüro *n*	pay office	bureau de la paye *m*	ufficio paga *m*	—
departamento técnico (Es)	technische Abteilung *f*	engineering department	service technique *m*	reparto tecnico *m*	—
départ gare (F)	ab Bahnhof	ex rail/free on rail	—	franco stazione	puesto en estación
departmental expense account (E)	Kostenstelle *f*	—	compte de frais par secteur *m*	posizione costi *f*	posición de costes *f*
department organization (E)	Abteilungs-organisation *f*	—	organisation du service *f*	organizzazione reparto *f*	organización de sección *f*
department store (E)	Waren-, Kaufhaus *n*	—	grand magasin *m*	grande magazzino *m*	gran almacén *m*
départ navire (F)	ab Schiff	ex ship	—	franco bordo	ex vapor
départ quai (F)	ab Kai	ex quay	—	franco banchina	ex muelle
départ usine (F)	ab Werk	ex works	—	franco fabbrica	ex fábrica
depending on the cyclical trend (E)	konjunkturanfällig	—	sensible aux oscillations de la conjoncture	soggetto ad influssi congiunturali	sensible a las fluctuaciones coyunturales
dépenses[1] (F)	Aufwand *m*	expenditure	—	spese *f pl*	gastos *m pl*
dépenses[2] (F)	Aufwendung *f*	expenditure	—	spese *f pl*	gasto *m*
dépenses[3] (F)	Ausgaben *pl*	expenses	—	spese *f pl*	gastos *m pl*
dépense spéciale (F)	Sonderausgaben *pl*	special expenses	—	spese straordinarie *f pl*	gastos extraordinarios *m pl*
dépenses en matériels (F)	Materialaufwand *m*	material expenditure	—	spese materiale *f pl*	coste de material *m*
dépenses publiques[1] (F)	Staatsausgaben *pl*	public spending	—	spese pubbliche *f pl*	gastos públicos *m pl*
dépenses publiques[2] (F)	öffentliche Ausgaben *pl*	public spending	—	spesa pubblica *f*	gastos públicos *m pl*
dépenses retardées (F)	Ausgaben-verzögerung *f*	expenditure delay	—	dilazione delle spese *f*	aplazamiento de gastos *m*
deperibile (I)	verderblich	perishable	périssable	—	perecedero
depliant (I)	Broschüre *f*	brochure	prospectus *m*	—	folleto *m*
de point en point (F)	Zug um Zug	concurrent	—	contestualmente	punto por punto
dépollution (F)	Entsorgung *f*	waste disposal	—	smaltimento *m*	eliminación *f*

	D	E	F	I	Es
deposit[1] (E)	Einlagen *pl*	—	dépôt *m*	depositi bancari *m pl*	depósitos bancarios *m pl*
deposit[2] (E)	Anzahlung *f*	—	acompte *m*	pagamento in acconto *m*	pago a cuenta *m*
deposit[3] (E)	Depot *n*	—	dépôt *m*	deposito *m*	depósito *m*
deposit[4] (E)	Hinterlegung *f*	—	dépôt *m*	deposito *m*	depósito *m*
depositi bancari (I)	Einlagen *pl*	deposit	dépôt *m*	—	depósitos bancarios *m pl*
deposit banking (E)	Depotgeschäft *n*	—	garde des titres *f*	operazione di deposito *f*	custodia de valores *f*
depositi di risparmio (I)	Spareinlagen *pl*	savings deposits	dépôt d'épargne *m*	—	imposiciones de ahorro *f pl*
depósitio de acciones (Es)	Aktiendepot *n*	share deposit	dépôt d'actions *m*	deposito di azioni *m*	—
depositi privati (I)	Privateinlagen *pl*	private contribution	apport personnel *m*	—	depósitos privados *m pl*
depósito[1] (Es)	Depot *n*	deposit	dépôt *m*	deposito *m*	—
depósito[2] (Es)	Hinterlegung *f*	deposit	dépôt *m*	deposito *m*	—
deposito[1] (I)	Hinterlegung *f*	deposit	dépôt *m*	—	depósito *m*
deposito[2] (I)	Depot *n*	deposit	dépôt *m*	—	depósito *m*
depósito a plazo (Es)	Festgeld *n*	fixed deposit	argent immobilisé *m*	denaro vincolato *m*	—
depósito de aduana (Es)	Zollagerung *f*	customs warehouse procedure	dépôt en entrepôt sous douane *m*	immagazzinamento doganale *m*	—
depósito de importación (Es)	Importdepot *n*	import deposit	dépôt d'importation *m*	deposito d'importazione *m*	—
depósito de mercancías (Es)	Warenlager *n*	stock room	stock de marchandises *m*	magazzino *m*	—
depósito de noche (Es)	Nachttresor *m*	night safe	dépôt de nuit *m*	cassa continua *f*	—
deposito di azioni (I)	Aktiendepot *n*	share deposit	dépôt d'actions *m*	—	depósitio de acciones *m*
deposito di consegna (I)	Auslieferungslager *n*	distribution centre	entrepôt de distribution *m*	—	almacén de entregas *m*
deposito d'importazione (I)	Importdepot *n*	import deposit	dépôt d'importation *m*	—	depósito de importación *m*
deposito vincolato (I)	Festgeldkonto *n*	time deposit account	compte de dépôt à terme *m*	—	cuenta a plazo *f*
depósitos bancarios (Es)	Einlagen *pl*	deposit	dépôt *m*	depositi bancari *m pl*	—
depósitos privados (Es)	Privateinlagen *pl*	private contribution	apport personnel *m*	depositi privati *m pl*	—
deposit transactions passive (E)	Passivgeschäft *n*	—	opération passive *f*	operazione passiva *f*	operación pasiva *f*
Depot (D)	—	deposit	dépôt *m*	deposito *m*	depósito *m*
dépôt[1] (F)	Depot *n*	deposit	—	deposito *m*	depósito *m*
dépôt[2] (F)	Einlagen *pl*	deposit/ contributed capital	—	depositi bancari *m pl*	depósitos bancarios *m pl*
dépôt[3] (F)	Hinterlegung *f*	deposit	—	deposito *m*	depósito *m*
dépôt[4] (F)	Verwahrung *f*	custody	—	custodia *f*	custodia *f*/ incautación *f*
dépôt d'actions (F)	Aktiendepot *n*	share deposit	—	deposito di azioni *m*	depósitio de acciones *m*
dépôt de nuit (F)	Nachttresor *m*	night safe	—	cassa continua *f*	depósito de noche *m*
dépôt d'épargne (F)	Spareinlagen *pl*	savings deposits	—	depositi di risparmio *m pl*	imposiciones de ahorro *f pl*
dépôt d'importation (F)	Importdepot *n*	import deposit	—	deposito d'importazione *m*	depósito de importación *m*
dépôl en entrepôt sous douane (F)	Zollagerung *f*	customs warehouse procedure	—	immagazzinamento doganale *m*	depósito de aduana *m*
Depotgeschäft (D)	—	deposit banking	garde des titres *f*	operazione di deposito *f*	custodia de valores *f*
depreciación[1] (Es)	Wertminderung *f*	decrease in value	diminution de la valeur *f*	riduzione di valore *f*	—
depreciación[2] (Es)	Wertverfall *m*	loss of value	dévalorisation *f*	deprezzamento *m*	—
depreciation (E)	Abschreibung *f*	—	amortissement *m*	ammortamento *m*	amortización *f*

	D	E	F	I	Es
dépréciation (F)	Abnutzung *f*	wear and tear	—	usura *f*	desgaste *m*
depreciation fund (E)	Abschreibungs-fonds *m*	—	fonds d'amortissement *m*	fondo ammortamenti *m*	fondo amortización *m*
de première qualité (F)	erstklassig	first class	—	di prima categoria	de primera calidad
depresión (Es)	Depression *f*	depression	dépression *f*	depressione *f*	—
Depression (D)	—	depression	dépression *f*	depressione *f*	depresión *f*
depression (E)	Depression *f*	—	dépression *f*	depressione *f*	depresión *f*
dépression[1] (F)	Abschwung *m*	down-swing	—	regresso *m*	baja *f*
dépression[2] (F)	Depression *f*	depression	—	depressione *f*	depresión *f*
depressione (I)	Depression *f*	depression	dépression *f*	—	depresión *f*
deprezzamento (I)	Wertverfall *m*	loss of value	dévalorisation *f*	—	depreciación *f*
de primera calidad (Es)	erstklassig	first class	de première qualité	di prima categoria	—
depuración de las aguas residuales (Es)	Abwasserreinigung *f*	purification of sewage	clarification des eaux usées *f*	depurazione delle acque di scarico *f*	—
depurazione delle acque di scarico (I)	Abwasserreinigung *f*	purification of sewage	clarification des eaux usées *f*	—	depuración de las aguas residuales *f*
deputy (E)	Stellvertreter *m*	—	adjoint *m*	sostituto *m*	sustituto *m*
derecho[1] (Es)	Recht *n*	law	droit *m*	diritto *m*	—
derecho[2] (Es)	Gebühr *f*	fee	taxe *f*	tassa *f*	—
derecho a indemnización por daños y perjuicios (Es)	Schadenersatz-ansprüche *pl*	claim for damages	droit à l'indemnité *m*	diritti al risarcimento danni *m pl*	—
derecho a voto (Es)	Stimmrecht *n*	right to vote	droit de vote *m*	diritto al voto *m*	—
derecho de devolución (Es)	Rückgaberecht *n*	right of redemption	droit à restitution *m*	diritto alla restituzione *m*	—
derecho de garantía real (Es)	Pfandrecht *n*	pledge	droit de gage *m*	diritto di pegno *m*	—
derecho de la competencia (Es)	Wettbewerbsrecht *n*	law on competition	législation en matière de concurrence commerciale *m*	diritto della concorrenza *m*	—
derecho del autor (Es)	Urheberrecht *n*	copyright	droit d'auteur *m*	diritto d'autore *m*	—
derecho de licencia (Es)	Lizenzgebühr *f*	royalty	taxe d'expoitation de licence *f*	tassa di licenza *f*	—
derecho de preferencia (Es)	Vorkaufsrecht *n*	preemption right	droit de préemption *m*	diritto di prelazione *m*	—
derecho de representación (Es)	Vertretungs-berechtigung *f*	authorized to represent	autorisation de représentation *f*	autorizzazione alla rappresentanza *f*	—
derecho de representación exclusiva (Es)	Alleinvertretungs-recht *n*	sole and exclusive agency right	droit exclusif de représentation *m*	diritto di rappresen-tanza esclusiva *m*	—
derecho de revocación (Es)	Widerrufsrecht *n*	right of revocation	droit de révocation *m*	diritto di revoca *m*	—
derecho de sociedades anónimas (Es)	Aktienrecht *n*	company law	loi sur les sociétés anonymes *f pl*	diritto azionario *m*	—
derecho de suministro adicional (Es)	Nachlieferungs-anspruch *m*	claim to subsequent delivery	droit à livraison complémentaire *m*	diritto alla fornitura supplementare *m*	—
derecho de tránsito (Es)	Transitzoll *m*	transit duty	droit de transit *m*	diritti di transito *m pl*	—
derecho económico (Es)	Wirtschaftsrecht *n*	economic law	législation économique *f*	diritto economico *m*	—
derecho laboral (Es)	Arbeitsrecht *n*	labour law	législation industrielle *f*	diritto di lavoro *m*	—
derecho minoritario (Es)	Minoritätsrecht *n*	minority right	droit de minorité *m*	diritto delle minoranze *m*	—
derecho pesquero (Es)	Fischereirecht *n*	fishing rights	droit de pêche *m*	diritto della pesca *m*	—
derecho preferente (Es)	Vorrecht *n*	privilege	prérogative *f*	privilegio *m*	—
derecho real (Es)	dingliches Recht *n*	real right	droit réel *m*	diritto reale *m*	—
derechos arancelarios (Es)	Zollgebühren *pl*	customs duties	droit de douane *m*	diritti doganali *m pl*	—
derechos de acarreo (Es)	Rollgeld *n*	haulage	camionnage *m*	spese di trasporto *f pl*	—
derechos de carga (Es)	Ladegebühren *pl*	loading charges	taxe de chargement *f*	spese di carico *f pl*	—
derechos de exportación (Es)	Ausfuhrzoll *m*	export duty	taxe de sortie *f*	dazio sull'esportazione *m*	—
derechos de giro (Es)	Ziehungsrechte *pl*	drawing rights	droits de tirage *m pl*	diritti di prelievo *m pl*	—

	D	E	F	I	Es
derechos de giro especial (Es)	Sonderziehungs-rechte *pl*	special drawing rights	droits de tirage spécial *m pl*	diritti speciali di prelievo *m pl*	—
derechos de soberanía nacional (Es)	nationale Souveränitätsrechte *pl*	national sovereignty rights	droits de souveraineté nationale *m pl*	diritti di sovranità nazionale *m pl*	—
derechos de timbre (Es)	Stempelgebühr *f*	stamp duty	droit de timbre *m*	tassa di bollo *f*	—
derechos portuarios (Es)	Hafengebühren *pl*	harbour dues	droits de port *m pl*	diritti di porto *m pl*	—
derechos prohibitivos (Es)	Prohibitivzoll *m*	prohibitive duty	droit prohibitif *m*	dazio proibitivo *m*	—
deregolazione (I)	Deregulierung *f*	deregulation	dérégularisation *f*	—	deregulación *f*
deregulación (Es)	Deregulierung *f*	deregulation	dérégularisation *f*	deregolazione *f*	—
dérégularisation (F)	Deregulierung *f*	deregulation	—	deregolazione *f*	deregulación *f*
deregulation (E)	Deregulierung *f*	—	dérégularisation *f*	deregolazione *f*	deregulación *f*
Deregulierung (D)	—	deregulation	dérégularisation *f*	deregolazione *f*	deregulación *f*
dernier cours (F)	Schlußkurs *m*	closing price	—	quotazione di chiusura *f*	cotización final *f*
déroulement de la fabrication (F)	Fertigungsprozess *m*	production procedure	—	processo produttivo *m*	proceso de producción *m*
derrumbamiento financiero (Es)	finanzieller Zusammenbruch *m*	financial failure	débâcle financière *f*	crollo finanziario *m*	—
desalojamiento (Es)	Räumung *f*	evacuation	évacuation *f*	evacuazione *f*	—
desarrollo (Es)	Entwicklung *f*	development	développement *m*	sviluppo *m*	—
désavantage (F)	Nachteil *m*	disadvantage	—	svantaggio *m*	desventaja *f*
descalabro financiero (Es)	Finanzdebakel *n*	financial debacle	débâcle fiancière *f*	dissesto finanziario *m*	—
descenso del empleo (Es)	Beschäftigungs-rückgang *m*	drop in employment	baisse de l'offre d'emploi *f*	calo dell'occupazione *m*	—
descentralización (Es)	Dezentralisierung *f*	decentralization	décentralisation *f*	decentralizzazione *f*	—
descripción del puesto de trabajo (Es)	Stellenbeschreibung *f*	job description	description de l'emploi *f*	descrizione d'impiego *f*	—
description de l'emploi (F)	Stellenbeschreibung *f*	job description	—	descrizione d'impiego *f*	descripción del puesto de trabajo *f*
descrizione d'impiego (I)	Stellenbeschreibung *f*	job description	description de l'emploi *f*	—	descripción del puesto de trabajo *f*
descubierto (Es)	Kontoüberziehung *f*	overdraft of an account	découvert de compte *m*	scoperto di conto *m*	—
descuendo por pago al contado[1] (Es)	Barzahlungs-nachlaß *m*	discount for cash payment	remise pour payement au comptant *f*	sconto per pagamento in contanti *m*	—
descuendo por pago al contado[2] (Es)	Barzahlungsrabatt *m*	cash discount	remise pour payement comptant *f*	ribasso per pagamento in contanti *m*	—
descuento[1] (Es)	Skonto *n*	discount	escompte *m*	sconto *m*	—
descuento[2] (Es)	Diskont *m*	discount	escompte *m*	sconto *m*	—
descuento[3] (Es)	Abschlag *m*	reduction	déduction *f*	detrazione *f*	—
descuento[4] (Es)	Preisabzug *m*	price deduction	réduction de prix *f*	riduzione del prezzo *f*	—
descuento de pago al contado (Es)	Barzahlungskonto *n*	cash discount	escompte de caisse *m*	sconto per pagamento in contanti *m*	—
descuento de suscripción (Es)	Vorbestellrabatt *m*	discount on advance orders	escompte de suscription *m*	ribasso per ordinazioni anticipate *m*	—
descuento de una letra aceptada (Es)	Akzepteinlösung *f*	honouring of an acceptance	honorer la traite acceptée	pagamento di un effetto *m*	—
descuento suplementario (Es)	Sonderrabatt *m*	special discount	ristourne exceptionnelle *f*	ribasso speciale *m*	—
descuido (Es)	Fahrlässigkeit *f*	negligence	négligence *f*	negligenza *f*	—
desechos (Es)	Abfall *m*	waste	déchet *m*	rifiuti *m pl*	—
desempleo (Es)	Arbeitslosigkeit *f*	unemployment	chômage *m*	disoccupazione *f*	—
desestacionalizado (Es)	saisonbereinigt	seasonally adjusted	corrigé du mouvement saisonnier	al netto degli influssi stagionali	—
desgaste (Es)	Abnutzung *f*	wear and tear	dépréciation *f*	usura *f*	—
desgravamen (Es)	Entlastung *f*	discharge	décharge *f*	sgravio *m*	—
Design (D)	—	design	design *m*	design *m*	diseño *m*
design (E)	Design *n*	—	design *m*	design *m*	diseño *m*
design (F)	Design *n*	design	—	design *m*	diseño *m*

	D	E	F	I	Es
design (I)	Design *n*	design	design *m*	—	diseño *m*
desk (E)	Schreibtisch *m*	—	bureau *m*	scrivania *f*	escritorio *m*
desnacionalización (Es)	Reprivatisierung *f*	reversion to private ownership	dénationalisation *f*	riprivatizzazione *f*	—
despacho (Es)	Abfertigung *f*	dispatch	expédition *f*	spedizione *f*	—
despacho de exportación (Es)	Ausfuhrabfertigung *f*	customs clearance of exports	formalités en douane à l'exportation *f pl*	sdoganamento delle esportazioni *m*	—
despido (Es)	Entlassung *f*	dismissal	licenciement *m*	licenziamento *m*	—
después de haber recibo la factura (Es)	nach Erhalt der Rechnung	on receipt of the invoice	après avoir reçu la facture	a ricevimento della fattura	—
destajo (Es)	Akkord *m*	piece work	convention de salaire à la tâche *f*	cottimo *m*	—
destinataire[1] (F)	Empfänger *m*	receiver	—	destinatario *m*	destinatario *m*
destinataire[2] (F)	Adressat *m*	addressee	—	destinatario *m*	destinatario *m*
destinatario[1] (Es)	Empfänger *m*	receiver	destinataire *m*	destinatario *m*	—
destinatario[2] (Es)	Adressat *m*	addressee	destinataire *m*	destinatario *m*	—
destinatario[1] (I)	Adressat *m*	addressee	destinataire *m*	—	destinatario *m*
destinatario[2] (I)	Empfänger *m*	receiver	destinataire *m*	—	destinatario *m*
desventaja (Es)	Nachteil *m*	disadvantage	désavantage *m*	svantaggio *m*	—
desviación standard (Es)	Standard-abweichung *f*	standard deviation	déviation standard *f*	scarto tipo *m*	—
détaillant (F)	Einzelhandels-kaufmann *m*	retail merchant	—	commerciante al dettaglio *m*	comerciante particular *m*
details of order (E)	Bestelldaten *pl*	—	références de commande *f pl*	dati delle ordinazioni *m pl*	datos de pedido *m pl*
deterioración (Es)	Beschädigung *f*	damage	endommagement *m*	danno *m*	—
détermination des cours (F)	Kursfestsetzung *f*	fixing of prices	—	fissazione dei corsi *f*	fijación de los cambios *f*
détermination du coût marginal (F)	Grenzkosten-rechnung *f*	marginal costing	—	conto dei costi limite *m*	cálculo de los costes marginales *m*
determinazione dell'ubicazione (I)	Standort-entscheidung *f*	location decision	décision de l'implantation *f*	—	decisión de ubicación *f*
déterminé par le facteur main-d'oeuvre (F)	arbeitsintensiv	labour-intensive	—	ad alta incidenza di lavoro	con gran intensidad de mano de obra
déterminé par le facteur salaire (F)	lohnintensiv	wage-intensive	—	ad alta incidenza salariale	con gran intensidad de costos salariales
détournement[1] (F)	Veruntreuung *f*	misappropriation	—	abuso di fiducia *m*	malversación *f*
détournement[2] (F)	Unterschlagung *f*	embezzlement	—	appropriazione indebita *f*	defraudación *f*
detracción privada (Es)	Privatentnahmen *pl*	personal withdrawals	prélèvement personnel *m*	prelevamento a titolo personale *m*	—
detrazione[1] (I)	Abschlag *m*	reduction	déduction *f*	—	descuento *m*
detrazione[2] (I)	Abzug *m*	deduction/discount	diminution *f*/ escompte *m*	—	deducción *f*/ descuento *m*
detrazione di sconto (I)	Skontoabzug *m*	discount deduction	déduction de l'escompte *f*	—	deducción del descuento *f*
detrazione porto (I)	Portoabzug *m*	postage deduction	déduction de port *f*	—	deducción de porte *f*
détritus spéciaux (F)	Sondermüll *m*	special refuse	—	rifiuti speciali *m pl*	basura especial *f*
dettagliante (I)	Einzelhändler *m*	retailer	commerçant détaillant *m*	—	minorista *m*
dettato (I)	Diktat *n*	dictation	dictée *f*	—	dictado *m*
dette (F)	Schuld *f*	debt	—	debito *m*	deuda *f*
dette foncière (F)	Grundschuld *f*	mortgage	—	debito fondiario *m*	hipoteca *f*
dettes (F)	Schulden *pl*	debts	—	debiti *m pl*	deudas *f pl*
dettes actives (F)	Außenstände *pl*	outstanding debts	—	crediti *m pl*	cobros pendientes *m pl*
dettes à l'étranger (F)	Auslandsschulden *pl*	foreign debts	—	debiti con l'estero *m pl*	deudas exteriores *f pl*
deuda (Es)	Schuld *f*	debt	dette *f*	debito *m*	—
deuda neta (Es)	Nettoverschuldung *f*	net indebtedness	endettement net *m*	indebitamento netto *m*	—
deudas (Es)	Schulden *pl*	debts	dettes *f pl*	debiti *m pl*	—

	D	E	F	I	Es
deudas exteriores (Es)	Auslandsschulden *pl*	foreign debts	dettes à l'étranger *f pl*	debiti con l'estero *m pl*	—
deudor[1] (Es)	Debitor *m*	debtors	débiteur *m*	debitore *m*	—
deudor[2] (Es)	Schuldner *m*	debtor	débiteur *m*	debitore *m*	—
deudor común (Es)	Gemeinschuldner *m*	adjudicated bankrupt	failli *m*	debitore fallito *m*	—
Deutsche Industrie-Norm (D)	—	German Industrial Standards	norme industrielle allemande *f*	norma tedesca di normalizzazione *f*	norma industrial alemana *f*
dévalorisation (F)	Wertverfall *m*	loss of value	—	deprezzamento *m*	depreciación *f*
devaluación (Es)	Abwertung *f*	devaluation	dévaluation *f*	svalutazione *f*	—
devaluation (E)	Abwertung *f*	—	dévaluation *f*	svalutazione *f*	devaluación *f*
dévaluation (F)	Abwertung *f*	devaluation	—	svalutazione *f*	devaluación *f*
development (E)	Entwicklung *f*	—	développement *m*	sviluppo *m*	desarrollo *m*
development aid (E)	Entwicklungshilfe *f*	—	aide au développement *f*	aiuto ai paesi in via di sviluppo *m*	ayuda al desarrollo *f*
development costs (E)	Entwicklungs-kosten *pl*	—	coûts de développement *m pl*	costi di sviluppo *m pl*	gastos de desarrollo *m pl*
development phase (E)	Aufbauphase *f*	—	phase d'organisation *f*	fase di costruzione *f*	fase de desarrollo *f*
développement (F)	Entwicklung *f*	development	—	sviluppo *m*	desarrollo *m*
deviación de dimensión (Es)	Größenabweichung *f*	deviation from size	déviation de dimension *f*	differenza di dimensione *f*	—
deviation (E)	Abweichung *f*	—	divergence *f*	deviazione *f*	diferencia *f*
déviation de dimension (F)	Größenabweichung *f*	deviation from size	—	differenza di dimensione *f*	deviación de dimensión *f*
deviation from quality (E)	Qualitäts-abweichung *f*	—	écart qualitatif *m*	differenza di qualità *f*	diferencia de calidad *f*
deviation from size (E)	Größenabweichung *f*	—	déviation de dimension *f*	differenza di dimensione *f*	deviación de dimensión *f*
déviation standard (F)	Standard-abweichung *f*	standard deviation	—	scarto tipo *m*	desviación standard *f*
deviazione (I)	Abweichung *f*	deviation	divergence *f*	—	diferencia *f*
devis (F)	Voranschlag *m*	estimate	—	preventivo *m*	presupuesto *m*
Devisen (D)	—	foreign exchange	devises *f pl*	divise *f pl*	divisas *f pl*
Devisenabfluß (D)	—	foreign exchange outflow	sortie de devises *f*	deflusso di divise *m*	drenaje de divisas *m*
Devisenarbitrage (D)	—	exchange arbitrage	arbitrage sur les devises *m*	arbitraggio valutario *m*	arbitraje de divisas *m*
Devisenausgleichs-abkommen (D)	—	foreign exchange offset agreement	accord de compen-sation de devises *m*	accordo di clearing valutario *m*	acuerdo de compen-sación de divisas *m*
Devisen-bewirtschaftung (D)	—	foreign exchange control	contrôle des devises *m*	controllo valutario *m*	control de divisas *m*
Devisenbilanz (D)	—	foreign exchange balance	compte de devises *m*	bilancia delle divise *f*	balanza de divisas *f*
Devisenbörse (D)	—	foreign exchange market	bourse de devises *f*	borsa valutaria *f*	bolsa de divisas *f*
Devisen-genehmigung (D)	—	foreign exchange authorization	autorisation de change *f*	autorizzazione valutaria *f*	certificado de divisas *m*
Devisenhandel (D)	—	foreign exchange dealings	marché des changes *m*	commercio delle divise *m*	operaciones de divisas *f pl*
Deviseninländer (D)	—	resident	résident *m*	persona residente *f*	residente *m*
Devisenkontrolle (D)	—	foreign exchange control	contrôle des changes *m*	controllo delle divise *m*	control de divisas *m*
Devisenkurs (D)	—	foreign exchange rate	taux de change *m*	cambio delle divise *m*	cambio *m*
Devisenmarkt (D)	—	foreign exchange market	marché des changes *m*	mercato valutario *m*	mercado de divisas *m*
Devisen-termingeschäft (D)	—	forward exchange dealings	opérations à terme sur les changes *f pl*	operazione valutaria a termine *f*	transacciones a tér-mino en divisas *f pl*
Devisenverkehr (D)	—	foreign exchange dealings	mouvement des devises *m*	commercio dei cambi *m*	tráfico de divisas *m*
devises (F)	Devisen *pl*	foreign exchange	—	divise *f pl*	divisas *f pl*
devis estimatif des frais (F)	Kostenvoranschlag *m*	estimate of cost	—	preventivo dei costi *m*	presupuesto de coste *m*
devolución (Es)	Rücksendung *f*	return	renvoi *m*	rispedizione *f*	—

	D	E	F	I	Es
Dezentralisierung (D)	—	decentralization	décentralisation *f*	decentralizzazione *f*	descentralización *f*
(día de) Año Nuevo (Es)	Neujahr *n*	New Year	Nouvel An *m*	Capodanno *m*	—
día de pago (Es)	Zahltag *m*	payday	jour de paye *m*	giorno di paga *m*	—
día de vencimiento (Es)	Verfalltag *m*	day of expiry	jour de l'échéance *m*	giorno di scadenza *m*	—
día laboral (Es)	Arbeitstag *m*	working day	jour de travail *m*	giorno lavorativo *m*	—
diagram (E)	Diagramm *n*	—	diagramme *m*	diagramma *m*	diagrama *m*
diagrama (Es)	Diagramm *n*	diagram	diagramme *m*	diagramma *m*	—
Diagramm (D)	—	diagram	diagramme *m*	diagramma *m*	diagrama *m*
diagramma[1] (I)	Diagramm *n*	diagram	diagramme *m*	—	diagrama *m*
diagramma[2] (I)	Schaubild *n*	graph	graphique *m*	—	cuadro *m*
diagramma flusso dati (I)	Datenflußplan *m*	data flow chart	organigramme de flux des données *m*	—	organigrama de flujo de datos *m*
diagramme (F)	Diagramm *n*	diagram	—	diagramma *m*	diagrama *m*
Diaprojektor (D)	—	slide projector	projecteur pour diapositives *m*	proiettore per diapositive *m*	projector de diapositivas *m*
diario (Es)	täglich	daily	quotidien	giornaliero	—
di buona fede (I)	gutgläubig	bona fide	de bonne foi	—	de buena fe
dichiarare (I)	deklarieren	declare	déclarer	—	declarar
dichiarazione dei redditi (I)	Steuererklärung *f*	tax return	déclaration d'impôts *f*	—	declaración a efectos fiscales *f*
dichiarazione del reddito (I)	Einkommens-erklärung *f*	income declaration	déclaration du revenu *f*	—	declaración de la renta *f*
dichiarazione di volontà (I)	Willenserklärung *f*	declaration of intent	déclaration de volonté *f*	—	declaración de la voluntad *f*
dichiarazione doganale[1] (I)	Zollerklärung *f*	customs declaration	déclaration en douane *f*	—	declaración arancelaria *f*
dichiarazione doganale[2] (I)	Zollanmeldung *f*	customs declaration	déclaration en douane *f*	—	declaración arancelaria *f*
dichiarazione doganale[3] (I)	Einfuhrerklärung *f*	import declaration	déclaration d'entrée *f*	—	declaración de importación *f*
dichiarazione giurata (I)	beeidigte Erklärung *f*	sworn statement	déclaration sous serment *f*	—	declaración jurada *f*
dichiarazione sostitutiva del giuramento (I)	eidesstattliche Erklärung *f*	declaration in lieu of an oath	déclaration formelle sans prestation de serment *f*	—	declaración bajo juramento *f*
dictado (Es)	Diktat *n*	dictation	dictée *f*	dettato *m*	—
dictamen (Es)	Stellungnahme *f*	comment	prise de position *f*	presa di posizione *f*	—
dictamen pericial (Es)	Expertise *f*	expert opinion	expertise *f*	perizia *f*	—
dictaphone (E)	Diktiergerät *n*	—	appareil à dicter *m*	dittafono *m*	máquina de dictar *f*
dictation (E)	Diktat *n*	—	dictée *f*	dettato *m*	dictado *m*
dictée (F)	Diktat *n*	dictation	—	dettato *m*	dictado *m*
di diritto pubblico (I)	öffentlich-rechtlich	under public law	de droit public	—	de derecho público
Diebstahl (D)	—	theft	vol *m*	furto *m*	robo *m*
Diebstahl-versicherung (D)	—	theft insurance	assurance contre le vol *f*	assicurazione contro il furto *f*	seguro contra el robo *m*
Dienst (D)	—	service	service *m*	servizio *m*	servicio *m*
Dienstgeheimnis (D)	—	official secret	secret de service *m*	segreto d'ufficio *m*	secreto profesional *m*
Dienstleistung (D)	—	service	prestation de service *f*	servizio *m*	prestación de servicio *m*
Dienstwagen (D)	—	official car	voiture de service *f*	vettura di servizio *f*	coche de servicio *m*
diferencia (Es)	Abweichung *f*	deviation	divergence *f*	deviazione *f*	—
diferenciación de los precios (Es)	Preisdifferenzierung *f*	price differentiation	différenciation de prix *f*	differenziazione dei prezzi *f*	—
diferencia de calidad (Es)	Qualitäts abweichung *f*	deviation from quality	écart qualitatif *m*	differenza di qualità *f*	—
diferencia de precios (Es)	Preisunterschied *m*	price difference	écart de prix *m*	differenza dei prezzi *f*	—
diferencia entre los tipos de interés (Es)	Zinsgefälle *n*	margin between interest rates	disparité des niveaux d'intérêts *f*	differenza dei tassi d'interesse *f*	—

	D	E	F	I	Es
diferencial entre precios y salarios (Es)	Lohnlag *m*	wage lag	décalage entre les prix et les salaires *m*	lag salariale *m*	—
difesa dei corsi (I)	Kursstützung *f*	price support	soutiens des cours *m*	—	sostén de las cotizaciones *m*
difettoso (I)	fehlerhaft	defective	défectueux	—	defectuoso
différenciation de prix (F)	Preisdifferenzierung *f*	price differentiation	—	differenziazione dei prezzi *f*	diferenciación de los precios *f*
differenza dei prezzi (I)	Preisunterschied *m*	price difference	écart de prix *m*	—	diferencia de precios *f*
differenza dei tassi d'interesse (I)	Zinsgefälle *n*	margin between interest rates	disparité des niveaux d'intérêts *f*	—	diferencia entre los tipos de interés *f*
differenza di dimensione (I)	Größenabweichung *f*	deviation from size	déviation de dimension *f*	—	deviación de dimensión *f*
differenza di qualità (I)	Qualitäts-abweichung *f*	deviation from quality	écart qualitatif *m*	—	diferencia de calidad *f*
differenziato (I)	gestaffelt	graduated	progressif	—	escalonado
differenziazione dei prezzi (I)	Preisdifferenzierung *f*	price differentiation	différenciation de prix *f*	—	diferenciación de los precios *f*
difficoltà di pagamento (I)	Zahlungs-schwierigkeit *f*	financial difficulties	difficultés financières *f pl*	—	dificultades de pago *f pl*
dificultades de pago (Es)	Zahlungs-schwierigkeit *f*	financial difficulties	difficultés financières *f pl*	difficoltà di pagamento *f*	—
difficultés financières (F)	Zahlungs-schwierigkeit *f*	financial difficulties	—	difficoltà di pagamento *f*	dificultades de pago *f pl*
Diktat (D)	—	dictation	dictée *f*	dettato *m*	dictado *m*
Diktatzeichen (D)	—	reference	références *f pl*	sigla *f*	referencias *f pl*
Diktiergerät (D)	—	dictaphone	appareil à dicter *m*	dittafono *m*	máquina de dictar *f*
dilatory (E)	säumig	—	retardataire	moroso	moroso
dilazione (I)	Stundung *f*	respite	prorogation *f*	—	moratoria *f*
dilazione del pagamento (I)	Zahlungsaufschub *m*	extension of time for payment	sursis de payement *m*	—	pago aplazado *m*
dilazione delle spese (I)	Ausgaben-verzögerung *f*	expenditure delay	dépenses retardées *f pl*	—	aplazamiento de gastos *m*
dimensión de la empresa (Es)	Unternehmens-größe *f*	size of the company	dimension de l'entreprise *f*	dimensione dell'impresa *f*	—
dimension de l'entreprise[1] (F)	Unternehmens-größe *f*	size of the company	—	dimensione dell'impresa *f*	dimensión de la empresa *f*
dimension de l'entreprise[2] (F)	Betriebsgröße *f*	size of the company	—	dimensione dell'azienda *f*	tamaño de la explotación *m*
dimensione dell'azienda (I)	Betriebsgröße *f*	size of the company	dimension de l'entreprise *f*	—	tamaño de la explotación *m*
dimensione dell'impresa (I)	Unternehmens-größe *f*	size of the company	dimension de l'entreprise *f*	—	dimensión de la empresa *f*
diminution[1] (F)	Minderung *f*	reduction	—	riduzione *f*	reducción *f*
diminution[2] (F)	Abzug *m*	deduction/discount	—	detrazione *f*/sconto *m*	deducción *f*/ descuento *m*
diminution de la valeur (F)	Wertminderung *f*	decrease in value	—	riduzione di valore *f*	depreciación *f*
diminution des coûts (F)	Kostensenkung *f*	cost reduction	—	ribasso dei costi *m*	reducción de coste *f*
diminution des dépenses (F)	Ausgabensenkung *f*	drop in expenditure	—	riduzione delle spese *f*	reducción de gastos *f*
diminution du capital (F)	Kapitalherabsetzung *f*	reduction of capital	—	riduzione del capitale *f*	reducción de capital *f*
diminution du taux de l'intérêt (F)	Zinssenkung *f*	reduction of interest	—	riduzione degli interessi *f*	reducción del tipo de interés *f*
diminuzione dei costi (I)	Kostenminimierung *f*	minimization of costs	minimalisation des coûts *f*	—	minimación de gastos *f*
dimisión (Es)	Rücktritt *m*	resignation	démission *f*	dimissioni *f pl*	—
dimissioni (I)	Rücktritt *m*	resignation	démission *f*	—	dimisión *f*
dinero (Es)	Geld *n*	money	argent *m*	denaro *m*	—
dinero bancario (Es)	Buchgeld *n*	money in account	monnaie de crédit *f*	moneta bancaria *f*	—
dinero barato (Es)	billiges Geld *n*	easy money	argent à bon marché *m*	crediti agevolati *m pl*	—

	D	E	F	I	Es
dinero de día a día (Es)	Tagesgeld *n*	day-to-day money	argent au jour le jour *m*	prestito giornaliero *m*	—
dinero efectivo (Es)	Bargeld *n*	cash	argent comptant *m*	denaro contante *m*	—
dinero metálico (Es)	Hartgeld *n*	specie	pièce de monnaie *f*	moneta metallica *f*	—
dinero tomado a préstamo (Es)	Geldaufnahme *f*	raising of money	emprunt *m*	accensione di un mutuo *f*	—
dingliche Sicherung (D)	—	real security	sécurité réelle *f*	garanzia reale *f*	garantía real *f*
dingliches Recht (D)	—	real right	droit réel *m*	diritto reale *m*	derecho real *m*
dipendente (I)	Untergebener *m*	subordinate	subalterne *m*	—	subordinado *m*
Diplom (D)	—	diploma	diplôme *m*	diploma *m*	diploma *m*
diploma (E)	Diplom *n*	—	diplôme *m*	diploma *m*	diploma *m*
diploma (Es)	Diplom *n*	diploma	diplôme *m*	diploma *m*	—
diploma (I)	Diplom *n*	diploma	diplôme *m*	—	diploma *m*
diplôme (F)	Diplom *n*	diploma	—	diploma *m*	diploma *m*
di prima categoria (I)	erstklassig	first class	de première qualité	—	de primera calidad
dirección[1] (Es)	Anschrift *f*	address	adresse *f*	indirizzo *m*	—
dirección[2] (Es)	Geschäftsleitung *f*	management	direction commerciale *f*	direzione *f*	—
dirección[3] (Es)	Adresse *f*	address	adresse *f*	indirizzo *m*	—
dirección[4] (Es)	Leitung *f*	management	direction *f*	direzione *f*	—
dirección de inversiones (Es)	Investitionslenkung *f*	investment control	politique d'investissement *f*	politica d'investimento *f*	—
dirección de la empresa[1] (Es)	Firmenanschrift *f*	company address	adresse de la maison *f*	indirizzo della ditta *m*	—
dirección de la empresa[2] (Es)	Unternehmens-leitung *f*	executive management	direction de l'entreprise *f*	direzione dell'impresa *f*	—
dirección de personal (Es)	Personalführung *f*	personnel management	direction du personnel *f*	gestione del personale *f*	—
direct cost (E)	direkte Kosten *pl*	—	coûts directs *m pl*	costi diretti *m pl*	coste directo *m*
direct selling (E)	Direktverkauf *m*	—	vente directe *f*	vendita diretta *f*	venta directa *f*
direct taxes (E)	direkte Steuern *pl*	—	impôts directs *m pl*	imposte dirette *f pl*	impuestos directos *m pl*
directeur (F)	Direktor *m*	director	—	direttore *m*	director *m*
directeur artistique (F)	Art-director *m*	art director	—	art director *m*	director artístico *m*
directeur d'agence (F)	Filialleiter *m*	branch manager	—	direttore della filiale *m*	jefe de sucursal *m*
directeur général (F)	Generaldirektor *m*	director managing	—	direttore generale *m*	director general *m*
direct insurer (E)	Erstversicherer *m*	—	assureur direct *m*	assicuratore diretto *m*	primer asegurador *m*
direct investments (E)	Direktinvestitionen *pl*	—	investissements directs *m pl*	investimenti diretti *m pl*	inversiones directas *f pl*
direction[1] (F)	Führung *f*	management	—	gestione *f*	gestión *f*
direction[2] (F)	Direktion *f*	board of directors	—	direzione *f*	junta directiva *f*
direction[3] (F)	Leitung *f*	management	—	direzione *f*	dirección *f*
direction commerciale (F)	Geschäftsleitung *f*	management	—	direzione *f*	dirección *f*
direction de l'entreprise (F)	Unternehmens-leitung *f*	executive management	—	direzione dell'impresa *f*	dirección de la empresa *f*
direction du personnel (F)	Personalführung *f*	personnel management	—	gestione del personale *f*	dirección de personal *f*
Direct-Marketing (D)	—	direct marketing	stratégie des ventes directes *f*	marketing in prima persona *m*	comercialización directa *f*
direct marketing (E)	Direct-Marketing *n*	—	stratégie des ventes directes *f*	marketing in prima persona *m*	comercialización directa *f*
direct means of advertising (E)	Direktwerbemittel *n*	—	moyens publicitaires directs *m pl*	mezzo pubblicitario diretto *m*	medios publicitarios directos *m pl*
director (E)	Direktor *m*	—	directeur *m*	direttore *m*	director *m*
director (Es)	Direktor *m*	director	directeur *m*	direttore *m*	—
director artístico (Es)	Art-director *m*	art director	directeur artistique *m*	art director *m*	—
direct ordering (E)	Direktbestellung *f*	—	commande directe *f*	ordinazione diretta *f*	pedido directo *m*
director general (E)	Generaldirektor *m*	—	directeur général *m*	direttore generale *m*	director general *m*

	D	E	F	I	Es
director general (Es)	Generaldirektor *m*	director general	directeur général *m*	direttore generale *m*	—
Direktbestellung (D)	—	direct ordering	commande directe *f*	ordinazione diretta *f*	pedido directo *m*
direkte Kosten (D)	—	direct cost	coûts directs *m pl*	costi diretti *m pl*	coste directo *m*
direkte Steuern (D)	—	direct taxes	impôts directs *m pl*	imposte dirette *f pl*	impuestos directos *m pl*
Direktinvestitionen (D)	—	direct investments	investissements directs *m pl*	investimenti diretti *m pl*	inversiones directas *f pl*
Direktion (D)	—	board of directors	direction *f*	direzione *f*	junta directiva *f*
Direktor (D)	—	director	directeur *m*	direttore *m*	director *m*
Direktverkauf (D)	—	direct selling	vente directe *f*	vendita diretta *f*	venta directa *f*
Direktwerbemittel (D)	—	direct means of advertising	moyens publicitaires directs *m pl*	mezzo pubblicitario diretto *m*	medios publicitarios directos *m pl*
direttore (I)	Direktor *m*	director	directeur *m*	—	director *m*
direttore della filiale (I)	Filialleiter *m*	branch manager	directeur d'agence *m*	—	jefe de sucursal *m*
direttore di vendita regionale (I)	Gebietsverkaufs-leiter *m*	area sales manager	chef de vente régionale *m*	—	jefe de venta regional *m*
direttore generale (I)	Generaldirektor *m*	director managing	directeur général *m*	—	director general *m*
direzione[1] (I)	Leitung *f*	management	direction *f*	—	dirección *f*
direzione[2] (I)	Geschäftsleitung *f*	management	direction commerciale *f*	—	dirección *f*
direzione[3] (I)	Direktion *f*	board of directors	direction *f*	—	junta directiva *f*
direzione dell'impresa (I)	Unternehmens-leitung *f*	executive management	direction de l'entreprise *f*	—	dirección de la empresa *f*
dirigente (I)	Führungsperson *f*	executive	cadre *m*	—	ejecutivo *m*
dirigir (Es)	adressieren	address	adresser	indirizzare	—
dirigisme (F)	Dirigismus *m*	controlled economy	—	dirigismo *m*	dirigismo *m*
dirigismo (Es)	Dirigismus *m*	controlled economy	dirigisme *m*	dirigismo *m*	—
dirigismo (I)	Dirigismus *m*	controlled economy	dirigisme *m*	—	dirigismo *m*
Dirigismus (D)	—	controlled economy	dirigisme *m*	dirigismo *m*	dirigismo *m*
diritti al risarcimento danni (I)	Schadenersatz-ansprüche *m pl*	claim for damages	droit à l'indemnité *m*	—	derecho a indemniza-ción por daños y perjuicios *m*
diritti di conto (I)	Kontogebühren *pl*	bank charges	frais de tenue de compte *m pl*	—	gastos de administración de una cuenta *m pl*
diritti di porto (I)	Hafengebühren *pl*	harbour dues	droits de ports *m pl*	—	derechos portuarios *m pl*
diritti di prelievo (I)	Ziehungsrechte *pl*	drawing rights	droits de tirage *m pl*	—	derechos de giro *m pl*
diritti di sovranità nazionale (I)	nationale Souveräni-tätsrechte *pl*	national sovereignty rights	droits de souveraine-té nationale *m pl*	—	derechos de sobe-ranía nacional *m pl*
diritti di transito (I)	Transitzoll *m*	transit duty	droit de transit *m*	—	derecho de tránsito *m*
diritti doganali (I)	Zollgebühren *pl*	customs duties	droit de douane *m*	—	derechos arancelarios *m pl*
diritti speciali di prelievo (I)	Sonderziehungs-rechte *pl*	special drawing rights	droits de tirage spécial *m pl*	—	derechos de giro especial *m pl*
diritto (I)	Recht *n*	law	droit *m*	—	derecho *m*
diritto alla fornitura supplementare (I)	Nachlieferungs-anspruch *m*	claim to subsequent delivery	droit à livraison complémentaire *m*	—	derecho de suminis-tro adicional *m*
diritto alla restituzione (I)	Rückgaberecht *n*	right of redemption	droit à restitution *m*	—	derecho de devolución *m*
diritto al voto (I)	Stimmrecht *n*	right to vote	droit de vote *m*	—	derecho a voto *m*
diritto azionario (I)	Aktienrecht *n*	company law	loi sur les sociétés anonymes *f pl*	—	derecho de socieda-des anónimas *m*
diritto d'asta (I)	Auktionsgebühr *f*	auction fees	droits de vente aux enchères *m pl*	—	gastos de subasta *m pl*
diritto d'autore (I)	Urheberrecht *n*	copyright	droit d'auteur *m*	—	derecho del autor *m*
diritto della concorrenza (I)	Wettbewerbsrecht *n*	law on competition	législation en matière de concurrence commerciale *m*	—	derecho de la competencia *m*
diritto della pesca (I)	Fischereirecht *n*	fishing rights	droit de pêche *m*	—	derecho pesquero *m*
diritto delle minoranze (I)	Minoritätsrecht *n*	minority right	droit de minorité *m*	—	derecho minoritario *m*

	D	E	F	I	Es
diritto di firma (I)	Zeichnungs-berechtigung *f*	authority to sign	autorisation de signer *f*	—	facultad de firma *f*
diritto di lavoro (I)	Arbeitsrecht *n*	labour law	législation industrielle *f*	—	derecho laboral *m*
diritto di pegno (I)	Pfandrecht *n*	piedge	droit de gage *m*	—	derecho de garantía real *m*
diritto di prelazione (I)	Vorkaufsrecht *n*	preemption right	droit de préemption *m*	—	derecho de preferencia *m*
diritto di rappresentanza esclusiva (I)	Alleinvertretungs-recht *n*	sole and exclusive agency right	droit exclusif de représentation *m*	—	derecho de representación exclusiva *m*
diritto di revoca (I)	Widerrufsrecht *n*	right of revocation	droit de révocation *m*	—	derecho de revocación *m*
diritto di servizio (I)	Bedienungsgeld *n*	tip	pourboire *m*	—	propina *f*
diritto di sovranità (I)	Hoheitsrecht *n*	sovereign right	droit de souveraineté *m*	—	soberanía *f*
diritto economico (I)	Wirtschaftsrecht *n*	economic law	législation économique *f*	—	derecho económico *m*
diritto reale (I)	dingliches Recht *n*	real right	droit réel *m*	—	derecho real *m*
disability for work (E)	Erwerbsunfähigkeit *f*	—	incapacité d'exercer toute activité professionnelle *f*	inabilità al lavoro *f*	incapacidad profesional *f*
disadvantage (E)	Nachteil *m*	—	désavantage *m*	svantaggio *m*	desventaja *f*
disaggio (I)	Disagio *n*	disagio	disagio *m*	—	disagio *m*
Disagio (D)	—	disagio	disagio *m*	disaggio *m*	disagio *m*
disagio (E)	Disagio *n*	—	disagio *m*	disaggio *m*	disagio *m*
disagio (Es)	Disagio *n*	disagio	disagio *m*	disaggio *m*	—
disagio (F)	Disagio *n*	disagio	—	disaggio *m*	disagio *m*
disavanzo della bilancia dei pagamenti (I)	Zahlungsbilanz-defizit *n*	deficit in the balance of payments	balance des payements déficitaire *f*	—	déficit en la balanza de pagos *m*
discharge (E)	Entlastung *f*	—	décharge *f*	sgravio *m*	desgravamen *m*
discharging expenses[1] (E)	Löschgebühren *pl*	—	droit de déchargement *m*	spese di scarico *f pl*	gastos de descarga *m pl*
discharging expenses[2] (E)	Entladungskosten *pl*	—	coûts de déchargement *m pl*	spese di scaricamento *f pl*	gastos de descargo *m pl*
dischetto (I)	Diskette *f*	disk	disquette *f*	—	diskette *f*
disclosure (E)	Offenlegung *f*	—	révélation des derniers bilans du postulant d'un prêt *f*	pubblicità del bilancio *f*	publicidad para fines de inspección *f*
discount[1] (E)	Skonto *n*	—	escompte *m*	sconto *m*	descuento *m*
discount[2] (E)	Diskont *m*	—	escompte *m*	sconto *m*	descuento *m*
discount[3] (E)	Rabatt *m*	—	remise *f*	ribasso *m*	rebaja *f*
discount deduction (E)	Skontoabzug *m*	—	déduction de l'escompte *f*	detrazione di sconto *f*	deducción del descuento *f*
discount for cash payment (E)	Barzahlungs-nachlaß *m*	—	remise pour payement au comptant *f*	sconto per pagamento in contanti *m*	descuento por pago al contado *m*
discounting (E)	Abzinsung *f*	—	déduction des intérêts non courus *f*	deduzione di interessi *f*	deducción de intereses no acumulados *f*
discount on advance orders (E)	Vorbestellrabatt *m*	—	escompte de suscription *m*	ribasso per ordinazioni anticipate *m*	descuento de suscripción *m*
discount policy (E)	Diskontpolitik *f*	—	politique d'escompte *f*	politica di sconto *f*	política de descuento *f*
discount rate (E)	Diskontsatz *m*	—	taux d'escompte *m*	saggio di sconto *m*	tasa de descuento *f*
discreción (Es)	Diskretion *f*	confidentiality	discrétion *f*	discrezione *f*	—
discrétion (F)	Diskretion *f*	confidentiality	—	discrezione *f*	discreción *f*
discrétion professionnelle (F)	Schweigepflicht *f*	professional discretion	—	obbligo del segreto professionale *m*	secreto profesional *m*
discrezione (I)	Diskretion *f*	confidentiality	discrétion *f*	—	discreción *f*
discriminación (Es)	Diskriminierung *f*	discrimination	discrimination *f*	discriminazione *f*	—
discrimination (E)	Diskriminierung *f*	—	discrimination *f*	discriminazione *f*	discriminación *f*
discrimination (F)	Diskriminierung *f*	discrimination	—	discriminazione *f*	discriminación *f*
discriminazione (I)	Diskriminierung *f*	discrimination	discrimination *f*	—	discriminación *f*
discussion[1] (E)	Besprechung *f*	—	conférence *f*	colloquio *m*	conferencia *f*

	D	E	F	I	Es
discussion[2] (E)	Unterredung *f*	—	entretien *m*	colloquio *m*	conversación *f*
disdetta (I)	Kündigung *f*	notice of termination	résiliation *f*	—	rescisión *f*
disdire (I)	kündigen	terminate/give notice	dénoncer/résilier	—	denunciar/dar aviso de despido
diseño (Es)	Design *n*	design	design *m*	design *m*	—
diseño del producto (Es)	Produktgestaltung *f*	product design	présentation d'un produit *f*	creazione del prodotto *f*	—
disk (E)	Diskette *f*	—	disquette *f*	dischetto *m*	diskette *f*
Diskette (D)	—	disk	disquette *f*	dischetto *m*	diskette *f*
diskette (Es)	Diskette *f*	disk	disquette *f*	dischetto *m*	—
Diskont (D)	—	discount	escompte *m*	sconto *m*	descuento *m*
Diskontpolitik (D)	—	discount policy	politique d'escompte *f*	politica di sconto *f*	política de descuento *f*
Diskontsatz (D)	—	discount rate	taux d'escompte *m*	saggio di sconto *m*	tasa de descuento *f*
Diskretion (D)	—	confidentiality	discrétion *f*	discrezione *f*	discreción *f*
Diskriminierung (D)	—	discrimination	discrimination *f*	discriminazione *f*	discriminación *f*
disminución de costes (Es)	Kostendämpfung *f*	combatting rising costs	réduction des coûts *f*	contenimento dei costi *m*	—
disminución de la cifra de facturación (Es)	Umsatzrückgang *m*	decrease of turnover	recul du chiffre d'affaires *m*	calo del fatturato *m*	—
disminución en la demanda (Es)	Nachfrage-rückgang *m*	decrease in demand	recul de la demande *m*	flessione della domanda *f*	—
dismissal (E)	Entlassung *f*	—	licenciement *m*	licenziamento *m*	despido *m*
disoccupazione (I)	Arbeitslosigkeit *f*	unemployment	chômage *m*	—	desempleo *m*
disoccupazione stagionale (I)	saisonale Arbeitslosigkeit *f*	seasonal unemployment	chômage saisonnier *m*	—	paro estacional *m*
disoccupazione strutturale (I)	strukturelle Arbeitslosigkeit *f*	structural unemployment	chômage structurel *m*	—	paro estructural *m*
disolución (Es)	Auflösung *f*	dissolution	liquidation *f*	scioglimento *m*	—
disparité des niveaux d'intérêts (F)	Zinsgefälle *n*	margin between interest rates	—	differenza dei tassi d'interesse *f*	diferencia entre los tipos de interés *f*
dispatch[1] (E)	Abfertigung *f*	—	expédition *f*	spedizione *f*	despacho *m*
dispatch[2] (E)	Absendung *f*	—	expédition *f*	spedizione *f*	expedición *f*
dispatch[3] (E)	Versand *m*	—	expédition *f*	spedizione *f*	envío *m*
dispatch department (E)	Versandabteilung *f*	—	service des expéditions *m*	reparto spedizioni *m*	departamento de expedición *m*
dispensé de l'impôt (F)	steuerfrei	tax-free	—	esente da imposte	libre de impuesto
display (E)	Auslage *f*	—	étalage *f*	vetrina *f*	vitrina *f*
disponibile (I)	lieferbar	deliverable	livrable	—	suministrable
disponible (F)	abholbereit	ready for collection	—	pronto per il ritiro	listo para la recogida
disposable income (E)	verfügbares Einkommen *n*	—	revenu disponible *m*	introito disponibile *m*	ingresos disponibles *m pl*
disposal[1] (E)	Disposition *f*	—	disposition *f*	disposizione *f*	disposición *f*
disposal[2] (E)	Verfügung *f*	—	disposition *f*/acte de disposition *m*	disposizione *f*/ ordinanza *f*	disposición *f*/ decreto *m*
disposal of waste oil (E)	Altölbeseitigung *f*	—	élimination d'huile usée *f*	smaltimento dell'olio usato *m*	eliminación de petróleo usado *f*
disposición[1] (Es)	Verfügung *f*	disposal/order	disposition *f*/acte de disposition *m*	disposizione *f*/ ordinanza *f*	—
disposición[2] (Es)	Disposition *f*	disposal	disposition *f*	disposizione *f*	—
disposición a comprar (Es)	Kaufbereitschaft *f*	buying intention	propension à l'achat *f*	propensione all'acquisto *f*	—
Disposition (D)	—	disposal	disposition *f*	disposizione *f*	disposición *f*
disposition[1] (F)	Verfügung *f*	disposal/order	—	disposizione *f*/ ordinanza *f*	disposición *f*/ decreto *m*
disposition[2] (F)	Disposition *f*	disposal	—	disposizione *f*	disposición *f*
disposition de l'annonce (F)	Anzeigenplazierung *f*	placing of an advertisement	—	collocamento dell'inserzione *m*	colocación del anuncio *f*
dispositions d'exportation (F)	Ausfuhr-bestimmungen *pl*	export regulations	—	disposizioni per le esportazioni *f pl*	reglamiento de exportación *m*
disposizione[1] (I)	Disposition *f*	disposal	disposition *f*	—	disposición *f*

	D	E	F	I	Es
disposizione² (I)	Verfügung *f*	disposal/order	disposition *f*/acte de disposition *m*	—	disposición *f*/ decreto *m*
disposizioni per le esportazioni (I)	Ausfuhr-bestimmungen *pl*	export regulations	dispositions d'exportation *f pl*	—	reglamiento de exportación *m*
dispute concerning an inheritance (E)	Erbstreit *m*	—	action successorale *f*	causa ereditaria *f*	litigio hereditario *m*
disquette (F)	Diskette *f*	disk	—	dischetto *m*	diskette *f*
dissesto finanziario (I)	Finanzdebakel *n*	financial debacle	débâcle fiancière *f*	—	descalabro financiero *m*
dissimulation en matière fiscale (F)	Steuerhinterziehung *f*	tax evasion	—	evasione fiscale *f*	defraudación fiscal *f*
dissolution (E)	Auflösung *f*	—	liquidation *f*	scioglimento *m*	disolución *f*
distance (E)	Abstand *m*	—	distance *f*	distanza *f*	distancia *f*
distance (F)	Abstand *m*	distance	—	distanza *f*	distancia *f*
distancia (Es)	Abstand *m*	distance	distance *f*	distanza *f*	—
distanza (I)	Abstand *m*	distance	distance *f*	—	distancia *f*
distribución¹ (Es)	Vertrieb *m*	distribution	distribution *f*	distribuzione *f*	—
distribución² (Es)	Verteilung *f*	distribution	distribution *f*	distribuzione *f*	—
distribución de beneficios (Es)	Gewinn-ausschüttung *f*	distribution of profits	distribution de bénéfices *f*	ripartizione dell'utile *f*	—
distribución de la renta¹ (Es)	Einkommens-verteilung *f*	distribution of income	distribution du revenu *f*	distribuzione dei redditi *f*	—
distribución de la renta² (Es)	Einkommens-verwendung *f*	appropriation of income	utilisation du revenu *f*	impiego dei redditi *m*	—
distribución exclusiva (Es)	Alleinvertrieb *m*	exclusive distribution	vente exclusive *f*	vendita esclusiva *f*	—
distribuidor automático¹ (Es)	Automat *m*	vending machine	appareil automatique *m*	distributore automatico *m*	—
distribuidor automático² (Es)	Verkaufsautomat *m*	vending machine	distributeur automatique *m*	distributore automatico *m*	—
distributeur (F)	Vertriebsfirma *f*	distributor	—	ditta di distribuzione *f*	compañía distribuidora *f*
distributeur automatique (F)	Verkaufsautomat *m*	vending machine	—	distributore automatico *m*	distribuidor automático *m*
Distribution (D)	—	distribution	distribution *f*	distribuzione *f*	distribución *f*
distribution¹ (E)	Vertrieb *m*	—	distribution *f*	distribuzione *f*	distribución *f*
distribution² (E)	Verteilung *f*	—	distribution *f*	distribuzione *f*	distribución *f*
distribution³ (E)	Distribution *f*	—	distribution *f*	distribuzione *f*	distribución *f*
distribution¹ (F)	Vertrieb *m*	distribution	—	distribuzione *f*	distribución *f*
distribution² (F)	Distribution *f*	distribution	—	distribuzione *f*	distribución *f*
distribution³ (F)	Verteilung *f*	distribution	—	distribuzione *f*	distribución *f*
distribution centre (E)	Auslieferungslager *n*	—	entrepôt de distribution *m*	deposito di consegna *m*	almacén de entregas *m*
distribution channel (E)	Vertriebsweg *m*	—	canal de distribution *m*	rete di distribuzione *f*	circuito de distribución *f*
distribution de bénéfices (F)	Gewinn-ausschüttung *f*	distribution of profits	—	ripartizione dell'utile *f*	distribución de beneficios *f*
distribution du revenu (F)	Einkommens-verteilung *f*	distribution of income	—	distribuzione dei redditi *f*	distribución de la renta *f*
distribution of income (E)	Einkommens-verteilung *f*	—	distribution du revenu *f*	distribuzione dei redditi *f*	distribución de la renta *f*
distribution of profits¹ (E)	Gewinnverteilung *f*	—	répartition des bénéfices *f*	ripartizione dell'utile *f*	reparto de beneficios *m*
distribution of profits² (E)	Gewinn-ausschüttung *f*	—	distribution de bénéfices *f*	ripartizione dell'utile *f*	distribución de beneficios *f*
distribution of wealth (E)	Vermögens-verteilung *f*	—	repartition du patrimoine *f*	ripartizione del patrimonio *f*	reparto de la riqueza *m*
distribution policy (E)	Verteilungspolitik *f*	—	politique de répartition *f*	politica della distribuzione *f*	política de distribución *f*
distributor (E)	Vertriebsfirma *f*	—	distributeur *m*	ditta di distribuzione *f*	compañía distribuidora *f*
distributore automatico¹ (I)	Automat *m*	vending machine	appareil automatique *m*	—	distribuidor automático *m*

	D	E	F	I	Es
distributore automatico[2] (I)	Verkaufsautomat *m*	vending machine	distributeur automatique *m*	—	distribuidor automático *m*
distribuzione[1] (I)	Verteilung *f*	distribution	distribution *f*	—	distribución *f*
distribuzione[2] (I)	Vertrieb *m*	distribution	distribution *f*	—	distribución *f*
distribuzione dei redditi (I)	Einkommens-verteilung *f*	distribution of income	distribution du revenu *f*	—	distribución de la renta *f*
distrito aduanero (Es)	Zollgebiet *n*	customs territory	territoire douanier *m*	territorio doganale *m*	—
ditta concorrente (I)	Konkurrenzfirma *f*	competing firm	maison concurrente *f*	—	empresa competidora *f*
ditta di distribuzione (I)	Vertriebsfirma *f*	distributor	distributeur *m*	—	compañía distribuidora *f*
dittafono (I)	Diktiergerät *n*	dictaphone	appareil à dicter *m*	—	máquina de dictar *f*
divergence (F)	Abweichung *f*	deviation	—	deviazione *f*	diferencia *f*
diversificación (Es)	Diversifikation *f*	diversification	diversification *f*	diversificazione *f*	—
diversification (E)	Diversifikation *f*	—	diversification *f*	diversificazione *f*	diversificación *f*
diversification (F)	Diversifikation *f*	diversification	—	diversificazione *f*	diversificación *f*
diversificazione (I)	Diversifikation *f*	diversification	diversification *f*	—	diversificación *f*
Diversifikation (D)	—	diversification	diversification *f*	diversificazione *f*	diversificación *f*
dividend (E)	Dividende *f*	—	dividende *m*	dividendo *m*	dividendo *m*
dividend-bearing shares (E)	Dividendenpapiere *pl*	—	titre donnant droit à des dividendes *m*	titoli a reddito variabile *m pl*	títulos de renta variable *m pl*
Dividende (D)	—	dividend	dividende *m*	dividendo *m*	dividendo *m*
dividende (F)	Dividende *f*	dividend	—	dividendo *m*	dividendo *m*
Dividendenpapiere (D)	—	dividend-bearing shares	titre donnant droit à des dividendes *m*	titoli a reddito variabile *m pl*	títulos de renta variable *m pl*
dividendo (Es)	Dividende *f*	dividend	dividende *m*	dividendo *m*	—
dividendo (I)	Dividende *f*	dividend	dividende *m*	—	dividendo *m*
divieto di concorrenza (I)	Wettbewerbsverbot *n*	prohibition of competition	interdiction en matière de concurrence *f*	—	prohibición de competencia *f*
divieto di pubblicità (I)	Werbeverbot *n*	ban on advertising	défense de publicité *f*	—	prohibición de publicidad *f*
divisas (Es)	Devisen *pl*	foreign exchange	devises *f pl*	divise *f pl*	—
divise (I)	Devisen *pl*	foreign exchange	devises *f pl*	—	divisas *f pl*
division (E)	Abteilung *f*	—	service *m*	reparto *m*	sección *f*
división del trabajo (Es)	Arbeitsteilung *f*	division of labour	division du travail *f*	divisione del lavoro *f*	—
division du travail (F)	Arbeitsteilung *f*	division of labour	—	divisione del lavoro *f*	división del trabajo *f*
divisione del lavoro (I)	Arbeitsteilung *f*	division of labour	division du travail *f*	—	división del trabajo *f*
division of labour (E)	Arbeitsteilung *f*	—	division du travail *f*	divisione del lavoro *f*	división del trabajo *f*
document[1] (E)	Urkunde *f*	—	document *m*	documento *m*	documento *m*
document[2] (E)	Dokument *n*	—	document *m*	documento *m*	documento *m*
document[1] (F)	Dokument *n*	document	—	documento *m*	documento *m*
document[2] (F)	Urkunde *f*	document	—	documento *m*	documento *m*
documentary acceptance credit (E)	Rembourskredit *m*	—	crédit documentaire confirmé *m*	credito di rimborso *m*	crédito de reembolso *m*
documentary letter of credit (E)	Dokumenten-akkreditiv *n*	—	crédit documentaire *m*	apertura di credito documentario *f*	crédito documentario *m*
documenti commerciali (I)	Geschäftspapiere *pl*	business papers	papiers d'affaires *m pl*	—	documentos comerciales *m pl*
documenti della domanda d'impiego (I)	Bewerbungs-unterlagen *pl*	application documents	dossier de candidature *m*	—	documentos de solicitud *m pl*
documenti d'esportazione (I)	Ausfuhrpapiere *pl*	export documents	documents d'exportation *m pl*	—	documentos de exportación *m pl*
documenti di trasporto (I)	Transportpapiere *pl*	documents covering transportation	documents de transport *m pl*	—	documentos de transporte *m pl*
documenti doganali (I)	Zollpapiere *pl*	customs documents	documents douaniers *m pl*	—	documentos aduaneros *m pl*
documento[1] (Es)	Urkunde *f*	document	document *m*	documento *m*	—
documento[2] (Es)	Dokument *n*	document	document *m*	documento *m*	—
documento[3] (Es)	Akte *f*	file	dossier *m*	pratica *f*	—
documento[1] (I)	Urkunde *f*	document	document *m*	—	documento *m*

	D	E	F	I	Es
documento[2] (I)	Dokument *n*	document	document *m*	—	documento *m*
documento di spedizione (I)	Versanddokument *n*	shipping document	documents d'expédition *m pl*	—	documentos de expedición *m pl*
documentos adjuntos (Es)	Begleitpapiere *pl*	accompanying documents	pièces accompagnant l'envoi *f pl*	bolle di accompagnamento *f pl*	—
documentos aduaneros (Es)	Zollpapiere *pl*	customs documents	documents douaniers *m pl*	documenti doganali *m pl*	—
documentos comerciales (Es)	Geschäftspapiere *pl*	business papers	papiers d'affaires *m pl*	documenti commerciali *m pl*	—
documentos de expedición (Es)	Versanddokument *n*	shipping document	documents d'expédition *m pl*	documento di spedizione *m*	—
documentos de exportación (Es)	Ausfuhrpapiere *pl*	export documents	documents d'exportation *m pl*	documenti d'esportazione *m pl*	—
documentos de importación (Es)	Einfuhrpapiere *pl*	import documents	documents d'importation *m pl*	bollette doganali *f pl*	—
documentos de solicitud (Es)	Bewerbungsunterlagen *pl*	application documents	dossier de candidature *m*	documenti della domanda d'impiego *m pl*	—
documentos de transporte (Es)	Transportpapiere *pl*	documents covering transportation	documents de transport *m pl*	documenti di trasporto *m pl*	—
documents against payments (E)	Dokumente gegen Zahlung *pl*	—	documents contre payement *m pl*	pagamento contro documenti *m*	al contado contra documentos
documents contre payement (F)	Dokumente gegen Zahlung *pl*	documents against payments	—	pagamento contro documenti *m*	al contado contra documentos
documents covering transportation (E)	Transportpapiere *pl*	—	documents de transport *m pl*	documenti di trasporto *m pl*	documentos de transporte *m pl*
documents de transport (F)	Transportpapiere *pl*	documents covering transportation	—	documenti di trasporto *m pl*	documentos de transporte *m pl*
documents d'expédition (F)	Versanddokument *n*	shipping document	—	documento di spedizione *m*	documentos de expedición *m pl*
documents d'exportation (F)	Ausfuhrpapiere *pl*	export documents	—	documenti d'esportazione *m pl*	documentos de exportación *m pl*
documents d'importation (F)	Einfuhrpapiere *pl*	import documents	—	bollette doganali *f pl*	documentos de importación *m pl*
documents douaniers (F)	Zollpapiere *pl*	customs documents	—	documenti doganali *m pl*	documentos aduaneros *m pl*
dogana (I)	Zoll *m*	customs/ customs duty	douane *f*/ droit de douane *m*	—	aduana *f*/ arancel *m*
doit (F)	Soll *m*	debit/target/quota	—	passivo *m*	debe *m*
Dokument (D)	—	document	document *m*	documento *m*	documento *m*
Dokumente gegen Zahlung (D)	—	documents against payments	documents contre payement *m pl*	pagamento contro documenti *m*	al contado contra documentos
Dokumentenakkreditiv (D)	—	documentary letter of credit	crédit documentaire *m*	apertura di credito documentario *f*	crédito documentario *m*
dollar clause (E)	Dollarklausel *f*	—	clause dollar *f*	clausola dollaro *f*	cláusula dólar *f*
Dollarklausel (D)	—	dollar clause	clause dollar *f*	clausola dollaro *f*	cláusula dólar *f*
Dolmetscher (D)	—	interpreter	interprète *m*	interprete *m*	intérprete *m*
domanda[1] (I)	Antrag *m*	application	demande *f*	—	solicitud *f*
domanda[2] (I)	Nachfrage *f*	demand	demande *f*	—	demanda *f*
domanda di capitale (I)	Kapitalbedarf *m*	capital requirements	besoin en capital *m*	—	necesidad de capital *f*
domanda di denaro (I)	Geldnachfrage *f*	demand for money	demande sur le marché monétaire *f*	—	demanda monetaria *f*
domanda di dichiarazione del fallimento (I)	Konkursantrag *m*	bankruptcy petition	demande en déclaration de faillite *f*	—	petición de quiebra *f*
domanda di lavoro (I)	Arbeitsnachfrage *f*	job demand	demande d'emploi *f*	—	demanda de trabajo *f*
domanda d'impiego[1] (I)	Bewerbungsschreiben *n*	letter of application	lettre de demande d'emploi *f*	—	carta de solicitud *f*
domanda d'impiego[2] (I)	Bewerbung *f*	application	candidature *f*	—	candidatura *f*
domanda d'impiego[3] (I)	Stellengesuch *n*	situation wanted/ application for a job	demande d'emploi *f*	—	solicitud de colocación *f*
domanda di sdoganamento (I)	Zollantrag *m*	customs application	demande de dédouanement *f*	—	solicitud de aduana *f*
domanda estera (I)	Auslandsnachfrage *f*	foreign demand	demande en provenance de l'étranger *f*	—	demanda exterior *m*
domanda interna (I)	Inlandsnachfrage *f*	home demand	demande intérieure *f*	—	demanda interior *f*

	D	E	F	I	Es
domestic customs territory (E)	Zollinland *n*	—	territoire douanier national *m*	territorio doganale nazionale *m*	territorio aduanero interior *m*
domestic economy (E)	Binnenwirtschaft *f*	—	économie nationale *f*	economia nazionale *f*	economía interior *f*
domestic establishment (E)	Inlands-niederlassung *f*	—	succursale à l'intérieur *f*	succursale nazionale *f*	sucursal en el interior *f*
domestic trade (E)	Binnenhandel *m*	—	commerce intérieur *m*	commercio nazionale *m*	comercio interior *m*
domicile of the company (E)	Firmensitz *m*	—	siège social *m*	sede *f*	sede social *f*
domiciliary bill (E)	Domizilwechsel *m*	—	effet domicilier *m*	cambiale domiciliata *f*	letra domiciliada *f*
Domizilwechsel (D)	—	domiciliary bill	effet domicilier *m*	cambiale domiciliata *f*	letra domiciliada *f*
dommage (F)	Schaden *m*	damage	—	danno *m*	daño *m*
dommage au cours d'un transport (F)	Transportschaden *m*	damage in transit	—	danno di trasporto *m*	daño de transporte *m*
dommage causé par l'eau (F)	Wasserschaden *m*	damage caused by water	—	danno dovuto all'acqua *m*	daño causado por el agua *m*
dommage consécutif (F)	Folgeschäden *pl*	consequential damages	—	danni indiretti *m pl*	daño consecuencial *m*
dommage immatériel (F)	immaterieller Schaden *m*	non-material damage	—	danno immateriale *m*	daño inmaterial *m*
dommage mineur (F)	Bagatellschaden *m*	minimal damage	—	danno piccolo *m*	siniestro leve *m*
dommages-intérêts (F)	Schadensersatz *m*	compensation for loss suffered	—	risarcimento danni *m*	indemnización *f*
dommage total (F)	Totalschaden *m*	total loss	—	danno totale *m*	daño total *m*
donación (Es)	Schenkung *f*	donation	donation *f*	donazione *f*	—
donation (E)	Schenkung *f*	—	donation *f*	donazione *f*	donación *f*
donation (F)	Schenkung *f*	donation	—	donazione *f*	donación *f*
donazione (I)	Schenkung *f*	donation	donation *f*	—	donación *f*
données (F)	Daten *f*	data	—	dati *m pl*	datos *m pl*
données sur le marché (F)	Marktdaten *pl*	market details	—	dati di mercato *m pl*	datos del mercado *m pl*
donneur de leasing (F)	Leasing-Geber *m*	lessor	—	concedente del leasing *m*	arrendatario financiero *m*
doppelte Buchführung (D)	—	double entry bookkeeping	comptabilité en partie double *f*	contabilità a partita doppia *f*	contabilidad por doble partida *f*
dormant partnership (E)	stille Gesellschaft *f*	—	association commerciale en participation *f*	associazione in partecipazione *f*	sociedad en participación *f*
dossier (F)	Akte *f*	file	—	pratica *f*	documento *m*
dossier à échantillons (F)	Mustermappe *f*	sample bag	—	cartella campioni *f*	muestrario *m*
dossier de candidature (F)	Bewerbungs-unterlagen *pl*	application documents	—	documenti della domanda d'impiego *m pl*	documentos de solicitud *m pl*
dotación (Es)	Dotierung *f*	endowment	dotation *f*	dotazione *f*	—
dotación en capital (F)	Kapitalausstattung *f*	capital resources	—	dotazione di capitale *f*	dotación de capital *f*
dotation (F)	Dotierung *f*	endowment	—	dotazione *f*	dotación *f*
dotation de capital (Es)	Kapitalausstattung *f*	capital resources	dotation en capital *f*	dotazione di capitale *f*	—
dotazione (I)	Dotierung *f*	endowment	dotation *f*	—	dotación *f*
dotazione di capitale (I)	Kapitalausstattung *f*	capital resources	dotation en capital *f*	—	dotación de capital *f*
Dotierung (D)	—	endowment	dotation *f*	dotazione *f*	dotación *f*
douane (F)	Zoll *m*	customs/ customs duty	—	dogana *f*/dazio *m*	aduana *f*/arancel *m*
double entry bookkeeping (E)	doppelte Buchführung *f*	—	comptabilité en partie double *f*	contabilità a partita doppia *f*	contabilidad por doble partida *f*
doubtful account (E)	zweifelhafte Forderung *f*	—	créance douteuse *f*	credito dubbio *m*	créditos dudosos *m pl*
Dow-Jones-Index (D)	—	Dow-Jones Industrial Average	indice Dow-Jones *m*	indice Dow-Jones *m*	Indice Dow Jones *m*
Dow-Jones Industrial Average (E)	Dow-Jones-Index *m*	—	indice Dow-Jones *m*	indice Dow-Jones *m*	Indice Dow Jones *m*
down-swing (E)	Abschwung *m*	—	dépression *f*	regresso *m*	baja *f*
downward trend (E)	Abwärtstrend *m*	—	baisse *f*	tendenza al ribasso *f*	tendencia bajista *f*

	D	E	F	I	Es
draft (E)	Entwurf *m*	—	projet *m*	progetto *m*	proyecto *m*
drawback (Es)	Rückzoll *m*	customs drawback	ristourne des droits de douane *f*	restituzione di dazi *f*	—
drawee (E)	Bezogener *m*	—	tiré *m*	trattario *m*	librado *m*
drawing rights (E)	Ziehungsrechte *pl*	—	droits de tirage *m pl*	diritti di prelievo *m pl*	derechos de giro *m pl*
Dreiecksgeschäft (D)	—	triangular transaction	opération commerciale triangulaire *f*	operazione triangolare *f*	operación triangular *f*
Dreimonatspapier (D)	—	three months papers	titre à trois mois *m*	titolo trimestrale *m*	títulos a tres meses *m*
drenaje de divisas (Es)	Devisenabfluß *m*	foreign exchange outflow	sortie de devises *f*	deflusso di divise *m*	—
Drittländer (D)	—	third countries	pays tiers *m pl*	paesi terzi *m pl*	terceros países *m pl*
droit (F)	Recht *n*	law	—	diritto *m*	derecho *m*
droit à l'indemnité (F)	Schadenersatzansprüche *pl*	claim for damages	—	diritti al risarcimento danni *m pl*	derecho a indemnización por daños y perjuicios *m*
droit à livraison complémentaire (F)	Nachlieferungsanspruch *m*	claim to subsequent delivery	—	diritto alla fornitura supplementare *m*	derecho de suministro adicional *m*
droit à restitution (F)	Rückgaberecht *n*	right of redemption	—	diritto alla restituzione *m*	derecho de devolución *m*
droit d'auteur (F)	Urheberrecht *n*	copyright	—	diritto d'autore *m*	derecho del autor *m*
droit de déchargement (F)	Löschgebühren *pl*	discharging expenses	—	spese di scarico *f pl*	gastos de descarga *m pl*
droit de douane (F)	Zollgebühren *pl*	customs duties	—	diritti doganali *m pl*	derechos arancelarios *m pl*
droit de douane par quantité (F)	Mengenzoll *m*	specific duty	—	dazio di quantità *m*	arancel aduanero cuantitativo *m*
droit de gage (F)	Pfandrecht *n*	pledge	—	diritto di pegno *m*	derecho de garantía real *m*
droit de minorité (F)	Minoritätsrecht *n*	minority right	—	diritto delle minoranze *m*	derecho minoritario *m*
droit d'entrée (F)	Einfuhrzoll *m*	import duty	—	dazio d'importazione *m*	arancel de importación *m*
droit de pêche (F)	Fischereirecht *n*	fishing rights	—	diritto della pesca *m*	derecho pesquero *m*
droit de préemption (F)	Vorkaufsrecht *n*	preemption right	—	diritto di prelazione *m*	derecho de preferencia *m*
droit de protection (F)	Schutzzoll *m*	protective duty	—	dazio protettivo *m*	aduana proteccionista *f*
droit de révocation (F)	Widerrufsrecht *n*	right of revocation	—	diritto di revoca *m*	derecho de revocación *m*
droit de souveraineté (F)	Hoheitsrecht *n*	sovereign right	—	diritto di sovranità *m*	soberanía *f*
droit de timbre (F)	Stempelgebühr *f*	stamp duty	—	tassa di bollo *f*	derechos de timbre *m pl*
droit de transaction sur les opérations boursières (F)	Börsenumsatzsteuer *f*	stock exchange turnover tax	—	imposta sulle operazioni di borsa *f*	impuesto de negociación bursátil *m*
droit de transit (F)	Transitzoll *m*	transit duty	—	diritti di transito *m pl*	derecho de tránsito *m*
droit de vote (F)	Stimmrecht *n*	right to vote	—	diritto al voto *m*	derecho a voto *m*
droit exclusif de représentation (F)	Alleinvertretungsrecht *n*	sole and exclusive agency right	—	diritto di rappresentanza esclusiva *m*	derecho de representación exclusiva *m*
droit d'exploitation (F)	Betriebserlaubnis *f*	operating permit	—	autorizzazione per l'esercizio *f*	autorización de funcionamiento *f*
droit prohibitif (F)	Prohibitivzoll *m*	prohibitive duty	—	dazio proibitivo *m*	derechos prohibitivos *m pl*
droit réel (F)	dingliches Recht *n*	real right	—	diritto reale *m*	derecho real *m*
droits de ports (F)	Hafengebühren *pl*	harbour dues	—	diritti di porto *m pl*	derechos portuarios *m pl*
droits de souveraineté nationale (F)	nationale Souveränitätsrechte *pl*	national sovereignty rights	—	diritti di sovranità nazionale *m pl*	derechos de soberanía nacional *m pl*
droits de tirage (F)	Ziehungsrechte *pl*	drawing rights	—	diritti di prelievo *m pl*	derechos de giro *m pl*
droits de tirage spécial (F)	Sonderziehungsrechte *pl*	special drawing rights	—	diritti speciali di prelievo *m pl*	derechos de giro especial *m pl*
droits de vente aux enchères (F)	Auktionsgebühr *f*	auction fees	—	diritto d'asta *m*	gastos de subasta *m pl*

	D	E	F	I	Es
droit unique (F)	Einheitszoll *m*	uniform duty	—	dazio unitario *m*	aduanas uniformes *f pl*
drop in employment (E)	Beschäftigungs-rückgang *m*	—	baisse de l'offre d'emploi *f*	calo dell'occupazione *m*	descenso del empleo *m*
drop in expenditure (E)	Ausgabensenkung *f*	—	diminution des dépenses *f*	riduzione delle spese *f*	reducción de gastos *f*
Drucker (D)	—	printer	imprimante *f*	stampante *f*	impresora *f*
Drucksache (D)	—	printed matter	imprimé *m*	stampa *f*	impreso *m*
dualism (E)	Dualismus *m*	—	dualisme *m*	dualismo *m*	dualismo *m*
dualisme (F)	Dualismus *m*	dualism	—	dualismo *m*	dualismo *m*
dualismo (Es)	Dualismus *m*	dualism	dualisme *m*	dualismo *m*	—
dualismo (I)	Dualismus *m*	dualism	dualisme *m*	—	dualismo *m*
Dualismus (D)	—	dualism	dualisme *m*	dualismo *m*	dualismo *m*
ducroire (F)	Delkredere *n*	del credere	—	star del credere *m*	delcrédere *m*
due payment reserved (E)	Eingang vorbehalten	—	sauf bonne fin	salvo buon fine	salvo buen cobro *m*
duplicado de la carta de porte (Es)	Frachtbriefdoppel *n*	duplicate consignment note	duplicata de la lettre de voiture *m*	duplicato della lettera di vettura *m*	—
duplicata de la lettre de voiture (F)	Frachtbriefdoppel *n*	duplicate consignment note	—	duplicato della lettera di vettura *m*	duplicado de la carta de porte *m*
duplicate consignment note (E)	Frachtbriefdoppel *n*	—	duplicata de la lettre de voiture *m*	duplicato della lettera di vettura *m*	duplicado de la carta de porte *m*
duplicato della lettera di vettura (I)	Frachtbriefdoppel *n*	duplicate consignment note	duplicata de la lettre de voiture *m*	—	duplicado de la carta de porte *m*
durable consumer goods (E)	Gebrauchsgüter *pl*	—	biens d'utilisation courante *m pl*	beni di consumo durevoli *m pl*	bienes de consumo duradero *m pl*
duración del contrato (Es)	Vertragsdauer *f*	contract period	durée du contrat *f*	durata del contratto *f*	—
duración mínima (Es)	Mindestdauer *f*	minimum length/ minimum duration	durée minimum *f*	durata minima *f*	—
durata del contratto (I)	Vertragsdauer *f*	contract period	durée du contrat *f*	—	duración del contrato *f*
durata del finanziamento (I)	Finanzierungsdauer *f*	period of financing	durée du financement *f*	—	período de financiación *m*
durata della protezione (I)	Schutzfrist *f*	term of protection	délai de protection *m*	—	plazo de protección *m*
durata minima (I)	Mindestdauer *f*	minimum length/ minimum duration	durée minimum *f*	—	duración mínima *m*/ plazo mínimo *m*
durata probabile della vita (I)	Lebenserwartung *f*	expectation of life	espérance de vie *f*	—	expectativa de vida *f*
duration of credit (E)	Kreditlaufzeit *f*	—	durée de l'allocation de crédit *f*	scadenza del credito *f*	período concesional de un crédito *m*
Durchführung (D)	—	realization	réalisation *f*	esecuzione *f*	ejecución *m*
Durchgangsschein (D)	—	transit certificate	acquit de transit *m*	bolletta di transito *f*	pasavante *m*
Durchschnitt (D)	—	average	moyenne *f*	media *f*	promedio *m*
Durchschnitts-kosten (D)	—	average costs	coût moyen *m*	costi medi *m pl*	gastos medios *m pl*
Durchsetzungs-vermögen (D)	—	capability of asserting one's right	capacité de se faire valoir *f*	capacità di imposizione *f*	capacidad de imponerse *f*
durée (F)	Laufzeit *f*	term	—	scadenza *f*/durata *f*	plazo de vencimiento *m*
durée de l'allocation de crédit (F)	Kreditlaufzeit *f*	duration of credit	—	scadenza del credito *f*	período concesional de un crédito *m*
durée du contrat (F)	Vertragsdauer *f*	contract period	—	durata del contratto *f*	duración del contrato *f*
durée du financement (F)	Finanzierungsdauer *f*	period of financing	—	durata del finanziamento *f*	período de financiación *m*
durée minimum (F)	Mindestdauer *f*	minimum length/ minimum duration	—	durata minima *f*	duración mínima *f*/ plazo mínimo *m*
durée restante (F)	Restlaufzeit *f*	residual time to maturity	—	scadenza residua *f*	plazo de vencimiento restante *m*
duty in kind (E)	Naturalabgabe *f*	—	taxe acquittée en nature *f*	imposta in natura *f*	impuesto en especie *m*
duty of supervision (E)	Aufsichtspflicht *f*	—	obligation de surveillance *f*	obbligo di sorveglianza *m*	obligación de vigilancia *f*

	D	E	F	I	Es
duty paid (E)	verzollt	—	dédouané	sdoganato	pagado
duty to supply (E)	Belieferungspflicht *f*	—	obligation de livraison *f*	obbligo di fornitura *m*	obligación de suministro *f*
duty unpaid (E)	unverzollt	—	non dédouané	non sdoganato	aduana aparte
earning capacity (E)	Ertragskraft *f*	—	force productive *f*	redditività *f*	rentabilidad *f*
earnings (E)	Bezüge *pl*	—	émoluments *m pl*	entrate *f pl*	retribuciones *f pl*
earning situation (E)	Ertragslage *f*	—	niveau du rendement *m*	situazione economica *f*	situación del beneficio *f*
East-West trade (E)	Ost-West-Handel *m*	—	commerce Est-Ouest *m*	scambio est-ovest *m*	comercio este-oeste *m*
easy money (E)	billiges Geld *n*	—	argent bon marché *m*	crediti agevolati *m pl*	dinero barato *m*
eaux côtières (F)	Küstengewässer *n*	coastal waters	—	acque territoriali *f pl*	zona costera *f*
eaux résiduelles (F)	Abwasser *n*	waste water	—	acque di scarico *f pl*	aguas residuales *f pl*
écart de prix (F)	Preisunterschied *m*	price difference	—	differenza dei prezzi *f*	diferencia de precios *f*
écart qualitatif (F)	Qualitäts-abweichung *f*	deviation from quality	—	differenza di qualità *f*	diferencia de calidad *f*
eccedenza (I)	Überschuß *m*	excess	excédent *m*	—	excedente *m*
eccedenza commerciale (I)	Handelsüberschuß *m*	trade surplus	excédent commercial *m*	—	excedente comercial *m*
eccedenza della bilancia dei pagamenti (I)	Zahlungsbilanz-überschuß *m*	surplus in the balance of payments	balance des payements excédentaire *f*	—	superávit en la balanza de pagos *m*
eccedenza delle esportazioni (I)	Exportüberschuß *m*	export surplus	excédent d'exportation *m*	—	excedente de exportación *m*
eccedenza di liquidità (I)	Liquiditäts-überschuß *m*	excess liquidity	excédent de liquidité *m*	—	exceso de liquidez *m*
eccedenza d'offerta (I)	Angebotsüberhang *m*	excess of supply over demand	excès de l'offre *m*	—	exceso de oferta *m*
eccedenze agricole (I)	Agrarüberschüsse *pl*	agricultural surpluses	excédents agricoles *m pl*	—	excedentes agrícolas *m pl*
eccessivo (I)	übermäßig	excessive	excessif	—	excesivo
échange[1] (F)	Umtausch *m*	exchange	—	cambio *m*	cambio *m*/ conversión *f*
échange[2] (F)	Tausch *m*	exchange/barter	—	scambio *m*/baratto *m*	cambio *m*/ trueque *m*
échanges commerciaux[1] (F)	Handelsverkehr *m*	commercial intercourse	—	circolazione delle merci *f*	comercio *m*
échanges commerciaux[2] (F)	Warenaustausch *m*	exchange of goods	—	scambio merci *m*	intercambio de mercancías *m*
échantillon[1] (F)	Probepackung *f*	trial package	—	confezione campione *f*	muestra *f*
échantillon[2] (F)	Muster *n*	sample/pattern	—	campione *m*/ disegno *m*	muestra *f*/dibujo *m*
échantillon[3] (F)	Warenprobe *f*	sample	—	campione di merce *m*	muestra de mercancía *f*
échantillon sans valeur (F)	Muster ohne Wert *n*	sample, no commercial value	—	campione senza valore *m*	muestra sin valor *f*
école (F)	Schule *f*	school	—	scuola *f*	escuela *f*
ecología (Es)	Ökologie *f*	ecology	écologie *f*	ecologia *f*	—
ecologia (I)	Ökologie *f*	ecology	écologie *f*	—	ecología *f*
ecologico (I)	umweltfreundlich	beneficial to the environment	favorable à l'environnement	—	no contaminante
écologie (F)	Ökologie *f*	ecology	—	ecologia *f*	ecología *f*
ecology (E)	Ökologie *f*	—	écologie *f*	ecologia *f*	ecología *f*
economía[1] (Es)	Wirtschaft *f*	economy	économie *f*	economia *f*	—
economía[2] (Es)	Ökonomie *f*	economy	économie *f*	economia *f*	—
economia[1] (I)	Wirtschaft *f*	economy	économie *f*	—	economía *f*
economia[2] (I)	Ökonomie *f*	economy	économie *f*	—	economía *f*
economía agraria (Es)	Agrarwirtschaft *f*	farming	économie agricole *f*	economia agraria *f*	—
economia agraria (I)	Agrarwirtschaft *f*	farming	économie agricole *f*	—	economía agraria *f*
economia aziendale (I)	Betriebs-wirtschaftslehre *f*	business administration	(science de la) gestion industrielle et commerciale *f*	—	teoría de la empresa *f*

	D	E	F	I	Es
economía de distribución (Es)	Absatzwirtschaft *f*	marketing	commercialisation *f*	marketing *m*	—
economía de mercado (Es)	Marktwirtschaft *f*	market economy	économie de marché *f*	economia di mercato *f*	—
economía de mercado social (Es)	soziale Marktwirtschaft *f*	social market economy	économie sociale du marché *f*	economia sociale di mercato *f*	—
economia di mercato (I)	Marktwirtschaft *f*	market economy	économie de marché *f*	—	economía de mercado *f*
economía doméstica[1] (Es)	privater Haushalt *m*	private household	ménage privé *m*	famiglia *f*	—
economía doméstica[2] (Es)	Haushalt *m*	private household/ budget	ménage de particuliers *m*/budget *m*	economia domestica *f*/bilancio *m*	—
economia domestica (I)	Haushalt *m*	private household/ budget	ménage de particuliers *m*/budget *m*	—	economía doméstica *f*/presupuesto *m*
economia forestale (I)	Forstwirtschaft *f*	forestry	économie forestière *f*	—	silvicultura *f*
economía interior (Es)	Binnenwirtschaft *f*	domestic economy	économie nationale *f*	economia nazionale *f*	—
economía internacional (Es)	Weltwirtschaft *f*	world economy	économie mondiale *f*	economia mondiale *f*	—
economia mondiale (I)	Weltwirtschaft *f*	world economy	économie mondiale *f*	—	economía internacional *f*
economía nacional[1] (Es)	Nationalökonomie *f*	economics	économie nationale *f*	economia nazionale *f*	—
economía nacional[2] (Es)	Volkswirtschaft *f*	national economy	économie nationale *f*	economia politica *f*	—
economia nazionale[1] (I)	Nationalökonomie *f*	economics	économie nationale *f*	—	economía nacional *f*
economia nazionale[2] (I)	Binnenwirtschaft *f*	domestic economy	économie nationale *f*	—	economía interior *f*
economía planificada (Es)	Planwirtschaft *f*	planned economy	économie planifiée *f*	economia pianificata *f*	—
economía planificada central (Es)	zentrale Planwirtschaft *f*	centrally controlled economy	économie planifiée centrale *f*	economia pianificata *f*	—
economia pianificata[1] (I)	zentrale Planwirtschaft *f*	centrally controlled economy	économie planifiée centrale *f*	—	economía planificada central *f*
economia pianificata[2] (I)	Planwirtschaft *f*	planned economy	économie planifiée *f*	—	economía planificada *f*
economia politica[1] (I)	Volkswirtschaft *f*	national economy	économie nationale *f*	—	economía nacional *f*
economia politica[2] (I)	Volkswirtschaftslehre *f*	economics	économie politique *f*	—	ciencias económicas *f pl*
economía privada (Es)	Privatwirtschaft *f*	private sector of the economy	économie privée *f*	economia privata *f*	—
economia privata (I)	Privatwirtschaft *f*	private sector of the economy	économie privée *f*	—	economía privada *f*
economia pubblica (I)	öffentliche Wirtschaft *f*	public sector of the economy	économie publique *f*	—	economía pública *f*
economía pública (Es)	öffentliche Wirtschaft *f*	public sector of the economy	économie publique *f*	economia pubblica *f*	—
economia sociale di mercato (I)	soziale Marktwirtschaft *f*	social market economy	économie sociale de marché *f*	—	economía de mercado social *f*
economic account (E)	Wirtschaftsrechnung *f*	—	comptabilisation économique *f*	conto economico *m*	contabilización económica *f*
economic analysis[1] (E)	Konjunkturanalyse *f*	—	analyse de la conjoncture *f*	analisi congiunturale *f*	análisis de la situación económica *m*
economic analysis[2] (E)	Wirtschaftsanalyse *f*	—	analyse de l'économie *f*	analisi economica *f*	análisis económico *m*
economic boycott (E)	Wirtschaftsboykott *m*	—	boycottage économique *m*	boicottaggio economico *m*	boicot económico *m*
economic community (E)	Wirtschaftsgemeinschaft *f*	—	communauté économique *f*	comunità economica *f*	comunidad económica *f*
economic concentration (E)	Wirtschaftskonzentration *f*	—	concentration économique *f*	concentrazione economica *f*	concentración económica *f*
economic crisis (E)	Wirtschaftskrise *f*	—	crise économique *f*	crisi economica *f*	crisis económica *f*
economic cycle (E)	Wirtschaftskreislauf *m*	—	circuit économique *m*	circuito economico *m*	circuito económico *m*
economic efficiency (E)	Wirtschaftlichkeit *f*	—	rentabilité *f*	economicità *f*	rentabilidad *f*
economic expert (E)	Wirtschaftsexperte *m*	—	expert économique *m*	esperto in materia economica *m*	economista *m*

	D	E	F	I	Es
economic geography (E)	Wirtschafts-geographie *f*	—	géographie économique *f*	geografia economica *f*	geografía económica *f*
economic good (E)	Wirtschaftsgut *n*	—	bien économique *m*	bene economico *m*	bien económico *m*
economic growth (E)	Wirtschafts-wachstum *n*	—	croissance économique *f*	crescita economica *f*	crecimiento económico *m*
economic history (E)	Wirtschafts-geschichte *f*	—	histoire économique *f*	storia economica *f*	historia económica *f*
economic integration (E)	wirtschaftliche Integration *f*	—	intégration économique *f*	integrazione economica *f*	integración económica *f*
economicità (I)	Wirtschaftlichkeit *f*	economic efficiency	rentabilité *f*	—	rentabilidad *f*
economic law (E)	Wirtschaftsrecht *n*	—	législation économique *f*	diritto economico *m*	derecho económico *m*
economic order (E)	Wirtschaftsordnung *f*	—	ordre économique *m*	ordinamento economico *m*	orden económico *m*
economic plan (E)	Wirtschaftsplan *m*	—	plan économique *m*	piano economico *m*	plan económico *m*
economic policy[1] (E)	Konjunkturpolitik *f*	—	politique de conjoncture *f*	politica congiunturale *f*	política de coyuntura *f*
economic policy[2] (E)	Wirtschaftspolitik *f*	—	politique économique *f*	politica economica *f*	política económica *f*
economics[1] (E)	Wirtschaftswissen-schaften *pl*	—	sciences économiques *f pl*	scienze economiche *f pl*	ciencias económicas *f pl*
economics[2] (E)	Nationalökonomie *f*	—	économie nationale *f*	economia nazionale *f*	economía nacional *f*
economics[3] (E)	Volkswirtschafts-lehre *f*	—	économie politique *f*	economia politica *f*	ciencias económicas *f pl*
economic structure (E)	Wirtschaftsstruktur *f*	—	structure économique *f*	struttura economica *f*	estructura económica *f*
economic theory (E)	Wirtschaftstheorie *f*	—	théorie économique *f*	teoria dell'economia *f*	teoría económica *f*
economic trend (E)	Konjunktur-entwicklung *f*	—	évolution de la conjoncture *f*	sviluppo congiunturale *m*	evolución de la coyuntura *f*
economic union (E)	Wirtschaftsunion *f*	—	union économique *f*	unione economica *f*	unión económica *f*
economic upturn (E)	Konjunkturbelebung *f*	—	relance économique *f*	ripresa congiunturale *f*	recuperación coyuntural *f*
economic use (E)	wirtschaftliche Nutzung *m*	—	utilisation économique *f*	utilizzo economico *m*	utilización económica *f*
economic war (E)	Wirtschaftskrieg *m*	—	guerre économique *f*	guerra economica *f*	guerra económica *f*
économie[1] (F)	Wirtschaft *f*	economy	—	economia *f*	economía *f*
économie[2] (F)	Ökonomie *f*	economy	—	economia *f*	economía *f*
économie agricole (F)	Agrarwirtschaft *f*	farming	—	economia agraria *f*	economía agraria *f*
économie de marché (F)	Marktwirtschaft *f*	market economy	—	economia di mercato *f*	economía de mercado *f*
économie forestière (F)	Forstwirtschaft *f*	forestry	—	economia forestale *f*	silvicultura *f*
économie mondiale (F)	Weltwirtschaft *f*	world economy	—	economia mondiale *f*	economía internacional *f*
économie nationale[1] (F)	Binnenwirtschaft *f*	domestic economy	—	economia nazionale *f*	economía interior *f*
économie nationale[2] (F)	Volkswirtschaft *f*	national economy	—	economia politica *f*	economía nacional *f*
économie nationale[3] (F)	Nationalökonomie *f*	economics	—	economia nazionale *f*	economía nacional *f*
économie planifiée (F)	Planwirtschaft *f*	planned economy	—	economia pianificata *f*	economía planificada *f*
économie planifiée centrale (F)	zentrale Planwirtschaft *f*	centrally controlled economy	—	economia pianificata *f*	economía planificada central *f*
économie politique (F)	Volkswirtschafts-lehre *f*	economics	—	economia politica *f*	ciencias económicas *f pl*
économie privée (F)	Privatwirtschaft *f*	private sector of the economy	—	economia privata *f*	economía privada *f*
économie publique (F)	öffentliche Wirtschaft *f*	public sector of the economy	—	economia pubblica *f*	economía pública *f*
économie sociale du marché (F)	soziale Marktwirtschaft *f*	social market economy	—	economia sociale di mercato *f*	economía de mercado social *f*
economista (Es)	Wirtschaftsexperte *m*	economic expert	expert économique *m*	esperto in materia economica *m*	—
economy[1] (E)	Ökonomie *f*	—	économie *f*	economia *f*	economía *f*
economy[2] (E)	Wirtschaft *f*	—	économie *f*	economia *f*	economía *f*
écran (F)	Bildschirm *m*	screen	—	video *m*	pantalla *f*

	D	E	F	I	Es
écriture de contre-passation (F)	Storno *n*	counter entry	—	storno *m*	extorno *m*
edilizia (I)	Bauwirtschaft *f*	building and construction industry	(industrie du) bâtiment *f*	—	ramo de la construcción *m*
edilizia abitativa (I)	Wohnungsbau *m*	housing construction	construction de logements *f*	—	construcción de viviendas *f*
éditeur (F)	Verleger *m*	publisher	—	editore *m*	editor *m*
editor (Es)	Verleger *m*	publisher	éditeur *m*	editore *m*	—
editore (I)	Verleger *m*	publisher	éditeur *m*	—	editor *m*
editorial (Es)	Verlag *m*	publishing house	maison d'édition *f*	casa editrice *f*	—
educación (Es)	Bildung *f*	education	formation *f*	formazione *f*	—
education (E)	Bildung *f*	—	formation *f*	formazione *f*	educación *f*
efectividad del anuncio (Es)	Anzeigenwirkung *f*	effectiveness of an advertisement	effet de l'annonce *m*	effetto dell'inserzione *m*	—
efecto bumerán (Es)	Bumerang-Effekt *m*	boomerang effect	effet boomerang *m*	effetto bumerang *m*	—
efecto invernadero (Es)	Treibhauseffekt *m*	global warming	effet de serre *m*	effetto serra *m*	—
efectos (Es)	Effekten *f*	securities	valeurs mobilières *f pl*	titoli *m pl*	—
efecto snob (Es)	Snob-Effekt *m*	snob effect	effet snob *m*	effetto snob *m*	—
effectif (F)	Aktivbestand *m*	assets	—	effettivo *m*	activo disponible *m*
effectif du personnel (F)	Personalsituation *f*	personnel situation	—	situazione occupazionale *f*	situación de personal *f*
effective (E)	in Kraft	—	en vigueur	in vigore	en vigor
effective interest (E)	Effektivzins *m*	—	intérêt effectif *m*	tasso d'interesse effettivo *m*	intereses reales *m pl*
effective interest yield (E)	Effektivverzinsung *f*	—	taux effectif (de l'intérêt) *m*	interessi effettivi *m pl*	interés efectivo *m*
effectiveness of an advertisement (E)	Anzeigenwirkung *f*	—	effet de l'annonce *m*	effetto dell'inserzione *m*	efectividad del anuncio *f*
Effekten (D)	—	securities	valeurs mobilières *f pl*	titoli *m pl*	efectos *m pl*
Effektenbörse (D)	—	stock exchange	bourse des titres et valeurs mobilières *f*	borsa valori *f*	Bolsa de valores *f*
Effektengeschäft (D)	—	securities business	commerce des valeurs mobilières *m*	operazione su titoli *f*	operación de valores *f*
effektive Verschuldung (D)	—	real indebtedness	endettement effectif *m*	indebitamento effettivo *m*	endeudamiento efectivo *m*
Effektivlohn (D)	—	actual wage	salaire effectif *m*	salario effettivo *m*	salario efectivo *m*
Effektivverzinsung (D)	—	effective interest yield	taux effectif (de l'intérêt) *m*	interessi effettivi *m pl*	interés efectivo *m*
Effektivzins (D)	—	effective interest	intérêt effectif *m*	tasso d'interesse effettivo *m*	intereses reales *m pl*
effet boomerang (F)	Bumerang-Effekt *m*	boomerang effect	—	effetto bumerang *m*	efecto bumerán *m*
effet de l'annonce (F)	Anzeigenwirkung *f*	effectiveness of an advertisement	—	effetto dell'inserzione *m*	efectividad del anuncio *f*
effet de serre (F)	Treibhauseffekt *m*	global warming	—	effetto serra *m*	efecto invernadero *m*
effet domicilier (F)	Domizilwechsel *m*	domiciliary bill	—	cambiale domiciliata *f*	letra domiciliada *f*
effet public (F)	Rentenanleihe *f*	annuity bonds	—	prestito a reddito fisso *m*	empréstito por anualidades *m*
effet snob (F)	Snob-Effekt *m*	snob effect	—	effetto snob *m*	efecto snob *m*
effettivo (I)	Aktivbestand *m*	assets	actif *m*	—	activo disponible *m*
effetto bumerang (I)	Bumerang-Effekt *m*	boomerang effect	effet boomerang *m*	—	efecto bumerán *m*
effetto dell'inserzione (I)	Anzeigenwirkung *f*	effectiveness of an advertisement	effet de l'annonce *m*	—	efectividad del anuncio *f*
effetto serra (I)	Treibhauseffekt *m*	global warming	effet de serre *m*	—	efecto invernadero *m*
effetto snob (I)	Snob-Effekt *m*	snob effect	effet snob *m*	—	efecto snob *m*
efficience¹ (F)	Effizienz *f*	efficiency	—	efficienza *f*	eficiencia *f*
efficience² (F)	Leistungsfähigkeit *f*	efficiency	—	efficienza *f*	capacidad productiva *f*
efficiency¹ (E)	Effizienz *f*	—	efficience *f*	efficienza *f*	eficiencia *f*
efficiency² (E)	Leistungsfähigkeit *f*	—	efficience *f*	efficienza *f*	capacidad productiva *f*

	D	E	F	I	Es
efficiency control (E)	Effizienzkontrolle *f*	—	contrôle de l'efficience *m*	controllo d'efficienza *m*	control de eficiencia *m*
efficienza[1] (I)	Leistungsfähigkeit *f*	efficiency	efficience *f*	—	capacidad productiva *f*
efficienza[2] (I)	Effizienz *f*	efficiency	efficience *f*	—	eficiencia *f*
Effizienz (D)	—	efficiency	efficience *f*	efficienza *f*	eficiencia *f*
Effizienzkontrolle (D)	—	efficiency control	contrôle de l'efficience *m*	controllo d'efficienza *m*	control de eficiencia *m*
eficiencia (Es)	Effizienz *f*	efficiency	efficience *f*	efficienza *f*	—
eichen (D)	—	gauge	jauger	tarare	contrastar
eidesstattliche Erklärung (D)	—	declaration in lieu of an oath	déclaration formelle sans prestation de serment *f*	dichiarazione sostitutiva del giuramento *f*	declaración bajo juramento *f*
Eigenfinanzierung (D)	—	self-financing	autofinancement *m*	autofinanziamento *m*	financiación propia *f*
Eigenkapital (D)	—	equity capital	capital propre *m*	capitale proprio *m*	capital propio *m*
Eigentum (D)	—	property	propriété *f*	proprietà *f*	propiedad *f*
Eigentumsverhältnisse (D)	—	property relations	régime de la propriété *m*	rapporti di proprietà *m pl*	régimen de tenencia *m*
Eigentumswohnung (D)	—	freehold flat	logement en propriété *m*	appartamento in condominio *m*	piso en propiedad *m*
Eigenverbrauch (D)	—	personal consumption	consommation personnelle *f*	consumo proprio *m*	consumo propio *m*
Eilbote (D)	—	express messenger	facteur spécial *m*	corriere *m*	expreso *m*
Eilbrief (D)	—	express letter	lettre par exprès *f*	lettera espresso *f*	carta urgente *f*
Eilgut (D)	—	goods sent by express	marchandise en grande vitesse *f*	merce a grande velocità *f*	mercancía en gran velocidad *f*
Eilpaket (D)	—	express parcel	colis exprès *m*	pacco espresso *m*	paquete urgente *m*
Eilzustellung (D)	—	express delivery	remise par exprès *f*	consegna per espresso *f*	entrega urgente *f*
Einarbeitung (D)	—	vocational adjustment	entraînement *m*	periodo d'adattamento *m*	entrenamiento *m*
Einbruchversicherung (D)	—	housebreaking insurance	assurance contre le vol avec effraction *f*	assicurazione contro il furto con scasso *f*	seguro contra robo con fractura *m*
Einflußbereich (D)	—	sphere of influence	sphère d'influence *f*	sfera d'influenza *f*	esfera de influencia *f*
Einfuhr (D)	—	import	importation *f*	importazione *f*	importación *f*
Einfuhrabgabe (D)	—	import duties	taxe à l'importation *f*	tassa d'importazione *f*	tasa a la importación *f*
Einfuhrbeschränkung (D)	—	import restriction	limitation des importations *f*	restrizione d'importazione *f*	restricción a la importación *f*
Einfuhrerklärung (D)	—	import declaration	déclaration d'entrée *f*	dichiarazione doganale *f*	declaración de importación *f*
Einfuhrgenehmigung (D)	—	import licence	autorisation d'importation *f*	permesso d'importazione *m*	permiso de importación *m*
Einfuhrpapiere (D)	—	import documents	documents d'importation *m pl*	bollette doganali *f pl*	documentos de importación *m pl*
Einführungsrabatt (D)	—	introductory discount	rabais d'introduction *m*	sconto di lancio *m*	rebaja de lanzamiento *f*
Einfuhrzoll (D)	—	import duty	droit d'entrée *m*	dazio d'importazione *m*	arancel de importación *m*
Eingang vorbehalten (D)	—	due payment reserved	sauf bonne fin	salvo buon fine	salvo buen cobro *m*
eingezahltes Kapital (D)	—	paid-up capital	capital versé *m*	capitale versato *m*	capitial desembolsado *m*
Einheitskurs (D)	—	spot price	cours unique *m*	cambio unitario *m*	cotización única *f*
Einheitspreis (D)	—	uniform price	prix unique *m*	prezzo unitario *m*	precio único *m*
Einheitstarif (D)	—	uniform tariff	tarif standard *m*	tariffa unitaria *f*	tarifa única *f*
Einheitswährung (D)	—	uniform currency	monométallisme *m*	moneta unitaria *f*	moneda única *f*
Einheitszoll (D)	—	uniform duty	droit unique *m*	dazio unitario *m*	aduanas uniformes *f pl*
Einkauf (D)	—	purchase	achat *m*	acquisto *m*	compra *f*
einkaufen (D)	—	buy	acheter	acquistare	comprar
Einkäufer (D)	—	buyer	acheteur *m*	acquirente *m*	comprador *m*

	D	E	F	I	Es
Einkaufs-bedingungen (D)	—	purchasing terms	conditions d'achat *f pl*	condizioni d'acquisto *f pl*	condiciones de compra *f pl*
Einkaufsland (D)	—	country of purchase	pays où l'on achète *m*	paese acquirente *m*	país de compra *m*
Einkaufspreis (D)	—	purchase price	prix d'achat *m*	prezzo d'acquisto *m*	precio de compra *m*
Einkommen (D)	—	income	revenu *m*	reddito *m*	ingresos *m pl*/renta *f*
Einkommens-erhöhung (D)	—	rise in income	augmentation du revenu *f*	aumento del reddito *m*	aumento de salario *m*
Einkommens-erklärung (D)	—	income declaration	déclaration du revenu *f*	dichiarazione del reddito *f*	declaración de la renta *f*
Einkommensteuer (D)	—	income tax	impôt sur le revenu *m*	imposta sui redditi *f*	impuesto sobre la renta de las personas físicas *m*
Einkommens-umverteilung (D)	—	redistribution of income	redistribution des revenus *f*	ridistribuzione dei redditi *f*	redistribución de la renta *f*
Einkommens-verteilung (D)	—	distribution of income	distribution du revenu *f*	distribuzione dei redditi *f*	distribución de la renta *f*
Einkommens-verwendung (D)	—	appropriation of income	utilisation du revenu *f*	impiego dei redditi *m*	distribución de la renta *f*
einladen (D)	—	invite	inviter	invitare	invitar
Einlagen (D)	—	deposit	dépôt *m*	depositi bancari *m pl*	depósitos bancarios *m pl*
Einlagerung (D)	—	storage	entreposage *m*	immagazzinamento *m*	almacenamiento *m*
Einlösung (D)	—	payment	payement *m*	pagamento *m*	pago *m*
Einnahmen (D)	—	receipts	revenu *m*	entrate *f pl*	ingresos *m pl*
Einschreibebrief (D)	—	registered letter	lettre recommandée *f*	lettera raccomandata *f*	carta certificada *f*
Einschreiben (D)	—	Registered	en recommandé	raccomandata *f*	certificado *m*
Einschreiben-Rückschein (D)	—	Recorded delivery letter (with advice)	lettre recommandée avec avis de réception *f*	lettera raccomandata con ricevuta di ritorno *f*	carta certificada con talón de recibo *f*
Einsichtnahme (D)	—	inspection	contrôle des livres comptables *m*	presa visione *f*	inspección *f*
Einstandspreis (D)	—	cost price	prix coûtant *m*	prezzo di costo *m*	precio de coste *m*
einstweilig (D)	—	temporary	provisoire	temporaneo	provisional
einstweilige Verfügung (D)	—	temporary injunction	ordonnance sur référé civil *f*	provvedimento temporaneo *m*	interdicto provisorio *m*
Eintrittskarte (D)	—	admission ticket	billet *m*	biglietto d'ingresso *m*	entrada *f*
Einwilligung (D)	—	consent	consentement *m*	consenso *m*	consentimiento *m*
Einwohner-meldeamt (D)	—	residents' registration office	bureau de déclaration de résidence *m*	ufficio anagrafe *m*	oficina del censo *f*
Einzelhandel (D)	—	retail trade	commerce de détail *m*	commercio al dettaglio *m*	comercio al por menor *m*
Einzelhandels-kaufmann (D)	—	retail merchant	détaillant *m*	commerciante al dettaglio *m*	comerciante particular *m*
Einzelhandels-spanne (D)	—	retail price margin	marge de détail *f*	margine del commercio al dettaglio *m*	margen del comercio al por menor *m*
Einzelhändler (D)	—	retailer	commerçant détaillant *m*	dettagliante *m*	minorista *m*
Eisenbahntarif (D)	—	railway tariff	tarif ferroviaire *m*	tariffa ferroviaria *f*	tarifa ferroviaria *f*
ejecución[1] (Es)	Vollstreckung *f*	enforcement	exécution *f*	esecuzione *f*	—
ejecución[2] (Es)	Durchführung *f*	realization	réalisation *f*	esecuzione *f*	—
ejecución[3] (Es)	Abwicklung *f*	settlement/ liquidation	exécution *f*/ liquidation *f*	esecuzione *f*	—
ejecución de pedidos (Es)	Auftragsabwicklung *f*	execution of the order	exécution d'une commande *f*	esecuzione ordini *f*	—
ejecución forzosa (Es)	Zwangs-vollstreckung *f*	judicial execution	exécution forcée *f*	esecuzione forzata *f*	—
ejecución por crédito documentario (Es)	Akkreditiv-abwicklung *f*	settlement by letter of credit	exécution par crédit documentaire *f*	procedura del credito documentario *f*	—
ejecutivo (Es)	Führungsperson *f*	executive	cadre *m*	dirigente *m*	—
ejecutor judicial (Es)	Gerichtsvollzieher *m*	bailiff	huissier de justice *m*	ufficiale giudiziario *m*	—
ejercicio[1] (Es)	Wirtschaftsjahr *n*	business year	exercice comptable *m*	esercizio *m*	—

	D	E	F	I	Es
ejercicio[2] (Es)	Rechnungsjahr *n*	financial year	exercice comptable *m*	anno d'esercizio *m*	—
ejercicio[3] (Es)	Haushaltsjahr *n*	financial year	exercice budgétaire *m*	anno finanziario *m*	—
ejercicio[4] (Es)	Geschäftsjahr *n*	financial year	exercice commerciale *m*	esercizio commerciale *m*	—
elaboración ulterior (Es)	Weiterverarbeitung *f*	further processing	transformation complémentaire *f*	trasformazione *f*	—
elaborar (Es)	aufbereiten	process/prepare	élaborer/traiter	elaborare/lavorare	—
elaborare (I)	aufbereiten	process/prepare	élaborer/traiter	—	elaborar/tratar
élaboration de texte (F)	Textverarbeitung *f*	word processing	—	elaborazione testi *f*	tratamiento de textos *m*
elaboratore elettronico di dati (I)	Datenverarbeitungs-anlage *f*	data processing system	installation de traite-ment électronique des informations *f*	—	ordenador *m*
elaborazione dati (I)	Datenverarbeitung *f*	data processing	traitement des information *m*	—	procesamiento de datos *m*
elaborazione testi (I)	Textverarbeitung *f*	word processing	élaboration de texte *f*	—	tratamiento de textos *m*
élaborer (F)	aufbereiten	process/prepare	—	elaborare/lavorare	elaborar/tratar
elección de la ubicación (Es)	Standortwahl *f*	choice of location	choix du lieu d'implantation *m*	scelta dell'ubicazione *f*	—
electric power (E)	Strom *m*	—	énergie électrique *f*	energia ellettrica *f*	energía *f*
electronic (E)	elektronisch	—	électronique	elettronico	electrónico
electrónica (Es)	Elektronik *f*	electronics	électronique *f*	elettronica *f*	—
electrónico (Es)	elektronisch	electronic	électronique	elettronico	—
electronics (E)	Elektronik *f*	—	électronique *f*	elettronica *f*	electrónica *f*
électronique[1] (F)	Elektronik *f*	electronics	—	elettronica *f*	electrónica *f*
électronique[2] (F)	elektronisch	electronic	—	elettronico	electrónico
Elektronik (D)	—	electronics	électronique *f*	elettronica *f*	electrónica *f*
elektronisch (D)	—	electronic	électronique	elettronico	electrónico
élément polluant (F)	Schadstoff *m*	pollutants	—	sostanza nociva *f*	substancia nociva *f*
éléments pouvant influencer la demande (F)	Bedarfsfaktoren *pl*	requirements factors	—	fattori del fabbisogno *m pl*	factores determinantes de las necesidades *m pl*
elettronica (I)	Elektronik *f*	electronics	électronique *f*	—	electrónica *f*
elettronico (I)	elektronisch	electronic	électronique	—	electrónico
élevage (F)	Tierzucht *f*	livestock breeding	—	zootecnia *f*	cría de animales *f*
eliminación (Es)	Entsorgung *f*	waste disposal	dépollution *f*	smaltimento *m*	—
eliminación de petróleo usado (Es)	Altölbeseitigung *f*	disposal of waste oil	élimination d'huile usée *f*	smaltimento dell'olio usato *m*	—
élimination de déchets (F)	Abfallbeseitigung *f*	waste disposal	—	smaltimento dei rifiuti *m*	evacuación de residuos *f*
élimination du pétrole usé (F)	Altölbeseitigung *f*	disposal of waste oil	—	smaltimento dell'olio usato *m*	eliminación de petróleo usado *f*
elocuencia (Es)	Redegewandtheit *f*	eloquence	élocution aisée *f*	eloquenza *f*	—
élocution aisée (F)	Redegewandtheit *f*	eloquence	—	eloquenza *f*	elocuencia *f*
eloquence (E)	Redegewandtheit *f*	—	élocution aisée *f*	eloquenza *f*	elocuencia *f*
eloquenza (I)	Redegewandtheit *f*	eloquence	élocution aisée *f*	—	elocuencia *f*
embalaje (Es)	Verpackung	packing	emballage *m*	imballaggio *m*	—
embalaje marítimo (Es)	seemäßige Verpackung *f*	seaproof packing	emballage maritime *m*	imballaggio marittimo *m*	—
emballage (F)	Verpackung	packing	—	imballaggio *m*	embalaje *m*
emballage maritime (F)	seemäßige Verpackung *f*	seaproof packing	—	imballaggio marittimo *m*	embalaje marítimo *m*
Embargo (D)	—	embargo	embargo *m*	embargo *m*	embargo *m*
embargo (E)	Embargo *n*	—	embargo *m*	embargo *m*	embargo *m*
embargo[1] (Es)	Embargo *n*	embargo	embargo *m*	embargo *m*	—
embargo[2] (Es)	Liefersperre *f*	delivery ban	blocage de livraisons *m*	blocco delle forniture *m*	—
embargo (F)	Embargo *n*	embargo	—	embargo *m*	embargo *m*
embargo (I)	Embargo *n*	embargo	embargo *m*	—	embargo *m*

	D	E	F	I	Es
embargo comercial (Es)	Handelsembargo *n*	trade embargo	embargo commercial *m*	embargo commerciale *m*	—
embargo commercial (F)	Handelsembargo *n*	trade embargo	—	embargo commerciale *m*	embargo comercial *m*
embargo commerciale (I)	Handelsembargo *n*	trade embargo	embargo commercial *m*	—	embargo comercial *m*
embargo de salario (Es)	Lohnpfändung *f*	attachment of earnings	saisie-arrêt sur le salaire *f*	pignoramento del salario *m*	—
embarque (Es)	Verschiffung *f*	shipment	embarquement *m*	imbarco *m*	—
embarquement (F)	Verschiffung *f*	shipment	—	imbarco *m*	embarque *m*
embezzlement (E)	Unterschlagung *f*	—	détournement *m*	appropriazione indebita *f*	defraudación *f*
emblema comercial(Es)	Markenzeichen *n*	trademark	marque déposée *f*	marchio *m*	—
emendamento di legge (I)	Gesetzesänderung *f*	amendment of a law	amendement d'une loi *m*	—	enmienda de la ley *f*
emisión (Es)	Emission *f*	issue	émission *f*	emissione *f*	—
emisión de acciones (Es)	Aktienemission *f*	share issue	émission d'actions *f*	emissione di azioni *f*	—
emisión parcial (Es)	Tranche *f*	tranche	tranche *f*	tranche *f*	—
Emission (D)	—	issue	émission *f*	emissione *f*	emisión *f*
émission (F)	Emission *f*	issue	—	emissione *f*	emisión *f*
émission d'actions (F)	Aktienemission *f*	share issue	—	emissione di azioni *f*	emisión de acciones *f*
émission publicitaire télévisée (F)	Fernsehwerbung *f*	television advertising	—	pubblicità televisiva *f*	publicidad televisiva *f*
emissione (I)	Emission *f*	issue	émission *f*	—	emisión *f*
emissione di assegno a vuoto (I)	Scheckbetrug *m*	cheque fraud	irrégularité en matière de chèque *f*	—	falsificación de cheques *f*
emissione di azioni (I)	Aktienemission *f*	share issue	émission d'actions *f*	—	emisión de acciones *f*
emissione di tratte incrociate (I)	Wechselreiterei *f*	kiteflying	tirage d'une traite de cavalerie *m*	—	libramiento de letras cruzadas *m*
Emissions-begrenzung (D)	—	issuing restriction	limitation d'émission *f*	limitazione d'emissione *f*	limitación de emisiones *f*
Emissionsgeschäft (D)	—	investment business	opération succédant à une émission *f*	operazione d'emissione *f*	operación de emisión *f*
Emissionskurs (D)	—	price of issue	cours d'émission *m*	prezzo d'emissione *m*	tipo de emisión *m*
émoluments (F)	Bezüge *pl*	earnings	—	entrate *f pl*	retribuciones *f pl*
empaque (Es)	Verpackungs-material *n*	packing material	matériel d'emballage *m*	materiale d'imballaggio *m*	—
Empfänger (D)	—	receiver	destinataire *m*	destinatario *m*	destinatario *m*
Empfangs-berechtigung (D)	—	authorization to receive	autorité pour recevoir *f*	autorizzazione di ricezione *f*	autorización de recibimiento *f*
Empfangs-bestätigung (D)	—	acknowledgement of receipt	accusé de réception *m*	ricevuta *f*	recibo *m*
Empfehlung (D)	—	recommendation	recommandation *f*	raccomandazione *f*	recomendación *f*
Empfehlungs-schreiben (D)	—	letter of recommendation	lettre de recommandation *f*	lettera di raccomandazione *f*	carta de recomendación *f*
empirical market research (E)	empirische Marktforschung *f*	—	étude de marché empirique *f*	ricerca di mercato empirica *f*	estudio del mercado empírico *m*
empirische Marktforschung (D)	—	empirical market research	étude de marché empirique *f*	ricerca di mercato empirica *f*	estudio del mercado empírico *m*
empleado[1] (Es)	Arbeitnehmer *m*	employee	salarié *m*	prestatore d'opera *m*	—
empleado[2] (Es)	Angestellter *m*	employee	employé *m*	impiegato *m*	—
emplear (Es)	anstellen	employ	employer	impiegare	—
empleo[1] (Es)	Stellung *f*	position	position *f*	posizione *f*	—
empleo[2] (Es)	Anstellung *f*	employment	emploi *m*	impiego *m*	—
empleo parcial (Es)	Teilzeit-beschäftigung *f*	part-time employment	emploi à temps partiel *m*	occupazione part-time *f*	—
empleo total (Es)	Vollbeschäftigung *f*	full employment	plein emploi *m*	piena occupazione *f*	—
emploi (F)	Anstellung *f*	employment	—	impiego *m*	empleo *m*
emploi à temps partiel (F)	Teilzeit-beschäftigung *f*	part-time employment	—	occupazione part-time *f*	empleo parcial *m*

	D	E	F	I	Es
emploi d'ordinateurs (F)	Computereinsatz *m*	use of a computer	—	impiego di computer *m*	utilización de ordenadores *f*
emploi vacant (F)	Arbeitsnachweis *m*	employment vacancies	—	informazioni sui posti vacanti *f pl*	servicio de colocación *m*
employ (E)	anstellen	—	employer	impiegare	emplear
employé (F)	Angestellte *pl*	employee	—	impiegati *m pl*	empleado *m*
employee[1] (E)	Arbeitnehmer *m*	—	salarié *m*	prestatore d'opera *m*	empleado *m*
employee[2] (E)	Angestellter *m*	—	employé *m*	impiegato *m*	empleado *m*
employee-employer relationship (E)	Arbeitsverhältnis *n*	—	rapport de travail *m*	rapporto di lavoro *m*	relación laboral *f*
employee-employer relationship on a trial basis (E)	Arbeitsverhältnis auf Probe *n*	—	contrat de travail convenu à l'essai *m*	rapporto di lavoro in prova *m*	relación laboral a prueba *f*
employer (E)	Arbeitgeber *m*	—	employeur *m*	datore di lavoro *m*	patrón *m*
employer (F)	anstellen	employ	—	impiegare	emplear
employers' association (E)	Unternehmer-verband *m*	—	association des chefs d'entreprise *f*	unione degli imprenditori *f*	asociación empresarial *f*
employeur (F)	Arbeitgeber *m*	employer	—	datore di lavoro *m*	patrón *m*
employment[1] (E)	Anstellung *f*	—	emploi *m*	impiego *m*	empleo *m*
employment[2] (E)	Beschäftigung *f*	—	occupation *f*	occupazione *f*	ocupación *f*
employment agency (E)	Arbeitsvermittlung *f*	—	bureau de placement *m*	ufficio di collocamento *m*	agencia laboral *f*
employment policy (E)	Beschäftigungs-politik *f*	—	politique d'emploi *f*	politica d'occupazione *f*	política de empleo *f*
employment protection (E)	Arbeitsschutz *m*	—	protection sociale du travail *f*	tutela del lavoro *f*	protección del trabajo *f*
employment theory (E)	Beschäftigungs-theorie *f*	—	théorie d'emploi *f*	teoria dell'occupazione *f*	teoría del empleo *f*
employment vacancies (E)	Arbeitsnachweis *m*	—	emploi vacant *m*	informazioni sui posti vacanti *f pl*	servicio de colocación *m*
empresa (Es)	Firma *f*	company	entreprise *f*	impresa *f*	—
empresa agrícola (Es)	Agrarbetrieb *m*	agricultural enterprise	entreprise agricole *f*	azienda agricola *f*	—
empresa competidora (Es)	Konkurrenzfirma *f*	competing firm	maison concurrente *f*	ditta concorrente *f*	—
empresa competitoria (Es)	Konkurrenz-unternehmen *n*	competitive undertaking	entreprise concurrente *f*	impresa concorrente *f*	—
empresa de beneficio común (Es)	gemeinnütziges Unternehmen *n*	public institution	entreprise d'utilité publique *f*	impresa di utilità pubblica *f*	—
empresa de explotación (Es)	Betriebsgesellschaft *f*	operating company	entreprise d'exploitation *f*	società d'esercizio *f*	—
empresa dominante (Es)	herrschendes Unternehmen *n*	controlling company	entreprise dirigeante *f*	impresa controllante *f*	—
empresa estatal (Es)	Regiebetrieb *m*	publicly owned enterprise	établissement en régie *m*	gestione in economia *f*	—
empresa ficticia (Es)	Briefkastenfirma *f*	bubble company	entreprise fantôme *f*	società bucalettere *f*	—
empresa industrial (Es)	gewerblicher Betrieb *m*	industrial undertaking	établissement commercial *m*	azienda commerciale *f*/azienda industriale *f*	—
empresa multinacional (Es)	multinationale Unternehmen *n*	multinational enterprise	entreprises multinationales *f pl*	imprese multinazionali *f pl*	—
empresa pública[1] (Es)	öffentliche Betriebe *pl*	public sector industrial enterpises	entreprises publiques *f pl*	aziende pubbliche *f pl*	—
empresa pública[2] (Es)	öffentliche Unternehmen *n*	public enterprises	entreprises publiques *f pl*	imprese pubbliche *f pl*	—
empresario[1] (Es)	Unternehmer *m*	entrepreneur	entrepreneur *m*	imprenditore *m*	—
empresario[2] (Es)	Unternehmen *n*	enterprise	entreprise *f*	impresa *f*	—
empresas públicas (Es)	staatliche Betriebe *pl*	state-owned enterprise	entreprise publique *f*	aziende statali *f pl*	—
empréstito (Es)	Anleihe *f*	loan	emprunt *m*	prestito *m*	—
empréstito estatal (Es)	Staatsanleihen *pl*	government loan	emprunt d'Etat *m*	titoli pubblici *m pl*	—
empréstito exterior (Es)	Auslandsanleihe *f*	foreign bond	emprunt extérieur *m*	prestito estero *m*	—
empréstito municipal (Es)	Kommunalanleihen *pl*	local authorities loan	emprunt communal *m*	prestiti comunali *m pl*	—

	D	E	F	I	Es
empréstito por anualidades[1] (Es)	Rentenanleihe *f*	annuity bonds	effet public *m*	prestito a reddito fisso *m*	—
empréstito por anualidades[2] (Es)	Annuitätendarlehen *n*	annuity loan	prêt amortissable par annuités *m*	prestito rimborsabile in annualità *m*	—
empréstito sobre obligaciones (Es)	Obligationsanleihe *f*	debenture loan	emprunt obligataire *m*	prestito obbligazionario *m*	—
emprunt[1] (F)	Anleihe *f*	loan	—	prestito *m*	empréstito *m*
emprunt[2] (F)	Geldaufnahme *f*	raising of money	—	accensione di un mutuo *f*	dinero tomado a préstamo *m*
emprunt communal (F)	Kommunalanleihen *pl*	local authorities loan	—	prestiti comunali *m pl*	empréstito municipal *m*
emprunt d'Etat (F)	Staatsanleihen *pl*	government loan	—	titoli pubblici *m pl*	empréstito estatal *m*
emprunt extérieur (F)	Auslandsanleihe *f*	foreign bond	—	prestito estero *m*	empréstito exterior *m*
emprunt obligataire (F)	Obligationsanleihe *f*	debenture loan	—	prestito obbligazionario *m*	empréstito sobre obligaciones *m*
empuje innovador (Es)	Innovationsschub *m*	technology push	animation d'innovation *f*	spinta innovativa *f*	—
enajenación (Es)	Veräußerung *f*	sale/alienation	aliénation *f*	alienazione *f*	—
en almacén (Es)	auf Lager	in stock	en stock	in magazzino	—
encabezamiento (Es)	Briefkopf *m*	letterhead	en-tête *m*	intestazione *f*	—
encarecimiento (Es)	Verteuerung *f*	rise in price	enchérissement *m*	rincaro *m*	—
encart non broché à la revue (F)	Beilage *f*	supplement	—	inserto *m*	suplemento *m*
enchérissement (F)	Verteuerung *f*	rise in price	—	rincaro *m*	encarecimiento *m*
enclosure (E)	Anlage *f*	—	pièce jointe *f*	allegato *m*	anexo *m*
encobro (Es)	Inkasso *n*	collection	recouvrement *m*	incasso *m*	—
en comisión (Es)	auf Kommissionsbasis	on a commission basis	en commission	in base commissionaria	—
en commission (F)	auf Kommissionsbasis	on a commission basis	—	in base commissionaria	en comisión
encouragement à l'exportation (F)	Ausfuhrförderung *f*	measures to encourage exports	—	promozione delle esportazioni *f*	fomento de la exportació *m*
encouragement à la vente (F)	Verkaufsförderung *f*	sales promotion	—	promozione di vendita *f*	promoción de las ventas *f*
encourir une peine (F)	straffällig	liable to prosecution	—	passibile di pena	criminal
encuesta (Es)	Befragung *f*	poll	enquête *f*	interrogazione *f*	—
encuesta entre los clientes (Es)	Kundenbefragung *f*	customer survey	enquête parmi les clients *f*	intervista ai clienti *f*	—
encuesta por muestreo (Es)	Stichproben-erhebung *f*	sample survey	enquête par sondage *f*	prelievo di campioni *m*	—
en deux exemplaires (F)	in zweifacher Ausfertigung	in duplicate	—	in due copie	por duplicado
en la fecha fijada (Es)	termingerecht	on schedule	dans les délais	puntuale	—
Endabnehmer (D)	—	ultimate buyer	preneur final *m*	acquirente finale *m*	comprador final *m*
endettement (F)	Verschuldung *f*	indebtedness	—	indebitamento *m*	endeudamiento *m*
endettement de l'Etat (F)	Staatsverschuldung *f*	state indebtedness	—	debito pubblico *m*	endeudamiento público *m*
endettement effectif (F)	effektive Verschuldung *f*	real indebtedness	—	indebitamento effettivo *m*	endeudamiento efectivo *m*
endettement net (F)	Nettoverschuldung *f*	net indebtedness	—	indebitamento netto *m*	deuda neta *m*
endeudamiento (Es)	Verschuldung *f*	indebtedness	endettement *m*	indebitamento *m*	—
endeudamiento efectivo (Es)	effektive Verschuldung *f*	real indebtedness	endettement effectif *m*	indebitamento effettivo *m*	—
endeudamiento público (Es)	Staatsverschuldung *f*	state indebtedness	endettement de l'Etat *m*	debito pubblico *m*	—
Endkontrolle (D)	—	final control	contrôle final *m*	controllo finale *m*	control final *m*
end of a quarter (E)	Quartalsende *n*	—	fin de trimestre *f*	fine trimestre *f*	final del trimestre *m*
end of the month (E)	Ultimo *n*	—	fin de mois *f*	fine mese *m*	fin de mes *m*
endommagement (F)	Beschädigung *f*	damage	—	danno *m*	deterioración *f*
endoso (Es)	Indossament *n*	endorsement	endossement *m*	girata *f*	—
endossement (F)	Indossament *n*	endorsement	—	girata *f*	endoso *m*

	D	E	F	I	Es
endowment (E)	Dotierung *f*	—	dotation *f*	dotazione *f*	dotación *f*
Endprodukt (D)	—	finished product	produit final *m*	prodotto finito *m*	producto final *m*
Endverbraucher (D)	—	ultimate consumer	consommateur final *m*	consumatore *m*	consumidor final *m*
en efectivo (Es)	in bar	in cash	comptant	in contanti	—
en el extranjero (Es)	im Ausland	abroad	à l'étranger	all'estero	—
en el término de (Es)	binnen	within	dans le délai de	entro	—
energía (Es)	Strom *m*	electric power	énergie électrique *f*	enrgia elettrica *f*	—
energia elettrica (I)	Strom *m*	electric power	énergie électrique *f*	—	energía *f*
energía eólica (Es)	Windenergie *f*	eolian energy	énergie éolienne *f*	energia eolica *f*	—
energia eolica (I)	Windenergie *f*	eolian energy	énergie éolienne *f*	—	energía eólica *f*
energía nuclear (Es)	Kernenergie *f*	nuclear energy	énergie nucléaire *f*	energia nucleare *f*	—
energia nucleare (I)	Kernenergie *f*	nuclear energy	énergie nucléaire *f*	—	energía nuclear *f*
energía primaria (Es)	Primärenergie *f*	primary energy	énergie primaire *f*	energia primaria *f*	—
energia primaria (I)	Primärenergie *f*	primary energy	énergie primaire *f*	—	energía primaria *f*
energia secondaria (I)	Sekundärenergie *f*	secondary energy	énergie secondaire *f*	—	energía secundaria *f*
energía secundaria (Es)	Sekundärenergie *f*	secondary energy	énergie secondaire *f*	energia secondaria *f*	—
énergie électrique (F)	Strom *m*	electric power	—	energia elettrica *f*	energía *f*
énergie éolienne (F)	Windenergie *f*	eolian energy	—	energia eolica *f*	energía eólica *f*
Energiekrise (D)	—	energy crisis	crise de l'énergie *f*	crisi energetica *f*	crisis energética *f*
énergie nucléaire (F)	Kernenergie *f*	nuclear energy	—	energia nucleare *f*	energía nuclear *f*
énergie primaire (F)	Primärenergie *f*	primary energy	—	energia primaria *f*	energía primaria *f*
énergie secondaire (F)	Sekundärenergie *f*	secondary energy	—	energia secondaria *f*	energía secundaria *f*
Energieversorgung (D)	—	energy supply	approvisionnement en énergie *m*	approvvigionamento d'energia *m*	abastecimiento energético *m*
energy crisis (E)	Energiekrise *f*	—	crise de l'énergie *f*	crisi energetica *f*	crisis energética *f*
energy supply (E)	Energieversorgung *f*	—	approvisionnement en énergie *m*	approvvigionamento d'energia *m*	abastecimiento energético *m*
enforcement (E)	Vollstreckung *f*	—	exécution *f*	esecuzione *f*	ejecución *f*
Engagement (D)	—	engagement/ commitment	engagement *m*	impegno *m*/ assunzione *f*	compromiso *m*
engagement (E)	Engagement *n*	—	engagement *m*	impegno *m*/ assunzione *f*	compromiso *m*
engagement[1] (F)	Engagement *n*	engagement/ commitment	—	impegno *m*/ assunzione *f*	compromiso *m*
engagement[2] (F)	Obligo *n*	liability	—	obbligo *m*	obligación *f*
engagement de garantie (F)	Garantie-verpflichtung *f*	guarantee obligation	—	obbligo di garanzia *m*	obligación de garantía *f*
engaño[1] (Es)	Schwindel *m*	swindle	tromperie *f*	truffa *f*	—
engaño[2] (Es)	Täuschung *f*	deceit	tromperie *f*	inganno *m*	—
engineer (E)	Ingenieur *m*	—	ingénieur *m*	ingegnere *m*	ingeniero *m*
engineering department (E)	technische Abteilung *f*	—	service technique *m*	reparto tecnico *m*	departamento técnico *m*
enmienda de la ley (Es)	Gesetzesänderung *f*	amendment of a law	amendement d'une loi *m*	emendamento di legge *m*	—
en nombre propio (Es)	im eigenen Namen	in one's own name	en nom propre	per nome proprio	—
en nom propre (F)	im eigenen Namen	in one's own name	—	per nome proprio	en nombre propio
en particular (Es)	im einzelnen	in particular	en particulier	in dettaglio	—
en particulier (F)	im einzelnen	in particular	—	in dettaglio	en particular
en recommandé (F)	Einschreiben *n*	Registered	—	raccomandata *f*	certificado *m*
enquête[1] (F)	Interview *n*	interview	—	intervista *f*	entrevista *f*
enquête[2] (F)	Befragung *f*	poll	—	interrogazione *f*	encuesta *f*
enquête par sondage (F)	Stichproben-erhebung *f*	sample survey	—	prelievo di campioni *m*	encuesta por muestreo *f*
enquête parmi les clients (F)	Kundenbefragung *f*	customer survey	—	intervista ai clienti *f*	encuesta entre los clientes *f*
ensayo (Es)	Probe *f*	trial/sample	essai *m*/ échantillon *m*	prova *f*/campione *m*	—

	D	E	F	I	Es
enseigne commerciale (F)	Firmenschild *n*	company's name plate	—	insegna dell'impresa *f*	letrero de establecimiento *m*
en stock (F)	auf Lager	in stock	—	in magazzino	en almacén
ente (I)	Körperschaft *f*	corporation	collectivité *f*	—	corporación *f*
Enteignung (D)	—	expropriation	expropriation *f*	espropriazione *f*	expropiación *f*
enterprise (E)	Unternehmen *n*	—	entreprise *f*	impresa *f*	empresario *m*
en-tête (F)	Briefkopf *m*	letterhead	—	intestazione *f*	encabezamiento *m*
entità (I)	Umfang *m*	volume	volume *m*	—	volumen *m*/ dimensión *f*
entità dell'inventario (I)	Bestandsgröße *f*	stock variable	stock variable *m*	—	magnitud *f*
Entladungskosten (D)	—	discharging expenses	coûts de déchargement *m pl*	spese di scaricamento *f pl*	gastos de descargo *m pl*
Entlassung (D)	—	dismissal	licenciement *m*	licenziamento *m*	despido *m*
Entlastung (D)	—	discharge	décharge *f*	sgravio *m*	desgravamen *m*
entrada (Es)	Eintrittskarte *f*	admission ticket	billet *m*	biglietto d'ingresso *m*	—
entrada de mercancías (Es)	Wareneingang *m*	arrival of goods	entrée de marchandises *f*	entrata merci *f*	—
entrada en el mercado (Es)	Markteintritt *m*	entry into the market	entrée dans le marché *f*	apertura di mercato *f*	—
entrada gratuita (Es)	Freikarte *f*	free ticket	billet de faveur *m*	biglietto gratuito *m*	—
entraînement (F)	Einarbeitung *f*	vocational adjustment	—	periodo d'adattamento *m*	entrenamiento *m*
entrata merci (I)	Wareneingang *m*	arrival of goods	entrée de marchandises *f*	—	entrada de mercancías *f*
entrate[1] (I)	Bezüge *pl*	earnings	émoluments *m pl*	—	retribuciones *f pl*
entrate[2] (I)	Einnahmen *pl*	receipts	revenu *m*	—	ingresos *m pl*
entrate pubbliche[1] (I)	Staatseinnahmen *pl*	public revenue	recettes de l'Etat *f pl*	—	ingresos del Estado *m pl*
entrate pubbliche[2] (I)	öffentliche Einnahmen *pl*	public revenues	recettes publiques *f pl*	—	ingresos públicos *m pl*
entrée[1] (F)	Input *m*	input	—	input *m*	insumo *m*
entrée[2] (F)	Zugang *m*	access	—	accesso *m*	acceso *m*
entrée dans le marché (F)	Markteintritt *m*	entry into the market	—	apertura di mercato *f*	entrada en el mercado *f*
entrée de marchandises (F)	Wareneingang *m*	arrival of goods	—	entrata merci *f*	entrada de mercancías *f*
entrega (Es)	Übergabe *f*	delivery	remise *f*	consegna *f*	—
entrega contra reembolso (Es)	Lieferung gegen Nachnahme *f*	cash on delivery	livraison contre remboursement *f*	consegna contro assegno *f*	—
entrega de reposición (Es)	Ersatzlieferung *f*	substitute delivery	livraison de remplacement *f*	fornitura di compensazione *f*	—
entrega inmediata (Es)	sofortige Lieferung *f*	immediate delivery	livraison immédiate *f*	consegna immediata *f*	—
entrega parcial (Es)	Teillieferung *f*	partial delivery	livraison partielle *f*	fornitura parziale *f*	—
entregar (Es)	abliefern	hand over	livrer	consegnare	—
entrega urgente (Es)	Eilzustellung *f*	express delivery	remise par exprès *f*	consegna per espresso *f*	—
entrenamiento[1] (Es)	Einarbeitung *f*	vocational adjustment	entraînement *m*	periodo d'adattamento *m*	—
entrenamiento[2] (Es)	Trainee *m*	trainee	apprenti *m*	trainee *m*	—
entreposage[1] (F)	Lagerverwaltung *f*	stockkeeping	—	amministrazione del magazzino *f*	administración de almacén *f*
entreposage[2] (F)	Lagerhaltung *f*	stockkeeping	—	magazzinaggio *m*	almacenaje *m*
entreposage[3] (F)	Einlagerung *f*	storage	—	immagazzinamento *m*	almacenamiento *m*
entrepôt de distribution (F)	Auslieferungslager *n*	distribution centre	—	deposito di consegna *m*	almacén de entregas *m*
entrepreneur (E)	Unternehmer *m*	—	entrepreneur *m*	imprenditore *m*	empresario *m*
entrepreneur (F)	Unternehmer *m*	entrepreneur	—	imprenditore *m*	empresario *m*
entrepreneur débutant (F)	Jungunternehmer *m*	young businessman	—	imprenditore giovane *m*	joven empresario *m*

	D	E	F	I	Es
entrepreneurial culture (E)	Unternehmenskultur *f*	—	culture de l'entreprise *f*	cultura imprenditoriale *f*	cultura empresarial *f*
entrepreneurial income (E)	Unternehmerlohn *m*	—	rémunération de l'entrepreneur *f*	retribuzione dell'imprenditore *f*	remuneración del empresario *f*
entreprise[1] (F)	Firma *f*	company	—	impresa *f*	empresa *f*
entreprise[2] (F)	Unternehmen *n*	enterprise	—	impresa *f*	empresario *m*
entreprise agricole (F)	Agrarbetrieb *m*	agricultural enterprise	—	azienda agricola *f*	empresa agrícola *f*
entreprise concurrente (F)	Konkurrenz-unternehmen *n*	competitive undertaking	—	impresa concorrente *f*	empresa competitoria *f*
entreprise d'exploitation (F)	Betriebsgesellschaft *f*	operating company	—	società d'esercizio *f*	empresa de explotación *f*
entreprise d'utilité publique (F)	gemeinnütziges Unternehmen *n*	public institution	—	impresa di utilità pubblica *f*	empresa de beneficio común *f*
entreprise dirigeante (F)	herrschendes Unternehmen *n*	controlling company	—	impresa controllante *f*	empresa dominante *f*
entreprise fantôme (F)	Briefkastenfirma *f*	bubble company	—	società bucalettere *f*	empresa ficticia *f*
entreprise industrielle (F)	Industriebetrieb *m*	industrial enterprise	—	azienda industriale *f*	establecimiento industrial *m*
entreprise publique (F)	staatliche Betriebe *pl*	state-owned enterprises	—	aziende statali *f pl*	empresas públicas *f pl*
entreprises multinationales (F)	multinationale Unternehmen *n*	multinational enterprises	—	imprese multinazionali *f pl*	empresa multinacional *f*
entreprises publiques[1] (F)	öffentliche Betriebe *pl*	public sector industrial enterprises	—	aziende pubbliche *f pl*	empresa pública *f*
entreprises publiques[2] (F)	öffentliche Unternehmen *n*	public enterprise	—	imprese pubbliche *f pl*	empresa pública *f*
entretien (F)	Unterredung *f*	discussion	—	colloquio *m*	conversación *f*
entrevista (Es)	Interview *n*	interview	enquête *f*	intervista *f*	—
entro (I)	binnen	within	dans le délai de	—	en el término de
entro il termine convenuto (I)	fristgerecht	timely	dans les délais	—	dentro del plazo fijado
entry into the market (E)	Markteintritt *m*	—	entrée dans le marché *f*	apertura di mercato *f*	entrada en el mercado *f*
Entschädigung (D)	—	compensation/ indemnification	indemnité *f*	indennità *f*	indemnización *f*/pago de compensación *m*
Entsorgung (D)	—	waste disposal	dépollution *f*	smaltimento *m*	eliminación *f*
Entwicklung (D)	—	development	développement *m*	sviluppo *m*	desarrollo *m*
Entwicklungshilfe (D)	—	development aid	aide au développement *f*	aiuto ai paesi in via di sviluppo *m*	ayuda al desarrollo *f*
Entwicklungskosten (D)	—	development costs	coûts de développement *m pl*	costi di sviluppo *m pl*	gastos de desarrollo *m pl*
Entwurf (D)	—	draft	projet *m*	progetto *m*	proyecto *m*
envelope[1] (E)	Briefumschlag *m*	—	enveloppe de lettre *f*	busta *f*	sobre *m*
envelope[2] (E)	Kuvert *n*	—	enveloppe *f*	busta *f*	sobre *m*
enveloppe (F)	Kuvert *n*	envelope	—	busta *f*	sobre *m*
enveloppe de lettre (F)	Briefumschlag *m*	envelope	—	busta *f*	sobre *m*
en vigor (Es)	in Kraft	effective/in force	en vigueur	in vigore	—
en vigueur (F)	in Kraft	effective/in force	—	in vigore	en vigor
envío[1] (Es)	Zustellung *f*	delivery	remise *f*	notifica f/recapito *m*	—
envío[2] (Es)	Versand *m*	dispatch	expédition *f*	spedizione *f*	—
envío[3] (Es)	Sendung *f*	consignment	envoi *m*	spedizione *f*	—
envío con valor declarado (Es)	Wertsendung *f*	consignment with value declared	envoi avec valeur déclarée *m*	spedizione con valore dichiarato *f*	—
envío de mercancías (Es)	Warensendung *f*	consignment of goods	expédition de marchandises *f*	spedizione di merci *f*	—
envío de muestras (Es)	Mustersendung *f*	sample consignment	envoi d'échantillons *m*	spedizione di campioni *f*	—
envío de prueba (Es)	Probelieferung *f*	trial shipment	livraison à titre d'essai *f*	fornitura a titolo di prova *f*	—
envío incompleto (Es)	Minderlieferung *f*	short delivery	livraison en quantité inférieure *f*	fornitura ridotta *f*	—
envío para inspección (Es)	Ansichtssendung *f*	consignment on approval	envoi à condition *m*	campione per esame *m*	—

	D	E	F	I	Es
envío perdido (Es)	verlorengegangene Sendung *f*	lost shipment	envoi perdu *m*	spedizione andata persa *f*	—
envío postal colectivo (Es)	Postwurfsendung *f*	printed papers or samples of merchandise posted in bulk	envoi publicitaire collectif *f*	spedizione postale cumulativa di stampati *f*	—
environmental pollution (E)	Umweltverschmutzung *f*	—	pollution de l'environnement *f*	inquinamento dell'ambiente *m*	contaminación del medio ambiente *f*
environmentally aware (E)	umweltbewußt	—	conscient de la réalité écologique	con rispetto dell'ambiente	consciente del medio ambiente
envoi (F)	Sendung *f*	consignment	—	spedizione *f*	envío *m*
envoi à condition (F)	Ansichtssendung *f*	consignment on approval	—	campione per esame *m*	envío para inspección *m*
envoi avec valeur déclarée (F)	Wertsendung *f*	consignment with value declared	—	spedizione con valore dichiarato *f*	envío con valor declarado *m*
envoi d'échantillons (F)	Mustersendung *f*	sample consignment	—	spedizione di campioni *f*	envío de muestras *m*
envoi par groupage (F)	Sammelladung *f*	collective consignment	—	carico a collettame *m*	carga colectiva *f*
envoi perdu (F)	verlorengegangene	lost shipment Sendung *f*	—	spedizione andata persa *f*	envío perdido *m*
envoi publicitaire collectif (F)	Postwurfsendung *f*	printed papers or samples of merchandise posted in bulk	—	spedizione postale cumulativa di stampati *f*	envío postal colectivo *m*
eolian energy (E)	Windenergie *f*	—	énergie éolienne *f*	energia eolica *f*	energía eólica *f*
épargne (F)	Ersparnis *f*	savings	—	risparmio *m*	ahorro *m*
épargne forcée (F)	Zwangssparen *n*	compulsory saving	—	risparmio coatto *m*	ahorro forzoso *m*
équilibrage du budget (F)	Budgetausgleich *m*	balancing of the budget	—	pareggio di bilancio *m*	balance del presupuesto *m*
équilibre (F)	Gleichgewicht *n*	balance	—	equilibrio *m*	equilibrio *m*
equilibrio (Es)	Gleichgewicht *n*	balance	équilibre *m*	equilibrio *m*	—
equilibrio (I)	Gleichgewicht *n*	balance	équilibre *m*	—	equilibrio *m*
equilibrio della bilancia dei pagamenti (I)	Zahlungsbilanzgleichgewicht *n*	equilibrium of the balance of payments	balance des payements équilibrée *f*	—	balanza de pagos equilibrada *f*
equilibrium of the balance of payments (E)	Zahlungsbilanzgleichgewicht *n*	—	balance des payements équilibrée *f*	equilibrio della bilancia dei pagamenti *m*	balanza de pagos equilibrada *f*
equilibrium price (E)	Gleichgewichtspreis *m*	—	prix équilibré *m*	prezzo d'equilibrio *m*	precio de equilibrio *m*
équipe de nuit (F)	Nachtschicht *f*	night shift	—	turno notturno *m*	turno de noche *m*
équipe de vente (F)	Verkaufsstab *m*	sales staff	—	staff di venditori *m*	equipo de venta *m*
équipe[1] (F)	Team *n*	team	—	équipe *f*	equipo *m*
équipe[2] (F)	Mannschaft *f*	team/crew	—	équipe *f*/ equipaggio *m*	equipo *m*/ tripulación *f*
équipe[1] (I)	Mannschaft *f*	team/crew	équipe *f*/équipage *m*	—	equipo *m*/ tripulación *f*
équipe[2] (I)	Team *n*	team	équipe *f*	—	equipo *m*
equipo[1] (Es)	Mannschaft *f*	team/crew	équipe *f*/équipage *m*	équipe *f*/equipaggio *m*	—
equipo[2] (Es)	Team *n*	team	équipe *f*	équipe *f*	—
equipo de venta (Es)	Verkaufsstab *m*	sales staff	équipe de vente *f*	staff di venditori *m*	—
equity capital (E)	Eigenkapital *n*	—	capital propre *m*	capitale proprio *m*	capital propio *m*
equivalent (E)	Gegenwert *m*	—	contre-valeur *f*	controvalore *m*	contravalor *m*
Erben (D)	—	heirs	héritiers *m pl*	eredi *m pl*	heredero *m*
Erbengemeinschaft (D)	—	community of heirs	communaute d'héritiers *f*	comunità degli eredi *f*	comunidad sucesoria *f*
Erbschaft (D)	—	inheritance	héritage *m*	eredità *f*	herencia *f*
Erbschaftsteuer (D)	—	inheritance tax	impôt sur les successions *m*	imposta di successione *f*	impuesto sobre sucesiones *m*
Erbstreit (D)	—	dispute concerning an inheritance	action successorale *f*	causa ereditaria *f*	litigio hereditario *m*
Erdgas (D)	—	natural gas	gaz naturel *m*	gas naturale *m*	gas natural *m*
Erdöl (D)	—	mineral oil	pétrole *m*	petrolio *m*	crudo *m*
eredi (I)	Erben *pl*	heirs	héritiers *m pl*	—	heredero *m*
eredità (I)	Erbschaft *f*	inheritance	héritage *m*	—	herencia *f*

	D	E	F	I	Es
Erfolgskonto (D)	—	profit account	compte de résultats *m*	conto profitti *m*	cuenta de beneficios y pérdidas *f*
erfolgsorientiert (D)	—	success-oriented	orienté vers le succès	orientato al successo	orientado hacia el éxito
Erfüllung (D)	—	compliance	acquittement *m*	adempimento *m*	cumplimiento *m*
Ergebnis (D)	—	result	résultat *m*	risultato *m*	resultado *m*
erkennen (D)	—	recognize	reconnaître	riconoscere	reconocer
Erklärung (D)	—	explanation/ declaration	explication *f*/ déclaration *f*	spiegazione *f*/ dichiarazione *f*	explicación *f*/ declaración *f*
Erlaubnis (D)	—	permission	permission *f*	permesso *m*	permiso *m*
Erlös (D)	—	proceeds	produit des ventes *m*	ricavo *m*	beneficio *m*
ermäßigte Tarife (D)	—	reduced tariffs	tarifs réduits *m pl*	tariffe ridotte *f pl*	tarifas reducidas *f pl*
Ermäßigung (D)	—	reduction	réduction *f*	riduzione *f*	reducción *f*
Ernennung (D)	—	apointment	nomination *f*	nomina *f*	nombramiento *m*
Eröffnungsbeschluß (D)	—	order opening a trial	arrêt de mise en accusation *m*	decreto di citazione in giudizio *m*	acuerdo de apertura *m*
Eröffnungsbilanz (D)	—	opening balance sheet	bilan d'ouverture *m*	bilancio d'apertura *m*	balance inicial *m*
erreur d'addition (F)	Additionsfehler *m*	adding mistake	—	errore di addizione *m*	error de adición *m*
erreur de calcul (F)	Rechenfehler *m*	miscalculation	—	errore di calcolo *m*	error de cálculo *m*
erreur de comptabilité (F)	Buchungsfehler *m*	bookkeeping error	—	errore di contabilità *m*	error contable *m*
erreur de droit (F)	Rechtsirrtum *m*	mistake of law	—	errore di diritto *m*	error de derecho *m*
erreur de transcription (F)	Übertragungsfehler *m*	transcription error	—	errore di trascrizione *m*	error de transcripción *m*
error (Es)	Fehler *m*	mistake	faute *f*	errore *m*	—
error contable (Es)	Buchungsfehler *m*	bookkeeping error	erreur de comptabilité *f*	errore di contabilità *m*	—
error de adición (Es)	Additionsfehler *m*	adding mistake	erreur d'addition *f*	errore di addizione *m*	—
error de cálculo (Es)	Rechenfehler *m*	miscalculation	erreur de calcul *f*	errore di calcolo *m*	—
error de derecho (Es)	Rechtsirrtum *m*	mistake of law	erreur de droit *m*	errore di diritto *m*	—
error de transcripción (Es)	Übertragungsfehler *m*	transcription error	erreur de transcription *f*	errore di trascrizione *m*	—
errore (I)	Fehler *m*	mistake	faute *f*	—	error *m*
errore di addizione (I)	Additionsfehler *m*	adding mistake	erreur d'addition *f*	—	error de adición *m*
errore di calcolo (I)	Rechenfehler *m*	miscalculation	erreur de calcul *f*	—	error de cálculo *m*
errore di contabilità (I)	Buchungsfehler *m*	bookkeeping error	erreur de comptabilité *f*	—	error contable *m*
errore di diritto (I)	Rechtsirrtum *m*	mistake of law	erreur de droit *m*	—	error de derecho *m*
errore di trascrizione (I)	Übertragungsfehler *m*	transcription error	erreur de transcription *f*	—	error de transcripción *m*
errors excepted (E)	Irrtum vorbehalten	—	sauf erreur	salvo errore	salvo error
Ersatzkauf (D)	—	substitute purchase	achat de remplacement *m*	acquisto di compensazione *m*	compra de sustitución *f*
Ersatzlieferung (D)	—	substitute delivery	livraison de remplacement *f*	fornitura di compensazione *f*	entrega de reposición *f*
Ersatzteil (D)	—	spare part	pièce de rechange *f*	pezzo di ricambio *m*	pieza de recambio *f*
Ersparnis (D)	—	savings	épargne *f*	risparmio *m*	ahorro *m*
erstklassig (D)	—	first class	de première qualité	di prima categoria	de primera calidad
Erstversicherer (D)	—	direct insurer	assureur direct *m*	assicuratore diretto *m*	primer asegurador *m*
Ertrag (D)	—	income/earnings	rendement *m*/ revenu *m*	reddito *m*/ rendimento *m*	rendimiento *m*/renta *f*
Ertragsbeteiligung (D)	—	participation in profits	participation aux bénéfices *f*	partecipazione al reddito *f*	participación en los resultados *f*
Ertragsfaktor (D)	—	income factor	facteur productif *m*	fattore reddito *m*	factor de beneficio *m*
Ertragskraft (D)	—	earning capacity	force productive *f*	redditività *f*	rentabilidad *f*
Ertragslage (D)	—	earning situation	niveau du rendement *m*	situazione economica *f*	situación del beneficio *f*
Ertragsrechnung (D)	—	profit and loss account	solde net de l'exploitation *m*	conto economico *m*	cuenta de ganancias *f pl*

	D	E	F	I	Es
Ertragsteuer (D)	—	tax on income	impôt assis sur le produit *m*	imposta cedolare *f*/ imposta sul reddito *f*	impuesto sobre beneficios *m*
Ertragswert (D)	—	capitalized value	valeur d'une chose *m*/mesurée à son rendement *f*	valore del reddito *m*	valor del rendimiento *m*
Erwerbsperson (D)	—	gainfully employed person	personne active *f*	persona attiva *f*	persona en activo *f*
Erwerbsquote (D)	—	activity rate	proportion de la population active *f*	quota della popolazione attiva *f*	proporción de la población activa *f*
erwerbstätig (D)	—	gainfully employed	actif	attivo	activo
Erwerbstätiger (D)	—	gainfully employed person	personne ayant un emploi *f*	persona attiva *f*	persona activa *f*
Erwerbsunfähigkeit (D)	—	disability for work	incapacité d'exercer toute activité professionnelle *f*	inabilità al lavoro *f*	incapacidad profesional *f*
Erzeuger (D)	—	manufacturer	producteur *m*	produttore *m*	productor *m*
Erzeugerpreis (D)	—	producer price	prix à la production *m*	prezzo di fabbrica *m*	precio de producción *m*
Erzeugerpreisindex (D)	—	producer price index	indice des prix à la production *m*	indice dei prezzi di fabbrica *m*	índice de precios de producción *m*
Erzeugnis (D)	—	product	produit *m*	prodotto *m*	producto *m*
esame (I)	Examen *n*	examination	examen *m*	—	examen *m*
escalonado (Es)	gestaffelt	graduated	progressif	differenziato	—
escaparate (Es)	Schaufenster *n*	shop-window	vitrine *f*	vetrina *f*	—
escape clause (E)	Rücktrittsklausel *f*	—	clause de résolution du contrat *f*	clausola di recesso *f*	cláusula de arrepentimiento *f*
escasez (Es)	Knappheit *f*	shortage	rareté *f*	scarsità *f*	—
escasez de capacidad (Es)	Kapazitätsengpaß *m*	bottleneck in capacity	goulot d'étranglement de capacité *m*	strettoia di capacità *f*	—
escasez de materias primas (Es)	Rohstoffknappheit *f*	raw materials shortage	pénurie de matières premières *f*	scarsità di materie prime *f*	—
escasez de mercancías (Es)	Warenknappheit *f*	shortage of goods	pénurie de marchandises *f*	scarsità di merci *f*	—
escaso (Es)	knapp	scarce	rare	scarso	—
escompte[1] (F)	Diskont *m*	discount	—	sconto *m*	descuento *m*
escompte[2] (F)	Skonto *n*	discount	—	sconto *m*	descuento *m*
escompte de caisse (F)	Barzahlungskonto *n*	cash discount	—	sconto per pagamento in contanti *m*	descuento de pago al contado *m*
escompte de suscription (F)	Vorbestellrabatt *m*	discount on advance orders	—	ribasso per ordinazioni anticipate *m*	descuento de suscripción *m*
escritorio (Es)	Schreibtisch *m*	desk	bureau *m*	scrivania *f*	—
escuela (Es)	Schule *f*	school	école *f*	scuola *f*	—
esecuzione[1] (I)	Vollstreckung *f*	enforcement	exécution *f*	—	ejecución *f*
esecuzione[2] (I)	Durchführung *f*	realization	réalisation *f*	—	ejecución *m*
esecuzione[3] (I)	Abwicklung *f*	settlement/liquidation	exécution *f*/ liquidation *f*	—	ejecución *f*
esecuzione forzata (I)	Zwangsvollstreckung *f*	judicial execution	exécution forcée *f*	—	ejecución forzosa *f*
esecuzione ordini[1] (I)	Auftragsabwicklung *f*	execution of the order	exécution d'une commande *f*	—	ejecución de pedidos *f*
esecuzione ordini[2] (I)	Auftragsbearbeitung *f*	order processing	réalisation d'une commande *f*	—	tramitación de pedidos *f*
esente da contributi (I)	abgabenfrei	tax-free/duty-free	exempt de taxes	—	exento de impuestos/ exento de derechos
esente da imposte (I)	steuerfrei	tax-free	dispensé de l'impôt	—	libre de impuesto
esente da vizi (I)	mangelfrei	free of defects	sans défaut	—	sin vicios
esercizio (I)	Wirtschaftsjahr *n*	business year	exercice comptable *m*	—	ejercicio *m*
esercizio commerciale (I)	Geschäftsjahr *n*	financial year	exercice commercial *m*	—	ejercicio *m*
esfera de influencia (Es)	Einflußbereich *m*	sphere of influence	sphère d'influence *f*	sfera d'influenza *f*	—
esistenza (I)	Existenz *f*	existence	existence *f*	—	existencia *f*
espace à bâtir (F)	Bauland *n*	building land	—	area edificabile *f*	terreno edificable *m*

	D	E	F	I	Es
espansione (I)	Expansion *f*	expansion	expansion *f*	—	expansión *f*
espansivo (I)	expansiv	expansive	tendant à l'expansion	—	expansivo
espanso (I)	Schaumstoff *m*	foam material	mousse synthétique *f*	—	espumaso plástico *m*
espèces en caisse (F)	Bargeldbestand *m*	cash in hand	—	denaro contante in cassa *m*	saldo en efectivo *m*
especialización (Es)	Spezialisierung *f*	specialization	spécialisation *f*	specializzazione *f*	—
especie (Es)	Sorte *f*	variety/foreign notes and coins	genre *m*/devises *f pl*	categoria *f*	—
especificación (Es)	Spezifikation *f*	specification	spécification *f*	specificazione *f*	—
especulación (Es)	Spekulation *f*	speculation	spéculation *f*	speculazione *f*	—
espérance de vie (F)	Lebenserwartung *f*	expectation of life	—	durata probabile della vita *f*	expectativa de vida *f*
esperto dei rifiuti (I)	Abfallexperte *m*	expert on waste products	expert en déchets *m*	—	experto de productos residuales *m*
esperto di pubblicità (I)	Werbefachmann *m*	advertising expert	technicien publicitaire *m*	—	perito publicitario *m*
esperto in materia economica (I)	Wirtschaftsexperte *m*	economic expert	expert économique *m*	—	economista *m*
esperto in materia monetaria (I)	Währungsexperte *m*	monetary expert	expert monétaire *m*	—	experto en materia monetaria *m*
espionage (E)	Spionage *f*	—	espionnage *m*	spionaggio *m*	espionaje *m*
espionaje (Es)	Spionage *f*	espionage	espionnage *m*	spionaggio *m*	—
espionaje industrial[1] (Es)	Werksspionage *f*	industrial espionage	espionnage industriel *m*	spionaggio aziendale *m*	—
espionaje industrial[2] (Es)	Industriespionage *f*	industrial espionage	espionnage industriel *m*	spionaggio industriale *m*	—
espionnage (F)	Spionage *f*	espionage	—	spionaggio *m*	espionaje *m*
espionnage industriel[1] (F)	Werksspionage *f*	industrial espionage	—	spionaggio aziendale *m*	espionaje industrial *m*
espionnage industriel[2] (F)	Industriespionage *f*	industrial espionage	—	spionaggio industriale *m*	espionaje industrial *m*
espiral inflacionista (Es)	Inflationsspirale *f*	inflationary spiral	spirale inflationniste *f*	spirale inflazionistica *f*	—
espiral salarios-precios (Es)	Lohn-Preis-Spirale *f*	wage-price spiral	course des prix et des salaires *f*	spirale prezzi-salari *f*	—
esplosione (I)	Explosion *f*	explosion	explosion *f*	—	explosión *f*
esplosione dei costi (I)	Kostenexplosion *f*	cost escalation	explosion des coûts *f*	—	incremento desmesurado de los costes *m*
esportazione (I)	Export *m*	export	exportation *f*	—	exportación *f*
esportazione agricola (I)	Agrarexport *m*	farm exports	exportation de produits agricoles *f*	—	exportación agrícola *f*
esportazione di capitale (I)	Kapitalexport *m*	capital export	exportation de capitaux *f*	—	exportación de capital *f*
esportazioni (I)	Exporthandel *m*	export trade	commerce d'exportation *m*	—	comercio de exportación *m*
espositore (I)	Aussteller *m*	exhibitor/issuer/ drawer	exposant *m*/ émetteur *m*/tireur *m*	—	expositor *m*/ emisor *m*/librador *m*
esposizione (I)	Ausstellung *f*	exhibition/making out/issue	exposition *f*/ émission *f*	—	exhibición *f*/ facturación *f*
esposizione specializzata (I)	Fachausstellung *f*	trade fair	exposition spécialisée *f*	—	exposición especializada *f*
espropriazione (I)	Enteignung *f*	expropriation	expropriation *f*	—	expropiación *f*
espumoso plástico (Es)	Schaumstoff *m*	foam material	mousse synthétique *f*	espanso *m*	—
essayer (F)	probieren	try	—	provare	probar
essence (F)	Benzin *n*	petrol	—	benzina *f*	gasolina *f*
essere degno di credito (I)	Kreditwürdigkeit *f*	creditworthiness	solvabilité *f*	—	crédito *m*
estabilidad (Es)	Stabilität *f*	stability	stabilité *f*	stabilità *f*	—
estabilidad de precios (Es)	Preisstabilität *f*	stability of prices	stabilité des prix *f*	stabilità dei prezzi *f*	—
estabilidad monetaria (Es)	Geldwertstabilität *f*	stability of the value of money	stabilité monétaire *f*	stabilità monetaria *f*	—
estabilización (Es)	Stabilisierung *f*	stabilization	stabilisation *f*	stabilizzazione *f*	—

	D	E	F	I	Es
establecimiento del presupuesto (Es)	Budgetierung *f*	budgeting	établissement du budget *m*	compilazione del bilancio *f*	—
establecimiento industrial (Es)	Industriebetrieb *m*	industrial enterprise	entreprise industrielle *f*	azienda industriale *f*	—
establishment (E)	Niederlassung *f*	—	succursale *f*	succursale *f*	sucursal *f*
estación de destino (Es)	Bestimmungs-bahnhof *m*	station of destination	gare destinataire *f*	stazione di destinazione *f*	—
estación satélite (Es)	Satellitenstation *f*	space station	station de satellite *f*	stazione satellite *f*	—
estadías (Es)	Liegetage *pl*	lay days	staries *f pl*	stallie *f pl*	—
estadística (Es)	Statistik *f*	statistics	statistique *f*	statistica *f*	—
estadística agrícola (Es)	Agrarstatistik *f*	agricultural statistics	statistique agricole *f*	statistica agraria *f*	—
estadística de la empresa (Es)	Betriebsstatistik *f*	operational statistics	statistique commerciale et industrielle *f*	statistica aziendale *f*	—
estadística de población (Es)	Bevölkerungs-statistik *f*	population statistics	statistique démographique *f*	statistica demografica *f*	—
estadística de ventas (Es)	Absatzstatistik *f*	sales statistics	statistique de la vente *f*	statistica delle vendite *f*	—
estadística del ramo (Es)	Branchenstatistik *f*	trade statistics	statistique sur les différentes branches économiques *f*	statistica di categoria *f*	—
estadística económica (Es)	Wirtschaftsstatistik *f*	housekeeping account	statistique économique *f*	statistica economica *f*	—
estado (Es)	Staat *m*	state	Etat *m*	stato *m*	—
estado agrario (Es)	Agrarstaat *m*	agricultural state	état agricole *m*	paese agrario *m*	—
estado de bienestar (Es)	Wohlfahrtsstaat *m*	welfare state	Etat social *m*	stato assistenziale *m*	—
estado del mercado (Es)	Marktsituation *f*	market situation	situation du marché *f*	situazione di mercato *f*	—
Estado social (Es)	Sozialstaat *m*	social state based on the rule of law	Etat social *m*	stato sociale *m*	—
estancamiento (Es)	Stagnation *f*	stagnation	stagnation *f*	stagnazione *f*	—
estándar (Es)	Standard *m*	standard	standard *m*	standard *m*	—
estandardizado (Es)	standardisiert	standardized	standardisé	standardizzato	—
estanflación (Es)	Stagflation *f*	stagflation	stagflation *f*	stagflazione *f*	—
estar pendiente (Es)	anstehen	be due	être échnu	essere scaduto	—
estatal (Es)	staatlich	state	de l'Etat	statale	—
estate agent (E)	Immobilienmakler *m*	—	courtier en affaires immoblières *m*	agente immobiliare *m*	agente de inmuebles *m*
estatuto (Es)	Satzung *f*	statutes	statut *m*	statuto *m*	—
esterno (I)	extern	external	extérieur	—	externo
estilo de compra (Es)	Käuferstil *m*	style of the purchaser	style des acheteurs *m*	stile dell'acquirente *m*	—
estimación (Es)	Schätzwert *m*	estimated value	valeur d'estimation *f*	valore stimato *m*	—
estimate (E)	Voranschlag *m*	—	devis *m*	preventivo *m*	presupuesto *m*
estimated value[1] (E)	Schätzwert *m*	—	valeur d'estimation *f*	valore stimato *m*	estimación *f*
estimated value[2] (E)	Taxwert *m*	—	valeur de taxation *f*	valore stimato *m*	valor de tasación *m*
estimate of cost (E)	Kostenvoranschlag *m*	—	devis estimatif des frais *m*	preventivo dei costi *m*	presupuesto de coste *m*
estimation of cost (E)	Vorkalkulation *f*	—	calcul des coûts a priori *m*	calcolo preventivo *m*	cálculo provisional *m*
estímulo a la inversión (Es)	Investitions-förderung *f*	investment promotion	promotion de l'investissement	promozione degli investimenti *f*	—
estrategia (Es)	Strategie *f*	strategy	stratégie *f*	strategia *f*	—
estrategia de personal (Es)	Personalstrategie *f*	personnel strategy	stratégie en matière de personnel *f*	strategia occupazionale *f*	—
estrategia de ventas (Es)	Absatzstrategie *f*	sales strategy	stratégie de vente *f*	strategia di vendita *f*	—
estrategia empresarial (Es)	Unternehmens-strategie *f*	corporate strategy	stratégie de l'entreprise *f*	strategia imprenditoriale *f*	—
estratégico (Es)	strategisch	strategic	stratégique	strategico	—
estratto conto (I)	Kontoauszug *m*	statement of account	extrait de compte *m*	—	extracto de cuenta *m*
estrés (Es)	Stress *m*	stress	stress *m*	stress *m*	—

	D	E	F	I	Es
estructura (Es)	Struktur *f*	structure	structure *f*	struttura *f*	—
estructura agraria (Es)	Agrarstruktur *f*	agricultural structure	structure agraire *f*	struttura agraria *f*	—
estructuración del anuncio (Es)	Anzeigengestaltung *f*	lay-out of an advertisement	arrangement de l'annonce *m*	tipo d'inserzione *m*	—
estructuración del texto (Es)	Textgestaltung *f*	text configuration	structure du texte *f*	redazione del testo *f*	—
estructura de distribución (Es)	Vertriebsstruktur *f*	structure of distribution	structure de distribution *f*	struttura della distribuzione *f*	—
estructura del consumo (Es)	Konsumstruktur *f*	consumption structure	structure de consommation	struttura del consumo *f*	—
estructura del ramo (Es)	Branchenstruktur *f*	trade structure	structure de la branche *f*	struttura di categoria *f*	—
estructura demográfica (Es)	Bevölkerungs-struktur *f*	population structure	structure démographique *f*	struttura demografica *f*	—
estructura económica (Es)	Wirtschaftsstruktur *f*	economic structure	structure économique *f*	struttura economica *f*	—
estructura territorial (Es)	Raumstruktur *f*	spatial structure	structure des espaces *f*	struttura territoriale *f*	—
estudio del mercado[1] (Es)	Marktforschung *f*	market research	étude de marché *f*	ricerca di mercato *f*	—
estudio del mercado[2] (Es)	Marktuntersuchung *f*	market survey	étude du marché *f*	analisi di mercato *f*	—
estudio del mercado empírico (Es)	empirische Marktforschung *f*	empirical market research	étude de marché empirique *f*	ricerca di mercato empirica *f*	—
estudio de tiempo (Es)	Zeitstudie *f*	time study	étude des temps *f*	analisi sul tempo impiegato *f*	—
établissement de crédit (F)	Kreditinstitut *n*	credit institution	—	istituto di credito *m*	instituto de crédito *m*
établissement du budget (F)	Budgetierung *f*	budgeting	—	compilazione del bilancio *f*	establecimiento del presupuesto *m*
établissement d'une facture (F)	Rechnungsstellung *f*	invoicing	—	fatturazione *f*	facturación *f*
établissement en régie (F)	Regiebetrieb *m*	publicly owned enterprise	—	gestione in economia *f*	empresa estatal *f*
établissement industriel (F)	gewerblicher Betrieb *m*	industrial undertaking	—	azienda commerciale, azienda industriale *f*	empresa industrial *f*
établissement secondaire (F)	Zweigbetrieb *m*	branch business	—	filiale *f*	sucursal *f*
étalage (F)	Auslage *f*	display	—	vetrina *f*	vitrina *f*
étalon or (F)	Goldstandard *m*	gold standard	—	gold standard *m*	patrón-oro *m*
Etat (D)	—	budget	budget *m*	bilancio *m*	presupuesto *m*
état[1] (F)	Status *m*	status	—	stato *m*	status *m*
état[2] (F)	Staat *m*	state	—	stato *m*	estado *m*
état agricole (F)	Agrarstaat *m*	agricultural state	—	paese agrario *m*	estado agrario *m*
état social[1] (F)	Sozialstaat *m*	social state based on the rule of law	—	stato sociale *m*	estado social *m*
état social[2] (F)	Wohlfahrtsstaat *m*	welfare state	—	stato assistenziale *m*	estado de bienestar *m*
eticchetta adesiva (I)	Aufkleber *m*	sticker	étiquette *f*	—	pegatina *f*
etichetta (I)	Etikett *n*	label	étiquette *f*	—	etiqueta *f*
Etikett (D)	—	label	étiquette *f*	etichetta *f*	etiqueta *f*
etiqueta (Es)	Etikett *n*	label	étiquette *f*	etichetta *f*	—
étiquette[1] (F)	Etikett *n*	label	—	etichetta *f*	etiqueta *f*
étiquette[2] (F)	Aufkleber *m*	sticker	—	eticchetta adesiva *f*	pegatina *f*
étranger (F)	Ausländer *m*	foreigner	—	straniero *m*	extranjero *m*
être échu (F)	anstehen	be due	—	essere scaduto	estar pendiente
étude (F)	Untersuchung *f*	examination	—	indagine *f*	inspección *f*
étude de marché empirique (F)	empirische Marktforschung *f*	empirical market research	—	ricerca di mercato empirica *f*	estudio del mercado empírico *m*
étude de marché (F)	Marktbeobachtung *f*	observation of markets	—	sondaggio del mercato *m*	observación del mercado *f*
étude des temps (F)	Zeitstudie *f*	time study	—	analisi sul tempo impiegato *f*	estudio de tiempo *m*

	D	E	F	I	Es
étude du marché (F)	Marktuntersuchung *f*	market survey	—	analisi di mercato *f*	estudio del mercado *m*
euroassegno (I)	Euroscheck *m*	Eurocheque	eurochèque *m*	—	eurocheque *m*
eurobon (F)	Eurobond *m*	Eurobond	—	eurobond *m*	euroemisión *f*
Eurobond (D)	—	Eurobond	eurobon *m*	eurobond *m*	euroemisión *f*
Eurobond (E)	Eurobond *m*	—	eurobon *m*	eurobond *m*	euroemisión *f*
eurobond (I)	Eurobond *m*	Eurobond	eurobon *m*	—	euroemisión *f*
Eurobrand (E)	Euro-Markenzeichen *n*	—	euromarque *f*	euromarchio *m*	euromarca *f*
Eurocheque (E)	Euroscheck *m*	—	eurochèque *m*	euroassegno *m*	eurocheque *m*
eurocheque (Es)	Euroscheck *m*	Eurocheque	eurochèque *m*	euroassegno *m*	—
eurochèque (F)	Euroscheck *m*	Eurocheque	—	euroassegno *m*	eurocheque *m*
Eurocredit (E)	Euro-Kredit *m*	—	eurocrédit *m*	eurocredito *m*	eurocrédito *m*
eurocrédit (F)	Euro-Kredit *m*	Eurocredit	—	eurocredito *m*	eurocrédito *m*
eurocrédito (Es)	Euro-Kredit *m*	Eurocredit	eurocrédit *m*	eurocredito *m*	—
eurocredito (I)	Euro-Kredit *m*	Eurocredit	eurocrédit *m*	—	eurocrédito *m*
Eurocurrency (E)	Eurogeld *n*	—	eurodevises *f pl*	euromoneta *f*	eurodinero *m*
eurodevises (F)	Eurogeld *n*	Eurocurrency	—	euromoneta *f*	eurodinero *m*
eurodinero (Es)	Eurogeld *n*	Eurocurrency	eurodevises *f pl*	euromoneta *f*	—
eurodólar (Es)	Euro-Dollar *m*	Eurodollar	eurodollar *m*	eurodollaro *m*	—
Euro-Dollar (D)	—	Eurodollar	eurodollar *m*	eurodollaro *m*	eurodólar *m*
Eurodollar (E)	Euro-Dollar *m*	—	eurodollar *m*	eurodollaro *m*	eurodólar *m*
eurodollar (F)	Euro-Dollar *m*	Eurodollar	—	eurodollaro *m*	eurodólar *m*
eurodollaro (I)	Euro-Dollar *m*	Eurodollar	eurodollar *m*	—	eurodólar *m*
euroemisión (Es)	Eurobond *m*	Eurobond	eurobon *m*	eurobond *m*	—
Eurogeld (D)	—	Eurocurrency	eurodevises *f pl*	euromoneta *f*	eurodinero *m*
Euro-Kredit (D)	—	Eurocredit	eurocrédit *m*	eurocredito *m*	eurocrédito *m*
euromarca (Es)	Euro-Markenzeichen *n*	Eurobrand	euromarque *f*	euromarchio *m*	—
euromarché (F)	Euromarkt *m*	Euromarket	—	euromercato *m*	euromercado *m*
euromarchio (I)	Euro-Markenzeichen *n*	Eurobrand	euromarque *f*	—	euromarca *f*
Euro-Markenzeichen (D)	—	Eurobrand	euromarque *f*	euromarchio *m*	euromarca *f*
Euromarket (E)	Euromarkt *m*	—	euromarché *m*	euromercato *m*	euromercado *m*
Euromarkt (D)	—	Euromarket	euromarché *m*	euromercato *m*	euromercado *m*
euromarque (F)	Euro-Markenzeichen *n*	Eurobrand	—	euromarchio *m*	euromarca *f*
euromercado (Es)	Euromarkt *m*	Euromarket	euromarché *m*	euromercato *m*	—
euromercato (I)	Euromarkt *m*	Euromarket	euromarché *m*	—	euromercado *m*
euromoneta (I)	Eurogeld *n*	Eurocurrency	eurodevises *f pl*	—	eurodinero *m*
Euronorm (D)	—	Eurostandard	euronorme *f*	euronorma *f*	euronorma *f*
euronorma (Es)	Euronorm *f*	Eurostandard	euronorme *f*	euronorma *f*	—
euronorma (I)	Euronorm *f*	Eurostandard	euronorme *f*	—	euronorma *f*
euronorme (F)	Euronorm *f*	Eurostandard	—	euronorma *f*	euronorma *f*
Europäische Gemeinschaft (D)	—	European Community	Communauté Européenne *f*	Comunità Europea *f*	Comunidad Europea *f*
Europäischer Gerichtshof (D)	—	European Court	Cour de Justice Européenne *f*	Corte di Giustizia Europea *f*	Tribunal de Justicia de las Comunidades Europeas *m*
Europäischer-Binnenmarkt (D)	—	Internal Market of the European Community	Marché Intérieur de la Communauté Européenne *m*	mercato unico *m*	Mercado Unico *m*
Europäisches Parlament (D)	—	European Parliament	Parlement européen *m*	Parlamento Europeo *m*	Parlamento Europeo *m*
Europäisches Patentamt (D)	—	European Patent Office	Office Européen de Brevets *f*	Ufficio Europeo Brevetti *m*	Oficina Europea de Patentes *f*
Europäische Währungseinheit (D)	—	European Currency Unit	unité de compte européenne *f*	unità monetaria europea *f*	unidad monetaria europea *f*

	D	E	F	I	Es
Europäische Zahlungsunion (D)	—	European Payments Union	union européenne des payements *f*	Unione Europea dei Pagamenti *f*	Unión Europea de Pagos *f*
Europäisches Währungssystem (D)	—	European Monetary System	Système Monétaire Européen *m*	Sistema Monetario Europeo *m*	Sistema Monetario Europeo *m*
europaleta (Es)	Euro-Palette *f*	Europallet	europalette *f*	europaletta *f*	—
europaletta (I)	Euro-Palette *f*	Europallet	europalette *f*	—	europaleta *f*
Euro-Palette (D)	—	Europallet	europalette *f*	europaletta *f*	europaleta *f*
europalette (F)	Euro-Palette *f*	Europallet	—	europaletta *f*	europaleta *f*
Europallet (E)	Euro-Palette *f*	—	europalette *f*	europaletta *f*	europaleta *f*
Europapatent (D)	—	European patent	brevet européen *m*	brevetto europeo *m*	patente europea *f*
European Communities (E)	Europäische Gemeinschaft *f*	—	Communauté Européenne *f*	Comunità Europea *f*	Comunidad Europea *f*
European Court (E)	Europäischer Gerichtshof *m*	—	Cour de Justice Européenne *f*	Corte di Giustizia Europea *f*	Tribunal de Justicia de las Comunidades Europeas *m*
European Currency Unit (E)	Europäische Währungseinheit *f*	—	unité de compte européenne *f*	unità monetaria europea *f*	unidad monetaria europea *f*
European Monetary System (E)	Europäisches Währungssystem *n*	—	Système Monétaire Européen *m*	Sistema Monetario Europeo *m*	Sistema Monetario Europeo *m*
European Parliament (E)	Europäisches Parlament *n*	—	Parlement européen *m*	Parlamento Europeo *m*	Parlamento Europeo *m*
European patent (E)	Europapatent *n*	—	brevet européen *m*	brevetto europeo *m*	patente europea *f*
European Patent Office (E)	Europäisches Patentamt *n*	—	Office Européen de Brevets *f*	Ufficio Europeo Brevetti *m*	Oficina Europea de Patentes *f*
European Payments Union (E)	Europäische Zahlungsunion *f*	—	union européenne des payements *f*	Unione Europea dei Pagamenti *f*	Unión Europea de Pagos *f*
Euroscheck (D)	—	Eurocheque	eurochèque *m*	euroassegno *m*	eurocheque *m*
Eurostandard (E)	Euronorm *f*	—	euronorme *f*	euronorma *f*	euronorma *f*
evacuación de residuos (Es)	Abfallbeseitigung *f*	waste disposal	élimination de déchets *f*	smaltimento dei rifiuti *m*	—
evacuation (E)	Räumung *f*	—	évacuation *f*	evacuazione *f*	desalojamiento *m*
évacuation (F)	Räumung *f*	evacuation	—	evacuazione *f*	desalojamiento *m*
evacuazione (I)	Räumung *f*	evacuation	évacuation *f*	—	desalojamiento *m*
evaluación aproximativa (Es)	vorsichtige Schätzung *f*	conservative estimate	évaluation approximative *f*	valutazione approssimativa *f*	—
evaluación del trabajo (Es)	Arbeitsbewertung *f*	job evaluation	qualification du travail *f*	valutazione del lavoro *f*	—
évaluation approximative (F)	vorsichtige Schätzung *f*	conservative estimate	—	valutazione approssimativa *f*	evaluación aproximativa *f*
évasion des capitaux (F)	Kapitalflucht *f*	flight of capital	—	fuga dei capitali *f*	fuga de capital *f*
evasione (I)	Hinterziehung *f*	evasion of taxes	fraude fiscale *f*	—	defraudación *f*
evasione fiscale (I)	Steuerhinterziehung *f*	tax evasion	dissimulation en matière fiscale *f*	—	defraudación fiscal *f*
evasion of taxes (E)	Hinterziehung *f*	—	fraude fiscale *f*	evasione *f*	defraudación *f*
event insured against (E)	Versicherungsfall *m*	—	sinistre *m*	caso di sinistro *m*	situación de siniestro *f*
evolución de la coyuntura (Es)	Konjunktur-entwicklung *f*	economic trend	évolution de la conjoncture *f*	sviluppo congiunturale *m*	—
evolución del volumen de facturación (Es)	Umsatzentwicklung *f*	turnover trend	évolution du chiffre d'affaires *f*	sviluppo del fatturato *m*	—
evolución económica (Es)	Wirtschaftsverlauf *m*	course of the economic evolution	évolution économique *f*	andamento dell'economia *m*	—
évolution de la conjoncture (F)	Konjunktur-entwicklung *f*	economic trend	—	sviluppo congiunturale *m*	evolución de la coyuntura *f*
évolution du chiffre d'affaires (F)	Umsatzentwicklung *f*	turnover trend	—	sviluppo del fatturato *m*	evolución del volumen de facturación *f*
évolution économique (F)	Wirtschaftsverlauf *m*	course of the economic evolution	—	andamento dell'economia *m*	evolución económica *f*
Examen (D)	—	examination	examen *m*	esame *m*	examen *m*
examen (Es)	Examen *n*	examination	examen *m*	esame *m*	—
examen (F)	Examen *n*	examination	—	esame *m*	examen *m*

	D	E	F	I	Es
examinación del mercado (Es)	Markttest *m*	market test	test du marché *m*	test di mercato *m*	—
examination[1] (E)	Untersuchung *f*	—	étude *f*	indagine *f*	inspección *f*
examination[2] (E)	Examen *n*	—	examen *m*	esame *m*	examen *m*
excédent[1] (F)	schwarze Zahlen *pl*	surplus	—	conti in nero *m pl*	superávit *m*
excédent[2] (F)	Überschuß *m*	excess	—	eccedenza *f*	excedente *m*
excédent annuel (F)	Jahresüberschuß *m*	annual surplus	—	surplus dell'anno *m*	superávit del ejercicio *m*
excédent commercial (F)	Handelsüberschuß *m*	trade surplus	—	eccedenza commerciale *f*	excedente comercial *m*
excédent de liquidité (F)	Liquiditätsüberschuß *m*	excess liquidity	—	eccedenza di liquidità *f*	exceso de liquidez *m*
excédent d'exportation (F)	Exportüberschuß *m*	export surplus	—	eccedenza delle esportazioni *f*	excedente de exportación *m*
excedente (Es)	Überschuß *m*	excess	excédent *m*	eccedenza *f*	—
excedente comercial (Es)	Handelsüberschuß *m*	trade surplus	excédent commercial *m*	eccedenza commerciale *f*	—
excedente de exportación (Es)	Exportüberschuß *m*	export surplus	excédent d'exportation *m*	eccedenza delle esportazioni *f*	—
excedentes agrícolas (Es)	Agrarüberschüsse *pl*	agricultural surpluses	excédents agricoles *m pl*	eccedenze agricole *f pl*	—
excédents agricoles (F)	Agrarüberschüsse *pl*	agricultural surpluses	—	eccedenze agricole *f pl*	excedentes agrícolas *m pl*
excès de l'offre (F)	Angebotsüberhang *m*	excess of supply over demand	—	eccedenza d'offerta *f*	exceso de oferta *m*
excesivo (Es)	übermäßig	excessive	excessif	eccessivo	—
exceso (Es)	Mehrlieferung *f*	additional delivery	livraison supplémentaire *f*	fornitura supplementare *f*	—
exceso de deudas (Es)	Überschuldung *f*	excessive indebtedness	surendettement *m*	indebitamento eccessivo *m*	—
exceso de empleo (Es)	Überbeschäftigung *f*	overcharge	surchargement *m*	occupazione eccedente *f*	—
exceso de liquidez (Es)	Liquiditätsüberschuß *m*	excess liquidity	excédent de liquidité *m*	eccedenza di liquidità *f*	—
exceso de oferta (Es)	Angebotsüberhang *m*	excess of supply over demand	excès de l'offre *m*	eccedenza d'offerta *f*	—
excess (E)	Überschuß *m*	—	excédent *m*	eccedenza *f*	excedente *m*
excessif (F)	übermäßig	excessive	—	eccessivo	excesivo
excessive (E)	übermäßig	—	excessif	eccessivo	excesivo
excessive indebtedness (E)	Überschuldung *f*	—	surendettement *m*	indebitamento eccessivo *m*	exceso de deudas *m*
excess liquidity (E)	Liquiditätsüberschuß *m*	—	excédent de liquidité *m*	eccedenza di liquidità *f*	exceso de liquidez *m*
excess of supply over demand (E)	Angebotsüberhang *m*	—	excès de l'offre *m*	eccedenza d'offerta *f*	exceso de oferta *m*
excess weight (E)	Übergewicht *n*	—	surcharge *f*	sovrappeso *m*	sobrepreso *m*
exchange[1] (E)	Tausch *m*	—	échange *m*/troc *m*	scambio *m*/baratto *m*	cambio *m*/ trueque *m*
exchange[2] (E)	Umtausch *m*	—	échange *m*	cambio *m*	cambio *m*/ conversión *f*
exchange arbitrage (E)	Devisenarbitrage *f*	—	arbitrage sur les devises *m*	arbitraggio valutario *m*	arbitraje de divisas *m*
exchange of goods (E)	Warenaustausch *m*	—	échanges commerciaux *m pl*	scambio merci *m*	intercambio de mercancías *m*
exchange rate[1] (E)	Kurs *m*	—	cours (du change) *m*	corso *m*/cambio *m*	cotización *f*/ tipo de cambio *m*
exchange rate[2] (E)	Wechselkurs *m*	—	cours du change *m*	cambio *m*	tipo de cambio *m*
exchangeable container (E)	Wechselbehälter *m*	—	conteneur interchangeable *m*	contenitore sostituibile *m*	contenedores intercambiables *m pl*
exclave aduanero (Es)	Zollausschluß *m*	territory inside political but outside customs frontier	territoire considéré hors frontière douanière nationale *m*	zona franca *f*	—
exclusive distribution (E)	Alleinvertrieb *m*	—	vente exclusive *f*	vendita esclusiva *f*	distribución exclusiva *f*

	D	E	F	I	Es
exclusivité territoriale (F)	Gebietsschutz *m*	territory protection	—	tutela territoriale *f*	protección territorial *f*
exécution[1] (F)	Abwicklung *f*	settlement/liquidation	—	esecuzione *f*	ejecución *f*
exécution[2] (F)	Vollstreckung *f*	enforcement	—	esecuzione *f*	ejecución *f*
exécution d'une commande (F)	Auftragsabwicklung *f*	execution of the order	—	esecuzione ordini *f*	ejecución de pedidos *f*
exécution forcée (F)	Zwangs-vollstreckung *f*	judicial execution	—	esecuzione forzata *f*	ejecución forzosa *f*
execution of the order (E)	Auftragsabwicklung *f*	—	exécution d'une commande *f*	esecuzione ordini *f*	ejecución de pedidos *f*
exécution par crédit documentaire (F)	Akkreditiv-abwicklung *f*	settlement by letter of credit	—	procedura del credito documentario *f*	ejecución por crédito documentario *f*
executive (E)	Führungsperson *f*	—	cadre *m*	dirigente *m*	ejecutivo *m*
executive level (E)	Führungsebene *f*	—	niveau de gestion *m*	quadri dirigenti *m*	nivel de dirección *m*
executive management (E)	Unternehmens-leitung *f*	—	direction de l'entreprise *f*	direzione dell'impresa *f*	dirección de la empresa *f*
exempt de frais de transport (F)	frachtfrei	freight paid	—	franco di nolo	franco de porte
exempt de taxes (F)	abgabenfrei	tax-free/duty-free	—	esente da contributi	exento de derechos
exento de impuestos (Es)	abgabenfrei	tax-free	exempt de taxes	esente da contributi	—
exercice budgétaire (F)	Haushaltsjahr *n*	financial year	—	anno finanziario *m*	ejercicio *m*
exercice commercial (F)	Geschäftsjahr *n*	financial year	—	esercizio commerciale *m*	ejercicio *m*
exercice comptable[1] (F)	Wirtschaftsjahr *n*	business year	—	esercizio *m*	ejercicio *m*
exercice comptable[2] (F)	Rechnungsjahr *n*	financial year	—	anno d'esercizio *m*	ejercicio *m*
ex fábrica (Es)	ab Werk	ex works	départ usine	franco fabbrica	—
exhibición (Es)	Ausstellung *f*	exhibition	exposition *f*	esposizione *f*	—
exhibition (E)	Ausstellung *f*	—	exposition *f*	esposizione *f*	exhibición *f*
exhibitor (E)	Aussteller *m*	—	exposant *m*	espositore *m*	expositor *m*
existence (E)	Existenz *f*	—	existence *f*	esistenza *f*	existencia *f*
existence (F)	Existenz *f*	existence	—	esistenza *f*	existencia *f*
existencia (Es)	Existenz *f*	existence	existence *f*	esistenza *f*	—
existencias[1] (Es)	Reserve *f*	reserve stock/ reserves	stocks de réserve *m pl*/réserve *f*	scorte *f pl*/riserva *f*	—
existencias[2] (Es)	Vorrat *m*	stock	stock *m*	scorte *f pl*	—
existencias de mercancías (Es)	Warenbestand *m*	stock	stock de marchandises *m*	scorte merci *f pl*	—
existencias iniciales (Es)	Anfangsbestand *m*	opening inventory	stock initial *m*	scorte iniziali *f pl*	—
Existenz (D)	—	existence	existence *f*	esistenza *f*	existencia *f*
Existenzgründung (D)	—	setting up of new business	fondation d'existence *f*	costituzione di un lavoro indipendente *f*	fundación de existencia *f*
Existenzminimum (D)	—	subsistence minimum	minimum vital *m*	minimo di esistenza *m*	mínimo vital *m*
ex muelle (Es)	ab Kai	ex quay	départ quai	franco banchina	—
exorbitant rent (E)	Mietwucher *m*	—	hausse illicite des loyers *f*	strozzinaggio sui canoni di locazione *m*	usura arrendaticia *f*
Expansion (D)	—	expansion	expansion *f*	espansione *f*	expansión *f*
expansion (E)	Expansion *f*	—	expansion *f*	espansione *f*	expansión *f*
expansión (Es)	Expansion *f*	expansion	expansion *f*	espansione *f*	—
expansion (F)	Expansion *f*	expansion	—	espansione *f*	expansión *f*
expansiv (D)	—	expansive	tendant à l'expansion	espansivo	expansivo
expansive (E)	expansiv	—	tendant à l'expansion	espansivo	expansivo
expansivo (Es)	expansiv	expansive	tendant à l'expansion	espansivo	—
expectation of life (E)	Lebenserwartung *f*	—	espérance de vie *f*	durata probabile della vita *f*	expectativa de vida *f*
expectativa de un futuro pago (Es)	Anwartschaft *f*	candidature	candidature *f*	candidatura *f*	—
expectativa de vida (Es)	Lebenserwartung *f*	expectation of life	espérance de vie *f*	durata probabile della vita *f*	—

	D	E	F	I	Es
expedición[1] (Es)	Verfrachtung *f*	carriage of goods by sea	affrètement *m*	trasporto marittimo *m*	—
expedición[2] (Es)	Absendung *f*	dispatch	expédition *f*	spedizione *f*	—
expedir[1] (Es)	verladen	load	charger	caricare	—
expedir[2] (Es)	verfrachten	freight/ship	fréter/embarquer	imbarcare	—
expéditeur (F)	Absender *m*	sender	—	mittente *m*	remitente *m*
expédition[1] (F)	Abfertigung *f*	dispatch/clearance	—	spedizione *f*/ sdoganamento *m*	despacho *m*/despacho de aduana *m*
expédition[2] (F)	Absendung *f*	dispatch	—	spedizione *f*	expedición *f*
expédition[3] (F)	Versand *m*	dispatch	—	spedizione *f*	envío *m*
expédition de marchandises (F)	Warensendung *f*	consignment of goods	—	spedizione di merci *f*	envío de mercancías *m*
expéditions de détail (F)	Stückgutverkehr *m*	general cargo trade	—	trasporto di collettame *m*	tráfico de mercanías en bultos sueltos *m*
expeditor (Es)	Spediteur *m*	forwarder	commissionnaire de transport *m*	spedizioniere *m*	—
expenditure[1] (E)	Aufwand *m*	—	charge *f*	spese *f pl*	gastos *m pl*
expenditure[2] (E)	Aufwendung *f*	—	dépenses *f pl*	spese *f pl*	gasto *m*
expenditure control (E)	Ausgabenkontrolle *f*	—	contrôle des dépenses *m*	controllo delle spese *m*	control de gastos *m*
expenditure delay (E)	Ausgaben-verzögerung *f*	—	dépenses retardées *f pl*	dilazione delle spese *f*	aplazamiento de gastos *m*
expenditure factor (E)	Aufwandsfaktor *m*	—	facteur des frais *m*	fattore spese *m*	factor de gastos *m*
expenditure minimization (E)	Aufwands-minimierung *f*	—	minimiser les frais	riduzione delle spese *f*	minimación de gastos *f*
expenditure of time (E)	Zeitaufwand *m*	—	temps passé *m*	tempo impiegato *m*	tiempo consagrado *m*
expenses[1] (E)	Spesen *pl*	—	frais *m pl*	spese *f pl*	gastos *m pl*
expenses[2] (E)	Ausgaben *pl*	—	dépenses *f pl*	spese *f pl*	gastos *m pl*
expert-comptable (F)	Betriebsprüfer *m*	auditor	—	revisore aziendale *m*	contador público *m*
expert comptable économique et financier (F)	Wirtschaftsprüfer *m*	auditor	—	revisore dei conti *m*	revisor de cuentas *m*/ experto contable *m*
expert de déchets (F)	Abfallexperte *m*	expert on waste products	—	esperto dei rifiuti *m*	experto de productos residuales *m*
expert économique (F)	Wirtschaftsexperte *m*	economic expert	—	esperto in materia economica *m*	economista *m*
expert monétaire (F)	Währungsexperte *m*	monetary expert	—	esperto in materia monetaria *m*	experto en materia monetaria *m*
experto de productos residuales (Es)	Abfallexperte *m*	expert on waste products	expert en déchets *m*	esperto dei rifiuti *m*	—
experto en materia monetaria (Es)	Währungsexperte *m*	monetary expert	expert monétaire *m*	esperto in materia monetaria *m*	—
expert on waste products (E)	Abfallexperte *m*	—	expert en déchets *m*	esperto dei rifiuti *m*	experto de productos residuales *m*
expert opinion (E)	Expertise *f*	—	expertise *f*	perizia *f*	dictamen pericial *m*
Expertise (D)	—	expert opinion	expertise *f*	perizia *f*	dictamen pericial *m*
expertise (F)	Expertise *f*	expert opinion	—	perizia *f*	dictamen pericial *m*
expiry date (E)	Verfallsdatum *n*	—	date d'échéance *f*	data di scadenza *f*	fecha de vencimiento *f*
explanation (E)	Erklärung *f*	—	explication *f*/ déclaration *f*	spiegazione *f*/ dichiarazione *f*	explicación *f*/ declaración *f*
explicación (Es)	Erklärung *f*	explanation/ declaration	explication *f*/ déclaration *f*	spiegazione *f*/ dichiarazione *f*	—
explication (F)	Erklärung *f*	explanation/ declaration	—	spiegazione *f*/ dichiarazione *f*	explicación *f*/ declaración *f*
exploitation abusive (F)	Raubbau *m*	ruinous exploitation	—	sfruttamento abusivo *m*	explotación abusiva *f*
Explosion (D)	—	explosion	explosion *f*	esplosione *f*	explosión *f*
explosion (E)	Explosion *f*	—	explosion *f*	esplosione *f*	explosión *f*
explosión (Es)	Explosion *f*	explosion	explosion *f*	esplosione *f*	—
explosion (F)	Explosion *f*	explosion	—	esplosione *f*	explosión *f*

	D	E	F	I	Es
explosion des coûts (F)	Kostenexplosion *f*	cost escalation	—	esplosione dei costi *f*	incremento desmesurado de los costes *m*
explotación abusiva (Es)	Raubbau *m*	ruinous exploitation	exploitation abusive *f*	sfruttamento abusivo *m*	—
Export (D)	—	export	exportation *f*	esportazione *f*	exportación *f*
export (E)	Ausfuhr *f*	—	exportation *f*	esportazione *f*	exportación *f*
Exportabteilung (D)	—	export department	service d'exportation *m*	reparto esportazioni *m*	departamento de exportación *m*
exportación (Es)	Ausfuhr *f*	export	exportation *f*	esportazione *f*	—
exportación agrícola (Es)	Agrarexport *m*	farm exports	exportation de produits agricoles *f*	esportazione agricola *f*	—
exportación de capital (Es)	Kapitalexport *m*	capital export	exportation de capitaux *f*	esportazione di capitale *f*	—
exportation (F)	Ausfuhr *f*	export	—	esportazione *f*	exportación *f*
exportation de capitaux (F)	Kapitalexport *m*	capital export	—	esportazione di capitale *f*	exportación de capital *f*
exportation de produits agricoles (F)	Agrarexport *m*	farm exports	—	esportazione agricola *f*	exportación agrícola *f*
Exportauftrag (D)	—	export order	commande d'exportation *f*	ordine d'esportazione *m*	pedido destinado a la exportación *m*
export business (E)	Exportgeschäft *n*	—	affaire d'exportation *f*	operazione d'esportazione *f*	operación de exportación *f*
export department (E)	Exportabteilung *f*	—	service d'exportation *m*	reparto esportazioni *m*	departamento de exportación *m*
export documents (E)	Ausfuhrpapiere *pl*	—	documents d'exportation *m pl*	documenti d'esportazione *m pl*	documentos de exportación *m pl*
export duty (E)	Ausfuhrzoll *m*	—	taxe de sortie *f*	dazio sull'esportazione *m*	derechos de exportación *m pl*
export factoring (E)	Export-Factoring *n*	—	factoring d'exportation *m*	factoring delle esportazioni *m*	facturing de exportación *m*
Export-Factoring (D)	—	export factoring	factoring d'exportation *m*	factoring delle esportazioni *m*	facturing de exportación *m*
export financing (E)	Ausfuhrfinanzierung *f*	—	financement de l'exportation *m*	finanziamento delle esportazioni *m*	financiación de la exportación *f*
Exportfinanzierung (D)	—	financing of exports	financement d'opéra-tion d'exportation *m*	finanziamento delle esportazioni *m*	financiación de exportación *f*
Exportgeschäft (D)	—	export business	affaire d'exportation *f*	operazione d'esportazione *f*	operación de exportación *f*
Exporthandel (D)	—	export trade	commerce d'exportation *m*	esportazioni *f pl*	comercio de exportación *m*
Exporthilfe (D)	—	export subsidy	subvention à l'exportatoin *f*	aiuto all'esportazione *m*	ayuda a la exportación *f*
export licence (E)	Ausfuhr-genehmigung *f*	—	autorisation d'exportation *f*	autorizzazione per le esportazioni *f*	licencia de exportación *f*
export market (E)	Exportmarkt *m*	—	marché d'exportation *m*	mercato delle esportazioni *m*	mercado de exportación *m*
Exportmarkt (D)	—	export market	marché d'exportation *m*	mercato delle esportazioni *m*	mercado de exportación *m*
export order (E)	Exportauftrag *m*	—	commande d'exportation *f*	ordine d'esportazione *m*	pedido destinado a la exportación *m*
Exportpreisliste (D)	—	export price list	liste des prix à l'exportation *f*	listino prezzi delle esportazioni *m*	lista de precios de exportación *f*
export price list (E)	Exportpreisliste *f*	—	liste des prix à l'exportation *f*	listino prezzi delle esportazioni *m*	lista de precios de exportación *f*
export quota (E)	Exportquote *f*	—	quota d'exportation *m*	contingente d'esportazione *m*	cupo de exportación *m*
Exportquote (D)	—	export quota	quota d'exportation *m*	contingente d'esportazione *m*	cupo de exportación *m*
export regulations (E)	Ausfuhr-bestimmungen *pl*	—	dispositions d'exportation *f pl*	disposizioni per le esportazioni *f pl*	reglamiento de exportación *m*
export restriction (E)	Ausfuhr-beschränkung *f*	—	contingentement de l'exportation *m*	restrizione delle esportazioni *f*	restricción a la exportación *f*
export subsidy (E)	Exporthilfe *f*	—	subvention à l'exportatoin *f*	aiuto all'esportazione *m*	ayuda a la exportación *f*
export surplus (E)	Exportüberschuß *m*	—	excédent d'exportation *m*	eccedenza delle esportazioni *f*	excedente de exportación *m*

	D	E	F	I	Es
export trade (E)	Exporthandel *m*	—	commerce d'exportation *m*	esportazioni *f pl*	comercio de exportación *m*
Exportüberschuß (D)	—	export surplus	excédent d'exportation *m*	eccedenza delle esportazioni *f*	excedente de exportación *m*
exposant (F)	Aussteller *m*	exhibitor	—	espositore *m*	expositor *m*
exposición especializada (Es)	Fachausstellung *f*	trade fair	exposition spécialisée *f*	esposizione specializzata *f*	—
exposition (F)	Ausstellung *f*	exhibition	—	esposizione *f*	exhibición *f*
exposition spécialisée (F)	Fachausstellung *f*	trade fair	—	esposizione specializzata *f*	exposición especializada *f*
expositor (Es)	Aussteller *m*	exhibitor	exposant *m*	espositore *m*	—
expreso (Es)	Eilbote *m*	express messenger	facteur spécial *m*	corriere *m*	—
express delivery (E)	Eilzustellung *f*	—	remise par exprès *f*	consegna per espresso *f*	entrega urgente *f*
express goods (E)	Expressgut *n*	—	colis express *m*	merce spedita per espresso *f*	carga por expreso *f*
express letter (E)	Eilbrief *m*	—	lettre par exprès *f*	lettera espresso *f*	carta urgente *f*
express messenger (E)	Eilbote *m*	—	facteur spécial *m*	corriere *m*	expreso *m*
express parcel (F)	Eilpaket *n*	—	colis exprès *m*	pacco espresso *m*	paquete urgente *m*
Expressgut (D)	—	express goods	colis express *m*	merce spedita per espresso *f*	carga por expreso *f*
expropiación (Es)	Enteignung *f*	expropriation	expropriation *f*	espropriazione *f*	—
expropriation (E)	Enteignung *f*	—	expropriation *f*	espropriazione *f*	expropiación *f*
expropriation (F)	Enteignung *f*	expropriation	—	espropriazione *f*	expropiación *f*
ex quay (E)	ab Kai	—	départ quai	franco banchina	ex muelle
ex rail (E)	ab Bahnhof	—	départ gare	franco stazione	puesto en estación
ex ship (E)	ab Schiff	—	départ navire	franco bordo	ex vapor
extension[1] (E)	Prolongation *f*	—	prolongation *f*	proroga *f*	prolongación *f*
extension[2] (E)	Verlängerung *f*	—	prolongation *f*	prolungamento *m*	prórroga *f*
extension de la capacité (F)	Kapazitätsausweitung *f*	increase in capacity	—	ampliamento delle capacità *m*	ampliación de la capacidad *f*
extension of time for payment (E)	Zahlungsaufschub *m*	—	sursis de payement *m*	dilazione del pagamento *f*	pago aplazado *m*
extérieur (F)	extern	external	—	esterno	externo
extern (D)	—	external	extérieur	esterno	externo
external (E)	extern	—	extérieur	esterno	externo
externo[1] (Es)	extern	external	extérieur	esterno	—
extorno[2] (Es)	Storno *n*	counter entry	écriture de contre-passation *f*	storno *m*	—
extra (E)	Zugabe *f*	—	prime *f*	aggiunta *f*	suplemento *m*
extra charge (E)	Zuschlag *m*	—	supplément *m*	supplemento *m*	suplemento *m*
extraction de matières premières (F)	Rohstoffgewinnung *f*	raw material production	—	produzione delle materie prime *f*	producción de materias primas *f*
extracto de cuenta (Es)	Kontoauszug *m*	statement of account	extrait de compte *m*	estratto conto *m*	—
extragiudiziale (I)	außergerichtlich	extrajudicial	extrajudiciaire	—	extrajudicial
extrait de compte (F)	Kontoauszug *m*	statement of account	—	estratto conto *m*	extracto de cuenta *m*
extrajudiciaire (F)	außergerichtlich	extrajudicial	—	extragiudiziale	extrajudicial
extrajudicial (E)	außergerichtlich	—	extrajudiciaire	extragiudiziale	extrajudicial
extrajudicial (Es)	außergerichtlich	extrajudicial	extrajudiciaire	extragiudiziale	—
extranjero (Es)	Ausländer *m*	foreigner	étranger *m*	straniero *m*	—
extraordinary expenses (E)	außergewöhnliche Belastung *f*	—	charges exceptionnelles *f pl*	oneri straordinari *m pl*	carga extraordinaria *f*
ex vapor (Es)	ab Schiff	ex ship	départ navire	franco bordo	—
ex works (E)	ab Werk	—	départ usine	franco fabbrica	ex fábrica
fabbisogno (I)	Bedarf *m*	need/demand	besoin *m*/demande *f*	—	necesidades *f*/demanda *f*
fabbisogno individuale (I)	Individualbedürfnis *n*	individual need	besoin individuel *m*	—	necesidades individuales *f pl*
fabbricazione di massa (I)	Massenfertigung *f*	mass production	production en série *f*	—	fabricación en masa *f*

	D	E	F	I	Es
fábrica (Es)	Betrieb *m*	factory	usine *f*	azienda *f*	—
fabricación en masa (Es)	Massenfertigung *f*	mass production	production en série *f*	fabbricazione di massa *f*	—
fabricación especial (Es)	Sonderanfertigung *f*	manufacture to customer's specifications	fabrication spéciale *f*	produzione fuori serie *f*	—
fabricant (F)	Hersteller *m*	producer	—	produttore *m*	fabricante *m*
fabricante (Es)	Hersteller *m*	producer	fabricant *m*	produttore *m*	—
fabrication en série (F)	Serienfertigung *f*	series production	—	produzione in serie *f*	producción en serie *f*
fabrication spéciale (F)	Sonderanfertigung *f*	manufacture to customer's specifications	—	produzione fuori serie *f*	fabricación especial *f*
Fachausstellung (D)	—	trade fair	exposition spécialisée *f*	esposizione specializzata *f*	exposición especializada *f*
Fachbuch (D)	—	technical book	livre technique *m*	libro specializzato *m*	libro técnico *m*
Fachwissen (D)	—	professional knowledge	connaissances professionnelles *f pl*	cognizioni professionali *f pl*	conocimientos especializados *m pl*
facilidad en lo negocios (Es)	Kulanz *f*	accommodation	souplesse en affaires *f*	correntezza *f*	—
facteur (F)	Postbote m	postman	—	portalettere m	cartero *m*
facteur des frais (F)	Aufwandsfaktor *m*	expenditure factor	—	fattore spese *m*	factor de gastos *m*
facteur productif (F)	Ertragsfaktor *m*	income factor	—	fattore reddito *m*	factor de beneficio *m*
facteurs de production (F)	Produktions-faktoren *pl*	factors of production	—	fattori di produzione *m pl*	factores de producción *m pl*
facteurs dépendant du lieu d'implantation (F)	Standortfaktoren *pl*	location factors	—	fattori d'ubicazione *m pl*	factores de ubicación *m pl*
facteur spécial (F)	Eilbote *m*	express messenger	—	corriere *m*	expreso
factor de beneficio (Es)	Ertragsfaktor *m*	income factor	facteur productif *m*	fattore reddito *m*	—
factor de gastos (Es)	Aufwandsfaktor *m*	expenditure factor	facteur des frais *m*	fattore spese *m*	—
factores de producción (Es)	Produktions-faktoren *pl*	factors of production	facteurs de production *m pl*	fattori di produzione *m pl*	—
factores determinantes de las necesidades (Es)	Bedarfsfaktoren *pl*	requirement factors	éléments pouvant influencer la demande *m pl*	fattori del fabbisogno *m pl*	—
factores de ubicación (Es)	Standortfaktoren *pl*	location factors	facteurs dépendant du lieu d'implantation *m pl*	fattori d'ubicazione *m pl*	—
factoring d'exportation (F)	Export-Factoring *n*	export factoring	—	factoring delle esportazioni *m*	facturing de exportación *m*
factoring delle esportazioni (I)	Export-Factoring *n*	export factoring	factoring d'exportation *m*	—	facturing de exportación *m*
factors of production (E)	Produktions-faktoren *pl*	—	facteurs de production *m pl*	fattori di produzione *m pl*	factores de producción *m pl*
factory (E)	Betrieb *m*	—	usine *f*	azienda *f*	fábrica *f*
factura[1] (Es)	Rechnung *f*	invoice	facture *f*	fattura *f*	—
factura[2] (Es)	Faktura *f*	invoice	facture *f*	fattura *f*	—
factura arancelaria (Es)	Zollfaktura *f*	customs invoice	facture douanière *f*	fattura doganale *f*	—
facturación[1] (Es)	Rechnungsstellung *f*	invoicing	établissement d'une facture *m*	fatturazione *f*	—
facturación[2] (Es)	Fakturierung *f*	making out an invoice	facturation *f*	fatturazione *f*	—
factura de aportación de fondos (Es)	Deckungsbeitrags-rechnung *f*	contribution costing	calcul de la propor-tion de garantie *m*	calcolo del contributo per copertura *m*	—
factura ficticia (Es)	fingierte Rechnung *f*	fictitious invoice	facture simulée *f*	fattura fittizia *f*	—
factura pendiente (Es)	offene Rechnung *f*	unsettled account	facture pas encore payée *f*	conto aperto *m*	—
factura proforma (Es)	Proforma-Rechnung *f*	pro forma invoice	facture pro forma *f*	fattura pro forma *f*	—
facturation (F)	Fakturierung *f*	making out an invoice	—	fatturazione *f*	facturación *f*
facture[1] (F)	Faktura *f*	invoice	—	fattura *f*	factura *f*
facture[2] (F)	Rechnung *f*	invoice	—	fattura *f*	factura *f*
facture douanière (F)	Zollfaktura *f*	customs invoice	—	fattura doganale *f*	factura arancelaria *f*
facture pas encore payée (F)	offene Rechnung *f*	unsettled account	—	conto aperto *m*	factura pendiente *f*

	D	E	F	I	Es
facture pro forma (F)	Proforma-Rechnung *f*	pro forma invoice	—	fattura pro forma *f*	factura proforma *f*
facture simulée (F)	fingierte Rechnung *f*	fictitious invoice	—	fattura fittizia *f*	factura ficticia *f*
facturing de exportación (Es)	Export-Factoring *n*	export factoring	factoring d'exportation *m*	factoring delle esportazioni *m*	—
facultad de firma (Es)	Zeichnungs-berechtigung *f*	authority to sign	autorisation de signer *f*	diritto di firma *m*	—
Fähigkeit (D)	—	ability	capacité *f*	capacità *f*	capacidad *f*
Fahrgeld (D)	—	fare	coût du voyage *m*	spese di trasferta *f pl*	precio de la travesía *m*
Fahrlässigkeit (D)	—	negligence	négligence *f*	negligenza *f*	descuido *m*
failli (F)	Gemeinschuldner *m*	adjudicated bankrupt	—	debitore fallito *m*	deudor común *m*
faillite (F)	Konkurs *m*	bankruptcy	—	fallimento *m*	quiebra *f*
failure to pay on due date (E)	Zahlungsverzug *m*	—	demeure du débiteur *f*	morosità di pagamento *f*	retraso en el pago *m*
fair (E)	Messe *f*	—	foire *f*	fiera *f*	feria *f*
faire la queue (F)	Schlange stehen	queue up	—	fare la coda	hacer la cola
faire un prélèvement à découvert (F)	überziehen	overdraw	—	mandare allo scoperto	sobrepasar
fair labour standards (E)	Arbeitsnorm *f*	—	norme de travail *f*	norma di lavoro *f*	norma de producción *f*
Faktura (D)	—	invoice	facture *f*	fattura *f*	factura *f*
Fakturierung (D)	—	making out an invoice	facturation *f*	fatturazione *f*	facturación *f*
fallimento (I)	Konkurs *m*	bankruptcy	faillite *f*	—	quiebra *f*
falsificación de cheques (Es)	Scheckbetrug *m*	cheque fraud	irrégularité en matière de chèque *f*	emissione di assegno a vuoto *f*	—
falta de liquidez (Es)	Illiquidität *f*	illiquidity	manque de trésorerie *f*	illiquidità *f*	—
falta de personal (Es)	Personalmangel *m*	shortage of staff	manque de personnel *m*	mancanza di personale *f*	—
famiglia (I)	privater Haushalt *m*	private household	ménage privé *m*	—	economía doméstica *f*
fardeau inacceptable (F)	unzumutbare Belastung *f*	unacceptable hardship	—	onere inammissibile *m*	carga no exigible *f*
fardo (Es)	Frachtstücke *pl*	packages	colis *m*	colli *m pl*	—
fardos (Es)	Stückgut *n*	mixed cargo	colis de détail *m*	collettame *m*	—
fare (E)	Fahrgeld *n*	—	coût du voyage *m*	spese di trasferta *f pl*	precio de la travesía *m*
fare la coda (I)	Schlange stehen	queue up	faire la queue	—	hacer la cola
farm exports (E)	Agrarexport *m*	—	exportation de produits agricoles *f*	esportazione agricola *f*	exportación agrícola *f*
farm imports (E)	Agrarimport *m*	—	importation de produits agricoles *f*	importazione agricola *f*	importación agrícola *f*
farming (E)	Agrarwirtschaft *f*	—	économie agricole *f*	economia agraria *f*	economía agraria *f*
farm produce (E)	Agrarprodukt *n*	—	produit agricole *m*	prodotto agricolo *m*	producto agrario *m*
fascia (I)	Streifband *f*	postal wrapper	bande étiquette *f*	—	precinto *m*
fase de desarrollo (Es)	Aufbauphase *f*	development phase	phase d'organisation *f*	fase di costruzione *f*	—
fase di costruzione (I)	Aufbauphase *f*	development phase	phase d'organisation *f*	—	fase de desarrollo *f*
fashion article (E)	Modeartikel *m*	—	article de mode *m*	articolo di moda *m*	artículos de moda *m pl*
fashion fair (E)	Modemesse *f*	—	foire de la mode *f*	fiera della moda *f*	feria de moda *f*
fattore reddito (I)	Ertragsfaktor *m*	income factor	facteur productif *m*	—	factor de beneficio *m*
fattore spese (I)	Aufwandsfaktor *m*	expenditure factor	facteur des frais *m*	—	factor de gastos *m*
fattori del fabbisogno (I)	Bedarfsfaktoren *pl*	requirement factors	éléments pouvant influencer la demande *m pl*	—	factores determinantes de las necesidades *m pl*
fattori di produzione (I)	Produktions-faktoren *pl*	factors of production	facteurs de production *m pl*	—	factores de producción *m pl*
fattori d'ubicazione (I)	Standortfaktoren *pl*	location factors	facteurs dépendant du lieu d'implantation *m pl*	—	factores de ubicación *m pl*

	D	E	F	I	Es
fattura[1] (I)	Rechnung *f*	invoice	facture *f*	—	factura *f*
fattura[2] (I)	Faktura *f*	invoice	facture *f*	—	factura *f*
fattura doganale (I)	Zollfaktura *f*	customs invoice	facture douanière *f*	—	factura arancelaria *f*
fattura fittizia (I)	fingierte Rechnung *f*	fictitious invoice	facture simulée *f*	—	factura ficticia *f*
fattura pro forma (I)	Proforma-Rechnung *f*	pro forma invoice	facture pro forma *f*	—	factura proforma *f*
fatturato (I)	Umsatz *m*	turnover	chiffre d'affaires *m*	—	volumen de ventas *m*
fatturato minimo (I)	Mindestumsatz *m*	minimum turnover	chiffre d'affaires minimum *m*	—	cifra de venta mínima *f*
fatturato netto (I)	Nettoumsatz *m*	net turnover	chiffre d'affaires net *m*	—	ventas netas *f pl*
fatturazione[1] (I)	Fakturierung *f*	making out an invoice	facturation *f*	—	facturación *f*
fatturazione[2] (I)	Rechnungsstellung *f*	invoicing	établissement d'une facture *m*	—	facturación *f*
faute (F)	Fehler *m*	mistake	—	errore *m*	error *m*
faute non intentionnelle (F)	Fahrlässigkeit *f*	negligence	—	negligenza *f*	descuido *m*
favorable à l'environnement (F)	umweltfreundlich	beneficial to the environment	—	ecologico	no contaminante
favorecido (Es)	Begünstigter *m*	beneficiary	bénéficiaire *m*	beneficiario *m*	—
fecha[1] (Es)	Datum *n*	date	date *f*	data *f*	—
fecha[2] (Es)	Termin *m*	deadline	date limite *f*	termine *m*	—
fecha de cita (Es)	Gesprächstermin *m*	appointment for a meeting	date de conversation *f*	appuntamento per un colloquio *m*	—
fecha de conferencia (Es)	Besprechungs-termin *m*	meeting date	date de la conférence *f*	termine del colloquio *m*	—
fecha de entrevista personal (Es)	Vorstellungstermin *m*	date of interview	rendez-vous de présentation *m*	appuntamento di presentazione *m*	—
fecha de liquidación (Es)	Abrechnungstag *m*	settling day	jour de la liquidation *m*	giorno di liquidazione *m*	—
fecha de llegada (Es)	Ankunftsdatum *n*	date of arrival	date d'arrivée *f*	data d'arrivo *f*	—
fecha de nacimiento (Es)	Geburtsdatum *n*	date of birth	date de naissance *f*	data di nascita *f*	—
fecha de partida (Es)	Abreisedatum *n*	date of departure	date de départ *f*	data di partenza *f*	—
fecha de vencimiento (Es)	Verfallsdatum *n*	expiry date	date d'échéance *f*	data di scadenza *f*	—
fee (E)	Gebühr *f*	—	taxe *f*	tassa *f*	derecho *m*
Feedback (D)	—	feedback	feed-back *m*	feedback *m*	repercusión *f*
feed-back (F)	Feedback *n*	feedback	—	feedback *m*	repercusión *f*
feedback (I)	Feedback *n*	feedback	feed-back *m*	—	repercusión *f*
feedback[1] (E)	Feedback *n*	—	feed-back *m*	feedback *m*	repercusión *f*
feedback[2] (E)	Rückkopplung *f*	—	accouplement réactif *m*	accoppiamento a reazione *m*	reacoplamiento *m*
Fehler (D)	—	mistake	faute *f*	errore *m*	error *m*
fehlerhaft (D)	—	defective	défectueux	difettoso	defectuoso
Fehlerprotokoll (D)	—	record of errors	protocole d'erreurs *m*	protocollo errori *m*	protocolo de errores *m*
Fehlinvestition (D)	—	misconceived capital projects	mauvais investissement *m*	investimento sbagliato *m*	inversión equivocada *f*
Feingehalt (D)	—	fine gold content	titre *m*	titolo *m*	ley *f*
Feingewicht (D)	—	weight of fine gold	poids de métal fin *m*	peso fino *m*	peso fino *m*
felicitaciónes (Es)	Glückwunsch *m*	congratulations	félicitations *f*	auguri *m pl*	—
félicitations (F)	Glückwunsch *m*	congratulations	—	auguri *m pl*	felicitaciónes *f*
feria (Es)	Messe *f*	fair	foire *f*	fiera *f*	—
feria comercial (Es)	Handelsmesse *f*	trade fair	foire commerciale *f*	fiera commerciale *f*	—
feria de moda (Es)	Modemesse *f*	fashion fair	foire de la mode *f*	fiera della moda *f*	—
feria de muestras (Es)	Mustermesse *f*	trade fair	foire d'échantillons *f*	fiera campionaria *f*	—
feria de otoño (Es)	Herbstmesse *f*	autumn fair	foire d'automne *f*	fiera autunnale *f*	—
ferie (I)	Urlaub *m*	annual holidays/ vacation	congé *m*/ vacances *f pl*	—	vacaciones *f pl*/ vacaciones colectivas de la empresa *f pl*

	D	E	F	I	Es
ferie aziendali (I)	Betriebsferien *pl*	annual holiday	clôture annuelle de l'établissement *f*	—	vacaciones de la empresa *f pl*
ferie non pagate (I)	unbezahlter Urlaub *m*	unpaid vacation	congé non payé *m*	—	vacaciones no pagadas *f pl*
ferie pagate (I)	bezahlter Urlaub *m*	paid vacation	congé payé *m*	—	vacaciones con goce de sueldo *f pl*
fermeture douanière (F)	Zollverschluß *m*	customs seal	—	sigillo doganale *m*	precinto aduanero *m*
fermo posta (I)	postlagernd	poste restante	poste restante	—	lista de correos *m*
Fernmeldeamt (D)	—	telephone exchange	service de télécommunication *m*	ufficio telecomunicazioni *m*	central interurbana *f*
Fernschreiber (D)	—	teleprinter	téléimprimeur *m*	telescrivente *m*	télex *m*
Fernsehwerbung (D)	—	television advertising	émission publicitaire télévisée *f*	pubblicità televisiva *f*	publicidad televisiva *f*
Fernsprecher (D)	—	telephone	appareil téléphonique *m*	telefono *m*	teléfono *m*
Fernverkehr (D)	—	long distance traffic	trafic sur longues distances *m*	traffico a grande distanza *m*	transporte a distancia *m*
Fertigprodukt (D)	—	finished product	produit fini *m*	prodotto finito *m*	producto acabado *m*
Fertigstellung (D)	—	completion	achèvement *m*	completamento *m*	terminación total *f*
Fertigungsmenge (D)	—	manufactured quantity	quantité fabriquée *f*	quantitativo di produzione *m*	cantidad producida *f*
Fertigungs-programm (D)	—	production programme	programme de fabrication *m*	programma di produzione *m*	programa de producción *m*
Fertigungsprozeß (D)	—	production procedure	déroulement de la fabrication *m*	processo produttivo *m*	proceso de producción *m*
Fertigungs-verfahren (D)	—	production process	méthode de production *f*	procedimento produttivo *m*	procedimiento de fabricación *m*
feste Wechselkurse (D)	—	fixed exchange rates	taux de change fixe *m*	cambi fissi *m pl*	tipos de cambio fijos *m pl*
Festeinkommen (D)	—	fixed income	revenu fixe *m*	reddito fisso *m*	salario fijo *m*
fester Zins (D)	—	fixed interest rate	intérêt fixe *m*	tasso d'interesse fisso *m*	interés fijo *m*
Festgeld (D)	—	fixed deposit	argent immobilisé *m*	denaro vincolato *m*	depósito a plazo *m*
Festgeldkonto (D)	—	time deposit account	compte de dépôt à terme *m*	deposito vincolato *m*	cuenta a plazo *f*
Festpreis (D)	—	fixed price	prix fixe *m*	prezzo fisso *m*	precio fijo *m*
Feuerversicherung (D)	—	fire insurance	assurance contre l'incendie *f*	assicurazione contro incendi *f*	seguro contra incendios *m*
feuille publicitaire (F)	Prospekt *m*	leaflet/prospectus	—	prospetto *m*	prospecto *m*/ folleto *m*
fiador (Es)	Bürge *m*	guarantor	garant *m*	fideiussore *m*	—
fianza (Es)	Bürgschaft *f*	guarantee	caution *f*	fideiussione *f*	—
fianza con beneficio de excusión (Es)	Ausfallbürgschaft *f*	deficiency guarantee	garantie de bonne fin *f*	fideiussione d'indennità *f*	—
fianza de contratista (Es)	Gewährleistungs-garantie *f*	guarantee for proper execution	caution de garantie *f*	garanzia di esecuzione *f*	—
fianza de puesta en libertad (Es)	Haftkaution *f*	bail	caution pour être mis en liberté *f*	cauzione per la scarcerazione *f*	—
ficha (Es)	Karteikarte *f*	index card	fiche *f*	scheda *f*	—
fiche (F)	Karteikarte *f*	index card	—	scheda *f*	ficha *f*
fichero (Es)	Kartei *f*	card-index	cartothèque	schedario *m*	—
fichier de données (F)	Datei *f*	file	—	file *m*	archivo de datos *m*
fictitious invoice (E)	fingierte Rechnung *f*	—	facture simulée *f*	fattura fittizia *f*	factura ficticia *f*
fictitious prices (E)	Mondpreise *pl*	—	prix fictifs *m pl*	prezzi alle stelle *m pl*	precios ficticios *m pl*
fictitious profit (E)	Scheingewinn *m*	—	gain fictif *m*	utile fittizio *m*	beneficio simulado *m*
fictitious transaction (E)	Scheingeschäft *n*	—	opération simulée *f*	negozio simulato *m*	operación ficticia *f*
fideiussione (I)	Bürgschaft *f*	guarantee	caution *f*	—	fianza *f*
fideiussione d'indennità (I)	Ausfallbürgschaft *f*	deficiency guarantee	garantie de bonne fin *f*	—	fianza con beneficio de excusión *f*
fideiussore (I)	Bürge *m*	guarantor	garant *m*	—	fiador *m*
fiduciary account (E)	Anderkonto *n*	—	compte de tiers *m*	conto per terzi *m*	cuenta fiduciaria de un abogado *f*

	D	E	F	I	Es
field of action (E)	Aktionsfeld *n*	—	champ d'action *m*	campo d'azione *m*	campo de acción *m*
field of activity (E)	Tätigkeitsfeld *n*	—	champ d'acitivité *m*	campo d'azione *m*	campo de actividad *m*
field of the economy (E)	Wirtschaftszweig *m*	—	secteur économique *m*	settore economico *m*	ramo económico *m*
field staff (E)	Außendienst-mitarbeiter *m*	—	personnel du service extérieur *m*	collaboratore del servizio esterno *m*	colaborador en el servicio exterior *m*
field work (E)	Außendienst *m*	—	service extérieur *m*	servizio esterno *m*	servicio exterior *m*
fiera (I)	Messe *f*	fair	foire *f*	—	feria *f*
fiera autunnale (I)	Herbstmesse *f*	autumn fair	foire d'automne *f*	—	feria de otoño *f*
fiera campionaria (I)	Mustermesse *f*	trade fair	foire d'échantillons *f*	—	feria de muestras *f*
fiera commerciale (I)	Handelsmesse *f*	trade fair	foire commerciale *f*	—	feria comercial *f*
fiera della moda (I)	Modemesse *f*	fashion fair	foire de la mode *f*	—	feria de moda *f*
fijación de los cambios (Es)	Kursfestsetzung *f*	fixing of prices	détermination des cours *f*	fissazione dei corsi *f*	—
fijo (Es)	Fixum *n*	fixed sum	somme fixe *f*	somma fissa *f*	—
fijo anual (Es)	Jahresfixum *n*	fixed annual salary	fixe annuel *m*	fisso annuale *m*	—
file[1] (E)	Datei *f*	—	fichier de données *m*	file *m*	archivo de datos *m*
file[2] (E)	Akte *f*	—	dossier *m*	pratica *f*	documento *m*
file[3] (E)	Ablage *f*	—	collection des dossiers *f*	archivio *m*	archivo *m*
file (I)	Datei *f*	file	fichier de données *m*	—	archivo de datos *m*
filial[1] (Es)	Zweigstelle *f*	branch	agence *f*	agenzia *f*	—
filial[2] (Es)	Filiale *f*	branch	agence *f*	filiale *f*	—
filial[3] (Es)	Zweigniederlassung *f*	branch office	succursale *f*	succursale *f*	—
filial[4] (Es)	Tochtergesellschaft *f*	subsidiary	société filiale *f*	società affiliata *f*	—
Filiale (D)	—	branch	agence *f*	filiale *f*	filial *f*
filiale[1] (I)	Zweigbetrieb *m*	branch business	établissement secondaire *m*	—	sucursal *f*
filiale[2] (I)	Filiale *f*	branch	agence *f*	—	filial *f*
filial en el exterior (Es)	Auslands-niederlassung *f*	branch abroad	succursale à l'étranger *f*	succursale estera *f*	—
Filialleiter (D)	—	branch manager	directeur d'agence *m*	direttore della filiale *m*	jefe de sucursal *m*
Filialnetz (D)	—	branch network	réseau de succursales *m*	rete delle filiali *f*	red de sucursales *f*
filing (E)	Aktenablage *f*	—	archives *f pl*	archivio delle pratiche *m*	archivo *m*
film pubblicitario (I)	Werbefilm *m*	advertising film	film publicitaire *m*	—	película promocional *f*
film publicitaire (F)	Werbefilm *m*	advertising film	—	film pubblicitario *m*	película promocional *f*
filosofia d'acquisto (I)	Kaufverhalten *n*	purchase pattern	comportement d'achat *m*	—	comportamiento de compra *m*
fils du partenaire (F)	Junior-Partner *m*	junior partner	—	junior partner *m*	socio menor *m*
final control (E)	Endkontrolle *f*	—	contrôle final *m*	controllo finale *m*	control final *m*
final del trimestre (Es)	Quartalsende *n*	end of a quarter	fin de trimestre *f*	fine trimestre *f*	—
financement (F)	Finanzierung *f*	financing	—	finanziamento *m*	financiación *f*
financement à la construction (F)	Baufinanzierung *f*	construction financing	—	finanziamento di costruzione *m*	financiación de la construcción *f*
financement de la vente à crédit (F)	Konsum-finanzierung *f*	financing of consumption	—	finanziamento del consumo *m*	financiación del consumo *f*
financement de l'exportation (F)	Ausfuhrfinanzierung *f*	export financing	—	finanziamento delle esportazioni *m*	financiación de la exportación *f*
financement des ventes (F)	Absatzfinanzierung *f*	sales financing	—	finanziamento delle vendite *m*	financiación de las ventas *f*
financement d'opération d'exportation (F)	Exportfinanzierung *f*	financing of exports	—	finanziamento delle esportazioni *m*	financiación de exportación *f*
financement du déficit (F)	Defizitfinanzierung *f*	deficit financing	—	finanziamento del deficit *m*	financiación del déficit *f*
financement du rachat (F)	Ablösungs-finanzierung *f*	redemption financing	—	finanziamento del rimborso *m*	financiamiento de amortización *m*

	D	E	F	I	Es
financement sans recours (F)	Forfaitierung *f*	non-recourse financing	—	forfetizzazione *f*	financiación sin recurso *f*
financement successif (F)	Anschluß-finanzierung *f*	follow-up financing	—	finanziamento successivo *m*	financiación sucesiva *f*
finances (E)	Finanzen *pl*	—	finances *f pl*	finanze *f pl*	finanzas *f pl*
finances (F)	Finanzen *pl*	finances	—	finanze *f pl*	finanzas *f pl*
financiación (Es)	Finanzierung *f*	financing	financement *m*	finanziamento *m*	—
financiación de exportación (Es)	Exportfinanzierung *f*	financing of exports	financement d'opération d'exportation *m*	finanziamento delle esportazioni *m*	—
financiación de la construcción (Es)	Baufinanzierung *f*	construction financing	financement à la construction *m*	finanziamento di costruzione *m*	—
financiación de la exportación (Es)	Ausfuhrfinanzierung *f*	export financing	financement de l'exportation *m*	finanziamento delle esportazioni *m*	—
financiación de las ventas (Es)	Absatzfinanzierung *f*	sales financing	financement des ventes *m*	finanziamento delle vendite *m*	—
financiación del comercio exterior (Es)	Außenhandels-finanzierung *f*	foreign trade financing	aide financière à l'exportation *m*	finanziamento del commercio estero *m*	—
financiación del consumo (Es)	Konsum-finanzierung *f*	financing of consumption	financement de la vente à crédit *m*	finanziamento del consumo *m*	—
financiación del déficit (Es)	Defizitfinanzierung *f*	deficit financing	financement du déficit *m*	finanziamento del deficit *m*	—
financiación externa (Es)	Fremdfinanzierung *f*	debt financing	constitution de capital par apport de tiers *f*	finanziamento passivo *m*	—
financiación propia (Es)	Eigenfinanzierung *f*	self-financing	autofinancement *m*	autofinanziamento *m*	—
financiación sin recurso (Es)	Forfaitierung *f*	non-recourse financing	financement sans recours *m*	forfetizzazione *f*	—
financiación sucesiva (Es)	Anschluß-finanzierung *f*	follow-up financing	financement successif *m*	finanziamento successivo *m*	—
financial accounting (E)	Finanzbuchhaltung *f*	—	comptabilité financière *f*	contabilità finanziaria *f*	contabilidad financiera *f*
financial assets (E)	Geldvermögen *n*	—	moyens financiers *m*	patrimonio monetario *m*	activo monetario *m*
financial backer (E)	Geldgeber *m*	—	bailleur de fonds *m*	finanziatore *m*	prestamista *m*
financial debacle (E)	Finanzdebakel *n*	—	débâcle fiancière *f*	dissesto finanziario *m*	descalabro financiero *m*
financial difficulties (E)	Zahlungs-schwierigkeit *f*	—	difficultés financières *f pl*	difficoltà di pagamento *f*	dificultades de pago *f pl*
financial equalization (E)	Finanzausgleich *m*	—	compensation financière *f*	compensazione finanziaria *f*	ajuste financiero *m*
financial failure (E)	finanzieller Zusammenbruch *m*	—	débâcle financière *f*	crollo finanziario *m*	derrumbamiento financiero *m*
financial plan (E)	Finanzplan *m*	—	plan financier *m*	piano finanziario *m*	presupuesto *m*
financial report (E)	Finanzbericht *m*	—	rapport financier *m*	relazione finanziaria *f*	informe financiero *m*
financial situation (E)	Vermögens-verhältnisse *pl*	—	situation financière *f*	situazione patrimoniale *f*	situación económica *f*
financial sovereignty (E)	Finanzhoheit *f*	—	souveraineté en matière budgétaire *f*	sovranità finanziaria *f*	soberanía financiera *f*
financial standing (E)	Kreditfähigkeit *f*	—	solvabilité *f*	capacità di credito *f*	crédito *m*
financial year[1] (E)	Geschäftsjahr *n*	—	exercice commercial *m*	esercizio commerciale *m*	ejercicio *m*
financial year[2] (E)	Rechnungsjahr *n*	—	exercice comptable *m*	anno d'esercizio *m*	ejercicio *m*
financial year[3] (E)	Haushaltsjahr *n*	—	exercice budgétaire *m*	anno finanziario *m*	ejercicio *m*
financiamiento de amortización (Es)	Ablösungs-finanzierung *f*	redemption financing	financement du rachat *m*	finanziamento del rimborso *m*	—
financing (E)	Finanzierung *f*	—	financement *m*	finanziamento *m*	financiación *f*
financing of consumption (E)	Konsum-finanzierung *f*	—	financement de la vente à crédit *m*	finanziamento del consumo *m*	financiación del consumo *f*
financing of exports (E)	Exportfinanzierung *f*	—	financement d'opération d'exportation *m*	finanziamento delle esportazioni *m*	financiación de exportación *f*
Finanzamt (D)	—	inland revenue office	service de contributions *m*	ufficio delle imposte *m*	Hacienda *f*
finanzas (Es)	Finanzen *pl*	finances	finances *f pl*	finanze *f pl*	—
Finanzausgleich (D)	—	financial equalization	compensation financière *f*	compensazione finanziaria *f*	ajuste financiero *m*

	D	E	F	I	Es
Finanzbericht (D)	—	financial report	rapport financier *m*	relazione finanziaria *f*	informe financiero *m*
Finanzbuchhaltung (D)	—	financial accounting	comptabilité financière *f*	contabilità finanziaria *f*	contabilidad financiera *f*
Finanzdebakel (D)	—	financial debacle	débâcle fiancière *f*	dissesto finanziario *m*	descalabro financiero *m*
finanze (I)	Finanzen *pl*	finances	finances *f pl*	—	finanzas *f pl*
Finanzen (D)	—	finances	finances *f pl*	finanze *f pl*	finanzas *f pl*
Finanzhoheit (D)	—	financial sovereignty	souveraineté en matière budgétaire *f*	sovranità finanziaria *f*	soberanía financiera *f*
finanziamento (I)	Finanzierung *f*	financing	financement *m*	—	financiación *f*
finanziamento del commercio estero (I)	Außenhandels-finanzierung *f*	foreign trade financing	aide financière à l'exportation *m*	—	financiación del comercio exterior *f*
finanziamento del consumo (I)	Konsum-finanzierung *f*	financing of consumption	financement de la vente à crédit *m*	—	financiación del consumo *f*
finanziamento del deficit (I)	Defizitfinanzierung *f*	deficit financing	financement du déficit *m*	—	financiación del déficit *f*
finanziamento delle esportazioni (I)	Exportfinanzierung *f*	financing of exports	financement d'opéra-tion d'exportation *m*	—	financiación de exportación *f*
finanziamento delle esportazioni (I)	Ausfuhrfinanzierung *f*	export financing	financement de l'exportation *m*	—	financiación de la exportación *f*
finanziamento delle vendite (I)	Absatzfinanzierung *f*	sales financing	financement des ventes *m*	—	financiación de las ventas *f*
finanziamento del rimborso (I)	Ablösungs-finanzierung *f*	redemption financing	financement du rachat *m*	—	financiamiento de amortización *m*
finanziamento di costruzione (I)	Baufinanzierung *f*	construction financing	financement à la construction *m*	—	financiación de la construcción *f*
finanziamento passivo (I)	Fremdfinanzierung *f*	debt financing	constitution de capital par apport de tiers *f*	—	financiación externa *f*
finanziamento successivo (I)	Anschluß-finanzierung *f*	follow-up financing	financement successif *m*	—	financiación sucesiva *f*
finanziatore (I)	Geldgeber *m*	financial backer	bailleur de fonds *m*	—	prestamista *m*
finanzieller Zusammenbruch (D)	—	financial failure	débâcle financière *f*	crollo finanziario *m*	derrumbamiento financiero *m*
Finanzierung (D)	—	financing	financement *m*	finanziamento *m*	financiación *f*
Finanzierungsdauer (D)	—	period of financing	durée du financement *f*	durata del finanziamento *f*	período de financiación *m*
Finanzierungs-rechnung (D)	—	flow-of-funds analysis	analyse des flux monétaires *f*	calcolo di finanziamento *m*	análisis de flujos monetarios *m*
Finanzkontrolle (D)	—	budgetary control	contrôle de financement *m*	controllo finanziario *m*	control financiero *m*
Finanzministerium (D)	—	Ministry of Finance	ministère des finances *m*	ministero delle Finanze *m*	Hacienda *f*
Finanzmonopol (D)	—	fiscal monopoly	monopole fiscal *m*	monopolio fiscale *m*	monopolio financiero *m*
Finanzplan (D)	—	financial plan	plan financier *m*	piano finanziario *m*	presupuesto *m*
Finanzpolitik (D)	—	fiscal policy	politique financière *f*	politica finanziaria *f*	política financiera *f*
fin de mes (Es)	Ultimo *n*	end of the month	fin de mois *f*	fine mese *m*	—
fin de mois (F)	Ultimo *n*	end of the month	—	fine mese *m*	fin de mes *m*
fin de trimestre (F)	Quartalsende *n*	end of a quarter	—	fine trimestre *f*	final del trimestre *m*
fin de venta (Es)	Absatzziel *n*	sales target	objectif de vente *m*	obbiettivo di vendita *m*	—
fine[1] (E)	Geldbuße *f*	—	amende *f*	pena pecuniaria *f*	multa *f*
fine[2] (E)	Geldstrafe *f*	—	peine pécuniaire *f*	multa *f*	multa *f*
fine gold content (E)	Feingehalt *m*	—	titre *m*	titolo *m*	ley *f*
fine mese (I)	Ultimo *n*	end of the month	fin de mois *f*	—	fin de mes *m*
fine trimestre (I)	Quartalsende *n*	end of a quarter	fin de trimestre *f*	—	final del trimestre *m*
fingierte Rechnung (D)	—	fictitious invoice	facture simulée *f*	fattura fittizia *f*	factura ficticia *f*
finished product[1] (E)	Fertigprodukt *n*	—	produit fini *m*	prodotto finito *m*	producto acabado *m*
finished product[2] (E)	Endprodukt *n*	—	produit final *m*	prodotto finito *m*	producto final *m*
finishing technique (E)	Abschlußtechnik *f*	—	technique de conclusion *f*	metodo di chiusura *m*	técnica de conclusión *f*
fire insurance (E)	Feuerversicherung *f*	—	assurance contre l'incendie *f*	assicurazione contro incendi *f*	seguro contra incendios *m*

	D	E	F	I	Es
Firma (D)	—	company	entreprise *f*	impresa *f*	empresa *f*
firma (Es)	Unterschrift *f*	signature	signature *f*	firma *f*	—
firma (I)	Unterschrift *f*	signature	signature *f*	—	firma *f*
firma en blanco (Es)	Blankounterschrift *f*	blank signature	signature en blanc *f*	firma in bianco *f*	—
firma in bianco (I)	Blankounterschrift *f*	blank signature	signature en blanc *f*	—	firma en blanco *f*
firmare (I)	unterschreiben	sign	signer	—	signar
Firmenanschrift (D)	—	company address	adresse de la maison *f*	indirizzo della ditta *m*	dirección de la empresa *f*
Firmenkonto (D)	—	company account	compte de maison *m*	conto intestato ad una ditta *m*	cuenta de la empresa *f*
Firmenname (D)	—	company name	nom de la maison *m*	denominazione *f*/ ragione sociale *f*	razón social *f*
Firmenschild (D)	—	company's name plate	enseigne commerciale *f*	insegna dell'impresa *f*	letrero de establecimiento *m*
Firmensitz (D)	—	domicile of the company	siège social *m*	sede *f*	sede social *f*
Firmenwagen (D)	—	company car	voiture appartenant à l'entreprise *f*	vettura aziendale *f*	coche de empresa *m*
Firmenwert (D)	—	goodwill	valeur commerciale *f*	goodwill *m*	fondo de comercio *m*
first class (E)	erstklassig	—	de première qualité	di prima categoria	de primera calidad
first class quality (E)	beste Qualität	—	première qualité *f*	qualità ottima *f*	primera calidad *f*
fiscal fraud (E)	Steuerbetrug *m*	—	fraude fiscale *f*	frode fiscale *f*	fraude fiscal *m*
fiscal monopoly (E)	Finanzmonopol *n*	—	monopole fiscal *m*	monopolio fiscale *m*	monopolio financiero *m*
fiscal policy (E)	Finanzpolitik *f*	—	politique financière *f*	politica finanziaria *f*	política financiera *f*
fiscal policy (E)	Steuerpolitik *f*	—	politique fiscale *f*	politica fiscale *f*	política fiscal *f*
Fischerei (D)	—	fishing	pêcherie *f*	pesca *f*	pesca *f*
Fischereirecht (D)	—	fishing rights	droit de pêche *m*	diritto della pesca *m*	derecho pesquero *m*
fishing (E)	Fischerei *f*	—	pêcherie *f*	pesca *f*	pesca *f*
fishing rights (E)	Fischereirecht *n*	—	droit de pêche *m*	diritto della pesca *m*	derecho pesquero *m*
fissazione dei corsi (I)	Kursfestsetzung *f*	fixing of prices	détermination des cours *f*	—	fijación de los cambios *f*
fisso annuale (I)	Jahresfixum *n*	fixed annual salary	fixe annuel *m*	—	fijo anual *m*
fixe annuel (F)	Jahresfixum *n*	fixed annual salary	—	fisso annuale *m*	fijo anual *m*
fixed annual salary (E)	Jahresfixum *n*	—	fixe annuel *m*	fisso annuale *m*	fijo anual *m*
fixed assets[1] (E)	Sachanlagen *pl*	—	immobilisations corporelles *f pl*	immobilizzazioni *f pl*	inmuebles y utillaje *m pl*
fixed assets[2] (E)	Anlagevermögen *n*	—	valeurs immobilisées *f pl*	attivo fisso *m*	activo fijo *m*
fixed costs (E)	Fixkosten *pl*	—	coûts fixes *m pl*	costi fissi *m pl*	gastos fijos *m pl*
fixed deposit (E)	Festgeld *n*	—	argent immobilisé *m*	denaro vincolato *m*	depósito a plazo *m*
fixed exchange (E)	Mengennotierung *f*	—	cotation de quantité *f*	cambio reale *m*	cotización real *f*
fixed exchange rates (E)	feste Wechselkurse *pl*	—	taux de change fixe *m*	cambi fissi *m pl*	tipos de cambio fijos *m pl*
fixed income (E)	Festeinkommen *n*	—	revenu fixe *m*	reddito fisso *m*	salario fijo *m*
fixed interest rate (E)	fester Zins *m*	—	intérêt fixe *m*	tasso d'interesse fisso *m*	interés fijo *m*
fixed price (E)	Festpreis *m*	—	prix fixe *m*	prezzo fisso *m*	precio fijo *m*
fixed sum (E)	Fixum *n*	—	somme fixe *f*	somma fissa *f*	fijo *m*
fixing of a quota (E)	Kontingentierung *f*	—	contingentement *m*	contingentamento *m*	contingentación *f*
fixing of prices (E)	Kursfestsetzung *f*	—	détermination des cours *f*	fissazione dei corsi *f*	fijación de los cambios *f*
Fixkosten (D)	—	fixed costs	coûts fixes *m pl*	costi fissi *m pl*	gastos fijos *m pl*
Fixum (D)	—	fixed sum	somme fixe *f*	somma fissa *f*	fijo *m*
flaconnage non consigné (F)	Einwegflasche *f*	one-way bottle	—	bottiglia a perdere *f*	botella de un solo uso *f*
flat rate amount (E)	Pauschalbetrag *m*	—	somme forfaitaire *f*	somma forfettaria *f*	suma global *f*
flessione della domanda (I)	Nachfrage-rückgang *m*	decrease in demand	recul de la demande *m*	—	disminución en la demanda *f*
flete aéreo (Es)	Luftfracht *f*	air freight	fret aérien *m*	nolo aereo *m*	—

	D	E	F	I	Es
flete pagado (Es)	Fracht bezahlt	freight paid	fret payé	nolo pagato	—
flexible exchange rate (E)	flexibler Wechselkurs *m*	—	taux de change flottant *m*	cambio flessibile *m*	tipo flotante de cambio *m*
flexibler Wechselkurs (D)	—	flexible exchange rate	taux de change flottant *m*	cambio flessibile *m*	tipo flotante de cambio *m*
flight of capital (E)	Kapitalflucht *f*	—	évasion des capitaux *f*	fuga dei capitali *f*	fuga de capital *f*
Floating (D)	—	floating	système des changes flottants *m*	floating *m*	flotación *f*
floating (E)	Floating *n*	—	système des changes flottants *m*	floating *m*	flotación *f*
floating (I)	Floating *n*	floating	système des changes flottants *m*	—	flotación *f*
floor price (E)	Niedrigstkurs *m*	—	cours le plus bas *m*	corso minimo *m*	cotización mínima *f*
flotación (Es)	Floating *n*	floating	système des changes flottants *m*	floating *m*	—
flow-of-funds analysis (E)	Finanzierungs-rechnung *f*	—	analyse des flux monétaires *f*	calcolo di finanziamento *m*	análisis de flujos monetarios *m*
fluctuación (Es)	Fluktuation *f*	fluctuation	fluctuation *f*	fluttuazione *f*	—
fluctuación de las necesidades (Es)	Bedarfsschwankung *f*	fluctuations in requirements	oscillations de demande *f pl*	oscillazioni del fabbisogno *f pl*	—
fluctuaciones en la producción (Es)	Produktions-schwankung *f*	fluctuations in production	fluctuation de la production *f pl*	oscillazione della produzione *f*	—
fluctuation (E)	Fluktuation *f*	—	fluctuation *f*	fluttuazione *f*	fluctuación *f*
fluctuation (F)	Fluktuation *f*	fluctuation	—	fluttuazione *f*	fluctuación *f*
fluctuation de la production (F)	Produktions-schwankung *f*	fluctuations in production	—	oscillazione della produzione *f*	fluctuaciones en la producción *f pl*
fluctuation des prix (F)	Preisschwankung *f*	price fluctuation	—	fluttuazione dei prezzi *f*	oscilación de precios *f*
fluctuations in production (E)	Produktions-schwankung *f*	—	fluctuation de la production *f pl*	oscillazione della produzione *f*	fluctuaciones en la producción *f pl*
fluctuations in requirements (E)	Bedarfsschwankung *f*	—	oscillations de demande *f pl*	oscillazioni del fabbisogno *f pl*	fluctuación de las necesidades *f*
Fluktuation (D)	—	fluctuation	fluctuation *f*	fluttuazione *f*	fluctuación *f*
Flurbereinigung (D)	—	compulsory consoli-dation of farmland	remembrement parcellaire *m*	ricomposizione fondiaria *f*	concentración parcelaria *f*
fluttuazione (I)	Fluktuation *f*	fluctuation	fluctuation *f*	—	fluctuación *f*
fluttuazione dei prezzi (I)	Preisschwankung *f*	price fluctuation	fluctuation des prix *f*	—	oscilación de precios *f*
foam material (E)	Schaumstoff *m*	—	mousse synthétique *f*	espanso *m*	espumoso plástico *m*
foire (F)	Messe *f*	fair	—	fiera *f*	feria *f*
foire commerciale (F)	Handelsmesse *f*	trade fair	—	fiera commerciale *f*	feria comercial *f*
foire d'automne (F)	Herbstmesse *f*	autumn fair	—	fiera autunnale *f*	feria de otoño *f*
foire d'échantillons (F)	Mustermesse *f*	trade fair	—	fiera campionaria *f*	feria de muestras *f*
foire de la mode (F)	Modemesse *f*	fashion fair	—	fiera della moda *f*	feria de moda *f*
Folgeauftrag (D)	—	follow-up order	commande consécutive *f*	ordine successivo *m*	orden sucesivo *f*
Folgeschäden (D)	—	consequential damages	dommage consécutif *m*	danni indiretti *m pl*	daño consecuencial *m*
folleto (Es)	Broschüre *f*	brochure	prospectus *m*	depliant *m*	—
follow-up financing (E)	Anschluß-finanzierung *f*	—	financement successif *m*	finanziamento successivo *m*	financiación sucesiva *f*
follow-up order (E)	Folgeauftrag *m*	—	commande consécutive *f*	ordine successivo *m*	orden sucesivo *f*
fomento de la exportació (Es)	Ausfuhrförderung *f*	measures to encourage exports	encouragement à l'exportation *m*	promozione delle esportazioni *f*	—
fonctionnaire (F)	Beamter *m*	official	—	funzionario *m*	funcionario *m*
fondation (F)	Stiftung *f*	foundation	—	fondazione *f*	fundación *f*
fondation d'existence (F)	Existenzgründung *f*	setting up of new business	—	costituzione di un lavoro indipendente *f*	fundación de existencia *f*
fondazione (I)	Stiftung *f*	foundation	fondation *f*	—	fundación *f*
fondé de procuration (F)	Prokurist *m*	"Prokurist" (authorized clerk)	—	procuratore *m*	apoderado general *m*

	D	E	F	I	Es
fondo (Es)	Fonds *m*	fund	fonds *m pl*	fondo *m*	—
fondo (I)	Fonds *m*	fund	fonds *m pl*	—	fondo *m*
fondo ammortamenti (I)	Abschreibungs-fonds *m*	depreciation fund	fonds d'amortissement *m*	—	fondo amortización *m*
fondo amortización (Es)	Abschreibungs-fonds *m*	depreciation fund	fonds d'amortissement *m*	fondo ammortamenti *m*	—
fondo de bonos (Es)	Rentenfonds *m*	pension fund	fonds d'Etat *m*/ effets publics *m pl*	fondo obbligazionario *m*	—
fondo de capital (Es)	Kapitalstock *m*	capital stock	réserve de capital *f*	riserva di capitale *f*	—
fondo de comercio (Es)	Firmenwert *m*	goodwill	valeur commerciale *f*	goodwill *m*	—
fondo de compensación (Es)	Ausgleichsfonds *m*	compensation fund	fonds de compensation *m*	fondo di compensazione *m*	—
fondo de inversión mobiliaria (Es)	Wertpapierfonds *m*	securities fund	fonds de valeurs mobilières *m*	fondo titoli *m*	—
fondo de inversiones (Es)	Investmentfonds *m*	unit trust	fonds commun de placement *m*	fondo d'investimento *m*	—
fondo de reserva (Es)	Reservefonds *m*	reserve fund	fonds de réserve *m*	fondo di riserva *m*	—
fondo di compensazione (I)	Ausgleichsfonds *m*	compensation fund	fonds de compensation *m*	—	fondo de compensaclón *m*
fondo d'investimento (I)	Investmentfonds *m*	unit trust	fonds commun de placement *m*	—	fondo de inversiones *m*
fondo di riserva (I)	Reservefonds *m*	reserve fund	fonds de réserve *m*	—	fondo de reserva *m*
fondo immobiliare (I)	Immobilienfonds *m*	real estate fund	fonds immobilier *m*	—	fondo inmobiliario *f*
fondo inmobiliario (Es)	Immobilienfonds *m*	real estate fund	fonds immobilier *m*	fondo immobiliare *m*	—
fondo obbligazionario (I)	Rentenfonds *m*	pension fund	fonds d'Etat *m*/ effets publics *m pl*	—	fondo de bonos *m*
fondos bloqueados (Es)	Sperrkonto *n*	blocked account	compte bloqué *m*	conto vincolato *m*	—
fondo titoli (I)	Wertpapierfonds *m*	securities fund	fonds de valeurs mobilières *m*	—	fondo de inversión mobiliaria *m*
Fonds (D)	—	fund	fonds *m pl*	fondo *m*	fondo *m*
fonds (F)	Fonds *m*	fund	—	fondo *m*	fondo *m*
fonds commun de placement (F)	Investmentfonds *m*	unit trust	—	fondo d'investimento *m*	fondo de inversiones *m*
fonds d'amortissement (F)	Abschreibungs-fonds *m*	depreciation fund	—	fondo ammortamenti *m*	fondo amortización *m*
fonds de compensation (F)	Ausgleichsfonds *m*	compensation fund	—	fondo di compensazione *m*	fondo de compensación *m*
fonds de réserve (F)	Reservefonds *m*	reserve fund	—	fondo di riserva *m*	fondo de reserva *m*
fonds d'Etat (F)	Rentenfonds *m*	pension fund	—	fondo obbligazionario *m*	fondo de bonos *m*
fonds de valeurs mobilières (F)	Wertpapierfonds *m*	securities fund	—	fondo titoli *m*	fondo de inversión mobiliaria *m*
fonds immobilier (F)	Immobilienfonds *m*	real estate fund	—	fondo immobiliare *m*	fondo inmobiliario *f*
fonds social (F)	Aktienkapital *n*	share capital	—	capitale azionario *m*	capital en acciones *m*
fonte d'acquisto (I)	Bezugsquelle *f*	source of supply	source d'approvi-sionnement *f*	—	fuente de suministro *f*
for account of a third party (E)	für fremde Rechnung	—	pour compte de tiers	per conto terzi	por cuenta ajena
forced sale (E)	Zwangsverkauf *m*	—	vente forcée *f*	vendita giudiziaria *f*	venta forzada *f*
force productive (F)	Ertragskraft *f*	earning capacity	—	redditività *f*	rentabilidad *f*
forces du marché (F)	Marktkräfte *pl*	market forces	—	forze di mercato *f pl*	fuerzas del mercado *f pl*
Förderlimit (D)	—	production limit	limite de production *f*	limite d'estrazione *m*	limite de producción *m*
Fördermenge (D)	—	output	quantité extraite *f*	quantitativo d'estrazione *m*	cantidad producida *f*
Förderquote (D)	—	production quota	quote-part de production *f*	quota d'estrazione *f*	cuota de producción *f*
forecast(ing) (E)	Prognose *f*	—	perspective *f*	prognosi *f*	pronóstico *m*
forecasting techniques (E)	Prognosetechnik *f*	—	technique de pronostic *f*	tecnica della prognosi *f*	técnica de pronóstico *f*
foreign account (E)	Auslandskonto *n*	—	compte d'étranger *m*	conto estero *m*	cuenta exterior *m*

	D	E	F	I	Es
foreign assets (E)	Auslandsvermögen *n*	—	avoirs à l'étranger *m pl*	patrimonio estero *m*	activo exterior *m*
foreign bill of exchange (E)	Auslandswechsel *n*	—	traite tirée sur l'étranger *f*	cambiale estera *f*	letra sobre el exterior *f*
foreign bond (E)	Auslandsanleihe *f*	—	emprunt extérieur *m*	prestito estero *m*	empréstito exterior *m*
foreign business (E)	Auslandsgeschäft *n*	—	opération avec l'étranger *f*	affare con l'estero *m*	negocio de exportación o importación *m*
foreign capital (E)	Auslandskapital *n*	—	capital étranger *m*	capitale estero *m*	capital extranjero *m*
foreign currency account (E)	Währungskonto *n*	—	compte en monnaies étrangères *m*	conto in valuta *m*	cuenta de moneda extranjera *f*
foreign customer (E)	Auslandskunde *f*	—	client étranger *m*	cliente estero *m*	cliente extranjero *m*
foreign customs territory (E)	Zollausland *n*	—	territoire hors du contrôle de la douane *m*	territorio doganale estero *m*	territorio aduanero exterior *m*
foreign debts (E)	Auslandsschulden *pl*	—	dettes à l'étranger *f pl*	debiti con l'estero *m pl*	deudas exteriores *f pl*
foreign demand (E)	Auslandsnachfrage *f*	—	demande en provenance de l'étranger *f*	domanda estera *f*	demanda exterior *m*
foreigner (E)	Ausländer *m*	—	étranger *m*	straniero *m*	extranjero *m*
foreign exchange and gold balance (E)	Gold- und Devisenbilanz *f*	—	balance d'or et de devises *f*	bilancia dell'oro e delle divise *f*	balanza de oro y divisas *f*
foreign exchange authorization (E)	Devisengenehmigung *f*	—	autorisation de change *f*	autorizzazione valutaria *f*	certificado de divisas *m*
foreign exchange balance (E)	Devisenbilanz *f*	—	compte de devises *m*	bilancia delle divise *f*	balanza de divisas *f*
foreign exchange control[1] (E)	Devisenkontrolle *f*	—	contrôle des changes *m*	controllo delle divise *m*	control de divisas *m*
foreign exchange control[2] (E)	Devisenbewirtschaftung *f*	—	contrôle des devises *m*	controllo valutario *m*	control de divisas *m*
foreign exchange dealings[1] (E)	Devisenhandel *m*	—	marché des changes *m*	commercio delle divise *m*	operaciones de divisas *f pl*
foreign exchange dealings[2] (E)	Devisenverkehr *m*	—	mouvement des devises *m*	commercio dei cambi *m*	tráfico de divisas *m*
foreign exchange market[1] (E)	Devisenmarkt *m*	—	marché des changes *m*	mercato valutario *m*	mercado de divisas *m*
foreign exchange market[2] (E)	Devisenbörse *f*	—	bourse de devises *f*	borsa valutaria *f*	Bolsa de divisas *f*
foreign exchange offset agreement (E)	Devisenausgleichsabkommen *n*	—	accord de compensation de devises *m*	accordo di clearing valutario *m*	acuerdo de compensación de divisas *m*
foreign exchange outflow (E)	Devisenabfluß *m*	—	sortie de devises *f*	deflusso di divise *m*	drenaje de divisas *m*
foreign exchange rate (E)	Devisenkurs *m*	—	taux de change *m*	cambio delle divise *m*	cambio *m*
foreign exchange[1] (E)	Devisen *pl*	—	devises *f pl*	divise *f pl*	divisas *f pl*
foreign exchange[2] (E)	Valuta *f*	—	monnaie étrangère *f*	valuta *f*/divise *f pl*	moneda extranjera *f*/divisas *f pl*/valuta *f*
foreign markets (E)	Auslandsmärkte *pl*	—	marchés extérieurs *m pl*	mercati esteri *m pl*	mercado exterior *m*
foreign trade (E)	Außenhandel *m*	—	commerce extérieur *m*	commercio estero *m*	comercio exterior *m*
foreign trade financing (E)	Außenhandelsfinanzierung *f*	—	aide financière à l'exportation *m*	finanziamento del commercio estero *m*	financiación del comercio exterior *f*
foreign trade monopoly (E)	Außenhandelsmonopol *n*	—	monopole du commerce extérieur *m*	monopolio del commercio estero *m*	monopolio del comercio exterior *m*
foreign trade policy (E)	Außenhandelspolitik *f*	—	politique de commerce extérieur *f*	politica del commercio estero *f*	política comercial exterior *f*
foreign worker (E)	ausländische Arbeitnehmer *m*	—	travailleur étranger *m*	prestatori d'opera stranieri *m pl*	trabajadores extranjeros *m*
forestry (E)	Forstwirtschaft *f*	—	économie forestière *f*	economia forestale *f*	silvicultura *f*
forfait de frais (F)	Spesenpauschale *f*	allowance for expenses	—	forfait di spese *m*	suma global de gastos *f*
forfait di spese (I)	Spesenpauschale *f*	allowance for expenses	forfait de frais *m*	—	suma global de gastos *f*
Forfaitierung (D)	—	non-recourse financing	financement sans recours *m*	forfetizzazione *f*	financiación sin recurso *f*
forfetizzazione (I)	Forfaitierung *f*	non-recourse financing	financement sans recours *m*	—	financiación sin recurso *f*

	D	E	F	I	Es
forged cheque (E)	gefälschter Scheck *m*	—	chèque maquillé *m*	assegno falsificato *m*	cheque falsificado *m*
form (E)	Formular *n*	—	formulaire *m*	modulo *m*	formulario *m*
formación de capital (Es)	Vermögensbildung *f*	capital formation	formation de capital *f*	formazione del patrimonio *f*	—
formación de carteles (Es)	Kartellbildung *f*	cartel formation	cartellisation *f*	costituzione di cartelli *f*	—
formación de los vendedores (Es)	Verkäuferschulung *f*	sales training	formation des vendeurs *f*	addestramento dei venditori *m*	—
formación de precios (Es)	Preisbildung *f*	formation of prices	formation des prix *f*	formazione dei prezzi *f*	—
formación de stocks (Es)	Vorratshaltung *f*	stockpiling	stockage *m*	gestione delle scorte *f*	—
formación profesional (Es)	Berufsausbildung *f*	professional training	formation professionelle *f*	formazione professionale *f*	—
forma de envío (Es)	Versandform *f*	manner of delivery	forme d'expéditoin *f*	tipo di spedizione *m*	—
forma de organización (Es)	Organisationsform *f*	pattern of organization	forme de l'organisation *f*	forma di organizzazione *f*	—
forma de organización empresarial (Es)	Unternehmensform *f*	form of business	forme de l'entreprise *f*	forma d'impresa *f*	—
forma de pago (Es)	Zahlungsform *f*	payment system	forme de payement *f*	tipo di pagamento *m*	—
forma d'impresa (I)	Unternehmensform *f*	form of business	forme de l'entreprise *f*	—	forma de organización empresarial *f*
forma di organizzazione (I)	Organisationsform *f*	pattern of organization	forme de l'organisation *f*	—	forma de organización *f*
forma escrita (Es)	Schriftform *f*	written form	forme par écrit *f*	forma scritta *f*	—
forma giuridica (I)	Rechtsform *f*	legal form	forme juridique *f*	—	forma jurídica *f*
forma jurídica (Es)	Rechtsform *f*	legal form	forme juridique *f*	forma giuridica *f*	—
forma scritta (I)	Schriftform *f*	written form	forme par écrit *f*	—	forma escrita *f*
formalidades aduaneras (Es)	Zollformalität *f*	customs formalities	formalité douanière *f*	formalità doganale *f*	—
formal identity (E)	Bilanzkontinuität *f*	—	identité des bilans successifs *f*	continuità di bilancio *f*	identidad de los balances sucsivos *f*
formalità doganale (I)	Zollformalität *f*	customs formalities	formalité douanière *f*	—	formalidades aduaneras *f pl*
formalité douanière (F)	Zollformalität *f*	customs formalities	—	formalità doganale *f*	formalidades aduaneras *f pl*
formalités en douane à l'exportation (F)	Ausfuhrabfertigung *f*	customs clearance of exports	—	sdoganamento delle esportazioni *m*	despacho de exportación *m*
formas del mercado (Es)	Marktformen *pl*	types of markets	formes du marché *f pl*	tipi di mercato *m pl*	—
format de l'annonce (F)	Anzeigenformat *n*	size of an advertisement	—	formato dell'inserzione *m*	tamaño del anuncio *m*
formatieren (D)	—	format	formatiser	formattare	formatizar
formation (E)	Gründung *f*	—	constitution *f*	costituzione *f*	fundación *f*
formation (F)	Bildung *f*	education	—	formazione *f*	educación *f*
formation de capital (F)	Vermögensbildung *f*	capital formation	—	formazione del patrimonio *f*	formación de capital *f*
formation des prix (F)	Preisbildung *f*	formation of prices	—	formazione dei prezzi *f*	formación de precios *f*
formation des vendeurs (F)	Verkäuferschulung *f*	sales training	—	addestramento dei venditori *m*	formación de los vendedores *f*
formation of prices (E)	Preisbildung *f*	—	formation des prix *f*	formazione dei prezzi *f*	formación de precios *f*
formation plan (E)	Gründungsplanung *f*	—	planification de fondation *f*	progettazione della costituzione *f*	planificación de la fundación *f*
formation professionelle (F)	Berufsausbildung *f*	professional training	—	formazione professionale *f*	formación profesional *f*
formation report (E)	Gründungsbericht *m*	—	procès-verbal de fondation *m*	relazione di costituzione *f*	informe de los fundadores *m*
formatiser (F)	formatieren	formatting	—	formattare	formatizar
formatizar (Es)	formatieren	formatting	formatiser	formattare	—
formato dell'inserzione (I)	Anzeigenformat *n*	size of an advertisement	format de l'annonce *m*	—	tamaño del anuncio *m*
formattare (I)	formatieren	format	formatiser	—	formatizar

	D	E	F	I	Es
formatting (E)	formatieren	—	formatiser	formattare	formatizar
formazione (I)	Bildung *f*	education	formation *f*	—	educación *f*
formazione dei prezzi (I)	Preisbildung *f*	formation of prices	formation des prix *f*	—	formación de precios *f*
formazione del patrimonio (I)	Vermögensbildung *f*	capital formation	formation de capital *f*	—	formación de capital *f*
formazione professionale (I)	Berufsausbildung *f*	professional training	formation professionelle *f*	—	formación profesional *f*
forme de l'entreprise (F)	Unternehmensform *f*	form of business	—	forma d'impresa *f*	forma de organización empresarial *f*
forme de l'organisation (F)	Organisationsform *f*	pattern of organization	—	forma di organizzazione *f*	forma de organización *f*
forme de payement (F)	Zahlungsform *f*	payment system	—	tipo di pagamento *m*	forma de pago *f*
forme d'expédition (F)	Versandform *f*	manner of delivery	—	tipo di spedizione *m*	forma de envío *f*
forme juridique (F)	Rechtsform *f*	legal form	—	forma giuridica *f*	forma jurídica *f*
forme par écrit (F)	Schriftform *f*	written form	—	forma scritta *f*	forma escrita *f*
formes du marché (F)	Marktformen *pl*	types of markets	—	tipi di mercato *m pl*	formas del mercado *f*
form of address (E)	Anrede *f*	—	début de lettre *m*	titolo *m*	tratamiento *m*
form of business (E)	Unternehmensform *f*	—	forme de l'entreprise *f*	forma d'impresa *f*	forma de organización empresarial *f*
formulaire (F)	Formular *n*	form	—	modulo *m*	formulario *m*
formulaire de demande (F)	Antragsformular *n*	application form	—	modulo di domanda *m*	formulario de solicitud *m*
Formular (D)	—	form	formulaire *m*	modulo *m*	formulario *m*
formulario (Es)	Formular *n*	form	formulaire *m*	modulo *m*	—
formulario de pedido (Es)	Bestellformular *n*	order form	bon de commande *m*	modulo d'ordinazione *m*	—
formulario de solicitud (Es)	Antragsformular *n*	application form	formulaire de demande *m*	modulo di domanda *m*	—
formulario en blanco (Es)	Blankoformular *n*	blank form	imprimé en blanc *m*	modulo in bianco *m*	—
fornitore[1] (I)	Lieferant *m*	supplier	fournisseur *m*	—	suministrador *m*
fornitore[2] (I)	Zulieferer *m*	supplier	sous-traitant *m*	—	abastecedor *m*
fornitura[3] (I)	Lieferung *f*	delivery	livraison *f*	—	suminstro *m*
fornitura a titolo di prova (I)	Probelieferung *f*	trial shipment	livraison à titre d'essai *f*	—	envío de prueba *m*
fornitura completa (I)	Gesamtlieferung *f*	total delivery	livraison totale *f*	—	suministro total *f*
fornitura di compensazione (I)	Ersatzlieferung *f*	substitute delivery	livraison de remplacement *f*	—	entrega de reposición *f*
fornitura parziale (I)	Teillieferung *f*	partial delivery	livraison partielle *f*	—	entrega parcial *f*
fornitura ridotta (I)	Minderlieferung *f*	short delivery	livraison en quantité inférieure *f*	—	envío incompleto *m*
fornitura supplementare (I)	Mehrlieferung *f*	additional delivery	livraison supplémentaire *f*	—	exceso *m*
foro competente (I)	Gerichtsstand *m*	jurisdiction	juridiction compétente *f*	—	tribunal competente *m*
for one's own account (E)	für eigene Rechnung	—	pour son propre compte	per conto proprio	por cuenta propia
for safekeeping (E)	zu treuen Händen	—	remettre en mains sûres	alla particolare attenzione	a la atención de
Forschung (D)	—	research	recherche *f*	ricerca *f*	investigación *f*
Forstwirtschaft (D)	—	forestry	économie forestière *f*	economia forestale *f*	silvicultura *f*
fortnight (E)	vierzehn Tage	—	quinze jours	quindici giorni	quince días *m pl*
forward contract (E)	Terminkontrakt *m*	—	contrat à terme *m*	contratto a termine *m*	contrato de entrega futura *m*
forwarder (E)	Spediteur *m*	—	commissionnaire de transport *m*	spedizioniere *m*	expeditor *m*
forward exchange dealings (E)	Devisentermin-geschäft *n*	—	opérations à terme sur les changes *f pl*	operazione valutaria a termine *f*	transacciones a tér-mino en divisas *f pl*
forwarding instruction (E)	Versandvorschrift *f*	—	prescriptions concer-nant l'expédition *f pl*	prescrizione per la spedizione *f*	instrucción para el envío *f*
forwarding merchandise (E)	Speditionsgut *n*	—	bien transporté *m*	merce spedita *f*	mercancía transportada *f*

	D	E	F	I	Es
forward price (E)	Terminkurs *m*	—	cours de bourse à terme *m*	corso a termine *m*	cambio a término *m*
forza d'argomentazione (I)	Argumentations-stärke *f*	talent for argumentation	capacité d'argumentation *f*	—	fuerza de argumentación *f*
forze di mercato (I)	Marktkräfte *pl*	market forces	forces du marché	—	fuerzas del mercado *f pl*
fosfato (Es)	Phosphat *n*	phosphate	phosphate *m*	fosfato *m*	—
fosfato (I)	Phosphat *n*	phosphate	phosphate *m*	—	fosfato *m*
fotocopia (Es)	Fotokopie *f*	photocopy	photocopie *f*	fotocopia *f*	—
fotocopia (I)	Fotokopie *f*	photocopy	photocopie *f*	—	fotocopia *f*
fotocopiadora (Es)	Fotokopierer *m*	photocopier	photocopieur *m*	copialettere *m*	—
Fotokopie (D)	—	photocopy	photocopie *f*	fotocopia *f*	fotocopia *f*
Fotokopierer (D)	—	photocopier	photocopieur *m*	copialettere *m*	fotocopiadora *f*
foundation (E)	Stiftung *f*	—	fondation *f*	fondazione *f*	fundación *f*
fournisseur (F)	Lieferant *m*	supplier	—	fornitore *m*	suministrador *m*
fourniture sous garantie (F)	Garantieleistung *f*	guarantee	—	prestazione di garanzia *f*	aplicación de la garantía *f*
Fracht (D)	—	freight	fret *m*	nolo *m*	carga *f*
Fracht bezahlt (D)	—	freight paid	fret payé	nolo pagato	flete pagado
Frachtbrief (D)	—	consignment note	lettre de voiture *f*	lettera di vettura *f*	carta de porte *f*
Frachtbriefdoppel (D)	—	duplicate consignment note	duplicata de la lettre de voiture *m*	duplicato della lettera di vettura *m*	duplicado de la carta de porte *m*
frachtfrei (D)	—	freight paid	exempt de frais de transport	franco di nolo	franco de porte
Frachtführer (D)	—	carrier	transporteur *m*	vettore *m*	transportista *m*
Frachtgut (D)	—	cargo	marchandise à transporter *f*	merce di trasporto *f*	mercancías en pe-queña velocidad *f pl*
Frachtkosten (D)	—	freight charges	frais de transport *m pl*	spese di trasporto *f pl*	gastos de transporte *m pl*
Frachtrate (D)	—	(freight) rate	taux de fret *m*	tariffa di nolo *f*	tipo de flete *m*
Frachtstücke (D)	—	packages	colis *m*	colli *m pl*	fardo *m*
Frachtvertrag (D)	—	freight contract	contrat d'affrètement *m*	contratto di trasporto *m*	contrato de transporte *m*
Frachtzuschlag (D)	—	additional freight charges	supplément de fret *m*	supplemento di nolo *m*	sobreporte *m*
fraction (E)	Bruchteil *m*	—	fraction *f*	frazione *f*	parte fraccionaria *f*
fraction (F)	Bruchteil *m*	fraction	—	frazione *f*	parte fraccionaria *f*
Fragebogen (D)	—	questionnaire	questionnaire *m*	questionario *m*	cuestionario *m*
frais (F)	Spesen *pl*	expenses	—	spese *f pl*	gastos *m pl*
frais d'acquisition (F)	Anschaffungs-kosten *pl*	purchase costs	—	costi d'acquisto *m pl*	coste de adquisición *m*
frais de banque (F)	Bankspesen *pl*	bank charges	—	commissioni bancarie *f pl*	gastos bancarios *m pl*
frais de commissions d'ouverture de crédit (F)	Kreditprovision *f*	credit commission	—	provvigione di credito *f*	comisión de apertura de crédito *f*
frais de fabrication (F)	Herstellungskosten *pl*	production costs	—	costi di produzione *m pl*	costo de la producción *m*
frais de fondation (F)	Gründungskosten *pl*	organization costs	—	costi della costituzione *m pl*	gastos de fundación *m pl*
frais de matériel (F)	Materialkosten *pl*	material costs	—	costi del materiale *m pl*	gastos de material *m pl*/coste de material *m*
frais de procédure (F)	Verfahrenskosten *pl*	costs of the proceedings	—	spese del procedimento *f pl*	costas *f pl*
frais de tenue de compte (F)	Kontogebühren *pl*	bank charges	—	diritti di conto *m pl*	gastos de administración de una cuenta *m pl*
frais de transport (F)	Frachtkosten *pl*	freight charges	—	spese di trasporto *f pl*	gastos de transporte *m pl*
frais de voyage[1] (F)	Reisespesen *pl*	travelling expenses	—	spese di viaggio *f pl*	gastos de viaje *m pl*
frais de voyage[2] (F)	Reisekosten *pl*	travelling expenses	—	costi di viaggio *m pl*	gastos de viaje *m pl*
frais judiciaires taxables exposés (F)	Gerichtskosten *pl*	legal costs	—	spese giudiziarie *f pl*	gastos judiciales *m pl*

	D	E	F	I	Es
Franchise (D)	—	franchise	franchise *f*	franchise *m*	franquicia *f*
franchise (E)	Franchise *f*	—	franchise *f*	franchise *m*	franquicia *f*
franchise (F)	Franchise *f*	franchise	—	franchise *m*	franquicia *f*
franchise (I)	Franchise *f*	franchise	franchise *f*	—	franquicia *f*
Franchisenehmer (D)	—	concessionary	concessionnaire *m*	concessionario *m*	concesionario *m*
Franchising (D)	—	franchising	franchising *m*	franchising *m*	franquicia *f*
franchising (E)	Franchising *n*	—	franchising *m*	franchising *m*	franquicia *f*
franchising (F)	Franchising *n*	franchising	—	franchising *m*	franquicia *f*
franchising (I)	Franchising *n*	franchising	franchising *m*	—	franquicia *f*
franco (Es)	frei Hafen	free port	franco port	franco porto	—
franco a bordo (I)	frei Schiff	free on board	franco sur navire	—	franco vapor
franco almacén (Es)	frei Lager	free warehouse	franco entrepôt	franco magazzino	—
franco banchina (I)	ab Kai	ex quay	départ quai	—	ex muelle
francobollo (I)	Briefmarke *f*	stamp	timbre-poste *m*	—	sello *m*
franco bordo (I)	ab Schiff	ex ship	départ navire	—	ex vapor
franco confine (I)	frei Grenze	free frontier	franco frontière	—	franco frontera
franco de port (F)	portofrei	post-free	—	franco di porto	porte pagado
franco de porte (Es)	frachtfrei	freight paid	exempt de frais de transport	franco di nolo	—
franco di nolo (I)	frachtfrei	freight paid	exempt de frais de transport	—	franco de porte
franco di porto (I)	portofrei	post-free	franco de port	—	porte pagado
franco domicile (F)	frei Haus	free domicile	—	franco domicilio	franco domicilio
franco domicilio (Es)	frei Haus	free domicile	franco domicile	franco domicilio	—
franco domicilio (I)	frei Haus	free domicile	franco domicile	—	franco domicilio
franco en gare (F)	frei Station	free station	—	franco stazione	franco estación
franco entrepôt (F)	frei Lager	free warehouse	—	franco magazzino	franco almacén
franco estación (Es)	frei Station	free station	franco en gare	franco stazione	—
franco fabbrica (I)	ab Werk	ex works	départ usine	—	ex fábrica
franco frontera (Es)	frei Grenze	free frontier	franco frontière	franco confine	—
franco frontière (F)	frei Grenze	free frontier	—	franco confine	franco frontera
franco magazzino (I)	frei Lager	free warehouse	franco entrepôt	—	franco almacén
franco port (F)	frei Hafen	free port	—	franco porto	franco
franco porto (I)	frei Hafen	free port	franco port	—	franco
franco stazione[1] (I)	frei Station	free station	franco en gare	—	franco estación
franco stazione[2] (I)	ab Bahnhof	ex rail/free on rail	départ gare	—	puesto en estación
franco sur navire (F)	frei Schiff	free on board	—	franco a bordo	franco vapor
franco sur wagon (F)	frei Waggon	free on rail	—	franco vagone	franco vagón
franco vagón (Es)	frei Waggon	free on rail	franco sur wagon	franco vagone	—
franco vagone (I)	frei Waggon	free on rail	franco sur wagon	—	franco vagón
franco vapor (Es)	frei Schiff	free on board	franco sur navire	franco a bordo	—
frankieren (D)	—	prepay the postage	affranchir	affrancare	franquear
franquear (Es)	frankieren	prepay the postage	affranchir	affrancare	—
franquicia[1] (Es)	Franchising *n*	franchising	franchising *m*	franchising *m*	—
franquicia[2] (Es)	Franchise *f*	franchise	franchise *f*	franchise *m*	—
fraud (E)	Betrug *m*	—	fraude *f*	frode *f*	fraude *m*
fraude (Es)	Betrug *m*	fraud	fraude *f*	frode *f*	—
fraude (F)	Betrug *m*	fraud	—	frode *f*	fraude *m*
fraude fiscal (Es)	Steuerbetrug *m*	fiscal fraud	fraude fiscale *f*	frode fiscale *f*	—
fraude fiscale[1] (F)	Steuerbetrug *m*	fiscal fraud	—	frode fiscale *f*	fraude fiscal *m*
fraude fiscale[2] (F)	Hinterziehung *f*	evasion of taxes	—	evasione *f*	defraudación *f*
fraudulent bankruptcy (E)	betrügerischer Bankrott *m*	—	banqueroute frauduleuse *f*	bancarotta fraudolenta *f*	quiebra frandulenta *f*
frazione (I)	Bruchteil *m*	fraction	fraction *f*	—	parte fraccionaria *f*

	D	E	F	I	Es
frecuencia de transbordo (Es)	Umschlags-häufigkeit *f*	transshipment frequencies	fréquence de transbordement *f*	velocità di rotazione *f*	—
frecuencia publicitaria (Es)	Werbefrequenz *f*	advertising frequency	fréquence publicitaire *f*	frequenza della pubblicità *f*	—
free domicile (E)	frei Haus	—	franco domicile	franco domicilio	franco domicilio
freedom of association (E)	Koalitionsfreiheit *f*	—	liberté d'association *f*	libertà di coalizione *f*	libertad de coalición *f*
freedom of consumption (E)	Konsumfreiheit *f*	—	liberté de consommation *f*	libertà di consumo *f*	libertad de consumo *f*
freedom of contract (E)	Vertragsfreiheit *f*	—	liberté de contracter *f*	libertà contrattuale *f*	libertad contractual *f*
freedom of trade (E)	Gewerbefreiheit *f*	—	liberté des professions industrielles et commerciales *f*	libertà d'industria *f*	libertad de industria *f*
free frontier (E)	frei Grenze	—	franco frontière	franco confine	franco frontera
freehold flat (E)	Eigentumswohnung *f*	—	logement en propriété *m*	appartamento in condominio *m*	piso en propiedad *m*
free movement of capital (E)	freier Kapitalverkehr *m*	—	libre circulation des capitaux *f*	libera circolazione dei capitali *f*	libre circulación de capitales
free of charge (E)	kostenlos	—	gratuit	gratuito	libre de gastos
free of charge (E)	unentgeltlich	—	à titre gracieux	gratuito	gratuito
free of defects (E)	mangelfrei	—	sans défaut	esente da vizi	sin vicios
free of phosphate (E)	phosphatfrei	—	sans phosphate	privo di fosfato	sin fosfato
free on board (E)	frei Schiff	—	franco sur navire	franco a bordo	franco vapor
free on rail (E)	frei Waggon	—	franco sur wagon	franco vagone	franco vagón
free port[1] (E)	frei Hafen	—	franco port	franco porto	franco
free port[2] (E)	Freihafen *m*	—	port franc *m*	porto franco *m*	puerto franco *m*
free station (E)	frei Station	—	franco en gare	franco stazione	franco estación
free ticket (E)	Freikarte *f*	—	billet de faveur *m*	biglietto gratuito *m*	entrada gratuita *f*
free trade[1] (E)	Freihandel *m*	—	commerce libre *m*	scambio libero *m*	librecambio *m*
free trade[2] (E)	Außenhandels-freiheit *f*	—	libre-échange *m*	libertà di commercio estero *f*	librecambio *m*
free trade area (E)	Freihandelszone *f*	—	zone de libre-échange *f*	zona di libero scambio *f*	zona de librecambio *f*
free warehouse (E)	frei Lager	—	franco entrepôt	franco magazzino	franco almacén
Freiberufler (D)	—	selfemployed person	personne exerçant une profession libérale *f*	libero professionista *m*	profesional *m*
freibleibend (D)	—	subject to confirmation	sans engagement	senza impegno	no vinculante
freier Kapitalverkehr (D)	—	free movement of capital	libre circulation des capitaux *f*	libera circolazione dei capitali *f*	libre circulación de capitales
freight[1] (E)	Fracht *f*	—	fret *m*	nolo *m*	carga *f*
freight[2] (E)	verfrachten	—	fréter/embarquer	imbarcare	expedir/fletar
freight[3] (E)	Ladung *f*	—	charge *f*	carico *m*	carga *f*
freight charges (E)	Frachtkosten *pl*	—	frais de transport *m pl*	spese di trasporto *f pl*	gastos de transporte *m pl*
freight contract (E)	Frachtvertrag *m*	—	contrat d'affrètement *m*	contratto di trasporto *m*	contrato de transporte *m*
freight paid[1] (E)	Fracht bezahlt	—	fret payé	nolo pagato	flete pagado
freight paid[2] (E)	frachtfrei	—	exempt de frais de transport	franco di nolo	franco de porte
(freight) rate (E)	Frachtrate *f*	—	taux de fret *m*	tariffa di nolo *f*	tipo de flete *m*
frei Grenze (D)	—	free frontier	franco frontière	franco confine	franco frontera
frei Hafen (D)	—	free port	franco port	franco porto	franco
Freihafen (D)	—	free port	port franc *m*	porto franco *m*	puerto franco *m*
Freihandel (D)	—	free trade	commerce libre *m*	scambio libero *m*	librecambio *m*
Freihandelszone (D)	—	free trade area	zone de libre-échange *f*	zona di libero scambio *f*	zona de librecambio *f*
frei Haus (D)	—	free domicile	franco domicile	franco domicilio	franco domicilio
Freikarte (D)	—	free ticket	billet de faveur *m*	biglietto gratuito *m*	entrada gratuita *f*
frei Lager (D)	—	free warehouse	franco entrepôt	franco magazzino	franco almacén

	D	E	F	I	Es
frei Schiff (D)	—	free on board	franco sur navire	franco a bordo	franco vapor
frei Station (D)	—	free station	franco en gare	franco stazione	franco estación
frei Waggon (D)	—	free on rail	franco sur wagon	franco vagone	franco vagón
Fremdfinanzierung (D)	—	debt financing	constitution de capital par apport de tiers *f*	finanziamento passivo *m*	financiación externa *f*
fréquence de transbordement (F)	Umschlags-häufigkeit *f*	transshipment frequencies	—	velocità di rotazione *f*	frecuencia de transbordo *f*
fréquence publicitaire (F)	Werbefrequenz *f*	advertising frequency	—	frequenza della pubblicità *f*	frecuencia publicitaria *f*
frequenza della pubblicità (I)	Werbefrequenz *f*	advertising frequency	fréquence publicitaire *f*	—	frecuencia publicitaria *f*
fret (F)	Fracht *f*	freight	—	nolo *m*	carga *f*
fret aérien (F)	Luftfracht *f*	air freight	—	nolo aereo *m*	flete aéreo *m*
fréter (F)	verfrachten	freight/to ship	—	imbarcare	expedir/fletar
fret par rail (F)	Bahnfracht *f*	rail freight	—	nolo ferroviario *m*	transporte ferroviario *m*
fret payé (F)	Fracht bezahlt	freight paid	—	nolo pagato	flete pagado
Frist (D)	—	period	délai *m*	termine *m*	plazo *m*
fristgerecht (D)	—	timely	dans les délais	entro il termine convenuto	dentro del plazo fijado
Fristgewährung (D)	—	granting a respite	octroi d'un délai *m*	concessione di un termine *f*	concesión de un plazo *f*
fristlos (D)	—	without prior notice	sans délai	senza preavviso	sin plazo
frode (I)	Betrug *m*	fraud	fraude *f*	—	fraude *m*
frode fiscale (I)	Steuerbetrug *m*	fiscal fraud	fraude fiscale *f*	—	fraude fiscal *m*
frontera aduanera (Es)	Zollgrenze *f*	customs frontier	frontière douanière *f*	confine doganale *m*	—
frontière douanière nationale (F)	Zollgrenze *f*	customs frontier	—	confine doganale *m*	frontera aduanera *f*
fuel (E)	Treibstoff *m*	—	carburant *m*	carburante *m*	combustible *m*
fuente de suministro (Es)	Bezugsquelle *f*	source of supply	source d'approvisionnement *f*	fonte d'acquisto *f*	—
fuerza de argumentación (Es)	Argumentations-stärke *f*	talent for argumentation	capacité d'argumentation *f*	forza d'argomentazione *f*	—
fuerzas del mercado (Es)	Marktkräfte *pl*	market forces	forces du marché	forze di mercato *f pl*	—
fuga de capital (Es)	Kapitalflucht *f*	flight of capital	évasion des capitaux *f*	fuga dei capitali *f*	—
fuga dei capitali (I)	Kapitalflucht *f*	flight of capital	évasion des capitaux *f*	—	fuga de capital *f*
Führung (D)	—	management	direction *f*	gestione *f*	gestión *f*
Führungsebene (D)	—	executive level	niveau de gestion *m*	quadri dirigenti *m*	nivel de dirección *m*
Führungsperson (D)	—	executive	cadre *m*	dirigente *m*	ejecutivo *m*
full employment (E)	Vollbeschäftigung *f*	—	plein emploi *m*	piena occupazione *f*	empleo total *m*
full power (E)	Vollmacht *f*	—	plein pouvoir *m*/ mandat *m*	autorizzazione *f*/ procura *f*	poder *m*/ autorización *f*/ escritura de poder *f*
funcionario (Es)	Beamter *m*	official	fonctionnaire *m*	funzionario *m*	—
fund (E)	Fonds *m*	—	fonds *m pl*	fondo *m*	fondo *m*
fundación[1] (Es)	Stiftung *f*	foundation	fondation *f*	fondazione *f*	—
fundación[2] (Es)	Gründung *f*	formation	constitution *f*	costituzione *f*	—
fundación de existencia (Es)	Existenzgründung *f*	setting up of new business	fondation d'existence *f*	costituzione di un lavoro indipendente *f*	—
fundación nueva (Es)	Neugründung *f*	new foundation	création d'une nouvelle société *f*	costituzione nuova *f*	—
fungibilidad (Es)	Fungibilität *f*	fungibility	qualité fongible *f* d'un bien	fungibilità *f*	—
fungibilità (I)	Fungibilität *f*	fungibility	qualité fongible d'un bien *f*	—	fungibilidad *f*
Fungibilität (D)	—	fungibility	qualité fongible d'un bien *f*	fungibilità *f*	fungibilidad *f*
fungibility (E)	Fungibilität *f*	—	qualité fongible d'un bien *f*	fungibilità *f*	fungibilidad *f*

	D	E	F	I	Es
Funkspruch (D)	—	radio message	message par radio *m*	radiotelefonata *f*	mensaje radiado *m*
funzionario (I)	Beamter *m*	official	fonctionnaire *m*	—	funcionario *m*
für eigene Rechnung (D)	—	for one's own account	pour son propre compte	per conto proprio	por cuenta propia
für fremde Rechnung (D)	—	for account of a third party	pour compte de tiers	per conto terzi	por cuenta ajena
further processing (E)	Weiterverarbeitung *f*	—	transformation complémentaire *f*	trasformazione *f*	elaboración ulterior *f*
furto (I)	Diebstahl *m*	theft	vol *m*	—	robo *m*
fusée (F)	Rakete *f*	rocket	—	missile *m*	cohete *m*
Fusion (D)	—	fusion	fusion *f*	fusione *f*	fusión *f*
fusion (E)	Fusion *f*	—	fusion *f*	fusione *f*	fusión *f*
fusión[1] (Es)	Fusion *f*	fusion	fusion *f*	fusione *f*	—
fusión[2] (Es)	Verschmelzung *f*	merger	fusion *f*	fusione *f*	—
fusion[1] (F)	Verschmelzung *f*	merger	—	fusione *f*	fusión *f*
fusion[2] (F)	Fusion *f*	fusion	—	fusione *f*	fusión *f*
fusión de empresas (Es)	Unternehmens-fusion *f*	merger of companies	fusion de sociétés *f*	fusione d'imprese *f*	—
fusion de sociétés (F)	Unternehmens-fusion *f*	merger of companies	—	fusione d'imprese *f*	fusión de empresas *f*
fusione[1] (I)	Fusion *f*	fusion	fusion *f*	—	fusión *f*
fusione[2] (I)	Verschmelzung *f*	merger	fusion *f*	—	fusión *f*
fusione d'imprese (I)	Unternehmens-fusion *f*	merger of companies	fusion de sociétés *f*	—	fusión de empresas *f*
Fusionskontrolle (D)	—	merger control	contrôle de fusion *m*	controllo delle fusioni *m*	control de fusiones *m*
future prospects (E)	Zukunftschance *f*	—	perspectives d'avenir *f pl*	prospettiva *f*	posibilidades futuras *f pl*
futures market (E)	Terminbörse *f*	—	bourse à terme *f*	mercato a termine *m*	bolsa de valores a término *f*
Gage (D)	—	salary	cachet *m*	onorario *m*	remuneración *f*
gain fictif (F)	Scheingewinn *m*	fictitious profit	—	utile fittizio *m*	beneficio simulado *m*
gainfully employed (E)	erwerbstätig	—	actif	attivo	activo
gainfully employed person[1] (E)	Erwerbstätiger *m*	—	personne ayant un emploi *f*	persona attiva *f*	persona activa *f*
gainfully employed person[2] (E)	Erwerbsperson *f*	—	personne active *f*	persona attiva *f*	persona en activo *f*
galloping inflation (E)	galoppierende Inflation *f*	—	inflation galopante *f*	inflazione galoppante *f*	inflación galopante *f*
galoppierende Inflation (D)	—	galloping inflation	inflation galopante *f*	inflazione galoppante *f*	inflación galopante *f*
gama de productos (Es)	Produktpalette *f*	range of products	gamme des produits *f*	gamma dei prodotti *f*	—
gamma dei prodotti (I)	Produktpalette *f*	range of products	gamme des produits *f*	—	gama de productos *f*
gamme (F)	Produktions-programm *n*	production programme	—	programma di produzione *m*	programa de producción *m*
gamme des produits (F)	Produktpalette *f*	range of products	—	gamma dei prodotti *f*	gama de productos *f*
ganancia bruta (Es)	Rohgewinn *m*	gross profit on sales	bénéfice brut *m*	utile lordo *m*	—
ganancia neta (Es)	Reingewinn *m*	net profit	bénéfice net *m*	utile netto *m*	—
ganancias de capital (Es)	Kapitaleinkommen *n*	unearned income	revenu du capital *m*	reddito del capitale *m*	—
garant (F)	Bürge *m*	guarantor	—	fideiussore *m*	fiador *m*
garantía[1] (Es)	Garantie *f*	warranty	garantie *f*	garanzia *f*	—
garantía[2] (Es)	Gewährleistung *f*	warranty	prestation de garantie *f*	garanzia *f*	—
garantía bancaria (Es)	Bankgarantie *f*	bank guarantee	garantie de banque *f*	garanzia bancaria *f*	—
garantía de comisión (Es)	Provisionsgarantie *f*	commission guarantee	garantie de commission *f*	garanzia di provvigione *f*	—
garantía de compra (Es)	Ankaufgarantie *f*	purchase guarantee	garantie d'achat *f*	garanzia d'acquisto *f*	—

	D	E	F	I	Es
garantía de la calidad (Es)	Qualitätssicherung *f*	quality assurance	garantie de la qualité *f*	garanzia di qualità *f*	—
garantía real (Es)	dingliche Sicherung *f*	real security	sécurité réelle *f*	garanzia reale *f*	—
Garantie (D)	—	warranty	garantie *f*	garanzia *f*	garantía *f*
garantie (F)	Garantie *f*	warranty	—	garanzia *f*	garantía *f*
garantie d'achat (F)	Ankaufgarantie *f*	purchase guarantee	—	garanzia d'acquisto *f*	garantía de compra *f*
garantie de banque (F)	Bankgarantie *f*	bank guarantee	—	garanzia bancaria *f*	garantía bancaria *f*
garantie de bonne fin (F)	Ausfallbürgschaft *f*	deficiency guarantee	—	fideiussione d'indennità *f*	fianza con beneficio de excusión *f*
garantie de commission (F)	Provisionsgarantie *f*	commission guarantee	—	garanzia di provvigione *f*	garantía de comisión *f*
garantie de la qualité (F)	Qualitätssicherung *f*	quality assurance	—	garanzia di qualità *f*	garantía de la calidad *f*
garantie des crénciers (F)	Gläubigerschutz *m*	protection of creditors	—	tutela del creditore *f*	protección de los acreedores *f*
Garantiekarte (D)	—	certificate of warranty	carte de garantie *f*	certificato di garanzia *m*	tarjeta de garantía *f*
Garantieleistung (D)	—	guarantee	fourniture sous garantie *f*	prestazione di garanzia *f*	aplicación de la garantía *f*
Garantie-verpflichtung (D)	—	guarantee obligation	engagement de garantie *m*	obbligo di garanzia *m*	obligación de garantía *f*
garanzia[1] (I)	Gewährleistung *f*	warranty	prestation de garantie *f*	—	garantía *f*
garanzia[2] (I)	Garantie *f*	warranty	garantie *f*	—	garantía *f*
garanzia bancaria (I)	Bankgarantie *f*	bank guarantee	garantie de banque *f*	—	garantía bancaria *f*
garanzia d'acquisto (I)	Ankaufgarantie *f*	purchase guarantee	garantie d'achat *f*	—	garantía de compra *f*
garanzia di esecuzione (I)	Gewährleistungs-garantie *f*	guarantee for proper execution	caution de garantie *f*	—	fianza de contratista *f*
garanzia di provvigione (I)	Provisionsgarantie *f*	commission guarantee	garantie de commission *f*	—	garantía de comisión *f*
garanzia di qualità (I)	Qualitätssicherung *f*	quality assurance	garantie de la qualité *f*	—	garantía de la calidad *f*
garanzia d'offerta (I)	Bietungsgarantie *f*	tender guarantee	cautionnement provisiore *m*	—	caución de licitación *f*
garanzia reale (I)	dingliche Sicherung *f*	real security	sécurité réelle *f*	—	garantía real *f*
garde des titres (F)	Depotgeschäft *n*	deposit banking	— deposito *f*	operazione di	custodia de valores *f*
gare destinataire (F)	Bestimmungs-bahnhof *m*	station of destination	—	stazione di destinazione *f*	estación de destino *f*
garzone (I)	Geselle *m*	journeyman	ouvrier artisan *m*	—	oficial *m*
gas natural (Es)	Erdgas *n*	natural gas	gaz naturel *m*	gas naturale *m*	—
gas naturale (I)	Erdgas *n*	natural gas	gaz naturel *m*	—	gas natural *m*
gasolina (Es)	Benzin *n*	petrol	essence *f*	benzina *f*	—
gasot (Es)	Aufwendung *f*	expenditure	dépenses *f pl*	spese *f pl*	—
gastos[1] (Es)	Kosten *pl*	costs	coût *m*	costi *m pl*	—
gastos[2] (Es)	Ausgaben *pl*	expenses	dépenses *f pl*	spese *f pl*	—
gastos[3] (Es)	Aufwand *m*	expenditure	charge *f*	spese *f pl*	—
gastos[4] (Es)	Spesen *pl*	expenses	frais *m pl*	spese *f pl*	—
gastos adicionales (Es)	Nebenkosten *pl*	ancillary costs	coûts accessoires *m pl*	costi accessori *m pl*	—
gastos bancarios (Es)	Bankspesen *pl*	bank charges	frais de banque *m pl*	commissioni bancarie *f pl*	—
gastos de administra-ción de una cuenta (Es)	Kontogebühren *pl*	bank charges	frais de tenue de compte *m pl*	diritti di conto *m pl*	—
gastos de adquisición (Es)	Bezugskosten *pl*	purchasing costs	coûts d'acquisition *m pl*	prezzo d'acquisto *m*	—
gastos de alojamiento (Es)	Übernachtungs-kosten *pl*	overnight expenses	coûts de nuitée *m pl*	spese di pernottamento *f pl*	—
gastos de carga (Es)	Verladekosten *pl*	loading charges	coût du chargement *m*	costi di caricamento *m pl*	—
gastos de desarrollo (Es)	Entwicklungs-kosten *pl*	development costs	coûts de développement *m pl*	costi di sviluppo *m pl*	—

	D	E	F	I	Es
gastos de descarga[1] (Es)	Löschgebühren *pl*	discharging expenses	droit de déchargement *m*	spese di scarico *f pl*	—
gastos de descargo[2] (Es)	Entladungskosten *pl*	discharging expenses	coûts de déchargement *m pl*	spese di scaricamento *f pl*	—
gastos de explotación[1] (Es)	Betriebsausgaben *f*	(current) operational expenses	charges d'exploitación *f pl*	spese aziendali *f pl*	—
gastos de explotación[2] (Es)	Betriebskosten *pl*	operating costs	charges d'exploitation *f pl*	spese d'esercizio *f pl*	—
gastos de fundación (Es)	Gründungskosten *pl*	organization costs	frais de fondation *m pl*	costi della costituzione *m pl*	—
gastos de información (Es)	Informations-kosten *pl*	information costs	coûts d'information *m pl*	costi d'informazione *m pl*	—
gastos de material (Es)	Materialkosten *pl*	material costs	frais de matériel *m pl*	costi del materiale *m pl*	—
gastos de producción (Es)	Produktionskosten *pl*	cost of production	coût de production *m*	costi produttivi *m pl*	—
gastos de readaptación (Es)	Anpassungskosten *pl*	adjustment costs	coûts d'adaptation *m pl*	costi d'adattamento *m pl*	—
gastos de reproducción (Es)	Reproduktions-kosten *pl*	reproduction cost	coût de reproduction *m*	costi di riproduzione *m pl*	—
gastos de saneamiento (Es)	Sanierungskosten *pl*	renewal costs	coûts d'assainisse-ment *m pl*	costi di risanamento *m pl*	—
gastos de subasta (Es)	Auktionsgebühr *f*	auction fees	droits de vente aux enchères *m pl*	diritto d'asta *m*	—
gastos de transporte (Es)	Frachtkosten *pl*	freight charges	frais de transport *m pl*	spese di trasporto *f pl*	—
gastos de utilización de capital (Es)	Kapitalnutzungs-kosten *pl*	costs of the utilization of capital	coûts d'utilisation de capital *m pl*	costo del capitale *m*	—
gastos de viaje (Es)	Reisespesen *pl*	travelling expenses	frais de voyage *m pl*	spese di viaggio *f pl*	—
gastos directos (Es)	Primäraufwand *m*	primary expenses	charge primaire *f*	spese primarie *f pl*	—
gastos efectivos (Es)	Istkosten *pl*	actual costs	coûts réels *m pl*	costi effettivi *m pl*	—
gastos extraordinarios (Es)	Sonderausgaben *pl*	special expenses	dépense spéciale *f*	spese straordinarie *f pl*	—
gastos fijos[1] (Es)	Fixkosten *pl*	fixed costs	coûts fixes *m pl*	costi fissi *m pl*	—
gastos fijos[2] (Es)	Bereitstellungs-kosten *pl*	commitment fee	coûts administratifs *m pl*	spese di stanziamento *f pl*	—
gastos fijos de utilización (Es)	Nutzkosten *pl*	utility costs	coûts fixes utiles *m pl*	costi fissi di utilizzo *m pl*	—
gastos generales[1] (Es)	Gesamtkosten *pl*	total costs	coût total *m*	costi totali *m pl*	—
gastos generales[2] (Es)	Gemeinkosten *pl*	overhead expenses	coûts indirects *m pl*	costi comuni *m pl*	—
gastos judiciales (Es)	Gerichtskosten *pl*	legal costs	frais judiciaires tax-ables exposés *m pl*	spese giudiziarie *f pl*	—
gastos medios (Es)	Durchschnitts-kosten *pl*	average costs	coût moyen *m*	costi medi *m pl*	—
gastos para aguas residuales (Es)	Abwasserkosten *pl*	sewage disposal costs	coûts de traitement des eaux usées *m pl*	costi per le acque di scarico *m pl*	—
gastos precalculados (Es)	Sollkosten *pl*	budgeted costs	coûts ex ante *m pl*	costi calcolati *m pl*	—
gastos públicos[1] (Es)	Staatsausgaben *pl*	public spending	dépenses publiques *f pl*	spese pubbliche *f pl*	—
gastos públicos[2] (Es)	öffentliche Ausgaben *pl*	public spending	dépenses publiques *f pl*	spesa pubblica *f*	—
gastos variables (Es)	variable Kosten *pl*	variable costs	coûts variables *m pl*	costi variabili *m pl*	—
gauge (E)	eichen	—	jauger	tarare	contrastar
gaz naturel (F)	Erdgas *n*	natural gas	—	gas naturale *m*	gas natural *m*
Gebäude-versicherung (D)	—	insurance on buildings	assurance des bâtiments *f*	assicurazione dei fabbricati *f*	seguro inmobiliario *m*
Gebietshoheit (D)	—	territorial jurisdiction	souveraineté territoriale *f*	sovranità territoriale *f*	soberanía territorial *f*
Gebietsschutz (D)	—	territory protection	exclusivité territoriale *f*	tutela territoriale *f*	protección territorial *f*
Gebiets-verkaufsleiter (D)	—	area sales manager	chef de vente régionale *m*	direttore di vendita regionale *m*	jefe de venta regional *m*
Gebietsvertreter (D)	—	area representative	représentant régional *m*	agente di zona *m*	representante regional *m*

	D	E	F	I	Es
Gebrauch (D)	—	use	utilisation *f*	uso *m*	uso *m*
Gebrauchsgüter (D)	—	durable consumer goods	biens d'utilisation courante *m pl*	beni di consumo durevoli *m pl*	bienes de consumo duradero *m pl*
Gebrauchtwagen (D)	—	used car	voiture d'occasion *f*	automobile usata *f*	coche de segunda mano *m*
Gebühr (D)	—	fee	taxe *f*	tassa *f*	derecho *m*
Geburtenrate (D)	—	birth rate	taux de natalité *m*	tasso di natalità *m*	tasa de natalidad *f*
Geburtsdatum (D)	—	date of birth	date de naissance *f*	data di nascita *f*	fecha de nacimiento *f*
Geburtsort (D)	—	place of birth	lieu de naissance *m*	luogo di nascita *m*	lugar de nacimiento *m*
Geburtstag (D)	—	birthday	anniversaire *m*	compleanno *m*	día de nacimiento *m*
Gefahr (D)	—	danger	danger *m*	pericolo *m*	peligro *m*
Gefahrenzulage (D)	—	danger money	prime de danger *f*	premio di rischio *m*	incremento por peligrosidad *m*
gefälschter Scheck (D)	—	forged cheque	chèque maquillé *m*	assegno falsificato *m*	cheque falsificado *m*
gegen Akkreditiv (D)	—	against letter of credit	contre accréditif	contro lettera di credito	con crédito documentario
gegen Barzahlung (D)	—	against cash	au comptant	contro pagamento in contanti	al contado
gegen Nachnahme (D)	—	cash on delivery	contre remboursement	contro assegno	contra rembolso
Gegenwert (D)	—	equivalent	contre-valeur *f*	controvalore *m*	contravalor *m*
Gegenzeichnung (D)	—	countersignature	contreseing *m*	controfirma *f*	contrafirma *f*
Gehalt (D)	—	salary	traitement *m*	stipendio *m*	sueldo *m*
Gehaltserhöhung (D)	—	increase in salary	augmentation du traitement *f*	aumento dello stipendio *m*	aumento de sueldo *m*
Gehaltskonto (D)	—	salary account	compte de domiciliation du salaire *m*	conto stipendi *m*	cuenta de salario *f*
geheim (D)	—	secret	secret	segreto	secreto
Geheimhaltung (D)	—	maintenance of secrecy	conservation du secret *f*	segretezza *f*	mantenimiento del secreto *m*
Geheimnis (D)	—	secret	secret *m*	segreto *m*	secreto *m*
gekreuzter Scheck (D)	—	crossed cheque	chèque barré *m*	assegno sbarrato *m*	cheque cruzado *m*
Geld (D)	—	money	argent *m*	denaro *m*	dinero *m*/efectivo *m*
Geldaufnahme (D)	—	raising of money	emprunt *m*	accensione di un mutuo *f*	dinero tomado a préstamo *m*
Geldbetrag (D)	—	amount of money	somme d'argent *f*	somma di denaro *f*	suma de dinero *f*
Geldbuße (D)	—	fine	amende *f*	pena pecuniaria *f*	multa *f*
Geldgeber (D)	—	financial backer	bailleur de fonds *m*	finanziatore *m*	prestamista *m*
Geldkurs (D)	—	demand price	cours de la demande *m*	prezzo di domanda *m*	cotización demandada *f*/precio ofrecido *m*
Geldmarkt (D)	—	money market	marché monétaire *m*	mercato monetario *m*	mercado monetario *m*
Geldmenge (D)	—	money supply	quantité de monnaie en circulation *f*	massa monetaria *f*	volumen monetario *m*
Geldnachfrage (D)	—	demand for money	demande sur le marché monétaire *f*	domanda di denaro *f*	demanda monetaria *f*
Geldpolitik (D)	—	monetary policy	politique monétaire *f*	politica monetaria *f*	política monetaria *f*
Geldschöpfung (D)	—	money creation	création de trésorerie *f*	creazione di denaro *f*	creación de dinero *f*
Geldstrafe (D)	—	fine	peine pécuniaire *f*	multa *f*	multa *f*
Geldtheorie (D)	—	monetary theory	théorie monétaire *f*	teoria del denaro *f*	teoría monetaria *f*
Geldumlauf (D)	—	circulation of money	circulation monétaire *f*	circolazione di denaro *f*	circulación monetaria *f*
Geldverknappung (D)	—	monetary restriction	pénurie d'argent *f*	riduzione del denaro *f*	restricción monetaria *f*
Geldvermögen (D)	—	financial assets	moyens financiers *m*	patrimonio monetario *m*	activo monetario *m*
Geldvolumen (D)	—	volume of money	masse monétaire *f*	volume monetario *m*	volumen monetario *m*
Geldwert (D)	—	value of money	valeur de l'argent *f*	valore monetario *m*	valor monetario *m*
Geldwertstabilität (D)	—	stability of the value of money	stabilité monétaire *f*	stabilità monetaria *f*	estabilidad monetaria *f*
Gemeinde (D)	—	community	commune *f*	comune *m*	comunidad *f*
Gemeineigentum (D)	—	public property	propriété publique *f*	proprietà collettiva *f*	propiedad común *m*

	D	E	F	I	Es
Gemeinkosten (D)	—	overhead expenses	coûts indirects *m pl*	costi comuni *m pl*	gastos generales *m pl*
gemeinnütziges Unternehmen (D)	—	public institution	entreprise d'utilité publique *f*	impresa di utilità pubblica *f*	empresa de beneficio común *f*
gemeinsamer Markt (D)	—	common market	marché commun *m*	mercato comune *m*	mercado común *m*
Gemeinschafts-eigentum (D)	—	collective property	propriété collective *f*	proprietà collettiva *f*	propiedad colectiva *f*
Gemeinschafts-werbung (D)	—	joint publicity	publicité collective *f*	pubblicità collettiva *f*	publicidad colectiva *f*
Gemeinschuldner (D)	—	adjudicated bankrupt	failli *m*	debitore fallito *m*	deudor común *m*
Genehmigung (D)	—	permission	autorisation *f*	autorizzazione *f*	autorización *f*
general agent (E)	Generalvertreter *m*	—	agent général *m*	rappresentante generale *m*	representante general *m*
general borrowing agreements (E)	allgemeine Kredit-vereinbarungen *f pl*	—	accords généraux de crédit *f pl*	condizioni generali di credito *f pl*	acuerdos generales de crédito *m pl*
general cargo trade (E)	Stückgutverkehr *m*	—	expéditions de détail *f*	trasporto di collettame *m*	tráfico de mercancías en bultos sueltos *m*
general director (E)	Generaldirektor *m*	—	directeur général *m*	direttore generale *m*	director general *m*
Generaldirektor (D)	—	director general	directeur général *m*	direttore generale *m*	director general *m*
generalità (I)	Personalien *pl*	personal data	identité *f*	—	datos personales *m pl*
general partner (E)	Komplementär *m*	—	commandité *m*	socio accomandatario *m*	socio colectivo *m*
general power (E)	Generalvollmacht *f*	—	pouvoir général *m*	procura generale *f*	poder general *m*
Generalstreik (D)	—	general strike	grève générale *f*	sciopero generale *m*	huelga general *f*
general strike (E)	Generalstreik *m*	—	grève générale *f*	sciopero generale *m*	huelga general *f*
general terms (E)	allgemeine Geschäfts-bedingungen *f pl*	—	conditions générales de contrat *f pl*	condizioni generali di contratto *f pl*	condiciones generales de contrato *f pl*
Generalpolice (D)	—	floating policy	police d'abonnement *f*	polizza generale *f*	póliza global *f*
Generalvertreter (D)	—	general agent	agent général *m*	rappresentante generale *m*	representante general *m*
Generalvollmacht (D)	—	general power	pouvoir général *m*	procura generale *f*	poder general *m*
generic product (E)	No-name-Produkt *n*	—	produit sans nom *m*	prodotto senza nome *m*	producto genérico *m*
genormt (D)	—	standardized	normalisé	standardizzato	normalizado
Genossenschaft (D)	—	co-operative	société coopérative *f*	cooperativa *f*	sociedad cooperativa *f*
genre (F)	Sorte *f*	variety	—	categoria *f*	especie *f*
geografía económica (Es)	Wirtschafts-geographie *f*	economic geography	géographie économique *f*	geografia economica *f*	—
geografia economica (I)	Wirtschafts-geographie *f*	economic geography	géographie économique *f*	—	geografía económica *f*
géographie économique (F)	Wirtschafts-geographie *f*	economic geography	—	geografia economica *f*	geografía económica *f*
gérant d'une affaire (F)	Geschäftsführer *m*	manager	—	amministratore *m*	gerente *m*
gerarchia (I)	Hierarchie *f*	hierarchy	hiérarchie *f*	—	jerarquía *f*
gerechtfertigt (D)	—	justified	justifié	giustificato	justificado
gerente (Es)	Geschäftsführer *m*	manager	gérant d'une affaire *m*	amministratore *m*	—
gerichtlich (D)	—	judicial	judiciaire	giudiziario	judicial
Gerichtskosten (D)	—	legal costs	frais judiciaires tax-ables exposés *m pl*	spese giudiziarie *f pl*	gastos judiciales *m pl*
Gerichtsstand (D)	—	jurisdiction	juridiction compétente *f*	foro competente *m*	tribunal competente *m*
Gerichtsvollzieher (D)	—	bailiff	huissier de justice *m*	ufficiale giudiziario *m*	ejecutor judicial *m*
German Industrial Standards (E)	Deutsche Industrie-Norm *f*	—	norme industrielle allemande *f*	norma tedesca di normalizzazione *f*	norma industrial alemana *f*
Gesamtkonzeption (D)	—	overall conception	conception générale *f*	concezione universale *f*	concepción general *f*
Gesamtkosten (D)	—	total costs	coût total *m*	costi totali *m pl*	gastos generales *m pl*
Gesamtlieferung (D)	—	total delivery	livraison totale *f*	fornitura completa *f*	suministro total *f*
Gesamtsumme (D)	—	total amount	montant total *m*	importo totale *m*	suma total *f*
Geschäft (D)	—	business	affaire *f*	negozio *m*	negocio *m*
Geschäftsabschluß (D)	—	conclusion of a deal	conclusion d'une affaire *f*	conclusione di un affare *f*	conclusión de un negocio *f*
Geschäftsanteil (D)	—	share	part sociale *f*	quota sociale *f*	participación *f*

	D	E	F	I	Es
Geschäftsbericht (D)	—	business report	rapport de gestion *m*	relazione sull'esercizio commerciale *f*	informe *m*
Geschäftsbeziehung (D)	—	business connections	relations d'affaires *f pl*	rapporti d'affari *m pl*	relaciones comerciales *f pl*
Geschäftsbücher (D)	—	account books	livres de commerce *m pl*	libri contabili *m pl*	libros de contabilidad *m pl*
Geschäftseröffnung (D)	—	opening of a business	ouverture d'une affaire *f*	apertura di un negozio *f*	apertura de los establecimientos *f*
Geschäftsfähigkeit (D)	—	capacity to enter into legal transactions	capacité d'accomplir des actes juridiques *f*	capacità di agire *f*	capacidad negocial *f*
Geschäftsfreund (D)	—	business friend	correspondant *m*	partner d'affari *m*	corresponsal *m*
Geschäftsführer (D)	—	manager	gérant d'une affaire *m*	amministratore *m*	gerente *m*
Geschäftsführung (D)	—	management	gestion *f*	amministrazione *f*	gestión *f*
Geschäftsgeheimnis (D)	—	business secret	secret d'affaires *m*	segreto commerciale *m*	secreto comercial *m*
Geschäftsjahr (D)	—	financial year	exercice commercial *m*	esercizio commerciale *m*	ejercicio *m*
Geschäftsjubiläum (D)	—	jubilee	anniversaire de l'entreprise *m*	anniversario aziendale *m*	aniversario de la empresa *m*
Geschäftsleitung (D)	—	management	direction commerciale *f*	direzione *f*	dirección *f*
Geschäftspapiere (D)	—	business papers	papiers d'affaires *m pl*	documenti commerciali *m pl*	documentos comerciales *m pl*
Geschäftspartner (D)	—	business partner	associé *m*	partner commerciale *m*	socio *m*
Geschäftsräume (D)	—	business premises	local à usage commercial *m*	locali commerciali *m pl*	local comercial *m*
Geschäftsstelle (D)	—	office	agence *f*	ufficio *m*	oficina *f*
Geschäfts-übernahme (D)	—	business acquisition	reprise d'une affaire *f*	acquisto di un'azienda *m*	adquisición de una empresa *f*
Geschäfts-verbindung (D)	—	business relation	relation d'affaires *f*	relazione d'affari *f*	relación comercial *f*
Geschäftswert (D)	—	goodwill	valeur commerciale *f*	valore d'avviamento *m*	valor comercial *m*
Geschäftszeit (D)	—	business hours	heures d'ouverture *f pl*	orario d'apertura *m*	hora de despacho *f pl*
Geselle (D)	—	journeyman	ouvrier artisan *m*	garzone *m*	oficial *m*
Gesellschafter (D)	—	partner	associé *m*	socio *m*	socio *m*
Gesellschafter-versammlung (D)	—	meeting of shareholders	réunion des associés *f*	assemblea dei soci *f*	junta social *f*
Gesellschaft mit beschränkter Haftung (D)	—	limited liability company	société à responsabilité limitée *f*	società a responsabilità limitata *f*	sociedad de responsabilidad limitada *f*
Gesellschafts-vermögen (D)	—	partnership assets	patrimoine social *m*	patrimonio sociale *m*	patrimonio social *m*
Gesellschafts-vertrag (D)	—	shareholder's agreement/partnership agreement	acte de société *m*	contratto di società *m*	contrato social *m*
Gesetz (D)	—	law	loi *f*	legge *f*	ley *f*
Gesetzesänderung (D)	—	amendment of a law	amendement d'une loi *m*	emendamento di legge *m*	enmienda de la ley *f*
Gesetzgebungs-hoheit (D)	—	legislative sovereignty	compétence législative *f*	sovranità legislativa *f*	soberanía legislativa *f*
gesetzliches Zahlungsmittel (D)	—	legal tender	monnaie légale *f*	mezzo di pagamento legale *m*	medio legal de pago *m*
gespaltene Wechselkurse (D)	—	two-tier exchange rate	cours du change multiple *m*	cambi multipli *m pl*	tipo de cambio múltiple *m*
gesperrtes Konto (D)	—	blocked account	compte bloqué *m*	conto bloccato *m*	cuenta congelada *f*
Gesprächstermin (D)	—	appointment for a meeting	date de conversation *f*	appuntamento per un colloquio *m*	fecha de cita *f*
gestaffelt (D)	—	graduated	progressif	differenziato	escalonado
gestión[1] (Es)	Geschäftsführung *f*	management	gestion *f*	amministrazione *f*	—
gestión[2] (Es)	Führung *f*	management	direction *f*	gestione *f*	—
gestion (F)	Geschäftsführung *f*	management	—	amministrazione *f*	gestión *f*
gestion d'un projet (F)	Projekt-Management *n*	project management	—	management di progetto *m*	administración del proyecto *f*

	D	E	F	I	Es
gestione (I)	Führung *f*	management	direction *f*	—	gestión *m*
gestione dei prezzi (I)	Preislenkung *f*	administration of prices	réglementation des prix *f*	—	reglamentación de precios *f*
gestione del personale (I)	Personalführung *f*	personnel management	direction du personnel *f*	—	dirección de personal *m*
gestione delle scorte (I)	Vorratshaltung *f*	stockpiling	stockage *m*	—	formación de stocks *f*
gestione in economia (I)	Regiebetrieb *m*	publicly owned enterprise	établissement en régie *m*	—	empresa estatal *f*
Gesundheitswesen (D)	—	public health	santé publique *f*	sanità *f*	sanidad *f*
Gesundheits-zeugnis (D)	—	health certificate	certificat de santé *m*	certificato sanitario *m*	certificado de sanidad *m*
Gewährleistung (D)	—	warranty	prestation de garantie *f*	garanzia *f*	garantía *f*
Gewährleistungs-garantie (D)	—	guarantee for proper execution	caution de garantie *f*	garanzia di esecuzione *f*	fianza de contratista *f*
Gewährleistungs-haftung (D)	—	liability for breach of warranty	responsabilité en matière de garantie *f*	responsabilità di garanzia *f*	responsabilidad de garantía *f*
Gewerbe (D)	—	trade/industry/craft	activité profession-nelle *f*/industrie *f*/ artisanat *m*	commercio *m*/ industria *f*/ artigianato *m*	industria *f*/ comercio *m*/ artesanía *f*
Gewerbefreiheit (D)	—	freedom of trade	liberté des profes-sions industrielles et commerciales *f*	libertà d'industria economica *f*	libertad de industria *f*
Gewerbesteuer (D)	—	trade tax	impôt sur les béné-fices des professions industrielles et commerciales *m*	imposta industriale *f*	impuesto industrial *m*
gewerblicher Betrieb (D)	—	industrial undertaking	établissement com-mercial *m*/établisse-ment industriel *m*	azienda commerciale/ azienda industriale *f*	empresa industrial *f*
Gewerkschaften (D)	—	trade union	syndicat *m*	sindacati *m pl*	sindicato *m*
Gewicht (D)	—	weight	poids *m*	peso *m*	peso *m*
Gewinn (D)	—	profit surplus	bénéfice *m*	utile *m*	beneficio *m*/ superávit *m*
Gewinnabführung (D)	—	transfer of profit	transfert du bénéfice *m*	trasferimento dell'utile *m*	tranferencia de beneficios *f*
Gewinnaufschlag (D)	—	profit mark-up	majoration de bénéfice *f*	maggiorazione dell'utile *f*	margen de benificio *f*
Gewinn-ausschüttung (D)	—	distribution of profits	distribution de bénéfices *f*	ripartizione dell'utile *f*	distribución de beneficios *f*
Gewinnbeteiligung (D)	—	participation in profits	participation auxbénéfices *f*	partecipazione all'utile *f*	participación en los beneficios *f*
Gewinnmarge (D)	—	profit margin	marge bénéficiaire *f*	margine dell'utile *m*	margen de beneficios *f*
Gewinn-maximierung (D)	—	maximization of profits	maximisation du gain *f*	massimizzazione dell'utile *f*	maximación de los beneficios *f*
Gewinnschwelle (D)	—	break-even point	seuil de rentabilité *m*	soglia dell'utile *f*	umbral de la rentabilidad *m*
Gewinnspanne (D)	—	margin of profit	marge de bénéfice *f*	margine dell'utile *m*	margen de beneficios *f*
Gewinn- und Verlustrechnung (D)	—	profit and loss account	compte de pertes et profits *m*	conto profitti e perdite *m*	cuenta de pérdidas y ganancias *f*
Gewinnverteilung (D)	—	distribution of profits	répartition des bénéfices *f*	ripartizione dell'utile *f*	reparto de beneficios *m*
Gewinnverwendung (D)	—	appropriation of net income	utilisation des bénéfices *f*	impiego dell'utile *m*	aplicación de los resultatods *f*
gift tax (E)	Schenkungssteuer *f*	—	impôt sur les donations *m*	imposta sulle donazioni *f*	impuesto sobre donaciones *m*
gioco di strategia imprenditoriale (I)	Planspiel *n*	management games	jeu d'entreprise *m*	—	juego de ensayo *m*
giornaliero (I)	täglich	daily	quotidien	—	diario
giorno di borsa (I)	Börsentag *m*	market day	jour de bourse *m*	—	sesión bursátil *f*
giorno di liquidazione (I)	Abrechnungstag *m*	settling day	jour de la liquidation *m*	—	fecha de liquidación *f*
giorno di paga (I)	Zahltag *m*	payday	jour de paye *m*	—	día de pago *m*
giorno di scadenza (I)	Verfalltag *m*	day of expiry	jour de l'échéance *m*	—	día de vencimiento *m*

	D	E	F	I	Es
giorno lavorativo (I)	Arbeitstag *m*	working day	jour de travail *m*	—	día laboral *m*
girata (I)	Indossament *n*	endorsement	endossement *m*	—	endoso *m*
Giro (D)	—	credit transfer	virement *m*	giro *m*	giro *m*
giro (Es)	Giro *n*	credit transfer	virement *m*	giro *m*	—
giro (I)	Giro *n*	credit transfer	virement *m*	—	giro *m*
giro di partite (I)	Umbuchung *f*	transfer of an entry	jeu d'écritures *m*	—	asiento en otra cuenta *m*
giro postal[1] (Es)	Postgiro *n*	postal giro	virement postal *m*	postagiro *m*	—
giro postal[2] (Es)	Postüberweisung *f*	postal remittance	virement postal *m*	bonifico postale *m*	—
giro telegráfico (Es)	Kabelüberweisung *f*	cable transfer	virement par câble *m*	bonifico telegrafico *m*	—
Girozentrale (D)	—	central giro institution	banque centrale de virement *f*	stanza centrale di compensazione *f*	central de giros *f*
giudice (I)	Richter *m*	judge	juge *m*	—	juez *m*
giudiziario (I)	gerichtlich	judicial	judiciaire	—	judicial
giurisprudenza (I)	Rechtsprechung *f*	administration of justice	jurisprudence *f*	—	jurisprudencia *f*
giustificato (I)	gerechtfertigt	justified	justifié	—	justificado
Gläubiger (D)	—	creditor	créancier *m*	creditore *m*	accreedor *m*
Gläubigerschutz (D)	—	protection of creditors	garantie des crénciers *f*	tutela del creditore *f*	protección de los acreedores *f*
Gläubiger-versammlung (D)	—	creditors' meeting	assemblée des créanciers *f*	riunione dei creditori *f*	junta de acreedores *f*
Gleichgewicht (D)	—	balance	équilibre *m*	equilibrio *m*	equilibrio *m*
Gleichgewichtspreis (D)	—	equilibrium price	prix équilibré *m*	prezzo d'equilibrio *m*	precio de equilibrio *m*
global assignment (E)	Globalzession *f*	—	cession globale *f*	cessione globale *f*	cesión en bloque *f*
global control (E)	Globalsteuerung *f*	—	régulation globale *f*	controllo globale *m*	regulación golbal *f*
Globalsteuerung (D)	—	global control	régulation globale *f*	controllo globale *m*	regulación golbal *f*
global warming (E)	Treibhauseffekt *m*	—	effet de serre *m*	effetto serra *m*	efecto invernadero *m*
Globalzession (D)	—	global assignment	cession globale *f*	cessione globale *f*	cesión en bloque *f*
Glückwunsch (D)	—	congratulations	félicitations *f pl*	auguri *m pl*	felicitación *f*
gobierno (Es)	Regierung *f*	government/Ministry	gouvernement *m*	governo *m*	—
Gold (D)	—	gold	or *m*	oro *m*	oro *m*
gold (E)	Gold *n*	—	or *m*	oro *m*	oro *m*
gold bar (E)	Goldbarren *m*	—	lingot d'ór *m*	lingotto d'oro *m*	lingote de oro *m*
Goldbarren (D)	—	gold bar	lingot d'ór *m*	lingotto d'oro *m*	lingote de oro *m*
gold currency (E)	Goldwährung *f*	—	monnaie à couverture or *f*	valuta aurea *f*	moneda oro *f*
gold in bars (E)	Barrengold *n*	—	or en lingot *m*	oro in lingotti *m*	oro en barras *m*
gold market (E)	Goldmarkt *m*	—	marché de l'ór *m*	mercato dell'oro *m*	mercado del oro *m*
Goldmarkt (D)	—	gold market	marché de l'ór *m*	mercato dell'oro *m*	mercado del oro *m*
Goldmine (D)	—	goldmine	mine d'or *f*	miniera d'oro *f*	mina de oro *f*
goldmine (E)	Goldmine *f*	—	mine d'or *f*	miniera d'oro *f*	mina de oro *f*
Goldparität (D)	—	gold parity	parité de l'or *f*	parità aurea *f*	paridad-oro *f*
gold parity (E)	Goldparität *f*	—	parité de l'or *f*	parità aurea *f*	paridad-oro *f*
Goldpreis (D)	—	gold price	prix de l'ór *m*	prezzo dell'oro *m*	precio del oro *m*
gold price (E)	Goldpreis *m*	—	prix de l'ór *m*	prezzo dell'oro *m*	precio del oro *m*
gold standard (E)	Goldstandard *m*	—	étalon or *m*	gold standard *m*	patrón-oro *m*
Goldstandard (D)	—	gold standard	étalon or *m*	gold standard *m*	patrón-oro *m*
gold standard (I)	Goldstandard *m*	gold standard	étalon or *m*	—	patrón-oro *m*
Gold- und Devisenbilanz (D)	—	foreign exchange and gold balance	balance d'or et de devises *f*	bilancia dell'oro e delle divise *f*	balanza de oro y divisas *f*
Goldwährung (D)	—	gold currency	monnaie à couverture or *f*	valuta aurea *f*	moneda oro *f*
goods[1] (E)	Ware *f*	—	marchandise *f*	merce *f*	mercancía *f*
goods[2] (E)	Güter *pl*	—	biens *m pl*	beni *m pl*	bienes *m pl*
goods for sale on commission (E)	Kommissionsgüter *pl*	—	marchandises en commssion *f pl*	beni in conto deposito *m pl*	mercancías en comisión *f pl*

	D	E	F	I	Es
goods sent by express (E)	Eilgut *n*	—	marchandise en grande vitesse *f*	merce a grande velocità *f*	mercancía en gran velocidad *f*
goodwill[1] (E)	Firmenwert *m*	—	valeur commerciale *f*	goodwill *m*	fondo de comercio *m*
goodwill[2] (E)	Geschäftswert *m*	—	valeur commerciale *f*	valore d'avviamento *m*	valor comercial *m*
goodwill (I)	Firmenwert *m*	goodwill	valeur commerciale *f*	—	fondo de comercio *m*
goulot d'étranglement de capacité (F)	Kapazitätsengpaß *m*	bottleneck in capacity	—	strettoia di capacità *f*	escasez de capacidad *f*
goulot d'étranglement dans la trésorerie (F)	Liquiditätsengpaß *m*	liquidity squeeze	—	strettoia di liquidità *f*	restricción de la liquidez *f*
gouvernement (F)	Regierung *f*	government/Ministry	—	governo *m*	gobierno *m*
government (E)	Regierung *f*	—	gouvernement *m*	governo *m*	gobierno *m*
government grant (E)	Staatszuschuß *m*	—	subvention de l'Etat *f*	sovvenzione pubblica *f*	subvenciones del Estado *f pl*
government loan (E)	Staatsanleihen *pl*	—	emprunt d'Etat *m*	titoli pubblici *m pl*	empréstito estatal *m*
governo (I)	Regierung *f*	government/Ministry	gouvernement *m*	—	gobierno *m*
grade[1] (E)	Handelsklasse *f*	—	catégorie de produits *f*	categoria commerciale *f*	clase *f*
grade[2] (E)	Güteklasse *f*	—	catégorie de qualité *f*	qualità *f*	categoría de calidad *f*
grado de empleo (Es)	Beschäftigungs-grad *m*	level of employment	taux d'emploi *m*	tasso d'occupazione *m*	—
grado de endeudamiento (Es)	Verschuldungsgrad *m*	debt ratio	niveau de l'endettement *m*	tasso d'indebitamento *m*	—
grado de utilización (Es)	Ausnutzungsgrad *m*	utilization rate	taux d'utilisation *m*	grado di utilizzazione *m*	—
grado di sfruttamento (I)	Auslastungsgrad *m*	capacity utilization rate	dégré de saturation *m*	—	tasa de utilización *f*
grado di utilizzazione (I)	Ausnutzungsgrad *m*	utilization rate	taux d'utilisation *m*	—	grado de utilización *m*
graduated (E)	gestaffelt	—	progressif	differenziato	escalonado
graduated price (E)	Staffelpreis *m*	—	prix échelonné *m*	prezzo differenziato *m*	precios escalonados *m pl*
graduated tariff (E)	Staffeltarif *m*	—	tarif échelonné *m*	tariffa differenziata *f*	tarifa diferencial *f*
gran almacén (Es)	Waren-, Kaufhaus *n*	department store	grand magasin *m*	grande magazzino *m*	—
gran contenedor (Es)	Großcontainer *m*	large container	conteneur à grand volume *m*	container di grande dimensione *m*	—
grande exploitation (F)	Großbetrieb *m*	large-scale operation	—	azienda di grande dimensione *f*	gran explotación *f*
grande magazzino (I)	Waren-, Kaufhaus *n*	department store	grand magasin *m*	—	gran almacén *m*
grand magasin (F)	Kaufhaus *n*	department store	—	grande magazzino *m*	gran almacén *m*
grand marché (F)	Großmarkt *m*	wholesale market	—	mercato all'ingrosso *m*	mercado central *m*
gran explotación (Es)	Großbetrieb *m*	large-scale operation	grande exploitation *f*	azienda di grande dimensione *f*	—
granting a respite (E)	Fristgewährung *f*	—	octroi d'un délai *m*	concessione di un termine *f*	concesión de un plazo *f*
grantor of a power of attorney (E)	Vollmachtgeber *m*	—	auteur de la procuration *m*	mandante *m*	poderdante *m*
graph (E)	Schaubild *n*	—	graphique *m*	diagramma *m*	cuadro *m*
graphique (F)	Schaubild *n*	graph	—	diagramma *m*	cuadro *m*
gratificación[1] (Es)	Prämie *f*	bonus/premium	prime *f*	premio *m*	—
gratificación[2] (Es)	Gratifikation *f*	bonus	gratification *f*	gratificazione *f*	—
gratificación[3] (Es)	Bonus *m*	bonus	bonification *f*	premio *m*	—
gratificación[4] (Es)	Zuwendung *f*	bestowal	affectation *f*	assegnazione *f*	—
gratificación[5] (Es)	Sondervergütung *f*	special remuneration	rémunération spéciale *f*	compenso straordinario *m*	—
gratification (F)	Gratifikation *f*	bonus	—	gratificazione *f*	gratificación *f*
gratificazione (I)	Gratifikation *f*	bonus	gratification *f*	—	gratificación *f*
Gratifikation (D)	—	bonus	gratification *f*	gratificazione *f*	gratificación *f*
gratuit (F)	kostenlos	free of charge	—	gratuito	libre de gastos
gratuito (Es)	unentgeltlich	free of charge	à titre gracieux	gratuito	—
gratuito[1] (I)	kostenlos	free of charge	gratuit	—	libre de gastos

	D	E	F	I	Es
gratuito[2] (I)	unentgeltlich	free of charge	à titre gracieux	—	gratuito
Grauer Markt (D)	—	grey market	marché gris *m*	mercato grigio *m*	mercado gris *m*
gravamen (Es)	Belastung *f*	load	charge *f*	addebito *m*	—
Grenzkontrolle (D)	—	border control	contrôle à la frontière *m*	controllo alla frontiera *m*	control fronterizo *m*
Grenzkosten-rechnung (D)	—	marginal costing	détermination du coût marginal *f*	conto dei costi limite *m*	cálculo de los costes marginales *m*
Grenzwert (D)	—	limiting value	valeur marginale *f*	valore limite *m*	valor límite *m*
grève (F)	Streik *m*	strike	—	sciopero *m*	huelga *f*
grève générale (F)	Generalstreik *m*	general strike	—	sciopero generale *m*	huelga general *f*
grey market (E)	Grauer Markt *m*	—	marché gris *m*	mercato grigio *m*	mercado gris *m*
Großabnehmer (D)	—	bulk buyer	acheteur en gros *m*	acquirente all'ingrosso *m*	comprador al por mayor *m*
Großauftrag (D)	—	large-scale order	grosse commande *f*	ordine di grandi quantità *m*	importante pedido *m*
Großbetrieb (D)	—	large-scale operation	grande exploitation *f*	azienda di grande dimensione *f*	gran explotación *f*
Großcontainer (D)	—	large container	conteneur à grand volume *m*	container di grande dimensione *m*	gran contenedor *m*
gross domestic product (E)	Bruttoinlands-produkt *n*	—	produit intérieur brut *m*	prodotto interno lordo *m*	producto interior bruto *m*
grosse commande (F)	Großauftrag *m*	large-scale order	—	ordine di grandi quantità *m*	importante pedido *m*
Größenabweichung (D)	—	deviation from size	déviation de dimension *f*	differenza di dimensione *f*	deviación de dimensión *f*
Großhandel (D)	—	wholesale trade	commerce de gros *m*	commercio all'ingrosso *m*	comercio mayorista *m*
Großhandelspreis (D)	—	wholesale prices	prix de gros *m*	prezzo all'ingrosso *m*	precio mayorista *m*
gross income (E)	Bruttoeinkommen *n*	—	revenu brut *m*	reddito lordo *m*	ingreso bruto *m*
Grossist (D)	—	wholesaler	grossiste *m*	grossista *m*	mayorista *m*
grossista (I)	Grossist *m*	wholesaler	grossiste *m*	—	mayorista *m*
grossiste (F)	Grossist *m*	wholesaler	—	grossista *m*	mayorista *m*
Großmarkt (D)	—	wholesale market	grand marché *m*	mercato all'ingrosso *m*	mercado central *m*
gross national product (E)	Bruttosozialprodukt *n*	—	produit national brut *m*	prodotto nazionale lordo *m*	producto nacional bruto *m*
gross pay (E)	Bruttolohn *m*	—	salaire brut *m*	salario lordo *m*	salario bruto *m*
gross price (E)	Bruttopreis *m*	—	prix brut *m*	prezzo lordo *m*	precio bruto *m*
gross proceeds (E)	Rohertrag *m*	—	produit brut *m*	reddito lordo *m*	producto bruto *m*
gross production (E)	Bruttoproduktion *f*	—	production brut *f*	produzione lorda *f*	producción bruta *m*
gross profit on sales (E)	Rohgewinn *m*	—	bénéfice brut *m*	utile lordo *m*	ganancia bruta *f*
gross register(ed) ton (E)	Bruttoregistertonne *f*	—	tonneau de jauge brut *m*	tonnellata di stazza lorda *f*	tonelada de registro bruto *f*
ground (E)	Boden *m*	—	sol *m*/terrain *m*	terra *f*/suolo *m*	suelo *m*/terreno *m*
group (E)	Konzern *m*	—	groupe industriel *m*	gruppo *m*	consorcio *m*
groupe de marchandises[1] (F)	Warengruppe *f*	product line	—	gruppo merci *m*	grupo de mercancías *m*
groupe de marchandises[2] (F)	Gütergruppe *f*	category of goods	—	gruppo di merci *m*	grupo de mercancías *m*
groupe de sociétaires (F)	Sozietät *f*	partnership	—	associazione *f*	sociedad *f*
groupe destinataire (F)	Zielgruppe *f*	target group	—	gruppo di riferimento *m*	grupo destinatario *m*
groupe d'âge (F)	Altersgruppe *f*	age group	—	gruppo d'età *m*	grupo según la edad *m*
groupe d'intérêts (F)	Interessengruppe *f*	interest group	—	gruppo d'interesse *m*	grupo de presión *m*
groupe industriel (F)	Konzern *m*	group/combine	—	gruppo *m*	consorcio *m*
groupe multinational (F)	multinationaler Konzern *m*	multinational group	—	gruppo multinazionale *m*	grupo multinacional *m*
growth (E)	Wachstum *n*	—	croissance *f*	crescita *f*	crecimiento *m*
growth impulse (E)	Wachstumsimpuls *m*	—	stimulation de l'accroissement *f*	impulso di crescita *m*	impulso de crecimiento *m*

	D	E	F	I	Es
growth policy (E)	Wachstumspolitik *f*	—	politique d'accroissement *f*	politica di crescita *f*	política de crecimiento económico *f*
Grundgehalt (D)	—	basic salary	traitement de base *m*	stipendio base *m*	salario base *m*
Grundkapital (D)	—	share capital	capital initial *m*	capitale sociale *m*	capital social *m*
Grundkenntnisse (D)	—	basic knowledge	connaissances fondamentales *f pl*	cognizioni elementari *f pl*	conocimientos básicos *m pl*
Grundrente (D)	—	basic pension	pension de base *f*	pensione base *f*	pensión básica *f*
Grundschuld (D)	—	mortgage	dette foncière *f*	debito fondiario *m*	hipoteca *f*
Grundstück (D)	—	real estate	terrain *m*	terreno *m*	terreno *m*
Gründung (D)	—	formation	constitution *f*	costituzione *f*	fundación *f*
Gründungsbericht (D)	—	formation report	procès-verbal de fondation *m*	relazione di costituzione *f*	informe de los fundadores *m*
Gründungskosten (D)	—	organization costs	frais de fondation *m pl*	costi della costituzione *m pl*	gastos de fundación *m pl*
Gründungsplanung (D)	—	formation plan	planification de fondation *f*	progettazione della costituzione *f*	planificación de la fundación *f*
grupo de mercancías[1] (Es)	Warengruppe *f*	product line	groupe de marchandises *m*	gruppo merci *m*	—
grupo de mercancías[2] (Es)	Gütergruppe *f*	category of goods	groupe de marchandises *m*	gruppo di merci *m*	—
grupo de presión[1] (Es)	Lobby *f*	lobbying group	lobby *m*	lobby *m*	—
grupo de presión[2] (Es)	Interessengruppe *f*	interest group	groupe d'intérêts *m*	gruppo d'interesse *m*	—
grupo destinatario (Es)	Zielgruppe *f*	target group	groupe destinataire *m*	gruppo di riferimento *m*	—
grupo multinacional (Es)	multinationaler Konzern *m*	multinational group	groupe multinational *m*	gruppo multinazionale *m*	—
grupo según la edad (Es)	Altersgruppe *f*	age group	groupe d'âge *m*	gruppo d'età *m*	—
gruppo (I)	Konzern *m*	group/combine	groupe industriel *m*	—	consorcio *m*
gruppo d'età (I)	Altersgruppe *f*	age group	groupe d'âge *m*	—	grupo según la edad *m*
gruppo d'interesse (I)	Interessengruppe *f*	interest group	groupe d'intérêts *m*	—	grupo de presión *m*
gruppo di merci (I)	Gütergruppe *f*	category of goods	groupe de marchandises *m*	—	grupo de mercancías *m*
gruppo di riferimento (I)	Zielgruppe *f*	target group	groupe destinataire *m*	—	grupo destinatario *m*
gruppo merci (I)	Warengruppe *f*	product line	groupe de marchandises *m*	—	grupo de mercancías *m*
gruppo multinazionale (I)	multinationaler Konzern *m*	multinational group	groupe multinational *m*	—	grupo multinacional *m*
guarantee[1] (E)	Garantieleistung *f*	—	fourniture sous garantie *f*	prestazione di garanzia *f*	aplicación de la garantía *f*
guarantee[2] (E)	Bürgschaft *f*	—	caution *f*	fideiussione *f*	fianza *f*
guarantee for proper execution (E)	Gewährleistungs-garantie *f*	—	caution de garantie *f*	garanzia di esecuzione *f*	fianza de contratista *f*
guarantee obligation (E)	Garantie-verpflichtung *f*	—	engagement de garantie *m*	obbligo di garanzia *m*	obligación de garantía *f*
guarantee of a bill (E)	Aval *m*	—	aval *m*	avallo *m*	aval *m*
guarantor (E)	Bürge *m*	—	garant *m*	fideiussore *m*	fiador *m*
guerra comercial (Es)	Handelskrieg *m*	trade war	guerre commerciale *f*	guerra commerciale *f*	—
guerra commerciale (I)	Handelskrieg *m*	trade war	guerre commerciale *f*	—	guerra comercial *f*
guerra económica (Es)	Wirtschaftskrieg *m*	economic war	guerre économique *f*	guerra economica *f*	—
guerra economica (I)	Wirtschaftskrieg *m*	economic war	guerre économique *f*	—	guerra económica *f*
guerre commerciale (F)	Handelskrieg *m*	trade war	—	guerra commerciale *f*	guerra comercial *f*
guerre économique (F)	Wirtschaftskrieg *m*	economic war	—	guerra economica *f*	guerra económica *f*
guide price (E)	Orientierungspreis *m*	—	prix d'orientation *m*	prezzo d'orientamento *m*	precio de orientación *m*
günstigstes Angebot (D)	—	most favourable offer	offre favorable *f*	offerta vantaggiosa *f*	oferta favorable *f*
Güteklasse (D)	—	grade	catégorie de qualité *f*	qualità *f*	categoría de calidad *f*
Güter (D)	—	goods	biens *m pl*	beni *m pl*	bienes *m pl*
Güterbeförderung (D)	—	carriage of goods	transport de marchandises *m*	trasporto di merci *m*	transporte de mercancías *m*

	D	E	F	I	Es
Gütergruppe (D)	—	category of goods	groupe de marchandises *m*	gruppo di merci *m*	grupo de mercancías *m*
Gütertarif (D)	—	trade tariff	tarif marchandises *m*	tariffa merci *f*	tarifa de transporte *f*
gutgläubig (D)	—	bona fide	de bonne foi	di buona fede	de buena fe
Guthaben (D)	—	money owed	avoir *m*	saldo attivo *m*	haber *m*
gutschreiben (D)	—	credit	créditer	accreditare	abonar en cuenta
Gutschrift (D)	—	credit	crédit *m*	accredito *m*	abono *m*
Gutschriftsanzeige (D)	—	credit advice	avis de crédit *m*	nota di accredito *f*	aviso de abono *m*
Haben (D)	—	credit side	avoir m	attivo m	haber m
Habenzinsen (D)	—	credit interest	intérêts créditeur *m*	interessi creditori *m pl*	intereses acreedores *m pl*
haber[1] (Es)	Haben *n*	credit side	avoir *m*	attivo *m*	—
haber[2] (Es)	Guthaben *n*	money owed	avoir *m*	saldo attivo *m*	—
haber social repartible (Es)	Liquidationserlös *m*	remaining assets after liquidation	produit de la liquidation *m*	ricavo della liquidazione *m*	—
habileté en matière de négociations (F)	Verhandlungs-geschick *n*	negotiation skills	—	abilità nel trattare *f*	tino de negociar *m*
habitude de payement (F)	Zahlungs-gewohnheit *f*	practice of payment	—	consuetudine di pagamento *f*	práctica de pago *f*
hacer la cola (Es)	Schlange stehen	queue up	faire la queue	fare la coda	—
hacer quincalla (Es)	verschrotten	scrap	mettre à la ferraille	ridurre a rottame	—
Hacienda[1] (Es)	Finanzamt *n*	inland revenue office	service de contributions *m*	ufficio delle imposte *m*	—
Hacienda[2] (Es)	Finanzministerium *n*	Ministry of Finance	ministère des finances *m*	ministero delle Finanze *m*	—
Hafen (D)	—	port	port *m*	porto *m*	puerto *m*
Hafengebühren (D)	—	harbour dues	droits de ports *m pl*	diritti di porto *m pl*	derechos portuarios *m pl*
Haftkaution (D)	—	bail	caution pour être mis en liberté *f*	cauzione per la scarcerazione *f*	fianza de puesta en libertad *f*
Haftpflicht-versicherung (D)	—	third party liability insurance	assurance responsa-bilité civile *f*	assicurazione della responsabilità civile *f*	seguro de responsa-bilidad civil *m*
Haftung (D)	—	liability	responsabilité *f*	responsabilità *f*	responsabilidad *f*
Halberzeugnis (D)	—	semi-finished good	produit demi-fini *m*	prodotto semifinito *m*	producto semielaborado *m*
halbjährlich (D)	—	half-yearly	semestriel	semestrale	semestral
half-yearly (E)	halbjährlich	—	semestriel	semestrale	semestral
halle de dépôt (F)	Lagerraum *m*	storage space	—	magazzino *m*	almacén *m*
hand over (E)	abliefern	—	livrer	consegnare	entregar
Handarbeit (D)	—	manual work	travail manuel *m*	lavoro manuale *m*	trabajo a mano *m*
Handbuch (D)	—	manual	manuel *m*	manuale *m*	manual *m*
Handel (D)	—	trade	commerce *m*	commercio *m*	comercio *m*
Handelsbank (D)	—	merchant bank	banque de commerce *f*	banca commerciale *f*	banco comercial *m*
Handels-bedingungen (D)	—	trading conditions	conditions commerciales *f pl*	condizioni commerciali *f pl*	condiciones comerciales *f pl*
Handels-beschränkungen (D)	—	trade restrictions	restrictions au commerce *f pl*	restrizioni commerciali *f pl*	restricciones commerciales *f pl*
Handels-beziehungen (D)	—	trade relations	relations commerciales *f pl*	rapporti commerciali *m pl*	relaciones comerciales *f pl*
Handelsbilanz (D)	—	balance of trade	balance des opérations en marchandises *f*	bilancia commerciale *f*	balanza comercial *f*
Handelsbrauch (D)	—	business practice	usage commercial *m*	usanza commerciale *f*	uso comercial *m*
Handelsembargo (D)	—	trade embargo	embargo commercial *m*	embargo commerciale *m*	embargo comercial *m*
Handelsfaktura (D)	—	commercial invoice	facture commerciale *f*	fattura commerciale *f*	factura comercial *f*
Handelsgesellschaft (D)	—	trading company	société commerciale *f*	società commerciale *f*	sociedad comercial *f*
Handelsgesetzbuch (D)	—	Commercial Code	code de commerce *m*	codice commerciale *m*	código mercantil *m*
Handelskammer (D)	—	Chamber of Commerce	chambre de commerce *f*	camera di commercio *f*	cámara de comercio *f*

	D	E	F	I	Es
Handelsklasse (D)	—	grade	catégorie de produits *f*	categoria commerciale *f*	clase *f*
Handelsklausel (D)	—	trade terms	clause commerciale *f*	clausola commerciale *f*	cláusula comercial *f*
Handelskreditbrief (D)	—	commercial letter of credit	lettre de crédit commercial *f*	lettera di credito commerciale *f*	carta de crédito comercial *f*
Handelskrieg (D)	—	trade war	guerre commerciale *f*	guerra commerciale *f*	guerra comercial *f*
Handelsmesse (D)	—	trade fair	foire commerciale *f*	fiera commerciale *f*	feria comercial *f*
Handelsmission (D)	—	trade mission	mission commerciale *f*	missione commerciale *f*	misión comercial *f*
Handelspartner (D)	—	trading partner	partenaire commercial *m*	partner commerciale *m*	socio comercial *m*
Handelsplatz (D)	—	trade centre	place marchande *f*	piazza commerciale *f*	plaza comercial *f*
Handelspolitik (D)	—	commercial policy	politique commerciale *f*	politica commerciale *f*	política comercial *f*
Handelsregister (D)	—	commercial register	registre du commerce *m*	registro commerciale *m*	registro mercantil *m*
Handelsspanne (D)	—	trading margin	bénéfice brut *m*	margine commerciale *m*	margen comercial *f*
Handelsüberschuß (D)	—	trade surplus	excédent commercial *m*	eccedenza commerciale *f*	excedente comercial *m*
Handelsusancen (D)	—	trade practice	usages commerciaux *m pl*	usanze commerciali *f pl*	usos comerciales *m pl*
Handelsverkehr (D)	—	commercial intercourse	échanges commerciaux *m pl*	circolazione delle merci *f*	comercio *m*
Handelsvertreter (D)	—	commercial agent	représentant de commerce *m*	rappresentante commerciale *m*	representante comercial *m*
Handelsvertretung (D)	—	commercial agency	représentation commerciale *f*	rappresentanza commerciale *f*	representación comercial *f*
handgeschriebener Lebenslauf (D)	—	hand-written curriculum vitae	curriculum vitae écrit à la main *m*	curriculum vitae scritto a mano *m*	curriculum vitae escrito a mano *m*
Handicrafts Regulation Act (E)	Handwerksordnung *f*	—	code de l'artisanat *m*	codice dell'artigianato *m*	reglamento del artesanado *m*
Händler (D)	—	trader	commerçant *m*	commerciante *m*	comerciante *m*
Handlungs-bevollmächtigter (D)	—	commercial agent	personne ayant le pouvoir commercial *f*	mandatario commerciale *m*	apoderado especial *m*
Handwerk (D)	—	craft trade	artisanat *m*	artigianato *m*	artesanía *f*
Handwerkskammer (D)	—	chamber of handicrafts	chambre artisanale *f*	camera dell'artigianato *f*	cámara de artesanía *f*
Handwerksordnung (D)	—	Handicrafts Regulation Act	code de l'artisanat *m*	codice dell'artigianato *m*	reglamento del artesanado *m*
handwork (E)	Handarbeit *f*	—	travail manuel *m*	lavoro manuale *m*	trabajo a mano *m*
hand-written curriculum vitae (E)	handgeschriebener Lebenslauf *m*	—	curriculum vitae écrit à la main *m*	curriculum vitae scritto a mano *m*	curriculum vitae escrito a mano *m*
harbour dues (E)	Hafengebühren *pl*	—	droits de port *m pl*	diritti di porto *m pl*	derechos portuarios *m pl*
hard coal (E)	Steinkohle *f*	—	houille *f*	carbone fossile *m*	hulla *f*
hard currency (E)	harte Währung *f*	—	monnaie solide *f*	moneta forte *f*	moneda dura *f*
harte Währung (D)	—	hard currency	monnaie solide *f*	moneta forte *f*	moneda dura *f*
Hartgeld (D)	—	specie	pièce de monnaie *f*	moneta metallica *f*	dinero metálico *m*
haulage (E)	Rollgeld *n*	—	camionnage *m*	spese di trasporto *f pl*	derechos de acarreo *m pl*
Hauptspeicher (D)	—	main memory	mémoire principale *f*	memoria principale *f*	memoria principal *f*
Hausbank (D)	—	company's bank	banque habituelle *f*	banca di preferenza *f*	banco particular *m*
Hausbesitzer (D)	—	home property owner	propriétaire d'immeuble *m*	possessore di casa *m*	propietario de una casa *m*
Hauseigentümer (D)	—	owner of a house	propriétaire d'une maison *m*	proprietario di casa *m*	propietario de una casa *m*
Haushalt (D)	—	budget	budget *m*	bilancio *m*	presupuesto *m*
Haushaltsdefizit (D)	—	budgetary deficit	déficit budgétaire *m*	deficit del bilancio *m*	déficit presupuestario *m*
Haushaltsjahr (D)	—	financial year	exercice budgétaire *m*	anno finanziario *m*	ejercicio *m*
Haushaltsplan (D)	—	budget	budget *m*	bilancio preventivo *m*	presupuesto *m*

	D	E	F	I	Es
Hausse (D)	—	boom	hausse *f*	rialzo *m*	alza *f*
hausse[1] (F)	Hausse *f*	boom	—	rialzo *m*	alza *f*
hausse[2] (F)	Kurssteigerung *f*	price advance	—	aumento dei corsi *m*	alza de las cotizaciones *f*
hausse[3] (F)	Aufschlag *m*	surcharge	—	aggiunta *f*	recargo *m*
hausse (I)	Hausse *f*	boom	hausse *f*	—	alza *f*
hausse des prix (F)	Preissteigerung *f*	price increase	—	aumento dei prezzi *m*	aumento de precios *m*
hausse illicite des loyers (F)	Mietwucher *m*	exorbitant rent	—	strozzinaggio sui canoni di locazione *m*	usura arrendaticia *f*
Haussier (D)	—	bull	haussier *m*	speculatore al rialzo *m*	alcista *m*
haussier (F)	Haussier *m*	bull	—	speculatore al rialzo *m*	alcista *m*
haussier (I)	Haussier *m*	bull	haussier *m*	—	alcista *m*
haute autorité (F)	hohe Behörde *f*	high authority	—	alta autorità *f*	Alta Autoridad *f*
haute conjoncture (F)	Hochkonjunktur *f*	boom	—	alta congiuntura *f*	alta coyuntura *f*
Havarie (D)	—	damage by sea	avarie *f*	avaria *f*	avería *m*
Havariezertifikat (D)	—	damage report	certificat d'avarie *m*	certificato d'avaria *m*	certificado de avería *m*
have in stock (E)	auf Lager haben	—	avoir en stock	avere in magazzino	tener en almacén
head (E)	Chef *m*	—	chef *m*	capo *m*	jefe *m*
head of department (E)	Abteilungsleiter *m*	—	chef de service *m*	capo reparto *m*	jefe de sección *m*
health certificate (E)	Gesundheits-zeugnis *n*	—	certificat de santé *m*	certificato sanitario *m*	certificado de sanidad *m*
health insurance (E)	Kranken-versicherung *f*	—	assurance maladie *f*	assicurazione contro le malattie *f*	seguro de enfermedad *m*
heavy freight (E)	Schwergut *n*	—	produit pondéreux *m*	carico pesante *m*	mercancía pesada *f*
heavy metal (E)	Schwermetall *n*	—	métal lourd *m*	metallo pesante *m*	metal pesado *m*
hebdomadaire (F)	wöchentlich	weekly	—	settimanale	semanal
hecho a medida (Es)	maßgefertigt	manufactured to measure	travaillé sur mesure	prodotto su misura	—
Heimarbeit (D)	—	homework	travail à domicile *m*	lavoro a domicilio *m*	trabajo a domicilio *m*
heirs (E)	Erben *pl*	—	héritiers *m pl*	eredi *m pl*	heredero *m*
Herbstmesse (D)	—	autumn fair	foire d'automne *f*	fiera autunnale *f*	feria de otoño *f*
heredero (Es)	Erben *pl*	heirs	héritiers *m pl*	eredi *m pl*	—
herencia (Es)	Erbschaft *f*	inheritance	héritage *m*	eredità *f*	—
héritage (F)	Erbschaft *f*	inheritance	—	eredità *f*	herencia *f*
héritiers (F)	Erben *pl*	heirs	—	eredi *m pl*	heredero *m*
Herkunftsland (D)	—	country of origin	pays de provenance *m*	paese d'origine *m*	país de origen *m*
herrschendes Unternehmen (D)	—	controlling company	entreprise dirigeante *f*	impresa controllante *f*	empresa dominante *f*
Herstellen-oder-zukaufen (D)	—	produce or buy in addition	produire ou acheter additionnellement	produrre o comprare in aggiunta	producir o comprar adicionalmente
Hersteller (D)	—	producer	fabricant *m*	produttore *m*	fabricante *m*
Herstellungskosten (D)	—	production costs	frais de fabrication *m pl*	costi di produzione *m pl*	costo de la producción *m*
Herstellungswert (D)	—	production value	prix de revient *m*	valore di produzione *m*	valor de fabricación *m*
heures d'ouverture (F)	Geschäftszeit *f*	business hours	—	orario d'apertura *m*	hora de despacho *f pl*
heures de travail (F)	Arbeitszeit *f*	working hours	—	orario di lavoro *m*	jornada laboral *f*
heure supplémentaire (F)	Überstunde *f*	overtime	—	ora straordinaria *f*	hora extraordinaria *f*
hidden reserves (E)	stille Reserve *f*	—	réserve cachée *f*	riserva occulta *f*	reserva tácita *f*
Hierarchie (D)	—	hierarchy	hiérarchie *f*	gerarchia *f*	jerarquía *f*
hiérarchie (F)	Hierarchie *f*	hierarchy	—	gerarchia *f*	jerarquía *f*
hierarchy (E)	Hierarchie *f*	—	hiérarchie *f*	gerarchia *f*	jerarquía *f*
high authority (E)	hohe Behörde *f*	—	haute autorité *f*	alta autorità *f*	Alta Autoridad *f*
highest rate (E)	Höchstkurs *m*	—	cours le plus haut *m*	corso massimo *m*	cotización máxima *f*
Hinterlegung (D)	—	deposit	dépôt *m*	deposito *m*	depósito *m*
Hinterziehung (D)	—	evasion of taxes	fraude fiscale *f*	evasione *f*	defraudación *f*

	D	E	F	I	Es
hiperinflación (Es)	Hyperinflation *f*	hyperinflation	hyperinflation *f*	iperinflazione *f*	—
hipoteca[1] (Es)	Hypothek *f*	mortgage	hypothéque *f*	ipoteca *f*	—
hipoteca[2] (Es)	Grundschuld *f*	mortgage	dette foncière *f*	debito fondiario *m*	—
hipótesis (Es)	Hypothese *f*	hypothesis	hypothèse *f*	ipotesi *f*	—
hired car (E)	Leihwagen *m*	—	voiture de location *f*	vettura da noleggio *f*	coche de alquiler *m*
hire purchase transaction (E)	Abzahlungsgeschäft *n*	—	achat à tempérament *m*	operazione con pagamento a rate *f*	venta a plazos *f*
hire-purchase transaction (E)	Ratenkauf *m*	—	achat à tempérament *m*	acquisto a rate *m*	compra a plazo *f*
hiring of personnel (E)	Personalwerbung *f*	—	recrutement de personnel *m*	reclutazione di personale *f*	reclutamiento de personal *m*
histoire économique (F)	Wirtschafts-geschichte *f*	economic history	—	storia economica *f*	historia económica *f*
historia económica (Es)	Wirtschafts-geschichte *f*	economic history	histoire économique *f*	storia economica *f*	—
historical costing (E)	Nachkalkulation *f*	—	calcul des coûts a posteriori *m*	computisteria *f*	cálculo de costes a posteriori *m*
Hochkonjunktur (D)	—	boom	haute conjoncture *f*	alta congiuntura *f*	alta coyuntura *f*
Höchstkurs (D)	—	highest rate	cours le plus haut *m*	corso massimo *m*	cotización máxima *f*
Höchstpreis (D)	—	top price	prix plafond *m*	prezzo massimo *m*	precio máximo *m*
hohe Behörde (D)	—	high authority	haute autorité *f*	alta autorità *f*	Alta Autoridad *f*
Hoheitsrecht (D)	—	sovereign right	droit de souveraineté *m*	diritto di sovranità *m*	soberanía *f*
hoja de pedido (Es)	Bestellschein *m*	order form	bulletin de commande *m*	bolletta d'ordinazione *f*	—
holding company (E)	Dachgesellschaft *f*	—	société holding *f*	società finanziaria *f*	sociedad holding *f*
holiday allowance (E)	Urlaubsgeld *n*	—	prime de vacances *f*	indennità di ferie *f*	retribución por vacaciones *f*
home demand (E)	Inlandsnachfrage *f*	—	demande intérieure *f*	domanda interna *f*	demanda interior *f*
home market (E)	Binnenmarkt *m*	—	marché national *m*	mercato nazionale *m*	mercado interior *m*
home property owner (E)	Hausbesitzer *m*	—	propriétaire d'immeuble *m*	possessore di casa *m*	propietario de una casa *m*
homework (E)	Heimarbeit *f*	—	travail à domicile *m*	lavoro a domicilio *m*	trabajo a domicilio *m*
homogeneidad (Es)	Homogenität *f*	homogeneity	homogénéité *f*	omogeneità *f*	—
homogeneity (E)	Homogenität *f*	—	homogénéité *f*	omogeneità *f*	homogeneidad *f*
homogénéité (F)	Homogenität *f*	homogeneity	—	omogeneità *f*	homogeneidad *f*
Homogenität (D)	—	homogeneity	homogénéité *f*	omogeneità *f*	homogeneidad *f*
honoraires (F)	Honorar *n*	professional fee	—	onorario *m*	honorario *m*
Honorar (D)	—	professional fee	honoraires *m pl*	onorario *m*	honorario *m*
honorario (Es)	Honorar *n*	professional fee	honoraires *m pl*	onorario *m*	—
honorary consul (E)	Wahlkonsul *m*	—	consul honoraire *m*	console onorario *m*	cónsul honorario *m*
honorer la traite acceptée (F)	Akzepteinlösung *f*	honouring of an acceptance	—	pagamento di un effetto *m*	descuento de una letra aceptada *m*
honouring of an acceptance (E)	Akzepteinlösung *f*	—	honorer la traite acceptée	pagamento di un effetto *m*	descuento de una letra aceptada *m*
hora de despacho (Es)	Geschäftszeit *f*	business hours	heures d'ouverture *f pl*	orario d'apertura *m*	—
hora extraordinaria (Es)	Überstunde *f*	overtime	heure supplémentaire *f*	ora straordinaria *f*	—
hospedaje (Es)	Bewirtung *f*	hospitality/catering	hospitalité *f*/accueil *m*	ospitalità *f*/servizio *m*	—
hospitalité (F)	Bewirtung *f*	hospitality/catering	—	ospitalità *f*/servizio *m*	hospedaje *m*/atenciones *f pl*
hospitality (E)	Bewirtung *f*	—	hospitalité *f*/accueil *m*	ospitalità *f*/servizio *m*	hospedaje *m*/atenciones *f pl*
houille (F)	Steinkohle *f*	hard coal	—	carbone fossile *m*	hulla *f*
hourly wage (E)	Stundenlohn *m*	—	salaire horaire *m*	salario ad ora *m*	salario-hora *m*
housebreaking insurance (E)	Einbruch-versicherung *f*	—	assurance contre le vol avec effraction *f*	assicurazione contro il furto con scasso *f*	seguro contra robo con fractura *m*
housekeeping account (E)	Wirtschaftsstatistik *f*	—	statistique économique *f*	statistica economica *f*	estadística económica *f*

	D	E	F	I	Es
housing construction (E)	Wohnungsbau *m*	—	construction de logements *f*	edilizia abitativa *f*	construcción de viviendas *f*
Huckepackverkehr (D)	—	piggyback service	transport pick-a-back *m*	trasporto strada-rotaia *m*	transporte combinado ferrocarril-carretera *m*
Huckepackwerbung (D)	—	piggyback advertisement	publicité pick-a-back *f*	pubblicità per il trasporto strada-rotaia *f*	publicidad combinada ferrocarril-carretera *f*
huelga (Es)	Streik *m*	strike	grève *f*	sciopero *m*	—
huelga general (Es)	Generalstreik *m*	general strike	grève générale *f*	sciopero generale *m*	—
huile usée (F)	Altöl *n*	waste oil	—	olio usato *m*	aceite usado *m*
huissier de justice (F)	Gerichtsvollzieher *m*	bailiff	—	ufficiale giudiziario *m*	ejecutor judicial *m*
hulla (Es)	Steinkohle *f*	hard coal	houille *f*	carbone fossile *m*	—
Hyperinflation (D)	—	hyperinflation	hyperinflation *f*	iperinflazione *f*	hiperinflación *f*
hyperinflation (E)	Hyperinflation *f*	—	hyperinflation *f*	iperinflazione *f*	hiperinflación *f*
hyperinflation (F)	Hyperinflation *f*	hyperinflation	—	iperinflazione *f*	hiperinflación *f*
Hypothek (D)	—	mortgage	hypothéque *f*	ipoteca *f*	hipoteca *f*
Hypothekenbank (D)	—	mortgage bank	banque hypothécaire *f*	banca ipotecaria *f*	banco hipotecario *m*
hypothéque (F)	Hypothek *f*	mortgage	—	ipoteca *f*	hipoteca *f*
Hypothese (D)	—	hypothesis	hypothèse *f*	ipotesi *f*	hipótesis *f*
hypothèse (F)	Hypothese *f*	hypothesis	—	ipotesi *f*	hipótesis *f*
hypothesis (E)	Hypothese *f*	—	hypothèse *f*	ipotesi *f*	hipótesis *f*
idea (E)	Idee *f*	—	idée *f*	idea *f*	idea *f*
idea (Es)	Idee *f*	idea	idée *f*	idea *f*	—
idea (I)	Idee *f*	idea	idée *f*	—	idea *f*
Idee (D)	—	idea	idée *f*	idea *f*	idea *f*
idée (F)	Idee *f*	idea	—	idea *f*	idea *f*
identidad de los balances sucsivos (Es)	Bilanzkontinuität *f*	formal identity	identité des bilans successifs *f*	continuità di bilancio *f*	—
identité (F)	Personalien *pl*	personal data	—	generalità *f pl*	datos personales *m pl*
identité des bilans successifs (F)	Bilanzkontinuität *f*	formal identity	—	continuità di bilancio *f*	identidad de los balances sucsivos *f*
identity card (E)	Personalausweis *m*	—	pièce d'identité *f*	carta d'identità *f*	carné de identidad *m*
ilegal (Es)	ungesetzlich	illegal	contraire à la loi	illegale	—
illegal (E)	ungesetzlich	—	contraire à la loi	illegale	ilegal
illegale (I)	ungesetzlich	illegal	contraire à la loi	—	ilegal
illicit trade (E)	Schwarzhandel *m*	—	commerce clandestin *m*	commercio abusivo *m*	comercio clandestino *m*
illicit work (E)	Schwarzarbeit *f*	—	travail noir *m*	lavoro abusivo *m*	trabajo clandestino *m*
illiquidità (I)	Illiquidität *f*	illiquidity	manque de trésorerie *f*	—	falta de liquidez *f*
Illiquidität (D)	—	illiquidity	manque de trésorerie *f*	illiquidità *f*	falta de liquidez *f*
illiquidity (E)	Illiquidität *f*	—	manque de trésorerie *f*	illiquidità *f*	falta de liquidez *f*
Image (D)	—	image	image *f*	immagine *f*	imagen *f*
image (E)	Image *n*	—	image *f*	immagine *f*	imagen *f*
image (F)	Image *n*	image	—	immagine *f*	imagen *f*
imagen (Es)	Image *n*	image	image *f*	immagine *f*	—
im Auftrag (D)	—	by order	par ordre	per ordine	por poder
im Ausland (D)	—	abroad	à l'étranger	all'estero	en el extranjero
imballaggio (I)	Verpackung	packing	emballage *m*	—	embalaje *m*
imballaggio marittimo (I)	seemäßige Verpackung *f*	seaproof packing	emballage maritime *m*	—	embalaje marítimo *m*
imbarcare (I)	verfrachten	freight/ship	fréter/embarquer	—	expedir/fletar
imbarco (I)	Verschiffung *f*	shipment	embarquement *m*	—	embarque *m*
im eigenen Namen (D)	—	in one's own name	en nom propre	per nome proprio	en nombre propio
im Einvernehmen mit (D)	—	in agreement with	d'accord avec	d'accordo con	de conformidad con
im einzelnen (D)	—	in particular	en particulier	in dettaglio	en particular
imitación (Es)	Imitation *f*	imitation	imitation *f*	imitazione *f*	—
Imitation (D)	—	imitation	imitation *f*	imitazione *f*	imitación *f*

	D	E	F	I	Es
imitation (E)	Imitation *f*	—	imitation *f*	imitazione *f*	imitación *f*
imitation (F)	Imitation *f*	imitation	—	imitazione *f*	imitación *f*
imitazione (I)	Imitation *f*	imitation	imitation *f*	—	imitación *f*
immagazzinamento (I)	Einlagerung *f*	storage	entreposage *m*	—	almacenamiento *m*
immagazzinamento doganale (I)	Zollagerung *f*	customs warehouse storage	dépôt en entrepôt sous douane *m*	—	depósito de aduana *m*
immagine (I)	Image *n*	image	image *f*	—	imagen *f*
immaterieller Schaden (D)	—	non-material damage	dommage immatériel *m*	danno immateriale *m*	daño inmaterial *m*
immediate delivery (E)	sofortige Lieferung *f*	—	livraison immédiate *f*	consegna immediata *f*	entrega inmediata *f*
immediate(ly) (E)	umgehend	—	immédiatement	immediatamente	inmediatamente
immédiatement (F)	umgehend	immediate(ly)	—	immediatamente	inmediatamente
immediate payment (E)	sofortige Zahlung *f*	—	payement immédiat *m*	pagamento immediato *m*	pago inmediato *m*
immediato (I)	umgehend	immediate(ly)	immédiatement	—	inmediatamente
immobile (I)	Immobilie *f*	item of real estate	bien immobilier *m*	—	inmueble *m*
Immobilie (D)	—	item of real estate	bien immobilier *m*	immobile *m*	inmueble *m*
Immobilienfonds (D)	—	real estate fund	fonds immobilier *m*	fondo immobiliare *m*	fondo inmobiliario *f*
Immobiliengeschäft (D)	—	property transactions	affaire immobilière *f*	operazione immobiliare *f*	negocio de inmuebles *m*
Immobilien-Leasing (D)	—	leasing of real estate	leasing de biens immobiliers *m*	leasing immobiliare *m*	leasing de inmuebles *m*
Immobilienmakler (D)	—	estate agent	courtier en affaires immoblières *m*	agente immobiliare *m*	agente de inmuebles *m*
immobilisations corporelles (F)	Sachanlagen *pl*	fixed assets	—	immobilizzazioni *f pl*	inmuebles y utillaje *m pl*
immobilizzazioni (I)	Sachanlagen *pl*	fixed assets	immobilisations corporelles *f pl*	—	inmuebles y utillaje *m pl*
impegno (I)	Engagement *n*	engagement/ commitment	engagement *m*	—	compromiso *m*
impegno di copertura (I)	Deckungszusage *f*	confirmation of cover	acceptation de prendre le risque en charge *f*	—	nota de cobertura *f*
impersonal taxes (E)	Realsteuern *pl*	—	impôt réel *m*	imposte reali *f pl*	impuestos reales *m pl*
impianti di produzione (I)	Produktions-anlagen *pl*	production facilities	installations industrielles *f pl*	—	instalaciones de producción *f pl*
impianto industriale (I)	Industrieanlage *f*	industrial plant	installation industrielle *f*	—	planta industrial *f*
impiegare (I)	anstellen	employ	employer	—	emplear
impiegati (I)	Angestellter *m*	employee	employé *m pl*	—	empleado *m*
impiego (I)	Anstellung *f*	employment	emploi *m*	—	empleo *m*
impiego dei redditi (I)	Einkommens-verwendung *f*	appropriation of income	utilisation du revenu *f*	—	distribución de la renta *f*
impiego dell'utile (I)	Gewinnverwendung *f*	appropriation of net income	utilisation des bénéfices *f*	—	aplicación de los resultatods *f*
impiego di computer (I)	Computereinsatz *m*	use of a computer	emploi d'ordinateurs *m*	—	utilización de ordenadores *f*
Import (D)	—	import	importation *f*	importazione *f*	importación *f*
import[1] (E)	Einfuhr *f*	—	importation *f*	importazione *f*	importación *f*
import[2] (E)	Import *m*	—	importation *f*	importazione *f*	importación *f*
importación[1] (Es)	Import *m*	import	importation *f*	importazione *f*	—
importación[2] (Es)	Einfuhr *f*	import	importation *f*	importazione *f*	—
importación agrícola (Es)	Agrarimport *m*	farm imports	importation de produits agricoles *f*	importazione agricola *f*	—
importación de capital (Es)	Kapitalimport *m*	capital import	importation de capitaux *f*	importazione di capitali *f*	—
importante (Es)	relevant	relevant	significatif	rilevante	—
importante pedido (Es)	Großauftrag *m*	large-scale order	grosse commande *f*	ordine di grandi quantità *m*	—
importation[1] (F)	Einfuhr *f*	import	—	importazione *f*	importación *f*
importation[2] (F)	Import *m*	import	—	importazione *f*	importación *f*

	D	E	F	I	Es
importation de capitaux (F)	Kapitalimport *m*	capital import	—	importazione di capitali *f*	importación de capital *f*
importation de l'inflation (F)	Inflationsimport *m*	import of inflation	—	importazione di inflazione *f*	inflación importada *f*
importation de produits agricoles (F)	Agrarimport *m*	farm imports	—	importazione agricola *f*	importación agrícola *f*
importazione[1] (I)	Import *m*	import	importation *f*	—	importación *f*
importazione[2] (I)	Einfuhr *f*	import	importation *f*	—	importación *f*
importazione agricola (I)	Agrarimport *m*	farm imports	importation de produits agricoles *f*	—	importación agrícola *f*
importazione di capitali (I)	Kapitalimport *m*	capital import	importation de capitaux *f*	—	importación de capital *f*
importazione di inflazione (I)	Inflationsimport *m*	import of inflation	importation de l'inflation *f*	—	inflación importada *f*
import declaration (E)	Einfuhrerklärung *f*	—	déclaration d'entrée *f*	dichiarazione doganale *f*	declaración de importación *f*
import deposit (E)	Importdepot *n*	—	dépôt d'importation *m*	deposito d'importazione *m*	depósito de importación *m*
Importdepot (D)	—	import deposit	dépôt d'importation *m*	deposito d'importazione *m*	depósito de importación *m*
import documents (E)	Einfuhrpapiere *pl*	—	documents d'importation *m pl*	bollette doganali *f pl*	documentos de importación *m pl*
import duties (E)	Einfuhrabgabe *f*	—	taxe à l'importation *f*	tassa d'importazione *f*	tasa a la importación *f*
import duty (E)	Einfuhrzoll *m*	—	droit d'entrée *m*	dazio d'importazione *m*	arancel de importación *m*
importe de la factura (Es)	Rechnungsbetrag *m*	amount of invoice	montant de la facture *m*	ammontare della fattura *m*	—
imported inflation (E)	importierte Inflation *f*	—	inflation importée *f*	inflazione importata *f*	inflación importada *f*
Importhandel (D)	—	import trade	commerce d'importation *m*	commercio delle importazioni *m*	comercio de importación *m*
importierte Inflation (D)	—	imported inflation	inflation importée *f*	inflazione importata *f*	inflación importada *f*
import licence (E)	Einfuhr-genehmigung *f*	—	autorisation d'importation *f*	permesso d'importazione *m*	permiso de importación *m*
importo (I)	Betrag *m*	amount	montant *m*	—	suma *f*
importo del credito documentario (I)	Akkreditivsumme *f*	amount of the letter of credit	montant de l'accréditif *m*	—	suma del crédito documentario *f*
importo della fattura (I)	Rechnungssumme *f*	invoice amount	montant de la facture *m*	—	suma de la factura *f*
importo di rimborso (I)	Ablösesumme *f*	redemption sum	montant de rachat *m*	—	suma de amortización *f*
import of inflation (E)	Inflationsimport *m*	—	importation de l'inflation *f*	importazione di inflazione *f*	inflación importada *f*
importo minimo (I)	Mindesthöhe *f*	minimum amount	montant minimum *m*	—	cantidad mínima *f*
importo nominale (I)	Nominalbetrag *m*	nominal amount	montant nominal *m*	—	montante nominal *m*
importo nominale minimo (I)	Mindestnennbetrag *m*	minimum nominal amount	montant nominal minimum *m*	—	valor nominal mínimo *m*
importo totale (I)	Gesamtsumme *f*	total amout	montant total *m*	—	suma total *f*
Importquote (D)	—	import quota	contingent d'importation *m*	quota d'importazione *f*	cuota de importación *f*
import quota (E)	Importquote *f*	—	contingent d'importation *m*	quota d'importazione *f*	cuota de importación *f*
import restriction (E)	Einfuhr-beschränkung *f*	—	limitation des importations *f*	restrizione d'importazione *f*	restricción a la importación *f*
import trade (E)	Importhandel *m*	—	commerce d'importation *m*	commercio delle importazioni *m*	comercio de importación *m*
imposiciones de ahorro (Es)	Spareinlagen *pl*	savings deposits	dépôt d'épargne *m*	depositi di risparmio *m pl*	—
imposición separada e igual de los cónyuges (Es)	Splitting *n*	splitting	péréquation fiscale des revenus des deux époux *f*	splittaggio *m*	—
imposta[1] (I)	Abgabe *f*	tax/duty	taxe *f*	—	impuesto *m*/arancel *m*
imposta[2] (I)	Steuer *f*	tax	impôt *m*	—	impuesto *m*
imposta cedolare (I)	Ertragsteuer *f*	tax on income	impôt assis sur le produit *m*	—	impuesto sobre beneficios *m*

	D	E	F	I	Es
imposta di successione (I)	Erbschaftsteuer *f*	inheritance tax	impôt sur les successions *m*	—	impuesto sobre sucesiones *m*
imposta generale sulle entrate (I)	Umsatzsteuer *f*	turnover tax	impôt sur le chiffre d'affaires *m*	—	impuesto sobre el volumen de ventas *m*
imposta industriale (I)	Gewerbesteuer *f*	trade tax	patente *f*	—	impuesto industrial *m*
imposta in natura (I)	Naturalabgabe *f*	duty in kind	taxe acquittée en nature *f*	—	impuesto en especie *m*
imposta sugli alcolici (I)	Alkoholsteuer *f*	tax on alcohol	impôt sur l'alcool *m*	—	impuesto sobre el alcohol *m*
imposta sugli investimenti (I)	Investitionssteuer *f*	investment tax	impôt sur les investissements *m*	—	impuesto sobre las inversiones *m*
imposta sugli olii minerali (I)	Mineralölsteuer *f*	mineral oil tax	taxe sur les carburants *f*	—	impuesto sobre la gasolina *m*
imposta sui consumi di lusso (I)	Luxussteuer *f*	luxury tax	taxe de luxe *f*	—	impuesto de lujo *m*
imposta sui redditi (I)	Einkommensteuer *f*	income tax	impôt sur le revenu *m*	—	impuesto sobre la renta de las personas físicas *m*
imposta sui salari (I)	Lohnsteuer *f*	wages tax	impôt sur les traitements et salaires *m*	—	impuesto sobre los rendimientos del trabajo personal *f*
imposta sul fatturato d'acquisto (I)	Vorsteuer *f*	input tax	impôt perçu en amont *m*	—	impuesto sobre el valor añadido deducible *m*
imposta sul reddito delle società (I)	Körperschaftsteuer *f*	corporation tax	taxe sur les sociétés *f*	—	impuesto de corporaciones *m*
imposta sul valore aggiunto (I)	Mehrwertsteuer *f*	value-added tax	taxe à la valeur ajoutée *f*	—	impuesto sobre el valor añadido *m*
imposta sulla circolazione degli autoveicoli (I)	Kraftfahrzeugsteuer *f*	motor vehicle tax	taxe sur les véhicules à moteur *f*	—	impuesto sobre vehículos *m*
imposta sulla rendita del capitale (I)	Kapitalertragsteuer *f*	tax on investment income	impôt sur le revenue du capital *m*	—	impuesto sobre la renta del capital *m*
imposta sulle donazioni (I)	Schenkungssteuer *f*	gift tax	impôt sur les donations *m*	—	impuesto sobre donaciones *m*
imposta sulle operazioni di borsa (I)	Börsen-umsatzsteuer *f*	stock exchange turnover tax	droit de transaction sur les opérations boursières *m*	—	impuesto de negociación bursátil *m*
imposte dirette (I)	direkte Steuern *pl*	direct taxes	impôts directs *m pl*	—	impuestos directos *m pl*
imposte indirette (I)	indirekte Steuern *pl*	indirect taxes	impôts indirects *m*	—	impuestos indirectos *m pl*
imposte reali (I)	Realsteuern *pl*	impersonal taxes	impôt réel *m*	—	impuestos reales *m pl*
impôt (F)	Steuer *f*	tax	—	imposta *f*	impuesto *m*
impôt assis sur le produit (F)	Ertragsteuer *f*	tax on income	—	imposta cedolare *f*/ imposta sul reddito *f*	impuesto sobre beneficios *m*
impôt perçu en amont (F)	Vorsteuer *f*	input tax	—	imposta sul fatturato d'acquisto *f*	impuesto sobre el valor añadido deducible *m*
impôt réel (F)	Realsteuern *pl*	impersonal taxes	—	imposte reali *f pl*	impuestos reales *m pl*
impôts directs (F)	direkte Steuern *pl*	direct taxes	—	imposte dirette *f pl*	impuestos directos *m pl*
impôts indirects (F)	indirekte Steuern *pl*	indirect taxes	—	imposte indirette *f pl*	impuestos indirectos *m pl*
impôt sur l'alcool (F)	Alkoholsteuer *f*	tax on alcohol	—	imposta sugli alcolici *f*	impuesto sobre el alcohol *m*
impôt sur le chiffre d'affaires (F)	Umsatzsteuer *f*	turnover tax	—	imposta generale sulle entrate *f*	impuesto sobre el volumen de ventas *m*
impôt sur le revenu (F)	Einkommensteuer *f*	income tax	—	imposta sui redditi *f*	impuesto sobre la renta de las personas físicas *m*
impôt sur le revenu du capital (F)	Kapitalertragsteuer *f*	tax on investment income	—	imposta sulla rendita del capitale *f*	impuesto sobre la renta del capital *m*
impôt sur les donations (F)	Schenkungssteuer *f*	gift tax	—	imposta sulle donazioni *f*	impuesto sobre donaciones *m*
impôt sur les investissements (F)	Investitionssteuer *f*	investment tax	—	imposta sugli investimenti *f*	impuesto sobre las inversiones *m*

	D	E	F	I	Es
impôt sur les successions (F)	Erbschaftsteuer *f*	inheritance tax	—	imposta di successione *f*	impuesto sobre sucesiones *m*
impôt sur les traitements et salaires (F)	Lohnsteuer *f*	wages tax	—	imposta sui salari *f*	impuesto sobre los rendimientos del trabajo personal *f*
im Preis inbegriffen (D)	—	included in the price	inclus dans le prix	incluso nel prezzo	incluido
imprenditore (I)	Unternehmer *m*	entrepreneur	entrepreneur *m*	—	empresario *m*
imprenditore giovane (I)	Jungunternehmer *m*	young businessman	entrepreneur débutant *m*	—	joven empresario *m*
impresa (I)	Unternehmen *n*	enterprise	entreprise *f*	—	empresario *m*
impresa concorrente (I)	Konkurrenz-unternehmen *n*	competitive undertaking	entreprise concurrente *f*	—	empresa competitoria *f*
impresa controllante (I)	herrschendes Unternehmen *n*	controlling company	entreprise dirigeante *f*	—	empresa dominante *f*
impresa di utilità pubblica (I)	gemeinnütziges Unternehmen *n*	public institution	entreprise d'utilité publique *f*	—	empresa de beneficio común *f*
imprese multinazionali (I)	multinationale Unternehmen *n*	multinational enterprise	entreprises multinationales	—	empresa multinacional *f*
imprese pubbliche (I)	öffentliche Unternehmen *n*	public enterprise	entreprises publiques *f*	—	empresa pública *f*
impresión offset (Es)	Offsetdruck *m*	offset (printing)	offset *m*	stampa offset *f*	—
impreso[1] (Es)	Drucksache *f*	printed matter	imprimé *m*	stampa *f*	—
impreso[2] (Es)	Vordruck *m*	printed form	imprimé *m*	modulo *m*	—
impresora (Es)	Drucker *m*	printer	imprimante *f*	stampante *f*	—
impresora laser (Es)	Laserdrucker *m*	laser printer	imprimante au laser *f*	stampante laser *f*	—
Impressum (D)	—	imprint	mention des responsables de l'édition *f*	impressum *m*	pie de imprenta *m*
impressum (I)	Impressum *n*	imprint	mention des responsables de l'édition *f*	—	pie de imprenta *m*
imprimante (F)	Drucker *m*	printer	—	stampante *f*	impresora *f*
imprimante au laser (F)	Laserdrucker *m*	laser printer	—	stampante laser *f*	impresora laser *m*
imprimé[1] (F)	Vordruck *m*	printed form	—	modulo *m*	impreso *m*
imprimé[2] (F)	Drucksache *f*	printed matter	—	stampa *f*	impreso *m*
imprimé en blanc (F)	Blankoformular *n*	blank form	—	modulo in bianco *m*	formulario en blanco *m*
imprint (E)	Impressum *n*	—	mention des responsables de l'édition *f*	impressum *m*	pie de imprenta *m*
improper (E)	unsachgemäß	—	non adéquat	non idoneo	con falta de objetividad
impuesto[1] (Es)	Steuer *f*	tax	impôt *m*	imposta *f*	—
impuesto[2] (Es)	Abgabe *f*	tax/duty	taxe *f*	imposta *f*/dazio *m*	—
impuesto de corporaciones (Es)	Körperschaftsteuer *f*	corporation tax	taxe sur les sociétés *f*	imposta sul reddito delle società *f*	—
impuesto de lujo (Es)	Luxussteuer *f*	luxury tax	taxe de luxe *f*	imposta sui consumi di lusso *f*	—
impuesto de negociación bursátil (Es)	Börsenumsatzsteuer *f*	stock exchange turnover tax	droit de transaction sur les opérations boursières *m*	imposta sulle operazioni di borsa *f*	—
impuesto en especie (Es)	Naturalabgabe *f*	duty in kind	taxe acquittée en nature *f*	imposta in natura *f*	—
impuesto industrial (Es)	Gewerbesteuer *f*	trade tax	patente *f*	imposta industriale *f*	—
impuestos adelantados (Es)	Steuer-vorauszahlung *f*	advanced payment of taxes	acompte provisionnel sur l'imposition *m*	pagamento anticipato delle imposte *m*	—
impuestos directos (Es)	direkte Steuern *pl*	direct taxes	impôts directs *m pl*	imposte dirette *f pl*	—
impuestos indirectos (Es)	indirekte Steuern *pl*	indirect taxes	impôts indirects *m*	imposte indirette *f pl*	—
impuesto sobre beneficios (Es)	Ertragsteuer *f*	tax on income	impôt assis sur le produit *m*	imposta cedolare *f*/ imposta sul reddito *f*	—
impuesto sobre donaciones (Es)	Schenkungssteuer *f*	gift tax	impôt sur les donations *m*	imposta sulle donazioni *f*	—
impuesto sobre el alcohol (Es)	Alkoholsteuer *f*	tax on alcohol	impôt sur l'alcool *m*	imposta sugli alcolici *f*	—

	D	E	F	I	Es
impuesto sobre el valor añadido (Es)	Mehrwertsteuer *f*	value-added tax	taxe à la valeur ajoutée *f*	imposta sul valore aggiunto *f*	—
impuesto sobre el valor añadido deducible (Es)	Vorsteuer *f*	input tax	impôt perçu en amont *m*	imposta sul fatturato d'acquisto *f*	—
impuesto sobre el volumen de ventas (Es)	Umsatzsteuer *f*	turnover tax	impôt sur le chiffre d'affaires *m*	imposta generale sulle entrate *f*	—
impuesto sobre la gasolina (Es)	Mineralölsteuer *f*	mineral oil tax	taxe sur les carburants *f*	imposta sugli olii minerali *f*	—
impuesto sobre la renta de las personas físicas (Es)	Einkommensteuer *f*	income tax	impôt sur le revenu *m*	imposta sui redditi *f*	—
impuesto sobre la renta del capital (Es)	Kapitalertragsteuer *f*	tax on investment income	impôt sur le revenu du capital *m*	imposta sulla rendita del capitale *f*	—
impuesto sobre las inversiones (Es)	Investitionssteuer *f*	investment tax	impôt sur les investissements *m*	imposta sugli investimenti *f*	—
impuesto sobre los rendimientos del trabajo personal (Es)	Lohnsteuer *f*	wages tax	impôt sur les traitements et salaires *m*	imposta sui salari *f*	—
impuesto sobre sucesiones (Es)	Erbschaftsteuer *f*	inheritance tax	impôt sur les successions *m*	imposta di successione *f*	—
impuesto sobre vehículos (Es)	Kraftfahrzeugsteuer *f*	motor vehicle tax	taxe sur les véhicules à moteur *f*	imposta sulla circolazione degli autoveicoli *f*	—
impuestos reales (Es)	Realsteuern *pl*	impersonal taxes	impôt réel *m*	imposte reali *f pl*	—
impulse buying (E)	Impulskauf *m*	—	achat d'impulsion *m*	acquisto impulsivo *m*	compra espontánea *f*
Impulskauf (D)	—	impulse buying	achat d'impulsion *m*	acquisto impulsivo *m*	compra espontánea *f*
impulso de crecimiento (Es)	Wachstumsimpuls *m*	growth impulse	stimulation de l'accroissement *f*	impulso di crescita *m*	—
impulso di crescita (I)	Wachstumsimpuls *m*	growth impulse	stimulation de l'accroissement *f*	—	impulso de crecimiento *m*
inabilità al lavoro (I)	Erwerbsunfähigkeit *f*	disability for work	incapacité d'exercer toute activité professionnelle *f*	—	incapacidad profesional *f*
inadempienza (I)	Nichterfüllung *f*	non-performance	inexécution *f*	—	incumplimiento *m*
in agreement with (E)	im Einvernehmen mit	—	d'accord avec	d'accordo con	de conformidad con
in aumento (I)	steigend	rising	croissant(e)	—	ascendente
in bar (D)	—	in cash	comptant	in contanti	en efectivo
in base commissionaria (I)	auf Kommissionsbasis	on a commission basis	en commission	—	en comisión
incapacidad profesional (Es)	Erwerbsunfähigkeit *f*	disability for work	incapacité d'exercer toute activité professionnelle *f*	inabilità al lavoro *f*	—
incapacité d'exercer toute activité professionnelle (F)	Erwerbsunfähigkeit *f*	disability for work	—	inabilità al lavoro *f*	incapacidad profesional *f*
in cash (E)	in bar	—	comptant	in contanti	en efectivo
incasso (I)	Inkasso *n*	collection	recouvrement *m*	—	encobro *m*
incentive (E)	Anreiz *m*	—	incitation *f*	incentivo *m*	incentivo *m*
incentive system (E)	Anreizsystem *n*	—	système d'incitation *m*	sistema d'incentivo *m*	sistema de incentivos *m*
incentivo (Es)	Anreiz *m*	incentive	incitation *f*	incentivo *m*	—
incentivo (I)	Anreiz *m*	incentive	incitation *f*	—	incentivo *m*
inchiesta tributaria (I)	Steuerfahndung *f*	investigation into suspected tax offences	recherche de la fraude fiscale *f*	—	investigación tributaria *f*
incineration (E)	Verbrennung *f*	—	combustion *f*	combustione *f*	combustión *f*
incitation (F)	Anreiz *m*	incentive	—	incentivo *m*	incentivo *m*
included in the price (E)	im Preis inbegriffen	—	inclus dans le prix	incluso nel prezzo	incluido
incluido (Es)	im Preis inbegriffen	included in the price	inclus dans le prix	incluso nel prezzo	—
inclus dans le prix (F)	im Preis inbegriffen	included in the price	—	incluso nel prezzo	incluido
inclusive (E)	inklusiv	—	inclusivement	incluso	incluso
inclusivement (F)	inklusiv	inclusive	—	incluso	incluso
incluso (Es)	inklusiv	inclusive	inclusivement	incluso	—
incluso (I)	inklusiv	inclusive	inclusivement	—	incluso

	D	E	F	I	Es
incluso nel prezzo (I)	im Preis inbegriffen	included in the price	inclus dans le prix	—	incluido
income[1] (E)	Einkommen *n*	—	revenu *m*	reddito *m*	ingresos *m pl*/renta *f*
income[2] (E)	Ertrag *m*	—	rendement *m*/ revenu *m*	reddito *m*/ rendimento *m*	rendimiento *m*/ renta *f*
income declaration (E)	Einkommens-erklärung *f*	—	déclaration du revenu *f*	dichiarazione del reddito *f*	declaración de la renta *f*
income factor (E)	Ertragsfaktor *m*	—	facteur productif *m*	fattore reddito *m*	factor de beneficio *m*
income from capital (E)	Kapitalertrag *m*	—	produit du capital *m*	rendita del capitale *f*	rendimiento del capital *m*
income tax (E)	Einkommensteuer *f*	—	impôt sur le revenu *m*	imposta sui redditi *f*	impuesto sobre la renta de las personas físicas *m*
incompatibilità degli obiettivi (I)	Zielkonflikt *m*	conflicting goals	conflit d'objectifs *m*	—	conflicto de objectivos *m*
incomplet (F)	unvollständig	incomplete	—	incompleto	incompleto
incomplete (E)	unvollständig	—	incomplet	incompleto	incompleto
incompleto (Es)	unvollständig	incomplete	incomplet	incompleto	—
incompleto (I)	unvollständig	incomplete	incomplet	—	incompleto
in conformity with market conditions (E)	marktkonform	—	conforme au marché	conforme al mercato	conforme al mercado
in contanti[1] (I)	bar	cash	comptant	—	al contado
in contanti[2] (I)	in bar	in cash	comptant	—	en efectivo
increase (E)	Zulage *f*	—	prime *f*/complément de salaire *m*	premio *m*/indennità *f*	suplemento *m*/plus *m*
increase in capacity (E)	Kapazitäts-ausweitung *f*	—	extension de la capacité *f*	ampliamento delle capacità *m*	ampliación de la capacidad *f*
increase in efficiency (E)	Leistungssteigerung *f*	—	amélioration du rendement *f*	aumento della produttività *m*	incremento del rendimiento *m*
increase in population (E)	Bevölkerungs-wachstum *m*	—	accroissement de la population *m*	incremento demografico *m*	crecimiento vegetativo *m*
increase in salary (E)	Gehaltserhöhung *f*	—	augmentation du traitement *f*	aumento dello stipendio *m*	aumento de sueldo *m*
increase in wages (E)	Lohnerhöhung *f*	—	augmentation du salaire *f*	aumento salariale *m*	aumento de salario *m*
increase of taxes (E)	Steuererhöhung *f*	—	relèvement des impôts *m*	aumento delle imposte *m*	aumento de los impuestos *m*
increase of the share capital (E)	Kapitalerhöhung *f*	—	augmentation de capital *f*	aumento del capitale *m*	aumento de capital *m*
incremento del rendimiento (Es)	Leistungs-steigerung *f*	increase in efficiency	amélioration du rendement *f*	aumento della produttività *m*	—
incremento demografico (I)	Bevölkerungs-wachstum *m*	increase in population	accroissement de la population *m*	—	crecimiento vegetativo *m*
incremento desmesurado de los costes (Es)	Kostenexplosion *f*	cost escalation	explosion des coûts *f*	esplosione dei costi *f*	—
incremento di valore (I)	Wertzuwachs *m*	appreciation	accroissement de valeur *m*	—	plusvalía *f*
incremento por peligrosidad (Es)	Gefahrenzulage *f*	danger money	prime de danger *f*	premio di rischio *m*	—
incumplimiento (Es)	Nichterfüllung *f*	non-performance	inexécution *f*	inadempienza *f*	—
indagine[1] (I)	Nachforschung *f*	investigation	recherche *f*	—	pesquisas *f pl*
indagine[2] (I)	Untersuchung *f*	examination	étude *f*	—	inspección *f*
indebitamento (I)	Verschuldung *f*	indebtedness	endettement *m*	—	endeudamiento *m*
indebitamento eccessivo (I)	Überschuldung *f*	excessive indebtedness	surendettement *m*	—	exceso de deudas *m*
indebitamento effettivo (I)	effektive Verschuldung *f*	real indebtedness	endettement effectif *m*	—	endeudamiento efectivo *m*
indebitamento netto (I)	Nettoverschuldung *f*	net indebtedness	endettement net *m*	—	deuda neta *m*
indebtedness (E)	Verschuldung *f*	—	endettement *m*	indebitamento *m*	endeudamiento *m*
indemnité[1] (F)	Abfindung *f*	indemnity/ compensation	—	indennità *f*/ compensazione *f*	indemnización *f*/ compensación *f*
indemnité[2] (F)	Entschädigung *f*	compensation/ indemnification	—	indennità *f*	indemnización *f*/pago de compensación *m*
indemnité de chômage (F)	Arbeitslosen-unterstützung *f*	unemployment benefit	—	sussidio di disoccupazione *m*	prestaciones por desempleo *m*

	D	E	F	I	Es
indemnité en capital (F)	Kapitalabfindung *f*	lump sum settlement	—	indennità in capitale *f*	indemnización en capital *f*
indemnité par kilomètre (F)	Kilometergeld *n*	allowance per kilometre	—	indennità per chilometro *f*	kilometraje *m*
indemnity (E)	Abfindung *f*	—	indemnité *f*/ compensation *f*	indennità *f*/ compensazione *f*	indemnización *f*/ compensación *f*
indemnización[1] (Es)	Schadensersatz *m*	compensation for loss suffered	dommages-intérêts *m pl*	risarcimento danni *m*	—
indemnización[2] (Es)	Abfindung *f*	indemnity/ compensation	indemnité *f*/ compensation *f*	indennità *f*/ compensazione *f*	—
indemnización[3] (Es)	Entschädigung *f*	compensation/ indemnification	indemnité *f*	indennità *f*	—
indemnización en capital (Es)	Kapitalabfindung *f*	lump sum settlement	indemnité en capital *f*	indennità in capitale *f*	—
indennità[1] (I)	Entschädigung *f*	compensation/ indemnification	indemnité *f*	—	indemnización *f*/pago de compensación *m*
indennità[2] (I)	Abfindung *f*	indemnity/ compensation	indemnité *f*/ compensation *f*	—	indemnización *f*/ compensación *f*
indennità di ferie (I)	Urlaubsgeld *n*	holiday allowance	prime de vacances *f*	—	retribución por vacaciones *f*
indennità in capitale (I)	Kapitalabfindung *f*	lump sum settlement	indemnité en capital *f*	—	indemnización de capital *f*
indennità per chilometro (I)	Kilometergeld *n*	allowance per kilometre	indemnité par kilomètre *f*	—	kilometraje *m*
indépendance (F)	Unabhängigkeit *f*	independence	—	indipendenza *f*	independencia *f*
indépendant (F)	selbständig	independent	—	indipendente	independiente/no asalariado/autónomo
independence (E)	Unabhängigkeit *f*	—	indépendance *f*	indipendenza *f*	independencia *f*
independencia (Es)	Unabhängigkeit *f*	independence	indépendance *f*	indipendenza *f*	—
independent (E)	selbständig	—	indépendant	indipendente	independiente/no asalariado/autónomo
independiente (Es)	selbständig	independent	indépendant	indipendente	—
in dettaglio (I)	im einzelnen	in particular	en particulier	—	en particular
Index (D)	—	index	indice *m*	indice *m*	índice *m*
index (E)	Index *m*	—	indice *m*	indice *m*	índice *m*
indexation (F)	Indizierung *f*	putting on the index	—	indicizzazione *f*	indiciación *f*
index card (E)	Karteikarte *f*	—	fiche *f*	scheda *f*	ficha *f*
index clause (E)	Indexklausel *f*	—	clause d'indexation *f*	clausola dell'indice *f*	cláusula de índice variable *f*
Indexklausel (D)	—	index clause	clause d'indexation *f*	clausola dell'indice *f*	cláusula de índice variable *f*
index-linked wages (E)	Indexlohn *m*	—	salaire indexé *m*	salario indicizzato *m*	salario-índice *m*
Indexlohn (D)	—	index-linked wages	salaire indexé *m*	salario indicizzato *m*	salario-índice *m*
indicación de cantidades (Es)	Mengenangabe *f*	indication of quantity	indication de la quantité *f*	indicazione della quantità *f*	—
indicación de precios (Es)	Preisauszeichnung *f*	pricemarking	affichage des prix *f*	indicazione del prezzo *f*	—
indication de la quantité (F)	Mengenangabe *f*	indication of quantity	—	indicazione della quantità *f*	indicación de cantidades *f*
indication of quantity (E)	Mengenangabe *f*	—	indication de la quantité *f*	indicazione della quantità *f*	indicación de cantidades *f*
indicazione del prezzo (I)	Preisauszeichnung *f*	pricemarking	affichage des prix *f*	—	indicación de precios *f*
indicazione della quantità (I)	Mengenangabe *f*	indication of quantity	indication de la quantité *f*	—	indicación de cantidades *f*
índice (Es)	Index *m*	index	indice *m*	indice *m*	—
indice[1] (F)	Index *m*	index	—	indice *m*	índice *m*
indice[2] (F)	Kennziffern *pl*	code numbers	—	cifre d'identificazione *f pl*	cifras índice *f pl*
indice (I)	Index *m*	index	indice *m*	—	índice *m*
indice azionario (I)	Aktienindex *m*	share index	indice du cours des actions *m*	—	índice de cotización de acciones *m*
índice bursátil (Es)	Börsenindex *m*	stock exchange index	indice des cours des actions *m*	indice delle quotazioni *m*	—

	D	E	F	I	Es
índice de cotización de acciones (Es)	Aktienindex *m*	share index	indice du cours des actions *m*	indice azionario *m*	—
índice de precios (Es)	Preisindex *m*	price index	indice des prix *m*	indice dei prezzi *m*	—
índice de precios de producción (Es)	Erzeugerpreisindex *m*	producer price index	indice des prix à la production *m*	indice dei prezzi di fabbrica *m*	—
indice dei prezzi (I)	Preisindex *m*	price index	indice des prix *m*	—	ínidce de precios *m*
indice dei prezzi di fabbrica (I)	Erzeugerpreisindex *m*	producer price index	indice des prix à la production *m*	—	índice de precios de producción *m*
indice delle quotazioni (I)	Börsenindex *m*	stock exchange index	indice des cours des actions *m*	—	índice bursátil *m*
indice des cours des actions (F)	Börsenindex *m*	stock exchange index	—	indice delle quotazioni *m*	índice bursátil *m*
indice des prix (F)	Preisindex *m*	price index	—	indice dei prezzi *m*	ínidce de precios *m*
indice des prix à la production (F)	Erzeugerpreisindex *m*	producer price index	—	indice dei prezzi di fabbrica *m*	índice de precios de producción *m*
Indice Dow Jones (Es)	Dow-Jones-Index *m*	Dow-Jones Industrial Average	indice Dow-Jones *m*	indice Dow-Jones *m*	—
indice Dow-Jones (F)	Dow-Jones-Index *m*	Dow-Jones Industrial Average	—	indice Dow-Jones *m*	Indice Dow Jones *m*
indice Dow-Jones (I)	Dow-Jones-Index *m*	Dow-Jones Industrial Average	indice Dow-Jones *m*	—	Indice Dow Jones *m*
indice du cours des actions (F)	Aktienindex *m*	share index	—	indice azionario *m*	índice de cotización de acciones *m*
indiciación (Es)	Indizierung *f*	putting on the index	indexation *f*	indicizzazione *f*	—
indicizzazione (I)	Indizierung *f*	putting on the index	indexation *f*	—	indiciación *f*
indipendente (I)	selbständig	independent	indépendant	—	independiente/no asalariado/autónomo
indipendenza (I)	Unabhängigkeit *f*	independence	indépendance *f*	—	independencia *f*
indirect taxes (E)	indirekte Steuern *pl*	—	impôts indirects *m*	imposte indirette *f pl*	impuestos indirectos *m pl*
indirekte Steuern (D)	—	indirect taxes	impôts indirects *m*	imposte indirette *f pl*	impuestos indirectos *m pl*
indirizzare (I)	adressieren	address	adresser	—	dirigir
indirizzo (I)	Adresse *f*	address	adresse *f*	—	dirección *f*
indirizzo della ditta (I)	Firmenanschrift *f*	company address	adresse de la maison *f*	—	dirección de la empresa *f*
Individualbedürfnis (D)	—	individual need	besoin individuel *m*	fabbisogno individuale *m*	necesidades individuales *f pl*
Indizierung (D)	—	putting on the index	indexation *f*	indicizzazione *f*	indiciación *f*
indorsement (E)	Indossament *n*	—	endossement *m*	girata *f*	endoso *m*
Indossament (D)	—	indorsement	endossement *m*	girata *f*	endoso *m*
in due copie (I)	in zweifacher Ausfertigung	in duplicate	en deux exemplaires	—	por duplicado
in duplicate (E)	in zweifacher Ausfertigung	—	en deux exemplaires	in due copie	por duplicado
industria (Es)	Gewerbe *n*	trade/industry/craft	activité profession-nelle *f*/industrie *f*/ artisanat *m*	commercio *m*/ industria *f*/ artigianato *m*	—
industria de bienes de consumo (Es)	Konsumgüter-industrie *f*	consumer goods industry	industrie des biens de consommation *f*	industria dei beni di consumo *f*	—
industria de bienes de producción (Es)	Produktionsgüter-Industrie *f*	producer goods industry	industrie des biens de production *f*	industria dei beni strumentali *f*	—
industria de desperdicios (Es)	Abfallwirtschaft *f*	waste management	industrie de déchets *f*	industria dei rifiuti *f*	—
industria dei beni di consumo (I)	Konsumgüter-industrie *f*	consumer goods industry	industrie des biens de consommation *f*	—	industria de bienes de consumo *f*
industria dei beni strumentali (I)	Produktionsgüter-Industrie *f*	producer goods industry	industrie des biens de production *f*	—	industria de bienes de producción *f*
industria dei rifiuti (I)	Abfallwirtschaft *f*	waste management	industrie de déchets *f*	—	industria de desperdicios *f*
industria de la construcción (Es)	Bauindustrie *f*	construction industry	industrie de sous-traitance du bâtiment *f*	industria edile *f*	—
industria di trasformazione (I)	verarbeitende Industrie *f*	manufacturing industry	industrie transformatrice *f*	—	industria transformadora *f*

	D	E	F	I	Es
industria edile (I)	Bauindustrie *f*	construction industry	industrie de sous-traitance du bâtiment *f*	—	industria de la construcción *f*
industrial area (E)	Industriegebiet *n*	—	région industrielle *f*	zona industriale *f*	región industrial *f*
industrial bonds (E)	Industrie-obligationen *pl*	—	obligations de l'industrie *f pl*	obbligazioni industriali *f pl*	obligaciónes industriales *f pl*
industrial enterprise (E)	Industriebetrieb *m*	—	entreprise industrielle *f*	azienda industriale *f*	establecimiento industrial *m*
industrial espionage[1] (E)	Industriespionage *f*	—	espionnage industriel *m*	spionaggio industriale *m*	espionaje industrial *m*
industrial espionage[2] (E)	Werkspionage *f*	—	espionnage industriel *m*	spionaggio aziendale *m*	espionaje industrial *m*
industrial espionage[3] (E)	Betriebsspionage *f*	—	espionnage dans l'entreprise	spionaggio aziendale *m*	espionaje industrial *m*
industrial injury (E)	Arbeitsunfall *m*	—	accident du travail *m*	infortunio sul posto di lavoro *m*	accidente profesional *m*
industrial plant (E)	Industrieanlage *f*	—	installation industrielle *f*	impianto industriale *m*	planta industrial *f*
industrial psychology (E)	Arbeitspsychologie *f*	—	psychologie de travail *f*	psicologia del lavoro *f*	psicología laboral *f*
industrial undertaking (E)	Industrie-unternehmen *n*	—	entreprise industrielle *f*	impresa industriale *f*	empresa industrial *f*
industria minera (Es)	Montanindustrie *f*	mining industry	industrie minière *f*	industria mineraria e siderurgica *f*	—
industria mineraria (I)	Bergbau *m*	mining	industrie extractive *f*	—	minería *f*
industria mineraria e siderurgica (I)	Montanindustrie *f*	mining industry	industrie minière *f*	—	industria minera *f*
industria transformadora (Es)	verarbeitende Industrie *f*	manufacturing industry	industrie transformatrice *f*	industria di trasformazione *f*	—
Industrieanlage (D)	—	industrial plant	installation industrielle *f*	impianto industriale *m*	planta industrial *f*
Industriebetrieb (D)	—	industrial enterprise	entreprise industrielle *f*	azienda industriale *f*	establecimiento industrial *m*
industrie de déchets (F)	Abfallwirtschaft *f*	waste management	—	industria dei rifiuti *f*	industria de desperdicios *f*
industrie des biens de consommation (F)	Konsumgüter-industrie *f*	consumer goods industry	—	industria dei beni di consumo *f*	industria de bienes de consumo *f*
industrie des biens de production (F)	Produktionsgüter-Industrie *f*	producer goods industry	—	industria dei beni strumentali *f*	industria de bienes de producción *f*
industrie de sous-traitance du bâtiment (F)	Bauindustrie *f*	construction industry	—	industria edile *f*	industria de la construcción *f*
(industrie du) bâtiment (F)	Bauwirtschaft *f*	building and construction industry	—	edilizia *f*	ramo de la construcción *m*
industrie extractive (F)	Bergbau *m*	mining	—	industria mineraria *f*	minería *f*
Industriegebiet (D)	—	industrial area	région industrielle *f*	zona industriale *f*	región industrial *f*
industrie minière (F)	Montanindustrie *f*	mining industry	—	industria mineraria e siderurgica *f*	industria minera *f*
Industrieobligation (D)	—	industrial bond	obligation de l'industrie *f pl*	obbligazioni industriali *f pl*	obligaciones industriales *f pl*
Industriespionage (D)	—	industrial espionage	espionnage industriel *m*	spionaggio industriale *m*	espionaje industrial *m*
industrie transformatrice (F)	verarbeitende Industrie *f*	manufacturing industry	—	industria di trasformazione *f*	industria transformadora *f*
Industrie- und Handelskammer (D)	—	Chamber of Industry and Commerce	chambre de commerce et d'industrie *f*	camera di commercio e industria *f*	cámara de industria y comercio *f*
inexécution (F)	Nichterfüllung *f*	non-performance	—	inadempienza *f*	incumplimiento *m*
inferiore Güter (D)	—	inferior goods	biens inférieurs *m pl*	beni inferiori *m pl*	bienes inferiores *m pl*
inferior goods (E)	inferiore Güter *pl*	—	biens inférieurs *m pl*	beni inferiori *m pl*	bienes inferiores *m pl*
inflación (Es)	Inflation *f*	inflation	inflation *f*	inflazione *f*	—
inflación galopante (Es)	galoppierende Inflation *f*	galloping inflation	inflation galopante *f*	inflazione galoppante *f*	—
inflación importada[1] (Es)	Inflationsimport *m*	import of inflation	importation de l'inflation *f*	importazione di inflazione *f*	—
inflación importada[2] (Es)	importierte Inflation *f*	imported inflation	inflation importée *f*	inflazione importata *f*	—

	D	E	F	I	Es
inflación latente (Es)	schleichende Inflation *f*	creeping inflation	inflation rampante *f*	inflazione strisciante *f*	—
Inflation (D)	—	inflation	inflation *f*	inflazione *f*	inflación *f*
inflation (E)	Inflation *f*	—	inflation *f*	inflazione *f*	inflación *f*
inflation (F)	Inflation *f*	inflation	—	inflazione *f*	inflación *f*
inflationary spiral (E)	Inflationsspirale *f*	—	spirale inflationniste *f*	spirale inflazionistica *f*	espiral inflacionista *m*
inflationary theory (E)	Inflationstheorie *f*	—	théorie d'inflation *f*	teoria dell'inflazione *f*	teoría inflacionista *f*
inflation galopante (F)	galoppierende Inflation *f*	galloping inflation	—	inflazione galoppante *f*	inflación galopante *f*
inflation importée (F)	importierte Inflation *f*	imported inflation	—	inflazione importata *f*	inflación importada *f*
inflation rampante (F)	schleichende Inflation *f*	creeping inflation	—	inflazione strisciante *f*	inflación latente *f*
Inflationsimport (D)	—	import of inflation	importation de l'inflation *f*	importazione di inflazione *f*	inflación importada *f*
Inflationsrate (D)	—	rate of inflation	taux d'inflation *m*	tasso d'inflazione *m*	tasa de inflación *f*
Inflationsspirale (D)	—	inflationary spiral	spirale inflationniste *f*	spirale inflazionistica *f*	espiral inflacionista *m*
Inflationstheorie (D)	—	inflationary theory	théorie d'inflation *f*	teoria dell'inflazione *f*	teoría inflacionista *f*
inflazione (I)	Inflation *f*	inflation	inflation *f*	—	inflación *f*
inflazione galoppante (I)	galoppierende Inflation *f*	galloping inflation	inflation galopante *f*	—	inflación galopante *f*
inflazione importata (I)	importierte Inflation *f*	imported inflation	inflation importée *f*	—	inflación importada *f*
inflazione strisciante (I)	schleichende Inflation *f*	creeping inflation	inflation rampante *f*	—	inflación latente *f*
influençable (F)	beeinflußbar	be influenced	—	influenzabile	sugestionable
influenzabile (I)	beeinflußbar	be influenced	influençable	—	sugestionable
información[1] (Es)	Information *f*	information	information *f*	informazione *f*	—
información[2] (Es)	Auskunft *f*	information	renseignement *m*	informazione *f*	—
información a los comsumidores (Es)	Konsumenten-information *f*	consumer information	information des consommateurs *f*	informazione per i consumatori *f*	—
información básica (Es)	Basisinformation *f*	basic information	information de base *f*	informazione base *f*	—
información de consumidores (Es)	Verbraucher-information *f*	consumer information	information des consommateurs *f*	informazione per i consumatori *f*	—
información de sí mismo (Es)	Selbstauskunft *f*	voluntary disclosure	renseignement fourni par l'intéressé lui-même *m*	informazione volontaria *f*	—
informaciones privilegiadas (Es)	Insider-Informationen *pl*	insider information	informations d'initiés *f pl*	informazioni per gli addetti al lavoro *f pl*	—
informática (Es)	Informatik *f*	data processing	informatique *f*	informatica *f*	—
informatica (I)	Informatik *f*	data processing	informatique *f*	—	informática *f*
Informatik (D)	—	data processing	informatique *f*	informatica *f*	informática *f*
Information (D)	—	information	information *f*	informazione *f*	información *f*
information[1] (E)	Auskunft *f*	—	renseignement *m*	informazione *f*	información *f*
information[2] (E)	Mitteilung *f*	—	notification *f*	comunicazione *f*	aviso *m*
information[3] (E)	Information *f*	—	information *f*	informazione *f*	información *f*
information (F)	Information *f*	information	—	informazione *f*	información *f*
information bureau (E)	Auskunftei *f*	—	agence de renseignements *f*	agenzia d'informazioni *f*	oficina de información *f*
information costs (E)	Informations-kosten *pl*	—	coûts d'information *m pl*	costi d'informazione *m pl*	gastos de información *m pl*
information de base (F)	Basisinformation *f*	basic information	—	informazione base *f*	información básica *f*
information des consommateurs[1] (F)	Konsumenten-information *f*	consumer information	—	informazione per i consumatori *f*	información a los comsumidores *f*
information des consommateurs[2] (F)	Verbraucher-information *f*	consumer information	—	informazione per i consumatori *f*	información de consumidores *f*
informations d'initiés (F)	Insider-Informationen *pl*	insider information	—	informazioni per gli addetti al lavoro *f pl*	informaciones privilegiadas *f pl*
Informationsbedarf (D)	—	requirement of information	besoin d'information *m*	bisogno d'informazioni *m*	necesidad de información *f*
Informationskosten (D)	—	information costs	coûts d'information *m pl*	costi d'informazione *m pl*	gastos de información *m pl*

	D	E	F	I	Es
Informationssystem (D)	—	information system	système d'information *m*	sistema d'informazione *m*	sistema de información *m*
Informations-technologie (D)	—	information technology	technologie d'information *f*	tecnologia d'informazione *f*	tecnología de información *f*
Informationstheorie (D)	—	information theory	théorie d'information *f*	teoria dell'informazione *f*	teoría de la información *f*
information system (E)	Informationssystem *n*	—	système d'information *m*	sistema d'informazione *m*	sistema de información *m*
information technology (E)	Informations-technologie *f*	—	technologie d'information *f*	tecnologia d'informazione *f*	tecnología de información *f*
information theory (E)	Informationstheorie *f*	—	théorie d'information *f*	teoria dell'informazione *f*	teoría de la información *f*
informatique (F)	Informatik *f*	data processing	—	informatica *f*	informática *f*
informazione[1] (I)	Information *f*	information	information *f*	—	información *f*
informazione[2] (I)	Auskunft *f*	information	renseignement *m*	—	información *f*
informazione per i consumatori (I)	Konsumenten-information *f*	consumer's information	information des consommateurs *f*	—	información a los comsumidores *f*
informazione base (I)	Basisinformation *f*	basic information	information de base *f*	—	información básica *f*
informazione per i consumatori (I)	Verbraucher-information *f*	consumer information	information des consommateurs *f*	—	información de consumidores *f*
informazione volontaria (I)	Selbstauskunft *f*	voluntary disclosure	renseignement fourni par l'intéressé lui-même *m*	—	información de sí mismo *f*
informazioni per gli addetti al lavoro (I)	Insider-Informationen *pl*	insider information	informations d'initiés *f pl*	—	informaciones privilegiadas *f pl*
informazioni sui posti vacanti (I)	Arbeitsnachweis *m*	employment vacancies	emploi vacant *m*	—	servicio de colocación *m*
informe[1] (Es)	Geschäftsbericht *m*	business report	rapport de gestion *m*	relazione sull'esercizio commerciale *f*	—
informe[2] (Es)	Report *m*	report	rapport *m*	rapporto *m*	—
informe de los fundadores (Es)	Gründungsbericht *m*	formation report	procès-verbal de fondation *m*	relazione di costituzione *f*	—
informe de venta (Es)	Verkaufsbericht *m*	sales report	rapport de vente *m*	rapporto sulle vendite *m*	—
informe económico anual (Es)	Jahreswirtschafts-bericht *m*	Annual Economic Report	compte rendu d'activité économique annuel *m*	relazione generale sulla situazione economica *f*	—
informe financiero (Es)	Finanzbericht *m*	financial report	rapport financier *m*	relazione finanziaria *f*	—
infortunio sul posto di lavoro (I)	Arbeitsunfall *m*	industrial injury	accident du travail *m*	—	accidente profesional *m*
infraestructura (Es)	Infrastruktur *f*	infrastructure	infrastructure *f*	infrastruttura *f*	—
infraseguro (Es)	Unterversicherung *f*	underinsurance	insuffisance d'assurance *f*	sottassicurazione *f*	—
infrastructural measures (E)	Infrastruktur-maßnahmen *f*	—	mesures pour l'amélioration de l'infractructure *f pl*	misure per l'infrastruttura *f pl*	medidas de infraestructura *f pl*
infrastructure (E)	Infrastruktur *f*	—	infrastructure *f*	infrastruttura *f*	infraestructura *f*
infrastructure (F)	Infrastruktur *f*	infrastructure	—	infrastruttura *f*	infraestructura *f*
Infrastruktur (D)	—	infrastructure	infrastructure *f*	infrastruttura *f*	infraestructura *f*
Infrastruktur-maßnahmen (D)	—	infrastructural measures	mesures pour l'amélioration de l'infrastructure *f pl*	misure per l'infrastruttura *f pl*	medidas de infraestructura *f pl*
infrastruttura (I)	Infrastruktur *f*	infrastructure	infrastructure *f*	—	infraestructura *f*
inganno (I)	Täuschung *f*	deceit	tromperie *f*	—	engaño *m*
ingegnere (I)	Ingenieur *m*	engineer	ingénieur *m*	—	ingeniero *m*
ingeniero (Es)	Ingenieur *m*	engineer	ingénieur *m*	ingegnere *m*	—
Ingenieur (D)	—	engineer	ingénieur *m*	ingegnere *m*	ingeniero *m*
ingénieur (F)	Ingenieur *m*	engineer	—	ingegnere *m*	ingeniero *m*
ingiunzione di pagamento (I)	Zahlungsbefehl *m*	order for payment	ordre de payement *m*	—	mandamiento de pago *m*
ingreso bruto (Es)	Bruttoeinkommen *n*	gross income	revenu brut *m*	reddito lordo *m*	—
ingreso neto (Es)	Nettoeinkommen *n*	net income	revenu net *m*	reddito netto *m*	—
ingreso real (Es)	Realeinkommen *n*	real income	revenu réel *m*	reddito reale *m*	—

	D	E	F	I	Es
ingresos[1] (Es)	Einnahmen *pl*	receipts	revenu *m*	entrate *f pl*	—
ingresos[2] (Es)	Einkommen *n*	income	revenu *m*	reddito *m*	—
ingresos del Estado (Es)	Staatseinnahmen *pl*	public revenue	recettes de l'Etat *f pl*	entrate pubbliche *f pl*	—
ingresos disponibles (Es)	verfügbares Einkommen *n*	disposable income	revenu disponible *m*	introito disponibile *m*	—
ingresos nominales (Es)	Nominaleinkommen *n*	nominal income	revenu nominal *m*	reddito nominale *m*	—
ingresos públicos (Es)	öffentliche Einnahmen *pl*	public revenues	recettes publiques *f pl*	entrate pubbliche *f pl*	—
Inhaber (D)	—	proprietor	propriétaire *m*	proprietario *m*	propietario *m*
Inhaberaktie (D)	—	bearer shares	action au porteur *f*	azione al portatore *f*	acción al portador *f*
Inhaberpapier (D)	—	bearer instrument	titre souscrit au porteur *m*	titolo al portatore *m*	título al portador *m*
Inhaberscheck (D)	—	cheque payable to bearer	chèque au porteur *m*	assegno al portatore *m*	cheque al portador *m*
inheritance (E)	Erbschaft *f*	—	héritage *m*	eredità *f*	herencia *f*
inheritance tax (E)	Erbschaftsteuer *f*	—	impôt sur les successions *m*	imposta di successione *f*	impuesto sobre sucesiones *m*
initial contribution (E)	Stammeinlage *f*	—	apport social *m*	quota sociale *f*	capital suscrito *m*
initial period (E)	Anlaufperiode *f*	—	période de mise en marche *f*	periodo iniziale *m*	período de puesta en marcha *m*
Inkasso (D)	—	collection	recouvrement *m*	incasso *m*	encobro *m*
inkassoberechtigt (D)	—	authorized to under-take the collection	autorisé à l'encaissement	autorizzato all'incasso	autorizado al encobro
inklusiv (D)	—	inclusive	inclusivement	incluso	incluso
in Kraft (D)	—	effective/in force	en vigueur	in vigore	en vigor
inland navigation (E)	Binnenschiffahrt *f*	—	navigation fluviale *f*	navigazione interna *f*	navegación fluvial *f*
inland revenue office (E)	Finanzamt *n*	—	service de contributions *m*	ufficio delle imposte *m*	Hacienda *f*
Inländer (D)	—	national resident	national *m*	persona residente *f*	residente *m*
Inlandsnachfrage (D)	—	home demand	demande intérieure *f*	domanda interna *f*	demanda interior *f*
Inlands-niederlassung (D)	—	domestic establishment	succursale à l'intérieur *f*	succursale nazionale *f*	sucursal en el interior *f*
in lieu of payment (E)	zahlungsstatt	—	à titre de payement	a titolo di pagamento	a título de pago
in magazzino (I)	auf Lager	in stock	en stock	—	en almacén
inmediatamente (Es)	umgehend	immediate(ly)	immédiatement	immediatamente	—
inmueble (Es)	Immobilie *f*	item of real estate	bien immobilier *m*	immobile *m*	—
inmuebles y utillaje (Es)	Sachanlagen *pl*	fixed assets	immobilisations corporelles *f pl*	immobilizzazioni *f pl*	—
innovación (Es)	Innovation *f*	innovation	innovation *f*	innovazione *f*	—
Innovation (D)	—	innovation	innovation *f*	innovazione *f*	innovación *f*
innovation (E)	Innovation *f*	—	innovation *f*	innovazione *f*	innovación *f*
innovation (F)	Innovation *f*	innovation	—	innovazione *f*	innovación *f*
Innovationsfähigkeit (D)	—	capability to innovate	capacité d'innovation *f*	capacità innovativa *f*	capacidad de innovación *f*
Innovationsschub (D)	—	technology push	animation d'innovation *f*	spinta innovativa *f*	empuje innovador *m*
innovazione (I)	Innovation *f*	innovation	innovation *f*	—	innovación *f*
in one's own name (E)	im eigenen Namen	—	en nom propre	per nome proprio	en nombre propio
in particular (E)	im einzelnen	—	en particulier	in dettaglio	en particular
in plico a parte (I)	mit getrennter Post	under separate cover	sous pli séparé	—	por correo aparte
in prova (I)	auf Probe	on trial	à l'essai	—	a prueba
Input (D)	—	input	entrée *f*	input *m*	insumo *m*
input (E)	Input *m*	—	entrée *f*	input *m*	insumo *m*
input (I)	Input *m*	input	entrée *f*	—	insumo *m*
input tax (E)	Vorsteuer *f*	—	impôt perçu en amont *m*	imposta sul fatturato d'acquisto *f*	impuesto sobre el valor añadido deducible *m*
Input-Output-Analyse (D)	—	input-output analysis	tableau économique input-output *m*	analisi input-output *f*	análisis de input-output *m*

	D	E	F	I	Es
input-output analysis (E)	Input-Output-Analyse *f*	—	tableau économique input-output *m*	analisi input-output *f*	análisis de input-output *m*
inquilino (Es)	Mieter *m*	tenant	locataire *m*	locatario *m*	—
inquinamento dell'ambiente (I)	Umwelt-verschmutzung *f*	environmental damage	pollution de l'environnement *f*	—	contaminación del medio ambiente *f*
inquinamento delle acque (I)	Wasser-verschmutzung *f*	water pollution	contamination des eaux *f*	—	contaminación del agua *f*
inquinante (I)	umweltschädlich	causing pollution	nuisible à l'environnement	—	contaminante
inquiry (E)	Anfrage *f*	—	demande *f*	richiesta *f*	demanda *f*
inscription (F)	Anmeldung *f*	registration/ declaration	—	avviso *m*/ dichiarazione *f*	solicitud *f*/ declaración *f*
insécurité (F)	Unsicherheit *f*	uncertainty	—	insicurezza *f*	inseguridad *f*
insegna dell'impresa (I)	Firmenschild *n*	company's name plate	enseigne commerciale *f*	—	letrero de establecimiento *m*
inseguridad (Es)	Unsicherheit *f*	uncertainty	insécurité *f*	insicurezza *f*	—
insensible aux influences de la crise économique (F)	krisenfest	slump-proof	—	resistente alle crisi	a prueba de crisis
inserción del anuncio (Es)	Anzeigenschaltung *f*	insertion of an advertisement	placement de l'annonce *m*	posizionamento dell'inserzione *m*	—
insertion of an advertisement (E)	Anzeigenschaltung *f*	—	placement de l'annonce *m*	posizionamento dell'inserzione *m*	inserción del anuncio *f*
inserto (I)	Beilage *f*	supplement	encart non broché à la revue *m*	—	suplemento *m*
inserzione (I)	Anzeige *f*	advertisement	annonce *f*	—	anuncio *m*
inserzione d'impiego (I)	Stellenanzeige *f*	position offered	annonce d'emploi *f*	—	anuncio de empleo *m*
inserzione in cifra (I)	Chiffre-Anzeige *f*	advertisement under a box number	annonce chiffrée *f*	—	anuncio codificado *m*
inserzione sul giornale (I)	Zeitungsanzeige *f*	advertisement	annonce de journal *f*	—	anuncio de prensa *m*
insicurezza (I)	Unsicherheit *f*	uncertainty	insécurité *f*	—	inseguridad *f*
insider information (E)	Insider-Informationen *pl*	—	informations d'initiés *f pl*	informazioni per gli addetti al lavoro *f pl*	informaciones privilegiadas *f pl*
Insider-Informationen (D)	—	insider information	informations d'initiés *f pl*	informazioni per gli addetti al lavoro *f pl*	informaciones privilegiadas *f pl*
insolvabilité[1] (F)	Insolvenz *f*	insolvency	—	insolvenza *f*	insolvencia *f*
insolvabilité[2] (F)	Zahlungsunfähigkeit *f*	insolvency	—	insolvenza *f*	insolvencia *f*
insolvencia[1] (Es)	Zahlungsunfähigkeit *f*	insolvency	insolvabilité *f*	insolvenza *f*	—
insolvencia[2] (Es)	Insolvenz *f*	insolvency	insolvabilité *f*	insolvenza *f*	—
insolvency[1] (E)	Insolvenz *f*	—	insolvabilité *f*	insolvenza *f*	insolvencia *f*
insolvency[2] (E)	Zahlungsunfähigkeit *f*	—	insolvabilité *f*	insolvenza *f*	insolvencia *f*
Insolvenz (D)	—	insolvency	insolvabilité *f*	insolvenza *f*	insolvencia *f*
insolvenza[1] (I)	Insolvenz *f*	insolvency	insolvabilité *f*	—	insolvencia *f*
insolvenza[2] (I)	Zahlungsunfähigkeit *f*	insolvency	insolvabilité *f*	—	insolvencia *f*
inspección de la explotación (Es)	Betriebsprüfung *f*	investigation by the tax authorities	vérification des livres de l'entreprise *f*	revisione aziendale *f*	—
inspección[1] (Es)	Aufsicht *f*	supervision	surveillance *f*	sorveglianza *f*	—
inspección[2] (Es)	Untersuchung *f*	examination	étude *f*	indagine *f*	—
inspección[3] (Es)	Einsichtnahme *f*	inspection	contrôle des livres comptables *m*	presa visione *f*	—
inspection[1] (E)	Prüfung *f*	—	vérification *f*/ examen *m*	controllo *m*/esame *m*	verificación *f*/ examen *m*
inspection[2] (E)	Einsichtnahme *f*	—	contrôle des livres comptables *m*	presa visione *f*	inspección *f*
instalaciones de producción (Es)	Produktions-anlagen *pl*	production facilities	installations industrielles *f pl*	impianti di produzione *m pl*	—
installation (E)	Montage *f*	—	montage *m*	montaggio *m*	montaje *m*
installation de traitement électronique des informations (F)	Datenverarbeitungs-anlage *f*	data processing system	—	elaboratore elettronico di dati *m*	ordenador *m*
installation industrielle (F)	Industrieanlage *f*	industrial plant	—	impianto industriale *m*	planta industrial *f*

	D	E	F	I	Es
installations industrielles (F)	Produktionsanlagen *pl*	production facilities	—	impianti di produzione *m pl*	instalaciones de producción *f pl*
instalment (E)	Rate *f*	—	acompte *m*	rata *f*	plazo *m*
instalment sale transaction (E)	Ratengeschäft *n*	—	vente à tempérament *f*	vendita a rate *f*	venta a plazo *f*
instance (E)	Instanz *f*	—	instance *f*	istanza *f*	instancia *f*
instance (F)	Instanz *f*	instance	—	istanza *f*	instancia *f*
instancia (Es)	Instanz *f*	instance	instance *f*	istanza *f*	—
Instanz (D)	—	instance	instance *f*	istanza *f*	instancia *f*
institución de prevision (Es)	Versorgungseinrichtung *f*	pension scheme	institution de retraite *f*	istituto previdenziale *m*	—
institut bancaire d'épargne (F)	Sparkasse *f*	savings bank	—	cassa di risparmio *f*	caja de ahorros *f*
institut d'études de marché (F)	Marktforschungsinstitut *n*	market research institute	—	istituto della ricerca di mercato *m*	instituto de investigación del mercado *m*
institution de retraite (F)	Versorgungseinrichtung *f*	pension scheme	—	istituto previdenziale *m*	institución de previsión *f*
instituto de crédito (Es)	Kreditinstitut *n*	credit institution	établissement de crédit *m*	istituto di credito *m*	—
instituto de investigación del mercado (Es)	Marktforschungsinstitut *n*	market research institute	institut d'études de marché *m*	istituto della ricerca di mercato *m*	—
in stock (E)	auf Lager	—	en stock	in magazzino	en almacén
instrucción (Es)	Anleitung *f*	instructions	instruction *f*	istruzione *f*	—
instrucción de reparación (Es)	Reparaturanleitung *f*	repair instructions	instruction de réparation *f*	istruzione per la riparazione *f*	—
instrucción para el envío (Es)	Versandvorschrift *f*	forwarding instruction	prescriptions concernant l'expédition *f pl*	prescrizione per la spedizione *f*	—
instructeur (F)	Ausbilder *m*	trainer	—	istruttore *m*	instructor *m*
instruction (F)	Anleitung *f*	instructions	—	istruzione *f*	instrucción *f*
instruction de réparation (F)	Reparaturanleitung *f*	repair instructions	—	istruzione per la riparazione *f*	instrucción de reparación *m*
instructions (E)	Anleitung *f*	—	instruction *f*	istruzione *f*	instrucción *f*
instructor (Es)	Ausbilder *m*	trainer	instructeur *m*	istruttore *m*	—
Instrument (D)	—	instrument	instrument *m*	strumento *m*	instrumento *m*
instrument (E)	Instrument *n*	—	instrument *m*	strumento *m*	instrumento *m*
instrument (F)	Instrument *n*	instrument	—	strumento *m*	instrumento *m*
instrumento *m*	Instrument *n*	instrument	instrument *m*	strumento *m*	—
instrumentos de medida (Es)	Meßgeräte *pl*	measuring instruments	instrument de mesure *m*	strumenti di misura *m pl*	—
instruments (made out) to order (E)	Orderpapier *n*	—	papier à ordre *m*	titolo all'ordine *m*	título a la orden *m*
insuffisance d'assurance (F)	Unterversicherung *f*	underinsurance	—	sottassicurazione *f*	infraseguro *m*
insumo (Es)	Input *m*	input	entrée *f*	input *m*	—
insurance (E)	Versicherung *f*	—	assurance *f*	assicurazione *f*	seguro *m*
insurance agent (E)	Versicherungsagent *m*	—	agent d'assurance *m*	agente d'assicurazione *m*	agente de seguros *m*
insurance broker (E)	Versicherungsmakler *m*	—	courtier en assurance *m*	mediatore d'assicurazione *m*	corredor de seguros *m*
insurance company (E)	Versicherungsgesellschaft *f*	—	société d'assurance *f*	compagnia di assicurazione *f*	sociedad de seguros *f*
insurance contract (E)	Versicherungsvertrag *m*	—	contrat d'assurance *m*	contratto d'assicurazione *m*	contrato de seguro *m*
insurance cover (E)	Versicherungsschutz *m*	—	couverture de l'assurance *f*	copertura assicurativa *f*	cobertura de seguro *f*
insurance of persons (E)	Personenversicherung *f*	—	assurance des personnes *f*	assicurazione di persone *f*	seguro personal *m*
insurance on buildings (E)	Gebäudeversicherung *f*	—	assurance des bâtiments *f*	assicurazione dei fabbricati *f*	seguro inmobiliario *m*
insurance policy (E)	Versicherungspolice *f*	—	police d'assurance *f*	polizza d'assicurazione *f*	seguro *m*
insurance premium (E)	Versicherungsprämie *f*	—	prime d'assurance *f*	premio d'assicurazione *m*	prima de seguro *f*

	D	E	F	I	Es
insurance sum (E)	Versicherungs-summe *f*	—	montant de l'assurance *m*	somma assicurata *f*	suma asegurada *f*
insured letter (E)	Wertbrief *m*	—	lettre avec valeur déclarée *f*	lettera con valore dichiarato *f*	letra con valor declarado *f*
insured person (E)	Versicherungs-nehmer *m*	—	souscripteur d'une assurance *m*	assicurato *m*	asegurado *m*
integración (Es)	Integration *f*	integration	intégration *f*	integrazione *f*	—
integración económica (Es)	wirtschaftliche Integration *f*	economic integration	intégration économique *f*	integrazione economica *f*	—
integral part (E)	wesentliche Bestandteile *pl*	—	parties constitutives essentielles *f pl*	componenti essenziali *f pl*	partes integrantes esencial *f pl*
Integration (D)	—	integration	intégration *f*	integrazione *f*	integración *f*
integration (E)	Integration *f*	—	intégration *f*	integrazione *f*	integración *f*
intégration (F)	Integration *f*	integration	—	integrazione *f*	integración *f*
intégration économique (F)	wirtschaftliche Integration *f*	economic integration	—	integrazione economica *f*	integración económica *f*
integrazione (I)	Integration *f*	integration	intégration *f*	—	integración *f*
integrazione economica (I)	wirtschaftliche Integration *f*	economic integration	intégration économique *f*	—	integración económica *f*
interbank rate (E)	Interbankrate *f*	—	taux interbancaire *m*	tasso interbancario *m*	tipo interbancario *m*
Interbankrate (D)	—	interbank rate	taux interbancaire *m*	tasso interbancario *m*	tipo interbancario *m*
intercambio de mercancías (Es)	Warenaustausch *m*	exchange of goods	échanges commerciaux *m pl*	scambio merci *m*	—
interchangeable (F)	substituierbar	replaceable	—	sostituibile	sustituible
interdépendance (F)	Interdependenz *f*	interdependence	—	interdipendenza *f*	interdependencia *f*
interdependence (E)	Interdependenz *f*	—	interdépendance *f*	interdipendenza *f*	interdependencia *f*
interdependencia (Es)	Interdependenz *f*	interdependence	interdépendance *f*	interdipendenza *f*	—
Interdependenz (D)	—	interdependence	interdépendance *f*	interdipendenza *f*	interdependencia *f*
interdiction en matière de concurrence (F)	Wettbewerbsverbot *n*	prohibition of competition	—	divieto di concorrenza *m*	prohibición de competencia *f*
interdicto provisorio (Es)	einstweilige Verfügung *f*	temporary injunction	ordonnance sur référé civil *f*	provvedimento temporaneo *m*	—
interdipendenza (I)	Interdependenz *f*	interdependence	interdépendance *f*	—	interdependencia *f*
interés[1] (Es)	Zins *m*	interest	intérêt *m*	interessi *m pl*	—
interés[2] (Es)	Interesse *n*	interest	intérêt *m*	interesse *m*	—
interesado (Es)	Interessent *m*	person interested	intéressé *m*	interessato *m*	—
interés compuesto (Es)	Zinseszins *m*	compound interest	intérêt composé *m*	interessi composti *m pl*	—
interés de disponibilidad (Es)	Bereitstellungs-zinsen *pl*	commitment interests	intérêts de disponibilité *m pl*	interessi per lo stanziamento *m pl*	—
interés efectivo (Es)	Effektivverzinsung *f*	effective interest yield	taux effectif (de l'intérêt) *m*	interessi effettivi *m pl*	—
intereses acreedores (Es)	Habenzinsen *pl*	credit interest	intérêts créditeur *m*	interessi creditori *m pl*	—
intereses de demora (Es)	Verzugszinsen *pl*	default interest	intérêts moratoires *m pl*	interessi di mora *m pl*	—
intereses deudores (Es)	Sollzinsen *pl*	debtor interest rates	intérêt débiteur *m*	interessi debitori *m pl*	—
intereses por fracción de período (Es)	Stückzinsen *f*	broken period interest	intérêts courus *m pl*	interessi maturati *m pl*	—
intereses reales (Es)	Effektivzins *m*	effective interest	intérêt effectif *m*	tasso d'interesse effettivo *m*	—
interés fijo (Es)	fester Zins *m*	fixed interest rate	intérêt fixe *m*	tasso d'interesse fisso *m*	—
interés real (Es)	Realzins *m*	real (rate of) interest	rendement réel *m*	tasso d'interesse reale *m*	—
interessato (I)	Interessent *m*	person interested	intéressé *m*	—	interesado *m*
Interesse (D)	—	interest	intérêt *m*	interesse *m*	interés *m*
intéressé (F)	Interessent *m*	person interested	—	interessato *m*	interesado *m*
interesse[1] (I)	Anteilnahme *f*	sympathy	participation *f*	—	participación *f*
interesse[2] (I)	Interesse *n*	interest	intérêt *m*	—	interés *m*
interesse del capitale (I)	Kapitalzins *m*	interest on capital	intérêt du capital *m*	—	renta del capital *f*

	D	E	F	I	Es
Interessengruppe (D)	—	interest group	groupe d'intérêts *m*	gruppo d'interesse *m*	grupo de presión *m*
Interessent (D)	—	person interested	intéressé *m*	interessato *m*	interesado *m*
Interessen-vertretung (D)	—	representation of interests	représentation des intérêts *f*	rappresentanza degli interessi *f*	representación de intereses *f*
interessi (I)	Zins *m*	interest	intérêt *m*	—	interés *m*
interessi composti (I)	Zinseszins *m*	compound interest	intérêt composé *m*	—	interés compuesto *m*
interessi creditori (I)	Habenzinsen *pl*	credit interest	intérêts créditeur *m*	—	intereses acreedores *m pl*
interessi debitori (I)	Sollzinsen *pl*	debtor interest rates	intérêt débiteur *m*	—	intereses deudores *m pl*
interessi di mora (I)	Verzugszinsen *pl*	default interest	intérêts moratoires *m pl*	—	intereses de demora *m pl*
interessi effettivi (I)	Effektivverzinsung *f*	effective interest yield	taux effectif (de l'intérêt) *m*	—	interés efectivo *m*
interessi maturati (I)	Stückzinsen *f*	broken period interest	intérêts courus *m pl*	—	intereses por fracción de período *m pl*
interessi per lo stanziamento (I)	Bereitstellungs-zinsen *pl*	commitment interests	intérêts de disponibilité *m pl*	—	interés de disponibilidad *m*
interest[1] (E)	Zins *m*	—	intérêt *m*	interessi *m pl*	interés *m*
interest[2] (E)	Interesse *n*	—	intérêt *m*	interesse *m*	interés *m*
interest account (E)	Zinsrechnung *f*	—	calcul des intérêts *m*	conteggio degli interessi *m*	cómputo de intereses *m*
interest group (E)	Interessengruppe *f*	—	groupe d'intérêts *m*	gruppo d'interesse *m*	grupo de presión *m*
interest margin (E)	Zinsmarge *f*	—	marge entre les taux d'intérêt créditeur et débiteur *f*	margine degli interessi *m*	margen de interés *m*
interest on capital (E)	Kapitalzins *m*	—	intérêt du capital *m*	interesse del capitale *m*	renta del capital *f*
interest rate (E)	Zinsfuß *m*	—	taux d'intérêt *m*	tasso d'interesse *m*	tipo de interés *m*
interest rate level (E)	Zinsniveau *n*	—	niveau du taux d'intérêt *m*	livello degli interessi *m*	nivel de interés *m*
interest rate policy (E)	Zinspolitik *f*	—	politique en matière d'intérêts *f*	politica dei tassi d'interesse *f*	política en materia de intereses *f*
interest service (E)	Zinsendienst *m*	—	service de l'intérêt *m*	servizio degli interessi *m*	servicio de intereses *m*
interés variable (Es)	variabler Zins *m*	variable rate of interest	intérêt variable *m*	tasso d'interesse variabile *m*	—
intérêt[1] (F)	Interesse *n*	interest	—	interesse *m*	interés *m*
intérêt[2] (F)	Zins *m*	interest	—	interessi *m pl*	interés *m*
intérêt composé (F)	Zinseszins *m*	compound interest	—	interessi composti *m pl*	interés compuesto *m*
intérêt débiteur (F)	Sollzinsen *pl*	debtor interest rates	—	interessi debitori *m pl*	intereses deudores *m pl*
intérêt du capital (F)	Kapitalzins *m*	interest on capital	—	interesse del capitale *m*	renta del capital *f*
intérêt effectif (F)	Effektivzins *m*	effective interest	—	tasso d'interesse effettivo *m*	intereses reales *m pl*
intérêt fixe (F)	fester Zins *m*	fixed interest rate	—	tasso d'interesse fisso *m*	interés fijo *m*
intérêts courus (F)	Stückzinsen *f*	broken period interest	—	interessi maturati *m pl*	intereses por fracción de período *m pl*
intérêts créditeur (F)	Habenzinsen *pl*	credit interest	—	interessi creditori *m pl*	intereses acreedores *m pl*
intérêts de disponibilité (F)	Bereitstellungs-zinsen *pl*	commitment interests	—	interessi per lo stanziamento *m pl*	interés de disponibilidad *m*
intérêts moratoires (F)	Verzugszinsen *pl*	default interest	—	interessi di mora *m pl*	intereses de demora *m pl*
intérêt variable (F)	variabler Zins *m*	variable rate of interest	—	tasso d'interesse variabile *m*	interés variable *m*
interim account (E)	Zwischenkonto *n*	—	compte provisoire *m*	conto transitorio *m*	cuenta provisional *f*
interim balance sheet (E)	Zwischenbilanz *f*	—	bilan intermédiaire *m*	bilancio provvisorio *m*	balance intermedio *m*
interim report (E)	Zwischenzeugnis *n*	—	certificat provisoire *m*	certificato provvisorio *m*	certificado provisional *m*
Interimslösung (D)	—	interim solution	solution intérimaire *f*	soluzione ad interim *f*	solución interina *f*

	D	E	F	I	Es
interim solution (E)	Interimslösung *f*	—	solution intérimaire *f*	soluzione ad interim *f*	solución interina *f*
intermédiaire (F)	Zwischenhändler *m*	middleman	—	intermediario *m*	intermediario *m*
intermediario (Es)	Zwischenhändler *m*	middleman	intermédiaire *m*	intermediario *m*	—
intermediario (I)	Zwischenhändler *m*	middleman	intermédiaire *m*	—	intermediario *m*
intermediate purchase (E)	Zwischenabnahme *f*	—	achat intermédiaire *m*	acquisto intermediario *m*	compra intermediaria *f*
intermediazione di crediti (I)	Kreditvermittlung *f*	arranging for a credit	médiation du crédit *f*	—	mediación de créditos *f*
intern (D)	—	internal	interne	interno	interno
internal (E)	intern	—	interne	interno	interno
Internal Market of the European Community (E)	EG-Binnenmarkt *m*	—	Marché Intérieur de la Communauté Européenne *m*	mercato unico *m*	Mercado Unico *m*
International Commodity Agreements (E)	Rohstoff-abkommen *n*	—	accord sur les matières premières *m*	accordo sulle materie prime *m*	acuerdo de materias primas *m*
international economic order (E)	Weltwirtschafts-ordnung *f*	—	ordre économique mondial *m*	sistema economico mondiale *m*	orden económico mundial *m*
international monetary system (E)	Weltwährungs-system *n*	—	système monétaire international *m*	sistema monetario internazionale *m*	sistema monetario internacional *m*
(international) price system (E)	Preiszusammen-hang *m*	—	système des prix *m*	contesto dei prezzi *m*	sistema de precios *m*
interne (F)	intern	internal	—	interno	interno
interno (Es)	intern	internal	interne	interno	—
interno (I)	intern	internal	interne	—	interno
inter-office sale (E)	Telefonverkauf *m*	—	vente par téléphone *f*	vendita per telefono *f*	venta por teléfono *f*
intérprete (Es)	Dolmetscher *m*	interpreter	interprète *m*	interprete *m*	—
interprète (F)	Dolmetscher *m*	interpreter	—	interprete *m*	intérprete *m*
interprete (I)	Dolmetscher *m*	interpreter	interprète *m*	—	intérprete *m*
interpreter (E)	Dolmetscher *m*	—	interprète *m*	interprete *m*	intérprete *m*
interrogazione (I)	Befragung *f*	poll	enquête *f*	—	encuesta *f*
intervención (Es)	Intervention *f*	intervention	intervention *f*	intervento *m*	—
Intervention (D)	—	intervention	intervention *f*	intervento *m*	intervención *f*
intervention (E)	Intervention *f*	—	intervention *f*	intervento *m*	intervención *f*
intervention (F)	Intervention *f*	intervention	—	intervento *m*	intervención *f*
intervention buying (E)	Interventionskäufe *pl*	—	achats d'intervention *m pl*	acquisti d'intervento *m pl*	compras de intervención *f pl*
intervention point (E)	Interventionspunkt *m*	—	point d'intervention *m*	punto d'intervento *m*	punto de intervención *m*
Interventionskäufe (D)	—	intervention buying	achats d'intervention *m pl*	acquisti d'intervento *m pl*	compras de intervención *f pl*
Interventionspflicht (D)	—	obligation to intervene	obligation d'intervention *f*	obbligo d'intervento *m*	obligación de intervención *f*
Interventionspunkt (D)	—	intervention point	point d'intervention *m*	punto d'intervento *m*	punto de intervención *m*
intervento (I)	Intervention *f*	intervention	intervention *f*	—	intervención *f*
Interview (D)	—	interview	enquête *f*	intervista *f*	entrevista *f*
interview (E)	Interview *n*	—	enquête *f*	intervista *f*	entrevista *f*
intervista (I)	Interview *n*	interview	enquête *f*	—	entrevista *f*
intervista ai clienti (I)	Kundenbefragung *f*	customer survey	enquête parmi les clients *f*	—	encuesta entre los clientes *f*
intestazione (I)	Briefkopf *m*	letterhead	en-tête *m*	—	encabezamiento *m*
(in) the red (E)	rote Zahlen *pl*	—	chiffres en déficit *m pl*	conti in rosso *m pl*	cifras rojas *f pl*
intransmisible (Es)	nicht übertragbar	non-assignable	ne pas transférable	non trasferibile	—
introductory discount (E)	Einführungsrabatt *m*	—	rabais d'introduction *m*	sconto di lancio *m*	rebaja de lanzamiento *f*
introiti base (I)	Basiseinkommen *n*	basic income	revenu de base *m*	—	salario base *m*
introito disponibile (I)	verfügbares Einkommen *n*	disposable income	revenu disponible *m*	—	ingresos disponibles *m pl*
inutilizzato (I)	ungenutzt	unused	pas utilisé	—	no utilizado
inventaire[1] (F)	Inventur *f*	taking of the inventory	—	redazione d'inventario *f*	inventario *m*

	D	E	F	I	Es
invoicing (E)	Rechnungsstellung *f*	—	établissement d'une facture *m*	fatturazione *f*	facturación *f*
in vigore (I)	in Kraft	effective/in force	en vigueur	—	en vigor
in visione (I)	zur Ansicht	on approval	à vue	—	para examen
in zweifacher Ausfertigung (D)	—	in duplicate	en deux exemplaires	in due copie	por duplicado
iperinflazione (I)	Hyperinflation *f*	hyperinflation	hyperinflation *f*	—	hiperinflación *f*
ipermercato (I)	Verbrauchermarkt *m*	consumer market	marché des consommateurs *m*	—	mercado favorable al consumidor *m*
ipoteca (I)	Hypothek *f*	mortgage	hypothéque *f*	—	hipoteca *f*
ipotesi (I)	Hypothese *f*	hypothesis	hypothèse *f*	—	hipótesis *f*
irregolarità (I)	Unregelmäßigkeit *f*	irregularity	irrégularité *f*	—	irregularidad *f*
irregularidad (Es)	Unregelmäßigkeit *f*	irregularity	irrégularité *f*	irregolarità *f*	—
irrégularité (F)	Unregelmäßigkeit *f*	irregularity	—	irregolarità *f*	irregularidad *f*
irrégularité en matière de chèque (F)	Scheckbetrug *m*	cheque fraud	—	emissione di assegno a vuoto *f*	falsificación de cheques *f*
irregularity (E)	Unregelmäßigkeit *f*	—	irrégularité *f*	irregolarità *f*	irregularidad *f*
irrevocable letter of credit (E)	unwiderrufliches Akkreditiv *n*	—	accréditif irrévocable *m*	apertura di credito documentario irrevocabile *f*	crédito documentario irrevocable *m*
Irrtum vorbehalten (D)	—	errors excepted	sauf erreur	salvo errore	salvo error
issue (E)	Emission *f*	—	émission *f*	emissione *f*	emisión *f*
issuing restriction (E)	Emissions-begrenzung *f*	—	limitation d'émission *f*	limitazione d'emissione *f*	limitación de emisiones *f*
istanza (I)	Instanz *f*	instance	instance *f*	—	instancia *f*
istituto della ricerca di mercato (I)	Marktforschungs-institut *n*	market research institute	institut d'études de marché *m*	—	instituto de investiga-ción del mercado *m*
istituto di credito (I)	Kreditinstitut *n*	credit institution	établissement de crédit *m*	—	instituto de crédito *m*
istituto previdenziale (I)	Versorgungs-einrichtung *f*	pension scheme	institution de retraite *f*	—	institución de prevision *f*
istituzione a finalità mutualistiche (I)	Selbsthilfe-einrichtung *f*	mutual assistance institution	organisation d'assistance mutuelle *f*	—	organización de asistencia mutua *f*
Istkosten (D)	—	actual costs	coûts réels *m pl*	costi effettivi *m pl*	gastos efectivos *m pl*
istruttore (I)	Ausbilder *m*	trainer	instructeur *m*	—	instructor *m*
istruzione (I)	Anleitung *f*	instructions	instruction *f*	—	instrucción *f*
istruzione per la riparazione (I)	Reparaturanleitung *f*	repair instructions	instruction de réparation *f*	—	instrucción de reparación *m*
Istzahlen (D)	—	actual figures	résultats effectifs *m pl*	dati effettivi *m pl*	cifras efectivas *f pl*
item of real estate (E)	Immobilie *f*	—	bien immobilier *m*	immobile *m*	inmueble *m*
itinéraire[1] (F)	Reiseroute *f*	route	—	itinerario *m*	itinerario *m*
itinéraire[2] (F)	Tourenplan *m*	tour schedule	—	programma dell'itinerario *m*	itinerario *m*
itinerant trade (E)	ambulantes Gewerbe *n*	—	commerce ambulant *m*	commercio ambulante *m*	comercio ambulante *m*
itinerario[1] (Es)	Reiseroute *f*	route	itinéraire *m*	itinerario *m*	—
itinerario[2] (Es)	Tourenplan *m*	tour schedule	itinéraire *m*	programma dell'itinerario *m*	—
itinerario (I)	Reiseroute *f*	route	itinéraire *m*	—	itinerario *m*
Jahresabschluß (D)	—	annual accounts	clôture annuelle des comptes *f*	chiusura d'esercizio *f*	cierre de cuentas *m*
Jahresarbeitszeit (D)	—	annual hours of work	temps de travail annuel *m*	orario di lavoro annuale *m*	jornada anual *f*
Jahresbedarf (D)	—	annual need	besoin annuel *m*	bisogno annuale *m*	necesidad anual *f*
Jahreseinkommen (D)	—	annual income	revenu annuel *m*	reddito annuale *m*	renta anual *f*
Jahresfixum (D)	—	fixed annual salary	fixe annuel *m*	fisso annuale *m*	fijo anual *m*
Jahresgewinn (D)	—	annual profit	bénéfice annuel *m*	utile dell'anno *m*	beneficio del ejercicio *m*
Jahreshaupt-versammlung (D)	—	annual meeting of shareholders	assemblée générale annuelle *f*	assemblea generale annuale *f*	junta general anual *f*

	D	E	F	I	Es
Jahresüberschuß (D)	—	annual surplus	excédent annuel *m*	surplus dell'anno *m*	superávit del ejercicio *m*
Jahreswirtschafts-bericht (D)	—	Annual Economic Report	compte rendu d'activité économique annuel *m*	relazione generale sulla situazione economica *f*	informe económico anual *m*
jährlich (D)	—	annual	annuel	annuale	anual
jauger (F)	eichen	gauge	—	tarare	contrastar
jefe (Es)	Chef *m*	head	chef *m*	capo *m*	—
jefe del departamento de expedición (Es)	Versandleiter *m*	manager of shipping department	chef du service des expéditions *m*	capo reparto spedizioni *m*	—
jefe de personal (Es)	Personalleiter *m*	staff manager	chef du personnel *m*	capo reparto personale *m*	—
jefe de sección (Es)	Abteilungsleiter *m*	head of department	chef de service *m*	capo reparto *m*	—
jefe de sucursal (Es)	Filialleiter *m*	branch manager	directeur d'agence *m*	direttore della filiale *m*	—
jefe de venta regional (Es)	Gebietsverkaufs-leiter *m*	area sales manager	chef de vente régionale *m*	direttore di vendita regionale *m*	—
jerarquía (Es)	Hierarchie *f*	hierarchy	hiérarchie *f*	gerarchia *f*	—
jeu d'écritures (F)	Umbuchung *f*	transfer of an entry	—	giro di partite *m*	asiento en otra cuenta *m*
jeu d'entreprise (F)	Planspiel *n*	management games	—	gioco di strategia imprenditoriale *m*	juego de ensayo *m*
job demand (E)	Arbeitsnachfrage *f*	—	demande d'emploi *f*	domanda di lavoro *f*	demanda de trabajo *f*
job description (E)	Stellenbeschreibung *f*	—	description de l'emploi *f*	descrizione d'impiego *f*	descripción del puesto de trabajo *f*
job evaluation (E)	Arbeitsbewertung *f*	—	qualification du travail *f*	valutazione del lavoro *f*	evaluación del trabajo *f*
job preparation (E)	Arbeitsvorbereitung *f*	—	préparation du travail *f*	preparazione del lavoro *f*	preparación laboral *f*
job satisfaction (E)	Arbeitszufriedenheit *f*	—	satisfaction de travail *f*	soddisfazione del lavoro *f*	satisfacción en el trabajo *f*
joint publicity (E)	Gemeinschafts-werbung *f*	—	publicité collective *f*	pubblicità collettiva *f*	publicidad colectiva *f*
joint stock company (E)	Aktiengesellschaft *f*	—	société anonyme *f*	società per azioni *f*	sociedad anónima *f*
jornada anual (Es)	Jahresarbeitszeit *f*	annual hours of work	temps de travail annuel *m*	orario di lavoro annuale *m*	—
jornada laboral (Es)	Arbeitszeit *f*	working hours	heures de travail *f pl*	orario di lavoro *m*	—
jour de bourse (F)	Börsentag *m*	market day	—	giorno di borsa *m*	sesión bursátil *f*
jour de la liquidation (F)	Abrechnungstag *m*	settling day	—	giorno di liquidazione *m*	fecha de liquidación *f*
jour de l'échéance (F)	Verfalltag *m*	day of expiry	—	giorno di scadenza *m*	día de vencimiento *m*
jour de paye (F)	Zahltag *m*	payday	—	giorno di paga *m*	día de pago *m*
jour de travail (F)	Arbeitstag *m*	working day	—	giorno lavorativo *m*	día laboral *m*
journal destiné à la clientèle (F)	Kundenzeitschrift *f*	customer magazine	—	periodico per i clienti *m*	revista para los clientes *f*
journeyman (E)	Geselle *m*	—	ouvrier artisan *m*	garzone *m*	oficial *m*
joven empresario (Es)	Jungunternehmer *m*	young businessman	entrepreneur débutant *m*	imprenditore giovane *m*	—
jubilee (E)	Geschäftsjubiläum *n*	—	anniversaire de l'entreprise *m*	anniversario aziendale *m*	aniversario de la empresa *m*
judge (E)	Richter *m*	—	juge *m*	giudice *m*	juez *m*
judiciaire (F)	gerichtlich	judicial	—	giudiziario	judicial
judicial (E)	gerichtlich	—	judiciaire	giudiziario	judicial
judicial (Es)	gerichtlich	judicial	judiciaire	giudiziario	—
judicial execution (E)	Zwangs-vollstreckung *f*	—	exécution forcée *f*	esecuzione forzata *f*	ejecución forzosa *f*
juego de ensayo (Es)	Planspiel *n*	management games	jeu d'entreprise *m*	gioco di strategia imprenditoriale *m*	—
juez (Es)	Richter *m*	judge	juge *m*	giudice *m*	—
juge (F)	Richter *m*	judge	—	giudice *m*	juez *m*
Jungunternehmer (D)	—	young businessman	entrepreneur débutant *m*	imprenditore giovane *m*	joven empresario *m*
junior partner (E)	Junior-Partner *m*	—	fils du partenaire *m*	junior partner *m*	socio menor *m*

	D	E	F	I	Es
junior partner (I)	Junior-Partner *m*	junior partner	fils du partenaire *m*	—	socio menor *m*
Junior-Partner (D)	—	junior partner	fils du partenaire *m*	junior partner *m*	socio menor *m*
junta de acreedores (Es)	Gläubiger-versammlung *f*	creditors' meeting	assemblée des créanciers *f*	riunione dei creditori *f*	—
junta directiva (Es)	Direktion *f*	board of directors	direction *f*	direzione *f*	—
junta general anual (Es)	Jahreshaupt-versammlung *f*	annual meeting of shareholders	assemblée générale annuelle *f*	assemblea generale annuale *f*	—
junta social (Es)	Gesellschafter-versammlung *f*	meeting of shareholders	réunion des associés *f*	assemblea dei soci *f*	—
jurídicamente capaz (Es)	rechtsfähig	capable of acting in law	capable de jouir des droits	avendo capacità giuridica *f*	—
juridiction compétente (F)	Gerichtsstand *m*	jurisdiction	—	foro competente *m*	tribunal competente *m*
jurisdiction (E)	Gerichtsstand *m*	—	juridiction compétente *f*	foro competente *m*	tribunal competente *m*
jurisprudence (F)	Rechtsprechung *f*	administration of justice	—	giurisprudenza *f*	jurisprudencia *f*
jurisprudencia (Es)	Rechtsprechung *f*	administration of justice	jurisprudence *f*	giurisprudenza *f*	—
juristische Person (D)	—	legal person	personne juridique *f*	persona giuridica *f*	persona jurídica *f*
justificado (Es)	gerechtfertigt	justified	justifié	giustificato	—
justificatif (F)	Beleg *m*	voucher	—	quietanza *f*	justificativo *m*
justificativo (Es)	Beleg *m*	voucher	justificatif *m*	quietanza *f*	—
justifié (F)	gerechtfertigt	justified	—	giustificato	justificado
justified (E)	gerechtfertigt	—	justifié	giustificato	justificado
Kabelfernsehen (D)	—	cable television	télévision par câble *f*	televisione via cavo *f*	televisión por cable *f*
Kabeltelegramm (D)	—	cablegram	câblogramme *m*	cablogramma *m*	cablegrama *f*
Kabelüberweisung (D)	—	cable transfer	virement par câble *m*	bonifico telegrafico *m*	giro telegráfico *m*
Kalenderjahr (D)	—	calendar year	année civile *f*	anno solare *m*	año civil *m*
Kalkulation (D)	—	calculation	calcul *m*	calcolazione *f*	calculación *f*
Kampagne (D)	—	campaign	campagne *f*	campagna *f*	campaña *f*
Kapazität (D)	—	capacity	capacité *f*	capacità *f*	capacidad *f*
Kapazitätsaus-lastung (D)	—	utilization of capacity	utilisation de la capacité *f*	sfruttamento delle capacità *m*	utilización de las capacidades *f*
Kapazitäts-ausweitung (D)	—	increase in capacity	extension de la capacité *f*	ampliamento delle capacità *m*	ampliación de la capacidad *f*
Kapazitätsengpaß (D)	—	bottleneck in capacity	goulot d'étranglement de capacité *m*	strettoia di capacità *f*	escasez de capacidad *f*
Kapital (D)	—	capital	capital *m*	capitale *m*	capital *m*
Kapitalabfindung (D)	—	lump sum settlemnt	indemnité en capital *f*	indennità in capitale *f*	indemnización en capital *f*
Kapitalanlage (D)	—	capital investment	investissement de capitaux *m*	investimento di capitale *m*	inversión de capital *f*
Kapitalanteil (D)	—	share in capital	part de capital *f*	quota di capitale *f*	participación en el capital *f*
Kapitalausstattung (D)	—	capital resources	dotation en capital *f*	dotazione di capitale *f*	dotación de capital *f*
Kapitalbasis (D)	—	capital base	base de capital *f*	base di capitale *f*	base de capital *f*
Kapitalbedarf (D)	—	capital requirements	besoin en capital *m*	domanda di capitale *m*	necesidad de capital *f*
Kapitalbilanz (D)	—	balance of capital transactions	balance des opéra-tions en capital *f*	bilancia dei capitali *f*	balanza de capitales *f*
Kapitaleinkommen (D)	—	unearned income	revenu du capital *m*	reddito del capitale *m*	ganancias de capital *f pl*
Kapitalerhöhung (D)	—	increase of the share capital	augmentation de capital *f*	aumento del capitale *m*	aumento de capital *m*
Kapitalertrag (D)	—	income from capital	produit du capital *m*	rendita del capitale *f*	rendimiento del capital *m*
Kapitalertragsteuer (D)	—	tax on investment income	impôt sur le revenu du capital *m*	imposta sulla rendita del capitale *f*	impuesto sobre la renta del capital *m*
Kapitalexport (D)	—	capital export	exportation de capitaux *f*	esportazione di capitale *f*	exportación de capital *f*
Kapitalflucht (D)	—	flight of capital	évasion des capitaux *f*	fuga dei capitali *f*	fuga de capital *f*

	D	E	F	I	Es
Kapitalgesellschaft (D)	—	company limited by shares	société de capitaux *f*	società di capitale *f*	sociedad capitalista *f*
Kapitalherabsetzung (D)	—	reduction of capital	diminution du capital *f*	riduzione del capitale *f*	reducción de capital *f*
Kapitalhilfe (D)	—	capital aid	aide financière *f*	aiuto finanziario *m*	ayuda financiera *f*
Kapitalimport (D)	—	capital import	importation de capitaux *f*	importazione di capitali *f*	importación de capital *f*
kapitalintensiv (D)	—	capital-intensive	avec grande intensité de capital	ad alta incidenza di capitale	con gran intensidad de capital
Kapitalisierung (D)	—	capitalization	capitalisation *f*	capitalizzazione *f*	capitalización *f*
Kapitalismus (D)	—	capitalism	capitalisme *m*	capitalismo *m*	capitalismo *m*
Kapitalmarkt (D)	—	capital market	marché des capitaux *m*	mercato finanziario *m*	mercado financiero *m*
Kapitalproduktivität (D)	—	productivity of capital	productivité du capital *f*	produttività del capitale *f*	productividad del capital *f*
Kapitalrentabilität (D)	—	return on investment	rentabilité du capital *f*	redditività del capitale *f*	rentabilidad del capital *f*
Kapitalstock (D)	—	capital stock	réserve de capital *f*	riserva di capitale *f*	fondo de capital *m*
Kapitaltheorie (D)	—	capital theory	théorie du capital *f*	teoria del capitale *f*	teoría financiera *f*
Kapitalumschlag (D)	—	capital turnover	roulement des capitaux *m*	rotazione del capitale *f*	rotación del capital *f*
Kapitalverkehr (D)	—	capital transactions	mouvement des capitaux *m*	movimento dei capitali *m*	circulación de capitales *f*
Kapitalwert (D)	—	capital value	valeur en capital *f*	valore del capitale *m*	valor capitalizado *m*
Kapitalzins (D)	—	interest on capital	intérêt du capital *m*	interesse del capitale *m*	renta del capital *f*
Karat (D)	—	carat	carat *m*	carato *m*	quilate *m*
Karenzzeit (D)	—	qualifying period	délai de carence *m*	periodo d'attesa *m*	período carencial *m*
Kartei (D)	—	card-index	cartothèque	schedario *m*	fichero *m*
Karteikarte (D)	—	index card	fiche *f*	scheda *f*	ficha *f*
Kartell (D)	—	cartel	cartel *m*	cartello *m*	cártel *m*
Kartellbehörde (D)	—	cartel authority	office de surveillance des cartels et ententes *m*	autorità antimonopoli *f pl*	oficina de cártels *f*
Kartellbildung (D)	—	cartel formation	cartellisation *f*	costituzione di cartelli *f*	formación de carteles *f*
Kartellgesetz (D)	—	Cartel Law	loi sur les cartels *f*	legge sui cartelli *f*	ley relativa a los cártels *f*
Kaskoversicherung (D)	—	comprehensive insurance	assurance tous risques *f*	assicurazione corpi del ramo trasporto *f*	seguro de casco *m*
Kassakurs (D)	—	spot price	cours au comptant *m*	corso a pronti *m*	cotización al contado *f*
Kassenbuch (D)	—	cash book	compte de caisse *m*	libro di cassa *m*	libro de caja *m*
Kassierer (D)	—	cashier	caissier *m*	cassiere *m*	cajero *m*
Katalog (D)	—	catalogue	catalogue *m*	catalogo *m*	catálogo *m*
Katalysator (D)	—	catalytic converter	catalyseur *m*	catalizzatore *m*	catalizador *m*
Kataster (D)	—	cadaster	cadastre *m*	catasto *m*	catastro *m*
Kauf (D)	—	purchase	achat *m*	acquisto *m*	compra *f*
Kaufabschluß (D)	—	conclusion of a sales contract	conclusion du marché *f*	conclusione d'acquisto *f*	convenio de compra *m*
Kaufanlaß (D)	—	buying motive	motif d'achat *m*	motivo d'acquisto *m*	motivo de compra *m*
Kauf auf Probe (D)	—	sale on approval	achat à l'éssai *m*	acquisto a titolo di prova *m*	compra a prueba *f*
Kaufbereitschaft (D)	—	buying intention	propension à l'achat *f*	propensione all'acquisto *f*	disposición a comprar *f*
kaufen (D)	—	buy	acheter	acquistare	comprar
Kaufentscheidung (D)	—	decision to purchase	décision d'acheter *f*	decisione d'acquisto *f*	decisión de compra *f*
Käufer (D)	—	purchaser	acheteur *m*	acquirente *m*	adquirente *m*
Käufermarkt (D)	—	buyer's market	marché d'acheteurs *m*	mercato favorevole all'acquirente *m*	mercado favorable al comprador *m*
Käuferprovision (D)	—	buyer's commission	commission d'acheteur *f*	provvigione dell'acquirente *f*	comisión al comprador *f*
Käuferstil (D)	—	style of the purchaser	style des acheteurs *m*	stile dell'acquirente *m*	estilo de compra *m*

	D	E	F	I	Es
Kaufhaus (D)	—	department store	grand magasin *m*	grande magazzino *m*	gran almacén *m*
Kaufkraft (D)	—	purchasing power	pouvoir d'achat *m*	potere d'acquisto *m*	poder adquisitivo *m*
Kaufkraftanalyse (D)	—	spending capacity analysis	analyse du pouvoir d'achat *f*	analisi del potere d'acquisto *f*	análisis del poder adquisitivo *m*
Kaufkraftänderung (D)	—	changes in the purchasing power	modification du pouvoir d'achat *f*	mutamento del potere d'acquisto *m*	cambio en el poder adquisitivo *m*
Kaufleute (D)	—	businessmen	commerçants *m pl*	commercianti *m pl*	comerciantes *m pl*
Kaufmann (D)	—	businessman	négociant *m*	commerciante *m*	comerciante *m*
kaufmännische Lehre (D)	—	commercial apprenticeship	apprentissage commercial *m*	apprendistato di commercio *m*	aprendizaje comercial *m*
Kaufpreis (D)	—	purchase price	prix d'achat *m*	prezzo d'acquisto *m*	precio de compra *m*
Kaufverhalten (D)	—	purchase pattern	comportement d'achat *m*	filosofia d'acquisto *f*	comportamiento de compra *m*
Kaufvertrag (D)	—	contract of sale	contrat de vente *m*	contratto di compravendita *m*	contrato de compraventa *m*
Kaution (D)	—	security/bond	caution *f*	cauzione *f*	caución f garantía *f*
keeping of an account (E)	Kontoführung *f*	—	tenue de compte *f*	tenuta di un conto *f*	administración de una cuenta *f*
Kennzahlen (D)	—	code numbers	numéros de référence *m pl*	numeri d'identificazione *m pl*	números índice *m pl*
Kennziffern (D)	—	code numbers	indice *m*	cifre d'identificazione *f pl*	cifras índice *f pl*
Kernenergie (D)	—	nuclear energy	énergie nucléaire *f*	energia nucleare *f*	energía nuclear *f*
keyboard (E)	Tastatur *f*	—	clavier *m*	tastiera *f*	teclado *m*
key currency (E)	Leitwährung *f*	—	monnaie-clé *f*	valuta guida *f*	moneda de referencia *f*
key rate (E)	Leitzins *m*	—	taux-clé d'intérêt bancaire	tasso d'interesse guida *m*	tipos de referencia *m pl*
key word (E)	Schlüsselwort *n*	—	mot-clé *m*	parola chiave *f*	palabra clave *f*
Kilometergeld (D)	—	allowance per kilometre	indemnité par kilomètre *f*	indennità per chilometro *f*	kilometraje *m*
kilometraje (Es)	Kilometergeld *n*	allowance per kilometre	indemnité par kilomètre *f*	indennità per chilometro *f*	—
Kiste (D)	—	box	caisse *f*	cassa *f*	caja *f*
kiteflying (E)	Wechselreiterei *f*	—	tirage d'une traite de cavalerie *m*	emissione di tratte incrociate *f*	libramiento de letras cruzadas *m*
Klage (D)	—	legal action	action en justice *f*	citazione in giudizio *f*	demanda *f*
Klausel (D)	—	clause	clause *f*	clausola *f*	cláusula *f*
Kleincontainer (D)	—	small container	petit conteneur *m*	mini container *m*	pequeño contenedor *m*
Kleinpalette (D)	—	small pallet	petite palette *f*	mini paletta *f*	pequña paleta *f*
Klein- und Mittelbetriebe (D)	—	small and medium-sized enterprises	petites et moyennes entreprises *f pl*	piccole e medie imprese *f pl*	pequeñas y medianas empresas *f pl*
Klientel (D)	—	clientele	clients *m pl*	clientela *f*	clientela *f*
knapp (D)	—	scarce	rare	scarso	escaso
Knappheit (D)	—	shortage	rareté *f*	scarsità *f*	escasez *f*
know-how (E)	Sachkenntnis *f*	—	compétence *f*	competenza *f*	conocimiento de causa *m*
Koalitionsfreiheit (D)	—	freedom of association	liberté d'association *f*	libertà di coalizione *f*	libertad de coalición *f*
Kollektiv (D)	—	collective	collectif *m*	collettivo *m*	colectivo *m*
Kollektivgüter (D)	—	collective goods	biens collectifs *m pl*	beni collettivi *m pl*	bienes sociales *m pl*
Kollektivismus (D)	—	collectivism	collectivisme *m*	collettivismo *m*	colectivismo *m*
Kommanditgesellschaft (D)	—	limited partnership	société en commandite *f*	società in accomandita semplice *f*	sociedad comanditaria *f*
Kommanditgesellschaft auf Aktien (D)	—	partnership limited by shares	société en commandite par action *f*	società in accomandita per azioni *f*	sociedad comanditaria por acciones *f*
Kommanditist (D)	—	limited partner	commanditaire *m*	socio accomandante *m*	comanditario *m*
Kommerz (D)	—	commerce	commerce *m*	commercio *m*	comercio *m*
Kommission (D)	—	commission	commission *f*	commissione *f*	comisión *f*
Kommissionär (D)	—	commission agent	commissionnaire *m*	commissionario *m*	comisionista *m*

	D	E	F	I	Es
Kommissionsgeschäft (D)	—	commission business	affaire en commission	operazione di commissione *f*	operación de comisión *f*
Kommissionsgüter (D)	—	goods for sale on commission	marchandises en commssion *f pl*	beni in conto deposito *m pl*	mercancías en comisión *f pl*
Kommissionshandel (D)	—	commission trade	commissionnage *m*	commercio di commissione *m*	comercio de comisión *m*
Kommunalanleihen (D)	—	local authorities loan	emprunt communal *m*	prestiti comunali *m pl*	empréstito municipal *m*
Kommunalobligation (D)	—	corporation stock	obligation communale *f*	obbligazioni comunali *f pl*	obligación comunal *f*
Kommune (D)	—	municipality	commune *f*	comune *m*	municipalidad *f*
Kompensation (D)	—	compensation	compensation *f*	compensazione *f*	compensación *f*
Kompensationsgeschäft (D)	—	barter transaction	affaire de compensation *f*	operazione di compensazione *f*	operacion de compensación *f*
Kompetenz (D)	—	competence	compétence *f*	competenza *f*	competencia *f*
Komplementär (D)	—	general partner	commandité *m*	socio accomandatario *m*	socio colectivo *m*
komplementäre Güter (D)	—	complementary goods	produits de complément *m pl*	beni complementari *m pl*	bienes complementarios *m pl*
Kondition (D)	—	condition	condition *f*	condizione *f*	condición *f*
Konferenz (D)	—	conference	conférence *f*	conferenza *f*	conferencia *f*
Konferenzraum (D)	—	conference room	salle de conférences *f*	sala conferenze *f*	sala de conferencia *f*
Konjunktur (D)	—	business cycle	conjoncture *f*	congiuntura *f*	conyuntura *f*
Konjunkturanalyse (D)	—	economic analysis	analyse de la conjoncture *f*	analisi congiunturale *f*	análisis de la situación económica *m*
konjunkturanfällig (D)	—	depending on the cyclical trend	sensible aux oscillations de la conjoncture	soggetto ad influssi congiunturali	sensible a las fluctuaciones coyunturales
Konjunkturbelebung (D)	—	economic upturn	relance économique *f*	ripresa congiunturale *f*	recuperación coyuntural *f*
Konjunkturentwicklung (D)	—	economic trend	évolution de la conjoncture *f*	sviluppo congiunturale *m*	evolución de la coyuntura *f*
Konjunkturpolitik (D)	—	economic policy	politique de conjoncture *f*	politica congiunturale *f*	política de coyuntura *f*
Konjunkturzyklus (D)	—	business cycle	cycle conjoncturel *m*	ciclo congiunturale *m*	ciclo económico *m*
Konkurrent (D)	—	competitor	concurrent *m*	concorrente *m*	competidor *m*
Konkurrenz (D)	—	competition	concurrence *f*	concorrenza *f*	competencia *f*
Konkurrenzbeobachtung (D)	—	observation of the competitors	observation de la concurrence *f*	studio della concorrenza *m*	observación de la competencia *f*
Konkurrenzfirma (D)	—	competing firm	maison concurrente *f*	ditta concorrente *f*	empresa competidora *f*
konkurrenzlos (D)	—	without competition	défiant toute concurrence	senza concorrenza	sin competencia
Konkurrenzsituation (D)	—	competitive situation	situation de concurrence *f*	situazione concorrenziale *f*	situación de competencia *f*
Konkurrenzunternehmen (D)	—	competing undertaking	entreprise concurrente *f*	impresa concorrente *f*	empresa competitoria *f*
Konkurs (D)	—	bankruptcy	faillite *f*	fallimento *m*	quiebra *f*
Konkursantrag (D)	—	bankruptcy petition	demande en déclaration de faillite *f*	domanda di dichiarazione del fallimento *f*	petición de quiebra *f*
Konkursgericht (D)	—	bankruptcy court	tribunal de la faillite *m*	tribunale fallimentare *m*	tribunal de quiebras *m*
Konkursgläubiger (D)	—	bankrupt's creditor	créancier de la faillite *m*	creditore della massa fallimentare *m*	acreedor de la quiebra *m*
Konkursmasse (D)	—	bankrupt's estate	masse de la faillite *f*	massa fallimentare *f*	masa de la quiebra *f*
Konkursordnung (D)	—	Bankruptcy Act	régime juridique de la faillite *m*	legge fallimentare *f*	ley de las quiebras *f*
Konkursverfahren (D)	—	proceedings in bankruptcy	procédure de faillite *f*	procedura fallimentare *f*	procedimiento de quiebra *m*
Konkursverwalter (D)	—	administrator in bankruptcy proceedings	liquidateur de la faillite *m*	curatore fallimentare *m*	síndico de quiebra *m*
Konnossement (D)	—	bill of lading	connaissement *m*	polizza di carico *f*	conocimiento *m*
konsolidierte Bilanz (D)	—	consolidated balance sheet	bilan consolidé *m*	bilancio consolidato *m*	balance consolidado *m*
Konsolidierung (D)	—	consolidation	consolidation *f*	consolidamento *m*	consolidación *f*

	D	E	F	I	Es
Konsortium (D)	—	consortium	consortium *m*	consorzio *m*	consorcio *m*
Konsul (D)	—	consul	consul *m*	console *m*	cónsul *m*
Konsulat (D)	—	consulate	consulat *m*	consolato *m*	consulado *m*
Konsum (D)	—	consumption	consommation *f*	consumo *m*	consumo *m*
Konsument (D)	—	consumer	consommateur *m*	consumatore *m*	consumidor *m*
Konsumenten-information (D)	—	consumer information	information des consommateurs *f*	informazione per i consumatori *f*	información a los comsumidores *f*
Konsum-finanzierung (D)	—	financing consumption	financement de la vente à crédit *m*	finanziamento del consumo *m*	financiación del consumo *f*
Konsumfreiheit (D)	—	freedom of consumption	liberté de consommation *f*	libertà di consumo *f*	libertad de consumo *f*
Konsumgüter (D)	—	consumer goods	biens de consommation *m pl*	beni di consumo *m pl*	bienes de consumo *m pl*
Konsumgüter-industrie (D)	—	consumer goods industry	industrie des biens de consommation *f*	industria dei beni di consumo *f*	industria de bienes de consumo *f*
konsumieren (D)	—	consume	consommer	consumare	consumir
Konsumkredit (D)	—	consumer credit	crédit à la consommation *m*	credito al consumatore *m*	crédito de consumo *m*
Konsumstruktur (D)	—	consumption structure	structure de la consommation	struttura del consumo *f*	estructura del consumo *f*
Konsumverzicht (D)	—	voluntary constraint in consumption	renonciation à la consommation *f*	rinuncia al consumo *f*	renuncia al consumo *f*
Kontaktfähigkeit (D)	—	capability to establish public relations	capacité d'entrer en contact *f*	comunicativa *f*	capacidad de anudar contactos *f*
Kontamination (D)	—	contamination	contamination *f*	contaminazione *f*	contaminación *f*
Kontingent (D)	—	quota	contingent *m*	contingente *m*	contingente *m*
Kontingentierung (D)	—	fixing of a quota	contingentement *m*	contingentamento *m*	contingentación *f*
Konto (D)	—	account	compte *m*	conto *m*	cuenta *f*
Kontoausgleich (D)	—	settlement of an account	solde de compte *m*	liquidazione del conto *f*	saldo de cuenta *m*
Kontoauszug (D)	—	statement of account	extrait de compte *m*	estratto conto *m*	extracto de cuenta *m*
Kontobuch (D)	—	account book	livre de compte *m*	libro dei conti *m*	libro de cuentas *m*
Kontoeröffnung (D)	—	opening of an account	ouverture de compte *f*	apertura di un conto *f*	apertura de una cuenta *f*
Kontoführung (D)	—	keeping of an account	tenue de compte *f*	tenuta di un conto *f*	administración de una cuenta *f*
Kontogebühren (D)	—	bank charges	frais de tenue de compte *m pl*	diritti di conto *m pl*	gastos de administración de una cuenta *m pl*
Kontoinhaber (D)	—	account holder	titulaire d'un compte *m*	titolare del conto *m*	titular de una cuenta *m*
Kontokorrent (D)	—	account current	compte courant *m*	conto corrente *m*	cuenta corriente *f*
Kontokorrentkonto (D)	—	current account	compte tenu en compte courant *m*	conto corrente *m*	cuenta corriente *f*
Kontokorrentkredit (D)	—	current account credit	crédit en compte courant *m*	credito in conto corrente *m*	crédito en cuenta corriente *m*
Kontonummer (D)	—	account number	numéro de compte *m*	numero di conto *m*	número de cuenta *m*
Kontoüberziehung (D)	—	overdraft of an account	découvert d'un compte *m*	scoperto di conto *m*	descubierto *m*
Kontrakt (D)	—	contract	contrat *m*	contratto *m*	contrato *m*
Kontrolle (D)	—	control	contrôle *m*	controllo *m*	control *m*
Konventionalstrafe (D)	—	contractual penalty	pénalité *f*	penalità convenzionale *f*	pena convencional *f*
konvertibel (D)	—	convertible	convertible	convertibile	convertible
Konvertibilität (D)	—	convertibility	convertibilité *f*	convertibilità *f*	convertibilidad *f*
Konzentration (D)	—	concentration	concentration *f*	concentrazione *f*	concentración *f*
Konzept (D)	—	concept	brouillon *m*	piano *m*	bosquejo *m*
Konzeption (D)	—	conception	conception *f*	concezione *f*	concepción *f*
konzeptionelles Denken (D)	—	conceptional thinking	penser conceptionnel *m*	mentalità concezionale *f*	pensar concepcional *m*
Konzern (D)	—	group/combine	groupe industriel *m*	gruppo *m*	consorcio *m*

	D	E	F	I	Es
Konzernbilanz (D)	—	balance sheet of a group	bilan consolidé d'un groupement de sociétés *m*	bilancio del gruppo *m*	balance del consorcio *m*
Konzession (D)	—	licence	concession *f*	concessione *f*	concesión *f*
Kooperation (D)	—	cooperation	coopération *f*	cooperazione *f*	cooperación *f*
kooperativ (D)	—	cooperative	coopératif	cooperativo	cooperativo
Koordination (D)	—	coordination	coordination *f*	coordinazione *f*	coordinación *f*
Kopie (D)	—	copy	copie *f*	copia *f*	copia *f*
Koppelproduktion (D)	—	tied production	production couplée *f*	produzione abbinata *f*	coproducción *f*
Kopplungsgeschäft (D)	—	tie-in transaction	affaire couplée *f*	operazione abbinata *f*	negocio acoplado *m*
Körperschaft (D)	—	corporation	collectivité *f*	ente *m*	corporación *f*
Körperschaftsteuer (D)	—	corporation tax	taxe sur les sociétés *f*	imposta sul reddito delle società *f*	impuesto de corporaciones *m*
Korrelation (D)	—	correlation	corrélation *f*	correlazione *f*	correlación *f*
korrigieren (D)	—	correct	corriger	correggere	corrigir
Kosten (D)	—	costs	coût *m*	costi *m pl*	gastos *m pl*
Kostenarten (D)	—	cost types	coûts par nature *m pl*	tipi di costi *m pl*	clases de costes *f pl*
Kostendämpfung (D)	—	combatting rising costs	réduction des coûts *f*	contenimento dei costi *m*	disminución de costes *f*
Kostendegression (D)	—	cost degression	dégressivité des coûts *f*	riduzione dei costi *f*	reducción de costes *f*
Kostenexplosion (D)	—	cost escalation	explosion des coûts *f*	esplosione dei costi *f*	incremento desmesurado de los costes *m*
kostenlos (D)	—	free of charge	gratuit	gratuito	libre de gastos
Kostenminimierung (D)	—	minimization of costs	minimalisation des coûts *f*	diminuzione dei costi *f*	minimación de gastos *f*
Kosten-Nutzen-Analyse (D)	—	cost-benefit analysis	analyse du ratio coût à profit *f*	analisi costi-benefici *f*	análisis de coste-beneficio *m*
Kostenplan (D)	—	cost schedule	planning des coûts *m*	piano dei costi *m*	planilla de costas *f*
Kostenrechnungssystem (D)	—	cost accounting system	méthode de calcul des coûts *f*	sistema dei costi *m*	sistema de costes *m*
Kostensenkung (D)	—	cost reduction	diminution des coûts *f*	ribasso dei costi *m*	reducción de coste
Kostenstelle (D)	—	departmental expense account	compte de frais par secteurs *m*	posizione costi *f*	posición de costes *f*
Kostenträger (D)	—	unit assuming costs	poste de production absorbant des coûts *m*	chi si assume i costi	que sufraga los costes
Kostenverrechung (D)	—	cost allocation	répartition des frais *f*	repartizione dei costi *f*	repartición de costes *f*
Kostenvoranschlag (D)	—	estimate of cost	devis estimatif des frais *m*	preventivo dei costi *m*	presupuesto de coste *m*
Kostenvorteil (D)	—	cost advantage	avantage de coût *m*	vantaggio di costo *m*	ventaja de costes *f*
Kraftfahrzeug (D)	—	motor vehicle	véhicule à moteur *m*	automobile *f*	automóvil *m*
Kraftfahrzeugsteuer (D)	—	motor vehicle tax	taxe sur les véhicules à moteur *f*	imposta sulla circolazione degli autoveicoli *f*	impuesto sobre vehículos *m*
Kraftfahrzeugversicherung (D)	—	motor insurance	assurance responsabilité civile automobile *f*	assicurazione autoveicoli *f*	seguro de automóviles *m*
Krankenversicherung (D)	—	health insurance	assurance maladie *f*	assicurazione contro le malattie *f*	seguro de enfermedad *m*
kreativ (D)	—	creative	créatif	creativo	creativo
kreatives Denken (D)	—	creative thinking	créativité conceptionnelle *f*	mentalità creativa *f*	creatividad concepcional *f*
Kredit (D)	—	credit	crédit *m*	credito *m*	crédito *m*
Kreditbank (D)	—	commercial bank	banque de crédit *f*	banca di credito *f*	banco de crédito *m*
Kreditbeschaffungskosten (D)	—	cost of borrowing	coûts d'obtention de crédits *m pl*	spese d'approvvigionamento di credito *f pl*	costes de apelación al crédito *m pl*
Kreditbrief (D)	—	letter of credit	lettre de crédit *f*	lettera di credito *f*	carta de crédito *f*
Kreditfähigkeit (D)	—	financial standing	solvabilité *f*	capacità di credito *f*	crédito *m*
Kreditgeschäft (D)	—	credit business	achat à crédit *m*	operazione di credito *f*	operaciones de crédito *f pl*

	D	E	F	I	Es
Kreditinstitut (D)	—	credit institution	établissement de crédit *m*	istituto di credito *m*	instituto de crédito *m*
Kreditkarte (D)	—	credit card	carte accréditive *f*	carta di credito *f*	tarjeta de crédito *f*
Kreditkauf (D)	—	credit purchase	achat à crédit *m*	acquisto a credito *m*	compra de crédito *f*
Kreditlaufzeit (D)	—	duration of credit	durée de l'allocation de crédit *f*	scadenza del credito *f*	período concesional de un crédito *m*
Kreditlimit (D)	—	borrowing limit	plafond du crédit alloué *m*	limite di credito *m*	límite de crédito *m*
Kreditlinie (D)	—	credit line	plafond du crédit accordé *m*	linea creditizia *f*	línea de crédito *f*
Kreditnehmer (D)	—	borrower	bénéficiaire d'un crédit *m*	beneficiario del credito *m*	prestatario *m*
Kreditor (D)	—	creditor	créditeur *m*	creditore *m*	acreedor *m*
Kreditpolitik (D)	—	credit policy	politique favorisant le crédit *f*	politica creditizia *f*	política de crédito *f*
Kreditprovision (D)	—	credit commission	frais de commissions d'ouverture de crédit *m pl*	provvigione di credito *f*	comisión de apertura de crédito *f*
Kreditrahmen (D)	—	credit margin	marge de crédit accordé *f*	plafond di credito *m*	margen de crédito *m*
Kreditrestriktion (D)	—	credit restriction	restriction du crédit *f*	restrizione creditizia *f*	restricción de créditos *f*
Kreditvermittlung (D)	—	arranging for a credit	médiation du crédit *f*	intermediazione di crediti *f*	mediación de créditos *f*
Kreditversicherung (D)	—	credit insurance	assurance crédit *f*	assicurazione dei crediti *f*	seguro crediticio *m*
kreditwürdig (D)	—	creditworthy	solvable	degno di credito	solvente
Kreditwürdigkeit (D)	—	creditworthiness	solvabilité *f*	essere degno di credito	crédito *m*
Kreditzusage (D)	—	promise of credit	promesse de crédit *f*	consenso di credito *m*	promesa de créditos *f*
Krise (D)	—	crisis	crise *f*	crisi *f*	crisis *f*
krisenfest (D)	—	slump-proof	insensible aux influences de la crise économique	resistente alle crisi	a prueba de crisis
Kühlwagen (D)	—	cold storage lorry	wagon frigorifique *m*	vagone frigorifero *m*	vagón frigorífico *m*
kulant (D)	—	accommodating	arrangeant	corrente	de fácil avenencia
Kulanz (D)	—	accommodation	souplesse en affaires *f*	correntezza *f*	facilidad en los negocios *f*
kündbar (D)	—	redeemable/callable	résiliable/ remboursable	risolubile/redimibile	revocable/rescindible
Kunde (D)	—	customer	client *m*	cliente *m*	cliente *m*
Kundenbefragung (D)	—	customer survey	enquête parmi les clients *f*	intervista ai clienti *f*	encuesta entre los clientes *f*
Kundendienst (D)	—	after-sales service	service après vente *m*	servizio d'assistenza *m*	servicio posventa *m*
Kundendienst-organisation (D)	—	service organization	organisation du service après vente *f*	organizzazione del servizio d'assistenza *f*	organización de servicio posventa *f*
Kundenkreis (D)	—	clientele	clientèle *f*	clientela *f*	clientela *f*
Kundennummer (D)	—	customer's reference number	numéro de référence du client *m*	numero di cliente *m*	número del cliente *m*
Kundenstamm (D)	—	regular customers	clients en portefeuille *m pl*	clientela fissa *f*	clientela fija *f*
Kundenzeitschrift (D)	—	customer magazine	journal destiné à la clientèle *m*	periodico per i clienti *m*	revista para los clientes *f*
kündigen (D)	—	terminate	résilier	disdire	denunciar/dar aviso de despido
Kündigung (D)	—	notice of termination	résiliation *f*	disdetta *f*	rescisión *f*
Kündigungsfrist (D)	—	period of notice	délai de préavis *m*	termine di preavviso per la disdetta *m*	plazo de preaviso *m*
Kündigungsschutz (D)	—	protection against dismissal	protection en matière de licenciement *f*	protezione contro il licenziamento *f*	protección contra el despido *f*
Kündigungsschutz-gesetz (D)	—	Termination of Employment Act	loi sur le délai-congé en matière de licenciement *f*	legge sulla tutela contro il licenziamento *f*	ley de protección contra el despido *f*

	D	E	F	I	Es
Kundschaft (D)	—	clientele	clientèle *f*	clientela *f*	clientela *f*
Kurs (D)	—	exchange rate	cours (du change) *m*	corso *m*/cambio *m*	cotización *f*/tipo de cambio *m*
Kursfestsetzung (D)	—	fixing of prices	détermination des cours *f*	fissazione dei corsi *f*	fijación de los cambios *f*
Kurs-Gewinn-Verhältnis (D)	—	price-earnings ratio	relation cours-bénéfice *f*	rapporto corso-profitto *m*	relación cotización-ganancia *f*
Kursmakler (D)	—	stock broker/ exchange broker	courtier en bourse *m*	agente di borsa *m*	agente cambio y bolsa *m*/corredor de cambios *m*
Kursnotierung (D)	—	quotation of prices	cotation *f*	quotazione dei corsi *f*	cotización *m*
Kurspflege (D)	—	price nursing	soutien des cours *m*	sostegno dei corsi *m*	compras de sostén *f pl*
Kursrisiko (D)	—	price risk	risque de change *m*	rischio di cambio *m*	riesgo de cambio *m*
Kurssteigerung (D)	—	price advance	hausse *f*	aumento dei corsi *m*	alza de las cotizaciones *f*
Kursstützung (D)	—	price support	soutiens des cours *m*	difesa dei corsi *f*	sostén de las cotizaciones *m*
Kursvergleich (D)	—	comparison of prices	comparaison des cours *f*	confronto dei corsi *m*	comparación de las cotizaciones *f*
Kursverlust (D)	—	loss in exchange	perte sur les cours *f*	perdita sul cambio *f*	pérdida en bolsa *f*
Kurszettel (D)	—	stock exchange list	bulletin des cours *m*	listino di borsa *m*	boletín de bolsa *m*
Kurszusammen-bruch (D)	—	collapse of prices	chute des cours *f*	crollo delle quotazioni *m*	caída de los cambios *f*
Kurzarbeit (D)	—	short-time work	travail à temps réduit *m*	lavoro ad orario ridotto *m*	trabajo reducido *m*
kurzfristig (D)	—	short-term	à court terme	a breve scadenza	a corto plazo
kurzfristiger Kredit (D)	—	short-term credit	crédit à court terme *m*	credito a breve scadenza *m*	crédito a corto plazo *m*
Küstengewässer (D)	—	coastal waters	eaux côtières *f pl*	acque territoriali *f pl*	zona costera *f*
Kuvert (D)	—	envelope	enveloppe *f*	busta *f*	sobre *m*
Kybernetik (D)	—	cybernetics	cybernétique *f*	cibernetica *f*	cibernética *f*
label (E)	Etikett *n*	—	étiquette *f*	etichetta *f*	etiqueta *f*
labour-intensive (E)	arbeitsintensiv	—	déterminé par le facteur main-d'œuvre	ad alta incidenza di lavoro	con gran intensidad de mano de obra
labour law (E)	Arbeitsrecht *n*	—	législation industrielle *f*	diritto di lavoro *m*	derecho laboral *m*
labour market (E)	Arbeitsmarkt *m*	—	marché du travail *m*	mercato del lavoro *m*	mercado laboral *m*
lacuna di mercato (I)	Marktlücke *f*	market gap	créneau du marché *m*	—	sector del mercado no abarcado por la oferta *m*
Ladegebühren (D)	—	loading charges	taxe de chargement *f*	spese di carico *f pl*	derechos de carga *m pl*
Ladenpreis (D)	—	retail price	prix de vente *m*	prezzo di vendita *m*	precio de venta *m*
Ladeschein (D)	—	bill of lading	avis de chargement *m*	bolletta di carico *f*	póliza de carga *f*
Ladung (D)	—	freight	charge *f*	carico *m*	carga *f*
Lager (D)	—	warehouse	magasin *m*	magazzino *m*	almacén *m*
Lagerhaltung (D)	—	stockkeeping	entreposage *m*	magazzinaggio *m*	almacenaje *m*
Lagerkapazität (D)	—	storage capacity	capacité de stockage *f*	capacità di magazzino *f*	capacidad de almacenaje *f*
Lagermiete (D)	—	warehouse rent	location d'une surface pour magasinage *f*	spese di magazzinaggio *f pl*	alquiler de almacenaje *m*
Lagerraum (D)	—	storage space	halle de dépôt *f*	magazzino *m*	almacén *m*
Lagerschein (D)	—	warehouse warrant	certificat de dépot *m*	ricevuta di deposito *f*	resguardo de almacén *m*
Lagerung (D)	—	storage	stockage *m*	magazzinaggio *m*	almacenaje *m*
Lagerverwaltung (D)	—	stockkeeping	entreposage *m*	amministrazione del magazzino *f*	administración de almacén *f*
Lagerzyklus (D)	—	stock cycle	cycle de stockage *m*	ciclo di magazzinaggio *m*	período de almacenaje *m*
lag salariale (I)	Lohnlag *m*	wage lag	décalage entre les prix et les salaires *m*	—	diferencial entre precios y salarios *m*
lanciare sul mercato (I)	vermarkten	market	commercialiser	—	comercializar
land policy (E)	Bodenpolitik *f*	—	politique de la terre *f*	politica del suolo *f*	política de suelo *f*

	D	E	F	I	Es
land price (E)	Bodenpreis *m*	—	prix du terrain *m*	prezzo del suolo *m*	precio de suelo *m*
land reform (E)	Bodenreform *f*	—	réforme agraire *f*	riforma agraria *f*	reforma agraria *f*
Landweg (D)	—	overland transportation	voie de terre *f*	via terra *f*	vía terrestre *m*
Landwirtschafts-ministerium (D)	—	Ministry of Agriculture	ministère de l'agriculture *m*	ministero dell'agricoltura *m*	minsterio de Agricultura, Pesca y Alimentación *m*
langage de programmation (F)	Programmier-sprache *f*	common business-oriented language	—	linguaggio di programmazione *m*	lenguaje de programación *m*
langfristig (D)	—	long-term	à long terme	a lunga scadenza	a largo plazo
langfristiger Kredit (D)	—	long-term credit	crédit à long terme *m*	credito a lunga scadenza *m*	crédito a largo plazo *m*
langfristiges Kapital (D)	—	long-term capital	capital à long terme *m*	capitale a lungo termine *m*	capital a largo plazo *m*
large container (E)	Großcontainer *m*	—	conteneur à grand volume *m*	container di grande dimensione *m*	gran contenedor *m*
large-scale operation (E)	Großbetrieb *m*	—	grande exploitation *f*	azienda di grande dimensione *f*	gran explotación *f*
large-scale order (E)	Großauftrag *m*	—	grosse commande *f*	ordine di grandi quantità *m*	importante pedido *m*
Lärmbekämpfung (D)	—	noise abatement	lutte contre le bruit *f*	lotta contro i rumori *f*	lucha contra el ruido *f*
Laserdrucker (D)	—	laser printer	imprimante au laser *f*	stampante laser *f*	impresora laser *m*
laser printer (E)	Laserdrucker *m*	—	imprimante au laser *f*	stampante laser *f*	impresora laser *m*
Lastschrift (D)	—	debit note	note de débit *f*	addebito *m*	cargo en cuenta *m*
last will (E)	Testament *n*	—	testament *m*	testamento *m*	testamento *m*
latent funds (E)	stille Rücklage *f*	—	réserve cachée *f*	riserva latente *m*	reserva tácita *f*
laufende Rechnung (D)	—	current account	compte courant *m*	conto corrente *m*	cuenta corriente *f*
Laufzeit (D)	—	term	durée *f*	scadenza *f*/durata *f*	plazo de vencimiento *m*
lavabo (Es)	Toilette *f*	toilet	toilettes *f pl*	toilette *f*	—
lavora a cottimo (I)	Akkordarbeit *f*	piecework	travail à la tâche *m*	—	trabajo a destajo *m*
lavorazione (I)	Verarbeitung *f*	processing	transformation *f*	—	transformación *f*
lavoro (I)	Arbeit *f*	work	travail *m*	—	trabajo *m*
lavoro abusivo (I)	Schwarzarbeit *f*	illicit work	travail noir *m*	—	trabajo clandestino *m*
lavoro a domicilio (I)	Heimarbeit *f*	homework	travail à domicile *m*	—	trabajo a domicilio *m*
lavoro ad orario ridotto (I)	Kurzarbeit *f*	short-time work	travail à temps réduit *m*	—	trabajo reducido *m*
lavoro d'équipe (I)	Teamarbeit *f*	team work	travail d'équipe *m*	—	trabajo en equipo *m*
lavoro domenicale (I)	Sonntagsarbeit *f*	Sunday work	travail du dimanche *m*	—	trabajo dominical *m*
lavoro manuale (I)	Handarbeit *f*	handwork	travail manuel *m*	—	trabajo a mano *m*
lavoro part-time (I)	Teilzeitarbeit *f*	part-time work	travail à temps partiel *m*	—	trabajo a tiempo parcial *m*
lavoro supplementare (I)	Mehrarbeit *f*	additional work	travail supplémentaire *m*	—	trabajo extraordinario *m*
lavoro video (I)	Bildschirmarbeit *f*	screen work	travail à l'écran	—	trabajo de pantalla *m*
law[1] (E)	Recht *n*	—	droit *m*	diritto *m*	derecho *m*
law[2] (E)	Gesetz *n*	—	loi *f*	legge *f*	ley *f*
Law on Collective Agreements (E)	Tarifvertragsgesetz *n*	—	loi réglant les conventions collectives *f*	legge sui contratti salariali *f pl*	ley de convenios colectivos *f*
law on competition (E)	Wettbewerbsrecht *n*	—	législation en matière de concurrence commerciale *m*	diritto della concorrenza *m*	derecho de la competencia *m*
lawyer[1] (E)	Anwalt *m*	—	avocat *m*	avvocato *m*	abogado *m*
lawyer[2] (E)	Rechtsanwalt *m*	—	avocat *m*	avvocato *m*	abogado *m*
lawyer's office (E)	Anwaltskanzlei *f*	—	cabinet d'avocat *m*	studio d'avvocato *m*	bufete de abogado *m*
lay days (E)	Liegetage *pl*	—	staries *f pl*	stallie *f pl*	estadías *f pl*
Layout (D)	—	layout	maquette *f*	layout *m*	layout *m*
layout (E)	Layout *n*	—	maquette *f*	layout *m*	layout *m*
layout (Es)	Layout *n*	layout	maquette *f*	layout *m*	—
layout (I)	Layout *n*	layout	maquette *f*	—	layout *m*

	D	E	F	I	Es
lay-out of an advertisement (E)	Anzeigengestaltung *f*	—	arrangement de l'annonce *m*	tipo d'inserzione *m*	estructuración del anuncio *f*
leader (E)	Anführer *m*	—	chef *m*	leader *m*	líder *m*
leader (I)	Anführer *m*	leader	chef *m*	—	líder *m*
leader en matière de prix (F)	Preisführerschaft *f*	price leadership	—	leader in materia di prezzi *m*	precio hegemónico *m*
leader in materia di prezzi (I)	Preisführerschaft *f*	price leadership	leader en matière de prix *m*	—	precio hegemónico *m*
leaflet (E)	Prospekt *m*	—	feuille publicitaire *f*/ prospectus *m*	prospetto *m*/ dépliant *m*	prospecto *m*/ folleto *m*
Leasing (D)	—	leasing	crédit-bail *m*	leasing *m*	leasing *m*
leasing (E)	Leasing *n*	—	crédit-bail *m*	leasing *m*	leasing *m*
leasing (Es)	Leasing *n*	leasing	crédit-bail *m*	leasing *m*	—
leasing (I)	Leasing *n*	leasing	crédit-bail *m*	—	leasing *m*
leasing company (E)	Leasing-Gesellschaft *f*	—	société de leasing *f*	società di leasing *f*	sociedad de leasing *f*
leasing contract (E)	Leasing-Vertrag *m*	—	contrat de leasing *m*	contratto leasing *m*	contrato de arrendamiento financiero *m*
leasing de biens immobiliers (F)	Immobilien-Leasing *n*	leasing of real estate	—	leasing immobiliare *m*	leasing de inmuebles *m*
leasing de inmuebles (Es)	Immobilien-Leasing *n*	leasing of real estate	leasing de biens immobiliers *m*	leasing immobiliare *m*	—
leasing de personal (Es)	Personal-Leasing *n*	personnel leasing	leasing de personnel *m*	leasing di personale *m*	—
leasing de personnel (F)	Personal-Leasing *n*	personnel leasing	—	leasing di personale *m*	leasing de personal *m*
leasing di personale (I)	Personal-Leasing *n*	personnel leasing	leasing de personnel *m*	—	leasing de personal *m*
Leasing-Geber (D)	—	lessor	donneur de leasing *m*	concedente del leasing *m*	arrendatario financiero *m*
Leasing-Gesellschaft (D)	—	leasing company	société de leasing *f*	società di leasing *f*	sociedad de leasing *f*
leasing immobiliare (I)	Immobilien-Leasing *n*	leasing of real estate	leasing de biens immobiliers *m*	—	leasing de inmuebles *m*
Leasing-Nehmer (D)	—	lessee	preneur de leasing *m*	utente del leasing *m*	arrendatante financiero *m*
leasing object (E)	Leasing-Objekt *n*	—	objet de leasing *m*	oggetto del leasing *m*	objeto de leasing *m*
Leasing-Objekt (D)	—	leasing object	objet de leasing *m*	oggetto del leasing *m*	objeto de leasing *m*
leasing of real estate (E)	Immobilien-Leasing *n*	—	leasing de biens immobiliers *m*	leasing immobiliare *m*	leasing de inmuebles *m*
leasing payment (E)	Leasing-Rate *f*	—	taux de leasing *m*	rata leasing *f*	plazo de arrendamiento financiero *m*
Leasing-Rate (D)	—	leasing payment	taux de leasing *m*	rata leasing *f*	plazo de arrendamiento financiero *m*
Leasing-Vertrag (D)	—	leasing contract	contrat de leasing *m*	contratto leasing *m*	contrato de arrendamiento financiero *m*
Lebenserwartung (D)	—	expectation of life	espérance de vie *f*	durata probabile della vita *f*	expectativa de vida *f*
Lebenslauf (D)	—	curriculum vitae	curriculum vitae *m*	curriculum vitae *m*	curriculum vitae *m*
Lebensqualität (D)	—	quality of life	qualité de la vie *f*	qualità di vita *f*	calidad de vida *m*
Lebensstandard (D)	—	standard of living	niveau de vie *m*	tenore di vita *m*	nivel de vida *m*
Lebensversicherung (D)	—	life insurance	assurance vie *f*	assicurazione sulla vita *f*	seguro de vida *m*
Lebenszyklus (D)	—	life cycle	cycle de vie *m*	ciclo di vita *m*	ciclo de vida *m*
Leerverkauf (D)	—	bear sale	vente à découvert *f*	vendita allo scoperto *f*	venta al descubierto *f*
legal action[1] (E)	Rechtsstreit *m*	—	litige *m*	causa *f*	conflicto jurídico *m*
legal action[2] (E)	Klage *f*	—	action en justice *f*	citazione in giudizio *f*	demanda *f*
legal adviser (E)	Syndikus	—	syndic *m*	consulente legale *m*	síndico *m*
legal capacity (E)	Rechtsfähigkeit *f*	—	capacité de jouissance des droits *f*	capacità giuridica *f*	capacidad jurídica *f*
legal claim (E)	Rechtsanspruch *m*	—	titre *m*	pretesa giuridica *f*	pretensión legal *f*
legal costs (E)	Gerichtskosten *pl*	—	frais judiciaires taxables exposés *m pl*	spese giudiziarie *f pl*	gastos judiciales *m pl*
legal department (E)	Rechtsabteilung *f*	—	bureau juridique *m*	ufficio legale *m*	sección jurídica *f*

	D	E	F	I	Es
legal form (E)	Rechtsform *f*	—	forme juridique *f*	forma giuridica *f*	forma jurídica *f*
legalización (Es)	Beglaubigung *f*	authentication	certification *f*	autenticazione *f*	—
legal norm (E)	Rechtsnorm *f*	—	règle de droit *f*	norma giuridica *f*	norma jurídica *f*
legal person (E)	juristische Person *f*	—	personne juridique *f*	persona giuridica *f*	persona jurídica *f*
legal relationship (E)	Rechtsverhältnis *n*	—	rapport juridique *m*	rapporto giuridico *m*	relación jurídica *f*
legal responsibility (E)	Rechtshaftung *f*	—	responsabilité légale *f*	responsabilità giuridica *f*	responsabilidad jurídica *f*
legal situation (E)	Rechtslage *f*	—	situation juridique *f*	situazione giuridica *f*	situación jurídica *f*
legal tender (E)	gesetzliches Zahlungsmittel *n*	—	monnaie légale *f*	mezzo di pagamento legale *m*	medio legal de pago *m*
legal transaction (E)	Rechtsgeschäft *n*	—	acte juridique *m*	negozio giuridico *m*	negocio jurídico *m*
legge (I)	Gesetz *n*	law	loi *f*	—	ley *f*
legge fallimentare (I)	Konkursordnung *f*	Bankruptcy Act	régime juridique de la faillite *m*	—	ley de las quiebras *f*
legge sui cartelli (I)	Kartellgesetz *n*	Cartel Law	loi sur les cartels *f*	—	ley relativa a los cártels *f*
legge sulla tutela contro il licenziamento (I)	Kündigungs-schutzgesetz *n*	Termination of Employment Act	loi sur le délai-congé en matière de licenciement *f*	—	ley de protección contra el despido *f*
legge sulla tutela dei dati (I)	Datenschutzgesetz *n*	Data Protection Act	loi sur l'informatique *f*	—	ley de protección de datos *f*
legge sulle società per azioni (I)	Aktiengesetz *n*	Companies Act	loi sur les sociétés par actions *f*	—	ley sobre sociedades anónimas *f*
législation économique (F)	Wirtschaftsrecht *n*	economic law	—	diritto economico *m*	derecho económico *m*
législation en matière de concurrence commerciale (F)	Wettbewerbsrecht *n*	law on competition	—	diritto della concorrenza *m*	derecho de la competencia *m*
législation industrielle (F)	Arbeitsrecht *n*	labour law	—	diritto di lavoro *m*	derecho laboral *m*
legislative sovereignty (E)	Gesetzgebungs-hoheit *f*	—	compétence législative *f*	sovranità legislativa *f*	soberanía legislativa *f*
Leihwagen (D)	—	hired car	voiture de location *f*	vettura da noleggio *f*	coche de alquiler *m*
Leistung (D)	—	performance	rendement *m*	rendimento *m*	rendimiento *m*
Leistungsbilanz (D)	—	balance of goods and services	balance des opéra-tions courantes *f*	bilancia delle partite correnti *f*	balanza por cuenta corriente *f*
Leistungsfähigkeit (D)	—	efficiency	efficience *f*	efficienza *f*	capacidad productiva *f*
Leistungslohn (D)	—	payment by result	salaire au rendement *m*	salario a rendimento *m*	salario por rendimiento *m*
leistungsorientiert (D)	—	performance-oriented	orienté vers le rendement	orientato al rendimento	orientado hacia el rendimiento
Leistungssteigerung (D)	—	increase in efficiency	amélioration du rendement *f*	aumento della produttività *m*	incremento del rendimiento *m*
Leitkurs (D)	—	central rate	taux central *m*	parità centrale *f*	tipo pivote *m*
Leitung (D)	—	management	direction *f*	direzione *f*	dirección *f*
Leitwährung (D)	—	key currency	monnaie-clé *f*	valuta guida *f*	moneda de referencia *f*
Leitzins (D)	—	key rate	taux-clé d'intérêt bancaire	tasso d'interesse guida *m*	tipos de referencia *m pl*
lending on securities (E)	Lombardgeschäft *n*	—	prêt sur gage *m*	anticipazioni *f pl*	operaciones de pignoración *f pl*
lenguaje de programación (Es)	Programmier-sprache *f*	common business-oriented language	langage de programmation *m*	linguaggio di programmazione *m*	—
le plus vite possible (F)	schnellstmöglich	as quickly as possible	—	al più presto possibile	tan rápido como sea posible
lessee (E)	Leasing-Nehmer *m*	—	preneur de leasing *m*	utente del leasing *m*	arrendatante financiero *m*
lessor (E)	Leasing-Geber *m*	—	donneur de leasing *m*	concedente del leasing *m*	arrendatario financiero *m*
letra comercial (Es)	Warenwechsel *m*	commercial bill	traite commerciale *f*	cambiale commerciale *f*	—
letra con valor declarado (Es)	Wertbrief *m*	insured letter	lettre avec valeur déclarée *f*	lettera con valore dichiarato *f*	—
letra de cambio (Es)	Wechsel *m*	bill of exchange	lettre de change *f*	cambiale *f*	—

	D	E	F	I	Es
letra domiciliada (Es)	Domizilwechsel *m*	domiciliary bill	effet domicilier *m*	cambiale domiciliata *f*	—
letra sobre el exterior (Es)	Auslandswechsel *n*	foreign bill of exchange	traite tirée sur l'étranger *f*	cambiale estera *f*	—
letrero de establecimiento (Es)	Firmenschild *n*	company's name plate	enseigne commerciale *f*	insegna dell'impresa *f*	—
letter (E)	Brief *m*	—	lettre *f*	lettera *f*	carta *f*
lettera (I)	Brief *m*	letter	lettre *f*	—	carta *f*
lettera con valore dichiarato (I)	Wertbrief *m*	insured letter	lettre avec valeur déclarée *f*	—	letra con valor declarado *f*
lettera di conferma (I)	Schlußbrief *m*	fixing letter	lettre de confirmation des conditions *f*	—	carta de confirmación *f*
lettera di credito commerciale (I)	Handelskreditbrief *m*	commercial letter of credit	lettre de crédit commercial *f*	—	carta de crédito comercial *f*
lettera di credito[1] (I)	Bankakkreditiv *n*	bank letter of credit	accréditif bancaire *m*	—	carta de crédito bancaria *f*
lettera di credito[2] (I)	Kreditbrief *m*	letter of credit	lettre de crédit *f*	—	carta de crédito *f*
lettera di raccomandazione (I)	Empfehlungs-schreiben *n*	letter of recommendation	lettre de recommandation *f*	—	carta de recomendación *f*
lettera di ringraziamento (I)	Dankschreiben *n*	letter of thanks	lettre de remerciement *f*	—	carta de agradecimiento *f*
lettera di sollecito (I)	Mahnbrief *m*	reminder	lettre d'avertissement *f*	—	carta (ad)monitoria *f*
lettera di trasporto aereo (I)	Luftfrachtbrief *m*	air waybill	lettre de transport aérien *f*	—	transporte aéreo *m*
lettera di vettura (I)	Frachtbrief *m*	consignment note	lettre de voiture *f*	—	carta de porte *f*
lettera espresso (I)	Eilbrief *m*	express letter	lettre par exprès *f*	—	carta urgente *f*
lettera pubblicitaria (I)	Werbebrief *m*	advertising letter	lettre publicitaire *f*	—	circular de publicidad *m*
lettera raccomandata (I)	Einschreibebrief *m*	registered letter	lettre recommandée *f*	—	carta certificada *f*
lettera raccomandata con ricevuta di ritorno (I)	Einschreiben-Rückschein *m*	recorded delivery letter with advice	lettre recommandée avec avis de réception *f*	—	carta certificada con talón de recibo *f*
letterhead (E)	Briefkopf *m*	—	en-tête *m*	intestazione *f*	encabezamiento *m*
letter of application (E)	Bewerbungs-schreiben *n*	—	lettre de demande d'emploi *f*	domanda d'impiego *f*	carta de solicitud *f*
letter of confirmation (E)	Schlußbrief *m*	—	lettre de confirmation des conditions *f*	lettera di conferma *f*	carta de confirmación *f*
letter of credit[1] (E)	Kreditbrief *m*	—	lettre de crédit *f*	lettera di credito *f*	carta de crédito *f*
letter of credit[2] (E)	Akkreditiv *n*	—	accréditif *m*	credito documentario *m*	crédito documentario *m*
letter of credit clause (E)	Akkreditivklausel *f*	—	clause de payement par accréditif *f*	clausola del credito documentario *f*	cláusula de crédito documentario *f*
letter of recommendation (E)	Empfehlungs-schreiben *n*	—	lettre de recommandation *f*	lettera di raccomandazione *f*	carta de recomendación *f*
letter of thanks (E)	Dankschreiben *n*	—	lettre de remerciement *f*	lettera di ringraziamento *f*	carta de agradecimiento *f*
letter scales (E)	Briefwaage *f*	—	pèse-lettres *m*	bilancia per corrispondenza *f*	pesacartas *m*
lettre (F)	Brief *m*	letter	—	lettera *f*	carta *f*
lettre avec valeur déclarée (F)	Wertbrief *m*	insured letter	—	lettera con valore dichiarato *f*	letra con valor declarado *f*
lettre circulaire (F)	Rundschreiben *n*	circular (letter)	—	circolare *f*	circular *m*
lettre d'avertissement (F)	Mahnbrief *m*	reminder	—	lettera di sollecito *f*	carta (ad)monitoria *f*
lettre de change (F)	Wechsel *m*	bill of exchange	—	cambiale *f*	letra de cambio *f*
lettre de confirmation des conditions (F)	Schlußbrief *m*	letter of confirmation	—	lettera di conferma *f*	carta de confirmación *f*
lettre de crédit (F)	Kreditbrief *m*	letter of credit	—	lettera di credito *f*	carta de crédito *f*
lettre de crédit commercial (F)	Handelskreditbrief *m*	commercial letter of credit	—	lettera di credito commerciale *f*	carta de crédito comercial *f*
lettre de demande d'emploi (F)	Bewerbungs-schreiben *n*	letter of application	—	domanda d'impiego *f*	carta de solicitud *f*
lettre de recommandation (F)	Empfehlungs-schreiben *n*	letter of recommendation	—	lettera di raccomandazione *f*	carta de recomendación *f*

	D	E	F	I	Es
lettre de remerciement (F)	Dankschreiben *n*	letter of thanks	—	lettera di ringraziamento *f*	carta de agradecimiento *f*
lettre de transport aérien (F)	Luftfrachtbrief *m*	air waybill	—	lettera di trasporto aereo *f*	transporte aéreo *m*
lettre de voiture (F)	Frachtbrief *m*	consignment note	—	lettera di vettura *f*	carta de porte *f*
lettre par exprès (F)	Eilbrief *m*	express letter	—	lettera espresso *f*	carta urgente *f*
lettre publicitaire (F)	Werbebrief *m*	advertising letter	—	lettera pubblicitaria *f*	circular de publicidad *m*
lettre recommandée (F)	Einschreibebrief *m*	registered letter	—	lettera raccomandata *f*	carta certificada *f*
lettre recommandée avec avis de réception (F)	Einschreiben-Rückschein *m*	recorded delivery letter with advice	—	lettera raccomandata con ricevuta di ritorno *f*	carta certificada con talón de recibo *f*
Leumund (D)	—	reputation	réputation *f*	reputazione *f*	reputación *f*
level of employment (E)	Beschäftigungs-grad *m*	—	taux d'emploi *m*	tasso d'occupazione *m*	grado de empleo *m*
ley[1] (Es)	Feingehalt *m*	fine gold content	titre *m*	titolo *m*	—
ley[2] (Es)	Gesetz *n*	law	loi *f*	legge *f*	—
ley de las quiebras (Es)	Konkursordnung *f*	Bankruptcy Act	régime juridique de la faillite *m*	legge fallimentare *f*	—
ley de protección contra el despido (Es)	Kündigungsschutz-gesetz *n*	Termination of Employment Act	loi sur le délai-congé en matière de licenciement *f*	legge sulla tutela contro il licenziamento *f*	—
ley de protección de datos (Es)	Datenschutzgesetz *n*	Data Protection Act	loi sur l'informatique	legge sulla tutela dei dati *f*	—
ley relativa a los cártels (Es)	Kartellgesetz *n*	Cartel Law	loi sur les cartels *f*	legge sui cartelli *f*	—
ley sobre sociedades anónimas (Es)	Aktiengesetz *n*	Companies Act	loi sur les sociétés par actions *f*	legge sulle società per azioni *f*	—
liabilities (E)	Passiva *n*	—	passif *m*	passivo *m*	pasivo *m*
liability[1] (E)	Obligo *n*	—	engagement *m*	obbligo *m*	obligación *f*
liability[2] (E)	Verbindlichkeiten *pl*	—	obligation *f*/ dettes *f pl*	obblighi *m pl*/ debiti *m pl*	obligaciónes *f pl*/ deudas *f pl*/créditos pasivos *m pl*
liability[3] (E)	Haftung *f*	—	responsabilité *f*	responsabilità *f*	responsabilidad *f*
liability for breach of warranty (E)	Gewährleistungs-haftung *f*	—	responsabilité en matière de garantie *f*	responsabilità di garanzia *f*	responsabilidad de garantía *f*
liability for damages (E)	Schadensersatz-pflicht *f*	—	obligation de dédommager *f*	obbligo di risarcimento danni *m*	obligación indemnizatoria *f*
liability to insure (E)	Versicherungspflicht *f*	—	assujettissement obligatoire à l'assurance *m*	obbligo d'assicurazione *m*	obligatoriedad del seguro *f*
liable to prosecution (E)	straffällig	—	encourir une peine	passibile di pena	criminal
liable to tax (E)	abgabenpflichtig	—	soumis à l'impôt	soggetto a contributi	sujeto a impuestos
libbra (I)	Pfund *n*	pound	livre *f*	—	libra *f*
libera circolazione dei capitali (I)	freier Kapitalverkehr *m*	free movement of capital	libre circulation des capitaux *f*	—	libre circulación de capitales
liberalism (E)	Liberalismus *m*	—	libéralisme *m*	liberalismo *m*	liberalismo *m*
libéralisme (F)	Liberalismus *m*	liberalism	—	liberalismo *m*	liberalismo *m*
liberalismo (Es)	Liberalismus *m*	liberalism	libéralisme *m*	liberalismo *m*	—
liberalismo (I)	Liberalismus *m*	liberalism	libéralisme *m*	—	liberalismo *m*
Liberalismus (D)	—	liberalism	libéralisme *m*	liberalismo *m*	liberalismo *m*
libero professionista (I)	Freiberufler *m*	self-employed person	personne exerçant une profession libérale *f*	—	profesional *m*
libertà contrattuale (I)	Vertragsfreiheit *f*	freedom of contract	liberté de contracter *f*	—	libertad contractual *f*
libertad contractual (Es)	Vertragsfreiheit *f*	freedom of contract	liberté de contracter *f*	libertà contrattuale *f*	—
libertad de coalición (Es)	Koalitionsfreiheit *f*	freedom of association	liberté d'association *f*	libertà di coalizione *f*	—
libertad de consumo (Es)	Konsumfreiheit *f*	freedom of consumption	liberté de consommation *f*	libertà di consumo *f*	—
libertad de industria (Es)	Gewerbefreiheit *f*	freedom of trade	liberté des professions industrielles et commerciales *f*	libertà d'industria *f*	—

	D	E	F	I	Es
libertà di coalizione (I)	Koalitionsfreiheit *f*	freedom of association	liberté d'association *f*	—	libertad de coalición *f*
libertà di commercio estero (I)	Außenhandelsfreiheit *f*	free trade	libre-échange *m*	—	librecambio *m*
libertà di consumo (I)	Konsumfreiheit *f*	freedom of consumption	liberté de consommation *f*	—	libertad de consumo *f*
libertà d'industria (I)	Gewerbefreiheit *f*	freedom of trade	liberté des professions industrielles et commerciales *f*	—	libertad de industria *f*
liberté d'association (F)	Koalitionsfreiheit *f*	freedom of association	—	libertà di coalizione *f*	libertad de coalición *f*
liberté de consommation (F)	Konsumfreiheit *f*	freedom of consumption	—	libertà di consumo *f*	libertad de consumo *f*
liberté de contracter (F)	Vertragsfreiheit *f*	freedom of contract	—	libertà contrattuale *f*	libertad contractual *f*
liberté des professions industrielles et commerciales (F)	Gewerbefreiheit *f*	freedom of trade	—	libertà d'industria *f*	libertad de industria *f*
libra (Es)	Pfund *n*	pound	livre *f*	libbra *f*	—
librado (Es)	Bezogener *m*	drawee	tiré *m*	trattario *m*	—
libramiento de letras cruzados (Es)	Wechselreiterei *f*	kitoflying	tirage d'une traite de cavalerie *m*	emissione di tratte incrociate *f*	—
librecambio[1] (Es)	Außenhandelsfreiheit *f*	free trade	libre-échange *m*	libertà di commercio estero *f*	—
librecambio[2] (Es)	Freihandel *m*	free trade	commerce libre *m*	scambio libero *m*	—
libre circulación de capitales (Es)	freier Kapitalverkehr *m*	free movement of capital	libre circulation des capitaux *f*	libera circolazione dei capitali *f*	—
libre circulation des capitaux (F)	freier Kapitalverkehr *m*	free movement of capital	—	libera circolazione dei capitali *f*	libre circulación de capitales *f*
libre de gastos (Es)	kostenlos	free of charge	gratuit	gratuito	—
libre de impuesto (Es)	steuerfrei	tax-free	dispensé de l'impôt	esente da imposte	—
libre-échange (F)	Außenhandelsfreiheit *f*	free trade	—	libertà di commercio estero *f*	librecambio *m*
libreta de cheques (Es)	Scheckheft *n*	cheque book	carnet de chèques *m*	carnet degli assegni *m*	—
libretto degli assegni (I)	Scheckbuch *n*	cheque book	livre d'enregistrement des chéques *m*	—	libro de cheques *m*
libri contabili (I)	Geschäftsbücher *pl*	account books	livres de commerce *m pl*	—	libros de contabilidad *m pl*
libro de caja (Es)	Kassenbuch *n*	cash book	compte de caisse *m*	libro di cassa *m*	—
libro de cheques (Es)	Scheckbuch *n*	cheque book	livre d'enregistrement des chéques *m*	libretto degli assegni *m*	—
libro de cuentas (Es)	Kontobuch *n*	account book	livre de compte *m*	libro dei conti *m*	—
libro dei conti (I)	Kontobuch *n*	account book	livre de compte *m*	—	libro de cuentas *m*
libro di cassa (I)	Kassenbuch *n*	cash book	compte de caisse *m*	—	libro de caja *m*
libros de contabilidad (Es)	Geschäftsbücher *pl*	account books	livres de commerce *m pl*	libri contabili *m pl*	—
libro specializzato (I)	Fachbuch *n*	technical book	livre technique *m*	—	libro técnico *m*
libro técnico (Es)	Fachbuch *n*	technical book	livre technique *m*	libro specializzato *m*	—
licence[1] (E)	Konzession *f*	—	concession *f*	concessione *f*	concesión *f*
licence[2] (E)	Lizenzen *pl*	—	licence *f*	licenze *f pl*	licencias *f pl*
licence agreement (E)	Lizenzvertrag *m*	—	contrat de concession de licence *m*	contratto di licenza *m*	contrato de licencia *m*
licence de brevet (F)	Patentlizenz *f*	patent licence	—	licenza di brevetto *f*	licencia de patente *f*
licences (F)	Lizenzen *pl*	licence	—	licenze *f pl*	licencias *f pl*
licencia de exportación (Es)	Ausfuhrgenehmigung *f*	export licence	autorisation d'exportation *f*	autorizzazione per le esportazioni *f*	—
licencia de patente (Es)	Patentlizenz *f*	patent licence	licence de brevet *f*	licenza di brevetto *f*	—
licenciado (Es)	Lizenznehmer *m*	licensee	preneur d'une licence *m*	concessionario di licenza *m*	—
licencias (Es)	Lizenzen *pl*	licence	licences *f*	licenze *f pl*	—
licenciement (F)	Entlassung *f*	dismissal	—	licenziamento *m*	despido *m*
licensee (E)	Lizenznehmer *m*	—	preneur d'une licence *m*	concessionario di licenza *m*	licenciado *m*

	D	E	F	I	Es
licenser (E)	Lizenzgeber *m*	—	concédant de licence *m*	concedente di licenza *m*	licitador *m*
licenza di brevetto (I)	Patentlizenz *f*	patent licence	licence de brevet *f*	—	licencia de patente *f*
licenze (I)	Lizenzen *pl*	licence	licences *f*	—	licencias *f pl*
licenziamento (I)	Entlassung *f*	dismissal	licenciement *m*	—	despido *m*
licitador (Es)	Lizenzgeber *m*	licenser	concédant de licence *m*	concedente di licenza *m*	—
líder (Es)	Anführer *m*	leader	chef *m*	leader *m*	—
Liebhaberpreis (D)	—	connoisseur's price	prix d'amateur *m*	prezzo d'affezione *m*	precio afectivo *m*
Lieferant (D)	—	supplier	fournisseur *m*	fornitore *m*	suministrador *m*
Lieferantenkredit (D)	—	supplier's credit	crédit de fournisseurs *m*	credito al fornitore *m*	crédito comercial *m*
lieferbar (D)	—	deliverable	livrable	disponibile	suministrable
Lieferbedingungen (D)	—	terms of delivery	conditions de livraison *f pl*	condizioni di consegna *f pl*	condiciones de suminstro *f pl*
Lieferfrist (D)	—	time for delivery	délai de livraison *m*	termine di consegna *m*	plazo de entrega *m*
Lieferkapazität (D)	—	delivery capacity	capacité de livraison *f*	capacità di fornitura *f*	capacidad de entrega *f*
Lieferklausel (D)	—	delivery clause	clause de livraison *f*	clausola di fornitura *f*	cláusulas comerciales *f pl*
Lieferprogramm (D)	—	delivery programme	programme de livraison *m*	programma di fornitura *m*	programa de entrega *m*
Lieferschein (D)	—	delivery note	bulletin de livraison *m*	bolletta di consegna *f*	recibo de entrega *m*
Liefersperre (D)	—	delivery ban	blocage de livraisons *m*	blocco delle forniture *m*	embargo *m*
Liefertermin (D)	—	date of delivery	délai de livraison *m*	termine di consegna *m*	plazo de entrega *m*
Lieferung (D)	—	delivery	livraison *f*	fornitura *f*/consegna *f*	suminstro *m*
Lieferung gegen Nachnahme (D)	—	cash on delivery	livraison contre remboursement *f*	consegna contro assegno *f*	entrega contra reembolso *f*
Lieferungs-verzögerung (D)	—	delay in delivery	retard dans la livraison *m*	ritardo della consegna *m*	demora en la entrega *f*
Liefervertrag (D)	—	supply contract	contrat de fourniture *m*	contratto di consegna *m*	contrata *f*
Lieferverzug (D)	—	delay in delivery	demeure du fournisseur *f*	mora nella consegna *f*	demora en la entrega *f*
Liegetage (D)	—	lay days	staries *f pl*	stallie *f pl*	estadías *f pl*
lieu de destination (F)	Bestimmungsort *m*	place of destination	—	luogo di destinazione *m*	lugar de de destino *m*
lieu de naissance (F)	Geburtsort *m*	place of birth	—	luogo di nascita *m*	lugar de nacimiento *m*
lieu de travail (F)	Arbeitsraum *m*	workroom	—	locale di lavoro *m*	sala de trabajo *f*
lieu d'implantation (F)	Standort *m*	location	—	ubicazione *f*	ubicación *f*
life cycle (E)	Lebenszyklus *m*	—	cycle de vie *m*	ciclo di vita *m*	ciclo de vida *m*
life insurance (E)	Lebensversicherung *f*	—	assurance vie *f*	assicurazione sulla vita *f*	seguro de vida *m*
ligne des produits (F)	Produktlinie *f*	production scheduling	—	linea dei prodotti *f*	línea de productos *f*
lignite (F)	Braunkohle *f*	brown coal	—	lignite *f*	lignito *m*
lignite (I)	Braunkohle *f*	brown coal	lignite *m*	—	lignito *m*
lignito (Es)	Braunkohle *f*	brown coal	lignite *m*	lignite *f*	—
Limit (D)	—	limit	limite *f*	limite *m*	límite *m*
limit (E)	Limit *n*	—	limite *f*	limite *m*	límite *m*
limitación de cultivos (Es)	Anbau-beschränkung *f*	restriction on cultivation	limitation des cultures *f*	restrizione di coltivazione *f*	—
limitación de emisiones (Es)	Emissions-begrenzung *f*	issuing restriction	limitation d'émission *f*	limitazione d'emissione *f*	—
limitación de precios[1] (Es)	Preisbindung *f*	obligation to main-tain fixed prices	obligation de respecter les prix *f*	obbligo di mantenere il prezzo fissato *m*	—
limitación de precios[2] (Es)	Preisstopp *m*	price stop	blocage des prix *m*	blocco dei prezzi *m*	—
limitation d'émission (F)	Emissions-begrenzung *f*	issuing restriction	—	limitazione d'emissione *f*	limitación de emisiones *f*

	D	E	F	I	Es
limitation des cultures (F)	Anbau-beschränkung *f*	restriction on cultivation	—	restrizione di coltivazione *f*	limitación de cultivos *f*
limitation des importations (F)	Einfuhr-beschränkung *f*	import restriction	—	restrizione d'importazione *f*	restricción a la importación *f*
limitation of actions (E)	Verjährung *f*	—	prescription *f*	prescrizione *f*	prescripción *f*
limitazione d'emissione (I)	Emissions-begrenzung *f*	issuing restriction	limitation d'émission *f*	—	limitación de emisiones *f*
límite (Es)	Limit *n*	limit	limite *f*	limite *m*	—
limite (F)	Limit *n*	limit	—	limite *m*	límite *m*
limite (I)	Limit *n*	limit	limite *f*	—	límite *m*
limite d'âge (F)	Altersgrenze *f*	age limit	—	limite d'età *m*	limite de edad *m*
límite de crédito (Es)	Kreditlimit *n*	borrowing limit	plafond du crédit alloué *m*	limite di credito *m*	—
limite de edad (Es)	Altersgrenze *f*	age limit	limite d'âge *f*	limite d'età *m*	—
limite de producción (Es)	Förderlimit *n*	production limit	limite de production *f*	limite d'estrazione *m*	—
limite de production (F)	Förderlimit *n*	production limit	—	limite d'estrazione *m*	limite de producción *m*
limite d'estrazione (I)	Förderlimit *n*	production limit	limite de production *f*	—	limite de producción *m*
limite d'età (I)	Altersgrenze *f*	age limit	limite d'âge *f*	—	limite de edad *m*
limite di credito (I)	Kreditlimit *n*	borrowing limit	plafond du crédit alloué *m*	—	límite de crédito *m*
limited liability company (E)	Gesellschaft mit beschränkter Haftung *f*	—	société à responsabilité limitée *f*	società a responsabilità limitata *f*	sociedad de responsabilidad limitada *f*
limited partner (E)	Kommanditist *m*	—	commanditaire *m*	socio accomandante *m*	comanditario *m*
limited partnership (E)	Kommandit-gesellschaft *f*	—	société en commandite *f*	società in accomandita semplice *f*	sociedad comanditaria *f*
límite inferior de los precios (Es)	Preisuntergrenze *f*	price floor	plancher des prix *m*	limite inferiore di prezzo *m*	—
límite inferior de rentabilidad (Es)	Rentabilitätschwelle *f*	break-even point	seuil de rentabilité *m*	soglia di redditività *f*	—
limite inferiore di prezzo (I)	Preisuntergrenze *f*	price floor	plancher des prix *m*	—	límite inferior de los precios *m*
limite massimo di prezzo (I)	Preisobergrenze *f*	price ceiling	limite supérieur des prix *f*	—	límite superior de los precios *m*
límite máximo (Es)	Plafond *m*	ceiling	plafond *m*	plafond *m*	—
limite supérieur des prix (F)	Preisobergrenze *f*	price ceiling	—	limite massimo di prezzo *m*	límite superior de los precios *m*
límite superior de los precios (Es)	Preisobergrenze *f*	price ceiling	limite supérieur des prix *f*	limite massimo di prezzo *m*	—
limiting value (E)	Grenzwert *m*	—	valeur marginale *f*	valore limite *m*	valor límite *m*
linea creditizia (I)	Kreditlinie *f*	credit line	plafond du crédit accordé *m*	—	línea de crédito *f*
línea de crédito (Es)	Kreditlinie *f*	credit line	plafond du crédit accordé *m*	linea creditizia *f*	—
linea dei prodotti (I)	Produktlinie *f*	production scheduling	ligne des produits *f*	—	línea de productos *f*
línea de productos (Es)	Produktlinie *f*	production scheduling	ligne des produits *f*	linea dei prodotti *f*	—
linear depreciation (E)	lineare Abschreibung *f*	—	amortissement constant *m*	ammortamento lineare *m*	amortización constante *f*
lineare Abschreibung (D)	—	linear depreciation	amortissement constant *m*	ammortamento lineare *m*	amortización constante *f*
lineare Programmierung (D)	—	linear programmation	programmation linéaire *f*	programmazione lineare *f*	programación lineal *f*
lineares Wachstum (D)	—	linear growth	accroissement constant *m*	crescita lineare *f*	crecimiento lineal *m*
linear growth (E)	lineares Wachstum *n*	—	accroissement constant *m*	crescita lineare *f*	crecimiento lineal *m*
linear programmation (E)	lineare Programmierung *f*	—	programmation linéaire *f*	programmazione lineare *f*	programación lineal *f*
line of business (E)	Branche *f*	—	branche *f*	categoria *f*	ramo *m*
lingot d'or (F)	Goldbarren *m*	gold bar	—	lingotto d'oro *m*	lingote de oro *m*

	D	E	F	I	Es
lingote de oro (Es)	Goldbarren *m*	gold bar	lingot d'ór *m*	lingotto d'oro *m*	—
lingotto d'oro (I)	Goldbarren *m*	gold bar	lingot d'ór *m*	—	lingote de oro *m*
linguaggio di programmazione (I)	Programmier-sprache *f*	common business-oriented language	langage de programmation *m*	—	lenguaje de programación *m*
liquid (E)	liquide	—	solvable	liquido	líquido
liquidación[1] (Es)	Ausverkauf *m*	clearance sale	soldes *m pl*	svendita *f*	—
liquidación[2] (Es)	Abrechnung *f*	settlement of accounts	règlement *m*	liquidazione *f*	—
liquidación[3] (Es)	Liquidation *f*	liquidation	liquidation *f*	liquidazione *f*	—
liquidación de gastos (Es)	Spesenabrechung *f*	statement of expenses	décompte des frais *m*	conteggio delle spese *m*	—
liquidación de impuestas (Es)	Steuerbescheid *m*	notice of assessment	avis d'imposition *m*	cartella delle imposte *f*	—
liquidación de la comisión (Es)	Provisions-abrechnung *f*	statement of a commission	compte des commissions *m*	conteggio delle provvigioni *m*	—
liquidación de los gastos de viaje (Es)	Reisekosten-abrechnung *f*	travel expense accounting	règlement des frais de voyage *m*	conteggio dei costi di viaggio *m*	—
liquidador[1] (Es)	Liquidator *m*	liquidator	liquidateur *m*	liquidatore *m*	—
liquidador[2] (Es)	Abwickler *m*	liquidator	liquidateur *m*	liquidatore *m*	—
liquidar (Es)	liquidieren	liquidate	liquider	liquidare	—
liquidare (I)	liquidieren	liquidate	liquider	—	liquidar
liquidate (E)	liquidieren	—	liquider	liquidare	liquidar
liquidateur[1] (F)	Liquidator *m*	liquidator	—	liquidatore *m*	liquidador *m*
liquidateur[2] (F)	Abwickler *m*	liquidator	—	liquidatore *m*	liquidador *m*
liquidateur de la faillite (F)	Konkursverwalter *m*	administrator in bankruptcy proceedings	—	curatore fallimentare *m*	síndico de quiebra *m*
Liquidation (D)	—	liquidation	liquidation *f*	liquidazione *f*	liquidación *f*
liquidation (E)	Liquidation *f*	—	liquidation *f*	liquidazione *f*	liquidación *f*
liquidation[1] (F)	Auflösung *f*	dissolution	—	scioglimento *m*	disolución *f*
liquidation[2] (F)	Liquidation *f*	liquidation	—	liquidazione *f*	liquidación *f*
liquidation des commissions (F)	Provisions-abrechnung *f*	statement of a commission	—	conteggio delle provvigioni *m*	liquidación de la comisión *f*
liquidation des stocks (F)	Räumungsverkauf *m*	clearance sale	—	liquidazione totale *f*	venta total *f*
Liquidationserlös (D)	—	remaining assets after liquidation	produit de la liquidation *m*	ricavo della liquidazione *m*	haber social repartible *m*
Liquidator (D)	—	liquidator	liquidateur *m*	liquidatore *m*	liquidador *m*
liquidator[1] (E)	Liquidator *m*	—	liquidateur *m*	liquidatore *m*	liquidador *m*
liquidator[2] (E)	Abwickler *m*	—	liquidateur *m*	liquidatore *m*	liquidador *m*
liquidatore[1] (I)	Liquidator *m*	liquidator	liquidateur *m*	—	liquidador *m*
liquidatore[2] (I)	Abwickler *m*	liquidator	liquidateur *m*	—	liquidador *m*
liquidazione[1] (I)	Abrechnung *f*	settlement of accounts	règlement *m*	—	liquidación *f*
liquidazione[2] (I)	Liquidation *f*	liquidation	liquidation *f*	—	liquidación *f*
liquidazione del conto (I)	Kontoausgleich *m*	settlement of an account	solde de compte *m*	—	saldo de cuenta *m*
liquidazione totale (I)	Räumungsverkauf *m*	clearance sale	liquidation des stocks *f*	—	venta total *f*
liquide (D)	—	liquid	solvable	liquido	líquido
liquider (F)	liquidieren	liquidate	—	liquidare	liquidar
liquidez (Es)	Liquidität *f*	liquidity	liquidité *f*	liquidità *f*	—
liquidieren (D)	—	liquidate	liquider	liquidare	liquidar
liquidità (I)	Liquidität *f*	liquidity	liquidité *f*	—	liquidez *f*
Liquidität (D)	—	liquidity	liquidité *f*	liquidità *f*	liquidez *f*
Liquiditätsengpaß (D)	—	liquidity squeeze	goulot d'étranglement dans la trésorerie	strettoia di liquidità *f*	restricción de la liquidez *f*
Liquiditätsplan (D)	—	cash forecasting plan	plan de liquidité *m*	piano della liquidità *m*	plan de liquidez *m*
Liquiditätsrechnung (D)	—	liquidity calculation	compte de liquidité *m*	calcolo della liquidità *m*	cálculo de liquidez *m*

	D	E	F	I	Es
Liquiditätsreserve (D)	—	liquidity reserves	réserves de liquidité *f pl*	riserva di liquidità *f*	reserva de liquidez *f*
Liquiditäts-überschuß (D)	—	excess liquidity	excédent de liquidité *m*	eccedenza di liquidità *f*	exceso de liquidez *m*
liquidité (F)	Liquidität *f*	liquidity	—	liquidità *f*	liquidez *f*
liquidity (E)	Liquidität *f*	—	liquidité *f*	liquidità *f*	liquidez *f*
liquidity calculation (E)	Liquiditätsrechnung *f*	—	compte de liquidité *m*	calcolo della liquidità *m*	cálculo de liquidez *m*
liquidity reserves (E)	Liquiditätsreserve *f*	—	réserves de liquidité *f pl*	riserva di liquidità *f*	reserva de liquidez *f*
liquidity squeeze (E)	Liquiditätsengpaß *m*	—	goulot d'étranglement dans la trésorerie	strettoia di liquidità *f*	restricción de la liquidez *f*
líquido (Es)	liquide	liquid	solvable	liquido	—
liquido (I)	liquide	liquid	solvable	—	líquido
lista de control (Es)	Checkliste *f*	checklist	liste de contrôle *f*	lista di controllo *f*	—
lista de correos (Es)	postlagernd	poste restante	poste restante	fermo posta *m*	—
lista dei partecipanti (I)	Teilnehmerliste *f*	list of participants	liste des participants *f*	—	lista de participantes *f*
lista de participantes (Es)	Teilnehmerliste *f*	list of participants	liste des participants *f*	lista dei partecipanti *f*	—
lista de precios (Es)	Preisliste *f*	price list	liste des prix *f*	listino prezzi *m*	—
lista de precios de exportación (Es)	Exportpreisliste *f*	export price list	liste des prix à l'exportation *f*	listino prezzi delle esportazioni *m*	—
lista di controllo (I)	Checkliste *f*	checklist	liste de contrôle *f*	—	lista de control *f*
liste de contrôle (F)	Checkliste *f*	checklist	—	lista di controllo *f*	lista de control *f*
liste des participants (F)	Teilnehmerliste *f*	list of participants	—	lista dei partecipanti *f*	lista de participantes *f*
liste des prix (F)	Preisliste *f*	price list	—	listino prezzi *m*	lista de precios *f*
liste des prix à l'exportation (F)	Exportpreisliste *f*	export price list	—	listino prezzi delle esportazioni *m*	lista de precios de exportación *f*
Listenpreis (D)	—	list price	prix du tarif *m*	prezzo di listino *m*	precio-lista *m*
listino di borsa (I)	Kurszettel *m*	stock exchange list	bulletin des cours *m*	—	boletín de bolsa *m*
listino prezzi (I)	Preisliste *f*	price list	liste des prix *f*	—	lista de precios *f*
listino prezzi delle esportazioni (I)	Exportpreisliste *f*	export price list	liste des prix à l'exportation *f*	—	lista de precios de exportación *f*
list of participants (E)	Teilnehmerliste *f*	—	liste des participants *f*	lista dei partecipanti *f*	lista de participantes *f*
listo para la recogida (Es)	abholbereit	ready for collection	disponible	pronto per il ritiro	—
listo para ser expedido (Es)	versandbereit	ready for dispatch	prêt à être expédié	pronto per la spedizione	—
list price (E)	Listenpreis *m*	—	prix du tarif *m*	prezzo di listino *m*	precio-lista *m*
litige (F)	Rechtsstreit *m*	legal action	—	causa *f*	conflicto jurídico *m*
litigio hereditario (Es)	Erbstreit *m*	dispute concerning an inheritance	action successorale *f*	causa ereditaria *f*	—
livello degli interessi (I)	Zinsniveau *n*	interest rate level	niveau du taux d'intérêt *m*	—	nivel de interés *m*
livello dei prezzi (I)	Preisniveau *n*	price level	niveau des prix *m*	—	nivel de precios *m*
livestock breeding (E)	Tierzucht *f*	—	élevage *m*	zootecnia *f*	cría de animales *f*
livrable (F)	lieferbar	deliverable	—	disponibile	suministrable
livraison (F)	Lieferung *f*	delivery	—	fornitura *f*/consegna *f*	suminstro *m*
livraison à titre d'essai (F)	Probelieferung *f*	trial shipment	—	fornitura a titolo di prova *f*	envío de prueba *m*
livraison contre remboursement (F)	Lieferung gegen Nachnahme *f*	cash on delivery	—	consegna contro assegno *f*	entrega contra reembolso *f*
livraison de remplacement (F)	Ersatzlieferung *f*	substitute delivery	—	fornitura di compensazione *f*	entrega de reposición *f*
livraison en quantité inférieure (F)	Minderlieferung *f*	short delivery	—	fornitura ridotta *f*	envío incompleto *m*
livraison immédiate (F)	sofortige Lieferung *f*	immediate delivery	—	consegna immediata *f*	entrega inmediata *f*
livraison partielle (F)	Teillieferung *f*	partial delivery	—	fornitura parziale	entrega parcial *f*
livraison supplémentaire (F)	Mehrlieferung *f*	additional delivery	—	fornitura supplementare *f*	exceso *m*

	D	E	F	I	Es
livraison totale (F)	Gesamtlieferung *f*	total delivery	—	fornitura completa *f*	suministro total *m*
livre (F)	Pfund *n*	pound	—	libbra *f*	libra *f*
livre de compte (F)	Kontobuch *n*	account book	—	libro dei conti *m*	libro de cuentas *m*
livre d'enregistrement des chèques (F)	Scheckbuch *n*	cheque book	—	libretto degli assegni *m*	libro de cheques *m*
livrer (F)	abliefern	hand over	—	consegnare	entregar
livres de commerce (F)	Geschäftsbücher *pl*	account books	—	libri contabili *m pl*	libros de contabilidad *m pl*
livre technique (F)	Fachbuch *n*	technical book	—	libro specializzato *m*	libro técnico *m*
Lizenzen (D)	—	licence	licences *f pl*	licenze *f pl*	licencias *f pl*
Lizenzgeber (D)	—	licenser	concédant de licence *m*	concedente di licenza *m*	licitador *m*
Lizenzgebühr (D)	—	royalty	taxe d'expoitation de licence *f*	tassa di licenza *f*	derecho de licencia *m*
Lizenznehmer (D)	—	licensee	preneur d'une licence *m*	concessionario di licenza *m*	licenciado *m*
Lizenzvertrag (D)	—	licence agreement	contrat de concession de licence *m*	contratto di licenza *m*	contrato de licencia *m*
llamada en causa (Es)	Beiladung *f*	summons to interested parties/ additional load	assignation en intervention *f*/complément de fret *m*	intervento per ordine del giudice *m*/spedizione in collettame *f*	—
lluvia ácida (Es)	saurer Regen *m*	acid rain	pluie acide *f*	pioggia acida *f*	—
load[1] (E)	verladen	—	charger	caricare	expedir
load[2] (E)	Belastung *f*	—	charge *f*	addebito *m*	gravamen *m*
load[3] (E)	belasten	—	débiter	addebitare	cargar/adeudar
loading charges[1] (E)	Ladegebühren *pl*	—	taxe de chargement *f*	spese di carico *f pl*	derechos de carga *m pl*
loading charges[2] (E)	Verladekosten *pl*	—	coût du chargement *m*	costi di caricamento *m pl*	gastos de carga *m pl*
loan[1] (E)	Anleihe *f*	—	emprunt *m*	prestito *m*	empréstito *m*
loan[2] (E)	Darlehen *n*	—	prêt *m*	mutuo *m*	préstamo *m*
Lobby (D)	—	lobbying group	lobby *m*	lobby *m*	grupo de presión *m*
lobby (F)	Lobby *f*	lobbying group	—	lobby *m*	grupo de presión *m*
lobby (I)	Lobby *f*	lobbying group	lobby *m*	—	grupo de presión *m*
local agent (E)	Bezirksvertreter *m*	—	agent local *m*	rappresentante di zona *m*	agente regional *m*
local à usage commercial (F)	Geschäftsräume *pl*	business premises	—	locali commerciali *m pl*	local comercial *m*
local authorities loan (E)	Kommunalanleihen *pl*	—	emprunt communal *m*	prestiti comunali *m pl*	empréstito municipal *m*
local comercial (Es)	Geschäftsräume *pl*	business premises	local à usage commercial *m*	locali commerciali *m pl*	—
locale di lavoro (I)	Arbeitsraum *m*	workroom	lieu de travail *m*	—	sala de trabajo *f*
locali commerciali (I)	Geschäftsräume *pl*	business premises	local à usage commercial *m*	—	local comercial *m*
locataire (F)	Mieter *m*	tenant	—	locatario *m*	inquilino *m*/ arrendatario *m*
locatario (I)	Mieter *m*	tenant	locataire *m*	—	inquilino *m*/ arrendatario *m*
location (E)	Standort *m*	—	lieu d'implantation *m*	ubicazione *f*	ubicación *f*
location (F)	Miete *f*	rent	—	canone di locazione *m*	alquiler *m*
location decision (E)	Standortentscheidung *f*	—	décision de l'implantation *f*	determinazione dell'ubicazione *f*	decisión de ubicación *f*
location d'une surface pour magasinage (F)	Lagermiete *f*	warehouse rent	—	spese di magazzinaggio *f pl*	alquiler de almacenaje *m*
location factors (E)	Standortfaktoren *pl*	—	facteurs dépendant du lieu d'implantation *m pl*	fattori d'ubicazione *m pl*	factores de ubicación *m pl*
lock-down period for interest rates (E)	Zinsbindungsfrist *f*	—	délai d'engagement sur le taux d'intérêt accordé *m*	scadenza degli interessi vincolati *f*	plazo de vinculación al tipo de interés pactado *m*
lockout (E)	Aussperrung *f*	—	lock-out *m*	serrata *f*	cierre patronal *m*
lock-out (F)	Aussperrung *f*	lockout	—	serrata *f*	cierre patronal *m*

	D	E	F	I	Es
logement en propriété (F)	Eigentumswohnung *f*	freehold flat	—	appartamento in condominio *m*	piso en propiedad *m*
logística (Es)	Logistik *f*	logistics	logistique *f*	logistica *f*	—
logistica (I)	Logistik *f*	logistics	logistique *f*	—	logística *f*
logistics (E)	Logistik *f*	—	logistique *f*	logistica *f*	logística *f*
Logistik (D)	—	logistics	logistique *f*	logistica *f*	logística *f*
logistique (F)	Logistik *f*	logistics	—	logistica *f*	logística *f*
Logo (D)	—	logo	logotype *m*	logo *m*	logo *m*
logo (E)	Logo *n*	—	logotype *m*	logo *m*	logo *m*
logo (Es)	Logo *n*	logo	logotype *m*	logo *m*	—
logo (I)	Logo *n*	logo	logotype *m*	—	logo *m*
logotype (F)	Logo *n*	logo	—	logo *m*	logo *m*
Lohn (D)	—	wage	salaire *m*	salario *m*	salario *m*
Lohnbüro (D)	—	pay office	bureau de la paye *m*	ufficio paga *m*	departamento de nóminas *m*
Lohnerhöhung (D)	—	increase in wages	augmentation du salaire *f*	aumento salariale *m*	aumento de salario *m*
Lohnforderung (D)	—	wage claim	revendication de salaire *f*	rivendicazione salariale *f*	reivindicación salarial *f*
lohnintensiv (D)	—	wage-intensive	déterminé par le facteur salaire	ad alta incidenza salariale	con gran intensidad de costos salariales
Lohnkosten (D)	—	cost of wages	coût du travail *m*	costo del lavoro *m*	coste de salarios *m*
Lohnlag (D)	—	wage lag	décalage entre les prix et les salaires *m*	lag salariale *m*	diferencial entre precios y salarios *m*
Lohnnebenkosten (D)	—	ancillary wage costs	charges salariales annexes *f pl*	costi complementari del lavoro *m pl*	cargas salariales accesorias *f pl*
Lohnpfändung (D)	—	attachment of earnings	saisie-arrêt sur le salaire *f*	pignoramento del salario *m*	embargo de salario *m*
Lohnpolitik (D)	—	wage policy	politique des salaires *f*	politica salariale *f*	política salarial *f*
Lohn-Preis-Spirale (D)	—	wage-price spiral	course des prix et des salaires *f*	spirale prezzi-salari *f*	espiral salarios-precios *m*
Lohnsteuer (D)	—	wage tax	impôt sur les traitements et salaires *m*	imposta sui salari *f*	impuesto sobre los rendimientos del trabajo personal *f*
Lohnstopp (D)	—	wage freeze	blocage des salaires *m*	blocco dei salari *m*	congelación salarial *f*
Lohnvereinbarung (D)	—	wage agreement	accord de salaires *m*	accordo salariale *m*	pacto salarial *m*
loi (F)	Gesetz *n*	law	—	legge *f*	ley *f*
loi sur le délai-congé en matière de licenciement (F)	Kündigungsschutzgesetz *n*	Termination of Employment Act	—	legge sulla tutela contro il licenziamento *f*	ley de protección contra el despido *f*
loi sur les cartels (F)	Kartellgesetz *n*	Cartel Law	—	legge sui cartelli *f*	ley relativa a los cártels *f*
loi sur les sociétés anonymes (F)	Aktienrecht *n*	company law	—	diritto azionario *m*	derecho de sociedades anónimas *m*
loi sur les sociétés par actions (F)	Aktiengesetz *n*	Companies Act	—	legge sulle società per azioni *f*	ley sobre sociedades anónimas *f*
loi sur l'informatique (F)	Datenschutzgesetz *n*	Data Protection Act	—	legge sulla tutela dei dati *f*	ley de protección de datos *f*
Lombardgeschäft (D)	—	lending on securities	prêt sur gage *m*	anticipazioni *f pl*	operaciones de pignoración *f pl*
Lombardkredit (D)	—	credit against securities	crédit garanti par nantissement *m*	credito su pegno *m*	crédito pignoraticio *m*
Lombardpolitik (D)	—	policy of advances on securities	politique des prêts sur gages *f*	politica delle anticipazioni *f*	política de pignoración *f*
Lombardsatz (D)	—	rate for advances on securities	taux d'intérêt de l'argent prêté sur gage *m*	tasso sulle anticipazioni *m*	tipo de pignoración *m*
long distance traffic (E)	Fernverkehr *m*	—	trafic sur longues distances *m*	traffico a grande distanza *m*	transporte a distancia *m*
long-term (E)	langfristig	—	à long terme	a lunga scadenza	a largo plazo
long-term capital (E)	langfristiges Kapital *n*	—	capital à long terme *m*	capitale a lungo termine *m*	capital a largo plazo *m*

	D	E	F	I	Es
long-term credit (E)	langfristiger Kredit *m*	—	crédit à long terme *m*	credito a lunga scadenza *m*	crédito a largo plazo *m*
lorryload (E)	Wagenladung *f*	—	charge de voiture *f*	carico di autocarro *m*	carga de un vagón *f*
Löschgebühren (D)	—	discharging expenses	droit de déchargement *m*	spese di scarico *f pl*	gastos de descarga *m pl*
losing business (E)	Verlustgeschäft *n*	—	affaire déficitaire *f*	affare in perdita *m*	venta con pérdida *f*
loss (E)	Verlust *m*	—	perte *f*	perdita *f*	pérdida *f*
loss in exchange (E)	Kursverlust *m*	—	perte sur les cours *f*	perdita sul cambio *f*	pérdida en bolsa *f*
loss of production (E)	Produktionsausfall *m*	—	perte dans la production *f*	perdita di produzione *f*	pérdida de producción *f*
loss of value (E)	Wertverfall *m*	—	dévalorisation *f*	deprezzamento *m*	depreciación *f*
loss prevention (E)	Schadenverhütung *f*	—	mesure préventive contre les sinistres *f*	prevenzione danni *f*	prevención de siniestros *f*
lost shipment (E)	verlorengegangene Sendung *f*	—	envoi perdu *m*	spedizione andata persa *f*	envío perdido *m*
lot (E)	Posten *m*	—	lot de merchandises *m*	partita *f*	partida *f*
lot restant (F)	Restposten *m*	remnants	—	rimanenze *f pl*	partida restante *f*
lotería (Es)	Lotterie *f*	lottery	loterie *f*	lotteria *f*	—
loterie (F)	Lotterie *f*	lottery	—	lotteria *f*	lotería *f*
lotta contro i rumori (I)	Lärmbekämpfung *f*	noise abatement	lutte contre le bruit *f*	—	lucha contra el ruido *f*
lotteria (I)	Lotterie *f*	lottery	loterie *f*	—	lotería *f*
Lotterie (D)	—	lottery	loterie *f*	lotteria *f*	lotería *f*
lottery (E)	Lotterie *f*	—	loterie *f*	lotteria *f*	lotería *f*
lubricants (E)	Schmierstoffe *pl*	—	lubrifiants *m pl*	lubrificanti *m pl*	lubrificantes *m pl*
lubrifiants (F)	Schmierstoffe *pl*	lubricants	—	lubrificanti *m pl*	lubrificantes *m pl*
lubrificantes (Es)	Schmierstoffe *pl*	lubricants	lubrifiants *m pl*	lubrificanti *m pl*	—
lubrificanti (I)	Schmierstoffe *pl*	lubricants	lubrifiants *m pl*	—	lubrificantes *m pl*
lucha contra el ruido (Es)	Lärmbekämpfung *f*	noise abatement	lutte contre le bruit *f*	lotta contro i rumori *f*	—
Luftfracht (D)	—	air freight	fret aérien *m*	nolo aereo *m*	flete aéreo *m*
Luftfrachtbrief (D)	—	air waybill	lettre de transport aérien *f*	lettera di trasporto aereo *f*	transporte aéreo *m*
Luftfrachtführer (D)	—	air carrier	voiturier aérien *m*	vettore aereo *m*	transportista *m*
Luftfrachtverkehr (D)	—	air freight traffic	transport aérien des marchandises *m*	traffico aereo commerciale *m*	tráfico de flete aéreo *m*
Luftpost (D)	—	air mail	par avion	posta aerea *f*	correo aéreo *m*
Luftweg (D)	—	air route	voie aérienne *f*	via aerea *f*	vía aérea *f*
lugar de destino (Es)	Bestimmungsort *m*	place of destination	lieu de destination *m*	luogo di destinazione *m*	—
lugar de la cita (Es)	Treffpunkt *m*	meeting place	rendez-vous *m*	punto d'incontro *m*	—
lugar de nacimiento (Es)	Geburtsort *m*	place of birth	lieu de naissance *m*	luogo di nascita *m*	—
lujo (Es)	Luxus *m*	luxury	luxe *m*	lusso *m*	—
lump sum settlement (E)	Kapitalabfindung *f*	—	indemnité en capital *f*	indennità in capitale *f*	indemnización en capital *f*
luogo di destinazione (I)	Bestimmungsort *m*	place of destination	lieu de destination *m*	—	lugar de de destino *m*
luogo di nascita (I)	Geburtsort *m*	place of birth	lieu de naissance *m*	—	lugar de nacimiento *m*
lusso (I)	Luxus *m*	luxury	luxe *m*	—	lujo *m*
lutte contre le bruit (F)	Lärmbekämpfung *f*	noise abatement	—	lotta contro i rumori *f*	lucha contra el ruido *f*
luxe (F)	Luxus *m*	luxury	—	lusso *m*	lujo *m*
luxury (E)	Luxus *m*	—	luxe *m*	lusso *m*	lujo *m*
luxury goods (E)	Luxusgüter *pl*	—	produits de luxe *m pl*	beni di lusso *m pl*	bienes de lujo *m pl*
luxury tax (E)	Luxussteuer *f*	—	taxe de luxe *f*	imposta sui consumi di lusso *f*	impuesto de lujo *m*
Luxus (D)	—	luxury	luxe *m*	lusso *m*	lujo *m*
Luxusgüter (D)	—	luxury goods	produits de luxe *m pl*	beni di lusso *m pl*	bienes de lujo *m pl*
Luxussteuer (D)	—	luxury tax	taxe de luxe *f*	imposta sui consumi di lusso *f*	impuesto de lujo *m*

	D	E	F	I	Es
macchina (I)	Maschine *f*	machine	machine *f*	—	máquina *f*
machine (E)	Maschine *f*	—	machine *f*	macchina *f*	máquina *f*
machine (F)	Maschine *f*	machine	—	macchina *f*	máquina *f*
machine insurance (E)	Maschinen-versicherung *f*	—	assurance des machines *f*	assicurazione delle macchine *f*	seguro de maquinaria *m*
macroeconomía (Es)	Makroökonomie *f*	macroeconomics	macroéconomie *f*	macroeconomia *m*	—
macroeconomia (I)	Makroökonomie *f*	macroeconomics	macroéconomie *f*	—	macroeconomía *f*
macroeconomics (E)	Makroökonomie *f*	—	macroéconomie *f*	macroeconomia *m*	macroeconomía *f*
macroéconomie (F)	Makroökonomie *f*	macroeconomics	—	macroeconomia *m*	macroeconomía *f*
maestranza (I)	Belegschaft *f*	staff	personnel *m*	—	plantilla *f*
magasin (F)	Lager *n*	warehouse	—	magazzino *m*	almacén *m*
magasins de test (F)	Testläden *pl*	test shops	—	negozi pilota *m pl*	tiendas piloto *f pl*
magazzinaggio[1] (I)	Lagerhaltung *f*	stockkeeping	entreposage *m*	—	almacenaje *m*
magazzinaggio[2] (I)	Lagerung *f*	storage	stockage *m*	—	almacenaje *m*
magazzino[1] (I)	Lagerraum *m*	storage space	halle de dépôt *f*	—	almacén *m*
magazzino[2] (I)	Lager *n*	warehouse	magasin *m*	—	almacén *m*
magazzino[3] (I)	Warenlager *n*	stock room	stock de marchandises *m*	—	depósito de mercancías *m*
maggioranza (I)	Majorität *f*	majority	majorité *f*	—	mayoría *f*
maggioranza dei voti (I)	Stimmenmehrheit *f*	majority of votes	majorité des voix *f*	—	mayoría de votos *f*
maggioranza delle azioni (I)	Aktienmehrheit *f*	majority of shares	majorité d'actions *f*	—	mayoría de acciones *f*
maggiorazione dell'utile (I)	Gewinnaufschlag *m*	profit mark-up	majoration de bénéfice *f*	—	margen de benificio *f*
magnitud (Es)	Bestandsgröße *f*	stock variable	stock variable *m*	entità dell'inventario *f*	—
Mahnbrief (D)	—	reminder	lettre d'avertissement *f*	lettera di sollecito *f*	carta (ad)monitoria *f*
Mahnung (D)	—	demand for payment	mise en demeure *f*	sollecito *m*	(ad)monición *f*
mail box (E)	Briefkasten *m*	—	boîte aux lettres *f*	cassetta postale *f*	buzón *m*
mail order business (E)	Versandhandel *m*	—	commerce de vente au détail par correspondance *m*	vendita per corrispondenza *f*	venta por correspondencia *f*
main memory (E)	Hauptspeicher *m*	—	mémoire principale *f*	memoria principale *f*	memoria principal *f*
maintained (E)	behauptet	—	affirmé	affermato	sostenido
maintaining the real value (E)	Substanzerhaltung *f*	—	maintien de la substance *m*	mantenimento della sostanza *m*	conservación de la sustancia *f*
maintenance of secrecy (E)	Geheimhaltung *f*	—	conservation du secret *f*	segretezza *f*	mantenimiento del secreto *m*
maintien de la substance (F)	Substanzerhaltung *f*	maintaining the real value	—	mantenimento della sostanza *m*	conservación de la sustancia *f*
maison concurrente (F)	Konkurrenzfirma *f*	competing firm	—	ditta concorrente *f*	empresa competidora *f*
maison d'édition (F)	Verlag *m*	publishing house	—	casa editrice *f*	editorial *f*
maison mère[1] (F)	Mutterhaus *n*	mother house	—	casa madre *f*	casa matriz *f*
maison mère[2] (F)	Stammhaus *n*	parent company	—	casa madre *f*	casa matriz *f*
majoration de bénéfice (F)	Gewinnaufschlag *m*	profit mark-up	—	maggiorazione dell'utile *f*	margen de benificio *f*
Majorität (D)	—	majority	majorité *f*	maggioranza *f*	mayoría *f*
majorité (F)	Majorität *f*	majority	—	maggioranza *f*	mayoría *f*
majorité d'actions (F)	Aktienmehrheit *f*	majority of shares	—	maggioranza delle azioni *f*	mayoría de acciones *f*
majorité des voix (F)	Stimmenmehrheit *f*	majority of votes	—	maggioranza dei voti *f*	mayoría de votos *f*
majority (E)	Majorität *f*	—	majorité *f*	maggioranza *f*	mayoría *f*
majority of shares (E)	Aktienmehrheit *f*	—	majorité d'actions *f*	maggioranza delle azioni *f*	mayoría de acciones *f*
majority of votes (E)	Stimmenmehrheit *f*	—	majorité des voix *f*	maggioranza dei voti *f*	mayoría de votos *f*
majority-ownership (E)	Mehrheitsbesitz *m*	—	possession majoritaire *f*	possesso maggioritario *m*	mayoría *f*
making out an invoice (E)	Fakturierung *f*	—	facturation *f*	fatturazione *f*	facturación *f*

	D	E	F	I	Es
Makler (D)	—	broker	courtier *m*	mediatore *m*	corredor *m*
Makroökonomie (D)	—	macroeconomics	macroéconomie *f*	macroeconomia *m*	macroeconomía *f*
mala calidad (Es)	schlechte Qualität *f*	poor quality	mauvaise qualité *f*	qualità scadente *f*	—
malnutrition (E)	Unterernährung *f*	—	sous-alimentation *f*	denutrizione *f*	subalimentación *f*
malversación (Es)	Veruntreuung *f*	misappropriation	détournement *m*	abuso di fiducia *m*	—
Management (D)	—	management	management *m*	management *m*	alta dirección *f*
management[1] (E)	Leitung *f*	—	direction *f*	direzione *f*	dirección *f*
management[2] (E)	Führung *f*	—	direction *f*	gestione *f*	gestión *f*
management[3] (E)	Geschäftsleitung *f*	—	direction commerciale *f*	direzione *f*	dirección *f*
management[4] (E)	Management *n*	—	management *m*	management *m*	alta dirección *f*
management[5] (E)	Geschäftsführung *f*	—	gestion *f*	amministrazione *f*	gestión *f*
management (F)	Management *n*	management	—	management *m*	alta dirección *f*
management (I)	Management *n*	management	management *m*	—	alta dirección *f*
management di progetto (I)	Projekt-Management *n*	project management	gestion d'un projet *f*	—	administración del proyecto *f*
management games (E)	Planspiel *n*	—	jeu d'entreprise *m*	gioco di strategia imprenditoriale *m*	juego de ensayo *m*
Manager (D)	—	manager	manager *m*	manager *m*	alto directivo *m*
manager[1] (E)	Geschäftsführer *m*	—	gérant d'une affaire *m*	amministratore *m*	gerente *m*
manager[2] (E)	Manager *m*	—	manager *m*	manager *m*	alto directivo *m*
manager (F)	Manager *m*	manager	—	manager *m*	alto directivo *m*
manager (I)	Manager *m*	manager	manager *m*	—	alto directivo *m*
manager of shipping department (E)	Versandleiter *m*	—	chef du service des expéditions *m*	capo reparto spedizioni *m*	jefe del departamento de expedición *m*
mancanza di personale (I)	Personalmangel *m*	shortage of staff	manque de personnel *m*	—	falta der personal *f*
mandamiento de pago (Es)	Zahlungsbefehl *m*	order for payment	ordre de payement *m*	ingiunzione di pagamento *f*	—
mandante (Es)	Auftraggeber *m*	client	commettant *m*	committente *m*	—
mandante (I)	Vollmachtgeber *m*	grantor of a power of attorney	auteur de la procuration *m*	—	poderdante *m*
mandare allo scoperto (I)	überziehen	overdraw	faire un prélèvement à découvert	—	sobrepasar
mandat (F)	Anweisung *f*	transfer	—	ordine di pagamento *m*	transferencia *f*
mandatario commerciale (I)	Handlungsbevoll-mächtigter *m*	commercial agent	personne ayant le pouvoir commercial *f*	—	apoderado especial *m*
mandat-carte (F)	Zahlkarte *f*	money order	—	modulo di versamento *m*	carta de pago *f*
mandat de payement (F)	Zahlungsanweisung *f*	order to pay	—	ordine di pagamento *m*	orden de pago *f*
mandat-poste (F)	Postanweisung *f*	postal money order	—	vaglia postale *m*	vale postal *m*
mandat télégraphique (F)	telegrafische Anweisung *f*	telegraphic payment order	—	vaglia telegrafico *m*	orden telegráfica *f*
Mangel (D)	—	defect	défaut *m*	vizio *m*	defecto *m*/vicio *m*
Mängelanzeige (D)	—	notice of defect	notification d'un vice *f*	denuncia dei vizi	aviso de vicios *m*
mangelfrei (D)	—	free of defects	sans défaut	esente da vizi	sin vicios
manifattura (I)	Manufaktur *f*	manufactory	manufacture *f*	—	manufactura *f*
manifesto (I)	Plakat *n*	poster	affiche *f*	—	cartel *m*
manifesto promozionale (I)	Aktionsplakat *n*	advertising bill	affiche d'action *f*	—	cartel de acción *m*
manner of delivery (E)	Versandform *f*	—	forme d'expédition *f*	tipo di spedizione *m*	forma de envío *f*
Mannschaft (D)	—	team/crew	équipe *f*/équipage *m*	équipe *f*/ equipaggio *m*	equipo *m*/tripulación *f*
man of straw (E)	Strohmann *m*	—	prête-nom *m*	prestanome *m*	testaferro *m*
mano pubblica (I)	öffentliche Hand *f*	public authorities	secteur public *m*	—	sector público *m*
manque de personnel (F)	Personalmangel *m*	shortage of staff	—	mancanza di personale *f*	falta de personal *f*
manque de trésorerie (F)	Illiquidität *f*	illiquidity	—	illiquidità *f*	falta de liquidez *f*

	D	E	F	I	Es
mantenimento della sostanza (I)	Substanzerhaltung *f*	maintaining the real value	maintien de la substance *m*	—	conservación de la sustancia *f*
mantenimiento del secreto (Es)	Geheimhaltung *f*	maintenance of secrecy	conservation du secret *f*	segretezza *f*	—
manual (E)	Handbuch *n*	—	manuel *m*	manuale *m*	manual *m*
manual (Es)	Handbuch *n*	manual	manuel *m*	manuale *m*	—
manuale (I)	Handbuch *n*	manual	manuel *m*	—	manual *m*
manuel (F)	Handbuch *n*	manual	—	manuale *m*	manual *m*
manufactory (E)	Manufaktur *f*	—	manufacture *f*	manifattura *f*	manufactura *f*
manufactura (Es)	Manufaktur *f*	manufactory	manufacture *f*	manifattura *f*	—
manufacture (F)	Manufaktur *f*	manufactory	—	manifattura *f*	manufactura *f*
manufactured quantity (E)	Fertigungsmenge *f*	—	quantité fabriquée *f*	quantitativo di produzione *m*	cantidad producida *f*
manufactured to measure (E)	maßgefertigt	—	travaillé sur mesure	prodotto su misura	hecho a medida
manufacturer (E)	Erzeuger *m*	—	producteur *m*	produttore *m*	productor *m*
manufacture to customer's specifications (E)	Sonderanfertigung *f*	—	fabrication spéciale *f*	produzione fuori serie *f*	fabricación especial *f*
manufacturing industry (E)	verarbeitende Industrie *f*	—	industrie transformatrice *f*	industria di trasformazione *f*	industria transformadora *f*
Manufaktur (D)	—	manufactory	manufacture *f*	manifattura *f*	manufactura *f*
maquette (F)	Layout *n*	layout	—	layout *m*	layout *m*
máquina (Es)	Maschine *f*	machine	machine *f*	macchina *f*	—
máquina de dictar (Es)	Diktiergerät *n*	dictaphone	appareil à dicter *m*	dittafono *m*	—
marca (Es)	Warenzeichen *n*	trade mark	marque *f*	marchio *m*	—
marca (I)	Marke *f*	mark	marque *f*	—	característica *f*
marchandise (F)	Ware *f*	goods	—	merce *f*	mercancía *f*
marchandise à transporter (F)	Frachtgut *n*	cargo	—	merce di trasporto *f*	mercancías en pequeña velocidad *f pl*
marchandise en grande vitesse (F)	Eilgut *n*	goods sent by express	—	merce a grande velocità *f*	mercancía en gran velocidad *f*
marchandises en commission (F)	Kommissionsgüter *pl*	goods for sale on commission	—	beni in conto deposito *m pl*	mercancías en comisión *f pl*
marchandises en vrac (F)	Massengüter *pl*	bulk goods	—	beni di massa *m pl*	productos a granel *m pl*
marché (F)	Markt *m*	market	—	mercato *m*	mercado *m*
marché agricole (F)	Agrarmarkt *m*	agricultural market	—	mercato agrario *m*	mercado agrícola *m*
marché avant le marché officiel (F)	Vorbörse *f*	before hours dealing	—	mercato preborsistico *m*	operaciones antes de la apertura de la bolsa *f pl*
marché commun (F)	gemeinsamer Markt *m*	common market	—	mercato comune *m*	mercado común *m*
marché d'acheteurs (F)	Käufermarkt *m*	buyer's market	—	mercato favorevole all'acquirente *m*	mercado favorable al comprador *m*
marché de l'ór (F)	Goldmarkt *m*	gold market	—	mercato dell'oro *m*	mercado del oro *m*
marché des capitaux (F)	Kapitalmarkt *m*	capital market	—	mercato finanziario *m*	mercado financiero *m*
marché des changes[1] (F)	Devisenhandel *m*	foreign exchange dealings	—	commercio delle divise *m*	operaciones de divisas *f pl*
marché des changes[2] (F)	Devisenmarkt *m*	foreign exchange market	—	mercato valutario *m*	mercado de divisas *m*
marché des consommateurs (F)	Verbrauchermarkt *m*	consumer market	—	ipermercato *m*	mercado favorable al consumidor *m*
marché des effets publics (F)	Rentenmarkt *m*	bond market	—	mercato dei titoli a reddito fisso *m*	mercado de títulos de renta fija *m*
marché de test (F)	Testmarkt *m*	test market	—	mercato pilota *m*	mercado piloto *m*
marché de vendeurs (F)	Verkäufermarkt *m*	seller's market	—	mercato favorevole ai venditori *m*	mercado favorable al vendedor *m*
marché d'exportation (F)	Exportmarkt *m*	export market	—	mercato delle esportazioni *m*	mercado de exportación *m*
marché du travail (F)	Arbeitsmarkt *m*	labour market	—	mercato del lavoro *m*	mercado laboral *m*
marché en disponible (F)	Spotmarkt *m*	spot market	—	mercato spot *m*	mercado de operaciones al contado y de entrega inmediata *m*

	D	E	F	I	Es
marché gris (F)	Grauer Markt *m*	grey market	—	mercato grigio *m*	mercado gris *m*
Marché Intérieur de la Communauté Européenne (F)	EG-Binnenmarkt *m*	Internal Market of the European Community	—	mercato unico *m*	Mercado Unico *m*
marché monétaire (F)	Geldmarkt *m*	money market	—	mercato monetario *m*	mercado monetario *m*
marché national (F)	Binnenmarkt *m*	home market	—	mercato nazionale *m*	mercado interior *m*
marché noir (F)	Schwarzmarkt *m*	black market	—	mercato nero *m*	mercado negro *m*
marchés des matières premières (F)	Rohstoffmarkt *m*	commodity market	—	mercato delle materie prime *m*	mercado de materias primas *m*
marchés extérieurs (F)	Auslandsmärkte *pl*	foreign markets	—	mercati esteri *m pl*	mercado exterior *m*
marchio[1] (I)	Markenzeichen *n*	trademark	marque déposée *f*	—	emblema comercial *m*/marca registrada *f*
marchio[2] (I)	Warenzeichen *n*	trade mark	marque *f*	—	marca *f*
Marge (D)	—	margin	marge *f*	margine *m*	margen *m*
marge[1] (F)	Marge *f*	margin	—	margine *m*	margen *m*
marge[2] (F)	Bandbreite *f*	margin	—	margine *m*	margen de fluctuación *f*
marge[3] (F)	Spanne *f*	margin	—	margine *m*	margen *f*
marge[4] (F)	Spielraum *m*	margin	—	tolleranza *f*	margen *f*
marge bénéficiaire (F)	Gewinnmarge *f*	profit margin	—	margine dell'utile *m*	margen de beneficios *f*
marge de bénéfice (F)	Gewinnspanne *f*	margin of profit	—	margine dell'utile *m*	margen de beneficios *f*
marge de crédit accordé (F)	Kreditrahmen *m*	credit margin	—	plafond di credito *m*	margen de crédito *m*
marge de détail (F)	Einzelhandels-spanne *f*	retail price margin	—	margine del commercio al dettaglio *m*	margen del comercio al por menor *m*
marge de la fluctuation (F)	Schwankungsbreite *f*	margin of fluctuation	—	margine d'oscillazione *m*	margen de fluctuación *f*
marge de sécurité (F)	Sicherheitsmarge *f*	margin	—	margine di sicurezza *m*	margen de seguridad *f*
marge entre les taux d'intérêt créditeur et débiteur (F)	Zinsmarge *f*	interest margin	—	margine degli interessi *m*	margen de interés *m*
margen[1] (Es)	Spielraum *m*	margin	marge *f*	tolleranza *f*	—
margen[2] (Es)	Marge *f*	margin	marge *f*	margine *m*	—
margen[3] (Es)	Spanne *f*	margin	marge *f*	margine *m*	—
margen comercial (Es)	Handelsspanne *f*	trading margin	bénéfice brut *m*	margine commerciale *m*	—
margen de beneficios[1] (Es)	Gewinnmarge *f*	profit margin	marge bénéficiaire *f*	margine dell'utile *m*	—
margen de beneficios[2] (Es)	Gewinnspanne *f*	margin of profit	marge de bénéfice *f*	margine dell'utile *m*	—
margen de benificio (Es)	Gewinnaufschlag *m*	profit mark-up	majoration de bénéfice *f*	maggiorazione dell'utile *f*	—
margen de crédito (Es)	Kreditrahmen *m*	credit margin	marge de crédit accordé *f*	plafond di credito *m*	—
margen de fluctuación[1] (Es)	Bandbreite *f*	margin	marge *f*	margine *m*	—
margen de fluctuación[2] (Es)	Schwankungsbreite *f*	margin of fluctuation	marge de la fluctuation *f*	margine d'oscillazione *m*	—
margen de interés (Es)	Zinsmarge *f*	interest margin	marge entre les taux d'intérêt créditeur et débiteur *f*	margine degli interessi *m*	—
margen del comercio al por menor (Es)	Einzelhandels-spanne *f*	retail price margin	marge de détail *f*	margine del commercio al dettaglio *m*	—
margen de seguridad (Es)	Sicherheitsmarge *f*	margin	marge de sécurité *f*	margine di sicurezza *m*	—
margin[1] (E)	Marge *f*	—	marge *f*	margine *m*	margen *m*
margin[2] (E)	Spielraum *m*	—	marge *f*	tolleranza *f*	margen *m*
margin[3] (E)	Spanne *f*	—	marge *f*	margine *m*	margen *m*
margin[4] (E)	Sicherheitsmarge *f*	—	marge de sécurité *f*	margine di sicurezza *m*	margen de seguridad *f*

	D	E	F	I	Es
margin[5] (E)	Bandbreite *f*	—	marge *f*	margine *m*	margen de fluctuación *f*
marginal costing (E)	Grenzkosten-rechnung *f*	—	détermination du coût marginal *f*	conto dei costi limite *m*	cálculo de los costes marginales *m*
marginal value (E)	Marginalwert *m*	—	valeur marginale *f*	valore marginale *m*	valor marginal *m*
Marginalwert (D)	—	marginal value	valeur marginale *f*	valore marginale *m*	valor marginal *m*
margin between interest rates (E)	Zinsgefälle *n*	—	disparité des niveaux d'intérêts *f*	differenza dei tassi d'interesse *f*	diferencia entre los tipos de interés *f*
margine[1] (I)	Spanne *f*	margin	marge *f*	—	margen *f*
margine[2] (I)	Bandbreite *f*	within a limit of	marge *f*	—	margen de fluctuación *f*
margine[3] (I)	Marge *f*	margin	marge *f*	—	margen f *m*
margine commerciale (I)	Handelsspanne *f*	trading margin	bénéfice brut *m*	—	margen comercial *f*
margine degli interessi (I)	Zinsmarge *f*	interest margin	marge entre les taux d'intérêt créditeur et débiteur *f*	—	margen de interés *m*
margine del commercio al dettaglio (I)	Einzelhandels-spanne *f*	retail price margin	marge de détail *f*	—	margen del comercio al por menor *m*
margine dell'utile[1] (I)	Gewinnmarge *f*	profit margin	marge bénéficiaire *f*	—	margen de beneficios *f*
margine dell'utile[2] (I)	Gewinnspanne *f*	margin of profit	marge de bénéfice *f*	—	margen de beneficios *f*
margine di sicurezza (I)	Sicherheitsmarge *f*	margin	marge de sécurité *f*	—	margen de seguridad *f*
margine d'oscillazione (I)	Schwankungsbreite *f*	margin of fluctuation	marge de la fluctuation *f*	—	margen de fluctuación *f*
margin of fluctuation (E)	Schwankungsbreite *f*	—	marge de la fluctuation *f*	margine d'oscillazione *m*	margen de fluctuación *f*
margin of profit (E)	Gewinnspanne *f*	—	marge de bénéfice *f*	margine dell'utile *m*	margen de beneficios *f*
mark (E)	Marke *f*	—	marque *f*	marca *f*	característica *f*
Marke (D)	—	mark	marque *f*	marca *f*	característica *f*
Markenartikel (D)	—	brandname article	produit de marque *m*	articolo di marca *m*	artículo de marca *m*
Markenzeichen (D)	—	trademark	marque deposée *f*	marchio *m*	emblema comercial *m*/ marca registrada *f*
market[1] (E)	vermarkten	—	commercialiser	lanciare sul mercato	comercializar
market[2] (E)	Markt *m*	—	marché *m*	mercato *m*	mercado *m*
marketable (E)	marktfähig	—	vendable	smerciabile	comerciable
market analysis (E)	Marktanalyse *f*	—	analyse du marché *f*	analisi di mercato *f*	análisis de mercado *m*
market day (E)	Börsentag *m*	—	jour de bourse *m*	giorno di borsa *m*	sesión bursátil *f*
market details (E)	Marktdaten *pl*	—	données sur le marché *f pl*	dati di mercato *m pl*	datos del mercado *m pl*
market economy (E)	Marktwirtschaft *f*	—	économie de marché *f*	economia di mercato *f*	economía de mercado *f*
market forces (E)	Marktkräfte *pl*	—	forces du marché	forze di mercato *f pl*	fuerzas del mercado *f pl*
market gap (E)	Marktlücke *f*	—	créneau du marché *m*	lacuna di mercato *f*	sector del mercado no abarcado por la oferta *m*
Marketing (D)	—	marketing	marketing *m*	marketing *m*	organización de ventas *f*
marketing[1] (E)	Marketing *n*	—	marketing *m*	marketing *m*	organización de ventas *f*
marketing[2] (E)	Absatzwirtschaft *f*	—	commercialisation *f*	marketing *m*	economía de distribución *f*
marketing (F)	Marketing *n*	marketing	—	marketing *m*	organización de ventas *f*
marketing[1] (I)	Marketing *n*	marketing	marketing *m*	—	organización de ventas *f*
marketing[2] (I)	Absatzwirtschaft *f*	marketing	commercialisation *f*	—	economía de distribución *f*
Marketingabteilung (D)	—	marketing department	bureau de marketing *m*	reparto marketing *m*	departamento de mercadeo *m*

	D	E	F	I	Es
Marketingberater (D)	—	marketing consultant	conseiller de marketing *m*	consulente di marketing *m*	asesor de marketing *m*
marketing consultant (E)	Marketingberater *m*	—	conseiller de marketing *m*	consulente di marketing *m*	asesor de marketing *m*
marketing department (E)	Marketingabteilung *f*	—	bureau de marketing *m*	reparto marketing *m*	departamento de mercadeo *m*
marketing in prima persona (I)	Direct-Marketing *n*	direct marketing	stratégie des ventes directes *f*	—	comercialización directa *f*
Marketing-Mix (D)	—	mixture of marketing strategies	mélange de marketing *f*	marketing-mix *m*	mezcla de marketing *f*
marketing-mix (I)	Marketing-Mix *m*	mixture of marketing strategies	mélange de marketing *f*	—	mezcla de marketing *f*
marketing-oriented (E)	Marketing-orientiert	—	orienté vers le marketing	orientato al marketing	orientado hacia el marketing
Marketing-orientiert (D)	—	marketing-oriented	orienté vers le marketing	orientato al marketing	orientado hacia el marketing
marketing planning (E)	Marketingplanung *f*	—	planning du marketing *m*	programmazione del marketing *f*	planificación de mercadeo *m*
Marketingplanung (D)	—	marketing planning	planning du marketing *m*	programmazione del marketing *f*	planificación de mercadeo *m*
marketing policy (E)	Absatzpolitik *f*	—	politique de vente *f*	politica di vendita *f*	política de ventas *f*
market organization (E)	Marktordnung *f*	—	organisation du marché *f*	ordinamento del mercato *m*	organización del mercado *f*
market position (E)	Marktposition *f*	—	position sur le marché *f*	posizione di mercato *f*	posición en el mercado *f*
market research (E)	Marktforschung *f*	—	recherche du marché *f*	ricerca di mercato *f*	estudio del mercado *m*
market research institute (E)	Marktforschungs-institut *n*	—	institut d'études de marché *m*	istituto della ricerca di mercato *m*	instituto de investiga-ción del mercado *m*
market share (E)	Marktanteil *m*	—	participation au marché *f*	quota di mercato *f*	cuota del mercado *f*
market situation (E)	Marktsituation *f*	—	situation du marché *f*	situazione di mercato *f*	estado del mercado *m*
market survey (E)	Marktuntersuchung *f*	—	étude du marché *f*	analisi di mercato *f*	estudio del mercado *m*
market test (E)	Markttest *m*	—	test du marché *m*	test di mercato *m*	examinación del mercado *f*
market transparency (E)	Markttransparenz *f*	—	transparence du marché *f*	trasparenza di mercato *f*	transparencia del mercado *f*
Markt (D)	—	market	marché *m*	mercato *m*	mercado *m*
Marktanalyse (D)	—	market analysis	analyse du marché *f*	analisi di mercato *f*	análisis de mercado *m*
Marktanteil (D)	—	market share	participation au marché *f*	quota di mercato *f*	cuota del mercado *f*
Marktbeobachtung (D)	—	observation of markets	étude de marché *f*	sondaggio del mercato *m*	observación del mercado *f*
Marktdaten (D)	—	market details	données sur le marché *f pl*	dati di mercato *m pl*	datos del mercado *m pl*
Markteintritt (D)	—	entry into the market	entrée dans le marché *f*	apertura di mercato *f*	entrada en el mercado *f*
marktfähig (D)	—	marketable	vendable	smerciabile	comerciable
Marktformen (D)	—	types of markets	formes du marché *f pl*	tipi di mercato *m pl*	formas del mercado *f*
Marktforschung (D)	—	market research	recherche du marché *f*	ricerca di mercato *f*	estudio del mercado *m*
Marktforschungs-institut (D)	—	market research institute	institut d'études de marché *m*	istituto della ricerca di mercato *m*	instituto de investigación del mercado *m*
marktkonform (D)	—	in conformity with market conditions	conforme au marché	conforme al mercato	conforme al mercado
Marktkräfte (D)	—	market forces	forces du marché	forze di mercato *f pl*	fuerzas del mercado *f pl*
Marktlage (D)	—	state of the market	situation du marché *f*	situazione di mercato *f*	condiciones del mercado *f pl*
Marktlücke (D)	—	market gap	créneau du marché *m*	lacuna di mercato *f*	sector del mercado no abarcado por la oferta *m*

	D	E	F	I	Es
Marktordnung (D)	—	market organization	organisation du marché *f*	ordinamento del mercato *m*	organización del mercado *f*
Marktposition (D)	—	market position	position sur le marché *f*	posizione di mercato *f*	posición en el mercado *f*
Marktsituation (D)	—	market situation	situation du marché *f*	situazione di mercato *f*	estado del mercado *m*
Markttest (D)	—	market test	test du marché *m*	test di mercato *m*	examinación del mercado *f*
Markttransparenz (D)	—	market transparency	transparence du marché *f*	trasparenza di mercato *f*	transparencia del mercado *f*
Marktübersicht (D)	—	overall view of the market	vue d'ensemble du marché *f*	quadro del mercato *m*	panorama de mercado *m*
Marktuntersuchung (D)	—	market survey	étude du marché *f*	analisi di mercato *f*	estudio del mercado *m*
Marktwirtschaft (D)	—	market economy	économie de marché *f*	economia di mercato *f*	economía de mercado *f*
marque[1] (F)	Warenzeichen *n*	trademark	—	marchio *m*	marca *f*
marque[2] (F)	Marke *f*	mark	—	marca *f*	característica *f*
marque déposée (F)	Markenzeichen *n*	trademark	—	marchio *m*	emblema comercial *m*/ marca registrada *f*
masa de la quiebra (Es)	Konkursmasse *f*	bankrupt's estate	masse de la faillite *f*	massa fallimentare *f*	—
masa pasiva (Es)	Schuldenmasse *f*	total of indebtedness	passif *m*	massa passiva *f*	—
Maschine (D)	—	machine	machine *f*	macchina *f*	máquina *f*
maschinell (D)	—	by machine	mécanique	a macchina	a máquina
Maschinen-versicherung (D)	—	machine insurance	assurance des machines *f*	assicurazione delle macchine *f*	seguro de maquinaria *m*
Maß (D)	—	measure	mesure *f*	misura *f*	medida *f*
massa fallimentare (I)	Konkursmasse *f*	bankrupt's estate	masse de la faillite *f*	—	masa de la quiebra *f*
massa monetaria (I)	Geldmenge *f*	money supply	quantité de monnaie en circulation *f*	—	volumen monetario *m*
massa passiva (I)	Schuldenmasse *f*	total of indebtedness	passif *m*	—	masa pasiva *f*
masse active (F)	Aktiva *pl*	assets	—	attivo *m*	activo *m*
masse de la faillite (F)	Konkursmasse *f*	bankrupt's estate	—	massa fallimentare *f*	masa de la quiebra *f*
masse héréditaire (F)	Erbengemeinschaft *f*	community of heirs	—	comunità degli eredi *f*	comunidad sucesoria *f*
masse monétaire (F)	Geldvolumen *n*	volume of money	—	volume monetario *m*	volumen monetario *m*
Massenfertigung (D)	—	mass production	production en série *f*	fabbricazione di massa *f*	fabricación en masa *f*
Massengüter (D)	—	bulk goods	marchandises en vrac *f pl*	beni di massa *m pl*	productos a granel *m pl*
Massenproduktion (D)	—	mass production	production en grandes séries *f*	produzione di massa *f*	producción en masa *f*
maßgefertigt (D)	—	manufactured to measure	travaillé sur mesure	prodotto su misura	hecho a medida
massimizzazione dell'utile (I)	Gewinn-maximierung *f*	maximization of profits	maximisation du gain *f*	—	maximación de los beneficios *f*
massimo (I)	Maximum *n*	maximum	maximum *m*	—	máximo *m*
mass production[1] (E)	Massenfertigung *f*	—	production en série *f*	fabbricazione di massa *f*	fabricación en masa *f*
mass production[2] (E)	Massenproduktion *f*	—	production en grandes séries *f*	produzione di massa *f*	producción en masa *f*
Material (D)	—	material	matériel *m*	materiale *m*	material *m*
material (E)	Material *n*	—	matériel *m*	materiale *m*	material *m*
material (Es)	Material *n*	material	matériel *m*	materiale *m*	—
material assets (E)	Sachvermögen *n*	—	biens corporels *m pl*	capitale reale *m*	patrimonio real *m*
Materialaufwand (D)	—	material expenditure	dépenses en matières *f pl*	spese materiale *f pl*	coste de material *m*
material costs (E)	Materialaufwand *m*	—	dépenses en matériels *f pl*	spese materiale *f pl*	coste de material *m*
materiale (I)	Material *n*	material	matériel *m*	—	material *m*
materiale d'imballaggio (I)	Verpackungs-material *n*	packing material	matériel d'emballage *m*	—	empaque *m*
material expenditures (E)	Materialkosten *pl*	—	frais de matériel *m pl*	costi del materiale *m pl*	gastos de ma-terial *m pl*/coste de material *m*

	D	E	F	I	Es
Materialkosten (D)	—	material costs	frais de matériel *m pl*	costi del materiale *m pl*	gastos de material *m pl*/coste de material *m*
Materialkostenanteil (D)	—	share in the material costs	proportion des frais de matériel *f*	quota dei costi del materiale *f*	parte de los gastos de material *m*
materia prima (Es)	Rohstoff *m*	raw materials	matière première *f*	materia prima *f*	—
materia prima (I)	Rohstoff *m*	raw materials	matière première *f*	—	materia prima *f*
matériel (F)	Material *n*	material	—	materiale *m*	material *m*
matériel d'emballage (F)	Verpackungsmittel *n*	means of packing	—	mezzi d'imballaggio *m pl*	medios de embalaje *m pl*
matière première (F)	Rohstoff *m*	raw materials	—	materia prima *f*	materia prima *f*
mauvaise qualité (F)	schlechte Qualität *f*	poor quality	—	qualità scadente *f*	mala calidad *f*
mauvais investissement (F)	Fehlinvestition *f*	misconceived capital projects	—	investimento sbagliato *m*	inversión equivocada *f*
maximación de los beneficios (Es)	Gewinnmaximierung *f*	maximization of profits	maximisation du gain *f*	massimizzazione dell'utile *f*	—
maximisation du gain (F)	Gewinnmaximierung *f*	maximization of profits	—	massimizzazione dell'utile *f*	maximación de los beneficios *f*
maximization of profits (E)	Gewinnmaximierung *f*	—	maximisation du gain *f*	massimizzazione dell'utile *f*	maximación de los beneficios *f*
máximo (Es)	Maximum *n*	maximum	maximum *m*	massimo *m*	—
Maximum (D)	—	maximum	maximum *m*	massimo *m*	máximo *m*
maximum (E)	Maximum *n*	—	maximum *m*	massimo *m*	máximo *m*
maximum (F)	Maximum *n*	maximum	—	massimo *m*	máximo *m*
mayoría (Es)	Majorität *f*	majority	majorité *f*	maggioranza *f*	—
mayoría de acciones (Es)	Aktienmehrheit *f*	majority of shares	majorité d'actions *f*	maggioranza delle azioni *f*	—
mayoría de votos (Es)	Stimmenmehrheit *f*	majority of votes	majorité des voix *f*	maggioranza dei voti *f*	—
mayorista (Es)	Grossist *m*	wholesaler	grossiste *m*	grossista *m*	—
means (E)	Mittel *n*	—	moyen *m*	mezzo *m*	medio *m*/recurso *m*
means of payment (E)	Zahlungsmittel *n*	—	moyen de payement *m*	mezzo di pagamento *m*	medio de pago *m*
means of transport (E)	Transportmittel *n*	—	moyen de transport *m*	mezzo di trasporto *m*	medio de transporte *m*
measure (E)	Maß *n*	—	mesure *f*	misura *f*	medida *f*
measurements (E)	Meßwerte *pl*	—	valeurs mesurées *f pl*	valori misurati *m pl*	valor de medida *m*
measures to encourage exports (E)	Ausfuhrförderung *f*	—	encouragement à l'exportation *m*	promozione delle esportazioni *f*	fomento de la exportación *m*
measuring (E)	Messung *f*	—	mesurage *m*	misurazione *f*	medición *f*
mécanicien (F)	Mechaniker *m*	mechanic	—	meccanico *m*	mecánico *m*
mecánico (Es)	Mechaniker *m*	mechanic	mécanicien *m*	meccanico *m*	—
mécanique (F)	maschinell	by machine	—	a macchina	a máquina
mécanisme des prix (F)	Preismechanismus *m*	price mechanism	—	meccanismo dei prezzi *m*	mecanismo de precios *m*
mecanismo de precios (Es)	Preismechanismus *m*	price mechanism	mécanisme des prix *m*	meccanismo dei prezzi *m*	—
meccanico (I)	Mechaniker *m*	mechanic	mécanicien *m*	—	mecánico *m*
meccanismo dei prezzi (I)	Preismechanismus *m*	price mechanism	mécanisme des prix *m*	—	mecanismo de precios *m*
mechanic (E)	Mechaniker *m*	—	mécanicien *m*	meccanico *m*	mecánico *m*
Mechaniker (D)	—	mechanic	mécanicien *m*	meccanico *m*	mecánico *m*
media (I)	Durchschnitt *m*	average	moyenne *f*	—	promedio *m*
mediación (Es)	Vermittlung *f*	mediation	médiation *f*	mediazione *f*	—
mediación de créditos (Es)	Kreditvermittlung *f*	arranging for a credit	médiation du crédit *f*	intermediazione di crediti *f*	—
mediante assegno (I)	bargeldlos	non-cash	par virement	—	por transferencia
média publicitaires (F)	Werbemedien *pl*	advertising media	—	mezzi pubblicitari *m pl*	medios de publicidad *m pl*
mediation (E)	Vermittlung *f*	—	médiation *f*	mediazione *f*	mediación *f*/ conciliación *f*
médiation (F)	Vermittlung *f*	mediation	—	mediazione *f*	mediación *f*/ conciliación *f*

	D	E	F	I	Es
médiation du crédit (F)	Kreditvermittlung *f*	arranging for a credit	—	intermediazione di crediti *f*	mediación de créditos *f*
mediatore (I)	Makler *m*	broker	courtier *m*	—	corredor *m*
mediatore d'assicurazione (I)	Versicherungs-makler *m*	insurance broker	courtier en assurance *m*	—	corredor de seguros *m*
mediazione (I)	Vermittlung *f*	mediation	médiation *f*	—	mediación *f*/ conciliación *f*
medición (Es)	Messung *f*	measuring	mesurage *m*	misurazione *f*	—
medida (Es)	Maß *n*	measure	mesure *f*	misura *f*	—
medidas de infraestructura (Es)	Infrastruktur-maßnahmen *f*	infrastructural measures	mesures pour l'amélioration de l'infrastructure *f pl*	misure per l'infrastruttura *f pl*	—
medio (Es)	Mittel *n*	means	moyen *m*	mezzo *m*	—
medio de datos (Es)	Datenträger *m*	data medium	porteur des données *m*	supporto dati *m*	—
medio de pago (Es)	Zahlungsmittel *n*	means of payment	moyen de payement *m*	mezzo di pagamento *m*	—
medio de publicidad (Es)	Werbeträger *m*	advertising medium	support publicitaire *m*	veicolo pubblicitario *m*	—
medio de transporte (Es)	Transportmittel *n*	means of transport	moyen de transport *m*	mezzo di trasporto *m*	—
medio de venta (Es)	Absatzweg *m*	channel of distribution	canal de distribution *m*	via della distribuzione *f*	—
medio legal de pago (Es)	gesetzliches Zahlungsmittel *n*	legal tender	monnaie légale *f*	mezzo di pagamento legale *m*	—
medio publicitario (Es)	Werbemittel *n*	advertising aids	moyen publicitaire *m*	mezzo pubblicitario *m*	—
medios de publicidad (Es)	Werbemedien *pl*	advertising media	média publicitaires *m pl*	mezzi pubblicitari *m pl*	—
medios publicitarios directos (Es)	Direktwerbemittel *n*	direct means of advertising	moyens publicitaires directs *m pl*	mezzo pubblicitario diretto *m*	—
medium-term (E)	mittelfristig	—	à moyen terme	a media scadenza	a medio plazo
medium-term credit (E)	mittelfristiger Kredit *m*	—	crédit à moyen terme *m*	credito a media scadenza *m*	crédito a medio plazo *m*
meeting (E)	Tagung *f*	—	congrès *m*	convegno *m*	reunión *f*
meeting date (E)	Besprechungs-termin *m*	—	date de la conférence *f*	termine del colloquio *m*	fecha de conferencia *f*
meeting of shareholders (E)	Gesellschafter-versammlung *f*	—	réunion des associés *f*	assemblea dei soci *f*	junta social *f*
meeting place (E)	Treffpunkt *m*	—	rendez-vous *m*	punto d'incontro *m*	lugar de la cita *m*
Mehrarbeit (D)	—	additional work	travail supplémentaire *m*	lavoro supplementare *m*	trabajo extraordinario *m*
Mehrbelastung (D)	—	additional burden	surcharge *f*	onere supplementare *m*	carga suplementaria *f*
Mehrlieferung (D)	—	additional delivery	livraison supplémentaire *f*	fornitura supplementare *f*	exceso *m*
Mehrwert (D)	—	value added	valeur ajoutée *f*	valore aggiunto *m*	plusvalía *f*
Mehrwertsteuer (D)	—	value-added tax	taxe à la valeur ajoutée *f*	imposta sul valore aggiunto *f*	impuesto sobre el valor añadido *m*
Meile (D)	—	mile	mille *m*	miglio *m*	milla *f*
Meinung (D)	—	opinion	opinion *f*	opinione *f*	opinión *f*
Meinungskäufe (D)	—	speculative buying	achats spéculatifs *m pl*	acquisti speculativi *m pl*	compras especulativas *f pl*
Meistbegünstigungs-klausel (D)	—	most-favoured nation clause	clause de la nation la plus favorisée *f*	clausola della na-zione più favorita *f*	cláusula de nación más favorecida *f*
mélange de marketing (F)	Marketing-Mix *m*	mixture of marketing strategies	—	marketing-mix *m*	mezcla de marketing *f*
member (E)	Mitglied *n*	—	membre *m*	membro *m*	miembro *m*
member of the European Commission (E)	EG-Kommissar *m*	—	commissaire européen *m*	commissario CEE *m*	comisario de la Comunidad Europea *m*
member of the managing board (E)	Vorstandsmitglied *n*	—	membre du comité de direction *m*	membro del consiglio di amministrazione *m*	consejero directivo *m*
membre (F)	Mitglied *n*	member	—	membro *m*	miembro *m*
membre du comité de direction (F)	Vorstandsmitglied *n*	member of the managing board	—	membro del consiglio di amministrazione *m*	consejero directivo *m*

	D	E	F	I	Es
membro (I)	Mitglied *n*	member	membre *m*	—	miembro *m*
membro del consiglio di amministrazione (I)	Vorstandsmitglied *n*	member of the managing board	membre du comité de direction *m*	—	consejero directivo *m*
mémoire principale (F)	Hauptspeicher *m*	main memory	—	memoria principale *f*	memoria principal *f*
memorandum (E)	Aktennotiz *f*	—	note *f*	annotazione *f*	nota *f*
memoria principal (Es)	Hauptspeicher *m*	main memory	mémoire principale *f*	memoria principale *f*	—
memoria principale (I)	Hauptspeicher *m*	main memory	mémoire principale *f*	—	memoria principal *f*
ménage privé (F)	privater Haushalt *m*	private household	—	famiglia *f*	economía doméstica *f*
Menge (D)	—	quantity	quantité *f*	quantità *f*	cantidad *f*
Mengenangabe (D)	—	indication of quantity	indication de la quantité *f*	indicazione della quantità *f*	indicación de cantidades *f*
Mengeneinheit (D)	—	quantity unit	unité de quantité *f*	unità quantitativa *f*	unidad cuantitativa *f*
Mengenkonjunktur (D)	—	quantitative boom	conjoncture de quantité *f*	congiuntura quantitativa *f*	coyuntura cuantitativa *f*
Mengenkontingent (D)	—	quantity quota	contingent de marchandises *m*	contingente di quantità *m*	contingente cuantitativo *m*
Mengennotierung (D)	—	fixed exchange	cotation de quantité *f*	cambio reale *m*	cotización real *f*
Mengenrabatt (D)	—	quantity discount	remise de quantité *f*	sconto di quantità *m*	rebaja de cantidad *f*
Mengenzoll (D)	—	specific duty	droit de douane par quantité *m*	dazio di quantità *m*	arancel aduanero cuantitativo *m*
menor de edad (Es)	minderjährig	under age	mineur	minorenne	—
mensaje publicitario (Es)	Werbebotschaft *f*	sales message	message publicitaire *m*	messaggio pubblicitario *m*	—
mensaje radiado (Es)	Funkspruch *m*	radio message	message par radio *m*	radiotelefonata *f*	—
mensile (I)	monatlich	monthly	par mois	—	mensual
mensual (Es)	monatlich	monthly	par mois	mensile	—
mensualité d'un achat à tempérament (F)	Teilzahlungsrate *f*	monthly instalment	—	rata *f*	plazo *m*
mentalità concezionale (I)	konzeptionelles Denken *n*	conceptional thinking	penser conceptionnel *m*	—	pensar concepcional *m*
mentalità creativa (I)	kreatives Denken *n*	creative thinking	créativité conceptionnelle *f*	—	creatividad concepcional *f*
mention des respons-ables de l'édition (F)	Impressum *n*	imprint	—	impressum *m*	pie de imprenta *m*
mercado (Es)	Markt *m*	market	marché *m*	mercato *m*	—
mercado agrícola (Es)	Agrarmarkt *m*	agricultural market	marché agricole *m*	mercato agrario *m*	—
mercado central (Es)	Großmarkt *m*	wholesale market	grand marché *m*	mercato all'ingrosso *m*	—
mercado común (Es)	gemeinsamer Markt *m*	common market	marché commun *m*	mercato comune *m*	—
mercado de divisas (Es)	Devisenmarkt *m*	foreign exchange market	marché des changes *m*	mercato valutario *m*	—
mercado de exportación (Es)	Exportmarkt *m*	export market	marché d'exportation *m*	mercato delle esportazioni *m*	—
mercado del oro (Es)	Goldmarkt *m*	gold market	marché de l'ór *m*	mercato dell'oro *m*	—
mercado de materias primas (Es)	Rohstoffmarkt *m*	commodity market	marchés des matières premières *m*	mercato delle materie prime *m*	—
mercado de operacio-nes al contado y de entrega inmediata (Es)	Spotmarkt *m*	spot market	marché en disponible *m*	mercato spot *m*	—
mercado de títulos de renta fija (Es)	Rentenmarkt *m*	bond market	marché des effets publics *m*	mercato dei titoli a reddito fisso *m*	—
mercado de valores (Es)	Wertpapierbörse *f*	securities market	bourse des titres et valeurs *f*	borsa valori *f*	—
mercado exterior (Es)	Auslandsmärkte *pl*	foreign markets	marchés extérieurs *m pl*	mercati esteri *m pl*	—
mercado favorable al comprador (Es)	Käufermarkt *m*	buyer's market	marché d'acheteurs *m*	mercato favorevole all'acquirente *m*	—
mercado favorable al consumidor (Es)	Verbrauchermarkt *m*	consumer market	marché des consommateurs *m*	ipermercato *m*	—
mercado favorable al vendedor (Es)	Verkäufermarkt *m*	seller's market	marché de vendeurs *m*	mercato favorevole ai venditori *m*	—
mercado financiero (Es)	Kapitalmarkt *m*	capital market	marché des capitaux *m*	mercato finanziario *m*	—
mercado gris (Es)	Grauer Markt *m*	grey market	marché gris *m*	mercato grigio *m*	—

	D	E	F	I	Es
mercado interior (Es)	Binnenmarkt *m*	home market	marché national *m*	mercato nazionale *m*	—
mercado laboral (Es)	Arbeitsmarkt *m*	labour market	marché du travail *m*	mercato del lavoro *m*	—
mercado monetario (Es)	Geldmarkt *m*	money market	marché monétaire *m*	mercato monetario *m*	—
mercado negro (Es)	Schwarzmarkt *m*	black market	marché noir *m*	mercato nero *m*	—
mercado piloto (Es)	Testmarkt *m*	test market	marché de test *m*	mercato pilota *m*	—
Mercado Unico (Es)	EG-Binnenmarkt *m*	Internal Market of the European Community	Marché Intérieur de la Communauté Européenne *m*	mercato unico *m*	—
mercancía (Es)	Ware *f*	goods	marchandise *f*	merce *f*	—
mercancía almacenada (Es)	Markenartikel *m*	branded article	produit de marque *m*	articolo di marca *m*	—
mercancía en gran velocidad (Es)	Eilgut *n*	goods sent by express	marchandise en grande vitesse *f*	merce a grande velocità *f*	—
mercancía pesada (Es)	Schwergut *n*	heavy freight	produit pondéreux *m*	carico pesante *m*	—
mercancías en comisión (Es)	Kommissionsgüter *pl*	goods for sale on commission	marchandises en commission *f pl*	beni in conto deposito *m pl*	—
mercancías en pequeña velocidad (Es)	Frachtgut *n*	cargo	marchandise à transporter *f*	merce di trasporto *f*	—
mercancía transportada (Es)	Speditionsgut *n*	forwarding merchandise	bien transporté *m*	merce spedita *f*	—
mercantile system (E)	Merkantilismus *m*	—	mercantilisme *m*	mercantilismo *m*	mercantilismo *m*
mercantilisme (F)	Merkantilismus *m*	mercantile system	—	mercantilismo *m*	mercantilismo *m*
mercantilismo (Es)	Merkantilismus *m*	mercantile system	mercantilisme *m*	mercantilismo *m*	—
mercantilismo (I)	Merkantilismus *m*	mercantile system	mercantilisme *m*	—	mercantilismo *m*
mercati esteri (I)	Auslandsmärkte *pl*	foreign markets	marchés extérieurs *m pl*	—	mercado exterior *m*
mercato (I)	Markt *m*	market	marché *m*	—	mercado *m*
mercato agrario (I)	Agrarmarkt *m*	agricultural market	marché agricole *m*	—	mercado agrícola *m*
mercato all'ingrosso (I)	Großmarkt *m*	wholesale market	grand marché *m*	—	mercado central *m*
mercato a termine (I)	Terminbörse *f*	futures market	bourse à terme *f*	—	bolsa de valores a término *f*
mercato comune (I)	gemeinsamer Markt *m*	common market	marché commun *m*	—	mercado común *m*
mercato dei titoli a reddito fisso (I)	Rentenmarkt *m*	bond market	marché des effets publics *m*	—	mercado de títulos de renta fija *m*
mercato del lavoro (I)	Arbeitsmarkt *m*	labour market	marché du travail *m*	—	mercado laboral *m*
mercato delle esportazioni (I)	Exportmarkt *m*	export market	marché d'exportation *m*	—	mercado de exportación *m*
mercato delle materie prime (I)	Rohstoffmarkt *m*	commodity market	marchés des matières premières *m*	—	mercado de materias primas *m*
mercato dell'oro (I)	Goldmarkt *m*	gold market	marché de l'ór *m*	—	mercado del oro *m*
mercato favorevole ai venditori (I)	Verkäufermarkt *m*	seller's market	marché de vendeurs *m*	—	mercado favorable al vendedor *m*
mercato favorevole all'acquirente (I)	Käufermarkt *m*	buyer's market	marché d'acheteurs *m*	—	mercado favorable al comprador *m*
mercato finanziario (I)	Kapitalmarkt *m*	capital market	marché des capitaux *m*	—	mercado financiero *m*
mercato grigio (I)	Grauer Markt *m*	grey market	marché gris *m*	—	mercado gris *m*
mercato monetario (I)	Geldmarkt *m*	money market	marché monétaire *m*	—	mercado monetario *m*
mercato nazionale (I)	Binnenmarkt *m*	home market	marché national *m*	—	mercado interior *m*
mercato nero (I)	Schwarzmarkt *m*	black market	marché noir *m*	—	mercado negro *m*
mercato pilota (I)	Testmarkt *m*	test market	marché de test *m*	—	mercado piloto *m*
mercato preborsistico (I)	Vorbörse *f*	before hours dealing	marché avant le marché officiel *m*	—	operaciones antes de la apertura de la bolsa *f pl*
mercato spot (I)	Spotmarkt *m*	spot market	marché en disponible *m*	—	mercado de operaciones al contado y de entrega inmediata *m*
mercato unico CEE (I)	EG-Binnenmarkt *m*	Internal Market of the European Community	Marché Intérieur de la Communauté Européenne *m*	—	Mercado Unico *m*
mercato valutario (I)	Devisenmarkt *m*	foreign exchange market	marché des changes *m*	—	mercado de divisas *m*

	D	E	F	I	Es
merce (I)	Ware *f*	goods	marchandise *f*	—	mercancía *f*
merce a grande velocità (I)	Eilgut *n*	goods sent by express	marchandise en grande vitesse *f*	—	mercancía en gran velocidad *f*
merce di trasporto (I)	Frachtgut *n*	cargo	marchandise a'transporter *f*	—	mercancías en pequeña velocidad *f pl*
merce immagazzinata (I)	Stapelware *f*	staple commodities	produit de stockage *m*	—	mercancía almacenada *f*
merce spedita (I)	Speditionsgut *n*	forwarding merchandise	bien transporté *m*	—	mercancía transportada *f*
merce spedita per espresso (I)	Expressgut *n*	express goods	colis express *m*	—	carga por expreso *f*
merchant bank (E)	Handelsbank *f*	—	banque de commerce *f*	banca commerciale *f*	banco comercial *m*
merger (E)	Verschmelzung *f*	—	fusion *f*	fusione *f*	fusión *f*
merger control (E)	Fusionskontrolle *f*	—	contrôle de fusion *m*	controllo delle fusioni *m*	control de fusiones *m*
merger of companies (E)	Unternehmensfusion *f*	—	fusion de sociétés *f*	fusione d'imprese *f*	fusión de empresas *f*
Merkantilismus (D)	—	mercantile system	mercantilisme *m*	mercantilismo *m*	mercantilismo *m*
message par radio (F)	Funkspruch *m*	radio message	—	radiotelefonata *f*	mensaje radiado *m*
message publicitaire (F)	Werbebotschaft *f*	sales message	—	messaggio pubblicitario *m*	mensaje publicitario *m*
messaggio pubblicitario (I)	Werbebotschaft *f*	sales message	message publicitaire *m*	—	mensaje publicitario *m*
Messe (D)	—	fair	foire *f*	fiera *f*	feria *f*
Messung (D)	—	measuring	mesurage *m*	misurazione *f*	medición *f*
Meßwerte (D)	—	measurements	valeurs mesurées *f pl*	valori misurati *m pl*	valor de medida *m*
mesure[1] (F)	Messung *f*	measuring	—	misurazione *f*	medición *f*
mesure[2] (F)	Maß *n*	measure	—	misura *f*	medida *f*
mesure préventive contre les sinistres (F)	Schadenverhütung *f*	loss prevention	—	prevenzione danni *f*	prevención de siniestros *f*
mesures pour l'amélioration de l'infrastructure (F)	Infrastrukturmaßnahmen *f*	infrastructural measures	—	misure per l'infrastruttura *f pl*	medidas de infraestructura *f pl*
metallo pesante (I)	Schwermetall *n*	heavy metal	métal lourd *m*	—	metal pesado *m*
métal lourd (F)	Schwermetall *n*	heavy metal	—	metallo pesante *m*	metal pesado *m*
metal pesado (Es)	Schwermetall *n*	heavy metal	métal lourd *m*	metallo pesante *m*	—
method (E)	Methode *f*	—	méthode *f*	metodo *m*	método *m*
Methode (D)	—	method	méthode *f*	metodo *m*	método *m*
méthode[1] (F)	Methode *f*	method	—	metodo *m*	método *m*
méthode[2] (F)	Verfahren *n*	procedure/process	—	procedimento *m*/ procedura *f*	proceso *m*/ procedimiento *m*
méthode de calcul des coûts (F)	Kostenrechnungssystem *n*	cost accounting system	—	sistema dei costi *m*	sistema de costes *m*
méthode de l'apurement des comptes (F)	Abrechnungsverfahren *n*	settling procedure	—	metodo di liquidazione *m*	operaciones de descuento *f pl*
méthode d'enquête par sondage (F)	Stichprobeverfahren *n*	sampling procedure	—	metodo del campionamento *m*	muestreo *m*
méthode de production (F)	Fertigungsverfahren *n*	production process	—	procedimento produttivo *m*	procedimiento de fabricación *m*
méthodes de vente (F)	Verkaufsmethoden *pl*	sales strategy	—	metodi di vendita *m pl*	métodos de venta *m pl*
metodi di vendita (I)	Verkaufsmethoden *pl*	sales strategy	méthodes de vente *f pl*	—	métodos de venta *m pl*
método (Es)	Methode *f*	method	méthode *f*	metodo *m*	—
metodo (I)	Methode *f*	method	méthode *f*	—	método *m*
metodo del campionamento (I)	Stichprobeverfahren *n*	sampling procedure	méthode d'enquête par sondage *f*	—	muestreo *m*
metodo di chiusura (I)	Abschlußtechnik *f*	finishing technique	technique de conclusion *f*	—	técnica de conclusión *f*
metodo di liquidazione (I)	Abrechnungsverfahren *n*	settling procedure	méthode de l'apurement des comptes	—	operaciones de descuento *f pl*
métodos de venta (Es)	Verkaufsmethoden *pl*	sales strategy	méthodes de vente *f pl*	metodi di vendita *m pl*	—

	D	E	F	I	Es
mettre à la ferraille (F)	verschrotten	scrap	—	ridurre a rottame	hacer quincalla/ desguazar
mezcla de marketing (Es)	Marketing-Mix *m*	mixture of marketing strategies	mélange de marketing *f*	marketing-mix *m*	—
mezzi pubblicitari (I)	Werbemedien *pl*	advertising media	média publicitaires *m pl*	—	medios de publicidad *m pl*
mezzo (I)	Mittel *n*	means	moyen *m*	—	medio *m*/recurso *m*
mezzo di pagamento (I)	Zahlungsmittel *n*	means of payment	moyen de payement *m*	—	medio de pago *m*
mezzo di pagamento legale (I)	gesetzliches Zahlungsmittel *n*	legal tender	monnaie légale *f*	—	medio legal de pago *m*
mezzo di trasporto (I)	Transportmittel *n*	means of transport	moyen de transport *m*	—	medio de transporte *m*
mezzo pubblicitario (I)	Werbemittel *n*	advertising aids	moyen publicitaire *m*	—	medio publicitario *m*
mezzo pubblicitario diretto (I)	Direktwerbemittel *n*	direct means of advertising	moyens publicitaires directs *m pl*	—	medios publicitarios directos *m pl*
microchip (E)	Mikrochip *m*	—	microplaquette *f*	microchip *m*	microchip *m*
microchip (Es)	Mikrochip *m*	microchip	microplaquette *f*	microchip *m*	—
microchip (I)	Mikrochip *m*	microchip	microplaquette *f*	—	microchip *m*
microeconomía (Es)	Mikroökonomie *f*	microeconomics	microéconomie *f*	microeconomia *f*	—
microeconomia (I)	Mikroökonomie *f*	microeconomics	microéconomie *f*	—	microeconomía *f*
microeconomics (E)	Mikroökonomie *f*	—	microéconomie *f*	microeconomia *f*	microeconomía *f*
microéconomie (F)	Mikroökonomie *f*	microeconomics	—	microeconomia *f*	microeconomía *f*
microplaquette (F)	Mikrochip *m*	microchip	—	microchip *m*	microchip *m*
microprocesor (Es)	Mikroprozessor *m*	microprocessor	microprocesseur *m*	microprocessore *m*	—
microprocesseur (F)	Mikroprozessor *m*	microprocessor	—	microprocessore *m*	microprocesor *m*
microprocessor (E)	Mikroprozessor *m*	—	microprocesseur *m*	microprocessore *m*	microprocesor *m*
microprocessore (I)	Mikroprozessor *m*	microprocessor	microprocesseur *m*	—	microprocesor *m*
middle class(es) (E)	Mittelstand *m*	—	classe moyenne *f*	ceto medio *m*	clase media *f*
middleman (E)	Zwischenhändler *m*	—	intermédiaire *m*	intermediario *m*	intermediario *m*
miembro (Es)	Mitglied *n*	member	membre *m*	membro *m*	—
Miete (D)	—	rent	location *f*	canone di locazione *m*	alquiler *m*
Mieter (D)	—	tenant	locataire *m*	locatario *m*	inquilino *m*/ arrendatario *m*
Mieterschutz (D)	—	protection of tenants	protection en matière de location *f*	tutela del locatario *f*	protección al arrendatario *f*
Mietwucher (D)	—	exorbitant rent	hausse illicite des loyers *f*	strozzinaggio sui canoni di locazione *m*	usura arrendaticia *f*
Mietzins (D)	—	rent	prix de location *m*	canone di locazione *m*	arrendamiento *m*
miglio (I)	Meile *f*	mile	mille *m*	—	milla *f*
miglio marino (I)	Seemeile *f*	nautical mile	mille nautique *m*	—	milla marina *f*
Mikrochip (D)	—	microchip	microplaquette *f*	microchip *m*	microchip *m*
Mikroökonomie (D)	—	microeconomics	microéconomie *f*	microeconomia *f*	microeconomía *f*
Mikroprozessor (D)	—	microprocessor	microprocesseur *m*	microprocessore *m*	microprocesor *m*
mile (E)	Meile *f*	—	mille *m*	miglio *m*	milla *f*
milla (Es)	Meile *f*	mile	mille *m*	miglio *m*	—
milla marina (Es)	Seemeile *f*	nautical mile	mille nautique *m*	miglio marino *m*	—
mille (F)	Meile *f*	mile	—	miglio *m*	milla *f*
mille nautique (F)	Seemeile *f*	nautical mile	—	miglio marino *m*	milla marina *f*
mina de oro (Es)	Goldmine *f*	goldmine	mine d'or *f*	miniera d'oro *f*	—
minderjährig (D)	—	under age	mineur	minorenne	menor de edad
Minderlieferung (D)	—	short delivery	livraison en quantité inférieure *f*	fornitura ridotta *f*	envío incompleto *m*
Minderung (D)	—	reduction	diminution *f*	riduzione *f*	reducción *f*
Mindestabnahme (D)	—	minimum purchase	achat d'une quantité minimum *m*	quantitativo minimo di fornitura *m*	recogida mínima *f*
Mindest-bestellmenge (D)	—	minimum quantity order	quantité commandée minimum *f*	quantitativo minimo di ordine *m*	cantidad mínima de pedido *f*
Mindestdauer (D)	—	minimum length/ minimum duration	durée minimum *f*	durata minima *f*	duración mínima *m*/ plazo mínimo *m*

	D	E	F	I	Es
Mindest-einfuhrpreise (D)	—	minimum import price	prix minimum d'importation *m pl*	prezzi minimi all'import *m pl*	precio mínimo a la importación *m*
Mindesthöhe (D)	—	minimum amount	montant minimum *m*	importo minimo *m*	cantidad mínima *f*
Mindestkapital (D)	—	minimum capital	capital minimum *m*	capitale minimo *m*	capital mínimo *m*
Mindestlohn (D)	—	minimum wage	salaire minimum *m*	salario minimo *m*	salario mínimo *m*
Mindestmenge (D)	—	minimum quantity	quantité minimum *f*	quantitativo minimo *m*	cantidad mínima *f*
Mindestpreis (D)	—	minimum price	prix minimum *m*	prezzo minimo *m*	precio mínimo *m*
Mindestreserve (D)	—	minimum reserves	réserve minimum *f*	riserva minima obbligatoria *f*	reserva mínima *f*
mine d'or (F)	Goldmine *f*	goldmine	—	miniera d'oro *f*	mina de oro *f*
Mineral (D)	—	mineral	minéral *m*	minerale *m*	mineral *m*
mineral (E)	Mineral *n*	—	minéral *m*	minerale *m*	mineral *m*
mineral (Es)	Mineral *n*	mineral	minéral *m*	minerale *m*	—
minéral (F)	Mineral *n*	mineral	—	minerale *m*	mineral *m*
minerale (I)	Mineral *n*	mineral	minéral *m*	—	mineral *m*
mineral oil (E)	Erdöl *n*	—	pétrole *m*	petrolio *m*	crudo *m*
mineral oil tax (E)	Mineralölsteuer *f*	—	taxe sur les carburants *f*	imposta sugli olii minerali *f*	impuesto sobre la gasolina *m*
Mineralölsteuer (D)	—	mineral oil tax	taxe sur les carburants *f*	imposta sugli olii minerali *f*	impuesto sobre la gasolina *m*
minería (Es)	Bergbau *m*	mining	industrie extractive *f*	industria mineraria *f*	—
mineur (F)	minderjährig	under age	—	minorenne	menor de edad
mini container (I)	Kleincontainer *m*	small container	petit conteneur *m*	—	pequeño contenedor *m*
miniera d'oro (I)	Goldmine *f*	goldmine	mine d'or *f*	—	mina de oro *f*
minimación de gastos[1] (Es)	Kostenminimierung *f*	minimization of costs	minimalisation des coûts *f*	diminuzione dei costi *f*	—
minimación de gastos[2] (Es)	Aufwands-minimierung *f*	expenditure minimization	minimiser les frais	riduzione delle spese *f*	—
minimal damage (E)	Bagatellschaden *m*	—	dommage mineur *m*	danno piccolo *m*	siniestro leve *m*
minimalisation des coûts (F)	Kostenminimierung *f*	minimization of costs	—	diminuzione dei costi *f*	minimación de gastos *f*
minimiser les frais (F)	Aufwands-minimierung *f*	expenditure minimization	—	riduzione delle spese *f*	minimación de gastos *f*
minimization of costs (E)	Kostenminimierung *f*	—	minimalisation des coûts *f*	diminuzione dei costi *f*	minimación de gastos *f*
minimo di esistenza (I)	Existenzminimum *n*	subsistence minimum	minimum vital *m*	—	minimo vital *m*
minimo vital (Es)	Existenzminimum *n*	subsistence minimum	minimum vital *m*	minimo di esistenza *m*	—
minimum amount (E)	Mindesthöhe *f*	—	montant minimum *m*	importo minimo *m*	cantidad mínima *f*
minimum capital (E)	Mindestkapital *n*	—	capital minimum *m*	capitale minimo *m*	capital mínimo *m*
minimum import price (E)	Mindest-einfuhrpreise *pl*	—	prix minimum d'importation *m pl*	prezzi minimi all'import *m pl*	precio mínimo a la importación *m*
minimum length (E)	Mindestdauer *f*	—	durée minimum *f*	durata minima *f*	duración mínima *m*/ plazo mínimo *m*
minimum nominal amount (E)	Mindestnennbetrag *m*	—	montant nominal minimum *m*	importo nominale minimo *m*	valor nominal mínimo *m*
minimum price (E)	Mindestpreis *m*	—	prix minimum *m*	prezzo minimo *m*	precio mínimo *m*
minimum purchase (E)	Mindestabnahme *f*	—	achat d'une quantité minimum *m*	quantitativo minimo di fornitura *m*	recogida mínima *f*
minimum quantity (E)	Mindestmenge *f*	—	quantité minimum *f*	quantitativo minimo *m*	cantidad mínima *f*
minimum quantity order (E)	Mindest-bestellmenge *f*	—	quantité commandée minimum *f*	quantitativo minimo di ordine *m*	cantidad mínima de pedido *f*
minimum reserves (E)	Mindestreserve *f*	—	réserve minimum *f*	riserva minima obbligatoria *f*	reserva mínima *f*
minimum turnover (E)	Mindestumsatz *m*	—	chiffre d'affaires minimum *m*	fatturato minimo *m*	cifra de venta mínima *f*
minimum vital (F)	Existenzminimum *n*	subsistence minimum	—	minimo di esistenza *m*	minimo vital *m*
minimum wage (E)	Mindestlohn *m*	—	salaire minimum *m*	salario minimo *m*	salario mínimo *m*
mining (E)	Bergbau *m*	—	industrie extractive *f*	industria mineraria *f*	minería *f*

	D	E	F	I	Es
mining industry (E)	Montanindustrie *f*	—	industrie minière *f*	industria mineraria e siderurgica *f*	industria minera *f*
mini paletta (I)	Kleinpalette *f*	small pallet	petite palette *f*	—	pequña paleta *f*
ministère de l'agriculture (F)	Landwirtschafts-ministerium *n*	Ministry of Agriculture	—	ministero dell'agricoltura *m*	minsterio de Agricultura, Pesca y Alimentación *m*
ministère des finances (F)	Finanzministerium *n*	Ministry of Finance	—	ministero delle Finanze *m*	Hacienda *f*
ministerio de Agricultura, Pesca y Alimentación (Es)	Landwirtschafts-ministerium *n*	Ministry of Agriculture	ministère de l'agriculture *m*	ministero dell'agricoltura *m*	—
ministero dell'agricoltura (I)	Landwirtschafts-ministerium *n*	Ministry of Agriculture	ministère de l'agriculture *m*	—	minsterio de Agricultura, Pesca y Alimentación *m*
ministero delle Finanze (I)	Finanzministerium *n*	Ministry of Finance	ministère des finances *m*	—	Hacienda *f*
Ministry of Agriculture (E)	Landwirtschafts-ministerium *n*	—	ministère de l'agriculture *m*	ministero dell'agricoltura *m*	minsterio de Agricultura, Pesca y Alimentación *m*
Ministry of Finance (E)	Finanzministerium *n*	—	ministère des finances *m*	ministero delle Finanze *m*	Hacienda *f*
minoration de l'intérêt (F)	Zinserleichterung *f*	reduction of interest	—	agevolazione sugli interessi *f*	reducción de intereses *f*
minorenne (I)	minderjährig	under age	mineur	—	menor de edad
minoría de bloqueo (Es)	Sperrminorität *f*	blocking minority	minorité suffisante pour bloquer qch. *f*	sindacato di blocco *m*	—
minorista (Es)	Einzelhändler *m*	retailer	commerçant détaillant *m*	dettagliante *m*	—
minorité suffisante pour bloquer qch. (F)	Sperrminorität *f*	blocking minority	—	sindacato di blocco *m*	minoría de bloqueo *f*
misappropriation (E)	Veruntreuung *f*	—	détournement *m*	abuso di fiducia *m*	malversación *f*
miscalculation (E)	Rechenfehler *m*	—	erreur de calcul *f*	errore di calcolo *m*	error de cálculo *m*
misconceived capital projects (E)	Fehlinvestition *f*	—	mauvais investissement *m*	investimento sbagliato *m*	inversión equivocada *f*
mise à profit (F)	Nutzung *f*	use/utilization	—	utilizzazione *f*	utilización *f*
mise au concours d'une place (F)	Stellen-ausschreibung *f*	advertisement of a vacancy	—	bando di concorso per impiegati *m*	convocatoria de oposiciones *f*
mise en demeure (F)	Mahnung *f*	demand for payment	—	sollecito *m*	(ad)monición *f*
mise en gage (F)	Verpfändung *f*	pledge	—	pignoramento *m*	pignoración *f*
misión comercial (Es)	Handelsmission *f*	trade mission	mission commerciale *f*	missione commerciale *f*	—
mission commerciale (F)	Handelsmission *f*	trade mission	—	missione commerciale *f*	misión comercial *f*
missione commerciale (I)	Handelsmission *f*	trade mission	mission commerciale *f*	—	misión comercial *f*
mistake (E)	Fehler *m*	—	faute *f*	errore *m*	error *m*
mistake of law (E)	Rechtsirrtum *m*	—	erreur de droit *m*	errore di diritto *m*	error de derecho *m*
misura (I)	Maß *n*	measure	mesure *f*	—	medida *f*
misurazione (I)	Messung *f*	measuring	mesurage *m*	—	medición *f*
misure per l'infrastruttura (I)	Infrastruktur-maßnahmen *f*	infrastructural measures	mesures pour l'amélioration de l'infrastructure *f pl*	—	medidas de infraestructura *f pl*
Mitarbeit (D)	—	collaboration	collaboration *f*	collaborazione *f*	colaboración *f*
Mitbestimmung (D)	—	codetermination of labour	cogestion *f*	cogestione *f*	cogestión *f*
Mitbewerber (D)	—	competitor	concurrent *m*	competitore *m*	contendiente *m*
Miteigentum (D)	—	co-ownership	copropriété *f*	comproprietà *f*	copropiedad *f*
mit getrennter Post (D)	—	under separate cover	sous pli séparé	in plico a parte	por correo aparte
Mitglied (D)	—	member	membre *m*	membro *m*	miembro *m*
Mitteilung (D)	—	information	notification *f*	comunicazione *f*	aviso *m*
Mittel (D)	—	means	moyen *m*	mezzo *m*	medio *m*/recurso *m*
mittelfristig (D)	—	medium-term	à moyen terme	a media scadenza	a medio plazo
mittelfristiger Kredit (D)	—	medium-term credit	crédit à moyen terme *m*	credito a media scadenza *m*	crédito a medio plazo *m*

	D	E	F	I	Es
Mittelstand (D)	—	middle class(es)	classe moyenne *f*	ceto medio *m*	clase media *f*
mittente (I)	Absender *m*	sender	envoyeur *m*	—	remitente *m*
mixed cargo (E)	Stückgut *n*	—	colis de détail *m*	collettame *m*	fardos *m pl*
mixture of marketing strategies (E)	Marketing-Mix *m*	—	mélange de marketing *f*	marketing-mix *m*	mezcla de marketing *f*
mobilidad (Es)	Mobilität *f*	mobility	mobilité *f*	mobilità *f*	—
mobilità (I)	Mobilität *f*	mobility	mobilité *f*	—	mobilidad *f*
Mobilität (D)	—	mobility	mobilité *f*	mobilità *f*	mobilidad *f*
mobilité (F)	Mobilität *f*	mobility	—	mobilità *f*	mobilidad *f*
mobility (E)	Mobilität *f*	—	mobilité *f*	mobilità *f*	mobilidad *f*
Modeartikel (D)	—	fashion article	article de mode *m*	articolo di moda *m*	artículos de moda *m pl*
Modemesse (D)	—	fashion fair	foire de la mode *f*	fiera della moda *f*	feria de moda *f*
modificación de contrato (Es)	Vertragsänderung *f*	modification of a contract	modification du contrat *f*	modificazione del contratto *f*	—
modificación de los estatutos (Es)	Satzungsänderung *f*	amendment of the statutes	modification des statuts *f*	modificazione dello statuto *f*	—
modification des statuts (F)	Satzungsänderung *f*	amendment of the statutes	—	modificazione dello statuto *f*	modificación de los estatutos *f*
modification du contrat (F)	Vertragsänderung *f*	modification of a contract	—	modificazione del contratto *f*	modificación de contrato *f*
modification du pouvoir d'achat (F)	Kaufkraftänderung *f*	changes in the purchasing power	—	mutamento del potere d'acquisto *m*	cambio en el poder adquisitivo *m*
modification of a contract (E)	Vertragsänderung *f*	—	modification du contrat *f*	modificazione del contratto *f*	modificación de contrato *f*
modificazione del contratto (I)	Vertragsänderung *f*	modification of a contract	modification du contrat *f*	—	modificación de contrato *f*
modificazione dello statuto (I)	Satzungsänderung *f*	amendment of the statutes	modification des statuts *f*	—	modificación de los estatutos *f*
modulo[1] (I)	Formular *n*	form	formulaire *m*	—	formulario *m*
modulo[2] (I)	Vordruck *m*	printed form	imprimé *m*	—	impreso *m*
modulo di domanda (I)	Antragsformular *n*	application form	formulaire de demande *m*	—	formulario de solicitud *m*
modulo di versamento (I)	Zahlkarte *f*	money order	mandat-carte *m*	—	carta de pago *f*
modulo d'ordinazione (I)	Bestellformular *n*	order form	bon de commande *m*	—	formulario de pedido *m*
modulo in bianco (I)	Blankoformular *n*	blank form	imprimé en blanc *m*	—	formulario en blanco *m*
monatlich (D)	—	monthly	par mois	mensile	mensual
moneda[1] (Es)	Münze *f*	coin	monnaie *f*	moneta *f*	—
moneda[2] (Es)	Währung *f*	currency	monnaie *f*	valuta *f*/moneta *f*	—
moneda blanda (Es)	weiche Währung *f*	soft currency	monnaie faible *f*	moneta debole *f*	—
moneda de referencia (Es)	Leitwährung *f*	key currency	monnaie-clé *f*	valuta guida *f*	—
moneda de reserva (Es)	Reservewährung *f*	reserve currency	monnaie de réserve *f*	valuta di riserva *f*	—
moneda dura (Es)	harte Währung *f*	hard currency	monnaie solide *f*	moneta forte *f*	—
moneda extranjera (Es)	Valuta *f*	foreign exchange/value	monnaie étrangère *f*	valuta *f*/divise *f pl*	—
moneda oro (Es)	Goldwährung *f*	gold currency	monnaie à couverture or *f*	valuta aurea *f*	—
moneda única (Es)	Einheitswährung *f*	uniform currency	monométallisme *m*	moneta unitaria *f*	—
moneta (I)	Münze *f*	coin	monnaie *f*	—	moneda *f*
moneta bancaria (I)	Buchgeld *n*	money in account	monnaie de crédit *f*	—	dinero bancario *m*
moneta debole (I)	weiche Währung *f*	soft currency	monnaie faible *f*	—	moneda blanda *f*
moneta forte (I)	harte Währung *f*	hard currency	monnaie solide *f*	—	moneda dura *f*
moneta metallica (I)	Hartgeld *n*	specie	pièce de monnaie *f*	—	dinero metálico *m*
moneta unitaria (I)	Einheitswährung *f*	uniform currency	monométallisme *m*	—	moneda única *f*
monétaire (F)	monetär	monetary	—	monetario	monetario
monetär (D)	—	monetary	monétaire	monetario	monetario
monetario (Es)	monetär	monetary	monétaire	monetario	—

	D	E	F	I	Es
monetario (I)	monetär	monetary	monétaire	—	monetario
monetarism (E)	Monetarismus *m*	—	monétarisme *m*	monetarismo *m*	monetarismo *m*
monétarisme (F)	Monetarismus *m*	monetarism	—	monetarismo *m*	monetarismo *m*
monetarismo (Es)	Monetarismus *m*	monetarism	monétarisme *m*	monetarismo *m*	—
monetarismo (I)	Monetarismus *m*	monetarism	monétarisme *m*	—	monetarismo *m*
Monetarismus (D)	—	monetarism	monétarisme *m*	monetarismo *m*	monetarismo *m*
monetary (E)	monetär	—	monétaire	monetario	monetario
monetary authority (E)	Währungsbehörde *f*	—	autorité monétaire *f*	autorità monetaria *f*	autoridad monetaria *f*
monetary expert (E)	Währungsexperte *m*	—	expert monétaire *m*	esperto in materia monetaria *m*	experto en materia monetaria *m*
monetary policy[1] (E)	Währungspolitik *f*	—	politique monétaire *f*	politica monetaria *f*	política monetaria *f*
monetary policy[2] (E)	Geldpolitik *f*	—	politique monétaire *f*	politica monetaria *f*	política monetaria *f*
monetary restriction (E)	Geldverknappung *f*	—	pénurie d'argent *f*	riduzione del denaro *f*	restricción monetaria *f*
monetary theory (E)	Geldtheorie *f*	—	théorie monétaire *f*	teoria del denaro *f*	teoría monetaria *f*
monetary union (E)	Währungsunion *f*	—	union monétaire *f*	unione monetaria *f*	uníon monetaria *f*
money (E)	Geld *n*	—	argent *m*	denaro *m*	dinero *m*/efectivo *m*
money creation (E)	Geldschöpfung *f*	—	création de trésorerie *f*	creazione di denaro *f*	creación de dinero *f*
money in account (E)	Buchgeld *n*	—	monnaie de crédit *f*	moneta bancaria *f*	dinero bancario *m*
money market (E)	Geldmarkt *m*	—	marché monétaire *m*	mercato monetario *m*	mercado monetario *m*
money order (E)	Zahlkarte *f*	—	mandat-carte *m*	modulo di versamento *m*	carta de pago *f*
money owed (E)	Guthaben *n*	—	avoir *m*	saldo attivo *m*	haber *m*
money supply (E)	Geldmenge *f*	—	quantité de monnaie en circulation *f*	massa monetaria *f*	volumen monetario *m*
monnaie[1] (F)	Währung *f*	currency	—	valuta *f*/moneta *f*	moneda *f*
monnaie[2] (F)	Münze *f*	coin	—	moneta *f*	moneda *f*
monnaie à couverture or (F)	Goldwährung *f*	gold currency	—	valuta aurea *f*	moneda oro *f*
monnaie-clé (F)	Leitwährung *f*	key currency	—	valuta guida *f*	moneda de referencia *f*
monnaie de crédit (F)	Buchgeld *n*	money in account	—	moneta bancaria *f*	dinero bancario *m*
monnaie de papier (F)	Papiergeld *n*	paper money	—	banconote *f pl*	papel-moneda *m*
monnaie de réserve (F)	Reservewährung *f*	reserve currency	—	valuta di riserva *f*	moneda de reserva *f*
monnaie étrangère (F)	Valuta *f*	foreign exchange	—	divise *f pl*	moneda extranjera *f*/ divisas *f pl*
monnaie faible (F)	weiche Währung *f*	soft currency	—	moneta debole *f*	moneda blanda *f*
monnaie légale (F)	gesetzliches Zahlungsmittel *n*	legal tender	—	mezzo di pagamento legale *m*	medio legal de pago *m*
monnaie solide (F)	harte Währung *f*	hard currency	—	moneta forte *f*	moneda dura *f*
monocoltura (I)	Monokultur *f*	monoculture	monoculture *f*	—	monocultivo *m*
monocultivo (Es)	Monokultur *f*	monoculture	monoculture *f*	monocoltura *f*	—
monoculture (E)	Monokultur *f*	—	monoculture *f*	monocoltura *f*	monocultivo *m*
monoculture (F)	Monokultur *f*	monoculture	—	monocoltura *f*	monocultivo *m*
Monokultur (D)	—	monoculture	monoculture *f*	monocoltura *f*	monocultivo *m*
monométallisme (F)	Einheitswährung *f*	uniform currency	—	moneta unitaria *f*	moneda única *f*
Monopol (D)	—	monopoly	monopole *m*	monopolio *m*	monopolio *m*
monopole (F)	Monopol *n*	monopoly	—	monopolio *m*	monopolio *m*
monopole du commerce extérieur (F)	Außenhandels-monopol *n*	foreign trade monopoly	—	monopolio del commercio estero *m*	monopolio del comercio exterior *m*
monopole fiscal (F)	Finanzmonopol *n*	fiscal monopoly	—	monopolio fiscale *m*	monopolio financiero *m*
monopolio (Es)	Monopol *n*	monopoly	monopole *m*	monopolio *m*	—
monopolio (I)	Monopol *n*	monopoly	monopole *m*	—	monopolio *m*
monopolio del comercio exterior (Es)	Außenhandels-monopol *n*	foreign trade monopoly	monopole du commerce extérieur *m*	monopolio del commercio estero *m*	—
monopolio del commercio estero (I)	Außenhandels-monopol *n*	foreign trade monopoly	monopole du commerce extérieur *m*	—	monopolio del comercio exterior *m*

	D	E	F	I	Es
monopolio financiero (Es)	Finanzmonopol *n*	fiscal monopoly	monopole fiscal *m*	monopolio fiscale *m*	—
monopolio fiscale (I)	Finanzmonopol *n*	fiscal monopoly	monopole fiscal *m*	—	monopolio financiero *m*
monopoly (E)	Monopol *n*	—	monopole *m*	monopolio *m*	monopolio *m*
Montage (D)	—	installation	montage *m*	montaggio *m*	montaje *m*
montage (F)	Montage *f*	installation	—	montaggio *m*	montaje *m*
montaggio (I)	Montage *f*	installation	montage *m*	—	montaje *m*
montaje (Es)	Montage *f*	installation	montage *m*	montaggio *m*	—
Montanindustrie (D)	—	mining industry	industrie minière *f*	industria mineraria e siderurgica *f*	industria minera *f*
montant (F)	Betrag *m*	amount	—	importo *m*	suma *f*
montant de l'accréditif (F)	Akkreditivsumme *f*	amount of the letter of credit	—	importo del credito documentario *m*	suma del crédito documentario *f*
montant de la facture[1] (F)	Rechnungssumme *f*	invoice amount	—	importo della fattura *m*	suma de la factura *f*
montant de la facture[2] (F)	Rechnungsbetrag *m*	amount of invoice	—	ammontare della fattura *m*	importe de la factura *m*
montant de la garantie (F)	Beleihungswert *m*	value as security for a loan	—	valore finanziabile *m*	valor para préstamos *m*
montant de l'assurance (F)	Versicherungs-summe *f*	insurance sum	—	somma assicurata *f*	suma asegurada *f*
montant de rachat (F)	Ablösesumme *f*	redemption sum	—	importo di rimborso *m*	suma de amortización *f*
montante nominal (Es)	Nominalbetrag *m*	nominal amount	montant nominal *m*	importo nominale *m*	—
montant minimum (F)	Mindesthöhe *f*	minimum amount	—	importo minimo *m*	cantidad mínima *f*
montant nominal (F)	Nominalbetrag *m*	nominal amount	—	importo nominale *m*	montante nominal *m*
montant nominal minimum (F)	Mindestnennbetrag *m*	minimum nominal amount	—	importo nominale minimo *m*	valor nominal mínimo *m*
montant total (F)	Gesamtsumme *f*	total amout	—	importo totale *m*	suma total *f*
monthly (E)	monatlich	—	par mois	mensile	mensual
monthly instalment (E)	Teilzahlungsrate *f*	—	mensualité d'un achat à tempérament *f*	rata *f*	plazo *m*
mora (I)	Verzug *m*	delay	demeure *f*	—	retraso *m*/demora *f*
mora nella consegna (I)	Lieferverzug *m*	delay in delivery	demeure du fournisseur *f*	—	demora en la entrega *f*
moratoria (Es)	Stundung *f*	respite	prorogation *f*	dilazione *f*/proroga *f*	—
morosità di pagamento[1] (I)	Zahlungsverzug *m*	failure to pay on due date	demeure du débiteur *f*	—	retraso en el pago *m*
morosità di pagamento[2] (I)	Zahlungsrückstand *m*	payment in arrears	arriéré de payement *m*	—	pago atrasado *m*
moroso (Es)	säumig	dilatory	retardataire	moroso	—
moroso (I)	säumig	dilatory	retardataire	—	moroso
mortgage[1] (E)	Hypothek *f*	—	hypothéque *f*	ipoteca *f*	hipoteca *f*
mortgage[2] (E)	Grundschuld *f*	—	dette foncière *f*	debito fondiario *m*	hipoteca *f*
mortgage bank (E)	Hypothekenbank *f*	—	banque hypothécaire *f*	banca ipotecaria *f*	banco hipotecario *m*
mortgage bond (E)	Pfandbrief *m*	—	obligation hypothécaire *f*	titolo ipotecario *m*	cédula hipotecaria *f*
most favourable offer (E)	günstigstes Angebot *n*	—	offre favorable *f*	offerta vantaggiosa *f*	oferta favorable *f*
most-favoured nation clause (E)	Meistbegünstigungs-klausel *f*	—	clause de la nation la plus favorisée *f*	clausola della nazione più favorita *f*	cláusula de la nación más favorecida *f*
mot-clé (F)	Schlüsselwort *n*	key word	—	parola chiave *f*	palabra clave *f*
mot de code (F)	Codewort *n*	code	—	parola di codice *f*	palabra de clave *f*
mother house (E)	Mutterhaus *n*	—	maison mère *f*	casa madre *f*	casa matriz *f*
motif (F)	Motiv *n*	motive	—	motivo *m*	motivo *m*
motif d'achat (F)	Kaufanlaß *m*	buying motive	—	motivo d'acquisto *m*	motivo de compra *m*
Motiv (D)	—	motive	motif *m*	motivo *m*	motivo *m*
motivación (Es)	Motivation *f*	motivation	motivation *f*	motivazione *f*	—
Motivation (D)	—	motivation	motivation *f*	motivazione *f*	motivación *f*

	D	E	F	I	Es
motivation (E)	Motivation *f*	—	motivation *f*	motivazione *f*	motivación *f*
motivation (F)	Motivation *f*	motivation	—	motivazione *f*	motivación *f*
motivazione (I)	Motivation *f*	motivation	motivation *f*	—	motivación *f*
motive (E)	Motiv *n*	—	motif *m*	motivo *m*	motivo *m*
motivo (Es)	Motiv *n*	motive	motif *m*	motivo *m*	—
motivo (I)	Motiv *n*	motive	motif *m*	—	motivo *m*
motivo d'acquisto (I)	Kaufanlaß *m*	buying motive	motif d'achat *m*	—	motivo de compra *m*
motivo de compra (Es)	Kaufanlaß *m*	buying motive	motif d'achat *m*	motivo d'acquisto *m*	—
motor insurance (E)	Kraftfahrzeug-versicherung *f*	—	assurance responsabilité civile automobile *f*	assicurazione autoveicoli *f*	seguro de automóviles *m*
motor vehicle (E)	Kraftfahrzeug *n*	—	véhicule à moteur *m*	automobile *f*	automóvil *m*
motor vehicle tax (E)	Kraftfahrzeugsteuer *f*	—	taxe sur les véhicules à moteur *f*	imposta sulla circolazione degli autoveicoli *f*	impuesto sobre vehículos *m*
mousse synthétique (F)	Schaumstoff *m*	foam material	—	espanso *m*	plástico espumoso *m*
mouvement ascendant (F)	Aufwärtstrend *m*	upward trend	—	tendenza al rialzo *f*	tendencia alcista *f*
mouvement des capitaux (F)	Kapitalverkehr *m*	capital transactions	—	movimento dei capitali *m*	circulación de capitales *f*
mouvement des devises (F)	Devisenverkehr *m*	foreign exchange dealings	—	commercio dei cambi *m*	tráfico de divisas *m*
mouvements dans le personnel (F)	Personalwechsel *m*	staff changes	—	cambio del personale *m*	cambio de personal *m*
mouvements saisonniers (F)	Saison-schwankungen *pl*	seasonal fluctuations	—	oscillazioni stagionali *f pl*	oscilaciones estacionales *f pl*
movable goods (E)	bewegliche Güter *pl*	—	biens meubles *m pl*	beni mobili *m pl*	bienes muebles *m pl*
movimento dei capitali (I)	Kapitalverkehr *m*	capital transactions	mouvement des capitaux *m*	—	circulación de capitales *f*
moyen (F)	Mittel *n*	means	—	mezzo *m*	medio *m*/recurso *m*
moyen de payement (F)	Zahlungsmittel *n*	means of payment	—	mezzo di pagamento *m*	medio de pago *m*
moyen de transport (F)	Transportmittel *n*	means of transport	—	mezzo di trasporto *m*	medio de transporte *m*
moyenne (F)	Durchschnitt *m*	average	—	media *f*	promedio *m*
moyen publicitaire (F)	Werbemittel *n*	advertising aids	—	mezzo pubblicitario *m*	medio publicitario *m*
moyens financiers (F)	Geldvermögen *n*	financial assets	—	patrimonio monetario *m*	activo monetario *m*
moyens publicitaires directs (F)	Direktwerbemittel *n*	direct means of advertising	—	mezzo pubblicitario diretto *m*	medios publicitarios directos *m pl*
mudanza (Es)	Umzug *m*	change of residence	déménagement *m*	trasferimento *m*	—
muestra[1] (Es)	Probepackung *f*	trial package	échantillon *m*	confezione campione *f*	—
muestra[2] (Es)	Warenprobe *f*	sample	échantillon *m*	campione *m*	—
muestrario (Es)	Mustermappe *f*	sample bag	dossier à échantillons *m*	cartella campioni *f*	—
muestra sin valor (Es)	Muster ohne Wert *n*	sample, no commercial value	échantillon sans valeur *m*	campione senza valore *m*	—
muestreo (Es)	Stichprobe-verfahren *n*	sampling procedure	méthode d'enquête par sondage *f*	metodo del campionamento *m*	—
multa[1] (Es)	Geldbuße *f*	fine	amende *f*	pena pecuniaria *f*	—
multa[2] (Es)	Bußgeld *n*	administration fee	amende *f*	pena pecuniaria *f*	—
multa[3] (Es)	Geldstrafe *f*	fine	peine pécuniaire *f*	multa *f*	—
multa (I)	Geldstrafe *f*	fine	peine pécuniaire *f*	—	multa *f*
multilateral (D)	—	multilateral	multilatéral	multilaterale	multilateral
multilateral (E)	multilateral	—	multilatéral	multilaterale	multilateral
multilateral (Es)	multilateral	multilateral	multilatéral	multilaterale	—
multilatéral (F)	multilateral	multilateral	—	multilaterale	multilateral
multilaterale (I)	multilateral	multilateral	multilatéral	—	multilateral
multinational enterprise (E)	multinationale Unternehmen *n*	—	entreprises multinationales *f pl*	imprese multinazionali *f pl*	empresa multinacional *f*

	D	E	F	I	Es
multinationaler Konzern (D)	—	multinational group	groupe multinational *m*	gruppo multinazionale *m*	grupo multinacional *m*
multinationale Unternehmen (D)	—	multinational enterprise	entreprises multinationales *f pl*	imprese multinazionali *f pl*	empresa multinacional *f*
multinational group (E)	multinationaler Konzern *m*	—	groupe multinational *m*	gruppo multinazionale *m*	grupo multinacional *m*
mündlich (D)	—	verbal	verbal	verbale	oral
municipalidad (Es)	Kommune *f*	municipality	commune *f*	comune *m*	—
municipality (E)	Kommune *f*	—	commune *f*	comune *m*	municipalidad *f*
Münze (D)	—	coin	monnaie *f*	moneta *f*	moneda *f*
Muster (D)	—	sample	échantillon *m*	campione *m*	muestra *f*/dibujo *m*
Mustermappe (D)	—	sample bag	dossier à échantillons *m*	cartella campioni *f*	muestrario *m*
Mustermesse (D)	—	trade fair	foire d'échantillons *f*	fiera campionaria *f*	feria de muestras *f*
Muster ohne Wert (D)	—	sample, no commercial value	échantillon sans valeur *m*	campione senza valore *m*	muestra sin valor *f*
Mustersendung (D)	—	sample consignment	envoi d'échantillons *m*	spedizione di campioni *f*	envío de muestras *m*
mutamento del potere d'acquisto (I)	Kaufkraftänderung *f*	changes in the purchasing power	modification du pouvoir d'achat *f*	—	cambio en el poder adquisitivo *m*
Mutmaßung (D)	—	conjecture	présomption *f*	presunzione *f*	suposición *f*
Muttergesellschaft (D)	—	parent company	société mère *f*	società madre *f*	sociedad matriz *f*
Mutterhaus (D)	—	mother house	maison mère *f*	casa madre *f*	casa matriz *f*
Mutterschutz (D)	—	protection for motherhood	protection maternelle et infantile *f*	tutela della maternità *f*	protección de la madre *f*
mutua assicurazione (I)	Versicherung auf Gegenseitigkeit *f*	mutual insurance	assurance mutuelle *f*	—	caja de socorros mutuos *f*
mutual insurance (E)	Versicherung auf Gegenseitigkeit *f*	—	assurance mutuelle *f*	mutua assicurazione *f*	caja de socorros mutuos *f*
mutuo (I)	Darlehen *n*	loan	prêt *m*	—	préstamo *m*
mutuo residuo (I)	Restdarlehen *n*	purchase-money loan	prêt restant *m*	—	restante de un préstamo *m*
nach Erhalt der Rechnung (D)	—	on receipt of the invoice	après avoir réçu la facture	a ricevimento della fattura	después de haber recibo la factura
Nachbereitung (D)	—	aftertreatment	remise en ordre *f*	rielaborazione *f*	tratamiento ulterior *m*
Nachbestellung (D)	—	repeat order	nouvel ordre *m*	ordinazione supplementare *f*	pedido suplementario *m*
nachdatiert (D)	—	postdated	postdaté	postdatato	pos(t)datado
Nachforschung (D)	—	investigation	recherche *f*	indagine *f*	pesquisas *f pl*
Nachfrage (D)	—	demand	demande *f*	domanda *f*	demanda *f*
Nachfragerückgang (D)	—	decrease in demand	recul de la demande *m*	flessione della domanda *f*	disminución en la demanda *f*
Nachfrist (D)	—	additional period	prolongation *f*	termine supplementare *m*	plazo de gracia *m*
Nachkalkulation (D)	—	historical costing	calcul des coûts a posteriori *m*	computisteria *f*	cálculo de costes a posteriori *m*
Nachlaß (D)	—	inheritance	héritage *m*	eredità *f*	herencia *f*
Nachlaßverwalter (D)	—	administrator of the deceased's estate	administrateur de la succession *m*	amministratore dell'eredità *m*	administrador de la herencia *m*
Nachlieferungs-anspruch (D)	—	claim to subsequent delivery	droit à livraison complémentaire *m*	diritto alla fornitura supplementare *m*	derecho de suministro adicional *m*
Nachnahme (D)	—	cash on delivery	remboursement *m*	contrassegno *m*	reembolso *m*
Nachprüfung (D)	—	reexamination	vérification *f*	revisione *f*	revisión *f*
Nachricht (D)	—	news	avis *m*/nouvelle *f*	notizia *f*	noticia *f*
Nachteil (D)	—	disadvantage	désavantage *m*	svantaggio *m*	desventaja *f*
Nachtschicht (D)	—	night shift	équipe de nuit *f*	turno notturno *m*	turno de noche *m*
Nachttresor (D)	—	night safe	dépôt de nuit *m*	cassa continua *f*	depósito de noche *m*
Nachzahlung (D)	—	supplementary payment	versement complémentaire *m*	pagamento supplementare *m*	pago suplementario *m*
nacionalización (Es)	Verstaatlichung *f*	nationalization	nationalisaiton *f*	nazionalizzazione *f*	—
Namensaktie (D)	—	registered shares	action nominative *f*	azione nominativa *f*	acción nominal *f*

	D	E	F	I	Es
Natale (I)	Weihnachten *n*	Christmas	Noël *m*	—	Navidad *f*
national (F)	Inländer *m*	national resident	—	persona residente *f*	residente *m*
national accounting (E)	Volkswirtschaftliche Gesamtrechnung *f*	—	comptabilité nationale *f*	contabilità nazionale *f*	contabilidad nacional *f*
national economy (E)	Volkswirtschaft *f*	—	économie nationale *f*	economia politica *f*	economía nacional *f*
nationale Souveränitätsrechte (D)	—	national sovereignty rights	droits de souveraineté nationale *m pl*	diritti di sovranità nazionale *m pl*	derechos de soberanía nacional *m pl*
national income (E)	Volkseinkommen *n*	—	revenu national *m*	reddito nazionale *m*	renta nacional *f*
nationalisation (F)	Verstaatlichung *f*	nationalization	—	nazionalizzazione *f*	nacionalización *f*
nationalization (E)	Verstaatlichung *f*	—	nationalisation *f*	nazionalizzazione *f*	nacionalización *f*
Nationalökonomie (D)	—	economics	économie nationale *f*	economia nazionale *f*	economía nacional *f*
national product (E)	Sozialprodukt *n*	—	produit national *m*	prodotto nazionale *m*	producto nacional *m*
national resident (E)	Inländer *m*	—	habitant du pays *m*	persona residente *f*	residente *m*
national sovereignty rights (E)	nationale Souveränitätsrechte *pl*	—	droits de souveraineté nationale *m pl*	diritti di sovranità nazionale *m pl*	derechos de soberanía nacional *m pl*
Naturalabgabe (D)	—	duty in kind	taxe acquittée en nature *f*	imposta in natura *f*	impuesto en especie *m*
natural gas (E)	Erdgas *n*	—	gaz naturel *m*	gas naturale *m*	gas natural *m*
Naturallohn (D)	—	wages (paid) in kind	rémunérarion du travail en nature *f*	remunerazione in natura *f*	salario en especie *m*
natural person (E)	natürliche Person *f*	—	personne physique *f*	persona fisica *f*	persona natural *f*
natürliche Person (D)	—	natural person	personne physique *f*	persona fisica *f*	persona natural *f*
nautical mile (E)	Seemeile *f*	—	mille nautique *m*	miglio marino *m*	milla marina *f*
naval blockade (E)	Seeblockade *f*	—	blocus maritime *m*	blocco marittimo *m*	bloqueo marítimo *m*
navegable (Es)	schiffbar	navigable	navigable	navigabile	—
navegación fluvial (Es)	Binnenschiffahrt *f*	inland navigation	navigation fluviale *f*	navigazione interna *f*	—
Navidad (Es)	Weihnachten *n*	Christmas	Noël *m*	Natale *m*	—
navigabile (I)	schiffbar	navigable	navigable	—	navegable
navigable (E)	schiffbar	—	navigable	navigabile	navegable
navigable (F)	schiffbar	navigable	—	navigabile	navegable
navigation fluviale (F)	Binnenschiffahrt *f*	inland navigation	—	navigazione interna *f*	navegación fluvial *f*
navigazione interna (I)	Binnenschiffahrt *f*	inland navigation	navigation fluviale *f*	—	navegación fluvial *f*
nazionalizzazione (I)	Verstaatlichung *f*	nationalization	nationalisation *f*	—	nacionalización *f*
Nebenkosten (D)	—	ancillary costs	coûts accessoires *m pl*	costi accessori *m pl*	gastos adicionales *m pl*
Nebenprodukt (D)	—	by-product	produit dérivé *m*	prodotto secondario *m*	producto accesorio *m*
necesidad (Es)	Bedürfnis *n*	need	besoin *m*	bisogno *m*	—
necesidad anual (Es)	Jahresbedarf *m*	annual need	besoin annuel *m*	bisogno annuale *m*	—
necesidad de capital (Es)	Kapitalbedarf *m*	capital requirements	besoin en capital *m*	domanda di capitale *m*	—
necesidad de información (Es)	Informationsbedarf *m*	requirement of information	besoin d'information *m*	bisogno d'informazioni *m*	—
necesidades (Es)	Bedarf *m*	need/demand	besoin *m*/demande *f*	fabbisogno *m*/ domanda *f*	—
necesidades individuales (Es)	Individualbedürfnis *n*	individual need	besoin individuel *m*	fabbisogno individuale *m*	—
need[1] (E)	Bedürfnis *n*	—	besoin *m*	bisogno *m*	necesidad *f*
need[2] (E)	Bedarf *m*	—	besoin *m*/demande *f*	fabbisogno *m*/ domanda *f*	necesidades *f*/ demanda *f*
negativa (Es)	Absage *f*	refusal	refus *m*	risposta negativa *f*	—
negligence (E)	Fahrlässigkeit *f*	—	négligence *f*	negligenza *f*	descuido *m*
negligenza (I)	Fahrlässigkeit *f*	negligence	négligence *f*	—	descuido *m*
negociación (Es)	Verhandlung *f*	negotiation	négociation *f*	trattativa *f*	—
negociación bursátil (Es)	Börsenhandel *m*	stock exchange transactions	transactions boursiaires *f pl*	commercio in borsa *m*	—
négociant (F)	Kaufmann *m*	businessman	—	commerciante *m*	comerciante *m*
négociation (F)	Verhandlung *f*	negotiation	—	trattativa *f*	negociación *f*
négociation des actions (F)	Aktienhandel *m*	dealing in shares	—	commercio azionario *m*	constratación de acciones *f pl*

	D	E	F	I	Es
negocio (Es)	Geschäft *n*	business	affaire *f*	negozio *m*	—
negocio acoplado (Es)	Kopplungsgeschäft *n*	tie-in transaction	affaire couplée *f*	operazione abbinata *f*	—
negocio de exportación o importación (Es)	Auslandsgeschäft *n*	foreign business	opération avec l'étranger *f*	affare con l'estero *m*	—
negocio de inmuebles (Es)	Immobilien-geschäft *n*	property transactions	affaire immobilière *f*	operazione immobiliare *f*	—
negocio jurídico (Es)	Rechtsgeschäft *n*	legal transaction	acte juridique *m*	negozio giuridico *m*	—
negocios de transporte (Es)	Beförderungs-geschäfte *pl*	transport services	transports *m pl*	operazioni di trasporto *f pl*	—
negotiation (E)	Verhandlung *f*	—	négociation *f*	trattativa *f*	negociación *f*
negotiation skills (E)	Verhandlungs-geschick *n*	—	habileté en matière de négociations *f*	abilità nel trattare *f*	tino de negociar *m*
negozi pilota (I)	Testläden *pl*	test shops	magasins de test *m pl*	—	tiendas piloto *f pl*
negozio (I)	Geschäft *n*	business	affaire *f*	—	negocio *m*
negozio giuridico (I)	Rechtsgeschäft *n*	legal transaction	acte juridique *m*	—	negocio jurídico *m*
negozio simulato (I)	Scheingeschäft *n*	fictitious transaction	opération simulée *f*	—	operación ficticia *f*
Nennwert (D)	—	nominal value	valeur nominale *f*	valore nominale *m*	valor nominal *m*
ne pas transférable (F)	nicht übertragbar	non-assignable	—	non trasferibile	intransmisible
net (E)	netto	—	net	netto	neto
net (F)	netto	net	—	netto	neto
net assets[1] (E)	Reinvermögen *n*	—	avoir net *m*	patrimonio netto *m*	patrimonio neto *m*
net assets[2] (E)	Nettovermögen *n*	—	patrimoine net *m*	patrimonio netto *m*	patrimonio neto *m*
net earnings (E)	Nettoertrag *m*	—	produit net *m*	ricavo netto *m*	producto neto *m*
net income (E)	Nettoeinkommen *n*	—	revenu net *m*	reddito netto *m*	ingreso neto *m*
net income percentage of turnover (E)	Umsatzrendite *f*	—	rendement du chiffre d'affaires *m*	rendita del fatturato *f*	rédito de la cifra de ventas *m*
net indebtedness (E)	Nettoverschuldung *f*	—	endettement net *m*	indebitamento netto *m*	deuda neta *m*
net investment (E)	Nettoinvestition *f*	—	investissement net *m*	investimento netto *m*	inversión neta *f*
net national product (E)	Nettosozialprodukt *n*	—	produit national net *m*	prodotto nazionale netto *m*	producto nacional neto *m*
neto (Es)	netto	net	net	netto	—
net price (E)	Nettopreis *m*	—	prix net *m*	prezzo netto *m*	precio neto *m*
net production (E)	Nettoproduktion *f*	—	production nette *f*	produzione netta *f*	producción neta *f*
net profit (E)	Reingewinn *m*	—	bénéfice net *m*	utile netto *m*	ganancia neta *f*
netto (D)	—	net	net	netto	neto
netto (I)	netto	net	net	—	neto
Nettoeinkommen (D)	—	net income	revenu net *m*	reddito netto *m*	ingreso neto *m*
Nettoertrag (D)	—	net earnings	produit net *m*	ricavo netto *m*	producto neto *m*
Nettoinvestition (D)	—	net investment	investissement net *m*	investimento netto *m*	inversión neta *f*
Nettolohn (D)	—	take-home pay	salaire net *m*	salario netto *m*	salario neto *m*
Nettopreis (D)	—	net price	prix net *m*	prezzo netto *m*	precio neto *m*
Nettoproduktion (D)	—	net production	production nette *f*	produzione netta *f*	producción neta *f*
Nettosozialprodukt (D)	—	net national product	produit national net *m*	prodotto nazionale netto *m*	producto nacional neto *m*
Nettoumsatz (D)	—	net turnover	chiffre d'affaires net *m*	fatturato netto *m*	ventas netas *f pl*
Nettovermögen (D)	—	net assets	patrimoine net *m*	patrimonio netto *m*	patrimonio neto *m*
Nettoverschuldung (D)	—	net indebtedness	endettement net *m*	indebitamento netto *m*	deuda neta *m*
net turnover (E)	Nettoumsatz *m*	—	chiffre d'affaires net *m*	fatturato netto *m*	ventas netas *f pl*
network (E)	Netzwerk *n*	—	réseau *m*	rete *f*	red *f*
network planning (E)	Netzplan *m*	—	réseau linéaire pour planification *m*	pianificazione reticolare *f*	planificación reticular *f*
Netzplan (D)	—	network planning	réseau linéaire pour planification *m*	pianificazione reticolare *f*	planificación reticular *f*
Netzwerk (D)	—	network	réseau *m*	rete *f*	red *f*
Neugründung (D)	—	new foundation	création d'une nouvelle société *f*	costituzione nuova *f*	fundación nueva *f*

	D	E	F	I	Es
Neujahr (D)	—	New Year	Nouvel An *m*	Capodanno *m*	(día de) Año Nuevo *m*
new foundation (E)	Neugründung *f*	—	création d'une nouvelle société *f*	costituzione nuova *f*	fundación nueva *f*
newly industrialized countries (E)	Schwellenland *n*	—	pays dans le seuil à l'industrialisation *m*	paese emergente *m*	país en el umbral hacia la industrialización *m*
news (E)	Nachricht *f*	—	nouvelle *f*	notizia *f*	noticia *f*
newspaper and magazine advertising (E)	Anzeigenwerbung *f*	—	publicité par la presse *f*	pubblicità per inserzione *f*	publicidad por anuncios *f*
New Year (E)	Neujahr *n*	—	Nouvel An *m*	Capodanno *m*	(día de) Año Nuevo *m*
Nichterfüllung (D)	—	non-performance	inexécution *f*	inadempienza *f*	incumplimiento *m*
nichtig (D)	—	void	non valable	nullo	nulo
nicht übertragbar (D)	—	non-assignable	ne pas transférable	non trasferibile	intransmisible
Niederlassung (D)	—	establishment	succursale *f*	succursale *f*	sucursal *f*
Niedrigstkurs (D)	—	floor price	cours le plus bas *m*	corso minimo *m*	cotización mínima *f*
Nießbrauch (D)	—	usufruct	usufruit *m*	usufrutto *m*	usufructo *m*
night safe (E)	Nachttresor *m*	—	dépôt de nuit *m*	cassa continua *f*	depósito de noche *m*
night shift (E)	Nachtschicht *f*	—	équipe de nuit *f*	turno notturno *m*	turno de noche *m*
nil tariff (E)	Nulltarif *m*	—	tarif gratuit *m*	tariffa zero *f*	tarifa gratuita *f*
nitric oxide (E)	Stickoxid *n*	—	oxyde azotique *m*	ossido di azoto *m*	óxido nítrico *m*
niveau de gestion (F)	Führungsebene *f*	executive level	—	quadri dirigenti *m*	nivel de dirección *m*
niveau de l'endettement (F)	Verschuldungsgrad *m*	debt ratio	—	tasso d'indebitamento *m*	grado de endeudamiento *m*
niveau des prix (F)	Preisniveau *n*	price level	—	livello dei prezzi *m*	nivel de precios *m*
niveau de vie (F)	Lebensstandard *m*	standard of living	—	tenore di vita *m*	nivel de vida *m*
niveau du rendement (F)	Ertragslage *f*	earning situation	—	situazione economica *f*	situación del beneficio *f*
niveau du taux d'intérêt (F)	Zinsniveau *n*	interest rate level	—	livello degli interessi *m*	nivel de interés *m*
nivel de dirección (Es)	Führungsebene *f*	executive level	niveau de gestion *m*	quadri dirigenti *m*	—
nivel de interés (Es)	Zinsniveau *n*	interest rate level	niveau du taux d'intérêt *m*	livello degli interessi *m*	—
nivel de precios (Es)	Preisniveau *n*	price level	niveau des prix *m*	livello dei prezzi *m*	—
nivel de vida (Es)	Lebensstandard *m*	standard of living	niveau de vie *m*	tenore di vita *m*	—
no asegurado (Es)	ungesichert	unsecured	non garanti	non assicurato	—
no contaminante (Es)	umweltfreundlich	beneficial to the environment	favorable à l'environnement	ecologico	—
Noël (F)	Weihnachten *n*	Christmas	—	Natale *m*	Navidad *f*
no en efectivo (Es)	unbar	non cash	non comptant	non in contanti	—
noise abatement (E)	Lärmbekämpfung *f*	—	lutte contre le bruit *f*	lotta contro i rumori *f*	lucha contra el ruido *f*
nolo (I)	Fracht *f*	freight	fret *m*	—	carga *f*
nolo aereo (I)	Luftfracht *f*	air freight	fret aérien *m*	—	flete aéreo *m*
nolo ferroviario (I)	Bahnfracht *f*	rail freight	fret par rail *m*	—	transporte ferroviario *m*
nolo pagato (I)	Fracht bezahlt	freight paid	fret payé	—	flete pagado
nombramiento (Es)	Ernennung *f*	apointment	nomination *f*	nomina *f*	—
nombre (F)	Zahl *f*	number/figure	—	numero *m*/cifra *f*	número *m*/cifra *f*
nom de la maison (F)	Firmenname *m*	company name	—	denominazione *f*/ ragione sociale *f*	razón social *f*
nomina (I)	Ernennung *f*	apointment	nomination *f*	—	nombramiento *m*
nominal amount (E)	Nominalbetrag *m*	—	montant nominal *m*	importo nominale *m*	montante nominal *m*
Nominalbetrag (D)	—	nominal amount	montant nominal *m*	importo nominale *m*	montante nominal *m*
Nominaleinkommen (D)	—	nominal income	revenu nominal *m*	reddito nominale *m*	ingresos nominales *m*
nominal income (E)	Nominaleinkommen *n*	—	revenu nominal *m*	reddito nominale *m*	ingresos nominales *m*
Nominallohn (D)	—	nominal wage	salaire nominal *m*	salario nominale *m*	salario nominal *m*
nominal value (E)	Nennwert *m*	—	valeur nominale *f*	valore nominale *m*	valor nominal *m*
nominal wage (E)	Nominallohn *m*	—	salaire nominal *m*	salario nominale *m*	salario nominal *m*
nomination[1] (F)	Beförderung *f*	promotion	—	promozione *f*	ascenso *m*

	D	E	F	I	Es
nomination[2] (F)	Ernennung *f*	apointment	—	nomina *f*	nombramiento *m*
non adéquat (F)	unsachgemäß	improper	—	non idoneo	con falta de objetividad
No-name-Produkt (D)	—	generic product	produit sans nom *m*	prodotto senza nome *m*	producto genérico *m*
non assicurato (I)	ungesichert	unsecured	non garanti	—	no asegurado
non-assignable (E)	nicht übertragbar	—	ne pas transférable	non trasferibile	intransmisible
non cash (E)	unbar	—	non comptant	non in contanti	no en efectivo
non-cash (E)	bargeldlos	—	par virement	mediante assegno	por transferencia
non comptant (F)	unbar	non cash	—	non in contanti	no en efectivo
non dédouané (F)	unverzollt	duty unpaid	—	non sdoganato	aduana aparte
non garanti (F)	ungesichert	unsecured	—	non assicurato	no asegurado
non idoneo (I)	unsachgemäß	improper	non adéquat	—	con falta de objetividad
non imballato (I)	unverpackt	unpacked	sans emballage	—	sin embalar
non in contanti (I)	unbar	non cash	non comptant	—	no en efectivo
non-material damage (E)	immaterieller Schaden *m*	—	dommage immatériel *m*	danno immateriale *m*	daño inmaterial *m*
non-performance (E)	Nichterfüllung *f*	—	inexécution *f*	inadempienza *f*	incumplimiento *m*
non-recourse financing (E)	Forfaitierung *f*	—	financement sans recours *m*	forfetizzazione *f*	financiación sin recurso *f*
non sdoganato (I)	unverzollt	duty unpaid	non dédouané	—	aduana aparte
non trasferibile (I)	nicht übertragbar	non-assignable	ne pas transférable	—	intransmisible
non valable (F)	nichtig	void	—	nullo	nulo
Norm (D)	—	standard	standard *m*	norma *f*	norma *f*
norma (Es)	Norm *f*	standard	standard *m*	norma *f*	—
norma (I)	Norm *f*	standard	standard *m*	—	norma *f*
norma de producción (Es)	Arbeitsnorm *f*	fair labour standards	norme de travail *f*	norma di lavoro *f*	—
norma di lavoro (I)	Arbeitsnorm *f*	fair labour standards	norme de travail *f*	—	norma de producción *f*
norma giuridica (I)	Rechtsnorm *f*	legal norm	règle de droit *f*	—	norma jurídica *f*
norma industrial alemana (Es)	Deutsche Industrie-Norm *f*	German Industrial Standards	norme industrielle allemande *f*	norma tedesca di normalizzazione *f*	—
norma jurídica (Es)	Rechtsnorm *f*	legal norm	règle de droit *f*	norma giuridica *f*	—
normalisé (F)	genormt	standardized	—	standardizzato	normalizado
normalización (Es)	Normung *f*	standardization	standardisation *f*	standardizzazione *f*	—
normalizado (Es)	genormt	standardized	normalisé	standardizzato	—
normas técnicas (Es)	technische Normen *pl*	technical standards	normes techniques *f pl*	norme tecniche *f pl*	—
norma tedesca di normalizzazione (I)	Deutsche Industrie-Norm *f*	German Industrial Standards	norme industrielle allemande *f*	—	norma industrial alemana *f*
norme de travail (F)	Arbeitsnorm *f*	fair labour standards	—	norma di lavoro *f*	norma de producción *f*
norme industrielle allemande (F)	Deutsche Industrie-Norm *f*	German Industrial Standards	—	norma tedesca di normalizzazione *f*	norma industrial alemana *f*
normes techniques (F)	technische Normen *pl*	technical standards	—	norme tecniche *f pl*	normas técnicas *f pl*
norme tecniche (I)	technische Normen *pl*	technical standards	normes techniques *f pl*	—	normas técnicas *f pl*
Normung (D)	—	standardization	standardisation *f*	standardizzazione *f*	normalización *f*
nota[1] (Es)	Aktennotiz *f*	memorandum	note *f*	annotazione *f*	—
nota[2] (Es)	Vermerk *m*	note	remarque *f*	annotazione *f*	—
nota de cobertura (Es)	Deckungszusage *f*	confirmation of cover	acceptation de prendre le risque en charge *f*	impegno di copertura *m*	—
nota de prensa (Es)	Pressenotiz *f*	press report	note de presse *f*	notizia stampa *f*	—
nota di accredito (I)	Gutschriftsanzeige *f*	credit advice	avis de crédit *m*	—	aviso de abono *m*
notaio (I)	Notar *m*	(public) notary	notaire *m*	—	notario *m*
notaire (F)	Notar *m*	(public) notary	—	notaio *m*	notario *m*
Notar (D)	—	(public) notary	notaire *m*	notaio *m*	notario *m*
notario (Es)	Notar *m*	(public) notary	notaire *m*	notaio *m*	—
not binding (E)	unverbindlich	—	sans obligation	senza impegno	sin compromiso

	D	E	F	I	Es
note[1] (E)	Vermerk *m*	—	remarque *f*	annotazione *f*	nota *f*
note[2] (E)	Notiz *f*	—	note *f*	annotazione *f*	noticia *f*
note[1] (F)	Notiz *f*	note	—	annotazione *f*	noticia *f*
note[2] (F)	Aktennotiz *f*	memorandum	—	annotazione *f*	nota *f*
note de débit (F)	Lastschrift *f*	debit entry	—	addebito *m*	cargo en cuenta *m*
note de presse (F)	Pressenotiz *f*	press report	—	notizia stampa *f*	nota de prensa *f*
Notenbank (D)	—	central bank	banque d'émission *f*	banca d'emissione *f*	banco emisor *m*
Notenumlauf (D)	—	notes in circulation	circulation fiduciaire *f*	circolazione delle banconote *f*	circulación fiduciaria *f*
notes in circulation (E)	Notenumlauf *m*	—	circulation fiduciaire *f*	circolazione delle banconote *f*	circulación fiduciaria *f*
notice of assessment (E)	Steuerbescheid *m*	—	avis d'imposition *m*	cartella delle imposte *f*	liquidación de impuestos *f*
notice of defect (E)	Mängelanzeige *f*	—	notification d'un vice *f*	denuncia dei vizi	aviso de vicios *m*
notice of termination (E)	Kündigung *f*	—	résiliation *f*	disdetta *f*	rescisión *f*
noticia[1] (Es)	Notiz *f*	note	note *f*	annotazione *f*	—
noticia[2] (Es)	Nachricht *f*	news	nouvelle *f*	notizia *f*	—
Notierung (D)	—	quotation	cotation *f*	quotazione *f*	cotización *f*
notifica (I)	Zustellung *f*	delivery	remise *f*	—	envío *m*
notification (F)	Mitteilung *f*	information	—	comunicazione *f*	aviso *m*
notification d'un vice (F)	Mängelanzeige *f*	notice of defect	—	denuncia dei vizi *f*	aviso de vicios *m*
notification of damage (E)	Schadensmeldung *f*	—	déclaration du sinistre *f*	avviso di danni *m*	aviso de siniestro *m*
Notiz (D)	—	note	note *f*	annotazione *f*	noticia *f*
notizia (I)	Nachricht *f*	news	nouvelle *f*	—	noticia *f*
notizia stampa (I)	Pressenotiz *f*	press report	note de presse *f*	—	nota de prensa *f*
no utilizado (Es)	ungenutzt	unused	pas utilisé	inutilizzato	—
Nouvel An (F)	Neujahr *n*	New Year	—	Capodanno *m*	(día de) Año Nuevo *m*
nouvel ordre (F)	Nachbestellung *f*	repeat order	—	ordinazione supplementare *f*	pedido suplementario *m*
no vinculante (Es)	freibleibend	subject to confirmation	sans engagement	senza impegno	—
nuclear energy (E)	Kernenergie *f*	—	énergie nucléaire *f*	energia nucleare *f*	energía nuclear *f*
nuclear power plant (E)	Atomkraftwerk *n*	—	centrale nucléaire *f*	centrale nucleare *f*	central nuclear *f*
nuisible à l'environnement (F)	umweltschädlich	causing environmental damages	—	inquinante	contaminante
nullo (I)	nichtig	void	non valable	—	nulo
Nulltarif (D)	—	nil tariff	tarif gratuit *m*	tariffa zero *f*	tarifa gratuita *f*
Nullwachstum (D)	—	zero growth	croissance zéro *f*	crescita zero *f*	crecimiento cero *m*
nulo (Es)	nichtig	void	non valable	nullo	—
number (E)	Zahl *f*	—	nombre *m*/chiffre *m*	numero *m*/cifra *f*	número *m*/cifra *f*
numbered account (E)	Nummernkonto *n*	—	compte anonyme *m*	conto cifrato *m*	cuenta cifrada *f*
numeri d'identificazione (I)	Kennzahlen *pl*	code numbers	numéros de référence *m pl*	—	números índice *m pl*
número (Es)	Zahl *f*	number/figure	nombre *m*/chiffre *m*	numero *m*/cifra *f*	—
numero (I)	Zahl *f*	number/figure	nombre *m*/chiffre *m*	—	número *m*/cifra *f*
numéro de commande (F)	Auftragsnummer *f*	order number	—	numero d'ordine *m*	número de pedido *m*
numéro de compte (F)	Kontonummer *f*	account number	—	numero di conto *m*	número de cuenta *m*
número de cuenta (Es)	Kontonummer *f*	account number	numéro de compte *m*	numero di conto *m*	—
número de la factura (Es)	Rechnungsnummer *f*	invoice number	numéro de la facture *m*	numero della fattura *m*	—
numéro de la facture (F)	Rechnungsnummer *f*	invoice number	—	numero della fattura *m*	número de la factura *m*
número del cliente (Es)	Kundennummer *f*	customer's reference number	numéro de référence du client *m*	numero di cliente *m*	—
numero della fattura (I)	Rechnungsnummer *f*	invoice number	numéro de la facture *m*	—	número de la factura *m*

	D	E	F	I	Es
número de pedido (Es)	Auftragsnummer *f*	order number	numéro de commande *m*	numero d'ordine *m*	—
numéro de référence du client (F)	Kundennummer *f*	customer's reference number	—	numero di cliente *m*	número del cliente *m*
número de telefax (Es)	Telefaxnummer *f*	telefax number	numéro de téléfax *m*	numero telefax *m*	—
numéro de téléfax (F)	Telefaxnummer *f*	telefax number	—	numero telefax *m*	número de telefax *m*
número de teléfono (Es)	Telefonnummer *f*	telephone number	numéro de téléphone *m*	numero di telefono *m*	—
numéro de téléphone (F)	Telefonnummer *f*	telephone number	—	numero di telefono *m*	número de teléfono *m*
número de téletex (Es)	Teletexnummer *f*	teletex number	numéro de télétex *m*	numero teletex *m*	—
numéro de télétex (F)	Teletexnummer *f*	teletex number	—	numero teletex *m*	número de téletex *m*
número de télex (Es)	Telexnummer *f*	telex number	numéro de télex *m*	numero telex *m*	—
numéro de télex (F)	Telexnummer *f*	telex number	—	numero telex *m*	número de télex *m*
numero di cliente (I)	Kundennummer *f*	customer's reference number	numéro de référence du client *m*	—	número del cliente *m*
numero di conto (I)	Kontonummer *f*	account number	numéro de compte *m*	—	número de cuenta *m*
numero di telefono (I)	Telefonnummer *f*	telephone number	numéro de téléphone *m*	—	número de teléfono *m*
numero d'ordine (I)	Auftragsnummer *f*	order number	numéro de commande *m*	—	número de pedido *m*
numéros de référence (F)	Kennzahlen *pl*	code numbers	—	numeri d'identificazione *m pl*	números índice *m pl*
números índice (Es)	Kennzahlen *pl*	code numbers	numéros de référence *m pl*	numeri d'identificazione *m pl*	—
numero telefax (I)	Telefaxnummer *f*	telefax number	numéro de téléfax *m*	—	número de telefax *m*
numero teletex (I)	Teletexnummer *f*	teletex number	numéro de télétex *m*	—	número de téletex *m*
numero telex (I)	Telexnummer *f*	telex number	numéro de télex *m*	—	número de télex *m*
Nummernkonto (D)	—	numbered account	compte anonyme *m*	conto cifrato *m*	cuenta cifrada *f*
Nutzen (D)	—	utility	utilité *f*	utilità *f*	utilidad *f*
Nutzkosten (D)	—	utility costs	coûts fixes utiles *m pl*	costi fissi di utilizzo *m pl*	gastos fijos de utilización *m pl*
Nutzung (D)	—	use/utilization	mise à profit *f*	utilizzazione *f*	utilización *f*
oasi fiscale (I)	Steueroase *f*	tax haven	oasis fiscale *f*	—	oasis fiscal *m*
oasis fiscal (Es)	Steueroase *f*	tax haven	oasis fiscale *f*	oasi fiscale *f*	—
oasis fiscale (F)	Steueroase *f*	tax haven	—	oasi fiscale *f*	oasis fiscal *m*
obbligazione (I)	Schuld-verschreibung *f*	debenture stock	obligation *f*	—	obligación *f*
obbligazione convertibile (I)	Wandelschuld-verschreibung *f*	convertible bonds	obligation convertible *f*	—	obligaciones convertibles *f pl*
obbligazione perpetua (I)	Dauerschuld-verschreibung *f*	unredeemable bond	obligation perpétuelle *f*	—	obligación perpetua *f*
obbligazioni comunali (I)	Kommunal-obligation *f*	corporation stock	obligation communale *f*	—	obligación comunal *f*
obbligazioni industriali (I)	Industrie-obligationen *pl*	industrial bonds	obligations de l'industrie *f pl*	—	obligaciones industriales *f pl*
obblighi (I)	Verbindlichkeiten *pl*	liability/debts	obligation *f*/dettes *f pl*	—	obligaciónes *f pl*/ deudas *f pl*/créditos pasivos *m pl*
obbligo (I)	Obligo *n*	liability	engagement *m*	—	obligación *f*
obbligo d'assicurazione (I)	Versicherungs-pflicht *f*	liability to insure	assujettissement obligatoire à l'assurance *m*	—	obligatoriedad del seguro *f*
obbligo del segreto professionale (I)	Schweigepflicht *f*	professional discretion	discretion professionnelle *f*	—	secreto profesional *m*
obbligo di accettare la consegna (I)	Abnahmepflicht *f*	obligation to accept delivery	obligation d'acceptation de la marchandise *f*	—	obligación de recepción *f*
obbligo di conservazione (I)	Aufbewahrungs-pflicht *f*	obligation to preserve records	obligation de conservation *f*	—	deber de conservación *m*
obbligo di fornitura (I)	Belieferungspflicht *f*	duty to supply	obligation de livraison *f*	—	obligación de suministro *f*
obbligo di garanzia (I)	Garantie-verpflichtung *f*	guarantee obligation	engagement de garantie *m*	—	obligación de garantía *f*

	D	E	F	I	Es
obbligo di mantenere il prezzo fissato (I)	Preisbindung *f*	obligation to maintain fixed prices	obligation de respecter les prix *f*	—	limitación de precios *f*
obbligo d'intervento (I)	Interventionspflicht *f*	obligation to intervene	obligation d'intervention *f*	—	obligación de intervención *f*
obbligo di relazione (I)	Berichtspflicht *f*	obligation to report	obligation d'information *f*	—	obligación de información *f*
obbligo di risarcimento danni (I)	Schadensersatzpflicht *f*	liability for damages	obligation de dédommager *f*	—	obligación indemnizatoria *f*
obbligo di sorveglianza (I)	Aufsichtspflicht *f*	duty of supervision	obligation de surveillance *f*	—	obligación de vigilancia *f*
obiettivi pubblicitari (I)	Werbeziele *pl*	advertising objective	objectifs publicitaires *m pl*	—	objetivos de la publicidad *m pl*
obiettivo (I)	Ziel *n*	objective	but *m*	—	objetivo *m*
obiettivo della politica economica (I)	wirtschaftspolitische Zielsetzung *f*	economy policy objectives	objectifs commandés par une politique économique *m pl*	—	objetivos de la política económica *m pl*
obiettivo di vendita (I)	Absatzziel *n*	sales target	objectif de vente *m*	—	fin de venta *m*
obiettivo imprenditoriale (I)	Unternehmensziel *n*	company objective	objectif de l'entreprise *m*	—	objetivo empresarial *m*
objectif de l'entreprise (F)	Unternehmensziel *n*	company objective	—	obiettivo imprenditoriale *m*	objetivo empresarial *m*
objectif de vente (F)	Absatzziel *n*	sales target	—	obbiettivo di vendita *m*	fin de venta *m*
objectifs commandés par une politique économique (F)	wirtschaftspolitische Zielsetzung *f*	economy policy objectives	—	obiettivo della politica economica *m*	objetivos de la política económica *m pl*
objectifs publicitaires (F)	Werbeziele *pl*	advertising objective	—	obiettivi pubblicitari *m pl*	objetivos de la publicidad *m pl*
objection (F)	Beanstandung *f*	objection	—	reclamo *m*	queja *f*
objection[1] (E)	Beanstandung *f*	—	objection *f*	reclamo *m*	queja *f*
objection[2] (E)	Protest *m*	—	protestation *f*/ protêt *m*	opposizione *f*/ protesta *f*	oposición *f*/protesta *f*
objective (E)	Ziel *n*	—	but *m*	obiettivo *m*	objetivo *m*
objectivo de facturación (Es)	Umsatzplan *m*	turnover plan	plan du chiffre d'affaires *m*	programma del fatturato *m*	—
object of depreciation (E)	Abschreibungsobjekt *n*	—	objet d'amortissement *m*	oggetto da ammortizzare *m*	objeto de amortización *m*
object of speculation (E)	Spekulationsobjekt *n*	—	objet de spéculation *m*	oggetto di speculazioni *m*	objeto de especulación *m*
objet d'amortissement (F)	Abschreibungsobjekt *n*	object of depreciation	—	oggetto da ammortizzare *m*	objeto de amortización *m*
objet de leasing (F)	Leasing-Objekt *n*	leasing object	—	oggetto del leasing *m*	objeto de leasing *m*
objet de spéculation (F)	Spekulationsobjekt *n*	object of speculation	—	oggetto di speculazioni *m*	objeto de especulación *m*
objetivo (Es)	Ziel *n*	objective	but *m*	obiettivo *m*	—
objetivo empresarial (Es)	Unternehmensziel *n*	company objective	objectif de l'entreprise *m*	obiettivo imprenditoriale *m*	—
objetivos de la política económica (Es)	wirtschaftspolitische Zielsetzung *f*	economy policy objectives	objectifs commandés par une politique économique *m pl*	obiettivo della politica economica *m*	—
objetivos de la publicidad (Es)	Werbeziele *pl*	advertising objective	objectifs publicitaires *m pl*	obiettivi pubblicitari *m pl*	—
objeto de amortización (Es)	Abschreibungsobjekt *n*	object of depreciation	objet d'amortissement *m*	oggetto da ammortizzare *m*	—
objeto de especulación (Es)	Spekulationsobjekt *n*	object of speculation	objet de spéculation *m*	oggetto di speculazioni *m*	—
objeto de leasing (Es)	Leasing-Objekt *n*	leasing object	objet de leasing *m*	oggetto del leasing *m*	—
obligación[1] (Es)	Obligo *n*	liability	engagement *m*	obbligo *m*	—
obligación[2] (Es)	Schuldverschreibung *f*	debenture stock	obligation *f*	obbligazione *f*	—
obligación comunal (Es)	Kommunalobligation *f*	corporation stock	obligation communale *f*	obbligazioni comunali *f pl*	—
obligación de garantía (Es)	Garantieverpflichtung *f*	guarantee obligation	engagement de garantie *m*	obbligo di garanzia *m*	—
obligación de información (Es)	Berichtspflicht *f*	obligation to report	obligation d'information *f*	obbligo di relazione *m*	—

	D	E	F	I	Es
obligación de intervención (Es)	Interventionspflicht *f*	obligation to intervene	obligation d'intervention *f*	obbligo d'intervento *m*	—
obligación de recepción (Es)	Abnahmepflicht *f*	obligation to accept delivery	obligation d'acceptation de la marchandise *f*	obbligo di accettare la consegna *m*	—
obligación de suministro (Es)	Belieferungspflicht *f*	duty to supply	obligation de livraison *f*	obbligo di fornitura *m*	—
obligación de vigilancia (Es)	Aufsichtspflicht *f*	duty of supervision	obligation de surveillance *f*	obbligo di sorveglianza *m*	—
obligaciones (Es)	Verbindlichkeiten *pl*	liability/debts	obligation *f*/ dettes *f pl*	obblighi *m pl*/ debiti *m pl*	—
obligaciones convertibles (Es)	Wandelschuld-verschreibung *f*	convertible bonds	obligation convertible *f*	obbligazione convertibile *f*	—
obligaciones industriales (Es)	Industrie-obligationen *pl*	industrial bonds	obligations de l'industrie *f pl*	obbligazioni industriali *f pl*	—
obligación indemnizatoria (Es)	Schadens-ersatzpflicht *f*	liability for damages	obligation de dédommager *f*	obbligo di risarcimento danni *m*	—
obligación perpetua (Es)	Dauerschuld-verschreibung *f*	unredeemable bond	obligation perpétuelle *f*	obbligazione perpetua *f*	—
obligation[1] (F)	Schuld-verschreibung *f*	debenture stock	—	obbligazione *f*	obligación *f*
obligation[2] (F)	Verbindlichkeiten *pl*	liability/debts	—	obblighi *m pl*/ debiti *m pl*	obligaciónes *f pl*/ deudas *f pl*/créditos pasivos *m pl*
obligation communale (F)	Kommunal-obligation *f*	corporation stock	—	obbligazioni comunali *f pl*	obligación comunal *f*
obligation convertible (F)	Wandelschuld-verschreibung *f*	convertible bonds	—	obbligazione convertibile *f*	obligaciones convertibles *f pl*
obligation d'acceptation de la marchandise (F)	Abnahmepflicht *f*	obligation to accept delivery	—	obbligo di accettare la consegna *m*	obligación de recepción *f*
obligation de conservation (F)	Aufbewahrungs-pflicht *f*	obligation to preserve records	—	obbligo di conservazione *m*	deber de conservación *m*
obligation de dédommager (F)	Schadensersatz-pflicht *f*	liability for damages	—	obbligo di risarcimento danni *m*	obligación indemnizatoria *f*
obligation de livraison (F)	Belieferungspflicht *f*	duty to supply	—	obbligo di fornitura *m*	obligación de suministro *f*
obligation de respecter les prix (F)	Preisbindung *f*	obligation to maintain fixed prices	—	obbligo di mantenere il prezzo fissato *m*	limitación de precios *f*
obligation de surveillance (F)	Aufsichtspflicht *f*	duty of supervision	—	obbligo di sorveglianza *m*	obligación de vigilancia *f*
obligation d'information (F)	Berichtspflicht *f*	obligation to report	—	obbligo di relazione *m*	obligación de información *f*
obligation d'intervention (F)	Interventionspflicht *f*	obligation to intervene	—	obbligo d'intervento *m*	obligación de intervención *f*
obligation hypothécaire (F)	Pfandbrief *m*	mortgage bond	—	titolo ipotecario *m*	cédula hipotecaria *f*
obligation perpétuelle (F)	Dauerschuld-verschreibung *f*	unredeemable bond	—	obbligazione perpetua *f*	obligación perpetua *f*
Obligationsanleihe (D)	—	debenture loan	emprunt obligataire *m*	prestito obbligazionario *m*	empréstito sobre obligaciones *m*
obligations de l'industrie (F)	Industrie-obligationen *pl*	industrial bonds	—	obbligazioni industriali *f pl*	obligaciones industriales *f pl*
obligation to accept delivery (E)	Abnahmepflicht *f*	—	obligation d'acceptation de la marchandise *f*	obbligo di accettare la consegna *m*	obligación de recepción *f*
obligation to intervene (E)	Interventionspflicht *f*	—	obligation d'intervention *f*	obbligo d'intervento *m*	obligación de intervención *f*
obligation to maintain fixed prices (E)	Preisbindung *f*	—	obligation de respecter les prix *f*	obbligo di mantenere il prezzo fissato *m*	limitación de precios *f*
obligation to preserve records (E)	Aufbewahrungs-pflicht *f*	—	obligation de conservation *f*	obbligo di conservazione *m*	deber de conservación *m*
obligation to report (E)	Berichtspflicht *f*	—	obligation d'information *f*	obbligo di relazione *m*	obligación de información *f*
obligatoriedad del seguro (Es)	Versicherungs-pflicht *f*	liability to insure	assujettissement obligatoire à l'assurance *m*	obbligo d'assicurazione *m*	—
Obligo (D)	—	liability	engagement *m*	obbligo *m*	obligación *f*

	D	E	F	I	Es
observación de la competencia (Es)	Konkurrenz-beobachtung *f*	observation of the competitors	observation de la concurrence *f*	studio della concorrenza *m*	—
observación del mercado (Es)	Marktbeobachtung *f*	observation of markets	recherche du marché *f*	sondaggio del mercato *m*	—
observation de la concurrence (F)	Konkurrenz-beobachtung *f*	observation of the competitors	—	studio della concorrenza *m*	observación de la competencia *f*
observation of markets (E)	Marktbeobachtung *f*	—	étude de marché *f*	sondaggio del mercato *m*	observación del mercado *f*
observation of the competitors (E)	Konkurrenz-beobachtung *f*	—	observation de la concurrence *f*	studio della concorrenza *m*	observación de la competencia *f*
occupation (F)	Beschäftigung *f*	employment	—	occupazione *f*	ocupación *f*
occupational hazard (E)	Berufsrisiko *n*	—	risque professionnel *m*	rischio professionale *m*	riesgo profesional *m*
occupazione (I)	Beschäftigung *f*	employment	occupation *f*	—	ocupación *f*
occupazione eccedente (I)	Überbeschäftigung *f*	overcharge	surchargement *m*	—	exceso de empleo *m*/ superempleo *m*
occupazione part-time (I)	Teilzeit-beschäftigung *f*	part-time employment	emploi à temps partiel *m*	—	empleo parcial *m*
octroi d'un délai (F)	Fristgewährung *f*	granting a respite	—	concessione di un termine *f*	concesión de un plazo *f*
ocupación (Es)	Beschäftigung *f*	employment	occupation *f*	occupazione *f*	—
oferta (Es)	Offerte *f*	offer	offre *f*	offerta *f*	—
oferta de empleo (Es)	Stellenangebot *n*	offer of employment	offre d'emploi *f*	offerta d'impiego *f*	—
oferta de indemnización (Es)	Abfindungsangebot *n*	compensation offer	offre d'indemnité *f*	offerta d'indennità *f*	—
oferta especial (Es)	Sonderangebot *n*	special offer	offre spéciale *f*	offerta speciale *f*	—
oferta favorable[1] (Es)	preisgünstiges Angebot *n*	well-priced offer	offre à un prix avantageux *f*	offerta a buon prezzo *f*	—
oferta favorable[2] (Es)	günstigstes Angebot *n*	most favourable offer	offre favorable *f*	offerta vantaggiosa *f*	—
offene Rechnung (D)	—	unsettled account	facture pas encore payée *f*	conto aperto *m*	factura pendiente *f*
Offenlegung (D)	—	disclosure	révélation des derniers bilans du postulant d'un prêt *f*	pubblicità del bilancio *f*	publicidad para fines de inspección *f*
öffentliche Ausgaben (D)	—	public spending	dépenses publiques *f pl*	spesa pubblica *f*	gastos públicos *m pl*
öffentliche Betriebe (D)	—	public sector industrial enterprises	entreprises publiques *f pl*	aziende pubbliche *f pl*	empresa pública *f*
öffentliche Einnahmen (D)	—	public revenues	recettes publiques *f pl*	entrate pubbliche *f pl*	ingresos públicos *m pl*
öffentliche Güter (D)	—	public goods	biens publics *m pl*	beni pubblici *m pl*	bienes públicos *m pl*
öffentliche Hand (D)	—	public authorities	secteur public *m*	mano pubblica *f*	sector público *m*
öffentliche Unternehmen (D)	—	public enterprise	entreprises publiques *f pl*	imprese pubbliche *f pl*	empresa pública *f*
öffentliche Wirtschaft (D)	—	public sector of the economy	économie publique *f*	economia pubblica *f*	economía pública *f*
Öffentlichkeits-arbeit (D)	—	public relations (work)	relations publiques *f pl*	relazioni pubbliche *f pl*	relaciones públicas *f pl*
öffentlich-rechtlich (D)	—	under public law	de droit public	di diritto pubblico	de derecho público
offer[1] (E)	Angebot *n*	—	proposition *f*	offerta *f*	oferta *f*
offer[2] (E)	Offerte *f*	—	offre *f*	offerta *f*	oferta *f*
offer[3] (E)	anbieten	—	offrir	offrire	ofrecer
offer of employment (E)	Stellenangebot *n*	—	offre d'emploi *f*	offerta d'impiego *f*	oferta de empleo *f*
offerta[1] (I)	Offerte *f*	offer	offre *f*	—	oferta *f*
offerta[2] (I)	Angebot *n*	offer	proposition *f*	—	oferta *f*
offerta a buon prezzo (I)	preisgünstiges Angebot *n*	well-priced offer	offre à un prix avantageux *f*	—	oferta favorable *f*
offerta d'impiego (I)	Stellenangebot *n*	offer of employment	offre d'emploi *f*	—	oferta de empleo *f*
offerta d'indennità (I)	Abfindungsangebot *n*	compensation offer	offre d'indemnité *f*	—	oferta de indemniza-ción *f*
offerta pubblica d'acquisto (I)	Tenderverfahren *n*	tender procedure	offre d'emprunts pour la régulation monétaire *f*	—	subasta de prestamos de regulación monetaria *f*

	D	E	F	I	Es
offerta speciale (I)	Sonderangebot *n*	special offer	offre spéciale *f*	—	oferta especial *f*
offerta vantaggiosa (I)	günstigstes	most favourable offer Angebot *n*	offre favorable *f*	—	oferta favorable *f*
Offerte (D)	—	offer	offre *f*	offerta *f*	oferta *f*
office de surveillance des cartels et ententes (F)	Kartellbehörde *f*	cartel authority	—	autorità antimonopoli *f pl*	oficina de cártels *f*
office des brevets (F)	Patentamt *n*	Patent Office	—	ufficio brevetti *m*	oficina del registro de patentes *f*
Office Européen de Brevets (F)	Europäisches Patentamt *n*	European Patent Office	—	Ufficio Europeo Brevetti *m*	Oficina Europea de Patentes *f*
office[1] (E)	Amt *n*	—	bureau *m*	ufficio *m*	cargo *m*
office[2] (E)	Geschäftsstelle *f*	—	agence *f*	ufficio *m*	oficina *f*
official (E)	Beamter *m*	—	fonctionnaire *m*	funzionario *m*	funcionario *m*
official car (E)	Dienstwagen *m*	—	voiture de service *f*	vettura di servizio *f*	coche de servicio *m*
official secret (E)	Dienstgeheimnis *n*	—	secret de service *m*	segreto d'ufficio *m*	secreto profesional *m*
offre (F)	Offerte *f*	offer	—	offerta *f*	oferta *f*
offre à un prix avantageux (F)	preisgünstiges Angebot *n*	well-priced offer	—	offerta a buon prezzo *f*	oferta favorable *f*
offre d'emploi (F)	Stellenangebot *n*	offer of employment	—	offerta d'impiego *f*	oferta de empleo *f*
offre d'emprunts pour la régulation monétaire (F)	Tenderverfahren *n*	tender procedure	—	offerta pubblica d'acquisto *f*	subasta de prestamos de regulación monetaria *f*
offre d'indemnité (F)	Abfindungsangebot *n*	compensation offer	—	offerta d'indennità *f*	oferta de indemnización *f*
offre favorable (F)	günstigstes Angebot *n*	most favourable offer	—	offerta vantaggiosa *f*	oferta favorable *f*
offre spéciale (F)	Sonderangebot *n*	special offer	—	offerta speciale *f*	oferta especial *f*
offrir (F)	anbieten	offer	—	offrire	ofrecer
offrire (I)	anbieten	offer	offrir	—	ofrecer
offset (F)	Offsetdruck *m*	offset (printing)	—	stampa offset *f*	impresión offset *f*
Offsetdruck (D)	—	offset (printing)	offset *m*	stampa offset *f*	impresión offset *f*
offset (printing) (E)	Offsetdruck *m*	—	offset *m*	stampa offset *f*	impresión offset *f*
oficial (Es)	Geselle *m*	journeyman	ouvrier artisan *m*	garzone *m*	—
oficina (Es)	Geschäftsstelle *f*	office	agence *f*	ufficio *m*	—
oficina de aduanas (Es)	Zollstelle *f*	customs office	bureau de douane *m*	posto di dogana *m*	—
oficina de cártels (Es)	Kartellbehörde *f*	cartel authority	office de surveillance des cartels et ententes *m*	autorità antimonopoli *f pl*	—
oficina de cheques postales (Es)	Postscheckamt *n*	postal giro centre	bureau de chèques postaux *m*	ufficio dei conti correnti postali *m*	—
oficina de información (Es)	Auskunftei *f*	information bureau	agence de renseignements *f*	agenzia d'informazioni *f*	—
oficina del censo (Es)	Einwohnermelde-amt *n*	residents' registration office	bureau de déclaration de résidence *m*	ufficio anagrafe *m*	—
oficina del registro de patentes (Es)	Patentamt *n*	Patent Office	office des brevets *m*	ufficio brevetti *m*	—
oficina de personal (Es)	Personalbüro *n*	personnel office	bureau du personnel *m*	ufficio del personale *m*	—
Oficina Europea de Patentes (Es)	Europäisches Patentamt *n*	European Patent Office	Office Européen de Brevets *f*	Ufficio Europeo Brevetti *m*	—
ofrecer (Es)	anbieten	offer	offrir	offrire	—
oggetto da ammortizzare (I)	Abschreibungs-objekt *n*	object of depreciation	objet d'amortissement *m*	—	objeto de amortización *m*
oggetto del leasing (I)	Leasing-Objekt *n*	leasing object	objet de leasing *m*	—	objeto de leasing *m*
oggetto di speculazioni (I)	Spekulationsobjekt *n*	object of speculation	objet de spéculation *m*	—	objeto de especulación *m*
ohne Dividende (D)	—	with non-distributed dividend	sans dividende *m*	senza dividendo	sin dividendo
ohne Gewähr (D)	—	without garanty	sous toute réserve	senza garanzia	sin garantía
ohne Obligo (D)	—	without obligation	sans engagement	senza obbligo	sin obligación
Ökologie (D)	—	ecology	écologie *f*	ecologia *f*	ecología *f*

	D	E	F	I	Es
Ökonomie (D)	—	economy	économie *f*	economia *f*	economía *f*
old age insurance (E)	Altersversicherung *f*	—	assurance-vieillesse *f*	assicurazione per la vecchiaia *f*	seguro de vejez *m*
old-age pension insurance (E)	Rentenversicherung *f*	—	assurance sociale invalidité-vieillesse *f*	assicurazione invalidità e vecchiaia *f*	seguro de pensiones *m*
Oligopol (D)	—	oligopoly	oligopole *m*	oligopolio *m*	oligopolio *m*
oligopole (F)	Oligopol *m*	oligopoly	—	oligopolio *m*	oligopolio *m*
oligopolio (Es)	Oligopol *m*	oligopoly	oligopole *m*	oligopolio *m*	—
oligopolio (I)	Oligopol *m*	oligopoly	oligopole *m*	—	oligopolio *m*
oligopoly (E)	Oligopol *m*	—	oligopole *m*	oligopolio *m*	oligopolio *m*
olio usato (I)	Altöl *n*	waste oil	huile usée *f*	—	aceite usado *m*
oltremare (I)	Übersee	oversea(s)	outre-mer	—	ultramar *m*
omaggio pubblicitario (I)	Werbegeschenk *n*	advertising gift	cadeau publicitaire *m*	—	regalo publicitario *m*
omogeneità (I)	Homogenität *f*	homogeneity	homogénéité *f*	—	homogeneidad *f*
on account of payment (E)	zahlungshalber	—	pour raison de payement	a titolo di pagamento	a título de pago
on a commission basis[1] (E)	auf Provisionsbasis	—	à la commission	a provvigione	a comisión
on a commission basis[2] (E)	auf Kommissionsbasis	—	en commission	in base commissionaria	en comisión
on approval (E)	zur Ansicht	—	à vue	in visione	para examen
on call (E)	auf Abruf	—	à convenance	su richiesta	a requerimiento
onere di prova (I)	Beweislast *f*	burden of proof	charge de la preuve *f*	—	carga de la prueba *f*
onere supplementare (I)	Mehrbelastung *f*	additional burden	surcharge *f*	—	carga suplementaria *f*
oneri straordinari (I)	außergewöhnliche Belastung *f*	extraordinary expenses	charges exceptionnelles *f pl*	—	carga extraordinaria *f*
onorario[1] (I)	Gage *f*	salary	cachet *m*	—	remuneración
onorario[2] (I)	Honorar *n*	professional fee	honoraires *m pl*	—	honorario *m*
on receipt of the invoice (E)	nach Erhalt der Rechnung	—	après avoir réçu la facture	a ricevimento della fattura	después de haber recibo la factura
on schedule (E)	termingerecht	—	dans les délais	puntuale	en la fecha fijada
on trial (E)	auf Probe	—	à l'essai	in prova	a prueba
opción (Es)	Option *f*	option	option *f*	opzione *f*	—
opción de venta (Es)	Verkaufsoption *f*	option to sell	option de vente *f*	opzione di vendita *f*	—
open cheque (E)	Barscheck *m*	—	chèque non barré *m*	assegno circolare *m*	cheque de caja *m*
open credit (E)	Blankokredit *m*	—	crédit en compte courant *m*	credito scoperto *m*	crédito en blanco *m*
opening balance sheet (E)	Eröffnungsbilanz *f*	—	bilan d'ouverture *m*	bilancio d'apertura *m*	balance inicial *m*
opening capital (E)	Anfangskapital *n*	—	capital initial *m*	capitale iniziale *m*	capital inicial *m*
opening inventory (E)	Anfangsbestand *m*	—	stock initial *m*	scorte iniziali *f pl*	existencias iniciales *f pl*
opening of a business (E)	Geschäftseröffnung *f*	—	ouverture d'une affaire *f*	apertura di un negozio *f*	apertura de los establecimientos *f*
opening of a letter of credit (E)	Akkreditiveröffnung *f*	—	ouverture d'un accréditif *f*	apertura del credito documentario *f*	apertura de un crédito documentario *f*
opening of an account (E)	Kontoeröffnung *f*	—	ouverture de compte *f*	apertura di un conto *f*	apertura de una cuenta *f*
opening of the will (E)	Testaments-eröffnung *f*	—	ouverture du testament *f*	apertura del testamento *f*	apertura de testamento *f*
open price (E)	Preis freibleibend	—	prix sans engagement *m*	prezzo non vincolante *m*	precio sin compromiso *m*
operación al contado (Es)	Tagesgeschäft *n*	day-to-day operations	affaire au comptant *f*	contratto a contanti *m*	—
operación a plazo[1] (Es)	Termingeschäft *n*	time bargain	opération à terme *f*	operazione a termine *f*	—
operación a plazo[2] (Es)	Teilzahlungs-geschäft *n*	partial payment transaction	achat à tempérament *m*	vendita a rate *f*	—
operación a plazo de mercancías (Es)	Warentermin-geschäft *n*	commodity forward transaction	opération de livraison à terme *f*	operazione a termine su merci *f*	—

	D	E	F	I	Es
operación bursátil (Es)	Börsengeschäfte *pl*	stock market transactions	opérations de bourse *f pl*	operazioni di borsa *f pl*	—
operación con valores (Es)	Wertpapiergeschäft *n*	securities business	opérations sur titres *f pl*	operazioni su titoli *f pl*	—
operación de comisión (Es)	Kommissionsgeschäft *n*	commission business	affaire en commission *f*	operazione di commissione *f*	—
operacion de compensación (Es)	Kompensationsgeschäft *n*	barter transaction	affaire de compensation *f*	operazione di compensazione *f*	—
operación de emisión (Es)	Emissionsgeschäft *n*	investment business	opération succédant à une émission *f*	operazione d'emissione *f*	—
operación de especulación (Es)	Spekulationsgeschäft *n*	speculative operations	affaire spéculative *f*	operazione speculativa *f*	—
operación de exportación (Es)	Exportgeschäft *n*	export business	affaire d'exportation *f*	operazione d'esportazione *f*	—
operación de moneda extranjera (Es)	Sortenhandel *m*	dealing in foreign notes and coins	commerce de change *m*	cambio valuta *m*	—
operacion de valores (Es)	Effektengeschäft *n*	securities business	commerce des valeurs mobilières *m*	operazione su titoli *f*	—
operaciones activas (Es)	Aktivgeschäft *n*	credit transaction	opération active *f*	operazione attiva *f*	—
operaciones antes de la apertura de la bolsa (Es)	Vorbörse *f*	before hours dealing	marché avant le marché officiel *m*	mercato preborsistico *m*	—
operaciones de crédito (Es)	Kreditgeschäft *n*	credit business	achat à crédit *m*	operazione di credito *f*	—
operaciones de descuento (Es)	Abrechnungsverfahren *n*	settling procedure	méthode de l'apurement des comptes	metodo di liquidazione *m*	—
operaciones de divisas (Es)	Devisenhandel *m*	foreign exchange dealings	marché des changes *m*	commercio delle divise *m*	—
operaciones de pignoración (Es)	Lombardgeschäft *n*	lending on securities	prêt sur gage *m*	anticipazioni *f pl*	—
operación ficticia (Es)	Scheingeschäft *n*	fictitious transaction	opération simulée *f*	negozio simulato *m*	—
operación pasiva (Es)	Passivgeschäft *n*	passive deposit transactions	opération passive *f*	operazione passiva *f*	—
operación swap (Es)	Swapgeschäft *n*	swap transaction	opération swap *f*	operazione swap *f*	—
operación triangular (Es)	Dreiecksgeschäft *n*	triangular transaction	opération commerciale triangulaire *f*	operazione triangolare *f*	—
operaio (I)	Arbeiter *m*	worker	travailleur *m*	—	trabajador *m*
operating company (E)	Betriebsgesellschaft *f*	—	entreprise d'exploitation *f*	società d'esercizio *f*	empresa de explotación *f*
operating costs (E)	Betriebskosten *pl*	—	charges d'exploitation *f pl*	spese d'esercizio *f pl*	gastos de explotación *m pl*
operating permit (E)	Betriebserlaubnis *f*	—	droit d'exploitation *m*	autorizzazione per l'esercizio *f*	autorización de funcionamiento *f*
opération active (F)	Aktivgeschäft *n*	credit transaction	—	operazione attiva *f*	operaciones activas *f pl*
operational statistics (E)	Betriebsstatistik *f*	—	statistique commerciale et industrielle *f*	statistica aziendale *f*	estadística de la empresa *f*
operation analysis (E)	Betriebsanalyse *f*	—	situation analytique de l'expoitation *f*	analisi aziendale *f*	análisis de la empresa *m*
opération à terme (F)	Termingeschäft *n*	time bargain	—	operazione a termine *f*	operación a plazo *f*
opération avec l'étranger (F)	Auslandsgeschäft *n*	foreign business	—	affare con l'estero *m*	negocio de exportación o importación *m*
opération commerciale triangulaire (F)	Dreiecksgeschäft *n*	triangular transaction	—	operazione triangolare *f*	operación triangular *f*
opération de livraison à terme (F)	Warentermingeschäft *n*	commodity forward transaction	—	operazione a termine su merci *f*	operación a plazo de mercancías *f*
opération passive (F)	Passivgeschäft *n*	passive deposit transactions	—	operazione passiva *f*	operación pasiva *m*
opérations à terme sur les changes (F)	Devisentermingeschäft *n*	forward exchange dealings	—	operazione valutaria a termine *f*	transacciones a término en divisas *f pl*
opérations de bourse (F)	Börsengeschäfte *pl*	stock market transactions	—	operazioni di borsa *f pl*	operación bursátil *f*
opérations de payement (F)	Zahlungsverkehr *m*	payment transactions	—	operazioni di pagamento *f pl*	servicio de pagos *m pl*
opération simulée (F)	Scheingeschäft *n*	fictitious transaction	—	negozio simulato *m*	operación ficticia *f*

	D	E	F	I	Es
opérations sur titres (F)	Wertpapiergeschäft *n*	securities business	—	operazioni su titoli *f pl*	operación con valores *f*
opération succédant à une émission (F)	Emissionsgeschäft *n*	investment business	—	operazione d'emissione *f*	operación de emisión *f*
opération swap (F)	Swapgeschäft *n*	swap transaction	—	operazione swap *f*	operación swap *f*
operazione abbinata (I)	Kopplungsgeschäft *n*	tie-in transaction	affaire couplée *f*	—	negocio acoplado *m*
operazione a termine (I)	Termingeschäft *n*	time bargain	opération à terme *f*	—	operación a plazo *f*
operazione a termine su merci (I)	Warentermin-geschäft *n*	commodity forward transaction	opération de livraison à terme *f*	—	operación a plazo de mercancías *f*
operazione attiva (I)	Aktivgeschäft *n*	credit transaction	opération active *f*	—	operaciones activas *f pl*
operazione con pagamento a rate (I)	Abzahlungs-geschäft *n*	hire purchase transaction	achat à tempérament *m*	—	venta a plazos *f*
operazione d'emissione (I)	Emissionsgeschäft *n*	investment business	opération succédant à une émission *f*	—	operación de emisión *f*
operazione d'esportazione (I)	Exportgeschäft *n*	export business	affaire d'exportation *f*	—	operación de exportación *f*
operazione di commissione (I)	Kommissions-geschäft *n*	commission business	affaire en commission *f*	—	operación de comisión *f*
operazione di compensazione (I)	Kompensations-geschäft *n*	barter transaction	affaire de compensation *f*	—	operacion de compensación *f*
operazione di credito (I)	Kreditgeschäft *n*	credit business	achat à crédit *m*	—	operaciones de crédito *f pl*
operazione di deposito (I)	Depotgeschäft *n*	deposit banking	garde des titres *f*	—	custodia de valores *f*
operazione immobiliare (I)	Immobiliengeschäft *n*	property transactions	affaire immobiliée *f*	—	negocio de inmuebles *m*
operazione passiva (I)	Passivgeschäft *n*	passive deposit transactions	opération passive *f*	—	operación pasiva *m*
operazione speculativa (I)	Spekulations-geschäft *n*	speculative operations	affaire spéculative *f*	—	operación de especulación *f*
operazione su titoli (I)	Effektengeschäft *n*	securities business	commerce des valeurs mobilières *m*	—	operacion de valores *f*
operazione swap (I)	Swapgeschäft *n*	swap transaction	opération swap *f*	—	operación swap *f*
operazione triangolare (I)	Dreiecksgeschäft *n*	triangular transaction	opération commer-ciale triangulaire *f*	—	operación triangular *f*
operazione valutaria a termine (I)	Devisentermin-geschäft *n*	forward exchange dealings	opérations à terme sur les changes *f pl*	—	transacciones a tér-mino en divisas *f pl*
operazioni a termine su merci (I)	Warenterminhandel *m*	commodity forward dealing	commerce d'opéra-tions à terme *m*	—	tráfico de futuro *m*
operazioni di borsa (I)	Börsengeschäfte *pl*	stock market transactions	opérations de bourse *f pl*	—	operación bursátil *f*
operazioni di pagamento (I)	Zahlungsverkehr *m*	payment transactions	opérations de payement *f pl*	—	servicio de pagos *m pl*
operazioni di trasporto (I)	Beförderungs-geschäfte *pl*	transport services	transports *m pl*	—	negocios de transporte *m pl*
operazioni su titoli (I)	Wertpapiergeschäft *n*	securities business	opérations sur titres *f pl*	—	operación con valores *f*
opinion (E)	Meinung *f*	—	opinion *f*	opinione *f*	opinión *f*
opinión (Es)	Meinung *f*	opinion	opinion *f*	opinione *f*	—
opinion (F)	Meinung *f*	opinion	—	opinione *f*	opinión *f*
opinione (I)	Meinung *f*	opinion	opinion *f*	—	opinión *f*
oposición (Es)	Protest *m*	objection/protest	protestation *f*/ protêt *m*	opposizione *f*/ protesta *f*	—
opportunity costs (E)	Alternativkosten *pl*	—	coûts alternatifs *m pl*	costi alternativi *m pl*	coste alternativo *m*
opposition au paye-ment d'un chèque (F)	Schecksperrung *f*	stopping payment of cheque	—	blocco d'assegno *m*	bloqueo de un cheque *m*
opposizione (I)	Protest *m*	objection/protest	protestation *f*/protêt *m*	—	oposición *f*/protesta *f*
optima (E)	Optimum *n*	—	optimum *m*	optimum *m*	óptimo *m*
Optimierung (D)	—	optimization	optimisation *f*	ottimizzazione *f*	optimización *f*
optimisation (F)	Optimierung *f*	optimization	—	ottimizzazione *f*	optimización *f*
optimización (Es)	Optimierung *f*	optimization	optimisation *f*	ottimizzazione *f*	—
optimization (E)	Optimierung *f*	—	optimisation *f*	ottimizzazione *f*	optimización *f*

	D	E	F	I	Es
óptimo (Es)	Optimum *n*	optima	optimum *m*	optimum *m*	—
Optimum (D)	—	optima	optimum *m*	optimum *m*	óptimo *m*
optimum (F)	Optimum *n*	optima	—	optimum *m*	óptimo *m*
optimum (I)	Optimum *n*	optima	optimum *m*	—	óptimo *m*
Option (D)	—	option	option *f*	opzione *f*	opción *f*
option (E)	Option *f*	—	option *f*	opzione *f*	opción *f*
option (F)	Option *f*	option	—	opzione *f*	opción *f*
option de vente (F)	Verkaufsoption *f*	option to sell	—	opzione di vendita *f*	opción de venta *f*
option to sell (E)	Verkaufsoption *f*	—	option de vente *f*	opzione di vendita *f*	opción de venta *f*
opzione (I)	Option *f*	option	option *f*	—	opción *f*
opzione di vendita (I)	Verkaufsoption *f*	option to sell	option de vente *f*	—	opción de venta *f*
or (F)	Gold *n*	gold	—	oro *m*	oro *m*
oral (Es)	mündlich	verbal	verbal	verbale	—
orario d'apertura (I)	Geschäftszeit *f*	business hours	heures d'ouverture *f pl*	—	hora de despacho *f pl*
orario di lavoro (I)	Arbeitszeit *f*	working hours	heures de travail *f pl*	—	jornada laboral *f*
orario di lavoro annuale (I)	Jahresarbeitszeit *f*	annual hours of work	temps de travail annuel *m*	—	jornada anual *f*
ora straordinaria (I)	Überstunde *f*	overtime	heure supplémentaire *f*	—	hora extraordinaria *f*
orden[1] (Es)	Anordnung *f*	order/arrangement	ordre *m*/disposition *f*	ordine *m*/ disposizione *f*	—
orden[2] (Es)	Ordnung *f*	order	ordre *m*	ordinamento *m*	—
ordenación del territorio (Es)	Raumordnung *f*	regional policy	aménagement des espaces *m*	ordinamento territoriale *m*	—
ordenador[1] (Es)	Computer *m*	computer	ordinateur *m*	computer *m*	—
ordenador[2] (Es)	Datenverarbeitungs-anlage *f*	data processing system	installation de traite-ment électronique des informations *f*	elaboratore elettro-nico di dati *m*	—
ordenador[3] (Es)	Rechner *m*	computer/calculator	ordinateur *m*/cal-culateur de poche *m*	calcolatore *m*	—
ordenador personal (Es)	Personalcomputer *m*	personal computer	ordinateur individuel *m*	personal computer *m*	—
orden al mejor cambio posible (Es)	Bestensorder	order at best	ordre non limité *m*	ordine al miglior corso *m*	—
ordenanza (Es)	Verordnung *f*	decree	décret *m*	regolamento *m*	—
orden de pago (Es)	Zahlungsanweisung *f*	order to pay	mandat de payement *m*	ordine di pagamento *m*	—
orden económico (Es)	Wirtschaftsordnung *f*	economic order	ordre économique *m*	ordinamento economico *m*	—
orden económico mundial (Es)	Weltwirtschafts-ordnung *f*	international economic order	ordre économique mondial *m*	sistema economico mondiale *m*	—
órden permanente (Es)	Dauerauftrag *m*	standing order	ordre régulier *m*	ordine permanente *m*	—
orden sucesivo (Es)	Folgeauftrag *m*	follow-up order	commande consécutive *f*	ordine successivo *m*	—
orden telegráfica (Es)	telegrafische Anweisung *f*	telegraphic payment order	mandat télégraphique *m*	vaglia telegrafico *m*	—
Order (D)	—	order	ordre *m*	ordine *m*	pedido *m*
order[1] (E)	Anordnung *f*	—	ordre *m*/disposition *f*	ordine *m*/ disposizione *f*	orden *f*/disposición *f*
order[2] (E)	Ordnung *f*	—	ordre *m*	ordinamento *m*	orden *m*/leyes *f pl*
order[3] (E)	Order *f*	—	ordre *m*	ordine *m*	pedido *m*
order[4] (E)	Bestellung *f*	—	commande *f*	ordinazione *f*	pedido *m*
order[5] (E)	Auftrag *m*	—	commande *f*	ordine *m*	pedido *m*
order at best (E)	Bestensorder	—	ordre non limité *m*	ordine al miglior corso *m*	orden al mejor cambio posible *f*
order cheque (E)	Orderscheck *m*	—	chèque à ordre *m*	assegno all'ordine *m*	cheque a la orden *m*
order form[1] (E)	Bestellschein *m*	—	bulletin de commande *m*	bolletta d'ordinazione *f*	hoja de pedido *f*
order form[2] (E)	Bestellformular *n*	—	bon de commande *m*	modulo d'ordinazione *m*	formulario de pedido *m*

	D	E	F	I	Es
order for payment (E)	Zahlungsbefehl *m*	—	ordre de payement *m*	ingiunzione di pagamento *f*	mandamiento de pago *m*
ordering quantity (E)	Bestellmenge *f*	—	quantité commandée *f*	quantità d'ordinazione *f*	cantidad pedida *f*
orderly (E)	ordnungsgemäß	—	correct(e)	regolare	debidamente
order number (E)	Auftragsnummer *f*	—	numéro de commande *m*	numero d'ordine *m*	número de pedido *m*
order opening a trial (E)	Eröffnungs-beschluß *m*	—	arrêt de mise en accusation *m*	decreto di citazione in giudizio *m*	acuerdo de apertura *m*
Orderpapier (D)	—	instruments (made out) to order	papier à ordre *m*	titolo all'ordine *m*	título a la orden *m*
order processing (E)	Auftragsbearbeitung *f*	—	réalisation d'une commande *f*	esecuzione ordini *f*	tramitación de pedidos *f*
Orderscheck (D)	—	order cheque	chèque à ordre *m*	assegno all'ordine *m*	cheque a la orden *m*
order scheduling (E)	Auftragsplanung *f*	—	planification des commandes *f*	pianificazione degli ordini *f*	planificación de la ejecución de pedidos *f*
order to pay (E)	Zahlungsanweisung *f*	—	mandat de payement *m*	ordine di pagamento *m*	orden de pago *f*
ordinamento (I)	Ordnung *f*	order	ordre *m*	—	orden *m*/leyes *f pl*
ordinamento del mercato (I)	Marktordnung *f*	market organization	organisation du marché *f*	—	organización del mercado *f*
ordinamento economico (I)	Wirtschaftsordnung *f*	economic order	ordre économique *m*	—	orden económico *m*
ordinamento territoriale (I)	Raumordnung *f*	regional policy	aménagement des espaces *m*	—	ordenación del territorio *f*
ordinary shares (E)	Stammaktie *f*	—	action ordinaire *f*	azione ordinaria *f*	acción ordinaria *f*
ordinateur[1] (F)	Computer *m*	computer	—	computer *m*	ordenador *m*
ordinateur[2] (F)	Rechner *m*	computer/calculator	—	calcolatore *m*	ordenador *m*/cal-culadora de bolsillo *f*
ordinateur individuel (F)	Personalcomputer *m*	personal computer	—	personal computer *m*	ordenador personal *m*
ordinazione[1] (I)	Auftragserteilung *f*	placing of an order	passation d'une commande *f*	—	otorgamiento de un pedido *m*
ordinazione[2] (I)	Bestellung *f*	order	commande *f*	—	pedido *m*
ordinazione anticipata (I)	Vorbestellung *f*	reservation	commande préalable *f*	—	pedidio anticipado *m*
ordinazione diretta (I)	Direktbestellung *f*	direct ordering	commande directe *f*	—	pedido directo *m*
ordinazione supplementare (I)	Nachbestellung *f*	repeat order	nouvel ordre *m*	—	pedido suplementario *m*
ordine[1] (I)	Auftrag *m*	order	commande *f*	—	pedido *m*
ordine[2] (I)	Order *f*	order	ordre *m*	—	pedido *m*
ordine[3] (I)	Anordnung *f*	order/arrangement	ordre *m*/disposition *f*	—	orden *f*/disposición *f*
ordine al miglior corso (I)	Bestensorder	order at best	ordre non limité *m*	—	orden al mejor cambio posible *f*
ordine a titolo di prova (I)	Probeauftrag *m*	trial order	ordre d'essai *m*	—	pedido de prueba *m*
ordine d'esportazione (I)	Exportauftrag *m*	export order	commande d'exportation *f*	—	pedido destinado a la exportación *m*
ordine di grandi quantità (I)	Großauftrag *m*	large-scale order	grosse commande *f*	—	importante pedido *m*
ordine di pagamento (I)	Zahlungsanweisung *f*	order to pay	mandat de payement *m*	—	orden de pago *f*
ordine permanente (I)	Dauerauftrag *m*	standing order	ordre régulier *m*	—	órden permanente *f*
ordine successivo (I)	Folgeauftrag *m*	follow-up order	commande consécutive *f*	—	orden sucesivo *f*
Ordnung (D)	—	order	ordre *m*	ordinamento *m*	orden *m*/leyes *f pl*
ordnungsgemäß (D)	—	orderly	correct(e)	regolare	debidamente
ordonnance sur référé civil (F)	einstweilige Verfügung *f*	temporary injunction	—	provvedimento temporaneo *m*	interdicto provisorio *m*
ordre[1] (F)	Anordnung *f*	order/arrangement	—	ordine *m*/ disposizione *f*	orden *f*/disposición *f*
ordre[2] (F)	Order *f*	order	—	ordine *m*	pedido *m*
ordre[3] (F)	Ordnung *f*	order	—	ordinamento *m*	orden *m*/leyes *f pl*

	D	E	F	I	Es
ordre de payement (F)	Zahlungsbefehl *m*	order for payment	—	ingiunzione di pagamento *f*	mandamiento de pago *m*
ordre d'essai (F)	Probeauftrag *m*	trial order	—	ordine a titolo di prova *m*	pedido de prueba *m*
ordre économique (F)	Wirtschaftsordnung *f*	economic order	—	ordinamento economico *m*	orden económico *m*
ordre économique mondial (F)	Weltwirtschafts-ordnung *f*	international economic order	—	sistema economico mondiale *m*	orden económico mundial *m*
ordre non limité (F)	Bestensorder	order at best	—	ordine al miglior corso *m*	orden al mejor cambio posible *f*
ordre régulier (F)	Dauerauftrag *m*	standing order	—	ordine permanente *m*	órden permanente *f*
or en lingot (F)	Barrengold *n*	gold in bars	—	oro in lingotti *m*	oro en barras *m*
organigrama de flujo de datos (Es)	Datenflußplan *m*	data flow chart	organigramme de flux des données *m*	diagramma flusso dati *m*	—
organigramme de flux des données (F)	Datenflußplan *m*	data flow chart	—	diagramma flusso dati *m*	organigrama de flujo de datos *m*
Organisation (D)	—	organization	organisation *f*	organizzazione *f*	organización *f*
organisation (F)	Organisation *f*	organization	—	organizzazione *f*	organización *f*
organisation de service après vente (F)	Kundendienst-organisation *f*	service organization	—	organizzazione del servizio d'assistenza *f*	organización de servicio posventa *f*
organisation des consommateurs (F)	Verbraucher-organisation *f*	consumer protection organization	—	organizzazione dei consumatori *f*	orgnización de defensa del consumidor *f*
organisation de vente (F)	Absatzorganisation *f*	sales organization	—	organizzazione di vendita *f*	organización de ventas *f*
organisation des marchés agricoles (F)	Agrarmarktordnung *f*	agricultural market organization	—	regolamento del mercato agrario *m*	reglamentación del mercado agrícola *f*
organisation du marché (F)	Marktordnung *f*	market organization	—	ordinamento del mercato *m*	organización del mercado *f*
organisation du service (F)	Abteilungs-organisation *f*	department organization	—	organizzazione reparto *f*	organización de sección *f*
organisation fonction-nelle de l'éntreprise (F)	Ablauforganisation *f*	scheduling organization	—	organizzazione del lavoro *f*	organización funcional *f*
Organisationsform (D)	—	pattern of organization	forme de l'organisation *f*	forma di organizzazione *f*	forma de organización *f*
organización (Es)	Organisation *f*	organization	organisation *f*	organizzazione *f*	—
organización de defen-sa del consumidor (Es)	Verbraucher-organisation *f*	consumer protection organization	organisation des consommateurs *f*	organizzazione dei consumatori *f*	—
organización del mercado (Es)	Marktordnung *f*	market organization	organisation du marché *f*	ordinamento del mercato *m*	—
organización de sección (Es)	Abteilungs-organisation *f*	department organization	organisation du service *f*	organizzazione reparto *f*	—
organización de servicio posventa (Es)	Kundendienst-organisation *f*	service organization	organisation de service après-vente *f*	organizzazione del servizio d'assistenza *f*	—
organización de ventas[1] (Es)	Absatzorganisation *f*	sales organization	organisation de vente *f*	organizzazione di vendita *f*	—
organización de ventas[2] (Es)	Marketing *n*	marketing	marketing *m*	marketing *m*	—
organización funcional (Es)	Ablauforganisation *f*	scheduling organization	organisation fonction-nelle de l'éntreprise *f*	organizzazione del lavoro *f*	—
organization (E)	Organisation *f*	—	organisation *f*	organizzazione *f*	organización *f*
organization costs (E)	Gründungskosten *pl*	—	frais de fondation *m pl*	costi della costituzione *m pl*	gastos de fundación *m pl*
organizzazione (I)	Organisation *f*	organization	organisation *f*	—	organización *f*
organizzazione dei consumatori (I)	Verbraucher-organisation *f*	consumer protection organization	organisation des consommateurs *f*	—	orgnización de defen-sa del consumidor *f*
organizzazione del lavoro (I)	Ablauforganisation *f*	scheduling organization	organisation fonction-nelle de l'éntreprise *f*	—	organización funcional *f*
organizzazione del servizio d'assistenza (I)	Kundendienst-organisation *f*	service organization	organisation de service après vente *f*	—	organización de servicio posventa *f*
organizzazione di vendita (I)	Absatzorganisation *f*	sales organization	organisation de vente *f*	—	organización de ventas *f*
organizzazione reparto (I)	Abteilungs-organisation *f*	department organization	organisation du service *f*	—	organización de sección *f*
orientado hacia el éxito (Es)	erfolgsorientiert	success-oriented	orienté vers le succès	orientato al successo	—

	D	E	F	I	Es
orientado hacia el marketing (Es)	Marketing-orientiert	marketing-oriented	orienté vers le marketing	orientato al marketing	—
orientado hacia el rendimiento (Es)	leistungsorientiert	performance-oriented	orienté vers le rendement	orientato al rendimento	—
orientato al marketing (I)	Marketing-orientiert	marketing-oriented	orienté vers le marketing	—	orientado hacia el marketing
orientato al rendimento (I)	leistungsorientiert	performance-oriented	orienté vers le rendement	—	orientado hacia el rendimiento
orientato al successo (I)	erfolgsorientiert	success-oriented	orienté vers le succès	—	orientado hacia el éxito
orienté vers le marketing (F)	Marketing-orientiert	marketing-oriented	—	orientato al marketing	orientado hacia el marketing
orienté vers le rendement (F)	leistungsorientiert	performance-oriented	—	orientato al rendimento	orientado hacia el rendimiento
orienté vers le succès (F)	erfolgsorientiert	success-oriented	—	orientato al successo	orientado hacia el éxito
Orientierungspreis (D)	—	guide price	prix d'orientation *m*	prezzo d'orientamento *m*	precio de orientación *m*
oro (Es)	Gold *n*	gold	or *m*	oro *m*	—
oro (I)	Gold *n*	gold	or *m*	—	oro *m*
oro en barras (Es)	Barrengold *n*	gold in bars	or en lingot *m*	oro in lingotti *m*	—
oro in lingotti (I)	Barrengold *n*	gold in bars	or en lingot *m*	—	oro en barras *m*
oscilación de precios (Es)	Preisschwankung *f*	price fluctuation	fluctuation des prix *f*	fluttuazione dei prezzi *f*	—
oscilaciones estacionales (Es)	Saison-schwankungen *pl*	seasonal fluctuations	mouvements saisonniers *m pl*	oscillazioni stagionali *f pl*	—
oscillations de la demande (F)	Bedarfsschwankung *f*	fluctuations in requirements	—	oscillazioni del fabbisogno *f pl*	fluctuación de las necesidades *f*
oscillazione della produzione (I)	Produktions-schwankung *f*	fluctuations in production	fluctuation de la production *f pl*	—	fluctuaciones en la producción *f pl*
oscillazioni del fabbisogno (I)	Bedarfsschwankung *f*	fluctuations in requirements	oscillations de la demande *f pl*	—	fluctuación de las necesidades *f*
oscillazioni stagionali (I)	Saison-schwankungen *pl*	seasonal fluctuations	mouvements saisonniers *m pl*	—	oscilaciones estacionales *f pl*
ospitalità (I)	Bewirtung *f*	hospitality/catering	hospitalité *f*/accueil *m*	—	hospedaje *m*/atenciones *f pl*
ossido di azoto (I)	Stickoxid *n*	nitric oxide	oxyde azotique *m*	—	óxido nítrico *m*
Ost-West-Handel (D)	—	East-West trade	commerce Est-Ouest *m*	scambio est-ovest *m*	comercio este-oeste *m*
otorgamiento de un pedido (Es)	Auftragserteilung *f*	placing of an order	passation d'une commande *f*	ordinazione *f*	—
ottimizzazione (I)	Optimierung *f*	optimization	optimisation *f*	—	optimización *f*
ottimo (I)	bestens	at best	au mieux	—	al mejor cambio
outdoor publicity (E)	Außenwerbung *f*	—	publicité extérieure *f*	pubblicità all'aperto *f*	publicitad al aire libre *f*
outgoing goods (E)	Warenausgang *m*	—	sortie de marchandieses *f*	uscita merci *f*	salida de mercancías *f*
Output (D)	—	output/production	output *m*/production totale *f*	output *m*/produzione totale *f*	output *m*/producción total *f*
output (Es)	Output *n*	output/production	output *m*/production totale *f*	output *m*/produzione totale *f*	—
output (F)	Output *n*	output/production	—	output *m*/produzione totale *f*	output *m*/producción total *f*
output (I)	Output *n*	output/production	output *m*/production totale *f*	—	output *m*/producción total *f*
output[1] (E)	Fördermenge *f*	—	quantité extraite *f*	quantitativo d'estrazione *m*	cantidad producida *f*
output[2] (E)	Output *n*	—	output *m*/production totale *f*	output *m*/produzione totale *f*	output *m*/producción total *f*
outre-mer (F)	Übersee	oversea(s)	—	oltremare *m*	ultramar *m*
outstanding debts (E)	Außenstände *pl*	—	dettes actives *f pl*	crediti *m pl*	cobros pendientes *m pl*
ouverture de compte (F)	Kontoeröffnung *f*	opening of an account	—	apertura di un conto *f*	apertura de una cuenta *f*
ouverture d'un accréditif (F)	Akkreditiveröffnung *f*	opening of a letter of credit	—	apertura del credito documentario *f*	apertura de un crédito documentario *f*

	D	E	F	I	Es
ouverture d'une affaire (F)	Geschäftseröffnung *f*	opening of a business	—	apertura di un negozio *f*	apertura de los establecimientos *f*
ouverture du testament (F)	Testaments-eröffnung *f*	opening of the will	—	apertura del testamento *f*	apertura de testamento *f*
ouvrier artisan (F)	Geselle *m*	journeyman	—	garzone *m*	oficial *m*
overall conception (E)	Gesamtkonzeption *f*	—	conception générale *f*	concezione universale *f*	concepción general *f*
overall view of the market (E)	Marktübersicht *f*	—	vue d'ensemble du marché *f*	quadro del mercato *m*	panorama de mercado *m*
overcapacity (E)	Überkapazität *f*	—	surcapacité *f*	capacità eccessiva *f*	supercapacidad *f*
overcapitalization (E)	Überkapitalisierung *f*	—	surcapitalisation *f*	sovracapitalizzazione *f*	sobrecapitalización *f*
overcharge (E)	Überbeschäftigung *f*	—	surchargement *m*	occupazione eccedente *f*	exceso de empleo *m*/ superempleo *m*
overdraft of an account (E)	Kontoüberziehung *f*	—	découvert de compte *m*	scoperto di conto *m*	descubierto *m*
overdraw (E)	überziehen	—	faire un prélèvement à découvert	mandare allo scoperto	sobrepasar
overhead expenses (E)	Gemeinkosten *pl*	—	coûts indirects *m pl*	costi comuni *m pl*	gastos generales *m pl*
overinsurance (E)	Überversicherung *f*	—	surassurance *f*	soprassicurazione *f*	sobreseguro *m*
overland transportation (E)	Landweg *m*	—	voie de terre *f*	via terra *f*	vía terrestre *m*
overnight expenses (E)	Übernachtungs-kosten *pl*	—	coûts de nuitée *m pl*	spese di pernottamento *f pl*	gastos de alojamiento *m pl*
overpopulation (E)	Überbevölkerung *f*	—	surpopulation *f*	sovrappopolazione *f*	superpoblación *f*
overproduction (E)	Überproduktion *f*	—	surproduction *f*	produzione eccessiva *f*	sobreproducción *f*
oversea(s) (E)	Übersee	—	outre-mer	oltremare *m*	ultramar *m*
oversea(s) trade (E)	Überseehandel *m*	—	commerce d'outre-mer *m*	commercio d'oltremare *m*	comercio de ultramar *m*
overtime (E)	Überstunde *f*	—	heure supplémentaire *f*	ora straordinaria *f*	hora extraordinaria *f*
overvaluation (E)	Überbewertung *f*	—	surestimation *f*	sopravvalutazione *f*	sobrevaloración *f*
owner of a house (E)	Hauseigentümer *m*	—	propriétaire de maison *m*	proprietario di casa *m*	propietario de una casa *m*
ownership of a flat (E)	Wohnungs-eigentum *n*	—	propriété du logement *f*	proprietà edilizia *f*	propiedad de vivienda *f*
óxido nítrico (Es)	Stickoxid *n*	nitric oxide	oxyde azotique *m*	ossido di azoto *m*	—
oxyde azotique (F)	Stickoxid *n*	nitric oxide	—	ossido di azoto *m*	óxido nítrico *m*
ozone layer (E)	Ozonschicht *f*	—	ozonosphère *f*	strato d'ozono *m*	capa del ozono *f*
ozonosphère (F)	Ozonschicht *f*	ozone layer	—	strato d'ozono *m*	capa del ozono *f*
Ozonschicht (D)	—	ozone layer	ozonosphère *f*	strato d'ozono *m*	capa del ozono *f*
pacchetto (I)	Päckchen *n*	small package	petit paquet *m*	—	pequeño paquete *m*
pacchetto delle azioni (I)	Aktienpaket *n*	block of shares	paquet d'actions *m*	—	paquete de acciones *m*
pacco (I)	Paket *n*	parcel	colis *m*	—	bulto *m*
pacco espresso (I)	Eilpaket *n*	express parcel	colis exprès *m*	—	paquete urgente *m*
packages (E)	Frachtstücke *pl*	—	colis *m*	colli *m pl*	fardo *m*
Päckchen (D)	—	small package	petit paquet *m*	pacchetto *m*	pequeño paquete *m*
packing (E)	Verpackung	—	emballage *m*	imballaggio *m*	embalaje *m*
packing instructions (E)	Verpackungs-vorschriften *pl*	—	prescriptions concernant l'emballage *f pl*	prescrizioni per l'imballaggio *f pl*	prescripciones de embalaje *f pl*
packing material (E)	Verpackungs-material *n*	—	matériel d'emballage *m*	materiale d'imballaggio *m*	empaque *m*
packing unit (E)	Verpackungseinheit *f*	—	unité d'emballage *f*	unità d'imballaggio *f*	unidad de embalaje *f*
pacto salarial (Es)	Lohnvereinbarung *f*	wage agreement	accord de salaires *m*	accordo salariale *m*	—
paese acquirente[1] (I)	Einkaufsland *n*	country of purchase	pays où l'on achète *m*	—	país de compra *m*
paese acquirente[2] (I)	Abnehmerland *n*	buyer country	pays acheteur *m*	—	país comprador *m*
paese agrario (I)	Agrarstaat *m*	agricultural state	état agricole *m*	—	estado agrario *m*
paese d'origine[1] (I)	Ursprungsland *n*	country of origin	pays d'origine *m*	—	país de origen *m*
paese d'origine[2] (I)	Herkunftsland *n*	country of origin	pays de provenance *m*	—	país de origen *m*

	D	E	F	I	Es
paese emergente (I)	Schwellenland *n*	newly industrialized countries	pays dans le seuil à l'industrialisation *m*	—	país en el umbral hacia la industrialización *m*
paesi debitori (I)	Schuldnerländer *pl*	debtor countries	pays débiteurs *m pl*	—	países deudores *m pl*
paesi sottosviluppati (I)	unterentwickelte Länder *pl*	less-developed countries	pays sous-développé *m pl*	—	países subdesarrolla-dos *m pl*
paesi terzi (I)	Drittländer *pl*	third countries	pays tiers *m pl*	—	terceros países *m pl*
pagabile (I)	zahlbar	payable	payable	—	pagable
pagable (Es)	zahlbar	payable	payable	pagabile	—
pagado (Es)	verzollt	duty paid	dédouané	sdoganato	—
pagamento[1] (I)	Auszahlung *f*	paying out	payement *m*	—	pago *m*
pagamento[2] (I)	Einlösung *f*	payment	payement *m*	—	pago *m*
pagamento[3] (I)	Zahlung *f*	payment	payement *m*	—	pago *m*
pagamento a conto (I)	a-conto-Zahlung *f*	payment on account	payement acompte *m*	—	pago a cuenta *m*
pagamento anticipato (I)	Vorauszahlung *f*	payment in advance	payement anticipé *m*	—	adelanto *m*
pagamento anticipato delle imposte (I)	Steuervoraus-zahlung *f*	advanced payment of taxes	acompte provisionnel sur l'imposition *m*	—	impuestos adelantados *m pl*
pagamento a rate[1] (I)	Teilzahlung *f*	partial payment	payement partiel *m*	—	pago parcial *m*
pagamento a rate[2] (I)	Abschlagszahlung *f*	partial payment/ payment on account	premier versement *m*/ acompte *m*	—	pago parcial *m*/ pago a cuenta *m*
pagamento arretrato delle imposte (I)	Steuernachzahlung *f*	additional payment of taxes	payement d'un rappel d'impôt *m*	—	pago de impuestos atrasados *m*
pagamento contro assegno (I)	Zahlung per Nachnahme *f*	cash on delivery	payement contre remboursement *m*	—	pago contra reembolso *m*
pagamento contro credito documentario (I)	Akkreditivzahlung *f*	payment by letter of credit	payement par accréditif *m*	—	pago por crédito documentario *m*
pagamento contro documenti (I)	Dokumente gegen Zahlung *pl*	documents against payments	documents contre payement *m pl*	—	al contado contra documentos
pagamento delle imposte (I)	Steuerzahlung *f*	payment of taxes	payement de l'impôt *m*	—	tributación *f*
pagamento di provvigione (I)	Provisionszahlung *f*	commission payment	payement de commission *m*	—	pago de comisión *m*
pagamento di un effetto (I)	Akzepteinlösung *f*	honouring of an acceptance	honorer la traite acceptée	—	descuento de una letra aceptada *m*
pagamento immediato (I)	sofortige Zahlung *f*	immediate payment	payement immédiat *m*	—	pago inmediato *m*
pagamento in acconto (I)	Anzahlung *f*	deposit	acompte *m*	—	pago a cuenta *m*
pagamento in contanti (I)	Barzahlung *f*	cash payment	payement comptant *m*	—	pago al contado *m*
pagamento rateale (I)	Ratenzahlung *f*	payment by instalments	payement par verse-ments fractionnés *m*	—	pago a plazos *m*
pagamento sotto protesta (I)	Zahlung unter Protest *f*	payment supra protest	payement sous protêt *m*	—	pago bajo protesta *m*
pagamento supplementare (I)	Nachzahlung *f*	supplementary payment	versement complémentaire *m*	—	pago suplementario *m*
pagamento totale (I)	vollständige Bezahlung *f*	payment in full	payement complet *m*	—	pago íntegro *m*
pagaré[1] (Es)	Schuldschein *m*	certificate of indebtedness	billet de créance *m*	certificato di debito *m*	—
pagaré[2] (Es)	Solawechsel *m*	promissory note	seule lettre de change *f*	pagherò *m*	—
pagare a rate (I)	abzahlen	pay off	régler par acompte	—	pagar por cuotas
pagare interessi (I)	verzinsen	pay interest on	compter des intérêts	—	pagar interés
pagar interés (Es)	verzinsen	pay interest on	compter des intérêts	pagare interessi	—
pagar por cuotas (Es)	abzahlen	pay off	régler par acompte	pagare a rate	—
pagella (I)	Zeugnis *n*	school report	certificat scolaire *m*	—	certificado de escuela *m*
pagherò (I)	Solawechsel *m*	promissory note	seule lettre de change *f*	—	pagaré *m*
pago[1] (Es)	Auszahlung *f*	paying out	payement *m*	pagamento *m*	—
pago[2] (Es)	Einlösung *f*	payment	payement *m*	pagamento *m*	—

	D	E	F	I	Es
pago[3] (Es)	Zahlung *f*	payment	payement *m*	pagamento *m*	—
pago a cuenta[1] (Es)	a-conto-Zahlung *f*	payment on account	payement acompte *m*	pagamento a conto *m*	—
pago a cuenta[2] (Es)	Anzahlung *f*	deposit	acompte *m*	pagamento in acconto *m*	—
pago al contado (Es)	Barzahlung *f*	cash payment	payement comptant *m*	pagamento in contanti *m*	—
pago aplazado (Es)	Zahlungsaufschub *m*	extension of time for payment	sursis de payement *m*	dilazione del pagamento *f*	—
pago a plazos (Es)	Ratenzahlung *f*	payment by instalments	payement par versements fractionnés *m*	pagamento rateale *m*	—
pago atrasado[1] (Es)	Rückstand *m*	arrear	arriéré *m*	arretrato *m*	—
pago atrasado[2] (Es)	Zahlungsrückstand *m*	payment in arrearse	arriéré de payement *m*	morosità di pagamento *f*	—
pago bajo protesta (Es)	Zahlung unter Protest *f*	payment supra protest	payement sous protêt *m*	pagamento sotto protesta *m*	—
pago contra reembolso (Es)	Zahlung per Nachnahme *f*	cash on delivery	payement contre remboursement *m*	pagamento contro assegno *m*	—
pago de comisión (Es)	Provisionszahlung *f*	commission payment	payement de commission *m*	pagamento di provvigione *m*	—
pago de compensación (Es)	Ausgleichszahlung *f*	compensation payment	payement pour solde de compte *m*	conguaglio *m*	—
pago de impuestos atrasados (Es)	Steuernachzahlung *f*	additional payment of taxes	payement d'un rappel d'impôt *m*	pagamento arretrato delle imposte *m*	—
pago inmediato (Es)	sofortige Zahlung *f*	immediate payment	payement immédiat *m*	pagamento immediato *m*	—
pago íntegro (Es)	vollständige Bezahlung *f*	payment in full	payement complet *m*	pagamento totale *m*	—
pago parcial[1] (Es)	Teilzahlung *f*	partial payment	payement partiel *m*	pagamento a rate *m*	—
pago parcial[2] (Es)	Abschlagszahlung *f*	partial payment/ payment on account	premier versement *m*/ acompte *m*	pagamento a rate *m*/ pagamento in acconto *m*	—
pago por crédito documentario (Es)	Akkreditivzahlung *f*	payment by letter of credit	payement par accréditif *m*	pagamento contro credito documentario *m*	—
pago suplementario (Es)	Nachzahlung *f*	supplementary payment	versement complémentaire *m*	pagamento supplementare *m*	—
paid-up capital (E)	eingezahltes Kapital *n*	—	capital versé *m*	capitale versato *m*	capital desembolsado *m*
paid vacation (E)	bezahlter Urlaub *m*	—	congé payé *m*	ferie pagate *f pl*	vacaciones con goce de sueldo *f pl*
país comprador (Es)	Abnehmerland *n*	buyer country	pays acheteur *m*	paese acquirente *m*	—
país de compra (Es)	Einkaufsland *n*	country of purchase	pays où l'on achète *m*	paese acquirente *m*	—
país de origen[1] (Es)	Ursprungsland *n*	country of origin	pays d'origine *m*	paese d'origine *m*	—
país de origen[2] (Es)	Herkunftsland *n*	country of origin	pays de provenance *m*	paese d'origine *m*	—
país en el umbral hacia la industrialización (Es)	Schwellenland *n* countries	newly industrialized l'industrialisation *m*	pays dans le seuil à	paese emergente *m*	—
países deudores (Es)	Schuldnerländer *pl*	debtor countries	pays débiteurs *m pl*	paesi debitori *m pl*	—
países subdesarrollados (Es)	unterentwickelte Länder *pl*	less developed countries	pays sous-développés *m pl*	paesi sottosviluppati *m pl*	—
Paket (D)	—	parcel	colis *m*	pacco *m*	bulto *m*
palabra clave (Es)	Schlüsselwort *n*	key word	mot-clé *m*	parola chiave *f*	—
palabra de clave (Es)	Codewort *n*	code	mot de code *m*	parola di codice *f*	—
paleta (Es)	Palette *f*	pallet	palette *f*	paletta *f*	—
paletta (I)	Palette *f*	pallet	palette *f*	—	paleta *m*
Palette (D)	—	pallet	palette *f*	paletta *f*	paleta *m*
palette (F)	Palette *f*	pallet	—	paletta *f*	paleta *m*
pallet (E)	Palette *f*	—	palette *f*	paletta *f*	paleta *m*
panorama de mercado (Es)	Marktübersicht *f*	overall view of the market	vue d'ensemble du marché *f*	quadro del mercato *m*	—
pantalla (Es)	Bildschirm *m*	screen	écran *m*	video *m*	—
papel-moneda (Es)	Papiergeld *n*	paper money	monnaie de papier *f*	banconote *f pl*	—

	D	E	F	I	Es
paper money (E)	Papiergeld *n*	—	monnaie de papier *f*	banconote *f pl*	papel-moneda *m*
papier à ordre (F)	Orderpapier *n*	instruments (made out) to order	—	titolo all'ordine *m*	título a la orden *m*
Papiergeld (D)	—	paper money	monnaie de papier *f*	banconote *f pl*	papel-moneda *m*
papiers d'affaires (F)	Geschäftspapiere *pl*	business papers	—	documenti commerciali *m pl*	documentos comerciales *m pl*
paquet d'actions (F)	Aktienpaket *n*	block of shares	—	pacchetto delle azioni *m*	paquete de acciones *m*
paquete de acciones (Es)	Aktienpaket *n*	block of shares	paquet d'actions *m*	pacchetto delle azioni *m*	—
paquete urgente (Es)	Eilpaket *n*	express parcel	colis exprès *m*	pacco espresso *m*	—
para examen (Es)	zur Ansicht	on approval	à vue	in visione	—
Parameter (D)	—	parameter	paramètre *m*	parametro *m*	parámetro *m*
parameter (E)	Parameter *m*	—	paramètre *m*	parametro *m*	parámetro *m*
paramètre (F)	Parameter *m*	paramotor	—	parametro *m*	parámetro *m*
paramètre d'action (F)	Aktionsparameter *m*	action parameter	—	parametro d'azione *m*	parámetro de acción *m*
parámetro (Es)	Parameter *m*	parameter	paramètre *m*	parametro *m*	—
parametro (I)	Parameter *m*	parameter	paramètre *m*	—	parámetro *m*
parametro d'azione (I)	Aktionsparameter *m*	action parameter	paramètre d'action *m*	—	parámetro de acción *m*
parámetro de acción (Es)	Aktionsparameter *m*	action parameter	paramètre d'action *m*	parametro d'azione *m*	—
par avion (F)	Luftpost *f*	air mail	—	posta aerea *f*	correo aéreo *m*
par camion (F)	per Lastkraftwagen	by lorry	—	per autocarro	por camión
parcel (E)	Paket *n*	—	colis *m*	pacco *m*	bulto *m*
par écrit (F)	schriftlich	written	—	per iscritto	por escrito
pareggio di bilancio (I)	Budgetausgleich *m*	balancing of the budget	équilibrage du budget *m*	—	balance del presupuesto *m*
parent company[1] (E)	Muttergesellschaft *f*	—	société mère *f*	società madre *f*	sociedad matriz *f*
parent company[2] (E)	Stammhaus *n*	—	maison mère *f*	casa madre *f*	casa matriz *f*
par exprès (F)	per Express	by express (mail)	—	per espresso	por expreso
paridad (Es)	Parität *f*	parity	parité *f*	parità *f*	—
paridad adquisitiva (Es)	Kaufkraftparität *f*	purchasing power parity	parité du pouvoir d'achat *f*	parità del potere d'acquisto *f*	—
paridad-oro (Es)	Goldparität *f*	gold parity	parité de l'or *f*	parità aurea *f*	—
parità (I)	Parität *f*	parity	parité *f*	—	paridad *f*
parità aurea (I)	Goldparität *f*	gold parity	parité de l'or *f*	—	paridad-oro *f*
parità centrale (I)	Leitkurs *m*	central rate	taux central *m*	—	tipo pivote *m*
parità del potere d'acquisto (I)	Kaufkraftparität *f*	purchasing power parity	parité du pouvoir d'achat *f*	—	paridad adquisitiva *f*
Parität (D)	—	parity	parité *f*	parità *f*	paridad *f*
parité (F)	Parität *f*	parity	—	parità *f*	paridad *f*
parité de l'or (F)	Goldparität *f*	gold parity	—	parità aurea *f*	paridad-oro *f*
parité du pouvoir d'achat (F)	Kaufkraftparität *f*	purchasing power parity	—	parità del potere d'acquisto *f*	paridad adquisitiva *f*
parity (E)	Parität *f*	—	parité *f*	parità *f*	paridad *f*
Parlamento Europeo (Es)	Europäisches Parlament *n*	European Parliament	Parlement européen *m*	Parlamento Europeo *m*	—
Parlamento Europeo (I)	Europäisches Parlament *n*	European Parliament	Parlement européen *m*	—	Parlamento Europeo *m*
Parlement européen (F)	Europäisches Parlament *n*	European Parliament	—	Parlamento Europeo *m*	Parlamento Europeo *m*
par mois (F)	monatlich	monthly	—	mensile	mensual
paro estacional (Es)	saisonale Arbeitslosigkeit *f*	seasonal unemployment	chômage saisonnier *m*	disoccupazione stagionale *f*	—
paro estructural (Es)	strukturelle Arbeitslosigkeit *f*	structural unemployment	chômage structurel *m*	disoccupazione strutturale *f*	—
parola chiave (I)	Schlüsselwort *n*	key word	mot-clé *m*	—	palabra clave *f*
parola di codice (I)	Codewort *n*	code	mot de code *m*	—	palabra de clave *f*
par ordre (F)	im Auftrag	by order	—	per ordine	por poder

	D	E	F	I	Es
par procuration (F)	per procura	by procuration	—	per procura	por poder
par retour du courrier (F)	postwendend	by return of post	—	a giro di posta	a vuelta de correo
part de capital (F)	Kapitalanteil *m*	share in capital	—	quota di capitale *f*	participación en el capital *f*
partecipante (I)	Teilnehmer *m*	participant	participant *m*	—	participante *m*
partecipazione (I)	Beteiligung *f*	participation	participation *f*	—	participación *f*
partecipazione all'utile (I)	Gewinnbeteiligung *f*	participation in profits	participation aux bénéfices *f*	—	participación en los beneficios *f*
partecipazione al reddito (I)	Ertragsbeteiligung *f*	participation in profits	participation aux bénéfices *f*	—	participación en los resultados *f*
partecipazione dei prestatori d'opera (I)	Arbeitnehmer-beteiligung *f*	worker participation	participation du personnel *f*	—	participación de los empleados *f*
parte contratante en un convenio colectivo (Es)	Tarifpartner *m*	parties to a collective agreement	signataire d'une convention collective *m*	parti sociali *f pl*	—
parte de los gastos de material (Es)	Materialkosten-anteil *m*	share in the material costs	proportion des frais de matériel *f*	quota dei costi del materiale *f*	—
parte fraccionaria (Es)	Bruchteil *m*	fraction	fraction *f*	frazione *f*	—
partenaire (F)	Partner *m*	partner	—	partner *m*	socio *m*
partenaire commercial (F)	Handelspartner *m*	trading partner	—	partner commerciale *m*	socio comercial *m*
partes integrantes esencial (Es)	wesentliche Bestandteile *pl*	integral part	parties constitutives essentielles *f pl*	componenti essenziali *f pl*	—
par tête d'habitant (F)	pro Kopf	per capita	—	pro capite	per cápita
partial analysis (E)	Teil-Analyse *f*	—	analyse partielle *f*	analisi parziale *f*	análisis parcial *m*
partial balance sheet (E)	Teilbilanz *f*	—	bilan partiel *m*	bilancio parziale *m*	balance parcial *m*
partial delivery (E)	Teillieferung *f*	—	livraison partielle *f*	fornitura parziale	entrega parcial *f*
partial denationalization (E)	Teilprivatisierung *f*	—	privatisation partielle *f*	privatizzazione parziale *f*	privatización parcial *f*
partial edition (E)	Teilauflage *f*	—	édition partielle *f*	emissione parziale *f*	emisión parcial *f*
partial loss (E)	Teilverlust *m*	—	perte partielle *f*	perdita parziale *f*	pérdida parcial *f*
partial payment[1] (E)	Teilzahlung *f*	—	payement partiel *m*	pagamento a rate *m*	pago parcial *m*
partial payment[2] (E)	Abschlagszahlung *f*	—	premier versement *m*/ acompte *m*	pagamento a rate *m*/ pagamento in acconto *m*	pago parcial *m*/ pago a cuenta *m*
partial payment price (E)	Teilzahlungspreis *m*	—	prix d'un achat à tempérament *m*	prezzo rateale *m*	precio de compras a plazo *m*
partial payment transaction (E)	Teilzahlungs-geschäft *n*	—	achat à tempérament *m*	vendita a rate *f*	operación a plazo *f*
partial value (E)	Teilwert *m*	—	valeur partielle *f*	valore parziale *m*	valor parcial *m*
participación[1] (Es)	Anteilnahme *f*	sympathy	participation *f*	interesse *m*	—
participación[2] (Es)	Geschäftsanteil *m*	share	part sociale *f*	quota sociale *f*	—
participación[3] (Es)	Beteiligung *f*	participation	participation *f*	partecipazione *f*	—
participación de los empleados (Es)	Arbeitnehmer-beteiligung *f*	worker participation	participation du personnel *f*	partecipazione dei prestatori d'opera *f*	—
participación en el capital (Es)	Kapitalanteil *m*	share in capital	part de capital *f*	quota di capitale *f*	—
participación en los beneficios (Es)	Gewinnbeteiligung *f*	participation in profits	participation aux bénéfices *f*	partecipazione all'utile *f*	—
participación en los resultados (Es)	Ertragsbeteiligung *f*	participation in profits	participation aux bénéfices *f*	partecipazione al reddito *f*	—
participant (E)	Teilnehmer *m*	—	participant *m*	partecipante *m*	participante *m*
participant (F)	Teilnehmer *m*	participant	—	partecipante *m*	participante *m*
participante (Es)	Teilnehmer *m*	participant	participant *m*	partecipante *m*	—
participation (E)	Beteiligung *f*	—	participation *f*	partecipazione *f*	participación *f*
participation[1] (F)	Anteilnahme *f*	sympathy	—	interesse *m*	participación *f*
participation[2] (F)	Beteiligung *f*	participation	—	partecipazione *f*	participación *f*
participation au marché (F)	Marktanteil *m*	market share	—	quota di mercato *f*	cuota del mercado *f*
participation aux bénéfices[1] (F)	Ertragsbeteiligung *f*	participation in profits	—	partecipazione al reddito *f*	participación en los resultados *f*

	D	E	F	I	Es
participation aux bénéfices[2] (F)	Gewinnbeteiligung *f*	participation in profits	—	partecipazione all'utile *f*	participación en los beneficios *f*
participation du personnel (F)	Arbeitnehmer-beteiligung *f*	worker participation	—	partecipazione dei prestatori d'opera *f*	participación de los empleados *f*
participation in profits[1] (E)	Gewinnbeteiligung *f*	—	participation aux bénéfices *f*	partecipazione all'utile *f*	participación en los beneficios *f*
participation in profits[2] (E)	Ertragsbeteiligung *f*	—	participation aux bénéfices *f*	partecipazione al reddito *f*	participación en los resultados *f*
participations (F)	Beiträge *pl*	contributions	—	contributi *m pl*	contribuciones *f pl*
partida restante (Es)	Restposten *m*	remnants	lot restant *m*	rimanenze *f pl*	—
parties constitutives essentielles (F)	wesentliche Bestandteile *pl*	integral part	—	componenti essenziali *f pl*	partes integrantes esencial *f pl*
parties to a collective agreement (E)	Tarifpartner *m*	—	signataire d'une convention collective *m*	parti sociali *f pl*	parte contratante en un convenio colectivo *f*
parti sociali (I)	Tarifpartner *m*	parties to a collective agreement	signataire d'une convention collective *m*	—	parte contratante en un convenio colectivo *f*
Partner (D)	—	partner	partenaire *m*	partner *m*	socio *m*
partner[1] (E)	Teilhaber *m*	—	associé *m*	socio *m*	socio *m*
partner[2] (E)	Partner *m*	—	partenaire *m*	partner *m*	socio *m*
partner[3] (E)	Gesellschafter *m*	—	associé *m*	socio *m*	socio *m*
partner (I)	Partner *m*	partner	partenaire *m*	—	socio *m*
partner commerciale[1] (I)	Handelspartner *m*	trading partner	partenaire commercial *m*	—	socio comercial *m*
partner commerciale[2] (I)	Geschäftspartner *m*	business partner	associé *m*	—	socio *m*
partner d'affari (I)	Geschäftsfreund *m*	business friend	correspondant *m*	—	corresponsal *m*
partnership[1] (E)	Sozietät *f*	—	groupe de sociétaires *m*	associazione *f*	sociedad *f*
partnership[2] (E)	Personen-gesellschaft *n*	—	société de personnes *f*	società di persone *f*	sociedad personalista *f*
partnership assets (E)	Gesellschafts-vermögen *n*	—	patrimoine social *m*	patrimonio sociale *m*	patrimonio social *m*
partnership limited by shares (E)	Kommanditgesell-schaft auf Aktien *f*	—	société en commandite par action *f*	società in accomandita per azioni *f*	sociedad comandita-ria por acciones *f*
part sociale (F)	Geschäftsanteil *m*	share	—	quota sociale *f*	participación *f*
part-time employment (E)	Teilzeit-beschäftigung *f*	—	emploi à temps partiel *m*	occupazione part-time *f*	empleo parcial *m*
part-time job (E)	Teilzeitstelle *f*	—	poste à temps partiel *m*	posto di lavoro part-time *m*	puesto de trabajo a tiempo parcial *m*
part-time work (E)	Teilzeitarbeit *f*	—	travail à temps partiel *m*	lavoro part-time *m*	trabajo a tiempo parcial *m*
par virement (F)	bargeldlos	non-cash	—	mediante assegno	por transferencia
pasavante (Es)	Durchgangs-schein *m*	transit certificate	acquit de transit *m*	bolletta di transito *f*	—
pasivo (Es)	Passiva *n*	liabilities	passif *m*	passivo *m*	—
passation d'une commande (F)	Auftragserteilung *f*	placing of an order	—	ordinazione *f*	otorgamiento de un pedido *m*
passibile di pena (I)	straffällig	liable to prosecution	encourir une peine	—	criminal
passif[1] (F)	Schuldenmasse *f*	total of indebtedness	—	massa passiva *f*	masa pasiva *f*
passif[2] (F)	Passiva *n*	liabilities	—	passivo *m*	pasivo *m*
passing on (E)	Überwälzung *f*	—	répercussion *f*	accollamento *m*	traslación *f*
Passiva (D)	—	liabilities	passif *m*	passivo *m*	pasivo *m*
Passivgeschäft (D)	—	passive deposit transactions	opération passive *f*	operazione passiva *f*	operación pasiva *m*
passivo[1] (I)	Soll *m*	debit	doit *m*	—	debe *m*
passivo[2] (I)	Passiva *pl*	liabilities	passif *m*	—	pasivo *m*
pas utilisé (F)	ungenutzt	unused	—	inutilizzato	no utilizado
Patent (D)	—	patent	brevet d'invention *m*	brevetto *m*	patente *f*
patent (E)	Patent *n*	—	brevet d'invention *m*	brevetto *m*	patente *f*
Patentamt (D)	—	Patent Office	office des brevets *m*	ufficio brevetti *m*	oficina del registro de patentes *f*

	D	E	F	I	Es
patent document (E)	Patenturkunde *f*	—	certificat d'attestation du brevet d'invention *m*	brevetto *m*	patente *f*
patente[1] (Es)	Patent *n*	patent	brevet d'invention *m*	brevetto *m*	—
patente[2] (Es)	Patenturkunde *f*	patent document	certificat d'attestation du brevet d'invention *m*	brevetto *m*	—
patente (F)	Gewerbesteuer *f*	trade tax	—	imposta industriale *f*	impuesto industrial *m*
patente europea (Es)	Europapatent *n*	European patent	brevet européen *m*	brevetto europeo *m*	—
patent licence (E)	Patentlizenz *f*	—	licence de brevet *f*	licenza di brevetto *f*	licencia de patente *f*
Patentlizenz (D)	—	patent licence	licence de brevet *f*	licenza di brevetto *f*	licencia de patente *f*
Patent Office (E)	Patentamt *n*	—	office des brevets *m*	ufficio brevetti *m*	oficina del registro de patentes *f*
patent pool (E)	Patentpool *m*	—	pool de brevet *m*	pool dei brevetti *m*	pool de patentes *m*
Patentpool (D)	—	patent pool	pool de brevet *m*	pool dei brevetti *m*	pool de patentes *m*
Patenturkunde (D)	—	patent document	certificat d'attestation du brevet d'invention *m*	brevetto *m*	patente *f*
patriarcal (Es)	patriarchalisch	patriarchal	patriarcal	patriarcale	—
patriarcal (F)	patriarchalisch	patriarchal	—	patriarcale	patriarcal
patriarcale (I)	patriarchalisch	patriarchal	patriarcal	—	patriarcal
patriarchal (E)	patriarchalisch	—	patriarcal	patriarcale	patriarcal
patriarchalisch (D)	—	patriarchal	patriarcal	patriarcale	patriarcal
patrimoine (F)	Vermögen *n*	property	—	patrimonio *m*	patrimonio *m*
patrimoine net (F)	Nettovermögen *n*	net assets	—	patrimonio netto *m*	patrimonio neto *m*
patrimoine réel (F)	Realvermögen *n*	real wealth	—	patrimonio reale *m*	activo inmobiliario *m*
patrimoine social (F)	Gesellschafts-vermögen *n*	partnership assets	—	patrimonio sociale *m*	patrimonio social *m*
patrimonio (Es)	Vermögen *n*	property	patrimoine *m*	patrimonio *m*	—
patrimonio (I)	Vermögen *n*	property	patrimoine *m*	—	patrimonio *m*
patrimonio circolante (I)	Umlaufvermögen *n*	current assets/ floating assets	capital de roulement *m*	—	capital circulante *m*
patrimonio estero (I)	Auslandsvermögen *n*	foreign assets	avoirs à l'étranger *m pl*	—	activo exterior *m*
patrimonio in contanti (I)	Barvermögen *n*	cash assets	valeurs réalisables à court terme ou disponibles *f pl*	—	activo efectivo *m*
patrimonio monetario (I)	Geldvermögen *n*	financial assets	moyens financiers *m*	—	activo monetario *m*
patrimonio neto[1] (Es)	Nettovermögen *n*	net assets	patrimoine net *m*	patrimonio netto *m*	—
patrimonio neto[2] (Es)	Reinvermögen *n*	net assets	avoir net *m*	patrimonio netto *m*	—
patrimonio netto[1] (I)	Reinvermögen *n*	net assets	avoir net *m*	—	patrimonio neto *m*
patrimonio netto[2] (I)	Nettovermögen *n*	net assets	patrimoine net *m*	—	patrimonio neto *m*
patrimonio productivo (Es)	Produktivvermögen *n*	productive property	capital productif *m*	patrimonio produttivo *m*	—
patrimonio produttivo (I)	Produktivvermögen *n*	productive property	capital productif *m*	—	patrimonio productivo *m*
patrimonio público (Es)	Staatseigentum *n*	public ownership	propriété d'Etat *f*	proprietà demaniale *f*	—
patrimonio real (Es)	Sachvermögen *n*	material assets	biens corporels *m pl*	capitale reale *m*	—
patrimonio reale (I)	Realvermögen *n*	real wealth	patrimoine réel *m*	—	activo inmobiliario *m*
patrimonio social (Es)	Gesellschafts-vermögen *n*	partnership assets	patrimoine social *m*	patrimonio sociale *m*	—
patrimonio sociale (I)	Gesellschafts-vermögen *n*	partnership assets	patrimoine social *m*	—	patrimonio social *m*
patrón (Es)	Arbeitgeber *m*	employer	employeur *m*	datore di lavoro *m*	—
patrón-oro (Es)	Goldstandard *m*	gold standard	étalon or *m*	gold standard *m*	—
pattern of organization (E)	Organisationsform *f*	—	forme de l'organisation *f*	forma di organizzazione *f*	forma de organización *f*
paupérisme (F)	Massenarmut *f*	pauperism	—	pauperismo *m*	pauperismo *m*
pauperismo (Es)	Massenarmut *f*	pauperism	paupérisme *m*	pauperismo *m*	—
pauperismo (I)	Massenarmut *f*	pauperism	paupérisme *m*	—	pauperismo *m*

	D	E	F	I	Es
Pauschalbetrag (D)	—	flat rate amount	somme forfaitaire *f*	somma forfettaria *f*	suma global *f*
pay (E)	Besoldung *f*	—	rétribution *f*	retribuzione *f*	sueldo *m*
payable (E)	zahlbar	—	payable	pagabile	pagable
payable (F)	zahlbar	payable	—	pagabile	pagable
payday (E)	Zahltag *m*	—	jour de paye *m*	giorno di paga *m*	día de pago *m*
payee (E)	Remittent *m*	—	remettant *m*	beneficiario *m*	remitente *m*
payement[1] (F)	Einlösung *f*	payment	—	pagamento *m*	pago *m*
payement[2] (F)	Zahlung *f*	payment	—	pagamento *m*	pago *m*
payement[3] (F)	Auszahlung *f*	paying out	—	pagamento *m*	pago *m*
payement acompte (F)	a-conto-Zahlung *f*	payment on account	—	pagamento a conto *m*	pago a cuenta *m*
payement anticipé (F)	Vorauszahlung *f*	payment in advance	—	pagamento anticipato *m*	adelanto *m*
payement complet (F)	vollständige Bezahlung *f*	payment in full	—	pagamento totale *m*	pago íntegro *m*
payement comptant (F)	Barzahlung *f*	cash payment	— contanti *m*	pagamento in	pago al contado *m*
payement contre remboursement (F)	Zahlung per Nachnahme *f*	cash on delivery	—	pagamento contro assegno *m*	pago contra reembolso *m*
payement de commission (F)	Provisionszahlung *f*	commission payment	—	pagamento di provvigione *m*	pago de comisión *m*
payement de l'impôt (F)	Steuerzahlung *f*	payment of taxes	—	pagamento delle imposte *m*	tributación *f*
payement d'un rappel d'impôt (F)	Steuernachzahlung *f*	additional payment of taxes	—	pagamento arretrato delle imposte *m*	pago de impuestos atrasados *m*
payement immédiat (F)	sofortige Zahlung *f*	immediate payment	—	pagamento immediato *m*	pago inmediato *m*
payement par accréditif (F)	Akkreditivzahlung *f*	payment by letter of credit	—	pagamento contro credito documentario *m*	pago por crédito documentario *m*
payement partiel (F)	Teilzahlung *f*	partial payment	—	pagamento a rate *m*	pago parcial *m*
payement par versements fractionnés (F)	Ratenzahlung *f*	payment by instalments	—	pagamento rateale *m*	pago a plazos *m*
payement pour solde de compte (F)	Ausgleichszahlung *f*	compensation payment	—	conguaglio *m*	pago de compensación *m*
payement sous protêt (F)	Zahlung unter Protest *f*	payment supra protest	—	pagamento sotto protesta *m*	pago bajo protesta *m*
paying out (E)	Auszahlung *f*	—	payement *m*	pagamento *m*	pago *m*
pay interest on (E)	verzinsen	—	compter des intérêts	pagare interessi	pagar interés
payment[1] (E)	Einlösung *f*	—	payement *m*	pagamento *m*	pago *m*
payment[2] (E)	Zahlung *f*	—	payement *m*	pagamento *m*	pago *m*
payment by instalments (E)	Ratenzahlung *f*	—	payement par versements fractionnés *m*	pagamento rateale *m*	pago a plazos *m*
payment by letter of credit (E)	Akkreditivzahlung *f*	—	payement par accréditif *m*	pagamento contro credito documentario *m*	pago por crédito documentario *m*
payment by result (E)	Leistungslohn *m*	—	salaire au rendement *m*	salario a rendimento *m*	salario por rendimiento *m*
payment in advance (E)	Vorauszahlung *f*	—	payement anticipé *m*	pagamento anticipato *m*	adelanto *m*
payment in arrears (E)	Zahlungsrückstand *m*	—	arriéré de payement *m*	morosità di pagamento *f*	pago atrasado *m*
payment in full (E)	vollständige Bezahlung *f*	—	payement complet *m*	pagamento totale *m*	pago íntegro *m*
payment of taxes (E)	Steuerzahlung *f*	—	payement de l'impôt *m*	pagamento delle imposte *m*	tributación *f*
payment on account (E)	a-conto-Zahlung *f*	—	payement acompte *m*	pagamento in acconto *m*	pago a cuenta *m*
payments arrangement (E)	Zahlungsabkommen *n*	—	accord de payement *m*	accordo di pagamento *m*	acuerdo de pagos *m*
payment supra protest (E)	Zahlung unter Protest *f*	—	payement sous protêt *m*	pagamento sotto protesta *m*	pago bajo protesta *m*
payment system (E)	Zahlungsform *f*	—	forme de payement *f*	tipo di pagamento *m*	forma de pago *f*
payment transactions (E)	Zahlungsverkehr *m*	—	opérations de payement *f pl*	operazioni di pagamento *f pl*	servicio de pagos *m pl*

	D	E	F	I	Es
pay off (E)	abzahlen	—	régler par acompte	pagare a rate	pagar por cuotas
pay office (E)	Lohnbüro *n*	—	bureau de la paye *m*	ufficio paga *m*	departamento de nóminas *m*
pays acheteur (F)	Abnehmerland *n*	buyer country	—	paese acquirente *m*	país comprador *m*
pays dans le seuil à l'industrialisation (F)	Schwellenland *n*	newly industrialized countries	—	paese emergente *m*	país en el umbral hacia la industrialización *m*
pays débiteurs (F)	Schuldnerländer *pl*	debtor countries	—	paesi debitori *m pl*	países deudores *m pl*
pays de provenance (F)	Herkunftsland *n*	country of origin	—	paese d'origine *m*	país de origen *m*
pays d'origine (F)	Ursprungsland *n*	country of origin	—	paese d'origine *m*	país de origen *m*
pays où l'on achète (F)	Einkaufsland *n*	country of purchase	—	paese acquirente *m*	país de compra *m*
pays sous-développé (F)	unterentwickelte Länder *pl*	less developed countries	—	paesi sottosviluppati *m pl*	países subdesarrolla-dos *m pl*
pays tiers (F)	Drittländer *pl*	third countries	—	paesi terzi *m pl*	terceros países *m pl*
pêcherie (F)	Fischerei *f*	fishing	—	pesca *f*	pesca *f*
pedido[1] (Es)	Auftrag *m*	order	commande *f*	ordine *m*	—
pedido[2] (Es)	Order *f*	order	ordre *m*	ordine *m*	—
pedido[3] (Es)	Bestellung *f*	order	commande *f*	ordinazione *f*	—
pedido anticipado (Es)	Vorbestellung *f*	reservation	commande préalable *f*	ordinazione anticipata *f*	—
pedido de prueba (Es)	Probeauftrag *m*	trial order	ordre d'essai *m*	ordine a titolo di prova *m*	—
pedido destinado a la exportación (Es)	Exportauftrag *m*	export order	commande d'exportation *f*	ordine d'esportazione *m*	—
pedido directo (Es)	Direktbestellung *f*	direct ordering	commande directe *f*	ordinazione diretta *f*	—
pedido suplementario (Es)	Nachbestellung *f*	repeat order	nouvel ordre *m*	ordinazione supplementare *f*	—
pegatina (Es)	Aufkleber *m*	sticker	étiquette *f*	eticchetta adesiva *f*	—
peine pécuniaire (F)	Geldstrafe *f*	fine	—	multa *f*	multa *f*
película promocional (Es)	Werbefilm *m*	advertising film	film publicitaire *m*	film pubblicitario *m*	—
peligro (Es)	Gefahr *f*	danger	danger *m*	pericolo *m*	—
pena convencional (Es)	Konventionalstrafe *f*	contractual penalty	pénalité *f*	penalità convenzionale *f*	—
penalità convenzionale (I)	Konventionalstrafe *f*	contractual penalty	pénalité *f*	—	pena convencional *f*
pénalité (F)	Konventionalstrafe *f*	contractual penalty	—	penalità convenzionale *f*	pena convencional *f*
pena pecuniaria[1] (I)	Geldbuße *f*	fine	amende *f*	—	multa *f*
pena pecuniaria[2] (I)	Bußgeld *n*	administration fee	amende *f*	—	multa *f*
Pendelverkehr (D)	—	shuttle service	trafic de va-et-vient *m*	traffico pendolare *m*	vaivén *m*
pensar concepcional (Es)	konzeptionelles Denken *n*	conceptional thinking	penser conceptionnel *m*	mentalità concezionale *f*	—
penser conceptionnel (F)	konzeptionelles Denken *n*	conceptional thinking	—	mentalità concezionale *f*	pensar concepcional *m*
pensión básica (Es)	Grundrente *f*	basic pension	pension de base *f*	pensione base *f*	—
pension de base (F)	Grundrente *f*	basic pension	—	pensione base *f*	pensión básica *f*
pensione base (I)	Grundrente *f*	basic pension	pension de base *f*	—	pensión básica *f*
pension fund (E)	Rentenfonds *m*	—	fonds d'Etat *m*/ effets publics *m pl*	fondo obbligazionario *m*	fondo de bonos *m*
pension scheme (E)	Versorgungs-einrichtung *f*	—	institution de retraite *f*	istituto previdenziale *m*	institución de previsión *f*
pénurie d'argent (F)	Geldverknappung *f*	monetary restriction	—	riduzione del denaro *f*	restricción monetaria *f*
pénurie de marchandises (F)	Warenknappheit *f*	shortage of goods	—	scarsità di merci *f*	escasez de mercancías *f*
pénurie de matières premières (F)	Rohstoffknappheit *f*	raw materials shortage	—	scarsità di materie prime *f*	escasez de materias primas *f*
pequeña paleta (Es)	Kleinpalette *f*	small pallet	petite palette *f*	mini paletta *f*	—
pequeñas y medianas empresas (Es)	Klein- und Mittelbetriebe *pl*	small and medium-sized enterprises	petites et moyennes entreprises *f pl*	piccole e medie imprese *f pl*	—

	D	E	F	I	Es
pequeño contenedor (Es)	Kleincontainer *m*	small container	petit conteneur *m*	mini container *m*	—
pequeño paquete (Es)	Päckchen *n*	small package	petit paquet *m*	pacchetto *m*	—
per autocarro (I)	per Lastkraftwagen	by lorry	par camion	—	por camión
per capita (E)	pro Kopf	—	par tête d'habitant	pro capite	per cápita
per cápita (Es)	pro Kopf	per capita	par tête d'habitant	pro capite	—
per cent (E)	Prozent *n*	—	pour-cent *m*	percento *m*	por ciento *m*
percentage[1] (E)	Prozentsatz *m*	—	pourcentage *m*	percentuale *f*	porcentaje *m*
percentage[2] (E)	Tantieme *f*	—	tantième *m*	percentuale *f*	tanto por ciento *m*
percento (I)	Prozent *n*	per cent	pour-cent *m*	—	por ciento *m*
percentuale[1] (I)	Tantieme *f*	percentage	tantième *m*	—	tanto por ciento *m*
percentuale[2] (I)	Prozentsatz *m*	percentage	pourcentage *m*	—	porcentaje *m*
percepciónes en especie (Es)	Sachbezüge *pl*	remuneration in kind	prestations en nature *f pl*	retribuzioni in natura *f pl*	—
per conto proprio (I)	für eigene Rechnung	for one's own account	pour son propre compte	—	por cuenta propia
per conto terzi (I)	für fremde Rechnung	for account of a third party	pour compte de tiers	—	por cuenta ajena
pérdida[1] (Es)	Verlust *m*	loss	perte *f*	perdita *f*	—
pérdida[2] (Es)	Damnum *n*	damnum	perte *f*	perdita *f*	—
pérdida de valor (Es)	Werteinbuße *f*	loss of value	perte de valeur *f*	perdita di valore *f*	—
pérdida en bolsa (Es)	Kursverlust *m*	loss in exchange	baisse sur les cours *f*	perdita sul cambio *f*	—
perdita[1] (I)	Verlust *m*	loss	perte *f*	—	pérdida *f*
perdita[2] (I)	Damnum *n*	damnum	perte *f*	—	pérdida *f*
perdita di valore (I)	Werteinbuße *f*	loss of value	perte de valeur *f*	—	pérdida de valor *f*
perdita sul cambio (I)	Kursverlust *m*	loss in exchange	baisse sur les cours *f*	—	pérdida en bolsa *f*
perecedero (Es)	verderblich	perishable	périssable	deperibile	—
per Einschreiben (D)	—	by registered post	sous pli recommandé	per raccomandata	certificado
péréquation fiscale des revenus des deux époux (F)	Splitting *n*	splitting	—	splittaggio *m*	imposición separada e igual de los conyúges *f*
per espresso (I)	per Express	by express (mail)	par exprès	—	por expreso
per Express (D)	—	by express (mail)	par exprès	per espresso	por expreso
perfeccionamiento (Es)	Veredelung *f*	processing	perfectionnement *m*	perfezionamento *m*	—
perfectionnement (F)	Veredelung *f*	processing	—	perfezionamento *m*	perfeccionamiento *m*
perfezionamento (I)	Veredelung *f*	processing	perfectionnement *m*	—	perfeccionamiento *m*
perforadora (Es)	Datentypistin *f*	terminal operator	perforatrice *f*	dattilografa *f*	—
perforatrice (F)	Datentypistin *f*	terminal operator	—	dattilografa *f*	perforadora *f*
performance (E)	Leistung *f*	—	rendement *m*	rendimento *m*	rendimiento *m*
performance-oriented (E)	leistungsorientiert	—	orienté vers le rendement	orientato al rendimento	orientado hacia el rendimiento
pericolo (I)	Gefahr *f*	danger	danger *m*	—	peligro *m*
period[1] (E)	Periode *f*	—	période *f*	periodo *m*	período *m*
period[2] (E)	Frist *f*	—	délai *m*	termine *m*	plazo *m*
Periode (D)	—	period	période *f*	periodo *m*	período *m*
période (F)	Periode *f*	period	—	periodo *m*	período *m*
période comptable (F)	Abrechnungszeitraum *m*	accounting period	—	periodo di liquidazione *m*	período contable *m*
période de base (F)	Basisperiode *f*	base period	—	periodo di base *m*	período básico *m*
période de mise en marche (F)	Anlaufperiode *f*	initial period	—	periodo iniziale *m*	período de puesta en marcha *m*
période d'essai (F)	Probezeit *f*	trial period	—	periodo di prova *m*	período de prueba *m*
period for payment (E)	Zahlungsziel *n*	—	délai de payement *m*	termine di pagamento *m*	plazo de pago *m*
periodico per i clienti (I)	Kundenzeitschrift *f*	customer magazine	journal destiné à la clientèle *m*	—	revista para los clientes *f*
período (Es)	Periode *f*	period	période *f*	periodo *m*	—
periodo (I)	Periode *f*	period	période *f*	—	período *m*

	D	E	F	I	Es
período básico (Es)	Basisperiode *f*	base period	période de base *f*	periodo di base *m*	—
período carencial (Es)	Karenzzeit *f*	qualifying period	délai de carence *m*	periodo d'attesa *m*	—
período concesional de un crédito (Es)	Kreditlaufzeit *f*	duration of credit	durée de l'allocation de crédit *f*	scadenza del credito *f*	—
período contable (Es)	Abrechnungszeitraum *m*	accounting period	période comptable *f*	periodo di liquidazione *m*	—
periodo d'adattamento (I)	Einarbeitung *f*	vocational adjustment	entraînement *m*	—	entrenamiento *m*
periodo d'attesa (I)	Karenzzeit *f*	qualifying period	délai de carence *m*	—	período carencial *m*
período de almacenaje (Es)	Lagerzyklus *m*	stock cycle	cycle de stockage *m*	ciclo di magazzinaggio *m*	—
período de financiación (Es)	Finanzierungsdauer *f*	period of financing	durée du financement *f*	durata del finanziamento *f*	—
período de prueba (Es)	Probezeit *f*	trial period	période d'essai *f*	periodo di prova *m*	—
período de puesta en marcha (Es)	Anlaufperiode *f*	initial period	période de mise en marche *f*	periodo iniziale *m*	—
periodo di base (I)	Basisperiode *f*	base period	période de base *f*	—	período básico *m*
periodo di liquidazione (I)	Abrechnungszeitraum *m*	accounting period	période comptable *f*	—	período contable *m*
periodo di prova (I)	Probezeit *f*	trial period	période d'essai *f*	—	período de prueba *m*
period of financing (E)	Finanzierungsdauer *f*	—	durée du financement *f*	durata del finanziamento *f*	período de financiación *m*
period of notice (E)	Kündigungsfrist *f*	—	délai de préavis *m*	termine di preavviso per la disdetta *m*	plazo de preaviso *m*
periodo iniziale (I)	Anlaufperiode *f*	initial period	période de mise en marche *f*	—	período de puesta en marcha *m*
per iscritto (I)	schriftlich	written	par écrit	—	por escrito
perishable (E)	verderblich	—	périssable	deperibile	perecedero
périssable (F)	verderblich	perishable	—	deperibile	perecedero
perito publicitario (Es)	Werbefachmann *m*	advertising expert	technicien publicitaire *m*	esperto di pubblicità *m*	—
perizia (I)	Expertise *f*	expert opinion	expertise *f*	—	dictamen pericial *m*
per Lastkraftwagen (D)	—	by lorry	par camion	per autocarro	por camión
permesso (I)	Erlaubnis *f*	permission	permission *f*	—	permiso *m*
permesso di lavoro (I)	Arbeitserlaubnis *f*	work permit	permis de travail *m*	—	permiso de trabajo *m*
permesso d'importazione (I)	Einfuhrgenehmigung *f*	import licence	autorisation d'importation *f*	—	permiso de importación *m*
permesso di soggiorno (I)	Aufenthaltserlaubnis *f*	residence permit	autorisation de séjour *f*	—	permiso de residencia *m*
permis de travail (F)	Arbeitserlaubnis *f*	work permit	—	permesso di lavoro *m*	permiso de trabajo *m*
permiso (Es)	Erlaubnis *f*	permission	permission *f*	permesso *m*	—
permiso de importación (Es)	Einfuhrgenehmigung *f*	import licence	autorisation d'importation *f*	permesso d'importazione *m*	—
permiso de residencia (Es)	Aufenthaltserlaubnis *f*	residence permit	autorisation de séjour *f*	permesso di soggiorno *m*	—
permiso de trabajo (Es)	Arbeitserlaubnis *f*	work permit	permis de travail *m*	permesso di lavoro *m*	—
permission (F)	Erlaubnis *f*	permission	—	permesso *m*	permiso *m*
permission[1] (E)	Genehmigung *f*	—	autorisation *f*	autorizzazione *f*	autorización *f*
permission[2] (E)	Erlaubnis *f*	—	permission *f*	permesso *m*	permiso *m*
per nome proprio (I)	im eigenen Namen	in one's own name	en nom propre	—	en nombre propio
per ordine (I)	im Auftrag	by order	par ordre	—	por poder
per procura (D)	—	by procuration	par procuration	per procura	por poder
per procura (I)	per procura	by procuration	par procuration	—	por poder
per raccomandata (I)	per Einschreiben	by registered post	sous pli recommandé	—	certificado
persona activa (Es)	Erwerbstätiger *m*	gainfully employed person	personne ayant un emploi *m*	persona attiva *f*	—
persona attiva[1] (I)	Erwerbstätiger *m*	gainfully employed person	personne ayant un emploi *m*	—	persona activa *f*
persona attiva[2] (I)	Erwerbsperson *f*	gainfully employed person	personne active *f*	—	persona en activo *f*

	D	E	F	I	Es
persona avente capacità giuridica (I)	rechtsfähig	capable to act in law	capable de jouir des droits	—	jurídicamente capaz
persona en activo (Es)	Erwerbsperson *f*	gainfully employed person	personne active *f*	persona attiva *f*	—
persona fisica (I)	natürliche Person *f*	natural person	personne physique *f*	—	persona natural *f*
persona giuridica (I)	juristische Person *f*	legal person	personne juridique *f*	—	persona jurídica *f*
persona jurídica (Es)	juristische Person *f*	legal person	personne juridique *f*	persona giuridica *f*	—
Personal (D)	—	staff	personnel *m*	personale *m*	personal *m*
personal (Es)	Personal *n*	staff	personnel *m*	personale *m*	—
Personalabbau (D)	—	reduction of staff	réduction de personnel *f*	riduzione del personale *f*	reducción de personal *f*
personal accident insurance (E)	Unfallversicherung *f*	—	assurance accidents corporels *f*	assicurazione contro infortuni *f*	seguro de accidentes *m*
Personalausweis (D)	—	identity card	pièce d'identité *f*	carta d'identità *f*	carné de identidad *m*
Personalbüro (D)	—	personnel office	bureau du personnel *m*	ufficio del personale *m*	oficina de personal *f*
Personalcomputer (D)	—	personal computer	ordinateur individuel *m*	personal computer *m*	ordenador personal *m*
personal computer (E)	Personalcomputer *m*	—	ordinateur individuel *m*	personal computer *m*	ordenador personal *m*
personal computer (I)	Personalcomputer *m*	personal computer	ordinateur individuel *m*	—	ordenador personal *m*
personal consumption (E)	Eigenverbrauch *m*	—	consommation personnelle *f*	consumo proprio *m*	consumo propio *m*
personal conversation (E)	persönliches Gespräch *n*	—	conversation personnelle *f*	colloquio personale *m*	conversación personal *f*
personal data (E)	Personalien *pl*	—	identité *f*	generalità *f pl*	datos personales *m pl*
personal de formación (Es)	Schulungspersonal *n*	training staff	personnel d'instruction *m*	personale d'addestramento *m*	—
personal drawings (E)	Privatentnahmen *pl*	—	prélèvement personnel *m*	prelevamento a titolo personale *m*	detracción privada *f*
personale (I)	Personal *n*	staff	personnel *m*	—	personal *m*
personale d'addestramento (I)	Schulungspersonal *n*	training staff	personnel d'instruction *m*	—	personal de formación *m*
Personalführung (D)	—	personnel management	direction du personnel *f*	gestione del personale *f*	dirección de personal *m*
Personalien (D)	—	personal data	identité *f*	generalità *f pl*	datos personales *m pl*
Personalkredit (D)	—	personal loan	crédit personnel *m*	credito al personale *m*	crédito personal *m*
Personal-Leasing (D)	—	personnel leasing	leasing de personnel *m*	leasing di personale *m*	leasing de personal *m*
Personalleiter (D)	—	staff manager	chef du personnel *m*	capo reparto personale *m*	jefe de personal *m*
personal loan (E)	Personalkredit *m*	—	crédit personnel *m*	credito al personale *m*	crédito personal *m*
Personalmangel (D)	—	shortage of staff	manque de personnel *m*	mancanza di personale *f*	falta der personal *f*
Personalsituation (D)	—	personnel situation	effectif du personnel *m*	situazione occupazionale *f*	situación de personal *f*
Personalstrategie (D)	—	personnel strategy	stratégie en matière de personnel *f*	strategia occupazionale *f*	estrategia de personal *f*
Personalwechsel (D)	—	staff changes	mouvements dans le personnel *m pl*	cambio del personale *m*	cambio de personal *m*
Personalwerbung (D)	—	hiring of personnel	recrutement de personnel *m*	reclutazione di personale *f*	reclutamiento de personal *m*
persona natural (Es)	natürliche Person *f*	natural person	personne physique *f*	persona fisica *f*	—
persona residente[1] (I)	Deviseninländer *m*	resident	résident *m*	—	residente *m*
persona residente[2] (I)	Inländer *m*	national resident	national *m*	—	residente *m*
Personenbeförderung (D)	—	carriage of passengers	transport de personnes *m*	trasporto di persone *m*	transporte de personas *m*
Personengesellschaft (D)	—	partnership	société de personnes *f*	società di persone *f*	sociedad personalista *f*
Personenversicherung (D)	—	insurance of persons	assurance des personnes *f*	assicurazione di persone *f*	seguro personal *m*
person interested (E)	Interessent *m*	—	intéressé *m*	interessato *m*	interesado *m*
persönliches Gespräch (D)	—	personal conversation	conversation personelle *f*	colloquio personale *m*	conversación personal *f*

	D	E	F	I	Es
personne ayant le pouvoir commercial (F)	Handlungsbevollmächtigter *m*	commercial agent	—	mandatario commerciale *m*	apoderado especial *m*
personne ayant un emploi (F)	Erwerbsperson *f*	gainfully employed person	—	persona attiva *f*	persona en activo *f*
personne exerçant une profession libérale (F)	Freiberufler *m*	selfemployed person	—	libero professionista *m*	profesional *m*
personne juridique (F)	juristische Person *f*	legal person	—	persona giuridica *f*	persona jurídica *f*
personnel[1] (F)	Personal *n*	staff	—	personale *m*	personal *m*
personnel[2] (F)	Belegschaft *f*	staff	—	maestranza *f*	plantilla *f*
personnel d'instruction (F)	Schulungspersonal *n*	training staff	—	personale d'addestramento *m*	personal de formación *m*
personnel du service extérieur (F)	Außendienstmitarbeiter *m*	field staff	—	collaboratore del servizio esterno *m*	colaborador en el servicio exterior *m*
personnel leasing (E)	Personal-Leasing *n*	—	leasing de personnel *m*	leasing di personale *m*	leasing de personal *m*
personnel management (E)	Personalführung *f*	—	direction du personnel *f*	gestione del personale *f*	dirección de personal *m*
personnel office (E)	Personalbüro *n*	—	bureau du personnel *m*	ufficio del personale *m*	oficina de personal *f*
personnel situation (E)	Personalsituation *f*	—	effectif du personnel *m*	situazione occupazionale *f*	situación de personal *f*
personnel strategy (E)	Personalstrategie *f*	—	stratégie en matière de personnel *f*	strategia occupazionale *f*	estrategia de personal *f*
personne physique (F)	natürliche Person *f*	natural person	—	persona fisica *f*	persona natural *f*
perspective (F)	Prognose *f*	forecast(ing)	—	prognosi *f*	pronóstico *m*
perspectives d'avenir (F)	Zukunftschance *f*	future prospects	—	prospettiva *f*	posibilidades futuras *f pl*
perspectives de promotion (F)	Aufstiegsmöglichkeit *f*	promotion possibility	—	possibilità di carriera *f*	posibilidades de ascenso *f pl*
perte[1] (F)	Verlust *m*	loss	—	perdita *f*	pérdida *f*
perte[2] (F)	Damnum *n*	damnum	—	perdita *f*	pérdida *f*
perte dans la production (F)	Produktionsausfall *m*	loss of production	—	perdita di produzione *f*	pérdida de producción *f*
pesacartas (Es)	Briefwaage *f*	letter scales	pèse-lettres *m*	bilancia per corrispondenza *f*	—
pesca (Es)	Fischerei *f*	fishing	pêcherie *f*	pesca *f*	—
pesca (I)	Fischerei *f*	fishing	pêcherie *f*	—	pesca *f*
pèse-lettres (F)	Briefwaage *f*	letter scales	—	bilancia per corrispondenza *f*	pesacartas *m*
peso (Es)	Gewicht *n*	weight	poids *m*	peso *m*	—
peso (I)	Gewicht *n*	weight	poids *m*	—	peso *m*
peso de descarga (Es)	Abladegewicht *n*	shipping (delivered) weight	poids au déchargement *m*	peso di scarico *m*	—
peso di scarico (I)	Abladegewicht *n*	shipping (delivered) weight	poids au déchargement *m*	—	peso de descarga *m*
peso fino (Es)	Feingewicht *n*	weight of fine gold	poids de métal fin *m*	peso fino *m*	—
peso fino (I)	Feingewicht *n*	weight of fine gold	poids de métal fin *m*	—	peso fino *m*
pesquisas (Es)	Nachforschung *f*	investigation	recherche *f*	indagine *f*	—
petición de quiebra (Es)	Konkursantrag *m*	bankruptcy petition	demande en déclaration de faillite *f*	domanda di dichiarazione del fallimento *f*	—
petit conteneur (F)	Kleincontainer *m*	small container	—	mini container *m*	pequeño contenedor *m*
petite palette (F)	Kleinpalette *f*	small pallet	—	mini paletta *f*	pequña paleta *f*
petites et moyennes entreprises (F)	Klein- und Mittelbetriebe *pl*	small and medium-sized enterprises	—	piccole e medie imprese *f pl*	pequeñas y medianas empresas *f pl*
petit paquet (F)	Päckchen *n*	small package	—	pacchetto *m*	pequeño paquete *m*
petrol (E)	Benzin *n*	—	essence *f*	benzina *f*	gasolina *f*
pétrole (F)	Erdöl *n*	mineral oil	—	petrolio *m*	crudo *m*
pétrole brut (F)	Rohöl *n*	crude oil	—	petrolio greggio *m*	crudo *m*
petrolio (I)	Erdöl *n*	mineral oil	pétrole *m*	—	crudo *m*
petrolio greggio (I)	Rohöl *n*	crude oil	pétrole brut *m*	—	crudo *m*
petrol voucher (E)	Benzingutscheine *pl*	—	bon d'essence *m*	coupons *m pl*	bono de gasolina *m*

	D	E	F	I	Es
pezzo di ricambio (I)	Ersatzteil *n*	spare part	pièce de rechange *f*	—	pieza de recambio *f*
Pfandbrief (D)	—	mortgage bond	obligation hypothécaire *f*	titolo ipotecario *m*	cédula hipotecaria *f*
Pfandrecht (D)	—	pledge	droit de gage *m*	diritto di pegno *m*	derecho de garantía real *m*
Pfändung (D)	—	seizure	saisie *f*	pignoramento *m*	pignoración *f*
Pfund (D)	—	pound	livre *f*	libbra *f*	libra *f*
phase d'organisation (F)	Aufbauphase *f*	development phase	—	fase di costruzione *f*	fase de desarrollo *f*
Phosphat (D)	—	phosphate	phosphate *m*	fosfato *m*	fosfato *m*
phosphate (E)	Phosphat *n*	—	phosphate *m*	fosfato *m*	fosfato *m*
phosphate (F)	Phosphat *n*	phosphate	—	fosfato *m*	fosfato *m*
phosphatfrei (D)	—	free of phosphate	sans phosphate	privo di fosfato	sin fosfato
photocopie (F)	Fotokopie *f*	photocopy	—	fotocopia *f*	fotocopia *f*
photocopier (E)	Fotokopierer *m*	—	photocopieur *m*	copialettere *m*	fotocopiadora *f*
photocopieur (F)	Fotokopierer *m*	photocopier	—	copialettere *m*	fotocopiadora *f*
photocopy (E)	Fotokopie *f*	—	photocopie *f*	fotocopia *f*	fotocopia *f*
pianificazione (I)	Planifikation *f*	planning	planification *f*	—	planificación *f*
pianificazione alternativa (I)	Alternativplanung *f*	alternative planning	planification alternative *f*	—	planificación alternativa *f*
pianificazione degli ordini (I)	Auftragsplanung *f*	order scheduling	planification des commandes *f*	—	planificación de la ejecución de pedidos *f*
pianificazione delle vendite (I)	Absatzplanung *f*	sales planning	planning de la distribution *m*	—	planificación de ventas *f*
pianificazione finanziaria a media scadenza (I)	mittelfristige Finanzplanung *f*	medium-term fiscal planning	gestion financière à moyen terme *f*	—	planificación financiera a medio plazo
pianificazione regionale (I)	Regionalplanung *f*	regional planning	aménagement régional *m*	—	planificación regional *f*
pianificazione reticolare (I)	Netzplan *m*	network planning	réseau linéaire pour planification *m*	—	planificación reticular *f*
pianificazione territoriale (I)	Raumplanung *f*	regional planning	plan d'aménagement des espaces *m*	—	planificación del espacio *m*
piano (I)	Konzept *n*	concept	brouillon *m*	—	bosquejo *m*
piano dei costi (I)	Kostenplan *m*	cost schedule	planning des coûts *m*	—	planilla de costas *f*
piano della liquidità (I)	Liquiditätsplan *m*	cash forecasting plan	plan de liquidité *m*	—	plan de liquidez *m*
piano d'investimento (I)	Investitionsplan *m*	investment scheme	plan des investissements *m*	—	plan de inversión *m*
piano di produzione (I)	Produktionsplan *m*	production plan	plan de production *m*	—	plan de producción *m*
piano economico (I)	Wirtschaftsplan *m*	economic plan	plan économique *m*	—	plan económico *m*
piano finanziario (I)	Finanzplan *m*	financial plan	plan financier *m*	—	presupuesto *m*
piano imprenditoriale (I)	Unternehmenskonzept *n*	business concept	stratégie de l'entreprise *f*	—	concepto comercial *m*
piazza (I)	Börsenplatz *m*	stock exchange centre	place boursière *f*	—	plaza bursátil *f*
piazza commerciale (I)	Handelsplatz *m*	trade centre	place marchande *f*	—	plaza comercial *f*
piccole e medie imprese (I)	Klein- und Mittelbetriebe *pl*	small and medium-sized enterprises	petites et moyennes entreprises *f pl*	—	pequeñas y medianas empresas *f pl*
pièce de monnaie (F)	Hartgeld *n*	specie	—	moneta metallica *f*	dinero metálico *m*
pièce de rechange (F)	Ersatzteil *n*	spare part	—	pezzo di ricambio *m*	pieza de recambio *f*
pièce d'identité (F)	Personalausweis *m*	identity card	—	carta d'identità *f*	carné de identidad *m*
pièce d'identité de l'entreprise (F)	Betriebsausweis *m*	staff identification card	—	tessera aziendale *f*	carné de empresa *f*
pièce jointe (F)	Anlage *f*	enclosure	—	allegato *m*	anexo *m*
pièces accompagnant l'envoi (F)	Begleitpapiere *pl*	accompanying documents	—	bolle di accompagnamento *f pl*	documentos adjuntos *m pl*
piece time (E)	Stückzeit *f*	—	temps par pièce *m*	tempo pezzo *m*	tiempo por unidad *m*
piecework (E)	Akkordarbeit *f*	—	travail à la tâche *m*	lavora a cottimo *m*	trabajo a destajo *m*
piece work (E)	Akkord *m*	—	convention de salaire à la tâche *f*	cottimo *m*	destajo *m*
piece work pay (E)	Stücklohn *m*	—	salaire à la tâche *m*	salario a cottimo *m*	salario a destajo *m*

	D	E	F	I	Es
piece work system (E)	Akkordsystem *n*	—	système du travail aux pièces *m*	sistema del lavoro a cottimo *m*	régimen de trabajo a destajo *m*
piece work wages (E)	Akkordlohn *m*	—	salaire à la pièce *m*	retribuzione per il lavoro a cottimo *f*	salario a destajo *m*
pie de imprenta (Es)	Impressum *n*	imprint	mention des responsables de l'édition *f*	impressum *m*	—
piena occupazione (I)	Vollbeschäftigung *f*	full employment	plein emploi *m*	—	empleo total *m*
pieza de recambio (Es)	Ersatzteil *n*	spare part	pièce de rechange *f*	pezzo di ricambio *m*	—
pig cycle (E)	Schweinezyklus *m*	—	cycle de porc *m*	teorema cobweb sul ciclo produttivo *m*	ciclo de puerco *m*
piggyback advertisement (E)	Huckepackwerbung *f*	—	publicité pick-a-back *f*	pubblicità per il trasporto strada-rotaia *f*	publicidad combinada ferrocarril-carretera *f*
piggyback service (E)	Huckepackverkehr *m*	—	transport pick-a-back *m*	trasporto strada-rotaia *m*	transporte combinado ferrocarril-carretera *m*
pignoración[1] (Es)	Verpfändung *f*	pledge	mise en gage *f*	pignoramento *m*	—
pignoración[2] (Es)	Pfändung *f*	seizure	saisie *f*	pignoramento *m*	—
pignoramento[1] (I)	Verpfändung *f*	pledge	mise en gage *f*	—	pignoración *f*
pignoramento[2] (I)	Pfändung *f*	seizure	saisie *f*	—	pignoración *f*
pignoramento del salario (I)	Lohnpfändung *f*	attachment of earnings	saisie-arrêt sur le salaire *f*	—	embargo de salario *m*
pioggia acida (I)	saurer Regen *m*	acid rain	pluie acide *f*	—	lluvia ácida *f*
pirating (E)	Abwerbung *f*	—	débauchage *m*	accaparramento *m*	sonsacamiento *m*
piso en propiedad (Es)	Eigentumswohnung *f*	freehold flat	logement en propriété *m*	appartamento in condominio *m*	—
place (E)	plazieren	—	placer	collocare	colocar
place boursière (F)	Börsenplatz *m*	stock exchange centre	—	piazza *f*	plaza bursátil *f*
place marchande (F)	Handelsplatz *m*	trade centre	—	piazza commerciale *f*	plaza comercial *f*
placement (E)	Plazierung *f*	—	placement *m*	collocamento *m*	colocación
placement (F)	Plazierung *f*	placing	—	collocamento *m*	colocación *f*
placement de l'annonce (F)	Anzeigenschaltung *f*	insertion of an advertisement	—	posizionamento dell'inserzione *m*	inserción del anuncio *f*
placement of an advertisement (E)	Anzeigenplazierung *f*	—	disposition de l'annonce *f*	collocamento dell'inserzione *m*	colocación del anuncio *f*
place of birth (E)	Geburtsort *m*	—	lieu de naissance *m*	luogo di nascita *m*	lugar de nacimiento *m*
place of destination (E)	Bestimmungsort *m*	—	lieu de destination *m*	luogo di destinazione *m*	lugar de de destino *m*
place of employment (E)	Arbeitsplatz *m*	—	poste de travail *m*	posto di lavoro *m*	puesto de trabajo *m*
placer (F)	plazieren	place	—	collocare	colocar
placing (E)	Plazierung *f*	—	placement *m*	collocamento *m*	colocación *f*
placing of an order (E)	Auftragserteilung *f*	—	passation d'une commande *f*	ordinazione *f*	otorgamiento de un pedido *m*
Plafond (D)	—	ceiling	plafond *m*	plafond *m*	límite máximo *m*
plafond (F)	Plafond *m*	ceiling	—	plafond *m*	límite máximo *m*
plafond (I)	Plafond *m*	ceiling	plafond *m*	—	límite máximo *m*
plafond di credito (I)	Kreditrahmen *m*	credit margin	marge de crédit accordé *f*	—	margen de crédito *m*
plafond du crédit accordé (F)	Kreditlinie *f*	credit line	—	linea creditizia *f*	línea de crédito *f*
plafond du crédit alloué (F)	Kreditlimit *n*	borrowing limit	—	limite di credito *m*	límite de crédito *m*
Plakat (D)	—	poster	affiche *f*	manifesto *m*	cartel *m*
plancher des prix (F)	Preisuntergrenze *f*	price floor	—	limite inferiore di prezzo *m*	límite inferior de los precios *m*
plan d'aménagement des espaces (F)	Raumplanung *f*	regional planning	—	pianificazione territoriale *f*	planificación del espacio *m*
plan de inversión (Es)	Investitionsplan *m*	investment scheme	plan des investissements *m*	piano d'investimento *m*	—
plan de liquidez (Es)	Liquiditätsplan *m*	cash forecasting plan	plan de liquidité *m*	piano della liquidità *m*	—
plan de liquidité (F)	Liquiditätsplan *m*	cash forecasting plan	—	piano della liquidità *m*	plan de liquidez *m*
plan de producción (Es)	Produktionsplan *m*	production plan	plan de production *m*	piano di produzione *m*	—

	D	E	F	I	Es
plan de production (F)	Produktionsplan *m*	production plan	—	piano di produzione *m*	plan de producción *m*
plan des investissements (F)	Investitionsplan *m*	investment scheme	—	piano d'investimento *m*	plan de inversión *m*
plan du chiffre d'affaires (F)	Umsatzplan *m*	turnover plan	—	programma del fatturato *m*	objectivo de facturación *m*
plan económico (Es)	Wirtschaftsplan *m*	economic plan	plan économique *m*	piano economico *m*	—
plan économique (F)	Wirtschaftsplan *m*	economic plan	—	piano economico *m*	plan económico *m*
plan financier (F)	Finanzplan *m*	financial plan	—	piano finanziario *m*	presupuesto *m*
planificación¹ (Es)	Planifikation *f*	planning	planification *f*	pianificazione *f*	—
planificación² (Es)	Planung *f*	planning	planning *m*	programmazione *f*	—
planificación alternativa (Es)	Alternativplanung *f*	alternative planning	planification alternative *f*	pianificazione alternativa *f*	—
planificación de la ejecución de pedidos (Es)	Auftragsplanung *f*	order scheduling	planification des commandes *f*	pianificazione degli ordini *f*	—
planificación de la fundación (Es)	Gründungsplanung *f*	formation plan	planification de fondation *f*	progettazione della costituzione *f*	—
planificación de las vacaciones (Es)	Urlaubsplanung *f*	vacation scheduling	planification des vacances *f*	programmazione delle ferie *f*	—
planificación del espacio (Es)	Raumplanung *f*	regional planning	plan d'aménagement des espaces *m*	pianificazione territoriale *f*	—
planificación del presupuesto (Es)	Budgetplanung *f*	budgetary planning	planification du budget *f*	programmazione del bilancio *f*	—
planificación de mercadeo (Es)	Marketingplanung *f*	marketing planning	planning du marketing *m*	programmazione del marketing *f*	—
planificación de plazos (Es)	Terminplanung *f*	scheduling	planning de rendez-vous *m*	programmazione dei termini *f*	—
planificación de ventas (Es)	Absatzplanung *f*	sales planning	planning de la distribution *m*	pianificazione delle vendite *f*	—
planificación regional (Es)	Regionalplanung *f*	regional planning	aménagement régional *m*	pianificazione regionale *f*	—
planificación reticular (Es)	Netzplan *m*	network planning	réseau linéaire pour planification *m*	pianificazione reticolare *f*	—
planification (F)	Planifikation *f*	planning	—	pianificazione *f*	planificación *f*
planification alternative (F)	Alternativplanung *f*	alternative planning	—	pianificazione alternativa *f*	planificación alternativa *f*
planification de fondation (F)	Gründungsplanung *f*	formation plan	—	progettazione della costituzione *f*	planificación de la fundación *f*
planification des commandes (F)	Auftragsplanung *f*	order scheduling	—	pianificazione degli ordini *f*	planificación de la ejecución de pedidos *f*
planification des vacances (F)	Urlaubsplanung *f*	vacation scheduling	—	programmazione delle ferie *f*	planificación de las vacaciones *f*
planification du budget (F)	Budgetplanung *f*	budgetary planning	—	programmazione del bilancio *f*	planificación del presupuesto *m*
Planifikation (D)	—	planning	planification *f*	pianificazione *f*	planificación *f*
planilla de costas (Es)	Kostenplan *m*	cost schedule	planning des coûts *m*	piano dei costi *m*	—
Plankalkulation (D)	—	target calculation	calcul des coûts prévisionnels *m*	calcolo pianificato *m*	cálculo de los objetivos *m*
Plankostenrechnung (D)	—	calculation of the budget costs	calcul de l'écart sur cadence de fabrication *m*	calcolo dei costi pianificati *m*	cálculo de costes normalizados *m*
planned economy (E)	Planwirtschaft *f*	—	économie planifiée *f*	economia pianificata *f*	economía planificada *f*
planning¹ (E)	Planifikation *f*	—	planification *f*	pianificazione *f*	planificación *f*
planning² (E)	Planung *f*	—	planning *m*	programmazione *f*	planificación *f*
planning (F)	Planung *f*	planning	—	programmazione *f*	planificación *f*
planning control (E)	Planungskontrolle *f*	—	contrôle de la planification *f*	controllo della programmazione *m*	contol de planificación *m*
planning de la distribution (F)	Absatzplanung *f*	sales planning	—	pianificazione delle vendite *f*	planificación de ventas *f*
planning de rendez-vous (F)	Terminplanung *f*	scheduling	—	programmazione dei termini *f*	planificación de plazos *f*
planning des coûts (F)	Kostenplan *m*	cost schedule	—	piano dei costi *m*	planilla de costas *f*
planning du marketing (F)	Marketingplanung *f*	marketing planning	—	programmazione del marketing *f*	planificación de mercadeo *m*

	D	E	F	I	Es
planning figures (E)	Planwerte *pl*	—	valeurs prévisionnelles *f pl*	valori pianificati *m pl*	valores previstos *m pl*
Planrevision (D)	—	budget adjustment	révision des coûts marginaux *f*	revisione del piano *f*	ajuste presupuestario *m*
Planspiel (D)	—	management games	jeu d'entreprise *m*	gioco di strategia imprenditoriale *m*	juego de ensayo *m*
plant (E)	Werk *n*	—	usine *f*	stabilimento *m*	planta *f*
planta (Es)	Werk *n*	plant	usine *f*	stabilimento *m*	—
planta industrial (Es)	Industrieanlage *f*	industrial plant	installation industrielle *f*	impianto industriale *m*	—
plantilla (Es)	Belegschaft *f*	staff	personnel *m*	maestranza *f*	—
Planung (D)	—	planning	planning *m*	programmazione *f*	planificación *f*
Planungskontrolle (D)	—	planning control	contrôle de la planification *f*	controllo della programmazione *m*	contol de planificación *m*
Planwerte (D)	—	planning figures	valeurs prévisionnelles *f pl*	valori pianificati *m pl*	valores previstos *m pl*
Planwirtschaft (D)	—	planned economy	économie planifiée *f*	economia pianificata *f*	economía planificada *f*
plata (Es)	Silber *n*	silver	argent *m*	argento *m*	—
plaza bursátil (Es)	Börsenplatz *m*	stock exchange centre	place boursière *f*	piazza *f*	—
plaza comercial (Es)	Handelsplatz *m*	trade centre	place marchande *f*	piazza commerciale *f*	—
plazieren (D)	—	place	placer	collocare	colocar
Plazierung (D)	—	placing	placement *m*	collocamento *m*	colocación *f*
plazo[1] (Es)	Teilzahlungsrate *f*	monthly instalment	mensualité d'un achat à tempérament *f*	rata *f*	—
plazo[2] (Es)	Rate *f*	instalment	acompte *m*	rata *f*	—
plazo[3] (Es)	Frist *f*	period	délai *m*	termine *m*	—
plazo de arrendamiento financiero (Es)	Leasing-Rate *f*	leasing payment	taux de leasing *m*	rata leasing *f*	—
plazo de entrega[1] (Es)	Lieferfrist *f*	time for delivery	délai de livraison *m*	termine di consegna *m*	—
plazo de entrega[2] (Es)	Liefertermin *m*	date of delivery	délai de livraison *m*	termine di consegna *m*	—
plazo de gracia (Es)	Nachfrist *f*	additional period	prolongation *f*	termine supplementare *m*	—
plazo de pago[1] (Es)	Zahlungsziel *n*	period for payment	délai de payement *m*	termine di pagamento *m*	—
plazo de pago[2] (Es)	Zahlungstermin *m*	date of payment	terme du payement *m*	termine di pagamento *m*	—
plazo de pago[3] (Es)	Zahlungsfrist *f*	terms of payment	délai de payement *f*	scadenza di pagamento *f*	—
plazo de preaviso (Es)	Kündigungsfrist *f*	period of notice	délai de préavis *m*	termine di preavviso per la disdetta *m*	—
plazo de protección (Es)	Schutzfrist *f*	term of protection	délai de protection *m*	durata della protezione *f*	—
plazo de solicitud (Es)	Anmeldefrist *f*	time for application	délai de déclaration *m*	termine di denuncia *m*	—
plazo de vencimiento (Es)	Laufzeit *f*	term	durée *f*	scadenza *f*/durata *f*	—
plazo de vencimiento restante (Es)	Restlaufzeit *f*	residual time to maturity	durée restante *f*	scadenza residua *f*	—
plazo de vinculación al tipo de interés pactado (Es)	Zinsbindungsfrist *f*	lock-down period for interest rates	délai d'engagement sur le taux d'intérêt accordé *m*	scadenza degli interessi vincolati *f*	—
pledge[1] (E)	Verpfändung *f*	—	mise en gage *f*	pignoramento *m*	pignoración *f*
pledge[2] (E)	Pfandrecht *n*	—	droit de gage *m*	diritto di pegno *m*	derecho de garantía real *m*
plein emploi (F)	Vollbeschäftigung *f*	full employment	—	piena occupazione *f*	empleo total *m*
plein pouvoir (F)	Vollmacht *f*	full power/ power of attorney	—	autorizzazione *f*/ procura *f*	poder *m*/ autorización *f* /escritura de poder *f*
pluie acide (F)	saurer Regen *m*	acid rain	—	pioggia acida *f*	lluvia ácida *f*
plusvalía[1] (Es)	Mehrwert *m*	value added	valeur ajoutée *f*	valore aggiunto *m*	—

	D	E	F	I	Es
plusvalía² (Es)	Wertzuwachs *m*	appreciation	accroissement de valeur *m*	incremento di valore *m*	—
población (Es)	Bevölkerung *f*	population	population *f*	popolazione *f*	—
poder (Es)	Vollmacht *f*	full power/power of attorney	plein pouvoir *m*/ mandat *m*	autorizzazione *f*/ procura *f*	—
poder adquisitivo (Es)	Kaufkraft *f*	purchasing power	pouvoir d'achat *m*	potere d'acquisto *m*	—
poderdante (Es)	Vollmachtgeber *m*	grantor of a power of attorney	auteur de la procuration *m*	mandante *m*	—
poder general¹ (Es)	Prokura *f*	Prokura (procuration)	procuration commerciale générale *f*	procura *f*	—
poder general² (Es)	Generalvollmacht *f*	general power	pouvoir général *m*	procura generale *f*	—
poids (F)	Gewicht *n*	weight	—	peso *m*	peso *m*
poids au déchargement (F)	Abladegewicht *n*	shipping (delivered) weight	—	peso di scarico *m*	peso de descarga *m*
poids de métal fin (F)	Feingewicht *n*	weight of fine gold	—	peso fino *m*	peso fino *m*
point d'intervention (F)	Interventionspunkt *m*	intervention point	—	punto d'intervento *m*	punto de intervención *m*
Police (D)	—	policy	police *f*	polizza *f*	póliza *f*
police (F)	Police *f*	policy	—	polizza *f*	póliza *f*
police certificate of good conduct (E)	polizeiliches Führungszeugnis *n*	—	certificat de bonnes vie et moeurs *m*	certificato di buona condotta *m*	certificado policial *m*
police d'assurance (F)	Versicherungspolice *f*	insurance policy	—	polizza d'assicurazione *f*	seguro *m*
policía de la empresa (Es)	Werkschutz *m*	works protection force	corps de sécurité d'entreprise *m*	servizio di sorveglianza aziendale *m*	—
policy (E)	Police *f*	—	police *f*	polizza *f*	póliza *f*
policy of advances on securities (E)	Lombardpolitik *f*	—	politique des prêts sur gages *f*	politica delle anticipazioni *f*	política de pignoración *f*
policy relating to capital formation (E)	Vermögenspolitik *f*	—	politique financière *f*	politica patrimoniale *f*	política de los patrimonios *f*
política (Es)	Politik *f*	politics	politique *f*	politica *f*	—
politica (I)	Politik *f*	politics	politique *f*	—	política *f*
politica agraria (I)	Agrarpolitik *f*	agricultural policy	politique agricole *f*	—	política agrícola *f*
política agrícola (Es)	Agrarpolitik *f*	agricultural policy	politique agricole *f*	politica agraria *f*	—
política comercial (Es)	Handelspolitik *f*	commercial policy	politique commerciale *f*	politica commerciale *f*	—
política comercial exterior (Es)	Außenhandelspolitik *f*	foreign trade policy	politique de commerce extérieur *f*	politica del commercio estero *f*	—
politica commerciale (I)	Handelspolitik *f*	commercial policy	politique commerciale *f*	—	política comercial *f*
politica concorrenziale (I)	Wettbewerbspolitik *f*	competition policy	politique de concurrence *f*	—	política de competencia *f*
politica congiunturale (I)	Konjunkturpolitik *f*	economic policy	politique de conjoncture *f*	—	política de coyuntura *f*
politica creditizia (I)	Kreditpolitik *f*	credit policy	politique favorisant le crédit *f*	—	política de crédito *f*
política de competencia (Es)	Wettbewerbspolitik *f*	competition policy	politique de concurrence *f*	politica concorrenziale *f*	—
política de coyuntura (Es)	Konjunkturpolitik *f*	economic policy	politique de conjoncture *f*	politica congiunturale *f*	—
política de crecimiento económico (Es)	Wachstumspolitik *f*	growth policy	politique d'accroissement *f*	politica di crescita *f*	—
política de crédito (Es)	Kreditpolitik *f*	credit policy	politique favorisant le crédit *f*	politica creditizia *f*	—
política de descuento (Es)	Diskontpolitik *f*	discount policy	politique d'escompte *f*	politica di sconto *f*	—
política de distribución (Es)	Verteilungspolitik *f*	distribution policy	politique de répartition *f*	politica della distribuzione *f*	—
política de empleo (Es)	Beschäftigungspolitik *f*	employment policy	politique d'emploi *f*	politica d'occupazione *f*	—
política de estabilidad económica (Es)	Stabilitätspolitik *f*	stability policy	politique de stabilité *f*	politica di consolidamento *f*	—
politica dei prezzi (I)	Preispolitik *f*	price policy	politiques des prix *f*	—	política de precios *f*

	D	E	F	I	Es
politica dei tassi d'interesse (I)	Zinspolitik *f*	interest rate policy	politique en matière d'intérêts *f*	—	política en materia de intereses *f*
politica del commercio estero (I)	Außenhandelspolitik *f*	foreign trade policy	politique de commerce extérieur *f*	—	política comercial exterior *f*
politica della bilancia dei pagamenti (I)	Zahlungsbilanzpolitik *f*	balance of payments policy	politique en matière de la balance des payements *f*	—	política en materia de balanza de pagos *f*
politica della distribuzione (I)	Verteilungspolitik *f*	distribution policy	politique de répartition *f*	—	política de distribución *f*
politica dell'assortimento (I)	Sortimentspolitik *f*	assortment policy	politique de sortiment *f*	—	política de surtido *f*
politica delle anticipazioni (I)	Lombardpolitik *f*	policy of advances on securities	politique des prêts sur gages *f*	—	política de pignoración *f*
política de los patrimonios (Es)	Vermögenspolitik *f*	policy relating to capital formation	politique financière *f*	politica patrimoniale *f*	—
politica del suolo (I)	Bodenpolitik *f*	land policy	politique de la terre *f*	—	política de suelo *f*
politica del traffico (I)	Verkehrspolitik *f*	transport policy	politique des transports *f*	—	política de transportes *f*
política demográfica (Es)	Bevölkerungspolitik *f*	population policy	politique démographique populationniste *f*	politica demografica *f*	—
politica demografica (I)	Bevölkerungspolitik *f*	population policy	politique démographique populationniste *f*	—	política demográfica *f*
política de pignoración (Es)	Lombardpolitik *f*	policy of advances on securities	politique des prêts sur gages *f*	politica delle anticipazioni *f*	—
política de precios (Es)	Preispolitik *f*	price policy	politiques des prix *f*	politica dei prezzi *f*	—
política de suelo (Es)	Bodenpolitik *f*	land policy	politique de la terre *f*	politica del suolo *f*	—
política de surtido (Es)	Sortimentspolitik *f*	assortment policy	politique de sortiment *f*	politica dell'assortimento *f*	—
política de transportes (Es)	Verkehrspolitik *f*	transport policy	politique des transports *f*	politica del traffico *f*	—
política de ventas (Es)	Absatzpolitik *f*	marketing policy	politique de vente *f*	politica di vendita *f*	—
politica di bilancio (I)	Bilanzpolitik *f*	balance policy	politique du bilan *f*	—	política en materia de balanzas *f*
politica di consolidamento (I)	Stabilitätspolitik *f*	stability policy	politique de stabilité *f*	—	política de estabilidad económica *f*
politica di crescita (I)	Wachstumspolitik *f*	growth policy	politique d'accroissement *f*	—	política de crecimiento económico *f*
politica d'investimento (I)	Investitionslenkung *f*	investment control	politique d'investissement *f*	—	dirección de inversiones *f*
politica di sconto (I)	Diskontpolitik *f*	discount policy	politique d'escompte *f*	—	política de descuento *f*
politica di vendita (I)	Absatzpolitik *f*	marketing policy	politique de vente *f*	—	política de ventas *f*
politica d'occupazione (I)	Beschäftigungspolitik *f*	employment policy	politique d'emploi *f*	—	política de empleo *f*
política económica (Es)	Wirtschaftspolitik *f*	economic policy	politique économique *f*	politica economica *f*	—
politica economica (I)	Wirtschaftspolitik *f*	economic policy	politique économique *f*	—	política económica *f*
política en materia de balanza de pagos (Es)	Zahlungsbilanzpolitik *f*	balance of payments policy	politique en matière de la balance des payements *f*	politica della bilancia dei pagamenti *f*	—
política en materia de balanzas (Es)	Bilanzpolitik *f*	balance policy	politique du bilan *f*	politica di bilancio *f*	—
política en materia de intereses (Es)	Zinspolitik *f*	interest rate policy	politique en matière d'intérêts *f*	politica dei tassi d'interesse *f*	—
política estructural (Es)	Strukturpolitik *f*	structural policy	politique structurelle *f*	politica strutturale *f*	—
política financiera (Es)	Finanzpolitik *f*	fiscal policy	politique financière *f*	politica finanziaria *f*	—
politica finanziaria (I)	Finanzpolitik *f*	fiscal policy	politique financière *f*	—	política financiera *f*
política fiscal (Es)	Steuerpolitik *f*	fiscal policy	politique fiscale *f*	politica fiscale *f*	—
politica fiscale (I)	Steuerpolitik *f*	fiscal policy	politique fiscale *f*	—	política fiscal *f*
política monetaria[1] (Es)	Geldpolitik *f*	monetary policy	politique monétaire *f*	politica monetaria *f*	—
política monetaria[2] (Es)	Währungspolitik *f*	monetary policy	politique monétaire *f*	politica monetaria *f*	—
politica monetaria[1] (I)	Geldpolitik *f*	monetary policy	politique monétaire *f*	—	política monetaria *f*
politica monetaria[2] (I)	Währungspolitik *f*	monetary policy	politique monétaire *f*	—	política monetaria *f*

	D	E	F	I	Es
politica patrimoniale (I)	Vermögenspolitik *f*	policy relating to capital formation	politique financière *f*	—	política de los patrimonios *f*
política regional (Es)	Regionalpolitik *f*	regional policy	politique régionale *f*	politica regionale *f*	—
politica regionale (I)	Regionalpolitik *f*	regional policy	politique régionale *f*	—	política regional *f*
política salarial (Es)	Lohnpolitik *f*	wage policy	politique des salaires *f*	politica salariale *f*	—
politica salariale (I)	Lohnpolitik *f*	wage policy	politique des salaires *f*	—	política salarial *f*
política social (Es)	Sozialpolitik *f*	social policy	politique sociale *f*	politica sociale *f*	—
politica sociale (I)	Sozialpolitik *f*	social policy	politique sociale *f*	—	política social *f*
politica strutturale (I)	Strukturpolitik *f*	structural policy	politique structurelle *f*	—	política estructural *f*
politics (E)	Politik *f*	—	politique *f*	politica *f*	política *f*
Politik (D)	—	politics	politique *f*	politica *f*	política *f*
politique (F)	Politik *f*	politics	—	politica *f*	política *f*
politique agricole (F)	Agrarpolitik *f*	agricultural policy	—	politica agraria *f*	política agrícola *f*
politique commerciale (F)	Handelspolitik *f*	commercial policy	—	politica commerciale *f*	política comercial *f*
politique d'accroissement (F)	Wachstumspolitik *f*	growth policy	—	politica di crescita *f*	política de crecimiento económico *f*
politique de commerce extérieur (F)	Außenhandelspolitik *f*	foreign trade policy	—	politica del commercio estero *f*	política comercial exterior *f*
politique de concurrence (F)	Wettbewerbspolitik *f*	competition policy	—	politica concorrenziale *f*	política de competencia *f*
politique de conjoncture (F)	Konjunkturpolitik *f*	economic policy	—	politica congiunturale *f*	política de coyuntura *f*
politique de l'assortiment (F)	Sortimentspolitik *f*	assortment policy	—	politica dell'assortimento *f*	política de surtido *f*
politique de la terre (F)	Bodenpolitik *f*	land policy	—	politica del suolo *f*	política de suelo *f*
politique démographique populationniste (F)	Bevölkerungspolitik *f*	population policy	—	politica demografica *f*	política demográfica *f*
politique d'emploi (F)	Beschäftigungspolitik *f*	employment policy	—	politica d'occupazione *f*	política de empleo *f*
politique de répartition (F)	Verteilungspolitik *f*	distribution policy	—	politica della distribuzione *f*	política de distribución *f*
politique d'escompte (F)	Diskontpolitik *f*	discount policy	—	politica di sconto *f*	política de descuento *f*
politique des prêts sur gages (F)	Lombardpolitik *f*	policy of advances on securities	—	politica delle anticipazioni *f*	política de pignoración *f*
politique des salaires (F)	Lohnpolitik *f*	wage policy	—	politica salariale *f*	política salarial *f*
politique de stabilité (F)	Stabilitätspolitik *f*	stability policy	—	politica di consolidamento *f*	política de estabilidad económica *f*
politique des transports (F)	Verkehrspolitik *f*	transport policy	—	politica del traffico *f*	política de transportes *f*
politique de vente (F)	Absatzpolitik *f*	marketing policy	—	politica di vendita *f*	política de ventas *f*
politique d'investissement (F)	Investitionslenkung *f*	investment control	—	politica d'investimento *f*	dirección de inversiones *f*
politique du bilan (F)	Bilanzpolitik *f*	balance policy	—	politica di bilancio *f*	política en materia de balanzas *f*
politique économique (F)	Wirtschaftspolitik *f*	economic policy	—	politica economica *f*	política económica *f*
politique en matière de la balance des payements (F)	Zahlungsbilanzpolitik *f*	balance of payments policy	—	politica della bilancia dei pagamenti *f*	política en materia de balanza de pagos *f*
politique en matière d'intérêts (F)	Zinspolitik *f*	interest rate policy	—	politica dei tassi d'interesse *f*	política en materia de intereses *f*
politique favorisant le crédit (F)	Kreditpolitik *f*	credit policy	—	politica creditizia *f*	política de crédito *f*
politique financière[1] (F)	Finanzpolitik *f*	fiscal policy	—	politica finanziaria *f*	política financiera *f*
politique financière[2] (F)	Vermögenspolitik *f*	policy relating to capital formation	—	politica patrimoniale *f*	política de los patrimonios *f*
politique fiscale (F)	Steuerpolitik *f*	fiscal policy	—	politica fiscale *f*	política fiscal *f*
politique monétaire[1] (F)	Geldpolitik *f*	monetary policy	—	politica monetaria *f*	política monetaria *f*
politique monétaire[2] (F)	Währungspolitik *f*	monetary policy	—	politica monetaria *f*	política monetaria *f*

	D	E	F	I	Es
politique régionale (F)	Regionalpolitik *f*	regional policy	—	politica regionale *f*	política regional *f*
politiques des prix (F)	Preispolitik *f*	price policy	—	politica dei prezzi *f*	política de precios *f*
politique sociale (F)	Sozialpolitik *f*	social policy	—	politica sociale *f*	política social *f*
politique structurelle (F)	Strukturpolitik *f*	structural policy	—	politica strutturale *f*	política estructural *f*
póliza[1] (Es)	Seefrachtbrief *m*	bill of lading	connaissement maritime *m*	polizza di carico *f*	—
póliza[2] (Es)	Police *f*	policy	police *f*	polizza *f*	—
póliza de carga (Es)	Ladeschein *m*	bill of lading	avis de chargement *m*	bolletta di carico *f*	—
polizeiliches Führungszeugnis (D)	—	police certificate of good conduct	certificat de bonnes vie et moeurs *m*	certificato di buona condotta *m*	certificado policial *m*
polizza (I)	Police *f*	policy	police *f*	—	póliza *f*
polizza d'assicurazione (I)	Versicherungspolice *f*	insurance policy	police d'assurance *f*	—	seguro *m*
polizza di carico[1] (I)	Konnossement *n*	bill of lading	connaissement *m*	—	conocimiento *m*
polizza di carico[2] (I)	Seefrachtbrief *m*	bill of lading	connaissement maritime *m*	—	póliza *f*
poll (E)	Befragung *f*	—	enquête *f*	interrogazione *f*	encuesta *f*
pollutants (E)	Schadstoff *m*	—	élément polluant *m*	sostanza nociva *f*	substancia nociva *f*
polluter pays principle (E)	Verursacherprinzip *n*	—	principe du pollueur payeur *m*	principio della colpa oggettiva *m*	principio contamina-dor-pagador *m*
pollution de l'environnement (F)	Umwelt-verschmutzung *f*	environmental pollution	—	inquinamento dell'ambiente *m*	contaminación del medio ambiente *f*
polvere secondaria (I)	Sekundärstaub *m*	secondary dust	poussière secondaire *f*	—	polvo secundario *m*
polvo secundario (Es)	Sekundärstaub *m*	secondary dust	poussière secondaire *f*	polvere secondaria *f*	—
Pool (D)	—	pool	pool *m*	pool *m*	pool *m*
pool (E)	Pool *m*	—	pool *m*	pool *m*	pool *m*
pool (Es)	Pool *m*	pool	pool *m*	pool *m*	—
pool (F)	Pool *m*	pool	—	pool *m*	pool *m*
pool (I)	Pool *m*	pool	pool *m*	—	pool *m*
pool de brevet (F)	Patentpool *m*	patent pool	—	pool dei brevetti *m*	pool de patentes *m*
pool dei brevetti (I)	Patentpool *m*	patent pool	pool de brevet *m*	—	pool de patentes *m*
pool de patentes (Es)	Patentpool *m*	patent pool	pool de brevet *m*	pool dei brevetti *m*	—
pool d'imprese (I)	Unternehmens-konzentration *f*	business concentration	concentration d'entreprises *f*	—	concentración de empresas *f*
poor quality (E)	schlechte Qualität *f*	—	mauvaise qualité *f*	qualità scadente *f*	mala calidad *f*
popolazione (I)	Bevölkerung *f*	population	population *f*	—	población *f*
population (E)	Bevölkerung *f*	—	population *f*	popolazione *f*	población *f*
population (F)	Bevölkerung *f*	population	—	popolazione *f*	población *f*
population policy (E)	Bevölkerungspolitik *f*	—	politique démo-graphique populationniste *f*	politica demografica *f*	política demográfica *f*
population statistics (E)	Bevölkerungs-statistik *f*	—	statistique démographique *f*	statistica demografica *f*	estadística de población *f*
population structure (E)	Bevölkerungs-struktur *f*	—	structure démographique *f*	struttura demografica *f*	estructura demográfica *f*
por camión (Es)	per Lastkraftwagen	by lorry	par camion	per autocarro	—
porcentaje (Es)	Prozentsatz *m*	percentage	pourcentage *m*	percentuale *f*	—
por ciento (Es)	Prozent *n*	per cent	pour-cent *m*	percento *m*	—
por correo aparte (Es)	mit getrennter Post	under separate cover	sous pli séparé	in plico a parte	—
por cuenta ajena (Es)	für fremde Rechnung	for account of a third party	pour compte de tiers	per conto terzi	—
por cuenta propia (Es)	für eigene Rechnung	for one's own account	pour son propre compte	per conto proprio	—
por duplicado (Es)	in zweifacher	in duplicate Ausfertigung	en deux exemplaires	in due copie	—
por escrito (Es)	schriftlich	written	par écrit	per iscritto	—
por expreso (Es)	per Express	by express (mail)	par exprès	per espresso	—
por poder[1] (Es)	per procura	by procuration	par procuration	per procura	—

	D	E	F	I	Es
por poder² (Es)	im Auftrag	by order	par ordre p.o.	per ordine	—
port (E)	Hafen *m*	—	port *m*	porto *m*	puerto *m*
port¹ (F)	Hafen *m*	port	—	porto *m*	puerto *m*
port² (F)	Porto *n*	postage	—	porto *m*	porte *m*
portador (Es)	Überbringer *m*	bearer	porteur *m*	portatore *m*	—
portafoglio (I)	Portfolio *n*	portfolio	portefeuille *m*	—	cartera *f*
portafoglio di azioni (I)	Aktienbestand *m*	shareholding	portefeuille d'actions *m*	—	cartera de acciones *f*
portalettere (I)	Postbote *m*	postman	facteur *m*	—	cartero *m*
portatore (I)	Überbringer *m*	bearer	porteur *m*	—	portador *m*
porte (Es)	Porto *n*	postage	port *m*	porto *m*	—
portefeuille (F)	Portfolio *n*	portfolio	—	portafoglio *m*	cartera *f*
portefeuille d'actions (F)	Aktienbestand *m*	shareholding	—	portafoglio di azioni *m*	cartera de acciones *f*
porte pagado (Es)	portofrei	post-free	franco de port	franco di porto	—
porteur (F)	Überbringer *m*	bearer	—	portatore *m*	portador *m*
porteur des données (F)	Datenträger *m*	data medium	—	supporto dati *m*	medio de datos *m*
Portfolio (D)	—	portfolio	portefeuille *m*	portafoglio *m*	cartera *f*
portfolio (E)	Portfolio *n*	—	portefeuille *m*	portafoglio *m*	cartera *f*
port franc (F)	Freihafen *m*	free port	—	porto franco *m*	puerto franco *m*
Porto (D)	—	postage	port *m*	porto *m*	porte *m*
porto¹ (I)	Porto *n*	postage	port *m*	—	porte *m*
porto² (I)	Hafen *m*	port	port *m*	—	puerto *m*
Portoabzug (D)	—	postage deduction	déduction de port *f*	detrazione porto *f*	deducción de porte *f*
porto franco (I)	Freihafen *m*	free port	port franc *m*	—	puerto franco *m*
portofrei (D)	—	post-free	franco de port	franco di porto	porte pagado
por transferencia (Es)	bargeldlos	non-cash	par virement	mediante assegno	—
poscritto (I)	Postskriptum *n*	postscript	post-scriptum *m*	—	pos(t)data *m*
posesión (Es)	Besitz *m*	possession	possession *f*	possesso *m*	—
posibilidades de ascenso (Es)	Aufstiegs-möglichkeit *f*	promotion possibility	perspectives de promotion *f pl*	possibilità di carriera *f*	—
posibilidades de venta¹ (Es)	Verkaufschance *f*	sales possibilities	possibilité de vente *f*	prospettiva dello smercio *f*	—
posibilidades de venta² (Es)	Absatzchance *f*	sales prospects	possibilités de réussite des ventes *f pl*	prospettive di smercio *f pl*	—
posibilidades futuras (Es)	Zukunftschance *f*	future prospects	perspectives d'avenir *f pl*	prospettiva *f*	—
posición de costes (Es)	Kostenstelle *f*	departmental expense account	compte de frais par secteurs *m*	posizione costi *f*	—
posición en el mercado (Es)	Marktposition *f*	market position	position sur le marché *f*	posizione di mercato *f*	—
position (E)	Stellung *f*	—	position *f*	posizione *f*	empleo *m*
position (F)	Stellung *f*	position	—	posizione *f*	empleo *m*
position offered (E)	Stellenanzeige *f*	—	annonce d'emploi *f*	inserzione d'impiego *f*	anuncio de empleo *m*
position sur le marché (F)	Marktposition *f*	market position	—	posizione di mercato *f*	posición en el mercado *f*
posizionamento dell'inserzione (I)	Anzeigenschaltung *f*	insertion of an advertisement	placement de l'annonce *m*	—	inserción del anuncio *f*
posizione (I)	Stellung *f*	position	position *f*	—	empleo *m*
posizione costi (I)	Kostenstelle *f*	departmental expense account	compte des frais por secteurs *m*	—	posición de costes *f*
posizione di mercato (I)	Marktposition *f*	market position	position sur le marché *f*	—	posición en el mercado *f*
possession (E)	Besitz *m*	—	possession *f*	possesso *m*	posesión *f*
possession (F)	Besitz *m*	possession	—	possesso *m*	posesión *f*
possesso (I)	Besitz *m*	possession	possession *f*	—	posesión *f*
possessore di casa (I)	Hausbesitzer *m*	home property owner	propriétaire d'immeuble *m*	—	propietario de una casa *m*

	D	E	F	I	Es
possibilità di carriera (I)	Aufstiegs-möglichkeit *f*	promotion possibility	perspectives de promotion *f pl*	—	posibilidades de ascenso *f pl*
possibilité de vente (F)	Verkaufschance *f*	sales possibilities	—	prospettiva dello smercio *f*	posibilidades de venta *f pl*
possibilités de réussite des ventes (F)	Absatzchance *f*	sales prospects	—	prospettive di smercio *f pl*	posibilidades de venta *f pl*
posta aerea (I)	Luftpost *f*	air mail	par avion	—	correo aéreo *m*
postage (E)	Porto *n*	—	port *m*	porto *m*	porte *m*
postage deduction (E)	Portoabzug *m*	—	déduction de port *f*	detrazione porto *f*	deducción de porte *f*
postagiro (I)	Postgiro *n*	postal giro	virement postal *m*	—	giro postal *m*
postal code (E)	Postleitzahl *f*	—	chiffre de code postal *m*	codice d'avviamento postale *m*	código postal *m*
postal giro[1] (E)	Postscheck *m*	—	chèque postal *m*	assegno postale *m*	cheque postal *m*
postal giro[2] (E)	Postgiro *n*	—	virement postal *m*	postagiro *m*	giro postal *m*
(postal) giro account (E)	Postscheckkonto *n*	—	compte chèque postal *m*/compte courant postal *m*	conto corrente postale *m*	cuenta corriente postal *f*
postal giro centre (E)	Postscheckamt *n*	—	bureau de chèques postaux *m*	ufficio dei conti correnti postali *m*	oficina de cheques postales *f*
postal money order (E)	Postanweisung *f*	—	mandat-poste *m*	vaglia postale *m*	vale postal *m*
postal remittance (E)	Postüberweisung *f*	—	virement postal *m*	bonifico postale *m*	giro postal *m*
postal wrapper (E)	Streifband *f*	—	bande étiquette *f*	fascia *f*	precinto *m*
Postamt (D)	—	post office	bureau de poste *m*	ufficio postale *m*	correos *m pl*
Postanweisung (D)	—	postal money order	mandat-poste *m*	vaglia postale *m*	vale postal *m*
Postbote (D)	—	postman	facteur *m*	portalettere *m*	cartero *m*
postcard (E)	Postkarte *f*	—	carte postale *f*	cartolina postale *f*	tarjeta postal *f*
pos(t)data (Es)	Postskriptum *n*	postscript	post-scriptum *m*	poscritto *m*	—
pos(t)datado (Es)	nachdatiert	postdated	postdaté	postdatato	—
postdatato (I)	nachdatiert	postdated	postdaté	—	pos(t)datado
postdaté (F)	nachdatiert	antedated	—	postdatato	pos(t)datado
postdated (E)	nachdatiert	—	postdaté	postdatato	pos(t)datado
poste (F)	Posten *m*	item/lot	—	voce *f*/partita *f*	puesto *m*/partida *f*
poste à temps partiel (F)	Teilzeitstelle *f*	part-time job	—	posto di lavoro part-time *m*	puesto de trabajo a tiempo parcial *m*
poste de production absorbant des coûts (F)	Kostenträger *m*	unit assuming costs	—	chi si assume i costi	que sufraga los costes
poste de travail (F)	Arbeitsplatz *m*	place of employment	—	posto di lavoro *m*	puesto de trabajo *m*
poste de travail à l'écran (F)	Bildschirmarbeits-platz *m*	screen job	—	posto di lavoro video *m*	puesto de trabajo de pantalla *m*
Posten (D)	—	item/lot	poste *m*/lot de marchandieses *m*	voce *f*/partita *f*	puesto *m*/partida *f*
poster (E)	Plakat *n*	—	affiche *f*	manifesto *m*	cartel *m*
poste restante[1] (E)	postlagernd	—	poste restante	fermo posta	lista de correos *m*
poste restante[2] (F)	postlagernd	poste restante	—	fermo posta	lista de correos *m*
Postfach (D)	—	post office box	boîte postale *f*	casella postale *f*	apartado postal *m*
post-free (E)	portofrei	—	franco de port	franco di porto	porte pagado
Postgeheimnis (D)	—	secrecy of the post	secret postal *m*	segreto postale *m*	secreto postal *m*
Postgiro (D)	—	postal giro	virement postal *m*	postagiro *m*	giro postal *m*
Postkarte (D)	—	postcard	carte postale *f*	cartolina postale *f*	tarjeta postal *f*
postlagernd (D)	—	poste restante	poste restante	fermo posta	lista de correos *m*
Postleitzahl (D)	—	postal code	chiffre de code postal *m*	codice d'avviamento postale *m*	código postal *m*
postman (E)	Postbote *m*	—	facteur *m*	portalettere *m*	cartero *m*
postmark (E)	Poststempel *m*	—	cachet de la poste *m*	timbro postale *m*	sello postal *m*
posto di dogana (I)	Zollstelle *f*	customs office	bureau de douane *m*	—	oficina de aduanas *f*
posto di lavoro (I)	Arbeitsplatz *m*	place of employment	poste de travail *m*	—	puesto de trabajo *m*
posto di lavoro part-time (I)	Teilzeitstelle *f*	part-time job	poste à temps partiel *m*	—	puesto de trabajo a tiempo parcial *m*

	D	E	F	I	Es
posto di lavoro video (I)	Bildschirm-arbeitsplatz *m*	screen job	poste de travail à l'écran *f*	—	puesto de trabajo de pantalla *m*
post office (E)	Postamt *n*	—	bureau de poste principal *m*	ufficio postale *m*	correos *m pl*
post office box (E)	Postfach *n*	—	boîte postale *f*	casella postale *f*	apartado postal *m*
postpone (E)	Vertagung *f*	—	ajournement *m*	rinvio *m*	aplazamiento *m*/ suspensión *f*
postponement (E)	Aufschiebung *f*	—	remise *f*	rinvio *m*	aplazamiento *m*
Postscheck (D)	—	postal giro	chèque postal *m*	assegno postale *m*	cheque postal *m*
Postscheckamt (D)	—	postal giro centre	bureau de chèques postaux *m*	ufficio dei conti correnti postali *m*	oficina de cheques postales *f*
Postscheckkonto (D)	—	(postal) giro account	compte chèque postal *m*	conto corrente postale *m*	cuenta corriente postal *f*
postscript (E)	Postskriptum *n*	—	post-scriptum *m*	poscritto *m*	pos(t)data *m*
post-scriptum (F)	Postskriptum *n*	postscript	—	poscritto *m*	pos(t)data *m*
Postskriptum (D)	—	postscript	post-scriptum *m*	poscritto *m*	pos(t)data *m*
Poststempel (D)	—	postmark	cachet de la poste *m*	timbro postale *m*	sello postal *m*
Postüberweisung (D)	—	postal remittance	virement postal *m*	bonifico postale *m*	giro postal *m*
postwendend (D)	—	by return of post	par retour du courrier	a giro di posta	a vuelta de correo
Postwurfsendung (D)	—	printed papers or samples of merchandise posted in bulk	envoi publicitaire collectif *m*	spedizione postale cumulativa di stampati *f*	envío postal colectivo *m*
potencial productivo (Es)	Produktions-potential *n*	production potential	potentiel de production *m*	potenziale produttivo *m*	—
potentiel de production (F)	Produktions-potential *n*	production potential	—	potenziale produttivo *m*	potencial productivo *m*
potenziale produttivo (I)	Produktions-potential *n*	production potential	potentiel de production *m*	—	potencial productivo *m*
potere d'acquisto (I)	Kaufkraft *f*	purchasing power	pouvoir d'achat *m*	—	poder adquisitivo *m*
pound (E)	Pfund *n*	—	livre *f*	libbra *f*	libra *f*
pouperism (E)	Massenarmut *f*	—	paupérisme *m*	paupersimo *m*	pauperismo *m*
pourboire (F)	Bedienungsgeld *n*	tip	—	diritto di servizio *m*	propina *f*
pour-cent (F)	Prozent *n*	per cent	—	percento *m*	por ciento *m*
pourcentage (F)	Prozentsatz *m*	percentage	—	percentuale *f*	porcentaje *m*
pour compte de tiers (F)	für fremde Rechnung	for account of a third party	—	per conto terzi	por cuenta ajena
pour raison de payement (F)	zahlungshalber	on account of payment	—	a titolo di pagamento	título de pago
pour son propre compte (F)	für eigene Rechnung	for one's own account	—	per conto proprio	por cuenta propia
poussière secondaire (F)	Sekundärstaub *m*	secondary dust	—	polvere secondaria *f*	polvo secundario *m*
pouvoir[1] (F)	Bevollmächtigung *f*	authorization	—	autorizzazione *f*	apoderamiento *m*
pouvoir[2] (F)	Befugnis *f*	authorization	—	prerogativa *f*	autorización *f*
pouvoir d'achat (F)	Kaufkraft *f*	purchasing power	—	potere d'acquisto *m*	poder adquisitivo *m*
pouvoir général (F)	Generalvollmacht *f*	general power	—	procura generale *f*	poder general *m*
power of administration (E)	Verwaltungshoheit *f*	—	autonomie d'administration *f*	sovranità amministrativa *f*	soberanía administrativa *f*
power station (E)	Kraftwerk *n*	—	centrale électrique *f*	centrale elettrica *f*	circulación de automóviles *f*
práctica de pago (Es)	Zahlungs-gewohnheit *f*	practice of payment	habitude de payement *f*	consuetudine di pagamento *f*	—
practice of payment (E)	Zahlungs-gewohnheit *f*	—	habitude de payement *f*	consuetudine di pagamento *f*	práctica de pago *f*
Präferenz (D)	—	preference	préférence *f*	preferenza *f*	preferencia *f*
Präferenzzoll (D)	—	preferential duty	taxe préférentielle de douane *f*	dazio preferenziale *m*	aduanas preferenciales *f pl*
Prämie (D)	—	bonus/premium	prime *f*	premio *m*	gratificación *f*/prima *f*
Prämiensystem (D)	—	bonus system	système de primes *m*	sistema dei premi *m*	sistema de primas *m*
Prämisse (D)	—	premise	prémisse *f*	premessa *f*	premisa *f*
pranzo di lavoro (I)	Arbeitsessen *n*	working lunch	déjeuner de travail *m*	—	comida de trabajo *f*
Präsentation (D)	—	presentation	présentation *f*	presentazione *f*	presentación *f*

	D	E	F	I	Es
Präsident (D)	—	president	président *m*	presidente *m*	presidente *m*
pratica (I)	Akte *f*	file	dossier *m*	—	documento *m*
précieux (F)	wertvoll	valuable	—	prezioso	precioso
precinto (Es)	Streifband *f*	postal wrapper	bande étiquette *f*	fascia *f*	—
precinto aduanero (Es)	Zollverschluß *m*	customs seal	fermeture douanière *f*	sigillo doganale *m*	—
precio (Es)	Preis *m*	price	prix *m*	prezzo *m*	—
precio afectivo (Es)	Liebhaberpreis *m*	connoisseur's price	prix d'amateur *m*	prezzo d'affezione *m*	—
precio agrícola (Es)	Agrarpreis *m*	prices of farm products	prix agricole *m*	prezzo agrario *m*	—
precio-base (Es)	Schwellenpreis *m*	threshold price	prix de seuil *m*	prezzo soglia *m*	—
precio bruto (Es)	Bruttopreis *m*	gross price	prix brut *m*	prezzo lordo *m*	—
precio de compra (Es)	Einkaufspreis *m*	purchase price	prix d'achat *m*	prezzo d'acquisto *m*	—
precio de compras a plazo (Es)	Teilzahlungspreis *m*	partial payment price	prix d'un achat à tempérament *m*	prezzo rateale *m*	—
precio de coste[1] (Es)	Selbstkostenpreis *m*	cost price	prix coûtant *m*	prezzo di costo *m*	—
precio de coste[2] (Es)	Einstandspreis *m*	cost price	prix coûtant *m*	prezzo di costo *m*	—
precio de equilibrio (Es)	Gleichgewichts-preis *m*	equilibrium price	prix équilibré *m*	prezzo d'equilibrio *m*	—
precio de la travesía (Es)	Fahrgeld *n*	fare	coût du voyage *m*	spese di trasferta *f pl*	—
precio del crudo (Es)	Rohölpreis *m*	crude oil price	prix du pétrole brut *m*	prezzo del petrolio greggio *m*	—
precio del mercado mundial (Es)	Weltmarktpreis *m*	world market price	prix du marché mondial *m*	prezzo di mercato mondiale *m*	—
precio del oro (Es)	Goldpreis *m*	gold price	prix de l'ór *m*	prezzo dell'oro *m*	—
precio de orientación (Es)	Orientierungspreis *m*	guide price	prix d'orientation *m*	prezzo d'orientamento *m*	—
precio de producción (Es)	Erzeugerpreis *m*	producer price	prix à la production *m*	prezzo di fabbrica *m*	—
precio de reventa (Es)	Wiederverkaufs-preis *m*	resale price	prix de revente *m*	prezzo di rivendita *m*	—
precio de suelo (Es)	Bodenpreis *m*	land price	prix du terrain *m*	prezzo del terreno *m*	—
precio de venta (Es)	Ladenpreis *m*	retail price	prix de vente *m*	prezzo di vendita *m*	—
precio fijo (Es)	Festpreis *m*	fixed price	prix fixe *m*	prezzo fisso *m*	—
precio hegemónico (Es)	Preisführerschaft *f*	price leadership	leader en matière de prix *m*	leader in materia di prezzi *m*	—
precio indicativo (Es)	Richtpreis *m*	recommended retail price	prix indicatif *m*	prezzo indicativo *m*	—
precio-lista (Es)	Listenpreis *m*	list price	prix au tarif *m*	prezzo di listino *m*	—
precio máximo (Es)	Höchstpreis *m*	top price	prix plafond *m*	prezzo massimo *m*	—
precio mayorista (Es)	Großhandelspreise *pl*	wholesale prices	prix de gros *m*	prezzo all'ingrosso *m*	—
precio mínimo (Es)	Mindestpreis *m*	minimum price	prix minimum *m*	prezzo minimo *m*	—
precio mínimo a la importación (Es)	Mindesteinfuhr-preise *pl*	minimum import price	prix minimum d'importation *m pl*	prezzi minimi all'importazione *m pl*	—
precio neto (Es)	Nettopreis *m*	net price	prix net *m*	prezzo netto *m*	—
precio recomendado (Es)	Preisempfehlung *f*	price recommendation	recommendation de prix *f*	suggerimento di prezzo *m*	—
precios administrados (Es)	administrierte Preise *pl*	administered prices	prix administrés *m pl*	prezzi amministrati *m pl*	—
precios escalonados (Es)	Staffelpreis *m*	graduated price	prix échelonné *m*	prezzo differenziato *m*	—
precios ficticios (Es)	Mondpreise *pl*	ficticious prices	prix fictifs *m pl*	prezzi alle stelle *m pl*	—
precio sin compromiso (Es)	Preis freibleibend	open price	prix sans engagement	prezzo non vincolante *m*	—
precioso (Es)	wertvoll	valuable	précieux	prezioso	—
precio único (Es)	Einheitspreis *m*	uniform price	prix unique *m*	prezzo unitario *m*	—
precondition (E)	Voraussetzung *f*	—	condition préalable *f*	presupposto *m*	condición previa *f*
preemption right (E)	Vorkaufsrecht *n*	—	droit de préemption *m*	diritto di prelazione *m*	derecho de preferencia *m*
preference (E)	Präferenz *f*	—	préférence *f*	preferenza *f*	preferencia *f*
préférence (F)	Präferenz *f*	preference	—	preferenza *f*	preferencia *f*

	D	E	F	I	Es
preference share (E)	Vorzugsaktie *f*	—	action privilégiée *f*	azione privilegiata *f*	acción preferente *f*
preferencia (Es)	Präferenz *f*	preference	préférence *f*	preferenza *f*	—
preferential discount (E)	Vorzugsrabatt *m*	—	remise de faveur *f*	ribasso preferenziale *m*	rebaja preferencial *f*
preferential duty (E)	Präferenzzoll *m*	—	taxe préférentielle de douane *f*	dazio preferenziale *m*	aduanas preferenciales *f pl*
preferenza (I)	Präferenz *f*	preference	préférence *f*	—	preferencia *f*
Preis (D)	—	price	prix *m*	prezzo *m*	precio *m*
Preisabsprache (D)	—	price fixing	accord sur les prix *m*	accordo sui prezzi *m*	acuerdo de precios *m*
Preisabzug (D)	—	price deduction	réduction de prix *f*	riduzione del prezzo *f*	descuento *m*
Preisanstieg (D)	—	price rise	hausse des prix *f*	aumento del prezzo *m*	aumento de precios *m*
Preisauszeichnung (D)	—	pricemarking	affichage des prix *f*	indicazione del prezzo *f*	indicación de precios *f*
Preisbildung (D)	—	formation of prices	formation des prix *f*	formazione dei prezzi *f*	formación de precios *f*
Preisbindung (D)	—	obligation to maintain fixed prices	obligation de respecter les prix *f*	obbligo di mantenere il prezzo fissato *m*	limitación de precios *f*
Preisdifferenzierung (D)	—	price differentiation	différenciation de prix *f*	differenziazione dei prezzi *f*	diferenciación de los precios *f*
Preisempfehlung (D)	—	price recommendation	recommendation de prix *f*	suggerimento di prezzo *m*	precio recomendado *m*
Preiserhöhung (D)	—	price increase	augmentation des prix *f*	rialzo dei prezzi *m*	aumento de precios *m*
Preis freibleibend (D)	—	open price	prix sans engagement	prezzo non vincolante *m*	precio sin compromiso *m*
Preisführerschaft (D)	—	price leadership	leader en matière de prix *m*	leader in materia di prezzi *m*	precio hegemónico *m*
preisgünstiges Angebot (D)	—	well-priced offer	offre à un *f* prix avantageux	offerta a buon prezzo *f*	oferta favorable *f*
Preisindex (D)	—	price index	indice des prix *m*	indice dei prezzi *m*	ínidce de precios *m*
Preiskontrolle (D)	—	price control	contrôle des prix *m*	controllo dei prezzi *m*	control de precios *m*
Preislenkung (D)	—	administration of prices	réglementation des prix *f*	gestione dei prezzi *f*	reglamentación de precios *f*
Preisliste (D)	—	price list	liste des prix *f*	listino prezzi *m*	lista de precios *f*
Preismechanismus (D)	—	price mechanism	mécanisme des prix *m*	meccanismo dei prezzi *m*	mecanismo de precios *m*
Preisnachlaß (D)	—	price reduction	remise sur le prix *f*	ribasso del prezzo *m*	rebaja *f*
Preisniveau (D)	—	price level	niveau des prix *m*	livello dei prezzi *m*	nivel de precios *m*
Preisnotierung (D)	—	prices quoted	cotation des prix *f*	quotazione dei prezzi *f*	cotización de precios *f*
Preisobergrenze (D)	—	price ceiling	limite supérieure des prix *f*	limite massimo di prezzo *m*	límite superior de los precios *m*
Preispolitik (D)	—	price policy	politiques des prix *f*	politica dei prezzi *f*	política de precios *f*
Preisschwankung (D)	—	price fluctuation	fluctuation des prix *f*	fluttuazione dei prezzi *f*	oscilación de precios *f*
Preisschwelle (D)	—	threshold price	seuil du prix *m*	soglia dei prezzi *f*	umbral de precios *m*
Preissenkung (D)	—	price reduction	réduction des prix *f*	riduzione dei prezzi *f*	reducción de precios *f*
Preisstabilität (D)	—	stability of prices	stabilité des prix *f*	stabilità dei prezzi *f*	estabilidad de precios *f*
Preissteigerung (D)	—	price increase	hausse des prix *f*	aumento dei prezzi *m*	aumento de precios *m*
Preisstopp (D)	—	price stop	blocage des prix *m*	blocco dei prezzi *m*	limitación de precios *f*
Preistheorie (D)	—	theory of prices	théorie des prix *f*	teoria del prezzo *f*	teoría de los precios *f*
Preisuntergrenze (D)	—	price floor	plancher des prix *m*	limite inferiore di prezzo *m*	límite inferior de los precios *m*
Preisunterschied (D)	—	price difference	écart de prix *m*	differenza dei prezzi *f*	diferencia de precios *f*
Preisverfall (D)	—	decline in prices	chute des prix *f*	caduta dei prezzi *f*	caída de precios *f*
Preiswettbewerb (D)	—	competition in prices	concurrence des prix *f*	competizione dei prezzi *f*	competencia de precios *f*
prelevamento a titolo personale (I)	Privatentnahmen *pl*	personal drawings	prélèvement personnel *m*	—	detracción privada *f*
prélèvement personnel (F)	Privatentnahmen *pl*	personal drawings	—	prelevamento a titolo personale *m*	detracción privada *f*

	D	E	F	I	Es
prelievo di campioni (I)	Stichprobenerhebung *f*	sample survey	enquête par sondage *f*	—	encuesta por muestreo *f*
premessa (I)	Prämisse *f*	premise	prémisse *f*	—	premisa *f*
première qualité (F)	beste Qualität	first class quality	—	qualità ottima *f*	primera calidad *f*
premier versement (F)	Abschlagszahlung *f*	partial payment/ payment on account	—	pagamento a rate *m*/ pagamento in acconto *m*	pago parcial *m*/ pago a cuenta *m*
premio[1] (I)	Bonus *m*	bonus	bonification *f*	—	gratificación *f*
premio[2] (I)	Prämie *f*	bonus/premium	prime *f*	—	gratificación *f*/prima *f*
premio[3] (I)	Zulage *f*	increase/ additional pay	prime *f*/complément de salaire *m*	—	suplemento *m*/plus *m*
premio d'assicurazione (I)	Versicherungsprämie *f*	insurance premium	prime d'assurance *f*	—	prima de seguro *f*
premio d'investimento (I)	Investitionszulage *f*	investment grant	prime d'investissement *f*	—	prima a la inversión *f*
premio di rischio[1] (I)	Risikoprämie *f*	risk premium	prime de risque *f*	—	prima de riesgo *f*
premio di rischio[2] (I)	Gefahrenzulage *f*	danger money	prime de danger *f*	—	incremento por peligrosidad *m*
premisa (Es)	Prämisse *f*	premise	prémisse *f*	premessa *f*	—
premise (E)	Prämisse *f*	—	prémisse *f*	premessa *f*	premisa *f*
prémisse (F)	Prämisse *f*	premise	—	premessa *f*	premisa *f*
preneur de leasing (F)	Leasing-Nehmer *m*	lessee	—	utente del leasing *m*	arrendatante financiero *m*
preneur d'une licence (F)	Lizenznehmer *m*	licensee	—	concessionario di licenza *m*	licenciado *m*
preneur final (F)	Endabnehmer *m*	ultimate buyer	—	acquirente finale *m*	comprador final *m*
prenotazione (I)	Reservierung *f*	reservation	réservation *f*	—	reservación *f*
prensa (Es)	Presse *f*	press	presse *f*	stampa *f*	—
preparación (Es)	Vorbereitung *f*	preparation	préparation *f*	preparazione *f*	—
preparación laboral (Es)	Arbeitsvorbereitung *f*	job preparation	préparation du travail *f*	preparazione del lavoro *f*	—
preparation (E)	Vorbereitung *f*	—	préparation *f*	preparazione *f*	preparación *f*
préparation (F)	Vorbereitung *f*	preparation	—	preparazione *f*	preparación *f*
préparation du travail (F)	Arbeitsvorbereitung *f*	job preparation	—	preparazione del lavoro *f*	preparación laboral *f*
preparazione (I)	Vorbereitung *f*	preparation	préparation *f*	—	preparación *f*
preparazione del lavoro (I)	Arbeitsvorbereitung *f*	job preparation	préparation du travail *f*	—	preparación laboral *f*
prepay the postage (E)	frankieren	—	affranchir	affrancare	franquear
prerogativa (I)	Befugnis *f*	authorization	pouvoir *m*	—	autorización *f*
prérogative (F)	Vorrecht *n*	privilege	—	privilegio *m*	derecho preferente *m*
presa di posizione (I)	Stellungnahme *f*	comment	prise de position *f*	—	dictamen *m*
presa visione (I)	Einsichtnahme *f*	inspection	contrôle des livres comptables *m*	—	inspección *f*
prescripción (Es)	Verjährung *f*	limitation of actions	prescription *f*	prescrizione *f*	—
prescripciones de embalaje (Es)	Verpackungsvorschriften *pl*	packing instructions	prescriptions concernant l'emballage *f pl*	prescrizioni per l'imballaggio *f pl*	—
prescription (F)	Verjährung *f*	limitation of actions	—	prescrizione *f*	prescripción *f*
prescriptions concernant l'emballage (F)	Verpackungsvorschriften *pl*	packing instructions	—	prescrizioni per l'imballaggio *f pl*	prescripciones de embalaje *f pl*
prescriptions concernant l'expédition (F)	Versandvorschrift *f*	forwarding instructions	—	prescrizione per la spedizione *f*	instrucción para el envío *f*
prescrizione (I)	Verjährung *f*	limitation of actions	prescription *f*	—	prescripción *f*
prescrizione per la spedizione (I)	Versandvorschrift *f*	forwarding instructions	prescriptions concernant l'expédition *f pl*	—	instrucción para el envío *f*
prescrizioni per l'imballaggio (I)	Verpackungsvorschriften *pl*	packing instructions	prescriptions concernant l'emballage *f pl*	—	prescripciones de embalaje *f pl*
presentación (Es)	Präsentation *f*	presentation	présentation *f*	presentazione *f*	—
presentation (E)	Präsentation *f*	—	présentation *f*	presentazione *f*	presentación *f*
présentation (F)	Präsentation *f*	presentation	—	presentazione *f*	presentación *f*

	D	E	F	I	Es
présentation d'un produit (F)	Produktgestaltung *f*	product design	—	creazione del prodotto *f*	diseño del producto *m*
presentazione (I)	Präsentation *f*	presentation	présentation *f*	—	presentación *f*
présidence (F)	Vorsitz *m*	chairmanship	—	presidenza *f*	presidencia *f*
presidencia (Es)	Vorsitz *m*	chairmanship	présidence *f*	presidenza *f*	—
president (E)	Präsident *m*	—	président *m*	presidente *m*	presidente *m*
président (F)	Präsident *m*	president	—	presidente *m*	presidente *m*
président du comité de direction (F)	Vorstands-vorsitzender *m*	chairman of the board	—	presidente del consiglio di amministrazione *m*	presidente del consejo *m*
président du conseil de surveillance (F)	Aufsichtsrats-vorsitzender *m*	chairman of the supervisory board	—	presidente del consiglio di sorveglianza *m*	presidente del consejo devigilancia *m*
presidente (Es)	Präsident *m*	president	président *m*	presidente *m*	—
presidente (I)	Präsident *m*	president	président *m*	—	presidente *m*
presidente del consejo (Es)	Vorstands-vorsitzender *m*	chairman of the board	président du comité de direction *m*	presidente del consiglio di amministrazione *m*	—
presidente del consejo devigilancia (Es)	Aufsichtsrats-vorsitzender *m*	chairman of the supervisory board	président du conseil de surveillance *m*	presidente del consiglio di sorveglianza *m*	—
presidente del consiglio di amministrazione (I)	Vorstands-vorsitzender *m*	chairman of the board	président du comité de direction *m*	—	presidente del consejo *m*
presidente del consiglio di sorveglianza (I)	Aufsichtsrats-vorsitzender *m*	chairman of the supervisory board	président du conseil de surveillance *m*	—	presidente del consejo devigilancia *m*
presidenza (I)	Vorsitz *m*	chairmanship	présidence *f*	—	presidencia *f*
présomption (F)	Mutmaßung *f*	conjecture	—	presunzione *f*	suposición *f*
press (E)	Presse *f*	—	presse *f*	stampa *f*	prensa *f*
press campaign (E)	Presseaktion *f*	—	action de presse *f*	azione stampa *f*	campaña de prensa *f*
press conference (E)	Pressekonferenz *f*	—	conférence de presse *f*	conferenza stampa *f*	rueda de prensa *f*
Presse (D)	—	press	presse *f*	stampa *f*	prensa *f*
presse (F)	Presse *f*	press	—	stampa *f*	prensa *f*
Presseaktion (D)	—	press campaign	action de presse *f*	azione stampa *f*	campaña de prensa *f*
Pressekonferenz (D)	—	press conference	conférence de presse *f*	conferenza stampa *f*	rueda de prensa *f*
Pressemitteilung (D)	—	press release	commentaire de presse *m*	comunicazione stampa *f*	remitido a la prensa *m*
Pressenotiz (D)	—	press report	note de presse *f*	notizia stampa *f*	nota de prensa *f*
press release (E)	Pressemitteilung *f*	—	commentaire de presse *m*	comunicazione stampa *f*	remitido a la prensa *m*
press report (E)	Pressenotiz *f*	—	note de presse *f*	notizia stampa *f*	nota de prensa *f*
pressure group (E)	Lobby *f*	—	lobby *m*	lobby *m*	grupo de presión *m*
prestación de servicio (Es)	Dienstleistung *f*	service	prestation de service *f*	servizio *m*	—
prestaciones por desempleo (Es)	Arbeitslosen-unterstützung *f*	unemployment benefits	indemnité de chômage *f*	sussidio di disoccupazione *m*	—
prestación social (Es)	Sozialleistung *f*	social services	prestations des caisses d'assurance sociale *f pl*/ prestation sociale *f*	prestazione sociale *f*	—
prestamista (Es)	Geldgeber *m*	financial backer	bailleur de fonds *m*	finanziatore *m*	—
préstamo (Es)	Darlehen *n*	loan	prêt *m*	mutuo *m*	—
prestanome (I)	Strohmann *m*	man of straw/ dummy	prête-nom *m*	—	testaferro *m*
prestatario (Es)	Kreditnehmer *m*	borrower	bénéficiaire d'un crédit *m*	beneficiario del credito *m*	—
prestation de garantie (F)	Gewährleistung *f*	warranty	—	garanzia *f*	garantía *f*
prestation de service (F)	Dienstleistung *f*	service	—	servizio *m*	prestación de servicio *m*
prestations des caisses d'assurance sociale (F)	Sozialleistung *f*	social services	—	prestazione sociale *f*	prestacion social *f*/ seguridad social *f*

	D	E	F	I	Es
prestations en nature (F)	Sachbezüge *pl*	remuneration in kind	—	retribuzioni in natura *f pl*	percepciónes en especie *f pl*
prestatore d'opera (I)	Arbeitnehmer *m*	employee	salarié *m*	—	empleado *m*
prestatori d'opera stranieri (I)	ausländische Arbeitnehmer *m*	foreign worker	travailleur étranger *m*	—	trabajadores extranjeros *m*
prestazione di garanzia (I)	Garantieleistung *f*	guarantee	fourniture sous garantie *f*	—	aplicación de la garantía *f*
prestazione sociale (I)	Sozialleistung *f*	social services	prestations des caisses d'assurance sociale *f pl*/ prestation sociale *f*	—	prestacion social *f*/ seguridad social *f*
prestiti comunali (I)	Kommunalanleihen *pl*	local authorities loan	emprunt communal *m*	—	empréstito municipal *m*
prestito (I)	Anleihe *f*	loan	emprunt *m*	—	empréstito *m*
prestito a reddito fisso (I)	Rentenanleihe *f*	annuity bonds	effet public *m*	—	empréstito por anualidades *m*
prestito estero (I)	Auslandsanleihe *f*	foreign bond	emprunt extérieur *m*	—	empréstito exterior *m*
prestito giornaliero (I)	Tagesgeld *n*	day-to-day money	argent au jour le jour *m*	—	dinero de día a día *m*
prestito obbligazionario (I)	Obligationsanleihe *f*	debenture loan	emprunt obligataire *m*	—	empréstito sobre obligaciones *m*
prestito rimborsabile in annualità (I)	Annuitätendarlehen *n*	annuity loan	prêt amortissable par annuités *m*	—	empréstito por anualidades *m*
presunzione (I)	Mutmaßung *f*	conjecture	présomption *f*	—	suposición *f*
presupposto (I)	Voraussetzung *f*	precondition	condition préalable *f*	—	condición previa *f*
presupuesto[1] (Es)	Haushaltsplan *m*	budget	budget *m*	bilancio preventivo *m*	—
presupuesto[2] (Es)	Budget *n*/Etat *m*	budget	budget *m*	bilancio *m*	—
presupuesto[3] (Es)	Finanzplan *m*	financial plan	plan financier *m*	piano finanziario *m*	—
presupuesto[4] (Es)	Voranschlag *m*	estimate	devis *m*	preventivo *m*	—
presupuesto de coste (Es)	Kostenvoranschlag *m*	estimate of cost	devis estimatif des frais *m*	preventivo dei costi *m*	—
presupuesto publicitario (Es)	Werbebudget *n*	advertising budget	budget de publicité *m*	budget pubblicitario *m*	—
prêt (F)	Darlehen *n*	loan	—	mutuo *m*	préstamo *m*
prêt à être expédié (F)	versandbereit	ready for dispatch	—	pronto per la spedizione	listo para ser expedido
prêt amortissable par annuités (F)	Annuitätendarlehen *n*	annuity loan	—	prestito rimborsabile in annualità *m*	empréstito por anualidades *m*
prête-nom (F)	Strohmann *m*	man of straw/ dummy	—	prestanome *m*	testaferro *m*
pretensión de indemnización (Es)	Schadensforderung *f*	claim for damages	prétention à dommages-intérêts *f*	credito da danni *m*	—
pretensión legal (Es)	Rechtsanspruch *m*	legal claim	titre *m*	pretesa giuridica *f*	—
prétention (F)	Anspruch *m*	claim	—	pretesa *f*	reivindicación *f*
prétention à dommages-intérêts (F)	Schadensforderung *f*	claim for damages	—	credito da danni *m*	pretensión de indemnización *f*
pretesa (I)	Anspruch *m*	claim	prétention *f*	—	reivindicación *f*
pretesa giuridica (I)	Rechtsanspruch *m*	legal claim	titre *m*	—	pretensión legal *f*
prêt restant (F)	Restdarlehen *n*	purchase-money loan	—	mutuo residuo *m*	restante de un préstamo *m*
prêt sur gage (F)	Lombardgeschäft *n*	lending on securities	—	anticipazioni *f pl*	operaciones de pignoración *f pl*
preuve (F)	Beweis *m*	proof	—	prova *f*	prueba *f*
prevención de siniestros (Es)	Schadenverhütung *f*	loss prevention	mesure préventive contre les sinistres *f*	prevenzione danni *f*	—
preventivo (I)	Voranschlag *m*	estimate	devis *m*	—	presupuesto *m*
preventivo dei costi (I)	Kostenvoranschlag *m*	estimate of cost	devis estimatif des frais *m*	—	presupuesto de coste *m*
prevenzione danni (I)	Schadenverhütung *f*	loss prevention	mesure préventive contre les sinistres *f*	—	prevención de siniestros *f*
previdenza per la vecchiaia (I)	Altersversorgung *f*	provision for old age	prévoyance vieillesse *f*	—	previsión para la vejez *f*
previdenza sociale (I)	Sozialversicherung *f*	social insurance	assurance sociale *m*	—	seguro social *m*

	D	E	F	I	Es
previsión de la evolución del volumen de ventas (Es)	Umsatzprognose *f*	turnover forecast	prévision de l'évolution du chiffre d'affaires *f*	prognosi del fatturato *f*	—
prévision de l'évolution du chiffre d'affaires (F)	Umsatzprognose *f*	turnover forecast	—	prognosi del fatturato *f*	previsión de la evolución del volumen de ventas *f*
previsión para la vejez (Es)	Altersversorgung *f*	provision for old age	prévoyance vieillesse *f*	previdenza per la vecchiaia *f*	—
prévoyance vieillesse (F)	Altersversorgung *f*	provision for old age	—	previdenza per la vecchiaia *f*	previsión para la vejez *f*
prezioso (I)	wertvoll	valuable	précieux	—	precioso
prezzi alle stelle (I)	Mondpreise *pl*	ficticious prices	prix fictifs *m pl*	—	precios ficticios *m pl*
prezzi amministrati (I)	administrierte Preise *pl*	administered prices	prix administrés *m pl*	—	precios administrados *m pl*
prezzi minimi all'importaz (I)	Mindest-einfuhrpreise *pl*	minimum import price	prix minimum d'importation *m pl*	—	precio mínimo a la importación *m*
prezzo (I)	Preis *m*	price	prix *m*	—	precio *m*
prezzo agrario (I)	Agrarpreis *m*	prices of farm products	prix agricole *m*	—	precio agrícola *m*
prezzo all'ingrosso (I)	Großhandelspreise *pl*	wholesale prices	prix de gros *m*	—	precio mayorista *m*
prezzo d'acquisto[1] (I)	Einkaufspreis *m*	purchase price	prix d'achat *m*	—	precio de compra *m*
prezzo d'acquisto[2] (I)	Bezugskosten *f pl*	purchasing costs	coûts d'acquisition *m pl*	—	gastos de adquisición *m pl*
prezzo d'affezione (I)	Liebhaberpreis *m*	connoisseur's price	prix d'amateur *m*	—	precio afectivo *m*
prezzo dell'oro (I)	Goldpreis *m*	gold price	prix de l'ór *m*	—	precio del oro *m*
prezzo del petrolio greggio (I)	Rohölpreis *m*	crude oil price	prix du pétrole brut *m*	—	precio del crudo *m*
prezzo del suolo (I)	Bodenpreis *m*	land price	prix du terrain *m*	—	precio de suelo *m*
prezzo d'emissione (I)	Emissionskurs *m*	price of issue	cours d'émission *m*	—	tipo de emisión *m*
prezzo d'equilibrio (I)	Gleichgewichts-preis *m*	equilibrium price	prix équilibré *m*	—	precio de equilibrio *m*
prezzo di costo[1] (I)	Selbstkostenpreis *m*	cost price	prix coûtant *m*	—	precio de coste *m*
prezzo di costo[2] (I)	Einstandspreis *m*	cost price	prix coûtant *m*	—	precio de coste *m*
prezzo di domanda (I)	Geldkurs *m*	demand price	cours de la demande *m*	—	cotización demandada *f*/precio ofrecido *m*
prezzo di fabbrica (I)	Erzeugerpreis *m*	producer price	prix à la production *m*	—	precio de producción *m*
prezzo differenziato (I)	Staffelpreis *m*	graduated price	prix échelonné *m*	—	precios escalonados *m pl*
prezzo di listino (I)	Listenpreis *m*	list price	prix au tarif *m*	—	precio-lista *m*
prezzo di mercato mondiale (I)	Weltmarktpreis *m*	world market price	prix du marché mondial *m*	—	precio del mercado mundial *m*
prezzo di rivendita (I)	Wiederverkaufs-preis *m*	resale price	prix de revente *m*	—	precio de reventa *m*
prezzo di vendita (I)	Ladenpreis *m*	retail price	prix de vente *m*	—	precio de venta *m*
prezzo d'offerta (I)	Briefkurs *m*	ask price	cours de vente *m*	—	cotización ofrecida *f*
prezzo d'orientamento (I)	Orientierungspreis *m*	guide price	prix d'orientation *m*	—	precio de orientación *m*
prezzo fisso (I)	Festpreis *m*	fixed price	prix fixe *m*	—	precio fijo *m*
prezzo indicativo (I)	Richtpreis *m*	recommended retail price	prix indicatif *m*	—	precio indicativo *m*
prezzo lordo (I)	Bruttopreis *m*	gross price	prix brut *m*	—	precio bruto *m*
prezzo massimo (I)	Höchstpreis *m*	top price	prix plafond *m*	—	precio máximo *m*
prezzo minimo (I)	Mindestpreis *m*	minimum price	prix minimum *m*	—	precio mínimo *m*
prezzo netto (I)	Nettopreis *m*	net price	prix net *m*	—	precio neto *m*
prezzo non vincolante (I)	Preis freibleibend	open price	prix sans engagement	—	precio sin compromiso *m*
prezzo rateale (I)	Teilzahlungspreis *m*	partial payment price	prix d'un achat à tempérament *m*	—	precio de compras a plazo *m*
prezzo soglia (I)	Schwellenpreis *m*	threshold price	prix de seuil *m*	—	precio-base *m*
prezzo unitario (I)	Einheitspreis *m*	uniform price	prix unique *m*	—	precio único *m*
price (E)	Preis *m*	—	prix *m*	prezzo *m*	precio *m*

	D	E	F	I	Es
price advance (E)	Kurssteigerung *f*	—	hausse *f*	aumento dei corsi *m*	alza de las cotizaciones *f*
price calculation (E)	Preiskalkulation *f*	—	calcul des prix *m*	calcolo dei prezzi *m*	cálculo de precios *m*
price ceiling (E)	Preisobergrenze *f*	—	limite supérieure des prix *f*	limite massimo di prezzo *m*	límite superior de los precios *m*
price control (E)	Preiskontrolle *f*	—	contrôle des prix *m*	controllo dei prezzi *m*	control de precios *m*
price deduction (E)	Preisabzug *m*	—	réduction de prix *f*	riduzione del prezzo *f*	descuento *m*
price difference (E)	Preisunterschied *m*	—	écart de prix *m*	differenza dei prezzi *f*	diferencia de precios *f*
price differentiation (E)	Preisdifferenzierung *f*	—	différenciation de prix *f*	differenziazione dei prezzi *f*	diferenciación de los precios *f*
price-earnings ratio (E)	Kurs-Gewinn-Verhältnis *n*	—	relation cours-bénéfice *f*	rapporto corso-profitto *m*	relación cotización-ganancia *f*
price fixing (E)	Preisabsprache *f*	—	accord sur les prix *m*	accordo sui prezzi *m*	acuerdo de precios *m*
price floor (E)	Preisuntergrenze *f*	—	plancher des prix *m*	limite inferiore di prezzo *m*	límite inferior de los precios *m*
price fluctuation (E)	Preisschwankung *f*	—	fluctuation des prix *f*	fluttuazione dei prezzi *f*	oscilación de precios *f*
price increase[1] (E)	Preissteigerung *f*	—	hausse des prix *f*	aumento dei prezzi *m*	aumento de precios *m*
price increase[2] (E)	Preiserhöhung *f*	—	augmentation des prix *f*	rialzo dei prezzi *m*	aumento de precios *m*
price index (E)	Preisindex *m*	—	indice des prix *m*	indice dei prezzi *m*	ínidce de precios *m*
price leadership (E)	Preisführerschaft *f*	—	leader en matière de prix *m*	leader in materia di prezzi *m*	precio hegemónico *m*
price level (E)	Preisniveau *n*	—	niveau des prix *m*	livello dei prezzi *m*	nivel de precios *m*
price list (E)	Preisliste *f*	—	liste des prix *f*	listino prezzi *m*	lista de precios *f*
pricemarking (E)	Preisauszeichnung *f*	—	affichage des prix *f*	indicazione del prezzo *f*	indicación de precios *f*
price mechanism (E)	Preismechanismus *m*	—	mécanisme des prix *m*	meccanismo dei prezzi *m*	mecanismo de precios *m*
price nursing (E)	Kurspflege *f*	—	soutien des cours *m*	sostegno dei corsi *m*	compras de sostén *f pl*
price of issue (E)	Emissionskurs *m*	—	cours d'émission *m*	prezzo d'emissione *m*	tipo de emisión *m*
price policy (E)	Preispolitik *f*	—	politiques des prix *f*	politica dei prezzi *f*	política de precios *f*
price recommendation (E)	Preisempfehlung *f*	—	recommendation de prix *f*	suggerimento di prezzo *m*	precio recomendado *m*
price reduction[1] (E)	Preisnachlaß *m*	—	remise sur le prix *f*	ribasso del prezzo *m*	rebaja *f*
price reduction[2] (E)	Preissenkung *f*	—	réduction des prix *f*	riduzione dei prezzi *f*	reducción de precios *f*
price rise (E)	Preisanstieg *m*	—	hausse des prix *f*	aumento del prezzo *m*	aumento de precios *m*
price risk (E)	Kursrisiko *n*	—	risque de change *m*	rischio di cambio *m*	riesgo de cambio *m*
prices of farm products (E)	Agrarpreis *m*	—	prix agricole *m*	prezzo agrario *m*	precio agrícola *m*
prices quoted (E)	Preisnotierung *f*	—	cotation des prix *f*	quotazione dei prezzi *f*	cotización de precios *f*
price stop (E)	Preisstopp *m*	—	blocage des prix *m*	blocco dei prezzi *m*	limitación de precios *f*
price support (E)	Kursstützung *f*	—	soutiens des cours *m*	difesa dei corsi *f*	sostén de las cotizaciones *m*
prima a la inversión (Es)	Investitionszulage *f*	investment grant	prime d'investissement *f*	premio d'investimento *m*	—
prima de riesgo (Es)	Risikoprämie *f*	risk premium	prime de risque *f*	premio di rischio *m*	—
prima de seguro (Es)	Versicherungsprämie *f*	insurance premium	prime d'assurance *f*	premio d'assicurazione *m*	—
Primäraufwand (D)	—	primary expenses	charge primaire *f*	spese primarie *f pl*	gastos directos *m pl*
Primärenergie (D)	—	primary energy	énergie primaire *f*	energia primaria *f*	energía primaria *f*
Primärhaftung (D)	—	primary responsibility	responsabilité primaire *f*	responsabilità primaria *f*	responsabilidad primaria *f*
primary energy (E)	Primärenergie *f*	—	énergie primaire *f*	energia primaria *f*	energía primaria *f*
primary expenses (E)	Primäraufwand *m*	—	charge primaire *f*	spese primarie *f pl*	gastos directos *m pl*
primary responsibility (E)	Primärhaftung *f*	—	responsabilité primaire *f*	responsabilità primaria *f*	responsabilidad primaria *f*
prime[1] (F)	Aufgeld *n*	agio	—	aggio *m*	agio *m*
prime[2] (F)	Prämie *f*	bonus/premium	—	premio *m*	gratificación *f*/prima *f*

	D	E	F	I	Es
prime[3] (F)	Zugabe *f*	extra	—	aggiunta *f*	suplemento *m*
prime[4] (F)	Zulage *f*	increase/ additional pay	—	premio *m*/indennità *f*	suplemento *m*/plus *m*
prime d'assurance (F)	Versicherungs-prämie *f*	insurance premium	—	premio d'assicurazione *m*	prima de seguro *f*
prime de danger (F)	Gefahrenzulage *f*	danger money	—	premio di rischio *m*	incremento por peligrosidad *m*
prime de risque (F)	Risikoprämie *f*	risk premium	—	premio di rischio *m*	prima de riesgo *f*
prime de vacances (F)	Urlaubsgeld *n*	holiday allowance	—	indennità di ferie *f*	retribución por vacaciones *f*
prime d'investissement (F)	Investitionszulage *f*	investment grant	—	premio d'investimento *m*	prima a la inversión *f*
primera calidad (Es)	beste Qualität	first class quality	première qualité *f*	qualità ottima *f*	—
primer asegurador (Es)	Erstversicherer *m*	direct insurer	assureur direct *m*	assicuratore diretto *m*	—
principe d'accélération (F)	Akzelerations-prinzip *n*	acceleration principle	—	principio di accelerazione *m*	principio de aceleracaión *m*
principe du pollueur payeur (F)	Verursacherprinzip *n*	polluter pays principle	—	principio della colpa oggettiva *m*	principio contamina-dor-pagador *m*
principes budgétaires (F)	Budgetgrundsätze *f*	budget principles	—	principi di bilancio *m pl*	principios presupues-tarios *m pl*
principi di bilancio (I)	Budgetgrundsätze *f*	budget principles	principes budgétaires *m pl*	—	principios presupuestarios *m pl*
principio contamina-dor-pagador (Es)	Verursacherprinzip *n*	polluter pays principle	principe du pollueur payeur *m*	principio della colpa oggettiva *m*	—
principio de aceleración (Es)	Akzelerations-prinzip *n*	acceleration principle	principe d'accélération *m*	principio di accelerazione *m*	—
principio della colpa oggettiva (I)	Verursacherprinzip *n*	polluter pays principle	principe du pollueur payeur *m*	—	principio contamina-dor-pagador *m*
principio di accelerazione (I)	Akzelerations-prinzip *n*	acceleration principle	principe d'accélération *m*	—	principio de aceleración *m*
principios presupuestarios (Es)	Budgetgrundsätze *f*	budget principles	principes budgétaires *m pl*	principi di bilancio *m pl*	—
printed form (E)	Vordruck *m*	—	imprimé *m*	modulo *m*	impreso *m*
printed matter (E)	Drucksache *f*	—	imprimé *m*	stampa *f*	impreso *m*
printed papers or samples of merchan-dise posted in bulk (E)	Postwurfsendung *f*	—	envoi publicitaire collectif *m*	spedizione postale cumulativa di stampati *f*	envío postal colectivo *m*
printer (E)	Drucker *m*	—	imprimante *f*	stampante *f*	impresora *f*
prise de position (F)	Stellungnahme *f*	comment	—	presa di posizione *f*	dictamen *m*
private account (E)	Privatkonto *n*	—	compte privé *m*	conto privato *m*	cuenta particular *f*
private contribution (E)	Privateinlagen *pl*	—	apport personnel *m*	depositi privati *m pl*	depósitos privados *m pl*
private household (E)	privater Haushalt *m*	—	ménage privé *m*	famiglia *f*	economía doméstica *f*
Privateigentum (D)	—	private property	propriété privée *f*	proprietà privata *f*	propiedad privada *f*
Privateinlagen (D)	—	private contribution	apport personnel *m*	depositi privati *m pl*	depósitos privados *m pl*
private insurance (E)	Privatversicherung *f*	—	assurance privée *f*	assicurazione privata *f*	seguro privado *m*
Privatentnahmen (D)	—	personal drawings	prélèvement personnel *m*	prelevamento a titolo personale *m*	detracción privada *f*
private property (E)	Privateigentum *n*	—	propriété privée *f*	proprietà privata *f*	propiedad privada *f*
privater Haushalt (D)	—	private household	ménage privé *m*	famiglia *f*	economía doméstica *f*
private sector of the economy (E)	Privatwirtschaft *f*	—	économie privée *f*	economia privata *f*	economía privada *f*
privatisation (F)	Privatisierung *f*	denationalization	—	privatizzazione *f*	privatización *f*
privatisation partielle (F)	Teilprivatisierung *f*	partial denationalization	—	privatizzazione parziale *f*	privatización parcial *f*
Privatisierung (D)	—	denationalization	privatisation *f*	privatizzazione *f*	privatización *f*
privatización (Es)	Privatisierung *f*	denationalization	privatisation *f*	privatizzazione *f*	—
privatización parcial (Es)	Teilprivatisierung *f*	partial denationalization	privatisation partielle *f*	privatizzazione parziale *f*	—
privatizzazione (I)	Privatisierung *f*	denationalization	privatisation *f*	—	privatización *f*

	D	E	F	I	Es
privatizzazione parziale (I)	Teilprivatisierung *f*	partial denationalization	privatisation partielle *f*	—	privatización parcial *f*
Privatkonto (D)	—	private account	compte privé *m*	conto privato *m*	cuenta particular *f*
Privatversicherung (D)	—	private insurance	assurance privée *f*	assicurazione privata *f*	seguro privado *m*
Privatwirtschaft (D)	—	private sector of the economy	économie privée *f*	economia privata *f*	economía privada *f*
privilege (E)	Vorrecht *n*	—	prérogative *f*	privilegio *m*	derecho preferente *m*
privilegio (I)	Vorrecht *n*	privilege	prérogative *f*	—	derecho preferente *m*
privo di fosfato (I)	phosphatfrei	free of phosphate	sans phosphate	—	sin fosfato
prix (F)	Preis *m*	price	—	prezzo *m*	precio *m*
prix administrés (F)	administrierte Preise *pl*	administered prices	—	prezzi amministrati *m pl*	precios administrados *m pl*
prix agricole (F)	Agrarpreis *m*	prices of farm products	—	prezzo agrario *m*	precio agrícola *m*
prix à la production (F)	Erzeugerpreis *m*	producer price	—	prezzo di fabbrica *m*	precio de producción *m*
prix au tarif (F)	Listenpreis *m*	list price	—	prezzo di listino *m*	precio-lista *m*
prix brut (F)	Bruttopreis *m*	gross price	—	prezzo lordo *m*	precio bruto *m*
prix coûtant[1] (F)	Einstandspreis *m*	cost price	—	prezzo di costo *m*	precio de coste *m*
prix coûtant[2] (F)	Selbstkostenpreis *m*	cost price	—	prezzo di costo *m*	precio de coste *m*
prix d'achat (F)	Einkaufspreis *m*	purchase price	—	prezzo d'acquisto *m*	precio de compra *m*
prix d'amateur (F)	Liebhaberpreis *m*	connoisseur's price	—	prezzo d'affezione *m*	precio afectivo *m*
prix de gros (F)	Großhandelspreise *pl*	wholesale prices	—	prezzo all'ingrosso *m*	precio mayorista *m*
prix de location (F)	Mietzins *m*	rent	—	canone di locazione *m*	arrendamiento *m*
prix de l'ór (F)	Goldpreis *m*	gold price	—	prezzo dell'oro *m*	precio del oro *m*
prix de revente (F)	Wiederverkaufspreis *m*	resale price	—	prezzo di rivendita *m*	precio de reventa *m*
prix de revient (F)	Herstellungswert *m*	production value	—	valore di produzione *m*	valor de fabricación *m*
prix de seuil (F)	Schwellenpreis *m*	threshold price	—	prezzo soglia *m*	precio-base *m*
prix de vente (F)	Ladenpreis *m*	retail price	—	prezzo di vendita *m*	precio de venta *m*
prix d'orientation (F)	Orientierungspreis *m*	guide price	—	prezzo d'orientamento *m*	precio de orientación *m*
prix du marché mondial (F)	Weltmarktpreis *m*	world market price	—	prezzo di mercato mondiale *m*	precio del mercado mundial *m*
prix d'un achat à tempérament (F)	Teilzahlungspreis *m*	partial payment price	—	prezzo rateale *m*	precio de compras a plazo *m*
prix du pétrole brut (F)	Rohölpreis *m*	crude oil price	—	prezzo del petrolio greggio *m*	precio del crudo *m*
prix du terrain (F)	Bodenpreis *m*	land price	—	prezzo del suolo *m*	precio de suelo *m*
prix échelonné (F)	Staffelpreis *m*	graduated price	—	prezzo differenziato *m*	precios escalonados *m pl*
prix équilibré (F)	Gleichgewichtspreis *m*	equilibrium price	—	prezzo d'equilibrio *m*	precio de equilibrio *m*
prix fictifs (F)	Mondpreise *pl*	ficticious prices	—	prezzi alle stelle *m pl*	precios ficticios *m pl*
prix fixe (F)	Festpreis *m*	fixed price	—	prezzo fisso *m*	precio fijo *m*
prix indicatif (F)	Richtpreis *m*	recommended retail price	—	prezzo indicativo *m*	precio indicativo *m*
prix minimum (F)	Mindestpreis *m*	minimum price	—	prezzo minimo *m*	precio mínimo *m*
prix minimum d'importation (F)	Mindesteinfuhrpreise *pl*	minimum import price	—	prezzi minimi all'importazione *m pl*	precio mínimo a la importación *m*
prix net (F)	Nettopreis *m*	net price	—	prezzo netto *m*	precio neto *m*
prix plafond (F)	Höchstpreis *m*	top price	—	prezzo massimo *m*	precio máximo *m*
prix sans engagement (F)	Preis freibleibend	open price	—	prezzo non vincolante *m*	precio sin compromiso *m*
prix unique (F)	Einheitspreis *m*	uniform price	—	prezzo unitario *m*	precio único *m*
probar (Es)	probieren	try	essayer	provare	—
Probeauftrag (D)	—	trial order	ordre d'essai *m*	ordine a titolo di prova *m*	pedido de prueba *m*
Probelieferung (D)	—	trial shipment	livraison à titre d'essai *f*	fornitura a titolo di prova *f*	envío de prueba *m*

	D	E	F	I	Es
Probepackung (D)	—	trial package	échantillon *m*	confezione campione *f*	muestra *f*
Probezeit (D)	—	trial period	période d'essai *f*	periodo di prova *m*	período de prueba *m*
probieren (D)	—	try	essayer	provare	probar
pro capite (I)	pro Kopf	per capita	par tête d'habitant	—	per cápita
procedimento[1] (I)	Verfahren *n*	procedure/process	méthode *f*/ procédure *f*	—	proceso *m*/ procedimiento *m*
procedimento[2] (I)	Prozeß *m*	process	processus *m*	—	proceso *m*
procedimento produttivo (I)	Fertigungs-verfahren *n*	production process	méthode de production *f*	—	procedimiento de fabricación *m*
procedimiento conciliatorio (Es)	Vergleichs-verfahren *n*	composition proceedings	procédure de conciliation *f*	procedura di concordato *f*	—
procedimiento de fabricación (Es)	Fertigungs-verfahren *n*	production process	méthode de production *f*	procedimento produttivo *m*	—
procedimiento de quiebra (Es)	Konkursverfahren *n*	proceedings in bankruptcy	procédure de faillite *f*	procedura fallimentare *f*	—
procedura d'ammis-sione in franchigia (I)	Zollfreischreibungs-verfahren *n*	procedure of duty free admission	régime de l'admission en franchise *m*	—	régimen de admisión en franquicia *m*
procedura del credito documentario (I)	Akkreditiv-abwicklung *f*	settlement by letter of credit	exécution par crédit documentaire *f*	—	ejecución por crédito documentario *f*
procedura di concordato (I)	Vergleichsverfahren *n*	composition proceedings	procédure de conciliation *f*	—	procedimiento conciliatorio *m*
procedura fallimentare (I)	Konkursverfahren *n*	proceedings in bankruptcy	procédure de faillite *f*	—	procedimiento de quiebra *m*
procédure de conciliation (F)	Vergleichsverfahren *n*	composition proceedings	—	procedura di concordato *f*	procedimiento conciliatorio *m*
procédure de faillite (F)	Konkursverfahren *n*	proceedings in bankruptcy	—	procedura fallimentare *f*	procedimiento de quiebra *m*
procedure doganali (I)	Zollverkehr *m*	customs procedure	régime douanier *m*	—	régimen aduanero de mercancías *m*
procedure of duty free admission (E)	Zollfreischreibungs-verfahren *n*	—	régime de l'admission en franchise *m*	procedura d'ammis-sione in franchigia *f*	régimen de admisión en franquicia *m*
proceedings in bankruptcy (E)	Konkursverfahren *n*	—	procédure de faillite *f*	procedura fallimentare *f*	procedimiento de quiebra *m*
proceeds (E)	Erlös *m*	—	produit des ventes *m*	ricavo *m*	beneficio *m*
procesamiento de datos (Es)	Datenverarbeitung *f*	data processing	traitement des information *m*	elaborazione dati *f*	—
proceso[1] (Es)	Prozeß *m*	process	processus *m*	procedimento *m*	—
proceso[2] (Es)	Verfahren *n*	procedure/process	méthode *f*/ procédure *f*	procedimento *m*/ procedura *f*	—
proceso de producción[1] (Es)	Fertigungsprozeß *m*	production procedure	déroulement de la fabrication *m*	processo produttivo *m*	—
proceso de producción[2] (Es)	Produktionsprozeß *m*	process of production	processus de production *m*	processo produttivo *m*	—
process[1] (E)	Prozeß *m*	—	processus *m*	procedimento *m*	proceso *m*
process[2] (E)	aufbereiten	—	élaborer/traiter	elaborare/lavorare	elaborar/tratar
processing[1] (E)	Veredelung *f*	—	perfectionnement *m*	perfezionamento *m*	perfeccionamiento *m*
processing[2] (E)	Verarbeitung *f*	—	transformation *f*	lavorazione *f*	transformación *f*
process of production (E)	Produktionsprozeß *m*	—	processus de production *m*	processo produttivo *m*	proceso de producción *m*
processo produttivo[1] (I)	Fertigungsprozeß *m*	production procedure	déroulement de la fabrication *m*	—	proceso de producción *m*
processo produttivo[2] (I)	Produktionsprozeß *m*	process of production	processus de production *m*	—	proceso de producción *m*
processus (F)	Prozeß *m*	process	—	procedimento *m*	proceso *m*
processus de production (F)	Produktionsprozeß *m*	process of production	—	processo produttivo *m*	proceso de producción *m*
procès-verbal (F)	Protokoll *n*	record/minutes	—	protocollo *m*/ verbale *m*	protocolo *m*/acta *f*
procès-verbal de fondation (F)	Gründungsbericht *m*	formation report	—	relazione di costituzione *f*	informe de los fundadores *m*
procura (I)	Prokura *f*	Prokura (procuration)	procuration commer-ciale générale *f*	—	poder general *m*
procura generale (I)	Generalvollmacht *f*	general power	pouvoir général *m*	—	poder general *m*

	D	E	F	I	Es
procuration commerciale générale (F)	Prokura *f*	Prokura (procuration)	—	procura *f*	poder general *m*
procuratore (I)	Prokurist *m*	Prokurist (authorized clerk)	fondé de procuration *m*	—	apoderado general *m*
prodotto (I)	Produkt *n*	product	produit *m*	—	producto *m*
prodotto agricolo[1] (I)	Agrarprodukt *n*	farm produce	produit agricole *m*	—	producto agrario *m*
prodotto agricolo[2] (I)	Agrarerzeugnis *n*	agricultural produce	produit agricole *m*	—	producto agrícola *m*
prodotto finito[1] (I)	Endprodukt *n*	finished product	produit final *m*	—	producto final *m*
prodotto finito[2] (I)	Fertigprodukt *n*	finished product	produit fini *m*	—	producto acabado *m*
prodotto interno lordo (I)	Bruttoinlandsprodukt *n*	gross domestic product	produit intérieur brut *m*	—	producto interior bruto *m*
prodotto nazionale (I)	Sozialprodukt *n*	national product	produit national *m*	—	producto nacional *m*
prodotto nazionale lordo (I)	Bruttosozialprodukt *n*	gross national product	produit national brut *m*	—	producto nacional bruto *m*
prodotto nazionale netto (I)	Nettosozialprodukt *n*	net national product	produit national net *m*	—	producto nacional neto *m*
prodotto secondario (I)	Nebenprodukt *n*	by-product	produit dérivé *m*	—	producto accesorio *m*
prodotto semifinito (I)	Halberzeugnis *n*	semi-finished product	produit demi-fini *m*	—	producto semielaborado *m*
prodotto senza nome (I)	No-name-Produkt *n*	generic product	produit sans nom *m*	—	producto genérico *m*
prodotto su misura (I)	maßgefertigt	manufactured to measure	travaillé sur mesure	—	hecho a medida
producción (Es)	Produktion *f*	production	production *f*	produzione *f*	—
producción bruta (Es)	Bruttoproduktion *f*	gross production	production brutte *f*	produzione lorda *f*	—
producción de materias primas (Es)	Rohstoffgewinnung *f*	raw material production	extraction de matières premières *f*	produzione delle materie prime *f*	—
producción en masa (Es)	Massenproduktion *f*	mass production	production en grandes séries *f*	produzione di massa *f*	—
producción en serie (Es)	Serienfertigung *f*	series production	fabrication de série *f*	produzione in serie *f*	—
producción neta (Es)	Nettoproduktion *f*	net production	production nette *f*	produzione netta *f*	—
produce or to buy in addition (E)	Herstellen-oder-Zukaufen	—	produire ou acheter additionnellement	produrre o comprare in aggiunta	producir o comprar adicionalmente
producer[1] (E)	Hersteller *m*	—	fabricant *m*	produttore *m*	fabricante *m*
producer[2] (E)	Produzent *m*	—	producteur *m*	produttore *m*	productor *m*
producer goods industry (E)	Produktionsgüter-Industrie *f*	—	industrie des biens de production *f*	industria dei beni strumentali *f*	industria de bienes de producción *f*
producer price (E)	Erzeugerpreis *m*	—	prix à la production *m*	prezzo di fabbrica *m*	precio de producción *m*
producer price index (E)	Erzeugerpreisindex *m*	—	indice des prix à la production *m*	indice dei prezzi di fabbrica *m*	índice de precios de producción *m*
producer's cooperative (E)	Produktionsgenossenschaft *f*	—	société coopérative de production *f*	cooperativa di produzione *f*	cooperativa de producción *f*
producer's surplus (E)	Produzentenrente *f*	—	rente du vendeur *f*	rendita del produttore *f*	superávit del productor *m*
producir o comprar adicionalmente (Es)	Herstellen-oder-Zukaufen	produce or to buy in addition	produire ou acheter additionnellement	produrre o comprare in aggiunta	—
product (E)	Produkt *n*	—	produit *m*	prodotto *m*	producto *m*
product design (E)	Produktgestaltung *f*	—	présentation d'un produit *f*	creazione del prodotto *f*	diseño del producto *m*
producteur[1] (F)	Erzeuger *m*	manufacturer	—	produttore *m*	productor *m*
producteur[2] (F)	Produzent *m*	producer	—	produttore *m*	productor *m*
production (E)	Produktion *f*	—	production *f*	produzione *f*	producción *f*
production (F)	Produktion *f*	production	—	produzione *f*	producción *f*
production agricole (F)	Ackerbau *m*	agriculture	—	agricoltura *f*	agricultura *f*
production brutte (F)	Bruttoproduktion *f*	gross production	—	produzione lorda *f*	producción bruta *m*
production capacity (E)	Produktionskapazität *f*	—	capacité de production *f*	capacità produttiva *f*	capacidad de producción *f*
production control (E)	Produktionskontrolle *f*	—	contrôle de la production *m*	controllo della produzione *m*	control de producción *m*
production costs (E)	Herstellungskosten *pl*	—	frais de fabrication *m pl*	costi di produzione *m pl*	costo de la producción *m*

	D	E	F	I	Es
production couplée (F)	Koppelproduktion *f*	tied production	—	produzione abbinata *f*	coproducción *f*
production en grandes séries (F)	Massenproduktion *f*	mass production	—	produzione di massa *f*	producción en masa *f*
production en série (F)	Massenfertigung *f*	mass production	—	fabbricazione di massa *f*	fabricación en masa *f*
production facilities (E)	Produktions-anlagen *pl*	—	installations industrielles *f pl*	impianti di produzione *m pl*	instalaciones de producción *f pl*
production limit (E)	Förderlimit *n*	—	limite de production *f*	limite d'estrazione *m*	limite de producción *m*
production nette (F)	Nettoproduktion *f*	net production	—	produzione netta *f*	producción neta *f*
production plan (E)	Produktionsplan *m*	—	plan de production *m*	piano di produzione *m*	plan de producción *m*
production potential (E)	Produktions-potential *n*	—	potentiel de production *m*	potenziale produttivo *m*	potencial productivo *m*
production procedure (E)	Fertigungs-prozeß *m*	—	déroulement de la fabrication *m*	processo produttivo *m*	proceso de producción *m*
production process (E)	Fertigungsverfahren *n*	—	méthode de production *f*	procedimento produttivo *m*	procedimiento de fabricación *m*
production programme[1] (E)	Produktions-programm *n*	—	gamme *f*	programma di produzione *m*	programa de producción *m*
production programme[2] (E)	Fertigungs-programm *n*	—	programme de fabrication *m*	programma di produzione *m*	programa de producción *m*
production quota (E)	Förderquote *f*	—	quote-part de production *f*	quota d'estrazione *f*	cuota de producción *f*
production scheduling (E)	Produktlinie *f*	—	ligne des produits *f*	linea dei prodotti *f*	línea de productos *f*
production theory (E)	Produktionstheorie *f*	—	théorie de la production *f*	teoria della produzione *f*	teoría de producción *f*
production value[1] (E)	Produktionswert *m*	—	valeur de production *f*	valore produttivo *m*	valor de la producción *m*
production value[2] (E)	Herstellungswert *m*	—	prix de revient *m*	valore di produzione *m*	valor de fabricación *m*
productive property (E)	Produktivvermögen *n*	—	capital productif *m*	patrimonio produttivo *m*	patrimonio productivo *m*
productividad[1] (Es)	Produktivität *f*	productivity	productivité *f*	produttività *f*	—
productividad[2] (Es)	Arbeitsleistung *f*	productivity	rendement *m*	produttività *f*	—
productividad del capital (Es)	Kapitalproduktivität *f*	productivity of capital	productivité du capital *f*	produttività del capitale *f*	—
productivité (F)	Produktivität *f*	productivity	—	produttività *f*	productividad *f*
productivité du capital (F)	Kapitalproduktivität *f*	productivity of capital	—	produttività del capitale *f*	prodicutividad del capital *f*
productivity[1] (E)	Produktivität *f*	—	productivité *f*	produttività *f*	productividad *f*
productivity[2] (E)	Arbeitsleistung *f*	—	rendement *m*	produttività *f*	productividad *f*
productivity of capital (E)	Kapitalproduktivität *f*	—	productivité du capital *f*	produttività del capitale *f*	prodicutividad del capital *f*
product liability[1] (E)	Produkthaftung *f*	—	responsabilité du fabricant *f*	responsabilità prodotto *f*	responsabilidad del productor *f*
product liability[2] (E)	Produzentenhaftung *f*	—	responsabilité du producteur *f*	responsabilità di produttore *f*	responsabilidad civil del fabricante *f*
product line (E)	Warengruppe *f*	—	groupe de marchandises *m*	gruppo merci *m*	grupo de mercancías *m*
producto (Es)	Produkt *n*	product	produit *m*	prodotto *m*	—
producto acabado (Es)	Fertigprodukt *n*	finished product	produit fini *m*	prodotto finito *m*	—
producto accesorio (Es)	Nebenprodukt *n*	by-product	produit dérivé *m*	prodotto secondario *m*	—
producto agrario (Es)	Agrarprodukt *n*	farm produce	produit agricole *m*	prodotto agricolo *m*	—
producto agrícola (Es)	Agrarerzeugnis *n*	agricultural produce	produit agricole *m*	prodotto agricolo *m*	—
producto bruto (Es)	Rohertrag *m*	gross proceeds	produit brut *m*	reddito lordo *m*	—
producto de la venta (Es)	Verkaufserlös *m*	sale proceeds	produit des ventes *m*	ricavo delle vendite *m*	—
producto final (Es)	Endprodukt *n*	finished product	produit final *m*	prodotto finito *m*	—
producto genérico (Es)	No-name-Produkt *n*	generic product	produit sans nom *m*	prodotto senza nome *m*	—

	D	E	F	I	Es
producto interior bruto (Es)	Bruttoinlandsprodukt *n*	gross domestic product	produit intérieur brut *m*	prodotto interno lordo *m*	—
producto nacional (Es)	Sozialprodukt *n*	national product	produit national *m*	prodotto nazionale *m*	—
producto nacional bruto (Es)	Bruttosozialprodukt *n*	gross national product	produit national brut *m*	prodotto nazionale lordo *m*	—
producto nacional neto (Es)	Nettosozialprodukt *n*	net national product	produit national net *m*	prodotto nazionale netto *m*	—
producto neto (Es)	Nettoertrag *m*	net earnings	produit net *m*	ricavo netto *m*	—
productor[1] (Es)	Erzeuger *m*	manufacturer	producteur *m*	produttore *m*	—
productor[2] (Es)	Produzent *m*	producer	producteur *m*	produttore *m*	—
productos a granel (Es)	Massengüter *pl*	bulk goods	marchandises en vrac *f pl*	beni di massa *m pl*	—
producto semielaborado (Es)	Halberzeugnis *n*	semi-finished good	produit demi-fini *m*	prodotto semifinito *m*	—
produire ou acheter additionnellement (F)	Herstellen-oder-Zukaufen	produce or to buy in addition	—	produrre o comprare in aggiunta	producir o comprar adicionalmente
produit (F)	Produkt *n*	product	—	prodotto *m*	producto *m*
produit agricole[1] (F)	Agrarprodukt *n*	farm produce	—	prodotto agricolo *m*	producto agrario *m*
produit agricole[2] (F)	Agrarerzeugnis *n*	agricultural produce	—	prodotto agricolo *m*	producto agrícola *m*
produit brut (F)	Rohertrag *m*	gross proceeds	—	reddito lordo *m*	producto bruto *m*
produit de la liquidation (F)	Liquidationserlös *m*	remaining assets after liquidation	—	ricavo della liquidazione *m*	haber social repartible *m*
produit de marque (F)	Markenartikel *m*	brandname article	—	articolo di marca *m*	artículo de marca *m*
produit demi-fini (F)	Halberzeugnis *n*	semi-finished product	—	prodotto semifinito *m*	producto semielaborado *m*
produit dérivé (F)	Nebenprodukt *n*	by-product	—	prodotto secondario *m*	producto accesorio *m*
produit de stockage (F)	Stapelware *f*	staple commodities	—	merce immagazzinata *f*	mercancía almacenada *f*
produit des ventes[1] (F)	Verkaufserlös *m*	sale proceeds	—	ricavo delle vendite *m*	producto de la venta *m*
produit des ventes[2] (F)	Erlös *m*	proceeds	—	ricavo *m*	beneficio *m*
produit du capital (F)	Kapitalertrag *m*	income from capital	—	rendita del capitale *f*	rendimiento del capital *m*
produit final (F)	Endprodukt *n*	finished product	—	prodotto finito *m*	producto final *m*
produit fini (F)	Fertigprodukt *n*	finished product	—	prodotto finito *m*	producto acabado *m*
produit intérieur brut (F)	Bruttoinlandsprodukt *n*	gross domestic product	—	prodotto interno lordo *m*	producto interior brutom
produit national (F)	Sozialprodukt *n*	national product	—	prodotto nazionale *m*	producto nacional *m*
produit national brut (F)	Bruttosozialprodukt *n*	gross national product	—	prodotto nazionale lordo *m*	producto nacional bruto *m*
produit national net (F)	Nettosozialprodukt *n*	net national product	—	prodotto nazionale netto *m*	producto nacional neto *m*
produit net (F)	Nettoertrag *m*	net earnings	—	ricavo netto *m*	producto neto *m*
produit pondéreux (F)	Schwergut *n*	heavy freight	—	carico pesante *m*	mercancía pesada *f*
produits agricoles (F)	Agrargüter *pl*	agricultural goods	—	beni agricoli *m pl*	bienes agrícolas *m pl*
produit sans nom (F)	No-name-Produkt *n*	generic product	—	prodotto senza nome *m*	producto genérico *m*
produits de complément (F)	komplementäre Güter *pl*	complementary goods	—	beni complementari *m pl*	bienes complementarios *m pl*
produits de luxe (F)	Luxusgüter *pl*	luxury goods	—	beni di lusso *m pl*	bienes de lujo *m pl*
Produkt (D)	—	product	produit *m*	prodotto *m*	producto *m*
Produktgestaltung (D)	—	product design	présentation d'un produit *f*	creazione del prodotto *f*	diseño del producto *m*
Produkthaftung (D)	—	product liability	responsabilité du fabricant *f*	responsabilità prodotto *f*	responsabilidad del productor *f*
Produktion (D)	—	production	production *f*	produzione *f*	producción *f*
Produktionsanlagen (D)	—	production facilities	installations industrielles *f pl*	impianti di produzione *m pl*	instalaciones de producción *f pl*
Produktionsausfall (D)	—	loss of production	perte dans la production *f*	perdita di produzione *f*	pérdida de producción *f*
Produktionsfaktoren (D)	—	factors of production	facteurs de production *m pl*	fattori di produzione *m pl*	factores de producción *m pl*

	D	E	F	I	Es
Produktions-genossenschaft (D)	—	producer's cooperative	société coopérative de production *f*	cooperativa di produzione *f*	cooperativa de producción *f*
Produktionsgüter-Industrie (D)	—	producer goods industry	industrie des biens de production *f*	industria dei beni strumentali *f*	industria de bienes de producción *f*
Produktions-kapazität (D)	—	production capacity	capacité de production *f*	capacità produttiva *f*	capacidad de producción *f*
Produktions-kontrolle (D)	—	production control	contrôle de la production *m*	controllo della produzione *m*	control de producción *m*
Produktionskosten (D)	—	cost of production	coût de production *m*	costi produttivi *m pl*	gastos de producción *m pl*
Produktionsplan (D)	—	production plan	plan de production *m*	piano di produzione *m*	plan de producción *m*
Produktions-potential (D)	—	production potential	potentiel de production *m*	potenziale produttivo *m*	potencial productivo *m*
Produktions-programm (D)	—	production programme	gamme *f*	programma di produzione *m*	programa de producción *m*
Produktionsprozeß (D)	—	process of production	processus de production *m*	processo produttivo *m*	proceso de producción *m*
Produktions-schwankung (D)	—	fluctuations in production	fluctuation de la production *f pl*	oscillazione della produzione *f*	fluctuaciones en la producción *f pl*
Produktionstheorie (D)	—	production theory	théorie de la production *f*	teoria della produzione *f*	teoría de producción *f*
Produktionswert (D)	—	production value	valeur de production *f*	valore produttivo *m*	valor de la producción *m*
Produktivität (D)	—	productivity	productivité *f*	produttività *f*	productividad *f*
Produktivvermögen (D)	—	productive property	capital productif *m*	patrimonio produttivo *m*	patrimonio productivo *m*
Produktlinie (D)	—	production scheduling	ligne des produits *f*	linea dei prodotti *f*	línea de productos *f*
Produktpalette (D)	—	range of products	gamme des produits *f*	gamma dei prodotti *f*	gama de productos *f*
produrre o comprare in aggiunta (I)	Herstellen-oder-Zukaufen	produce or buy in addition	produire ou acheter additionnellement	—	producir o comprar adicionalmente
produttività[1] (I)	Produktivität *f*	productivity	productivité *f*	—	productividad *f*
produttività[2] (I)	Arbeitsleistung *f*	productivity	rendement *m*	—	productividad *f*
produttività del capitale (I)	Kapitalproduktivität *f*	productivity of capital	productivité du capital *f*	—	prodicutividad del capital *f*
produttore[1] (I)	Erzeuger *m*	manufacturer	producteur *m*	—	productor *m*
produttore[2] (I)	Hersteller *m*	producer	fabricant *m*	—	fabricante *m*
produttore[3] (I)	Produzent *m*	producer	producteur *m*	—	productor *m*
Produzent (D)	—	producer	producteur *m*	produttore *m*	productor *m*
Produzentenhaftung (D)	—	product liability	responsabilité du producteur *f*	responsabilità di produttore *f*	responsabilidad civil del fabricante *f*
Produzentenrente (D)	—	producer's surplus	rente du vendeur *f*	rendita del produttore *f*	superávit del productor *m*
produzione (I)	Produktion *f*	production	production *f*	—	producción *f*
produzione abbinata (I)	Koppelproduktion *f*	tied production	production couplée *f*	—	coproducción *f*
produzione delle materie prime (I)	Rohstoffgewinnung *f*	raw material production	extraction de matières premières *f*	—	producción de materias primas *f*
produzione di massa (I)	Massenproduktion *f*	mass production	production en grandes séries *f*	—	producción en masa *f*
produzione eccessiva (I)	Überproduktion *f*	overproduction	surproduction *f*	—	sobreproducción *f*
produzione fuori serie (I)	Sonderanfertigung *f*	manufacture to customer's specifications	fabrication spéciale *f*	—	fabricación especial *f*
produzione in serie (I)	Serienfertigung *f*	series production	fabrication de série *f*	—	producción en serie *f*
produzione lorda (I)	Bruttoproduktion *f*	gross production	production brutte *f*	—	producción bruta *m*
produzione netta (I)	Nettoproduktion *f*	net production	production nette *f*	—	producción neta *f*
profesión (Es)	Beruf *m*	profession	profession *f*	professione *f*	—
profesional (Es)	Freiberufler *m*	self-employed person	personne exerçant une profession libérale *f*	libero professionista *m*	—
profession (E)	Beruf *m*	—	profession *f*	professione *f*	profesión *f*
profession (F)	Beruf *m*	profession	—	professione *f*	profesión *f*

	D	E	F	I	Es
professional discretion (E)	Schweigepflicht *f*	—	discretion professionnelle *f*	obbligo del segreto professionale *m*	secreto profesional *m*
professional fee (E)	Honorar *n*	—	honoraires *m pl*	onorario *m*	honorario *m*
professional knowledge (E)	Fachwissen *n*	—	connaissances professionnelles *f pl*	cognizioni professionali *f pl*	conocimientos especializados *m pl*
professional secret (E)	Berufsgeheimnis *n*	—	secret professionnel *m*	segreto professionale *m*	secreto profesional *m*
professional training (E)	Berufsausbildung *f*	—	formation professionnelle *f*	formazione professionale *f*	formación profesional *f*
professione (I)	Beruf *m*	profession	profession *f*	—	profesión *f*
Profit (D)	—	profit	profit *m*	profitto *m*	beneficio *m*
profit[1] (E)	Gewinn *m*	—	bénéfice *m*	utile *m*	beneficio *m*/ superávit *m*
profit[2] (E)	Profit *m*	—	profit *m*	profitto *m*	beneficio *m*
profit (F)	Profit *m*	profit	—	profitto *m*	beneficio *m*
profitability (E)	Rentabilität *f*	—	rentabilité *f*	redditività *f*	rentabilidad *f*
profit account (E)	Erfolgskonto *n*	—	compte de résultats *m*	conto profitti *m*	cuenta de beneficios y pérdidas *f*
profit and loss account[1] (E)	Ertragsrechnung *f*	—	solde net de l'exploitation *m*	conto economico *m*	cuenta de ganancias *f pl*
profit and loss account[2] (E)	Gewinn- und Verlustrechnung *f*	—	compte de pertes et profits *m*	conto profitti e perdite *m*	cuenta de pérdidas y ganancias *f*
profit de rationalisation (F)	Rationalisierungsgewinn *m*	rationalization profit	—	profitto di razionalizzazione *m*	beneficio de racionalización *m*
profit margin (E)	Gewinnmarge *f*	—	marge bénéficiaire *f*	margine dell'utile *m*	margen de beneficios *f*
profit mark-up (E)	Gewinnaufschlag *m*	—	majoration de bénéfice *f*	maggiorazione dell'utile *f*	margen de benificio *f*
profit of the enterprise (E)	Unternehmensgewinn *m*	—	bénéfice d'exploitation *m*	utile d'impresa *m*	beneficio empresarial *m*
Profitrate (D)	—	profit rate	taux de profit *m*	tasso di profitto *m*	tasa de beneficio *f*
profit rate (E)	Profitrate *f*	—	taux de profit *m*	tasso di profitto *m*	tasa de beneficio *f*
profitto (I)	Profit *m*	profit	profit *m*	—	beneficio *m*
profitto di razionalizzazione (I)	Rationalisierungsgewinn *m*	rationalization profit	profit de rationalisation *m*	—	beneficio de racionalización *m*
pro forma invoice (E)	Proforma-Rechnung *f*	—	facture pro forma *f*	fattura pro forma *f*	factura proforma *f*
Proforma-Rechnung (D)	—	pro forma invoice	facture pro forma *f*	fattura pro forma *f*	factura proforma *f*
progettazione della costituzione (I)	Gründungsplanung *f*	formation plan	planification de fondation *f*	—	planificación de la fundación *f*
progetto (I)	Entwurf *m*	draft	projet *m*	—	proyecto *m*
Prognose (D)	—	forecast(ing)	perspective *f*	prognosi *f*	pronóstico *m*
Prognosetechnik (D)	—	forecasting techniques	technique de pronostic *f*	tecnica della prognosi *f*	técnica de pronóstico *f*
prognosi (I)	Prognose *f*	forecast(ing)	perspective *f*	—	pronóstico *m*
prognosi del fatturato (I)	Umsatzprognose *f*	turnover forecast	prévision de l'évolution du chiffre d'affaires *f*	—	previsión de la evolución del volumen de ventas *f*
programa (Es)	Programm *n*	programme	programme *m*	programma *m*	—
programación (Es)	Programmierung *f*	programming	programmation *f*	programmazione *f*	—
programación lineal (Es)	lineare Programmierung *f*	linear programmation	programmation linéaire *f*	programmazione lineare *f*	—
programa de entrega (Es)	Lieferprogramm *n*	delivery programme	programme de livraison *m*	programma di fornitura *m*	—
programa de producción[1] (Es)	Fertigungsprogramm *n*	production programme	programme de fabrication *m*	programma di produzione *m*	—
programa de producción[2] (Es)	Produktionsprogramm *n*	production programme	gamme *f*	programma di produzione *m*	—
programa de venta (Es)	Verkaufsprogramm *n*	sales programme	programme de vente *m*	programma di vendita *m*	—
programador (Es)	Programmierer *m*	programmer	programmeur *m*	programmatore *m*	—
Programa Europeo de Recuperación (Es)	Europäisches Wiederaufbauprogramm *n*	European Recovery Programme	Programme Européen de Récupération *m*	Programma di Ricostruzione Europea *m*	—
Programm (D)	—	programme	programme *m*	programma *m*	programa *m*

	D	E	F	I	Es
programma (I)	Programm *n*	programme	programme *m*	—	programa *m*
programma del fatturato (I)	Umsatzplan *m*	turnover plan	plan du chiffre d'affaires *m*	—	objectivo de facturación *m*
programma dell'itinerario (I)	Tourenplan *m*	tour schedule	itinéraire *m*	—	itinerario *m*
programma di fornitura (I)	Lieferprogramm *n*	delivery programme	programme de livraison *m*	—	programa de entrega *m*
programma di produzione[1] (I)	Produktions-programm *n*	production programme	gamme *f*	—	programa de producción *m*
programma di produzione[2] (I)	Fertigungs-programm *n*	production programme	programme de fabrication *m*	—	programa de producción *m*
programma di vendita (I)	Verkaufsprogramm *n*	sales programme	programme de vente *m*	—	programa de venta *m*
programmation (F)	Programmierung *f*	programming	—	programma-zione *f*	programación *f*
programmation linéaire (F)	lineare Programmierung *f*	linear programmation	—	programmazione lineare *f*	programación lineal *f*
programmatore (I)	Programmierer *m*	programmer	programmeur *m*	—	programador *m*
programmazione[1] (I)	Planung *f*	planning	planning *m*	—	planificación *f*
programmazione[2] (I)	Programmierung *f*	programming	programmation *f*	—	programación *f*
programmazione dei termini (I)	Terminplanung *f*	scheduling	planning de rendez-vous *m*	—	planificación de plazos *f*
programmazione del bilancio (I)	Budgetplanung *f*	budgetary planning	planification du budget *f*	—	planificación del presupuesto *m*
programmazione delle ferie (I)	Urlaubsplanung *f*	vacation scheduling	planification des vacances *f*	—	planificación de las vacaciones *f*
programmazione del marketing (I)	Marketingplanung *f*	marketing planning	planning du marketing *m*	—	planificación de mercadeo *m*
programmazione lineare (I)	lineare Programmierung *f*	linear programmation	programmation linéaire *f*	—	programación lineal *f*
programme (E)	Programm *n*	—	programme *m*	programma *m*	programa *m*
programme (F)	Programm *n*	programme	—	programma *m*	programa *m*
programme de fabrication (F)	Fertigungs-programm *n*	production programme	—	programma di produzione *m*	programa de producción *m*
programme de livraison (F)	Lieferprogramm *n*	delivery programme	—	programma di fornitura *m*	programa de entrega *m*
programme de vente (F)	Verkaufsprogramm *n*	sales programme	—	programma di vendita *m*	programa de venta *m*
programmer (E)	Programmierer *m*	—	programmeur *m*	programmatore *m*	programador *m*
programmeur (F)	Programmierer *m*	programmer	—	programmatore *m*	programador *m*
Programmierer (D)	—	programmer	programmeur *m*	programmatore *m*	programador *m*
Programmier-sprache (D)	—	common business-oriented language	langage de programmation *m*	linguaggio di programmazione *m*	lenguaje de programación *m*
Programmierung (D)	—	programming	programmation *f*	programmazione *f*	programación *f*
programming (E)	Programmierung *f*	—	programmation *f*	programmazione *f*	programación *f*
progresión (Es)	Progression *f*	progression	progression *f*	progressione *f*	—
progressif (F)	gestaffelt	graduated	—	differenziato	escalonado
Progression (D)	—	progression	progression *f*	progressione *f*	progresión *f*
progression (E)	Progression *f*	—	progression *f*	progressione *f*	progresión *f*
progression (F)	Progression *f*	progression	—	progressione *f*	progresión *f*
progressione (I)	Progression *f*	progression	progression *f*	—	progresión *f*
progressive Abschreibung (D)	—	progressive depreciation	amortissement progressif *m*	ammortamento progressivo *m*	amortización progresiva *f*
progressive depreciation (E)	progressive Abschreibung *f*	—	amortissement progressif *m*	ammortamento progressivo *m*	amortización progresiva *f*
prohibición de competencia (Es)	Wettbewerbsverbot *n*	prohibition of competition	interdiction en matière de concurrence *f*	divieto di concorrenza *m*	—
prohibición de publicidad (Es)	Werbeverbot *n*	ban on advertising	défense de publicité *f*	divieto di pubblicità *m*	—
prohibition of competition (E)	Wettbewerbsverbot *n*	—	interdiction en matière de concurrence *f*	divieto di concorrenza *m*	prohibición de competencia *f*
prohibitive duty (E)	Prohibitivzoll *m*	—	droit prohibitif *m*	dazio proibitivo *m*	derechos prohibitivos *m pl*

	D	E	F	I	Es
Prohibitivzoll (D)	—	prohibitive duty	droit prohibitif *m*	dazio proibitivo *m*	derechos prohibitivos *m pl*
proiettore per diapositive (I)	Diaprojektor *m*	slide projector	projecteur pour diapositives *m*	—	projector de diapositivas *m*
proiezione (I)	Projektion *f*	projection	projection *f*	—	proyección *f*
proiezione degli obiettivi (I)	Zielprojektion *f*	target projection	projection d'objectifs *f*	—	proyección de objetivos *f*
projecteur pour diapositives (F)	Diaprojektor *m*	slide projector	—	proiettore per diapositive *m*	projector de diapositivas *m*
projection (E)	Projektion *f*	—	projection *f*	proiezione *f*	proyección *f*
projection (F)	Projektion *f*	projection	—	proiezione *f*	proyección *f*
projection d'objectifs (F)	Zielprojektion *f*	target projection	—	proiezione degli obiettivi *f*	proyección de objetivos *f*
project management (E)	Projekt-Management *n*	—	gestion d'un projet *f*	management di progetto *m*	administración del proyecto *f*
projector de diapositivas (Es)	Diaprojektor *m*	slide projector	projecteur pour diapositives *m*	proiettore per diapositive *m*	—
project write-off company (E)	Abschreibungs-gesellschaft *f*	—	société d'amortissement *f*	società di ammortamento *f*	sociedad de amortización *f*
Projektion (D)	—	projection	projection *f*	proiezione *f*	proyección *f*
Projekt-Management (D)	—	project management	gestion d'un projet *f*	management di progetto *m*	administración del proyecto *f*
projet (F)	Entwurf *m*	draft	—	progetto *m*	proyecto *m*
pro Kopf (D)	—	per capita	par tête d'habitant	pro capite	per cápita
Prokura (D)	—	Prokura (procuration)	procuration commerciale générale *f*	procura *f*	poder general *m*
Prokura (E)	Prokura *f*	—	procuration commerciale générale *f*	procura *f*	poder general *m*
Prokurist (D)	—	Prokurist (authorized clerk)	fondé de procuration *m*	procuratore *m*	apoderado general *m*
Prokurist (E)	Prokurist *m*	—	fondé de procuration *m*	procuratore *m*	apoderado general *m*
prolongación (Es)	Prolongation *f*	extension/ prolongation	prolongation *f*/ report *m*	proroga *f*/riporto *m*	—
Prolongation (D)	—	extension/ prolongation	prolongation *f*/ report *m*	proroga *f*/riporto *m*	prolongación *f*/renovación *f*/prórroga *f*
prolongation[1] (F)	Nachfrist *f*	additional period	—	termine supplementare *m*	plazo de gracia *m*
prolongation[2] (F)	Prolongation *f*	extension/ prolongation	—	proroga *f*/riporto *m*	prolongación *f*/renovación *f*/prórroga *f*
prolongation[3] (F)	Verlängerung *f*	extension	—	prolungamento *m*	prórroga *f*
prolungamento (I)	Verlängerung *f*	extension	prolongation *f*	—	prórroga *f*
promedio (Es)	Durchschnitt *m*	average	moyenne *f*	media *f*	—
promesa (Es)	Zusage *f*	promise	promesse *f*	conferma *f*	—
promesa de créditos (Es)	Kreditzusage *f*	promise of credit	promesse de crédit *f*	consenso di credito *m*	—
promesse (F)	Zusage *f*	promise	—	conferma *f*	promesa *f*
promesse de crédit (F)	Kreditzusage *f*	promise of credit	—	consenso di credito *m*	promesa de créditos *f*
promise (E)	Zusage *f*	—	promesse *f*	conferma *f*	promesa *f*
promise of credit (E)	Kreditzusage *f*	—	promesse de crédit *f*	consenso di credito *m*	promesa de créditos *f*
promissory note (E)	Solawechsel *m*	—	seule lettre de change *f*	pagherò *m*	pagaré *m*
promoción comercial (Es)	Absatzförderung *f*	sales promotion	promotion des ventes *f*	promozione dello smercio *f*	—
promoción de las ventas (Es)	Verkaufsförderung *f*	sales promotion	encouragement à la vente *m*	promozione di vendita *f*	—
promotion (E)	Beförderung *f*	—	nomination *f*	promozione *f*	ascenso *m*
promotion de l'investissement (F)	Investitions-förderung *f*	investment promotion	—	promozione degli investimenti *f*	estímulo a la inversión *m*
promotion des ventes (F)	Absatzförderung *f*	sales promotion	—	promozione dello smercio *f*	promoción comercial *f*
promotion possibility (E)	Aufstiegs-möglichkeit *f*	—	perspectives de promotion *f pl*	possibilità di carriera *f*	posibilidades de ascenso *f pl*

	D	E	F	I	Es
promozione (I)	Beförderung *f*	promotion	nomination *f*	—	ascenso *m*
promozione degli investimenti (I)	Investitions-förderung *f*	investment promotion	promotion de l'investissement *f*	—	estímulo a la inversión *m*
promozione delle esportazioni (I)	Ausfuhrförderung *f*	measures to encourage exports	encouragement à l'exportation *m*	—	fomento de la exportació *m*
promozione dello smercio (I)	Absatzförderung *f*	sales promotion	promotion des ventes *f*	—	promoción comercial *f*
promozione di vendita (I)	Verkaufsförderung *f*	sales promotion	encouragement à la vente *m*	—	promoción de las ventas *f*
pronóstico (Es)	Prognose *f*	forecast(ing)	perspective *f*	prognosi *f*	—
pronto per il ritiro (I)	abholbereit	ready for collection	disponible	—	listo para la recogida
pronto per la spedizione (I)	versandbereit	ready for dispatch	prêt à être expédié	—	listo para ser expedido
proof (E)	Beweis *m*	—	preuve *f*	prova *f*	prueba *f*
propension à l'achat (F)	Kaufbereitschaft *f*	buying intention	—	propensione all'acquisto *f*	disposición a comprar *f*
propensione all'acquisto (I)	Kaufbereitschaft *f*	buying intention	propension à l'achat *f*	—	disposición a comprar *f*
property[1] (E)	Eigentum *n*	—	propriété *f*	proprietà *f*	propiedad *f*
property[2] (E)	Vermögen *n*	—	patrimoine *m*	patrimonio *m*	patrimonio *m*
property insurance (E)	Sachversicherung *f*	—	assurance de choses *f*	assicurazione di cose *f*	seguro de cosas *m*
property relations (E)	Eigentums-verhältnisse *pl*	—	régime de la propriété *m*	rapporti di proprietà *m pl*	régimen de tenencia *m*
property transactions (E)	Immobiliengeschäft *n*	—	affaire immobilière *f*	operazione immobiliare *f*	negocio de inmuebles *m*
propiedad (Es)	Eigentum *n*	property	propriété *f*	proprietà *f*	—
propiedad colectiva (Es)	Gemeinschafts-eigentum *n*	collective property	propriété collective *f*	proprietà collettiva *f*	—
propiedad común (Es)	Gemeineigentum *n*	public property	propriété publique *f*	proprietà collettiva *f*	—
propiedad del Estado (Es)	Staatsbesitz *m*	government property	propriété de l'Etat *f*	demanio *m*	—
propiedad de vivienda (Es)	Wohnungseigentum *n*	ownership of a flat	propriété du logement *f*	proprietà edilizia *f*	—
propiedad privada (Es)	Privateigentum *n*	private property	propriété privée *f*	proprietà privata *f*	—
propietario (Es)	Inhaber *m*	proprietor	propriétaire *m*	proprietario *m*	—
propietario de una casa[1] (Es)	Hausbesitzer *m*	home property owner	propriétaire d'immeuble *m*	possessore di casa *m*	—
propietario de una casa[2] (Es)	Hauseigentümer *m*	owner of a house	propriétaire d'une maison *m*	proprietario di casa *m*	—
propietario exclusivo (Es)	Alleininhaber *m*	sole owner	seul propriétaire *m*	titolare unico *m*	—
propina (Es)	Bedienungsgeld *n*	tip	pourboire *m*	diritto di servizio *m*	—
proporción de la población activa (Es)	Erwerbsquote *f*	activity rate	proportion de la population active *f*	quota della popolazione attiva *f*	—
proportion (E)	Verhältnis *n*	—	relation *f*	rapporto *m*	relación *f*
proportion de garantie (F)	Deckungsbeitrag *m*	contribution margin	—	contributo per copertura *m*	aportación de cobertura *f*
proportion de la population active (F)	Erwerbsquote *f*	activity rate	—	quota della popolazione attiva *f*	proporción de la población activa *f*
proportion des frais afférents aux matières (F)	Materialkosten-anteil *m*	share in the material costs	—	quota della popolazione attiva *f*	parte de los gastos de material *m*
proposal (E)	Vorschlag *m*	—	proposition *f*	proposta *f*	proposición *f*
proposición (Es)	Vorschlag *m*	proposal	proposition *f*	proposta *f*	—
proposition[1] (F)	Angebot *n*	offer	—	offerta *f*	oferta *f*
proposition[2] (F)	Vorschlag *m*	proposal	—	proposta *f*	proposición *f*
proposition d'amélioration (F)	Verbesserungs-vorschlag *m*	suggestion for improvement	—	proposta di miglioramento *f*	propuesta de mejora *f*
proposta (I)	Vorschlag *m*	proposal	proposition *f*	—	proposición *f*
proposta di miglioramento (I)	Verbesserungs-vorschlag *m*	suggestion for improvement	proposition d'amélioration *f*	—	propuesta de mejora *f*
proprietà (I)	Eigentum *n*	property	propriété *f*	—	propiedad *f*

	D	E	F	I	Es
proprietà collettiva[1] (I)	Gemeineigentum *n*	public property	propriété publique *f*	—	propiedad común *m*
proprietà collettiva[2] (I)	Gemeinschafts-eigentum *n*	collective property	propriété collective *f*	—	propiedad colectiva *f*
proprietà demaniale (I)	Staatseigentum *n*	public ownership	propriété d'Etat *f*	—	patrimonio público *m*
proprietà edilizia (I)	Wohnungs-eigentum *n*	ownership of a flat	propriété du logement *f*	—	propiedad de vivienda *f*
propriétaire (F)	Inhaber *m*	proprietor	—	proprietario *m*	propietario *m*
propriétaire d'immeuble (F)	Hausbesitzer *m*	home property owner	—	possessore di casa *m*	propietario de una casa *m*
propriétaire d'une maison (F)	Hauseigentümer *m*	owner of a house	—	proprietario di casa *m*	propietario de una casa *m*
proprietà privata (I)	Privateigentum *n*	private property	propriété privée *f*	—	propiedad privada *f*
proprietario (I)	Inhaber *m*	proprietor	propriétaire *m*	—	propietario *m*
proprietario di casa (I)	Hauseigentümer *m*	owner of a house	propriétaire d'une maison *m*	—	propietario de una casa *m*
propriété (F)	Eigentum *n*	property	—	proprietà *f*	propiedad *f*
propriété collective (F)	Gemeinschafts-eigentum *n*	collective property	—	proprietà collettiva *f*	propiedad colectiva *f*
propriété d'Etat (F)	Staatseigentum *n*	public ownership	—	proprietà demaniale *f*	patrimonio público *m*
propriété du logement (F)	Wohnungseigentum *n*	ownership of a flat	—	proprietà edilizia *f*	propiedad de vivienda *f*
propriété privée (F)	Privateigentum *n*	private property	—	proprietà privata *f*	propiedad privada *f*
propriété publique (F)	Gemeineigentum *n*	public property	—	proprietà collettiva *f*	propiedad común *m*
proprietor (E)	Inhaber *m*	—	propriétaire *m*	proprietario *m*	propietario *m*
propuesta de mejora (Es)	Verbesserungs-vorschlag *m*	suggestion for improvement	proposition d'amélioration *f*	proposta di miglioramento *f*	—
proroga (I)	Prolongation *f*	extension/ prolongation	prolongation *f*/ report *m*	—	prolongación *f*/ renovación *f*/ prórroga *f*
prorogation (F)	Stundung *f*	respite	—	dilazione *f*/proroga *f*	moratoria *f*
prórroga (Es)	Verlängerung *f*	extension	prolongation *f*	prolungamento *m*	—
prospecto (Es)	Prospekt *m*	leaflet/prospectus	feuille publicitaire *f*/ prospectus *m*	prospetto *m*/ dépliant *m*	—
prospectus (F)	Broschüre *f*	brochure	—	dépliant *m*	folleto *m*
Prospekt (D)	—	leaflet/prospectus	feuille publicitaire *f*/ prospectus *m*	prospetto *m*/ dépliant *m*	prospecto *m*/ folleto *m*
prospérité (F)	Wohlstand *m*	prosperity	—	benessere *m*	bienestar *m*
prosperity (E)	Wohlstand *m*	—	prospérité *f*	benessere *m*	bienestar *m*
prospettiva (I)	Zukunftschance *f*	future prospects	perspectives d'avenir *f pl*	—	posibilidades futuras *f pl*
prospettiva dello smercio (I)	Verkaufschance *f*	sales possibilities	possibilité de vente *f*	—	posibilidades de venta *f pl*
prospettive di smercio (I)	Absatzchance *f*	sales prospects	possibilités de réussite des ventes *f pl*	—	posibilidades de venta *f pl*
prospetto (I)	Prospekt *m*	leaflet/prospectus	feuille publicitaire *f*/ prospectus *m*	—	prospecto *m*/ folleto *m*
protección (Es)	Protektion *f*	protection	protection *f*	protezione *f*	—
protección al arrendatario (Es)	Mieterschutz *m*	protection of tenants	protection en matière de location *f*	tutela del locatario *f*	—
protección contra el despido (Es)	Kündigungsschutz *m*	protection against dismissal	protection en matière de licenciement *f*	protezione contro il licenziamento *f*	—
protección contra incendios (Es)	Brandschutz *m*	protection against fire	protection contre l'incendie *f*	protezione antincendio *f*	—
protección de datos (Es)	Datensicherung *f*	data protection	protection de données *f*	protezione dei dati *f*	—
protección de la madre (Es)	Mutterschutz *m*	protection of motherhood	protection maternelle et infantile *f*	tutela della maternità *f*	—
protección del medio ambiente (Es)	Umweltschutz *m*	protection of the environment	protection de l'environnement *f*	tutela dell'ambiente *f*	—
protección de los acreedores (Es)	Gläubigerschutz *m*	protection of creditors	garantie des créanciers *f*	tutela del creditore *f*	—
protección de los consumidores[1] (Es)	Konsumenten-schutz *m*	consumer protection	protection des consommateurs *f*	tutela del consumatore *f*	—

	D	E	F	I	Es
protección de los consumidores[2] (Es)	Verbraucherschutz *m*	consumer protection	protection des consommateurs *f*	tutela dei consumatori *f*	—
protección de los datos (Es)	Datenschutz *m*	data securing	sauvegarde des données *f*	tutela dei dati *f*	—
protección del trabajo (Es)	Arbeitsschutz *m*	employment protection	protection sociale du travail *f*	tutela del lavoro *f*	—
proteccionismo (Es)	Protektionismus *m*	protectionism	protectionnisme *m*	protezionismo *m*	—
protección territorial (Es)	Gebietsschutz *m*	territory protection	exclusivité territoriale *f*	tutela territoriale *f*	—
protection (E)	Protektion *f*	—	protection *f*	protezione *f*	protección *f*
protection (F)	Protektion *f*	protection	—	protezione *f*	protección *f*
protection against dismissal (E)	Kündigungsschutz *m*	—	protection en matière de licenciement *f*	protezione contro il licenziamento *f*	protección contra el despido *f*
protection against fire (E)	Brandschutz *m*	—	protection contre l'incendie *f*	protezione antincendio *f*	protección contra incendios *f*
protection contre l'incendie (F)	Brandschutz *m*	protection against fire	—	protezione antincendio *f*	protección contra incendios *f*
protection de données (F)	Datensicherung *f*	data protection	—	protezione dei dati *f*	protección de datos *f*
protection de l'environnement (F)	Umweltschutz *m*	protection of the environment	—	tutela dell'ambiente *f*	protección del medio ambiente *f*
protection des consommateurs (F)	Verbraucherschutz *m*	consumer protection	—	tutela dei consumatori *f*	protección de los consumidores *f*
protection en matière de licenciement (F)	Kündigungsschutz *m*	protection against dismissal	—	protezione contro il licenziamento *f*	protección contra el despido *f*
protection en matière de location (F)	Mieterschutz *m*	protection of tenants	—	tutela del locatario *f*	protección al arrendatario *f*
protectionism (E)	Protektionismus *m*	—	protectionnisme *m*	protezionismo *m*	proteccionismo *m*
protection maternelle et infantile (F)	Mutterschutz *m*	protection of motherhood	—	tutela della maternità *f*	protección de la madre *f*
protectionnisme (F)	Protektionismus *m*	protectionism	—	protezionismo *m*	proteccionismo *m*
protection of creditors (E)	Gläubigerschutz *m*	—	garantie des créanciers *f*	tutela del creditore *f*	protección de los acreedores *f*
protection of endangered species (E)	Artenschutz *m*	—	protection d'espèces *f*	protezione delle speci *f*	protección de la especie *f*
protection of motherhood (E)	Mutterschutz *m*	—	protection maternelle et infantile *f*	tutela della maternità *f*	protección de la madre *f*
protection of tenants (E)	Mieterschutz *m*	—	protection en matière de location *f*	tutela del locatario *f*	protección al arrendatario *f*
protection of the environment (E)	Umweltschutz *m*	—	protection de l'environnement *f*	tutela dell'ambiente *f*	protección del medio ambiente *f*
protection sociale du travail (F)	Arbeitsschutz *m*	employment protection	—	tutela del lavoro *f*	protección del trabajo *f*
protective duty (E)	Schutzzoll *m*	—	droit de protection *m*	dazio protettivo *m*	aduana proteccionista *f*
Protektion (D)	—	protection	protection *f*	protezione *f*	protección *f*
Protektionismus (D)	—	protectionism	protectionnisme *m*	protezionismo *m*	proteccionismo *m*
Protest (D)	—	objection/protest	protestation *f*/ protêt *m*	opposizione *f*/ protesta *f*	oposición *f*/protesta *f*
protest (E)	Wechselprotest *m*	—	protêt de traite *m*	protesto cambiario *m*	protesto de letra *m*
protesta (I)	Beschwerde *f*	complaint	réclamation *f*	—	recurso *m*
protestation (F)	Protest *m*	objection/protest	—	opposizione *f*/ protesta *f*	oposición *f*/protesta *f*
protesto cambiario (I)	Wechselprotest *m*	protest	protêt de traite *m*	—	protesto de letra *m*
protesto de letra (Es)	Wechselprotest *m*	protest	protêt de traite *m*	protesto cambiario *m*	—
protêt de traite (F)	Wechselprotest *m*	protest	—	protesto cambiario *m*	protesto de letra *m*
protezione (I)	Protektion *f*	protection	protection *f*	—	protección *f*
protezione antincendio (I)	Brandschutz *m*	protection against fire	protection contre l'incendie *f*	—	protección contra incendios *f*
protezione contro il licenziamento (I)	Kündigungsschutz *m*	protection against dismissal	protection en matière de licenciement *f*	—	protección contra el despido *f*
protezione dei dati (I)	Datensicherung *f*	data protection	protection de données *f*	—	protección de datos *f*
protezionismo (I)	Protektionismus *m*	protectionism	protectionnisme *m*	—	proteccionismo *m*

	D	E	F	I	Es
protocole d'erreurs (F)	Fehlerprotokoll *n*	record of errors	—	protocollo errori *m*	protocolo de errores *m*
protocollo (I)	Protokoll *n*	record/minutes	procès-verbal *m*/ compte-rendu *m*	—	protocolo *m*/acta *f*
protocollo errori (I)	Fehlerprotokoll *n*	record of errors	protocole d'erreurs *m*	—	protocolo de errores *m*
protocolo (Es)	Protokoll *n*	record/minutes	procès-verbal *m*/ compte-rendu *m*	protocollo *m*/ verbale *m*	—
protocolo de errores (Es)	Fehlerprotokoll *n*	record of errors	protocole d'erreurs *m*	protocollo errori *m*	—
Protokoll (D)	—	record/minutes	procès-verbal *m*/ compte-rendu *m*	protcollo *m*/verbale *m*	protocolo *m*/acta *f*
prototipo (Es)	Prototyp *m*	prototype	prototype *m*	prototipo *m*	—
prototipo (I)	Prototyp *m*	prototype	prototype *m*	—	prototipo *m*
Prototyp (D)	—	prototype	prototype *m*	prototipo *m*	prototipo *m*
prototype (E)	Prototyp *m*	—	prototype *m*	prototipo *m*	prototipo *m*
prototype (F)	Prototyp *m*	prototype	—	prototipo *m*	prototipo *m*
prova (I)	Beweis *m*	proof	preuve *f*	—	prueba *f*
provare (I)	probieren	try	essayer	—	probar
Provision (D)	—	commission	commission *f*	provvigione *f*	comisión *f*/ corretaje *m*
provisional (Es)	einstweilig	temporary	provisoire	temporaneo	—
provision for old age (E)	Altersversorgung *f*	—	prévoyance vieillesse *f*	previdenza per la vecchiaia *f*	previsión para la vejez *f*
provisioning with raw materials (E)	Rohstoffversorgung *f*	—	approvisionnement de matières premières *m*	approvvigionamento di materie prime *m*	aprovisionamiento de materias primas *m*
provision pour pertes et charges (F)	Rückstellung *f*	reserves	—	accantonamento *m*	reserva *f*
Provisions-abrechnung (D)	—	statement of a commission	liquidation des commissions *f*	conteggio delle provvigioni *m*	liquidación de la comisión *f*
Provisionsgarantie (D)	—	commission guarantee	garantie de commission *f*	garanzia di provvigione *f*	garantía de comisión *f*
Provisionszahlung (D)	—	commission payment	payement de commission *m*	pagamento di provvigione *m*	pago de comisión *m*
provisiore (F)	einstweilig	temporary	—	temporaneo	provisional
provvedimento temporaneo (I)	einstweilige Verfügung *f*	temporary injunction	ordonnance sur référé civil *f*	—	interdicto provisorio *m*
provvigione (I)	Provision *f*	commission	commission *f*	—	comisión *f*/corretaje *m*
provvigione dell'acquirente (I)	Käuferprovision *f*	buyer's commission	commission d'acheteur *f*	—	comisión al comprador *f*
provvigione dello star del credere (I)	Delkredereprovision *f*	del credere commission	commission ducroire *f*	—	comisión de garantía *f*
provvigione di credito (I)	Kreditprovision *f*	credit commission	frais de com-missions d'ouverture de crédit *m pl*	—	comisión de apertura de crédito *f*
provvigione del venditore (I)	Verkäuferprovision *f*	sales commission	commission sur les ventes *f*	—	comisión sobre la venta *f*
provvigione sul fatturato (I)	Umsatzprovision *f*	commission on turnover	commission sur le chiffre d'affaires *f*	—	comisión sobre la cifra de ventas *f*
proyección (Es)	Projektion *f*	projection	projection *f*	proiezione *f*	—
proyección de objetivos (Es)	Zielprojektion *f*	target projection	projection d'objectifs *f*	proiezione degli obiettivi *f*	—
proyecto (Es)	Entwurf *m*	draft	projet *m*	progetto *m*	—
Prozent (D)	—	per cent	pour-cent *m*	percento *m*	por ciento *m*
Prozentsatz (D)	—	percentage	pourcentage *m*	percentuale *f*	porcentaje *m*
Prozeß (D)	—	process	processus *m*	procedimento *m*	proceso *m*
prueba (Es)	Beweis *m*	proof	preuve *f*	prova *f*	—
prueba por sondeo (Es)	Stichproben *pl*	random test	sondage *m*	campioni *m pl*	—
Prüfung (D)	—	inspection/ examination	vérification *f*/ examen *m*	controllo *m*/ esame *m*	verificación *f*/ examen *m*
pseudoditta (I)	Scheinfirma *f*	bogus firm	raison sociale imaginaire *f*	—	casa ficticia *f*
psicologia del lavoro (I)	Arbeitspsychologie *f*	industrial psychology	psychologie de travail *f*	—	psicología laboral *f*

	D	E	F	I	Es
psicología industrial (Es)	Industrie-psychologie *f*	psychology of industry	psychologie industrielle *f*	psicologia industriale *f*	—
psicologia industriale (I)	Industrie-psychologie *f*	psychology of industry	psychologie industrielle *f*	—	psicología industrial
psicología laboral (Es)	Arbeitspsychologie *f*	industrial psychology	psychologie de travail *f*	psicologia del lavoro *f*	—
psychologie de travail (F)	Arbeitspsychologie *f*	industrial psychology	—	psicologia del lavoro *f*	psicología laboral *f*
psychologie industrielle (F)	Industrie-psychologie *f*	psychology of industry	—	psicologia industriale *f*	psicología industrial
psychology of industry (E)	Industrie-psychologie *f*	—	psychologie industrielle *f*	psicologia industriale *f*	psicología industrial
pubblicazione (I)	Veröffentlichung *f*	publication	publication *f*	—	publicación *f*
pubblicità (I)	Werbung *f*	publicity	publicité *f*	—	publicidad *f*
pubblicità all'aperto (I)	Außenwerbung *f*	outdoor publicity	publicité extérieure *f*	—	publicitad al aire libre *f*
pubblicità collettiva[1] (I)	Gemeinschafts-werbung *f*	joint publicity	publicité collective *f*	—	publicidad colectiva *f*
pubblicità collettiva[2] (I)	Sammelwerbung *f*	collective advertisement	publicité groupée *f*	—	publicidad colectiva *f*
pubblicità comparativa (I)	vergleichende Werbung *f*	comparative advertising	publicité comparative *f*	—	publicidad comparativa *f*
pubblicità del bilancio (I)	Offenlegung *f*	disclosure	révélation des derniers bilans du postulant d'un prêt *f*	—	publicidad para fines de inspección *f*
pubblicità per il trasporto strada-rotaia (I)	Huckepackwerbung *f*	piggyback advertisement	publicité pick-a-back *f*	—	publicidad combinada ferrocarril-carretera *f*
pubblicità per inserzione (I)	Anzeigenwerbung *f*	newspaper and magazine advertising	publicité par la presse *f*	—	publicidad por anuncios *f*
pubblicità radiofonica (I)	Rundfunkwerbung *f*	radio advertising	publicité à la radio *f*	—	publicidad radiada *f*
pubblicità televisiva (I)	Fernsehwerbung *f*	television advertising	émission publicitaire télévisée *f*	—	publicidad televisiva *f*
publicación (Es)	Veröffentlichung *f*	publication	publication *f*	pubblicazione *f*	—
public assistance (E)	Sozialhilfe *f*	—	aide sociale *f*	assistenza sociale *f*	ayuda social *f*
publication (E)	Veröffentlichung *f*	—	publication *f*	pubblicazione *f*	publicación *f*
publication (F)	Veröffentlichung *f*	publication	—	pubblicazione *f*	publicación *f*
public authorities (E)	öffentliche Hand *f*	—	secteur public *m*	mano pubblica *f*	sector público *m*
public enterprise (E)	öffentliche Unternehmen *n*	—	entreprises publiques *f pl*	imprese pubbliche *f pl*	empresa pública *f*
public goods (E)	öffentliche Güter n *pl*	—	biens publics *m pl*	beni pubblici *m pl*	bienes públicos *m pl*
public health (E)	Gesundheitswesen *n*	—	santé publique *f*	sanità *f*	sanidad *f*
publicidad[1] (Es)	Werbung *f*	publicity	publicité *f*	pubblicità *f*	—
publicidad[2] (Es)	Reklame *f*	advertising	publicité *f*	réclame *f*	—
publicidad al aire libre (Es)	Außenwerbung *f*	outdoor publicity	publicité extérieure *f*	pubblicità all'aperto *f*	—
publicidad colectiva[1] (Es)	Sammelwerbung *f*	collective advertisement	publicité groupée *f*	pubblicità collettiva *f*	—
publicidad colectiva[2] (Es)	Gemeinschafts-werbung *f*	joint publicity	publicité collective *f*	pubblicità collettiva *f*	—
publicidad combinada ferrocarril-carretera (Es)	Huckepackwerbung *f*	piggyback advertisement	publicité pick-a-back *f*	pubblicità per il trasporto strada-rotaia *f*	—
publicidad comparativa (Es)	vergleichende Werbung *f*	comparative advertising	publicité comparative *f*	pubblicità comparativa *f*	—
publicidad para fines de inspección (Es)	Offenlegung *f*	disclosure	révélation des derniers bilans du postulant d'un prêt *f*	pubblicità del bilancio *f*	—
publicidad por anuncios (Es)	Anzeigenwerbung *f*	newspaper and magazine advertising	publicité par la presse *f*	pubblicità per inserzione *f*	—
publicidad radiada (Es)	Rundfunkwerbung *f*	radio advertising	publicité à la radio *f*	pubblicità radiofonica *f*	—
publicidad televisiva (Es)	Fernsehwerbung *f*	television advertising	émission publicitaire télévisée *f*	pubblicità televisiva *f*	—
public institution (E)	gemeinnütziges Unternehmen *n*	—	entreprise d'utilité publique *f*	impresa di utilità pubblica *f*	empresa de beneficio común *f*

	D	E	F	I	Es
publicité[1] (F)	Reklame *f*	advertising	—	réclame *f*	publicidad *f*
publicité[2] (F)	Werbung *f*	publicity	—	pubblicità *f*	publicidad *f*
publicité à la radio (F)	Rundfunkwerbung *f*	radio advertising	—	pubblicità radiofonica *f*	publicidad radiada *f*
publicité collective (F)	Gemeinschafts-werbung *f*	joint publicity	—	pubblicità collettiva *f*	publicidad colectiva *f*
publicité comparative (F)	vergleichende Werbung *f*	comparative advertising	—	pubblicità comparativa *f*	publicidad comparativa *f*
publicité extérieure (F)	Außenwerbung *f*	outdoor publicity	—	pubblicità all'aperto *f*	publicitad al aire libre *f*
publicité groupée (F)	Sammelwerbung *f*	collective advertisement	—	pubblicità collettiva *f*	publicidad colectiva *f*
publicité par la presse (F)	Anzeigenwerbung *f*	newspaper and magazine advertising	—	pubblicità per inserzione *f*	publicidad por anuncios *f*
publicité pick-a-back (F)	Huckepackwerbung *f*	piggyback advertisement	—	pubblicità per il trasporto strada-rotaia *f*	publicidad combinada ferrocarril-carretera *f*
publicity[1] (E)	Publizität *f*	—	publicité *f*	pubblicità *f*	publicidad *f*
publicity[2] (E)	Werbung *f*	—	publicité *f*	pubblicità *f*	publicidad *f*
publicity department (E)	Werbeabteilung *f*	—	service de publicité *m*	reparto pubblicità *m*	sección de publicidad *f*
publicly owned enterprise (E)	Regiebetrieb *m*	—	établissement en régie *m*	gestione in economia *f*	empresa estatal *f*
(public) notary (E)	Notar *m*	—	notaire *m*	notaio *m*	notario *m*
public opinion research (E)	Demoskopie *f*	—	sondage de l'opinion publique *m*	demoscopia *f*	demoscopia *f*
public ownership (E)	Staatseigentum *n*	—	propriété d'Etat *f*	proprietà demaniale *f*	patrimonio público *m*
public property (E)	Gemeineigentum *n*	—	propriété publique *f*	proprietà collettiva *f*	propiedad común *m*
Public Relations (D)	—	public relations	relations publiques *f pl*	public relations *f pl*	relaciones públicas *f pl*
public relations (E)	Public Relations	—	relations publiques *f pl*	public relations *f pl*	relaciones públicas *f pl*
public relations (I)	Public Relations	public relations	relations publiques *f pl*	—	relaciones públicas *f pl*
public relations (work) (E)	Öffentlichkeitsarbeit *f*	—	relations publiques *f pl*	relazioni pubbliche *f pl*	relaciones públicas *f pl*
public revenue (E)	Staatseinnahmen *pl*	—	recettes de l'Etat *f pl*	entrate pubbliche *f pl*	ingresos del Estado *m pl*
public revenues (E)	öffentliche Einnahmen *pl*	—	recettes publiques *f pl*	entrate pubbliche *f pl*	ingresos públicos *m pl*
public sector industrial enterprise (E)	öffentliche Betriebe *pl*	—	entreprises publiques *f pl*	aziende pubbliche *f pl*	empresa pública *f*
public sector of the economy (E)	öffentliche Wirtschaft *f*	—	économie publique *f*	economia pubblica *f*	economía pública *f*
public spending[1] (E)	Staatsausgaben *pl*	—	dépenses publiques *f pl*	spese pubbliche *f pl*	gastos públicos *m pl*
public spending[2] (E)	öffentliche Ausgaben *pl*	—	dépenses publiques *f pl*	spesa pubblica *f*	gastos públicos *m pl*
public supervision of banking (E)	Bankenaufsicht *f*	—	contrôle des banques *m*	commissione bancaria *f*	supervisión bancaria *f*
(public) utility (E)	Versorgungs-betrieb *m*	—	services publics de distribution urbaine *m pl*	impresa di pubblici servizi *f*	empresa de suministros *f*
public welfare (E)	Allgemeinwohl *n*	—	bien général *m*	benestare pubblico *m*	bienestar público *m*
publisher (E)	Verleger *m*	—	éditeur *m*	editore *m*	editor *m*
publishing house (E)	Verlag *m*	—	maison d'édition *f*	casa editrice *f*	editorial *f*
puerto (Es)	Hafen *m*	port	port *m*	porto *m*	—
puerto franco (Es)	Freihafen *m*	free port	port franc *m*	porto franco *m*	—
puesto (Es)	Posten *m*	item	poste *m*	voce *f*	—
puesto de trabajo (Es)	Arbeitsplatz *m*	place of employment	poste de travail *m*	posto di lavoro *m*	—
puesto de trabajo a tiempo parcial (Es)	Teilzeitstelle *f*	part-time job	poste à temps partiel *m*	posto di lavoro part-time *m*	—
puesto de trabajo de pantalla (Es)	Bildschirm-arbeitsplatz *m*	screen job	poste de travail à l'écran *f*	posto di lavoro video *m*	—

	D	E	F	I	Es
puesto en estación (Es)	ab Bahnhof	ex rail	départ gare	franco stazione	—
punibile (I)	strafbar	punishable	punissable	—	punible
punible (Es)	strafbar	punishable	punissable	punibile	—
punishable (E)	strafbar	—	punissable	punibile	punible
punissable (F)	strafbar	punishable	—	punibile	punible
punto de intervención (Es)	Interventionspunkt *m*	intervention point	point d'intervention *m*	punto d'intervento *m*	—
punto d'incontro (I)	Treffpunkt *m*	meeting place	rendez-vous *m*	—	lugar de la cita *m*
punto d'intervento (I)	Interventionspunkt *m*	intervention point	point d'intervention *m*	—	punto de intervención *m*
punto por punto (Es)	Zug um Zug	concurrent	de point en point	contestualmente	—
puntuale (I)	termingerecht	on schedule	dans les délais	—	en la fecha fijada
purchase¹ (E)	Einkauf *m*	—	achat *m*	acquisto *m*	compra *f*
purchase² (E)	Kauf *m*	—	achat *m*	acquisto *m*	compra *f*
purchase costs (E)	Anschaffungs-kosten *pl*	—	frais d'acquisition *m pl*	costi d'acquisto *m pl*	coste de adquisición *m*
purchased quantity (E)	Abnahmemenge *f*	—	quantité commercialisée *f*	quantità d'acquisto *f*	cantidad de compra *f*
purchase guarantee (E)	Ankaufgarantie *f*	—	garantie d'achat *f*	garanzia d'acquisto *f*	garantía de compra *f*
purchase-money loan (E)	Restdarlehen *n*	—	prêt restant *m*	mutuo residuo *m*	restante de un préstamo *m*
purchase on credit (E)	Zielkauf *m*	—	achat à terme *m*	acquisto a termine *m*	compra a plazos *m*
purchase pattern (E)	Kaufverhalten *n*	—	comportement d'achat *m*	filosofia d'acquisto *f*	comportamiento de compra *m*
purchase price¹ (E)	Kaufpreis *m*	—	prix d'achat *m*	prezzo d'acquisto *m*	precio de compra *m*
purchase price² (E)	Einkaufspreis *m*	—	prix d'achat *m*	prezzo d'acquisto *m*	precio de compra *m*
purchaser (E)	Käufer *m*	—	acheteur *m*	acquirente *m*	adquirente *m*
purchasing costs (E)	Bezugskosten *pl*	—	coûts d'acquisition *m pl*	prezzo d'acquisto *m*	gastos de adquisición *m pl*
purchasing power (E)	Kaufkraft *f*	—	pouvoir d'achat *m*	potere d'acquisto *m*	poder adquisitivo *m*
purchasing power parity (E)	Kaufkraftparität *f*	—	parité du pouvoir d'achat *f*	parità del potere d'acquisto *f*	paridad adquisitiva *f*
purchasing terms (E)	Einkaufs-bedingungen *pl*	—	conditions d'achat *f pl*	condizioni d'acquisto *f pl*	condiciones de compra *f pl*
purification of sewage (E)	Abwasserreinigung *f*	—	clarification des eaux usées *f*	depurazione delle acque di scarico *f*	depuración de las aguas residuales *f*
putting on the index (E)	Indizierung *f*	—	indexation *f*	indicizzazione *f*	indiciación *f*
quadri dirigenti (I)	Führungsebene *f*	executive level	niveau de gestion *m*	—	nivel de dirección *m*
quadro del mercato (I)	Marktübersicht *f*	overall view of the market	vue d'ensemble du marché *f*	—	panorama de mercado *m*
qualification (E)	Qualifikation *f*	—	qualification *f*	qualificazione *f*	cualificación *f*
qualification (F)	Qualifikation *f*	qualification	—	qualificazione *f*	cualificación *f*
qualification du travail (F)	Arbeitsbewertung *f*	job evaluation	—	valutazione del lavoro *f*	evaluación del trabajo *f*
qualificazione (I)	Qualifikation *f*	qualification	qualification *f*	—	cualificación *f*
Qualifikation (D)	—	qualification	qualification *f*	qualificazione *f*	cualificación *f*
qualifying period (E)	Karenzzeit *f*	—	délai de carence *m*	periodo d'attesa *m*	período carencial *m*
qualità¹ (I)	Güteklasse *f*	grade	catégorie de qualité *f*	—	categoría de calidad *f*
qualità² (I)	Qualität *f*	quality	qualité *f*	—	calidad *f*
qualità dell'acqua potabile (I)	Trinkwasserqualität *f*	drinking water quality	qualité de l'eau potable *f*	—	calidad del agua potable *f*
qualità di vita (I)	Lebensqualität *f*	quality of life	qualité de la vie *f*	—	calidad de vida *m*
qualità ottima (I)	beste Qualität	first class quality	première qualité *f*	—	primera calidad *f*
qualità scadente (I)	schlechte Qualität *f*	poor quality	mauvaise qualité *f*	—	mala calidad *f*
Qualität (D)	—	quality	qualité *f*	qualità *f*	calidad *f*
qualitatif (F)	qualitativ	qualitative	—	qualitativo	cualitativo
qualitativ (D)	—	qualitative	qualitatif	qualitativo	cualitativo
qualitative (E)	qualitativ	—	qualitatif	qualitativo	cualitativo
qualitativo (I)	qualitativ	qualitative	qualitatif	—	cualitativo

	D	E	F	I	Es
Qualitätsabweichung (D)	—	deviation from quality	écart qualitatif *m*	differenza di qualità *f*	diferencia de calidad *f*
Qualitätskontrolle (D)	—	quality control	contrôle de la qualité *m*	controllo di qualità *m*	verificación de la calidad *f*
Qualitätssicherung (D)	—	quality assurance	garantie de la qualité *f*	garanzia di qualità *f*	garantía de la calidad *f*
qualité (F)	Qualität *f*	quality	—	qualità *f*	calidad *f*
qualité de la vie (F)	Lebensqualität *f*	quality of life	—	qualità di vita *f*	calidad de vida *m*
qualité de l'eau potable (F)	Trinkwasserqualität *f*	drinking water quality	—	qualità dell'acqua potabile *f*	calidad del agua potable *f*
qualité fongible d'un bien (F)	Fungibilität *f*	fungibility	—	fungibilità *f*	fungibilidad *f*
qualité promise (F)	zugesicherte Eigenschaften *pl*	warranted characteristics	—	caratteristiche promesse *f pl*	calidades aseguradas *f pl*
quality (E)	Qualität *f*	—	qualité *f*	qualità *f*	calidad *f*
quality assurance (E)	Qualitätssicherung *f*	—	garantie de la qualité *f*	garanzia di qualità *f*	garantía de la calidad *f*
quality control (E)	Qualitätskontrolle *f*	—	contrôle de la qualité *m*	controllo di qualità *m*	verificación de la calidad *f*
quality of life (E)	Lebensqualität *f*	—	qualité de la vie *f*	qualità di vita *f*	calidad de vida *m*
quantità (I)	Menge *f*	quantity	quantité *f*	—	cantidad *f*
quantità d'acquisto (I)	Abnahmemenge *f*	purchased quantity	quantité commercialisée *f*	—	cantidad de compra *f*
quantità d'ordinazione (I)	Bestellmenge *f*	ordering quantity	quantité commandée *f*	—	cantidad pedida *f*
quantitatif (F)	quantitativ	quantitative	—	quantitativo	cuantitativo
quantitativ (D)	—	quantitative	quantitatif	quantitativo	cuantitativo
quantitative (E)	quantitativ	—	quantitatif	quantitativo	cuantitativo
quantitative boom (E)	Mengenkonjunktur *f*	—	conjoncture de quantité *f*	congiuntura quantitativa *f*	coyuntura cuantitativa *f*
quantitativo (I)	quantitativ	quantitative	quantitatif	—	cuantitativo
quantitativo d'estrazione (I)	Fördermenge *f*	output	quantité extraite *f*	—	cantidad producida *f*
quantitativo di produzione (I)	Fertigungsmenge *f*	manufactured quantity	quantité fabriquée *f*	—	cantidad producida *f*
quantitativo minimo (I)	Mindestmenge *f*	minimum quantity	quantité minimum *f*	—	cantidad mínima *f*
quantitativo minimo di fornitura (I)	Mindestabnahme *f*	minimum purchase	achat d'une quantité minimum *m*	—	recogida mínima *f*
quantitativo minimo di ordine (I)	Mindestbestellmenge *f*	minimum quantity order	quantité commandée minimum *f*	—	cantidad mínima de pedido *f*
quantité (F)	Menge *f*	quantity	—	quantità *f*	cantidad *f*
quantité commandée (F)	Bestellmenge *f*	ordering quantity	—	quantità d'ordinazione *f*	cantidad pedida *f*
quantité commandée minimum (F)	Mindestbestellmenge *f*	minimum quantity order	—	quantitativo minimo di ordine *m*	cantidad mínima de pedido *f*
quantité commercialisée (F)	Abnahmemenge *f*	purchased quantity	—	quantità d'acquisto *f*	cantidad de compra *f*
quantité de monnaie en circulation (F)	Geldmenge *f*	money supply	—	massa monetaria *f*	volumen monetario *m*
quantité extraite (F)	Fördermenge *f*	output	—	quantitativo d'estrazione *m*	cantidad producida *f*
quantité fabriquée (F)	Fertigungsmenge *f*	manufactured quantity	—	quantitativo di produzione *m*	cantidad producida *f*
quantité minimum (F)	Mindestmenge *f*	minimum quantity	—	quantitativo minimo *m*	cantidad mínima *f*
quantity (E)	Menge *f*	—	quantité *f*	quantità *f*	cantidad *f*
quantity discount (E)	Mengenrabatt *m*	—	remise de quantité *f*	sconto di quantità *m*	rebaja de cantidad *f*
quantity quota (E)	Mengenkontingent *n*	—	contingent de marchandises *m*	contingente di quantità *m*	contingente cuantitativo *m*
quantity unit (E)	Mengeneinheit *f*	—	unité de quantité *f*	unità quantitativa *f*	unidad cuantitativa *f*
Quartal (D)	—	quarter	trimestre *m*	trimestre *m*	trimestre *m*
Quartalsende (D)	—	end of a quarter	fin de trimestre *f*	fine trimestre *f*	final del trimestre *m*
Quartalsrechnung (D)	—	quarterly invoice	compte trimestriel *m*	conto trimestrale *m*	cuenta trimestral *f*

	D	E	F	I	Es
quarter (E)	Quartal *n*	—	trimestre *m*	trimestre *m*	trimestre *m*
quarterly (E)	vierteljährlich	—	trimestriel	trimestrale	trimestral
quarterly invoice (E)	Quartalsrechnung *f*	—	compte trimestriel *m*	conto trimestrale *m*	cuenta trimestral *f*
queja (Es)	Beanstandung *f*	objection	objection *f*	reclamo *m*	—
que sofrage los costes (Es)	Kostenträger *m*	assuming unit costs	poste de production absorbant des coûts *m*	chi si assume i costi	—
questionario (I)	Fragebogen *m*	questionnaire	questionnaire *m*	—	cuestionario *m*
questionnaire (E)	Fragebogen *m*	—	questionnaire *m*	questionario *m*	cuestionario *m*
questionnaire (F)	Fragebogen *m*	questionnaire	—	questionario *m*	cuestionario *m*
queue up (E)	Schlange stehen	—	faire la queue	fare la coda	hacer la cola
quiebra[1] (Es)	Konkurs *m*	bankruptcy	faillite *f*	fallimento *m*	—
quiebra[2] (Es)	Bankrott *m*	bankruptcy	banqueroute *f*	bancarotta	—
quietanza[1] (I)	Quittung *f*	receipt	quittance *f*	—	recibo *m*
quietanza[2] (I)	Beleg *m*	voucher	justificatif *m*	—	justificativo *m*
quilate (Es)	Karat *n*	carat	carat *m*	carato *m*	—
química (Es)	Chemie *f*	chemistry	chimie *f*	chimica *f*	—
quince días (Es)	vierzehn Tage	fortnight	quinze jours	quindici giorni	—
quindici giorni (I)	vierzehn Tage	fortnight	quinze jours	—	quince días *m pl*
quinze jours (F)	vierzehn Tage	fortnight	—	quindici giorni	quince días *m pl*
quittance (F)	Quittung *f*	receipt	—	quietanza *f*	recibo *m*
Quittung (D)	—	receipt	quittance *f*	quietanza *f*	recibo *m*
quota[1] (E)	Quote *f*	—	quota *m*	quota *f*	cuota *f*
quota[2] (E)	Kontingent *n*	—	contingent *m*	contingente *m*	contingente *m*
quota (F)	Quote *f*	quota	—	quota *f*	cuota *f*
quota (I)	Quote *f*	quota	quota *m*	—	cuota *f*
quota dei costi del materiale (I)	Materialkosten-anteil *m*	share in the material costs	proportion des frais de matériel *f*	—	parte de los gastos de material *m*
quota della popolazione attiva (I)	Erwerbsquote *f*	activity rate	proportion de la population active *f*	—	proporción de la población activa *f*
quota d'estrazione (I)	Förderquote *f*	production quota	quote-part de production *f*	—	cuota de producción *f*
quota d'exportation (F)	Exportquote *f*	export quota	—	contingente d'esportazione *m*	cupo de exportación *m*
quota di capitale (I)	Kapitalanteil *m*	share in capital	part de capital *f*	—	participación en el capital *f*
quota di mercato (I)	Marktanteil *m*	market share	participation au marché *f*	—	cuota del mercado *f*
quota d'importazione (I)	Importquote *f*	import quota	contingent d'importation *m*	—	cuota de importación *f*
quota di risparmio (I)	Sparquote *f*	savings ratio	quote-part de revenu réservée à des fins d'épargne *f*	—	cuota de ahorro *f*
quota sociale[1] (I)	Stammeinlage *f*	initial contribution	apport social *m*	—	capital suscrito *m*
quota sociale[2] (I)	Geschäftsanteil *m*	share	part sociale *f*	—	participación *f*
quota system (E)	Quotensystem *n*	—	système de quote-parts *m*	sistema di contingentamento *m*	sistema de cuotas *m*
quotation (E)	Notierung *f*	—	cotation *f*	quotazione *f*	cotización *f*
quotation of prices (E)	Kursnotierung *f*	—	cotation *f*	quotazione dei corsi *f*	cotización *m*
quotation on the stock exchange[1] (E)	Börsennotierung *f*	—	cotation des cours en bourse *f*	quotazione di borsa *f*	cotización de bolsa *f*
quotation on the stock exchange[2] (E)	Börsenkurs *m*	—	cours de bourse *m pl*	corso di borsa *m*	cotización en bolsa *f*
quotazione (I)	Notierung *f*	quotation	cotation *f*	—	cotización *f*
quotazione dei corsi (I)	Kursnotierung *f*	quotation of prices	cotation *f*	—	cotización *m*
quotazione dei prezzi (I)	Preisnotierung *f*	prices quoted	cotation des prix *f*	—	cotización de precios *f*
quotazione delle azioni (I)	Aktiennotierung *f*	share quotation	cotation des actions *f*	—	cotización de acciones *f*
quotazione di borsa (I)	Börsennotierung *f*	quotation on the stock exchange	cotation des cours en bourse *f*	—	cotización de bolsa *f*

	D	E	F	I	Es
quotazione di chiusura (I)	Schlußkurs *m*	closing price	dernier cours *m*	—	cotización final *f*
Quote (D)	—	quota	quota *m*	quota *f*	cuota *f*
Quotensystem (D)	—	quota system	système de quote-parts *m*	sistema di contingentamento *m*	sistema de cuotas *m*
quote-part de production (F)	Förderquote *f*	production quota	—	quota d'estrazione *f*	cuota de producción *f*
quote-part de revenu réservée à des fins d'épargne (F)	Sparquote *f*	savings ratio	—	quota di risparmio *f*	cuota de ahorro *f*
quotidien (F)	täglich	daily	—	giornaliero	diario
Quotient (D)	—	quotient	quotient *m*	quoziente *m*	cociente *m*
quotient (E)	Quotient *m*	—	quotient *m*	quoziente *m*	cociente *m*
quotient (F)	Quotient *m*	quotient	—	quoziente *m*	cociente *m*
quoziente (I)	Quotient *m*	quotient	quotient *m*	—	cociente *m*
rabais d'introduction (F)	Einführungsrabatt *m*	introductory discount	—	sconto di lancio *m*	rebaja de lanzamiento *f*
Rabatt (D)	—	discount	remise *f*	ribasso *m*	rebaja *f*
raccolta dati (I)	Datenerfassung *f*	data collection	saisie des données informatiques *f*	—	recogida de datos *f*
raccomandata (I)	Einschreiben *n*	Registered	en recommandé	—	certificado *m*
raccomandazione (I)	Empfehlung *f*	recommendation	recommandation *f*	—	recomendación *f*
racionalización (Es)	Rationalisierung *f*	rationalization	rationalisation *f*	razionalizzazione *f*	—
racionamiento (Es)	Rationierung *f*	rationing	rationnement *m*	razionamento *m*	—
radio advertising (E)	Rundfunkwerbung *f*	—	publicité à la radio *f*	pubblicità radiofonica *f*	publicidad radiada *f*
radio message (E)	Funkspruch *m*	—	message par radio *m*	radiotelefonata *f*	mensaje radiado *m*
radiotelefonata (I)	Funkspruch *m*	radio message	message par radio *m*	—	mensaje radiado *m*
raggio d'azione della pubblicità (I)	Werbereichweite *f*	scope of advertising effect	zone de rayonnement de la publicité *f*	—	alcance publicitario *m*
ragioneria (I)	Rechnungswesen *n*	accounting system	comptabilité *f*	—	contabilidad *f*
ragioniere (I)	Buchhalter *m*	bookkeeper	comptable *m*	—	tenedor de libros *m*
rail freight (E)	Bahnfracht *f*	—	fret par rail *m*	nolo ferroviario *m*	transporte ferroviario *m*
railway tariff (E)	Eisenbahntarif *m*	—	tarif ferroviaire *m*	tariffa ferroviaria *f*	tarifa ferroviaria *f*
raising of money (E)	Geldaufnahme *f*	—	emprunt *m*	accensione di un mutuo *f*	dinero tomado a préstamo *m*
raison sociale imaginaire (F)	Scheinfirma *f*	bogus firm	—	pseudoditta *f*	casa ficticia *f*
ramo (Es)	Branche *f*	line of business	branche *f*	categoria *f*	—
ramo de la construcción (Es)	Bauwirtschaft *f*	building and construction industry	(industrie du) bâtiment *f*	edilizia *f*	—
ramo económico (Es)	Wirtschaftszweig *m*	field of the economy	secteur économique *m*	settore economico *m*	—
random test (E)	Stichproben *pl*	—	sondage *m*	campioni *m pl*	prueba por sondeo *f*
range of production (E)	Produktionspalette *f*	—	gamme de production *f*	gamma di produzione *f*	gama de producción *f*
rapport (F)	Report *m*	report	—	rapporto *m*	informe *m*
rapport de confiance (F)	Vertrauens-verhältnis *n*	confidential relationship	—	rapporto di fiducia *m*	relación de confianza *f*
rapport de gestion (F)	Geschäftsbericht *m*	business report	—	relazione sull'esercizio commerciale *f*	informe *m*
rapport de travail (F)	Arbeitsverhältnis *n*	employee-employer relationship	—	rapporto di lavoro *m*	relación laboral *f*
rapport de vente (F)	Verkaufsbericht *m*	sales report	—	rapporto sulle vendite *m*	informe de venta *m*
rapport financier (F)	Finanzbericht *m*	financial report	—	relazione finanziaria *f*	informe financiero *m*
rapporti commerciali (I)	Handels-beziehungen *pl*	trade relations	relations commerciales *f pl*	—	relaciones comerciales *f pl*
rapporti d'affari (I)	Geschäfts-beziehung *f*	business relation	relations d'affaires *f pl*	—	relaciones comerciales *f pl*
rapporti di proprietà (I)	Eigentums-verhältnisse *pl*	property relations	régime de la propriété *m*	—	régimen de tenencia *m*

	D	E	F	I	Es
rapport juridique (F)	Rechtsverhältnis *n*	legal relationship	—	rapporto giuridico *m*	relación jurídica *f*
rapporto[1] (I)	Verhältnis *n*	proportion	relation *f*	—	relación *f*
rapporto[2] (I)	Report *m*	report	rapport *m*	—	informe *m*
rapporto corso-profitto (I)	Kurs-Gewinn-Verhältnis *n*	price-earnings ratio	relation cours-bénéfice *f*	—	relación cotización-ganancia *f*
rapporto di fiducia (I)	Vertrauens-verhältnis *n*	confidential relationship	rapport de confiance *m*	—	relación de confianza *f*
rapporto di lavoro (I)	Arbeitsverhältnis *n*	employee-employer relationship	rapport de travail *m*	—	relación laboral *f*
rapporto di lavoro in prova (I)	Arbeitsverhältnis auf Probe *n*	employee-employer relationship on a trial basis	contrat de travail convenu à l'essai *m*	—	relación laboral a prueba *f*
rapporto giuridico (I)	Rechtsverhältnis *n*	legal relationship	rapport juridique *m*	—	relación jurídica *f*
rapporto sulle vendite (I)	Verkaufsbericht *m*	sales report	rapport de vente *m*	—	informe de venta *m*
rappresaglia (I)	Repressalie *f*	reprisals	représaille *f*	—	represalia *f*
rappresentante (I)	Vertreter *m*	representative	représentant *m*	—	representante *m*
rappresentante commerciale (I)	Handelsvertreter *m*	commercial agent	représentant de commerce *m*	—	representante comercial *m*
rappresentante di zona (I)	Bezirksvertreter *m*	local agent	agent local *m*	—	agente regional *m*
rappresentante esclusivo (I)	Alleinvertreter *m*	sole agent	agent exclusive *m*	—	representante exclusivo *m*
rappresentante generale (I)	Generalvertreter *m*	general agent	agent général *m*	—	representante general *m*
rappresentanza (I)	Vertretung *f*	representation	représentation *f*	—	representación *f*
rappresentanza commerciale (I)	Handelsvertretung *f*	commercial agency	représentation commerciale *f*	—	representación comercial *f*
rappresentanza degli interessi (I)	Interessen-vertretung *f*	representation of interests	représentation des intérêts *f*	—	representación de intereses *f*
rappresentanza esclusiva (I)	Alleinvertretung *f*	sole agency	agence exclusive *f*	—	representación exclusiva *f*
rappresentanza estera (I)	Auslandsvertretung *f*	agency abroad	agence à l'étranger *f*	—	representación en el exterior *f*
rare (F)	knapp	scarce	—	scarso	escaso
rareté (F)	Knappheit *f*	shortage	—	scarsità *f*	escasez *f*
rata[1] (I)	Rate *f*	instalment	acompte *m*	—	plazo *m*
rata[2] (I)	Teilzahlungsrate *f*	monthly instalment	mensualité d'un achat à tempérament *f*	—	plazo *m*
rata leasing (I)	Leasing-Rate *f*	leasing payment	taux de leasing *m*	—	plazo de arrenda-miento financiero *m*
Rate (D)	—	instalment	acompte *m*	rata *f*/tasso *m*	plazo *m*
rate for advances on securities (E)	Lombardsatz *m*	—	taux d'intérêt de l'argent prêté sur gage *m*	tasso sulle anticipazioni *m*	tipo de pignoración *m*
rate for foreign notes and coin (E)	Sortenkurs *m*	—	cours des monnaies étrangères *m*	corso dei cambi *m*	tipo de cambio de billetes y monedas extranjeras *m*
ratei e risconti (I)	Rechnungs-abgrenzung *f*	apportionment of payments between accounting periods	délimitation des comptes non encore soldés *f*	—	ajuste de cuentas *m*
Ratengeschäft (D)	—	instalment sale transaction	vente à tempérament *f*	vendita a rate *f*	venta a plazo *f*
Ratenkauf (D)	—	hire-purchase transaction	achat à tempérament *m*	acquisto a rate *m*	compra a plazo *f*
Ratenzahlung (D)	—	payment by instalments	payement par verse-ments fractionnés *m*	pagamento rateale *m*	pago a plazos *m*
rate of conversion (E)	Umrechnungskurs *m*	—	cours de conversion *m*	corso di cambio *m*	tasa de cambio *f*
rate of growth (E)	Wachstumsrate *f*	—	taux d'accroissement *m*	tasso di crescita *m*	tasa de crecimiento *f*
rate of inflation (E)	Inflationsrate *f*	—	taux d'inflation *m*	tasso d'inflazione *m*	tasa de inflación *f*
ratificación (Es)	Ratifikation *f*	ratification	ratification *f*	ratificazione *f*	—
ratification (E)	Ratifikation *f*	—	ratification *f*	ratificazione *f*	ratificación *f*
ratification (F)	Ratifikation *f*	ratification	—	ratificazione *f*	ratificación *f*

	D	E	F	I	Es
ratificazione (I)	Ratifikation *f*	ratification	ratification *f*	—	ratificación *f*
Ratifikation (D)	—	ratification	ratification *f*	ratificazione *f*	ratificación *f*
ratio de perte (F)	Ausfallquote *f*	default rate	—	tasso di perdita *m*	cuota de pérdida *f*
rational behaviour (E)	Rationalverhalten *n*	—	comportement rationnel *m*	atteggiamento razionale *m*	comportamiento racional *m*
rationalisation (F)	Rationalisierung *f*	rationalization	—	razionalizzazione *f*	racionalización *f*
Rationalisierung (D)	—	rationalization	rationalisation *f*	razionalizzazione *f*	racionalización *f*
Rationalisierungsgewinn (D)	—	rationalization profit	profit de rationalisation *m*	profitto di razionalizzazione *m*	beneficio de racionalización *m*
rationalization (E)	Rationalisierung *f*	—	rationalisation *f*	razionalizzazione *f*	racionalización *f*
rationalization profit (E)	Rationalisierungsgewinn *m*	—	profit de rationalisation *m*	profitto di razionalizzazione *m*	beneficio de racionalización *m*
Rationalverhalten (D)	—	rational behaviour	comportement rationnel *m*	atteggiamento razionale *m*	comportamiento racional *m*
Rationierung (D)	—	rationing	rationnement *m*	razionamento *m*	racionamiento *m*
rationing (E)	Rationierung *f*	—	rationnement *m*	razionamento *m*	racionamiento *m*
rationnement (F)	Rationierung *f*	rationing	—	razionamento *m*	racionamiento *m*
Raubbau (D)	—	ruinous exploitation	exploitation abusive *f*	sfruttamento abusivo *m*	explotación abusiva *f*
Raumforschung (D)	—	space research	recherches spatiales *f pl*	ricerche spaziali *f pl*	investigación espacial *f*
Raumordnung (D)	—	regional policy	aménagement des espaces *m*	ordinamento territoriale *m*	ordenación del territorio *f*
Raumplanung (D)	—	regional planning	plan d'aménagement des espaces *m*	pianificazione territoriale *f*	planificación del espacio *m*
Raumstruktur (D)	—	spatial structure	structure des espaces *f*	struttura territoriale *f*	estructura territorial *f*
Räumung (D)	—	evacuation	évacuation *f*	evacuazione *f*	desalojamiento *m*
Räumungsverkauf (D)	—	clearance sale	liquidation des stocks *f*	liquidazione totale *f*	venta total *f*
raw material production (E)	Rohstoffgewinnung *f*	—	extraction de matières premières *f*	produzione delle materie prime *f*	producción de materias primas *f*
raw materials (E)	Rohstoff *m*	—	matière première *f*	materia prima *f*	materia prima *f*
raw materials marketing (E)	Rohstoffvermarktung *f*	—	commercialisation des matières premières *f*	smercio delle materie prime *m*	comercialización de las materias primas *f*
raw materials shortage (E)	Rohstoffknappheit *f*	—	pénurie de matières premières *f*	scarsità di materie prime *f*	escasez de materias primas *f*
razionalizzazione (I)	Rationalisierung *f*	rationalization	rationalisation *f*	—	racionalización *f*
razionamento (I)	Rationierung *f*	rationing	rationnement *m*	—	racionamiento *m*
razón social (Es)	Firmenname *m*	company name	nom de la maison *m*	denominazione *f*/ ragione sociale *f*	—
reacción (Es)	Reaktion *f*	reaction	réaction *f*	reazione *f*	—
reacoplamiento (Es)	Rückkopplung *f*	feedback	accouplement réactif *m*	accoppiamento a reazione *m*	—
reaction (E)	Reaktion *f*	—	réaction *f*	reazione *f*	reacción *f*
réaction (F)	Reaktion *f*	reaction	—	reazione *f*	reacción *f*
readaptación profesional (Es)	Umschulung *f*	retraining	rééducation professionnelle *f*	riqualificazione professionale *f*	—
ready for collection (E)	abholbereit	—	disponible	pronto per il ritiro	listo para la recogida
ready for dispatch (E)	versandbereit	—	prêt à être expédié	pronto per la spedizione	listo para ser expedido
Reaktion (D)	—	reaction	réaction *f*	reazione *f*	reacción *f*
real account (E)	Bestandskonto *n*	—	compte d'existences *m*	conto merci *m*	cuenta de existencias *f*
real capital (E)	Realkapital *n*	—	biens corporels immobilisés *m pl*	capitale reale *m*	capital real *m*
Realeinkommen (D)	—	real income	revenu réel *m*	reddito reale *m*	ingreso real *m*
real estate (E)	Grundstück *n*	—	terrain *m*	terreno *m*	terreno *m*
real estate fund (E)	Immobilienfonds *m*	—	fonds immobilier *m*	fondo immobiliare *m*	fondo inmobiliario *f*
real income (E)	Realeinkommen *n*	—	revenu réel *m*	reddito reale *m*	ingreso real *m*
real indebtedness (E)	effektive Verschuldung *f*	—	endettement effectif *m*	indebitamento effettivo *m*	endeudamiento efectivo *m*

	D	E	F	I	Es
real (rate of) interest (E)	Realzins *m*	—	rendement réel *m*	tasso d'interesse reale *m*	interés real *m*
réalisation (F)	Durchführung *f*	realization	—	esecuzione *f*	ejecución *f*
réalisation d'une commande (F)	Auftragsbearbeitung *f*	order processing	—	esecuzione ordini *f*	tramitación de pedidos *f*
realization (E)	Durchführung *f*	—	réalisation *f*	esecuzione *f*	ejecución *f*
Realkapital (D)	—	real capital	biens corporels immobilisés *m pl*	capitale reale *m*	capital real *m*
Realkredit (D)	—	credit secured by real property	crédit sur gage mobilier *m*	credito reale *m*	crédito real *m*
Reallohn (D)	—	real wage	salaire réel *m*	salario reale *m*	salario real *m*
real right (E)	dingliches Recht *n*	—	droit réel *m*	diritto reale *m*	derecho real *m*
real security (E)	dingliche Sicherung *f*	—	sécurité réelle *f*	garanzia reale *f*	garantía real *f*
Realsteuern (D)	—	impersonal taxes	impôt réel *m*	imposte reali *f pl*	impuestos reales *m pl*
real value (E)	Sachwert *m*	—	valeur matérielle *f*	valore reale *m*	valor real *m*
Realvermögen (D)	—	real wealth	patrimoine réel *m*	patrimonio reale *m*	activo inmobiliario *m*
real wage (E)	Reallohn *m*	—	salaire réel *m*	salario reale *m*	salario real *m*
real wealth (E)	Realvermögen *n*	—	patrimoine réel *m*	patrimonio reale *m*	activo inmobiliario *m*
Realzins (D)	—	real (rate of) interest	rendement réel *m*	tasso d'interesse reale *m*	interés real *m*
réapprovisionnement (F)	Wiederbeschaffung *f*	replacement	—	riapprovvigionamento *m*	reposición *f*
reaseguro (Es)	Rückversicherung *f*	reinsurance	réassurance *f*	riassicurazione *f*	—
réassurance (F)	Rückversicherung *f*	reinsurance	—	riassicurazione *f*	reaseguro *m*
reazione (I)	Reaktion *f*	reaction	réaction *f*	—	reacción *f*
rebaja[1] (Es)	Rabatt *m*	discount	remise *f*	ribasso *m*	—
rebaja[2] (Es)	Preisnachlaß *m*	price reduction	remise sur le prix *f*	ribasso del prezzo *m*	—
rebaja de cantidad (Es)	Mengenrabatt *m*	quantity discount	remise de quantité *f*	sconto di quantità *m*	—
rebaja de lanzamiento (Es)	Einführungsrabatt *m*	introductory discount	rabais d'introduction *m*	sconto di lancio *m*	—
rebaja preferencial (Es)	Vorzugsrabatt *m*	preferential discount	remise de faveur *f*	ribasso preferenziale *m*	—
rebajas de invierno (Es)	Winterschlußverkauf *m*	winter clearance sale	solde d'hiver *m*	svendita di fine inverno *f*	—
recargo (Es)	Aufschlag *m*	surcharge	hausse *f*	aggiunta *f*	—
receipt (E)	Quittung *f*	—	quittance *f*	quietanza *f*	recibo *m*
receipt for payment (E)	Zahlungsbestätigung *f*	—	confirmation de payement *f*	conferma di pagamento *f*	confirmación de pago *f*
receipts (E)	Einnahmen *pl*	—	revenu *m*	entrate *f pl*	ingresos *m pl*
receiver (E)	Empfänger *m*	—	destinataire *m*	destinatario *m*	destinatario *m*
receivership (E)	Zwangsverwaltung *f*	—	séquestre judiciare *m*	amministrazione giudiziaria *f*	administración forzosa *f*
recensement démographique (F)	Volkszählung *f*	census of population	—	censimento *m*	censo *m*
réception (F)	Abnahme *f*	acceptance/decrease	—	accettazione *f*/ riduzione *f*	aceptación *f*/ disminución *f*
recesión (Es)	Rezession *f*	recession	récession *f*	recessione *f*	—
recession (E)	Rezession *f*	—	récession *f*	recessione *f*	recesión *f*
récession (F)	Rezession *f*	recession	—	recessione *f*	recesión *f*
recessione (I)	Rezession *f*	recession	récession *f*	—	recesión *f*
recettes de l'Etat (F)	Staatseinnahmen *pl*	public revenue	—	entrate pubbliche *f pl*	ingresos del Estado *m pl*
recettes publiques (F)	öffentliche Einnahmen *pl*	public revenues	—	entrate pubbliche *f pl*	ingresos públicos *m pl*
Recheneinheit (D)	—	calculation unit	unité de calcul *f*	unità di conteggio *f*	unidad de cuenta *f*
Rechenfehler (D)	—	miscalculation	erreur de calcul *f*	errore di calcolo *m*	error de cálculo *m*
Rechenzentrum (D)	—	computer centre	centre de calcul *m*	centro da computer *m*	centro de computación *m*
recherche[1] (F)	Forschung *f*	research	—	ricerca *f*	investigación *f*
recherche[2] (F)	Nachforschung *f*	investigation	—	indagine *f*	pesquisas *f pl*

	D	E	F	I	Es
recherche de la fraude fiscale (F)	Steuerfahndung *f*	investigation into suspected tax offences	—	inchiesta tributaria *f*	investigación tributaria *f*
recherches spatiales (F)	Raumforschung *f*	space research	—	ricerche spaziali *f pl*	investigación espacial *f*
Rechner (D)	—	computer/calculator	ordinateur *m*/calculateur de poche *m*	computer *m*/ calcolatore *m*	ordenador *m*/calculadora de bolsillo *f*
Rechnung (D)	—	invoice/calculation	facture *f*/calcul *m*	fattura *f*/calcolo *m*	factura *f*/cálculo *m*
Rechnungsbetrag (D)	—	amount of invoice	montant de la facture *m*	ammontare della fattura *m*	importe de la factura *m*
Rechnungseinheit (D)	—	unit of account	unité de compte *f*	unità di conto *f*	unidad de cuenta *f*
Rechnungsjahr (D)	—	financial year	exercice comptable *m*	anno d'esercizio *m*	ejercicio *m*
Rechnungsnummer (D)	—	invoice number	numéro de la facture *m*	numero della fattura *m*	número de la factura *m*
Rechnungsprüfer (D)	—	auditor	commissaire aux comptes *m*	revisore dei conti *m*	revisor contable *m*
Rechnungsstellung (D)	—	invoicing	établissement d'une facture *m*	fatturazione *f*	facturación *f*
Rechnungssumme (D)	—	invoice amount	montant de la facture *m*	importo della fattura *m*	suma de la factura *f*
Rechnungswesen (D)	—	accounting system	comptabilité *f*	ragioneria *f*	contabilidad *f*
Recht (D)	—	law	droit *m*	diritto *m*	derecho *m*
Rechtsabteilung (D)	—	legal department	bureau juridique *m*	ufficio legale *m*	sección jurídica *f*
Rechtsanspruch (D)	—	legal claim	titre *m*	pretesa giuridica *f*	pretensión legal *f*
Rechtsanwalt (D)	—	lawyer	avocat *m*	avvocato *m*	abogado *m*
rechtsfähig (D)	—	capable to act in law	capable de jouir des droits	persona avente capacità giuridica *f*	jurídicamente capaz
Rechtsfähigkeit (D)	—	legal capacity	capacité de jouissance des droits *f*	capacità giuridica *f*	capacidad jurídica *f*
Rechtsform (D)	—	legal form	forme juridique *f*	forma giuridica *f*	forma jurídica *f*
Rechtsgeschäft (D)	—	legal transaction	acte juridique *m*	negozio giuridico *m*	negocio jurídico *m*
Rechtshaftung (D)	—	legal responsibility	responsabilité légale *f*	responsabilità giuridica *f*	responsabilidad jurídica *f*
Rechtsirrtum (D)	—	mistake of law	erreur de droit *m*	errore di diritto *m*	error de derecho *m*
Rechtslage (D)	—	legal situation	situation juridique *f*	situazione giuridica *f*	situación jurídica *f*
Rechtsnorm (D)	—	legal norm	règle de droit *f*	norma giuridica *f*	norma jurídica *f*
Rechtsprechung (D)	—	administration of justice	jurisprudence *f*	giurisprudenza *f*	jurisprudencia *f*
Rechtsstreit (D)	—	legal action	litige *m*	causa *f*	conflicto jurídico *m*
Rechtsverhältnis (D)	—	legal relationship	rapport juridique *m*	rapporto giuridico *m*	relación jurídica *f*
recibo[1] (Es)	Quittung *f*	receipt	quittance *f*	quietanza *f*	—
recibo[2] (Es)	Empfangsbestätigung *f*	acknowledgement of receipt	accusé de réception *m*	ricevuta *f*	—
recibo de entrega (Es)	Lieferschein *m*	delivery note	bulletin de livraison *m*	bolletta di consegna *f*	—
reciclaje (Es)	Recycling *n*	recycling	recyclage *m*	riciclaggio *m*	—
reciprocidad (Es)	Reziprozität *f*	reciprocity	réciprocité *f*	reciprocità *f*	—
reciprocità (I)	Reziprozität *f*	reciprocity	réciprocité *f*	—	reciprocidad *f*
réciprocité (F)	Reziprozität *f*	reciprocity	—	reciprocità *f*	reciprocidad *f*
reciprocity (E)	Reziprozität *f*	—	réciprocité *f*	reciprocità *f*	reciprocidad *f*
reclamación (Es)	Reklamation *f*	complaint	réclamation *f*	reclamo *m*	—
reclamación de la entrega de un pedido (Es)	Abruf *m*	call	appel *m*	richiesta *f*	—
réclamation[1] (F)	Reklamation *f*	complaint	—	reclamo *m*	reclamación *f*
réclamation[2] (F)	Beschwerde *f*	complaint	—	protesta *f*	recurso *m*
réclame (I)	Reklame *f*	advertising	publicité *f*	—	publicidad *f*
reclamo[1] (I)	Reklamation *f*	complaint	réclamation *f*	—	reclamación *f*
reclamo[2] (I)	Beanstandung *f*	objection	objection *f*	—	queja *f*
reclutamento (I)	Anwerbung *f*	recruitment	recrutement *m*	—	contratación *f*
reclutamiento de personal (Es)	Personalwerbung *f*	hiring of personnel	recrutement de personnel *m*	reclutazione di personale *f*	—

	D	E	F	I	Es
reclutazione di personale (I)	Personalwerbung *f*	hiring of personnel	recrutement de personnel *m*	—	reclutamiento de personal *m*
recogida de datos (Es)	Datenerfassung *f*	data collection	saisie des données informatiques *f*	raccolta dati *f*	—
recogida mínima (Es)	Mindestabnahme *f*	minimum purchase	achat d'une quantité minimum *m*	quantitativo minimo di fornitura *m*	—
recognize (E)	erkennen	—	reconnaître	riconoscere	reconocer
recomendación (Es)	Empfehlung *f*	recommendation	recommandation *f*	raccomandazione *f*	—
recommandation (F)	Empfehlung *f*	recommendation	—	raccomandazione *f*	recomendación *f*
recommendation (E)	Empfehlung *f*	—	recommandation *f*	raccomandazione *f*	recomendación *f*
recommendation de prix (F)	Preisempfehlung *f*	price recommendation	—	suggerimento di prezzo *m*	precio recomendado *m*
recommended retail price (E)	Richtpreis *m*	—	prix indicatif *m*	prezzo indicativo *m*	precio indicativo *m*
reconnaissance de dette (F)	Schuldanerkennung *f*	acknowledgement of a debt	—	riconoscimento del debito *m*	reconocimiento de la deuda *m*
reconnaître (F)	erkennen	recognize	—	riconoscere	reconocer
reconocer (Es)	erkennen	recognize	reconnaître	riconoscere	—
reconocimiento de la deuda (Es)	Schuldanerkennung *f*	acknowledgement of a debt	reconnaissance de dette *f*	riconoscimento del debito *m*	—
reconstrucción (Es)	Wiederaufbau *m*	reconstruction	reconstruction *f*	ricostruzione *f*	—
reconstruction (E)	Wiederaufbau *m*	—	reconstruction *f*	ricostruzione *f*	reconstrucción *f*
reconstruction (F)	Wiederaufbau *m*	reconstruction	—	ricostruzione *f*	reconstrucción *f*
record (E)	Protokoll *n*	—	procès-verbal *m*/ compte-rendu *m*	protocollo *m*/ verbale *m*	protocolo *m*/acta *f*
recorded delivery letter (with advice) (E)	Einschreiben-Rückschein *m*	—	lettre recommandée avec avis de réception *f*	lettera raccomandata con ricevuta di ritorno *f*	carta certificada con talón de recibo *f*
record of errors (E)	Fehlerprotokoll *n*	—	protocole d'erreurs *m*	protocollo errori *m*	protocolo de errores *m*
recours[1] (F)	Regreß *m*	recourse	—	regresso *m*	regreso *m*
recours[2] (F)	Rückgriff *m*	recourse	—	regresso *m*	recurso *m*
recourse[1] (E)	Rückgriff *m*	—	recours *m*	regresso *m*	recurso *m*
recourse[2] (E)	Regreß *m*	—	recours *m*	regresso *m*	regreso *m*
recouvrement (F)	Inkasso *n*	collection	—	incasso *m*	encobro *m*
recruitment (E)	Anwerbung *f*	—	recrutement *m*	reclutamento *m*	contratación *f*
recrutement (F)	Anwerbung *f*	recruitment	—	reclutamento *m*	contratación *f*
recrutement de personnel (F)	Personalwerbung *f*	hiring of personnel	—	reclutazione di personale *f*	reclutamiento de personal *m*
rectificación (Es)	Berichtigung *f*	correction	rectification *f*	correzione *f*	—
rectificación de valor (Es)	Wertberichtigung *f*	value adjustment	réévaluation *f*	rettifica del valore *f*	—
rectification (F)	Berichtigung *f*	correction	—	correzione *f*	rectificación *f*
recul de la demande (F)	Nachfrage-rückgang *m*	decrease in demand	—	flessione della domanda *f*	disminución en la demanda *f*
recul du chiffre d'affaires (F)	Umsatzrückgang *m*	decrease of turnover	—	calo del fatturato *m*	disminución de la cifra de facturación *f*
recuperable (Es)	wiederverwertbar	recyclable	réutilisable	riutilizzabile	—
recuperación coyuntural (Es)	Konjunkturbelebung *f*	economic upturn	relance économique *f*	ripresa congiunturale *f*	—
recurso[1] (Es)	Beschwerde *f*	complaint	réclamation *f*	protesta *f*	—
recurso[2] (Es)	Ressource *f*	resources	ressource *f*	risorsa *f*	—
recurso[3] (Es)	Rückgriff *m*	recourse	recours *m*	regresso *m*	—
recusación (Es)	Ablehnung *f*	refusal/rejection	refus *m*/rejet *m*	rifiuto *m*/rigetto *m*	—
recyclable (E)	wiederverwertbar	—	réutilisable	riutilizzabile	recuperable
recyclage (F)	Recycling *n*	recycling	—	riciclaggio *m*	reciclaje *m*
Recycling (D)	—	recycling	recyclage *m*	riciclaggio *m*	reciclaje *m*
recycling (E)	Recycling *n*	—	recyclage *m*	riciclaggio *m*	reciclaje *m*
recycling exchange (E)	Abfallbörse *f*	—	bourse de recyclage *f*	borsa dei rifiuti *f*	bolsa de reciclaje *f*
red (Es)	Netzwerk *n*	network	réseau *m*	rete *f*	—

	D	E	F	I	Es
redazione del testo (I)	Textgestaltung *f*	text configuration	structure du texte *f*	—	estructuración del texto *f*
redazione d'inventario (I)	Inventur *f*	taking of the inventory	inventaire *m*	—	inventario *m*
red de carreteras (Es)	Straßennetz *n*	road network	réseau routier *m*	rete stradale *f*	—
red de sucursales (Es)	Filialnetz *n*	branch network	réseau de succursales *m*	rete delle filiali *f*	—
redditività[1] (I)	Ertragskraft *f*	earning capacity	force productive *f*	—	rentabilidad *f*
redditività[2] (I)	Rentabilität *f*	profitability	rentabilité *f*	—	rentabilidad *f*
redditività del capitale (I)	Kapitalrentabilität *f*	return on investment	rentabilité du capital *f*	—	rentabilidad del capital *f*
reddito[1] (I)	Einkommen *n*	income	revenu *m*	—	ingresos *m pl*/ renta *f*
reddito[2] (I)	Ertrag *m*	income/earnings	rendement *m*/ revenu *m*	—	producto *m*/ rendimiento *m*/ renta *f*
reddito annuale (I)	Jahreseinkommen *n*	annual income	revenu annuel *m*	—	renta anual *f*
reddito da possesso (I)	Besitzeinkommen *n*	unearned income	revenu du patrimoine *m*	—	renta de la propiedad *f*
reddito del capitale (I)	Kapitaleinkommen *n*	unearned income	revenu du capital *m*	—	ganancias de capital *f pl*
reddito fisso (I)	Festeinkommen *n*	fixed income	revenu fixe *m*	—	salario fijo *m*
reddito lordo[1] (I)	Rohertrag *m*	gross proceeds	produit brut *m*	—	producto bruto *m*
reddito lordo[2] (I)	Bruttoeinkommen *n*	gross income	revenu brut *m*	—	ingreso bruto *m*
reddito nazionale (I)	Volkseinkommen *n*	national income	revenu national *m*	—	renta nacional *f*
reddito netto (I)	Nettoeinkommen *n*	net income	revenu net *m*	—	ingreso neto *m*
reddito nominale (I)	Nominal-einkommen *n*	nominal income	revenu nominal *m*	—	ingresos nominales *m*
reddito reale (I)	Realeinkommen *n*	real income	revenu réel *m*	—	ingreso real *m*
redeem (E)	ablösen	—	amortir	rimborsare	amortizar
Redegewandtheit (D)	—	eloquence	élocution aisée *f*	eloquenza *f*	elocuencia *f*
redemption (E)	Tilgung *f*	—	amortissement *m*	ammortamento *m*	amortización *f*
redemption financing (E)	Ablösungs-finanzierung *f*	—	financement du rachat *m*	finanziamento del rimborso *m*	financiamiento de amortización *m*
redemption sum (E)	Ablösesumme *f*	—	montant de rachat *m*	importo di rimborso *m*	suma de amortización *f*
redescontar (Es)	rediskontieren	rediscount	réescompter	riscontare	—
rediscount (E)	rediskontieren	—	réescompter	riscontare	redescontar
rediskontieren (D)	—	rediscount	réescompter	riscontare	redescontar
redistribución (Es)	Redistribution *f*	redistribution	redistribution *f*	ridistribuzione *f*	—
redistribución de la renta (Es)	Einkommens-umverteilung *f*	redistribution of income	redistribution des revenus *f pl*	ridistribuzione dei redditi *f*	—
Redistribution (D)	—	redistribution	redistribution *f*	ridistribuzione *f*	redistribución *f*
redistribution (E)	Redistribution *f*	—	redistribution *f*	ridistribuzione *f*	redistribución *f*
redistribution (F)	Redistribution *f*	redistribution	—	ridistribuzione *f*	redistribución *f*
redistribution des revenues (F)	Einkommens-umverteilung *f*	redistribution of income	—	ridistribuzione dei redditi *f*	redistribución de la renta *f*
redistribution of income (E)	Einkommens-umverteilung *f*	—	redistribution des revenus *f pl*	ridistribuzione dei redditi *f*	redistribución de la renta *f*
rédito de la cifra de ventas (Es)	Umsatzrendite *f*	net income percent-age of turnover	rendement du chiffre d'affaires *m*	rendita del fatturato *f*	—
redondance (F)	Redundanz *f*	redundancy	—	ridondanza *f*	redundancia *f*
reducción[1] (Es)	Abbau *m*	reduction/lay off	réduction *f*/ diminution *f*	riduzione *f*/ diminuzione *f*	—
reducción[2] (Es)	Ermäßigung *f*	reduction	réduction *f*	riduzione *f*	—
reducción[3] (Es)	Minderung *f*	reduction	diminution *f*	riduzione *f*	—
reducción de capital (Es)	Kapitalherabsetzung *f*	reduction of capital	diminution du capital *f*	riduzione del capitale *f*	—
reducción de coste (Es)	Kostensenkung *f*	cost reduction	diminution des coûts *f*	ribasso dei costi *m*	—
reducción de costes (Es)	Kostendegression *f*	cost degression	dégressivité des coûts *f*	riduzione dei costi *f*	—

	D	E	F	I	Es
reducción de gastos (Es)	Ausgabensenkung *f*	drop in expenditure	diminution des dépenses *f*	riduzione delle spese *f*	—
reducción de intereses (Es)	Zinserleichterung *f*	reduction of interest	minoration de l'intérêt *m*	agevolazione sugli interessi *f*	—
reducción de las subvenciones (Es)	Subventionsabbau *m*	reduction of subsidy	réduction des subventions *f*	riduzione delle sovvenzioni *f*	—
reducción del tipo de interés (Es)	Zinssenkung *f*	reduction of interest	diminution du taux de l'intérêt *f*	riduzione degli interessi *f*	—
reducción de personal (Es)	Personalabbau *m*	reduction of staff	réduction de personnel *f*	riduzione del personale *f*	—
reducción de precios (Es)	Preissenkung *f*	price reduction	réduction des prix *f*	riduzione dei prezzi *f*	—
reduced tariffs (E)	ermäßigte Tarife *pl*	—	tarifs reduits *m pl*	tariffe ridotte *f pl*	tarifas reducidas *f pl*
reduction[1] (E)	Abschlag *m*	—	déduction *f*	detrazione *f*	descuento *m*
reduction[2] (E)	Abbau *m*	—	réduction *f*/ diminution *f*	riduzione *f*/ diminuzione *f*	reducción *f*/ disminución *f*
reduction[3] (E)	Minderung *f*	—	diminution *f*	riduzione *f*	reducción *f*
réduction[1] (F)	Abbau *m*	reduction/lay off	—	riduzione *f*/ diminuzione *f*	reducción *f*/ disminución *f*
réduction[2] (F)	Ermäßigung *f*	reduction	—	riduzione *f*	reducción *f*
réduction de prix (F)	Preisabzug *m*	price deduction	—	riduzione del prezzo *f*	descuento *m*
réduction des coûts (F)	Kostendämpfung *f*	combatting rising costs	—	contenimento dei costi *m*	disminución de costes *f*
réduction des prix (F)	Preissenkung *f*	price reduction	—	riduzione dei prezzi *f*	reducción de precios *f*
réduction des subventions (F)	Subventionsabbau *m*	reduction of subsidy	—	riduzione delle sovvenzioni *f*	reducción de las subvenciones *f*
réduction du prix (F)	Verbilligung *f*	cheapening	—	ribasso *m*	abaratamiento *m*
reduction of capital (E)	Kapitalherabsetzung *f*	—	diminution du capital *f*	riduzione del capitale *f*	reducción de capital *f*
reduction of interest[1] (E)	Zinssenkung *f*	—	diminution du taux de l'intérêt *f*	riduzione degli interessi *f*	reducción del tipo de interés *f*
reduction of interest[2] (E)	Zinserleichterung *f*	—	minoration de l'intérêt *m*	agevolazione sugli interessi *f*	reducción de intereses *f*
reduction of staff (E)	Personalabbau *m*	—	réduction de personnel *f*	riduzione del personale *f*	reducción de personal *f*
reduction of subsidy (E)	Subventionsabbau *m*	—	réduction des subventions *f*	riduzione delle sovvenzioni *f*	reducción de las subvenciones *f*
redundancia (Es)	Redundanz *f*	redundancy	redondance *f*	ridondanza *f*	—
redundancy (E)	Redundanz *f*	—	redondance *f*	ridondanza *f*	redundancia *f*
Redundanz (D)	—	redundancy	redondance *f*	ridondanza *f*	redundancia *f*
Reeder (D)	—	shipowner	armateur *m*	armatore *m*	armador *m*
Reederei (D)	—	shipping company	société d'armateurs *f pl*	compagnia armatoriale *f*	compañía naviera *f*
rééducation professionnelle (F)	Umschulung *f*	retraining	—	riqualificazione professionale *f*	readaptación profesional *f*
reembolso (Es)	Nachnahme *f*	cash on delivery	remboursement *m*	contrassegno *m*	—
reempaquetar (Es)	umpacken	repack	remballer	rifare l'imballaggio	—
réescompter (F)	rediskontieren	rediscount	—	riscontare	redescontar
reestructuración (Es)	Umstrukturierung *f*	restructuring	restructuration *f*	ristrutturazione *f*	—
réévaluation (F)	Wertberichtigung *f*	value adjustment	—	rettifica del valore *f*	rectificación de valor *f*
reexamination (E)	Nachprüfung *f*	—	vérification *f*	revisione *f*	revisión *f*
reexportación (Es)	Wiederausfuhr *f*	reexportation	réexportation *f*	riesportazione *f*	—
reexportation (E)	Wiederausfuhr *f*	—	réexportation *f*	riesportazione *f*	reexportación *f*
réexportation (F)	Wiederausfuhr *f*	reexportation	—	riesportazione *f*	reexportación *f*
reference[1] (E)	Referenz *f*	—	référence *f*	referenza *f*	referencia *f*
reference[2] (E)	Diktatzeichen *n*	—	références *f pl*	sigla *f*	referencias *f pl*
reference[3] (E)	Bezug *m*	—	référence *f*	riferimento *m*	referencia *f*
référence[1] (F)	Referenz *f*	reference	—	referenza *f*	referencia *f*
référence[2] (F)	Bezug *m*	reference	—	riferimento *m*	referencia *f*
références (F)	Diktatzeichen *n*	reference	—	sigla *f*	referencias *f pl*

	D	E	F	I	Es
références de commande (F)	Bestelldaten *pl*	details of order	—	dati delle ordinazioni *m pl*	datos de pedido *m pl*
referencia[1] (Es)	Bezug *m*	reference	référence *f*	riferimento *m*	—
referencia[2] (Es)	Referenz *f*	reference	référence *f*	referenza *f*	—
referencias (Es)	Diktatzeichen *n*	reference	références *f pl*	sigla *f*	—
Referenz (D)	—	reference	référence *f*	referenza *f*	referencia *f*
referenza (I)	Referenz *f*	reference	référence *f*	—	referencia *f*
referring to (E)	bezugnehmend	—	se référant (à)	con riferimento	con referencia a
refinancement (F)	Refinanzierung *f*	refinancing	—	rifinanziamento *m*	refinanciación *f*
refinanciación (Es)	Refinanzierung *f*	refinancing	refinancement *m*	rifinanziamento *m*	—
refinancing (E)	Refinanzierung *f*	—	refinancement *m*	rifinanziamento *m*	refinanciación *f*
Refinanzierung (D)	—	refinancing	refinancement *m*	rifinanziamento *m*	refinanciación *f*
reforma agraria (Es)	Bodenreform *f*	land reform	réforme agraire *f*	riforma agraria *f*	—
réforme agraire (F)	Bodenreform *f*	land reform	—	riforma agraria *f*	reforma agraria *f*
refus[1] (F)	Absage *f*	refusal	—	risposta negativa *f*	negativa *f*
refus[2] (F)	Ablehnung *f*	refusal/rejection	—	rifiuto *m*/rigetto *m*	recusación *f*/repulsa *f*
refus d'acceptation (F)	Annahmeverweigerung *f*	refusal of delivery	—	rifiuto d'accettazione *m*	rehuso de aceptación *m*
refusal[1] (E)	Absage *f*	—	refus *m*	risposta negativa *f*	negativa *f*
refusal[2] (E)	Ablehnung *f*	—	refus *m*/rejet *m*	rifiuto *m*/rigetto *m*	recusación *f*/repulsa *f*
refusal of delivery (E)	Annahmeverweigerung *f*	—	refus d'acceptation *m*	rifiuto d'accettazione *m*	rehuso de aceptación *m*
regalo publicitario (Es)	Werbegeschenk *n*	advertising gift	cadeau publicitaire *m*	omaggio pubblicitario *m*	—
Regiebetrieb (D)	—	publicly owned enterprise	établissement en régie *m*	gestione in economia *f*	empresa estatal *m*
Regierung (D)	—	government/Ministry	gouvernement *m*	governo *m*	gobierno *m*
régime de l'admission en franchise (F)	Zollfreischreibungsverfahren *n*	procedure of duty free admission	—	procedura d'ammissione in franchigia *f*	régimen de admisión en franquicia *m*
régime de la propriété (F)	Eigentumsverhältnisse *pl*	property relations	—	rapporti di proprietà *m pl*	régimen de tenencia *m*
regime di prelievo (I)	Abschöpfungssystem *n*	absorption system	système d'absorption *m*	—	sistema de gravámenes *m*
régime douanier (F)	Zollverkehr *m*	customs procedure	—	procedure doganali *f pl*	régimen aduanero de mercancías *m*
régime juridique de la faillite (F)	Konkursordnung *f*	Bankruptcy Act	—	legge fallimentare *f*	ley de las quiebras *f*
régime monétaire international (F)	internationale Währungsordnung *f*	international monetary system	—	regolamento valutario internazionale *m*	régimen monetario internacional *m*
régimen aduanero de mercancías (Es)	Zollverkehr *m*	customs procedure	régime douanier *m*	procedure doganali *f pl*	—
régimen de admisión en franquicia (Es)	Zollfreischreibungsverfahren *n*	procedure of duty-free admission	régime de l'admission en franchise *m*	procedura d'ammissione in franchigia *f*	—
régimen de tenencia (Es)	Eigentumsverhältnisse *pl*	property relations	régime de la propriété *m*	rapporti di proprietà *m pl*	—
régimen de trabajo a destajo (Es)	Akkordsystem *n*	piece work system	système du travail aux pièces *m*	sistema del lavoro a cottimo *m*	—
régimen monetario internacional (Es)	internationale Währungsordnung *f*	international monetary system	régime monétaire international *m*	regolamento valutario internazionale *m*	—
Regionalbank (D)	—	regional bank	banque régionale *f*	banca regionale *f*	banco regional *m*
regional bank (E)	Regionalbank *f*	—	banque régionale *f*	banca regionale *f*	banco regional *m*
regional planning[1] (E)	Raumplanung *f*	—	plan d'aménagement des espaces *m*	pianificazione territoriale *f*	planificación del espacio *m*
regional planning[2] (E)	Regionalplanung *f*	—	aménagement régional *m*	pianificazione regionale *f*	planificación regional *f*
Regionalplanung (D)	—	regional planning	aménagement régional *m*	pianificazione regionale *f*	planificación regional *f*
regional policy[1] (E)	Raumordnung *f*	—	aménagement des espaces *m*	ordinamento territoriale *m*	ordenación del territorio *f*
regional policy[2] (E)	Regionalpolitik *f*	—	politique régionale *f*	politica regionale *f*	política regional *f*
Regionalpolitik (D)	—	regional policy	politique régionale *f*	politica regionale *f*	política regional *f*
región industrial (Es)	Industriegebiet *n*	industrial area	région industrielle *f*	zona industriale *f*	—

	D	E	F	I	Es
région industrielle (F)	Industriegebiet *n*	industrial area	—	zona industriale *f*	región industrial *f*
Register (D)	—	register	registre *m*	registro *m*	registro *m*
register (E)	Register *n*	—	registre *m*	registro *m*	registro *m*
Registered (E)	Einschreiben *n*	—	en recommandé	raccomandata *f*	certificado *m*
Registered-Advice of Delivery (E)	Einschreiben-Rückschein *m*	—	lettre recommandée avec avis de réception *f*	lettera raccommandata con ricevuta di ritorno *f*	carta certificada con talón de recibo *f*
registered letter (E)	Einschreibebrief *m*	—	lettre recommandée *f*	lettera raccomandata *f*	carta certificada *f*
registered shares (E)	Namensaktie *f*	—	action nominative *f*	azione nominativa *f*	acción nominal *f*
register of ships (E)	Schiffsregister *n*	—	répertoire des navires *m*	registro navale *m*	registro marítimo *m*
register ton (E)	Registertonne *f*	—	tonneau de jauge *m*	tonnellata di registro *f*	tonelada de registro *f*
Registertonne (D)	—	register ton	tonneau de jauge *m*	tonnellata di registro *f*	tonelada de registro *f*
registration (E)	Anmeldung *f*	—	inscription *f*/ déclaration *f*	avviso *m*/ dichiarazione *f*	solicitud *f*/ declaración *f*
registre (F)	Register *n*	register	—	registro *m*	registro *m*
registre du commerce (F)	Handelsregister *n*	commercial register	—	registro commerciale *m*	registro mercantil *m*
registro (Es)	Register *n*	register	registre *m*	registro *m*	—
registro (I)	Register *n*	register	registre *m*	—	registro *m*
registro commerciale (I)	Handelsregister *n*	commercial register	registre du commerce *m*	—	registro mercantil *m*
registro marítimo (Es)	Schiffsregister *n*	register of ships	répertoire des navires *m*	registro navale *m*	—
registro mercantil (Es)	Handelsregister *n*	commercial register	registre du commerce *m*	registro commerciale *m*	—
registro navale (I)	Schiffsregister *n*	register of ships	répertoire des navires *m*	—	registro marítimo *m*
reglamentación del mercado agrícola (Es)	Agrarmarktordnung *f*	agricultural market organization	organisation des marchés agricoles *f*	regolamento del mercato agrario *m*	—
reglamentación de precios (Es)	Preislenkung *f*	administration of prices	réglementation des prix *f*	gestione dei prezzi *f*	—
reglamento de exportación (Es)	Ausfuhr-bestimmungen *pl*	export regulations	dispositions d'exportation *f pl*	disposizioni per le esportazioni *f pl*	—
reglamento del artesanado (Es)	Handwerksordnung *f*	Handicrafts Regulation Act	code de l'artisanat *m*	codice dell'artigianato *m*	—
règle de droit (F)	Rechtsnorm *f*	legal norm	—	norma giuridica *f*	norma jurídica *f*
règlement (F)	Abrechnung *f*	settlement of accounts	—	liquidazione *f*	liquidación *f*
réglementation des prix (F)	Preislenkung *f*	administration of prices	—	gestione dei prezzi *f*	reglamentación de precios *f*
règlement des frais de voyage (F)	Reisekosten-abrechnung *f*	travel expense accounting	—	conteggio dei costi di viaggio *m*	liquidación de los gastos de viaje *f*
règlement immédiat (F)	sofortige Regulierung *f*	settlement with immediate effect	—	regolazione immediata *f*	regulación inmediata *f*
règlement transitoire (F)	Übergangsregelung *f*	transitional arrangement	—	regolamento transitorio *m*	regulación transitoria *f*
régler par compte (F)	abzahlen	pay off	—	pagare a rate	pagar por cuotas
regolamento (I)	Verordnung *f*	decree	décret *m*	—	ordenanza *f*
regolamento del mercato agrario (I)	Agrarmarktordnung *f*	agricultural market organization	organisation des marchés agricoles *f*	—	reglamentación del mercado agrícola *f*
regolamento transitorio (I)	Übergangsregelung *f*	transitional arrangement	règlement transitoire *m*	—	regulación transitoria *f*
regolamento valutario internazionale (I)	internationale Währungsordnung *f*	international monetary system	régime monétaire international *m*	—	régimen monetario internacional *m*
regolare (I)	ordnungsgemäß	orderly	correct(e)	—	debidamente
regolazione immediata (I)	sofortige Regulierung *f*	settlement with immediate effect	règlement immédiat *m*	—	regulación inmediata *f*
regreso (Es)	Regreß *m*	recourse	recours *m*	regresso *m*	—
Regreß (D)	—	recourse	recours *m*	regresso *m*	regreso *m*
regresso[1] (I)	Rückgriff *m*	recourse	recours *m*	—	recurso *m*
regresso[2] (I)	Abschwung *m*	down-swing	dépression *f*	—	baja *f*

	D	E	F	I	Es
regresso[3] (I)	Regreß *m*	recourse	recours *m*	—	regreso *m*
regulación global (Es)	Globalsteuerung *f*	global control	régulation globale *f*	controllo globale *m*	—
regulación inmediata (Es)	sofortige Regulierung *f*	settlement with immediate effect	règlement immédiat *m*	regolazione immediata *f*	—
regulación transitoria (Es)	Übergangsregelung *f*	transitional arrangement	règlement transitoire *m*	regolamento transitorio *m*	—
regular customer (E)	Stammkunde *f*	—	client habituel *m*	cliente fisso *m*	cliente habitual *m*
regular customers (E)	Kundenstamm *m*	—	clients en portefeuille *m pl*	clientela fissa *f*	clientela fija *f*
regular meeting (E)	ordentliche Versammlung *f*	—	assemblée ordinaire *f*	assemblea ordinaria *f*	asamblea ordinaria *f*
régulation globale (F)	Globalsteuerung *f*	global control	—	controllo globale *m*	regulación golbal *f*
rehuso de aceptación (Es)	Annahme-verweigerung *f*	refusal of delivery	refus d'acceptation *m*	rifiuto d'accettazione *m*	—
Re-Import (D)	—	reimportation	réimportation *f*	reimportazione *f*	reimportación *f*
reimportación (Es)	Re-Import *m*	reimportation	réimportation *f*	reimportazione *f*	—
reimportation (E)	Re-Import *m*	—	réimportation *f*	reimportazione *f*	reimportación *f*
réimportation (F)	Re-Import *m*	reimportation	—	reimportazione *f*	reimportación *f*
reimportazione (I)	Re-Import *m*	reimportation	réimportation *f*	—	reimportación *f*
Reingewinn (D)	—	net profit	bénéfice net *m*	utile netto *m*	ganancia neta *f*
reinsurance (E)	Rückversicherung *f*	—	réassurance *f*	riassicurazione *f*	reaseguro *m*
reintegro (Es)	Abzahlung *f*	hire purchase	payement par acomptes *m*	pagamento a rate *m*	—
Reinvermögen (D)	—	net assets	avoir net *m*	patrimonio netto *m*	patrimonio neto *m*
reinversión (Es)	Reinvestition *f*	reinvestment	réinvestissement *m*	reinvestimento *m*	—
reinvestimento (I)	Reinvestition *f*	reinvestment	réinvestissement *m*	—	reinversión *f*
réinvestissement (F)	Reinvestition *f*	reinvestment	—	reinvestimento *m*	reinversión *f*
Reinvestition (D)	—	reinvestment	réinvestissement *m*	reinvestimento *m*	reinversión *f*
reinvestment (E)	Reinvestition *f*	—	réinvestissement *m*	reinvestimento *m*	reinversión *f*
Reisebüro (D)	—	travel agency	agence de voyages *f*	ufficio viaggi *m*	agencia de viajes *f*
Reisegepäck-versicherung (D)	—	baggage insurance	assurance des bagages *f*	assicurazione del bagaglio *f*	seguro de equipajes *m*
Reisekosten-abrechnung (D)	—	travel expense accounting	règlement des frais de voyage *m*	conteggio dei costi di viaggio *m*	liquidación de los gastos de viaje *f*
Reiseroute (D)	—	route	itinéraire *m*	itinerario *m*	itinerario *m*
Reiserücktritts-versicherung (D)	—	travel cancellation insurance	assurance de résilia-tion du voyage *f*	assicurazione reces-sione viaggio *f*	seguro de rescisión del viaje *m*
Reisescheck (D)	—	traveller's cheque	chèque de voyage *m*	assegno turistico *m*	cheque de viaje *m*
Reisespesen (D)	—	travel(l)ing expenses	frais de voyage *m pl*	spese di viaggio *f pl*	gastos de viaje *m pl*
reivindicación (Es)	Anspruch *m*	claim	prétention *f*	pretesa *f*	—
reivindicación salarial (Es)	Lohnforderung *f*	wage claim	revendication de salaire *f*	rivendicazione salariale *f*	—
Reklamation (D)	—	complaint	réclamation *f*	reclamo *m*	reclamación *f*
Reklame (D)	—	advertising	publicité *f*	réclame *f*	publicidad *f*
relación[1] (Es)	Relation *f*	relation	relation *f*	relazione *f*	—
relación[2] (Es)	Verhältnis *n*	proportion	relation *f*	rapporto *m*	—
relación comercial (Es)	Geschäfts-verbindung *f*	business relation	relation d'affaires *f*	relazione d'affari *f*	—
relación cotización-ganancia (Es)	Kurs-Gewinn-Verhältnis *n*	price-earnings ratio	relation cours-bénéfice *f*	rapporto corso-profitto *m*	—
relación de confianza (Es)	Vertrauens-verhältnis *n*	confidential relationship	rapport de confiance *m*	rapporto di fiducia *m*	—
relaciones comerciales[1] (Es)	Handels-beziehungen *pl*	trade relations	relations commerciales *f pl*	rapporti commerciali *m pl*	—
relaciones comerciales[2] (Es)	Geschäftsbeziehung *f*	business relation	relations d'affaires *f pl*	rapporti d'affari *m pl*	—
relaciones públicas[1] (Es)	Öffentlichkeitsarbeit *f*	public relations (work)	relations publiques *f pl*	relazioni pubbliche *f pl*	—
relaciones públicas[2] (Es)	Public Relations	public relations	relations publiques *f pl*	public relations *f pl*	—
relación jurídica (Es)	Rechtsverhältnis *n*	legal relationship	rapport juridique *m*	rapporto giuridico *m*	—

	D	E	F	I	Es
relación laboral (Es)	Arbeitsverhältnis *n*	employee-employer relationship	rapport de travail *m*	rapporto di lavoro *m*	—
relación laboral a prueba (Es)	Arbeitsverhältnis auf Probe *n*	employee-employer relationship on a trial basis	contrat de travail convenu à l'essai *m*	rapporto di lavoro in prova *m*	—
relance économique (F)	Konjunkturbelebung *f*	economic upturn	—	ripresa congiunturale *f*	recuperación coyuntural *f*
Relation (D)	—	relation	relation *f*	relazione *f*	relación *f*
relation (E)	Relation *f*	—	relation *f*	relazione *f*	relación *f*
relation[1] (F)	Verhältnis *n*	proportion	—	rapporto *m*	relación *f*
relation[2] (F)	Relation *f*	relation	—	relazione *f*	relación *f*
relation cours-bénéfice (F)	Kurs-Gewinn-Verhältnis *n*	price-earnings ratio	—	rapporto corso-profitto *m*	relación cotización-ganancia *f*
relation d'affaires (F)	Geschäfts-verbindung *f*	business relation	—	relazione d'affari *f*	relación comercial *f*
relations commerciales (F)	Handels-beziehungen *pl*	trade relations	—	rapporti commerciali *m pl*	relaciones comerciales *f pl*
relations d'affaires (F)	Geschäfts-beziehung *f*	business relation	—	rapporti d'affari *m pl*	relaciones comerciales *f pl*
relations publiques (F)	Öffentlichkeitsarbeit *f*	public relations (work)	—	relazioni pubbliche *f pl*	relaciones públicas *f pl*
relazione[1] (I)	Berichterstattung *f*	reporting	compte rendu *m*	—	reportaje *m*
relazione[2] (I)	Relation *f*	relation	relation *f*	—	relación *f*
relazione d'affari (I)	Geschäfts-verbindung *f*	business relation	relation d'affaires *f*	—	relación comercial *f*
relazione di costituzione (I)	Gründungsbericht *m*	formation report	procès-verbal de fondation *m*	—	informe de los fundadores *m*
relazione finanziaria (I)	Finanzbericht *m*	financial report	rapport financier *m*	—	informe financiero *m*
relazione generale sulla situazione economica (I)	Jahreswirtschafts-bericht *m*	Annual Economic Report	compte rendu d'activité économique annuel *m*	—	informe económico anual *m*
relazione sull'esercizio commerciale (I)	Geschäftsbericht *m*	business report	rapport de gestion *m*	—	informe *m*
relazioni pubbliche (I)	Öffentlichkeitsarbeit *f*	public relations (work)	relations publiques *f pl*	—	relaciones públicas *f pl*
relevant (D)	—	relevant	significatif	rilevante	importante
relevant (E)	relevant	—	significatif	rilevante	importante
relève d'équipe (F)	Schichtwechsel *m*	change of shift	—	cambio di turno *m*	cambio del equipo de obreros *m*
relèvement des impôts (F)	Steuererhöhung *f*	increase of taxes	—	aumento delle imposte *m*	aumento de los impuestos *m*
reliable (E)	zuverlässig	—	de confiance	affidabile	de confianza
remaining assets after liquidation (E)	Liquidationserlös *m*	—	produit de la liquidation *m*	ricavo della liquidazione *m*	haber social repartible *m*
remarque (F)	Vermerk *m*	note	—	annotazione *f*	nota *f*
remballer (F)	umpacken	repack	—	rifare l'imballaggio	reempaquetar
remboursement[1] (F)	Abzahlung *f*	repayment/ hire purchase	—	rimborso *m*/ pagamento a rate *m*	reintegro *m*/ pago a plazos *m*
remboursement[2] (F)	Rückerstattung *f*	repayment	—	rimborso *m*	restitución *f*
remboursement[3] (F)	Nachnahme *f*	cash on delivery	—	contrassegno *m*	reembolso *m*
Rembourskredit (D)	—	documentary acceptance credit	crédit documentaire confirmé *m*	credito di rimborso *m*	crédito de reembolso *m*
remembrement parcellaire (F)	Flurbereinigung *f*	compulsory consoli-dation of farmland	—	ricomposizione fondiaria *f*	concentración parcelaria *f*
remesa (Es)	Rimesse *f*	remittance	remise *f*	rimessa *f*	—
remettant (F)	Remittent *m*	payee	—	beneficiario *m*	remitente *m*
remettre en mains sûres (F)	zu treuen Händen	for safekeeping	—	alla particolare attenzione	a la atención
reminder (E)	Mahnbrief *m*	—	lettre d'avertissement *f*	lettera di sollecito *f*	carta (ad)monitoria *f*
remise[1] (F)	Übergabe *f*	delivery	—	consegna *f*	entrega *f*
remise[2] (F)	Rimesse *f*	remittance	—	rimessa *f*	remesa *f*
remise[3] (F)	Zustellung *f*	delivery	—	notifica *f*/recapito *m*	envío *m*

	D	E	F	I	Es
remise[4] (F)	Rabatt *m*	discount	—	ribasso *m*	rebaja *f*
remise[5] (F)	Aufschiebung *f*	postponement	—	rinvio *m*	aplazamiento *m*
remise de faveur (F)	Vorzugsrabatt *m*	preferential discount	—	ribasso preferenziale *m*	rebaja preferencial *f*
remise de quantité (F)	Mengenrabatt *m*	quantity discount	—	sconto di quantità *m*	rebaja de cantidad *f*
remise en ordre (F)	Nachbereitung *f*	aftertreatment	—	rielaborazione *f*	tratamiento ulterior *m*
remise par exprès (F)	Eilzustellung *f*	express delivery	—	consegna per espresso *f*	entrega urgente *f*
remise pour payement au comptant (F)	Barzahlungs-nachlaß *m*	discount for cash payment	—	sconto per pagamento in contanti *m*	descuento por pago al contado *m*
remise pour payement comptant (F)	Barzahlungsrabatt *m*	cash discount	—	ribasso per pagamento in contanti *m*	descuento por pago al contado *m*
remise sur le prix (F)	Preisnachlaß *m*	price reduction	—	ribasso del prezzo *m*	rebaja *f*
remitente[1] (Es)	Remittent *m*	payee	remettant *m*	beneficiario *m*	—
remitente[2] (Es)	Absender *m*	sender	envoyeur *m*	mittente *m*	—
remitido a la prensa (Es)	Pressemitteilung *f*	press release	commentaire de presse *m*	comunicazione stampa *f*	—
remittance[1] (E)	Überweisung *f*	—	virement *m*	rimessa *f*	transferencia *f*
remittance[2] (E)	Rimesse *f*	—	remise *f*	rimessa *f*	remesa *f*
Remittent (D)	—	payee	remettant *m*	beneficiario *m*	remitente *m*
remnants (E)	Restposten *m*	—	lot restant *m*	rimanenze *f pl*	partida restante *f*
remote data transmission (E)	Datenfern-übertragung *f*	—	télétransmission des données informatiques *f*	teletrasmissione dati *f*	transmisión de datos *f*
remuneración[1] (Es)	Gage *f*	salary	cachet *m*	onorario *m*	—
remuneración[2] (Es)	Vergütung *f*	remuneration	rémunération *f*	ricompensa *f*	—
remuneración del empresario (Es)	Unternehmerlohn *m*	entrepreneurial income	rémunération de l'entrepreneur *f*	retribuzione dell'imprenditore *f*	—
remuneration (E)	Vergütung *f*	—	rémunération *f*	ricompensa *f*	remuneración *f*
rémunération (F)	Vergütung *f*	remuneration	—	ricompensa *f*	remuneración *f*
rémunération de l'entrepreneur (F)	Unternehmerlohn *m*	entrepreneurial income	—	retribuzione dell'imprenditore *f*	remuneración del empresario *f*
rémunération du travail en nature (F)	Naturallohn *m*	wages (paid) in kind	—	remunerazione in natura *f*	salario en especie *m*
remuneration in kind (E)	Sachbezüge *pl*	—	prestations en nature *f pl*	retribuzioni in natura *f pl*	percepciónes en especie *f pl*
rémunération spéciale (F)	Sondervergütung *f*	special remuneration	—	compenso straordinario *m*	gratificación *f*
remunerazione in natura (I)	Naturallohn *m*	wages (paid) in kind	rémunérarion du travail en nature *f*	—	salario en especie *m*
rendement[1] (F)	Leistung *f*	performance	—	rendimento *m*	rendimiento *m*
rendement[2] (F)	Arbeitsleistung *f*	productivity	—	produttività *f*	productividad *f*
rendement[3] (F)	Rendite *f*	yield	—	rendita *f*	rentabilidad *f*
rendement du chiffre d'affaires (F)	Umsatzrendite *f*	net income percentage of turnover	—	rendita del fatturato *f*	rédito de la cifra de ventas *m*
rendement du travail (F)	Arbeitsertrag *m*	work performed	—	rendimento del lavoro *m*	rendimiento del trabajo *m*
rendement réel (F)	Realzins *m*	real (rate of) interest	—	tasso d'interesse reale *m*	interés real *m*
rendez-vous (F)	Treffpunkt *m*	meeting place	—	punto d'incontro *m*	lugar de la cita *m*
rendez-vous de présentation (F)	Vorstellungstermin *m*	date of interview	—	appuntamento di presentazione *m*	fecha de entrevista personal *f*
rendimento (I)	Leistung *f*	performance	rendement *m*	—	rendimiento *m*
rendimento del lavoro (I)	Arbeitsertrag *m*	work performed	rendement du travail *m*	—	rendimiento del trabajo *m*
rendimiento del capital (Es)	Kapitalertrag *m*	income from capital	produit du capital *m*	rendita del capitale *f*	—
rendimiento del trabajo (Es)	Arbeitsertrag *m*	work performed	rendement du travail *m*	rendimento del lavoro *m*	—
rendita (I)	Rendite *f*	yield	rendement *m*	—	rentabilidad *f*
rendita del capitale (I)	Kapitalertrag *m*	income from capital	produit du capital *m*	—	rendimiento del capital *m*

	D	E	F	I	Es
rendita del fatturato (I)	Umsatzrendite *f*	net income percentage of turnover	rendement du chiffre d'affaires *m*	—	rédito de la cifra de ventas *m*
rendita del produttore (I)	Produzentenrente *f*	producer's surplus	rente du vendeur *f*	—	superávit del productor *m*
Rendite (D)	—	yield	rendement *m*	rendita *f*	rentabilidad *f*
renewal costs (E)	Sanierungskosten *pl*	—	coûts d'assainissement *m pl*	costi di risanamento *m pl*	gastos de saneamiento *m pl*/ gastos de rehabilitación *m pl*
renonciation à la consommation (F)	Konsumverzicht *m*	voluntary constraint in consumption	—	rinuncia al consumo *f*	renuncia al consumo *f*
renseignement (F)	Auskunft *f*	information	—	informazione *f*	información *f*
renseignement fourni par l'intéressé lui-même (F)	Selbstauskunft *f*	voluntary disclosure	—	informazione volontaria *f*	información de sí mismo *f*
rent¹ (E)	Mietzins *m*	—	prix de location *m*	canone di locazione *m*	arrendamiento *m*
rent² (E)	Miete *f*	—	location *f*	canone di locazione *m*	alquiler *m*
renta (Es)	Rente *f*	annuity	rente *f*	rendita *f*	—
rentabilidad¹ (Es)	Ertragskraft *f*	earning capacity	force productive *f*	redditività *f*	—
rentabilidad² (Es)	Wirtschaftlichkeit *f*	economic efficiency	rentabilité *f*	economicità *f*	—
rentabilidad³ (Es)	Rendite *f*	yield	rendement *m*	rendita *f*	—
rentabilidad⁴ (Es)	Rentabilität *f*	profitability	rentabilité *f*	redditività *f*	—
rentabilidad del capital (Es)	Kapitalrentabilität *f*	return on investment	rentabilité du capital *f*	redditività del capitale *f*	—
Rentabilität (D)	—	profitability	rentabilité *f*	redditività *f*	rentabilidad *f*
Rentabilitätschwelle (D)	—	break-even point	seuil de rentabilité *m*	soglia di redditività *f*	límite inferior de rentabilidad *m*
rentabilité¹ (F)	Rentabilität *f*	profitability	—	redditività *f*	rentabilidad *f*
rentabilité² (F)	Wirtschaftlichkeit *f*	economic efficiency	—	economicità *f*	rentabilidad *f*
rentabilité du capital (F)	Kapitalrentabilität *f*	return on investment	—	redditività del capitale *f*	rentabilidad del capital *f*
renta del capital (Es)	Kapitalzins *m*	interest on capital	intérêt du capital *m*	interesse del capitale *m*	—
renta de la propiedad (Es)	Besitzeinkommen *n*	unearned income	revenu du patrimoine *m*	reddito da possesso *m*	—
Rente (D)	—	annuity	rente *f*	rendita *f*	renta *f*
rente (F)	Rente *f*	annuity	—	rendita *f*	renta *f*
rente du vendeur (F)	Produzentenrente *f*	producer's surplus	—	rendita del produttore *f*	superávit del productor *m*
Rentenanleihe (D)	—	annuity bonds	effet public *m*	prestito a reddito fisso *m*	empréstito por anualidades *m*
Rentenfonds (D)	—	pension fund	fonds d'Etat *m*/ effets publics *m pl*	fondo obbligazionario *m*	fondo de bonos *m*
Rentenmarkt (D)	—	bond market	marché des effets publics *m*	mercato dei titoli a reddito fisso *m*	mercado de títulos de renta fija *m*
Rentenpapiere (D)	—	bonds	titres de rente *m pl*	titoli a reddito fisso *m pl*	títulos de renta fija *m pl*
Rentenversicherung (D)	—	old-age pension insurance	assurance sociale invalidité-vieillesse *f*	assicurazione invalidità e vecchiaia *f*	seguro de pensiones *m*
renuncia al consumo (Es)	Konsumverzicht *m*	voluntary constraint in consumption	renonciation à la consommation *f*	rinuncia al consumo *f*	—
renvoi (F)	Rücksendung *f*	return	—	rispedizione *f*	devolución *f*
repack (E)	umpacken	—	remballer	rifare l'imballaggio	reempaquetar
repair¹ (E)	reparieren	—	réparer	riparare	reparar
repair² (E)	Reparatur *f*	—	réparation *f*	riparazione *f*	reparación *f*
repair instructions (E)	Reparaturanleitung *f*	—	instruction de réparation *f*	istruzione per la riparazione *f*	instrucción de reparación *f*
reparación (Es)	Reparatur *f*	repair	réparation *f*	riparazione *f*	—
reparar (Es)	reparieren	repair	réparer	riparare	—
réparation (F)	Reparatur *f*	repair	—	riparazione *f*	reparación *f*
Reparatur (D)	—	repair	réparation *f*	riparazione *f*	reparación *f*
Reparaturanleitung (D)	—	repair instructions	instruction de réparation *f*	istruzione per la riparazione *f*	instrucción de reparación *f*

	D	E	F	I	Es
réparer (F)	reparieren	repair	—	riparare	reparar
reparieren (D)	—	repair	réparer	riparare	reparar
répartition[1] (F)	Umlage *f*	charge levied	—	ripartizione *f*	reparto *m*
répartition[2] (F)	Zuteilung *f*	allocation	—	attribuzione *f*/ ripartizione *f*	asignación *f*
répartition des bénéfices (F)	Gewinnverteilung *f*	distribution of profits	—	ripartizione dell'utile *f*	reparto de beneficios *m*
répartition du patrimoine (F)	Vermögens-verteilung *f*	distribution of wealth	—	ripartizione del patrimonio *f*	reparto de la riqueza *m*
reparto (I)	Abteilung *f*	division/department	service *m*	—	sección *f*
reparto de beneficios (Es)	Gewinnverteilung *f*	distribution of profits	répartition des bénéfices *f*	ripartizione dell'utile *f*	—
reparto de la riqueza (Es)	Vermögens-verteilung *f*	distribution of wealth	repartition du patrimoine *f*	ripartizione del patrimonio *f*	—
reparto esportazioni (I)	Exportabteilung *f*	export department	service d'exportation *m*	—	departamento de exportación *m*
reparto marketing (I)	Marketingabteilung *f*	marketing department	bureau de marketing *m*	—	departamento de mercadeo *m*
reparto pubblicità (I)	Werbeabteilung *f*	publicity department	service de publicité *m*	—	sección de publicidad *f*
reparto spedizioni (I)	Versandabteilung *f*	dispatch department	service des expéditions *m*	—	departamento de expedición *m*
reparto tecnico (I)	technische Abteilung *f*	engineering department	service technique *m*	—	departamento técnico *m*
repayment[1] (E)	Abzahlung *f*	—	remboursement *m*/ payement par acomptes *m*	rimborso *m*/ pagamento a rate *m*	reintegro *m*/ pago a plazos *m*
repayment[2] (E)	Rückerstattung *f*	—	rembourse-ment *m*	rimborso *m*	restitución *f*
repeat (E)	Reprise *f*	—	tendance à la hausse *f*	ripresa *f*	segunda lectura en el corro *f*
repeat order (E)	Nachbestellung *f*	—	nouvel ordre *m*	ordinazione supplementare *f*	pedido suplementario *m*
repercusión (Es)	Feedback *n*	feedback	feed-back *m*	feedback *m*	—
répercussion (F)	Überwälzung *f*	passing on	—	accollamento *m*	traslación *f*
répertoire des navires (F)	Schiffsregister *n*	register of ships	—	registro navale *m*	registro marítimo *m*
replaceable (E)	substituierbar	—	interchangeable	sostituibile	sustituible
replacement (E)	Wiederbeschaffung *f*	—	réapprovisionne-ment *m*	riapprovvigiona-mento *m*	reposición *f*
reply (E)	Antwort *f*	—	réponse *f*	risposta *f*	respuesta *f*
répondeur automatique (F)	Anrufbeantworter *m*	answering machine	—	segreteria telefonica *f*	contestador de llamadas *m*
réponse (F)	Antwort *f*	reply	—	risposta *f*	respuesta *f*
Report (D)	—	report	rapport *m*	rapporto *m*	informe *m*
report (E)	Report *m*	—	rapport *m*	rapporto *m*	informe *m*
reportaje (Es)	Berichterstattung *f*	reporting	compte rendu *m*	relazione *f*	—
reporting (E)	Berichterstattung *f*	—	compte rendu *m*	relazione *f*	reportaje *m*
reposición (Es)	Wiederbeschaffung *f*	replacement	réapprovisionne-ment *m*	riapprovvigiona-mento *m*	—
Repräsentant (D)	—	representative	représentant *m*	rappresentante *m*	representante *m*
représaille (F)	Repressalie *f*	reprisals	—	rappresaglia *f*	represalia *f*
represalia (Es)	Repressalie *f*	reprisals	représaille *f*	rappresaglia *f*	—
representación (Es)	Vertretung *f*	representation	représentation *f*	rappresentanza *f*	—
representación comercial (Es)	Handelsvertretung *f*	commercial agency	représentation commerciale *f*	rappresentanza commerciale *f*	—
representación de intereses (Es)	Interessen-vertretung *f*	representation of interests	représentation des intérêts *f*	rappresentanza degli interessi *f*	—
representación en el exterior (Es)	Auslandsvertretung *f*	agency abroad	agence à l'étranger *f*	rappresentanza estera *f*	—
representación exclusiva (Es)	Alleinvertretung *f*	sole agency	agence exclusive *f*	rappresentanza esclusiva *f*	—
représentant (F)	Vertreter *m*	representative	—	rappresentante *m*	representante *m*

	D	E	F	I	Es
représentant de commerce (F)	Handelsvertreter *m*	commercial agent	—	rappresentante commerciale *m*	representante comercial *m*
representante (Es)	Vertreter *m*	representative	représentant *m*	rappresentante *m*	—
representante comercial (Es)	Handelsvertreter *m*	commercial agent	représentant de commerce *m*	rappresentante commerciale *m*	—
representante general (Es)	Generalvertreter *m*	general agent	agent général *m*	rappresentante generale *m*	—
representante regional (Es)	Gebietsvertreter *m*	area representative	représentant régional *m*	agente di zona *m*	—
représentant régional (F)	Gebietsvertreter *m*	area representative	—	agente di zona *m*	representante regional *m*
representation (E)	Vertretung *f*	—	représentation *f*	rappresentanza *f*	representación *f*
représentation (F)	Vertretung *f*	representation	—	rappresentanza *f*	representación *f*
représentation commerciale (F)	Handelsvertretung *f*	commercial agency	—	rappresentanza commerciale *f*	representación comercial *f*
représentation des intérêts (F)	Interessen-vertretung *f*	representation of interests		rappresentanza degli interessi *f*	representación de intereses *f*
representation of interests (E)	Interessen-vertretung *f*	—	représentation des intérêts *f*	rappresentanza degli interessi *f*	representación de intereses *f*
representative (E)	Vertreter *m*	—	représentant *m*	rappresentante *m*	representante *m*
Repressalie (D)	—	reprisals	représaille *f*	rappresaglia *f*	represalia *f*
reprisals (E)	Repressalie *f*	—	représaille *f*	rappresaglia *f*	represalia *f*
Reprise (D)	—	repeat	tendance à la hausse *f*	ripresa *f*	segunda lectura en el corro *f*
reprise d'une affaire (F)	Geschäfts-übernahme *f*	business acquisition	—	acquisto di un'azienda *m*	adquisición de una empresa *f*
Reprivatisierung (D)	—	reversion to private ownership	dénationalisation *f*	riprivatizzazione *f*	desnacionalización *f*
reproducción (Es)	Vervielfältigung *f*	reproduction	reproduction *f*	riproduzione *f*	—
reproduction (E)	Vervielfältigung *f*	—	reproduction *f*	riproduzione *f*	reproducción *f*/ multiplicación *f*
reproduction (F)	Vervielfältigung *f*	reproduction	—	riproduzione *f*	reproducción *f*/ multiplicación *f*
reproduction cost (E)	Reproduktions-kosten *pl*	—	coût de reproduction *m*	costi di riproduzione *m pl*	gastos de reprducción *m pl*
reproduction value (E)	Reproduktionswert *m*	—	valeur de remplacement *f*	valore di riproduzione *m*	valor de reproducción *m*
Reproduktion (D)	—	reproduction	reproduction *f*	riproduzione *f*	reproducción *f*
Reproduktions-kosten (D)	—	reproduction cost	coût de reproduction *m*	costi di riproduzione *m pl*	gastos de reprducción *m pl*
Reproduktionswert (D)	—	reproduction value	valeur de remplacement *f*	valore di riproduzione *m*	valor de reproducción *m*
reputación (Es)	Leumund *m*	reputation	réputation *f*	reputazione *f*	—
reputation (E)	Leumund *m*	—	réputation *f*	reputazione *f*	reputación *f*
réputation (F)	Leumund *m*	reputation	—	reputazione *f*	reputación *f*
reputazione (I)	Leumund *m*	reputation	réputation *f*	—	reputación *f*
requirement characteristics (E)	Anforderungs-merkmal *n*	—	caractéristique d'exigences *f*	caratteristica richiesta *f*	característica de requisitos *f*
requirement factors (E)	Bedarfsfaktoren *pl*	—	éléments pouvant influencer la demande *m pl*	fattori del fabbisogno *m pl*	factores determinantes de las necesidades *m pl*
requirement of information (E)	Informationsbedarf *m*	—	besoin d'information *m*	bisogno d'informazioni *m*	necesidad de información *f*
resale price (E)	Wieder-verkaufspreis *m*	—	prix de revente *m*	prezzo di rivendita *m*	precio de reventa *m*
rescisión (Es)	Kündigung *f*	notice of termination (of employment)	licenciement *m*	licenziamento *m*	—
rescission (E)	Rücktritt *m*	—	démission *f*/résolution du contrat *f*	recesso *m*	rescisión *f*
research (E)	Forschung *f*	—	recherche *f*	ricerca *f*	investigación *f*
réseau (F)	Netzwerk *n*	network	—	rete *f*	red *f*
réseau de succursales (F)	Filialnetz *n*	branch network	—	rete delle filiali *f*	red de sucursales *f*

	D	E	F	I	Es
réseau linéaire pour planification (F)	Netzplan *m*	network planning	—	pianificazione reticolare *f*	planificación reticular *f*
réseau routier (F)	Straßennetz *n*	road network	—	rete stradale *f*	red de carreteras *f*
reseller (E)	Wiederverkäufer *m*	—	revendeur *m*	rivenditore *m*	revendedor *m*
reserva (Es)	Rückstellung *f*	reserves	provision pour pertes et charges *f*	accantonamento *m*	—
reservación (Es)	Reservierung *f*	reservation	réservation *f*	prenotazione *f*	—
reserva de liquidez (Es)	Liquiditätsreserve *f*	liquidity reserves	réserves de liquidité *f pl*	riserva di liquidità *f*	—
reserva mínima (Es)	Mindestreserve *f*	minimum reserves	réserve minimum *f*	riserva minima obbligatoria *f*	—
reservas (Es)	Rücklagen *pl*	reserves	réserve *f*	riserve *f pl*	—
reserva tácita[1] (Es)	stille Rücklage *f*	latent funds	réserve cachée *f*	riserva latente *m*	—
reserva tácita[2] (Es)	stille Reserve *f*	hidden reserves	réserve cachée *f*	riserva occulta *f*	—
reservation[1] (E)	Vorbestellung *f*	—	commande préalable *f*	ordinazione anticipata *f*	pedidio anticipado *m*
reservation[2] (E)	Reservierung *f*	—	réservation *f*	prenotazione *f*	reservación *f*
réservation (F)	Reservierung *f*	reservation	—	prenotazione *f*	reservación *f*
reservation confirmation (E)	Reservierungs-bestätigung *f*	—	confirmation de réservation *f*	conferma della prenotazione *f*	confirmación de la reservación *f*
Reserve (D)	—	reserve stock/ reserves	stocks de ré-serve *m pl*/réserve *f*	scorte *f pl*/ riserva *f*	existencias *f pl*/ reserva *f*
réserve (F)	Rücklagen *pl*	reserves	—	riserve *f pl*	reservas *f pl*
réserve cachée[1] (F)	stille Rücklage *f*	latent funds	—	riserva latente *m*	reserva tácita *f*
réserve cachée[2] (F)	stille Reserve *f*	hidden reserves	—	riserva occulta *f*	reserva tácita *f*
reserve currency (E)	Reservewährung *f*	—	monnaie de réserve *f*	valuta di riserva *f*	moneda de reserva *f*
réserve de capital (F)	Kapitalstock *m*	capital stock	—	riserva di capitale *f*	fondo de capital *m*
Reservefonds (D)	—	reserve fund	fonds de réserve *m*	fondo di riserva *m*	fondo de reserva *m*
reserve fund (E)	Reservefonds *m*	—	fonds de réserve *m*	fondo di riserva *m*	fondo de reserva *m*
réserve minimum (F)	Mindestreserve *f*	minimum reserves	—	riserva minima obbligatoria *f*	reserva mínima *f*
reserves[1] (E)	Rücklagen *pl*	—	réserve *f*	riserve *f pl*	reservas *f pl*
reserves[2] (E)	Rückstellung *f*	—	provision pour pertes et charges *f*	accantonamento *m*	reserva *f*
réserves de liquidité (F)	Liquiditätsreserve *f*	liquidity reserves	—	riserva di liquidità *f*	reserva de liquidez *f*
reserve stock (E)	Reserve *f*	—	stocks de ré-serve *m pl*/réserve *f*	scorte *f pl*/ riserva *f*	existencias *f pl*/ reserva *f*
Reservewährung (D)	—	reserve currency	monnaie de réserve *f*	valuta di riserva *f*	moneda de reserva *f*
Reservierung (D)	—	reservation	réservation *f*	prenotazione *f*	reservación *f*
Reservierungs-bestätigung (D)	—	reservation confirmation	confirmation de réservation *f*	conferma della prenotazione *f*	confirmación de la reservación *f*
resguardo de almacén (Es)	Lagerschein *m*	warehouse warrant	certificat de dépôt *m*	ricevuta di deposito *f*	—
residence permit (E)	Aufenthaltserlaubnis *f*	—	autorisation de séjour *f*	permesso di soggiorno *m*	permiso de residencia *m*
resident (E)	Deviseninländer *m*	—	résident *m*	persona residente *f*	residente *m*
résident (F)	Deviseninländer *m*	resident	—	persona residente *f*	residente *m*
residente (Es)	Deviseninländer *m*	resident	résident *m*	persona residente *f*	—
residents' registration office (E)	Einwohnermelde-amt *n*	—	bureau de déclaration de résidence *m*	ufficio anagrafe *m*	oficina del censo *f*
residual time to maturity (E)	Restlaufzeit *f*	—	durée restante *f*	scadenza residua *f*	plazo de vencimiento restante *m*
residual value (E)	Restwert *m*	—	valeur résiduelle *f*	valore rimanente *m*	valor residual *m*/ valor contable residual *m*
residues (E)	Rückstände *pl*	—	déchet *m*	residui *m pl*	residuos *m pl*
residui (I)	Rückstände *pl*	residues	déchet *m*	—	residuos *m pl*
residuos (Es)	Rückstände *pl*	residues	déchet *m*	residui *m pl*	—
résiliation (F)	Kündigung *f*	notice of termination	—	disdetta *f*	rescisión *f*

	D	E	F	I	Es
resistente alle crisi (I)	krisenfest	slump-proof	insensible aux influences de la crise économique	—	a prueba de crisis
resolución (Es)	Resolution *f*	resolution	résolution *f*	risoluzione *f*	—
Resolution (D)	—	resolution	résolution *f*	risoluzione *f*	resolución *f*
resolution (E)	Resolution *f*	—	résolution *f*	risoluzione *f*	resolución *f*
résolution (F)	Resolution *f*	resolution	—	risoluzione *f*	resolución *f*
resources (E)	Ressource *f*	—	ressource *f*	risorsa *f*	recurso *m*
respite (E)	Stundung *f*	—	prorogation *f*	dilazione *f*/proroga *f*	moratoria *f*
responsabilidad (Es)	Haftung *f*	liability	responsabilité *f*	responsabilità *f*	—
responsabilidad civil del fabricante (Es)	Produzentenhaftung *f*	product liability	responsabilité du producteur *f*	responsabilità di produttore *f*	—
responsabilidad de garantía (Es)	Gewährleistungs-haftung *f*	liability for breach of warranty	responsabilité en matière de garantie *f*	responsabilità di garanzia *f*	—
responsabilidad del productor (Es)	Produkthaftung *f*	product liability	responsabilité du fabricant *f*	responsabilità prodotto *f*	—
responsabilidad jurídica (Es)	Rechtshaftung *f*	legal responsibility	responsabilité légale *f*	responsabilità giuridica *f*	—
responsabilidad primaria (Es)	Primärhaftung *f*	primary responsibility	responsabilité primaire *f*	responsabilità primaria *f*	—
responsabilità (I)	Haftung *f*	liability	responsabilité *f*	—	responsabilidad *f*
responsabilità di garanzia (I)	Gewährleistungs-haftung *f*	liability for breach of warranty	responsabilité en matière de garantie *f*	—	responsabilidad de garantía *f*
responsabilità di produttore (I)	Produzentenhaftung *f*	product liability	responsabilité du producteur *f*	—	responsabilidad civil del fabricante *f*
responsabilità giuridica (I)	Rechtshaftung *f*	legal responsibility	responsabilité légale *f*	—	responsabilidad jurídica *f*
responsabilità primaria (I)	Primärhaftung *f*	primary responsibility	responsabilité primaire *f*	—	responsabilidad primaria *f*
responsabilità prodotto (I)	Produkthaftung *f*	product liability	responsabilité du fabricant *f*	—	responsabilidad del productor *f*
responsabilité (F)	Haftung *f*	liability	—	responsabilità *f*	responsabilidad *f*
responsabilité du fabricant (F)	Produkthaftung *f*	product liability	—	responsabilità prodotto *f*	responsabilidad del productor *f*
responsabilité du producteur (F)	Produzentenhaftung *f*	product liability	—	responsabilità di produttore *f*	responsabilidad civil del fabricante *f*
responsabilité en matière de garantie (F)	Gewährleistungs-haftung *f*	liability for breach of warranty	—	responsabilità di garanzia *f*	responsabilidad de garantía *f*
responsabilité légale (F)	Rechtshaftung *f*	legal responsibility	—	responsabilità giuridica *f*	responsabilidad jurídica *f*
responsabilité primaire (F)	Primärhaftung *f*	primary responsibility	—	responsabilità primaria *f*	responsabilidad primaria *f*
respuesta (Es)	Antwort *f*	reply	réponse *f*	risposta *f*	—
Ressource (D)	—	resources	ressource *f*	risorsa *f*	recurso *m*
ressource (F)	Ressource *f*	resources	—	risorsa *f*	recurso *m*
Restdarlehen (D)	—	purchase-money loan	prêt restant *m*	mutuo residuo *m*	restante de un préstamo *m*
restitución[1] (Es)	Rückgabe *f*	return	restitution *f*	restituzione *f*	—
restitución[2] (Es)	Rückerstattung *f*	repayment	remboursement *m*	rimborso *m*	—
restitution (F)	Rückgabe *f*	return	—	restituzione *f*	restitución *f*
restituzione (I)	Rückgabe *f*	return	restitution *f*	—	restitución *f*
Restlaufzeit (D)	—	residual time to maturity	durée restante *f*	scadenza residua *f*	plazo de vencimiento restante *m*
Restposten (D)	—	remnants	lot restant *m*	rimanenze *f pl*	partida restante *f*
restraint of competition (E)	Wettbewerbs-beschränkung *f*	—	restriction apportée à la concurrence *f*	restrizione della concorrenza *f*	restricciones a la competencia *f pl*
restricción (Es)	Restriktion *f*	restriction	restriction *f*	restrizione *f*	—
restricción a la exportación (Es)	Ausfuhr-beschränkung *f*	export restriction	contingentement de l'exportation *m*	restrizione delle esportazioni *f*	—
restricción a la importación (Es)	Einfuhr-beschränkung *f*	import restriction	limitation des importations *f*	restrizione d'importazione *f*	—
restricción de créditos (Es)	Kreditrestriktion *f*	credit restriction	restriction du crédit *f*	restrizione creditizia *f*	—

	D	E	F	I	Es
restricción de la liquidez (Es)	Liquiditätsengpaß *m*	liquidity squeeze	goulot d'étranglement dans la trésorerie	strettoia di liquidità *f*	—
restricciones a la competencia (Es)	Wettbewerbsbeschränkung *f*	restraint of competition	restriction apportée à la concurrence *f*	restrizione della concorrenza *f*	—
restricciones commerciales (Es)	Handelsbeschränkungen *pl*	trade restrictions	restrictions au commerce *f pl*	restrizioni commerciali *f pl*	—
restricción monetaria (Es)	Geldverknappung *f*	monetary restriction	pénurie d'argent *f*	riduzione del denaro *f*	—
restriction (E)	Restriktion *f*	—	restriction *f*	restrizione *f*	restricción *f*
restriction (F)	Restriktion *f*	restriction	—	restrizione *f*	restricción *f*
restriction apportée à la concurrence (F)	Wettbewerbsbeschränkung *f*	restraint of competition	—	restrizione della concorrenza *f*	restricciones a la competencia *f pl*
restriction du crédit (F)	Kreditrestriktion *f*	credit restriction	—	restrizione creditizia *f*	restricción de créditos *f*
restriction on cultivation (E)	Anbaubeschränkung *f*	—	limitation des cultures *f*	restrizione di coltivazione *f*	limitación de cultivos *f*
restrictions au commerce (F)	Handelsbeschränkungen *pl*	trade restrictions	—	restrizioni commerciali *f pl*	restricciones commerciales *f pl*
Restriktion (D)	—	restriction	restriction *f*	restrizione *f*	restricción *f*
Restrisiko (D)	—	acceptable risk	risque acceptable *m*	rischio rimanente *m*	riesgo aceptable *m*
restrizione (I)	Restriktion *f*	restriction	restriction *f*	—	restricción *f*
restrizione creditizia (I)	Kreditrestriktion *f*	credit restriction	restriction du crédit *f*	—	restricción de créditos *f*
restrizione della concorrenza (I)	Wettbewerbsbeschränkung *f*	restraint of competition	restriction apportée à la concurrence *f*	—	restricciones a la competencia *f pl*
restrizione delle esportazioni (I)	Ausfuhrbeschränkung *f*	export restriction	contingentement de l'exportation *m*	—	restricción a la exportación *f*
restrizione di coltivazione (I)	Anbaubeschränkung *f*	restriction on cultivation	limitation des cultures *f*	—	limitación de cultivos *f*
restrizione d'importazione (I)	Einfuhrbeschränkung *f*	import restriction	limitation des importations *f*	—	restricción a la importación *f*
restrizioni commerciali (I)	Handelsbeschränkungen *pl*	trade restrictions	restrictions au commerce *f pl*	—	restricciones commerciales *f pl*
restructuration (F)	Umstrukturierung *f*	restructuring	—	ristrutturazione *f*	reestructuración *f*
restructuring (E)	Umstrukturierung *f*	—	restructuration *f*	ristrutturazione *f*	reestructuración *f*
Restwert (D)	—	residual value/ net book value	valeur résiduelle *f*	valore rimanente *m*	valor residual *m*/valor contable residual *m*
result (E)	Ergebnis *n*	—	résultat *m*	risultato *m*	resultado *m*
resultado (Es)	Ergebnis *n*	result	résultat *m*	risultato *m*	—
résultat (F)	Ergebnis *n*	result	—	risultato *m*	resultado *m*
résultats effectifs (F)	Istzahlen *pl*	actual figures	—	dati effettivi *m pl*	cifras efectivas *f pl*
retailer (E)	Einzelhändler *m*	—	commerçant détaillant *m*	dettagliante *m*	minorista *m*
retail merchant (E)	Einzelhandelskaufmann *m*	—	détaillant *m*	commerciante al dettaglio *m*	comerciante particular *m*
retail price (E)	Ladenpreis *m*	—	prix de vente *m*	prezzo di vendita *m*	precio de venta *m*
retail price margin (E)	Einzelhandelsspanne *f*	—	marge de détail *f*	margine del commercio al dettaglio *m*	margen del comercio al por menor *m*
retail trade (E)	Einzelhandel *m*	—	commerce de détail *m*	commercio al dettaglio *m*	comercio al por menor *m*
retard (F)	Verspätung *f*	delay	—	ritardo *m*	retraso *m*
retardataire (F)	säumig	dilatory	—	moroso	moroso
retard d'adaptation (F)	Anpassungsverzögerung *f*	adjustment lag	—	ritardo d'adattamento *m*	retraso de adaptación *m*
retard dans la livraison (F)	Lieferungsverzögerung *f*	delay in delivery	—	ritardo della consegna *m*	demora en la entrega *f*
rete (I)	Netzwerk *n*	network	réseau *m*	—	red *f*
rete delle filiali (I)	Filialnetz *n*	branch network	réseau de succursales *m*	—	red de sucursales *f*
rete di distribuzione (I)	Vertriebsweg *m*	distribution channel	canal de distribution *m*	—	circuito de distribución *f*
rete stradale[1] (I)	Straßennetz *n*	road network	réseau routier *m*	—	red de carreteras *f*
rete stradale[2] (I)	Wegenetz *n*	road network	voirie *f*	—	comunicaciones *f pl*

	D	E	F	I	Es
retórica (Es)	Rhetorik *f*	rhetoric	rhétorique *f*	retorica *f*	—
retorica (I)	Rhetorik *f*	rhetoric	rhétorique *f*	—	retórica *f*
retraining (E)	Umschulung *f*	—	rééducation professionnelle *f*	riqualificazione professionale *f*	readaptación profesional *f*
retraso[1] (Es)	Verspätung *f*	delay	retard *m*	ritardo *m*	—
retraso[2] (Es)	Verzug *m*	delay	demeure *f*	mora *f*	—
retraso de adaptación (Es)	Anpassungs-verzögerung *f*	adjustment lag	retard d'adaptation *m*	ritardo d'adattamento *m*	—
retraso en el pago (Es)	Zahlungsverzug *m*	failure to pay on due date	demeure du débiteur *f*	morosità di pagamento *f*	—
retribuciones (Es)	Bezüge *pl*	earnings	émoluments *m pl*	entrate *f pl*	—
retribución por vacaciones (Es)	Urlaubsgeld *n*	holiday allowance	prime de vacances *f*	indennità di ferie *f*	—
retribuzione (I)	Besoldung *f*	pay	rétribution *f*	—	sueldo *m*
retribuzione dell'imprenditore (I)	Unternehmerlohn *m*	entrepreneurial income	salaire de l'entrepreneur *m*	—	remuneración del empresario *f*
retribuzione per il lavoro a cottimo (I)	Akkordlohn *m*	piece work wages	salaire à la pièce *m*	—	salario a destajo *m*
retribuzioni in natura (I)	Sachbezüge *pl*	remuneration in kind	prestations en nature *f pl*	—	percepciónes en especie *f pl*
rétroactif (F)	rückwirkend	retrospective	—	con effetto retroattivo	retroactivo
retroactivo (Es)	rückwirkend	retrospective	rétroactif	con effetto retroattivo	—
retrospective (E)	rückwirkend	—	rétroactif	con effetto retroattivo	retroactivo
rettifica del valore (I)	Wertberichtigung *f*	value adjustment	réévaluation *f*	—	rectificación de valor *f*
return[1] (E)	Rücksendung *f*	—	renvoi *m*	rispedizione *f*	devolución *f*
return[2] (E)	Rückgabe *f*	—	restitution *f*	restituzione *f*	restitución *f*
return on investment (E)	Kapitalrentabilität *f*	—	rentabilité du capital *f*	redditività del capitale *f*	rentabilidad del capital *f*
return ticket (E)	Rückfahrkarte *f*	—	billet d'aller et retour *m*	biglietto di andata e ritorno *m*	billete de ida y vuelta *m*
reunión (Es)	Tagung *f*	meeting	congrès *m*	convegno *m*	—
réunion des associés (F)	Gesellschafter-versammlung *f*	meeting of shareholders	—	assemblea dei soci *f*	junta social *f*
réutilisable (F)	wiederverwertbar	recyclable	—	riutilizzabile	recuperable
revalorisation (F)	Aufwertung *f*	revaluation	—	rivalutazione *f*	revalorización *f*
revalorización (Es)	Aufwertung *f*	revaluation	revalorisation *f*	rivalutazione *f*	—
revaluation (E)	Aufwertung *f*	—	revalorisation *f*	rivalutazione *f*	revalorización *f*
revendedor (Es)	Wiederverkäufer *m*	reseller	revendeur *m*	rivenditore *m*	—
revendeur (F)	Wiederverkäufer *m*	reseller	—	rivenditore *m*	revendedor *m*
revendication de salaire (F)	Lohnforderung *f*	wage claim	—	rivendicazione salariale *f*	reivindicación salarial *f*
revenu[1] (F)	Einkommen *n*	income	—	reddito *m*	ingresos *m pl*/renta *f*
revenu[2] (F)	Einnahmen *pl*	receipts	—	entrate *f pl*	ingresos *m pl*
revenu annuel (F)	Jahreseinkommen *n*	annual income	—	reddito annuale *m*	renta anual *f*
revenu brut (F)	Bruttoeinkommen *n*	gross income	—	reddito lordo *m*	ingreso bruto *m*
revenu de base (F)	Basiseinkommen *n*	basic income	—	introiti base *m pl*	salario base *m*
revenu disponible (F)	verfügbares Einkommen *n*	disposable income	—	introito disponibile *m*	ingresos disponibles *m pl*
revenu du capital (F)	Kapitaleinkommen *n*	unearned income	—	reddito del capitale *m*	ganancias de capital *f pl*
revenu du patrimoine (F)	Besitzeinkommen *n*	unearned income	—	reddito da possesso *m*	renta de la propiedad *f*
revenu fixe (F)	Festeinkommen *n*	fixed income	—	reddito fisso *m*	salario fijo *m*
revenu national (F)	Volkseinkommen *n*	national income	—	reddito nazionale *m*	renta nacional *f*
revenu net (F)	Nettoeinkommen *n*	net income	—	reddito netto *m*	ingreso neto *m*
revenu nominal (F)	Nominal-einkommen *n*	nominal income	—	reddito nominale *m*	ingresos nominales *m*
revenu réel (F)	Realeinkommen *n*	real income	—	reddito reale *m*	ingreso real *m*
reversion to private ownership (E)	Reprivatisierung *f*	—	dénationalisation *f*	riprivatizzazione *f*	desnacionalización *f*

	D	E	F	I	Es
Revision (D)	—	audit/examination	vérification *f*/ contrôle *m*	revisione *f*/verifica *f*	revisión *f*/ examinación *f*
revisión[1] (Es)	Nachprüfung *f*	reexamination	vérification *f*	revisione *f*	—
revisión[2] (Es)	Revision *f*	audit/examination	vérification *f*/ contrôle *m*	revisione *f*/verifica *f*	—
revisión contable (Es)	Abschlußprüfung *f*	audit	vérification des comptes *f*	revisione *f*	—
revisione[1] (I)	Revision *f*	audit/examination	vérification *f*/ contrôle *m*	—	revisión *f*/ examinación *f*
revisione[2] (I)	Nachprüfung *f*	reexamination	vérification *f*	—	revisión *f*
revisione[3] (I)	Wirtschaftsprüfung *f*	auditing	contrôle de la gestion et des comptes *m*	—	revisoría *f*
revisione[4] (I)	Abschlußprüfung *f*	audit	vérification des comptes *f*	—	revisión contable *f*
revisione aziendale (I)	Betriebsprüfung *f*	investigation by the tax authorities	vérification des livres de l'entreprise *f*	—	inspección de la explotación *f*
revisione del piano (I)	Planrevision *f*	budget adjustment	révision des coûts marginaux *f*	—	ajuste presupuestario *m*
revisor contable[1] (Es)	Rechnungsprüfer *m*	auditor	commissaire aux comptes *m*	revisore dei conti *m*	—
revisor contable[2] (Es)	Abschlußprüfer *m*	auditor	vérificateur des comptes *m*	revisore *m*	—
revisor de cuentas (Es)	Wirtschaftsprüfer *m*	auditor	expert comptable économique et financier *m*/commissaire aux comptes *m*	revisore dei conti *m*	—
revisore (I)	Abschlußprüfer *m*	auditor	vérificateur des comptes *m*	—	revisor contable *m*
revisore aziendale (I)	Betriebsprüfer *m*	auditor	expert-comptable *m*	—	contador público *m*
revisore dei conti[1] (I)	Rechnungsprüfer *m*	auditor	commissaire aux comptes *m*	—	revisor contable *m*
revisore dei conti[2] (I)	Wirtschaftsprüfer *m*	auditor	expert comptable économique et financier *m*	—	revisor de cuentas *m*/ experto contable *m*
revisoría (Es)	Wirtschaftsprüfung *f*	auditing	contrôle de la gestion et des comptes *m*	revisione *f*	—
revista para los clientes (Es)	Kundenzeitschrift *f*	customer magazine	journal destiné à la clientèle *m*	periodico per i clienti *m*	—
revocable (Es)	kündbar	redeemable/callable	résiliable/ remboursable	risolubile/redimibile	—
revocar (Es)	widerrufen	revoke	révoquer	revocare	—
revocare (I)	widerrufen	revoke	révoquer	—	revocar
revocation clause (E)	Widerrufsklausel *f*	—	clause de révocation *f*	clausola di revoca *f*	cláusula revocatoria *f*
revoke (E)	widerrufen	—	révoquer	revocare	revocar
revolving credit (E)	Revolving-Kredit *m*	—	crédit rotatif *m*	credito rotativo *m*	crédito rotativo *m*
Revolving-Kredit (D)	—	revolving credit	crédit rotatif *m*	credito rotativo *m*	crédito rotativo *m*
révoquer (F)	widerrufen	revoke	—	revocare	revocar
Rezession (D)	—	recession	récession *f*	recessione *f*	recesión *f*
Reziprozität (D)	—	reciprocity	réciprocité *f*	reciprocità *f*	reciprocidad *f*
rhetoric (E)	Rhetorik *f*	—	rhétorique *f*	retorica *f*	retórica *f*
Rhetorik (D)	—	rhetoric	rhétorique *f*	retorica *f*	retórica *f*
rhétorique (F)	Rhetorik *f*	rhetoric	—	retorica *f*	retórica *f*
rialzo dei prezzi (I)	Preiserhöhung *f*	price increase	augmentation des prix *f*	—	aumento de precios *m*
riapprovvigionamento (I)	Wiederbeschaffung *f*	replacement	réapprovisionnement *m*	—	reposición *f*
riassicurazione (I)	Rückversicherung *f*	reinsurance	réassurance *f*	—	reaseguro *m*
ribasso[1] (I)	Rabatt *m*	discount	remise *f*	—	rebaja *f*
ribasso[2] (I)	Verbilligung *f*	cheapening	réduction du prix *f*	—	abaratamiento *m*
ribasso dei costi (I)	Kostensenkung *f*	cost reduction	diminution des coûts *f*	—	reducción de coste *f*
ribasso del prezzo (I)	Preisnachlaß *m*	price reduction	remise sur le prix *f*	—	rebaja *f*

	D	E	F	I	Es
ribasso per ordinazioni anticipate (I)	Vorbestellrabatt *m*	discount on advance orders	escompte de suscription *m*	—	descuento de suscripción *m*
ribasso per pagamento in contanti (I)	Barzahlungsrabatt *m*	cash discount	remise pour payement comptant *f*	—	descento por pago al contado *m*
ribasso preferenziale (I)	Vorzugsrabatt *m*	preferential discount	remise de faveur *f*	—	rebaja preferencial *f*
ribasso speciale (I)	Sonderrabatt *m*	special discount	ristourne exceptionnelle *f*	—	descuento suplementario *m*
ricavo della liquidazione (I)	Liquidationserlös *m*	remaining assets after liquidation	produit de la liquidation *m*	—	haber social repartible *m*
ricavo delle vendite (I)	Verkaufserlös *m*	sale proceeds	produit des ventes *m*	—	producto de la venta *m*
ricavo netto (I)	Nettoertrag *m*	net earnings	produit net *m*	—	producto neto *m*
ricerca (I)	Forschung *f*	research	recherche *f*	—	investigación *f*
ricerca di mercato (I)	Marktforschung *f*	market research	recherche du marché *f*	—	estudio del mercado *m*
ricerca di mercato empirica (I)	empirische Marktforschung *f*	empirical market research	étude de marché empirique *f*	—	estudio del mercado empírico *m*
ricerche spaziali (I)	Raumforschung *f*	space research	recherches spatiales *f pl*	—	investigación espacial *f*
ricevuta (I)	Empfangsbestätigung *f*	acknowledgement of receipt	accusé de réception *m*	—	recibo *m*
ricevuta di deposito (I)	Lagerschein *m*	warehouse warrant	certificat de dépôt *m*	—	resguardo de almacén *m*
ricevuta di ritorno (I)	Rückschein *m*	advice of delivery	avis de réception *m*	—	acuse de recibo *m*
richiesta[1] (I)	Anfrage *f*	inquiry	demande *f*	—	demanda *f*
richiesta[2] (I)	Abruf *m*	call	appel *m*	—	reclamación de la entrega de un pedido *f*
Richter (D)	—	judge	juge *m*	giudice *m*	juez *m*
Richtpreis (D)	—	recommended retail price	prix indicatif *m*	prezzo indicativo *m*	precio indicativo *m*
riciclaggio (I)	Recycling *n*	recycling	recyclage *m*	—	reciclaje *m*
ricompensa (I)	Vergütung *f*	remuneration	rémunération *f*	—	remuneración *f*
ricomposizione fondiaria (I)	Flurbereinigung *f*	compulsory consolidation of farmland	remembrement parcellaire *m*	—	concentración parcelaria *f*
riconoscere (I)	erkennen	recognize	reconnaître	—	reconocer
riconoscimento del debito (I)	Schuldanerkennung *f*	acknowledgement of a debt	reconnaissance de dette *f*	—	reconocimiento de la deuda *m*
ricostruzione (I)	Wiederaufbau *m*	reconstruction	reconstruction *f*	—	reconstrucción *f*
ricupero (I)	Bergung *f*	salvage	sauvetage *m*	—	salvamento *m*
ridistribuzione (I)	Redistribution *f*	redistribution	redistribution *f*	—	redistribución *f*
ridistribuzione dei redditi (I)	Einkommensumverteilung *f*	redistribution of income	redistribution des revenus *f pl*	—	redistribución de la renta *f*
ridondanza (I)	Redundanz *f*	redundancy	redondance *f*	—	redundancia *f*
ridurre a rottame (I)	verschrotten	scrap	mettre à la ferraille	—	hacer quincalla desguazar
riduzione[1] (I)	Abbau *m*	reduction/lay off	réduction *f*/ diminution *f*	—	reducción *f*/ disminución *f*
riduzione[2] (I)	Ermäßigung *f*	reduction	réduction *f*	—	reducción *f*
riduzione[3] (I)	Minderung *f*	reduction	diminution *f*	—	reducción *f*
riduzione degli interessi (I)	Zinssenkung *f*	reduction of interest	diminution du taux de l'intérêt *f*	—	reducción del tipo de interés *f*
riduzione dei costi (I)	Kostendegression *f*	cost degression	dégressivité des coûts *f*	—	reducción de costes *f*
riduzione dei prezzi (I)	Preissenkung *f*	price reduction	baisse des prix *f*	—	reducción de precios *f*
riduzione del capitale (I)	Kapitalherabsetzung *f*	reduction of capital	diminution du capital *f*	—	reducción de capital *f*
riduzione del denaro (I)	Geldverknappung *f*	monetary restriction	pénurie d'argent *f*	—	restricción monetaria *f*
riduzione delle sovvenzioni (I)	Subventionsabbau *m*	reduction of subsidy	réduction des subventions *f*	—	reducción de las subvenciones *f*
riduzione delle spese[1] (I)	Aufwandsminimierung *f*	expenditure minimization	minimiser les frais	—	minimación de gastos *f*

	D	E	F	I	Es
riduzione delle spese[2] (I)	Ausgabensenkung *f*	drop in expenditure	diminution des dépenses *f*	—	reducción de gastos *f*
riduzione del personale (I)	Personalabbau *m*	reduction of staff	réduction de personnel *f*	—	reducción de personal *f*
riduzione del prezzo (I)	Preisabzug *m*	price deduction	réduction de prix *f*	—	descuento *m*
riduzione di valore (I)	Wertminderung *f*	decrease in value	diminution de la valeur *f*	—	depreciación *f*
rielaborazione (I)	Nachbereitung *f*	aftertreatment	remise en ordre *f*	—	tratamiento ulterior *m*
riesgo[1] (Es)	Wagnis *n*	venture	risque *m*	rischio *m*	—
riesgo[2] (Es)	Risiko *n*	risk	risque *m*	rischio *m*	—
riesgo aceptable (Es)	Restrisiko *n*	acceptable risk	risque acceptable *m*	rischio rimanente *m*	—
riesgo de cambio (Es)	Kursrisiko *n*	price risk	risque de change *m*	rischio di cambio *m*	—
riesgo de pago (Es)	Zahlungsrisiko *n*	risk of payment	risque de payement *m*	rischio di pagamento *m*	—
riesgo de pérdida (Es)	Ausfallrisiko *n*	default risk	risque de perte *m*	rischio di perdita *m*	—
riesgo de transferencia (Es)	Transferrisiko *n*	risk of transfer	risque de transfert *m*	rischio di trasferimento *m*	—
riesgo monetario (Es)	Währungsrisiko *n*	currency risk	risque de change *m*	rischio monetario *m*	—
riesgo profesional (Es)	Berufsrisiko *n*	occupational hazard	risque professionnel *m*	rischio professionale *m*	—
riesportazione (I)	Wiederausfuhr *f*	reexportation	réexportation *f*	—	reexportación *f*
rifare l'imballaggio (I)	umpacken	repack	remballer	—	reempaquetar
riferimento (I)	Referenz	reference	référence *f*	—	referencia *f*
rifinanziamento (I)	Refinanzierung *f*	refinancing	refinancement *m*	—	refinanciación *f*
rifiuti (I)	Abfall *m*	waste	déchet *m*	—	desechos *m pl*
rifiuti da imballaggi (I)	Verpackungsmüll *m*	packing waste	déchets d'emballage *m pl*	—	basura de embalaje *f*
rifiuti speciali (I)	Sondermüll *m*	special refuse	détritus spéciaux *m pl*	—	basura especial *f*
rifiuto (I)	Ablehnung *f*	refusal/rejection	refus *m*/rejet *m*	—	recusación *f*/repulsa *f*
rifiuto d'accettazione (I)	Annahme-verweigerung *f*	refusal of delivery	refus d'acceptation *m*	—	rehuso de aceptación *m*
riforma agraria (I)	Bodenreform *f*	land reform	réforme agraire *f*	—	reforma agraria *f*
right of redemption (E)	Rückgaberecht *n*	—	droit à restitution *m*	diritto alla restituzione *m*	derecho de devolución *m*
right of revocation (E)	Widerrufsrecht *n*	—	droit de révocation *m*	diritto di revoca *m*	derecho de revocación *m*
right to vote (E)	Stimmrecht *n*	—	droit de vote *m*	diritto al voto *m*	derecho a voto *m*
rilevante (I)	relevant	relevant	significatif	—	importante
rimanenze (I)	Restposten *m*	remnants	lot restant *m*	—	partida restante *f*
rimborsare (I)	ablösen	redeem	amortir	—	amortizar
rimborso[1] (I)	Rückerstattung *f*	repayment	remboursement *m*	—	restitución *f*
rimborso[2] (I)	Abzahlung *f*	repayment/ hire purchase	remboursement *m*/ payement par acomptes *m*	—	reintegro *m*/ pago a plazos *m*
rimessa[1] (I)	Rimesse *f*	remittance	remise *f*	—	remesa *f*
rimessa[2] (I)	Überweisung *f*	remittance	virement *m*	—	transferencia *f*
rimessa bancaria (I)	Banküberweisung *f*	bank transfer	virement bancaire *m*	—	transferencia bancaria *f*
Rimesse (D)	—	remittance	remise *f*	rimessa *f*	remesa *f*
rincaro (I)	Verteuerung *f*	rise in price	enchérissement *m*	—	encarecimiento *m*
rinuncia al consumo (I)	Konsumverzicht *m*	voluntary constraint in consumption	renonciation à la consommation *f*	—	renuncia al consumo *f*
rinvio[1] (I)	Vertagung *f*	postponement	ajournement *m*	—	aplazamiento *m*/ suspensión *f*
rinvio[2] (I)	Aufschiebung *f*	postponement	remise *f*	—	aplazamiento *m*
riparare (I)	reparieren	repair	réparer	—	reparar
riparazione (I)	Reparatur *f*	repair	réparation *f*	—	reparación *f*
ripartizione (I)	Umlage *f*	charge levied	répartition *f*	—	reparto *m*
ripartizione dell'utile[1] (I)	Gewinnverteilung *f*	distribution of profits	répartition des bénéfices *f*	—	reparto de beneficios *m*

	D	E	F	I	Es
ripartizione dell'utile[2] (I)	Gewinnausschüttung *f*	distribution of profits	distribution de bénéfices *f*	—	distribución de beneficios *f*
ripartizione del patrimonio (I)	Vermögensverteilung *f*	distribution of wealth	répartition du patrimoine *f*	—	reparto de la riqueza *m*
ripresa (I)	Reprise *f*	repeat	tendance à la hausse *f*	—	segunda lectura en el corro *f*
ripresa congiunturale (I)	Konjunkturbelebung *f*	economic upturn	relance économique *f*	—	recuperación coyuntural *f*
riprivatizzazione (I)	Reprivatisierung *f*	reversion to private ownership	dénationalisation *f*	—	desnacionalización *f*
riproduzione (I)	Vervielfältigung *f*	reproduction	reproduction *f*	—	reproducción *f*/ multiplicación *f*
riqualificazione professionale (I)	Umschulung *f*	retraining	rééducation professionnelle *f*	—	readaptación profesional *f*
risanamento (I)	Sanierung *f*	urban renewal/ reconstruction	assainissement *m*	—	saneamiento *m*/ rehabilitación *f*
risarcimento danni (I)	Schadensersatz *m*	compensation for loss suffered	dommages-intérêts *m pl*	—	indemnización *f*
rischio[1] (I)	Wagnis *n*	venture	risque *m*	—	riesgo *m*
rischio[2] (I)	Risiko *n*	risk	risque *m*	—	riesgo *m*
rischio di cambio (I)	Kursrisiko *n*	price risk	risque de change *m*	—	riesgo de cambio *m*
rischio di pagamento (I)	Zahlungsrisiko *n*	risk of payment	risque de payement *m*	—	riesgo de pago *m*
rischio di perdita (I)	Ausfallrisiko *n*	default risk	risque de perte *m*	—	riesgo de pérdida *m*
rischio di trasferimento (I)	Transferrisiko *n*	risk of transfer	risque de transfert *m*	—	riesgo de transferencia *m*
rischio monetario (I)	Währungsrisiko *n*	currency risk	risque de change *m*	—	riesgo monetario *m*
rischio professionale (I)	Berufsrisiko *n*	occupational hazard	risque professionnel *m*	—	riesgo profesional *m*
rischio rimanente (I)	Restrisiko *n*	acceptable risk	risque acceptable *m*	—	riesgo aceptable *m*
rischioso (I)	riskant	risky	risqué	—	arriesgado
riscontare (I)	rediskontieren	rediscount	réescompter	—	redescontar
rise in income (E)	Einkommenserhöhung *f*	—	augmentation du revenu *f*	aumento del reddito *m*	aumento de salario *m*
rise in price (E)	Verteuerung *f*	—	enchérissement *m*	rincaro *m*	encarecimiento *m*
riserva di capitale (I)	Kapitalstock *m*	capital stock	réserve de capital *f*	—	fondo de capital *m*
riserva di liquidità (I)	Liquiditätsreserve *f*	liquidity reserves	réserves de liquidité *f pl*	—	reserva de liquidez *f*
riserva latente (I)	stille Rücklage *f*	latent funds	réserve cachée *f*	—	reserva tácita *f*
riserva minima obbligatoria (I)	Mindestreserve *f*	minimum reserves	réserve minimum *f*	—	reserva mínima *f*
riserva occulta (I)	stille Reserve *f*	hidden reserves	réserve cachée *f*	—	reserva tácita *f*
riserve (I)	Rücklagen *pl*	reserves	réserve *f*	—	reservas *f pl*
Risiko (D)	—	risk	risque *m*	rischio *m*	riesgo *m*
Risiko-Lebensversicherung (D)	—	term life insurance	assurance-vie temporaire *f*	assicurazione rischio-vita *f*	seguro de vida temporal *m*
Risikoprämie (D)	—	risk premium	prime de risque *f*	premio di rischio *m*	prima de riesgo *f*
rising (E)	steigend	—	croissant(e)	in aumento	ascendente
risk (E)	Risiko *n*	—	risque *m*	rischio *m*	riesgo *m*
riskant (D)	—	risky	risqué	rischioso	arriesgado
risk of payment (E)	Zahlungsrisiko *n*	—	risque de payement *m*	rischio di pagamento *m*	riesgo de pago *m*
risk of transfer (E)	Transferrisiko *n*	—	risque de transfert *m*	rischio di trasferimento *m*	riesgo de transferencia *m*
risk premium (E)	Risikoprämie *f*	—	prime de risque *f*	premio di rischio *m*	prima de riesgo *f*
risky (E)	riskant	—	risqué	rischioso	arriesgado
risolubile (I)	kündbar	redeemable/callable	résiliable/ remboursable	—	revocable/rescindible
risoluzione (I)	Resolution *f*	resolution	résolution *f*	—	resolución *f*
risorsa (I)	Ressource *f*	resources	ressource *f*	—	recurso *m*
risparmio[1] (I)	Ersparnis *f*	savings	épargne *f*	—	ahorro *m*

	D	E	F	I	Es
risparmio² (I)	Sparen *n*	saving	épargne *f*	—	ahorro *m*
risparmio coatto (I)	Zwangssparen *n*	compulsory saving	épargne forcée *f*	—	ahorro forzoso *m*
rispedizione (I)	Rücksendung *f*	return	renvoi *m*	—	devolución *f*
risposta (I)	Antwort *f*	reply	réponse *f*	—	respuesta *f*
risposta negativa (I)	Absage *f*	refusal	refus *m*	—	negativa *f*
risque¹ (F)	Wagnis *n*	venture	—	rischio *m*	riesgo *m*
risque² (F)	Risiko *n*	risk	—	rischio *m*	riesgo *m*
risqué³ (F)	riskant	risky	—	rischioso	arriesgado
risque acceptable (F)	Restrisiko *n*	acceptable risk	—	rischio rimanente *m*	riesgo aceptable *m*
risque de change¹ (F)	Kursrisiko *n*	price risk	—	rischio di cambio *m*	riesgo de cambio *m*
risque de change² (F)	Währungsrisiko *n*	currency risk	—	rischio monetario *m*	riesgo monetario *m*
risque de payement (F)	Zahlungsrisiko *n*	risk of payment	—	rischio di pagamento *m*	riesgo de pago *m*
risque de perte (F)	Ausfallrisiko *n*	default risk	—	rischio di perdita *m*	riesgo de pérdida *m*
risque de transfert (F)	Transferrisiko *n*	risk of transfer	—	rischio di trasferimento *m*	riesgo de transferencia *m*
risque professionnel (F)	Berufsrisiko *n*	occupational hazard	—	rischio professionale *m*	riesgo profesional *m*
ristourne des droits de douane (F)	Rückzoll *m*	customs drawback	—	restituzione di dazi *f*	drawback *m*
ristourne exceptionnelle (F)	Sonderrabatt *m*	special discount	—	ribasso speciale *m*	descuento suplementario *m*
ristrutturazione (I)	Umstrukturierung *f*	restructuring	restructuration *f*	—	reestructuración *f*
risultato (I)	Ergebnis *n*	result	résultat *m*	—	resultado *m*
ritardo (I)	Verspätung *f*	delay	retard *m*	—	retraso *m*
ritardo d'adattamento (I)	Anpassungs-verzögerung *f*	adjustment lag	retard d'adaptation *m*	—	retraso de adaptación *m*
ritardo della consegna (I)	Lieferungs-verzögerung *f*	delay in delivery	retard dans la livraison *m*	—	demora en la entrega *f*
ritmo de trabajo (Es)	Arbeitsrhythmus *m*	work rhythm	rythme de travail *m*	ritmo di lavoro *m*	—
ritmo di lavoro (I)	Arbeitsrhythmus *m*	work rhythm	rythme de travail *m*	—	ritmo de trabajo *m*
riunione dei creditori (I)	Gläubiger-versammlung *f*	creditors' meeting	assemblée des créanciers *f*	—	junta de acreedores *f*
riutilizzabile (I)	wiederverwertbar	recyclable	réutilisable	—	recuperable
rival (E)	Rivale *m*	—	rival *m*	rivale *m*	rival *m*
rival (Es)	Rivale *m*	rival	rival *m*	rivale *m*	—
rival (F)	Rivale *m*	rival	—	rivale *m*	rival *m*
Rivale (D)	—	rival	rival *m*	rivale *m*	rival *m*
rivale (I)	Rivale *m*	rival	rival *m*	—	rival *m*
rivalutazione (I)	Aufwertung *f*	revaluation	revalorisation *f*	—	revalorización *f*
rivendicazione salariale (I)	Lohnforderung *f*	wage claim	revendication de salaire *f*	—	reivindicación salarial *f*
rivenditore (I)	Wiederverkäufer *m*	reseller	revendeur *m*	—	revendedor *m*
road network¹ (E)	Wegenetz *n*	—	voirie *f*	rete stradale *f*	comunicaciones *f pl*
road network² (E)	Straßennetz *n*	—	réseau routier *m*	rete stradale *f*	red de carreteras *f*
road traffic (E)	Straßenverkehr *m*	—	trafic routier *m*	traffico stradale *m*	circulación *f*
robo (Es)	Diebstahl *m*	theft	vol *m*	furto *m*	—
Rohgewinn (D)	—	gross profit on sales	bénéfice brut *m*	utile lordo *m*	ganancia bruta *f*
Rohöl (D)	—	crude oil	pétrole brut *m*	petrolio greggio *m*	crudo *m*
Rohölpreis (D)	—	crude oil price	prix du pétrole brut *m*	prezzo del petrolio greggio *m*	precio del crudo *m*
Rohstoff (D)	—	raw materials	matière première *f*	materia prima *f*	materia prima *f*
Rohstoffgewinnung (D)	—	raw material production	extraction de matières premières *f*	produzione delle materie prime *f*	producción de materias primas *f*
Rohstoffknappheit (D)	—	raw materials shortage	pénurie de matières premières *f*	scarsità di materie prime *f*	escasez de materias primas *f*
Rohstoffmarkt (D)	—	commodity market	marchés des matières premières *m*	mercato delle materie prime *m*	mercado de materias primas *m*

	D	E	F	I	Es
Rohstoff-vermarktung (D)	—	raw materials marketing	commercialisation des matières premières *f*	smercio delle materie prime *m*	comercialización de las materias primas *f*
Rohstoffversorgung (D)	—	provisioning with raw materials	approvisionnement de matières premières *m*	approvvigionamento di materie prime *m*	aprovisionamiento de materias primas *m*
Rollgeld (D)	—	haulage	camionnage *m*	spese di trasporto *f pl*	derechos de acarreo *m pl*
roll-over credit (E)	Roll-over-Kredit *m*	—	crédit roll-over *m*	credito roll-over *m*	crédito roll over *m*
Roll-over-Kredit (D)	—	roll-over credit	crédit roll-over *m*	credito roll-over *m*	crédito roll over *m*
room reservation (E)	Zimmerbestellung *f*	—	réservation de chambre *f*	prenotazione di una camera *f*	reservación *f*
rotación del capital (Es)	Kapitalumschlag *m*	capital turnover	roulement des capitaux *m*	rotazione del capitale *f*	—
rotazione del capitale (I)	Kapitalumschlag *m*	capital turnover	roulement des capitaux *m*	—	rotación del capital *f*
rote Zahlen (D)	—	(in) the red	chiffres en déficit *f pl*	conti in rosso *m pl*	cifras rojas *f pl*
roulement des capitaux (F)	Kapitalumschlag *m*	capital turnover	—	rotazione del capitale *f*	rotación del capital *f*
route (E)	Reiseroute *f*	—	itinéraire *m*	itinerario *m*	itinerario *m*
route of transportation (E)	Transportweg *m*	—	voie de transport *f*	via di trasporto *f*	vía de transporte *f*
royalty (E)	Lizenzgebühr *f*	—	taxe d'exploitation de licence *f*	tassa di licenza *f*	derecho de licencia *m*
Rückerstattung (D)	—	repayment	remboursement *m*	rimborso *m*	restitución *f*
Rückfahrkarte (D)	—	return ticket	billet d'aller et retour *m*	biglietto di andata e ritorno *m*	billete de ida y vuelta *m*
Rückgabe (D)	—	return	restitution *f*	restituzione *f*	restitución *f*
Rückgaberecht (D)	—	right of redemption	droit à restitution *m*	diritto alla restituzione *m*	derecho de devolución *m*
Rückgriff (D)	—	recourse	recours *m*	regresso *m*	recurso *m*
Rückkopplung (D)	—	feedback	accouplement réactif *m*	accoppiamento a reazione *m*	reacoplamiento *m*
Rücklagen (D)	—	reserves	réserve *f*	riserve *f pl*	reservas *f pl*
Rückschein (D)	—	advice of delivery	avis de réception *m*	ricevuta di ritorno *f*	acuse de recibo *m*
Rücksendung (D)	—	return	renvoi *m*	rispedizione *f*	devolución *f*
Rückstand (D)	—	arrear	arriéré *m*	arretrato *m*	pago atrasado *m*/ atraso *m*
Rückstände (D)	—	residues	déchet *m*	residui *m pl*	residuos *m pl*
Rückstellung (D)	—	reserves	provision pour pertes et charges *f*	accantonamento *m*	reserva *f*
Rücktritt (D)	—	rescission	résolution du contrat *f*	recesso *m*	rescisión *f*
Rücktrittsklausel (D)	—	escape clause	clause de résolution du contrat *f*	clausola di recesso *f*	cláusula de arrepentimiento *f*
Rückversicherung (D)	—	reinsurance	réassurance *f*	riassicurazione *f*	reaseguro *m*
rückwirkend (D)	—	retrospective	rétroactif	con effetto retroattivo	retroactivo
Rückzoll (D)	—	customs drawback	ristourne des droits de douane *f*	restituzione di dazi *f*	drawback *m*
rue (F)	Straße *f*	street/road	—	via *f*/strada *f*	calle *f*/carretera *f*
rueda de prensa (Es)	Pressekonferenz *f*	press conference	conférence de presse *f*	conferenza stampa *f*	—
ruinous exploitation (E)	Raubbau *m*	—	exploitation abusive *f*	sfruttamento abusivo *m*	explotación abusiva *f*
Rundfunkwerbung (D)	—	radio advertising	publicité à la radio *f*	pubblicità radiofonica *f*	publicidad radiada *f*
Rundschreiben (D)	—	circular (letter)	lettre circulaire *f*	circolare *f*	circular *m*
rythme de travail (F)	Arbeitsrhythmus *m*	work rhythm	—	ritmo di lavoro *m*	ritmo de trabajo *m*
Sabotage (D)	—	sabotage	sabotage *m*	sabotaggio *m*	sabotaje *m*
sabotage (E)	Sabotage *f*	—	sabotage *m*	sabotaggio *m*	sabotaje *m*
sabotage (F)	Sabotage *f*	sabotage	—	sabotaggio *m*	sabotaje *m*
sabotaggio (I)	Sabotage *f*	sabotage	sabotage *m*	—	sabotaje *m*
sabotaje (Es)	Sabotage *f*	sabotage	sabotage *m*	sabotaggio *m*	—
sac (F)	Sack *m*	sack	—	sacco *m*	saco *m*

	D	E	F	I	Es
sacco (I)	Sack *m*	sack	sac *m*	—	saco *m*
Sachanlagen (D)	—	fixed assets	immobilisations corporelles *f pl*	immobilizzazioni *f pl*	inmuebles y utillaje *m pl*
Sachbezüge (D)	—	remuneration in kind	prestations en nature *f pl*	retribuzioni in natura *f pl*	percepciónes en especie *f pl*
Sachkenntnis (D)	—	know-how	compétence *f*	competenza *f*	conocimiento de causa *m*
Sachvermögen (D)	—	material assets	biens corporels *m pl*	capitale reale *m*	patrimonio real *m*
Sachversicherung (D)	—	property insurance	assurance de choses *f*	assicurazione di cose *f*	seguro de cosas *m*
Sachwert (D)	—	real value	valeur matérielle *f*	valore reale *m*	valor real *m*
Sack (D)	—	sack	sac *m*	sacco *m*	saco *m*
sack (E)	Sack *m*	—	sac *m*	sacco *m*	saco *m*
saco (Es)	Sack *m*	sack	sac *m*	sacco *m*	—
Safe (D)	—	safe	coffre-fort *m*	cassetta di sicurezza *f*	caja de seguridad *f*
safe[1] (E)	Tresor *m*	—	coffre-fort *m*	cassaforte *f*	caja fuerte *f*
safe[2] (E)	Safe *m*	—	coffre-fort *m*	cassetta di sicurezza *f*	caja de seguridad *f*
safety at work (E)	Arbeitssicherheit *f*	—	sécurité du travail *f*	sicurezza del lavoro *f*	seguridad del trabajo *f*
saggio di sconto (I)	Diskontsatz *m*	discount rate	taux d'escompte *m*	—	tasa de descuento *f*
saisie[1] (F)	Beschlagnahme *f*	confiscation	—	sequestro *m*	confiscación *f*
saisie[2] (F)	Pfändung *f*	seizure	—	pignoramento *m*	pignoración *f*
saisie des données informatiques (F)	Datenerfassung *f*	data collection	—	raccolta dati *f*	recogida de datos *f*
saisie-arrêt sur le salaire (F)	Lohnpfändung *f*	attachment of earnings	—	pignoramento del salario *m*	embargo de salario *m*
Saison (D)	—	season	saison *f*	stagione *f*	temporada *f*
saison (F)	Saison *f*	season	—	stagione *f*	temporada *f*
saisonale Arbeitslosigkeit (D)	—	seasonal unemployment	chômage saisonnier *m*	disoccupazione stagionale *f*	paro estacional *m*
Saison-schwankungen (D)	—	seasonal fluctuations	mouvements saisonniers *m pl*	oscillazioni stagionali *f pl*	oscilaciones estacionales *f pl*
sala conferenze (I)	Konferenzraum *m*	conference room	salle de conférences *f*	—	sala de conferencia *f*
sala de conferencia[1] (Es)	Konferenzraum *m*	conference room	salle de conférences *f*	sala conferenze *f*	—
sala de conferencia[2] (Es)	Sitzungszimmer *n*	conference room	salle de réunion *f*	sala riunioni *f*	—
salaire (F)	Lohn *m*	wage	—	salario *m*	salario *m*
salaire à la pièce (F)	Akkordlohn *m*	piece work wages	—	retribuzione per il lavoro a cottimo *f*	salario a destajo *m*
salaire à la tâche (F)	Stücklohn *m*	piece work pay	—	salario a cottimo *m*	salario a destajo *m*
salaire au rendement (F)	Leistungslohn *m*	payment by result	—	salario a rendimento *m*	salario por rendimiento *m*
salaire au temps (F)	Zeitlohn *m*	time wage	—	salario a tempo *m*	salario por unidad de tiempo *m*
salaire brut (F)	Bruttolohn *m*	gross pay	—	salario lordo *m*	salario bruto *m*
salaire de référence (F)	Basislohn *m*	basic wage	—	salario base *m*	sueldo base *m*
salaire effectif (F)	Effektivlohn *m*	actual wage	—	salario effettivo *m*	salario efectivo *m*
salaire horaire (F)	Stundenlohn *m*	hourly wage	—	salario ad ora *m*	salario-hora *m*
salaire indexé (F)	Indexlohn *m*	index-linked wages	—	salario indicizzato *m*	salario-índice *m*
salaire initial (F)	Anfangsgehalt *n*	starting salary	—	stipendio iniziale *m*	salario inicial *m*
salaire maximum (F)	Spitzenlohn *m*	top wage	—	salario massimo *m*	salario máximo *m*
salaire minimum (F)	Mindestlohn *m*	minimum wage	—	salario minimo *m*	salario mínimo *m*
salaire net (F)	Nettolohn *m*	take-home pay	—	salario netto *m*	salario neto *m*
salaire nominal (F)	Nominallohn *m*	nominal wage	—	salario nominale *m*	salario nominal *m*
salaire réel (F)	Reallohn *m*	real wage	—	salario reale *m*	salario real *m*
salaire tarifaire (F)	Tariflohn *m*	standard wage	—	salario contrattuale *m*	salario tarifado *m*
salarié (F)	Arbeitnehmer *m*	employee	—	prestatore d'opera *m*	empleado *m*
Salaried Employees' Pension Insurance (E)	Angestellten-versicherung *f*	—	assurance invalidité-vieillesse des employés *f*	assicurazione degli impiegati *f*	seguro de empleados *m*

	D	E	F	I	Es
salario (Es)	Lohn *m*	wage	salaire *m*	salario *m*	—
salario (I)	Lohn *m*	wage	salaire *m*	—	salario *m*
salario a cottimo (I)	Stücklohn *m*	piece work pay	salaire à la tâche *m*	—	salario a destajo *m*
salario a destajo[1] (Es)	Akkordlohn *m*	piece work wages	salaire à la pièce *m*	retribuzione per il lavoro a cottimo *f*	—
salario a destajo[2] (Es)	Stücklohn *m*	piece work pay	salaire à la tâche *m*	salario a cottimo *m*	—
salario ad ora (I)	Stundenlohn *m*	hourly wage	salaire horaire *m*	—	salario-hora *m*
salario a rendimento (I)	Leistungslohn *m*	payment by result	salaire au rendement *m*	—	salario por rendimiento *m*
salario a tempo (I)	Zeitlohn *m*	time wage	salaire au temps *m*	—	salario por unidad de tiempo *m*
salario base (I)	Basislohn *m*	basic wage	salaire de référence *m*	—	sueldo base *m*
salario base[1] (Es)	Grundgehalt *n*	basic salary	traitement de base *m*	stipendio base *m*	—
salario base[2] (Es)	Basiseinkommen *n*	basic income	revenu de base *m*	introiti base *m pl*	
salario bruto (Es)	Bruttolohn *m*	gross pay	salaire brut *m*	salario lordo *m*	—
salario contrattuale (I)	Tariflohn *m*	standard wage	salaire tarifaire *m*	—	salario tarifado *m*
salario efectivo (Es)	Effektivlohn *m*	actual wage	salaire effectif *m*	salario effettivo *m*	—
salario effettivo (I)	Effektivlohn *m*	actual wage	salaire effectif *m*	—	salario efectivo *m*
salario en especie (Es)	Naturallohn *m*	wages (paid) in kind	rémunération du travail en nature *f*	remunerazione in natura *f*	—
salario fijo (Es)	Festeinkommen *n*	fixed income	revenu fixe *m*	reddito fisso *m*	—
salario-hora (Es)	Stundenlohn *m*	hourly wage	salaire horaire *m*	salario ad ora *m*	—
salario-índice (Es)	Indexlohn *m*	index-linked wages	salaire indexé *m*	salario indicizzato *m*	—
salario indicizzato (I)	Indexlohn *m*	index-linked wages	salaire indexé *m*	—	salario-índice *m*
salario inicial (Es)	Anfangsgehalt *n*	starting salary	salaire initial *m*	stipendio iniziale *m*	—
salario lordo (I)	Bruttolohn *m*	gross pay	salaire brut *m*	—	salario bruto *m*
salario massimo (I)	Spitzenlohn *m*	top wage	salaire maximum *m*	—	salario máximo *m*
salario máximo (Es)	Spitzenlohn *m*	top wage	salaire maximum *m*	salario massimo *m*	—
salario mínimo (Es)	Mindestlohn *m*	minimum wage	salaire minimum *m*	salario minimo *m*	—
salario minimo (I)	Mindestlohn *m*	minimum wage	salaire minimum *m*	—	salario mínimo *m*
salario neto (Es)	Nettolohn *m*	take-home pay	salaire net *m*	salario netto *m*	—
salario netto (I)	Nettolohn *m*	take-home pay	salaire net *m*	—	salario neto *m*
salario nominal (Es)	Nominallohn *m*	nominal wage	salaire nominal *m*	salario nominale *m*	—
salario nominale (I)	Nominallohn *m*	nominal wage	salaire nominal *m*	—	salario nominal *m*
salario por rendimiento (Es)	Leistungslohn *m*	payment by result	salaire au rendement *m*	salario a rendimento *m*	—
salario por unidad de tiempo (Es)	Zeitlohn *m*	time wage	salaire au temps *m*	salario a tempo *m*	—
salario real (Es)	Reallohn *m*	real wage	salaire réel *m*	salario reale *m*	—
salario reale (I)	Reallohn *m*	real wage	salaire réel *m*	—	salario real *m*
salario tarifado (Es)	Tariflohn *m*	standard wage	salaire tarifaire *m*	salario contrattuale *m*	—
sala riunioni (I)	Sitzungszimmer *n*	conference room	salle de réunion *f*	—	sala de conferencia *f*
salary[1] (E)	Gage *f*	—	cachet *m*	onorario *m*	remuneración *f*
salary[2] (E)	Gehalt *n*	—	traitement *m*	stipendio *m*	sueldo *m*
salary account (E)	Gehaltskonto *n*	—	compte de domiciliation du salaire *m*	conto stipendi *m*	cuenta de salario *f*
Saldo (D)	—	balance	solde *m*	saldo *m*	saldo *m*
saldo (Es)	Saldo *m*	balance	solde *m*	saldo *m*	—
saldo (I)	Saldo *m*	balance	solde *m*	—	saldo *m*
saldo activo (Es)	Aktivsaldo *m*	active balance	solde créditeur *m*	saldo attivo *m*	—
saldo attivo[1] (I)	Aktivsaldo *m*	active balance	solde créditeur *m*	—	saldo activo *m*
saldo attivo[2] (I)	Guthaben *n*	money owed	avoir *m*	—	haber *m*
saldo de cuenta (Es)	Kontoausgleich *m*	settlement of an account	solde de compte *m*	liquidazione del conto *f*	—
saldo en efectivo (Es)	Bargeldbestand *m*	cash in hand	espèces en caisse *f pl*	denaro contante in cassa *m*	—
sale[1] (E)	Verkauf *m*	—	vente *f*	vendita *f*	venta *f*

	D	E	F	I	Es
sale[2] (E)	Veräußerung *f*	—	aliénation *f*	alienazione *f*	enajenación *f*
sale[3] (E)	Absatz *m*	—	volume des ventes *m*	vendita *f*	cifra de ventas *f*
sale by court order (E)	Zwangs-versteigerung *f*	—	vente de biens par justice *f*	asta giudiziaria *f*	subasta forzosa *f*
sale on approval (E)	Kauf auf Probe *m*	—	achat à l'éssai *m*	acquisto a titolo di prova *m*	compra a prueba *f*
sale proceeds (E)	Verkaufserlös *m*	—	produit des ventes *m*	ricavo delle vendite *m*	producto de la venta *m*
sales analysis[1] (E)	Absatzanalyse *f*	—	analyse de la distribution *f*	analisi di mercato *f*	análisis de venta *m*
sales analysis[2] (E)	Verkaufsanalyse *f*	—	analyse des ventes *f*	analisi delle vendite *f*	análisis de las ventas *m*
sales campaign (E)	Verkaufskampagne *f*	—	campagne de vente *f*	campagna di vendita *f*	campaña de venta *f*
sales commission (E)	Verkäuferprovision *f*	—	commission sur les ventes *f*	provvigione del venditore *f*	comisión sobre la venta *f*
sales conception (E)	Verkaufskonzeption *f*	—	conception de vente *f*	concezione di vendita *f*	concepción de venta *f*
sales contract (E)	Verkaufsabschluß *m*	—	contrat de vente *m*	conclusione di vendita *f*	conclusión de la venta *f*
sales crisis (E)	Absatzkrise *f*	—	crise de vente *f*	crisi di mercato *f*	crisis en la venta *f*
sales financing (E)	Absatzfinanzierung *f*	—	financement des ventes *m*	finanziamento delle vendite *m*	financiación de las ventas *f*
sales meeting (E)	Vertretertagung *f*	—	réunion de représentants *f*	convegno dei rappresentanti *m*	conferencia de representantes *f*
sales message (E)	Werbebotschaft *f*	—	message publicitaire *m*	messaggio pubblicitario *m*	mensaje publicitario *m*
sales organization (E)	Absatzorganisation *f*	—	organisation de vente *f*	organizzazione di vendita *f*	organización de ventas *f*
sales planning (E)	Absatzplanung *f*	—	planning de la distribution *m*	pianificazione delle vendite *f*	planificación de ventas *f*
sales possibilities (E)	Verkaufschance *f*	—	possibilité de vente *f*	prospettiva dello smercio *f*	posibilidades de venta *f pl*
sales programme (E)	Verkaufsprogramm *n*	—	programme de vente *m*	programma di vendita *m*	programa de venta *m*
sales promotion[1] (E)	Verkaufsförderung *f*	—	encouragement à la vente *m*	promozione di vendita *f*	promoción de las ventas *f*
sales promotion[2] (E)	Absatzförderung *f*	—	promotion des ventes *f*	promozione dello smercio *f*	promoción comercial *f*
sales prospects (E)	Absatzchance *f*	—	possibilités de réussite des ventes *f pl*	prospettive di smercio *f pl*	posibilidades de venta *f pl*
sales report (E)	Verkaufsbericht *m*	—	rapport de vente *m*	rapporto sulle vendite *m*	informe de venta *m*
sales representative (E)	festangestellter Reisender *m*	—	voyageur de commerce *m*	commesso viaggiatore *m*	viajante *m*
sales segment (E)	Absatzsegment *n*	—	segment de vente *m*	segmento di vendita *m*	segmento de venta *m*
sales staff (E)	Verkaufsstab *m*	—	équipe de vente *f*	staff di venditori *m*	equipo de venta *m*
sales statistics (E)	Absatzstatistik *f*	—	statistique de la vente *f*	statistica delle vendite *f*	estadística de ventas *f*
sales strategy[1] (E)	Verkaufsmethoden *pl*	—	méthodes de vente *f pl*	metodi di vendita *m pl*	métodos de venta *m pl*
sales strategy[2] (E)	Absatzstrategie *f*	—	stratégie de vente *f*	strategia di vendita *f*	estrategia de ventas *f*
sales target (E)	Absatzziel *n*	—	objectif de vente *m*	obbiettivo di vendita *m*	fin de venta *m*
sales technique (E)	Verkaufstechnik *f*	—	art de vendre *m*	tecnica di vendita *f*	técnica de venta *f*
sales territory (E)	Verkaufsgebiet *n*	—	territoire de vente *m*	zona di vendita *f*	territorio de venta *m*
sales training (E)	Verkäuferschulung *f*	—	formation des vendeurs *f*	addestramento dei venditori *f*	formación de los vendedores *f*
sale talk (E)	Verkaufsgespräch *n*	—	conversation de vente *f*	colloquio di vendita *m*	conversación de venta *f*
salida de mercancías (Es)	Warenausgang *m*	outgoing goods	sortie de marchandieses *f*	uscita merci *f*	—
salle de conférences (F)	Konferenzraum *m*	conference room	—	sala conferenze *f*	sala de conferencia *f*

	D	E	F	I	Es
salle de réunion (F)	Sitzungszimmer *n*	conference room	—	sala riunioni *f*	sala de conferencia *f*
saludo (Es)	Begrüßung *f*	salutation	salutations *f pl*	saluto *m*	—
salutation (E)	Begrüßung *f*	—	salutations *f pl*	saluto *m*	saludo *m*
salutations (F)	Begrüßung *f*	salutation	—	saluto *m*	saludo *m*
saluto (I)	Begrüßung *f*	salutation	salutations *f pl*	—	saludo *m*
salvage (E)	Bergung *f*	—	sauvetage *m*	ricupero *m*	salvamento *m*
salvamento (Es)	Bergung *f*	salvage	sauvetage *m*	ricupero *m*	—
salvo buen cobro (Es)	Eingang vorbehalten	due payment reserved	sauf bonne fin	salvo buon fine	—
salvo buon fine (I)	Eingang vorbehalten	due payment reserved	sauf bonne fin	—	salvo buen cobro *m*
salvo error (Es)	Irrtum vorbehalten	errors excepted	sauf erreur	salvo errore	—
salvo errore (I)	Irrtum vorbehalten	errors excepted	sauf erreur	—	salvo error
Sammelladung (D)	—	collective consignment	envoi par groupage *m*	carico a collettame *m*	carga colectiva *f*
Sammeltransport (D)	—	collective transport	transport de groupage *m*	trasporto a collettame *m*	transporte colectivo *m*
Sammelwerbung (D)	—	collective advertisement	publicité groupée *f*	pubblicità collettiva *f*	publicidad colectiva *f*
sample[1] (E)	Muster *n*	—	échantillon *m*	campione *m*	muestra *f*
sample[2] (E)	Warenprobe *f*	—	échantillon *m*	campione *m*	muestra *f*
sample bag (E)	Mustermappe *f*	—	dossier à échantillons *m*	cartella campioni *f*	muestrario *m*
sample consignment (E)	Mustersendung *f*	—	envoi d'échantillons *m*	spedizione di campioni *f*	envío de muestras *m*
sample, no commercial value (E)	Muster ohne Wert *n*	—	échantillon sans valeur *m*	campione senza valore *m*	muestra sin valor *f*
sample survey (E)	Stichproben-erhebung *f*	—	enquête par sondage *f*	prelievo di campioni *m*	encuesta por muestreo *f*
sampling procedure (E)	Stichprobe-verfahren *n*	—	méthode d'enquête par sondage *f*	metodo del campionamento *m*	muestreo *m*
sanción (Es)	Sanktion *f*	sanction	sanction *f*	sanzione *f*	—
sanction (E)	Sanktion *f*	—	sanction *f*	sanzione *f*	sanción *f*
sanction (F)	Sanktion *f*	sanction	—	sanzione *f*	sanción *f*
saneamiento (Es)	Sanierung *f*	urban renewal/ reconstruction	assainissement *m*	risanamento *m*	—
sanidad (Es)	Gesundheitswesen *n*	public health	santé publique *f*	sanità *f*	—
Sanierung (D)	—	urban renewal/ reconstruction	assainissement *m*	risanamento *m*	saneamiento *m*
sanità (I)	Gesundheitswesen *n*	public health	santé publique *f*	—	sanidad *f*
Sanktion (D)	—	sanction	sanction *f*	sanzione *f*	sanción *f*
sans défaut (F)	mangelfrei	free of defects	—	esente da vizi	sin vicios
sans délai (F)	fristlos	without prior notice	—	senza preavviso	sin plazo
sans dividende (F)	ohne Dividende	with non-distributed dividend	—	senza dividendo	sin dividendo
sans emballage (F)	unverpackt	unpacked	—	non imballato/ alla rinfusa	sin embalar
sans engagement[1] (F)	freibleibend	subject to confirmation	—	senza impegno	no vinculante
sans engagement[2] (F)	ohne Obligo	without obligation	—	senza obbligo	sin obligación
sans obligation (F)	unverbindlich	not binding	—	senza impegno	sin compromiso
sans phosphate (F)	phosphatfrei	free of phosphate	—	privo di fosfato	sin fosfato
santé publique (F)	Gesundheitswesen *n*	public health	—	sanità *f*	sanidad *f*
sanzione (I)	Sanktion *f*	sanction	sanction *f*	—	sanción *f*
satélite (Es)	Satellit *m*	satellite	satellite *f*	satellite *m*	—
Satellit (D)	—	satellite	satellite *f*	satellite *m*	satélite *m*
satellite (E)	Satellit *m*	—	satellite *f*	satellite *m*	satélite *m*
satellite (F)	Satellit *m*	satellite	—	satellite *m*	satélite *m*
satellite (I)	Satellit *m*	satellite	satellite *f*	—	satélite *m*
Satellitenstation (D)	—	space station	station de satellite *f*	stazione satellite *f*	estación satélite *f*

	D	E	F	I	Es
satisfacción de las necesidades (Es)	Bedürfnis-befriedigung *f*	satisfaction of needs	satisfaction des besoins *f*	soddisfazione dei bisogni *f*	—
satisfacción en el trabajo (Es)	Arbeitszufriedenheit *f*	job satisfaction	satisfaction de travail *f*	soddisfazione del lavoro *f*	—
satisfaction des besoins (F)	Bedürfnis-befriedigung *f*	satisfaction of needs	—	soddisfazione dei bisogni *f*	satisfacción de las necesidades *f*
satisfaction de travail (F)	Arbeitszufriedenheit *f*	job satisfaction	—	soddisfazione del lavoro *f*	satisfacción en el trabajo *f*
satisfaction of needs (E)	Bedürfnis-befriedigung *f*	—	satisfaction des besoins *f*	soddisfazione dei bisogni *f*	satisfacción de las necesidades *f*
Sättigung (D)	—	saturation	saturation *f*	saturazione *f*	saturación *f*
saturazione (I)	Sättigung *f*	saturation	saturation *f*	—	saturación *f*
saturación (Es)	Sättigung *f*	saturation	saturation *f*	saturazione *f*	—
saturation (E)	Sättigung *f*	—	saturation *f*	saturazione *f*	saturación *f*
saturation (F)	Sättigung *f*	saturation	—	saturazione *f*	saturación *f*
Satzung (D)	—	statutes	statut *m*	statuto *m*	estatuto *m*
Satzungsänderung (D)	—	amendment of the statutes	modification des statuts *f*	modificazione dello statuto *f*	modificación de los estatutos *f*
sauf bonne fin (F)	Eingang vorbehalten	due payment reserved	—	salvo buon fine	salvo buen cobro *m*
sauf erreur (F)	Irrtum vorbehalten	errors excepted	—	salvo errore	salvo error
säumig (D)	—	dilatory	retardataire	moroso	moroso
sauvegarde des données (F)	Datenschutz *m*	data securing	—	tutela dei dati *f*	protección de los datos *f*
sauvetage (F)	Bergung *f*	salvage	—	ricupero *m*	salvamento *m*
saving (E)	Sparen *n*	—	épargne *f*	risparmio *m*	ahorro *m*
savings (E)	Ersparnis *f*	—	épargne *f*	risparmio *m*	ahorro *m*
savings bank (E)	Sparkasse *f*	—	institut bancaire d'épargne *m*	cassa di risparmio *f*	caja de ahorros *f*
savings deposits (E)	Spareinlagen *pl*	—	dépôt d'épargne *m*	depositi di risparmio *m pl*	imposiciones de ahorro *f pl*
savings ratio (E)	Sparquote *f*	—	quote-part de revenu réservée à des fins d'épargne *f*	quota di risparmio *f*	cuota de ahorro *f*
scadenza (I)	Laufzeit *f*	term	durée *f*	—	plazo de vencimiento *m*
scadenza degli interessi vincolati (I)	Zinsbindungsfrist *f*	lock-down period for interest rates	délai d'engagement sur le taux d'intérêt accordé *m*	—	plazo de vinculación al tipo de interés pactado *m*
scadenza del credito (I)	Kreditlaufzeit *f*	duration of credit	durée de l'allocation de crédit *f*	—	período concesional de un crédito *m*
scadenza di pagamento (I)	Zahlungsfrist *f*	terms of payment	délai de payement *f*	—	plazo de pago *m*
scadenza residua (I)	Restlaufzeit *f*	residual time to maturity	durée restante *f*	—	plazo de vencimiento restante *m*
scaduto (I)	anstehen	be due	échu	—	estar pendiente
scambio (I)	Tausch *m*	exchange/barter	échange *m*/troc *m*	—	cambio *m*/trueque *m*
scambio est-ovest (I)	Ost-West-Handel *m*	East-West trade	commerce Est-Ouest *m*	—	comercio este-oeste *m*
scambio libero (I)	Freihandel *m*	free trade	commerce libre *m*	—	librecambio *m*
scambio merci (I)	Warenaustausch *m*	exchange of goods	échanges commerciaux *m pl*	—	intercambio de mercancías *m*
scarce (E)	knapp	—	rare	scarso	escaso
scarsità (I)	Knappheit *f*	shortage	rareté *f*	—	escasez *f*
scarsità di materie prime (I)	Rohstoffknappheit *f*	raw materials shortage	pénurie de matières premières *f*	—	escasez de materias primas *f*
scarsità di merci (I)	Warenknappheit *f*	shortage of goods	pénurie de marchandises *f*	—	escasez de mercancías *f*
scarso (I)	knapp	scarce	rare	—	escaso
scarto tipo (I)	Standard-abweichung *f*	standard deviation	déviation standard *f*	—	desviación standard *f*
sceau (F)	Siegel *n*	seal	—	sigillo *m*	sello *m*
scelta dell'ubicazione (I)	Standortwahl *f*	choice of location	choix du lieu d'implantation *m*	—	elección de la ubicación *f*

	D	E	F	I	Es
Schaden (D)	—	damage	dommage *m*	danno *m*	daño *m*
Schadenersatz-ansprüche (D)	—	claim for damages	droit à l'indemnité *m*	diritti al risarcimento danni *m pl*	derecho a indemnización por daños y perjuicios *m*
Schadensersatz (D)	—	compensation for loss suffered	dommages-intérêts *m pl*	risarcimento danni *m*	indemnización *f*
Schadensersatz-klage (D)	—	action for damages	action en dommages-intérêts *f*	azione di risarcimento danni *f*	demanda de daños y perjuicios *f*
Schadensersatz-pflicht (D)	—	liability for damages	obligation de dédommager *f*	obbligo di risarcimento danni *m*	obligación indemnizatoria *f*
Schadensforderung (D)	—	claim for damages	prétention à dommages-intérêts *f*	credito da danni *m*	pretensión de indemnización *f*
Schadensmeldung (D)	—	notification of damage	déclaration du sinistre *f*	avviso di danni *m*	aviso de siniestro *m*
Schadenverhütung (D)	—	loss prevention	mesure préventive contre les sinistres *f*	prevenzione danni *f*	prevención de siniestros *f*
Schadstoff (D)	—	pollutants	élément polluant *m*	sostanza nociva *f*	substancia nociva *f*
Schatzamt (D)	—	Treasury	trésor *m*	tesoreria *f*	tesorería *f*
Schätzwert (D)	—	estimated value	valeur d'estimation *f*	valore stimato *m*	estimación *f*
Schaubild (D)	—	graph	graphique *m*	diagramma *m*	cuadro *m*
Schaufenster (D)	—	shop-window	vitrine *f*	vetrina *f*	escaparate *m*
Schaufenster-dekoration (D)	—	window dressing	décoration de vitrine *f*	allestimento di vetrina *m*	adorno del escaparate *m*
Schaumstoff (D)	—	foam material	mousse synthétique *f*	espanso *m*	plástico espumoso *m*
Scheck (D)	—	cheque	chèque *m*	assegno *m*	cheque *m*
Scheckbetrug (D)	—	cheque fraud	irrégularité en matière de chèque *f*	emissione di assegno a vuoto *f*	falsificación de cheques *f*
Scheckbuch (D)	—	cheque book	livre d'enregistrement des chéques *m*	libretto degli assegni *m*	libro de cheques *m*
Scheckheft (D)	—	cheque book	carnet de chèques *m*	carnet degli assegni *m*	libreta de cheques *f*
Scheckkarte (D)	—	cheque card	carte d'identité eurochèque *f*	carta assegni *f*	tarjeta de cheques *f*
Schecksperrung (D)	—	stopping payment of cheque	opposition au paye-ment d'un chèque *f*	blocco d'assegno *m*	bloqueo de un cheque *m*
scheda (I)	Karteikarte *f*	index card	fiche *f*	—	ficha *f*
schedario (I)	Kartei *f*	card-index	cartothèque	—	fichero *m*
scheduling (E)	Terminplanung *f*	—	planning de rendez-vous *m*	programmazione dei termini *f*	planificación de plazos *f*
scheduling organization (E)	Ablauforganisation *f*	—	organisation fonctionnelle de l'entreprise *f*	organizzazione del lavoro *f*	organización funcional *f*
Scheinfirma (D)	—	bogus firm	raison sociale imaginaire *f*	pseudoditta *f*	casa ficticia *f*
Scheingeschäft (D)	—	fictitious transaction	opération simulée *f*	negozio simulato *m*	operación ficticia *f*
Scheingewinn (D)	—	fictitious profit	gain fictif *m*	utile fittizio *m*	beneficio simulado *m*
Schenkung (D)	—	donation	donation *f*	donazione *f*	donación *f*
Schenkungssteuer (D)	—	gift tax	impôt sur les donations *m*	imposta sulle donazioni *f*	impuesto sobre donaciones *m*
Schichtwechsel (D)	—	change of shift	relève d'équipe *f*	cambio di turno *m*	cambio del equipo de obreros *m*
Schiedsgericht (D)	—	court of arbitration	tribunal d'arbitrage *m*	tribunale arbitrale *m*	tirbunal arbitral *m*
schiffbar (D)	—	navigable	navigable	navigabile	navegable
Schiffsmakler (D)	—	shipbroker	courtier maritime *m*	agente marittimo *m*	corredor marítimo *m*
Schiffsregister (D)	—	register of ships	répertoire des navires *m*	registro navale *m*	registro marítimo *m*
Schlange stehen (D)	—	queue up	faire la queue	fare la coda	hacer la cola
schlechte Qualität (D)	—	poor quality	mauvaise qualité *f*	qualità scadente *f*	mala calidad *f*
schleichende Inflation (D)	—	creeping inflation	inflation rampante *f*	inflazione strisciante *f*	inflación latente *f*
Schlußbilanz (D)	—	closing balance	bilan de clôture *m*	bilancio consuntivo *m*	balance final *m*/balanza de saldos definitivos *f*

	D	E	F	I	Es
Schlußbrief (D)	—	letter of confirmation	lettre de confirmation des conditions *f*	lettera di conferma *f*	carta de confirmación *f*
Schlußkurs (D)	—	closing price	dernier cours *m*	quotazione di chiusura *f*	cotización final *f*
Schlußverkauf (D)	—	seasonal sale	vente de fin de saison *f*	svendita di fine stagione *f*	venta de liquidación *f*
Schlüsselwort (D)	—	key word	mot-clé *m*	parola chiave *f*	palabra clave *f*
Schmierstoffe (D)	—	lubricants	lubrifiants *m pl*	lubrificanti *m pl*	lubrificantes *m pl*
Schmuggel (D)	—	smuggling	contrebande *f*	contrabbando *m*	contrabando *m*
Schneeballsystem (D)	—	snowball system	système de la boule de neige *m*	sistema di vendite a catena aperta *m*	venta en cadena *f*
schnellstmöglich (D)	—	as quickly as possible	le plus vite possible	al più presto possibile	tan rápido como sea posible
school (E)	Schule *f*	—	école *f*	scuola *f*	escuela *f*
school report (E)	Zeugnis *n*	—	certificat scolaire *m*	pagella *f*	certificado de escuela *m*
Schreibtisch (D)	—	desk	bureau *m*	scrivania *f*	escritorio *m*
Schriftform (D)	—	written form	forme par écrit *f*	forma scritta *f*	forma escrita *f*
schriftlich (D)	—	written	par écrit	per iscritto	por escrito
Schuld (D)	—	debt	dette *f*	debito *m*	deuda *f*
Schuldanerkennung (D)	—	acknowledgement of a debt	reconnaissance de dette *f*	riconoscimento del debito *m*	reconocimiento de la deuda *m*
Schulden (D)	—	debts	dettes *f pl*	debiti *m pl*	deudas *f pl*
Schuldendienst (D)	—	debt service	service de la dette *m*	servizio dei debiti *m*	servicio de la deuda *m*
Schuldenmasse (D)	—	total of indebtedness	passif *m*	massa passiva *f*	masa pasiva *f*
schuldhaft (D)	—	culpable	coupable	colposo	culpable
Schuldner (D)	—	debtor	débiteur *m*	debitore *m*	deudor *m*
Schuldnerländer (D)	—	debtor countries	pays débiteurs *m pl*	paesi debitori *m pl*	países deudores *m pl*
Schuldschein (D)	—	certificate of indebtedness	billet de créance *m*	certificato di debito *m*	pagaré *m*
Schuldverschreibung (D)	—	debenture stock	obligation *f*	obbligazione *f*	obligación *f*
Schule (D)	—	school	école *f*	scuola *f*	escuela *f*
Schulungspersonal (D)	—	training staff	personnel d'instruction *m*	personale d'addestramento *m*	personal de formación *m*
Schutzfrist (D)	—	term of protection	délai de protection *m*	durata della protezione *f*	plazo de protección *m*
Schutzzoll (D)	—	protective duty	droit de protection *m*	dazio protettivo *m*	aduana proteccionista *f*
Schwankungsbreite (D)	—	margin of fluctuation	marge de la fluctuation *f*	margine d'oscillazione *m*	margen de fluctuación *f*
Schwarzarbeit (D)	—	illicit work	travail noir *m*	lavoro abusivo *m*	trabajo clandestino *m*
schwarze Zahlen (D)	—	surplus	excédent *m*	conti in nero *m pl*	superávit *m*
Schwarzmarkt (D)	—	black market	marché noir *m*	mercato nero *m*	mercado negro *m*
Schweigepflicht (D)	—	professional discretion	discrétion professionnelle *f*	obbligo del segreto professionale *m*	secreto profesional *m*
Schwellenland (D)	—	newly industrialized countries	pays dans le seuil à l'industrialisation *m*	paese emergente *m*	país en el umbral hacia la industrialización *m*
Schwellenpreis (D)	—	threshold price	prix de seuil *m*	prezzo soglia *m*	precio-base *m*
Schwergut (D)	—	heavy freight	produit pondéreux *m*	carico pesante *m*	mercancía pesada *f*
Schwermetall (D)	—	heavy metal	métal lourd *m*	metallo pesante *m*	metal pesado *m*
Schwestergesellschaft (D)	—	affiliated company	société affiliée *f*	consorella *f*	compañía asociada *f*
Schwindel (D)	—	swindle	tromperie *f*	truffa *f*	engaño *m*
(science de la) gestion industrielle et commerciale (F)	Betriebswirtschaftslehre *f*	business administration	—	economia aziendale *f*	teoría de la empresa *f*
sciences économiques (F)	Wirtschaftswissenschaften *pl*	economics	—	scienze economiche *f pl*	ciencias económicas *f pl*
scienze economiche (I)	Wirtschaftswissenschaften *pl*	economics	sciences économiques *f pl*	—	ciencias económicas *f pl*

	D	E	F	I	Es
scioglimento (I)	Auflösung *f*	dissolution	liquidation *f*	—	disolución *f*
sciopero (I)	Streik *m*	strike	grève *f*	—	huelga *f*
sciopero generale (I)	Generalstreik *m*	general strike	grève générale *f*	—	huelga general *f*
sconto[1] (I)	Diskont *m*	discount	escompte *m*	—	descuento *m*
sconto[2] (I)	Skonto *n*	discount	escompte *m*	—	descuento *m*
sconto di lancio (I)	Einführungsrabatt *m*	introductory discount	rabais d'introduction *m*	—	rebaja de lanzamineto *f*
sconto di quantità (I)	Mengenrabatt *m*	quantity discount	remise de quantité *f*	—	rebaja de cantidad *f*
sconto per pagamento in contanti[1] (I)	Barzahlungs-nachlaß *m*	discount for cash payment	remise pour paye-ment au comptant *f*	—	descuento por pago al contado *m*
sconto per pagamento in contanti[2] (I)	Barzahlungskonto *n*	cash discount	escompte de caisse *m*	—	descuento de pago al contado *f*
scope of advertising effect (E)	Werbereichweite *f*	—	zone de rayonnement de la publicité *f*	raggio d'azione della pubblicità *m*	alcance publicitario *m*
scoperto di conto (I)	Kontoüberziehung *f*	overdraft of an account	découvert de compte *m*	—	descubierto *m*
scorte[1] (I)	Reserve *f*	reserve stock/ reserves	stocks de ré-serve *m pl*/réserve *f*	—	existencias *f pl*/ reserva *f*
scorte[2] (I)	Vorrat *m*	stock	stock *m*	—	existencias *f pl*
scorte iniziali (I)	Anfangsbestand *m*	opening inventory	stock initial *m*	—	existencias iniciales *f pl*
scorte merci (I)	Warenbestand *m*	stock	stock de marchandises *m*	—	existencias de mercancías *f pl*
scrap (E)	verschrotten	—	mettre à la ferraille	ridurre a rottame	hacer quincalla desguazar
screen (E)	Bildschirm *m*	—	écran *m*	video *m*	pantalla *f*
screen job (E)	Bildschirm-arbeitsplatz *m*	—	poste de travail à l'écran *f*	posto di lavoro video *m*	puesto de trabajo de pantalla *m*
screen work (E)	Bildschirmarbeit *f*	—	travail à l'écran	lavoro video *m*	trabajo de pantalla *m*
scrivania (I)	Schreibtisch *m*	desk	bureau *m*	—	escritorio *m*
scuola (I)	Schule *f*	school	école *f*	—	escuela *f*
sdoganamento delle esportazioni (I)	Ausfuhrabfertigung *f*	customs clearance of exports	formalités en douane à l'exportation *f pl*	—	despacho de exportación *m*
sdoganato (I)	verzollt	duty paid	dédouané	—	pagado
seal (E)	Siegel *n*	—	sceau *m*	sigillo *m*	sello *m*
séance extraordinaire (F)	Sondersitzung *f*	special meeting	—	seduta straordinaria *f*	sesión especial *f*
seaproof packing (E)	seemäßige Verpackung *f*	—	emballage maritime *m*	imballaggio marittimo *m*	embalaje marítimo *m*
season (E)	Saison *f*	—	saison *f*	stagione *f*	temporada *f*
sea route (E)	Seeweg *m*	—	voie maritime *f*	via marittima *f*	vía marítima *f*
seasonal fluctuations (E)	Saison-schwankungen *pl*	—	mouvements saisonniers *m pl*	oscillazioni stagionali *f pl*	oscilaciones estacionales *f pl*
seasonally adjusted (E)	saisonbereinigt	—	corrigé du mouve-ment saisonnier	al netto degli influssi stagionali	desestacionalizado
seasonal sale (E)	Schlußverkauf *m*	—	vente de fin de saison *f*	svendita di fine stagione *f*	venta de liquidación *f*
seasonal unemployment (E)	saisonale Arbeitslosigkeit *f*	—	chômage saisonnier *m*	disoccupazione stagionale *f*	paro estacional *m*
sección (Es)	Abteilung *f*	division/department	service *m*	reparto *m*	—
sección de publicidad (Es)	Werbeabteilung *f*	publicity department	service de publicité *m*	reparto pubblicità *m*	—
sección jurídica (Es)	Rechtsabteilung *f*	legal department	bureau juridique *m*	ufficio legale *m*	—
secondary dust (E)	Sekundärstaub *m*	—	poussière secondaire *f*	polvere secondaria *f*	polvo secundario *m*
secondary energy (E)	Sekundärenergie *f*	—	énergie secondaire *f*	energia secondaria *f*	energía secundaria *f*
secrecy of the post (E)	Postgeheimnis *n*	—	secret postal *m*	segreto postale *m*	secreto postal *m*
secret[1] (E)	geheim	—	secret	segreto	secreto
secret[2] (E)	Geheimnis *n*	—	secret *m*	segreto *m*	secreto *m*
secret[1] (F)	geheim	secret	—	segreto	secreto
secret[2] (F)	Geheimnis *n*	secret	—	segreto *m*	secreto *m*

	D	E	F	I	Es
secrétaire[1] (F)	Sekretärin *f*	secretary	—	segretaria *f*	secretaria *f*
secrétaire[2] (F)	Sekretär *m*	secretary	—	segretario *m*	secretario *m*
secretaria (Es)	Sekretärin *f*	secretary	secrétaire *f*	segretaria *f*	—
secretario (Es)	Sekretär *m*	secretary	secrétaire *m*	segretario *m*	—
secretary[1] (E)	Sekretär *m*	—	secrétaire *m*	segretario *m*	secretario *m*
secretary[2] (E)	Sekretärin *f*	—	secrétaire *f*	segretaria *f*	secretaria *f*
secret bancaire (F)	Bankgeheimnis *n*	banker's duty of secrecy	—	segreto bancario *m*	secreto bancario *m*
secret d'affaires (F)	Geschäftsgeheimnis *n*	business secret	—	segreto commerciale *m*	secreto comercial *m*
secret de service (F)	Dienstgeheimnis *n*	official secret	—	segreto d'ufficio *m*	secreto profesional *m*
secret d'exploitation (F)	Betriebsgeheimnis *n*	trade secret	—	segreto aziendale *m*	secreto empresarial *m*
secreto[1] (Es)	geheim	secret	secret	segreto	—
secreto[2] (Es)	Geheimnis *n*	secret	secret *m*	segreto *m*	—
secreto bancario (Es)	Bankgeheimnis *n*	banker's duty of secrecy	secret bancaire *m*	segreto bancario *m*	—
secreto comercial (Es)	Geschäftsgeheimnis *n*	business secret	secret d'affaires *m*	segreto commerciale *m*	—
secreto empresarial (Es)	Betriebsgeheimnis *n*	trade secret	secret d'exploitation *m*	segreto aziendale *m*	—
secreto postal (Es)	Postgeheimnis *n*	secrecy of the post	secret postal *m*	segreto postale *m*	—
secreto profesional[1] (Es)	Berufsgeheimnis *n*	professional secret	secret professionnel *m*	segreto professionale *m*	—
secreto profesional[2] (Es)	Schweigepflicht *f*	professional discretion	discrétion professionnelle *f*	obbligo del segreto professionale *m*	—
secreto profesional[3] (Es)	Dienstgeheimnis *n*	official secret	secret de service *m*	segreto d'ufficio *m*	—
secret postal (F)	Postgeheimnis *n*	secrecy of the post	—	segreto postale *m*	secreto postal *m*
secret professionnel (F)	Berufsgeheimnis *n*	professional secret	—	segreto professionale *m*	secreto profesional *m*
secteur (F)	Sektor *m*	sector	—	settore *m*	sector *m*
secteur économique (F)	Wirtschaftszweig *m*	field of the economy	—	settore economico *m*	ramo económico *m*
secteur public (F)	öffentliche Hand *f*	public authorities	—	mano pubblica *f*	sector público *m*
sector (E)	Sektor *m*	—	secteur *m*	settore *m*	sector *m*
sector (Es)	Sektor *m*	sector	secteur *m*	settore *m*	—
sector del mercado no abarcado por la oferta (Es)	Marktlücke *f*	market gap	créneau du marché *m*	lacuna di mercato *f*	—
sector público (Es)	öffentliche Hand *f*	public authorities	secteur public *m*	mano pubblica *f*	—
sécurité (F)	Sicherheit *f*	security	—	sicurezza *f*	seguridad *f*
sécurité du travail (F)	Arbeitssicherheit *f*	safety at work	—	sicurezza del lavoro *f*	seguridad del trabajo *f*
sécurité réelle (F)	dingliche Sicherung *f*	real security	—	garanzia reale *f*	garantía real *f*
sécurité sociale (F)	soziale Sicherheit *f*	social security	—	sicurezza sociale *f*	seguridad social *f*
securities (E)	Effekten *f*	—	valeurs mobilières *f pl*	titoli *m pl*	efectos *m pl*
securities business[1] (E)	Effektengeschäft *n*	—	commerce des valeurs mobilières *m*	operazione su titoli *f*	operacion de valores *f*
securities business[2] (E)	Wertpapiergeschäft *n*	—	opérations sur titres *f pl*	operazioni su titoli *f pl*	operación con valores *f*
securities fund (E)	Wertpapierfonds *m*	—	fonds de valeurs mobilières *m*	fondo titoli *m*	fondo de inversión mobiliaria *m*
securities market (E)	Wertpapierbörse *f*	—	bourse des titres et valeurs *f*	borsa valori *f*	mercado de valores *m*
security[1] (E)	Kaution *f*	—	caution *f*	cauzione *f*	caución *f*/garantía *f*
security[2] (E)	Wertpapier *n*	—	titre *m*/valeur *f*	titolo *m*	título *m*/valor *m*
security[3] (E)	Sicherheit *f*	—	sécurité *f*	sicurezza *f*	seguridad *f*
sede (I)	Firmensitz *m*	domicile of the company	siège social *m*	—	sede social *f*
sede social (Es)	Firmensitz *m*	domicile of the company	siège social *m*	sede *f*	—

	D	E	F	I	Es
seduta straordinaria (I)	Sondersitzung *f*	special meeting	séance extraordinaire *f*	—	sesión especial *f*
Seeblockade (D)	—	naval blockade	blocus maritime *m*	blocco marittimo *m*	bloqueo marítimo *m*
Seefrachtbrief (D)	—	bill of lading	connaissement maritime *m*	polizza di carico *f*	póliza *f*
seemäßige Verpackung (D)	—	seaproof packing	emballage maritime *m*	imballaggio marittimo *m*	embalaje marítimo *m*
Seemeile (D)	—	nautical mile	mille nautique *m*	miglio marino *m*	milla marina *f*
Seeweg (D)	—	sea route	voie maritime *f*	via marittima *f*	vía marítima *f*
segment de vente (F)	Absatzsegment *n*	sales segment	—	segmento di vendita *m*	segmento de venta *m*
segmento de venta (Es)	Absatzsegment *n*	sales segment	segment de vente *m*	segmento di vendita *m*	—
segmento di vendita (I)	Absatzsegment *n*	sales segment	segment de vente *m*	—	segmento de venta *m*
segretaria (I)	Sekretärin *f*	secretary	secrétaire *f*	—	secretaria *f*
segretario (I)	Sekretär *m*	secretary	secrétaire *m*	—	secretario *m*
segreteria telefonica (I)	Anrufbeantworter *m*	answering machine	répondeur automatique *m*	—	contestador de llamadas *m*
segretezza (I)	Geheimhaltung *f*	maintenance of secrecy	conservation du secret *f*	—	mantenimiento del secreto *m*
segreto[1] (I)	Geheimnis *n*	secret	secret *m*	—	secreto *m*
segreto[2] (I)	geheim	secret	secret	—	secreto
segreto aziendale (I)	Betriebsgeheimnis *n*	trade secret	secret d'exploitation *m*	—	secreto empresarial *m*
segreto bancario (I)	Bankgeheimnis *n*	banker's duty of secrecy	secret bancaire *m*	—	secreto bancario *m*
segreto commerciale (I)	Geschäfts-geheimnis *n*	business secret	secret d'affaires *m*	—	secreto comercial *m*
segreto d'ufficio (I)	Dienstgeheimnis *n*	official secret	secret de service *m*	—	secreto profesional *m*
segreto postale (I)	Postgeheimnis *n*	secrecy of the post	secret postal *m*	—	secreto postal *m*
segreto professionale (I)	Berufsgeheimnis *n*	professional secret	secret professionnel *m*	—	secreto profesional *m*
segunda lectura en el corro (Es)	Reprise *f*	repeat	tendance à la hausse *f*	ripresa *f*	—
según lo acordado (Es)	vereinbarungsgemäß	as agreed	comme convenu	come convenuto	—
seguridad (Es)	Sicherheit *f*	security	sécurité *f*	sicurezza *f*	—
seguridad del trabajo (Es)	Arbeitssicherheit *f*	safety at work	sécurité du travail *f*	sicurezza del lavoro *f*	—
seguridad social (Es)	soziale Sicherheit *f*	social security	sécurité sociale *f*	sicurezza sociale *f*	—
seguro[1] (Es)	Assekuranz *f*	assurance	assurance *f*	assicurazione *f*	—
seguro[2] (Es)	Versicherungspolice *f*	insurance policy	police d'assurance *f*	polizza d'assicurazione *f*	—
seguro[3] (Es)	Versicherung *f*	insurance	assurance *f*	assicurazione *f*	—
seguro contra el robo (Es)	Diebstahl-versicherung *f*	theft insurance	assurance contre le vol *f*	assicurazione contro il furto *f*	—
seguro contra incendios (Es)	Feuerversicherung *f*	fire insurance	assurance contre l'incendie *f*	assicurazione contro incendi *f*	—
seguro contra robo con fractura (Es)	Einbruch-versicherung *f*	housebreaking insurance	assurance contre le vol avec effraction *f*	assicurazione contro il furto con scasso *f*	—
seguro crediticio (Es)	Kreditversicherung *f*	credit insurance	assurance crédit *f*	assicurazione dei crediti *f*	—
seguro de accidentes (Es)	Unfallversicherung *f*	personal accident insurance	assurance accidents corporels *f*	assicurazione contro infortuni *f*	—
seguro de automóviles (Es)	Kraftfahrzeug-versicherung *f*	motor insurance	assurance responsabilité civile automobile *f*	assicurazione autoveicoli *f*	—
seguro de casco (Es)	Kaskoversicherung *f*	comprehensive insurance	assurance tous risques *f*	assicurazione corpi del ramo trasporto *f*	—
seguro de cosas (Es)	Sachversicherung *f*	property insurance	assurance de choses *f*	assicurazione di cose *f*	—
seguro de empleados (Es)	Angestellten-versicherung *f*	Salaried Employees' Pension Insurance	assurance invalidité-vieillesse des employés *f*	assicurazione degli impiegati *f*	—

	D	E	F	I	Es
seguro de enfermedad (Es)	Krankenversicherung *f*	health insurance	assurance maladie *f*	assicurazione contro le malattie	—
seguro de equipajes (Es)	Reisegepäckversicherung *f*	baggage insurance	assurance des bagages *f*	assicurazione del bagaglio *f*	—
seguro de maquinaria (Es)	Maschinenversicherung *f*	machine insurance	assurance des machines *f*	assicurazione delle macchine *f*	—
seguro de pensiones (Es)	Rentenversicherung *f*	old-age pension insurance	assurance sociale invalidité-vieillesse *f*	assicurazione invalidità e vecchiaia *f*	—
seguro de rescisión del viaje (Es)	Reiserücktrittsversicherung *f*	travel cancellation insurance	assurance de résiliation du voyage *f*	assicurazione recessione viaggio *f*	—
seguro de responsabilidad civil (Es)	Haftpflichtversicherung *f*	third party liability insurance	assurance responsabilité civile *f*	assicurazione della responsabilità civile *f*	—
seguro de transporte (Es)	Transportversicherung *f*	transportation insurance	assurance transports *f*	assicurazione dei trasporti *f*	—
seguro de vejez (Es)	Altersversicherung *f*	old age insurance	assurance-vieillesse *f*	assicurazione per la vecchiaia *f*	—
seguro de vida (Es)	Lebensversicherung *f*	life insurance	assurance vie *f*	assicurazione sulla vita *f*	—
seguro de vida temporal (Es)	Risiko-Lebensversicherung *f*	term life insurance	assurance-vie temporaire *f*	assicurazione rischio-vita *f*	—
seguro inmobiliario (Es)	Gebäudeversicherung *f*	insurance on buildings	assurance des bâtiments *f*	assicurazione dei fabbricati *f*	—
seguro personal (Es)	Personenversicherung *f*	insurance of persons	assurance des personnes *f*	assicurazione di persone *f*	—
seguro privado (Es)	Privatversicherung *f*	private security	assurance privée *f*	assicurazione privata *f*	—
seguro social (Es)	Sozialversicherung *f*	social insurance	assurance sociale *m*	previdenza sociale *f*	—
Sekretär (D)	—	secretary	secrétaire *m*	segretario *m*	secretario *m*
Sekretärin (D)	—	secretary	secrétaire *f*	segretaria *f*	secretaria *f*
Sektor (D)	—	sector	secteur *m*	settore *m*	sector *m*
Sekundärenergie (D)	—	secondary energy	énergie secondaire *f*	energia secondaria *f*	energía secundaria *f*
Sekundärstaub (D)	—	secondary dust	poussière secondaire *f*	polvere secondaria *f*	polvo secundario *m*
selbständig (D)	—	independent	indépendant	indipendente	independiente/no asalariado/autónomo
Selbstauskunft (D)	—	voluntary disclosure	renseignement fourni par l'intéressé lui-même *m*	informazione volontaria *f*	información de sí mismo *f*
Selbstbedienung (D)	—	self-service	self-service *m*	self service *m*	autoservicio *m*
Selbstfinanzierung (D)	—	self-financing	autofinancement *m*	autofinanziamento *m*	autofinanciación *f*
Selbstkosten (D)	—	cost	coût de revient *m*	spese vive *f pl*	costes propios *m pl*
Selbstkostenpreis (D)	—	cost price	prix coûtant *m*	prezzo di costo *m*	precio de coste *m*
selección (Es)	Selektion *f*	selection	sélection *f*	selezione *f*	—
sélectif (F)	selektiv	selective	—	selettivo	selectivo
selection (E)	Selektion *f*	—	sélection *f*	selezione *f*	selección *f*
sélection (F)	Selektion *f*	selection	—	selezione *f*	selección *f*
selective (E)	selektiv	—	sélectif	selettivo	selectivo
selectivo (Es)	selektiv	selective	sélectif	selettivo	—
Selektion (D)	—	selection	sélection *f*	selezione *f*	selección *f*
selektiv (D)	—	selective	sélectif	selettivo	selectivo
selettivo (I)	selektiv	selective	sélectif	—	selectivo
selezione (I)	Selektion *f*	selection	sélection *f*	—	selección *f*
selfemployed person (E)	Freiberufler *m*	—	personne exerçant une profession libérale *f*	libero professionista *m*	profesional *m*
self-financing (E)	Eigenfinanzierung *f*	—	autofinancement *m*	autofinanziamento *m*	financiación propia *f*
self-service (E)	Selbstbedienung *f*	—	self-service *m*	self service *m*	autoservicio *m*
self-service (F)	Selbstbedienung *f*	self-service	—	self service *m*	autoservicio *m*
self service (I)	Selbstbedienung *f*	self-service	self-service *m*	—	autoservicio *m*
sell (E)	verkaufen	—	vendre	vendere	vender
sellers competition (E)	Verkäuferwettbewerb *m*	—	compétition des vendeurs *f*	concorrenza dei venditori *f*	competición de vendedores *f*

	D	E	F	I	Es
seller's market (E)	Verkäufermarkt *m*	—	marché de vendeurs *m*	mercato favorevole ai venditori *m*	mercado favorable al vendedor *m*
sello[1] (Es)	Briefmarke *f*	stamp	timbre-poste *m*	francobollo *m*	—
sello[2] (Es)	Siegel *n*	seal	sceau *m*	sigillo *m*	—
sello postal (Es)	Poststempel *m*	postmark	cachet de la poste *m*	timbro postale *m*	—
semaine de travail (F)	Arbeitswoche *f*	working week	—	settimana lavorativa *f*	semana laboral *f*
semana laboral (Es)	Arbeitswoche *f*	working week	semaine de travail *f*	settimana lavorativa *f*	—
semestral (Es)	halbjährlich	half-yearly	semestriel	semestrale	—
semestrale (I)	halbjährlich	half-yearly	semestriel	—	semestral
semestriel (F)	halbjährlich	half-yearly	—	semestrale	semestral
semi-finished good (E)	Halberzeugnis *n*	—	produit demi-fini *m*	prodotto semifinito *m*	producto semielaborado *m*
semi-qualificato (I)	angelernt	semi-skilled	semi-qualifié	—	semicualificado
semi-qualifié (F)	angelernt	semi-skilled	—	semi-qualificato	semicualificado
semi-skilled (E)	angelernt	—	semi-qualifié	semi-qualificato	semicualificado
send a telegram (E)	telegrafieren	—	télégraphier	telegrafare	telegrafiar
sender (E)	Absender *m*	—	envoyeur *m*	mittente *m*	remitente *m*
Sendung (D)	—	consignment	envoi *m*	spedizione *f*	envío *m*
sensible a las fluctuaciones coyunturales (Es)	konjunkturanfällig	depending on the cyclical trend	sensible aux oscillations de la conjoncture	soggetto ad influssi congiunturali	—
sensible aux oscillations de la conjoncture (F)	konjunkturanfällig	depending on the cyclical trend	—	soggetto ad influssi congiunturali	sensible a las fluctuaciones coyunturales
senza concorrenza (I)	konkurrenzlos	without competition	défiant toute concurrence	—	sin competencia
senza dividendo (I)	ohne Dividende	with non-distributed dividend	sans dividende *m*	—	sin dividendo
senza garanzia (I)	ohne Gewähr	without garanty	sous toute réserve	—	sin garantía
senza impegno[1] (I)	unverbindlich	not binding	sans obligation	—	sin compromiso
senza impegno[2] (I)	freibleibend	subject to confirmation	sans engagement	—	no vinculante
senza obbligo (I)	ohne Obligo	without obligation	sans engagement	—	sin obligación
senza preavviso (I)	fristlos	without prior notice	sans délai	—	sin plazo
séquestre judiciare (F)	Zwangsverwaltung *f*	receivership	—	amministrazione giudiziaria *f*	administración forzosa *f*
sequestro (I)	Beschlagnahme *f*	confiscation	saisie *f*	—	confiscación *f*
se référant (F)	bezugnehmend	referring to	—	con riferimento	con referencia a
Serienfertigung (D)	—	series production	fabrication de série *f*	produzione in serie *f*	producción en serie *f*
series production (E)	Serienfertigung *f*	—	fabrication de série *f*	produzione in serie *f*	producción en serie *f*
serietà (I)	Seriosität *f*	seriousness	caractère sérieux *m*	—	buena reputación *f*
Seriosität (D)	—	seriousness	caractère sérieux *m*	serietà *f*	buena reputación *f*
seriousness (E)	Seriosität *f*	—	caractère sérieux *m*	serietà *f*	buena reputación *f*
serpente monetario (I)	Währungsschlange *f*	currency snake	serpent monétaire *m*	—	serpiente monetaria *f*
serpent monétaire (F)	Währungsschlange *f*	currency snake	—	serpente monetario *m*	serpiente monetaria *f*
serpiente monetaria (Es)	Währungsschlange *f*	currency snake	serpent monétaire *m*	serpente monetario *m*	—
serrata (I)	Aussperrung *f*	lock out	lock-out *m*	—	cierre patronal *m*
Service (D)	—	service	service *m*	servizio *m*	servicio *m*
service[1] (E)	Service *m*	—	service *m*	servizio *m*	servicio *m*
service[2] (E)	Dienst *m*	—	service *m*	servizio *m*	servicio *m*
service[3] (E)	Dienstleistung *f*	—	prestation de service *f*	servizio *m*	prestación de servicio *m*
service[1] (F)	Service *m*	service	—	servizio *m*	servicio *m*
service[2] (F)	Abteilung *f*	division/department	—	reparto *m*	sección *f*
service[3] (F)	Dienst *m*	service	—	servizio *m*	servicio *m*
service après vente (F).	Kundendienst *m*	after-sales service	—	servizio d'assistenza *m*	servicio posventa *m*

	D	E	F	I	Es
service de contributions (F)	Finanzamt *n*	inland revenue office	—	ufficio delle imposte *m*	Hacienda *f*
service de la dette (F)	Schuldendienst *m*	debt service	—	servizio dei debiti *m*	servicio de la deuda *m*
service de l'intérêt (F)	Zinsendienst *m*	interest service	—	servizio degli interessi *m*	servicio de intereses *m*
service de publicité (F)	Werbeabteilung *f*	publicity department	—	reparto pubblicità *m*	sección de publicidad *f*
service des expéditions (F)	Versandabteilung *f*	dispatch department	—	reparto spedizioni *m*	departamento de expedición *m*
service de télécommunication (F)	Fernmeldeamt *n*	telephone exchange	—	ufficio telecomunicazioni *m*	central interurbana *f*
service d'exportation (F)	Exportabteilung *f*	export department	—	reparto esportazioni *m*	departamento de exportación *m*
service du téléphone (F)	Telefondienst *m*	telephone service	—	servizio telefonico *m*	servicio telefónico *m*
service extérieur (F)	Außendienst *m*	field work	—	servizio esterno *m*	servicio exterior *m*
service organization (E)	Kundendienst-organisation *f*	—	organisation de service après-vente *f*	organizzazione del servizio d'assistenza *f*	organización de servicio posventa *f*
service technique (F)	technische Abteilung *f*	engineering department	—	reparto tecnico *m*	departamento técnico *m*
servicio¹ (Es)	Dienst *m*	service	service *m*	servizio *m*	—
servicio² (Es)	Service *m*	service	service *m*	servizio *m*	—
servicio de colocación (Es)	Arbeitsnachweis *m*	vacancies employment	emploi vacant *m*	informazioni sui posti vacanti *f pl*	—
servicio de intereses (Es)	Zinsendienst *m*	interest service	service de l'intérêt *m*	servizio degli interessi *m*	—
servicio de la deuda (Es)	Schuldendienst *m*	debt service	service de la dette *m*	servizio dei debiti *m*	—
servicio de pagos (Es)	Zahlungsverkehr *m*	payment transactions	opérations de payement *f pl*	operazioni di pagamento *f pl*	—
servicio exterior (Es)	Außendienst *m*	field work	service extérieur *m*	servizio esterno *m*	—
servicio posventa (Es)	Kundendienst *m*	after-sales service	service après vente *m*	servizio d'assistenza *m*	—
servicio telefónico (Es)	Telefondienst *m*	telephone service	service du téléphone *m*	servizio telefonico *m*	—
servizio¹ (I)	Service *m*	service	service *m*	—	servicio *m*
servizio² (I)	Dienst *m*	service	service *m*	—	servicio *m*
servizio³ (I)	Dienstleistung *f*	service	prestation de service *f*	—	prestación de servicio *m*
servizio d'assistenza (I)	Kundendienst *m*	after-sales service	service après vente *m*	—	servicio posventa *m*
servizio degli interessi (I)	Zinsendienst *m*	interest service	service de l'intérêt *m*	—	servicio de intereses *m*
servizio dei debiti (I)	Schuldendienst *m*	debt service	service de la dette *m*	—	servicio de la deuda *m*
servizio di sorveglianza aziendale (I)	Werkschutz *m*	works protection force	corps de sécurité d'entreprise *m*	—	policía de la empresa *f*
servizio esterno (I)	Außendienst *m*	field work	service extérieur *m*	—	servicio exterior *m*
servizio telefonico (I)	Telefondienst *m*	telephone service	service du téléphone *m*	—	servicio telefónico *m*
sesión bursátil (Es)	Börsentag *m*	market day	jour de bourse *m*	giorno di borsa *m*	—
sesión especial (Es)	Sondersitzung *f*	special meeting	séance extraordinaire *f*	seduta straordinaria *f*	—
set-off (E)	Aufrechnung *f*	—	compensation *f*	compensazione *f*	compensación *f*
settimana lavorativa (I)	Arbeitswoche *f*	working week	semaine de travail *f*	—	semana laboral *f*
settimanale (I)	wöchentlich	weekly	hebdomadaire	—	semanal
setting up of new business (E)	Existenzgründung *f*	—	fondation d'existence *f*	costituzione di un lavoro indipendente *f*	fundación de existencia *f*
settlement (E)	Abwicklung *f*	—	exécution *f*/ liquidation *f*	esecuzione *f*	ejecución *f*
settlement account (E)	Abwicklungskonto *n*	—	compte de liquidation *m*	conto di liquidazione *f*	cuenta de liquidación *f*
settlement by letter of credit (E)	Akkreditiv-abwicklung *f*	—	exécution par crédit documentaire *f*	procedura del credito documentario *f*	ejecución por crédito documentario *f*

	D	E	F	I	Es
settlement of accounts (E)	Abrechnung *f*	—	règlement *m*	liquidazione *f*	liquidación *f*
settlement of an account (E)	Kontoausgleich *m*	—	solde de compte *m*	liquidazione del conto *f*	saldo de cuenta *m*
settlement with immediate effect (E)	sofortige Regulierung *f*	—	règlement immédiat *m*	regolazione immediata *f*	regulación inmediata *f*
settling day (E)	Abrechnungstag *m*	—	jour de la liquidation *m*	giorno di liquidazione *m*	fecha de liquidación *f*
settling procedure (E)	Abrechnungs-verfahren *n*	—	méthode de l'apure-ment des comptes	metodo di liquidazione *m*	operaciones de descuento *f pl*
settore (I)	Sektor *m*	sector	secteur *m*	—	sector *m*
settore economico (I)	Wirtschaftszweig *m*	field of the economy	secteur économique *m*	—	ramo económico *m*
seuil de rentabilité[1] (F)	Gewinnschwelle *f*	break even point	—	soglia dell'utile *f*	umbral de la rentabilidad *m*
seuil de rentabilité[2] (F)	Rentabilitätschwelle *f*	break-even point	—	soglia di redditività *f*	límite inferior de rentabilidad *m*
seuil du prix (F)	Preisschwelle *f*	threshold price	—	soglia dei prezzi *f*	umbral de precios *m*
seule de change (F)	Solawechsel *m*	promissory note	—	pagherò *m*	pagaré *m*
seul propriétaire (F)	Alleininhaber *m*	sole owner	—	titolare unico *m*	propietario exclusivo *m*
sewage disposal costs (E)	Abwasserkosten *pl*	—	coûts de traitement des eaux usées *m pl*	costi per le acque di scarico *m pl*	gastos para aguas residuales *m pl*
sfruttamento abusivo (I)	Raubbau *m*	ruinous exploitation	exploitation abusive *f*	—	explotación abusiva *f*
sfruttamento delle capacità (I)	Kapazitäts-auslastung *f*	utilization of capacity	utilisation de la capacité *f*	—	utilización de las capacidades *f*
sgravio (I)	Entlastung *f*	discharge	décharge *f*	—	desgravamen *m*
share[1] (E)	Geschäftsanteil *m*	—	part sociale *f*	quota sociale *f*	participación *f*
share[2] (E)	Aktie *f*	—	action *f*	azione *f*	acción *f*
share capital[1] (E)	Grundkapital *n*	—	capital initial *m*	capitale sociale *m*	capital social *m*
share capital[2] (E)	Stammkapital *n*	—	capital social *m*	capitale sociale *m*	capital social *m*
share capital[3] (E)	Aktienkapital *n*	—	fonds social *m*	capitale azionario *m*	capital en acciones *m*
share deposit (E)	Aktiendepot *n*	—	dépôt d'actions *m*	deposito di azioni *m*	depósitio de acciones *m*
shareholder (E)	Aktionär *m*	—	actionnaire *m*	azionista *m*	accionista *m*
shareholder's agreement (E)	Gesellschafts-vertrag *m*	—	acte de société *m*	contratto di società *m*	contrato social *m*
shareholding (E)	Aktienbestand *m*	—	portefeuille d'actions *m*	portafoglio di azioni *m*	cartera de acciones *f*
share in capital (E)	Kapitalanteil *m*	—	part de capital *f*	quota di capitale *f*	participación en el capital *f*
share index (E)	Aktienindex *m*	—	indice du cours des actions *m*	indice azionario *m*	índice de cotización de acciones *m*
share in the material costs (E)	Materialkosten-anteil *m*	—	proportion des frais de matériel *f*	quota dei costi del materiale *f*	parte de los gastos de material *m*
share issue[1] (E)	Aktienemision *f*	—	émission d'actions *f*	emissione di azioni *f*	emisión de acciones *f*
share issue[2] (E)	Aktienausgabe *f*	—	émission d'actions *f*	emissione di azioni *f*	emisión de acciones *f*
share price (E)	Aktienkurs *m*	—	cours des actions *m*	corso delle azioni *m*	cotización de las acciones *f*
share quotation (E)	Aktiennotierung *f*	—	cotation des actions *f*	quotazione delle azioni *f*	cotización de acciones *f*
shares (E)	Aktien *pl*	—	actions *f pl*	azioni *f*	acciones *f pl*
shipbroker (E)	Schiffsmakler *m*	—	courtier maritime *m*	agente marittimo *m*	corredor marítimo *m*
shipment (E)	Verschiffung *f*	—	embarquement *m*	imbarco *m*	embarque *m*
shipowner (E)	Reeder *m*	—	armateur *m*	armatore *m*	armador *m*
shipping company (E)	Reederei *f*	—	société d'armateurs *f*	compagnia armatoriale *f*	compañía naviera *f*
shipping (delivered) weight (E)	Abladegewicht *n*	—	poids au déchargement *m*	peso di scarico *m*	peso de descarga *m*
shipping document (E)	Versanddokument *n*	—	documents d'expédition *m pl*	documento di spedizione *m*	documentos de expedición *m pl*
Shopping Center (D)	—	shopping centre	centre commercial *m*	centro commerciale *m*	centro comercial *m*
shopping centre (E)	Shopping Center *n*	—	centre commercial *m*	centro commerciale *m*	centro comercial *m*

	D	E	F	I	Es
shop-window (E)	Schaufenster *n*	—	vitrine *f*	vetrina *f*	escaparate *m*
shortage (E)	Knappheit *f*	—	rareté *f*	scarsità *f*	escasez *f*
shortage of goods (E)	Warenknappheit *f*	—	pénurie de marchandises *f*	scarsità di merci *f*	escasez de mercancías *f*
shortage of staff (E)	Personalmangel *m*	—	manque de personnel *m*	mancanza di personale *f*	falta der personal *f*
short delivery (E)	Minderlieferung *f*	—	livraison en quantité inférieure *f*	fornitura ridotta *f*	envío incompleto *m*
short distance traffic (E)	Nahverkehr *m*	—	transport à courte distance *m*	traffico a breve distanza *m*	tráfico a corta distancia *m*
short sale (E)	Blankoverkauf *m*	—	vente à découvert *f*	vendita allo scoperto *f*	venta al descubierto *f*
short-term (E)	kurzfristig	—	à court terme	a breve scadenza	a corto plazo
short-term credit (E)	kurzfristiger Kredit *m*	—	crédit à court terme *m*	credito a breve scadenza *m*	crédito a corto plazo *m*
short-time work (E)	Kurzarbeit *f*	—	travail à temps réduit *m*	lavoro ad orario ridotto *m*	trabajo reducido *m*
shuttle service (E)	Pendelverkehr *m*	—	trafic de va-et-vient *m*	traffico pendolare *m*	vaivén *m*
Sicherheit (D)	—	security	sécurité *f*	sicurezza *f*	seguridad *f*
Sicherheitsmarge (D)	—	margin	marge de sécurité *f*	margine di sicurezza *m*	margen de seguridad *f*
sicurezza (I)	Sicherheit *f*	security	sécurité *f*	—	seguridad *f*
sicurezza del lavoro (I)	Arbeitssicherheit *f*	safety at work	sécurité du travail *f*	—	seguridad del trabajo *f*
sicurezza sociale (I)	soziale Sicherheit *f*	social security	sécurité sociale *f*	—	seguridad social *f*
Siegel (D)	—	seal	sceau *m*	sigillo *m*	sello *m*
siège social (F)	Firmensitz *m*	domicile of the company	—	sede *f*	sede social *f*
sigillo (I)	Siegel *n*	seal	sceau *m*	—	sello *m*
sigillo doganale (I)	Zollverschluß *m*	customs seal	fermeture douanière *f*	—	precinto aduanero *m*
sigla (I)	Diktatzeichen *n*	reference	références *f pl*	—	referencias *f pl*
sign (E)	unterschreiben	—	signer	firmare	signar
signar (Es)	unterschreiben	sign	signer	firmare	—
signataire d'une convention collective (F)	Tarifpartner *m*	parties to a collective agreement	—	parti sociali *f pl*	parte contratante en un convenio colectivo *f*
signature (E)	Unterschrift *f*	—	signature *f*	firma *f*	firma *f*
signature (F)	Unterschrift *f*	signature	—	firma *f*	firma *f*
signature en blanc (F)	Blankounterschrift *f*	blank signature	—	firma in bianco *f*	firma en blanco *f*
signer (F)	unterschreiben	sign	—	firmare	signar
significatif (F)	relevant	relevant	—	rilevante	importante
Silber (D)	—	silver	argent *m*	argento *m*	plata *f*
silver (E)	Silber *n*	—	argent *m*	argento *m*	plata *f*
silvicultura (Es)	Forstwirtschaft *f*	forestry	économie forestière *f*	economia forestale *f*	—
simulación (Es)	Simulation *f*	simulation	simulation *f*	simulazione *f*	—
Simulation (D)	—	simulation	simulation *f*	simulazione *f*	simulación *f*
simulation (E)	Simulation *f*	—	simulation *f*	simulazione *f*	simulación *f*
simulation (F)	Simulation *f*	simulation	—	simulazione *f*	simulación *f*
simulazione (I)	Simulation *f*	simulation	simulation *f*	—	simulación *f*
sinceridad del balance (Es)	Bilanzwahrheit *f*	truth in the balance sheet	sincérité du bilan *f*	chiarezza di bilancio *f*	—
sincérité du bilan (F)	Bilanzwahrheit *f*	truth in the balance sheet	—	chiarezza di bilancio *f*	sinceridad del balance *f*
sin competencia (Es)	konkurrenzlos	without competition	défiant toute concurrence	senza concorrenza	—
sin compromiso (Es)	unverbindlich	not binding	sans obligation	senza impegno	—
sindacati (I)	Gewerkschaften *pl*	trade union	syndicat *m*	—	sindicato *m*
sindacato (I)	Syndikat *n*	syndicate	syndicat *m*	—	sindicato *m*
sindacato di blocco (I)	Sperrminorität *f*	blocking minority	minorité suffisante pour bloquer qch. *f*	—	minoría de bloqueo *f*
sindicación (Es)	Syndizierung *f*	syndication	syndication *f*	costituzione di un sindacato *f*	—

	D	E	F	I	Es
sindicato[1] (Es)	Gewerkschaften *pl*	trade union	syndicat *m*	sindacati *m pl*	—
sindicato[2] (Es)	Syndikat *n*	syndicate	syndicat *m*	sindacato *m*	—
síndico (Es)	Syndikus	legal adviser	syndic *m*	consulente legale *m*	—
síndico de quiebra (Es)	Konkursverwalter *m*	administrator in bankruptcy proceedings	liquidateur de la faillite *m*	curatore fallimentare *m*	—
sin dividendo (Es)	ohne Dividende	with non-distributed dividend	sans dividende *m*	senza dividendo	—
sin embalar (Es)	unverpackt	unpacked	sans emballage	non imballato/ alla rinfusa	—
sin fosfato (Es)	phosphatfrei	free of phosphate	sans phosphate	privo di fosfato	—
sin garantía (Es)	ohne Gewähr	without garanty	sous toute réserve	senza garanzia	—
sin obligación (Es)	ohne Obligo	without obligation	sans engagement	senza obbligo	—
siniestro leve (Es)	Bagatellschaden *m*	minimal damage	dommage mineur *m*	danno piccolo *m*	—
sinistre (F)	Versicherungsfall *m*	event insured against	—	caso di sinistro *m*	situación de siniestro *f*
sin plazo (Es)	fristlos	without prior notice	sans délai	senza preavviso	—
sin vicios (Es)	mangelfrei	free of defects	sans défaut	esente da vizi	—
sistema (Es)	System *n*	system	système *m*	sistema *m*	—
sistema (I)	System *n*	system	système *m*	—	sistema *m*
sistema de costes (Es)	Kostenrechnungs-system *n*	cost accounting system	méthode de calcul des coûts *f*	sistema dei costi *m*	—
sistema de cuotas (Es)	Quotensystem *n*	quota system	système de quote-parts *m*	sistema di contingentamento *m*	—
sistema de gravámenes (Es)	Abschöpfungs-system *n*	absorption system	système d'absorption *m*	regime di prelievo *m*	—
sistema dei costi (I)	Kostenrechnungs-system *n*	cost accounting system	méthode de calcul des coûts *f*	—	sistema de costes *m*
sistema de incentivos (Es)	Anreizsystem *n*	incentive system	système d'incitation *m*	sistema d'incentivo *m*	—
sistema de información (Es)	Informations-system *n*	information system	système d'information *m*	sistema d'informazione *m*	—
sistema de información asistido por ordenador (Es)	computergestützes Informations-system *n*	computer-aided information system	système d'informa-tion assisté par ordinateur *m*	sistema di informazione computerizzato *m*	—
sistema dei premi (I)	Prämiensystem *n*	bonus system	système de primes *m*	—	sistema de primas *m*
sistema del lavoro a cottimo (I)	Akkordsystem *n*	piece work system	système du travail aux pièces *m*	—	régimen de trabajo a destajo *m*
sistema de primas (Es)	Prämiensystem *n*	bonus system	système de primes *m*	sistema dei premi *m*	—
sistema di contingentamento (I)	Quotensystem *n*	quota system	système de quote-parts *m*	—	sistema de cuotas *m*
sistema di informazione computerizzato (I)	computergestützes Informations-system *n*	computer-aided information system	système d'informa-tion assisté par ordinateur *m*	—	sistema de informa-ción asistido por ordenador *m*
sistema d'incentivo (I)	Anreizsystem *n*	incentive system	système d'incitation *m*	—	sistema de incentivos *m*
sistema d'informazione (I)	Informations-system *n*	information system	système d'information *m*	—	sistema de información *m*
sistema di vendite a catena aperta (I)	Schneeballsystem *n*	snowball system	système de la boule de neige *m*	—	venta en cadena *f*
sistema economico mondiale (I)	Weltwirtschafts-ordnung *f*	international economic order	ordre économique mondial *m*	—	orden económico mundial *m*
sistema fiscal (Es)	Steuersystem *n*	system of taxation	système fiscal *m*	sistema fiscale *m*	—
sistema fiscale (I)	Steuersystem *n*	system of taxation	système fiscal *m*	—	sistema fiscal *m*
Sistema Monetario Europeo (Es)	Europäisches Währungssystem *n*	European Monetary System	Système Monétaire Européen *m*	Sistema Monetario Europeo *m*	—
Sistema Monetario Europeo (I)	Europäisches Währungssystem *n*	European Monetary System	Système Monétaire Européen *m*	—	Sistema Monetario Europeo *m*
sistema monetario internacional (Es)	Weltwährungs-system *n*	international monetary system	système monétaire international *m*	sistema monetario internazionale *m*	—
sistema monetario internazionale (I)	Weltwährungs-system *n*	international monetary system	système monétaire international *m*	—	sistema monetario internacional *m*
situación de competencia (Es)	Konkurrenzsituation *f*	competitive situation	situation de concurrence *f*	situazione concorrenziale *f*	—

	D	E	F	I	Es
situación del beneficio (Es)	Ertragslage *f*	earning situation	niveau du rendement *m*	situazione economica *f*	—
situación de personal (Es)	Personalsituation *f*	personnel situation	effectif du personnel *m*	situazione occupazionale *f*	—
situación de siniestro (Es)	Versicherungsfall *m*	event insured against	sinistre *m*	caso di sinistro *m*	—
situación económica (Es)	Vermögens-verhältnisse *pl*	financial situation	situation financière *f*	situazione patrimoniale *f*	—
situación jurídica (Es)	Rechtslage *f*	legal situation	situation juridique *f*	situazione giuridica *f*	—
situation analytique de l'expoitation (F)	Betriebsanalyse *f*	operation analysis	—	analisi aziendale *f*	análisis de la empresa *m*
situation de concurrence (F)	Konkurrenzsituation *f*	competitive situation	—	situazione concorrenziale *f*	situación de competencia *f*
situation du marché[1] (F)	Marktsituation *f*	market situation	—	situazione di mercato *f*	estado del mercado *m*
situation du marché[2] (F)	Marktlage *f*	state of the market	—	situazione di mercato *f*	condiciones del mercado *f pl*
situation financière (F)	Vermögens-verhältnisse *pl*	financial situation	—	situazione patrimoniale *f*	situación económica *f*
situation juridique (F)	Rechtslage *f*	legal situation	—	situazione giuridica *f*	situación jurídica *f*
situation wanted (E)	Stellengesuch *n*	—	demande d'emploi *f*	domanda d'impiego *f*	solicitud de colocación *f*
situazione concorrenziale (I)	Konkurrenz-situation *f*	competitive situation	situation de concurrence *f*	—	situación de competencia *f*
situazione di mercato[1] (I)	Marktsituation *f*	market situation	situation du marché *f*	—	estado del mercado *m*
situazione di mercato[2] (I)	Marktlage *f*	state of the market	situation du marché *f*	—	condiciones del mercado *f pl*
situazione economica (I)	Ertragslage *f*	earning situation	niveau du rendement *m*	—	situación del beneficio *f*
situazione giuridica (I)	Rechtslage *f*	legal situation	situation juridique *f*	—	situación jurídica *f*
situazione occupazionale (I)	Personalsituation *f*	personnel situation	effectif du personnel *m*	—	situación de personal *f*
situazione patrimoniale (I)	Vermögens-verhältnisse *pl*	financial situation	situation financière *f*	—	situación económica *f*
Sitzungszimmer (D)	—	conference room	salle de réunion *f*	sala riunioni *f*	sala de conferencia *f*
size of an advertisement (E)	Anzeigenformat *n*	—	format de l'annonce *m*	formato dell'inserzione *m*	tamaño del anuncio *m*
size of the company[1] (E)	Betriebsgröße *f*	—	dimension de l'entreprise *f*	dimensione dell'azienda *f*	tamaño de la explotación *m*
size of the company[2] (E)	Unternehmens-größe *f*	—	dimension de l'entreprise *f*	dimensione dell'impresa *f*	dimensión de la empresa *f*
Skonto (D)	—	discount	escompte *m*	sconto *m*	descuento *m*
Skontoabzug (D)	—	discount deduction	déduction de l'escompte *f*	detrazione di sconto *f*	deducción del descuento *f*
slide projector (E)	Diaprojektor *m*	—	projecteur pour diapositives *m*	proiettore per diapositive *m*	projector de dipositivas *m*
slump-proof (E)	krisenfest	—	insensible aux influences de la crise économique	resistente alle crisi	a prueba de crisis
small and medium-sized enterprises (E)	Klein- und Mittelbetriebe *pl*	—	petites et moyennes entreprises *f pl*	piccole e medie imprese *f pl*	pequeñas y medianas empresas *f pl*
small container (E)	Kleincontainer *m*	—	petit conteneur *m*	mini container *m*	pequeño contenedor *m*
small package (E)	Päckchen *n*	—	petit paquet *m*	pacchetto *m*	pequeño paquete *m*
small pallet (E)	Kleinpalette *f*	—	petite palette *f*	mini paletta *f*	pequña paleta *f*
smaltimento (I)	Entsorgung *f*	waste disposal	dépollution *f*	—	eliminación *f*
smaltimento dei rifiuti (I)	Abfallbeseitigung *f*	waste disposal	élimination de déchets *f*	—	evacuación de residuos *f*
smaltimento dell'olio usato (I)	Altölbeseitigung *f*	disposal of waste oil	élimination d'huile usée *f*	—	eliminación de petróleo usado *f*
smerciabile (I)	marktfähig	marketable	vendable	—	comerciable
smercio delle materie prime (I)	Rohstoff-vermarktung *f*	raw materials marketing	commercialisation des matières premières *f*	—	comercialización de las materias primas *f*
Smog (D)	—	smog	smog *m*	smog *m*	smog *m*
smog (E)	Smog *m*	—	smog *m*	smog *m*	smog *m*

	D	E	F	I	Es
smog (Es)	Smog *m*	smog	smog *m*	smog *m*	—
smog (F)	Smog *m*	smog	—	smog *m*	smog *m*
smog (I)	Smog *m*	smog	smog *m*	—	smog *m*
Smogalarm (D)	—	smog warning	alerte au smog *f*	allarme smog *m*	alarma de smog *f*
smog warning (E)	Smogalarm *m*	—	alerte au smog *f*	allarme smog *m*	alarma de smog *f*
smuggling (E)	Schmuggel *m*	—	contrebande *f*	contrabbando *m*	contrabando *m*
snob effect (E)	Snob-Effekt *m*	—	effet snob *m*	effetto snob *m*	efecto snob *m*
Snob-Effekt (D)	—	snob effect	effet snob *m*	effetto snob *m*	efecto snob *m*
snowball system (E)	Schneeballsystem *n*	—	système de la boule de neige *m*	sistema di vendite a catena aperta *m*	venta en cadena *f*
soberanía (Es)	Hoheitsrecht *n*	sovereign right	droit de souveraineté *m*	diritto di sovranità *m*	—
soberanía administrativa (Es)	Verwaltungshoheit *f*	power of administration	autonomie d'administration *f*	sovranità amministrativa *f*	—
soberanía financiera (Es)	Finanzhoheit *f*	financial sovereignty	souveraineté en matière budgétaire *f*	sovranità finanziaria *f*	—
soberanía legislativa (Es)	Gesetzgebungs-hoheit *f*	legislative sovereignty	compétence législative *f*	sovranità legislativa *f*	—
soberanía territorial (Es)	Gebietshoheit *f*	territorial jurisdiction	souveraineté territoriale *f*	sovranità territoriale *f*	—
soborno (Es)	Bestechung *f*	bribe	corruption *f*	corruzione *f*	—
sobre[1] (Es)	Kuvert *n*	envelope	enveloppe *f*	busta *f*	—
sobre[2] (Es)	Briefumschlag *m*	envelope	enveloppe de lettre *f*	busta *f*	—
sobrecapitaliza-ción (Es)	Überkapitalisierung *f*	overcapitalization	surcapitalisation *f*	sovracapitalizza-zione *f*	—
sobrepasar (Es)	überziehen	overdraw	faire un prélèvement à découvert	mandare allo scoperto	—
sobreporte (Es)	Frachtzuschlag *m*	additional freight charges	supplément de fret *m*	supplemento di nolo *m*	—
sobrepreso (Es)	Übergewicht *n*	excess weight	surcharge *f*	sovrappeso *m*	—
sobreproducción (Es)	Überproduktion *f*	overproduction	surproduction *f*	produzione eccessiva *f*	—
sobreseguro (Es)	Überversicherung *f*	overinsurance	surassurance *f*	soprassicurazione *f*	—
sobreseimiento del proceso (Es)	Verfahrens-einstellung *f*	abatement of an action	arrêt d'une procédure *m*	sospensione del procedimento *f*	—
sobrevaloración (Es)	Überbewertung *f*	overvaluation	surestimation *f*	sopravvalutazione *f*	—
social insurance (E)	Sozialversicherung *f*	—	assurance sociale *m*	previdenza sociale *f*	seguro social *m*
socialisation (F)	Sozialisierung *f*	socialization	—	socializzazione *f*	socialización *f*
socialización (Es)	Sozialisierung *f*	socialization	socialisation *f*	socializzazione *f*	—
socialization (E)	Sozialisierung *f*	—	socialisation *f*	socializzazione *f*	socialización *f*
socializzazione (I)	Sozialisierung *f*	socialization	socialisation *f*	—	socialización *f*
social market economy (E)	soziale Marktwirtschaft *f*	—	économie sociale du marché *f*	economia sociale di mercato *f*	economía de mercado social *f*
social policy (E)	Sozialpolitik *f*	—	politique sociale *f*	politica sociale *f*	política social *f*
social security (E)	soziale Sicherheit *f*	—	sécurité sociale *f*	sicurezza sociale *f*	seguridad social *f*
social services (E)	Sozialleistung *f*	—	prestation sociale *f*	prestazione sociale *f*	prestacion social *f*/ seguridad social *f*
social state based on the rule of law (E)	Sozialstaat *m*	—	Etat social *m*	stato sociale *m*	Estado social *m*
sociedad (Es)	Sozietät *f*	partnership	groupe de sociétaires *m*	associazione *f*	—
sociedad anónima (Es)	Aktiengesellschaft *f*	joint stock company	société anonyme *f*	società per azioni *f*	—
sociedad capitalista (Es)	Kapitalgesellschaft *f*	company limited by shares	société de capitaux *f*	società di capitale *f*	—
sociedad comanditaria (Es)	Kommandit-gesellschaft *f*	limited partnership	société en commandite *f*	società in accoman-dita semplice *f*	—
sociedad comanditaria por acciones (Es)	Kommanditgesell schaft auf Aktien *f*	partnership limited by shares	société en com-mandite par action *f*	società in accoman-dita per azioni *f*	—
sociedad comercial (Es)	Handelsgesellschaft *f*	trading company	société commerciale *f*	società commerciale *f*	—
sociedad controladora (Es)	Besitzgesellschaft *f*	controlling company	société contrôleuse *f*	società finanziaria *f*	—

	D	E	F	I	Es
sociedad cooperativa (Es)	Genossenschaft *f*	co-operative	société coopérative *f*	cooperativa *f*	—
sociedad de amortización (Es)	Abschreibungs-gesellschaft *f*	project write-off company	société d'amortissement *f*	società di ammortamento *f*	—
sociedad de bienestar (Es)	Wohlstands-gesellschaft *f*	affluent society	société de bien-être *f*	società del benessere *f*	—
sociedad de inversiones (Es)	Investment-gesellschaft *f*	investment company	société d'investissement *f*	società d'investimento *f*	—
sociedad de leasing (Es)	Leasing-Gesellschaft *f*	leasing company	société de leasing *f*	società di leasing *f*	—
sociedad de responsabilidad limitada (Es)	Gesellschaft mit beschränkter Haftung *f*	limited liability company	société à responsabilité limitée *f*	società a responsabilità limitata *f*	—
sociedad de seguros (Es)	Versicherungs-gesellschaft *f*	insurance company	société d'assurance *f*	compagnia di assicurazione *f*	—
sociedad en participación (Es)	stille Gesellschaft *f*	dorment partnership	association commerciale en participation *f*	associazione in partecipazione *f*	—
sociedad holding (Es)	Dachgesellschaft *f*	holding company	société holding *f*	società finanziaria *f*	—
sociedad matriz (Es)	Muttergesellschaft *f*	parent company	société mère *f*	società madre *f*	—
sociedad personalista (Es)	Personen-gesellschaft *n*	partnership	société de personnes *f*	società di persone *f*	—
società affiliata (I)	Tochtergesellschaft *f*	subsidiary	société filiale *f*	—	filial *f*
società a responsabilità limitata (I)	Gesellschaft mit beschränkter Haftung *f*	limited liability company	société à responsabilité limitée *f*	—	sociedad de responsabilidad limitada *f*
società bucalettere (I)	Briefkastenfirma *f*	bubble company	entreprise fantôme *f*	—	empresa ficticia *f*
società commerciale (I)	Handelsgesellschaft *f*	trading company	société commerciale *f*	—	sociedad comercial *f*
società del benessere (I)	Wohlstands-gesellschaft *f*	affluent society	société de bien-être *f*	—	sociedad de bienestar *f*
società d'esercizio (I)	Betriebsgesellschaft *f*	operating company	entreprise d'exploitation *f*	—	empresa de explotación *f*
società di ammortamento (I)	Abschreibungs-gesellschaft *f*	project write-off company	société d'amortissement *f*	—	sociedad de amortización *f*
società di capitale (I)	Kapitalgesellschaft *f*	company limited by shares	société de capitaux *f*	—	sociedad capitalista *f*
società di leasing (I)	Leasing-Gesellschaft *f*	leasing company	société de leasing *f*	—	sociedad de leasing *f*
società d'investimento (I)	Investment-gesellschaft *f*	investment company	société d'investissement *f*	—	sociedad de inversiones *f*
società di persone (I)	Personen-gesellschaft *n*	partnership	société de personnes *f*	—	sociedad personalista *f*
società finanziaria[1] (I)	Besitzgesellschaft *f*	controlling company	société contrôleuse *f*	—	sociedad controladora *f*
società finanziaria[2] (I)	Dachgesellschaft *f*	holding company	société holding *f*	—	sociedad holding *f*
società in accomandita per azioni (I)	Kommanditgesell-schaft auf Aktien *f*	partnership limited by shares	société en commandite par action *f*	—	sociedad comanditaria por acciones *f*
società in accomandita semplice (I)	Kommandit-gesellschaft *f*	limited partnership	société en commandite *f*	—	sociedad comanditaria *f*
società madre (I)	Muttergesellschaft *f*	parent company	société mère *f*	—	sociedad matriz *f*
società per azioni (I)	Aktiengesellschaft *f*	joint stock company	société anonyme *f*	—	sociedad anónima *f*
société affiliée (F)	Schwester-gesellschaft *f*	affiliated company	—	consorella *f*	compañía asociada *f*
société anonyme (F)	Aktiengesellschaft *f*	joint stock company	—	società per azioni *f*	sociedad anónima *f*
société à responsabilité limitée (F)	Gesellschaft mit beschränkter Haftung *f*	limited liability company	—	società a responsabilità limitata *f*	sociedad de responsabilidad limitada *f*
société commerciale (F)	Handelsgesellschaft *f*	trading company	—	società commerciale *f*	sociedad comercial *f*
société contrôleuse (F)	Besitzgesellschaft *f*	controlling company	—	società finanziaria *f*	sociedad controladora *f*
société coopérative (F)	Genossenschaft *f*	co-operative	—	cooperativa *f*	sociedad cooperativa *f*
société coopérative de production (F)	Produktions-genossenschaft *f*	producer's cooperative	—	cooperativa di produzione *f*	cooperativa de producción *f*
société d'amortissement (F)	Abschreibungs-gesellschaft *f*	project write-off company	—	società di ammortamento *f*	sociedad de amortización *f*

	D	E	F	I	Es
société d'assurance (F)	Versicherungs-gesellschaft *f*	insurance company	—	compagnia di assicurazione *f*	sociedad de seguros *f*
société de bien-être (F)	Wohlstands-gesellschaft *f*	affluent society	—	società del benessere *f*	sociedad de bienestar *f*
société de capitaux (F)	Kapitalgesellschaft *f*	company limited by shares	—	società di capitale *f*	sociedad capitalista *f*
société de leasing (F)	Leasing-Gesellschaft *f*	leasing company	—	società di leasing *f*	sociedad de leasing *f*
société de personnes (F)	Personen-gesellschaft *n*	partnership	—	società di persone *f*	sociedad personalista *f*
société d'investissement (F)	Investment-gesellschaft *f*	investment company	—	società d'investimento *f*	sociedad de inversiones *f*
société en commandite (F)	Kommandit-gesellschaft *f*	limited partnership	—	società in accomandita semplice *f*	sociedad comanditaria *f*
société en commandite par action (F)	Kommanditgesell-schaft auf Aktien *f*	partnership limited by shares	—	società in accomandita per azioni *f*	sociedad comanditaria por acciones *f*
société filiale (F)	Tochtergesellschaft *f*	subsidiary	—	società affiliata *f*	filial *f*
société holding (F)	Dachgesellschaft *f*	holding company	—	società finanziaria *f*	sociedad holding *f*
société mère (F)	Muttergesellschaft *f*	parent company	—	società madre *f*	sociedad matriz *f*
socio[1] (Es)	Teilhaber *m*	partner	associé *m*	socio *m*	—
socio[2] (Es)	Partner *m*	partner	partenaire *m*	partner *m*	—
socio[3] (Es)	Geschäftspartner *m*	business partner	associé *m*	partner commerciale *m*	—
socio[4] (Es)	Gesellschafter *m*	partner	associé *m*	socio *m*	—
socio[1] (I)	Teilhaber *m*	partner	associé *m*	—	socio *m*
socio[2] (I)	Gesellschafter *m*	partner	associé *m*	—	socio *m*
socio accomandante (I)	Kommanditist *m*	limited partner	associé *m*	—	comanditario *m*
socio accomandatario (I)	Komplementär *m*	general partner	commandité *m*	—	socio colectivo *m*
socio activo (Es)	aktiver Teilhaber *m*	active partner	associé prenant part à la gestion *m*	socio attivo *m*	—
socio attivo (I)	aktiver Teilhaber *m*	active partner	associé prenant part à la gestion *m*	—	socio activo *m*
socio colectivo (Es)	Komplementär *m*	general partner	commandité *m*	socio accomandatario *m*	—
socio comercial (Es)	Handelspartner *m*	trading partner	partenaire commercial *m*	partner commerciale *m*	—
socio menor (Es)	Junior-Partner *m*	junior partner	fils du partenaire *m*	junior partner *m*	—
soddisfazione dei bisogni (I)	Bedürfnis-befriedigung *f*	satisfaction of needs	satisfaction des besoins *f*	—	satisfacción de las necesidades *f*
soddisfazione del lavoro (I)	Arbeitszufriedenheit *f*	job satisfaction	satisfaction de travail *f*	—	satisfacción en el trabajo *f*
sofortige Lieferung (D)	—	immediate delivery	livraison immédiate *f*	consegna immediata *f*	entrega inmediata *f*
sofortige Regulierung (D)	—	settlement with immediate effect	règlement immédiat *m*	regolazione immediata *f*	regulación inmediata *f*
sofortige Zahlung (D)	—	immediate payment	payement immédiat *m*	pagamento immediato *m*	pago inmediato *m*
soft currency (E)	weiche Währung *f*	—	monnaie faible *f*	moneta debole *f*	moneda blanda *f*
soggetto a contributi (I)	abgabenpflichtig	liable to tax	soumis à l'impôt	—	sujeto a impuestos
soggetto ad influssi congiunturali (I)	konjunkturanfällig	depending on the cyclical trend	sensible aux oscillations de la conjoncture	—	sensible a las fluctuaciones coyunturales
soglia dei prezzi (I)	Preisschwelle *f*	threshold price	seuil du prix *m*	—	umbral de la rentabilidad *m*
soglia dell'utile (I)	Gewinnschwelle *f*	break-even point	seuil de rentabilité *m*	—	umbral de la rentabilidad *m*
soglia di redditività (I)	Rentabilitätschwelle *f*	break-even point	seuil de rentabilité *m*	—	límite inferior de rentabilidad *m*
sol (F)	Boden *m*	ground/soil	—	terra *f*/suolo *m*	suelo *m*/terreno *m*
Solawechsel (D)	—	promissory note	seule lettre de change *f*	pagherò *m*	pagaré *m*
solde (F)	Saldo *m*	balance	—	saldo *m*	saldo *m*
solde créditeur (F)	Aktivsaldo *m*	active balance	—	saldo attivo *m*	saldo activo *m*

	D	E	F	I	Es
solde de compte (F)	Kontoausgleich *m*	settlement of an account	—	liquidazione del conto *f*	saldo de cuenta *m*
solde d'hiver (F)	Winterschluß-verkauf *m*	winter clearance sale	—	svendita di fine inverno *f*	rebajas de invierno *f pl*
solde net de l'exploitation (F)	Ertragsrechnung *f*	profit and loss account	—	conto economico *m*	cuenta de ganancias *f pl*
soldes (F)	Ausverkauf *m*	clearance sale	—	svendita *f*	liquidación *f*
sole agency (E)	Alleinvertretung *f*	—	agence exclusive *f*	rappresentanza esclusiva *f*	representación exclusiva *f*
sole agent (E)	Alleinvertreter *m*	—	agent exclusif *m*	rappresentante esclusivo *m*	representante exclusivo *m*
sole and exclusive agency right (E)	Alleinvertretungs-recht *n*	—	droit exclusif de représentation *m*	diritto di rappresen-tanza esclusiva *m*	derecho de repre-sentación exclusiva *m*
sole owner (E)	Alleininhaber *m*	—	seul propriétaire *m*	titolare unico *m*	propietario exclusivo *m*
solicitud[1] (Es)	Anmeldung *f*	registration/ declaration	inscription *f*/ déclaration *f*	avviso *m*/ dichiarazione *f*	—
solicitud[2] (Es)	Antrag *m*	application	demande *f*	domanda *f*	—
solicitud de aduana (Es)	Zollantrag *m*	customs application	demande de dédouanement *f*	domanda di sdoganamento *f*	—
solicitud de colocación (Es)	Stellengesuch *n*	situation wanted/ application for a job	demande d'emploi *f*	domanda d'impiego *f*	—
Soll (D)	—	debit	doit *m*	passivo *m*	debe *m*
sollecito (I)	Mahnung *f*	demand for payment	mise en demeure *f*	—	(ad)monición *f*
Soll/Ist-Vergleich (D)	—	comparison of estimates with results	comparaison entre les résultats effectifs et les prévisions *f*	confronto costi calcolati/costi reali *m*	comparación entre los resultados efectivos y las previsiones *f*
Sollkosten (D)	—	budgeted costs	coûts ex ante *m pl*	costi calcolati *m pl*	gastos precalculados *m pl*
Sollzahlen (D)	—	target figures	chiffres prévisionnels *m pl*	cifre calcolate *f pl*	cifras e estimadas *f pl*
Sollzinsen (D)	—	debtor interest rates	intérêt débiteur *m*	interessi debitori *m pl*	intereses deudores *m pl*
solución interina (Es)	Interimslösung *f*	interim solution	solution intérimaire *f*	soluzione ad interim *f*	—
solution intérimaire (F)	Interimslösung *f*	interim solution	—	soluzione ad interim *f*	solución interina *f*
soluzione ad interim (I)	Interimslösung *f*	interim solution	solution intérimaire *f*	—	solución interina *f*
solvabilité[1] (F)	Kreditfähigkeit *f*	financial standing	—	capacità di credito *f*	crédito *m*
solvabilité[2] (F)	Bonität *f*	solvency	—	solvibilità *f*	solvencia *f*
solvabilité[3] (F)	Kreditwürdigkeit *f*	creditworthiness	—	essere degno di credito	crédito *m*
solvabilité[4] (F)	Zahlungsfähigkeit *f*	solvency	—	solvibilità *f*	solvencia *f*
solvable[1] (F)	liquide	liquid	—	liquido	líquido
solvable[2] (F)	zahlungsfähig	solvent	—	solvibile	solvente
solvable[3] (F)	kreditwürdig	creditworthy	—	degno di credito	solvente
solvencia (Es)	Bonität *f*	solvency	solvabilité *f*	solvibilità *f*	—
solvency (E)	Zahlungsfähigkeit *f*	—	solvabilité *f*	solvibilità *f*	solvencia *f*
solvent (E)	zahlungsfähig	—	solvable	solvibile	solvente
solvente (Es)	kreditwürdig	creditworthy	solvable	degno di credito	—
solvibile (I)	zahlungsfähig	solvent	solvable	—	solvente
solvibilità[1] (I)	Zahlungsfähigkeit *f*	solvency	solvabilité *f*	—	solvencia *f*
solvibilità[2] (I)	Bonität *f*	solvency	solvabilité *f*	—	solvencia *f*
somma assicurata (I)	Versicherungs-summe *f*	insurance sum	montant de l'assurance *m*	—	suma asegurada *f*
somma di denaro (I)	Geldbetrag *m*	amount of money	somme d'argent *f*	—	suma de dinero *f*
somma fissa (I)	Fixum *n*	fixed sum	somme fixe *f*	—	fijo *m*
somma forfettaria (I)	Pauschalbetrag *m*	flat rate amount	somme forfaitaire *f*	—	suma global *f*
somme d'argent (F)	Geldbetrag *m*	amount of money	—	somma di denaro *f*	suma de dinero *f*
somme fixe (F)	Fixum *n*	fixed sum	—	somma fissa *f*	fijo *m*
somme forfaitaire (F)	Pauschalbetrag *m*	flat rate amount	—	somma forfettaria *f*	suma global *f*
sondage (F)	Stichproben *pl*	random test	—	campioni *m pl*	prueba por sondeo *f*
sondage de l'opinion publique (F)	Demoskopie *f*	public opinion research	—	demoscopia *f*	demoscopia *f*

	D	E	F	I	Es
sondaggio del mercato (I)	Marktbeobachtung *f*	observation of markets	étude de marché *f*	—	observación del mercado *f*
Sonder-abschreibungen (D)	—	special depreciation	amortissement extraordinaire *m*	ammortamenti straordinari *m pl*	amortización extraordinaria *f*
Sonderaktion (D)	—	special action	action spéciale *f*	azione speciale *f*	acción especial *f*
Sonderanfertigung (D)	—	manufacture to customer's specifications	fabrication spéciale *f*	produzione fuori serie *f*	fabricación especial *f*
Sonderangebot (D)	—	special offer	offre spéciale *f*	offerta speciale *f*	oferta especial *f*
Sonderausgaben (D)	—	special expenses	dépense spéciale *f*	spese straordinarie *f pl*	gastos extraordinarios *m pl*
Sondermüll (D)	—	special refuse	détritus spéciaux *m pl*	rifiuti speciali *m pl*	basura especial *f*
Sonderrabatt (D)	—	special discount	ristourne exceptionnelle *f*	ribasso speciale *m*	descuento suplementario *m*
Sondersitzung (D)	—	special meeting	séance extraordinaire *f*	seduta straordinaria *f*	sesión especial *f*
Sondervereinbarung (D)	—	special agreement	accord particulier *m*	accordo speciale *m*	acuerdo especial *m*
Sondervergütung (D)	—	special remuneration	rémunération spéciale *f*	compenso straordinario *m*	gratificación *f*
Sonderziehungs-rechte (D)	—	special drawing rights	droits de tirage spécial *m pl*	diritti speciali di prelievo *m pl*	derechos de giro especial *m pl*
Sonntagsarbeit (D)	—	Sunday work	travail du dimanche *m*	lavoro domenicale *m*	trabajo dominical *m*
sonsacamiento (Es)	Abwerbung *f*	pirating	débauchage *m*	accaparramento *m*	—
soprassicurazione (I)	Überversicherung *f*	overinsurance	surassurance *f*	—	sobreseguro *m*
sopravvalutazione (I)	Überbewertung *f*	overvaluation	surestimation *f*	—	sobrevaloración *f*
Sorte (D)	—	variety/foreign notes and coins	genre *m*/ devises *f pl*	categoria *f*/ valuta estera *f*	especie *f*/calidad *f*/ marca *f*/ moneda extranjera *f*
Sortenhandel (D)	—	dealing in foreign notes and coins	commerce de change *m*	cambio valuta *m*	operación de moneda extranjera *f*
Sortenkurs (D)	—	rate for foreign notes and coins	cours des monnaies étrangères *m*	corso dei cambi *m*	tipo de cambio de billetes y monedas extranjeras *m*
sortie de devises (F)	Devisenabfluß *m*	foreign exchange outflow	—	deflusso di divise *m*	drenaje de divisas *m*
sortie de marchandieses (F)	Warenausgang *m*	outgoing goods	—	uscita merci *f*	salida de mercancías *f*
Sortiment (D)	—	assortment	assortiment *m*	assortimento *m*	surtido *m*
Sortimentsanalyse (D)	—	analysis of assortment	analyse d'assortiment *f*	analisi dell'assortimento *f*	análisis del surtido *m*
Sortiments-gestaltung (D)	—	assortment structuring	structure d'ssortiment *f*	composizione dell'assortimento *f*	configuración del surtido *f*
Sortimentspolitik (D)	—	assortment policy	politique d'assortiment *f*	politica dell'assortimento *f*	política de surtido *f*
sorveglianza (I)	Aufsicht *f*	supervision	surveillance *f*	—	inspección *f*
sorvegliare (I)	überwachen	supervise	surveiller	—	vigilar
sospensione del procedimento (I)	Verfahrens-einstellung *f*	abatement of an action	arrêt d'une procédure *m*	—	sobreseimiento del proceso *m*
sostanza (I)	Substanz *f*	substance	substance *f*	—	sustancia *f*
sostanza nociva (I)	Schadstoff *m*	pollutants	élément polluant *m*	—	substancia nociva *f*
sostegno dei corsi (I)	Kurspflege *f*	price nursing	soutien des cours *m*	—	compras de sostén *f pl*
sostén de las cotizaciones (Es)	Kursstützung *f*	price support	soutiens des cours *m*	difesa dei corsi *f*	—
sostenido (Es)	behauptet	maintained	affirmé	affermato	—
sostituibile (I)	substituierbar	replaceable	interchangeable	—	sustituible
sostituto (I)	Stellvertreter *m*	deputy	adjoint *m*	—	sustituto *m*
sottassicurazione (I)	Unterversicherung *f*	underinsurance	insuffisance d'assurance *f*	—	infraseguro *m*
sottoccupazione (I)	Unterbeschäftigung *f*	underemployment	sous-emploi *m*	—	subempleo *m*
sottoscrizione (I)	Suskription *f*	subscription	souscription *f*	—	suscripción *f*
sottovalutazione (I)	Unterbewertung *f*	undervaluation	sous-estimation *f*	—	subvaloración *f*
soumis à l'impôt (F)	abgabenpflichtig	liable to tax	—	soggetto a contributi	sujeto a impuestos
soumission (F)	Ausschreibung *f*	tender	—	appalto *m*	concurso-subasta *m*

	D	E	F	I	Es
source d'approvisionnement (F)	Bezugsquelle *f*	source of supply	—	fonte d'acquisto *f*	fuente de suministro *f*
source of supply (E)	Bezugsquelle *f*	—	source d'approvisionnement *f*	fonte d'acquisto *f*	fuente de suministro *f*
sous-agent (F)	Untervertreter *m*	subagent	—	subagente *m*	subagente *m*
sous-alimentation (F)	Unterernährung *f*	malnutrition	—	denutrizione *f*	subalimentación *f*
souscripteur d'une assurance (F)	Versicherungsnehmer *m*	insured person	—	assicurato *m*	asegurado *m*
souscription (F)	Suskription *f*	subscription	—	sottoscrizione *f*	suscripción *f*
sous-emploi (F)	Unterbeschäftigung *f*	underemployment	—	sottoccupazione *f*	subempleo *m*
sous-entrepreneur (F)	Subunternehmer *m*	subcontractor	—	subimprenditore *m*	subcontratista *m*
sous-estimation (F)	Unterbewertung *f*	undervaluation	—	sottovalutazione *f*	subvaloración *f*
sous-location (F)	Untervermietung *f*	subletting	—	subaffitto *m*	subalquiler *m*
sous pli recommandé (F)	per Einschreiben	by registered post	—	per raccomandata	certificado
sous pli séparé (F)	mit getrennter Post	under separate cover	—	in plico a parte	por correo aparte
sous toute réserve (F)	ohne Gewähr	without garanty	—	senza garanzia	sin garantía
sous-traitant (F)	Zulieferer *m*	supplier	—	fornitore *m*	abastecedor *m*
soutien des cours[1] (F)	Kurspflege *f*	price nursing	—	sostegno dei corsi *m*	compras de sostén *f pl*
soutien des cours[2] (F)	Kursstützung *f*	price support	—	difesa dei corsi *f*	sostén de las cotizaciones *m*
souveraineté en matière budgétaire (F)	Finanzhoheit *f*	financial sovereignty	—	sovranità finanziaria *f*	soberanía financiera *f*
souveraineté territoriale (F)	Gebietshoheit *f*	territorial jurisdiction	—	sovranità territoriale *f*	soberanía territorial *f*
sovereign right (E)	Hoheitsrecht *n*	—	droit de souveraineté *m*	diritto di sovranità *m*	soberanía *f*
sovracapitalizzazione (I)	Überkapitalisierung *f*	overcapitalization	surcapitalisation *f*	—	sobrecapitalización *f*
sovranità amministrativa (I)	Verwaltungshoheit *f*	power of administration	autonomie d'administration *f*	—	soberanía administrativa *f*
sovranità finanziaria (I)	Finanzhoheit *f*	financial sovereignty	souveraineté en matière budgétaire *f*	—	soberanía financiera *f*
sovranità legislativa (I)	Gesetzgebungshoheit *f*	legislative sovereignty	compétence législative *f*	—	soberanía legislativa *f*
sovranità territoriale (I)	Gebietshoheit *f*	territorial jurisdiction	souveraineté territoriale *f*	—	soberanía territorial *f*
sovrappeso (I)	Übergewicht *n*	excess weight	surcharge *f*	—	sobrepreso *m*
sovvenzione[1] (I)	Subvention *f*	subsidy	subvention *f*	—	subvención *f*
sovvenzione[2] (I)	Zuschuß *m*	allowance	allocation *f*	—	subvención *f*
sovvenzione pubblica (I)	Staatszuschuß *m*	government grant	subvention de l'Etat *f*	—	subvenciones del Estado *f pl*
sovvenzioni agrarie (I)	Agrarsubventionen *pl*	agricultural subsidies	subventions de l'agriculture *f pl*	—	subvención a la agricultura *f*
soziale Marktwirtschaft (D)	—	social market economy	économie sociale du marché *f*	economia sociale di mercato *f*	economía de mercado social *f*
soziale Sicherheit (D)	—	social security	sécurité sociale *f*	sicurezza sociale *f*	seguridad social *f*
Sozialhilfe (D)	—	public assistance	aide sociale *f*	assistenza sociale *f*	ayuda social *f*
Sozialisierung (D)	—	socialization	socialisation *f*	socializzazione *f*	socialización *f*
Sozialkosten (D)	—	social insurance costs	coûts sociaux *m pl*	costi sociali *m pl*	costo social *m*/ cargas sociales *f pl*
Sozialleistung (D)	—	social services	prestation sociale *f*	prestazione sociale *f*	prestacion social *f*/ seguridad social *f*
Sozialpolitik (D)	—	social policy	politique sociale *f*	politica sociale *f*	política social *f*
Sozialprodukt (D)	—	national product	produit national *m*	prodotto nazionale *m*	producto nacional *m*
Sozialversicherung (D)	—	social insurance	assurance sociale *m*	previdenza sociale *f*	seguro social *m*
Sozietät (D)	—	partnership	groupe de sociétaires *m*	associazione *f*	sociedad *f*
space research (E)	Raumforschung *f*	—	recherches spatiales *f pl*	ricerche spaziali *f pl*	investigación espacial *f*
space station (E)	Satellitenstation *f*	—	station de satellite *f*	stazione satellite *f*	estación satélite *f*
Spanne (D)	—	margin	marge *f*	margine *m*	margen *f*

	D	E	F	I	Es
Spareinlagen (D)	—	savings deposits	dépôt d'épargne *m*	depositi di risparmio *m pl*	imposiciones de ahorro *f pl*
Sparen (D)	—	saving	épargne *f*	risparmio *m*	ahorro *m*
spare part (E)	Ersatzteil *n*	—	pièce de rechange *f*	pezzo di ricambio *m*	pieza de recambio *f*
Sparkasse (D)	—	savings bank	institut bancaire d'épargne *m*	cassa di risparmio *f*	caja de ahorros *f*
Sparquote (D)	—	savings ratio	quote-part de revenu réservée à des fins d'épargne *f*	quota di risparmio *f*	cuota de ahorro *f*
spatial structure (E)	Raumstruktur *f*	—	structure des espaces *f*	struttura territoriale *f*	estructura territorial *f*
special action (E)	Sonderaktion *f*	—	action spéciale *f*	azione speciale *f*	acción especial *f*
special agreements (E)	Sondervereinbarung *f*	—	accord particulier *m*	accordo speciale *m*	acuerdo especial *m*
special depreciation (E)	Sonder-abschreibungen *f*	—	amortissement extraordinaire *m*	ammortamenti straordinari *m pl*	amortización extraordinaria *f*
special discount (E)	Sonderrabatt *m*	—	ristourne exceptionnelle *f*	ribasso speciale *m*	descuento suplementario *m*
special drawing rights (E)	Sonderziehungs-rechte *pl*	—	droits de tirage spécial *m pl*	diritti speciali di prelievo, DSP *m pl*	derechos de giro especial *m pl*
special expenses (E)	Sonderausgaben *pl*	—	dépense spéciale *f*	spese straordinarie *f pl*	gastos extraordinarios *m pl*
spécialisation (F)	Spezialisierung *f*	specialization	—	specializzazione *f*	especialización *f*
specialization (E)	Spezialisierung *f*	—	spécialisation *f*	specializzazione *f*	especialización *f*
specializzazione (I)	Spezialisierung *f*	specialization	spécialisation *f*	—	especialización *f*
special meeting (E)	Sondersitzung *f*	—	séance extraordinaire *f*	seduta straordinaria *f*	sesión especial *f*
special offer (E)	Sonderangebot *n*	—	offre spéciale *f*	offerta speciale *f*	oferta especial *f*
special purpose association (E)	Zweckverband *m*	—	association à but déterminé *f*	consorzio intercomunale *m*	asociación con un fin determinado *f*
special refuse (E)	Sondermüll *m*	—	détritus spéciaux *m pl*	rifiuti speciali *m pl*	basura especial *f*
special remuneration (E)	Sondervergütung *f*	—	rémunération spéciale *f*	compenso straordinario *m*	gratificación *f*
specie (E)	Hartgeld *n*	—	pièce de monnaie *f*	moneta metallica *f*	dinero metálico *m*
specification (E)	Spezifikation *f*	—	spécification *f*	specificazione *f*	especificación *f*
spécification (F)	Spezifikation *f*	specification	—	specificazione *f*	especificación *f*
specificazione (I)	Spezifikation *f*	specification	spécification *f*	—	especificación *f*
specific duty (E)	Mengenzoll *m*	—	droit de douane par quantité *m*	dazio di quantità *m*	arancel aduanero cuantitativo *m*
speculation (E)	Spekulation *f*	—	spéculation *f*	speculazione *f*	especulación *f*
spéculation (F)	Spekulation *f*	speculation	—	speculazione *f*	especulación *f*
speculative buying (E)	Meinungskäufe *pl*	—	achats spéculatifs *m pl*	acquisti speculativi *m pl*	compras especulativas *f pl*
speculative operations (E)	Spekulations-geschäft *n*	—	affaire spéculative *f*	operazione speculativa *f*	operación de especulación *f*
speculazione (I)	Spekulation *f*	speculation	spéculation *f*	—	especulación *f*
Spediteur (D)	—	forwarder	commissionnaire de transport *m*	spedizioniere *m*	expeditor *m*
Speditionsgut (D)	—	forwarding merchandise	bien transporté *m*	merce spedita *f*	mercancía transportada *f*
spedizione[1] (I)	Absendung *f*	dispatch	expédition *f*	—	expedición *f*
spedizione[2] (I)	Abfertigung *f*	dispatch/clearance	expédition *f*/expédition en douane *f*	—	despacho *m*/despacho de aduana *m*
spedizione[3] (I)	Sendung *f*	consignment	envoi *m*	—	envío *m*
spedizione[4] (I)	Versand *m*	dispatch	expédition *f*	—	envío *m*
spedizione andata persa (I)	verlorengegangene Sendung *f*	lost shipment	envoi perdu *m*	—	envío perdido *m*
spedizione con valore dichiarato (I)	Wertsendung *f*	consignment with value declared	envoi avec valeur déclarée *m*	—	envío con valor declarado *m*
spedizione di campioni (I)	Mustersendung *f*	sample consignment	envoi d'échantillons *m*	—	envío de muestras *m*
spedizione di merci (I)	Warensendung *f*	consignment of goods	expédition de marchandises *f*	—	envío de mercancías *m*

	D	E	F	I	Es
spedizione postale cumulativa di stampati (I)	Postwurfsendung *f*	printed papers or samples of merchandise posted in bulk	envoi publicitaire collectif *m*	—	envío postal colectivo *m*
spedizioniere (I)	Spediteur *m*	forwarder	commissionnaire de transport *m*	—	expeditor *m*
speedy (E)	beschleunigt	—	accéléré	accelerato	acelerado
Spekulation (D)	—	speculation	spéculation *f*	speculazione *f*	especulación *f*
Spekulationsgeschäft (D)	—	speculative operations	affaire spéculative *f*	operazione speculativa *f*	operación de especulación *f*
Spekulationsobjekt (D)	—	object of speculation	objet de spéculation *m*	oggetto di speculazioni *m*	objeto de especulación *m*
spending capacity analysis (E)	Kaufkraftanalyse *f*	—	analyse du pouvoir d'achat *f*	analisi del potere d'acquisto *f*	análisis del poder adquisitivo *m*
Sperrkonto (D)	—	blocked account	compte bloqué *m*	conto vincolato *m*	fondos bloqueados *m pl*
Sperrminorität (D)	—	blocking minority	minorité suffisante pour bloquer qch. *f*	sindacato di blocco *m*	minoría de bloqueo *f*
spesa pubblica (I)	öffentliche Ausgaben *pl*	public spending	dépenses publiques *f pl*	—	gastos públicos *m pl*
spese[1] (I)	Ausgaben *pl*	expenses	dépenses *f pl*	—	gastos *m pl*
spese[2] (I)	Aufwendung *f*	expenditure	dépenses *f pl*	—	gasot *m*
spese[3] (I)	Aufwand *m*	expenditure	charge *f*	—	gastos *m pl*
spese[4] (I)	Spesen *pl*	expenses	frais *m pl*	—	gastos *m pl*
spese aziendali (I)	Betriebsausgaben *f*	(current) operational expenses	charges d'exploitation *f pl*	—	gastos de explotación *m pl*
spese d'approvvigionamento di credito (I)	Kreditbeschaffungskosten *pl*	cost of borrowing	coûts d'obtention de crédits *m pl*	—	costes de apelación al crédito *m pl*
spese d'esercizio (I)	Betriebskosten *pl*	operating costs	charges d'exploitation *f pl*	—	gastos de explotación *m pl*
spese del procedimento (I)	Verfahrenskosten *pl*	costs of the proceedings	frais de procédure *m pl*	—	costas *f pl*
spese di carico (I)	Ladegebühren *pl*	loading charges	taxe de chargement *f*	—	derechos de carga *m pl*
spese di magazzinaggio (I)	Lagermiete *f*	warehouse rent	location d'une surface pour magasinage *f*	—	alquiler de almacenaje *m*
spese di pernottamento (I)	Übernachtungskosten *pl*	overnight expenses	coûts de nuitée *m pl*	—	gastos de alojamiento *m pl*
spese di scaricamento (I)	Entladungskosten *pl*	discharging expenses	coûts de déchargement *m pl*	—	gastos de descargo *m pl*
spese di scarico (I)	Löschgebühren *pl*	discharging expenses	droit de déchargement *m*	—	gastos de descarga *m pl*
spese di stanziamento (I)	Bereitstellungskosten *pl*	commitment fee	coûts administratifs *m pl*	—	gastos fijos *m pl*
spese di trasferta (I)	Fahrgeld *n*	fare	coût du voyage *m*	—	precio de la travesía *m*
spese di trasporto[1] (I)	Frachtkosten *pl*	freight charges	frais de transport *m pl*	—	gastos de transporte *m pl*
spese di trasporto[2] (I)	Rollgeld *n*	haulage	camionnage *m*	—	derechos de acarreo *m pl*
spese di viaggio (I)	Reisespesen *pl*	travelling expenses	frais de voyage *m pl*	—	gastos de viaje *m pl*
spese giudiziarie (I)	Gerichtskosten *pl*	legal costs	frais judiciaires taxabies exposés *m pl*	—	gastos judiciales *m pl*
spese materiale (I)	Materialaufwand *m*	material expenditure	dépenses en matières *f pl*	—	coste de material *m*
Spesen (D)	—	expenses	frais *m pl*	spese *f pl*	gastos *m pl*
Spesenabrechung (D)	—	statement of expenses	décompte des frais *m*	conteggio delle spese *m*	liquidación de gastos *f*
Spesenpauschale (D)	—	allowance for expenses	forfait de frais *m*	forfait di spese *m*	suma global de gastos *f*
spese primarie (I)	Primäraufwand *m*	primary expenses	charge primaire *f*	—	gastos directos *m pl*
spese pubbliche (I)	Staatsausgaben *pl*	public spending	dépenses publiques *f pl*	—	gastos públicos *m pl*
spese straordinarie (I)	Sonderausgaben *pl*	special expenses	dépense spéciale *f*	—	gastos extraordinarios *m pl*
spese vive (I)	Selbstkosten *pl*	cost	coût de revient *m*	—	costes propios *m pl*
Spezialisierung (D)	—	specialization	spécialisation *f*	specializzazione *f*	especialización *f*

	D	E	F	I	Es
Spezifikation (D)	—	specification	spécification *f*	specificazione *f*	especificación *f*
sphère d'influence (F)	Einflußbereich *m*	sphere of influence	—	sfera d'influenza *f*	esfera de influencia *f*
sphere of influence (E)	Einflußbereich *m*	—	sphère d'influence *f*	sfera d'influenza *f*	esfera de influencia *f*
Spielraum (D)	—	margin	marge *f*	tolleranza *f*	margen *m*
spinta innovativa (I)	Innovationsschub *m*	technology push	animation d'innovation *f*	—	empuje innovador *m*
Spionage (D)	—	espionage	espionnage *m*	spionaggio *m*	espionaje *m*
spionaggio (I)	Spionage *f*	espionage	espionnage *m*	—	espionaje *m*
spionaggio aziendale[1] (I)	Betriebsspionage *f*	industrial espionage	espionnage dans l'entreprise	—	espionaje industrial *m*
spionaggio aziendale[2] (I)	Werkspionage *f*	industrial espionage	espionnage industriel *m*	—	espionaje industrial *m*
spionaggio industriale (I)	Industriespionage *f*	industrial espionage	espionnage industriel *m*	—	espionaje industrial *m*
spirale inflationniste (F)	Inflationsspirale *f*	inflationary spiral	—	spirale inflazionistica *f*	espiral inflacionista *m*
spirale inflazionistica (I)	Inflationsspirale *f*	inflationary spiral	spirale inflationniste *f*	—	espiral inflacionista *m*
spirale prezzi-salari (I)	Lohn-Preis-Spirale *f*	wage-price spiral	course des prix et des salaires *f*	—	espiral salarios-precios *m*
Spitzenlohn (D)	—	top wage	salaire maximum *m*	salario massimo *m*	salario máximo *m*
splittaggio (I)	Splitting *n*	splitting	péréquation fiscale des revenus des deux époux *f*	—	imposición separada e igual de los cónyuges *f*
Splitting (D)	—	splitting	péréquation fiscale des revenus des deux époux *f*	splittaggio *m*	imposición separada e igual de los cónyuges *f*
splitting (E)	Splitting *n*	—	péréquation fiscale des revenus des deux époux *f*	splittaggio *m*	imposición separada e igual de los cónyuges *f*
spot market (E)	Spotmarkt *m*	—	marché en disponible *m*	mercato spot *m*	mercado de operaciones al contado y de entrega inmediata *m*
Spotmarkt (D)	—	spot market	marché en disponible *m*	mercato spot *m*	mercado de operaciones al contado y de entrega inmediata *m*
spot price[1] (E)	Einheitskurs *m*	—	cours unique *m*	cambio unitario *m*	cotización única *f*
spot price[2] (E)	Kassakurs *m*	—	cours au comptant *m*	corso a pronti *m*	cotización al contado *f*
spot pubblicitario (I)	Werbespot *m*	commercial	spot publicitaire *m*	—	spot publicitario *m*
spot publicitaire (F)	Werbespot *m*	commercial	—	spot pubblicitario *m*	spot publicitario *m*
spot publicitario (Es)	Werbespot *m*	commercial	spot publicitaire *m*	spot pubblicitario *m*	—
Staat (D)	—	state	Etat *m*	stato *m*	Estado *m*
staatlich (D)	—	state	de l'Etat	statale	estatal
staatliche Betriebe (D)	—	state-owned enterprise	entreprise publique *f*	aziende statali *f pl*	empresas públicas *f pl*
Staatsanleihen (D)	—	government loan	emprunt d'Etat *m*	titoli pubblici *m pl*	empréstito estatal *m*
Staatsausgaben (D)	—	public spending	dépenses publiques *f pl*	spese pubbliche *f pl*	gastos públicos *m pl*
Staatsbank (D)	—	state bank	banque nationale *f*	Banca Centrale *f*	banco del Estado *m*
Staatseigentum (D)	—	public ownership	propriété d'Etat *f*	proprietà demaniale *f*	patrimonio público *m*
Staatseinnahmen (D)	—	public revenue	recettes de l'Etat *f pl*	entrate pubbliche *f pl*	ingresos del Estado *m pl*
Staatstätigkeit (D)	—	state activity	activité de l'Etat *f*	attività pubblica *f*	actividad del Estado *f*
Staatsverschuldung (D)	—	state indebtedness	endettement de l'Etat *m*	debito pubblico *m*	endeudamiento público *m*
Staatszuschuß (D)	—	government grant	subvention de l'Etat *f*	sovvenzione pubblica *f*	subvenciones del Estado *f pl*
stabilimento (I)	Werk *n*	plant	usine *f*	—	planta *f*
stabilimento di lavorazione del rame (I)	Kupferhütte *f*	copper smelting work	cuivrerie *f*	—	fábrica metalúrgica de cobre *f*
Stabilisierung (D)	—	stabilization	stabilisation *f*	stabilizzazione *f*	estabilización *f*
stabilità (I)	Stabilität *f*	stability	stabilité *f*	—	estabilidad *f*
stabilità dei prezzi (I)	Preisstabilität *f*	stability of prices	stabilité des prix *f*	—	estabilidad de precios *f*

	D	E	F	I	Es
stabilità monetaria (I)	Geldwertstabilität *f*	stability of the value of money	stabilité monétaire *f*	—	estabilidad monetaria *f*
Stabilität (D)	—	stability	stabilité *f*	stabilità *f*	estabilidad *f*
Stabilitätspolitik (D)	—	stability policy	politique de stabilité *f*	politica di consolidamento *f*	política de estabilidad económica *f*
stabilité (F)	Stabilität *f*	stability	—	stabilità *f*	estabilidad *f*
stabilité des prix (F)	Preisstabilität *f*	stability of prices	—	stabilità dei prezzi *f*	estabilidad de precios *f*
stabilité monétaire (F)	Geldwertstabilität *f*	stability of the value of money	—	stabilità monetaria *f*	estabilidad monetaria *f*
stability (E)	Stabilität *f*	—	stabilité *f*	stabilità *f*	estabilidad *f*
stability of prices (E)	Preisstabilität *f*	—	stabilité des prix *f*	stabilità dei prezzi *f*	estabilidad de precios *f*
stability of the value of money (E)	Geldwertstabilität *f*	—	stabilité monétaire *f*	stabilità monetaria *f*	estabilidad monetaria *f*
stability policy (E)	Stabilitätspolitik *f*	—	politique de stabilité *f*	politica di consolidamento *f*	política de estabilidad económica *f*
stabilization (E)	Stabilisierung *f*	—	stabilisation *f*	stabilizzazione *f*	estabilización *f*
stabilizzazione (I)	Stabilisierung *f*	stabilization	stabilisation *f*	—	estabilización *f*
stable value clause (E)	Wertsicherungs-klausel *f*	—	clause de stabilité *f*	clausola di garanzia monetaria *f*	cláusula de índice variable *f*
Städtebau (D)	—	town planning	urbanisme *m*	urbanistica *f*	urbanización *f*
staff[1] (E)	Personal *n*	—	personnel *m*	personale *m*	personal *m*
staff[2] (E)	Belegschaft *f*	—	personnel *m*	maestranza *f*	plantilla *f*
staff changes (E)	Personalwechsel *m*	—	mouvements dans le personnel *m pl*	cambio del personale *m*	cambio de personal *m*
staff di venditori (I)	Verkaufsstab *m*	sales staff	équipe de vente *f*	—	equipo de venta *m*
Staffelpreis (D)	—	graduated price	prix échelonné *m*	prezzo differenziato *m*	precios escalonados *m pl*
Staffeltarif (D)	—	graduated tariff	tarif échelonné *m*	tariffa differenziata *f*	tarifa diferencial *f*
staff identification card (E)	Betriebsausweis *m*	—	pièce d'identité de l'entreprise *f*	tessera aziendale *f*	carné de empresa *f*
staff manager (E)	Personalleiter *m*	—	chef du personnel *m*	capo reparto personale *m*	jefe de personal *m*
Stagflation (D)	—	stagflation	stagflation *f*	stagflazione *f*	estanflación *f*
stagflation (E)	Stagflation *f*	—	stagflation *f*	stagflazione *f*	estanflación *f*
stagflation (F)	Stagflation *f*	stagflation	—	stagflazione *f*	estanflación *f*
stagflazione (I)	Stagflation *f*	stagflation	stagflation *f*	—	estanflación *f*
stagione (I)	Saison *f*	season	saison *f*	—	temporada *f*
Stagnation (D)	—	stagnation	stagnation *f*	stagnazione *f*	estancamiento *m*
stagnation (E)	Stagnation *f*	—	stagnation *f*	stagnazione *f*	estancamiento *m*
stagnation (F)	Stagnation *f*	stagnation	—	stagnazione *f*	estancamiento *m*
stagnazione (I)	Stagnation *f*	stagnation	stagnation *f*	—	estancamiento *m*
stallie (I)	Liegetage *pl*	lay days	staries *f pl*	—	estadías *f pl*
Stammaktie (D)	—	ordinary shares	action ordinaire *f*	azione ordinaria *f*	acción ordinaria *f*
Stammeinlage (D)	—	initial contribution	apport social *m*	quota sociale *f*	capital suscrito *m*
Stammhaus (D)	—	parent company	maison mère *f*	casa madre *f*	casa matriz *f*
Stammkapital (D)	—	share capital/ nominal capital	capital social *m*	capitale sociale *m*	capital social *m*
Stammkunde (D)	—	regular customer	client habituel *m*	cliente fisso *m*	cliente habitual *m*
stamp (E)	Briefmarke *f*	—	timbre-poste *m*	francobollo *m*	sello *m*
stampa[1] (I)	Presse *f*	press	presse *f*	—	prensa *f*
stampa[2] (I)	Drucksache *f*	printed matter	imprimé *m*	—	impreso *m*
stampante (I)	Drucker *m*	printer	imprimante *f*	—	impresora *f*
stampante laser (I)	Laserdrucker *m*	laser printer	imprimante au laser *f*	—	impresora laser *m*
stampa offset (I)	Offsetdruck *m*	offset (printing)	offset *m*	—	impresión offset *f*
stamp duty (E)	Stempelgebühr *f*	—	droit de timbre *m*	tassa di bollo *f*	derechos de timbre *m pl*
Standard (D)	—	standard	standard *m*	standard *m*	estándar *m*

	D	E	F	I	Es
standard[1] (E)	Norm *f*	—	standard *m*	norma *f*	norma *f*
standard[2] (E)	Standard *m*	—	standard *m*	standard *m*	estándar *m*
standard[1] (F)	Standard *m*	standard	—	standard *m*	estándar *m*
standard[2] (F)	Norm *f*	standard	—	norma *f*	norma *f*
standard (I)	Standard *m*	standard	standard *m*	—	estándar *m*
Standard-abweichung (D)	—	standard deviation	déviation standard *f*	scarto tipo *m*	desviación standard *f*
standard deviation (E)	Standard-abweichung *f*	—	déviation standard *f*	scarto tipo *m*	desviación standard *f*
standardisation (F)	Normung *f*	standardization	—	standardizzazione *f*	normalización *f*
standardisé (F)	standardisiert	standardized	—	standardizzato	estandardizado
standardisiert (D)	—	standardized	standardisé	standardizzato	estandardizado
standardization (E)	Normung *f*	—	standardisation *f*	standardizzazione *f*	normalización *f*
standardized[1] (E)	genormt	—	normalisé	standardizzato	normalizado
standardized[2] (E)	standardisiert	—	standardisé	standardizzato	estandardizado
standardized within the European Community (E)	EG-einheitlich	—	uniforme au niveau communautaire	uniforme all'interno della CEE	armonizado a nivel comunitario
standardizzato[1] (I)	standardisiert	standardized	standardisé	—	estandardizado
standardizzato[2] (I)	genormt	standardized	normalisé	—	normalizado
standardizzazione (I)	Normung *f*	standardization	standardisation *f*	—	normalización *f*
standard of living (E)	Lebensstandard *m*	—	niveau de vie *m*	tenore di vita *m*	nivel de vida *m*
standard technique (F)	technischer Standard *m*	technical standard	—	standard tecnico *m*	standard técnico *m*
standard técnico (Es)	technischer Standard *m*	technical standard	standard technique *m*	standard tecnico *m*	—
standard tecnico (I)	technischer Standard *m*	technical standard	standard technique *m*	—	standard técnico *m*
standard wage (E)	Tariflohn *m*	—	salaire tarifaire *m*	salario contrattuale *m*	salario tarifado *m*
Standardwerte (D)	—	standard values	valeur standard *f*	valori standard *m pl*	valores representativos *m pl*
stand-by credits (E)	Stand-by-Kredite *pl*	—	crédit stand-by *m*	crediti stand-by *m pl*	créditos stand-by *m pl*
Stand-by-Kredite (D)	—	stand-by credits	crédit stand-by *m*	crediti stand-by *m pl*	créditos stand-by *m pl*
standing order (E)	Dauerauftrag *m*	—	ordre régulier *m*	ordine permanente *m*	órden permanente *f*
Standort (D)	—	location	lieu d'implantation *m*	ubicazione *f*	ubicación *f*
Standort-entscheidung (D)	—	location decision	décision de l'implantation *f*	determinazione dell'ubicazione *f*	decisión de ubicación *f*
Standortfaktoren (D)	—	location factors	facteurs dépendant du lieu d'implantation *m pl*	fattori d'ubicazione *m pl*	factores de ubicación *m pl*
Standortwahl (D)	—	choice of location	choix du lieu d'implantation *m*	scelta dell'ubicazione *f*	elección de la ubicación *f*
stanza centrale di compensazione (I)	Girozentrale *f*	central giro institution	banque centrale de virement *f*	—	central de giros *f*
Stapelware (D)	—	staple commodities	produit de stockage *m*	merce immagazzinata *f*	mercancía almacenada *f*
staple commodities (E)	Stapelware *f*	—	produit de stockage *m*	merce immagazzinata *f*	mercancía almacenada *f*
star del credere (I)	Delkredere *n*	del credere	ducroire *m*	—	delcrédere *m*
staries (F)	Liegetage *pl*	lay days	—	stallie *f pl*	estadías *f pl*
starting salary (E)	Anfangsgehalt *n*	—	salaire initial *m*	stipendio iniziale *m*	salario inicial *m*
statale (I)	staatlich	state	de l'Etat	—	estatal
state[1] (E)	Staat *m*	—	Etat *m*	stato *m*	Estado *m*
state[2] (E)	staatlich	—	de l'Etat	statale	estatal
state activity (E)	Staatstätigkeit *f*	—	activité de l'Etat *f*	attività pubblica *f*	actividad del Estado *f*
state bank (E)	Staatsbank *f*	—	banque nationale *f*	Banca Centrale *f*	banco del Estado *m*
state indebtedness (E)	Staatsverschuldung *f*	—	endettement de l'Etat *m*	debito pubblico *m*	endeudamiento público *m*
statement of account (E)	Kontoauszug *m*	—	extrait de compte *m*	estratto conto *m*	extracto de cuenta *m*

	D	E	F	I	Es
statement of a commission (E)	Provisions-abrechnung *f*	—	liquidation des commissions *f*	conteggio delle provvigioni *m*	liquidación de la comisión *f*
statement of expenses (E)	Spesenabrechung *f*	—	décompte des frais *m*	conteggio delle spese *m*	liquidación de gastos *f*
state of the market (E)	Marktlage *f*	—	situation du marché *f*	situazione di mercato *f*	condiciones del mercado *f pl*
state-owned enterprise (E)	staatliche Betriebe *pl*	—	entreprise publique *f*	aziende statali *f pl*	empresas públicas *f pl*
station de satellite (F)	Satellitenstation *f*	space station	—	stazione satellite *f*	estación satélite *f*
station of destination (E)	Bestimmungs-bahnhof *m*	—	gare destinataire *f*	stazione di destinazione *f*	estación de destino *f*
statistica (I)	Statistik *f*	statistics	statistique *f*	—	estadística *f*
statistica agraria (I)	Agrarstatistik *f*	agricultural statistics	statistique agricole *f*	—	estadística agrícola *f*
statistica aziendale (I)	Betriebsstatistik *f*	operational statistics	statistique commer-ciale et industrielle *f*	—	estadística de la empresa *f*
statistica delle vendite (I)	Absatzstatistik *f*	sales statistics	statistique de la vente *f*	—	estadística de ventas *f*
statistica demografica (I)	Bevölkerungs-statistik *f*	population statistics	statistique démographique *f*	—	estadística de población *f*
statistica di categoria (I)	Branchenstatistik *f*	trade statistics	statistique sur les différentes branches économiques *f*	—	estadística del ramo *f*
statistica economica (I)	Wirtschaftsstatistik *f*	housekeeping account	statistique économique *f*	—	estadística económica *f*
statistics (E)	Statistik *f*	—	statistique *f*	statistica *f*	estadística *f*
Statistik (D)	—	statistics	statistique *f*	statistica *f*	estadística *f*
statistique (F)	Statistik *f*	statistics	—	statistica *f*	estadística *f*
statistique agricole (F)	Agrarstatistik *f*	agricultural statistics	—	statistica agraria *f*	estadística agrícola *f*
statistique commer-ciale et industrielle (F)	Betriebsstatistik *f*	operational statistics	—	statistica aziendale *f*	estadística de la empresa *f*
statistique de la vente (F)	Absatzstatistik *f*	sales statistics	—	statistica delle vendite *f*	estadística de ventas *f*
statistique démographique (F)	Bevölkerungs-statistik *f*	population statistics	—	statistica demografica *f*	estadística de población *f*
statistique économique (F)	Wirtschaftsstatistik *f*	housekeeping account	—	statistica economica *f*	estadística económica *f*
statistique sur les différentes branches économiques (F)	Branchenstatistik *f*	trade statistics	—	statistica di categoria *f*	estadística del ramo *f*
stato[1] (I)	Status *m*	status	état *m*	—	status *m*
stato[2] (I)	Staat *m*	state	Etat *m*	—	Estado *m*
stato assistenziale (I)	Wohlfahrtsstaat *m*	welfare state	Etat social *m*	—	estado de bienestar *m*
stato sociale (I)	Sozialstaat *m*	social state based on the rule of law	Etat social *m*	—	Estado social *m*
Status (D)	—	status	état *m*	stato *m*	status *m*
status (E)	Status *m*	—	état *m*	stato *m*	status *m*
status (Es)	Status *m*	status	état *m*	stato *m*	—
statut (F)	Satzung *f*	statutes	—	statuto *m*	constitución *f*/ estatuto *m*
statutes (E)	Satzung *f*	—	statut *m*	statuto *m*	estatuto *m*
statuto (I)	Satzung *f*	statutes	statut *m*	—	estatuto *m*
stazione di destinazione (I)	Bestimmungs-bahnhof *m*	station of destination	gare destinataire *f*	—	estación de destino *f*
stazione satellite (I)	Satellitenstation *f*	space station	station de satellite *f*	—	estación satélite *f*
steigend (D)	—	rising	croissant(e)	in aumento	ascendente
Steinkohle (D)	—	hard coal	houille *f*	carbone fossile *m*	hulla *f*
Stellenangebot (D)	—	offer of employment	offre d'emploi *f*	offerta d'impiego *f*	oferta de empleo *f*
Stellenanzeige (D)	—	position offered	annonce d'emploi *f*	inserzione d'impiego *f*	anuncio de empleo *m*
Stellen-ausschreibung (D)	—	advertisement of a vacancy	mise au concours d'une place *f*	bando di concorso per impiegati *m*	convocatoria de oposiciones *f*
Stellen-beschreibung (D)	—	job description	description de l'emploi *f*	descrizione d'impiego *f*	descripción del puesto de trabajo *f*

	D	E	F	I	Es
Stellengesuch (D)	—	situation wanted/ application for a job	demande d'emploi *f*	domanda d'impiego *f*	solicitud de colocación *f*
Stellung (D)	—	position	position *f*	posizione *f*	empleo *m*
Stellungnahme (D)	—	comment	prise de position *f*	presa di posizione *f*	dictamen *m*
Stellungswechsel (D)	—	change of employment	changement d'emploi *m*	cambiamento del posto di lavoro *m*	cambio de empleo *m*
Stellvertreter (D)	—	deputy	adjoint *m*	sostituto *m*	sustituto *m*
Stempelgebühr (D)	—	stamp duty	droit de timbre *m*	tassa di bollo *f*	derechos de timbre *m pl*
Steuer (D)	—	tax	impôt *m*	imposta *f*	impuesto *m*
Steuerbehörden (D)	—	tax authority	administration des contributions *f*	autorità fiscali *f pl*	administración de hacienda *f*
Steuerberater (D)	—	tax adviser	conseiller fiscal *m*	consulente fiscale *m*	asesor fiscal *m*
Steuerbescheid (D)	—	notice of assessment	avis d'imposition *m*	cartella delle imposte *f*	liquidación de impuestos *f*
Steuerbetrug (D)	—	fiscal fraud	fraude fiscale *f*	frode fiscale *f*	fraude fiscal *m*
Steuerbilanz (D)	—	tax balance-sheet	bilan fiscal *m*	bilancio fiscale *m*	balance impositivo *m*
Steuererhöhung (D)	—	increase of taxes	relèvement des impôts *m*	aumento delle imposte *m*	aumento de los impuestos *m*
Steuererklärung (D)	—	tax return	déclaration d'impôts *f*	dichiarazione dei redditi *f*	declaración a efectos fiscales *f*
Steuerfahndung (D)	—	investigation into suspected tax offences	recherche de la fraude fiscale *f*	inchiesta tributaria *f*	investigación tributaria *f*
steuerfrei (D)	—	tax-free	dispensé de l'impôt	esente da imposte	libre de impuesto
Steuer-hinterziehung (D)	—	tax evasion	dissimulation en matière fiscale *f*	evasione fiscale *f*	defraudación fiscal *f*
Steuernachzahlung (D)	—	additional payment of taxes	payement d'un rappel d'impôt *m*	pagamento arretrato delle imposte *m*	pago de impuestos atrasados *m*
Steueroase (D)	—	tax haven	oasis fiscale *f*	oasi fiscale *f*	oasis fiscal *m*
Steuerpolitik (D)	—	fiscal policy	politique fiscale *f*	politica fiscale *f*	política fiscal *f*
Steuersystem (D)	—	system of taxation	système fiscal *m*	sistema fiscale *m*	sistema fiscal *m*
Steuerung (D)	—	control	contrôle *m*	controllo *m*	control *m*
Steuerveranlagung (D)	—	tax assessment	taxation fiscale *f*	accertamento tributario *m*	tasación de los impuestos *f*
Steuervoraus-zahlung (D)	—	advanced payment of taxes	acompte provisionnel sur l'imposition *m*	pagamento anticipato delle imposte *m*	impuestos adelantados *m pl*
Steuerzahler (D)	—	taxpayer	contribuable *m*	contribuente *m*	contribuyente *m*
Steuerzahlung (D)	—	payment of taxes	payement de l'impôt *m*	pagamento delle imposte *m*	tributación *f*
Stichprobe (D)	—	random test	sondage *m*	campioni *pl*	prueba for sondeo *f*
Stichprobe-verfahren (D)	—	sampling procedure	méthode d'enquête par sondage *f*	metodo del campionamento *m*	muestreo *m*
sticker (E)	Aufkleber *m*	—	étiquette *f*	eticchetta adesiva *f*	pegatina *f*
Stickoxid (D)	—	nitric oxide	oxyde azotique *m*	ossido di azoto *m*	óxido nítrico *m*
Stiftung (D)	—	foundation	fondation *f*	fondazione *f*	fundación *f*
stile dell'acquirente (I)	Käuferstil *m*	style of the purchaser	style des acheteurs *m*	—	estilo de compra *m*
stille Gesellschaft (D)	—	dormant partnership	association commer-ciale en participation *f*	associazione in partecipazione *f*	sociedad en participación *f*
stille Reserve (D)	—	hidden reserves	réserve cachée *f*	riserva occulta *f*	reserva tácita *f*
stille Rücklage (D)	—	latent funds	réserve cachée *f*	riserva latente *m*	reserva tácita *f*
Stimmabgabe (D)	—	vote	vote *m*	votazione *f*	voto *m*
Stimme (D)	—	voting	voix *f*	voto *m*	voz *f*
Stimmenmehrheit (D)	—	majority of votes	majorité des voix *f*	maggioranza dei voti *f*	mayoría de votos *f*
Stimmrecht (D)	—	right to vote	droit de vote *m*	diritto al voto *m*	derecho a voto *m*
Stimmungs-barometer (D)	—	barometer of public opinion	baromètre de la tendance *m*	barometro economico *m*	barómetro de la opinión pública *m*
stimulation de l'accroissement (F)	Wachstumsimpuls *m*	growth impulse	—	impulso di crescita *m*	impulso de crecimiento *m*
stipendio (I)	Gehalt *n*	salary	traitement *m*	—	sueldo *m*
stipendio base (I)	Grundgehalt *n*	basic salary	traitement de base *m*	—	salario base *m*

	D	E	F	I	Es
stipendio iniziale (I)	Anfangsgehalt *n*	starting salary	salaire initial *m*	—	salario inicial *m*
stipulazione (I)	Abschluß *m*	conclusion/business deal/balancing	conclusion *f*/ règlement *m*/clôture *f*	—	contratación *f*/ conclusión *f*/cierre *m*
stipulazione del contratto (I)	Vertragsabschluß *m*	conclusion of a contract	conclusion du contrat *f*	—	conclusión de un contrato *f*
stock[1] (E)	Warenbestand *m*	—	stock de marchandises *m*	scorte merci *f pl*	existencias de mercancías *f pl*
stock[2] (E)	Vorrat *m*	—	stock *m*	scorte *f pl*	existencias *f pl*
stock (F)	Vorrat *m*	stock	—	scorte *f pl*	existencias *f pl*
stockage[1] (F)	Lagerung *f*	storage	—	magazzinaggio *m*	almacenaje *m*
stockage[2] (F)	Vorratshaltung *f*	stock piling	—	gestione delle scorte *f*	formación de stocks *f*
stockbroker (E)	Börsenmakler *m*	—	courtier en bourse *m*	agente di cambio *m*	corredor de bolsa *m*
stock broker (E)	Kursmakler *m*	—	courtier en bourse *m*	agente di borsa *m*	agente cambio y bolsa *m*/corredor de cambios *m*
stock cycle (E)	Lagerzyklus *m*	—	cycle de stockage *m*	ciclo di magazzinaggio *m*	período de almacenaje *m*
stock de marchandises[1] (F)	Warenbestand *m*	stock	—	scorte merci *f pl*	existencias de mercancías *f pl*
stock de marchandises[2] (F)	Warenlager *n*	stock room	—	magazzino *m*	depósito de mercancías *m*
(stock) exchange (E)	Börse *f*	—	bourse *f*	borsa *f*	bolsa *f*
stock exchange (E)	Effektenbörse *f*	—	bourse des titres et valeurs mobilières *f*	borsa valori *f*	Bolsa de valores *f*
stock exchange centre (E)	Börsenplatz *m*	—	place boursière *f*	piazza *f*	plaza bursátil *f*
stock exchange index (E)	Börsenindex *m*	—	indice des cours des actions *m*	indice delle quotazioni *m*	índice bursátil *m*
stock exchange list (E)	Kurszettel *m*	—	bulletin des cours *m*	listino di borsa *m*	boletín de bolsa *m*
stockkeeping[1] (E)	Lagerhaltung *f*	—	entreposage *m*	magazzinaggio *m*	almacenaje *m*
stockkeeping[2] (E)	Lagerverwaltung *f*	—	entreposage *m*	amministrazione del magazzino *f*	administración de almacén *f*
stockmarket crash (E)	Börsenkrach *m*	—	débâcle boursière *f*	crollo di borsa *m*	caída en picado de la bolsa *f*
stock exchange transactions (E)	Börsenhandel *m*	—	transactions boursiaires *f pl*	commercio in borsa *m*	negociación bursátil *f*
stock exchange turnover tax (E)	Börsenumsatz-steuer *f*	—	droit de transaction sur les opérations boursières *m*	imposta sulle operazioni di borsa *f*	impuesto de negociación bursátil *m*
stock initial (F)	Anfangsbestand *m*	opening inventory	—	scorte iniziali *f pl*	existencias iniciales *f pl*
stock market transactions (E)	Börsengeschäfte *pl*	—	opérations de bourse *f pl*	operazioni di borsa *f pl*	operación bursátil *f*
stock piling (E)	Vorratshaltung *f*	—	stockage *m*	gestione delle scorte *f*	formación de stocks *f*
stock room (E)	Warenlager *n*	—	stock de marchandises *m*	magazzino *m*	depósito de mercancías *m*
stock variable (F)	Bestandsgröße *f*	stock variable	—	entità dell'inventario *f*	magnitud *f*
stopping payment of cheque (E)	Schecksperrung *f*	—	opposition au paye-ment d'un chèque *f*	blocco d'assegno *m*	bloqueo de un cheque *m*
storage[1] (E)	Einlagerung *f*	—	entreposage *m*	immagazzinamento *m*	almacenamiento *m*
storage[2] (E)	Lagerung *f*	—	stockage *m*	magazzinaggio *m*	almacenaje *m*
storage capacity (E)	Lagerkapazität *f*	—	capacité de stockage *f*	capacità di magazzino *f*	capacidad de almacenaje *f*
storage space (E)	Lagerraum *m*	—	halle de dépôt *f*	magazzino *m*	almacén *m*
storia economica (I)	Wirtschafts-geschichte *f*	economic history	histoire économique *f*	—	historia económica *f*
Stornierung (D)	—	cancellation	annulation *f*	storno *m*	cancelación *f*/anula-ción *f*/contrapartida *f*
Storno (D)	—	counter entry	écriture de contre-passation *f*	storno *m*	extorno *m*
storno[1] (I)	Storno *n*	counter entry	écriture de contre-passation *f*	—	extorno *m*
storno[2] (I)	Stornierung *f*	cancellation	annulation *f*	—	cancelación *f*/anula-ción *f*/contrapartida *f*
strafbar (D)	—	punishable	punissable	punibile	punible

	D	E	F	I	Es
straffällig (D)	—	liable to prosecution	encourir une peine	passibile di pena	criminal
straniero (I)	Ausländer *m*	foreigner	étranger *m*	—	extranjero *m*
Straße (D)	—	street/road	rue *f*/route *f*	via *f*/strada *f*	calle *f*/carretera *f*
Straßenbahn (D)	—	tramway	tramway *m*	tram *m*	tranvía *m*
Straßennetz (D)	—	road network	réseau routier *m*	rete stradale *f*	red de carreteras *f*
Straßenverkehr (D)	—	road traffic	trafic routier *m*	traffico stradale *m*	circulación *f*
strategia (I)	Strategie *f*	strategy	stratégie *f*	—	estrategia *f*
strategia di vendita (I)	Absatzstrategie *f*	sales strategy	stratégie de vente *f*	—	estrategia de ventas *f*
strategia imprenditoriale (I)	Unternehmens-strategie *f*	corporate strategy	stratégie de l'entreprise *f*	—	estrategia empresarial *f*
strategia occupazionale (I)	Personalstrategie *f*	personnel strategy	stratégie en matière de personnel *f*	—	estrategia de personal *f*
strategic (E)	strategisch	—	stratégique	strategico	estratégico
strategico (I)	strategisch	strategic	stratégique	—	estratégico
Strategie (D)	—	strategy	stratégie *f*	strategia *f*	estrategia *f*
stratégie (F)	Strategie *f*	strategy	—	strategia *f*	estratogia *f*
stratégie de l'entreprise[1] (F)	Unternehmens-konzept *n*	business concept	—	piano imprenditoriale *m*	concepto comercial *m*
stratégie de l'entreprise[2] (F)	Unternehmens-strategie *f*	corporate strategy	—	strategia imprenditoriale *f*	estrategia empresarial *f*
stratégie des ventes directes (F)	Direct-Marketing *n*	direct marketing	—	marketing in prima persona *m*	comercialización directa *f*
stratégie de vente (F)	Absatzstrategie *f*	sales strategy	—	strategia di vendita *f*	estrategia de ventas *f*
stratégie en matière de personnel (F)	Personalstrategie *f*	personnel strategy	—	strategia occupazionale *f*	estrategia de personal *f*
stratégique (F)	strategisch	strategic	—	strategico	estratégico
strategisch (D)	—	strategic	stratégique	strategico	estratégico
strategy (E)	Strategie *f*	—	stratégie *f*	strategia *f*	estrategia *f*
strato d'ozono (I)	Ozonschicht *f*	ozone layer	ozonosphère *f*	—	capa del ozono *f*
street (E)	Straße *f*	—	rue *f*/route *f*	via *f*/strada *f*	calle *f*/carretera *f*
Streifband (D)	—	postal wrapper	bande étiquette *f*	fascia *f*	precinto *m*
Streik (D)	—	strike	grève *f*	sciopero *m*	huelga *f*
streng vertraulich (D)	—	strictly confidential	strictement confidentiel	strettamente confidenziale	absolutamente confidencial
Stress (D)	—	stress	stress *m*	stress *m*	estrés *m*
stress (E)	Stress *m*	—	stress *m*	stress *m*	estrés *m*
stress (I)	Stress *m*	stress	stress *m*	—	estrés *m*
strettamente confidenziale (I)	streng vertraulich	strictly confidential	strictement confidentiel	—	absolutamente confidencial
strettoia di capacità (I)	Kapazitätsengpaß *m*	bottleneck in capacity	goulot d'étrangle-ment de capacité *m*	—	escasez de capacidad *f*
strettoia di liquidità (I)	Liquiditätsengpaß *m*	liquidity squeeze	goulot d'étranglement dans la trésorerie	—	restricción de la liquidez *f*
strictement confidentiel (F)	streng vertraulich	strictly confidential	—	strettamente confidenziale	absolutamente confidencial
strictly confidential (E)	streng vertraulich	—	strictement confidentiel	strettamente confidenziale	absolutamente confidencial
strike (E)	Streik *m*	—	grève *f*	sciopero *m*	huelga *f*
Strohmann (D)	—	man of straw/dummy	prête-nom *m*	prestanome *m*	testaferro *m*
Strom (D)	—	current	courant *m*	corrente *f*	corriente *f*
strozzinaggio sui canoni di locazione (I)	Mietwucher *m*	exorbitant rent	hausse illicite des loyers *f*	—	usura arrendaticia *f*
structural change (E)	Strukturwandel *m*	—	changement dans les structures *m*	cambiamenti strutturali *m pl*	cambio de estructuras *m*
structural investments (E)	Bauinvestitionen *pl*	—	investissements à la construction *m pl*	investimenti edili *m pl*	inversión inmobiliaria *f*
structural policy (E)	Strukturpolitik *f*	—	politique structurelle *f*	politica strutturale *f*	política estructural *f*
structural unemployment (E)	strukturelle Arbeitslosigkeit *f*	—	chômage structurel *m*	disoccupazione strutturale *f*	paro estructural *m*
structure (E)	Struktur *f*	—	structure *f*	struttura *f*	estructura *f*

	D	E	F	I	Es
structure (F)	Struktur *f*	structure	—	struttura *f*	estructura *f*
structure agraire (F)	Agrarstruktur *f*	agricultural structure	—	struttura agraria *f*	estructura agraria *f*
structure d'assortiment (F)	Sortiments-gestaltung *f*	assortment structuring	—	composizione dell'assortimento *f*	configuración del surtido *f*
structure de la consommation (F)	Konsumstruktur *f*	consumption structure	—	struttura del consumo *f*	estructura del consumo *f*
structure de distribution (F)	Vertriebsstruktur *f*	structure of distribution	—	struttura della distribuzione *f*	estructura de distribución *f*
structure de la branche (F)	Branchenstruktur *f*	trade structure	—	struttura di categoria *f*	estructura del ramo *f*
structure démographique (F)	Bevölkerungs-struktur *f*	population structure	—	struttura demografica *f*	estructura demográfica *f*
structure des espaces (F)	Raumstruktur *f*	spatial structure	—	struttura territoriale *f*	estructura territorial *f*
structure du texte (F)	Textgestaltung *f*	text configuration	—	redazione del testo *f*	estructuración del texto *f*
structure économique (F)	Wirtschaftsstruktur *f*	economic structure	—	struttura economica *f*	estructura económica *f*
structure of distribution (E)	Vertriebsstruktur *f*	—	structure de distribution *f*	struttura della distribuzione *f*	estructura de distribución *f*
Struktur (D)	—	structure	structure *f*	struttura *f*	estructura *f*
strukturelle Arbeitslosigkeit (D)	—	structural unemployment	chômage structurel *m*	disoccupazione strutturale *f*	paro estructural *m*
Strukturpolitik (D)	—	structural policy	politique structurelle *f*	politica strutturale *f*	política estructural *f*
Strukturwandel (D)	—	structural change	changement dans les structures *m*	cambiamenti strutturali *m pl*	cambio de estructuras *m*
strumento (I)	Instrument *n*	instrument	instrument *m*	—	instrumento *m*
struttura (I)	Struktur *f*	structure	structure *f*	—	estructura *f*
struttura agraria (I)	Agrarstruktur *f*	agricultural structure	structure agraire *f*	—	estructura agraria *f*
struttura del consumo (I)	Konsumstruktur *f*	consumption structure	structure de la consommation	—	estructura del consumo *f*
struttura della distribuzione (I)	Vertriebsstruktur *f*	structure of distribution	structure de distribution *f*	—	estructura de distribución *f*
struttura demografica (I)	Bevölkerungs-struktur *f*	population structure	structure démographique *f*	—	estructura demográfica *f*
struttura di categoria (I)	Branchenstruktur *f*	trade structure	structure de la branche *f*	—	estructura del ramo *f*
struttura economica (I)	Wirtschaftsstruktur *f*	economic structure	structure économique *f*	—	estructura económica *f*
struttura territoriale (I)	Raumstruktur *f*	spatial structure	structure des espaces *f*	—	estructura territorial *f*
Stückgut (D)	—	mixed cargo	colis de détail *m*	collettame *m*	fardos *m pl*
Stückgutverkehr (D)	—	general cargo trade	expéditions de détail *f*	trasporto di collettame *m*	tráfico de mercanías en bultos sueltos *m*
Stückkosten (D)	—	costs per unit	coût unitaire de production *m*	costi unitari *m pl*	coste por unidad *m*
Stücklohn (D)	—	piece work pay	salaire à la tâche *m*	salario a cottimo *m*	salario a destajo *m*
Stückzeit (D)	—	piece time	temps par pièce *m*	tempo pezzo *m*	tiempo por unidad *m*
Stückzinsen (D)	—	broken period interest	intérêts courus *m pl*	interessi maturati *m pl*	intereses por fracción de período *m pl*
studio d'avvocato (I)	Anwaltskanzlei *f*	lawyer's office	cabinet d'avocat *m*	—	bufete de abogado *m*
studio della concorrenza (I)	Konkurrenz-beobachtung *f*	observation of the competitors	observation de la concurrence *f*	—	observación de la competencia *f*
Stundenlohn (D)	—	hourly wage	salaire horaire *m*	salario ad ora *m*	salario-hora *m*
Stundung (D)	—	respite	prorogation *f*	dilazione *f*/proroga *f*	moratoria *f*
Stützungskauf (D)	—	support buying	achat de soutien *m*	acquisto di sostegno *m*	compra para sostener precios *f*
style des acheteurs (F)	Käuferstil *m*	style of the purchaser	—	stile dell'acquirente *m*	estilo de compra *m*
style of the purchaser (E)	Käuferstil *m*	—	style des acheteurs *m*	stile dell'acquirente *m*	estilo de compra *m*
subaffitto (I)	Untervermietung *f*	subletting	sous-location *f*	—	subalquiler *m*
subagent (E)	Untervertreter *m*	—	sous-agent *m*	subagente *m*	subagente *m*
subagente (Es)	Untervertreter *m*	subagent	sous-agent *m*	subagente *m*	—

	D	E	F	I	Es
subagente (I)	Untervertreter *m*	subagent	sous-agent *m*	—	subagente *m*
subalimentación (Es)	Unterernährung *f*	malnutrition	sous-alimentation *f*	denutrizione *f*	—
subalquiler (Es)	Untervermietung *f*	subletting	sous-location *f*	subaffitto *m*	—
subalterne (F)	Untergebener *m*	subordinate	—	dipendente *m*	subordinado *m*
subasta¹ (Es)	Versteigerung *f*	auction	vente à l'enchère *f*	vendita all'asta *f*	—
subasta² (Es)	Auktion *f*	auction	vente à l'enchère *f*	asta *f*	—
subasta de préstamos de regulación monetaria (Es)	Tenderverfahren *n*	tender procedure	offre d'emprunts pour la régulation monétaire *f*	offerta pubblica d'acquisto *f*	—
subasta forzosa (Es)	Zwangs-versteigerung *f*	sale by court order	vente de biens par justice *f*	asta giudiziaria *f*	—
subcontractor (E)	Subunternehmer *m*	—	sous-entrepreneur *m*	subimprenditore *m*	subcontratista *m*
subcontratista (Es)	Subunternehmer *m*	subcontractor	sous-entrepreneur *m*	subimprenditore *m*	—
subempleo (Es)	Unterbeschäftigung *f*	underemployment	sous-emploi *m*	sottoccupazione *f*	—
subimprenditore (I)	Subunternehmer *m*	subcontractor	sous-entrepreneur *m*	—	subcontratista *m*
subject to confirmation (E)	freibleibend	—	sans engagement	senza impegno	no vinculante
subletting (E)	Untervermietung *f*	—	sous-location *f*	subaffitto *m*	subalquiler *m*
subordinado (Es)	Untergebener *m*	subordinate	subalterne *m*	dipendente *m*	—
subordinate (E)	Untergebener *m*	—	subalterne *m*	dipendente *m*	subordinado *m*
subscriber (E)	Abonnent *m*	—	abonné *m*	abbonato *m*	suscriptor *m*
subscription¹ (E)	Abonnement *n*	—	abonnement *m*	abbonamento *m*	suscripción *f*
subscription² (E)	Suskription *f*	—	souscription *f*	sottoscrizione *f*	suscripción *f*
subsidiary (E)	Tochtergesellschaft *f*	—	société filiale *f*	società affiliata *f*	filial *f*
subsidy (E)	Subvention *f*	—	subvention *f*	sovvenzione *f*	subvención *f*
subsistence minimum (E)	Existenzminimum *n*	—	minimum vital *m*	minimo di esistenza *m*	minimo vital *m*
Subkription (D)	—	subscription	souscription *f*	sottoscrizione *f*	suscripción *f*
substance (E)	Substanz *f*	—	substance *f*	sostanza *f*	sustancia *f*
substance (F)	Substanz *f*	substance	—	sostanza *f*	sustancia *f*
substancia nociva (Es)	Schadstoff *m*	pollutants	élément polluant *m*	sostanza nociva *f*	—
Substanz (D)	—	substance	substance *f*	sostanza *f*	sustancia *f*
Substanzerhaltung (D)	—	maintaining the real value	maintien de la substance *m*	mantenimento della sostanza *m*	conservación de la sustancia *f*
Substanzwert (D)	—	assets value	valeur de remplacement *f*	valore sostanziale *m*	valor sustancial *m*
substituierbar (D)	—	replaceable	interchangeable	sostituibile	sustituible
substitute delivery (E)	Ersatzlieferung *f*	—	livraison de remplacement *f*	fornitura di compensazione *f*	entrega de reposición *f*
substitute purchase (E)	Ersatzkauf *m*	—	achat de remplacement *m*	acquisto di compensazione *m*	compra de sustitución *f*
Subunternehmer (D)	—	subcontractor	sous-entrepreneur *m*	subimprenditore *m*	subcontratista *m*
subvaloración (Es)	Unterbewertung *f*	undervaluation	sous-estimation *f*	sottovalutazione *f*	—
subvención¹ (Es)	Subvention *f*	subsidy	subvention *f*	sovvenzione *f*	—
subvención² (Es)	Zuschuß *m*	allowance	allocation *f*	sovvenzione *f*	—
subvención a la agricultura (Es)	Agrarsubventionen *pl*	agricultural subsidies	subventions de l'agriculture *f pl*	sovvenzioni agrarie *f pl*	—
subvenciones del Estado (Es)	Staatszuschuß *m*	government grant	subvention de l'Etat *f*	sovvenzione pubblica *f*	—
Subvention (D)	—	subsidy	subvention *f*	sovvenzione *f*	subvención *f*
subvention (F)	Subvention *f*	subsidy	—	sovvenzione *f*	subvención *f*
subvention à l'exportatoin (F)	Exporthilfe *f*	export subsidy	—	aiuto all'esportazione *m*	ayuda a la exportación *f*
subvention de l'Etat (F)	Staatszuschuß *m*	government grant	—	sovvenzione pubblica *f*	subvenciones del Estado *f pl*
Subventionsabbau (D)	—	reduction of subsidy	réduction des subventions *f*	riduzione delle sovvenzioni *f*	reducción de las subvenciones *f*
subventions de l'agriculture (F)	Agrarsubventionen *pl*	agricultural subsidies	—	sovvenzioni agrarie *f pl*	subvención a la agricultura *f*

	D	E	F	I	Es
success-oriented (E)	erfolgsorientiert	—	orienté vers le succès	orientato al successo	orientado hacia el éxito
succursale[1] (F)	Niederlassung *f*	establishment	—	succursale *f*	sucursal *f*
succursale[2] (F)	Zweigniederlassung *f*	branch office	—	succursale *f*	filial *f*
succursale[1] (I)	Niederlassung *f*	establishment	succursale *f*	—	sucursal *f*
succursale[2] (I)	Zweigniederlassung *f*	branch office	succursale *f*	—	filial *f*
succursale à l'étranger (F)	Auslands-niederlassung *f*	branch abroad	—	succursale estera *f*	filial en el exterior *m*
succursale à l'intérieur (F)	Inlands-niederlassung *f*	domestic establishment	—	succursale nazionale *f*	sucursal en el interior *f*
succursale estera (I)	Auslands-niederlassung *f*	branch abroad	succursale à l'étranger *f*	—	filial en el exterior *m*
succursale nazionale (I)	Inlands-niederlassung *f*	domestic establishment	succursale à l'intérieur *f*	—	sucursal en el interior *f*
sucursal (Es)	Zweigbetrieb *m*	branch business	établissement secondaire *m*	filiale *f*	—
sucursal en el interior (Es)	Inlands-niederlassung *f*	domestic establishment	succursale à l'intérieur *f*	succursale nazionale *f*	—
sueldo[1] (Es)	Besoldung *f*	pay	rétribution *f*	retribuzione *f*	—
sueldo[2] (Es)	Gehalt *n*	salary	traitement *m*	stipendio *m*	—
sueldo base (Es)	Basislohn *m*	basic wage	salaire de référence *m*	salario base *m*	—
suelo (Es)	Boden *m*	ground/soil	sol *m*/terrain *m*	terra *f*/suolo *m*	—
sugestionable (Es)	beeinflußbar	be influenced	influençable	influenzabile	—
suggerimento di prezzo (I)	Preisempfehlung *f*	price recommendation	recommendation de prix *f*	—	precio recomendado *m*
suggestion for improvement (E)	Verbesserungs-vorschlag *m*	—	proposition d'amélioration *f*	proposta di miglioramento *f*	propuesta de mejora *f*
sujeto a impuestos (Es)	abgabenpflichtig	liable to tax	soumis à l'impôt	soggetto a contributi	—
suma (Es)	Betrag *m*	amount	montant *m*	importo *m*	—
suma asegurada (Es)	Versicherungs-summe *f*	insurance sum	montant de l'assurance *m*	somma assicurata *f*	—
suma de amortización (Es)	Ablösesumme *f*	redemption sum	montant de rachat *m*	importo di rimborso *m*	—
suma de dinero (Es)	Geldbetrag *m*	amount of money	somme d'argent *f*	somma di denaro *f*	—
suma de la factura (Es)	Rechnungssumme *f*	invoice amount	montant de la facture *m*	importo della fattura *m*	—
suma del crédito documentario (Es)	Akkreditivsumme *f*	amount of the letter of credit	montant de l'accréditif *m*	importo del credito documentario *m*	—
suma global (Es)	Pauschalbetrag *m*	flat rate amount	somme forfaitaire *f*	somma forfettaria *f*	—
suma global de gastos (Es)	Spesenpauschale *f*	allowance for expenses	forfait de frais *m*	forfait di spese *m*	—
sumar (Es)	addieren	add	additionner	addizionare	—
suma total (Es)	Gesamtsumme *f*	total amount	montant total *m*	importo totale *m*	—
suministrable (Es)	lieferbar	deliverable	livrable	disponibile	—
suministrador (Es)	Lieferant *m*	supplier	fournisseur *m*	fornitore *m*	—
suministro (Es)	Lieferung *f*	delivery	livraison *f*	fornitura *f*/consegna *f*	—
suministro total (Es)	Gesamtlieferung *f*	total delivery	livraison totale *f*	fornitura completa *f*	—
Sunday work (E)	Sonntagsarbeit *f*	—	travail du dimanche *m*	lavoro domenicale *m*	trabajo dominical *m*
superávit (Es)	schwarze Zahlen *pl*	surplus	excédent *m*	conti in nero *m pl*	—
superávit del ejercicio (Es)	Jahresüberschuß *m*	annual surplus	excédent annuel *m*	surplus dell'anno *m*	—
superávit del productor (Es)	Produzentenrente *f*	producer's surplus	rente du vendeur *f*	rendita del produttore *f*	—
superávit en la balanza de pagos (Es)	Zahlungsbilanz-überschuß *m*	surplus in the balance of payments	balance des payements excédentaire *f*	eccedenza della bilancia dei pagamenti *f*	—
supercapacidad (Es)	Überkapazität *f*	overcapacity	surcapacité *f*	capacità eccessiva *f*	—
superficie agrícola utilizada (Es)	Anbaufläche *f*	area under cultivation	surface plantée *f*	area coltivata *f*	—
supermarché (F)	Supermarkt *m*	supermarket	—	supermercato *m*	supermercado *m*
supermarket (E)	Supermarkt *m*	—	supermarché *m*	supermercato *m*	supermercado *m*
Supermarkt (D)	—	supermarket	supermarché *m*	supermercato *m*	supermercado *m*

	D	E	F	I	Es
supermercado (Es)	Supermarkt *m*	supermarket	supermarché *m*	supermercato *m*	—
supermercato (I)	Supermarkt *m*	supermarket	supermarché *m*	—	supermercado *m*
superpoblación (Es)	Überbevölkerung *f*	overpopulation	surpopulation *f*	sovrappopolazione *f*	—
supervision (E)	Aufsicht *f*	—	surveillance *f*	sorveglianza *f*	inspección *f*
supervisión bancaria (Es)	Bankenaufsicht *f*	public supervision of banking	contrôle des banques *m*	commissione bancaria *f*	—
supervisory board (E)	Aufsichtsrat *m*	—	conseil de surveillance *m*	consiglio di sorveglianza *m*	consejo de vigilancia *m*
suplemento[1] (Es)	Beilage *f*	supplement	encart non broché à la revue *m*	inserto *m*	—
suplemento[2] (Es)	Zugabe *f*	extra	prime *f*	aggiunta *f*	—
suplemento[3] (Es)	Zuschlag *m*	extra charge	supplément *m*	supplemento *m*/ premio *m*	—
suplemento[4] (Es)	Zulage *f*	increase/ additional pay	prime *f*/complément de salaire *m*	premio *m*/indennità *f*	—
suposición (Es)	Mutmaßung *f*	conjecture	présomption *f*	presunzione *f*	—
supplement (E)	Beilage *f*	—	encart non broché à la revue *m*	inserto *m*	suplemento *m*
supplément (F)	Zuschlag *m*	extra charge	—	supplemento *m*/ premio *m*	suplemento *m*/ prima *f*
supplementary payment (E)	Nachzahlung *f*	—	versement complémentaire *m*	pagamento supplementare *m*	pago suplementario *m*
supplément de fret (F)	Frachtzuschlag *m*	additional freight charges	—	supplemento di nolo *m*	sobreporte *m*
supplemento (I)	Zuschlag *m*	extra charge	supplément *m*	—	suplemento *m*/ prima *f*
supplemento di nolo (I)	Frachtzuschlag *m*	additional freight charges	supplément de fret *m*	—	sobreporte *m*
supplier[1] (E)	Zulieferer *m*	—	sous-traitant *m*	fornitore *m*	abastecedor *m*
supplier[2] (E)	Lieferant *m*	—	fournisseur *m*	fornitore *m*	suministrador *m*
supplier's credit (E)	Lieferantenkredit *m*	—	crédit de fournisseurs *m*	credito al fornitore *m*	crédito comercial *m*
supply (E)	Versorgung *f*	—	approvisionnement *m*	approvvigiona-mento *m*	abastecimiento *m*
supply contract (E)	Liefervertrag *m*	—	contrat de fourniture *m*	contratto di consegna *m*	contrata *f*
support buying (E)	Stützungskauf *m*	—	achat de soutien *m*	acquisto di sostegno *m*	compra para sostener precios *f*
supporto dati (I)	Datenträger *m*	data medium	porteur des données *m*	—	medio de datos *m*
support publicitaire (F)	Werbeträger *m*	advertising medium	—	veicolo pubblicitario *m*	medio de publicidad *m*
surassurance (F)	Überversicherung *f*	overinsurance	—	soprassicurazione *f*	sobreseguro *m*
surcapacité (F)	Überkapazität *f*	overcapacity	—	capacità eccessiva *f*	supercapacidad *f*
surcapitalisation (F)	Überkapitali-sierung *f*	overcapitalization	—	sovracapitalizzazione *f*	sobrecapitalización *f*
surcharge (E)	Aufschlag *m*	—	hausse *f*	aggiunta *f*	recargo *m*
surcharge[1] (F)	Übergewicht *n*	excess weight	—	sovrappeso *m*	sobrepreso *m*
surcharge[2] (F)	Mehrbelastung *f*	additional burden	—	onere supplementare *m*	carga suplementaria *f*
surchargement (F)	Überbeschäftigung *f*	overcharge	—	occupazione eccedente *f*	exceso de empleo *m*/ superempleo *m*
surendettement (F)	Überschuldung *f*	excessive indebtedness	—	indebitamento eccessivo *m*	exceso de deudas *m*
surestimation (F)	Überbewertung *f*	overvaluation	—	sopravvalutazione *f*	sobrevaloración *f*
surface plantée (F)	Anbaufläche *f*	area under cultivation	—	area coltivata *f*	superficie agrícola utilizada *f*
su richiesta (I)	auf Abruf	on call	à convenance	—	a requerimiento
surplus (E)	schwarze Zahlen *pl*	—	excédent *m*	conti in nero *m pl*	superávit *m*
surplus dell'anno (I)	Jahresüberschuß *m*	annual surplus	excédent annuel *m*	—	superávit del ejercicio *m*
surplus d'offres (F)	Angebotsüberhang *m*	excess of supply over demand	—	eccedenza d'offerta *f*	exceso de oferta *m*

	D	E	F	I	Es
surplus in the balance of payments (E)	Zahlungsbilanzüberschuß *m*	—	balance des payements excédentaires *f*	eccedenza della bilancia dei pagamenti *f*	superávit en la balanza de pagos *m*
surpopulation (F)	Überbevölkerung *f*	overpopulation	—	sovrappopolazione *f*	superpoblación *f*
surproduction (F)	Überproduktion *f*	overproduction	—	produzione eccessiva *f*	sobreproducción *f*
sursis de payement (F)	Zahlungsaufschub *m*	extension of time for payment	—	dilazione del pagamento *f*	pago aplazado *m*
surtido (Es)	Sortiment *n*	assortment	assortiment *m*	assortimento *m*	—
surveillance (F)	Aufsicht *f*	supervision	—	sorveglianza *f*	inspección *f*
surveiller (F)	überwachen	supervise	—	sorvegliare	vigilar
survey report (E)	Havariezertifikat *n*	—	certificat d'avarie *m*	certificato d'avaria *m*	certificado de avería *m*
suscripción[1] (Es)	Abonnement *n*	subscription	abonnement *m*	abbonamento *m*	—
suscripción[2] (Es)	Suskription *f*	subscription	souscription *f*	sottoscrizione *f*	—
suscriptor (Es)	Abonnent *m*	subscriber	abonné *m*	abbonato *m*	—
suspensión de pagos (Es)	Zahlungseinstellung *f*	cessation of payments	suspension de payement *f*	cessazione dei pagamenti *f*	—
suspension de payement (F)	Zahlungseinstellung *f*	cessation of payments	—	cessazione dei pagamenti *f*	suspensión de pagos *f*
sussidio di disoccupazione (I)	Arbeitslosenunterstützung *f*	unemployment benefits	indemnité de chômage *f*	—	prestaciones por desempleo *f pl*
sustancia (Es)	Substanz *f*	substance	substance *f*	sostanza *f*	—
sustituible (Es)	substituierbar	replaceable	interchangeable	sostituibile	—
sustituto (Es)	Stellvertreter *m*	deputy	adjoint *m*	sostituto *m*	—
svalutazione (I)	Abwertung *f*	devaluation	dévaluation *f*	—	devaluación *f*
svantaggio (I)	Nachteil *m*	disadvantage	désavantage *m*	—	desventaja *f*
svendita (I)	Ausverkauf *m*	clearance sale	soldes *m pl*	—	liquidación *f*
svendita di fine inverno (I)	Winterschlußverkauf *m*	winter clearance sale	solde d'hiver *m*	—	rebajas de invierno *f pl*
svendita di fine stagione (I)	Schlußverkauf *m*	seasonal sale	vente de fin de saison *f*	—	venta de liquidación *f*
sviluppo (I)	Entwicklung *f*	development	développement *m*	—	desarrollo *m*
sviluppo congiunturale (I)	Konjunkturentwicklung *f*	economic trend	évolution de la conjoncture *f*	—	evolución de la coyuntura *f*
sviluppo del fatturato (I)	Umsatzentwicklung *f*	turnover trend	évolution du chiffre d'affaires *f*	—	evolución del volumen de facturación *f*
Swapgeschäft (D)	—	swap transaction	opération swap *f*	operazione swap *f*	operación swap *f*
swap rate (E)	Swapsatz *m*	—	taux de swap *m*	tasso swap *m*	tasa swap *f*
Swapsatz (D)	—	swap rate	taux de swap *m*	tasso swap *m*	tasa swap *f*
swap transaction (E)	Swapgeschäft *n*	—	opération swap *f*	operazione swap *f*	operación swap *f*
swindle (E)	Schwindel *m*	—	tromperie *f*	truffa *f*	engaño *m*
Swing (D)	—	swing	swing *m*	swing *m*	swing *m*
swing (E)	Swing *m*	—	swing *m*	swing *m*	swing *m*
swing (Es)	Swing *m*	swing	swing *m*	swing *m*	—
swing (F)	Swing *m*	swing	—	swing *m*	swing *m*
swing (I)	Swing *m*	swing	swing *m*	—	swing *m*
sworn statement (E)	beeidigte Erklärung *f*	—	déclaration sous serment *f*	dichiarazione giurata *f*	declaración jurada *f*
sympathy (E)	Anteilnahme *f*	—	participation *f*	interesse *m*	participación *f*
syndic (F)	Syndikus	legal adviser	—	consulente legale *m*	síndico *m*
syndicat[1] (F)	Syndikat *n*	syndicate	—	sindacato *m*	sindicato *m*
syndicat[2] (F)	Gewerkschaften *pl*	trade union	—	sindacati *m pl*	sindicato *m*
syndicate (E)	Syndikat *n*	—	syndicat *m*	sindacato *m*	sindicato *m*
syndication (E)	Syndizierung *f*	—	syndication *f*	costituzione di un sindacato *f*	sindicación *f*
syndication (F)	Syndizierung *f*	syndication	—	costituzione di un sindacato *f*	sindicación *f*
Syndikat (D)	—	syndicate	syndicat *m*	sindacato *m*	sindicato *m*
Syndikus (D)	—	legal adviser	syndic *m*	consulente legale *m*	síndico *m*
Syndizierung (D)	—	syndication	syndication *f*	costituzione di un sindacato *f*	sindicación *f*

	D	E	F	I	Es
System (D)	—	system	système *m*	sistema *m*	sistema *m*
system (E)	System *n*	—	système *m*	sistema *m*	sistema *m*
Systemanalyse (D)	—	systems analysis	analyse du système *f*	analisi di sistema *f*	análisis de los sistemas *m*
system control (E)	Systemsteuerung *f*	—	contrôle du système *m*	controllo del sistema *m*	control del sistema *m*
système (F)	System *n*	system	—	sistema *m*	sistema *m*
système d'absorption (F)	Abschöpfungs-system *n*	absorption system	—	regime di prelievo *m*	sistema de gravámenes *m*
système de la boule de neige (F)	Schneeballsystem *n*	snowball system	—	sistema di vendite a catena aperta *m*	venta en cadena *f*
système de primes (F)	Prämiensystem *n*	bonus system	—	sistema dei premi *m*	sistema de primas *m*
système de quote-parts (F)	Quotensystem *n*	quota system	—	sistema di contingentamento *m*	sistema de cuotas *m*
système des changes flottants (F)	Floating *n*	floating	—	floating *m*	flotación *f*
système d'incitation (F)	Anreizsystem *n*	incentive system	—	sistema d'incentivo *m*	sistema de incentivos *m*
système d'information (F)	Informations-system *n*	information system	—	sistema d'informazione *m*	sistema de información *m*
système d'information assisté par ordinateur (F)	computergestütztes Informations-system *n*	computer-aided information system	—	sistema di informazione computerizzato *m*	sistema de información asistido por ordenador *m*
système du travail aux pièces (F)	Akkordsystem *n*	piece work system	—	sistema del lavoro a cottimo *m*	régimen de trabajo a destajo *m*
système fiscal (F)	Steuersystem *n*	system of taxation	—	sistema fiscale *m*	sistema fiscal *m*
Système Monétaire Européen (F)	Europäisches Währungssystem *n*	European Monetary System	—	Sistema Monetario Europeo *m*	Sistema Monetario Europeo *m*
système monétaire international (F)	Weltwährungs-system *n*	international monetary system	—	sistema monetario internazionale *m*	sistema monetario internacional *m*
systems analysis (E)	Systemanalyse *f*	—	analyse du système *f*	analisi di sistema *f*	análisis de los sistemas *m*
system of taxation (E)	Steuersystem *n*	—	système fiscal *m*	sistema fiscale *m*	sistema fiscal *m*
Systemsteuerung (D)	—	system control	contrôle du système *m*	controllo del sistema *m*	control del sistema *m*
tabella (I)	Tabelle *f*	table	tableau *m*	—	tabla *f*
Tabelle (D)	—	table	tableau *m*	tabella *f*	tabla *f*
tabla (Es)	Tabelle *f*	table	tableau *m*	tabella *f*	—
table (E)	Tabelle *f*	—	tableau *m*	tabella *f*	tabla *f*
tableau (F)	Tabelle *f*	table	—	tabella *f*	tabla *f*
tableau économique input-output (F)	Input-Output-Analyse *f*	input-output analysis	—	analisi input-output *f*	análisis de input-output *m*
Tagesgeld (D)	—	day-to-day money	argent au jour le jour *m*	prestito giornaliero *m*	dinero de día a día *m*
Tagesgeschäft (D)	—	day-to-day operations	affaire au comptant *f*	contratto a contanti *m*	operación al contado *f*
Tageswert (D)	—	current value	valeur du jour *f*	valore del giorno *m*	valor del día *m*
täglich (D)	—	daily	quotidien	giornaliero	diario
Tagung (D)	—	meeting	congrès *m*	convegno *m*	reunión *f*
taking of the inventory (E)	Inventur *f*	—	inventaire *m*	redazione d'inventario *f*	inventario *m*
talent for argumentation (E)	Argumentations-stärke *f*	—	capacité d'argumentation *f*	forza d'argomentazione *f*	fuerza de argumentación *f*
tamaño de la explotación (Es)	Betriebsgröße *f*	size of the company	dimension de l'entreprise *f*	dimensione dell'azienda *f*	—
tamaño del anuncio (Es)	Anzeigenformat *n*	size of an advertisement	format de l'annonce *m*	formato dell'inserzione *m*	—
tan rápido como sea posible (Es)	schnellstmöglich	as quickly as possible	le plus vite possible	al più presto possibile	—
Tantieme (D)	—	percentage	tantième *m*	percentuale *f*	tanto por ciento *m*
tantième (F)	Tantieme *f*	percentage	—	percentuale *f*	tanto por ciento *m*

	D	E	F	I	Es
tanto por ciento (Es)	Tantieme *f*	percentage	tantième *m*	percentuale *f*	—
Tara (D)	—	tare	tare *f*	tara *f*	tara *f*
tara (Es)	Tara *f*	tare	tare *f*	tara *f*	—
tara (I)	Tara *f*	tare	tare *f*	—	tara *f*
tarare (I)	eichen	gauge	jauger	—	contrastar
tare (E)	Tara *f*	—	tare *f*	tara *f*	tara *f*
tare (F)	Tara *f*	tare	—	tara *f*	tara *f*
target calculation (E)	Plankalkulation *f*	—	calcul des coûts prévisionnels *m*	calcolo pianificato *m*	cálculo de los objetivos *m*
target figures (E)	Sollzahlen *pl*	—	chiffres prévisionnels *m pl*	cifre calcolate *f pl*	cifras estimadas *f pl*
target group (E)	Zielgruppe *f*	—	groupe destinataire *m*	gruppo di riferimento *m*	grupo destinatario *m*
target projection (E)	Zielprojektion *f*	—	projection d'objectifs *f*	proiezione degli obiettivi *f*	proyección de objetivos *f*
Tarif (D)	—	tariff	tarif *m*	tariffa *f*	tarifa *f*
tarif (F)	Tarif *m*	tariff	—	tariffa *f*	tarifa *f*
tarifa (Es)	Tarif *m*	tariff	tarif *m*	tariffa *f*	—
tarifa arancelaria (Es)	Zolltarif *m*	customs tariff	tarif des douanes *m*	tariffa doganale *f*	—
tarifa de transporte (Es)	Gütertarif *m*	trade tariff	tarif marchandises *m*	tariffa merci *f*	—
tarifa diferencial (Es)	Staffeltarif *m*	graduated tariff	tarif échelonné *m*	tariffa differenziata *f*	—
tarifa ferroviaria (Es)	Eisenbahntarif *m*	railway tariff	tarif ferroviaire *m*	tariffa ferroviaria *f*	—
tarifas reducidas (Es)	ermäßigte Tarife *pl*	reduced tariffs	tarifs reduits *m pl*	tariffe ridotte *f pl*	—
tarifa única (Es)	Einheitstarif *m*	uniform tariff	tarif standard *m*	tariffa unitaria *f*	—
tarif des douanes (F)	Zolltarif *m*	customs tariff	—	tariffa doganale *f*	tarifa arancelaria *f*
tarif échelonné (F)	Staffeltarif *m*	graduated tariff	—	tariffa differenziata *f*	tarifa diferencial *f*
tariff (E)	Tarif *m*	—	tarif *m*	tariffa *f*	tarifa *f*
tariffa (I)	Tarif *m*	tariff	tarif *m*	—	tarifa *f*
tariffa differenziata (I)	Staffeltarif *m*	graduated tariff	tarif échelonné *m*	—	tarifa diferencial *f*
tariffa di nolo (I)	Frachtrate *f*	(freight) rate	taux de fret *m*	—	tipo de flete *m*
tariffa doganale (I)	Zolltarif *m*	customs tariff	tarif des douanes *m*	—	tarifa arancelaria *f*
tariffa ferroviaria (I)	Eisenbahntarif *m*	railway tariff	tarif ferroviaire *m*	—	tarifa ferroviaria *f*
tariffa merci (I)	Gütertarif *m*	trade tariff	tarif marchandises *m*	—	tarifa de transporte *f*
tariffa unitaria (I)	Einheitstarif *m*	uniform tariff	tarif standard *m*	—	tarifa única *f*
tariffa zero (I)	Nulltarif *m*	nil tariff	tarif gratuit *m*	—	tarifa gratuita *f*
tariffe ridotte (I)	ermäßigte Tarife *pl*	reduced tariffs	tarifs réduits *m pl*	—	tarifas reducidas *f pl*
tarif ferroviaire (F)	Eisenbahntarif *m*	railway tariff	—	tariffa ferroviaria *f*	tarifa ferroviaria *f*
tarif gratuit (F)	Nulltarif *m*	nil tariff	—	tariffa zero *f*	tarifa gratuita *f*
Tariflohn (D)	—	standard wage	salaire tarifaire *m*	salario contrattuale *m*	salario tarifado *m*
tarif marchandises (F)	Gütertarif *m*	trade tariff	—	tariffa merci *f*	tarifa de transporte *f*
Tarifpartner (D)	—	parties to a collective agreement	signataire d'une convention collective *m*	parti sociali *f pl*	parte contratante en un convenio colectivo *f*
tarifs reduits (F)	ermäßigte Tarife *pl*	reduced tariffs	—	tariffe ridotte *f pl*	tarifas reducidas *f pl*
tarif standard (F)	Einheitstarif *m*	uniform tariff	—	tariffa unitaria *f*	tarifa única *f*
Tarifvertrag (D)	—	collective agreement	convention collective *f*	contratto salariale *m*	contrato colectivo *m*
tarjeta de cheques (Es)	Scheckkarte *f*	cheque card	carte d'identité eurochèque *f*	carta assegni *f*	—
tarjeta de crédito (Es)	Kreditkarte *f*	credit card	carte accréditive *f*	carta di credito *f*	—
tarjeta de garantía (Es)	Garantiekarte *f*	certificate of warranty	carte de garantie *f*	certificato di garanzia *m*	—
tarjeta postal (Es)	Postkarte *f*	postcard	carte postale *f*	cartolina postale *f*	—
tasa a la importación (Es)	Einfuhrabgabe *f*	import duties	taxe à l'importation *f*	tassa d'importazione *f*	—

	D	E	F	I	Es
tasación de los impuestos (Es)	Steuerveranlagung *f*	tax assessment	taxation fiscale *f*	accertamento tributario *m*	—
tasa de beneficio (Es)	Profitrate *f*	profit rate	taux de profit *m*	tasso di profitto *m*	—
tasa de cambio (Es)	Umrechnungskurs *m*	rate of conversion	cours de conversion *m*	corso di cambio *m*	—
tasa de descuento (Es)	Diskontsatz *m*	discount rate	taux d'escompte *m*	saggio di sconto *m*	—
tasa de inflación (Es)	Inflationsrate *f*	rate of inflation	taux d'inflation *m*	tasso d'inflazione *m*	—
tasa de natalidad (Es)	Geburtenrate *f*	birth rate	taux de natalité *m*	tasso di natalità *m*	—
tasa de utilización (Es)	Auslastungsgrad *m*	capacity utilisation rate	dégré de saturation *m*	grado di sfruttamento *m*	—
tasa swap (Es)	Swapsatz *m*	swap rate	taux de swap *m*	tasso swap *m*	—
tassa (I)	Gebühr *f*	fee	taxe *f*	—	derecho *m*
tassa di bollo (I)	Stempelgebühr *f*	stamp duty	droit de timbre *m*	—	derechos de timbre *m pl*
tassa di licenza (I)	Lizenzgebühr *f*	royalty	taxe d'exploitation de licence *f*	—	derecho de licencia *m*
tassa d'importazione (I)	Einfuhrabgabe *f*	import duties	taxe à l'importation *f*	—	tasa a la importación *f*
tasso di crescita (I)	Wachstumsrate *f*	rate of growth	taux d'accroissement *m*	—	tasa de crecimiento *f*
tasso di natalità (I)	Geburtenrate *f*	birth rate	taux de natalité *m*	—	tasa de natalidad *f*
tasso d'indebitamento (I)	Verschuldungsgrad *m*	debt ratio	niveau de l'endettement *m*	—	grado de endeudamiento *m*
tasso d'inflazione (I)	Inflationsrate *f*	rate of inflation	taux d'inflation *m*	—	tasa de inflación *f*
tasso d'interesse (I)	Zinsfuß *m*	interest rate	taux d'intérêt *m*	—	tipo de interés *m*
tasso d'interesse effettivo (I)	Effektivzins *m*	effective interest	intérêt effectif *m*	—	intereses reales *m pl*
tasso d'interesse fisso (I)	fester Zins *m*	fixed interest rate	intérêt fixe *m*	—	interés fijo *m*
tasso d'interesse guida (I)	Leitzins *m*	key rate	taux-clé d'intérêt bancaire	—	tipos de referencia *m pl*
tasso d'interesse reale (I)	Realzins *m*	real (rate of) interest	rendement réel *m*	—	interés real *m*
tasso d'interesse variabile (I)	variabler Zins *m*	variable rate of interest	intérêt variable *m*	—	interés variable *m*
tasso di perdita (I)	Ausfallquote *f*	default rate	ratio de perte *m*	—	cuota de pérdida *f*
tasso di profitto (I)	Profitrate *f*	profit rate	taux de profit *m*	—	tasa de beneficio *f*
tasso d'occupazione (I)	Beschäftigungs-grad *m*	level of employment	taux d'emploi *m*	—	grado de empleo *m*
tasso interbancario (I)	Interbankrate *f*	interbank rate	taux interbancaire *m*	—	tipo interbancario *m*
tasso sulle anticipazioni (I)	Lombardsatz *m*	rate for advances on securities	taux d'intérêt de l'argent prêté sur gage *m*	—	tipo de pignoración *m*
tasso swap (I)	Swapsatz *m*	swap rate	taux de swap *m*	—	tasa swap *f*
Tastatur (D)	—	keyboard	clavier *m*	tastiera *f*	teclado *m*
tastiera (I)	Tastatur *f*	keyboard	clavier *m*	—	teclado *m*
Tätigkeitsfeld (D)	—	field of activity	champ d'acitivité *m*	campo d'azione *m*	campo de actividad *m*
Tausch (D)	—	exchange/barter	échange *m*/troc *m*	scambio *m*/baratto *m*	cambio *m*/trueque *m*
Täuschung (D)	—	deceit	tromperie *f*	inganno *m*	engaño *m*
taux central (F)	Leitkurs *m*	central rate	—	parità centrale *f*	tipo pivote *m*
taux-clé d'intérêt bancaire (F)	Leitzins *m*	key rate	—	tasso d'interesse guida *m*	tipos de referencia *m pl*
taux d'accroissement (F)	Wachstumsrate *f*	rate of growth	—	tasso di crescita *m*	tasa de crecimiento *f*
taux de change (F)	Devisenkurs *m*	foreign exchange rate	—	cambio delle divise *m*	cambio *m*
taux de change fixe (F)	feste Wechselkurse *pl*	fixed exchange rates	—	cambi fissi *m pl*	tipos de cambio fijos *m pl*
taux de change flottant (F)	flexibler Wechselkurs *m*	flexible exchange rate	—	cambio flessibile *m*	tipo flotante de cambio *m*
taux de fret (F)	Frachtrate *f*	(freight) rate	—	tariffa di nolo *f*	tipo de flete *m*

	D	E	F	I	Es
taux de leasing (F)	Leasing-Rate *f*	leasing payment	—	rata leasing *f*	plazo de arrendamiento financiero *m*
taux d'emploi (F)	Beschäftigungsgrad *m*	level of employment	—	tasso d'occupazione *m*	grado de empleo *m*
taux de natalité (F)	Geburtenrate *f*	birth rate	—	tasso di natalità *m*	tasa de natalidad *f*
taux de profit (F)	Profitrate *f*	profit rate	—	tasso di profitto *m*	tasa de beneficio *f*
taux d'escompte (F)	Diskontsatz *m*	discount rate	—	saggio di sconto *m*	tasa de descuento *f*
taux de swap (F)	Swapsatz *m*	swap rate	—	tasso swap *m*	tasa swap *f*
taux d'inflation (F)	Inflationsrate *f*	rate of inflation	—	tasso d'inflazione *m*	tasa de inflación *f*
taux d'intérêt (F)	Zinsfuß *m*	interest rate	—	tasso d'interesse *m*	tipo de interés *m*
taux d'intérêt de l'argent prêté sur gage (F)	Lombardsatz *m*	rate for advances on securities	—	tasso sulle anticipazioni *m*	tipo de pignoración *m*
taux d'utilisation (F)	Ausnutzungsgrad *m*	utilization rate	—	grado di utilizzazione *m*	grado de utilización *m*
taux effectif (de l'intérêt) (F)	Effektivverzinsung *f*	effective interest yield	—	interessi effettivi *m pl*	interés efectivo *m*
taux interbancaire (F)	Interbankrate *f*	interbank rate	—	tasso interbancario *m*	tipo interbancario *m*
tax[1] (E)	Steuer *f*	—	impôt *m*	imposta *f*	impuesto *m*
tax[2] (E)	Abgabe *f*	—	taxe *f*	imposta *f*/dazio *m*	impuesto *m*/ arancel *m*
tax adviser (E)	Steuerberater *m*	—	conseiller fiscal *m*	consulente fiscale *m*	asesor fiscal *m*
tax assessment (E)	Steuerveranlagung *f*	—	taxation fiscale *f*	accertamento tributario *m*	tasación de los impuestos *f*
taxation fiscale (F)	Steuerveranlagung *f*	tax assessment	—	accertamento tributario *m*	tasación de los impuestos *f*
tax authority (E)	Steuerbehörden *pl*	—	administration des contributions *f*	autorità fiscali *f pl*	administración de hacienda *f*
tax balance-sheet (E)	Steuerbilanz *f*	—	bilan fiscal *m*	bilancio fiscale *m*	balance impositivo *m*
taxe[1] (F)	Gebühr *f*	fee	—	tassa *f*	derecho *m*
taxe[2] (F)	Abgabe *f*	tax/duty	—	imposta *f*/dazio *m*	impuesto *m*/ arancel *m*
taxe acquittée en nature (F)	Naturalabgabe *f*	duty in kind	—	imposta in natura *f*	impuesto en especie *m*
taxe à la valeur ajoutée (F)	Mehrwertsteuer *f*	value-added tax	—	imposta sul valore aggiunto *f*	impuesto sobre el valor añadido *m*
taxe à l'importation (F)	Einfuhrabgabe *f*	import duties	—	tassa d'importazione *f*	tasa a la importación *f*
taxe de chargement (F)	Ladegebühren *pl*	loading charges	—	spese di carico *f pl*	derechos de carga *m pl*
taxe de douane ad valorem (F)	Wertzoll *m*	ad valorem duty	—	dazio ad valorem *m*	aduanas ad valorem *f pl*
taxe de luxe (F)	Luxussteuer *f*	luxury tax	—	imposta sui consumi di lusso *f*	impuesto de lujo *m*
taxe de sortie (F)	Ausfuhrzoll *m*	export duty	—	dazio sull'esportazione *m*	derechos de exportación *m pl*
taxe d'expoitation de licence (F)	Lizenzgebühr *f*	royalty	—	tassa di licenza *f*	derecho de licencia *m*
taxe préférentielle de douane (F)	Präferenzzoll *m*	preferential duty	—	dazio preferenziale *m*	aduanas preferenciales *f pl*
taxe sur les sociétés (F)	Körperschaftsteuer *f*	corporation tax	—	imposta sul reddito delle società *f*	impuesto de corporaciones *m*
taxe sur les véhicules à moteur (F)	Kraftfahrzeugsteuer *f*	motor vehicle tax	—	imposta sulla circolazione degli autoveicoli *f*	impuesto sobre vehículos *m*
tax evasion (E)	Steuerhinterziehung *f*	—	dissimulation en *f* matière fiscale	evasione fiscale *f*	defraudación fiscal *f*
tax-free[1] (E)	abgabenfrei	—	exempt de taxes	esente da contributi	exento de derechos
tax-free[2] (E)	steuerfrei	—	dispensé de l'impôt	esente da imposte	libre de impuesto
tax haven (E)	Steueroase *f*	—	oasis fiscale *f*	oasi fiscale *f*	oasis fiscal *m*
tax on alcohol (E)	Alkoholsteuer *f*	—	impôt sur l'alcool *m*	imposta sugli alcolici *f*	impuesto sobre el alcohol *m*

	D	E	F	I	Es
tax on income (E)	Ertragsteuer *f*	—	impôt assis sur le produit *m*	imposta cedolare *f*/ imposta sul reddito *f*	impuesto sobre beneficios *m*
tax on investment income (E)	Kapitalertragsteuer *f*	—	impôt sur le revenu du capital *m*	imposta sulla rendita del capitale *f*	impuesto sobre la renta del capital *m*
taxpayer (E)	Steuerzahler *m*	—	contribuable *m*	contribuente *m*	contribuyente *m*
tax return (E)	Steuererklärung *f*	—	déclaration d'impôts *f*	dichiarazione dei redditi *f*	declaración a efectos fiscales *f*
Taxwert (D)	—	estimated value	valeur de taxation *f*	valore stimato *m*	valor de tasación *m*
Team (D)	—	team	équipe *f*	équipe *f*	equipo *m*
team[1] (E)	Mannschaft *f*	—	équipe *f*/équipage *m*	équipe *f*/ equipaggio *m*	equipo *m*/ tripulación *f*
team[2] (E)	Team *n*	—	équipe *f*	équipe *f*	equipo *m*
Teamarbeit (D)	—	team work	travail d'équipe *m*	lavoro d'équipe *m*	trabajo en equipo *m*
team work (E)	Teamarbeit *f*	—	travail d'équipe *m*	lavoro d'équipe *m*	trabajo en equipo *m*
technical (E)	technisch	—	technique	tecnico	técnico
technical book (E)	Fachbuch *n*	—	livre technique *m*	libro specializzato *m*	libro técnico *m*
technical standard (E)	technischer Standard *m*	—	standard technique *m*	standard tecnico *m*	standard técnico *m*
technical standards (E)	technische Normen *pl*	—	normes norme techniques *f pl*	tecniche *f pl*	normas técnicas *f pl*
technicien publicitaire (F)	Werbefachmann *m*	advertising expert	—	esperto di pubblicità *m*	perito publicitario *m*
Technik (D)	—	technique	technique *f*	tecnica *f*	técnica *f*/método *m*
technique (E)	Technik *f*	—	technique *f*	tecnica *f*	técnica *f*/método *m*
technique[1] (F)	Technik *f*	technique	—	tecnica *f*	técnica *f*/método *m*
technique[2] (F)	technisch	technical	—	tecnico	técnico
technique de conclusion (F)	Abschlußtechnik *f*	finishing technique	—	metodo di chiusura *m*	técnica de conclusión *f*
technique de pronostic (F)	Prognosetechnik *f*	forecasting techniques	—	tecnica della prognosi *f*	técnica de pronóstico *f*
technique de travail (F)	Arbeitstechnik *f*	working technique	—	tecnica lavorativa *f*	técnica del trabajo *f*
technique informatique (F)	Computertechnik *f*	computer technology	—	tecnica dei computer *f*	técnica informática *f*
technisch (D)	—	technical	technique	tecnico	técnico
technische Abteilung (D)	—	engineering department	service technique *m*	reparto tecnico *m*	departamento técnico *m*
technische Normen (D)	—	technical standards	normes techniques *f pl*	norme tecniche *f pl*	normas técnicas *f pl*
technischer Standard (D)	—	technical standard	standard technique *m*	standard tecnico *m*	standard técnico *m*
Technologie (D)	—	technology	technologie *f*	tecnologia *f*	tecnología *f*
technologie (F)	Technologie *f*	technology	—	tecnologia *f*	tecnología *f*
technologie d'information (F)	Informations-technologie *f*	information technology	—	tecnologia d'informazione *f*	tecnología de información *f*
technology (E)	Technologie *f*	—	technologie *f*	tecnologia *f*	tecnología *f*
technology push (E)	Innovationsschub *m*	—	animation d'innovation *f*	spinta innovativa *f*	empuje innovador *m*
teclado (Es)	Tastatur *f*	keyboard	clavier *m*	tastiera *f*	—
técnica (Es)	Technik *f*	technique	technique *f*	tecnica *f*	—
tecnica (I)	Technik *f*	technique	technique *f*	—	técnica *f*/ método *m*
técnica de conclusión (Es)	Abschlußtechnik *f*	finishing technique	technique de conclusion *f*	metodo di chiusura *m*	—
tecnica dei computer (I)	Computertechnik *f*	computer technology	technique informatique *f*	—	técnica informática *f*
técnica del trabajo (Es)	Arbeitstechnik *f*	working technique	technique de travail *f*	tecnica lavorativa *f*	—
tecnica della prognosi (I)	Prognosetechnik *f*	forecasting techniques	technique de pronostic *f*	—	técnica de pronóstico *f*
técnica de pronóstico (Es)	Prognosetechnik *f*	forecasting techniques	technique de pronostic *f*	tecnica della prognosi *f*	—

	D	E	F	I	Es
técnica de venta (Es)	Verkaufstechnik *f*	sales technique	art de vendre *m*	tecnica di vendita *f*	—
tecnica di vendita (I)	Verkaufstechnik *f*	sales technique	art de vendre *m*	—	técnica de venta *f*
técnica informática (Es)	Computertechnik *f*	computer technology	technique informatique *f*	tecnica dei computer *f*	—
tecnica lavorativa (I)	Arbeitstechnik *f*	working technique	technique de travail *f*	—	técnica del trabajo *f*
técnico (Es)	technisch	technical	technique	tecnico	—
tecnico (I)	technisch	technical	technique	—	técnico
tecnología (Es)	Technologie *f*	technology	technologie *f*	tecnologia *f*	—
tecnologia (I)	Technologie *f*	technology	technologie *f*	—	tecnología *f*
tecnología de información (Es)	Informations technologie *f*	information technology	technologie d'information *f*	tecnologia d'informazione *f*	—
tecnologia d'informazione (I)	Informations-technologie *f*	information technology	technologie d'information *f*	—	tecnología de información *f*
Teilhaber (D)	—	partner	associé *m*	socio *m*	socio *m*
Teillieferung (D)	—	partial delivery	livraison partielle *f*	fornitura parziale *f*	entrega parcial *f*
Teilnehmer (D)	—	participant	participant *m*	partecipante *m*	participante *m*
Teilnehmerliste (D)	—	list of participants	liste des participants *f*	lista dei partecipanti *f*	lista de participantes *f*
Teilprivatisierung (D)	—	partial denationalization	privatisation partielle *f*	privatizzazione parziale *f*	privatización parcial *f*
Teilwert (D)	—	partial value	valeur partielle *f*	valore parziale *m*	valor parcial *m*
Teilzahlung (D)	—	partial payment	payement partiel *m*	pagamento a rate *m*	pago parcial *m*
Teilzahlungs-geschäft (D)	—	partial payment transaction	achat à tempérament *m*	vendita a rate *f*	operación a plazo *f*
Teilzahlungspreis (D)	—	partial payment price	prix d'un achat à tempérament *m*	prezzo rateale *m*	precio de compras a plazo *m*
Teilzahlungsrate (D)	—	monthly instalment	mensualité d'un achat à tempérament *f*	rata *f*	plazo *m*
Teilzeitarbeit (D)	—	part-time work	travail à temps partiel *m*	lavoro part-time *m*	trabajo a tiempo parcial *m*
Teilzeitstelle (D)	—	part-time job	poste à temps partiel *m*	posto di lavoro part-time *m*	puesto de trabajo a tiempo parcial *m*
telefax number (E)	Telefaxnummer *f*	—	numéro de téléfax *m*	numero telefax *m*	número de telefax *m*
Telefaxnummer (D)	—	telefax number	numéro de téléfax *m*	numero telefax *m*	número de telefax *m*
Telefon (D)	—	telephone	téléphone *m*	telefono *m*	teléfono *m*
telefonata (I)	Telefongespräch *n*	telephone conversation	conversation téléphonique *f*	—	conferencia telefónica *f*
Telefondienst (D)	—	telephone service	service du téléphone *m*	servizio telefonico *m*	servicio telefónico *m*
Telefongespräch (D)	—	telephone conversation	conversation téléphonique *f*	telefonata *f*	conferencia telefónica *f*
Telefonnummer (D)	—	telephone number	numéro de téléphone *m*	numero di telefono *m*	número de teléfono *m*
teléfono[1] (Es)	Fernsprecher *m*	telephone	appareil téléphonique *m*	telefono *m*	—
teléfono[2] (Es)	Telefon *n*	telephone	téléphone *m*	telefono *m*	—
telefono[1] (I)	Fernsprecher *m*	telephone	appareil téléphonique *m*	—	teléfono *m*
telefono[2] (I)	Telefon *n*	telephone	téléphone *m*	—	teléfono *m*
Telefonverkauf (D)	—	inter-office sale	vente par téléphone *f*	vendita per telefono *f*	venta por teléfono *f*
Telegraf (D)	—	telegraph	télégraphe *m*	telegrafo *m*	telégrafo *m*
telegrafare (I)	telegrafieren	send a telegram	télégraphier	—	telegrafiar
telegrafiar (Es)	telegrafieren	send a telegram	télégraphier	telegrafare	—
telegrafieren (D)	—	send a telegram	télégraphier	telegrafare	telegrafiar
telegrafische Anweisung (D)	—	telegraphic payment order	mandat télégraphique *m*	vaglia telegrafico *m*	orden telegráfica *f*
telégrafo (Es)	Telegraf *m*	telegraph	télégraphe *m*	telegrafo *m*	—
telegrafo (I)	Telegraf *m*	telegraph	télégraphe *m*	—	telégrafo *m*
telegram (E)	Telegramm *n*	—	télégramme *m*	telegramma *m*	telegrama *m*

	D	E	F	I	Es
telegrama (Es)	Telegramm *n*	telegram	télégramme *m*	telegramma *m*	—
Telegramm (D)	—	telegram	télégramme *m*	telegramma *m*	telegrama *m*
telegramma (I)	Telegramm *n*	telegram	télégramme *m*	—	telegrama *m*
télégramme (F)	Telegramm *n*	telegram	—	telegramma *m*	telegrama *m*
telegraph (E)	Telegraf *m*	—	télégraphe *m*	telegrafo *m*	telégrafo *m*
télégraphe (F)	Telegraf *m*	telegraph	—	telegrafo *m*	telégrafo *m*
telegraphic payment order (E)	telegrafische Anweisung *f*	—	mandat télégraphique *m*	vaglia telegrafico *m*	orden telegráfica *f*
télégraphier (F)	telegrafieren	send a telegram	—	telegrafare	telegrafiar
téléimprimeur (F)	Fernschreiber *m*	teleprinter	—	telescrivente *m*	télex *m*
telephone[1] (E)	Telefon *n*	—	téléphone *m*	telefono *m*	teléfono *m*
telephone[2] (E)	Fernsprecher *m*	—	appareil téléphonique *m*	telefono *m*	teléfono *m*
téléphone (F)	Telefon *n*	telephone	—	telefono *m*	teléfono *m*
telephone conversation (E)	Telefongespräch *n*	—	conversation téléphonique *f*	telefonata *f*	conferencia telefónica *f*
telephone exchange (E)	Fernmeldeamt *n*	—	service de télécommunication *m*	ufficio telecomunicazioni *m*	central interurbana *f*
telephone number (E)	Telefonnummer *f*	—	numéro de téléphone *m*	numero di telefono *m*	número de teléfono *m*
telephone service (E)	Telefondienst *m*	—	service du téléphone *m*	servizio telefonico *m*	servicio telefónico *m*
teleprinter (E)	Fernschreiber *m*	—	téléimprimeur *m*	telescrivente *m*	télex *m*
telescrivente (I)	Fernschreiber *m*	teleprinter	téléimprimeur *m*	—	télex *m*
teletex number (E)	Teletexnummer *f*	—	numéro de télétex *m*	numero teletex *m*	número de teletex *m*
Teletexnummer (D)	—	teletex number	numéro de télétex *m*	numero teletex *m*	número de teletex *m*
teletexto (Es)	Bildschirmtext *m*	videotext	videotex international *m*	videotex *m*	—
télétransmission des données informatiques (F)	Datenfern-übertragung *f*	remote data transmission	—	teletrasmissione dati *f*	transmisión de datos *f*
teletrasmissione dati (I)	Datenfern-übertragung *f*	remote data transmission	télétransmission des données informatiques *f*	—	transmisión de datos *f*
television advertising (E)	Fernsehwerbung *f*	—	émission publicitaire télévisée *f*	pubblicità televisiva *f*	publicidad televisiva *f*
televisione via cavo (I)	Kabelfernsehen *n*	cable television	télévision par câble *f*	—	televisión por cable *f*
télévision par câble (F)	Kabelfernsehen *n*	cable television	—	televisione via cavo *f*	televisión por cable *f*
televisión por cable (Es)	Kabelfernsehen *n*	cable television	télévision par câble *f*	televisione via cavo *f*	—
télex (Es)	Fernschreiber *m*	teleprinter	téléimprimeur *m*	telescrivente *m*	—
Telexanschluß (D)	—	telex connection	communication de télex *f*	collegamento telex *m*	comunicación de télex *f*
telex connection (E)	Telexanschluß *m*	—	communication de télex *f*	collegamento telex *m*	comunicación de télex *f*
telex number (E)	Telexnummer *f*	—	numéro de télex *m*	numero telex *m*	número de télex *m*
Telexnummer (D)	—	telex number	numéro de télex *m*	numero telex *m*	número de télex *m*
tempo d'attesa (I)	Wartezeit *f*	waiting time	temps d'attente *m*	—	tiempo de espera *m*
tempo impiegato (I)	Zeitaufwand *m*	expenditure of time	temps passé *m*	—	tiempo consagrado *m*
tempo pezzo (I)	Stückzeit *f*	piece time	temps par pièce *m*	—	tiempo por unidad *m*
temporada (Es)	Saison *f*	season	saison *f*	stagione *f*	—
temporaneo (I)	einstweilig	temporary	provisoire	—	provisional
temporary (E)	einstweilig	—	provisoire	temporaneo	provisional
temporary injunction (E)	einstweilige Verfügung *f*	—	ordonnance sur référé civil *f*	provvedimento temporaneo *m*	interdicto provisorio *m*
temps d'attente (F)	Wartezeit *f*	waiting time	—	tempo d'attesa *m*	tiempo de espera *m*
temps de travail annuel (F)	Jahresarbeitszeit *f*	annual hours of work	—	orario di lavoro annuale *m*	jornada anual *f*

	D	E	F	I	Es
temps par pièce (F)	Stückzeit *f*	piece time	—	tempo pezzo *m*	tiempo por unidad *m*
temps passé (F)	Zeitaufwand *m*	expenditure of time	—	tempo impiegato *m*	tiempo consagrado *m*
tenant (E)	Mieter *m*	—	locataire *m*	locatario *m*	inquilino *m*/ arrendatario *m*
tendance (F)	Tendenz *f*	tendency	—	tendenza *f*	tendencia *f*
tendance à la hausse (F)	Reprise *f*	repeat	—	ripresa *f*	segunda lectura en el corro *f*
tendance générale (F)	Trend *m*	trend	—	tendenza *f*	tendencia *f*
tendant à l'expansion (F)	expansiv	expansive	—	espansivo	expansivo
tendencia¹ (Es)	Tendenz *f*	tendency	tendance *f*	tendenza *f*	—
tendencia² (Es)	Trend *m*	trend	tendance générale *f*	tendenza *f*	—
tendencia alcista (Es)	Aufwärtstrend *m*	upward trend	mouvement ascendant *m*	tendenza al rialzo *f*	—
tendencia bajista (Es)	Abwärtstrend *m*	downward trend	baisse *f*	tendenza al ribasso *f*	—
tendency (E)	Tendenz *f*	—	tendance *f*	tendenza *f*	tendencia *f*
Tendenz (D)	—	tendency	tendance *f*	tendenza *f*	tendencia *f*
tendenza¹ (I)	Tendenz *f*	tendency	tendance *f*	—	tendencia *f*
tendenza² (I)	Trend *m*	trend	tendance générale *f*	—	tendencia *f*
tendenza al rialzo (I)	Aufwärtstrend *m*	upward trend	mouvement ascendant *m*	—	tendencia alcista *f*
tendenza al ribasso (I)	Abwärtstrend *m*	downward trend	baisse *f*	—	tendencia bajista *f*
tender (E)	Ausschreibung *f*	—	soumission *f*	appalto *m*	concurso-subasta *m*
tender guarantee (E)	Bietungsgarantie *f*	—	cautionnement provisoire *m*	garanzia d'offerta *f*	caución de licitación *f*
tender procedure (E)	Tenderverfahren *n*	—	offre d'emprunts pour la régulation monétaire *f*	offerta pubblica d'acquisto *f*	subasta de prestamos de regulación monetaria *f*
Tenderverfahren (D)	—	tender procedure	offre d'emprunts pour la régulation monétaire *f*	offerta pubblica d'acquisto *f*	subasta de prestamos de regulación monetaria *f*
tenedor de libros (Es)	Buchhalter *m*	bookkeeper	comptable *m*	ragioniere *m*	—
tener en almacén (Es)	auf Lager haben	have in stock	avoir en stock	avere in magazzino	—
tenore di vita (I)	Lebensstandard *m*	standard of living	niveau de vie *m*	—	nivel de vida *m*
tenue de compte (F)	Kontoführung *f*	keeping of an account	—	tenuta di un conto *f*	administración de una cuenta *f*
tenuta di un conto (I)	Kontoführung *f*	keeping of an account	tenue de compte *f*	—	administración de una cuenta *f*
teoría (Es)	Theorie *f*	theory	théorie *f*	teoria *f*	—
teoria (I)	Theorie *f*	theory	théorie *f*	—	teoría *f*
teoría de la empresa (Es)	Betriebswirtschafts-lehre *f*	business administration	(science de la) gestion industrielle et commerciale *f*	economia aziendale *f*	—
teoría de la información (Es)	Informationstheorie *f*	information theory	théorie d'information *f*	teoria dell'informazione *f*	—
teoria del capitale (I)	Kapitaltheorie *f*	capital theory	théorie du capital *f*	—	teoría financiera *f*
teoria del denaro (I)	Geldtheorie *f*	monetary theory	théorie monétaire *f*	—	teoría monetaria *f*
teoría del empleo (Es)	Beschäftigungs-theorie *f*	employment theory	théorie d'emploi *f*	teoria dell'occupazione *f*	—
teoria della produzione (I)	Produktionstheorie *f*	production theory	théorie de la production *f*	—	teoría de producción *f*
teoria dell'economia (I)	Wirtschaftstheorie *f*	economic theory	théorie économique *f*	—	teoría económica *f*
teoria dell'inflazione (I)	Inflationstheorie *f*	inflationary theory	théorie d'inflation *f*	—	teoría inflacionista *f*
teoria dell'informazione (I)	Informationstheorie *f*	information theory	théorie d'information *f*	—	teoría de la información *f*
teoria dell'occupazione (I)	Beschäftigungs-theorie *f*	employment theory	théorie d'emploi *f*	—	teoría del empleo *f*
teoría de los precios (Es)	Preistheorie *f*	theory of prices	théorie des prix *f*	teoria del prezzo *f*	—

	D	E	F	I	Es
teoria del prezzo (I)	Preistheorie *f*	theory of prices	théorie des prix *f*	—	teoría de los precios *f*
teoría de producción (Es)	Produktionstheorie *f*	production theory	théorie de la production *f*	teoria della produzione *f*	—
teoría económica (Es)	Wirtschaftstheorie *f*	economic theory	théorie économique *f*	teoria dell'economia *f*	—
teoría financiera (Es)	Kapitaltheorie *f*	capital theory	théorie du capital *f*	teoria del capitale *f*	—
teoría inflacionista (Es)	Inflationstheorie *f*	inflationary theory	théorie d'inflation *f*	teoria dell'inflazione *f*	—
teoría monetaria (Es)	Geldtheorie *f*	monetary theory	théorie monétaire *f*	teoria del denaro *f*	—
terceros países (Es)	Drittländer *pl*	third countries	pays tiers *m pl*	paesi terzi *m pl*	—
term (E)	Laufzeit *f*	—	durée *f*	scadenza *f*/durata *f*	plazo de vencimiento *m*
terme du payement (F)	Zahlungstermin *m*	date of payment	—	termine di pagamento *m*	plazo de pago *m*
Termin (D)	—	deadline	date limite *f*	termine *m*	fecha *f*/cita *f*/ plazo *m*
terminación total (Es)	Fertigstellung *f*	completion	achèvement *m*	completamento *m*	—
Terminal (D)	—	terminal	terminal *m*	terminale *m*	terminal *m*
terminal (E)	Terminal *m*	—	terminal *m*	terminale *m*	terminal *m*
terminal (Es)	Terminal *m*	terminal	terminal *m*	terminale *m*	—
terminal (F)	Terminal *m*	terminal	—	terminale *m*	terminal *m*
terminale (I)	Terminal *m*	terminal	terminal *m*	—	terminal *m*
terminal operator (E)	Datentypistin *f*	—	perforatrice *f*	dattilografa *f*	perforadora *f*
terminate (E)	kündigen	—	résilier	disdire	denunciar/dar aviso de despido
Termination of Employment Act (E)	Kündigungsschutz-gesetz *n*	—	loi sur le délai-congé en matière de licenciement *f*	legge sulla tutela contro il licenziamento *f*	ley de protección contra el despido *f*
Terminbörse (D)	—	futures market	bourse à terme *f*	mercato a termine *m*	bolsa de valores a término *f*
termine[1] (I)	Termin *m*	deadline	date limite *f*	—	fecha *f*/cita *f*/ plazo *m*
termine[2] (I)	Frist *f*	period	délai *m*	—	plazo *m*
termine del colloquio (I)	Besprechungs-termin *m*	meeting date	date de la conférence *f*	—	fecha de conferencia *f*
termine di consegna[1] (I)	Liefertermin *m*	date of delivery	délai de livraison *m*	—	plazo de entrega *m*
termine di consegna[2] (I)	Lieferfrist *f*	time for delivery	délai de livraison *m*	—	plazo de entrega *m*
termine di denuncia (I)	Anmeldefrist *f*	time for application	délai de déclaration *m*	—	plazo de solicitud *m*
termine di pagamento[1] (I)	Zahlungsziel *n*	period for payment	délai de payement *m*	—	plazo de pago *m*
termine di pagamento[2] (I)	Zahlungstermin *m*	date of payment	terme du payement *m*	—	plazo de pago *m*
termine di preavviso per la disdetta (I)	Kündigungsfrist *f*	period of notice	délai de préavis *m*	—	plazo de preaviso *m*
termine di scadenza (I)	Ablauffrist *f*	time limit	délai *m*	—	vencimiento *m*
termine supplementare (I)	Nachfrist *f*	additional period	prolongation *f*	—	plazo de gracia *m*
termingerecht (D)	—	on schedule	dans les délais	puntuale	en la fecha fijada
Termingeschäft (D)	—	time bargain	opération à terme *f*	operazione a termine *f*	operación a plazo *f*
Terminkontrakt (D)	—	forward contract	contrat à terme *m*	contratto a termine *m*	contrato de entrega futura *m*
Terminkurs (D)	—	forward price	cours de bourse à terme *m*	corso a termine *m*	cambio a término *m*
Terminplanung (D)	—	scheduling	planning de rendez-vous *m*	programmazione dei termini *f*	planificación de plazos *f*
term life insurance (E)	Risiko-Lebens-versicherung *f*	—	assurance-vie temporaire *f*	assicurazione rischio-vita *f*	seguro de vida temporal *m*
term of contract (E)	Vertragsbedingung *f*	—	condition du contrat *f*	condizione del contratto *f*	condiciones contractuales *f pl*

	D	E	F	I	Es
term of protection (E)	Schutzfrist *f*	—	délai de protection *m*	durata della protezione *f*	plazo de protección *m*
terms of conveyance (E)	Beförderungs-bedingungen *f*	—	conditions de transport *f pl*	condizioni di trasporto *f pl*	condiciones de transporte *f pl*
terms of delivery (E)	Lieferbedingungen *pl*	—	conditions de livraison *f pl*	condizioni di consegna *f pl*	condiciones de suminstro *f pl*
terms of payment[1] (E)	Zahlungsbedingung *f*	—	conditions de payement *f pl*	condizione di pagamento *f*	condiciones de pago *f pl*
terms of payment[2] (E)	Zahlungsfrist *f*	—	délai de payement *f*	scadenza di pagamento *f*	plazo de pago *m*
terra (I)	Boden *m*	ground/soil	sol *m*/terrain *m*	—	suelo *m*/ terreno *m*
terrain (F)	Grundstück *n*	real estate	—	terreno *m*	terreno *m*
terreno (Es)	Grundstück *n*	real estate	terrain *m*	terreno *m*	—
terreno (I)	Grundstück *n*	real estate	terrain *m*	—	terreno *m*
terreno edificable (Es)	Bauland *n*	building land	espace à bâtir *m*	area edificabile *f*	—
territoire considéré hors frontière douanière nationale (F)	Zollausschluß *m*	territory inside political but outside customs frontier	—	zona franca *f*	exclave aduanero *m*
territoire de surveil-lance douanière (F)	Zollgrenzgebiet *n*	customs frontier district	—	area doganale di confine *f*	territorio aduanero fronterizo *m*
territoire de vente (F)	Verkaufsgebiet *n*	sales territory	—	zona di vendita *f*	territorio de venta *m*
territoire douanier[1] (F)	Zollgebiet *n*	customs territory	—	territorio doganale *m*	distrito aduanero *m*
territoire douanier[2] (F)	Zollinland *n*	domestic customs territory	—	territorio doganale nazionale *m*	territorio aduanero interior *m*
territoire hors du con-trôle de la douane (F)	Zollausland *n*	foreign customs territory	—	territorio doganale estero *m*	territorio aduanero exterior *m*
territorial jurisdiction (E)	Gebietshoheit *f*	—	souveraineté territoriale *f*	sovranità territoriale *f*	soberanía territorial *f*
territorio aduanero exterior (Es)	Zollausland *n*	foreign customs territory	territoire hors du con-trôle de la douane *m*	territorio doganale estero *m*	—
territorio aduanero fronterizo (Es)	Zollgrenzgebiet *n*	customs frontier district	territoire de surveil-lance douanière *m*	area doganale di confine *f*	—
territorio aduanero interior (Es)	Zollinland *n*	domestic customs territory	territoire douanier national *m*	territorio doganale nazionale *m*	—
territorio de venta (Es)	Verkaufsgebiet *n*	sales territory	territoire de vente *m*	zona di vendita *f*	—
territorio doganale (I)	Zollgebiet *n*	customs territory	territoire douanier *m*	—	distrito aduanero *m*
territorio doganale estero (I)	Zollausland *n*	foreign customs territory	territoire hors du con trôle de la douane *m*	—	territorio aduanero exterior *m*
territorio doganale nazionale (I)	Zollinland *n*	domestic customs territory	territoire douanier national *m*	—	territorio aduanero interior *m*
territory inside political but outside customs frontier (E)	Zollausschluß *m*	—	territoire considéré hors frontière doua-nière nationale *m*	zona franca *f*	exclave aduanero *m*
territory protection (E)	Gebietsschutz *m*	—	exclusivité territoriale *f*	tutela territoriale *f*	protección territorial *f*
tesorería (Es)	Schatzamt *n*	Treasury	trésor *m*	tesoreria *f*	—
tesoreria (I)	Schatzamt *n*	Treasury	trésor *m*	—	tesorería *f*
tessera aziendale (I)	Betriebsausweis *m*	staff identification card	pièce d'identité de l'entreprise *f*	—	carné de empresa *f*
Test (D)	—	test	test *m*	test *m*	test *m*
test (E)	Test *m*	—	test *m*	test *m*	test *m*
test (Es)	Test *m*	test	test *m*	test *m*	—
test (F)	Test *m*	test	—	test *m*	test *m*
test (I)	Test *m*	test	test *m*	—	test *m*
testaferro (Es)	Strohmann *m*	man of straw/ dummy	prête-nom *m*	prestanome *m*	—
Testament (D)	—	last will	testament *m*	testamento *m*	testamento *m*
testament (F)	Testament *n*	last will	—	testamento *m*	testamento *m*
testamento (Es)	Testament *n*	last will	testament *m*	testamento *m*	—
testamento (I)	Testament *n*	last will	testament *m*	—	testamento *m*

	D	E	F	I	Es
Testaments-eröffnung (D)	—	opening of the will	ouverture du testament *f*	apertura del testamento *f*	apertura de testamento *f*
test di mercato (I)	Markttest *m*	market test	test du marché *m*	—	examinación del mercado *f*
test du marché (F)	Markttest *m*	market test	—	test di mercato *m*	examinación del mercado *f*
Testläden (D)	—	test shops	magasins de test *m pl*	negozi pilota *m pl*	tiendas piloto *f pl*
test market (E)	Testmarkt *m*	—	marché de test *m*	mercato pilota *m*	mercado piloto *m*
Testmarkt (D)	—	test market	marché de test *m*	mercato pilota *m*	mercado piloto *m*
testo pubblicitario (I)	Werbetext *m*	advertising copy	texte publicitaire *m*	—	texto publicitario *m*
test shops (E)	Testläden *pl*	—	magasins de test *m pl*	negozi pilota *m pl*	tiendas piloto *f pl*
text configuration (E)	Textgestaltung *f*	—	structure du texte *f*	redazione del testo *f*	estructuración del texto *f*
texte publicitaire (F)	Werbetext *m*	advertising copy	—	testo pubblicitario *m*	texto publicitario *m*
Textgestaltung (D)	—	text configuration	structure du texte *f*	redazione del testo *f*	estructuración del texto *f*
texto publicitario (Es)	Werbetext *m*	advertising copy	texte publicitaire *m*	testo pubblicitario *m*	—
Textverarbeitung (D)	—	word processing	élaboration de texte *f*	elaborazione testi *f*	tratamiento de textos *m*
theft (E)	Diebstahl *m*	—	vol *m*	furto *m*	robo *m*
Theorie (D)	—	theory	théorie *f*	teoria *f*	teoría *f*
théorie (F)	Theorie *f*	theory	—	teoria *f*	teoría *f*
théorie de la production (F)	Produktionstheorie *f*	production theory	—	teoria della produzione *f*	teoría de producción *f*
théorie d'emploi (F)	Beschäftigungs-theorie *f*	employment theory	—	teoria dell'occupazione *f*	teoría del empleo *f*
théorie des prix (F)	Preistheorie *f*	theory of prices	—	teoria del prezzo *f*	teoría de los precios *f*
théorie d'inflation (F)	Inflationstheorie *f*	inflationary theory	—	teoria dell'inflazione *f*	teoría inflacionista *f*
théorie d'information (F)	Informationstheorie *f*	information theory	—	teoria dell'informazione *f*	teoría de la información *f*
théorie du capital (F)	Kapitaltheorie *f*	capital theory	—	teoria del capitale *f*	teoría financiera *f*
théorie économique (F)	Wirtschaftstheorie *f*	economic theory	—	teoria dell'economia *f*	teoría económica *f*
théorie monétaire (F)	Geldtheorie *f*	monetary theory	—	teoria del denaro *f*	teoría monetaria *f*
theory (E)	Theorie *f*	—	théorie *f*	teoria *f*	teoría *f*
theory of prices (E)	Preistheorie *f*	—	théorie des prix *f*	teoria del prezzo *f*	teoría de los precios *f*
third countries (E)	Drittländer *pl*	—	pays tiers *m pl*	paesi terzi *m pl*	terceros países *m pl*
third party liability insurance (E)	Haftpflicht-versicherung *f*	—	assurance responsa-bilité civile *f*	assicurazione della responsabilità civile *f*	seguro de responsa-bilidad civil *m*
three months papers (E)	Dreimonatspapier *n*	—	titre à trois mois *m*	titolo trimestrale *m*	títulos a tres meses *m*
threshold price[1] (E)	Schwellenpreis *m*	—	prix de seuil *m*	prezzo soglia *m*	precio-base *m*
threshold price[2] (E)	Preisschwelle *f*	—	seuil du prix *m*	soglia dei prezzi *f*	umbral de precios *m*
tied production (E)	Koppelproduktion *f*	—	production couplée *f*	produzione abbinata *f*	coproducción *f*
tie-in transaction (E)	Kopplungsgeschäft *n*	—	affaire couplée *f*	operazione abbinata *f*	negocio acoplado *m*
tiempo consagrado (Es)	Zeitaufwand *m*	expenditure of time	temps passé *m*	tempo impiegato *m*	—
tiempo de espera (Es)	Wartezeit *f*	waiting time	temps d'attente *m*	tempo d'attesa *m*	—
tiendas piloto (Es)	Testläden *pl*	test shops	magasins de test *m pl*	negozi pilota *m pl*	—
Tierzucht (D)	—	livestock breeding	élevage *m*	zootecnia *f*	cría de animales *f*
Tilgung (D)	—	redemption	amortissement *m*	ammortamento *m*	amortización *f*
timbre-poste (F)	Briefmarke *f*	stamp	—	francobollo *m*	sello *m*

	D	E	F	I	Es
timbro postale (I)	Poststempel *m*	postmark	cachet de la poste *m*	—	sello postal *m*
time bargain (E)	Termingeschäft *n*	—	opération à terme *f*	operazione a termine *f*	operación a plazo *f*
time deposit account (E)	Festgeldkonto *n*	—	compte de dépôt à terme *m*	deposito vincolato *m*	cuenta a plazo *f*
time for application (E)	Anmeldefrist *f*	—	délai de déclaration *m*	termine di denuncia *m*	plazo de solicitud *m*
time for delivery (E)	Lieferfrist *f*	—	délai de livraison *m*	termine di consegna *m*	plazo de entrega *m*
time limit (E)	Ablauffrist *f*	—	délai *m*	termine di scadenza *m*	vencimiento *m*
timely (E)	fristgerecht	—	dans les délais	entro il termine convenuto	dentro del plazo fijado
time study (E)	Zeitstudie *f*	—	étude des temps *f*	analisi sul tempo impiegato *f*	estudio de tiempo *m*
time wage (E)	Zeitlohn *m*	—	salaire au temps *m*	salario a tempo *m*	salario por unidad de tiempo *m*
tino de negociar (Es)	Verhandlungs-geschick *n*	negotiation skills	habileté en matière de négociations *f*	abilità nel trattare *f*	—
tip (E)	Bedienungsgeld *n*	—	pourboire *m*	diritto di servizio *m*	propina *f*
tipi di costi (I)	Kostenarten *pl*	cost types	coûts par nature *m pl*	—	clases de costes *f pl*
tipi di mercato (I)	Marktformen *pl*	types of markets	formes du marché *f pl*	—	formas del mercado *f*
tipo de cambio (Es)	Wechselkurs *m*	exchange rate	cours du change *m*	cambio *m*	—
tipo de cambio de billetes y monedas extranjeras (Es)	Sortenkurs *m*	rate for foreign notes and coin	cours des monnaies étrangères *m*	corso dei cambi *m*	—
tipo de cambio múltiple (Es)	gespaltene Wechselkurse *pl*	two-tier exchange rate	cours du change multiple *m*	cambi multipli *m pl*	—
tipo de emisión (Es)	Emissionskurs *m*	price of issue	cours d'émission *m*	prezzo d'emissione *m*	—
tipo de flete (Es)	Frachtrate *f*	(freight) rate	taux de fret *m*	tariffa di nolo *f*	—
tipo de interés (Es)	Zinsfuß *m*	interest rate	taux d'intérêt *m*	tasso d'interesse *m*	—
tipo de pignoración (Es)	Lombardsatz *m*	rate for advances on securities	taux d'intérêt de l'argent prêté sur gage *m*	tasso sulle anticipazioni *m*	—
tipo di merce (I)	Warenart *f*	class of goods	catégorie de marchandise *f*	—	categoría de mercancías *f*
tipo d'inserzione (I)	Anzeigengestaltung *f*	lay out of an advertisement	arrangement de l'annonce *m*	—	estructuración del anuncio *f*
tipo di pagamento (I)	Zahlungsform *f*	payment system	forme de payement *f*	—	forma de pago *f*
tipo di spedizione (I)	Versandform *f*	manner of delivery	forme d'expéditoin *f*	—	forma de envío *f*
tipo flotante de cambio (Es)	flexibler Wechselkurs *m*	flexible exchange rate	taux de change flottant *m*	cambio flessibile *m*	—
tipo interbancario (Es)	Interbankrate *f*	interbank rate	taux interbancaire *m*	tasso interbancario *m*	—
tipo pivote (Es)	Leitkurs *m*	central rate	taux central *m*	parità centrale *f*	—
tipos de cambio fijos (Es)	feste Wechselkurse *pl*	fixed exchange rates	taux de change fixe *m*	cambi fissi *m pl*	—
tipos de referencia (Es)	Leitzins *m*	key rate	taux-clé d'intérêt bancaire	tasso d'interesse guida *m*	—
tirage d'une traite de cavalerie (F)	Wechselreiterei *f*	kiteflying	—	emissione di tratte incrociate *f*	libramiento de letras cruzadas *m*
tiré (F)	Bezogener *m*	drawee	—	trattario *m*	librado *m*
Titel (D)	—	title	titre *m*	titolo *m*	título *m*
title (E)	Titel *m*	—	titre *m*	titolo *m*	título *m*
titolare del conto (I)	Kontoinhaber *m*	account holder	titulaire d'un compte *m*	—	titular de una cuenta *m*
titolare unico (I)	Alleininhaber *m*	sole owner	seul propriétaire *m*	—	propietario exclusivo *m*
titoli (I)	Effekten *f*	securities	valeurs mobilières *f pl*	—	efectos *m pl*
titoli a reddito fisso (I)	Rentenpapiere *pl*	bonds	titres de rente *m pl*	—	títulos de renta fija *m pl*

	D	E	F	I	Es
titoli a reddito variabile (I)	Dividendenpapiere *pl*	dividend-bearing shares	titre donnant droit à des dividendes *m*	—	títulos de renta variable *m pl*
titoli d'investimento (I)	Anlagepapiere *pl*	investment securities	valeurs de placement *f*	—	valores de inversión *m pl*
titoli pubblici (I)	Staatsanleihen *pl*	government loan	emprunt d'Etat *m*	—	empréstito estatal *m*
titolo[1] (I)	Titel *m*	title	titre *m*	—	título *m*
titolo[2] (I)	Feingehalt *m*	fine gold content	titre *m*	—	ley *f*
titolo[3] (I)	Anrede *f*	form of address	début de lettre *m*	—	tratamiento *m*
titolo[4] (I)	Wertpapier *n*	security	titre *m*/valeur *f*	—	título *m*/valor *m*
titolo all'ordine (I)	Orderpapier *n*	instruments (made out) to order	papier à ordre *m*	—	título a la orden *m*
titolo al portatore (I)	Inhaberpapier *n*	bearer instrument	titre souscrit au porteur *m*	—	título al portador *m*
titolo ipotecario (I)	Pfandbrief *m*	mortgage bond	obligation hypothécaire *f*	—	cédula hipotecaria *f*
titolo trimestrale (I)	Dreimonatspapier *n*	three months papers	titre à trois mois *m*	—	títulos a tres meses *m*
titre[1] (F)	Titel *m*	title	—	titolo *m*	título *m*
titre[2] (F)	Rechtsanspruch *m*	legal claim	—	pretesa giuridica *f*	pretensión legal *f*
titre[3] (F)	Wertpapier *n*	security	—	titolo *m*	título *m*/valor *m*
titre à trois mois (F)	Dreimonatspapier *n*	three months papers	—	titolo trimestrale *m*	títulos a tres meses *m*
titre donnant droit à des dividendes (F)	Dividendenpapiere *pl*	dividend-bearing shares	—	titoli a reddito variabile *m pl*	títulos de renta variable *m pl*
titre souscrit au porteur (F)	Inhaberpapier *n*	bearer instrument	—	titolo al portatore *m*	título al portador *m*
titulaire d'un compte (F)	Kontoinhaber *m*	account holder	—	titolare del conto *m*	titular de una cuenta *m*
titular de una cuenta (Es)	Kontoinhaber *m*	account holder	titulaire d'un compte *m*	titolare del conto *m*	—
título[1] (Es)	Wertpapier *n*	security	titre *m*/valeur *f*	titolo *m*	—
título[2] (Es)	Titel *m*	title	titre *m*	titolo *m*	—
título al portador (Es)	Inhaberpapier *n*	bearer instrument	titre souscrit au porteur *m*	titolo al portatore *m*	—
títulos a tres meses (Es)	Dreimonatspapier *n*	three months papers	titre à trois mois *m*	titolo trimestrale *m*	—
títulos de renta fija (Es)	Rentenpapiere *pl*	bonds	titres de rente *m pl*	titoli a reddito fisso *m pl*	—
títulos de renta variable (Es)	Dividendenpapiere *pl*	dividend-bearing shares	titre donnant droit à des dividendes *m*	titoli a reddito variabile *m pl*	—
Tochter-gesellschaft (D)	—	subsidiary	société filiale *f*	società affiliata *f*	filial *f*
toilet (E)	Toilette *f*	—	toilettes *f pl*	toilette *f*	lavabo *m*
Toilette (D)	—	toilet	toilettes *f pl*	toilette *f*	lavabo *m*
toilette (I)	Toilette *f*	toilet	toilettes *f pl*	—	lavabo *m*
toilettes (F)	Toilette *f*	toilet	—	toilette *f*	lavabo *m*
tolleranza (I)	Spielraum *m*	margin	marge *f*	—	margen *f*
tomador (Es)	Abnehmer *m*	buyer/purchaser/ customer	acheteur *m*	acquirente *m*/ cliente *m*	—
tonelada de registro (Es)	Registertonne *f*	register ton	tonneau de jauge *m*	tonnellata di registro *f*	—
tonelada de registro bruto (Es)	Bruttoregistertonne *f*	gross register(ed) ton	tonneau de jauge brute *m*	tonnellata di stazza lorda *f*	—
tonneau de jauge (F)	Registertonne *f*	register ton	—	tonnellata di registro *f*	tonelada de registro *f*
tonneau de jauge brute (F)	Bruttoregistertonne *f*	gross register(ed) ton	—	tonnellata di stazza lorda *f*	tonelada de registro bruto *f*
tonnellata di registro (I)	Registertonne *f*	register ton	tonneau de jauge *m*	—	tonelada de registro *f*
tonnellata di stazza lorda (I)	Bruttoregistertonne *f*	gross register(ed) ton	tonneau de jauge	— brute *m*	tonelada de registro bruto *f*
top price (E)	Höchstpreis *m*	—	prix plafond *m*	prezzo massimo *m*	precio máximo *m*

	D	E	F	I	Es
top wage (E)	Spitzenlohn *m*	—	salaire maximum *m*	salario massimo *m*	salario máximo *m*
total amout (E)	Gesamtsumme *f*	—	montant total *m*	importo totale *m*	suma total *f*
total costs (E)	Gesamtkosten *pl*	—	coût total *m*	costi totali *m pl*	gastos generales *m pl*
total delivery (E)	Gesamtlieferung *f*	—	livraison totale *f*	fornitura completa *f*	suministro total *f*
total loss (E)	Totalschaden *m*	—	dommage total *m*	danno totale *m*	daño total *m*
total of indebtedness (E)	Schuldenmasse *f*	—	passif *m*	massa passiva *f*	masa pasiva *f*
Totalschaden (D)	—	total loss	dommage total *m*	danno totale *m*	daño total *m*
totes Kapital (D)	—	unproductive capital	capital improductif *m*	capitale infruttifero *m*	capital improductivo *m*
tour schedule (E)	Tourenplan *m*	—	itinéraire *m*	programma dell'itinerario *m*	itinerario *m*
Tourenplan (D)	—	tour schedule	itinéraire *m*	programma dell'itinerario *m*	itinerario *m*
town planning (E)	Städtebau *m*	—	urbanisme *m*	urbanistica *f*	urbanización *f*
trabajador (Es)	Arbeiter *m*	worker	travailleur *m*	operaio *m*	—
trabajadores extranjeros (Es)	ausländische Arbeitnehmer *m*	foreign workers	travailleurs étrangers *m*	prestatori d'opera stranieri *m pl*	—
trabajo (Es)	Arbeit *f*	work	travail *m*	lavoro *m*	—
trabajo a destajo (Es)	Akkordarbeit *f*	piecework	travail à la tâche *m*	lavora a cottimo *m*	—
trabajo a domicilio (Es)	Heimarbeit *f*	homework	travail à domicile *m*	lavoro a domicilio *m*	—
trabajo a mano (Es)	Handarbeit *f*	handwork	travail manuel *m*	lavoro manuale *m*	—
trabajo a tiempo parcial (Es)	Teilzeitarbeit *f*	part-time work	travail à temps partiel *m*	lavoro part-time *m*	—
trabajo clandestino (Es)	Schwarzarbeit *f*	illicit work	travail noir *m*	lavoro abusivo *m*	—
trabajo de pantalla (Es)	Bildschirmarbeit *f*	screen work	travail à l'écran	lavoro video *m*	—
trabajo dominical (Es)	Sonntagsarbeit *f*	Sunday work	travail du dimanche *m*	lavoro domenicale *m*	—
trabajo en equipo (Es)	Teamarbeit *f*	team work	travail d'équipe *m*	lavoro d'équipe *m*	—
trabajo extraordinario (Es)	Mehrarbeit *f*	additional work	travail supplément aire *m*	lavoro supplementare *m*	—
trabajo reducido (Es)	Kurzarbeit *f*	short-time work	travail à temps réduit *m*	lavoro ad orario ridotto *m*	—
trade[1] (E)	Gewerbe *n*	—	activité professionnelle *f*/industrie *f*/ arsanat *m*	commercio *m*/ industria *f*/ artigianato *m*	industria *f*/ comercio *m*/ artesanía *f*
trade[2] (E)	Handel *m*	—	commerce *m*	commercio *m*	comercio *m*
trade analysis (E)	Branchenanalyse *f*	—	analyse des branches *f*	analisi di categoria *f*	análisis del ramo *m*
trade association (E)	Wirtschaftsverband *m*	—	association économique *f*	associazione economica *f*	asociación económica *f*
trade centre (E)	Handelsplatz *m*	—	place marchande *f* commerciale *f*	piazza	plaza comercial *f*
trade comparison (E)	Branchenvergleich *m*	—	comparaison des différentes branches *f*	comparazione delle categorie *f*	comparación de ramos *f*
trade credit (E)	Warenkredit *m*	—	avance sur marchandises *f*	credito su merci *m*	crédito comercial *m*
trade deficit (E)	Außenhandelsdefizit *n*	—	déficit de la balance du commerce extérieur *m*	deficit del commercio estero *m*	déficit del comercio exterior *m*
trade embargo (E)	Handelsembargo *n*	—	embargo commercial *m*	embargo commerciale *m*	embargo comercial *m*
trade fair[1] (E)	Handelsmesse *f*	—	foire commerciale *f*	fiera commerciale *f*	feria comercial *f*
trade fair[2] (E)	Fachausstellung *f*	—	exposition spécialisée *f*	esposizione specializzata *f*	exposición especializada *f*
trade fair[3] (E)	Mustermesse *f*	—	foire d'échantillons *f*	fiera campionaria *f*	feria de muestras *f*
trade mark (E)	Warenzeichen *n*	—	marque *f*	marchio *m*	marca *f*
trade mission (E)	Handelsmission *f*	—	mission commerciale *f*	missione commerciale *f*	misión comercial *f*
trade practice (E)	Handelsusancen *pl*	—	usages commerciaux *m pl*	usanze commerciali *f pl*	usos comerciales *m pl*

	D	E	F	I	Es
trader (E)	Händler *m*	—	commerçant *m*	commerciante *m*	comerciante *m*
trade relations (E)	Handelsbeziehungen *pl*	—	relations commerciales *f pl*	rapporti commerciali *m pl*	relaciones comerciales *f pl*
trade restrictions (E)	Handelsbeschränkungen *pl*	—	restrictions au commerce *f pl*	restrizioni commerciali *f pl*	restricciones commerciales *f pl*
trade secret (E)	Betriebsgeheimnis *n*	—	secret d'exploitation *m*	segreto aziendale *m*	secreto empresarial *m*
trade statistics (E)	Branchenstatistik *f*	—	statistique sur les différentes branches économiques *f*	statistica di categoria *f*	estadística del ramo *f*
trade structure (E)	Branchenstruktur *f*	—	structure de la branche *f*	struttura di categoria *f*	estructura del ramo *f*
trade surplus (E)	Handelsüberschuß *m*	—	excédent commercial *m*	eccedenza commerciale *f*	excedente comercial *m*
trade tariff (E)	Gütertarif *m*	—	tarif marchandises *m*	tariffa merci *f*	tarifa de transporte *f*
trade tax (E)	Gewerbesteuer *f*	—	patente *f*	imposta industriale *f*	impuesto industrial *m*
trade terms (E)	Handelsklausel *f*	—	clause commerciale *f*	clausola commerciale *f*	cláusula comercial *f*
trade union (E)	Gewerkschaften *pl*	—	syndicat *m*	sindacati *m pl*	sindicato *m*
trade war (E)	Handelskrieg *m*	—	guerre commerciale *f*	guerra commerciale *f*	guerra comercial *f*
trading company (E)	Handelsgesellschaft *f*	—	société commerciale *f*	società commerciale *f*	sociedad comercial *f*
trading conditions (E)	Handelsbedingungen *pl*	—	conditions commerciales *f pl*	condizioni commerciali *f pl*	condiciones comerciales *f pl*
trading margin (E)	Handelsspanne *f*	—	bénéfice brut *m*	margine commerciale *m*	margen comercial *f*
trading partner (E)	Handelspartner *m*	—	partenaire commercial *m*	partner commerciale *m*	socio comercial *m*
traffic (E)	Verkehr *m*	—	circulation *f*	traffico *m*	circulación *f*
traffico (I)	Verkehr *m*	traffic	circulation *f*	—	circulación *f*
traffico a breve distanza (I)	Nahverkehr *m*	short distance traffic	transport à courte distance *m*	—	tráfico a corta distancia *m*
traffico aereo commerciale (I)	Luftfrachtverkehr *m*	air freight traffic	transport aérien des marchandises *m*	—	tráfico de flete aéreo *m*
traffico a grande distanza (I)	Fernverkehr *m*	long distance traffic	trafic sur longues distances *m*	—	transporte a distancia *m*
traffico pendolare (I)	Pendelverkehr *m*	shuttle service	trafic de va-et-vient *m*	—	vaivén *m*
traffico stradale (I)	Straßenverkehr *m*	road traffic	trafic routier *m*	—	circulación *f*
tráfico a corta distancia (Es)	Nahverkehr *m*	short distance traffic	transport à courte distance *m*	traffico a breve distanza *m*	—
tráfico de divisas (Es)	Devisenverkehr *m*	foreign exchange dealings	mouvement des devises *m*	commercio dei cambi *m*	—
tráfico de flete aéreo (Es)	Luftfrachtverkehr *m*	air freight traffic	transport aérien des marchandises *m*	traffico aereo commerciale *m*	—
tráfico de futuro (Es)	Warenterminhandel *m*	commodity forward dealing	commerce d'opérations à terme *m*	operazioni a termine su merci *f pl*	—
tráfico de mercanías en bultos sueltos (Es)	Stückgutverkehr *m*	general cargo trade	expéditions de détail *f*	trasporto di collettame *m*	—
trafic routier (F)	Straßenverkehr *m*	road traffic	—	traffico stradale *m*	circulación *f*
trafic sur longues distances (F)	Fernverkehr *m*	long distance traffic	—	traffico a grande distanza *m*	transporte a distancia *m*
Trainee (D)	—	trainee	apprenti *m*	trainee *m*	entrenamiento *m*
trainee (E)	Trainee *m*	—	apprenti *m*	trainee *m*	entrenamiento *m*
trainee (I)	Trainee *m*	trainee	apprenti *m*	—	entrenamiento *m*
trainer (E)	Ausbilder *m*	—	instructeur *m*	istruttore *m*	instructor *m*
training staff (E)	Schulungspersonal *n*	—	personnel d'instruction *m*	personale d'addestramento *m*	personal de formación *m*
traite acceptée (F)	Akzept *n*	accepted bill	—	accettazione *f*	aceptación *f*
traite commerciale (F)	Warenwechsel *m*	commercial bill	—	cambiale commerciale *f*	letra comercial *f*

	D	E	F	I	Es
traitement (F)	Gehalt *n*	salary	—	stipendio *m*	sueldo *m*
traitement de base (F)	Grundgehalt *n*	basic salary	—	stipendio base *m*	salario base *m*
traitement des informations (F)	Datenverarbeitung *f*	data processing	—	elaborazione dati *f*	procesamiento de datos *m*
traite tirée sur l'étranger (F)	Auslandswechsel *n*	foreign bill of exchange	—	cambiale estera *f*	letra sobre el exterior *f*
tram (I)	Straßenbahn *f*	tramway	tramway *m*	—	tranvía *m*
tramitación de pedidos (Es)	Auftragsbearbeitung *f*	order processing	réalisation d'une commande *f*	esecuzione ordini *f*	—
tramway (E)	Straßenbahn *f*	—	tramway *m*	tram *m*	tranvía *m*
tramway (F)	Straßenbahn *f*	tramway	—	tram *m*	tranvía *m*
Tranche (D)	—	tranche	tranche *f*	tranche *f*	emisión parcial *f*
tranche (E)	Tranche *f*	—	tranche *f*	tranche *f*	emisión parcial *f*
tranche (F)	Tranche *f*	tranche	—	tranche *f*	emisión parcial *f*
tranche (I)	Tranche *f*	tranche	tranche *f*	—	emisión parcial *f*
transacción (Es)	Transaktion *f*	transaction	transaction *f*	transazione *f*	—
transacciones a término en divisas (Es)	Devisentermingeschäft *n*	forward exchange dealings	opérations à terme sur les changes *f pl*	operazione valutaria a termine *f*	—
transaction (E)	Transaktion *f*	—	transaction *f*	transazione *f*	transacción *f*
transaction (F)	Transaktion *f*	transaction	—	transazione *f*	transacción *f*
transactions boursiaires (F)	Börsenhandel *m*	stock exchange transactions	—	commercio in borsa *m*	negociación bursátil *f*
Transaktion (D)	—	transaction	transaction *f*	transazione *f*	transacción *f*
transazione (I)	Transaktion *f*	transaction	transaction *f*	—	transacción *f*
transbordement (F)	Umschlag *m*	transshipment	—	trasbordo *m*	transbordo de carga *m*
transbordo de carga (Es)	Umschlag *m*	transshipment	transbordement *m*	trasbordo *m*	—
transcription error (E)	Übertragungsfehler *m*	—	erreur de transcription *f*	errore di trascrizione *m*	error de transcripción *m*
Transfer (D)	—	transfer	transfert *m*	trasferimento *m*	transferencia *f*
transfer[1] (E)	Anweisung *f*	—	mandat *m*	ordine di pagamento *m*	transferencia *f*
transfer[2] (E)	Transfer *m*	—	transfert *m*	trasferimento *m*	transferencia *f*
transferencia[1] (Es)	Transfer *m*	transfer	transfert *m*	trasferimento *m*	—
transferencia[2] (Es)	Anweisung *f*	transfer	mandat *m* pagamento *m*	ordine di	—
transferencia[3] (Es)	Überweisung *f*	remittance	virement *m*	rimessa *f*	—
transferencia bancaria (Es)	Banküberweisung *f*	bank transfer	virement bancaire *m*	rimessa bancaria *f*	—
transfer of an entry (E)	Umbuchung *f*	—	jeu d'écritures *m*	giro di partite *m*	asiento en otra
transfer of profit (E)	Gewinnabführung *f*	—	transfert du bénéfice *m*	trasferimento dell'utile *m*	tranferencia de beneficios *f*
transferencia de beneficios (Es)	Gewinnabführung *f*	transfer of profit	transfert du bénéfice *m*	trasferimento dell'utile *m*	—
Transferrisiko (D)	—	risk of transfer	risque de transfert *m*	rischio di trasferimento *m*	riesgo de transferencia *m*
transfert[1] (F)	Transfer *m*	transfer/transmission	—	trasferimento *m*/ trasmissione *f*	transferencia *f*
transfert[2] (F)	Übertragung *f*	transfer/transmission	—	trasferimento *m*/ trasmissione *f*	transmisión *f*
transfert de résidence (F)	Wohnungswechsel *m*	change of residence	—	cambiamento dell'abitazione *m*	cambio de vivienda *m*
transfert du bénéfice (F)	Gewinnabführung *f*	transfer of profit	—	trasferimento dell'utile *m*	tranferencia de beneficios *f*
transformación (Es)	Verarbeitung *f*	processing	transformation *f*	lavorazione *f*	—
transformation (F)	Verarbeitung *f*	processing	—	lavorazione *f*	transformación *f*
transformation complémentaire (F)	Weiterverarbeitung *f*	further processing	—	trasformazione *f*	elaboración ulterior *f*
Transit (D)	—	transit	transit *m*	transito *m*	tránsito *m*
transit (E)	Transit *m*	—	transit *m*	transito *m*	tránsito *m*

	D	E	F	I	Es
transit (F)	Transit *m*	transit	—	transito *m*	tránsito *m*
transit certificate (E)	Durchgangsschein *m*	—	acquit de transit *m*	bolletta di transito *f*	pasavante *m*
transit clause (E)	Transitklausel *f*	—	clause de transit *f*	clausola di transito *f*	cláusula de tránsito *f*
transit duty (E)	Transitzoll *m*	—	droit de transit *m*	diritti di transito *m pl*	derecho de tránsito *m*
Transithandel (D)	—	transit trade	commerce de transit *m*	commercio di transito *m*	comercio de tránsito *m*
transitional arrangement (E)	Übergangsregelung *f*	—	règlement transitoire *m*	regolamento transitorio *m*	regulación transitoria *f*
Transitklausel (D)	—	transit clause	clause de transit *f*	clausola di transito *f*	cláusula de tránsito *f*
tránsito (Es)	Transit *m*	transit	transit *m*	transito *m*	—
transito (I)	Transit *m*	transit	transit *m*	—	tránsito *m*
transit trade (E)	Transithandel *m*	—	commerce de transit *m*	commercio di transito *m*	comercio de tránsito *m*
Transitzoll (D)	—	transit duty	droit de transit *m*	diritti di transito *m pl*	derecho de tránsito *m*
transmisión (Es)	Übertragung *f*	transfer/transmission	transfert *m*/ transmission *f*	trasferimento *m*/ trasmissione *f*	—
transmisión de datos[1] (Es)	Datenübertragung *f*	data transmission	transmission de dates *f*	trasmissione dati *f*	—
transmisión de datos[2] (Es)	Datenfern-übertragung *f*	remote data transmission	télétransmission des données informatiques *f*	teletrasmissione dati *f*	—
transmission de dates (F)	Datenübertragung *f*	data transmission	—	trasmissione dati *f*	transmisión de datos *f*
transparence (F)	Transparenz *f*	transparency	—	trasparenza *f*	transparencia *f*
transparence du marché (F)	Markttransparenz *f*	market transparency	—	trasparenza di mercato *f*	transparencia del mercado *f*
transparencia (Es)	Transparenz *f*	transparency	transparence *f*	trasparenza *f*	—
transparencia del mercado (Es)	Markttransparenz *f*	market transparency	transparence du marché *f*	trasparenza di mercato *f*	—
transparency (E)	Transparenz *f*	—	transparence *f*	trasparenza *f*	transparencia *f*
Transparenz (D)	—	transparency	transparence *f*	trasparenza *f*	transparencia *f*
Transport (D)	—	transport	transport *m*	trasporto *m*	transporte *m*
transport (E)	Transport *m*	—	transport *m*	trasporto *m*	transporte *m*
transport (F)	Transport *m*	transport	—	trasporto *m*	transporte *m*
transport à courte distance (F)	Nahverkehr *m*	short distance traffic	—	traffico a breve distanza *m*	tráfico a corta distancia *m*
transport aérien des marchandises (F)	Luftfrachtverkehr *m*	air freight traffic	—	traffico aereo commerciale *m*	tráfico de flete aéreo *m*
transportación en contenedores (Es)	Behälterverkehr *m*	container transport	transport utilisant des containers *m*	trasporto container *m*	—
transport(ation) (E)	Transport-wesen *n*	—	transports *m pl*	trasporti *m pl*	transportes *m pl*
transportation insurance (E)	Transport-versicherung *f*	—	assurance transports *f*	assicurazione dei trasporti *f*	seguro de transporte *m*
transport de groupage (F)	Sammeltransport *m*	collective transport	—	trasporto a collettame *m*	transporte colectivo *m*
transport de marchandises (F)	Güterbeförderung *f*	carriage of goods	—	trasporto di merci *m*	transporte de mercancías *m*
transport de personnes (F)	Personen-beförderung *f*	carriage of passengers	—	trasporto di persone *m*	transporte de personas *m*
transporte (Es)	Transport *m*	transport	transport *m*	trasporto *m*	—
transporte a distancia (Es)	Fernverkehr *m*	long distance traffic	trafic sur longues distances *m*	traffico a grande distanza *m*	—
transporte aéreo (Es)	Luftfrachtbrief *m*	air waybill	lettre de transport aérien *f*	lettera di trasporto aereo *f*	—
transporte colectivo (Es)	Sammeltransport *m*	collective transport	transport de groupage *m*	trasporto a collettame *m*	—
transporte combinado ferrocarril-carretera (Es)	Huckepackverkehr *m*	piggyback service	transport pick-a-back *m*	trasporto strada-rotaia *m*	—

	D	E	F	I	Es
transporte de mercancías (Es)	Güterbeförderung *f*	carriage of goods	transport de marchandises *m*	trasporto di merci *m*	—
transporte de personas (Es)	Personenbeförderung *f*	carriage of passengers	transport de personnes *m*	trasporto di persone *m*	—
transporte ferroviario (Es)	Bahnfracht *f*	rail freight	fret par rail *m*	nolo ferroviario *m*	—
transporteur (F)	Frachtführer *m*	carrier	—	vettore *m*	transportista *m*
transportista[1] (Es)	Luftfrachtführer *m*	air carrier	voiturier aérien *m*	vettore aereo *m*	—
transportista[2] (Es)	Frachtführer *m*	carrier	transporteur *m*	vettore *m*	—
Transportmittel (D)	—	means of transport	moyen de transport *m*	mezzo di trasporto *m*	medio de transporte *m*
Transportpapiere (D)	—	documents covering transportation	documents de transport *m pl*	documenti di trasporto *m pl*	documentos de transporte *m pl*
transport pick-a-back (F)	Huckepackverkehr *m*	piggyback service	—	trasporto strada-rotaia *m*	transporte combinado ferrocarril-carretera *m*
transport policy (E)	Verkehrspolitik *f*	—	politique des transports *f*	politica del traffico *f*	política de transportes *f*
transports (F)	Beförderungsgeschäfte *pl*	transport services	—	operazioni di trasporto *f pl*	negocios de transporte *m pl*
Transportschaden (D)	—	damage to goods in transit	dommage au cours d'un transport *m*	danno di trasporto *m*	daño de transporte *m*
transport services (E)	Beförderungsgeschäfte *pl*	—	transports *m pl*	operazioni di trasporto *f pl*	negocios de transporte *m pl*
transport utilisant des containers (F)	Behälterverkehr *m*	container transport	—	trasporto container *m*	transportación en contenedores *f*
Transportversicherung (D)	—	transportation insurance	assurance transports *f*	assicurazione dei trasporti *f*	seguro de transporte *m*
Transportweg (D)	—	route of transportation	voie de transport *f*	via di trasporto *f*	vía de transporte *f*
transshipment (E)	Umschlag *m*	—	transbordement *m*	trasbordo *m*	transbordo de carga *m*
transshipment frequencies (E)	Umschlagshäufigkeit *f*	—	fréquence de transboredement *f*	velocità di rotazione *f*	frecuencia de transbordo *f*
tranvía (Es)	Straßenbahn *f*	tramway	tramway *m*	tram *m*	—
trasbordo (I)	Umschlag *m*	transshipment	transbordement *m*	—	transbordo de carga *m*
trasferimento[1] (I)	Umzug *m*	change of residence	déménagement *m*	—	mudanza *f*
trasferimento[2] (I)	Übertragung *f*	transfer/transmission	transfert *m*/ transmission *f*	—	transmisión *f*
trasferimento[3] (I)	Transfer *m*	transfer	transfert *m*	—	transferencia *f*
trasferimento dell'utile (I)	Gewinnabführung *f*	transfer of profit	transfert du bénéfice *m*	—	tranferencia de beneficios *f*
trasformazione (I)	Weiterverarbeitung *f*	further processing	transformation complémentaire *f*	—	elaboración ulterior *f*
traslación (Es)	Überwälzung *f*	passing on	répercussion *f*	accollamento *m*	—
trasmissione dati (I)	Datenübertragung *f*	data transmission	transmission de dates *f*	—	transmisión de datos *f*
trasparenza (I)	Transparenz *f*	transparency	transparence *f*	—	transparencia *f*
trasparenza di bilancio (I)	Bilanzklarheit *f*	balance transparency	clarté du bilan *f*	—	claridad del balance *f*
trasparenza di mercato (I)	Markttransparenz *f*	market transparency	transparence du marché *f*	—	transparencia del mercado *f*
trasporto (I)	Transport *m*	transport	transport *m*	—	transporte *m*
trasporto a collettame (I)	Sammeltransport *m*	collective transport	transport de groupage *m*	—	transporte colectivo *m*
trasporto container (I)	Behälterverkehr *m*	container transport	transport utilisant des containers *m*	—	transportación en contenedores *f*
trasporto di collettame (I)	Stückgutverkehr *m*	general cargo trade	expéditions de détail *f*	—	tráfico de mercanías en bultos sueltos *m*
trasporto di merci (I)	Güterbeförderung *f*	carriage of goods	transport de marchandises *m*	—	transporte de mercancías *m*
trasporto di persone (I)	Personenbeförderung *f*	carriage of passengers	transport de personnes *m*	—	transporte de personas *m*
trasporto marittimo (I)	Verfrachtung *f*	carriage of goods by sea	affrètement *m*	—	expedición *f*

	D	E	F	I	Es
trasporto strada-rotaia (I)	Huckepackverkehr *m*	piggyback service	transport pick-a-back *m*	—	transporte combinado ferrocarril-carretera *m*
tratamiento (Es)	Anrede *f*	form of address	début de lettre *m*	titolo *m*	—
tratamiento de textos (Es)	Textverarbeitung *f*	word processing	élaboration de texte *f*	elaborazione testi *f*	—
tratamiento ulterior (Es)	Nachbereitung *f*	aftertreatment	remise en ordre *f*	rielaborazione *f*	—
trattario (I)	Bezogener *m*	drawee	tiré *m*	—	librado *m*
trattativa (I)	Verhandlung *f*	negotiation	négociation *f*	—	negociación *f*
travail (F)	Arbeit *f*	work	—	lavoro *m*	trabajo *m*
travail à domicile (F)	Heimarbeit *f*	homework	—	lavoro a domicilio *m*	trabajo a domicilio *m*
travail à exécuter (F)	Arbeitsanfall *m*	volume of work	—	volume di lavoro *m*	volumen de trabajo *m*
travail à la tâche (F)	Akkordarbeit *f*	piecework	—	lavora a cottimo *m*	trabajo a destajo *m*
travail à l'écran (F)	Bildschirmarbeit *f*	screen work	—	lavoro video *m*	trabajo de pantalla *m*
travail à temps partiel (F)	Teilzeitarbeit *f*	part-time work	—	lavoro part-time *m*	trabajo a tiempo parcial *m*
travail à temps réduit (F)	Kurzarbeit *f*	short-time work	—	lavoro ad orario ridotto *m*	trabajo reducido *m*
travail d'équipe (F)	Teamarbeit *f*	team work	—	lavoro d'équipe *m*	trabajo en equipo *m*
travail du dimanche (F)	Sonntagsarbeit *f*	Sunday work	—	lavoro domenicale *m*	trabajo dominical *m*
travaillé sur mesure (F)	maßgefertigt	manufactured to measure	—	prodotto su misura	hecho a medida
travailleur (F)	Arbeiter *m*	worker	—	operaio *m*	trabajador *m*
travailleur ayant un emploi (F)	Erwerbstätiger *m*	gainfully employed person	—	persona attiva *f*	persona activa *f*
travailleurs étrangers (F)	ausländische Arbeitnehmer *m*	foreign workers	—	prestatori d'opera stranieri *m pl*	trabajadores extranjeros *m*
travail manuel (F)	Handarbeit *f*	handwork	—	lavoro manuale *m*	trabajo a mano *m*
travail noir (F)	Schwarzarbeit *f*	illicit work	—	lavoro abusivo *m*	trabajo clandestino *m*
travail supplémentaire (F)	Mehrarbeit *f*	additional work	—	lavoro supplementare *m*	trabajo extraordinario *m*
travel agency (E)	Reisebüro *n*	—	agence de voyages *f*	ufficio viaggi *m*	agencia de viajes *f*
travel cancellation insurance (E)	Reiserücktritts-versicherung *f*	—	assurance de résilia-tion du voyage *f*	assicurazione recessione viaggio *f*	seguro de rescisión del viaje *m*
traveller's cheque (E)	Reisescheck *m*	—	chèque de voyage *m*	assegno turistico *m*	cheque de viaje *m*
travel(l)ing expenses (E)	Reisespesen *pl*	—	frais de voyage *m pl*	spese di viaggio *f pl*	gastos de viaje *m pl*
Treasury (E)	Schatzamt *n*	—	trésor *m*	tesoreria *f*	tesorería *f*
Treffpunkt (D)	—	meeting place	rendez-vous *m*	punto d'incontro *m*	lugar de la cita *m*
Treibhauseffekt (D)	—	global warming	effet de serre *m*	effotto serra *m*	efecto invernadero *m*
Treibstoff (D)	—	fuel	carburant *m*	carburante *m*	combustible *m*
Trend (D)	—	trend	tendance générale *f*	tendenza *f*	tendencia *f*
trend (E)	Trend *m*	—	tendance générale *f*	tendenza *f*	tendencia *f*
Trendanalyse (D)	—	trend analysis	analyse de la tendance générale *f*	analisi delle tendenze *f*	análisis de tendencia *m*
trend analysis (E)	Trendanalyse *f*	—	analyse de la tendance générale *f*	analisi delle tendenze *f*	análisis de tendencia *m*
Tresor (D)	—	safe	coffre-fort *m*	cassaforte *f*	caja fuerte *f*
trésor (F)	Schatzamt *n*	Treasury	—	tesoreria *f*	tesorería *f*
trial order (E)	Probeauftrag *m*	—	ordre d'essai *m*	ordine a titolo di prova *m*	pedido de prueba *m*
trial package (E)	Probepackung *f*	—	échantillon *m*	confezione campione *f*	muestra *f*
trial period (E)	Probezeit *f*	—	période d'essai *f*	periodo di prova *m*	período de prueba *m*

	D	E	F	I	Es
trial shipment (E)	Probelieferung *f*	—	livraison à titre d'essai *f*	fornitura a titolo di prova *f*	envío de prueba *m*
triangular transaction (E)	Dreiecksgeschäft *n*	—	opération commerciale triangulaire *f*	operazione triangolare *f*	operación triangular *f*
tribunal arbitral (Es)	Schiedsgericht *n*	court of arbitration	tribunal d'arbitrage *m*	tribunale arbitrale *m*	—
tribunal competente (Es)	Gerichtsstand *m*	jurisdiction	juridiction compétente *f*	foro competente *m*	—
tribunal d'appel (F)	Berufungsgericht *n*	appeal court	—	corte d'appello *f*	tribunal de apelación *m*
tribunal d'arbitrage (F)	Schiedsgericht *n*	court of arbitration	—	tribunale arbitrale *m*	tirbunal arbitral *m*
tribunal de apelación (Es)	Berufungsgericht *n*	appeal court	tribunal d'appel *m*	corte d'appello *f*	—
Tribunal de Justicia de las Comunidades Europeas (Es)	Europäischer Gerichtshof *m*	European Court	Cour de Justice Européenne *f*	Corte di Giustizia Europea *f*	—
tribunal de la faillite (F)	Konkursgericht *n*	bankruptcy court	—	tribunale fallimentare *m*	tribunal de quiebras *m*
tribunal de quiebras (Es)	Konkursgericht *n*	bankruptcy court	tribunal de la faillite *m*	tribunale fallimentare *m*	—
tribunale arbitrale (I)	Schiedsgericht *n*	court of arbitration	tribunal d'arbitrage *m*	—	tirbunal arbitral *m*
tribunale fallimentare (I)	Konkursgericht *n*	bankruptcy court	tribunal de la faillite *m*	—	tribunal de quiebras *m*
tributación (Es)	Steuerzahlung *f*	payment of taxes	payement de l'impôt *m*	pagamento delle imposte *m*	—
trimestral (Es)	vierteljährlich	quarterly	trimestriel	trimestrale	—
trimestrale (I)	vierteljährlich	quarterly	trimestriel	—	trimestral
trimestre (Es)	Quartal *n*	quarter	trimestre *m*	trimestre *m*	—
trimestre (F)	Quartal *n*	quarter	—	trimestre *m*	trimestre *m*
trimestre (I)	Quartal *n*	quarter	trimestre *m*	—	trimestre *m*
trimestriel (F)	vierteljährlich	quarterly	—	trimestrale	trimestral
tromperie[1] (F)	Täuschung *f*	deceit	—	inganno *m*	engaño *m*
tromperie[2] (F)	Schwindel *m*	swindle	—	truffa *f*	engaño *m*
truffa (I)	Schwindel *m*	swindle	tromperie *f*	—	engaño *m*
Trust (D)	—	trust	trust *m*	trust *m*	trust *m*
trust (E)	Trust *m*	—	trust *m*	trust *m*	trust *m*
trust (Es)	Trust *m*	trust	trust *m*	trust *m*	—
trust (F)	Trust *m*	trust	—	trust *m*	trust *m*
trust (I)	Trust *m*	trust	trust *m*	—	trust *m*
truth in the balance sheet (E)	Bilanzwahrheit *f*	—	sincérité du bilan *f*	chiarezza di bilancio *f*	sinceridad del balance *f*
try (E)	probieren	—	essayer	provare	probar
turno de noche (Es)	Nachtschicht *f*	night shift	équipe de nuit *f*	turno notturno *m*	—
turno notturno (I)	Nachtschicht *f*	night shift	équipe de nuit *f*	—	turno de noche *m*
turnover (E)	Umsatz *m*	—	chiffre d'affaires *m*	fatturato *m*	volumen de ventas *m*
turnover forecast (E)	Umsatzprognose *f*	—	prévision de l'évolution du chiffre d'affaires *f*	prognosi del fatturato *f*	previsión de la evolución del volumen de ventas *f*
turnover increase (E)	Umsatzanstieg *m*	—	augmentation du chiffre d'affaires *f*	aumento del fatturato *m*	aumento del volumen de facturación *m*
turnover plan (E)	Umsatzplan *m*	—	plan du chiffre d'affaires *m*	programma del fatturato *m*	objectivo de facturación *m*
turnover tax (E)	Umsatzsteuer *f*	—	impôt sur le chiffre d'affaires *m*	imposta generale sulle entrate *f*	impuesto sobre el volumen de ventas *m*
turnover trend (E)	Umsatzentwicklung *f*	—	évolution du chiffre d'affaires *f*	sviluppo del fatturato *m*	evolución del volumen de facturación *f*
tutela dei consumatori (I)	Verbraucherschutz *m*	consumer protection	protection des consommateurs *f*	—	protección de los consumidores *f*
tutela dei dati (I)	Datenschutz *m*	data securing	sauvegarde des données *f*	—	protección de los datos *f*

	D	E	F	I	Es
tutela del creditore (I)	Gläubigerschutz *m*	protection of creditors	garantie des créanciers *f*	—	protección de los acreedores *f*
tutela dell'ambiente (I)	Umweltschutz *m*	protection of the environment	protection de l'environment *f*	—	protección del medio ambiente *f*
tutela della maternità (I)	Mutterschutz *m*	protection of motherhood	protection maternelle et infantile *f*	—	protección de la madre *f*
tutela del lavoro (I)	Arbeitsschutz *m*	employment protection	protection sociale du travail *f*	—	protección del trabajo *f*
tutela del locatario (I)	Mieterschutz *m*	protection of tenants	protection en matière de location *f*	—	protección al arrendatario *f*
tutela territoriale (I)	Gebietsschutz *m*	territory protection	exclusivité territoriale *f*	—	protección territorial *f*
two-tier exchange rate (E)	gespaltene Wechselkurse *pl*	—	cours du change multiple *m*	cambi multipli *m pl*	tipo de cambio múltiple *m*
types of markets (E)	Marktformen *pl*	—	formes du marché *f pl*	tipi di mercato *m pl*	formas del mercado *f*
Überbeschäftigung (D)	—	overcharge	surchargement *m*	occupazione eccedente *f*	exceso de empleo *m*/ superempleo *m*
Überbevölkerung (D)	—	overpopulation	surpopulation *f*	sovrappopolazione *f*	superpoblación *f*
Überbewertung (D)	—	overvaluation	surestimation *f*	sopravvalutazione *f*	sobrevaloración *f*
Überbringer (D)	—	bearer	porteur *m*	portatore *m*	portador *m*
Überbringerscheck (D)	—	bearer cheque	chèque au porteur *m*	assegno al portatore *m*	cheque al portador *m*
Überbrückungskredit (D)	—	bridging loan	crédit transitoire *m*	credito ponte *m*	crédito transitorio *m*
Überfremdung (D)	—	control by foreign capital	majorité d'étrangers *f*	inforestierimento *m*	extranjerización *f*
Übergabe (D)	—	delivery	remise *f*	consegna *f*	entrega *f*
Übergangsregelung (D)	—	transitional arrangement	règlement transitoire *m*	regolamento transitorio *m*	regulación transitoria *f*
Übergewicht (D)	—	excess weight	surcharge *f*	sovrappeso *m*	sobrepreso *m*
Überkapazität (D)	—	overcapacity	surcapacité *f*	capacità eccessiva *f*	supercapacidad *f*
Überkapitalisierung (D)	—	overcapitalization	surcapitalisation *f*	sovracapitalizzazione *f*	sobrecapitalización *f*
übermäßig (D)	—	excessive	excessif	eccessivo	excesivo
Übernachtungskosten (D)	—	overnight expenses	coûts de nuitée *m pl*	spese di pernottamento *f pl*	gastos de alojamiento *m pl*
Überproduktion (D)	—	overproduction	surproduction *f*	produzione eccessiva *f*	sobreproducción *f*
Überschuldung (D)	—	excessive indebtedness	surendettement *m*	indebitamento eccessivo *m*	exceso de deudas *m*
Überschuß (D)	—	excess	excédent *m*	eccedenza *f*	excedente *m*
Übersee (D)	—	oversea	outre-mer	oltremare *m*	ultramar *m*
Überseehandel (D)	—	oversea trade	commerce d'outre-mer *m*	commercio d'oltremare *m*	comercio de ultramar *m*
Überstunde (D)	—	overtime	heure supplémentaire *f*	ora straordinaria *f*	hora extraordinaria *f*
Übertragung (D)	—	transfer/transmission	transfert *m*/ transmission *f*	trasferimento *m*/ trasmissione *f*	transmisión *f*
Übertragungsfehler (D)	—	transcription error	erreur de transcription *f*	errore di trascrizione *m*	error de transcripción *m*
Überversicherung (D)	—	overinsurance	surassurance *f*	soprassicurazione *f*	sobreseguro *m*
überwachen (D)	—	supervise	surveiller	sorvegliare	vigilar
Überwälzung (D)	—	passing on	répercussion *f*	accollamento *m*	traslación *f*
Überweisung (D)	—	remittance	virement *m*	rimessa *f*	transferencia *f*
überziehen (D)	—	overdraw	faire un prélèvement à découvert	mandare allo scoperto	sobrepasar
ubicación (Es)	Standort *m*	location	lieu d'implantation *m*	ubicazione *f*	—
ubicazione (I)	Standort *m*	location	lieu d'implantation *m*	—	ubicación *f*
Überziehungskredit (D)	—	credit by way of overdraft	avance sur compte courant *f*	credito allo scoperto *m*	crédito en descubierto *m*

	D	E	F	I	Es
ufficiale giudiziario (I)	Gerichtsvollzieher *m*	bailiff	huissier de justice *m*	—	ejecutor judicial *m*
ufficio[1] (I)	Amt *n*	office	bureau *m*	—	cargo *m*
ufficio[2] (I)	Geschäftsstelle *f*	office	agence *f*	—	oficina *f*
ufficio anagrafe (I)	Einwohnermelde-amt *n*	residents' registration office	bureau de déclaration de résidence *m*	—	oficina del censo *f*
ufficio brevetti (I)	Patentamt *n*	Patent Office	office des brevets *m*	—	oficina del registro de patentes *f*
ufficio dei conti correnti postali (I)	Postscheckamt *n*	postal giro centre	bureau de chèques postaux *m*	—	oficina de cheques postales *f*
ufficio delle imposte (I)	Finanzamt *n*	inland revenue office	service de contributions *m*	—	Hacienda *f*
ufficio del personale (I)	Personalbüro *n*	personnel office	bureau du personnel *m*	—	oficina de personal *f*
ufficio di collocamento (I)	Arbeitsvermittlung *f*	employment agency	bureau de placement *m*	—	agencia laboral *f*
Ufficio Europeo Brevetti (I)	Europäisches Patentamt *n*	European Patent Office	Office Européen de Brevets *f*	—	Oficina Europea de Patentes *f*
ufficio legale (I)	Rechtsabteilung *f*	legal department	bureau juridique *m*	—	sección jurídica *f*
ufficio paga (I)	Lohnbüro *n*	pay office	bureau de la paye *m*	—	departamento de nóminas *m*
ufficio postale (I)	Postamt *n*	post office	bureau de poste *m*	—	correos *m pl*
ufficio tele-comunicazioni (I)	Fernmeldeamt *n*	telephone exchange	service de télécommunication *m*	—	central interurbana *f*
ufficio viaggi (I)	Reisebüro *n*	travel agency	agence de voyages *f*	—	agencia de viajes *f*
ultimate buyer (E)	Endabnehmer *m*	—	preneur final *m*	acquirente finale *m*	comprador final *m*
ultimate consumer (E)	Endverbraucher *m*	—	consommateur final *m*	consumatore finale *m*	consumidor final *m*
Ultimo (D)	—	end of the month	fin de mois *f*	fine mese *m*	fin de mes *m*
ultramar (Es)	Übersee	oversea(s)	outre-mer	oltremare *m*	—
umbral de precios (Es)	Preisschwelle *f*	threshold price	seuil du prix *m*	soglia dei prezzi *f*	—
Umbuchung (D)	—	transfer of an entry	jeu d'écritures *m*	giro di partite *m*	asiento en otra cuenta *m*
Umfang (D)	—	volume	volume *m*	volume *m*	volumen *m*/ dimensión *f*
umgehend (D)	—	immediate(ly)	immédiatement	immediato	inmediatamente
Umlage (D)	—	charge levied	répartition *f*	ripartizione *f*	reparto *m*
Umlaufvermögen (D)	—	current assets/ floating assets	capital de roulement *m*	patrimonio circolante *m*	capital circulante *m*
umpacken (D)	—	repack	remballer	rifare l'imballaggio	reempaquetar
Umrechnungskurs (D)	—	rate of conversion	cours de conversion *m*	corso di cambio *m*	tasa de cambio *f*
Umsatz (D)	—	turnover	chiffre d'affaires *m*	fatturato *m*	volumen de ventas *m*
Umsatzanstieg (D)	—	turnover increase	augmentation du chiffre d'affaires *f*	aumento del fatturato *m*	aumento del volumen de facturación *m*
Umsatzentwicklung (D)	—	turnover trend	évolution du chiffre d'affaires *f*	sviluppo del fatturato *m*	evolución del volu-men de facturación *f*
Umsatzplan (D)	—	turnover plan	plan du chiffre d'affaires *m*	programma del fatturato *m*	objectivo de facturación *m*
Umsatzprognose (D)	—	turnover forecast	prévision de l'évolution du chiffre d'affaires *f*	prognosi del fatturato *f*	previsión de la evo-lución del volumen de ventas *f*
Umsatzprovision (D)	—	commission on turnover	commission sur le chiffre d'affaires *f*	provvigione sul fatturato *f*	comisión sobre la cifra de ventas *f*
Umsatzrendite (D)	—	net income percentage of turnover	rendement du chiffre d'affaires *m*	rendita del fatturato *f*	rédito de la cifra de ventas *m*
Umsatzrückgang (D)	—	decrease of turnover	recul du chiffre d'affaires *m*	calo del fatturato *m*	disminución de la cifra de facturación *f*
Umsatzsteuer (D)	—	turnover tax	impôt sur le chiffre d'affaires *m*	imposta generale sulle entrate *f*	impuesto sobre el volumen de ventas *m*

	D	E	F	I	Es
Umschlag (D)	—	transshipment	transbordement *m*	trasbordo *m*	transbordo de carga *m*
Umschlags-häufigkeit (D)	—	transshipment frequencies	fréquence de transbordement *f*	frequenza di trasbordo *f*	frecuencia de transbordo *f*
Umschulung (D)	—	retraining	rééducation professionnelle *f*	riqualificazione professionale *f*	readaptación profesional *f*
Umstrukturierung (D)	—	restructuring	restructuration *f*	ristrutturazione *f*	reestructuración *f*
Umtausch (D)	—	exchange	échange *m*	cambio *m*	cambio *m*/ conversión *f*
umweltbewußt (D)	—	environmental-conscious	conscient de la réalité écologique	con rispetto dell'ambiente	consciente del medio ambiente
umweltfreundlich (D)	—	beneficial to the environment	favorable à l'environnement	ecologico	no contaminante
umweltschädlich (D)	—	causing environ-mental damages	nuisible à l'environnement	inquinante	contaminante
Umweltschutz (D)	—	protection of the environment	protection de l'environnement *f*	tutela dell'ambiente *f*	protección del medio ambiente *f*
Umwelt-verschmutzung (D)	—	environmental pollution	pollution de l'environnement *f*	inquinamento dell'ambiente *m*	contaminación del medio ambiente *f*
Umzug (D)	—	change of residence	déménagement *m*	trasferimento *m*	mudanza *f*
Unabhängigkeit (D)	—	independence	indépendance *f*	indipendenza *f*	independencia *f*
unbar (D)	—	non cash	non comptant	non in contanti	no en efectivo
unbezahlter Urlaub (D)	—	unpaid vacation	congé non payé *m*	ferie non pagate *f pl*	vacaciones no pagadas *f pl*
uncertainty (E)	Unsicherheit *f*	—	insécurité *f*	insicurezza *f*	inseguridad *f*
under age (E)	minderjährig	—	mineur	minorenne	menor de edad
underemployment (E)	Unter-beschäftigung *f*	—	sous-emploi *m*	sottoccupazione *f*	subempleo *m*
underinsurance (E)	Unterversicherung *f*	—	insuffisance d'assurance *f*	sottassicurazione *f*	infraseguro *m*
under public law (E)	öffentlich-rechtlich	—	de droit public	di diritto pubblico	de derecho público
under separate cover (E)	mit getrennter Post	—	sous pli séparé	in plico a parte	por correo aparte
undervaluation (E)	Unterbewertung *f*	—	sous-estimation *f*	sottovalutazione *f*	subvaloración *f*
unearned income[1] (E)	Kapitaleinkommen *n*	—	revenu du capital *m*	reddito del capitale *m*	ganancias de capital *f pl*
unearned income[2] (E)	Besitzeinkommen *n*	—	revenu du patrimoine *m*	reddito da possesso *m*	renta de la propiedad *f*
unemployment (E)	Arbeitslosigkeit *f*	—	chômage *m*	disoccupazione *f*	desempleo *m*
unemployment benefits (E)	Arbeitslosen-unterstützung *f*	—	indemnité de chômage *f*	sussidio di disoccupazione *m*	prestaciones por desempleo *m*
unentgeltlich (D)	—	free of charge	à titre gracieux	gratuito	gratuito
unfair competition (E)	unlauterer Wettbewerb *m*	—	concurrence déloyale *f*	concorrenza sleale *f*	competencia desleal *f*
Unfallversicherung (D)	—	personal accident insurance	assurance accidents corporels *f*	assicurazione contro infortuni *f*	seguro de accidentes *m*
ungenutzt (D)	—	unused	pas utilisé	inutilizzato	no utilizado
ungesetzlich (D)	—	illegal	contraire à la loi	illegale	ilegal
ungesichert (D)	—	unsecured	non garanti	non assicurato	no asegurado
unidad central (Es)	Zentraleinheit *f*	central unit	unité centrale *f*	unità centrale *f*	—
unidad cuantitativa (Es)	Mengeneinheit *f*	quantity unit	unité de quantité *f*	unità quantitativa *f*	—
unidad de compensación (Es)	Verrechnungs-einheit *f*	clearing unit	unité de compte *f*	unità di compensazione *f*	—
unidad de cuenta[1] (Es)	Recheneinheit *f*	calculation unit	unité de calcul *f*	unità di conteggio *f*	—
unidad de cuenta[2] (Es)	Rechnungseinheit *f*	unit of account	unité de compte *f*	unità di conto *f*	—
unidad de embalaje (Es)	Verpackungseinheit *f*	packing unit	unité d'emballage *f*	unità d'imballaggio *f*	—
unidad monetaria europea (Es)	Europäische Währungseinheit *f*	European Currency Unit	unité de compte européenne *f*	unità monetaria europea *f*	—
uniform currency (E)	Einheitswährung *f*	—	monométallisme *m*	moneta unitaria *f*	moneda única *f*

	D	E	F	I	Es
uniform duty (E)	Einheitszoll *m*	—	droit unique *m*	dazio unitario *m*	aduanas uniformes *f pl*
uniforme all'interno della CEE (I)	EG-einheitlich	standardized within the European Community	uniforme au niveau communautaire	—	armonizado a nivel comunitario
uniforme au niveau communautaire (F)	EG-einheitlich	standardized within the European Community	—	uniforme all'interno della CEE	armonizado a nivel comunitario
uniform price (E)	Einheitspreis *m*	—	prix unique *m*	prezzo unitario *m*	precio único *m*
uniform tariff (E)	Einheitstarif *m*	—	tarif standard *m*	tariffa unitaria *f*	tarifa única *f*
unión aduanera (Es)	Zollunion *f*	customs union	union douanière *f*	unione doganale *f*	—
unión agrícola (Es)	Agrarunion *f*	agricultural union	union agricole *f*	unione agraria *f*	—
union agricole (F)	Agrarunion *f*	agricultural union	—	unione agraria *f*	unión agrícola *f*
union douanière (F)	Zollunion *f*	customs union	—	unione doganale *f*	unión aduanera *f*
unione agraria (I)	Agrarunion *f*	agricultural union	union agricole *f*	—	unión agrícola *f*
unión económica (Es)	Wirtschaftsunion *f*	economic union	union économique *f*	unione economica *f*	—
union économique (F)	Wirtschaftsunion *f*	economic union	—	unione economica *f*	unión económica *f*
unione degli imprenditori (I)	Unternehmerverband *m*	employers' association	association des chefs d'entreprise *f*	—	asociación empresarial *f*
unione doganale (I)	Zollunion *f*	customs union	union douanière *f*	—	unión aduanera *f*
unione economica (I)	Wirtschaftsunion *f*	economic union	union économique *f*	—	unión económica *f*
Unione Europea dei Pagamenti (I)	Europäische Zahlungsunion *f*	European Payments Union	union européenne des payements *f*	—	Unión Europea de Pagos *f*
unione monetaria (I)	Währungsunion *f*	monetary union	union monétaire *f*	—	unìon monetaria *f*
Unión Europea de Pagos (Es)	Europäische Zahlungsunion *f*	European Payments Union	union européenne des payements *f*	Unione Europea dei Pagamenti *f*	—
union européenne des payements (F)	Europäische Zahlungsunion *f*	European Payments Union	—	Unione Europea dei Pagamenti *f*	Unión Europea de Pagos *f*
union monétaire (F)	Währungsunion *f*	monetary union	—	unione monetaria *f*	unìon monetaria *f*
unìon monetaria (Es)	Währungsunion *f*	monetary union	union monétaire *f*	unione monetaria *f*	—
unità centrale (I)	Zentraleinheit *f*	central unit	unité centrale *f*	—	unidad central *f*
unità di compensazione (I)	Verrechnungseinheit *f*	clearing unit	unité de compte *f*	—	unidad de compensación *f*
unità di conteggio (I)	Recheneinheit *f*	calculation unit	unité de calcul *f*	—	unidad de cuenta *f*
unità di conto (I)	Rechnungseinheit *f*	unit of account	unité de compte *f*	—	unidad de cuenta *f*
unità d'imballaggio (I)	Verpackungseinheit *f*	packing unit	unité d'emballage *f*	—	unidad de embalaje *f*
unità monetaria europea (I)	Europäische Währungseinheit *f*	European Currency Unit	unité de compte européenne *f*	—	unidad monetaria europea *f*
unità quantitativa (I)	Mengeneinheit *f*	quantity unit	unité de quantité *f*	—	unidad cuantitativa *f*
unité centrale (F)	Zentraleinheit *f*	central unit	—	unità centrale *f*	unidad central *f*
unité de calcul (F)	Recheneinheit *f*	calculation unit	—	unità di conteggio *f*	unidad de cuenta *f*
unité de compte[1] (F)	Rechnungseinheit *f*	unit of account	—	unità di conto *f*	unidad de cuenta *f*
unité de compte[2] (F)	Verrechnungseinheit *f*	clearing unit	—	unità di compensazione *f*	unidad de compensación *f*
unité de compte européenne (F)	Europäische Währungseinheit *f*	European Currency Unit	—	unità monetaria europea *f*	unidad monetaria europea *f*
unité d'emballage (F)	Verpackungseinheit *f*	packing unit	—	unità d'imballaggio *f*	unidad de embalaje *f*
unité de quantité (F)	Mengeneinheit *f*	quantity unit	—	unità quantitativa *f*	unidad cuantitativa *f*
unit of account (E)	Rechnungseinheit *f*	—	unité de compte *f*	unità di conto *f*	unidad de cuenta *f*
unit trust (E)	Investmentfonds *m*	—	fonds commun de placement *m*	fondo d'investimento *m*	fondo de inversiones *m*
universidad (Es)	Universität *f*	university	université *f*	università *f*	—

	D	E	F	I	Es
università (I)	Universität *f*	university	université *f*	—	universidad *f*
Universität (D)	—	university	université *f*	università *f*	universidad *f*
université (F)	Universität *f*	university	—	università *f*	universidad *f*
university (E)	Universität *f*	—	université *f*	università *f*	universidad *f*
unlauterer Wettbewerb (D)	—	unfair competition	concurrence déloyale *f*	concorrenza sleale *f*	competencia desleal *f*
unpacked (E)	unverpackt	—	sans emballage	non imballato/ alla rinfusa	sin embalar
unpaid vacation (E)	unbezahlter Urlaub *m*	—	congé non payé *m*	ferie non pagate *f pl*	vacaciones no pagadas *f pl*
unproductive capital (E)	totes Kapital *n*	—	capital improductif *m*	capitale infruttifero *m*	capital improductivo *m*
unredeemable bond (E)	Dauerschuld-verschreibung *f*	—	obligation perpétuelle *f*	obbligazione perpetua *f*	obligación perpetua *f*
Unregelmäßigkeit (D)	—	irregularity	irrégularité *f*	irregolarità *f*	irregularidad *f*
unsachgemäß (D)	—	improper	non adéquat	non idoneo	con falta de objetividad
unsecured (E)	ungesichert	—	non garanti	non assicurato	no asegurado
unsettled account (E)	offene Rechnung *f*	—	facture pas encore payée *f*	conto aperto *m*	factura pendiente *f*
Unsicherheit (D)	—	uncertainty	insécurité *f*	insicurezza *f*	inseguridad *f*
Unterbeschäftigung (D)	—	underemployment	insuffisance de charge *f*	sottoccupazione *f*	subempleo *m*
Unterbewertung (D)	—	undervaluation	sous-estimation *f*	sottovalutazione *f*	subvaloración *f*
unterentwickelte Länder (D)	—	underdeveloped countries	pays sous-développé *m pl*	paesi sottosviluppati *m pl*	países subdesa-rrollados *m pl*
Unterernährung (D)	—	malnutrition	sous-alimentation *f*	denutrizione *f*	subalimentación *f*
Untergebener (D)	—	subordinate	subalterne *m*	dipendente *m*	subordinado *m*
Unternehmen (D)	—	enterprise	entreprise *f*	impresa *f*	empresario *m*
Unternehmensform (D)	—	form of business	forme de l'entreprise *f*	forma d'impresa *f*	forma de organización empresarial *f*
Unternehmens-fusion (D)	—	merger of companies	fusion de sociétés *f*	fusione d'imprese *f*	fusión de empresas *f*
Unternehmens-gewinn (D)	—	profit of the enterprise	bénéfice d'exploitation *m*	utile d'impresa *m*	beneficio empresarial *m*
Unternehmens-größe (D)	—	size of the company	dimension de l'entreprise *f*	dimensione dell'impresa *f*	dimensión de la empresa *f*
Unternehmens-konzentration (D)	—	business concentration	concentration d'entreprises *f*	pool d'imprese *m*	concentración de empresas *f*
Unternehmens-konzept (D)	—	business concept	stratégie de l'entreprise *f*	piano imprenditoriale *m*	concepto comercial *m*
Unternehmens-kultur (D)	—	entrepreneurial culture	culture de l'entreprise *f*	cultura imprenditoriale *f*	cultura empresarial *f*
Unternehmens-leitung (D)	—	executive management	direction de l'entreprise *f*	direzione dell'impresa *f*	dirección de la empresa *f*
Unternehmens-strategie (D)	—	corporate strategy	stratégie de l'entreprise *f*	strategia imprenditoriale *f*	estrategia empresarial *f*
Unternehmensziel (D)	—	company objective	objectif de l'entreprise *m*	obiettivo i mprenditoriale *m*	objetivo empresarial *m*
Unternehmer (D)	—	entrepreneur	entrepreneur *m*	imprenditore *m*	empresario *m*
Unternehmerlohn (D)	—	entrepreneurial income	rémunération de l'entrepreneur *f*	retribuzione dell'imprenditore *f*	remuneración del empresario *f*
Unternehmer-verband (D)	—	employers' association	association des chefs d'entreprise *f*	unione degli imprenditori *f*	asociación empresarial *f*
Unterredung (D)	—	discussion	entretien *m*	colloquio *m*	conversación *f*
Unterschlagung (D)	—	embezzlement	détournement *m*	appropriazione indebita *f*	defraudación *f*
unterschreiben (D)	—	sign	signer	firmare	signar
Unterschrift (D)	—	signature	signature *f*	firma *f*	firma *f*
Untersuchung (D)	—	examination	étude *f*	indagine *f*	inspección *f*
Untervermietung (D)	—	subletting	sous-location *f*	subaffitto *m*	subalquiler *m*
Unterversicherung (D)	—	underinsurance	insuffisance d'assurance *f*	sottassicurazione *f*	infraseguro *m*

	D	E	F	I	Es
Untervertreter (D)	—	subagent	sous-agent *m*	subagente *m*	subagente *m*
unused (E)	ungenutzt	—	pas utilisé	inutilizzato	no utilizado
unverbindlich (D)	—	not binding	sans obligation	senza impegno	sin compromiso
unverpackt (D)	—	unpacked	sans emballage	non imballato/ alla rinfusa	sin embalar
unverzollt (D)	—	duty unpaid	non dédouané	non sdoganato	aduana aparte
unvollständig (D)	—	incomplete	incomplet	incompleto	incompleto
unwiderrufliches Akkreditiv (D)	—	irrevocable letter of credit	accréditif irrévocable *m*	apertura di credito documentario irrevocabile *f*	crédito documentario irrevocable *m*
upward trend (E)	Aufwärtstrend *m*	—	mouvement ascendant *m*	tendenza al rialzo *f*	tendencia alcista *f*
urban renewal (E)	Sanierung *f*	—	assainissement *m*	risanamento *m*	saneamiento *m*/ rehabilitación *f*
urbanisme (F)	Städtebau *m*	town planning	—	urbanistica *f*	urbanización *f*
urbanistica (I)	Städtebau *m*	town planning	urbanisme *m*	—	urbanización *f*
urbanización (Es)	Städtebau *m*	town planning	urbanisme *m*	urbanistica *f*	—
Urheberrecht (D)	—	copyright	droit d'auteur *m*	diritto d'autore *m*	derecho del autor *m*
Urkunde (D)	—	document	document *m*	documento *m*	documento *m*
Urlaub (D)	—	annual holidays/ vacation	congé *m*/ vacances *f pl*	ferie *f pl*/ vacanze *f pl*	vacaciones *f pl*
Urlaubsgeld (D)	—	holiday allowance	prime de vacances *f*	indennità di ferie *f*	retribución por vacaciones *f*
Urlaubsplanung (D)	—	vacation scheduling	planification des vacances *f*	programmazione delle ferie *f*	planificación de las vacaciones *f*
Ursprungsland (D)	—	country of origin	pays d'origine *m*	paese d'origine *m*	país de origen *m*
Ursprungszeugnis (D)	—	certificate of origin	certificat d'origine *m*	certificato d'origine *m*	certificado de origen *m*
usage (E)	Usancen *pl*	—	usages *m pl*	usanze *f pl*	usanza *f*
usage commercial (F)	Handelsbrauch *m*	business practice	—	usanza commerciale *f*	uso comercial *m*
usages (F)	Usancen *pl*	usage	—	usanze *f pl*	usanza *f*
usages commerciaux (F)	Handelsusancen *pl*	trade practice	—	usanze commerciali *f pl*	usos comerciales *m pl*
Usancen (D)	—	usage	usages *m pl*	usanze *f pl*	usanza *f*
usanza (Es)	Usancen *pl*	usage	usages *m pl*	usanze *f pl*	—
usanza commerciale (I)	Handelsbrauch *m*	business practice	usage commercial *m*	—	uso comercial *m*
usanze (I)	Usancen *pl*	usage	usages *m pl*	—	usanza *f*
usanze commerciali (I)	Handelsusancen *pl*	trade practice	usages commerciaux *m pl*	—	usos comerciales *m pl*
uscita merci (I)	Warenausgang *m*	outgoing goods	sortie de marchandises *f*	—	salida de mercancías *f*
use of a computer (E)	Computereinsatz *m*	—	emploi d'ordinateurs *m*	impiego di computer *m*	utilización de ordenadores *f*
use¹ (E)	Gebrauch *m*	—	utilisation *f*	uso *m*	uso *m*
use² (E)	Nutzung *f*	—	mise à profit *f*	utilizzazione *f*	utilización *f*
used car (E)	Gebrauchtwagen *m*	—	voiture d'occasion *f*	automobile usata *f*	coche de segunda mano *m*
usine¹ (F)	Betrieb *m*	factory	—	azienda *f*	fábrica *f*
usine² (F)	Werk *n*	plant	—	stabilimento *m*	planta *f*
uso (Es)	Gebrauch *m*	use	utilisation *f*	uso *m*	—
uso (I)	Gebrauch *m*	use	utilisation *f*	—	uso *m*
uso comercial (Es)	Handelsbrauch *m*	business practice	usage commercial *m*	usanza commerciale *f*	—
usos comerciales (Es)	Handelsusancen *pl*	trade practice	usages commerciaux *m pl*	usanze commerciali *f pl*	—
usuary (E)	Wucher *m*	—	usure *f*	usura *f*	usura *f*
usufruct (E)	Nießbrauch *m*	—	usufruit *m*	usufrutto *m*	usufructo *m*

	D	E	F	I	Es
usufructo (Es)	Nießbrauch *m*	usufruct	usufruit *m*	usufrutto *m*	—
usufruit (F)	Nießbrauch *m*	usufruct	—	usufrutto *m*	usufructo *m*
usufrutto (I)	Nießbrauch *m*	usufruct	usufruit *m*	—	usufructo *m*
usura (Es)	Wucher *m*	usuary	usure *f*	usura *f*	—
usura[1] (I)	Wucher *m*	usuary	usure *f*	—	usura *f*
usura[2] (I)	Abnutzung *f*	wear and tear	dépréciation *f*	—	desgaste *m*
usura arrendaticia (Es)	Mietwucher *m*	exorbitant rent	hausse illicite des loyers *f*	strozzinaggio sui canoni di locazione *m*	—
usure (F)	Wucher *m*	usuary	—	usura *f*	usura *f*
utente del leasing (I)	Leasing-Nehmer *m*	lessee	preneur de leasing *m*	—	arrendatante financiero *m*
utile (I)	Gewinn *m*	profit/surplus	bénéfice *m*	—	beneficio *m*/ superávit *m*
utile contabile (I)	Buchgewinn *m*	book profit	bénéfice comptable *m*	—	beneficio contable *m*
utile dell'anno (I)	Jahresgewinn *m*	annual profit	bénéfice annuel *m*	—	beneficio del ejercicio *m*
utile d'impresa (I)	Unternehmens-gewinn *m*	profit of the enterprise	bénéfice d'exploitation *m*	—	beneficio empresarial *m*
utile fittizio (I)	Scheingewinn *m*	ficticious profit	gain fictif *m*	—	beneficio simulado *m*
utile lordo (I)	Rohgewinn *m*	gross profit on sales	bénéfice brut *m*	—	ganancia bruta *f*
utile netto (I)	Reingewinn *m*	net profit	bénéfice net *m*	—	ganancia neta *f*
utilidad (Es)	Nutzen *m*	utility	utilité *f*	utilità *f*	—
utilisation (F)	Gebrauch *m*	use	—	uso *m*	uso *m*
utilisation de la capacité (F)	Kapazitäts-auslastung *f*	utilization of capacity	—	sfruttamento delle capacità *m*	utilización de las capacidades *f*
utilisation des bénéfices (F)	Gewinnverwendung *f*	appropriation of net income	—	impiego dell'utile *m*	aplicación de los resultados *f*
utilisation du revenu (F)	Einkommens-verwendung *f*	appropriation of income	—	impiego dei redditi *m*	distribución de la renta *f*
utilisation économique (F)	wirtschaftliche Nutzung *m*	economic use	—	utilizzo economico *m*	utilización económica *f*
utilité (F)	Nutzen *m*	utility	—	utilità *f*	utilidad *f*
utility (E)	Nutzen *m*	—	utilité *f*	utilità *f*	utilidad *f*
utility costs (E)	Nutzkosten *pl*	—	coûts fixes utiles *m pl*	costi fissi di utilizzo *m pl*	gastos fijos de utilización *m pl*
utilización (Es)	Nutzung *f*	use/utilization	mise à profit *f*	utilizzazione *f*	—
utilización de las capacidades (Es)	Kapazitäts-auslastung *f*	utilization of capacity	utilisation de la capacité *f*	sfruttamento delle capacità *m*	—
utilización de ordenadores (Es)	Computereinsatz *m*	use of a computer	emploi d'ordinateurs *m*	impiego di computer *m*	—
utilización económica (Es)	wirtschaftliche Nutzung *m*	economic use	utilisation économique *f*	utilizzo economico *m*	—
utilization of capacity (E)	Kapazitäts-auslastung *f*	—	utilisation de la capacité *f*	sfruttamento delle capacità *m*	utilización de las capacidades *f*
utilization rate (E)	Ausnutzungsgrad *m*	—	taux d'utilisation *m*	grado di utilizzazione *m*	grado de utilización *m*
utilizzazione (I)	Nutzung *f*	use/utilization	mise à profit *f*	—	utilización *f*
utilizzo economico (I)	wirtschaftliche Nutzung *m*	economic use	utilisation économique *f*	—	utilización económica *f*
vacaciones (Es)	Urlaub *m*	annual holidays/ vacation	congé *m*/ vacances *f pl*	ferie *f pl*/ vacanze *f pl*	—
vacaciones con goce de sueldo (Es)	bezahlter Urlaub *m*	paid vacation	congé payé *m*	ferie pagate *f pl*	—
vacaciones de la empresa (Es)	Betriebsferien *pl*	annual holiday	clôture annuelle de l'établissement *f*	ferie aziendali *f pl*	—
vacaciones no pagadas (Es)	unbezahlter Urlaub *m*	unpaid vacation	congé non payé *m*	ferie non pagate *f pl*	—
vacation scheduling (E)	Urlaubsplanung *f*	—	planification des vacances *f*	programmazione delle ferie *f*	planificación de las vacaciones *f*
vaglia postale (I)	Postanweisung *f*	postal money order	mandat-poste *m*	—	vale postal *m*

	D	E	F	I	Es
vaglia telegrafico (I)	telegrafische Anweisung *f*	telegraphic payment order	mandat télégraphique *m*	—	orden telegráfica *f*
vagone frigorifero (I)	Kühlwagen *m*	cold storage lorry	wagon frigorifique *m*	—	vagón frigorífico *m*
vagón frigorífico (Es)	Kühlwagen *m*	cold storage lorry	wagon frigorifique *m*	vagone frigorifero *m*	—
vale postal (Es)	Postanweisung *f*	postal money order	mandat-poste *m*	vaglia postale *m*	—
valeur (F)	Wert *m*	value	—	valore *m*	valor *m*
valeur ajoutée (F)	Mehrwert *m*	value added	—	valore aggiunto *m*	plusvalía *f*
valeur à une certaine date (F)	Zeitwert *m*	current market value	—	valore corrente *m*	valor actual *m*
valeur commerciale[1] (F)	Firmenwert *m*	goodwill	—	goodwill *m*	fondo de comercio *m*
valeur commerciale[2] (F)	Geschäftswert *m*	goodwill	—	valore d'avviamento *m*	valor comercial *m*
valeur comptable (F)	Buchwert *m*	book value	—	valore contabile *m*	valor contable *m*
valeur d'acquisition (F)	Anschaffungswert *m*	acquisition value	—	valore d'acquisto *m*	valor de adquisición *m*
valeur de l'argent (F)	Geldwert *m*	value of money	—	valore monetario *m*	valor monetario *m*
valeur de production (F)	Produktionswert *m*	production value	—	valore produttivo *m*	valor de la producción *m*
valeur de remplacement (F)	Substanzwert *m*	assets value	—	valore sostanziale *m*	valor sustancial *m*
valeur de remplacement (F)	Reproduktionswert *m*	reproduction value	—	valore di riproduzione *m*	valor de reproducción *m*
valeur d'estimation (F)	Schätzwert *m*	estimated value	—	valore stimato *m*	estimación *f*
valeur de taxation (F)	Taxwert *m*	estimated value	—	valore stimato *m*	valor de tasación *m*
valeur du jour (F)	Tageswert *m*	current value	—	valore del giorno *m*	valor del día *m*
valeur d'une chose mesurée à son rendement (F)	Ertragswert *m*	capitalized value	—	valore del reddito *m*	valor de rendimiento *m*
valeur en capital (F)	Kapitalwert *m*	capital value	—	valore del capitale *m*	valor capitalizado *m*
valeur immoblisée (F)	Anlagegüter *pl*	capital goods	—	beni d'investimento *m pl*	bienes de inversión *m pl*
valeur marginale[1] (F)	Grenzwert *m*	limiting value	—	valore limite *m*	valor límite *m*
valeur marginale[2] (F)	Marginalwert *m*	marginal value	—	valore marginale *m*	valor marginal *m*
valeur matérielle (F)	Sachwert *m*	real value	—	valore reale *m*	valor real *m*
valeur nominale (F)	Nennwert *m*	nominal value	—	valore nominale *m*	valor nominal *m*
valeur partielle (F)	Teilwert *m*	partial value	—	valore parziale *m*	valor parcial *m*
valeur résiduelle (F)	Restwert *m*	residual value/ net book value	—	valore rimanente *m*	valor residual *m*/ valor contable residual *m*
valeurs de placement (F)	Anlagepapiere *pl*	investment securities	—	titoli d'investimento *m pl*	valores de inversión *m pl*
valeurs immobilisées (F)	Anlagevermögen *n*	fixed assets	—	attivo fisso *m*	activo fijo *m*
valeurs mesurées (F)	Meßwerte *pl*	measurements	—	valori misurati *m pl*	valor de medida *m*
valeurs mobilières (F)	Effekten *f*	securities	—	titoli *m pl*	efectos *m pl*
valeurs prévisionnelles (F)	Planwerte *pl*	planning figures	—	valori pianificati *m pl*	valores previstos *m pl*
valeurs réalisables à court terme ou disponibles (F)	Barvermögen *n*	cash assets	—	patrimonio in contanti *m*	activo efectivo *m*
valeur standard (F)	Standardwerte *pl*	standard values	—	valori standard *m pl*	valores representativos *m pl*
valor (Es)	Wert *m*	value	valeur *f*	valore *m*	—
valoración (Es)	Bewertung *f*	valuation	valorisation *f*	valutazione *f*	—

	D	E	F	I	Es
valor actual (Es)	Zeitwert *m*	current market value	valeur à une certaine date *f*	valore corrente *m*	—
valor capitalizado (Es)	Kapitalwert *m*	capital value	valeur en capital *f*	valore del capitale *m*	—
valor comercial (Es)	Geschäftswert *m*	goodwill	valeur commerciale *f*	valore d'avviamento *m*	—
valor contable (Es)	Buchwert *m*	book value	valeur comptable *f*	valore contabile *m*	—
valor de adquisisción (Es)	Anschaffungswert *m*	acquisition value	valeur d'acquisition *f*	valore d'acquisto *m*	—
valor de fabricación (Es)	Herstellungswert *m*	production value	prix de revient *m*	valore di produzione *m*	—
valor de la producción (Es)	Produktionswert *m*	production value	valeur de production *f*	valore produttivo *m*	—
valor del día (Es)	Tageswert *m*	current value	valeur du jour *f*	valore del giorno *m*	—
valor de medida (Es)	Meßwerte *pl*	measurements	valeurs mesurées *f pl*	valori misurati *m pl*	—
valor de rendimiento (Es)	Ertragswert *m*	capitalized value	valeur d'une chose mesurée à son rendement *f*	valore del reddito *m*	—
valor de reproducción (Es)	Reproduktionswert *m*	reproduction value	valeur de remplacement *f*	valore di riproduzione *m*	—
valor de tasación (Es)	Taxwert *m*	estimated value	valeur de taxation *f*	valore stimato *m*	—
valore (I)	Wert *m*	value	valeur *f*	—	valor *m*
valore aggiunto[1] (I)	Mehrwert *m*	value added	valeur ajoutée *f*	—	plusvalía *f*
valore aggiunto[2] (I)	Wertschöpfung *f*	value added	création de valeurs *f*	—	creación de riqueza *f*
valore contabile (I)	Buchwert *m*	book value	valeur comptable *f*	—	valor contable *m*
valore corrente (I)	Zeitwert *m*	current market value	valeur à une certaine date *f*	—	valor actual *m*
valore d'acquisto (I)	Anschaffungswert *m*	acquisition value	valeur d'acquisition *f*	—	valor de adquisisción *m*
valore d'avviamento (I)	Geschäftswert *m*	goodwill	valeur commerciale *f*	—	valor comercial *m*
valore del capitale (I)	Kapitalwert *m*	capital value	valeur en capital *f*	—	valor capitalizado *m*
valore del giorno (I)	Tageswert *m*	current value	valeur du jour *f*	—	valor del día *m*
valore del reddito (I)	Ertragswert *m*	capitalized value	valeur d'une chose mesurée à son rendement *f*	—	valor de rendimiento *m*
valore di produzione (I)	Herstellungswert *m*	production value	prix de revient *m*	—	valor de fabricación *m*
valore di riproduzione (I)	Reproduktionswert *m*	reproduction value	valeur de remplacement *f*	—	valor de reproducción *m*
valore finanziabile (I)	Beleihungswert *m*	value as security for a loan	montant de la garantie *m*	—	valor para préstamos *m*
valore limite (I)	Grenzwert *m*	limiting value	valeur marginale *f*	—	valor límite *m*
valore marginale (I)	Marginalwert *m*	marginal value	valeur marginale *f*	—	valor marginal *m*
valore monetario (I)	Geldwert *m*	value of money	valeur de l'argent *f*	—	valor monetario *m*
valore nominale (I)	Nennwert *m*	nominal value	valeur nominale *f*	—	valor nominal *m*
valore parziale (I)	Teilwert *m*	partial value	valeur partielle *f*	—	valor parcial *m*
valore produttivo (I)	Produktionswert *m*	production value	valeur de production *f*	—	valor de la producción *m*
valore reale (I)	Sachwert *m*	real value	valeur matérielle *f*	—	valor real *m*
valore rimanente (I)	Restwert *m*	residual value/ net book value	valeur résiduelle *f*	—	valor residual *m*/valor contable residual *m*
valores de inversión (Es)	Anlagepapiere *pl*	investment securities	valeurs de placement *f*	titoli d'investimento *m pl*	—
valore sostanziale (I)	Substanzwert *m*	assets value	valeur de remplacement *f*	—	valor sustancial *m*
valores previstos (Es)	Planwerte *pl*	planning figures	valeurs prévisionnelles *f pl*	valori pianificati *m pl*	—
valore stimato[1] (I)	Taxwert *m*	estimated value	valeur de taxation *f*	—	valor de tasación *m*
valore stimato[2] (I)	Schätzwert *m*	estimated value	valeur d'estimation *f*	—	estimación *f*

	D	E	F	I	Es
valori misurati (I)	Meßwerte *pl*	measurements	valeurs mesurées *f pl*	—	valor de medida *m*
valori pianificati (I)	Planwerte *pl*	planning figures	valeurs prévisionnelles *f pl*	—	valores previstos *m pl*
valorisation (F)	Bewertung *f*	valuation	—	valutazione *f*	valoración *f*
valori standard (I)	Standardwerte *pl*	standard values	valeur standard *f*	—	valores representativos *m pl*
valor límite (Es)	Grenzwert *m*	limiting value	valeur marginale *f*	valore limite *m*	—
valor marginal (Es)	Marginalwert *m*	marginal value	valeur marginale *f*	valore marginale *m*	—
valor monetario (Es)	Geldwert *m*	value of money	valeur de l'argent *f*	valore monetario *m*	—
valor nominal (Es)	Nennwert *m*	nominal value	valeur nominale *f*	valore nominale *m*	—
valor nominal mínimo (Es)	Mindest-nennbetrag *m*	minimum nominal amount	montant nominal minimum *m*	importo nominale minimo *m*	—
valor para préstamos (Es)	Beleihungswert *m*	value as security for a loan	montant de la garantie *m*	valore finanziabile *m*	—
valor parcial (Es)	Teilwert *m*	partial value	valeur partielle *f*	valore parziale *m*	—
valor real (Es)	Sachwert *m*	real value	valeur matérielle *f*	valore reale *m*	—
valor residual (Es)	Restwert *m*	residual value/ net book value	valeur résiduelle *f*	valore rimanente *m*	—
valor sustancial (Es)	Substanzwert *m*	assets value	valeur de remplacement *f*	valore sostanziale *m*	—
valuable (E)	wertvoll	—	précieux	prezioso	precioso
value (E)	Wert *m*	—	valeur *f*	valore *m*	valor *m*
value added[1] (E)	Mehrwert *m*	—	valeur ajoutée *f*	valore aggiunto *m*	plusvalía *f*
value added[2] (E)	Wertschöpfung *f*	—	création de valeurs *f*	valore aggiunto *m*	creación de riqueza *f*
value-added tax (E)	Mehrwertsteuer *f*	—	taxe à la valeur ajoutée *f*	imposta sul valore aggiunto *f*	impuesto sobre el valor añadido *m*
value adjustment (E)	Wertberichtigung *f*	—	réévaluation *f*	rettifica del valore *f*	rectificación de valor *f*
value as security for a loan (E)	Beleihungswert *m*	—	montant de la garantie *m*	valore finanziabile *m*	valor para préstamos *m*
value of money (E)	Geldwert *m*	—	valeur de l'argent *f*	valore monetario *m*	valor monetario *m*
Valuta (D)	—	foreign exchange/ value	monnaie étrangère *f*	valuta *f*/divise *f pl*	moneda extranjera *f*/ divisas *f pl*/valuta *f*
valuta[1] (I)	Valuta *f*	foreign exchange/ value	monnaie étrangère *f*	—	moneda extranjera *f*/ divisas *f pl*/valuta *f*
valuta[2] (I)	Währung *f*	currency	monnaie *f*	—	moneda *f*
valuta aurea (I)	Goldwährung *f*	gold currency	monnaie à couverture or *f*	—	moneda oro *f*
valuta di riserva (I)	Reservewährung *f*	reserve currency	monnaie de réserve *f*	—	moneda de reserva *f*
valuta guida (I)	Leitwährung *f*	key currency	monnaie-clé *f*	—	moneda de referencia *f*
valutazione (I)	Bewertung *f*	valuation	valorisation *f*	—	valoración *f*
valutazione approssimativa (I)	vorsichtige Schätzung *f*	conservative estimate	évaluation approximative *f*	—	evaluación aproximativa *f*
valutazione del lavoro (I)	Arbeitsbewertung *f*	job evaluation	qualification du travail *f*	—	evaluación del trabajo *f*
vantaggio (I)	Vorteil *m*	advantage	avantage *m*	—	ventaja *f*
vantaggio concorrenziale (I)	Wettbewerbs-vorteil *m*	competitive advantage	avantage de concurrence *m*	—	ventaja de competencia *f*
vantaggio di costo (I)	Kostenvorteil *m*	cost advantage	avantage de coût *m*	—	ventaja de costes *f*
variabel (D)	—	variable	variable	variabile	variable
variabile (I)	variabel	variable	variable	—	variable
variable (E)	variabel	—	variable	variabile	variable
variable (Es)	variabel	variable	variable	variabile	—
variable (F)	variabel	variable	—	variabile	variable

	D	E	F	I	Es
variable costs (E)	variable Kosten *pl*	—	coûts variables *m pl*	costi variabili *m pl*	gastos variables *m pl*
variable Kosten (D)	—	variable costs	coûts variables *m pl*	costi variabili *m pl*	gastos variables *m pl*
variable rate of interest (E)	variabler Zins *m*	—	intérêt variable *m*	tasso d'interesse variabile *m*	interés variable *m*
variabler Zins (D)	—	variable rate of interest	intérêt variable *m*	tasso d'interesse variabile *m*	interés variable *m*
variety (E)	Sorte *f*	—	genre *m*	categoria *f*	especie *f*
véhicule à moteur (F)	Kraftfahrzeug *n*	motor vehicle	—	automobile *f*	automóvil *m*
veicolo pubblicitario (I)	Werbeträger *m*	advertising medium	support publicitaire *m*	—	medio de publicidad *m*
vencimiento (Es)	Ablauffrist *f*	time limit	délai *m*	termine di scadenza *m*	—
vendable (F)	marktfähig	marketable	—	smerciabile	comerciable
vender (Es)	verkaufen	sell	vendre	vendere	—
vendere (I)	verkaufen	sell	vendre	—	vender
vending machine[1] (E)	Verkaufsautomat *m*	—	distributeur automatique *m*	distributore automatico *m*	distribuidor automático *m*
vending machine[2] (E)	Automat *m*	—	appareil automatique *m*	distributore automatico *m*	distribuidor automático *m*
vendita[1] (I)	Absatz *m*	sale/distribution	volume des ventes *m*	—	cifra de ventas *f*
vendita[2] (I)	Verkauf *m*	sale	vente *f*	—	venta *f*
vendita all'asta (I)	Versteigerung *f*	auction	vente à l'enchère *f*	—	subasta *f*
vendita allo scoperto[1] (I)	Leerverkauf *m*	bear sale	vente à découvert *f*	—	venta al descubierto *f*
vendita allo scoperto[2] (I)	Blankoverkauf *m*	short sale	vente à découvert *f*	—	venta al descubierto *f*
vendita a rate[1] (I)	Teilzahlungs-geschäft *n*	partial payment transaction	achat à tempérament *m*	—	operación a plazo *f*
vendita a rate[2] (I)	Ratengeschäft *n*	instalment sale transaction	vente à tempérament *f*	—	venta a plazo *f*
vendita complementare (I)	Zusatzverkauf *m*	additional sale	vente additionnelle *f*	—	venta adicional *f*
vendita diretta (I)	Direktverkauf *m*	direct selling	vente directe *f*	—	venta directa *f*
vendita esclusiva (I)	Alleinvertrieb *m*	exclusive distribution	vente exclusive *f*	—	distribución exclusiva *f*
vendita giudiziaria (I)	Zwangsverkauf *m*	forced sale	vente forcée *f*	—	venta forzada *f*
vendita per corrispondenza (I)	Versandhandel *m*	mail order business	commerce de vente au détail par correspondance *m*	—	venta por correspondencia *f*
vendita per distributori automatici (I)	Automatenverkauf *m*	automatic vending	vente par distributeur automatique *f*	—	venta por distribuido-res automáticos *f*
vendita per telefono (I)	Telefonverkauf *m*	inter-office sale	vente par téléphone *f*	—	venta por teléfono *f*
vendre (F)	verkaufen	sell	—	vendere	vender
venta (Es)	Verkauf *m*	sale	vente *f*	vendita *f*	—
venta adicional (Es)	Zusatzverkauf *m*	additional sale	vente additionnelle *f*	vendita complementare *f*	—
venta al descubierto[1] (Es)	Blankoverkauf *m*	short sale	vente à découvert *f*	vendita allo scoperto *f*	—
venta al descubierto[2] (Es)	Leerverkauf *m*	bear sale	vente à découvert *f*	vendita allo scoperto *f*	—
venta a plazo (Es)	Ratengeschäft *n*	instalment sale transaction	vente à tempérament *f*	vendita a rate *f*	—
venta a plazos (Es)	Abzahlungs-geschäft *n*	hire purchase transaction	achat à tempérament *m*	operazione con pagamento a rate *f*	—
venta con pérdida (Es)	Verlustgeschäft *n*	losing business	affaire déficitaire *f*	affare in perdita *m*	—
venta de liquidación (Es)	Schlußverkauf *m*	seasonal sale	vente de fin de saison *f*	svendita di fine stagione *f*	—
venta directa (Es)	Direktverkauf *m*	direct selling	vente directe *f*	vendita diretta *f*	—

	D	E	F	I	Es
venta en cadena (Es)	Schneeballsystem *n*	snowball system	système de la boule de neige *m*	sistema di vendite a catena aperta *m*	—
venta forzada (Es)	Zwangsverkauf *m*	forced sale	vente forcée *f*	vendita giudiziaria *f*	—
ventaja (Es)	Vorteil *m*	advantage	avantage *m*	vantaggio *m*	—
ventaja de competencia (Es)	Wettbewerbs-vorteil *m*	competitive advantage	avantage de concurrence *m*	vantaggio concorrenziale *m*	—
ventaja de costes (Es)	Kostenvorteil *m*	cost advantage	avantage de coût *m*	vantaggio di costo *m*	—
venta por correspondencia (Es)	Versandhandel *m*	mail order business	commerce de vente au détail par correspondance *m*	vendita per corrispondenza *f*	—
venta por distribuidores automáticos (Es)	Automatenverkauf *m*	automatic vending	vente par distributeur automatique *f*	vendita per distributori automatici *f*	—
venta por teléfono (Es)	Telefonverkauf *m*	inter-office sale	vente par téléphone *f*	vendita per telefono *f*	—
ventas netas (Es)	Nettoumsatz *m*	net turnover	chiffre d'affaires net *m*	fatturato netto *m*	—
venta total (Es)	Räumungsverkauf *m*	clearance sale	liquidation des stocks *f*	liquidazione totale *f*	—
vente (F)	Verkauf *m*	sale	—	vendita *f*	venta *f*
vente additionnelle (F)	Zusatzverkauf *m*	additional sale	—	vendita complementare *f*	venta adicional *f*
vente à découvert[1] (F)	Blankoverkauf *m*	short sale	—	vendita allo scoperto *f*	venta al descubierto *f*
vente à découvert[2] (F)	Leerverkauf *m*	bear sale	—	vendita allo scoperto *f*	venta al descubierto *f*
vente à l'enchère[1] (F)	Versteigerung *f*	auction	—	vendita all'asta *f*	subasta *f*
vente à l'enchère[2] (F)	Auktion *f*	auction	—	asta *f*	subasta *f*
vente à tempérament (F)	Ratengeschäft *n*	instalment sale transaction	—	vendita a rate *f*	venta a plazo *f*
vente de biens par justice (F)	Zwangs-versteigerung *f*	sale by court order	—	asta giudiziaria *f*	subasta forzosa *f*
vente de fin de saison (F)	Schlußverkauf *m*	seasonal sale	—	svendita di fine stagione *f*	venta de liquidación *f*
vente directe (F)	Direktverkauf *m*	direct selling	—	vendita diretta *f*	venta directa *f*
vente exclusive (F)	Alleinvertrieb *m*	exclusive distribution	—	vendita esclusiva *f*	distribución exclusiva *f*
vente forcée (F)	Zwangsverkauf *m*	forced sale	—	vendita giudiziaria *f*	venta forzada *f*
vente par distributeur automatique (F)	Automatenverkauf *m*	automatic vending	—	vendita per distributori automatici *f*	venta por distribuidores automáticos *f*
vente par téléphone (F)	Telefonverkauf *m*	inter-office sale	—	vendita per telefono *f*	venta por teléfono *f*
venture (E)	Wagnis *n*	—	risque *m*	rischio *m*	riesgo *m*
verarbeitende Industrie (D)	—	manufacturing industry	industrie transformatrice *f*	industria di trasformazione *f*	industria transformadora *f*
Verarbeitung (D)	—	processing	transformation *f*	lavorazione *f*	transformación *f*
Veräußerung (D)	—	sale/alienation	aliénation *f*	alienazione *f*	enajenación *f*
verbale (I)	mündlich	verbal	verbal	—	oral
Verband (D)	—	association	association *f*	associazione *f*	asociación *f*
Verbesserungs-vorschlag (D)	—	suggestion for improvement	proposition d'amélioration *f*	proposta di miglioramento *f*	propuesta de mejora *f*
Verbilligung (D)	—	cheapening	réduction du prix *f*	ribasso *m*	abaratamiento *m*
Verbindlichkeiten (D)	—	liability/debts	obligation *f*/ dettes *f pl*	obblighi *m pl*/ debiti *m pl*	obligaciónes *f pl*/ deudas *f pl*/créditos pasivos *m pl*
Verbrauch (D)	—	consumption	consommation *f*	consumo *m*	consumo *m*
verbrauchen (D)	—	consume	consommer	consumare	consumir
Verbraucher (D)	—	consumer	consommateur *m*	consumatore *m*	consumidor *m*
Verbraucher-information (D)	—	consumer information	information des consommateurs *f*	informazione per i consumatori *f*	información de consumidores *f*
Verbrauchermarkt (D)	—	consumer market	marché des consommateurs *m*	ipermercato *m*	mercado favorable al consumidor *m*

	D	E	F	I	Es
Verbraucher-organisation (D)	—	consumer protection organization	organisation des consommateurs *f*	organizzazione dei consumatori *f*	orgnización de defensa del consumidor *f*
Verbraucherschutz (D)	—	consumer protection	protection des consommateurs *f*	tutela dei consumatori *f*	protección de los consumidores *f*
Verbrauchsgüter (D)	—	consumer goods	biens de consommation *m pl*	beni non durevoli *m pl*	bienes de consumo *m pl*
Verbrennung (D)	—	incineration	combustion *f*	combustione *f*	combustión *f*
verderblich (D)	—	perishable	périssable	deperibile	perecedero
Veredelung (D)	—	processing	perfectionnement *m*	perfezionamento *m*	perfeccionamiento *m*
Verein (D)	—	association	association *f*	associazione *f*	asociación *f*
vereinbarungs-gemäß (D)	—	as agreed	comme convenu	come convenuto	según lo acordado
Verfahren (D)	—	procedure/process	méthode *f*/ procédure *f*	procedimento *m*/ procedura *f*	proceso *m*/ procedimiento *m*
Verfahrens-einstellung (D)	—	abatement of an action	arrêt d'une procédure	sospensione del procedimento *f*	sobreseimiento del proceso *m*
Verfahrenskosten (D)	—	costs of the proceedings	frais de procédure *m pl*	spese del procedimento *f pl*	costas *f pl*
Verfallsdatum (D)	—	expiry date	date d'échéance *f*	data di scadenza *f*	fecha de vencimiento *f*
Verfalltag (D)	—	day of expiry	jour de l'échéance *m*	giorno di scadenza *m*	día de vencimiento *m*
verfrachten (D)	—	freight/ship	fréter/embarquer	imbarcare	expedir/fletar
Verfrachtung (D)	—	carriage of goods by sea	affrètement *m*	trasporto marittimo *m*	expedición *f*
verfügbares Einkommen (D)	—	disposable income	revenu disponible *m*	introito disponibile *m*	ingresos disponibles *m pl*
Verfügung (D)	—	disposal/order disposition *m*	disposition *f*/acte de	disposizione *f*/ ordinanza *f*	disposición *f*/ decreto *m*
Vergleich (D)	—	comparison	comparaison *f*	confronto *m*	comparación *f*
vergleichende Werbung (D)	—	comparative advertising	publicité comparative *f*	pubblicità comparativa *f*	publicidad comparativa *f*
Vergleichs-verfahren (D)	—	composition proceedings	procédure de conciliation *f*	procedura di concordato *f*	procedimiento conciliatorio *m*
Vergütung (D)	—	remuneration	rémunération *f*	ricompensa *f*	remuneración *f*
Verhältnis (D)	—	proportion	relation *f*	rapporto *m*	relación *f*
Verhandlung (D)	—	negotiation	négociation *f*	trattativa *f*	negociación *f*/ juicio *m*/ vista oral *f*
Verhandlungs-geschick (D)	—	negotiation skills	habileté de négociation *f*	abilità nel trattare *f*	tino de negociar *m*
verificación (Es)	Prüfung *f*	inspection/ examination	vérification *f*/ examen *m*	controllo *m*/ esame *m*	—
verificación de la calidad (Es)	Qualitätskontrolle *f*	quality control	contrôle de la qualité *m*	controllo di qualità *m*	—
vérificateur des comptes (F)	Abschlußprüfer *m*	auditor	—	revisore *m*	revisor contable *m*
vérification[1] (F)	Prüfung *f*	inspection/ examination	—	controllo *m*/ esame *m*	verificación *f*/ examen *m*
vérification[2] (F)	Nachprüfung *f*	reexamination	—	revisione *f*	revisión *f*
vérification des comptes (F)	Abschlußprüfung *f*	audit	—	revisione *f*	revisión contable *f*
vérification des livres de l'entreprise (F)	Betriebsprüfung *f*	investigation by the tax authorities	—	revisione aziendale *f*	inspección de la explotación *f*
Verjährung (D)	—	limitation of actions	prescription *f*	prescrizione *f*	prescripción *f*
Verkauf (D)	—	sale	vente *f*	vendita *f*	venta *f*
verkaufen (D)	—	sell	vendre	vendere	vender
Verkäufermarkt (D)	—	seller's market	marché de vendeurs *m*	mercato favorevole ai venditori *m*	mercado favorable al vendedor *m*
Verkäuferprovision (D)	—	sales commission	commission sur les ventes *f*	provvigione del venditore *f*	comisión sobre la venta *f*
Verkäuferschulung (D)	—	sales training	formation des vendeurs *f*	addestramento dei venditori *f*	formación de los vendedores *f*
Verkäufer-wettbewerb (D)	—	sellers competition	compétition des vendeurs *f*	concorrenza dei venditori *f*	competición de vendedores *f*

	D	E	F	I	Es
Verkaufsabschluß (D)	—	sales contract	contrat de vente *m*	conclusione di vendita *f*	conclusión de la venta *f*
Verkaufsanalyse (D)	—	sales analysis	analyse des ventes *f*	analisi delle vendite *f*	análisis de las ventas *m*
Verkaufsautomat (D)	—	vending machine	distributeur automatique *m*	distributore automatico *m*	distribuidor automático *m*
Verkaufsbericht (D)	—	sales report	rapport de vente *m*	rapporto sulle vendite *m*	informe de venta *m*
Verkaufschance (D)	—	sales possibilities	possibilité de vente *f*	prospettiva dello smercio *f*	posibilidades de venta *f pl*
Verkaufserlös (D)	—	sale proceeds	produit des ventes *m*	ricavo delle vendite *m*	producto de la venta *m*
Verkaufsförderung (D)	—	sales promotion	encouragement à la vente *m*	promozione di vendita *f*	promoción de las ventas *f*
Verkaufsgebiet (D)	—	sales territory	territoire de vente *m*	zona di vendita *f*	territorio de venta *m*
Verkaufsgespräch (D)	—	sale talk	conversation de vente *f*	colloquio di vendita *m*	conversación de venta *f*
Verkaufskampagne (D)	—	sales campaign	campagne de vente *f*	campagna di vendita *f*	campaña de venta *f*
Verkaufskonzeption (D)	—	sales conception	conception de vente *f*	concezione di vendita *f*	concepción de venta *f*
Verkaufsmethoden (D)	—	sales strategy	méthodes de vente *f pl*	metodi di vendita *m pl*	métodos de venta *m pl*
Verkaufsoption (D)	—	option to sell	option de vente *f*	opzione di vendita *f*	opción de venta *f*
Verkaufsprogramm (D)	—	sales programme	programme de vente *m*	programma di vendita *m*	programa de venta *m*
Verkaufsstab (D)	—	sales staff	équipe de vente *f*	staff di venditori *m*	equipo de venta *m*
Verkaufstechnik (D)	—	sales technique	art de vendre *m*	tecnica di vendita *f*	técnica de venta *f*
Verkehr (D)	—	traffic	circulation *f*	traffico *m*	circulación *f*
Verkehrspolitik (D)	—	transport policy	politique des transports *f*	politica del traffico *f*	política de transportes *f*
Verladekosten (D)	—	loading charges	coût du chargement *m*	costi di caricamento *m pl*	gastos de carga *m pl*
verladen (D)	—	load	charger	caricare	expedir
Verlag (D)	—	publishing house	maison d'édition *f*	casa editrice *f*	editorial *f*
Verlängerung (D)	—	extension	prolongation *f*	prolungamento *m*	prórroga *f*
Verleger (D)	—	publisher	éditeur *m*	editore *m*	editor *m*
verlorengegangene Sendung (D)	—	lost shipment	envoi perdu *m*	spedizione andata persa *f*	envío perdido *m*
Verlust (D)	—	loss	perte *f*	perdita *f*	pérdida *f*
Verlustgeschäft (D)	—	losing business	affaire déficitaire *f*	affare in perdita *m*	venta con pérdida *f*
vermarkten (D)	—	market	commercialiser	lanciare sul mercato	comercializar
Vermerk (D)	—	note	remarque *f*	annotazione *f*	nota *f*
Vermittlung (D)	—	mediation	médiation *f*	mediazione *f*	mediación *f*
Vermögen (D)	—	property	patrimoine *m*	patrimonio *m*	patrimonio *m*
Vermögensbildung (D)	—	capital formation	formation de capital *f*	formazione del patrimonio *f*	formación de capital *f*
Vermögenspolitik (D)	—	policy relating to capital formation	politique financière *f*	politica patrimoniale *f*	política de los patrimonios *f*
Vermögens-rechnung (D)	—	capital account	calcul du patrimoine *m*	calcolo del patrimonio *m*	cálculo del valor neto *m*
Vermögens-verhältnisse (D)	—	financial situation	situation financière *f*	situazione patrimoniale *f*	situación económica *f*
Vermögens-verteilung (D)	—	distribution of wealth	répartition du patrimoine *f*	ripartizione del patrimonio *f*	reparto de la riqueza *m*
Veröffentlichung (D)	—	publication	publication *f*	pubblicazione *f*	publicación *f*
Verordnung (D)	—	decree	décret *m*	regolamento *m*	ordenanza *f*
Verpackung (D)	—	packing	emballage *m*	imballaggio *m*	embalaje *m*
Verpackungseinheit (D)	—	packing unit	unité d'emballage *f*	unità d'imballaggio *f*	unidad de embalaje *f*

	D	E	F	I	Es
Verpackungs-material (D)	—	packing material	matériel d'emballage *m*	materiale d'imballaggio *m*	empaque *m*
Verpackungsmüll (D)	—	packing waste	déchets d'emballage *m pl*	rifiuti da imballaggi *m pl*	basura de embalaje *f*
Verpackungs-vorschriften (D)	—	packing instructions	prescriptions concernant l'emballage *f pl*	prescrizioni per l'imballaggio *f pl*	prescripciones de embalaje *f pl*
Verpfändung (D)	—	pledge	mise en gage *f*	pignoramento *m*	pignoración *f*
Verrechnung (D)	—	compensation	compensation *f*	compensazione *f*	compensación *f*
Verrechnungs-einheit (D)	—	clearing unit	unité de compte *f*	unità di compensazione *f*	unidad de compensación *f*
Verrechnungs-scheck (D)	—	crossed cheque	chèque à porter en compte *m*	assegno sbarrato *m*	cheque cruzado *m*
Versand (D)	—	dispatch	expédition *f*	spedizione *f*	envío *m*
Versandabteilung (D)	—	dispatch department	service des expéditions *m*	reparto spedizioni *m*	departamento de expedición *m*
Versandavis (D)	—	advice of dispatch	avis d'expédition *m*	avviso di spedizione *m*	aviso de envío *m*
versandbereit (D)	—	ready for dispatch	prêt à être expédié	pronto per la spedizione	listo para ser expedido
Versanddokument (D)	—	shipping document	documents d'expédition *m pl*	documento di spedizione *m*	documentos de expedición *m pl*
Versandform (D)	—	manner of delivery	forme d'expédition *f*	tipo di spedizione *m*	forma de envío *f*
Versandhandel (D)	—	mail order business	commerce de vente au détail par correspondance *m*	vendita per corrispondenza *f*	venta por correspondencia *f*
Versandleiter (D)	—	manager of shipping department	chef du service des expéditions *m*	capo reparto spedizioni *m*	jefe del departamento de expedición *m*
Versandvorschrift (D)	—	forwarding instruction	prescriptions concernant l'expédition *f pl*	prescrizione per la spedizione *f*	instrucción para el envío *f*
Verschiffung (D)	—	shipment	embarquement *m*	imbarco *m*	embarque *m*
Verschmelzung (D)	—	merger	fusion *f*	fusione *f*	fusión *f*
verschrotten (D)	—	scrap	mettre à la ferraille	ridurre a rottame	hacer quincalla u/c/ desguazar
Verschuldung (D)	—	indebtedness	endettement *m*	indebitamento *m*	endeudamiento *m*
Verschuldungsgrad (D)	—	debt ratio	niveau de l'endettement *m*	tasso d'indebitamento *m*	grado de endeudamiento *m*
versement complémentaire (F)	Nachzahlung *f*	supplementary payment	—	pagamento supplementare *m*	pago suplementario *m*
Versicherung (D)	—	insurance	assurance *f*	assicurazione *f*	seguro *m*
Versicherung auf Gegenseitigkeit (D)	—	mutual insurance	assurance mutuelle *f*	mutua assicurazione *f*	caja de socorros mutuos *f*
Versicherungsagent (D)	—	insurance agent	agent d'assurance *m*	agente d'assicurazione *m*	agente de seguros *m*
Versicherungsfall (D)	—	event insured against	sinistre *m*	caso di sinistro *m*	situación de siniestro *f*
Versicherungs-gesellschaft (D)	—	insurance company	société d'assurance *f*	compagnia di assicurazione *f*	sociedad de seguros *f*
Versicherungs-makler (D)	—	insurance broker	courtier en assurance *m*	mediatore d'assicurazione *m*	corredor de seguros *m*
Versicherungs-nehmer (D)	—	insured person	souscripteur d'une assurance *m*	assicurato *m*	asegurado *m*
Versicherungs-pflicht (D)	—	liability to insure	assujettissement obligatoire à l'assurance *m*	obbligo d'assicurazione *m*	obligatoriedad del seguro *f*
Versicherungs-police (D)	—	insurance policy	police d'assurance *f*	polizza d'assicurazione *f*	seguro *m*
Versicherungs-prämie (D)	—	insurance premium	prime d'assurance *f*	premio d'assicurazione *m*	prima de seguro *f*
Versicherungs-schutz (D)	—	insurance cover	couverture de l'assurance *f*	copertura assicurativa *f*	cobertura de seguro *f*
Versicherungs-summe (D)	—	insurance sum	montant de l'assurance *m*	somma assicurata *f*	suma asegurada *f*
Versicherungs-vertrag (D)	—	insurance contract	contrat d'assurance *m*	contratto d'assicurazione *m*	contrato de seguro *m*

	D	E	F	I	Es
Versorgung (D)	—	supply	approvisionnement *m*	approvvigionamento *m*	abastecimiento *m*
Versorgungseinrichtung (D)	—	pension scheme	institution de retraite *f*	istituto previdenziale *m*	insitución de previsón *f*
Verspätung (D)	—	delay	retard *m*	ritardo *m*	retraso *m*
Verstaatlichung (D)	—	nationalization	nationalisaiton *f*	nazionalizzazione *f*	nacionalización *f*
Versteigerung (D)	—	auction	vente à l'enchère *f*	vendita all'asta *f*	subasta *f*
Vertagung (D)	—	postponement	ajournement *m*	rinvio *m*	aplazamiento *m*/ suspensión *f*
Verteilung (D)	—	distribution	distribution *f*	distribuzione *f*	distribución *f*
Verteilungspolitik (D)	—	distribution policy	politique de répartition *f*	politica della distribuzione *f*	política de distribución *f*
Verteuerung (D)	—	rise in price	enchérissement *m*	rincaro *m*	encarecimiento *m*
Vertrag (D)	—	contract/treaty/ agreement	contrat *m*/traité *m*/ accord *m*	contratto *m*	contrato *m*/ tratado *m*/acuerdo *m*
Vertragsabschluß (D)	—	conclusion of a contract	conclusion du contrat *f*	stipulazione del contratto *f*	conclusión de un contrato *f*
Vertragsänderung (D)	—	modification of a contract	modification du contrat *f*	modificazione del contratto *f*	modificación de contrato *f*
Vertragsbedingung (D)	—	term of contract	condition du contrat *f*	condizione del contratto *f*	condiciones contractuales *f pl*
Vertragsdauer (D)	—	contract period	durée du contrat *f*	durata del contratto *f*	duración del contrato *f*
Vertragsfreiheit (D)	—	freedom of contract	liberté de contracter *f*	libertà contrattuale *f*	libertad contractual *f*
Vertragsstrafe (D)	—	contractual penalty	pénalité *f*	penalità convenzionale *f*	pena convencional *f*
Vertrauensverhältnis (D)	—	confidential relationship	rapport de confiance *m*	rapporto di fiducia *m*	relación de confianza *f*
vertraulich (D)	—	confidential	confidentiel	confidenziale	confidencial
Vertreter (D)	—	representative	représentant *m*	rappresentante *m*	representante *m*
Vertretertagung (D)	—	sales meeting	réunion de représentants *f*	convegno dei rappresentanti *m*	conferencia de representantes *f*
Vertretung (D)	—	representation	représentation *f*	rappresentanza *f*	representación *f*
Vertretungsberechtigung (D)	—	authorized to represent	autorisation de représentation *f*	autorizzazione alla rappresentanza *f*	derecho de representación *m*
Vertrieb (D)	—	distribution	distribution *f*	distribuzione *f*	distribución *f*
Vertriebsfirma (D)	—	distributor	distributeur *m*	ditta di distribuzione *f*	compañía distribuidora *f*
Vertriebsstruktur (D)	—	structure of distribution	structure de distribution *f*	struttura della distribuzione *f*	estructura de distribución *f*
Vertriebsweg (D)	—	distribution channel	canal de distribution *m*	rete di distribuzione *f*	circuito de distribución *f*
Veruntreuung (D)	—	misappropriation	détournement *m*	abuso di fiducia *m*	malversación *f*
Verursacherprinzip (D)	—	polluter pays principle	principe du pollueur payeur *m*	principio della colpa oggettiva *m*	principio contaminador-pagador *m*
Vervielfältigung (D)	—	reproduction	reproduction *f*	riproduzione *f*	reproducción *f*/ multiplicación *f*
Verwahrung (D)	—	custody	dépôt *m*	custodia *f*	custodia *f*/ incautación *f*
Verwalter (D)	—	administrator	administrateur *m*	amministratore *m*	administrador *m*
Verwaltung (D)	—	administration	administration *f*	amministrazione *f*	administración *f*
Verwaltungsakt (D)	—	administrative act	acte administratif *m*	atto amministrativo *m*	acto administrativo *m*
Verwaltungshoheit (D)	—	power of administration	autonomie d'administration *f*	sovranità amministrativa *f*	soberanía administrativa *f*
verzinsen (D)	—	pay interest on	compter des intérêts	pagare interessi	pagar interés
verzollt (D)	—	duty paid	dédouané	sdoganato	aranceles pagados
Verzug (D)	—	delay	demeure *f*	mora *f*	retraso *m*/demora *f*
Verzugszinsen (D)	—	default interest	intérêts moratoires *m pl*	interessi di mora *m pl*	intereses de demora *m pl*
vetrina[1] (I)	Schaufenster *n*	shop-window	vitrine *f*	—	escaparate *m*

	D	E	F	I	Es
vetrina[2] (I)	Auslage *f*	display/ expenditure	étalage *f*/ débours *m*	—	vitrina *f*/ gastos *m pl*
vettore (I)	Frachtführer *m*	carrier	transporteur *m*	—	transportista *m*
vettore aereo (I)	Luftfrachtführer *m*	air carrier	voiturier aérien *m*	—	transportista *m*
vettura aziendale (I)	Firmenwagen *m*	company car	voiture appartenant à l'entreprise *f*	—	coche de empresa *m*
vettura da noleggio (I)	Leihwagen *m*	hired car	voiture de location *f*	—	coche de alquiler *m*
vettura di servizio (I)	Dienstwagen *m*	official car	voiture de service *f*	—	coche de servicio *m*
via (I)	Straße *f*	street/road	rue *f*/route *f*	—	calle *f*/carretera *f*
vía aérea (Es)	Luftweg *m*	air route	voie aérienne *f*	via aerea *f*	—
via aerea (I)	Luftweg *m*	air route	voie aérienne *f*	—	vía aérea *f*
via d'acqua (I)	Wasserstraße *f*	waterway	voie d'eau *f*	—	vía navegable *f*
vía de transporte (Es)	Transportweg *m*	route of transportation	voie de transport *f*	via di trasporto *f*	—
via della distribuzione (I)	Absatzweg *m*	channel of distribution	canal de distribution *m*	—	medio de venta *f*
via di trasporto (I)	Transportweg *m*	route of transportation	voie de transport *f*	—	vía de transporte *f*
viajante (Es)	festangestellter Reisender *m*	sales representative	voyageur de commerce *m*	commesso viaggiatore *m*	—
vía marítima (Es)	Seeweg *m*	sea route	voie maritime *f*	via marittima *f*	—
via marittima (I)	Seeweg *m*	sea route	voie maritime *f*	—	vía marítima *f*
vía navegable (Es)	Wasserstraße *f*	waterway	voie d'eau *f*	via d'acqua *f*	—
via terra (I)	Landweg *m*	overland transportation	voie de terre *f*	—	vía terrestre *m*
vía terrestre (Es)	Landweg *m*	overland transportation	voie de terre *f*	via terra *f*	—
video (I)	Bildschirm *m*	screen	écran *m*	—	pantalla *f*
videotex (I)	Bildschirmtext *m*	videotext	videotex international *m*	—	teletexto *m*
videotex international (F)	Bildschirmtext *m*	videotext	—	videotex *m*	teletexto *m*
videotext (E)	Bildschirmtext *m*	—	videotex international *m*	videotex *m*	teletexto *m*
vierteljährlich (D)	—	quarterly	trimestriel	trimestrale	trimestral
vierzehn Tage (D)	—	fortnight	quinze jours	quindici giorni	quince días *m pl*
vigilar (Es)	überwachen	supervise	surveiller	sorvegliare	—
violación de las reglas de competencia (Es)	Wettbewerbs-verstoß *m*	violation of competition rules	violation de concurrence *f*	violazione delle regole di concorrenza *f*	—
violation de concurrence (F)	Wettbewerbs-verstoß *m*	violation of competition rules	—	violazione delle regole di concorrenza *f*	violación de las reglas de competencia *f*
violation of competition rules (E)	Wettbewerbs-verstoß *m*	—	violation de concurrence *f*	violazione delle regole di concorrenza *f*	violación de las reglas de competencia *f*
violazione delle regole di concorrenza (I)	Wettbewerbs-verstoß *m*	violation of competition rules	violation de concurrence *f*	—	violación de las reglas de competencia *f*
virement[1] (F)	Giro *n*	credit transfer	—	giro *m*	giro *m*
virement[2] (F)	Überweisung *f*	remittance	—	rimessa *f*	transferencia *f*
virement bancaire (F)	Banküberweisung *f*	bank transfer	—	rimessa bancaria *f*	transferencia bancaria *f*
virement par câble (F)	Kabelüberweisung *f*	cable transfer	—	bonifico telegrafico *m*	giro telegráfico *m*
virement postal[1] (F)	Postüberweisung *f*	postal remittance	—	bonifico postale *m*	giro postal *m*
virement postal[2] (F)	Postgiro *n*	postal giro	—	postagiro *m*	giro postal *m*
visa (E)	Visum *n*	—	visa *m*	visto *m*	visado *m*
visa (F)	Visum *n*	visa	—	visto *m*	visado *m*
visado (Es)	Visum *n*	visa	visa *m*	visto *m*	—
visto (I)	Visum *n*	visa	visa *m*	—	visado *m*
Visum (D)	—	visa	visa *m*	visto *m*	visado *m*
vitrine (F)	Schaufenster *n*	shop-window	—	vetrina *f*	escaparate *m*

	D	E	F	I	Es
vivienda (Es)	Wohnung *f*	apartment	appartement *m*	abitazione *f*	—
vizio (I)	Mangel *m*	defect	défaut *m*	—	defecto *m*/ vicio *m*
vocational adjustment (E)	Einarbeitung *f*	—	entraînement *m*	periodo d'adattamento *m*	entrenamiento *m*
voce (I)	Posten *m*	item	poste *m*	—	puesto *m*
void (E)	nichtig	—	non valable	nullo	nulo
voie aérienne (F)	Luftweg *m*	air route	—	via aerea *f*	vía aérea *f*
voie d'eau (F)	Wasserstraße *f*	waterway	—	via d'acqua *f*	vía navegable *f*
voie de terre (F)	Landweg *m*	overland transportation	—	via terra *f*	vía terrestre *m*
voie de transport (F)	Transportweg *m*	route of transportation	—	via di trasporto *f*	vía de transporte *f*
voie maritime (F)	Seeweg *m*	sea route	—	via marittima *f*	vía marítima *f*
voirie (F)	Wegenetz *n*	road network	—	rete stradale *f*	comunicaciones *f pl*
voiture appartenant à l'entreprise (F)	Firmenwagen *m*	company car	—	vettura aziendale *f*	coche de empresa *m*
voiture de location (F)	Leihwagen *m*	hired car	—	vettura da noleggio *f*	coche de alquiler *m*
voiture de service (F)	Dienstwagen *m*	official car	—	vettura di servizio *f*	coche de servicio *m*
voiture d'occasion (F)	Gebrauchtwagen *m*	used car	—	automobile usata *f*	coche de segunda mano *m*
voiturier aérien (F)	Luftfracht-führer *m*	air carrier	—	vettore aereo *m*	transportista *m*
voix (F)	Stimme *f*	voting	—	voto *m*	voz *f*
vol (F)	Diebstahl *m*	theft	—	furto *m*	robo *m*
vol charter (F)	Charterflug *m*	charter flight	—	volo charter *m*	vuelo fletado *m*
Volkseinkommen (D)	—	national income	revenu national *m*	reddito nazionale *m*	renta nacional *f*
Volkswirtschaft (D)	—	national economy	économie nationale *f*	economia politica *f*	economía nacional *f*
Volkswirtschaftliche Gesamtrechnung (D)	—	national accounting	comptabilité nationale *f*	contabilità nazionale *f*	contabilidad nacional *f*
Volkswirtschafts-lehre (D)	—	economics	économie politique *f*	economia politica *f*	ciencias económicas *f pl*
Volkszählung (D)	—	census of population	recensement démographique *m*	censimento *m*	censo *m*
Vollbeschäftigung (D)	—	full employment	plein emploi *m*	piena occupazione *f*	empleo total *m*
Vollmacht (D)	—	full power/power of attorney	plein pouvoir *m*/ mandat *m*	mandato *m*	poder *m*/ autorización *f*/ escritura de poder *f*
Vollmachtgeber (D)	—	grantor of a power of attorney	auteur de la procuration *m*	mandante *m*	poderdante *m*
vollständige Bezahlung (D)	—	payment in full	payement complet *m*	pagamento totale *m*	pago íntegro *m*
Vollstreckung (D)	—	enforcement	exécution *f*	esecuzione *f*	ejecución *f*
volo charter (I)	Charterflug *m*	charter flight	vol charter *m*	—	vuelo fletado *m*
volume[1] (E)	Umfang *m*	—	volume *m*	entità *f*	volumen *m*/ dimensión *f*
volume[2] (E)	Volumen *n*	—	volume *m*	volume *m*	volumen *m*
volume (F)	Volumen *n*	volume	—	volume *m*	volumen *m*
volume (I)	Volumen *n*	volume	volume *m*	—	volumen *m*
volume des ventes (F)	Absatz *m*	sale/distribution	—	vendita *f*	cifra de ventas *f*
volume di lavoro (I)	Arbeitsanfall *m*	volume of work	travail à exécuter *m*	—	volumen de trabajo *m*
volume monetario (I)	Geldvolumen *n*	volume of money	masse monétaire *f*	—	volumen monetario *m*
Volumen (D)	—	volume	volume *m*	volume *m*	volumen *m*
volumen (Es)	Volumen *n*	volume	volume *m*	volume *m*	—
volumen de trabajo (Es)	Arbeitsanfall *m*	volume of work	travail à exécuter *m*	volume di lavoro *m*	—
volumen de ventas (Es)	Umsatz *m*	turnover	chiffre d'affaires *m*	fatturato *m*	—

	D	E	F	I	Es
volumen monetario[1] (Es)	Geldvolumen *n*	volume of money	masse monétaire *f*	volume monetario *m*	—
volumen monetario[2] (Es)	Geldmenge *f*	money supply	quantité de monnaie en circulation *f*	massa monetaria *f*	—
volume of money (E)	Geldvolumen *n*	—	masse monétaire *f*	volume monetario *m*	volumen monetario *m*
volume of work (E)	Arbeitsanfall *m*	—	travail à exécuter *m*	volume di lavoro *m*	volumen de trabajo *m*
voluntary constraint in consumption (E)	Konsumverzicht *m*	—	renonciation à la consommation *f*	rinuncia al consumo *f*	renuncia al consumo *f*
voluntary disclo sure (E)	Selbstauskunft *f*	—	renseignement fourni lui-même *m*	informazione volontaria *f*	información de sí mismo *f*
Voranschlag (D)	—	estimate	devis *m*	preventivo *m*	presupuesto *m*
Voraussetzung (D)	—	precondition	condition préalable *f*	presupposto *m*	condición previa *f*
Vorauszahlung (D)	—	payment in advance	payement anticipé *m*	pagamento anticipato *m*	adelanto *m*
Vorbereitung (D)	—	preparation	préparation *f*	preparazione *f*	preparación *f*
Vorbestellrabatt (D)	—	discount on advance orders	escompte de suscription *m*	ribasso per ordinazioni anticipate *m*	descuento de suscripción *m*
Vorbestellung (D)	—	reservation	commande préalable *f*	ordinazione anticipata *f*	pedidio anticipado *m*
Vorbörse (D)	—	before hours dealing	marché avant le marché officiel *m*	mercato preborsistico *m*	operaciones antes de la apertura de la bolsa *f pl*
vordatierter Scheck (D)	—	antidated cheque	chèque antidaté *m*	assegno antidatato *m*	cheque de fecha adelantada *m*
Vordruck (D)	—	printed form	imprimé *m*	modulo *m*	impreso *m*
Vorkalkulation (D)	—	estimation of cost	calcul des coûts a priori *m*	calcolo preventivo *m*	cálculo provisional *m*
Vorkaufsrecht (D)	—	preemption right	droit de préemption *m*	diritto di prelazione *m*	derecho de preferencia *m*
Vorrat (D)	—	stock	stock *m*	scorte *f pl*	existencias *f pl*
Vorratshaltung (D)	—	stockpiling	stockage *m*	gestione delle scorte *f*	formación de stocks *f*
Vorrecht (D)	—	privilege	prérogative *f*	privilegio *m*	derecho preferente *m*
Vorschlag (D)	—	proposal	proposition *f*	proposta *f*	proposición *f*
Vorschuß (D)	—	advance	avance *f*	anticipo *m*	anticipo *m*
vorsichtige Schätzung (D)	—	conservative estimate	évaluation approximative *f*	valutazione approssimativa *f*	evaluación aproximativa *f*
Vorsitz (D)	—	chairmanship	présidence *f*	presidenza *f*	presidencia *f*
Vorstand (D)	—	board	comité directeur *m*	consiglio di amministrazione *m*	consejo de dirección *m*
Vorstandsmitglied (D)	—	member of the managing board	membre du comité de direction *m*	membro del consiglio di amministrazione *m*	consejero directivo *m*
Vorstandsvorsitzender (D)	—	chairman of the board	président du comité de direction *m*	presidente del consiglio di amministrazione *m*	presidente del consejo *m*
Vorstellungstermin (D)	—	date of interview	rendez-vous de présentation *m*	appuntamento di presentazione *m*	fecha de entrevista personal *f*
Vorsteuer (D)	—	input tax	impôt perçu en amont *m*	imposta sul fatturato d'acquisto *f*	impuesto sobre el valor añadido deducible *m*
Vorteil (D)	—	advantage	avantage *m*	vantaggio *m*	ventaja *f*
Vorzugsaktie (D)	—	preference share	action privilégiée *f*	azione privilegiata *f*	acción preferente *f*
Vorzugsrabatt (D)	—	preferential discount	remise de faveur *f*	ribasso preferenziale *m*	rebaja preferencial *f*
votazione (I)	Stimmabgabe *f*	vote	vote *m*	—	voto *m*
vote (E)	Stimmabgabe *f*	—	vote *m*	votazione *f*	voto *m*
vote (F)	Stimmabgabe *f*	vote	—	votazione *f*	voto *m*
voting (E)	Stimme *f*	—	voix *f*	voto *m*	voz *f*
voto (Es)	Stimmabgabe *f*	vote	vote *m*	votazione *f*	—
voto (I)	Stimme *f*	voting	voix *f*	—	voz *f*
voucher[1] (E)	Beleg *m*	—	justificatif *m*	quietanza *f*	justificativo *m*

	D	E	F	I	Es
voucher² (E)	Bon *m*	—	bon *m*	buono *m*	bono *m*
voyageur de commerce (F)	festangestellter Reisender *m*	sales representative	—	commesso viaggiatore *m*	viajante *m*
voz (Es)	Stimme *f*	voting	voix *f*	voto *m*	—
vue d'ensemble du marché (F)	Marktübersicht *f*	overall view of the market	—	quadro del mercato *m*	panorama de mercado *m*
vuelo fletado (Es)	Charterflug *m*	charter flight	vol charter *m*	volo charter *m*	—
Wachstum (D)	—	growth	croissance *f*	crescita *f*	crecimiento *m*
Wachstumsimpuls (D)	—	growth impulse	stimulation de l'accroissement *f*	impulso di crescita *m*	impulso de crecimiento *m*
Wachstumspolitik (D)	—	growth policy	politique d'accroissement *f*	politica di crescita *f*	política de creci-miento económico *f*
Wachstumsrate (D)	—	rate of growth	taux d'accroissement *m*	tasso di crescita *m*	tasa de crecimiento *f*
wage (E)	Lohn *m*	—	salaire *m*	salario *m*	salario *m*
wage agreement (E)	Lohnvereinbarung *f*	—	accord de salaires *m*	accordo salariale *m*	pacto salarial *m*
wage claim (E)	Lohnforderung *f*	—	revendication de salaire *f*	rivendicazione salariale *f*	reivindicación salarial *f*
wage freeze (E)	Lohnstopp *m*	—	blocage des salaires *m*	blocco dei salari *m*	congelación salarial *f*
wage-intensive (E)	lohnintensiv	—	déterminé par le facteur salaire	ad alta incidenza salariale	con gran intensidad de costos salariales
wage lag (E)	Lohnlag *m*	—	décalage entre les prix et les salaires *m*	lag salariale *m*	diferencial entre precios y salarios *m*
Wagenladung (D)	—	cartload	charge de voiture *f*	carico di autocarro *m*	carga de un vagón *f*
wage policy (E)	Lohnpolitik *f*	—	politique des salaires *f*	politica salariale *f*	política salarial *f*
wage-price spiral (E)	Lohn-Preis-Spirale *f*	—	course des prix et des salaires *f*	spirale prezzi-salari *f*	espiral salarios-precios *m*
wages (paid) in kind (E)	Naturallohn *m*	—	rémunérarion du travail en nature *f*	remunerazione in natura *f*	salario en especie *m*
wage tax (E)	Lohnsteuer *f*	—	impôt sur les traite-ments et salaires *m*	imposta sui salari *f*	impuesto sobre los rendimientos del trabajo personal *f*
Wagnis (D)	—	venture	risque *m*	rischio *m*	riesgo *m*
wagon frigorifique (F)	Kühlwagen *m*	cold storage lorry	—	vagone frigorifero *m*	vagón frigorífico *m*
Wahlkonsul (D)	—	honorary consul	consul honoraire *m*	console onorario *m*	cónsul honorario *m*
Wahrscheinlichkeits-rechnung (D)	—	calculation of probabilities	calcul des probabilités *m*	calcolo della probabilità *m*	cálculo de probabilidades *m*
Währung (D)	—	currency	monnaie *f*	valuta *f*/moneta *f*	moneda *f*
Währungs-abkommen (D)	—	currency agreement	accord monétaire *m*	accordo monetario *m*	acuerdo monetario *m*
Währungsbehörde (D)	—	monetary authority	autorité monétaire *f*	autorità monetaria *f*	autoridad monetaria *f*
Währungsexperte (D)	—	monetary expert	expert monétaire *m*	esperto in materia monetaria *m*	experto en materia monetaria *m*
Währungsgebiet (D)	—	currency area	zone monétaire *f*	area monetaria *f*	área monetaria *f*
Währungsklausel (D)	—	currency clause	clause monétaire *f*	clausola monetaria *f*	cláusula monetaria *f*
Währungskonto (D)	—	currency account	compte en monnaies étrangères *m*	conto in valuta *m*	cuenta de moneda extranjera *f*
Währungspolitik (D)	—	monetary policy	politique monétaire *f*	politica monetaria *f*	política monetaria *f*
Währungsrisiko (D)	—	currency risk	risque de change *m*	rischio monetario *m*	riesgo monetario *m*
Währungsschlange (D)	—	currency snake	serpent monétaire *m*	serpente monetario *m*	serpiente monetaria *f*
Währungsunion (D)	—	monetary union	union monétaire *f*	unione monetaria *f*	unión monetaria *f*
Währungszone (D)	—	currency zone	zone monétaire *f*	zona monetaria *f*	zona monetaria *f*
waiting time (E)	Wartezeit *f*	—	temps d'attente *m*	tempo d'attesa *m*	tiempo de espera *m*
Wandelschuld-verschreibung (D)	—	convertible bonds	obligation convertible *f*	obbligazione convertibile *f*	obligaciones convertibles *f pl*

	D	E	F	I	Es
Ware (D)	—	goods	marchandise *f*	merce *f*	mercancía *f*
warehouse (E)	Lager *n*	—	magasin *m*	magazzino *m*	almacén *m*
warehouse rent (E)	Lagermiete *f*	—	location d'une surface pour magasinage *f*	spese di magazzinaggio *f pl*	alquiler de almacenaje *m*
warehouse warrant (E)	Lagerschein *m*	—	certificat de dépot *m*	ricevuta di deposito *f*	resguardo de almacén *m*
Warenart (D)	—	class of goods	catégorie de marchandise *f*	tipo di merce *m*	categoría de mercancías *f*
Warenausgang (D)	—	outgoing goods	sortie de marchandises *f*	uscita merci *f*	salida de mercancías *f*
Warenaustausch (D)	—	exchange of goods	échanges commerciaux *m pl*	scambio merci *m*	intercambio de mercancías *m*
Warenbestand (D)	—	stock	stock de marchandises *m*	scorte merci *f pl*	existencias de mercancías *f pl*
Warenbörse (D)	—	commodity exchange	bourse de marchandises *f*	borsa merci *f*	bolsa de mercancías *f*
Wareneingang (D)	—	arrival of goods	entrée de marchandises *f*	entrata merci *f*	entrada de mercancías *f*
Warengruppe (D)	—	product line	groupe de marchandises *m*	gruppo merci *m*	grupo de mercancías *m*
Warenhaus (D)	—	department store	grand magasin *m*	grande magazzino *m*	gran almacén *m*
Warenknappheit (D)	—	shortage of goods	pénurie de marchandises *f*	scarsità di merci *f*	escasez de mercancías *f*
Warenkredit (D)	—	trade credit	avance sur marchandises *f*	credito su merci *m*	crédito comercial *m*
Warenlager (D)	—	stock room	stock de marchandises *m*	magazzino *m*	depósito de mercancías *m*
Warenprobe (D)	—	sample	échantillon *m*	campione *m*	muestra *f*
Warensendung (D)	—	consignment of goods	expédition de marchandises *f*	spedizione di merci *f*	envío de mercancías *m*
Warenterminbörse (D)	—	commodity forward exchange	bourse d'opérations à livrer *f*	borsa merci a termine *f*	bolsa de mercancías a plazo *m*
Warentermin-geschäft (D)	—	commodity forward transaction	opération de livraison à terme *f*	operazione a termine su merci *f*	operación a plazo de mercancías *f*
Warenterminhandel (D)	—	commodity forward dealing	commerce d'opéra-tions à terme *m*	operazioni a termine su merci *f pl*	tráfico de futuro *m*
Warenwechsel (D)	—	commercial bill	traite commerciale *f*	cambiale commerciale *f*	letra comercial *f*
Warenzeichen (D)	—	trade mark	marque *f*	marchio *m*	marca *f*
warranted characteristics (E)	zugesicherte Eigenschaften *pl*	—	qualité promise *f*	caratteristiche promesse *f pl*	calidades aseguradas *f pl*
warranty[1] (E)	Garantie *f*	—	garantie *f*	garanzia *f*	garantía *f*
warranty[2] (E)	Gewährleistung *f*	—	prestation de garantie *f*	garanzia *f*	garantía *f*
Wartezeit (D)	—	waiting time	temps d'attente *m*	tempo d'attesa *m*	tiempo de espera *m*
Wasserschaden (D)	—	damage caused by water	dommage causé par l'eau *m*	danno dovuto all'acqua *m*	daño causado por el agua *m*
Wasserstraße (D)	—	waterway	voie d'eau *f*	via d'acqua *f*	vía navegable *f*
Wasser-verschmutzung (D)	—	water pollution	contamination des eaux *f*	inquinamento delle acque *m*	contaminación del agua *f*
waste (E)	Abfall *m*	—	déchet *m*	rifiuti *m pl*	desechos *m pl*
waste disposal[1] (E)	Abfallbeseitigung *f*	—	élimination de déchets *f*	smaltimento dei rifiuti *m*	evacuación de residuos *f*
waste disposal[2] (E)	Entsorgung *f*	—	dépollution *f*	smaltimento *m*	eliminación *f*
waste management (E)	Abfallwirtschaft *f*	—	industrie de déchets *f*	industria dei rifiuti *f*	industria de desperdicios *f*
waste oil (E)	Altöl *n*	—	huile usée *f*	olio usato *m*	aceite usado *m*
waste water (E)	Abwasser *n*	—	eaux résiduelles *f pl*	acque di scarico *f pl*	aguas residuales *f pl*
water pollution (E)	Wasser-verschmutzung *f*	—	contamination des eaux *f*	inquinamento delle acque *m*	contaminación del agua *f*
waterway (E)	Wasserstraße *f*	—	voie d'eau *f*	via d'acqua *f*	vía navegable *f*
wear and tear (E)	Abnutzung *f*	—	dépréciation *f*	usura *f*	desgaste *m*

	D	E	F	I	Es
Wechsel (D)	—	bill of exchange	lettre de change *f*	cambiale *f*	letra de cambio *f*
Wechselkredit (D)	—	acceptance credit	crédit d'escompte *m*	credito cambiario *m*	crédito cambiario *m*
Wechselkurs (D)	—	exchange rate	cours du change *m*	cambio *m*	tipo de cambio *m*
Wechselprotest (D)	—	protest	protêt de traite *m*	protesto cambiario *m*	protesto de letra *m*
Wechselreiterei (D)	—	kiteflying	tirage d'une traite de cavalerie *m*	emissione di tratte incrociate *f*	libramiento de letras cruzadas *m*
weekly (E)	wöchentlich	—	hebdomadaire	settimanale	semanal
Wegenetz (D)	—	road network	voirie *f*	rete stradale *f*	comunicaciones *f pl*
weiche Währung (D)	—	soft currency	monnaie faible *f*	moneta debole *f*	moneda blanda *f*
weight (E)	Gewicht *n*	—	poids *m*	peso *m*	peso *m*
weight of fine gold (E)	Feingewicht *n*	—	poids de métal fin *m*	peso fino *m*	peso fino *m*
Weihnachten (D)	—	Christmas	Noël *m*	Natale *m*	Navidad *f*
Weiterverarbeitung (D)	—	further processing	transformation complémentaire *f*	trasformazione *f*	elaboración ulterior *f*
welfare state (E)	Wohlfahrtsstaat *m*	—	Etat social *m*	stato assistenziale *m*	estado de bienestar *m*
well-price offer (E)	preisgünstiges Angebot *n*	—	offre à un avantageux *f*	offerta a buon prezzo *f*	oferta favorable *f*
Weltbank (D)	—	World Bank	banque mondiale *f*	Banca Mondiale *f*	Banco Mundial *m*
Welthandel (D)	—	world trade	commerce mondial *m*	commercio mondiale *m*	comercio internacional *m*
Weltmarktpreis (D)	—	world market price	prix du marché mondial *m*	prezzo di mercato mondiale *m*	precio del mercado mundial *m*
Weltwährungssystem (D)	—	international monetary system	système monétaire international *m*	sistema monetario internazionale *m*	sistema monetario internacional *m*
Weltwirtschaft (D)	—	world economy	économie mondiale *f*	economia mondiale *f*	economía internacional *f*
Weltwirtschaftskrise (D)	—	worldwide economic crisis	crise économique mondiale *f*	crisi dell'economia mondiale *f*	crisis económica internacional *f*
Weltwirtschaftsordnung (D)	—	international economic order	ordre économique mondial *m*	sistema economico mondiale *m*	orden económico mundial *m*
Werbeabteilung (D)	—	publicity department	service de publicité *m*	reparto pubblicità *m*	sección de publicidad *f*
Werbeagentur (D)	—	advertising agency	agence de publicité *f*	agenzia pubblicitaria *f*	agencia publicitaria *f*
Werbeaktion (D)	—	advertising activity	campagne publicitaire *f*	azione pubblicitaria *f*	campaña publicitaria *f*
Werbebotschaft (D)	—	sales message	message publicitaire *m*	messaggio pubblicitario *m*	mensaje publicitario *m*
Werbebrief (D)	—	advertising letter	lettre publicitaire *f*	lettera pubblicitaria *f*	circular de publicidad *m*
Werbebudget (D)	—	advertising budget	budget de publicité *m*	budget pubblicitario *m*	presupuesto publicitario *m*
Werbeerfolgskontrolle (D)	—	advertising control	contrôle du résultat de la publicité *m*	controllo del successo pubblicitario *m*	análisis del resultado publicitario *m*
Werbefachmann (D)	—	advertising expert	technicien publicitaire *m*	esperto di pubblicità *m*	perito publicitario *m*
Werbefilm (D)	—	advertising film	film publicitaire *m*	film pubblicitario *m*	película promocional *f*
Werbefrequenz (D)	—	advertising frequency	fréquence publicitaire *f*	frequenza della pubblicità *f*	frecuencia publicitaria *f*
Werbegeschenk (D)	—	advertising gift	cadeau publicitaire *m*	omaggio pubblicitario *m*	regalo publicitario *m*
Werbekampagne (D)	—	advertising campaign	campagne publicitaire *f*	campagna pubblicitaria *f*	campaña publicitaria *f*
Werbemedien (D)	—	advertising media	médias publicitaires *m pl*	mezzi pubblicitari *m pl*	medios de publicidad *m pl*
Werbemittel (D)	—	advertising aids	moyen publicitaire *m*	mezzo pubblicitario *m*	medio publicitario *m*
Werbereichweite (D)	—	scope of advertising effect	zone de rayonnement de la publicité *f*	raggio d'azione della pubblicità *m*	alcance publicitario *m*
Werbespot (D)	—	commercial	spot publicitaire *m*	spot pubblicitario *m*	spot publicitario *m*
Werbetext (D)	—	advertising copy	texte publicitaire *m*	testo pubblicitario *m*	texto publicitario *m*

	D	E	F	I	Es
Werbeträger (D)	—	advertising medium	support publicitaire *m*	veicolo pubblicitario *m*	medio de publicidad *m*
Werbeverbot (D)	—	ban on advertising	défense de publicité *f*	divieto di pubblicità *m*	prohibición de publicidad *f*
Werbeziele (D)	—	advertising objective	objectifs publicitaires *m pl*	obiettivi pubblicitari *m pl*	objetivos de la publicidad *m pl*
Werbung (D)	—	publicity	publicité *f*	pubblicità *f*	publicidad *f*
Werft (D)	—	shipyard	chantier naval *m*	cantiere navale *m*	astillero *m*
Werk (D)	—	plant	usine *f*	stabilimento *m*	planta *f*
Werkschutz (D)	—	works protection force	corps de sécurité d'entreprise *m*	servizio di sorve-glianza aziendale *m*	policía de la empresa *f*
Werkspionage (D)	—	industrial espionage	espionnage industriel *m*	spionaggio aziendale *m*	espionaje industrial *m*
Werkvertrag (D)	—	contract for work and services	contrat de louage d'ouvrage et d'industrie *m*	contratto d'appalto *m*	contrato de obra *m*
Wert (D)	—	value	valeur *f*	valore *m*	valor *m*
Wertberichtigung (D)	—	value adjustment	réévaluation *f*	rettifica del valore *f*	rectificación de valor *f*
Wertbrief (D)	—	insured letter	lettre avec valeur déclarée *f*	lettera con valore dichiarato *f*	letra con valor declarado *f*
Wertminderung (D)	—	decrease in value	diminution de la valeur *f*	riduzione di valore *f*	depreciación *f*
Wertpapier (D)	—	security	titre *m*/valeur *f*	titolo *m*	título *m*/valor *m*
Wertpapierbörse (D)	—	securities market	bourse des titres et valeurs *f*	borsa valori *f*	mercado de valores *m*
Wertpapierfonds (D)	—	securities fund	fonds de valeurs mobilières *m*	fondo titoli *m*	fondo de inversión mobiliaria *m*
Wertpapier-geschäft (D)	—	securities business	opérations sur titres *f pl*	operazioni su titoli *f pl*	operación con valores *f*
Wertschöpfung (D)	—	value added	création de valeurs *f*	valore aggiunto *m*	creación de riqueza *f*
Wertsendung (D)	—	consignment with value declared	envoi avec valeur déclarée *m*	spedizione con valore dichiarato *f*	envío con valor declarado *m*
Wertsicherungs-klausel (D)	—	stable value clause	clause de stabilité *f*	clausola di garanzia monetaria *f*	cláusula de índice variable *f*
Wertverfall (D)	—	loss of value	dévalorisation *f*	deprezzamento *m*	depreciación *f*
wertvoll (D)	—	valuable	précieux	prezioso	precioso
Wertzoll (D)	—	ad valorem duty	taxe de douane ad valorem *f*	dazio ad valorem *m*	aduanas ad valorem *f pl*
Wertzuwachs (D)	—	appreciation	accroissement de valeur *m*	incremento di valore *m*	plusvalía *f*
wesentliche Bestandteile (D)	—	integral part	parties constitutives essentielles *f pl*	componenti essenziali *f pl*	partes integrantes esencial *f pl*
Wettbewerb (D)	—	competition	compétition *f*	concorrenza *f*	competencia *f*
Wettbewerbs-beschränkung (D)	—	restraint of competition	restriction apportée à la concurrence *f*	restrizione della concorrenza *f*	restricciones a la competencia *f pl*
Wettbewerbs-fähigkeit (D)	—	competitiveness	compétitivité *f*	competitività *f*	competitividad *f*
Wettbewerbspolitik (D)	—	competition policy	politique de concurrence *f*	politica concorrenziale *f*	política de competencia *f*
Wettbewerbsrecht (D)	—	law on competition	législation en matière de concurrence commerciale *m*	diritto della concorrenza *m*	derecho de la competencia *m*
Wettbewerbsverbot (D)	—	prohibition of competition	interdiction en matière de concurrence *f*	divieto di concorrenza *m*	prohibición de competencia *f*
Wettbewerbs-verstoß (D)	—	violation of competition rules	violation de concurrence *f*	violazione delle regole di concorrenza *f*	violación de las reglas de competencia *f*
Wettbewerbsvorteil (D)	—	competitive advantage	avantage de concurrence *m*	vantaggio concorrenziale	ventaja de competencia *f*
white-collar crime (E)	Wirtschafts-kriminalität *f*	—	délinquance économique *f*	criminalità economica *f*	criminalidad económica *f*
white-collar delinquency (E)	White-collar-Kriminalität *f*	—	délinquance économique *f*	criminalità dei colletti bianchi *f*	criminalidad económica *f*

	D	E	F	I	Es
White-collar Kriminalität (D)	—	white-collar delinquency	délinquance économique *f*	criminalità dei colletti bianchi *f*	criminalidad económica *f*
wholesale prices (E)	Großhandels-preise *pl*	—	prix de gros *m*	prezzo all'ingrosso *m*	precio mayorista *m*
wholesaler (E)	Grossist *m*	—	grossiste *m*	grossista *m*	mayorista *m*
wholesale trade (E)	Großhandel *m*	—	commerce de gros *m*	commercio all'ingrosso *m*	comercio mayorista *m*
widerrufen (D)	—	revoke	révoquer	revocare	revocar
Widerrufsklausel (D)	—	revocation clause	clause de révocation *f*	clausola di revoca *f*	cláusula revocatoria *f*
Widerrufsrecht (D)	—	right of revocation	droit de révocation *m*	diritto di revoca *m*	derecho de revocación *m*
Wiederaufbau (D)	—	reconstruction	reconstruction *f*	ricostruzione *f*	reconstrucción *f*
Wiederausfuhr (D)	—	reexportation	réexportation *f*	riesportazione *f*	reexportación *f*
Wiederbeschaffung (D)	—	replacement	réapprovisionne-ment *m*	riapprovvigiona-mento *m*	reposición *f*
Wiederverkäufer (D)	—	reseller	revendeur *m*	rivenditore *m*	revendedor *m*
Wieder-verkaufspreis (D)	—	resale price	prix de revente *m*	prezzo di rivendita *m*	precio de reventa *m*
wiederverwertbar (D)	—	recyclable	réutilisable	riutilizzabile	recuperable
Willenserklärung (D)	—	declaration of intent	déclaration de volonté *f*	dichiarazione di volontà *f*	declaración de la voluntad *f*
Windenergie (D)	—	eolian energy	énergie éolienne *f*	energia eolica *f*	energía eólica *f*
window dressing (E)	Schaufenster-dekoration *f*	—	décoration de vitrine *f*	allestimento di vetrina *m*	adorno del escaparate *m*
Wirtschaft (D)	—	economy	économie *f*	economia *f*	economía *f*
wirtschaftliche Integration (D)	—	economic integration	intégration économique *f*	integrazione economica *f*	integración económica *f*
wirtschaftliche Nutzung (D)	—	economic use	utilisation économique *f*	utilizzo economico *m*	utilización económica *f*
wirtschaftliches Prinzip (D)	—	economic principle	principe économique *m*	principio economico *m*	principio económico *m*
Wirtschaftlichkeit (D)	—	economic efficiency	rentabilité *f*	economicità *f*	rentabilidad *f*
Wirtschaftsanalyse (D)	—	economic analysis	analyse de l'économie *f*	analisi economica *f*	análisis económico *m*
Wirtschaftsboykott (D)	—	economic boycott	boycottage économique *m*	boicottaggio economico *m*	boicot económico *m*
Wirtschaftsexperte (D)	—	economic expert	expert économique *m*	esperto in materia economica *m*	economista *m*
Wirtschafts-gemeinschaft (D)	—	economic community	communauté économique *f*	comunità economica *f*	comunidad económica *f*
Wirtschafts-geographie (D)	—	economic geography	géographie économique *f*	geografia economica *f*	geografía económica *f*
Wirtschafts-geschichte (D)	—	economic history	histoire économique *f*	storia economica *f*	historia económica *f*
Wirtschaftsgut (D)	—	economic good	bien économique *m*	bene economico *m*	bien económico *m*
Wirtschaftsjahr (D)	—	business year	exercice comptable *m*	esercizio *m*	ejercicio *m*
Wirtschafts-konzentration (D)	—	economic concentration	concentration économique *f*	concentrazione economica *f*	concentración económica *f*
Wirtschafts-kreislauf (D)	—	economic cycle	circuit économique *m*	circuito economico *m*	circuito económico *m*
Wirtschaftskrieg (D)	—	economic war	guerre économique *f*	guerra economica *f*	guerra económica *f*
Wirtschafts-kriminalität (D)	—	white-collar crime	délinquance économique *f*	criminalità economica *f*	criminalidad económica *f*
Wirtschaftskrise (D)	—	economic crisis	crise économique *f*	crisi economica *f*	crisis económica *f*
Wirtschaftsordnung (D)	—	economic order	ordre économique *m*	ordinamento economico *m*	orden económico *m*
Wirtschaftsplan (D)	—	economic plan	plan économique *m*	piano economico *m*	plan económico *m*
Wirtschaftspolitik (D)	—	economic policy	politique économique *f*	politica economica *f*	política económica *f*

	D	E	F	I	Es
wirtschaftspolitische Zielsetzung (D)	—	economy policy objectives	objectifs commandés par une politique économique *m pl*	obiettivo della politica economica *m*	objetivos de la política económica *m pl*
Wirtschaftsprüfer (D)	—	auditor	expert comptable économique et financier *m*	revisore dei conti *m*	revisor de cuentas *m*/ experto contable *m*
Wirtschaftsprüfung (D)	—	auditing	contrôle de la gestion et des comptes *m*	revisione *f*	revisoría *f*
Wirtschafts-rechnung (D)	—	economic account	comptabilisation économique *f*	conto economico *m*	contabilización económica *f*
Wirtschaftsrecht (D)	—	economic law	législation économique *f*	diritto economico *m*	derecho económico *m*
Wirtschaftsstatistik (D)	—	housekeeping account	statistique économique *f*	statistica economica *f*	estadística económica *f*
Wirtschaftsstruktur (D)	—	economic structure	structure économique *f*	struttura economica *f*	estructura económica *f*
Wirtschafts-theorie (D)	—	economic theory	théorie économique *f*	teoria dell'economia *f*	teoría económica *f*
Wirtschaftsunion (D)	—	economic union	union économique *f*	unione economica *f*	unión económica *f*
Wirtschaftsverband (D)	—	trade association	association économique *f*	associazione economica *f*	asociación económica *f*
Wirtschaftsverlauf (D)	—	course of the economic evolution	évolution économique *f*	andamento dell'economia *m*	evolución económica *f*
Wirtschafts-wachstum (D)	—	economic growth	croissance économique *f*	crescita economica *f*	crecimiento económico *m*
Wirtschafts-wissenschaften (D)	—	economics	sciences économiques *f pl*	scienze economiche *f pl*	ciencias económicas *f pl*
Wirtschaftszweig (D)	—	field of the economy	secteur économique *m*	settore economico *m*	ramo económico *m*
within (E)	binnen	—	dans le délai de	entro	en el término de
with non-distributed dividend (E)	ohne Dividende	—	sans dividende *m*	senza dividendo	sin dividendo
without competition (E)	konkurrenzlos	—	défiant toute concurrence	senza concorrenza	sin competencia
without obligation (E)	ohne Obligo	—	sans engagement	senza obbligo	sin obligación
without garanty (E)	ohne Gewähr	—	sous toute réserve	senza garanzia	sin garantía
without prior notice (E)	fristlos	—	sans délai	senza preavviso	sin plazo
wöchentlich (D)	—	weekly	hebdomadaire	settimanale	semanal
Wohlfahrtsstaat (D)	—	welfare state	Etat social *m*	stato assistenziale *m*	estado de bienestar *m*
Wohlstand (D)	—	prosperity	prospérité *f*	benessere *m*	bienestar *m*
Wohlstands-gesellschaft (D)	—	affluent society	société de bien-être *f*	società del benessere *f*	sociedad de bienestar *f*
Wohnung (D)	—	flab	appartement *m*	abitazione *f*	vivienda *f*
Wohnungsbau (D)	—	housing construction	construction de logements *f*	edilizia abitativa *f*	construcción de viviends *f*
Wohnungs-eigentum (D)	—	ownership of a flat	propriété du logement *f*	proprietà edilizia *f*	propiedad de vivienda *f*
Wohnungswechsel (D)	—	change of residence	transfert de résidence *m*	cambiamento dell'abitazione *m*	cambio de vivienda *m*
word processing (E)	Textverarbeitung *f*	—	élaboration de texte *f*	elaborazione testi *f*	tratamiento de textos *m*
work (E)	Arbeit *f*	—	travail *m*	lavoro *m*	trabajo *m*
worker (E)	Arbeiter *m*	—	travailleur *m*	operaio *m*	trabajador *m*
worker participation (E)	Arbeitnehmer-beteiligung *f*	—	participation du personnel *f*	partecipazione dei prestatori d'opera *f*	participación de los empleados *f*
working capital (E)	Betriebskapital *n*	—	capital de roulement *m*	capitale d'esercizio *m*	capital de explotación *m*
working class (E)	Arbeiterklasse *f*	—	classe ouvrière *f*	classe degli operai *f*	clase obrera *f*
working conditions and human relations (E)	Betriebsklima *n*	—	climat social *m*	atmosfera di lavoro *f*	ambiente de trabajo *m*
working day (E)	Arbeitstag *m*	—	jour de travail *m*	giorno lavorativo *m*	día laboral *m*

	D	E	F	I	Es
working hours (E)	Arbeitszeit *f*	—	heures de travail *f pl*	orario di lavoro *m*	jornada laboral *f*
working lunch (E)	Arbeitsessen *n*	—	déjeuner de travail *m*	pranzo di lavoro *m*	comida de trabajo *f*
working technique (E)	Arbeitstechnik *f*	—	technique de travail *f*	tecnica lavorativa *f*	técnica del trabajo *f*
working week (E)	Arbeitswoche *f*	—	semaine de travail *f*	settimana lavorativa *f*	semana laboral *f*
work performed (E)	Arbeitsertrag *m*	—	rendement du travail *m*	rendimento del lavoro *m*	rendimiento del trabajo *m*
work permit (E)	Arbeitserlaubnis *f*	—	permis de travail *m*	permesso di lavoro *m*	permiso de trabajo *m*
work rhythm (E)	Arbeitsrhythmus *m*	—	rythme de travail *m*	ritmo di lavoro *m*	ritmo de trabajo *m*
workroom (E)	Arbeitsraum *m*	—	lieu de travail *m*	locale di lavoro *m*	sala de trabajo *f*
works protection force (E)	Werkschutz *m*	—	corps de sécurité d'entreprise *m*	servizio di sorve-glianza aziendale *m*	policía de la empresa *f*
World Bank (E)	Weltbank *f*	—	banque mondiale *f*	Banca Mondiale *f*	Banco Mundial *m*
world economy (E)	Weltwirtschaft *f*	—	économie mondiale *f*	economia mondiale *f*	economía internacional *f*
world market price (E)	Weltmarktpreis *m*	—	prix du marché mondial *m*	prezzo di mercato mondiale *m*	precio del mercado mundial *m*
world trade (E)	Welthandel *m*	—	commerce mondial *m*	commercio mondiale *m*	comercio internacional *m*
worldwide economic crisis (E)	Weltwirtschaftskrise *f*	—	crise économique mondiale *f*	crisi dell'economia mondiale *f*	crisis económica internacional *f*
written (E)	schriftlich	—	par écrit	per iscritto	por escrito
written form (E)	Schriftform *f*	—	forme par écrit *f*	forma scritta *f*	forma escrita *f*
Wucher (D)	—	usuary	usure *f*	usura *f*	usura *f*
yield (E)	Rendite *f*	—	rendement *m*	rendita *f*	rentabilidad *f*
young businessman (E)	Jungunternehmer *m*	—	entrepreneur débutant *m*	imprenditore giovane *m*	joven empresario *m*
Zahl (D)	—	number/ figure	nombre *m*/ chiffre *m*	numero *m*/ cifra *f*	número *m*/ cifra *f*
zahlbar (D)	—	payable	payable	pagabile	pagable
Zahlkarte (D)	—	money order	mandat-carte *m*	modulo di versamento *m*	carta de pago *f*
Zahltag (D)	—	payday	jour de paye *m*	giorno di paga *m*	día de pago *m*
Zahlung (D)	—	payment	payement *m*	pagamento *m*	pago *m*
Zahlung per Nachnahme (D)	—	cash on delivery	payement contre remboursement *m*	pagamento contro assegno *m*	pago contra reembolso *m*
Zahlungs-abkommen (D)	—	payments arrangement	accord de payement *m*	accordo di pagamento *m*	acuerdo de pagos *m*
Zahlungsanweisung (D)	—	order to pay	mandat de payement *m*	ordine di pagamento *m*	orden de pago *f*
Zahlungsaufschub (D)	—	extension of time for payment	sursis de payement *m*	dilazione del pagamento *f*	pago aplazado *m*
Zahlungsbedingung (D)	—	terms of payment	conditions de payement *f pl*	condizione di pagamento *f*	condiciones de pago *f pl*
Zahlungsbefehl (D)	—	order for payment	ordre de payement *m*	ingiunzione di pagamento *f*	mandamiento de pago *m*
Zahlungs-berechtigter (D)	—	beneficiary of payment	bénéficiaire du payement *m*	beneficiario del pagamento *m*	beneficiario del pago *m*
Zahlungs-bestätigung (D)	—	receipt for payment	confirmation de payement *f*	conferma di pagamento *f*	confirmación de pago *f*
Zahlungsbilanz (D)	—	balance of payments	balance des payements *f*	bilancia dei pagamenti *f*	balanza de pagos *f*
Zahlungs-bilanzdefizit (D)	—	deficit in the balance of payments	balance des payements déficitaire *f*	disavanzo della bilancia dei pagamenti *m*	déficit en la balanza de pagos *m*
Zahlungsbilanz-gleichgewicht (D)	—	equilibrium of the balance of payments	balance des payements équilibrée *f*	equilibrio della bilancia dei pagamenti *m*	balanza de pagos equilibrada *f*
Zahlungsbilanz-politik (D)	—	balance of payments policy	politique en matière de la balance des payements *f*	politica della bilancia dei pagamenti *f*	política en materia de balanza de pagos *f*
Zahlungsbilanz-überschuß (D)	—	surplus in the balance of payments	balance des paye-ments excédentaire *f*	eccedenza della bilan-cia dei pagamenti *f*	superávit en la balanza de pagos *m*

	D	E	F	I	Es
Zahlungseinstellung (D)	—	cessation of payments	suspension de payement *f*	cessazione dei pagamenti *f*	suspensión de pagos *f*
zahlungsfähig (D)	—	solvent	solvable	solvibile	solvente
Zahlungsfähigkeit (D)	—	solvency	solvabilité *f*	solvibilità *f*	solvencia *f*
Zahlungsform (D)	—	payment system	forme de payement *f*	tipo di pagamento *m*	forma de pago *f*
Zahlungsfrist (D)	—	terms of payment	délai de payement *f*	scadenza di pagamento *f*	plazo de pago *m*
Zahlungsgewohnheit (D)	—	practice of payment	habitude de payement *f*	consuetudine di pagamento *f*	práctica de pago *f*
zahlungshalber (D)	—	on account of payment	pour raison de payement	a titolo di pagamento	a título de pago
Zahlungsmittel (D)	—	means of payment	moyen de payement *m*	mezzo di pagamento *m*	medio de pago *m*
Zahlungsrisiko (D)	—	risk of payment	risque de payement *m*	rischio di pagamento *m*	riesgo de pago *m*
Zahlungsrückstand (D)	—	payment in arrears	arriéré de payement *m*	morosità di pagamento *f*	pago atrasado *m*
Zahlungsschwierigkeit (D)	—	financial difficulties	difficultés financières *f pl*	difficoltà di pagamento *f*	dificultades de pago *f pl*
zahlungsstatt (D)	—	in lieu of payment	à titre de payement	a titolo di pagamento	a título de pago
Zahlungstermin (D)	—	date of payment	terme du payement *m*	termine di pagamento *m*	plazo de pago *m*
Zahlungsunfähigkeit (D)	—	insolvency	insolvabilité *f*	insolvenza *f*	insolvencia *f*
Zahlungsverkehr (D)	—	payment transaction	opérations de payement *f pl*	operazioni di pagamento *f pl*	servicio de pagos *m pl*
Zahlungsverzug (D)	—	failure to pay on due date	demeure du débiteur *f*	morosità di pagamento *f*	retraso en el pago *m*
Zahlungsziel (D)	—	period for payment	délai de payement *m*	termine di pagamento *m*	plazo de pago *m*
Zahlung unter Protest (D)	—	payment supra protest	payement sous protêt *m*	pagamento sotto protesta *m*	pago bajo protesta *m*
Zedent (D)	—	assignor	cédant *m*	cedente *m*	cedente *m*
Zeichnungsberechtigung (D)	—	authority to sign	autorisation de signer *f*	diritto di firma *m*	facultad de firma *f*
Zeitaufwand (D)	—	expenditure of time	temps passé *m*	tempo impiegato *m*	tiempo consagrado *m*
Zeitlohn (D)	—	time wage	salaire au temps *m*	salario a tempo *m*	salario por unidad de tiempo *m*
Zeitstudie (D)	—	time study	étude des temps *f*	analisi sul tempo impiegato *f*	estudio de tiempo *m*
Zeitungsanzeige (D)	—	advertisement	annonce de journal *f*	inserzione sul giornale *f*	anuncio de prensa *m*
Zeitwert (D)	—	current market value	valeur à une certaine date *f*	valore corrente *m*	valor actual *m*
Zentralbank (D)	—	central bank	banque centrale *f*	Banca Centrale *f*	banco emisor *m*
Zentralbankrat (D)	—	Central Bank Council	Conseil de la Banque Centrale *m*	consiglio superiore della Banca Centrale *m*	Consejo del Banco Central *m*
Zentraleinheit (D)	—	central unit	unité centrale *f*	unità centrale *f*	unidad central *f*
zentrale Planwirtschaft (D)	—	centrally controlled economy	économie planifiée centrale *f*	economia pianificata *f*	economía planificada central *f*
Zentralisierung (D)	—	centralization	centralisation *f*	centralizzazione *f*	centralización *f*
zero growth (E)	Nullwachstum *n*	—	croissance zéro *f*	crescita zero *f*	crecimiento cero *m*
Zertifikat (D)	—	certificate	certificat *m*	certificato *m*	certificado *m*
Zession (D)	—	assignment	cession *f*	cessione *f*	cesión *f*
Zessionar (D)	—	assignee	cessionnaire *m*	cessionario *m*	cesionario *m*
Zeugnis (D)	—	school report/ certificate/evidence	certificat scolaire *m*/ certificat *m*/ témoignage *m*	pagella *f*/ certificato *m*/ testimonianza *f*	certificado de escuela *m*/ certificado *m*/ testimonio *m*
Ziehungsrechte (D)	—	drawing rights	droits de tirage *m pl*	diritti di prelievo *m pl*	derechos de giro *m pl*

	D	E	F	I	Es
Ziel (D)	—	objective	but *m*	obiettivo *m*	objetivo *m*
Zielgruppe (D)	—	target group	groupe destinataire *m*	gruppo di riferimento *m*	grupo destinatario *m*
Zielkauf (D)	—	purchase on credit	achat à terme *m*	acquisto a termine *m*	compra a plazos *m*
Zielkonflikt (D)	—	conflicting goals	conflit d'objectifs *m*	incompatibilità degli obiettivi *f*	conflicto de objectivos *m*
Zielprojektion (D)	—	target projection	projection d'objectifs *f*	proiezione degli obiettivi *f*	proyección de objetivos *f*
Zins (D)	—	interest	intérêt *m*	interessi *m pl*	interés *m*
Zinsberechnung (D)	—	calculating the interest	calcul des intérêts *m*	calcolo degli interessi *m*	cálculo de intereses *m*
Zinsbindungsfrist (D)	—	lock-down period for interest rates	délai d'engagement sur le taux d'intérêt accordé *m*	scadenza degli interessi vincolati *f*	plazo de vinculación al tipo de interés pactado *f*
Zinsendienst (D)	—	interest service	service de l'intérêt *m*	servizio degli interessi *m*	servicio de intereses *m*
Zinserleichterung (D)	—	reduction of interest	minoration de l'intérêt *m*	agevolazione sugli interessi *f*	reducción de intereses *f*
Zinseszins (D)	—	compound interest	intérêt composé *m*	interessi composti *m pl*	interés compuesto *m*
Zinsfuß (D)	—	interest rate	taux d'intérêt *m*	tasso d'interesse *m*	tipo de interés *m*
Zinsgefälle (D)	—	margin between interest rates	disparité des niveaux d'intérêts *f*	differenza dei tassi d'interesse *f*	diferencia entre los tipos de interés *f*
Zinsmarge (D)	—	interest margin	marge entre les taux d'intérêt créditeur et débiteur *f*	margine degli interessi *m*	margen de interés *m*
Zinsniveau (D)	—	interest rate level	niveau du taux d'intérêt *m*	livello degli interessi *m*	nivel de interés *m*
Zinspolitik (D)	—	interest rate policy	politique en matière d'intérêts *f*	politica dei tassi d'interesse *f*	política en materia de intereses *f*
Zinsrechnung (D)	—	interest account	calcul des intérêts *m*	conteggio degli interessi *m*	cómputo de intereses *m*
Zinssatz (D)	—	interest rate	taux de l'intérêt *m*	tasso d'interesse *m*	tipo de interés *m*
Zinssenkung (D)	—	reduction of interest	diminution du taux de l'intérêt *f*	riduzione degli interessi *f*	reducción del tipo de interés *f*
Zoll (D)	—	customs/ customs duty	douane *f*/ droit de douane *m*	dogana *f*/dazio *m*	aduana *f*/arancel *m*
Zollabkommen (D)	—	customs convention	accord douanier *m* doganali *m*	accordo sulle tariffe	convenio aduanero *m*
Zollagerung (D)	—	customs warehouse procedure	dépôt en entrepôt sous douane *m*	immagazzinamento doganale *m*	depósito de aduana *m*
Zollanmeldung (D)	—	customs declaration	déclaration en douane *f*	dichiarazione doganale *f*	declaración arancelaria *f*
Zollantrag (D)	—	customs application	demande de dédouanement *f*	domanda di sdoganamento *f*	solicitud de aduana *f*
Zollausland (D)	—	foreign customs territory	territoire hors du contrôle de la douane *m*	territorio doganale estero *m*	territorio aduanero exterior *m*
Zollausschluß (D)	—	territory inside political but outside customs frontier	territoire considéré hors frontière douanière nationale *m*	zona franca *f*	exclave aduanero *m*
Zolleinfuhrschein (D)	—	bill of entry	acquit d'entrée *m*	bolletta d'entrata *m*	certificado de aduana *m*
Zollerklärung (D)	—	customs declaration	déclaration en douane *f*	dichiarazione doganale *f*	declaración arancelaria *f*
Zollfaktura (D)	—	customs invoice	facture douanière *f*	fattura doganale *f*	factura arancelaria *f*
Zollformalität (D)	—	customs formalities	formalité douanières *f*	formalità doganale *f*	formalidades aduaneras *f pl*
Zollfreischreibungsverfahren (D)	—	procedure of duty free admission	régime de l'admission en franchise *m*	procedura d'ammissione in franchigia *f*	régimen de admisión en franquicia *m*
Zollgebiet (D)	—	customs territory	territoire douanier *m*	territorio doganale *m*	distrito aduanero *m*
Zollgebühren (D)	—	customs duties	droit de douane *m*	diritti doganali *m pl*	derechos arancelarios *m pl*
Zollgrenze (D)	—	customs frontier	frontière douanière *f*	confine doganale *m*	frontera aduanera *f*

	D	E	F	I	Es
Zollgrenzgebiet (D)	—	customs frontier district	territoire de surveillance douanière *m*	area doganale di confine *f*	territorio aduanero fronterizo *m*
Zollinland (D)	—	domestic customs territory	territoire douanier national *m*	territorio doganale nazionale *m*	territorio aduanero interior *m*
Zollpapiere (D)	—	customs documents	documents douaniers *m pl*	documenti doganali *m pl*	documentos aduaneros *m pl*
Zollstelle (D)	—	customs office	bureau de douane *m*	posto di dogana *m*	oficina de aduanas *f*
Zolltarif (D)	—	customs tariff	tarif des douanes *m*	tariffa doganale *f*	tarifa arancelaria *f*
Zollunion (D)	—	customs union	union douanière *f*	unione doganale *f*	unión aduanera *f*
Zollverkehr (D)	—	customs procedure	régime douanier *m*	procedure doganali *f pl*	régimen aduanero de mercancías *m*
Zollverschluß (D)	—	customs seal	fermeture douanière *f*	sigillo doganale *m*	precinto aduanero *m*
zona (Es)	Zone *f*	zone	zone *f*	zona *f*	—
zona (I)	Zone *f*	zone	zone *f*	—	zona *f*
zona costera (Es)	Küstengewässer *n*	coastal waters	eaux côtières *f pl*	acque territoriali *f pl*	—
zona de librecambio (Es)	Freihandelszone *f*	free trade area	zone de libre-échange *f*	zona di libero scambio *f*	—
zona di libero scambio (I)	Freihandelszone *f*	free trade area	zone de libre-échange *f*	—	zona de librecambio *f*
zona di vendita (I)	Verkaufsgebiet *n*	sales territory	territoire de vente *m*	—	territorio de venta *m*
zona franca (I)	Zollausschluß *m*	territory inside political but outside customs frontier	territoire considéré hors frontière douanière nationale *m*	—	exclave aduanero *m*
zona industriale (I)	Industriegebiet *n*	industrial area	région industrielle *f*	—	región industrial *f*
zona monetaria (Es)	Währungszone *f*	currency zone	zone monétaire *f*	zona monetaria *f*	—
zona monetaria (I)	Währungszone *f*	currency zone	zone monétaire *f*	—	zona monetaria *f*
Zone (D)	—	zone	zone *f*	zona *f*	zona *f*
zone (E)	Zone *f*	—	zone *f*	zona *f*	zona *f*
zone (F)	Zone *f*	zone	—	zona *f*	zona *f*
zone de libre-échange (F)	Freihandelszone *f*	free trade area	—	zona di libero scambio *f*	zona de librecambio *f*
zone de rayonnement de la publicité (F)	Werbereichweite *f*	scope of advertising effect	—	raggio d'azione della pubblicità *m*	alcance publicitario *m*
zone monétaire[1] (F)	Währungszone *f*	currency zone	—	zona monetaria *f*	zona monetaria *f*
zone monétaire[2] (F)	Währungsgebiet *n*	currency area	—	area monetaria *f*	área monetaria *f*
zootecnia (I)	Tierzucht *f*	livestock breeding	élevage *m*	—	cría de animales *f*
Zugabe (D)	—	extra	prime *f*	aggiunta *f*	suplemento *m*
Zugang (D)	—	access	entrée *f*	accesso *m*	acceso *m*
zugesicherte Eigenschaften (D)	—	warranted characteristics	qualité promise *f*	caratteristiche promesse *f pl*	calidades aseguradas *f pl*
Zug um Zug (D)	—	concurrent	de point en point	contestualmente	punto por punto
Zukunftschance (D)	—	future prospects	perspectives d'avenir *f pl*	prospettiva *f*	posibilidades futuras *f pl*
Zulage (D)	—	increase/ additional pay	prime *f*/complément de salaire *m*	premio *m*/indennità *f*	suplemento *m*/plus *m*
Zulassung (D)	—	admission	admission *f*	ammissione *f*	admisión *f*
zu Lasten (D)	—	chargeable to	à la charge de qn	a carico di	a cargo de
Zulieferer (D)	—	supplier	sous-traitant *m*	fornitore *m*	abastecedor *m*
zur Ansicht (D)	—	on approval	à vue	in visione	para examen
Zusage (D)	—	promise	promesse *f*	conferma *f*	promesa *f*
Zusammenarbeit (D)	—	cooperation	collaboration *f*	collaborazione *f*	cooperación *f*
Zusatzverkauf (D)	—	additional sale	vente additionnelle *f*	vendita complementare *f*	venta adicional *f*
Zuschlag (D)	—	extra charge	supplément *m*	supplemento *m*/ premio *m*	suplemento *m*/ prima *f*
Zuschuß (D)	—	allowance	allocation *f*	sovvenzione *f*	subvención *f*
Zustellung (D)	—	delivery	remise *f*	notifica *f*/ recapito *m*	envío *m*

	D	E	F	I	Es
Zustimmung (D)	—	consent	accord *m*	consenso *m*	consentimiento *m*
Zuteilung (D)	—	allocation	répartition *f*	attribuzione *f*/ ripartizione *f*	asignación *f*
zu treuen Händen (D)	—	for safekeeping	remettre en mains sûres	alla particolare attenzione	a la atención
zuverlässig (D)	—	reliable	de confiance	affidabile	de confianza
Zuwendung (D)	—	bestowal	affectation *f*	assegnazione *f*	gratificación *f*
Zwangssparen (D)	—	compulsory saving	épargne forcée *f*	risparmio coatto *m*	ahorro forzoso *m*
Zwangsvergleich (D)	—	compulsory settlement	arrangement forcé *m*	concordato fallimentare *m*	convenio forzoso *m*
Zwangsverkauf (D)	—	forced sale	vente forcée *f*	vendita giudiziaria *f*	venta forzada *f*
Zwangs-versteigerung (D)	—	sale by court order	vente de biens par justice *f*	asta giudiziaria *f*	subasta forzosa *f*
Zwangsverwaltung (D)	—	receivership	séquestre judiciare *m*	amministrazione giudiziaria *f*	administración forzosa *f*
Zwangs-vollstreckung (D)	—	judicial execution	exécution forcée *f*	esecuzione forzata *f*	ejecución forzosa *f*
Zweckverband (D)	—	special purpose association	association à but déterminé *f*	consorzio intercomunale *m*	asociación con un fin determinado *f*
zweifelhafte Forderung (D)	—	doubtful account	créance douteuse *f*	credito dubbio *m*	créditos dudosos *m pl*
Zweigbetrieb (D)	—	branch business	établissement secondaire *m*	filiale *f*	sucursal *f*
Zweig-niederlassung (D)	—	branch office	succursale *f*	succursale *f*	filial *f*
Zweigstelle (D)	—	branch	agence *f*	agenzia *f*	filial *f*
Zwischenabnahme (D)	—	intermediate purchase	achat intermédiaire *m*	acquisto intermediario *m*	compra intermediaria *f*
Zwischenbilanz (D)	—	interim balance sheet	bilan intermédiaire *m*	bilancio provvisorio *m*	balance intermedio *m*
Zwischenhändler (D)	—	middleman	intermédiaire *m*	intermediario *m*	intermediario *m*
Zwischenkonto (D)	—	interim account	compte provisoire *m*	conto transitorio *m*	cuenta provisional *f*
Zwischenzeugnis (D)	—	interim report	certificat provisoire *m*	certificato provvisorio *m*	certificado provisional *m*
Zyklus (D)	—	cycle	cycle *m*	ciclo *m*	ciclo *m*

	D	E	F	I	Es
	Grundzahlen	**cardinal numbers**	**nombres cardinaux**	**numeri cardinali**	**números cardinales**
1	eins	one	un, une	uno	uno
2	zwei	two	deux	due	dos
3	drei	three	trois	tre	tres
4	vier	four	quatre	quattro	cuatro
5	fünf	five	cinq	cinque	cinco
6	sechs	six	six	sei	seis
7	sieben	seven	sept	sette	siete
8	acht	eight	huit	otto	ocho
9	neun	nine	neuf	nove	nueve
10	zehn	ten	dix	diece	diez
11	elf	eleven	onze	undici	once
12	zwölf	twelf	douze	dodici	doce
13	dreizehn	thirteen	treize	tredici	trece
14	vierzehn	fourteen	quatorze	quattordici	catorce
15	fünfzehn	fifteen	quinze	quindici	quince
16	sechzehn	sixteen	seize	seidici	dieciséis
17	siebzehn	seventeen	dix-sept	diciasette	diecisiete
18	achtzehn	eighteen	dix-huit	dicio	dieciocho
19	neunzehn	nineteen	dix-neuf	dicinove	diecinueve
20	zwanzig	twenty	vingt	venti	veinte
21	einundzwanzig	twenty-one	vingt et un	ventuno	veintiuno
22	zweiundzwanzig	twenty-two	vingt-deux	ventidue	veintidos
30	dreißig	thirty	trente	trenta	treinta
40	vierzig	forty	quarante	quaranta	cuarenta
50	fünfzig	fifty	cinquante	cinquanta	cincuenta
60	sechzig	sixty	soixante	settanta	sesanta
70	siebzig	seventy	soixante-dix	settanta	setenta
80	achtzig	eighty	quatre-vingts	ottanta	ochenta
90	neunzig	ninety	quatre-vingt-dix	novanta	noventa
100	hundert	(one) hundred	cent	cento	cien(to)
200	zweihundert	two hundred	deux cents	duecento	descientos, -as
300	dreihundert	three hundred	trois cents	trecento	trescientos, -as
400	vierhundert	four hundred	quatre cents	quattrocento	cuatrocientos, -as
500	fünfhundert	five hundred	cinq cents	cinquacento	quinientos, -as
600	sechshundert	six hundred	six cents	seicento	seiscientos, -as
700	siebenhundert	seven hundred	sept cents	settecento	setecientos, -as
800	achthundert	eight hundred	huit cents	ottocento	ochocientos, -as
900	neunhundert	nine hundred	neuf cents	novecento	novecientos, -as
1000	tausend	(one) thousand	mille	mille	mil
5000	fünftausend	five thousand	cinq mille	cinquemilla	cinco mil
10.000	zehntausend	ten thousand	dix mille	diecemilla	diez mil
100.000	hunderttausend	hundred thousand	cent mille	centomilla	cien mil
200.000	zweihundert-tausend	two hundred thousand	deux cents mille	duecentamilla	descientos mil
500.000	fünfhundert-tausend	five hundred thousand	cinq cents mille	cinquacentamilla	quinientos mil
1.000.000	eine Million	(one) million	un million	un millione	un millón

D	E	F	I	Es
Wochentage	**weekdays**	**jours de la semaine**	**giorni della settimana**	**días de semana**
Montag	Monday	lundi	lunedì	lunes
Dienstag	Tuesday	mardi	martedì	martes
Mittwoch	Wednesday	mercredi	mercoledì	miércoles
Donnerstag	Thursday	jeudi	giovedì	jueves
Freitag	Friday	vendredi	venerdì	viernes
Samstag	Saturday	samedi	sabato	sábado
Sonntag	Sunday	dimanche	domenica	domingo

Monate	**months**	**mois**	**mesi**	**meses**
Januar	January	janvier	gennoaio	enero
Februar	February	février	febbraio	febrero
März	March	mars	marzo	marzo
April	April	avril	aprile	abril
Mai	May	mai	maggio	mayo
Juni	June	juin	giugno	junio
Juli	July	juillet	luglio	julio
August	August	août	agosto	agosto
September	September	septembre	settembre	septiembre
Oktober	October	octobre	ottobre	octubre
November	November	novembre	novembre	noviembre
Dezember	December	décembre	dicembre	diciembre